W9-CDC-460

Modern Catholic Social Teaching

Modern Catholic Social Teaching

Commentaries and Interpretations

EDITOR
Kenneth R. Himes, O.F.M.

ASSOCIATE EDITORS
Lisa Sowle Cahill
Charles E. Curran
David Hollenbach, S.J.
Thomas A. Shannon

Georgetown University Press
Washington, D.C.

Georgetown University Press, Washington, D.C.

Printed in the United States of America

10 9 8 7 6 5 4 3 2 1 2004

This book is printed on acid-free paper meeting the requirements of the American National Standard for Permanence in Paper for Printed Library Materials.

Library of Congress Cataloging-in-Publication Data

Modern Catholic social teaching : commentaries and interpretations / Kenneth R. Himes, editor ; Lisa Sowle Cahill . . . [et al.] associate editors.

p. cm.

Includes bibliographical references and index.

ISBN 1-58901-053-1 (pbk. : alk. paper)—ISBN 1-58901-058-2 (cloth : alk. paper)

1. Christian sociology—Catholic Church. 2. Church and social problems—Catholic Church. 3. Catholic Church—United States—Doctrines. I. Himes, Kenneth R., 1950– II. Cahill, Lisa Sowle.

BX1753.M573 2005
261.8'088'282—dc22 2004023165

This book is dedicated to the memory of

ROBERT MARTIN FOLEY

who taught his children to
believe in social justice

CONTENTS

ACKNOWLEDGMENTS

A book of this nature and size is obviously not the work of any one person. I am grateful, first, to the authors who agreed to engage in this project. They gave far more time than is usual to writing an essay because they participated in a collaborative method that stretched over several years. Each contributor wrote and rewrote in response to comments by peers and editors. I thank the authors for their willingness to participate in a process that was truly a joint effort by editors, authors, and publisher.

Several people who have played a role in this project ought to be mentioned by name. The plan that was developed for it—two weekend meetings of all the authors and multiple drafts submitted to peer review and criticism over a period of three years—involved many committed individuals.

Charles Foley, a generous trustee of the Washington Theological Union (WTU) and supporter of theological education, provided the funding to make this book possible. I am deeply grateful to him for his trust, support, and encouragement in translating an idea for a project into an actual publication.

The administration and staff of the WTU provided wonderful assistance in hosting the meetings with authors as well as dealing with a variety of practical details. Vincent Cushing, Daniel McLellan, Joseph Lehman, Joseph LaGressa, Rita Gibbons, Alyce Korba, and Bob Allen all played a part in bringing this book to completion. Their work is much appreciated.

Lisa Sowle Cahill, Charles Curran, David Hollenbach, and Thomas Shannon have been immensely helpful and cooperative as associate editors. They were part of the planning of the volume as well as serving as conveners for groups of authors. The associate editors reviewed and read manuscripts, made many helpful suggestions, and did all that was asked of them. The merits of this book are in good measure the result of their work.

Daniel Grigassy came to the project in its later stages as assistant editor and improved virtually every single manuscript by his critical eye and astute judgment. He helped with formatting, literary style, and library research in preparing the manuscript for production. I am deeply grateful to him for his generous labor.

Richard Brown and the staff at Georgetown University Press have been cooperative beyond what I could have hoped for in a publisher. The sheer size, complexity, and duration of this project never caused them to doubt its worth, and it is a pleasure to have this volume published by such a distinguished university press.

INTERNET RESOURCE

Many collections of the documents of Catholic social teaching are available in published works. There is also online access to various sites that contain the documents studied in this volume.

The editor has established a web page that will provide easy access to the documents of modern Catholic social teaching in both English and Latin versions. Access to the paintings discussed by Michael Schuck in his exposition of pre-Leonine social thought is also available through the web page. To see the documents and artwork, go to http://www2.bc.edu/~khimes/publications/mcst/.

ABBREVIATIONS

AAS	*Acta apostolicis sedis*
ACCO	Association of Catholic Conscientious Objectors
ACLI	Associazioni Cristiane Lavoratori Italiani
CA	*Centesimus annus*
CAIP	Catholic Association for International Peace
CDF	Congregation for the Doctrine of the Faith
CELAM	Consejo Episcopal Latinoamericano
CHD	Campaign for Human Development
CP	*The Challenge of Peace*
CPC	Central Preparatory Committee (Vatican II)
CS	*Caritatis studium*
CSD	Catholic social doctrine
DH	*Dignitatis humanae*
DR	*Divini redemptoris*
EJA	*Economic Justice for All*
FC	*Familiaris consortio*
GS	*Gaudium et spes*
HV	*Humanae vitae*
JM	*Justitia in mundo*
JSOT	*Journal for the Study of the Old Testament*
LE	*Laborem exercens*
LG	*Lumen gentium*
LXX	Septuagint
MM	*Mater et magistra*
NAB	New American Bible
NCWC	National Catholic Welfare Conference
NFP	Natural Family Planning
NRSV	New Revised Standard Version
OA	*Octogesima adveniens*
OCCO	Ouevre des circles catholiques d'ouvriers
OR	Commission for Oriental Churches (Vatican II)
PP	*Populorum progressio*
PT	*Pacem in terris*
QA	*Quadragesimo anno*
RH	*Redemptor hominis*
RN	*Rerum novarum*
SAD	Social Action Department (of the NCWC)
SCU	Secretariat for Christian Unity (Vatican II)

SNTSMS	Society for New Testament Monograph Series
SRS	*Sollicitudo rei socialis*
ST	*Summa theologiae*
TC	Theological Commission (of Vatican II)
USCC	U.S. Catholic Conference
USCCB	U.S. Conference of Catholic Bishops
WCC	World Council of Churches

INTRODUCTION

KENNETH R. HIMES, O.F.M.

This is a large book, the work of many hands and minds. It is the end result of a process of extensive scholarly collaboration that took place over three years. The project and process began with the assembly of a board of associate editors that discussed the selection of authors and topics for an anthology that would serve as a standard reference work for the major documents of Catholic social teaching.

The editors and authors involved in this project attended two springtime meetings that were rewarding exercises in intellectual exchange. Prior to the initial meeting, authors submitted the first drafts of their manuscripts, which were read and commented upon by others in the group. At this meeting, detailed suggestions for revision of each manuscript were offered by the editors and fellow authors. One year later the entire group met again after submitting second drafts in advance of the meeting. Once more, reactions and comments were given that provided each author with guidance for additional revision.

Then in the autumn following the second meeting, the final version of each author's text was submitted to an editorial board member who reviewed the work to ensure that the author's text reflected the insights of the collaborative process. Following that review the entire manuscript was then closely edited and put into proper format for the production process. As a result this volume is truly a joint effort by twenty scholars who have worked to produce a book that distills their collective insights into a series of commentaries and essays on modern Catholic social teaching.

DESIGN OF THE BOOK

This volume is intended as a reference work for anyone interested in studying the key documents of Catholic social teaching. It is presumed that readers will not go through this book cover to cover but will dip into the material at various points to gain insight about some aspect of the Church's social teaching. That presumption has shaped the way the editors planned the present volume.

There are fourteen commentaries and seven essays included in this volume. Four essays comprise part I of the volume; each can be read profitably by both scholar and student alike. The first two essays (Donahue and Pope) provide assistance in understanding the biblical and philosophical underpinnings for Catholic social teaching. The third essay (Gaillardetz) addresses the ecclesiological issues that arise in discussion of the Church's social teaching.

Although this volume is focused on modern documents of the tradition, commonly dated as starting in 1891 with publication of Leo XIII's *Rerum novarum,* there is a rich vein of writing that precedes that landmark papal encyclical. The fourth essay (Schuck) offers a study of the social thought that preceded Leo's writing.

In part II of the book the reader will find fourteen commentaries on major documents of Catholic social teaching. The commentaries follow a similar format[1]:

- **Introduction**—briefly notes the document's significance and key points
- **Outline of the Document**—provides an overview of the entire document with short descriptions of subsections
- **Ecclesial and Social Context of the Document**—assists readers in understanding the historical setting of the document and what the climate was like in the Church and the world at the time it was written
- **Process of Formulation and Authorship**—describes who contributed to the writing of the document and what stages it went through prior to completion
- **Essay**—is the heart of the commentary, which develops the major themes, methodology, arguments, and conclusions of the text, explaining how it stands in relation to the broad tradition of Catholic social teaching
- **Excursus**—examines in detail some aspect(s) of the text that calls for more extensive analysis
- **Reactions to the Document**—details reactions of critics and supporters
- **Selected Bibliography**—is annotated to assist further research
- **Notes**—provides additional bibliographic information

Since each commentary is meant to be self-contained, there is a certain amount of repetition as one moves from commentary to commentary. For example, discussion of the context for a document written in early 1971 (*Octogesima adveniens*) will not differ all that greatly from the context for a document written later that same year (*Justitia in mundo*). The editor believes the risk of some repetitiveness is outweighed by the benefit of each commentary being able to stand alone as a comprehensive treatment of a document.

Part III of the volume contains three essays. Two of these essays (Curran and Whitmore) review how Catholic social teaching has been received in the United States. They also discuss how various Catholic leaders in the United States have articulated the social tradition for their particular time and place. One of the criticisms made of the social teaching expressed in papal writings is that it does not build upon and learn from the experience of local churches. Certainly, there are few references to documents issued by national and regional assemblies of bishops. Yet, the efforts of local church leaders to interpret and apply Catholic social teaching to a particular locale are a noteworthy aspect of the development of the tradition. The essays on the U.S. experience serve to highlight one local church experience.

The final essay (Coleman) in the volume looks to the future. It takes an informed look at needed developments and unresolved questions for the future of the tradition. One end of a tradition reaches back into the past, providing roots for a stable foundation, but the other end must be the "growing edge" whereby the tradition is retrieved and developed so that it continues to inform people living in new eras with new issues. The authors in this book believe that the tradition of Catholic social teaching remains a worthwhile object of study precisely because its rootedness in the past does not diminish but enhances its ability to provide insight and lessons for the future.

THE SUBJECT MATTER OF THE BOOK

The title of this volume, *Modern Catholic Social Teaching: Commentaries and Interpretations*, accurately portrays what the reader will find inside the cover. But the title deserves additional explanation. The designation of *modern* teaching is a customary way of dating those teachings that begin with the promulgation of *Rerum novarum* in 1891 by Leo XIII. As Michael Schuck, one of our contributors, has maintained here and elsewhere,[2] this dating is misleading if it gives the impression that prior to 1891 the papacy ignored social topics. Indeed, Leo himself issued a number of papal letters, called encyclicals, on political matters that predate *Rerum novarum*.

Without doubt, however, it was the 1891 encyclical that inspired a deeper and broader commitment by church members to the social questions of the time. It is for that reason—its impact on the wider Church as well as its subsequent commemoration by later popes—that an informal designation of *Rerum novarum* as the initial text of modern Catholic social teaching has arisen. While the essays of part I cover a wide range of materials prior to 1891, the commentaries of part II begin with *Rerum novarum* and follow the customary practice of using Leo's encyclical as a marker for the onset of *modern* social teaching.

The second word of this volume's title is *Catholic*, as in Roman Catholic. There are other branches of Catholicism but it is Roman Catholicism, the largest of the Catholic churches, that has produced a substantial body of literature on social questions. It is members of the hierarchy, either singly or collectively, who have issued the documents under study in this volume.

For the most part, the literature of Catholic social teaching has been written by a small group of people. Officially the authors are popes or bishops, but church leaders have relied upon a small band of ghostwriters, advisors, consultants, and pastoral ministers in the formulation of these documents. Usually, the circle of people involved in the production of a document has been composed mainly of European clerics.

To what extent the documents give voice to the actual sentiments and ideals of the wider Catholic population is difficult to assess. At times, some Catholics, in both the past and present, have expressed deep disagreement with one or another aspect of the teachings. Other Catholics, a committed but minority population, have used the writings as inspiration and guidance for social engagement. It is safe to say that the majority of Catholics have never read these documents in their entirety or even read any one of them from beginning to end. However, the importance of the material cannot be measured by the size of the readership. Its influence comes from how the texts have been "translated" into sermons, lectures, public programs, social movements, acts of charity, just deeds, and peacemaking.

What is certain is that the documents under review in this volume are the accepted expression of a social outlook that the Catholic tradition generates. There is a normative vision found in the writings that articulate the official position of the Catholic Church as promulgated by its hierarchical leadership. In this sense it is *Catholic* teaching.

A final clarification of the volume's title is the use of social *teaching* as distinct from social thought. As one might expect from such a sizable and diverse segment of humanity, Catholic men and women have contributed insightful and even brilliant ideas to the history of political, economic, and cultural thought. There is much to be learned from the historical tradition of Catholic social thought—from Tertullian's "Military Chaplet" to Clement of Alexandria's "Can a Rich Man Be Saved?"; from Marsilius of Padua's "Defender of Peace" to Thomas More's *Utopia*; from Aquinas's "Treatise on Law" in Ia IIae of the *Summa Theologica* to Francisco Suarez's *Laws and God the Lawgiver*. In more recent times Jacques Maritain's *Integral Humanism* and Dorothy Day's editorials in the *Catholic Worker* exemplify Catholic thinkers who address social questions of their time from the perspective of faith. All of this and more falls under the heading of Catholic social thought.

Catholic *teaching* refers more narrowly to the texts issued by those who hold an official teaching position within the Church by virtue of membership within the episcopal college. Contemporary Catholicism designates this official teaching office as the magisterium. Better appreciation and understanding of the authority and nature of this official teaching issued by the hierarchy of the Church is provided by Richard Gaillardetz's chapter in this volume.

There is also at present a disagreement about whether the material under study in this book is more appropriately described as social doctrine rather than social teaching. Several decades ago a French Dominican theologian, Marie-Dominique Chenu, wrote a book in which he used the term *doctrine* in a pejorative sense.[3] For Chenu, social doctrine was an ideology, an abstract theory to be universally applied that ignored inductive methods and empirical evidence that did not confirm the theory. He believed that elements of such an ideology infected the approach of pre–Vatican II social teaching. Chenu went on to endorse changes in Catholic social teaching that moved toward greater reliance upon an inductive reading of the signs of the times and use of the social sciences. For him Catholic social doctrine was a negative term and its demise was to be welcomed.

During the papacy of John Paul II there were instances where the term *social doctrine* was used, seemingly as a direct rebuttal to the Chenu thesis. To make his case, Chenu had to emphasize the discontinuity between pre- and postconciliar social teaching. In his writing John Paul II frequently stressed the continuity of the tradition and did not shy away from use of the word *doctrine* because he was unwilling to grant Chenu's premise of significant discontinuity within the tradition. Thus, one finds the expressions *social teaching, social doctrine*, and another expression, *social magisterium*, used virtually synonymously in the work of John Paul II. Since *social teaching* is used by both those who favor and those who challenge the Chenu thesis, it is an apt term for the title of this volume.

Properly understood, social teaching is not social ethics. Ethical discourse entails critical reflection aimed at achieving a systematic and especially methodological investigation. The papal and episcopal teaching under consideration in this volume exhibits a different intent—to enlighten, inspire, and guide moral reform on social matters.

It is the ambition of the authors in this volume to provide ethical reflection upon the hierarchical teaching, in both the commentaries and essays that are included. Catholic *social teaching*, as explained above, is much less broad than social thought or social ethics.

THE SELECTION OF TEXTS

There are fourteen commentaries in this volume. The editors had to decide which documents to include as subject matter for this volume since there is no established canon of Catholic social teaching. (As already noted, the use of *Rerum novarum* in 1891 as a starting date is customary but not indisputable.) There are a number of texts, such as John XXIII's *Pacem in terris* or Paul VI's *Populorum progressio*, that would be on any list of modern Catholic social teaching. Much of the material chosen as subject matter for commentary invited no disagreement. But other writings were a topic of debate among the editors.

Certain documents of papal social teaching have been important at the time but the intervening years have made them less significant for today. Pius XI issued an encyclical, *Divini redemptoris*, which condemned atheistic communism and stirred strong Catholic opposition to Stalinism and the political program of the Soviet Union. His letter to the bishops of Germany, *Mit Brennender Sorge*, opposed the ideology of Nazism and was a stern rebuke to Hitler's regime. While historically notable, neither of these writings appears to merit extended commentary in the present age.

Marriage and family life are key social institutions and they have been understood as being foundational to the Catholic vision of human society. Two papal encyclicals came to mind as a result. Paul VI's *Humanae vitae*, issued in 1968, was certainly of historical importance. The encyclical offered a very positive expression of a Christian view of human sexuality and marriage as well as occasioned a vigorous debate over artificial contraception. Much has changed since 1968 regarding family, marriage, and women's social roles. A more recent text than *Humanae vitae* that addresses these topics is John Paul II's *Familiaris consortio*. Including a commentary on that apostolic exhortation provides an opportunity to examine the importance of the "domestic church" in the Catholic vision of social life.

Another text issued by Paul VI, *Evangelii nuntiandi*, reflects upon the relationship between evangelization and the social agenda of human liberation. Explicating the relationship of the church's central religious mission and its social mission is an important theological concern but it is an issue that various documents of social teaching either implicitly or explicitly address. Furthermore, while *Evangelii nuntiandi* contains important ideas, it is not mainly devoted to Catholic social teaching. Because several of the other commentaries included in this volume examine the theological foundations of the Church's social mission, it was decided not to include one on *Evangelii nuntiandi*.

For whatever reason, the text of *Dignitatis humanae* is often not studied in treatments of Catholic social teaching. Why that is the case is surprising since the *Declaration on Religious Liberty* issued by Vatican II is a remarkable document. Not only does it squarely address the main issue of religious liberty, it is also fraught with implications for Catholic teaching on democracy, the nature of the state, civil law, and human rights in general. It is also the conciliar text most directly influenced by the thought and experience of Catholics in the United States. Members of the editorial board all agreed that a commentary on it should be included in this volume.

Ultimately, the editors decided that the fourteen commentaries included in this book should not only cover the major documents of Catholic social teaching, but also reflect a list of the popes who have been significant for modern Catholic social teaching. (Including the addresses of Pius XII was one way of incorporating the pope who has been the subject of much controversy with regard to his activities during the years of World War II and after.) There was also a concern that no one papal voice dominate the presentation of the entire modern tradition. This explains the decision not to include a fifteenth commentary on John Paul II's *Evangelium vitae* since four of his other writings are examined.

Of course, other scholars and church leaders might have their own list of suggested texts for modern Catholic social teaching. The editors believe that our list is a good and reasonably complete one, even if not beyond dispute.

THE GENRE OF CATHOLIC SOCIAL TEACHING

The writings under study are examples of the universal teaching authority of the Church. As such, they are attempts to speak to the broad audience of worldwide Catholicism and, even beyond the confines of the Catholic community, the global audience of "all people of good will." Consequently, one finds in this teaching few specifics and many broad general statements. The teaching does not delve into the specifics of proposed solutions but functions more at the level of values and perspectives by which to frame discussion of a problem and understand what is at stake. These are not documents that will satisfy all the requirements of social ethics or public policy analysis; nor are they meant to do so. There is more religious-moral content than methodological precision and programmatic detail in the Church's teaching.

Another facet of the genre is the confidence that church leaders exhibit that they can indeed fashion teaching that is universal. Due in large part to reliance upon the methodology and presuppositions of the natural law tradition, the Catholic Church has maintained it is possible to formulate teaching that really does speak to all people in all settings. This emphasis on the universal has on occasion blinded the proponents of Catholic social teaching to the partiality of the tradition. In various ways the claims of universality are too easily made in Catholic social teaching.

It is also the case that within the tradition certain themes receive a great deal of attention and other topics have been slighted. Labor, just wages, duties of the state, poverty, and human rights are examples of recurring topics. Racism, nationalism, anti-Semitism, and feminism are illustrations of topics that get insufficient attention. Another topic that is not adequately addressed is institutional self-criticism and how the Church's institutional self-interest may shape its teaching on social questions.

Readers will find that the various essayists and commentators quite properly point out the weaknesses as well as strengths of the social teaching.

AN AMERICAN CATHOLIC READING OF THE TRADITION

A final word must be said about the authors and editors of this volume. All of us are Roman Catholics living in the United States. Every author is a distinguished scholar who has studied Catholic social teaching as part of his or her academic career. This volume is self-consciously a work that reflects the perspective of American Catholicism.

Certainly, there are scholars from other countries who could have contributed to this book and there are advantages to having a book that represents the divergent experiences of Catholics from around the world as well as from different theological viewpoints. Nonetheless, there are also advantages to having a volume that reflects upon the tradition from a particular perspective. The authors in this book are part of the broad spectrum of progressive Catholicism that is committed to the ongoing renewal of the Church in the spirit of Vatican II. When other strands of the Catholic tradition are treated throughout the volume, an effort has been made to do so with respect and fairness.

The scholars involved in producing this book are aware that the U.S. Catholic Church is a complex reality and that it is only one region of a universal Church. The editors and authors do not imagine that they have said the final word on any of the topics they address. We do believe that we have produced an intellectually responsible and theologically faithful exposition and analysis of Catholic social teaching. Readers who utilize this volume can judge for themselves the accuracy of that claim, but the editors and authors sincerely hope that is the case. If our work serves to advance our readers' appreciation and understanding of the Catholic social tradition we will be satisfied.

All royalties from the sale of this volume will be donated to the Catholic Campaign for Human Development, a program sponsored by the bishops of the United States that assists the poor to help themselves.

NOTES

1. The one exception to the standard format is that of John Langan's commentary on the writings of Pius XII. Because this pope wrote no major social encyclical, he is often downplayed or omitted in studies dealing with Catholic social teaching. However, his lengthy papacy was a time of significant turmoil in the world and developments in the Church that ought not be overlooked. To find his social teaching one must explore not a single document but a series of addresses he delivered over Vatican radio. Langan's commentary, as a consequence, is not focused on a single text.

2. Michael Schuck, *That They Be One: The Social Teaching of the Papal Encyclicals 1740–1989* (Washington, D.C.: Georgetown University Press, 1991).

3. Marie Dominique Chenu, *La "doctrine sociale" de l'Église comme idéologie* (Paris: Cerf, 1979).

PART I

Foundations

CHAPTER 1

The Bible and Catholic Social Teaching: Will This Engagement Lead to Marriage?

JOHN R. DONAHUE, S.J.

INTRODUCTION

Over the last century the Catholic Church has responded to the changing social and economic challenges of the modern world with a wide variety of official teaching, beginning with the encyclical letter of Pope Leo XIII, *On the Condition of Labor* (*Rerum novarum*, 1891) and continuing through the pontificate of Pope John Paul II (1978 to 2005).[1] The same period that witnessed the rise of Catholic social teaching was also the century during which the magisterium cautiously accepted the methods and conclusions of modern biblical scholarship.[2] The social teaching was based almost exclusively on the Catholic natural law tradition mediated primarily through Scholastic philosophy and theology, though later enhanced by dialogue with contemporary social ethics. During the evolution of Catholic social teaching and the development of Catholic biblical studies, these two great streams of renewal flowed side by side rather than together.

Yet there were tentative beginnings of the use of scripture in the early social encyclicals, which often evoked biblical texts and themes that had a long history in the patristic tradition. *Rerum novarum* highlights the need to use worldly goods for the benefit of others and the obligation to give alms (citing Luke 11:41 and Acts 4:34, RN 19, 24) and the equal dignity of all human beings (citing Rom. 10:12, RN 37). *Quadragesimo anno*, while making comparatively little use of scripture, did invoke Matthew 11:28, "Come to me, all you who are weary and carrying heavy burdens," to call back those "who have deserted the camp of the Church and passed over to the ranks of socialism" (QA 123), and later used the Pauline image of the body (Rom. 12:5; 1 Cor. 12:24–25) to stress the importance of the common good (QA 137).[3]

A major change in the use of scripture was inaugurated by Vatican II, held twenty years after Pope Pius XII's encyclical, *Divino afflante Spiritu*, often called the "Magna Carta" of biblical studies.[4] Following in the footsteps of Pope Leo XIII, Vatican II mandated that scripture be the soul of sacred theology, and stressed that "special care should be given to the perfecting of moral theology, . . . whereby its scientific presentation should draw more fully on the teaching of Holy Scripture."[5] In the post–Vatican II period the social teaching of the magisterium, while never abandoning its debt to philosophical analysis, began to be more explicitly theological and scriptural. The documents did not engage in exegetical discussions but drew on the fruits of exegesis, especially by giving a more Christological thrust to moral teaching. J. Bryan Hehir has observed, "After the appearance of *Gaudium et spes*, however, the pressure for more biblically and theologically based social ethic came from within the ranks of Catholic theologians and advocates of social justice."[6]

Select writings of Pope John Paul II indicate ways in which scripture has been used for social justice. In his letter dealing with human work, *Laborem exercens* (September 19, 1981), John Paul II speaks of human dignity and human destiny in the first two chapters of Genesis and comments: "An analysis of these texts makes us aware that they express—sometimes in an archaic way of manifesting thought—the fundamental truths about humanity."[7] John Paul's most sustained use of the Bible occurs in his encyclical, *Sollicitudo rei socialis* (*On Social Concerns*; December 30, 1987), in commemoration of Pope Paul VI's encyclical, *Populorum progressio* (1967). Again the pope turns to Genesis 1 and 2 to stress that men and women are created in the image of God, and he further notes: "The story of the human race described by Sacred Scripture is, even after the fall into sin, a story of constant achievements which, although always called into question and threatened by sin, are nonetheless repeated, increased and extended in response to the divine vocation given from the beginning to man and woman (Gen. 1:26–28) and inscribed in the image they received" (SRS, 29).

The parable of the rich man and Lazarus (Luke 16:19–31) is one of the texts most often cited in modern social teaching. Vatican II cites the parable to show that "everyone must consider his [or her] neighbor without exception as another self," so as not to imitate the rich man who had no concern for the poor Lazarus (GS 27). In *Populorum progressio*, Pope Paul VI expressed a hope for "a world where freedom is not an empty word, and where the poor man Lazarus can sit down at the same table with the rich man" (47). In his world travels, Pope John Paul II has used the parable frequently, most notably in his address in Yankee Stadium on October 2, 1979, where he noted that the rich man was condemned because "he failed to take notice" of Lazarus who sat at his door. The pope further stated that this parable "must always be in our memory" and "form our conscience," and that Christ demands openness "from the rich, the affluent, the economically advantaged to the poor, the underdeveloped and the disadvantaged." He sees this as both an individual and national challenge.[8] The key words in the papal statement are "always be in our memory" and "form our conscience." The biblical material does not give direct precepts, but it is necessary to inform the Christian imagination and moral dispositions.[9]

Pope John Paul returns to this parable in *Sollicitudo rei socialis* (1987), stating, "it is essential to recognize each person's equal right to be seated at the common banquet instead of lying outside the door like Lazarus" (SRS 33). Though this use of the parable verges on the allegorical, I would argue that intertextually its use is legitimate and that it touches human imagination today in a way that can evoke a response to the parable analogous to that expected of Luke's original readers.

Other texts most frequently used are a number of references to Genesis 1–2, especially to Genesis 1:26, the creation of man and woman in the image of God, as a basis of human rights and human dignity, and, as one might expect, to the allegory of the sheep and the goats in Matthew 25:31–46, but interpreted in the universalistic sense that all the thirsty, the hungry, and people otherwise marginalized are brothers and sisters of Jesus.

In his *Centesimus annus* the pope makes sparing use of scripture, again invoking Genesis to undergird human dignity and the destination of the goods of the earth for common use. He also cites Matthew 25:31–46 (sheep and goats) and the parable of the good Samaritan (Luke 10:30–35) to stress that everyone is responsible for the well-being of his or her brother or sister (CA 51). More important than citation of specific texts is that the pope sees the whole Christian tradition as affirming "the option or love of preference for the poor" (CA 42), and says that it is because of "her *evangelical duty* [emphasis mine] that the Church feels called to take her stand beside the poor, to discern the justice of their requests" (CA 39).

The most sustained use of the Bible in any church document on social justice was in the 1986 pastoral letter of the U.S. bishops, *Economic Justice for All*.[10] Here the bishops recognize the difficulty of bringing the Bible to bear on complex economic and social issues, and call attention to "the Bible's deeper vision of God, of the purpose of creation, and of the dignity of human life in society" (EJA 29). While offering no sustained biblical argument, the bishops select six themes from the Bible that are judged especially pertinent to social issues today: (1) creation of all men and women in God's image, which stamps them with an inalienable dignity; (2) God's formation of a covenant community that lives in justice and mutual concern; (3) the proclamation of God's reign by Jesus, (4) along with his formation of a community of disciples that is (5) to be manifest in a special concern for the poor and marginal, and (6) that bequeaths to history a legacy of hope and courage even amid failure and suffering. Despite the cursory and selective nature of the biblical treatment and the criticism in some circles that the use of the Bible by the bishops softens the prophetic critique of injustice, the themes selected provide a foundation for further theological reflection. Also, as Benedictine Archbishop Rembert Weakland, the chair of the committee that drafted the economics pastoral, stressed, no matter how difficult the problems of interpretation and application of the biblical material, "*if the document was to influence preaching and daily church life*, there should be a scriptural section that would put people in touch with the major texts and social themes of the Bible."[11] Whatever the intellectual power and depth of papal teaching, the encyclicals rarely touch the lives of everyday Catholics. If Catholic social teaching is to form people's consciences, inspire their imaginations, and shape their lives, it must weave biblical theology into its presentations.

Though often the charge is made that church teaching simply uses the scripture for proof texting, this is not completely accurate. Catholic moral theologians have tended to base their teaching on a modified natural law theology as interpreted by a magisterial and theological tradition. Scripture is often used as "a moral reminder" or a way of motivating people to moral activity that is based on diverse sources.[12] Second, a distinction must be made between the use of scripture as intertextual reference and proof texting, strictly speaking.[13] Contemporary studies of intertextuality show that often texts evoke earlier texts and a whole history of associations in a community.[14] Much of the use of scripture in official documents is of this nature, and is in this sense quite legitimate. Neither usage is the same as crass proof texting, where there is neither a chain of traditional association nor little intrinsic connection between the scriptural reference and the doctrine to be "proved."

While this volume offers careful studies of the mainly magisterial documents that produced a coherent body of social doctrine, the biblical renewal is much less focused and comprises a myriad of methods, originally historical criticism, now supplemented by varieties of "criticisms," for example, redaction criticism, social science criticism, and literary criticism, all of which are enveloped by different hermeneutical approaches, for example, liberation and feminist hermeneutics, and a proliferation of "posts," postmodern readings, postfeminist readings, and postcolonial readings. Nor among biblical scholars themselves is there one consistent position on what makes a particular biblical text or theme authoritative or how they concretely influence church life and practice. An adequate presentation of the relation and relevance of biblical thought to Catholic social teaching would itself involve a multivolume work.

APPROACHING THE TEXTS: THE OLD TESTAMENT FOUNDATION

The Bible is not one book, but rather a collection of texts that themselves incorporate traditions ranging over a millennium. In contrast to the careful language of Catholic social teaching, couched mainly in the encyclical genre, the Bible is a mélange of different literary genres, historical and legendary narratives, epic tales, prophetic oracles, varied collections of wisdom sayings, religious poetry praising God and lamenting his absence, and apocalyptic visions. Until recently the Bible represented unexplored terrain for many Catholics and, even with the transformation of the Church after Vatican II into a Bible-reading and Bible-praying community, the relevance of these ancient texts to today's complex social world seems questionable.

In debt to the writings of Paul Ricoeur, as mediated primarily through Sandra Schneiders and Dorothy Lee, I propose an admittedly oversimplified approach to the biblical material.[15] Ricoeur argues that, "as readers, we begin to read a text naively, opening ourselves to its dynamic in the same way that children listen to stories; this first movement is a 'naive grasping of the meaning of the text as a whole.'"[16] For reflections on the biblical meaning of justice, this means that often, especially for Catholics not nurtured on the biblical tradition, simple exposure to biblical texts is a prerequisite to any significant use of these texts. Subsequent explanation and exegesis may simultaneously challenge and enrich this initial engagement, but always as a preparation for an appropriation that leads to individual and social transformation.

The next movement involves explanation of the text: "the reader steps back from the text and engages in the kind of research necessary for a deeper comprehension at a number of levels. Here the historical-critical method and related tools of biblical study play their part."[17] This movement also involves "distanciation," that is, the reader moves beyond preliminary and naive interpretations that arise from an initial engagement with the text, and then experiences a "second naiveté" that enables an informed explanation of the text.[18]

Ricoeur's insights also lead to the concept of the semantic autonomy of a text whereby its meaning is not *limited to* the "intention" of an original author. This autonomy, he stresses, does not imply that "authorial meaning has lost all significance." There will always be a dialectical relationship between authorial intention and subsequent meaning.[19] His insights on the "semantic autonomy" of texts, that texts are open to interpretations beyond their original context, are consistent with observations of biblical scholars about the development of traditions.[20] Texts engender traditions of interpretation that often involve genres and settings quite different from the originating discourse. For example, the exodus is celebrated, perhaps originally by the hymns at the sea (Exod. 15:1–18, 20–21), in psalms (Pss. 78, 105), and in the sagas of the "taking of the land" in Joshua and Judges (Josh. 3:14–17). The return from exile in Isaiah is seen as a second exodus from oppression to liberation,[21] and the exodus motif shapes much of New Testament theology.[22] The "effective history" (*Wirkungsgeschicte*) of texts and traditions continues beyond the canonical scriptures and influences subsequent interpretations and appropriations of the originating narratives.

The Bible is both historical document and canonical, sacred text for a believing community. It is proclaimed in liturgy and is "the soul of sacred theology."[23] Though virtually no one feels that the Bible offers concrete directives or solutions to today's complex social problems, the Bible is the foundation of a Judeo-Christian vision of life. It discloses *the kind of God* we love and worship. This God is interested in the world, in human history, and in the manner in which humans live in community. This theme is pervasive throughout both Testaments. In one sense, the "faith that does justice" is simply an application of the great command to love God with one's whole heart, mind, and soul, and the neighbor as one's self. What the Bible relentlessly affirms from the law of Moses to the Pauline summons "to bear another's burdens and in this way you will fulfill the law of Christ" (Gal. 6:2) is that the love of neighbor is manifest especially in care for the weak and the powerless. When such a pervasive motif is found in multiple biblical literary genres (law, prophets, wisdom teaching) that are handed on and reinterpreted over a millennium, it can be seen as central to biblical revelation.

An indispensable task is increased knowledge and close reading of pertinent biblical texts in their historical and literary context, but read with a concern for issues of social justice.[24] Feminist scholars have long called attention to the blindness of established interpreters regarding texts and motifs that challenge an androcentric reading of the Bible. Allied to this challenge is a "hermeneutics of suspicion" about interpretations that support individualized piety. Philip Esler states, for example, that Luke's writings are read through a layer of *embourgeoisment* to foster middle-class values.[25]

Equally important as the engagement with the meaning of the text is how the text forms the interpreter. James Gustafson, a leader in theological ethics over the past generation, has commented that the Bible does not offer revealed morality but revealed reality and tells us *the kinds of people we are to become* if we are to hear its message faithfully.[26] This approach leads to the present concern for virtue ethics, where the biblical narratives can form character and dispositions.

Some principle of analogy is helpful for application of the biblical texts to subsequent periods. Though the social and cultural situation of biblical texts is very different from our modern, postindustrial society, there are profound analogies, especially at the level of human behavior. The use of analogy also involves an appropriation of Gadamer's fusion of horizons, but in a sense in which the horizons are first seen in parallel structure.[27] For example, Amos's criticism of the ostentatiously rich (2:6–7; 4:1; 6:4–7), the plight of the poor man in Psalm 10, and the blindness of the wealthy to the needy at their gates (Luke 16:19–31) are hauntingly familiar to our own day, but do not provide clear moral guidelines. Paul's concern for the poorer churches of Palestine and even his collection strategy have relevance to a church in the United States increasingly divided along socioeconomic lines. Paul Tillich once defined the task of theology as one of correlation of the symbols of the faith (where symbol is understood as sacred text and sacred tradition) with the existential question of a given age.[28] David Tracy has extended this insight by arguing for a "critical correlation" whereby the theologian not only engages the existential questions but subjects their bases and formulation to critical appraisal, while engaged in self-critical reflection on the tradition in which he or she stands.[29] In our age, socioeconomic questions are the most pressing, and conversion, study, and imagination are necessary to achieve the task of critical correlation.

In approaching the biblical material initially I describe the diverse ways in which the term *justice* is used in the Bible, often in contrast to the more circumscribed and careful use in social ethics. Then I highlight those biblical themes that have not only de facto been part of the emerging dialogue between the Bible and social ethics, but also those that have been constantly invoked and reinterpreted in the Bible itself, as illustrated above by the continuing reappropriation of the exodus event. The surplus of meaning and potential for new appropriations arise *within the Bible itself.* The notes, often more bibliographical than discursive, offer resources for continued explanation and adaptation of the material by different readers in different settings.[30] I conclude with some reflections on the need for continued and critical reappropriation of the biblical material by the ecclesial community.

The Biblical Vocabulary of Justice

Biblical justice is similar to, but very different from, the necessary and precise understandings of justice that emerge from the philosophical tradition dating back to Aristotle and modified in Thomistic thought. Even though justice is at once a transcendental term and an analogous one that is applied differently in specific situations, some major understandings and distinctions are almost universally accepted. A fundamental difficulty is translation of the appropriate terms.

The Bible has a rich vocabulary of justice, and injustice, that does not yield to a one-to-one correspondence in English.[31] The two principal biblical terms are variations of the root *ṣdq* (used 523 times) and *mišpāṭ* (422 times), which are often used virtually interchangeably. Space does not allow adequate exploration of the labyrinth of other terms used for justice and their translations into

Greek, Latin, and contemporary versions, so the emphasis will be put on the above terms and a major translation problem. In most contemporary English versions, *ṣĕdāqāh* is translated "righteousness" and *mišpāṭ* "justice or judgment" which, as we will see, causes major problems.

Biblical terms do not have the precision of concepts based on philosophical analysis, so distinctions between "justice" and "charity," or "justice" and "holiness," are much murkier in the Bible. A classic instance of the larger semantic fields embraced by these terms is the famous covenant renewal text of Hosea 2:21–22 (in NAB; NRSV, 2:19–20).

I will espouse you to me forever;
I will espouse you in right and justice [*bĕ ṣedeq wĕ bĕ mišpāṭ*]
in love [*bĕ ḥesed*] and in mercy [*bĕ raḥămîm*]
I will espouse you in fidelity [*bĕ 'ĕmūnāh*],
and you shall know the Lord.
(Trans. NAB, 1970. See also Jer. 22:15–16, where the doing of justice is equated with knowledge of the Lord)

Another important example would be Isaiah 32:16–17:

Right [*mišpāṭ*] will dwell in the desert
and justice [*ṣĕdāqāh*] abide in the orchard
Justice will bring about peace [*šālôm*]
right will produce calm and security.

A major problem arises in English from the connotations of the terms *righteous* and *righteousness* (generally used to translate the *ṣdq* word group). The *Oxford English Dictionary* defines righteousness as "justice, uprightness, rectitude, conformity of life to the requirements of the divine moral law, virtue, and integrity." The term was first introduced into English biblical translations under the influence of Cloverdale (1535). The problem is that in most people's minds *righteousness* evokes primarily personal rectitude or personal virtue, and the social dimension of the original Hebrew is lost. This has resulted in a virtual "biblical dialect" in which righteousness is relegated to the sphere of religion and personal piety, while justice is more associated with the realm of public, secular discourse. Imagine, for instance, people's reaction if we had a national "department of righteousness" or we talked about "social righteousness."

The centrality as well as the richness of the biblical statements on justice is the very reason it is difficult to give a "biblical definition" of justice which, in the Bible, is a protean and many-faceted term. Justice is used in the legal codes to describe ordinances that regulate communal life (e.g., Exod. 21:1–23:10) and that prescribe restitution for injury done to person and property as well as for cultic regulations. The Hebrew terms for justice are applied to a wide variety of things. Scales or weights are called just when they give a fair measure, and paths are called just when they do what a path or way should do—lead to a goal. Laws are just, not because they conform to an external norm or constitution, but because they create harmony within the community. Acting justly consists in avoiding violence and fraud and other actions that destroy communal life and in pursuing that which sustains the life of the community. Yahweh is just not only as lawgiver and Lord of the covenant; his saving deeds are called "just deeds" because they restore the community when it has been threatened. The justice of Yahweh is not in contrast to other covenant qualities, such as steadfast love, mercy, or faithfulness, but, in many texts, is virtually equated with them.

In general terms the biblical idea of justice can be described as *fidelity to the demands of a relationship*.[32] God is just when he acts as a God should, defending or vindicating his people or punishing violations of the covenant. People are just when they are in right relationship to God and to other humans. In contrast to modern individualism the Israelite is in a world where "to live" is to be united with others in a social context either by bonds of family or by covenant relationships. This web of relationships—king with people, judge with complainants, family with tribe and kinfolk, the community with the resident aliens suffering in their midst, and all with the covenant God—constitutes the world in which life is played out. The demands of the differing relationships cannot be specified a priori but must be seen in the different settings of Israel's history.[33]

Recent commentators have also stressed the social dimension of *ṣedeq* and *mišpāṭ*. For example, Walter Brueggemann, arguably the premier Old Testament theologian today, describes *ṣdq* as "equitable, generative social relations."[34] In commenting on Amos 5:24, Barbara Johnson, author of two foundational studies of these terms, writes, "Here *ṣedeq* is understood as the normative principle and *mišpāṭ* as the principle of conduct which must conform to *ṣedeq* (cf. Ps. 119:160)."[35] Very significant, especially in Isaiah, is the conjunction of *ṣĕdāqāh* and *mišpāṭ* by hendiadys (two terms used to convey a single meaning) that many recent scholars interpret as "social justice" (e.g., Pss. 72:2; 89:14; Is. 1:27: 5:16; 9:7; 32:16; 56:1).[36]

A major implication of the wider semantic field of biblical understanding of justice is that "biblical justice" is not as clearly distinguished from "charity" or caritative activity as in contemporary social ethics. Actions such as confronting the oppressive power of the wealthy and alleviating the sufferings of the poor are ultimately ways of "doing right" and seeking right relationships between God and humanity, and among humans themselves. On the other hand, today the traditional works of mercy (e.g., feeding the hungry, caring for the imprisoned, welcoming strangers) are equated with "social justice ministry," often at both the parish and national levels. While such actions are certainly a hallmark of church life, a biblical concern for justice has three elements that supplement such actions: (1) biblical justice is embedded in those very narratives that form a people's self-identity; (2) actions that manifest concern for the weak and vulnerable become mandated in law and are not, as often thought today, supererogatory; and (3) biblical justice always has a "prophetic dimension," by virtue of entering into conflict with oppressive structures of injustice.

Though application of biblical teaching to theology and ethics has become a virtual subdiscipline within biblical studies, I would like to suggest, somewhat eclectically, that certain biblical themes can offer helpful but not exclusive resources for the appropriation of biblical material for concerns of social justice.

Central Biblical Themes and Their Significance

While the biblical literature evolved over centuries from diverse oral traditions to blocks of literature, its canonical shape was fixed rather late. Genesis 1–11 (creation and primeval history), though narrated "in the beginning" (Gen. 1:1) was appended to the national history (Exodus–Deuteronomy) only after the exile (586–536 B.C.), and the Torah receives its final shape only between 300 and 200 B.C.

The older positions of Gerhard Von Rad and Martin Noth still offer an excellent way to survey the Old Testament.[37] Von Rad argued that the Pentateuchal traditions developed from creedal formulas such as Deuteronomy 6:20–25, 26:1–12, and Joshua 24:2–13, which provided the fundamental themes of Israel's faith, where a "theme" is understood as a basic act of God by which the people are constituted. I offer some reflection and bibliography on certain themes that are part of Israel's faith and appear throughout the Bible, beginning with the creation story, which is an important overture to the salvation history of Genesis through Joshua.

A generation of Catholics was nurtured on two perspectives that are no longer helpful for understanding creation in the Bible. The first was that Genesis 1–3 (culminating in the fall and the expulsion of Adam and Eve from the garden) could be read as an independent block of material. This was undergirded by the use of these chapters primarily for the doctrine of original sin. The second was that the biblical creation narratives dealt with cosmology. This latter view was supported by debates over evolution. As Claus Westermann has strongly argued, the whole primeval history (Gen. 1–11) must be read as a unity, culminating in the tower of Babel. Theologically, creation is not concerned with the origin of the world and the universe, but rather with the situation in which later readers found themselves.[38] Technically, these narratives are "etiological"; they describe the causes of the yearning for God, the gap between God and humanity, and the divisions within humanity itself.

It is customary to see two major perspectives in the creation account. The preamble, or first account (1:1–2:4a), is attributed to the priestly tradition (P) and is the later of the two accounts. The second account, which narrates the creation of the man and the woman, their offspring, and the spread of civilization (2:4b–4:26), is attributed to J (the Yahwist).

Contemporary reflection on social justice often turns to these accounts to ground human dignity in the creation in God's image, to argue for the common claim of all humanity to the world's resources, and more frequently, for reflection on ecological issues. I now simply indicate elements in the text that are important.

The first account describes a primitive cosmology in rhythmic cadences marked off by a division into "days" with the frequent refrain that "it was good" (Gen. 1:4, 10, 12, 18, 21, 25), culminating in the final day when God views all creation as "very good" (v. 31). Claus Westermann, whose extensive writings on creation are the best resource for a proper biblical theology of creation, notes that these narratives reveal the Priestly stress that all events have their origin in God's commanding word. They prepare us for the revelation on Sinai when God's word forms the somewhat chaotic throng into a people.[39] He also notes that the author, by placing the separation of night and day through the creation of "light" before the creation of "space," stresses that human life is temporal and historical.

The goodness of creation is not something that men and women affirm but is a divine proclamation. By locating the creation story as a preamble to the whole sacred history, the Priestly writer proclaims the goodness of all creation even though the narrative that unfolds depicts the catastrophic results of sin on both nature and human history.[40] The proper response to creation is praise and thanksgiving even amid suffering and catastrophe, since God has affirmed that nature and its power are "good." Two obvious implications arise from Genesis 1:1–2:4a: first, the proper response to creation is reverence and praise, not exploitation, and second, humanity shares solidarity with both the inanimate and animate worlds in owing its existence to the Word of God.

The creation narrative of P reaches its summit in Genesis 1:26, "Let us make humankind in our image, according to our likeness and let them have dominion. . . ." This is then followed by the blessing of man and woman, the command to be fruitful and multiply, and God's resting on the seventh day. Man and woman created in the image of God is one of the most frequently cited texts to undergird human dignity and human rights. Created "in the image of God" in its original context does not mean some human quality (intellect or free will) or the possession of "sanctifying grace." Two interpretations enjoy some exegetical support today. One view is that just as ancient Near Eastern kings erected images of themselves in subject territory, so humans are God's representatives, to be given the same honor due God. Claus Westermann argues that the phrase means that humans were created to be God's counterparts, creatures analogous to God with whom God can speak and who will hear God's Word.[41] In either of these interpretations all men and women prior to identification by race, social status, religion, or sex are worthy of respect and reverence.

The term *have dominion* (see Gen. 2:15, "to till and to keep") has often been criticized by ecologists as the warrant for a utilitarian view of creation or as justification for the exploitation of creation for human convenience. In other places, the Hebrew term is used in reference to royal care that characterizes a king as God's vice regent (Pss. 72:8; 110:2; cf. 8:5–9). Like ancient kings, men and women are to be the mediators of prosperity and well-being.[42] In neither creation account is the human being given dominion over another human being. This is not part of the human constitution. Reverential care for God's creation rather than exploitation is the mandate given humanity in this section of Genesis.

The second and older creation story (2:4b–3:24) is more anthropomorphic and dramatic.

It may be composed of two originally different stories. One deals with the origin of the sexes. The original human one (*hā' ādām,* "from the clay of the earth") is now differentiated into *'îš* (man) and a complementary partner (*'iššā*). In her ground-breaking discussion of this section, Phyllis Trible has stressed that this narrative, while stressing differentiation among humans, does not imply derivation or subordination of woman to man, but both "owe the origin to divine mystery."[43] The other major theme, as Westermann stresses, which runs through Genesis 1–11 is the spread of sin (see also 4:1–6; 6:1–4, 6–9; 11:1–10). The former motif has dominated the history of exegesis of the creation account.

Two elements of the creation of "man" and "woman" are important for contemporary reflection. First, as a story of mythic beginnings (akin to other ancient myths of androgyny) the narrative stresses the complementarity of male and female. The "human" is male and female united as "one flesh" (2:24)—not understood simply as a description of marriage, but as a basic fact of prototypical human existence. On the anthropological level this calls for recognition of the presence of "male" and "female" in every human. On the social level it means that the human condition can never be defined or named in terms of the dominant characteristics or activity of one sex.[44]

Proper understanding of the fall or sin of the first parents also has implications for a theological grounding of social justice. Taking this narrative on its own terms requires a bracketing of its Pauline and post-Pauline interpretation (Rom. 5:12–20; 2 Cor. 11:3; 1 Tim. 2:13–15) and of the Augustinian doctrine of original sin as well. The narrative remains, however, a rich source for understanding human evil and alienation from God.

It explains the human potentiality for evil, no matter how gifted one may be. The human person, according to Genesis 2:4b–3:24, is created for life and knowledge. The ultimate test or temptation in this narrative is to "be like God" (3:5), knowing good and evil, which is "knowledge in a wide sense, inasmuch as it relates to the mastery of human existence."[45] The temptation is always to an autonomy that seeks this apart from the limits of being human, or divorced from life in community. Sin is overstepping the limits of the human condition by aspiring to divine power. It can take place through action (the woman) or through complicity (the man). Their desire to be like God sadly separates them from God.

After the fall the narrative relates the trial and the punishment (3:8–24). The expected punishment of 3:3 ("you shall die") does not occur. Instead, the harmony of their earlier status is destroyed. Desire for human autonomy leads to alienation and breakdown of community with nature and between man and woman. It is important to note that the subordinate position of woman (3:16–17), which reflects the de facto situation of women in ancient society, is not something that was to be part of the original blessing of creation but arises from human sinfulness. Alienation between the earth and humans (3:17–19) is likewise a result of sin. While the "work" of cultivating and caring for the earth is intrinsic to the human condition prior to sin, "toil" is its consequence.

The narratives of Genesis 4–11 capture the ambivalence of the human condition. As civilization grows through the multiplication of occupations (farmers and shepherds) and through the invention of elements of culture (4:19–22), sin is depicted as "crouched at the door" (4:7) and humans continually overstep their limits. This culminates in the tower of Babel, where humans attempt to invade the realm of God. Though a reprise of the attempt to be like God, the narrative has political ramifications. Though set in "primeval time," it receives its final form after the Babylonian exile. The fate of Babylon with its pretensions of world rule and its idolatrous self-exaltation, only to be split apart by the onslaught of Cyrus, is reflected in the tower of Babel. The spread of sin culminates in the idolatrous pretensions and ultimate destruction of national power.

The primeval history of Genesis 1–11 thus provides a rich resource for reflection on issues crucial to faith and justice. Men and women are God's representatives and conversation partners in the world, with a fundamental dignity that must be respected and fostered. They are to exist in interdependence and mutual support, and are to care for the world with respect, as for a gift received from God. Yet the human condition is flawed by a drive to overstep the limits of the human situation and to claim autonomous power. The result of this drive is violence (Cain and Abel) and idolatry (the tower of Babel). The Genesis narrative functions as both a normative description of the human condition before God and a critical principle against any power that distorts or usurps the dignity of humanity or God's claim over men and women.

Exodus: The Leading Out from Egypt

The primeval history is followed by the patriarchal history in Genesis 12–50 that begins with God's call and covenant with Abraham and Sarah (12:1–9; 15:1–21; 17:1–27) and constitutes the foundation narrative for the emergence of Israel as a people. The subsequent stories of the children of Abraham describe how God's promise is maintained through adversity. Though these narratives are foundational, it is the narratives of exodus and Sinai that constitute Israel's identity. I offer some reflections on the exodus and discuss covenant in the context of the Sinai covenant.

The exodus from Egypt (Exod. 1:1–15:21) has emerged as one of the most dominant biblical events for a biblical theology of liberation from evil and from unjust social structures.[46] There are two dangers here: the first, that a too generalized statement of its meaning absolves people from close attention to the rich theological dimensions of the text; the second, that the exodus is considered in isolation from other biblical themes. While liberation from oppression is a fundamental aspect of the exodus narrative, it is not simply *freedom from* that is important but *freedom for* the formation of a community that lives under the covenant. As Michael Walzer says, the journey of Israel is to a "bonded freedom."[47] Exodus and covenant, liberation and commitment, must be taken together as part of one process.

The description of Israel's bondage has become paradigmatic of oppression. In fulfillment of the promise to Abraham and through no action of their own, other than fulfilling God's command to be fruitful and multiply, the people grow numerous and become a threat to a dominant power. The initial response is one of massive forced labor. Maimonides (A.D. 1135–1204) described this as service without limits of time or purpose.[48] The second major threat, the killing of the male children, is in effect genocide. The people's identity will be slowly but surely destroyed. Theologically it is a challenge to the fidelity of God manifest in the promises to Abraham.

Though it is customary to mark the beginning of the liberation from the birth of Moses (Exod. 2:1–20), the "revolt of the midwives" (1:15–22) is an important paradigm of resistance to oppression.[49] It is described briefly: "But the midwives feared God; they did not do as the king of Egypt commanded them, but they let the boys live" (1:17). These women, daughters of Eve, the mother of all the living, commissioned to bring forth life in the world, reject the murderous command of Pharaoh. They do this in light of a higher law ("fearing God," 1:17, 21). Therefore, "God dealt well with the midwives, and the people multiplied and became very strong." On the narrative level they allow the promise to continue and also prepare for the rescue of Moses from death (2:1–10).

The process of liberation continues with the "liberation" of the liberator. The agent of liberation must suffer the same fate as that of the people (threat of death; life as an alien in an alien land, 2:15; 3:22). At the same time, the liberator must be equipped to meet the threat (3:1–11) and be the agent of a higher power (4:10–11). Liberation is a power struggle between humans and their oppressors, but more fundamentally between God and the powers opposed to God.

The theophany at the burning bush and the call of Moses proclaim that liberation is fundamentally an act of God. God's action begins in 2:24 ("God heard their groaning and remembered his covenant") and is detailed in 3:7–12, which is a virtual summary of the identity of Yahweh as the compassionate God who enters human history. Immediately after the revelation of his name, Yahweh says, "I have *observed* the misery of the people; I have *heard* their cry; indeed I *know* their sufferings; I have *come down to deliver them*" (3:7–8, emphasis added; cf. Luke 1:78, "by the tender mercy [compassion] of our God the dawn from on high will break upon us").

The liberation itself unfolds through the sequence of ten plagues divided into three triads and culminates in the killing of the Egyptian firstborn and the "passing over" of the firstborn of Israel. Nature itself turns against the Egyptians in the plagues, almost in revulsion for their oppression of God's people. As the plagues escalate, the issue again becomes the nature of God and the usurpation of divine power. In Exodus 9:16–17, God speaks through Moses to Pharaoh: "This is why I let you live: to show you my power, and to make my name resound through all the earth. You are still exalting yourself against my people."[50]

In the final plague, the Passover (11:1–13:16); the P source, 12:1–38 becomes prominent, which shows that the narrative had become "the cult legend" for the later celebration of Passover. Here the exodus receives the character of anamnesis, something to be represented and celebrated annually. Thus it continues to shape the identity of the people and reveal the nature of God.

I offer a few observations on the exodus as a paradigm of liberation, a power struggle in which the issues of oppression are progressively highlighted. Pharaoh begins with concern about the growth of an alien population, but the real issue is whether he will be their "god" or whether they will be free to worship the one who called their ancestors. Oppression and idolatry are never far apart. Liberation does not come from the most oppressed members of the community. Moses is nurtured at the center of Egypt's power and is equipped to enter its world. Through his own "conversion" and preparation by God he becomes a prophet, one who speaks for God and for a people without a voice (see Deut. 34:10, "never since has there arisen a prophet like Moses"). Yet, as I note below, "liberation" is but one aspect of a true concept of freedom. Israel's journey is "from liberation to freedom," which is the ultimate theme of the wilderness wandering and the covenant at Sinai.

Covenant, Law, and Justice

In contrast to a philosophical foundation for justice, biblical justice is mediated by God's self-disclosure and human response. Paradigmatic for this dynamic is the covenant between God and the people. When Israel is freed from the slavery of Egypt, this freedom, as Walzer has noted, is a bonded freedom, not simply freedom from external oppression but freedom expressed in commitments to God and others.

The distinctive understandings of justice are revealed in the law codes of Israel and especially in their concern for the powerless in the community. Though full examination of the history and scope of the law codes is beyond the purpose of this chapter, I mention a few things that are important for a biblical foundation of social justice today.[51]

The codes themselves comprise: (1) "Covenant Code" (Exod. 20:22–23:33), parts of which date from northern Israel in the ninth century B.C. and which reflect premonarchic rural life, though, like the rest of the Pentateuch, it receives its final shape after the exile; (2) the Decalogue, found in two versions (Exod. 20:1–17 and Deut. 5:6–21) that represent early covenant law; (3) the Deuteronomic code (Deut. 12–26), which embodies traditions from the seventh century B.C. and perhaps from Josiah's reform, but which was incorporated into the full-blown "Deuteronomic history" only after the exile; (4) the "Holiness Code" (Lev. 17–26), put together after the exile and often attributed to priestly circles.

Comments on the legal texts are confined to those sections that deal with the powerless (often made concrete as the "poor, the widow, the orphan, and the stranger in the land"). Norbert Lohfink, whom I follow extensively here, has cautioned against viewing concern for the poor as unique to Israel's faith. A survey of a number of Mesopotamian texts (such as the code of Hammurabi) and Egyptian wisdom texts shows a similar concern for *personae miserae*, with the exception of care for "the stranger in the land," which is distinctive to Israel.[52] While the content of concern is similar, the foundation and motivation are different. Care for such persons in Israel is part of the "contrast society" that is created through the exodus. In Israel this concern functions more as a critical principle against the misuse of power, while in some of the surrounding cultures it is a way in which those in power dampen down revolutionary tendencies of the people and thus maintain a divinely sanctioned hierarchy of power.[53] As Paul Hanson notes, in Israel responsibility for the well-being of such people devolves on the covenant community as a whole and not simply on the king.[54]

Concern for the powerless emerges first as part of the "Covenant Code" (see above). For our purposes the first important section is Exodus 22:21–27. Here God says, "You shall not wrong or oppress a resident alien, for you were aliens in the land of Egypt" (v. 21; note the motivation of a contrast society). The following verse proscribes abuse of the widow and the orphan, with the promise that God will heed their cry and "kill with the sword" their oppressors, and the section concludes with prohibiting the lending to the poor at interest and encouraging the restoring of a neighbor's coat taken in surety for a loan. Here also the motivation is God in his role as the protector of the poor: "And if your neighbor cries out to me, I will listen, for I am compassionate" (22:27). The next section contains a series of laws on the proper administration of justice. One of the first states: "You shall not side with the majority so as to pervert justice, nor shall you be partial to the poor in a lawsuit" (23:2). The prohibition of "partiality" to the poor in the specific context of a lawsuit does not contradict the concern for the marginal, since 23:6 immediately says that "you shall not pervert the justice due to the poor in their lawsuits" (there is no corresponding statement on the rich or powerful), and 23:9 repeats the protection of the resident alien. In verses 10–11, in a more cultic setting, the code mandates a Sabbath year of leaving land fallow "so that the poor may eat."

In discussing the Deuteronomic legislation of Deuteronomy 12–26, Norbert Lohfink points out that the ideal in the "Covenant Code" of a contrast society without oppression and poverty was in fact not realized, and locates Deuteronomy in this context.[55] While retaining an ideal that "there will be no one in need among you, because the LORD is sure to bless you" (15:4; cf. Acts 4:34), Deuteronomy realistically states: "there will never cease to be some in need on the earth," and commands, "open your hand to the poor and needy neighbor in the land" (15:11). More strongly than the other codes, Deuteronomy commands justice and compassion for the powerless (15:1–18; 24:10–15; 26:11–12). The historical significance of Deuteronomy is as evidence for a continuing concern in Israel's law for the *personae miserae* that attempts to institutionalize the covenant ideal through law and practice. The significance of Deuteronomy in its present canonical location is that it is cast in the form of farewell speeches from Moses to the people on the brink of the Promised Land. The land is God's gift on condition of fidelity to the covenant: "These are the statutes and ordinances that you must diligently observe in the land of the LORD, the God of your ancestors has given you to occupy" (12:1). When read *after the exile*, it can be seen as a warning against an infidelity that allows the kind of society to develop which is in opposition to the exodus event and the Sinai covenant.[56]

The "Holiness Code" (Lev. 17–26) contains provisions similar to Deuteronomy. In 19:9–10 and 23:22, gleanings from the harvest are to be left for "the poor and the alien," though as Lohfink points out, specific mention is not made of "the widow and the orphan," who now seem to be subsumed under "the poor." The "Holiness Code" has other provisions that spell out in detail provisions for the poor, very often those who have come suddenly upon hard times (25:35–42, 47–52). Leviticus is also more concerned with the details of repayment of debts and cultic offerings made by the poor (12:8; see Luke 2:24). The significance of Leviticus is twofold. First, though it is primarily a cultic code concerned with the holiness of the people and the means to assure that holiness, it manifests a practical concern for the poor in the land. As John Gammie has shown in his excellent study, there is no tension between Israel's concern to be a holy people consecrated to God and a people concerned about justice.[57] Second, and perhaps less positively, Leviticus seems to represent a relaxation of some of the earlier provisions for the poor. Lohfink argues that the stipulations of the Jubilee (25:8–17, 23–25; 27:16–25), where debts are canceled every fiftieth year, would hardly benefit the majority of people who lived in poverty and represent a step back from the Sabbath year legislation of Deuteronomy. The "Holiness Code" may also reflect the radically changed postexilic political situation, when the monarchy was extinct and people had limited ability to enshrine the ideals of the covenant in law. This period also represents the beginning of apocalyptic thought, when many groups projected the hope of God's justice and a society free of oppression and poverty to a new heaven and new earth that would be ushered in by cosmic cataclysm.

The events of salvation history, especially the leading out from Egypt and the covenant at Sinai, are thus the foundations in Israel of a society that seeks justice and manifests concern for the marginal. This concern is incorporated in law and custom that take different shapes in different historical circumstances stretching over five centuries. As founding documents not only of the historical people of Israel but of the Christian church, they offer a vision of life in society before God that is to inform religious belief and social practice. The laws of Israel have two great values. First, they show that religious belief must be translated into law and custom that guide life in community and protect the vulnerable. Paul Hanson states this well in describing Torah as "faith coming to expression in communal forms and structures."[58] In our contemporary pluralistic society, the Church and its episcopal and lay leadership rightly strive to infuse the legislative process with a vision of social justice.

Second, although these traditions do not offer concrete directives for our complex socioeconomic world, they offer a vision of a "contrast society," not ruled by power and greed but where the treatment of the marginal becomes the touchstone of "right relationship" to God. As Christians we today must ask soberly how our lives provide a contrast society, and whether, when we think of our "right relation" to God, the concerns of the marginal in our own time have been really made concrete in our attitudes and style of life.

Biblical Justice, the Poor, and the Prophetic Critique of Wealth

If there is one pervasive biblical motif in both Testaments it is concern for the poor and marginal, which has been the subject of an increasing number of important studies. The question of the poor raises many problems, from their identity (e.g., economically poor or spiritually poor) to the social location of statements concerning them to different evaluations of a response.[59] Since the biblical vocabulary for the poor is much richer than ours, at the risk of seeming overly technical I indicate some of these. There are five principal Hebrew terms for the poor: (1) *'ānî* (plural *'āniyyîm*), meaning "bent down" or "afflicted," which the Greek Old Testament most often translates as *ptōchos* (beggar or destitute person) and which is the prime New Testament term for "the poor"; (2) *'ānāw* (plural *'ānāwîm*), derived from the same root as *'ānî* and often confused by copyists, which is most often translated *tapeinos* and *praüs* (humble and lowly); (3) *'ebyôn* (the term *Ebionites* derives from this), from the root meaning "lack or need" or "wretched, miserable," used sixty-one times in the Old Testament, especially in the Psalms (twenty-three times); (4) *dal*, from the root that means "be bent over," "bend down," "miserable"; (5) *rāš*, poor in a derogatory sense with overtones of a lazy person responsible for his or her own poverty, found only in the Wisdom literature (e.g., Prov. 10:4; 13:23; 14:20; 19:7; 28:3).

The importance of the terminology is twofold. First, it shows that "poverty" was not itself a value. Even etymologically the poor are bent down, wretched, and beggars. While the

Bible has great concern for "the poor," poverty itself is an evil. Second, the terminology (as well as actual use) is a caution against misuse of the phrase *spiritually poor*. Though later literature (the Psalms and Dead Sea Scrolls) often equates the poor with the humble or meek, and though the poor are those people open to God in contrast to idolatrous or blind rich people, the prime analogue of the term is an economic condition. When the "poor in spirit" are praised as in Matthew 5:3, it is because in addition to their material poverty they are open to God's presence and love. Certain contemporary usages of "spiritual poverty," which allow it to be used of extremely wealthy people who are unhappy even amid prosperity, are not faithful to the biblical tradition. Nor is an idea of "spiritual poverty" as indifference to riches amid wealth faithful to the Bible. The "poor" in the Bible are almost without exception *powerless* people who experience economic and social deprivation. In both Isaiah and the Psalms the poor are often victims of the injustice of the rich and powerful. Isaiah tells us that the elders and princes "devour" the poor and grind their faces in the dust (3:14–15); they turn aside the needy from injustice to rob the poor of their rights (10:2); wicked people "ruin" the poor with lying words (32:7). In the Psalms the poor, often called "the downtrodden," are contrasted not simply to the rich but to the wicked and the powerful (10:2–10; 72:4, 12–14). Today, poverty is most often not simply an economic issue but arises when one group can exploit or oppress another.

The Prophets and the Call for Justice

When a people forgets its origins or loses sight of its ideals, figures arise who often speak a strident message to summon them to return to God. In Israel's history the prophetic movement represents such a phenomenon. The prophet, as the Greek etymology *prophēmi* suggests, speaks on behalf of another. This has a dual sense. The prophet speaks on behalf of God; he or she is a "forth teller," not simply a foreteller who also speaks on behalf of those who have no one to speak for them, specifically the powerless and poor in the land.[60] From the original social gospel movement to the present time, those concerned for social justice among Catholics, Protestants, and Jews have continually drawn on the powerful language of the great prophets of Israel, who castigate the abuse of justice by the powerful and give a voice to the voiceless poor. A few guidelines for reading the prophets as well some "snapshots" of this preaching can lead hopefully to a deeper engagement.

First, the prophets are generally "conservative" in the best sense of the word. They hearken back to the originating experiences of Israel to counter corrupting influences of urbanization and centralized power that developed under the monarchy, especially after the split between the northern kingdom (Israel) and the southern kingdom (Judea) after the death of Solomon (922 B.C.). Their works are also a collection of traditions, some going back to the originally named prophets, others additions by disciples and later editors. Much recent research has attempted to describe these levels of tradition.

Second, in assessing the prophetic texts on justice and concern for the marginal, careful attention must be given to the literary context of a given text, but more important to its historical context. Amos, for example, prophesied at the northern court shortly before the fall of Samaria to the Assyrians (721 B.C.). During this time, however, the northern kingdom experienced material prosperity. Under the reign of Solomon a more prosperous upper class had emerged. This created a class with a vested interest in the accumulation of land and goods as capital. The old emphasis on the land as the inheritance of every Israelite disappeared (see 1 Kings 21, story of Naboth's vineyard). James L. Mays describes this as "the shift of the primary social good, land, from the function of support to that of capital; the reorientation of social goals from personal values to personal profit; to subordination of judicial process to the interests of the entrepreneur."[61] Amos's harsh words against the prosperous must be set in this context. He laments the sins of Israel: "You who turn justice into bitterness and cast righteousness to the ground" (5:7), which is manifest when "they trample the head of the poor into the dust of the earth" (2:7) and through deceptive business practices "buy the poor for silver and the needy for a pair of sandals" (8:5–6). For Amos the root cause of these sins is the lavish lifestyle of the upper classes of the northern kingdom (3:15–4:3; 6:4–7).

A generation later, Isaiah of Jerusalem, himself from the upper classes, has easy access to the king and utters some of the harshest criticisms of injustice, calling the city once known for its justice and righteousness a "harlot" (1:21) and castigating the leaders because God looked for justice but found bloodshed, and for righteousness but heard rather a cry (5:7). In capsule form Isaiah captures the cause of the city's infidelity: because they "deprive the poor of their rights and withhold justice from the oppressed of my people, making widows their prey and robbing the fatherless" (10:2). As Amos also observed, the desire for ostentatious wealth drives the oppression of the poor by the rich (1:23; 5:8).

A century after Isaiah, beginning during the reign of the reforming king Josiah, Jeremiah, using vivid imagery, repeats the attack on the self-satisfied wealthy: "Like a basket full of birds, their houses are full of treachery; therefore they have become great and rich, they have grown fat and sleek. They know no bounds in deeds of wickedness; they judge not with justice the cause of the fatherless, to make it prosper, and they do not defend the rights of the needy" (5:27–29). More strongly than his predecessors, Jeremiah grounds the quest for justice in the very nature of God: "I am the LORD, who exercises kindness, justice and righteousness on earth, for in these I delight,' declares the LORD" (9:24). And in a phrase that had great influence on the 1971 Synod, Jeremiah describes the good king Josiah: "He judged the cause of the poor and needy; then it was well. Is not this to know me? says the LORD" (22:16). Though the context of the prophetic preaching changes, there is a continuity of defending the poor and powerless and attacking the unjust practices of the powerful and wealthy.

Third, the prophets are not opposed to cultic worship per se but to its corruption. Jeremiah was the son of a priest; Isaiah used cultic imagery associated with the Jerusalem temple; and Ezekiel was steeped in the cult. Recent research on Amos, often popularly portrayed as a "righteous peasant," has suggested some contact with the Jerusalem temple. Though Isaiah is eloquent on the demand for justice, the motivation is different from Amos or Hosea. The controlling principle of much of Isaiah's teaching was his conviction of the holiness and royal power of God. Oppression of the weaker members of the community offended Yahweh's holiness, so Isaiah vehemently criticizes injustice and distorted cultic worship.

Fourth, though the prophets criticize the misuse of power by those in authority, their message is reformist rather than revolutionary. They do not envision a community without a king or without laws and statutes. During the bulk of the postexilic period (especially after the codification of the law under Ezra and Nehemiah) when the people lack their own kings and live under the successive rule of the Persians, the successors of Alexander, and finally the Romans, prophecy as a movement with Judaism virtually ceases. Biblical prophecy required a shared heritage of values by the rulers and the ruled, even when those in power did not live up to these values. When a people have no control over their destiny and are subject to brutal power, prophecy can take the form only of protest, not of a call to reform. After the exile, prophetic protest leading to hope for reform is gradually supplanted by apocalyptic hopes for a new heaven and a new earth.

Israel after the Exile: A New Situation

Above I alluded to significant changes in Israelite life after the Babylonian exile (deportation of upper classes to Babylon in 597 B.C.; other deportations in 587 and 582; return under Cyrus in 539). The subsequent period is generally divided into the Persian period (539–332), the Hellenistic period (332–175), followed by a brief period of independence under the Hasmonean kings (175–63), which yielded to Roman rule under either client kings (Herod and his sons) or Roman prefects (in Judea). This period also witnesses the rise of a large corpus of "intertestamental writings" (apocrypha and pseudepigrapha), which are important for the history of ideas and as a background to the New Testament, even though most are not part of the Jewish and Christian canon.[62]

With conscious oversimplification I would like to highlight three considerations in regard to concern for the poor at the time. First, the sense of individual responsibility develops (Ezek. 18:1–32; 33:1–20) with the consequent focus on justice as the right relation *of the individual* to God. Second, there is the expansion of apocalyptic literature. Here the hope for God's saving justice is removed from history and reserved for the end of history when the wicked will be punished and the just rewarded. Allied to this are attacks on the wealthy with increasing invective and vehemence (e.g., 1 Enoch 92–105). The third consideration is the expansion of Wisdom literature (e.g., the Wisdom of Solomon; Ben Sirach [Ecclesiasticus]), couched in the form of maxims or sayings, many of which describe how to survive and succeed in everyday life. This literature shows a much stronger influence of Hellenism than the apocalyptic literature and may have originated among the growing number of city dwellers engaged in commerce and in the governmental bureaucracy. Only in the late Wisdom literature are certain poor blamed for their own condition (Prov. 10:4; 13:23), yet, as Alexander DiLella notes, social justice remained one of the prime concerns of Ben Sirach, who wrote at the beginning of the second century B.C.[63]

Again, risking the charge of oversimplification, I would like to propose some summary statements on rich and poor in the Bible.

First, the "poor" are primarily the sociologically poor. They are the economically destitute and the socially outcast, typified by the characteristic biblical figures of exploited powerlessness, "the widow, the orphan and the refugee."[64] In contemporary parlance the poor would better be described as "the powerless."

Second, the poor have a special claim on the community and its leaders; they are "just" because they do not follow the evil ways of the rich and powerful. Both the king and the whole people are obliged to seek justice, which involves being on the side of the poor and the powerless. This perspective informs all of Israel's traditions and at all stages in its history.

Third, riches are both a danger and an evil. Often they are associated with idolatry and oppression (see esp. Ps. 10). They present a temptation to secure one's life apart from God (see Luke 12:13–21) or cause blindness when faced with the needy neighbor (Luke 16:19–31).

SOCIAL JUSTICE AND THE NEW TESTAMENT: SOME DIRECTIONS

The canonical New Testament books emerged in less than a century and in social, political, and cultural contexts far less diverse than in the Old Testament and intertestamental literature. Yet many Christians today are somewhat like the second-century heretic Marcion, who rejected the Old Testament; they often want to ground their ethics in the New Testament to the neglect of the Hebrew Scriptures. I select several areas of consideration where there have been significant discussions of issues that lend themselves to questions of social justice. This means that the Gospel and letters of John are overlooked. Though there are significant sections, especially 1 John 3:11–18, which bear directly on issues of social justice, the Johannine writings thus far have not been the subject of intense discussion by those interested in New Testament social ethics. The areas I deal with are: aspects of the teaching and ministry of Jesus; Jewish Christianity as manifest in the Gospel of Matthew and in the letter of James; the Gospel of Luke and the Acts of the Apostles; and the letters of Paul.

The Teaching and Ministry of Jesus

It has become axiomatic to say that Jesus was not a social reformer; nonetheless, his teachings and actions had strong social implications during his lifetime and continue to shape the consciences of his followers today. A key to his life is his proclamation of the imminence of God's reign or kingdom through direct proclamation or in parable.[65] He also brings about the kingdom through acts of power (healings and exorcisms) and by his association with and offer of God's love to "the marginal" of his day, especially tax collectors and sinners.

Many scholars today locate Jesus' teaching in the wider context of different "restorationist" movements alive in Palestine. Jesus is seen as summoning people to a renewed dedication to the primacy of God in their lives and to a deepened concern for their neighbor (the dual command of love). This command of love is made perfect in love and forgiveness of enemies (Matt. 5:43–48). The God disclosed by Jesus makes his sun shine on the good and the bad. Jesus' teaching breaks down the proclivity people have for dividing the world into clearly identifiable friends and enemies, outsiders and insiders.

Like many of his contemporaries Jesus hoped for the intervention of God in history in the near future (imminent eschatology), yet he proclaimed that the reign of God has already begun in his teaching and action, and people are to live in response to it (eschatology in the process of realization). The eschatological thrust of Jesus' teaching (and later of Paul's) should not be invoked to undermine its effective impact (as if the nearness of the end makes ethical behavior superfluous), but is rather "a view from the future" of what life should be in the present. The fact that God's definitive reign is still in the future does not excuse us from living according to its norms and values in our everyday lives.

Jesus' teaching is a summons to conversion that is to affect the way people live in the world. In the Lord's Prayer (in the Matthean version, 6:9–10) Jesus prays that God's will be done and God's kingdom come *on earth.* In the Beatitudes, which are also in the Q source, with high claims of authenticity, Jesus calls the poor and the oppressed "blessed," not because their actual condition is such, but because the kingdom that he proclaims and enacts will confront those values and conditions that have made them marginal. This was the great value of the massive studies of Jacques Dupont on the Beatitudes, which are summarized in the essay mentioned above.[66] In all levels of this teaching from the early Q source through the Lukan writings, response to the kingdom demands complete reliance on God rather than on power or wealth.

The kingdom as proclaimed by Jesus challenged deep-seated expectations of his hearers. This is especially true in his parables, which contain frequent reversals: those who worked only one hour received the same wage as those who had worked all day; Jesus says that one should invite not friends but unknown strangers gathered from the highways to a banquet; the hated outsider, a Samaritan, teaches the true meaning of love of neighbor; the prodigal is accepted as readily as the dutiful. These reversals challenge deeply held values and invite people to enter imaginatively into a different world, providing a paradigm for the manner in which a new vision of social justice can be presented to people today.[67] Jesus' acceptance of marginal groups counters the evaluation of people by class and social status that was characteristic of first-century society. Also, by associating with those seen as ritually unclean and by his willingness to break the law on their behalf, Jesus alienates the religious establishment of his day in such a way that he is both a political and religious threat. By taking the side of these scorned people, Jesus, like the Old Testament prophets, gives a voice to the voiceless. Ultimately Jesus dies by a mode of execution reserved for those who were threats to the "public order" due to collusion between the Jerusalem temple authorities (whose power rested on proper subservience to Rome) and the Roman prefect, Pontius Pilate. Jesus' life is a paradigm of the cost of discipleship for those who take the side of the poor and the marginal.

The Gospel of Matthew and Jewish Christianity Represented by James

My reason for joining these two works together is that they reflect a similar background. Matthew, the most "Jewish" of the Gospels in its content, was written perhaps in opposition to Jewish movements at the end of the first century for a community composed of a great number of recent converts from Judaism. Similarly, James is directed at a Jewish Christian community with a theology heavily influenced by the Old Testament. They are also similar in that both stress that belief and discipleship should be translated into action on behalf of powerless and poor people.[68]

In Matthew this concern emerges in two ways. The long recognized similarities between Jesus and Moses in Matthew would suggest that Sinai and the formation of a covenant community of responsible care for each other are a concern of Matthew. Matthew's Jesus is also concerned about faith translated into action. At the end of the Sermon on the Mount, Jesus warns against people who simply say "Lord, Lord" or who prophesy and cast out demons but do not "bear fruit." The true disciple is the one "who listens to these words of mine and acts upon them" (7:24). In the scathing denunciations of the Pharisees, who may also be "Christian Pharisees" in Matthew's own community, Jesus contrasts external trappings of prestige and power with the service required of his disciples (23:1–11). The Pharisees are further castigated for stressing external observance or minutiae while neglecting the weightier things of the law, "justice, mercy and faith" (23:23; see Hos. 2:19, where three of these are qualities of the covenant).[69]

The section of Matthew most often invoked in a discussion of faith and justice by a wide spectrum of Christians and non-Christians is the "parable" of the sheep and the goats (25:31–46). Structurally this contains the final words of Jesus before his Passion and reaches backward in an arch to the very beginning of the Sermon on the Mount, where suffering and persecuted people are pronounced blessed by Jesus. The narrative is familiar. In a scene of apocalyptic judgment when the Son of man will return as king and summon all the nations of the world, they will be separated like sheep and goats, the former for eternal joy, the latter for eternal punishment. The criterion for judgment will be how they treated the king (Son of man) when he was hungry, thirsty, a stranger, naked, sick, or in prison. When both the elect and the condemned question when or how they came to the aid of the king in these circumstances he answers, "As often as you did this to the least of my brothers and sisters you did it to me" (my translation).

The story seems simple on first reading. Jesus is identified with suffering men and women, cares for them, with or without explicit Christological motivation, and brings them salvation. Yet in recent years a major debate has arisen between this "universalistic" reading and a "discipleship" reading proposed by a number of scholars and adopted by Daniel Harrington in his commentary on Matthew.[70] Based principally on the argument that the "little ones" in Matthew are Christian disciples and that "brother or sister" is similarly used, the parable is interpreted as a judgment on pagan nations that reject the proclamation of the missionary disciples who are to announce the teaching of Jesus "to all the nations" (28:16–20).[71] At present there are very competent scholars on both sides, with John Meier, among others, representing the "universalistic" view.[72] In both the universalistic and discipleship readings the important issue is that those who minister to the "least of the brothers and sisters of Jesus" are called "just" (Greek *dikaioi*). Actions that alleviate things such as hunger, thirst, and imprisonment are ways of manifesting "justice" to the world.[73]

The Jewish Christian letter of James presents a severe and pragmatic spirituality.[74] One of its early exhortations is "Be doers of the word and not hearers only, deluding yourselves" (1:22), which is followed by the definition of true religion as "to care for orphans and widows in their affliction and to keep oneself unstained by the world" (1:27). James exhorts his community to avoid partiality and in biting language mocks the deference shown to the rich and powerful, even though they are oppressing the community (2:1–7). He criticizes them for dishonoring a poor person, even though God chose the poor to become heirs of the kingdom. In line with being doers as well as hearers of the word, James says faith without works is dead and specifies one of the works as clothing and feeding a poor brother or sister (2:14–17). Near the end of the letter is one of the most violent denunciations of the rich found in the New Testament: "Come now, you rich, weep and wail over your impending miseries" (5:1). In addition to amassing gold and silver jewelry, the rich have withheld the wages of their harvesters and lived on earth in luxury and pleasure; thus "you have fattened your hearts for the day of slaughter" (5:2–6). Behind the words of James can be heard Amos of Tekoa, almost seven centuries earlier.

The Gospel of Luke and the Acts of the Apostles

The Lukan writings comprise about one-quarter of the whole New Testament. These writings, with the exception of James, contain the most explicit statements on wealth, poverty, and the use of resources.[75] Luke's special concern is manifest from his editing of the Markan tradition, and most important by the incorporation of L material (material found only in Luke), which is itself a combination of tradition and Lukan composition. Luke-Acts has also been that New Testament work most often invoked on issues of social justice and concern for the marginal.

The Lukan infancy narratives show a special concern for the *'ānāwîm,* people without money and power. In her *Magnificat* Mary praises a God who puts down the mighty from their thrones, fills the hungry with good things, and sends the rich away empty (Luke 1:52–53). The first proclamation of Jesus' birth is to people on the margin of society ("shepherds," 2:8–14); the sacrifice offered at the presentation is that determined by law for poor people (2:24); Simeon and Anna (a widow) represent faithful and just people (2:25–38). Luke begins the public ministry of Jesus not with the proclamation of the imminence of the kingdom (cf. Mark 1:15; Matt. 4:17), but with Jesus citing Isaiah 61:1–2, "the good news to the poor" (Luke 4:17–19; cf. 7:22).

Material found *only in Luke* shows concern for the poor and for the danger of wealth. In Luke it is simply "the poor" who are blessed and Luke adds woes against the rich and powerful. (6:20, 24–26). Luke presents Jesus in the form of an Old Testament prophet who takes the side of the widow (7:11–17; 18:1–8), the stranger in the land (10:25–37; 17:16), and those on the margins of society (14:12–13, 21). At the same time Luke articulates some of the harshest warnings about wealth found in the New Testament: the parables of the rich fool (12:13–21), of the unjust steward (16:1–8) and of the rich man and Lazarus (16:19–31). Though often called the "Gospel of the poor," Luke really contains far more warnings against the rich and the danger of wealth. There is no glorification or spiritualization of poverty. The good news to the poor is that wealth does not bring divine blessing, and that the fortunes of rich and poor will be reversed in the life to come. The Gospel might better be called "sad news for the wealthy."[76]

The Acts of the Apostles offers a somewhat different perspective. The early community is one that shares its goods in common and where there is no needy person (2:41–47; 4:32–37). Shared possession rather than dispossession is the goal, and almsgiving is stressed (10:2, 4, 31; 24:17). Lydia, "the seller of purple," who was a worshipper of God, shows Paul hospitality, an example of good use of resources (16:11–15), while upper-class women and men accept the gospel (17:12). In biblical terms almsgiving is not an exercise in optional charity, but an obligation in justice so much so that in later biblical thought justice is translated as "almsgiving."[77]

From this sketchy overview it is clear that the Lukan writings present a dilemma. In the Gospel, riches are evil when they become such a preoccupation that they dominate a person's whole life or when a person attempts to secure the future through them, as in the case of the rich fool (12:16–21). They are also evil, as in the parable of Dives and Lazarus (16:19–31), when they blind people to the suffering neighbor at their doorstep. Discipleship demands renunciation of one's goods and adoption of the itinerant lifestyle of Jesus. Acts does not develop the more radical statements of the Gospel. Here proper use of possessions through mutual sharing and almsgiving is commended rather than total dispossession. If hospitality to the missionary was such an important aspect of Acts (and Paul), there must have been a great number of Christians who retained their homes and resources. If almsgiving is praised, the community could not have been composed of the wandering dispossessed.

Many solutions have been proposed for this dilemma, ranging from the older view of a two-level morality, one for the committed disciple and one for the ordinary Christian, to views that Luke accurately portrays the difference between the teaching of the earthly Jesus and its accommodation in the ongoing life of a first-century church.[78] In the latter case the teaching of Jesus is only of historical interest and possesses no lasting value as a model or ideal for subsequent Christians.

I would suggest (somewhat tentatively) that attention to the social setting of the final composition of Luke-Acts offers guidelines for interpretation. Luke-Acts was put together most likely in a Hellenistic city between A.D. 85 and 95. At the time more and more people of relative means and higher social status were entering the church. As I noted earlier, economic difference in antiquity was accompanied by social discrimination and often scorn for "the lower classes." By stressing the radical poverty of Jesus and his first followers and by emphasizing their origins among people of low status, Luke reminds his community of their "roots." Though Jesus can be acclaimed as "Lord and Savior," titles normally reserved for the Roman emperor, he himself was of low status and died a criminal's death. His followers lived as a community without status and class division. At the same time in the Jewish tradition of almsgiving (Tobit 4:10: "For almsgiving delivers from death and keeps you from entering the darkness"), Luke exhorts his community to a proper use of wealth by putting it at the service of others. The old Deuteronomic ideal of a community where there are no needy persons has been resurrected by Luke (Deut. 15:4; Acts 4:34).

In surveying the biblical material, we have noted a consistent biblical concern for the poor and powerless, the traditional "works of mercy" (e.g., direct aid to the poor; sheltering the homeless, welcoming the stranger [immigrant], see Matt. 25:31–46). These have undoubtedly been a part of the Church's life from its infancy, although they do not exhaust the Church's ministry of social justice. Surveying the early centuries the distinguished early church historian Peter Brown has written:

> The Christian community suddenly came to appeal to men who felt deserted. At a time of inflation the Christians invested large sums of liquid capital in people; at a time of universal brutality the courage of Christian martyrs was impressive; during public emergencies such as plague or rioting, the Christian clergy were shown to be the only united group in the town, able to look after the burial of the dead and to organize food supplies.[79]

Today both nationally and internationally the Church is summoned to be a "light to the nations" in its direct response to the tattered cloak of suffering worn by such a mass of humanity.

At the same time the biblical context of statements on the poor most often involves a criticism of the abuses of the wealthy, frequently in vivid terms. The more difficult task is to appropriate the prophetic critique of wealth and injustice. The Church in the United States is an established and respected institution within a modern (or even postmodern) complex economic structure. The Church also depends on the resources and generosity of people of power and wealth. One of the most demanding ministries of church leaders today, is, like the author of Luke-Acts, to address people of means, helping them to recall their "roots" as a church and guiding them in proper use of resources. Church leaders can raise the consciousness of people about those very kinds of issues that have distinguished church teaching over the last century, and are called on to speak out as forcefully on issues of injustice as strongly as they have on protection of human life. This is certainly done by papal teaching and by the agencies of the U.S. Conference of Catholic Bishops, but often this teaching, because of its volume and complexity, is not appropriated or communicated to local churches. It is also inevitable that, as the Church really adopts the "option for the poor" and the powerless, it will alienate certain powerful groups and carry the cross of rejection. Throughout the world we continually see Catholics murdered because of their exposing of injustice and advocacy for the poor.

Pauline Theology and Concerns for Faith and Justice

A certain paradox confronts us when we approach Paul. On the one hand, no New Testament author uses the Greek term *dikaiosynē* (justice) more than Paul, nor does any other author link it so explicitly with issues of faith. Yet the contemporary concern for social justice has been most often based on Old Testament considerations (the exodus, the prophetic concern for the poor) or on the teaching of Jesus. Three principal reasons explain the neglect of Paul. First, the traditional theological debate over "faith and works" and justification by faith has given a radical individualistic bent to presentations of Pauline theology, often phrased in terms of how the individual sinner finds acceptance by God. Second, since Paul is the most "theological" of the New Testament writers, it is those portions of his letters that receive prime attention. The latter sections of most letters where Paul deals with practical problems facing the communities are rushed through, nor is their relation to the theological sections developed. Third, since Albert Schweitzer, Paul has been accused of teaching only an "interim ethic." Evidence for this would be in his exhortation to people not to change their marital or social status because "the time is short." Paul's eschatological view that the shape of the world is passing away and his own personal hope to be with the Lord has made some interpreters doubt whether Paul's ethics offer any help for Christians settling in for the long haul of history. I would like to offer some suggestions on how both Paul's theology and his pastoral engagement in the lives of his communities provide resources for the faith that does justice.

Central to Paul's thought is the proclamation of the Christ event, which Joseph A. Fitzmyer has described as "the meaning that the person and lordship of Jesus of Nazareth had and still has for human history and existence."[80] It is equivalent to "objective redemption" and comprises "the complex of decisive moments of the earthly and risen life of Jesus Christ," specifically, his Passion, death, and resurrection along with his burial, exaltation, and heavenly intercession. This Christ event as proclaimed and lived by Paul has a number of implications for issues of social justice.[81]

The Christ Event as the Foundation of Christian Faith Demands Responsibility for the World

Christian faith in the death and resurrection is not simply faith in the promise of eternal life, but faith in the *victory over death* achieved in Jesus. Through baptism Christians participate *already* in this victory: "We were buried therefore with him by baptism into death, so that as Christ was raised from the dead by the glory of the Father, we too might *walk in the newness of life*" (Rom. 6:4). Here in Romans, Paul does *not say*, as does the author of Colossians (3:1), that Christians "were raised with Christ." The resurrection has an ethical counterpart: "walking in the newness of life." Also in Paul, the Christian contrast is *not* between earth and heaven or between material and spiritual reality but between the "old age" and "the new" (see esp. Rom. 8; 2 Cor. 5:16–21). Fundamental to new life in Christ is the experience of "power": "With great power the Apostles gave testimony to the resurrection of the Lord Jesus" (Acts 4:32–37; cf. 1 Cor. 1:18–31; Phil. 3:10). The Christian is to be a *witness in mission* of the victory over death and the transforming power of the resurrection. To pursue the quest for justice in faith means that the Christian walks in confidence that evil is not Lord of life and that even death for the sake of others cannot separate a person from the love of God (Rom. 8:28–39).

Justification of the Sinner by God's Grace through Faith Results in a Personal and Communal Liberation That Enables People to Live for Others Rather Than for Self

Theologically, Paul states that the Christ event frees the Christian from sin, law, and death. Equally important as this "freedom from" is the Pauline notion of "freedom for." Paul states this succinctly: "For freedom Christ has set us free" (Gal. 5:1a). Freedom for Paul is liberation from the self-serving and self-destructive aspects of "striving" and "boasting" in human achievements in order to direct one's attention to the needs of others. In Galatians, which, along with Romans is his major theological statement on justification, after somewhat polemically rejecting those opponents who want to reimpose Jewish practices on Gentile Christians, Paul says: "For you were called for freedom, brothers and sisters. But do not use this freedom as an opportunity for self-indulgence ['flesh'], but through love become servants of one another" (5:13). Paul then goes on to describe "walking according to the spirit" and "walking according to the flesh" (5:16–21). The virtues and vices listed here for the most part either foster or destroy life in community. Paul then concludes this whole section with the statement: "Bear one another's burdens, and so you will fulfill the law of Christ" (6:2). Therefore, the justified and graced Christian is a person who seeks a community not of isolated individuals, but one in which concern for the weak and suffering is the touchstone of living according to the law of Christ.

Pauline Eschatology Does Not Warrant an "Interim Ethic," But Rather Summons Christians to Responsibility for Life in the World

Since Albert Schweitzer's challenge that Paul provided only an "interim ethic," significant research has been done on the social context and meaning of Paul's eschatology.[82] For Paul, the Christian lives between the "already" and the "not yet." Through Christ the evil powers have been subdued (Phil. 2:10–11) and Christians live in the new age (1 Cor. 10:11; 2 Cor. 5:17). Yet Paul has an eschatological reservation. All creation is groaning (Rom. 8:23), and Christians are to look forward to the final victory over death when the risen Christ hands over the kingdom to his Father (1 Cor. 15:51–54). Between the "already" and the "not yet," Christians are to walk in the newness of life and not let sin reign in their mortal bodies (Rom. 6:12). They should yield themselves to God so that they might become instruments and servants of justice (6:13, 18). Eschatology thus provides a *view from the end*, a vision of a restored creation and of the kind of community that should exist in the world, and summons Christians to implement this vision, however incomplete, in their individual and social lives.

Pastoral Practice

As he addresses issues that arise in his communities, Paul translates his theological vision into practice. Throughout his missionary career he organized collections for the poor churches of Judea (1 Cor. 16:1–4; 2 Cor. 8–9).[83] Peter Brown stresses that Paul (unlike the tradition of Jesus) did not advocate renunciation of property but "was convinced that the secret of the unity of believers lay in a steady circulation of goods among 'the brethren.'"[84] The collection is not simply an act of charity, but a way to affirm solidarity between the Greek churches and the Jerusalem mother church.

A second major issue was the dispute over the celebration of the Lord's Supper.[85] At Corinth the Eucharist was celebrated in the context of an ordinary meal, when Christians gathered in the evening at the end of an ordinary working day. The only place with enough space for a community gathering would normally have been the home of one of the more prosperous members of the community.

Paul states the problem starkly: "I heard that when you meet as a community [as a church], there are divisions among you." Then he gives his initial judgment on the situation: "When you meet in one place, then, *it is not to eat the Lord's supper*" (emphasis mine), for "in eating, each one goes ahead with their own supper and one goes hungry, while another gets drunk" (1 Cor. 11:22–23, NAB).

This community quarrel had social and ethical dimensions. Apparently the more prosperous members of the community simply became hungry and tired waiting for the small artisans and day laborers to arrive after a working day that stretched from dawn to dusk. They began the celebration of the Lord's Supper and also ate special food and drink that they had prepared for themselves rather than sharing it with others. Paul reacts strongly to this practice ("Do you not have houses in which you can eat or drink?" 11:22) and highlights the evil effect of this practice ("Do you show contempt for the church of God, and humiliate those who have nothing?" [the Greek here is literally "the have nots"]). Paul is, in effect, saying that those social distinctions between upper-class and lower-class people that are part of the fabric of the Hellenistic world have no place in the Christian assembly. One might recall here Paul's early statement to the Galatians that in Christ there is neither Jew nor Greek, slave nor free, male and female (3:26).

Paul then quotes the words of institution that make present again the self-offering of Christ: "my body for you." The "you" are all the Christians equally. As Paul has noted in other places, the death of Jesus is an example of one who did not choose his own benefit but that of others, and Christ died for the weak or marginal Christian brother or sister as well as for the powerful (see esp. Rom. 14:9; 1 Cor. 8:11–13). The practices of the Corinthians are a direct affront to the example of Christ. By preferring their own good and shaming other members of the community of lower social and economic status, they are making a mockery of the Eucharist. This explains Paul's harsh judgment that, in effect, the community is not really celebrating the Lord's Supper.

Paul's directives here show that issues of justice and concern for the more vulnerable members of the community enter into the most central act of Christian community, the celebration of the Lord's Supper. They also show Paul's constant concern for the weaker members of the community and for the creation of a community in which economic and social divisions do not invalidate the faith that the community as a whole professes. Contemporary Christians are faced with the challenge to join together worship and social action, to live in such a fashion that there is no gap between the faith they celebrate on Sunday and the way they live the other six days of the week.[86]

TOWARD APPROPRIATION OF THE BIBLICAL WITNESS

The purpose of this chapter thus far has been twofold: to call attention to those principal biblical texts that would inform the Christian conscience on issues of social and economic justice (Ricoeur's "first naiveté") and to present some explanation and interpretation of these texts, along with bibliographical resources for further study. Now I would like, again in debt to Ricoeur, to propose some suggestions for the continuing appropriation of the biblical tradition.

In a seminal essay Ricoeur states that "interpretation concerns essentially the power of the work to disclose a world"[87] and that interpretation "overcomes distanciation" and "actualizes the meaning of the text for the present reader."[88] He then notes that "appropriation is the concept which is suitable for the actualization of meaning as addressed to someone" and "as appropriation, interpretation becomes an event."[89] Ricoeur understands "appropriation" in the terms of the German *Aneigen*, which conveys the sense of making one's own what was initially "alien."[90] The English neologism *owning-ship* might well capture Ricoeur's understanding. Appropriation involves both dispossession and a new possession. It involves moving beyond both sedimented meanings of texts as well as the myth of subjectivity where the person "subjects" meaning to intention. Appropriation follows the "arrow of meaning" in a text and engenders a new self-understanding.[91] The cryptic phrase *arrow of meaning* is important since, throughout his works on biblical interpretation, Ricoeur speaks of the "surplus of meaning" of biblical texts and of following the direction of the text itself rather than literal reproduction. In areas of social justice the direction to which the text points opens ways to new applications and new appropriations.

Sandra Schneiders, who has herself appropriated carefully the methods of Paul Ricoeur and Hans Gadamer, describes the process of appropriation as primarily the "fusion of horizons," whereby "the world horizon of the reader fuses with the horizon of the world projected by the text."[92] She then states: "Appropriation of the meaning of a text, the transformative achievement of interpretation, is neither mastery of the text by the reader (an extraction of its meaning by the application of method) nor mastery of a reader by the text (a blind submission to what the text says) but an ongoing dialogue with the text about its subject matter."[93] If appropriation (making one's own) is to continue as part of the ecclesial praxis of the church, I would like to propose some elements that will foster ongoing appropriation.

First, if the Bible is to remain a dialogue partner with issues of social justice, a continuing task will be to maintain the power of the biblical renewal so that the people of God, pastoral ministers, and church leaders will continue to be enriched and challenged by biblical texts. There is constant need "to renew the renewal."[94] Yet, as Francis Moloney, the Katherine Drexel Professor of Religious Studies at The Catholic University of America and former member of the Vatican Theological Commission, has written recently: "There is every indication that the golden era of biblical enthusiasm in the Catholic Church is on the wane. There is a return to a new dogmatism."[95] This new dogmatism is shown in the tendency to prefer the *Catechism of the Catholic Church* over biblical teaching and to ground theology and ethics almost exclusively in magisterial statements.[96]

Such new dogmatism will stifle the continued exploration of the relation of the Bible to issues of justice, wider than those selected in this chapter. In this volume, following the magisterial tradition since Pope Leo XIII, "social justice" has been understood mainly in relation to socioeconomic issues, and the biblical themes chosen have followed this lead. Yet biblical justice, that is, forging right relationships between God and humanity and within the human family, must today confront a range of issues often more fundamental than socioeconomic ones. Issues of gender and of war and peace are glaring omissions from the present chapter, mainly because they have not been the central focus of the corpus of social teaching covered in this volume. Future concerns would bring the Bible to bear on the reconciliation of differences between groups that demonize each other, often over long suppressed hatreds, and the propensity toward lethal violence that often invokes the Bible itself as a warrant.[97] In these areas and others that will emerge, the biblical renewal must be continually renewed.

At the same time Catholic tradition and practice is not "biblicist," and the Bible will always be in dialogue with other sources. In a programmatic essay James Gustafson argued that "comprehensive and coherent theological ethics must be adequate with reference to the four following sources": (1) the Bible and Christian tradition; (2) philosophical methods, insights, and principles; (3) scientific information and methods that are relevant; and (4) human experience, broadly conceived.[98] Since each of these "reference points" has its own methods and challenges, dialogue between them must involve communities of interpretation that engage in multiple conversations between the disciplines themselves, as well as between sacred texts, traditions, and possible applications.[99] Today's application could easily become tomorrow's horror, as history sadly confirms.

Communities of interpretation must also be communities of faithful witness. A significant obstacle to the engagement of the Bible and issues of social justice is often the absence of integrity between proclamation and practice. Both the Old and New Testaments summon religious leaders and people of faith to an integrity of belief and practice (see esp. Isa. 9:1–6; Jer. 29:13–14, cited in Mark 7:6; Matt. 7:21–28; James 1:22). The social doctrine of the Church often seems produced for external consumption rather than internal appropriation. Though selection of the hierarchy is cloaked in secrecy, the average Catholic would be hard pressed to say that concern for social justice has been a major criterion in the appointment of bishops. There have been many instances where bishops, noted for their commitment to the poor and to their confrontation with powerful forces, are succeeded by those opposed to those very commitments.[100] Theologians are often stronger in articulating a prophetic vision than living it. The Church has been consistently one of the strongest world advocates for human rights and just treatment of all people, yet one can only wonder if these same concerns guide church authorities when dealing with internal issues.[101]

In conclusion, the engagement of biblical studies with Catholic social teaching, though relatively recent, offers much promise, especially in shaping the Catholic conscience and imagination, and also in forming communities of concern. One can only hope that this engagement will lead to a long and fruitful marriage.

NOTES

1. For helpful surveys, see John A. Coleman, ed., *One Hundred Years of Catholic Social Thought: Celebration and Challenge* (Maryknoll, N.Y.: Orbis, 1991); Charles E. Curran, *Catholic Social Teaching 1891–Present: A Historical, Theological and Ethical Analysis* (Washington, D.C.: Georgetown University Press, 2002); Michael J. Schuck, *That They Be One: The Social Teaching of the Papal Encyclicals, 1740–1989* (Washington, D.C.: Georgetown University Press, 1991); for Pope John Paul II, Gerard Biegel, *Faith and Social Justice in the Teaching of Pope John Paul II* (New York: Peter Lang, 1997); John Conley and Joseph Koterski, eds., *Prophecy and Diplomacy: The Moral Doctrine of John Paul II* (Bronx, N.Y.: Fordham University Press, 1999); and the essays in Charles E. Curran and Richard A. McCormick, eds., *John Paul II and Moral Theology* (Mahwah, N.J.: Paulist, 1998), 237–375.

2. Helpful surveys are Raymond F. Collins, *Introduction to the New Testament* (New York: Doubleday, 1983), 272–386; and Raymond E. Brown, "Church Pronouncements," in *The New Jerome Biblical Commentary*, ed. R. E. Brown, J. A. Fitzmyer, and R. E. Murphy (Englewood Cliffs, N.J.: Prentice Hall, 1990), 1166–75.

3. Unless otherwise noted all translations are from the New Revised Standard Version (New York: Oxford University Press, 1989) with occasional use of the New American Bible (New York: Catholic Book Publishing Co., 1970, 1986).

4. In Dean Bechard, ed. and trans., *The Scripture Documents: An Anthology of Official Catholic Teachings* (Collegeville, Minn.: Liturgical, 2002), 115–39.

5. *Dogmatic Constitution on Divine Revelation* (*Dei verbum*), number 24, and the *Decree on the Training of Priests* (*Optatum totius*), number 16, cites also Leo XIII, *Providentissimus Deus*, number 33, in *Scripture Documents*, number 50, and Benedict XV, *Spiritus Paraclitus*, number 14. All of these documents in ibid., 100.

6. "Forum," *Religion and American Culture* 10 (winter 2000): 25.

7. LE 4. See the important study of the use of scripture in LE by David Hollenbach, "Human Word and the Story of Creation: Theology and Ethics in *Laborem Exercens*," in *Catholic Social Thought and the New World Order*, ed. Oliver F. Williams and John W. Houck (Notre Dame, Ind.: University of Notre Dame Press, 1993), 59–77. While appreciative of the encyclical's use of scripture, Hollenbach notes certain defects, mainly the absence of a nuanced discussion of Genesis 1–11.

8. Pope John Paul II, "Special Sensitivity to Those in Distress," in *Justice in the Marketplace: Collected Statements of the Vatican and the U.S. Catholic Bishops on Economic Policy, 1891–1984*, ed. David M. Byers (Washington, D.C.: U.S. Catholic Conference, 1985), 351. The pope himself comments that he has used this parable "on various occasions."

9. See esp. James M. Gustafson, "The Changing Use of the Bible in Christian Ethics" and "The Place of Scripture in Christian Ethics: A Methodological Study," in *Readings in Moral Theology No. 4: The Use of Scripture in Moral Theology*, ed. C. Curran and R. McCormick (New York: Paulist, 1984), 133–78.

10. *Economic Justice for All: Pastoral Letter on Catholic Social Teaching and the U.S. Economy* (Washington, D.C.: National Conference of Catholic

Bishops, 1986). Also in David J. O'Brien and Thomas A. Shannon, eds., *Catholic Social Teaching: The Documentary Heritage* (Maryknoll, N.Y.: Orbis, 1998), 572–680.

11. Oral communication from Archbishop Rembert Weakland to the committee.

12. On scripture as a "moral reminder," esp. in the works of Josef Fuchs and Karl Rahner, see William C. Spohn, "Scripture as Moral Reminder," chap. 2 in *What Are They Saying About Scripture and Ethics*? 2d ed. (New York: Paulist, 1995).

13. Proof texting has its modern origin in the period of post-Reformation Lutheran orthodoxy, when collections of biblical texts (*dicta probantia*) were used to buttress theological positions.

14. Intertextuality, a concept appropriated from the work of the French literary theorist Julia Kristeva, "suggests that each text is situated for each reader in an ever-changing web composed of innumerable texts." Cited from E. Castelli et al., *The Postmodern Bible* (New Haven, Conn.: Yale University Press, 1995), 130.

15. Dorothy Lee, *Flesh and Glory: Symbol, Gender and Theology in the Gospel of John* (New York: Crossroad, 2002), 4–7; Sandra M. Schneiders, *The Revelatory Text: Interpreting the New Testament as Sacred Scripture*, 2d ed. (Collegeville, Minn.: Liturgical, 1999), esp. 132–56.

16. Paul Ricoeur, *Interpretation Theory: Discourse and the Surplus of Meaning* (Fort Worth: Texas Christian University Press, 1976), 24, as cited in Lee, *Flesh and Glory*, 6.

17. Lee, *Flesh and Glory*, 6.

18. Schneiders describes "criticism" as "the process of distancing the text, which results in a second naiveté." This involves a double distancing, first of the text itself so that its independence and intrinsic power can be recognized, and second, a distancing from the worldview of the authors. See *Revelatory Text*, 169–70.

19. Ricoeur, *Interpretation Theory*, 30.

20. On semantic autonomy, see Schneiders, *Revelatory Text,* 142–44; on developing traditions, see Michael Fishbane, *Biblical Interpretation in Ancient Israel* (New York: Oxford University Press, 1985).

21. Carroll Stuhlmueller calls the exodus the "controlling theme" of Second Isaiah. See "Deutero-Isaiah and Trito-Isaiah," *New Jerome Biblical Commentary*, 329–48.

22. Willard M. Swartley, *Israel's Scripture Traditions and the Synoptic Gospels: Story Shaping Story* (Peabody, Mass.: Hendrickson, 1994).

23. *Dei verbum*, number 24.

24. Though monographs on the Bible and social justice are relatively few, the following give fine overviews: Bruce C. Birch, *Let Justice Roll: The Old Testament, Ethics, and the Christian Life* (Louisville, Ky.: Westminster/John Knox, 1991) and *What Does The Lord Require? The Old Testament Call to Social Witness* (Philadelphia: Westminster, 1985); Anthony B. Ceresko, *Introduction to the Old Testament: A Liberation Perspective* (Maryknoll, N.Y.: Orbis, 1992); Stephen C. Mott, *Biblical Ethics and Social Change* (New York: Oxford University Press, 1982); J. David Pleins, *The Social Visions of the Hebrew Bible: A Theological Introduction* (Louisville, Ky.: Westminster/John Knox, 2001).

25. Philip Esler, *Community and Gospel in Luke-Acts: The Social and Political Motivation of Lucan Theology*, SNTSMS, no. 57 (Cambridge: Cambridge University Press, 1987), 53.

26. James F. Gustafson, *Can Ethics Be Christian*? (Chicago: University of Chicago Press, 1975), 48–81.

27. On Hans Gadamer, see Schneiders, *Revelatory Text*, esp. 42–43, 140–42, 172–76.

28. Paul Tillich, *Systematic Theology* (Chicago: University of Chicago Press, 1967), 1:59–66.

29. David Tracy, *The Analogical Imagination: Christian Theology and the Culture of Pluralism* (New York: Crossroad, 1981), 24–27, 60–61, 405–45.

30. For more extensive bibliography, see John R. Donahue, *What Does the Lord Require? A Bibliographical Essay on the Bible and Social Justice* (St. Louis, Mo.: Institute of Jesuit Sources, 2000).

31. The major studies are Eliezer Berkovits, "The Biblical Meaning of Justice," *Judaism* 18 (1969): 188–209; Pietro Bovati, *Re-establishing Justice: Legal Terms, Concepts and Procedures in the Hebrew Bible*, trans. M. J. Smith, *Journal for the Study of the Old Testament*, Supplement 105 (Sheffield, England: JSOT, 1994); Léon Epsztein, *Social Justice in the Ancient Near East and the People of the Bible* (London: SCM, 1986); Barbara Johnson, "*mišpāṭ*," in *Theological Dictionary of the Old Testament*, ed. G. Johannes Botterweck, H. Ringgren, and H.-J. Fabry (Grand Rapids, Mich.: Eerdmans, 2003), 9:86–98, and "*ṣĕdāqāh*," ibid., 12:239–64; G. Reventlow and Y. Hoffman, eds., *Justice and Righteousness: Biblical Themes and*

Their Influence, JSOT, Supplement, no. 137 (Sheffield, England: JSOT, 1992); J. Pedersen, *Israel: Its Life and Culture* (London: Oxford University Press, 1926), I–II 337–40; K. H.-J. Fahlgren, *Sedàkà, nahestehende und entgegengesetze Begriffe im Alten Testament* (Uppsala: Almquist und Wiksells, 1932), 81. Fahlgren describes justice as *Gemeinschafttreue*, that is, fidelity in communal life; Moshe Weinfeld, *Social Justice in Ancient Israel and in the Ancient Near East* (Minneapolis: Fortress; Jerusalem: Magnes, 1995).

32. I proposed this definition in "Biblical Perspectives on Justice," in *The Faith That Does Justice*, ed. John Haughey (New York: Paulist, 1977), 69. It is similar to the perspectives now described by Johnson, "*ṣĕdāqāh*," esp. 246–47. See also Joseph A. Fitzmyer, "What Do the Scriptures Say About Injustice?" in *Jesuit Education 21: Conference Proceedings on the Future of Jesuit Higher Education*, ed. Martin Tripole (Philadelphia: St. Joseph's University and Press, 2000), 99–112. Fitzmyer offers a careful philological discussion of the biblical terms for justice. In their responses Richard Clifford (ibid., 113–16) and Mark Smith (ibid., 119–22) extend the implications of Fitzmyer's remarks. See esp. Smith: "Accordingly Social Justice is embedded in the larger context of relations with God. Social Justice advances right relations with both the human and the divine" (122).

33. See also the important study of James M. Walsh, *The Mighty from Their Thrones* (Philadelphia: Fortress, 1987). Walsh describes *ṣedeq* as a "consensus which shapes God's people." He also studies the related concept of *nāqām,* "vengeance," which is not simply punishment but the restoration of justice.

34. Walter Brueggemann, *Isaiah 1–39*, *Westminster Bible Companion* (Louisville, Ky.: Westminster/John Knox, 1998), 48.

35. Johnson, "*mišpāṭ*," 93.

36. See esp. Thomas Leclerc, "*mispat*, Justice in the Book of Isaiah" (Ph.D. diss., Harvard University, 1998).

37. Martin Noth, "The Major Themes of the Tradition in the Pentateuch and Their Origin," in *A History of the Pentateuchal Traditions*, trans. B. Anderson (Englewood Cliffs, N.J.: Prentice Hall, 1972), 46–62; Gerhard Von Rad, *The Problem of the Hexateuch and Other Essays* (New York: McGraw Hill, 1966).

38. The presentation of creation here follows Claus Westermann, *Creation* (Philadelphia: Fortress, 1974); idem, *Genesis: A Practical Commentary* (Grand Rapids, Mich.: Eerdmans, 1987). Along with *Creation*, this offers a fine digest of Westermann's exegesis. See also Bernhard Anderson, ed., *Creation in the Old Testament* (Philadelphia: Fortress; London: SPCK, 1984), a collection of classic essays on creation.

39. Westermann, *Creation*, 42.

40. Westermann, *Genesis 1–11: A Commentary*, trans. J. Scullion (Minneapolis: Augsburg, 1984), 60–64.

41. Westermann, *Creation*, 10.

42. Westermann, *Genesis 1–11*, 51–53.

43. Phyllis Trible, *God and the Rhetoric of Sexuality* (Philadelphia: Fortress, 1978), 101–2.

44. Ibid., esp. 12–23, 72–105.

45. Westermann, *Creation*, 92–93.

46. Terence E. Fretheim, *Exodus, Interpretation: A Bible for Teaching and Preaching* (Louisville, Ky.: John Knox, 1991). Excellent commentary, esp. on Exod. 1–15, with sensitivity to issues of liberation and justice.

47. Michael Walzer, *Exodus and Revolution* (New York: Basic, 1985), 53, 73–90.

48. Ibid., 27.

49. Cheryl J. Exum, "'You Shall Let Every Daughter Live': A Study of Exodus 1:18–2:10," *Semeia* 28 (1983): 63–82; Tikva Frymer Kensky, *Reading the Women of the Bible* (New York: Schocken, 2002), 24–26.

50. See Terence Fretheim, "The Plagues as Ecological Signs of Historical Disaster," *Journal of Biblical Literature* 110 (fall 1991): 385–96. Fretheim argues that the plagues are signs that nature itself revolts against the moral injustice of Pharaoh's reign.

51. See the excellent treatments in Walter Harrelson, *The Ten Commandments and Human Rights* (Philadelphia: Fortress, 1980; reprint, Macon, Ga.: Mercer University Press, 1997); Pleins, *The Social Visions of the Hebrew Bible*, 41–91; and Norbert Lohfink, "Poverty in the Laws of the Ancient Near East and the Bible," *Theological Studies* 52 (1991): 34–50.

52. Norbert Lohfink, *Option for the Poor: The Basic Principle of Liberation Theology in Light of the Bible* (Berkeley, Calif.: Bibal, 1988).

53. In a recent study, *Injustice Made Legal: Deuteronomic Law and the Plight of Widows, Stangers,*

and Orphans in Ancient Israel (Grand Rapids, Mich.: Eerdmans, 2003), Harold V. Bennett employs a "critical theory" of law to argue that all law ultimately benefits those in power and applies this theory to Israelite laws concerning the disadvantaged. His argument ultimately rests on a select contemporary theory of law.

54. Paul D. Hanson, *The People Called: The Growth of Community in the Bible* (San Francisco: Harper and Row, 1986).

55. See Lohfink, "Poverty in the Laws."

56. On the social importance of covenant, see esp. Walter Brueggemann, *A Social Reading of the Old Testament*, ed. Patrick D. Miller (Minneapolis: Fortress, 1994), 43–69.

57. John G. Gammie, *Holiness in Israel* (Minneapolis: Fortress, 1989).

58. Hanson, *The People Called*, 47.

59. The literature on the poor in the Bible is immense. See esp. the articles in *The Theological Dictionary of the Old Testament*, ed. G. J. Botterwick and H. Ringgren (Grand Rapids, Mich.: Eerdmans, 1977–), "*'ebyôn*," 1:27–41; "*dal*," vol. 3:208–30; and in *The Theological Dictionary of the New Testament*, "*ptōchos*," 6:885–915; J. David Pleins, "Poor, Poverty (Old Testament)," in *The Anchor Bible Dictionary*, ed. David N. Freedman (New York: Doubleday, 1992), 5:403–14; F. C. Fensham, "Widow, Orphan and the Poor in Ancient Near Eastern Legal and Wisdom Literature," *Journal of Near Eastern Studies* 21 (1962): 129–39; A. George, ed., *Gospel Poverty: Essays in Biblical Theology* (Chicago: Franciscan Herald, 1977), a very important collection of essays by leading French biblical scholars. The essays by George on the Old Testament and Dupont on the New Testament are especially good; Robert Gnuse, *You Shall Not Steal: Community and Property in the Biblical Tradition* (Maryknoll, N.Y.: Orbis, 1985).

60. Helpful overviews of the prophets are found in Paul J. Achtemeier and James L. Mays, eds., *Interpreting the Prophets* (Philadelphia: Fortress, 1987), a series of articles originally published in *Interpretation*. They treat mainly literary and historical problems with the essays on Jeremiah by Brueggemann and Holladay especially helpful, as is the "Resources for Studying the Prophets" by J. Limburg; Walter Brueggemann, *The Prophetic Imagination* (Philadelphia: Fortress, 1978); Joseph Blenkinsopp, *A History of Prophecy in Israel*, rev. ed. (Louisville, Ky.: Westminster/John Knox, 1996), excellent standard introductions to all aspects of the prophets; Carol J. Dempsey, *The Prophets: A Liberation-Critical Reading* (Minneapolis: Fortress, 2000); Hemchand Gossai, *Justice, Righteousness, and the Social Critique of the Eighth-Century Prophets*, American University Studies, Series VII, Theology and Religion (New York: Peter Lang, 1993); James Limburg, *The Prophets and the Powerless* (Atlanta: John Knox, 1977); James L. Mays, "Justice: Perspectives from the Prophetic Tradition," in *Prophecy in Israel: Search for an Identity*, ed. David L. Peterson (Philadelphia: Fortress, 1987), 144–58; also in *Interpretation* 37 (1983): 5–17.

61. Mays, "Justice," 9.

62. The rise of apocalyptic literature and thought dates from the postexilic period. It involved significant transformation of Israel's thought and religion, and its implications for issues of social justice would require another chapter. Two characteristics are, however, noteworthy: first, the decline of prophecy and, second, the hope for a "new heaven and a new earth" rather than for a transformed society. Excellent studies are John J. Collins, *The Apocalyptic Imagination: An Introduction to Jewish Apocalyptic* (Grand Rapids, Mich.: Eerdmans, 1998); and Paul D. Hanson, *The Dawn of Apocalyptic* (Philadelphia: Fortress, 1975).

63. Alexander A. DiLella and Patrick Skehan, *The Wisdom of Ben Sira*, Anchor Bible, 39 (New York: Doubleday, 1987), 88–90.

64. Strongly emphasized by the Indian biblical scholar, the late George Soares-Prabhu; see "Class in the Bible: The Biblical Poor, A Social Class?" *Vidyajoti* 49 (1985): 322–46.

65. The literature on Jesus and the kingdom is encyclopedic. Some helpful studies are Bruce Chilton and J. H. McDonald, *Jesus and the Ethics of the Kingdom* (Grand Rapids, Mich.: Eerdmans, 1987); William R. Herzog II, *Jesus, Justice and the Reign of God: A Ministry of Liberation* (Louisville, Ky.: Westminster/John Knox, 1999); John Meier, *A Marginal Jew: Rethinking the Historical Jesus: Mentor, Message and Miracles* (Garden City, N.Y.: Doubleday, 1994), which treats extensively Jesus' relation to John, his kingdom proclamation, and miracles; S. C. Mott, *Jesus and Social Ethics*, Grove Booklets on Ethics, 55 (Malden, Mass.: Institute for Christian Renewal, 1984), also published in *Journal of Religious Ethics* 15, no. 2 (1987): 225–66; E. P. Sanders, *Jesus*

and Judaism (Philadelphia: Fortress, 1985), 123–245 (on kingdom) and *The Historical Figure of Jesus* (New York: Penguin, 1993), 169–204; N. T. Wright, *Jesus and the Victory of God* (Minneapolis: Fortress, 1996), 198–474. Some helpful articles are Ernst Käsemann, "The Eschatological Royal Reign of God," in *Your Kingdom Come: Mission Perspectives*, Commission on World Mission and Evangelism (Geneva: World Council of Churches, 1981); Norbert Lohfink, "The Kingdom of God and the Economy in the Bible," *Communio* 13 (1986): 216–31.

66. George, ed., *Gospel Poverty*.

67. See esp. Michael Cook, *Jesus' Parables and the Faith That Does Justice, Studies in the Spirituality of the Jesuits* 24, no. 5 (St. Louis, Mo.: Institute of Jesuit Sources, 1992); William R. Herzog II, *Parables as Subversive Speech: Jesus as Pedagogue of the Oppressed* (Louisville, Ky.: Westminster/John Knox, 1994).

68. Until recently studies of Matthew have not focused on the implications of the gospel for issues of social justice. Some helpful studies are David Balch, ed., *Social History of the Matthean Community: Cross Disciplinary Approaches* (Minneapolis: Fortress, 1991); Warren Carter, *Matthew and the Margins: A Sociopolitical and Religious Reading* (Maryknoll, N.Y.: Orbis, 2000) and idem, *Matthew and Empire: Initial Explorations* (Harrisburg, Pa.: Trinity Press International, 2001). Matthew's ethics, especially in concern for the poor, are very much part of his Jewish identity. See Anthony J. Saldarini, *Matthew's Christian-Jewish Community* (Chicago: University of Chicago Press, 1994). A very important study on social concerns in Judaism is Gildas Hamel, *Poverty and Charity in Roman Palestine, First Three Centuries C.E.* (Berkeley: University of California Press, 1990). An important scholarly study that will influence future research on the question of "rich and poor" in first-century Judaism is Catherine M. Murphy, *Wealth in the Dead Sea Scrolls and the Qumran Community* (Leiden: E. J. Brill, 2000).

69. See David Garland, *The Intention of Matthew 23, Novum Testamentum* Supplements, 52 (Leiden: E. J. Brill, 1979).

70. Daniel Harrington, *The Gospel of Matthew, Sacra Pagina*, 1 (Collegeville, Minn.: Liturgical, 1991), 355–60.

71. Lamar Cope, "Matthew XXV: 31–46, 'The Sheep and the Goats' Reinterpreted," *Novum Testamentum* 11 (1969): 32–44.

72. John Meier, *Matthew*, New Testament Message 3 (Wilmington, Del.: Michael Glazier, 1980), 301–6.

73. For the "discipleship" interpretation, see John R. Donahue, "The 'Parable' of the Sheep and the Goats: A Challenge to Christian Ethics," *Theological Studies* 47 (1986): 3–31; *The Gospel in Parable: Metaphor, Narrative and Theology in the Synoptic Gospels* (Philadelphia: Fortress, 1988), 109–25.

74. See esp. Pedrito U. Maynard-Reid, *Poverty and Wealth in James* (Maryknoll, N.Y.: Orbis, 1987); Greg Forster, *The Ethics of the Letter of James* (Cambridge: Grove, 2002).

75. The writings on Luke and economic questions are extensive. See esp. John R. Donahue, "Two Decades of Research on the Rich and the Poor in Luke-Acts," in *Justice and the Holy: Essays in Honor of Walter Harrelson*, ed. D. A. Knight and J. Paris (Atlanta: Scholars, 1989), 129–44; *The Gospel in Parable*, 162–80, on Luke's parables that deal with the danger of wealth and concern for the poor; Jacques Dupont, *Les béatitudes*, 3 vols. (Paris: Gabalda, 1969, 1973), esp. 2:19–142; 3:41–64, 151–206, 389–471, a classic study that revolutionized the study of the Beatitudes; "Community of Goods in the Early Church," in *The Salvation of the Gentiles: Studies in the Acts of the Apostles* (New York: Paulist, 1979), 85–102; "The Poor and Poverty in the Gospels," in *Gospel Poverty*, ed. A. George (Chicago: Franciscan Herald, 1971), 25–52; John Gillman, *Possessions and the Life of Faith: A Reading of Luke-Acts*, Zaccheus Studies (Collegeville, Minn.: Liturgical, 1991); Joel B. Green, "Good News to Whom? Jesus and the 'Poor' in the Gospel of Luke," in *Jesus of Nazareth: Lord and Christ*, ed. Joel B. Green and Max Turner (Grand Rapids, Mich.: Eerdmans, 1994), 59–74; Luke Johnson, *Sharing Possessions: Mandate and Symbol of Faith* (Philadelphia: Fortress, 1981); Walter E. Pilgrim, *Good News to the Poor: Wealth and Poverty in Luke-Acts* (Minneapolis: Augsburg, 1981), excellent overview; W. Stegemann, "The Following of Christ as Solidarity between Rich, Respected Christians and Poor, Despised Christians (Gospel of Luke)," in *Jesus and the Hope of the Poor*, ed. L. Schottroff and W. Stegemann (Maryknoll, N.Y.: Orbis, 1986), 67–120; W. Stegemann, *The Gospel and the Poor* (Philadelphia: Fortress, 1984), good for use in a pastoral setting.

76. See esp. Stegemann, "The Following of Christ."

77. Compare Prov. 10:2, "righteousness [*ṣĕdāqāh*] delivers from death," with Tobit 12:9 (LXX), "almsgiving [*eleēmosynē*] delivers from death."

78. Surveyed in Donahue, "Two Decades."

79. Peter Brown, *The World of Late Antiquity from Marcus Aurelius to Muhammed* (London: Thames and Hudson, 1971), 67. See also his important study, *Poverty and Leadership in the Late Roman Empire* (Hanover, N.H.: New England University Press, 2002).

80. Joseph A. Fitzmyer, "Pauline Theology," in *New Jerome Biblical Commentary*, 1389.

81. Select studies that integrate Paul's theology and issues of social justice are Elsa Tamez, *The Amnesty of Grace: Justification by Faith from a Latin American Perspective* (Nashville, Tenn.: Abingdon, 1993); Neil Elliott, *Liberating Paul: The Justice of God and the Politics of the Apostle* (Maryknoll, N.Y.: Orbis, 1994); and the essays in Richard A. Horsley, ed., *Paul and Empire: Religion and Power in Imperial Society* (Harrisburg, Pa.: Trinity Press International, 1997).

82. On Schweitzer's "interim ethics," see Victor Furnish, *Theology and Ethics in Paul* (Nashville, Tenn.: Abingdon, 1968), 258–59.

83. Dieter Georgi, *Remembering the Poor: The History of Paul's Collection for Jerusalem* (Nashville, Tenn.: Abingdon, 1992).

84. Brown, *Poverty and Leadership*, 18.

85. Gerd Theissen, *The Social Setting of Pauline Christianity: Essays on Corinth* (Philadelphia: Fortress, 1982), esp. chap. 4, "Social Integration and Sacramental Activity: An Analysis of 1 Corinthians 11:17–34."

86. Some helpful resources for integrating preaching, liturgy, and social justice are John F. Baldovin, "The Liturgical Year: Calendar for a Just Community," in *Liturgy and Spirituality in Context*, ed. E. Bernstein (Collegeville, Minn.: Liturgical, 1990), 98–114; Walter J. Burghardt, *Preaching the Just Word* (New Haven, Conn.: Yale University Press, 1996); James L. Empereur and Christopher Kiesling, *The Liturgy That Does Justice*, A Michael Glazier Book (Collegeville, Minn.: Liturgical, 1990); Anne Y. Koester, ed., *Liturgy and Justice: To Worship God in Spirit and Truth* (Collegeville, Minn.: Liturgical, 2002).

87. P. Ricoeur, *Hermeneutics and the Human Sciences: Essays on Language, Action and Interpretation*, ed. and trans. John S. Thompson (Cambridge: Cambridge University Press; Paris: Éditions de la Maison des Sciences de l'Homme, 1981), 182.

88. Ibid., 185.

89. Ibid. He further notes here that in texts "'revelation or disclosure' takes the place of ostensive reference in the dialogical situation."

90. Ibid.

91. Ibid., 192–93.

92. Schneiders, *The Revelatory Text*, 172.

93. Ibid., 177.

94. In an interview Cardinal Carlo M. Martini, recently retired archbishop of Milan who personally has used the study of the Bible to revitalize the Church, especially among young people in his diocese, remarked that there is still resistance to biblical renewal and suggests that a synod of bishops be called to consider how the Church has responded to *Dei verbum*. Gerald O'Connell, "A Pastor's Vision," *The Tablet* 247 (July 10, 1993): 876–78 at 877.

95. Francis Moloney, "Whither Catholic Biblical Studies?" *Australian Catholic Record* 66 (1989): 84.

96. In reviewing the *Catechism of the Catholic Church*, a leading Catholic exegete Luke Johnson observes "how completely this catechism ignores the results of biblical scholarship. The code for reading the Gospels is the same used by Augustine and Aquinas." See, "The Catechism: Four Responses," *Commonweal* 120 (May 7, 1993): 16–18 at 17. The *Catechism* treats social justice under the seventh commandment, thus giving the concept a limited and negative focus. Nor does the *Catechism* reference those prophetic texts that have so influenced issues of social justice, and while urging charity toward the poor and warning against greed, the phrase *option for the poor* never appears in the *Catechism*.

97. In a recent essay, when discussing justice toward others (philosophically understood) and love, P. Ricoeur writes, "Love presses justice to enlarge the circle of mutual recognition," and gives as examples "Gandhi, Martin Luther King, Jr., and others." See André LaCocque and Paul Ricoeur, *Thinking Biblically: Exegetical and Hermeneutical Studies* (Chicago: University of Chicago Press, 1998), 130. The understanding of biblical justice proposed in this chapter includes such love.

98. James Gustafson, *Protestant and Roman Catholic Ethics: Prospects for Rapprochement* (Chicago: University of Chicago Press, 1978), 142. Lisa Sowle Cahill has developed these in *Foundations for a Christian Ethics of Sexuality* (Philadelphia: Fortress; New York: Paulist, 1985), esp. 1–13. People have noted that these reference points have their origin in the Methodist "quadrilateral" of scripture, tradition, reason, and experience.

99. Ricoeur speaks of "a community of reading and of interpretation" and states, "It is in interpreting the Scriptures in question, that the community interprets itself." *Thinking Biblically*, xvi. A different model of communities of intepretation has been proposed by the South African theologian Gerald O. West: "The Bible must be read from the perspective of the poor and marginalized, that the Bible must be read together with the poor and marginalized, that Bible reading is related to social transformation, and, significantly, that the Bible must be read critically." *The Academy of the Poor: Towards a Dialogic Reading of the Bible* (Sheffield, England: Sheffield Academic, 1999), 106.

100. The most dramatic examples of this practice have been the appointment of the archconservative José Cardosa Sobrinho to the see of Recife, Brazil, after the resignation of Dom Helder Câmara in 1985, and of the Opus Dei Archbishop Fernando Sáenz Lacalle to the archdiocese of San Salvador after the death of Salesian Archbishop Arturo Rivera Damas in 1994, who himself followed the assassinated Archbishop Oscar Romero (d. March 24, 1980).

101. Most sobering is the late Bernhard Häring's painful recollection that he stood before Hitler's military court four times on life-and-death issues, and would have preferred that again to the manner in which he was treated by the members of the Congregation for the Doctrine of the Faith. Rather sadly, he notes, one major difference was that the Nazi accusations were true—he was not submissive to that regime—while the curial accusations were false. See Bernhard Häring, *My Witness for the Church*, ed. and trans. Leonard Swidler (New York: Paulist, 1992), 132–33. See also Cherie Booth, Q.C. (the wife of the British prime minister and herself a Catholic), "A Catholic Perspective on Human Rights," *The Tablet* (June 21, 2003): 4–7. While quite laudatory of the Church's influence on the international dialogue about human rights, Booth points out that "the Church sees its duty to speak out on human rights where it has considerable influence but has not direct power to effect change," but then she asks, "What about respect for human rights within the Church itself, where the Church has actual authority to make a difference?" (7).

SELECTED BIBLIOGRAPHY

Birch, Bruce C. *Let Justice Roll: The Old Testament, Ethics and The Christian Life*. Louisville, Ky.: Westminster/John Knox, 1991. Covers justice in the larger context of Old Testament ethics.

Blenkinsopp, Joseph. *A History of Prophecy in Israel*. Rev. ed. Louisville, KY: Westminster/John Knox, 1996. One of the best overviews of prophetic literature.

Bovati, Pietro. *Re-establishing Justice: Legal Terms, Concepts and Procedures in the Hebrew Bible*. Translated by Michael J. Smith. *Journal for the Study of the Old Testament*, Supplement Series 105. Sheffield, England: JSOT, 1994. Scholarly and important.

Burghardt, Walter J. *Preaching the Just Word*. New Haven, Conn.: Yale University Press, 1996. Excellent homilies by a master preacher who has dedicated fifteen years to reflection on how to preach about biblical justice.

———. *Justice: A Global Adventure*. Maryknoll, N.Y.: Orbis, 2004. The fruit of decades of reflection and preaching on justice, this work describes the biblical and theological foundations of social justice and addresses a wide variety of contemporary social issues.

Croatto, J. Severino. *Exodus: A Hermeneutics of Freedom*. Maryknoll, N.Y.: Orbis, 1981. Seminal work in liberation theology.

Donahue, John R. *What Does the Lord Require? A Bibliographical Essay on the Bible and Social Justice*. St. Louis, Mo.: Institute of Jesuit Sources, 2000. Helpful list of secondary readings with a short introduction to issues involved.

Epsztein, Léon. *Social Justice in the Ancient Near East and the People of the Bible*. London: SCM, 1986. Scholarly while eminently readable.

Esler, Philip F. *Community and Gospel in Luke-Acts: The Social and Political Motivations of Lucan*

Theology. SNTSMS 57. Cambridge: Cambridge University Press, 1987. Excellent on the Lukan community.

Gossai, Hemchand. *Justice, Righteousness, and the Social Critique of the Eighth-Century Prophets*. American University Studies, Series VII, Theology and Religion. New York: Peter Lang, 1993. Scholarly study of an important period in Israel's history.

Harrelson, Walter. *The Ten Commandments and Human Rights*. Philadelphia: Fortress, 1980. Repr. Macon, Ga.: Mercer University Press, 1997. Exposition of the Decalogue with sensitivity to contemporary issues.

Pilgrim, Walter E. *Good News to the Poor: Wealth and Poverty in Luke-Acts*. Minneapolis: Augsburg, 1981. Excellent overview.

Pleins, John David. *The Social Visions of the Hebrew Bible: A Theological Introduction*. Louisville, Ky.: Westminster/John Knox, 2000. Best study available in English.

Reventlow, H. G., and Y. Hoffman, eds. *Justice and Righteousness: Biblical Themes and Their Influence*. Journal for the Study of the Old Testament, Supplement Series 137. Sheffield, England: JSOT, 1992. Collection of important essays by biblical scholars.

Sandeen, Ernest, ed. *The Bible and Social Reform*. Chico, Calif.: Scholars, 1982. Fine overview of the impact of the Bible on social reform movements of the twentieth century.

CHAPTER

2 Natural Law in Catholic Social Teachings

STEPHEN J. POPE

INTRODUCTION

This chapter examines the meaning and uses of natural law within Catholic social teachings. It intends to provide a brief overview of natural law in Catholic social teachings and to inform readers of the issues with which natural law theologians typically grapple. It is organized into three major sections: the historical development of natural law reflection, its evolution in Catholic social teachings, and major challenges it faces in the twenty-first century.

HISTORICAL CONTEXT

We begin with a sketch of the historical origins and development of natural law ethics in order to understand the major influences and sources at work in this feature of Catholic social teachings.

Ancient and Medieval Origins

The remote origins of natural law ethics lie in Greek and Roman philosophy and law. Aristotle spoke of doing the right or the just act. He contrasted what is "just by nature" from what is "just by convention."[1] In the early second century before the common era, the Romans began to make a critically important distinction between the civil law (*ius civile*) that pertained to citizens of Rome and the law common to all nations (*ius gentium*) used to govern the peoples of Italy and the Roman provinces. Up until this time, the laws of the Roman state, like that of other ancient laws, applied only to its own citizens. This legal development resonated with a current Hellenistic philosophical and rhetorical distinction between the positive laws governing particular political communities and the natural law that exists everywhere prior to its official enactment by any particular state. The Stoics maintained that moral law is rooted in nature (*physis*) rather than only constructed by convention (*nomos*), and that moral virtues can be identified by reason reflecting on nature. Cicero (106–43 B.C.) understood true law as "right reason in agreement with nature" (*recta ratio naturae congruens*)[2] and to be universally binding for all places and times.

The Roman jurist Gaius (fl. A.D. 130–180) identified the natural law with the "law of nations" (*ius gentium*).[3] The influential legal theorist Ulpian (c. 170–228), however, defined natural law quite differently—as "that which nature teaches all animals" (*id quod natura omnia animalia docet*).[4] Thus he regarded the natural law not as something only common to all human beings but rather an ordering shared by humans and all other animals, for example, out of natural law comes marriage and the procreation and rearing of children.[5] Ambiguity and disagreement among the major legal authorities regarding the relation between the "natural law" and the "law of nations" would be passed on to medieval natural law and from there into Catholic social teachings.

The first Christians saw creation as the reflection of the Creator's wise governance. Scripture teaches that wisdom "reaches mightily from one end of the earth to the other and she orders all things well" (Wisdom 8:1, NRSV). Early Christian thinkers like the apologists Athenagoras (177) and Justin Martyr (165) found congenial the Stoic notion of a natural moral order grasped by reason and binding on all human beings.[6] Justin argued in his famous *Dialogue with Trypho* that God instructs every race about the content of justice and that this is why everyone grasps the evil of homicide, adultery, and other sins.[7]

The Church turned to natural law for two principal reasons. First, the central normative document of the faith, the sacred scripture, speaks in many different voices about moral and social issues. It provides neither a moral philosophy nor an extensive body of law with which to govern political communities. The distinguished historian Henry Chadwick actually considered it of "providential importance" that the writers of the New Testament did not attempt to "philosophize."[8] The fact that the gospel was not tied to any first-century speculative system, Chadwick pointed out, leaves it free alternatively to criticize and to draw from classical philosophies as needed. Some early Christians hated "the world," but others sought intellectual resources or "mediating languages" to help them think in a systematic way about the implications of faith for social, economic, and political matters. Natural law provided such a resource, particularly as Christians came to assimilate Roman culture and civil law.[9]

Second, Christians in the Roman Empire, not entirely unlike Christians today, faced the problem of communicating their convictions to citizens who did not necessarily share their religious convictions. Indeed, some were outwardly hostile to them. Natural law provided a conceptual vehicle for preserving, explaining, and reflecting on the moral requirements embedded in human nature and for expressing these claims to wider audiences. Early Christians drew from St. Paul's recognition that the Gentiles are able to know divine attributes from what God has made in the creation (Rom. 1:19–21). In what became the scriptural *locus classicus* for the natural law tradition, and a key text for the social encyclicals (e.g., PT 5), Paul observed that when Gentiles observe by nature the prescriptions of the law, they show that "the demands of the law are written in their hearts" (Rom. 2:14–15). Arguing against those who assume that possession of the covenantal law is sufficient, Paul argued that the conscience of the good pagan bears witness to the natural roots of the moral law. On this Pauline basis the great Alexandrian theologian Origen (185–254) could explain how reasonable pagans grasp the binding force of natural equity and the Golden Rule. Even a person who does not believe in Christ, he wrote, "may yet do good works, may keep justice and love mercy, preserve chastity and continence, keep modesty and gentleness, and do every good work."[10]

St. Augustine (354–430), engaged in a protracted anti-Manichean polemic, contrasted the changeable and flawed "temporal law" with the immutable "eternal law" through which God governs all of creation. God orders the material world through the eternal law, which in turn provides the ultimate basis for temporal law. From this root grew the principle used in twentieth-century civil disobedience movements that an unjust law is not binding. Augustine's tract *Contra Faustum* argued that the eternal law commands human beings to respect the natural order.[11] Just as God commanded the fleeing Hebrews to despoil the Egyptians, Augustine argued, so Christians ought to use the riches of pagan philosophy more effectively to preach the gospel.[12]

In the sixth century the first Byzantine emperor Justinian I (483–565) ordered the drafting of the massive *Corpus iuris civilis* to provide legal structures for the empire on the basis of ancient Roman law.[13] This work became the most influential treatment of Western law until the nineteenth century. The *Corpus* included the *Codex*, a collection and codification of earlier imperial statutes; the *Institutes*, an introductory textbook of law; and the *Digest*, a compilation of important legal opinions of Roman jurists. Justinian sponsored the assimilation of Ulpian's famous definition of natural law as what nature teaches all animals but, in contradiction to him, identified the law of nations with the natural law.[14] Justinian was more responsible than any other figure of the time for the handing down of natural law doctrine into the medieval period.

In the twelfth century the eminent legal scholar Gratian wrote the *Decretum* (completed by c. 1140), which became one of the most important texts on ecclesiastical law up until the promulgation of the Code of Canon Law in 1917. Gratian wanted to bring greater intelligibility and harmony to ecclesiastical law and to communicate it effectively to others. He defined natural law as what is contained in the "Law and the Gospels." The *Decretum* incorporated Isidore of Seville's doctrine of natural right as the law common to all peoples,[15] and taught that any provisions of human law that contradict natural law are "null and void."[16]

Natural law doctrine was gradually expanded to accommodate a new recognition of what have come to be called "subjective rights." Medieval canon lawyers began to speak of right (*ius*) as a "liberty," "power," or "faculty" possessed by an individual. A person, for example, has a "right" to marry under the law. Distinguishing natural law from customary law, Gratian thought of "right" primarily as objective law, but his later–twelfth-century followers Hugaccio (c. 1180) and Rufinus (c. 1160) expanded the term to include a new notion of "subjective rights," for example, regarding self-defense, marriage, and property (including the right of the poor to sustenance).[17] This usage was a precursor to the development of modern subjective "natural rights," but at the time it was subordinate to duties and considered secondary in importance to the natural law.[18]

St. Thomas Aquinas (1225–74) produced the most famous exposition of natural law ethics. He gave law its classical definition as "an ordinance of reason for the common good, promulgated by him who has care of the community."[19] Thomas regarded law—the "rule and measure of acts"[20]—as essentially the product of reason rather than the will. He underscored the inherent reasonableness of law rather than its enforcement by means of coercion.

Thomas developed a more systematic treatment of the distinction between different types of law than had any of his predecessors. He used the notion of law analogously to encompass physical, human, and divine affairs. He distinguished (1) the "eternal law" governing everything in the universe, (2) the "divine law" revealed first in the Old Law of the Hebrew Bible and then in the New Law, (3) the "natural law" that sets the fundamental moral standards for human conduct, and (4) the "human law" created by civil authorities who have care for the social order. Because the simple promptings of nature do not suffice to meet the typically very complex needs of human beings, reason is required to penetrate and extend the normative implications of natural law. Natural law requires acts to which nature does not spontaneously incline but which reason identifies as good.[21]

Thomas's synthetic theory of natural law was made possible by his adoption of the newly reintroduced Aristotelian philosophy of nature. Aristotle's *Physics* defined nature as "an intrinsic principle of motion and rest,"[22] that is, as *acting for an end* rather than randomly. A being's intrinsic "end" or "nature" is simply "what each thing is when fully developed"[23] and its extrinsic end concerns its proper place within the natural world. Human beings ought to live "according to nature" (*kata physin*),[24] that is, in such a way as to fulfill the intrinsic functions or purposes built into the structure of human nature. The intrinsic finality of human nature *inclines*, of course, but by no means *determines*, the will of a free human being to his or her proper end, namely, the human good.

Thomas associated the habit of *synderesis* with the Pauline law "written on the heart" (Rom. 2:15). Practical reason naturally orients each person to the good and away from evil, and so the first principle of practical reason is that we ought to seek good and avoid evil. The principal injunction "do good and avoid evil" receives concrete specification from natural human inclinations.[25] We share with other natural objects the inclination to preserve our existence; we share with other animals biological inclinations to food, water, sex, and the like; and we share within one another rational inclinations to know the truth about God and to live in political community.[26] In this way, Thomas coordinated Cicero's "right reason in agreement with nature" (*recta ratio naturae congruens*)[27] with Ulpian's "what nature teaches to all animals."[28] These levels move from the more elemental to the more distinctively human, with the former taken up and ordered by the latter. This framework later supports John XXIII's affirmation that "the common good touches the whole man, the need both of his body and his soul" (PT 57). In this way, natural law avoids the two opposite extremes of reductive materialism and otherworldly idealism.

This broad context enables one to make sense of Thomas's most famous description of the natural law as the "*rational* creature's participation in the eternal law."[29] The natural law is what governs beings who are rational, free, and spiritual and at the same time material and organic. Thomas understood the philosophical framework for ethics in primarily Aristotelian terms, but its theological framework in primarily Augustinian terms. Thomas concurred with Augustine's view of the cosmos as a perfectly ordered whole within which the lower parts are subordinated to the higher.[30] Augustine regarded the eternal ideas in the mind of God as constituting an immutable order or "eternal law" to which all that exists is subject. Human beings are subject to this order in a rational way, by means of our intelligence and freedom. Indeed, human beings take part in providence by providing for themselves and others and in this way partake in the eternal law in ways unavailable to other animals.

The cardinal virtues empower the person to act naturally and thereby to attain some degree of happiness in this life, but the theological virtues, animated by grace, order the person to the ultimate human end, the beatific vision. The ancient admonishment to "follow nature," then, did not prescribe imitating animal behavior but rather required acting in accord with the inner demands of one's own deepest desire for the good. Because human nature is rational, Thomas pointed out, it is *natural* for each person to take pleasure in the contemplation of truth and in the exercise of virtue.[31]

Later Catholic social teachings also built upon another fundamental element in Thomas's anthropology: its acknowledgment of the person as naturally social and political.[32] We exist by nature as parts of larger social wholes on which we depend for our existence and functioning, and these provide instrumental reasons for participating in political community.[33] Yet political community is also intrinsically valuable as the only context in which we can satisfy our natural inclination to mutual love and friendship. The person cannot be completely subordinated to the group, like the worker bee to the hive, since the person is not ordered to any particular temporal community as the highest end.[34] This is not because the person is an isolated monad, but because he or she is a member of a much larger and more important body, the universal community of all creation.[35] As ontologically prior, the person is ultimately served by the state rather than vice versa. Natural law thus sets the framework for the rejection of two extremes later opposed by Catholic social teachings: individualism, which values the part at the expense of the whole, and collectivism, which values the whole at the expense of the part.

Thomas interpreted justice in terms of natural ends. Right (*ius*) obtains when purposes are respected and fulfilled, for example, when parents care for their children. He thus understood "right" in human relations, objectively, as "the object of justice" and "the just thing itself," and not as a claim made by one individual over and against others (right as a moral faculty, the notion of "subjective right").[36] Thus the wrongfulness of the vice of usury, the unjust taking of interest, lies in its violation of the purpose of money,[37] and lying because "false signification" violates the natural purpose of human speech.[38] More positively, Thomas affirmed the inherent goodness of sexual intercourse when it fulfilled its natural purposes. Against the dualists of his day, he held that nothing genuinely natural can be innately sinful.[39]

Natural law learns about natural purposes from a variety of sources, including philosophy and science. Thomas used available scientific analyses of the order of nature to support normative claims regarding the human body,[40] the creation of women,[41] the nature of the passions,[42] and the like. Modern moralists criticize this reliance on Ulpian's "physicalism" on the grounds that it gives excessive priority to biological structures at the expense of distinctively rational capacities,[43] but at least it made clear that human nature should not be reduced to consciousness, rationality, and will.

Thomas believed the most basic moral standards could be, and in fact were, known by almost everyone. These include, in capsule form, the Golden Rule and, in somewhat more amplified form, the second table of the Decalogue. Yet he thought that revealed divine law was necessary, among other things, to make up for the deficiency of human judgment, to provide certain moral knowledge, especially in concrete matters,[44] and to give finite human beings knowledge of the highest good, the beatific vision. Reason is competent to grasp the precepts that promote imperfect happiness in this life, both the individual life of virtue and the more encompassing common good of the wider community. It suffers from obvious limitations but it nevertheless has broad competence to grasp the goods proper to human nature and to identify the virtues by which they are attained. Thomas even claimed that there would be no need for divine law if human beings were ordered only to their natural end rather than to a supernatural end.[45]

The Rise of Modern Natural Law

Historians trace the origins of the new modern theory of natural law to a number of major influences too complex to do more than simply acknowledge here. Four factors will be mentioned: nominalism, "second Scholasticism," international law, and the liberal rights theory of Hobbes and his intellectual heirs.

The emergence of nominalism inaugurated a movement away from the Thomistic attempt to base ethics on universal characteristics of human nature. Its shift of attention away from the general to the particular thereby inaugurated a new focus of attention on the individual and his or her subjective rights. The complementary development of voluntarism gave primacy to the will rather than the intellect and to the good, as distinct from the true.[46]

The English Franciscan William of Ockham (c. 1266–1349) replaced the will's finality to the good with a radical freedom to choose between opposites (the so-called freedom of indifference). This led to a new focus on obligation and law and to the displacement of virtue from the center of the moral life.[47] If God functions with divine "freedom of indifference," then moral obligations are products of the divine will rather than the divine understanding of the human good.[48] Since God's will is utterly free, God could have decreed, for example, adultery to be morally obligatory. Ockham subtly changed natural law theory by interpreting it in a way that gave new force to the subjective notion of right. He did so in part for practical reasons, both to support Franciscans who wanted to renounce their natural right to property, as well as to defend those who sought moral limits to the power of the pope. Ockham, however, continued to regard subjective right as subordinate to natural law.[49]

The rise of "second Scholasticism" in the Renaissance constituted another factor influencing the development of modern natural law theory. The Spanish Dominican Francisco de Vitoria (1483–1546) developed an account of universal human dignity in the course of mounting arguments to refute philosophical justifications offered for the European exploitation of the native peoples of the Americas. His *De Indis* argued from the basic humanity of the natives to their natural right of control and action (*dominium*) over their own bodies and possessions, the right to self-governance,[50] and the right to self-defense.[51]

The Spanish Jesuit Francisco Suárez (1548–1617), author of the massive *De legibus et legislatore Deo*, contributed significantly to the slow accretion of voluntaristic presuppositions into the natural law. Suárez understood morality primarily as conformity to law. Since law and moral obligation can only be produced by a will, human nature in itself can only be said to carry natural inclinations to the good but no morally obligatory force. On one level, Suárez concurred with Thomas's judgment that reason can discover the content of the human good, but unlike his famous forbear he held that its morally *binding force* comes only from the will of God.[52] Suárez moved from this moral voluntarism to develop an account of subjective right as a moral faculty in every individual. He assumed without argument the full compatibility of Thomistic natural law with the newer notion of subjective rights.[53]

The practical need to obtain greater stability in relations among the newly established European nation-states provided a third major stimulus for the development of modern natural law theory. The viciousness and length of the wars of religion in the sixteenth and seventeenth centuries underscored the need for a theory of law and political organization able to transcend confessional boundaries.

Dutch Protestant jurist Hugo Grotius (1585–1645), known as the "Father of International Law," constructed a version of rights-based natural law in order to provide a framework for ethics in his intensely combative and religiously divided age. Grotius's early work was occasioned by the seizure of a ship at sea in territory lying outside the boundaries controlled by law. His major work, *De iure belli et pacis* (1625), offered the first systematic attempt to regulate international conflict by means of just war criteria; many of its provisions were incorporated into later Geneva conventions.

Grotius understood natural law largely in terms of rights. In this way he anticipated developments in the twentieth century. Following the Spanish Scholastics, he understood rights to be qualities possessed by all human beings as such rather than as members of this or that particular political community. He held that the norms of natural law are established by reason and are universal: they bind morally even if, though impossible (*etiamsi daremus*), there were no God—a claim found neither in the earlier moral theology of Thomas Aquinas nor in later Catholic social teachings. Protection of these norms is morally necessary for any just social order. From this theoretical principle he could derive the practical conclusion that even parties at war are obligated to respect the rights of their enemies.

Natural law theories evolved in directions Grotius never intended. They came to regard the human predicament as essentially conflicted, apolitical, and even antisocial. The Peace of Westphalia (1648) established the modern system of international politics centered on the sovereign nation-state, the context for the political reflections of later Catholic social teachings in documents like *Pacem in terris* and *Dignitatis humanae.* Though Grotius was a sincere Christian with no desire to secularize natural law theory, he believed for the sake of agreement that it was necessary to abandon speculation on the highest good, the ideal regime, or anything more elevated than a minimal version of Christian belief. This period generated the first proposals to approach morality from a purely empirical perspective in order to establish a "science of morals." From this point on, the major theoreticians of natural law were lawyers and philosophers rather than theologians. Through the influence of Grotius, natural law was established as the dominant mode of moral reflection in the seventeenth and eighteenth centuries.

A fourth and definitively modern interpretation of natural law was developed by Thomas Hobbes (1588–1679) and his followers. Hobbes produced the first fully modern theory of rights-based natural law. His originality lay in part in the way he attempted to begin his analysis of human nature from the "new science" and to break completely with the classical Aristotelian teleological philosophy of nature that had permeated the writings of the "schoolmen." Modern science from the time of Bacon conceived of nature as a machine that can be analyzed sufficiently by reducing its wholes to simple parts and then investigating how they function via efficient and material causality. [54] Following Galileo, Hobbes held that all matter was in motion and would continue in motion unless resisted by other forces. He strove to apply the rules of Euclidean geometry and physics to human behavior for the joint purposes of explanation and control. Modern science was concerned with uniformity of operations or "natural necessity," which stood in sharp contrast to the classical notion of nature composed of Aristotelian finalities that act only "for the most part." "Only in a universe empty of *telos*," explains Michael Sandel, "is it possible to conceive a subject apart from and prior to its purposes and ends. Only a world ungoverned by a purposive order leaves principles of justice open to human construction and conceptions of the good to individual choice."[55] The coupling of the new mechanistic philosophy of nature with a voluntaristic philosophy of law led to a radical recasting of the meaning of natural law.

Politics and ethics, like science, seek to conquer and control nature. Hobbes held that each individual is first and foremost self-seeking, not naturally inclined to "do good and avoid evil." We are not naturally parts of larger social wholes, but rather artificially connected to them by choices based on calculating self-interest. He abandoned the classical admonition to "follow nature" and to cultivate the virtues appropriate to it. There are accordingly no natural duties to other people that correspond to natural rights. The "right of nature" is prior to the institution of morality. The "Right of Nature" (*ius naturale*) is "the Liberty each man hath, to use his own power, as he will himselfe, for the preservation of his own Nature; that is to say, of his own Life; and consequently, of doing any thing, which in his own Judgment, and Reason, hee shall conceive to be the aptest means thereunto."[56] In stark contrast to Thomas Aquinas, Hobbes separated right (*ius*) from law (*lex*): "right, consisteth in liberty to do, or forbeare; whereas Law, determineth, and bindeth to one them; so that Law, and Right, differ as much, as Obligation, and Liberty."[57] By nature individuals possess liberty without duty or intrinsic moral limits. Nothing could be further from Hobbes's view of humanity than the presumption of early Catholic social teachings that each person is, as Leo XIII put it, "the steward of God's providence, [and expected] to act for the benefit of others" (RN 22).

Hobbes derived a set of nineteen "natural laws" from the foundation of self-preservation: to seek peace, form a social contract, keep covenants, and so on. Only the will of the sovereign can impose political order on individuals who are naturally in a state of war with one another. Law is, and ought to be, nothing but the expression of the will of the sovereign. There is no higher moral law outside of positive law and the social contract, hence Hobbes's rather chilling inference that "no law can be unjust."[58]

Lutheran Samuel von Pufendorf (1632–94) is sometimes known as the "German Hobbes." *De iure naturae et gentium* (1672) followed the Hobbesian logic that individuals enter into society to obtain the security and order necessary for individual survival. Pufendorf believed nature to be fundamentally egoistic and therefore only made to serve higher purposes by the force of external compulsion. If the natural order is utterly amoral, God's will determines what is good and what is evil and then imposes it on humanity by divine command. We are commanded by God to be sociable and to obey out of fear of punishment. (Natural law would collapse, Pufendort believed, if theism were undermined.) Morality here is thus anything but living "according to nature"—on the contrary, natural law ethics combats the utter amorality of nature. Pufendorf, like Grotius, sought to provide international norms on the basis of natural law moral principles that are universally valid and acceptable whatever one's religious confession. It led the way to later attempts to construct a purely secular natural law moral theory.

John Locke (1632–1704), especially in his *Essays on the Law of Nature* (1676) and *Second Treatise on Civil Government* (1690), followed his predecessors' interest in limiting quarrels by establishing laws independent of both sectarian religious beliefs and controversial metaphysical claims about the highest good. Locke agreed with Hobbes that natural right exists in the presocial state of nature. Human beings abandon the anarchic state of nature and enter into the social contract for the sake of greater security. The purpose of government is then to protect "Lives, Liberties, and Estates."[59] When it fails to do so, the people have a right to seek a better regime. Lockean natural law functioned as the "foundation" of positive laws, the first of which is that "all mankind" is to be preserved,[60] and positive laws draw their binding power from this foundation.[61]

Modern natural lawyers came to agree on the individualistic basis of natural rights and their priority to natural law. Lockean natural right grounds religious toleration, a position only acceptable to Catholic social teachings (though on different grounds) with the promulgation of *Dignitatis humanae* in 1965. Since moral goodness was increasingly regarded as a private matter—what is good for one person might be bad for another—society could be expected only to protect the right of individuals to make up their own minds about the good life. The gradual dominance of modern ethics by legal language, and the eclipse of appeals to virtue, had an enormous influence on early Catholic social teachings.[62]

Lockean natural law had a profound influence on Rousseau, Hume, Jefferson, Kant, Montesquieu, and other influential modern social thinkers, but leading philosophers came in turn to subject modern natural law to a variety of significant criticisms. Immanuel Kant (1724–1805), to mention one important figure, regarded traditional natural law theory as fatally flawed in its understanding of both "nature" and "law." He judged Aristotelian philosophy of nature and ethics to be completely inadequate: if "nature" is "the sum of the objects of experience" that can be perceived through the senses and subject to experimentation by the natural sciences,[63] then it cannot generate moral obligations. If "ethics" is concerned about good will, then it cannot be built upon the foundation of human happiness or flourishing.

Kant regarded classical natural law as suffering from the fatal flaw of "heteronomy," that is, of leaving moral decisions to authority rather than requiring individuals to function as autonomous moral agents.[64] Kant held that since the will alone has moral worth, its rightness depends on the conformity of the agent's will to reason rather than on the practical consequences of his or her acts or their ability to produce happiness. An animal conforms to nature because it has no choice but to act from instinct, but the rational agent acts from the dictates of reason as determined by the "categorical imperative." Kant's understanding of the rational agent provided a powerful basis for an ethic based on "respect for persons," a doctrine of individual rights, and an affirmation of the dignity of the human person. Strains of Kant's ethics, mediated through both the negative and the positive ways in which it shaped phenomenology and personalism, came to influence the ethic of John Paul II. One does not find in the writings of John Paul II an agreement with Kant's belief in the sufficiency of reason, of course, but there is a recurrent emphasis on the dignity of the person, on the right of each person to "respect," and on the absolute centrality of human rights within any just social order.

In the nineteenth century, natural law was superseded by the utilitarianism of Jeremy Bentham (1748–1832) and John Stuart Mill (1806–73). Bentham attempted to base ethics on an account of nature—"nature has placed mankind under the governance of two sovereign masters, pain and pleasure"[65]—but he was adamantly opposed to natural law and dismissed natural rights as "fictions" that present obstacles to social reform. The primary opposition to natural law in the past two centuries has come from various forms of positivism that regarded morality as an attempt to codify and justify conventional social norms.

CATHOLIC SOCIAL TEACHINGS

Catholic social teachings from Leo XIII through John Paul II have been influenced in various ways, either by way of agreement or by way of disagreement, by these natural law traditions. They have selectively incorporated, sometimes to the consternation of purists, both modern natural rights theories as well as the older views of medieval jurists and Scholastic theologians. For purposes of convenience, Catholic social teachings are often divided into two main periods: one preceding *Gaudium et spes* and the second following from it. Literature from the former period was primarily philosophical and its theological claims generally drew from the doctrine of creation. It employed natural law argumentation in an explicit, direct, and fairly consistent manner; its philosophical framework was neoscholastic. Literature from the more recent period has been explicitly biblical and its claims are drawn more often from the doctrine of Christ; it presumes the existence of the natural law but uses it in a more restricted, indirect, and selective fashion. Its philosophical matrix has attempted to combine neoscholasticism with continental philosophy, and particularly existentialism, personalism, and phenomenology.

The term *neoscholasticism* refers to a philosophical movement in the nineteenth and early twentieth centuries to return to the medieval Scholastics and their commentators (particularly Jesuit and Dominican) in order to provide a comprehensive philosophical system that could counter regnant secular philosophies.

Leo XIII

The first encyclical of Leo XIII (1878–1903), *Aeterni patris* (August 4, 1879), called on the Church "to restore the golden wisdom of St. Thomas."[66] Leo was concerned from early in his papacy about the danger posed to civil society from socialism and communism. Adherents of these ideologies, he thought, refuse to obey higher powers, proclaim the absolute equality of all individuals, debase the natural union of man and wife, and assail the right to private property.

Leo XIII's 1885 encyclical *Immortale dei* (*On the Christian Constitution of States*) justified government as a natural institution against those extreme liberals who regarded it as a necessary evil.[67] Natural law gives the state certain moral obligations. Arguing against both the Catholic monarchists opposed to the French Republic and the disciples of the excommunicated egalitarian French journalist Robert Felicité de Lamennais (1782–1854), Leo insisted that natural law does not dictate one special form of government. Each society must determine its own political structures to meet its own needs and particular circumstances as long as they "bear in mind that God is the paramount ruler of the world, and must set Him before themselves as their exemplar and law in the administration of the State."[68] Against militant secular liberalism, Leo regarded atheism as a crime and support for the one true religion a moral requirement imposed on the state by natural law. True freedom is "freedom from error" and the modern freedoms of speech, conscience, and worship must be carefully interpreted. The Church is concerned with the salvation of souls, and the state with the political order, but both must work for the true common good.

Leo's 1888 encyclical *Libertas praestantissimum* (*The Nature of Human Liberty*) lamented forgetfulness of the natural law as a cause of massive moral disorder.[69] It singled out for particular criticism all forms of liberalism in politics and economics that would replace law with unregulated liberty on the basis of the principle that "every man is the law to himself."[70] Proper understanding of freedom and respect for law begin with recognition of God as the supreme legislator. Free will must be regulated by law, "a fixed rule of teaching what is to be done and what is to be left undone."[71] Reason "prescribes to the will what it should seek after or shun, in order to the eventual attainment of man's last end, for the sake of which all his actions ought to be performed."[72] The natural law is "engraved in the mind of every man" in the command to do right and avoid evil; each person will be rewarded or punished by God according to his or her conformity to the law.[73]

Leo applied these principles to the "social question" in *Rerum novarum* (1891). The destruction of the guilds in the modern period left members of the working class vulnerable to exploitation and predatory capitalism. The answer to this injustice, Leo held, included both a return to religion and respect for rights—private property, association (trade unions), a living wage, reasonable hours, sabbath rest, education, family life—all of which are rooted in natural law. Leo countered socialism, his major bête noire, with a threefold defense of private property. First, the argument from dominion (RN 6) echoes some of the language of the *Summa theologiae*, though without Thomas's emphasis on "use" rather than "ownership."[74] The second argument is based on the worker leaving "an impress of his personality" (RN 9) and resembles that found in Locke's *The Second Treatise of Government*.[75] The third and final argument bases private property on natural familial duties (RN 13); it is taken from Aristotle.[76]

The basic welfare of the working class is not a matter of almsgiving but of distributive justice, the virtue by which the "ruler" properly assigns the benefits and burdens to the various sectors of society (RN 33). Justice demands that workers proportionately share in the goods that they have helped to create (RN 14). The Leonine model of the orderly society was taken from what he took to be the order of nature—a position that had been abandoned by modern natural lawyers. Assuming a neoscholastic rather than Darwinian view of the natural world, Leo held that nature itself has ordained social inequalities. He denounced as foolish the utopian belief in social leveling, that is, nature is hierarchical and "all striving against nature is in vain" (RN 14). In response to the class antagonisms of the dialectical model of society, Leo offered an organic model of society, inspired by an image of medieval unity, within which classes live in mutually interdependent order and harmony. "Each needs the other: capital cannot do without labor, nor labor without capital" (RN 19; cf. LE 12). Observation of the precepts of justice would be sufficient to control social strife, Leo argued, but Christianity goes further in its claim that rich and poor should be bound to each other in friendship.

Natural law gives responsibilities to, but imposes limits on, the state. The state has "a special responsibility to protect the common good" and "to promote to the utmost the interests of the poor." The end of society is "to make men better," so the state has a duty to promote religion and morality (RN 32). Since the family is prior to the community and the state (RN 13), the latter have no sovereign control over the former. Anticipating Pius XI's "principle of subsidiarity" (QA 79–80), Leo taught that the state must intervene whenever the common good (including the good of any single class) is threatened with harm and no other solution is forthcoming (RN 36).

Pius XI

Pius XI (1922–39) wrote a number of encyclicals calling for a return to the proper principles of social order. In 1931, the "Fortieth Year" after *Rerum novarum*, he issued *Quadragesimo anno*, usually given the English title, *On Reconstructing the Social Order*. Pius XI used natural law to back a set of rights that were violated by fascism, Nazism, and communism. Rights were also invoked to underscore the moral limits to the power of the state. The right to private property, for example, comes directly from the Creator so that individuals can provide for themselves and their families and so that the goods of creation can be distributed throughout the entire human family. State appropriation of private property in violation of this right, even if authorized by positive law, contradicts the natural law and therefore is morally illegitimate.

Natural law includes the critically important "principle of subsidiarity." Based on the Latin *subsidium*, "support" or "assistance," subsidiarity holds that "one should not withdraw from individuals and commit to the community what they can accomplish by their own enterprise and industry" (QA 79).[77] Subsidiarity has a twofold function: negatively, it holds that high-level institutions should not usurp all social power and responsibility, and positively, it maintains that higher-level institutions need to support and encourage lower-level institutions. More "natural" social arrangements are built around the primary relations of marriage and family, and intermediate associations like neighborhoods, small businesses, and local communities. These primary and intermediate associations must help themselves and contribute to the common good. What parades as industrial progress can in fact destroy the social fabric. When it accords with the natural law, public authority works to ensure that the true requirements of the common good are being met. Natural law challenges radical individualism as well as socialism. While the state may not unjustly deprive citizens of their private property, it ought to bring private ownership into harmony with the needs of the common good. Nature strives to harmonize part and whole for the good of both.

Pius XI's *Casti connubii* (December 31, 1930), usually translated *On Christian Marriage*,[78] made more explicit appeals to natural law than did *Quadragesimo anno*. Natural law in this document gives precise ethical judgments about specific classes of acts such as sterilization, artificial birth control, and abortion. Pius XI condemned artificial contraception on the grounds that it is "intrinsically against nature." The "conjugal act" is designed by God for procreation, and the deliberate attempt to thwart this purpose is "intrinsically vicious."[79] Violation of this natural ordering is an insult to nature and a self-destructive attempt to thwart the will of the Creator. Individuals "are not free to destroy or mutilate their members, or in any other way render themselves unfit for their natural functions, except when no other provision can be made for the good of the whole body."[80] Because human beings have a social nature, marriage relations are not simply private contracts that can be dissolved at will.[81] Divorce cannot be permitted by civil law because of its harmful effects on both individual children and the entire social order.[82]

While not usually considered "social teaching," *Casti connubii* had powerful social and political implications. During Pius XI's pontificate the Nazis passed the "Law for the Protection of Hereditary Health" (July 14, 1933), calling for those determined to have one of eight categories of hereditary illness (ranging from schizophrenia to alcoholism) to undergo compulsory sterilization; a law authorizing the castration of "habitual offenders against public morals" (including the charge of "racial pollution"); and the Nuremberg Laws, including the "Law for the Protection of German Blood and German Honor" (1935). Between 1934 and 1939 about 400,000 people were victims of forced sterilization. At the time, natural law faced its most compelling opponent in racist naturalism.[83] Advocates of these laws justified them through a social Darwinian reading of nature: individuals and groups compete against one another and have variable worth. Only the strongest ought to survive, reproduce, and achieve cultural dominance. Hitler's brutal view of nature reinforced his equally brutal view of humanity: "He who wants to live should fight, therefore, and he who does not want to battle in this world of eternal struggle does not deserve to be alive!"[84]

Pius XI condemned as a violation of natural right both the practice of forced sterilization[85] and the policy of state prohibition of marriage to those at risk for bearing genetically defective children. Those who do have a high likelihood of giving birth to genetically defective children ought to be persuaded not to marry, argued the pope, but the state has no moral authority to restrict the natural right to marry.[86] He invoked Thomas's prohibition of the maiming of innocent people to support a right to bodily integrity that cannot be violated by the state for any utilitarian purposes, including the desire to avoid future social evils.[87]

Pius XII

Pius XII (1930–58) continued his predecessor's criticism of fascism and totalitarianism on the twofold ground that they attack the dignity of the person and overextend the power of the state. He was the first pope to extend Catholic social teaching beyond the nation-state and into a broader, more international context. His first encyclical, *Summi pontificatus* (October 27, 1939), attacked Nazi aggression in Poland.[88] Before becoming pope, Pacelli had a hand in formulating Pius XI's 1937 denunciation of Nazism, *Mit Brennender Sorge*.[89] This encyclical invoked the standard argument that positive law must be judged according to the standards of the natural law to which every rational person has access.[90] *Summi pontificatus* attacked Nazi racism for "forgetfulness of that law of human solidarity and charity which is dictated and imposed by our common origin, and by the equality of rational nature in all men, to whatever people they belong, and by the redeeming Sacrifice offered by Jesus Christ on the Altar of the Cross."[91] Human dignity comes not from blood or soil but, Pius XII argued, from our common human nature made in the image of God. The state must be ordered to the divine will and not treated as an end in itself. It must protect the person and the family, the first cell of society.

Pius XII had initially continued Pius XI's suspicion of liberalism and commitment to the ideal of a distinctive Catholic social order grounded in natural law, but he was more concerned about the dangers of communism than those of fascism and Nazism. The devastation of the war, however, gradually led him to an increased appreciation for the moral value of liberal democracy. His Christmas addresses called for an entirely new social order based on justice and peace. His 1944 Christmas address in particular acknowledged the apparent reasonableness of democracy as the political system best suited to protect the dignity of the person.[92] This step toward representative democracy, held at arm's length by previous popes, marked the beginning of a new way of interpreting natural law. It signaled a shift away from his immediate predecessor's organicist vision of the natural law with its corporatist model for the rightly ordered society. Since democracy has to allow for the free play of ideas and arguments, even this modest recognition of the moral superiority of democracy would soon lead the church to abandon policies of censorship in *Pacem in terris* (1963) and established religion in *Dignitatis humanae* (1965).

John XXIII

Pope John XXIII (1958–63) employed natural law in his attempt to address the compelling international issues of his day. *Mater et magistra*, his encyclical concerned with social and economic justice, repeated the fundamental teachings of his predecessors regarding the social nature of the person, society as oriented to civic friendship, and the state's obligation to promote the common good, but he did so by creatively wedding rights language with natural law.

Like his predecessor, John XXIII offered a philosophical analysis of the moral purposes that ought to govern human affairs, from interpersonal to international relations. He spoke of the "person" not as a unified Aristotelian substance composed of matter and substantial form with faculties of knowing and willing, but as a bearer of rights as well as duties. The *imago Dei* grounds a set of universal and inviolable rights and a profound call to moral responsibility for self and others. Whereas Leo XIII adopted the notion of rights within a neoscholastic vision that gave primacy to the natural law, John XXIII meshed the two languages in a much more extensive way and accorded much more centrality to the notion of human rights.[93]

Individual rights must be harmonized with the common good, "the sum total of those conditions of social living whereby men are enabled more fully and readily to achieve their own perfection" (MM 65; also PT 58). This implies support for wider democratic participation in decision making throughout society, a positive encouragement of "socialization" (MM 59), and a new level of appreciation for intermediary associations (PT 24). These emphases from the natural law tradition provide an important corrective to the exaggerated individualism of liberal rights theories. Interdependence is more pronounced in John than independence. Moral interdependence is not only to characterize relations within particular communities, but also the relations of states to one another (see PT 83). International relations, especially to resolve these conflicts, must be conducted with a desire to build on the common nature that all people share.

John XXIII's most famous encyclical, *Pacem in terris*, developed an extensive natural law framework for human rights as a response to issues raised in the Cuban missile crisis. John developed rights-based criteria for assessing the moral status of public policies. He applied them to particular questions regarding the foreign policies of states engaged in the cold war, and specifically to the work of international agencies, arms control and disarmament, and, of course, positive human rights legislation. The key principle of *Pacem in terris* is that "any human society, if it to be well ordered and productive, must lay down as a foundation this principle, namely, that every human being is a person, that is, his nature is endowed with intelligence and free will. Indeed, precisely because he is a person he has rights and obligations flowing directly and simultaneously from his very nature. And as these rights are universal and inviolable so they cannot in any way be surrendered" (PT 9).

Like Grotius, John XXIII believed that natural law provides a universal moral charter that transcends particular religious confessions. He also believed with Thomas Aquinas and Leo that the human conscience readily identifies the order imprinted by God the Creator into each human being. John XXIII was in general more positively inclined to the culture of his day than were Leo XIII and Pius XI to theirs, yet all affirmed that reason can identify the dignity proper to the person and acknowledge the rights that flow from it. Protestant ethicists lamented John's high level of confidence in moral reason, optimism about historical developments, and tendency not fully to face conflicting values and interests.[94]

John XXIII was the first pope to interpret natural law in the context of genuine social and political pluralism and to treat human rights as the standard against which every social order is evaluated. His doctrine of human rights proposed what David Hollenbach calls "a normative framework for a pluralistic world."[95] It represented a significant shift away from a natural law ethic promoting a specific model of society to one acknowledging the validity of multiple valid ways of structuring society provided they pass the test of human rights.[96] This expansion set the stage not only for distinguishing one culture from another but also for distinguishing one culture from human nature as such. *Pacem in terris* signaled a dawning recognition of the need for a moral framework that does not simply impose one particular and culturally specific interpretation of human nature onto all cultures.

John XXIII's position resonated with that developed by John Courtney Murray, for whom natural law functioned both to set the moral criteria for public policy debate and to provide principles for the development of an informed conscience. What Murray called the "tradition of reason" maintained that human reason can establish a minimum moral framework for public life that can provide criteria for assessing the justice of particular social practices and civil laws.

The development of the just war theory provides a helpful example of how this approach to natural law functions. It provides criteria for interpreting and analyzing the morality of aggression, noncombatant immunity, treatment of prisoners of war, targeting policies, and the like. Though the origin of the just war theory lay in antiquity and medieval theology, its principles were further developed by international law in the seventeenth and eighteenth centuries, and refined by lawyers, secular moral philosophers, and political theorists in the twentieth century. It continues to be subject to further examination and application in light of evolving concerns about humanitarian intervention, preemptive strikes against terrorists, and uses of weapons of mass destruction. The danger that it will be used to rationalize decisions made on nonmoral grounds is as real today as it was in the eighteenth century, but the "tradition of reason" at least offers some rational criteria for engaging in public debate over where to draw the ethical line between what is ethically permissible and what is not.

Vatican II: Gaudium et spes

John XXIII's attempt to "read the signs of the times"[97] was adopted by Vatican II (1962–65). *Gaudium et spes* began by declaring its intent to read "the signs of the times" in light of the gospel. These simple words signaled a very fundamental transformation of the character of Catholic social teachings that took place at the time. We can mention briefly four of its important features: a new openness to the modern world, a heightened attentiveness to historical context and development, a return to scripture and Christology, and a special emphasis on the dignity of the person.

First, the Council's openness to the modern world contrasted with the distance and sometimes strong suspicions of popes earlier in the century. It recognized "the proper autonomy of the creature," that "by the very nature of creation, all things are endowed with their own solidity, truth, and goodness, their own laws and logic" (GS 36). This fundamental affirmation of "created autonomy" expressed both the Council's reaffirmation of the substance of the classical natural law tradition and its ability to distinguish the core of the vital tradition from its naïve and outmoded particular expressions.[98] This principle led to the admission that "the church herself knows how richly she has profited by the history and development of humanity" (GS 44).

Second, the Council's use of the language of "times" signaled a profound attentiveness to history.[99] This focus was accompanied by a new sensitivity to possibilities for change, pluralism of values and philosophies, and willingness to acknowledge the deep social and economic roots of social divisions (see GS 63). The natural law theory employed by Catholic social teachings up to the Council had been crafted under the influence of ahistorical continental rationalism. The kind of method employed by Leo XIII and Pius XI developed a modern "morality of obligation" having its roots in the Council of Trent and the subsequent four centuries of moral manuals.[100] Whereas Leo tended to attribute philosophical and religious disagreements to ignorance, fear, faulty reasoning, and prejudice, the authors of *Gaudium et spes* were more attuned to the fact that not all human beings possess a univocal faculty called "reason" that leads to identical moral conclusions.

Third, a new awareness of historicity necessarily encouraged a deeper appreciation of the biblical and Christological identity of the Church and Christian life. Openness to engage in dialogue with the modern world (*aggiornamento*) was complemented by a "return to the sources" (*ressourcement*), especially the Word of God. The new biblical emphasis was reflected in the profoundly theological understanding of human nature developed by *Gaudium et spes*, or, more precisely, a "Christologically centered humanism."[101] Neoscholastic natural law tended to rely on the theology of creation but the Council taught that the inner meaning of humanity is revealed in Christ: "The truth," they wrote, "is that only in the mystery of the incarnate Word does the mystery of man take on light. . . . Christ, the final Adam, by the revelation of the mystery of the Father and His love, fully reveals man to man himself and makes his supreme calling clear . . ." (GS 22; see also GS 10, 38, and 45). *Gaudium et spes* thus focused on relating the gospel, rather than applying "social doctrine," to contemporary situations.[102]

The new emphasis on the scriptures led to a significant departure from the usual neoscholastic philosophical framework of Catholic social teaching. The moral significance of scripture was found not in its legal directives as "divine law" but in its depiction of the call of every Christian to be united with Christ and actively to participate in the social mission of the Church. The Council's "turn to history" encouraged a more existential understanding of the concrete dynamics of grace, nature, and sin in daily life, and away from the abstract neoscholastic tendency to place nature and grace "side by side."[103] Philosophical argumentation was to be balanced by a more theologically focused imagination, policy analysis with prophetic witness, and deductive logic with appeals to the concrete struggles of the Church.

Fourth, the council fathers continued John XXIII's focus on the dignity of the person, which they understood not only in terms of the *imago Dei* of Genesis but also, as we have seen, in light of Jesus Christ. The doctrine of the incarnation generates a powerful sense of the worth of each person. The Christian moral life is not simply directed by "right reason" but also by conformity to the paschal mystery. Instead of drawing on "divine law" to confirm conclusions drawn from natural law reasoning (as in RN 11), the Word of God provides the starting point for discernment, the moral core of ethical wisdom, and the ultimate court of appeal for Christian ethical judgment.

Focus on the dignity of the person was naturally accompanied by greater attention to conscience as a source of moral insight. Placed in the context of sacred history, human experience reinforces the claim that we are caught in a "dramatic struggle between good and evil." Acknowledging the dignity of the individual conscience encouraged the Church to endorse a more inductive style of moral discernment than was typically found in the methodology of neoscholastic natural law.[104] It accorded the laity greater responsibility for their own spiritual development and encouraged greater moral maturity on their part. In virtue of their baptism, all Christians are called to holiness. The laity was thus no longer simply expected to implement directives issued by the hierarchy. On the contrary, "the task of the *entire* People of God [is] to hear, distinguish and interpret the many voices of our age, and to judge them in light of the divine word" (GS 44, emphasis added; see also MM 233–60). Out of this soil grew the new theology of liberation in Latin America.

The council fathers did not reject natural law, but they did subsume it within a more explicitly Christological understanding of human nature. Standard natural law themes were retained. "In the depths of his conscience, man detects a law which he does not impose upon himself, but which holds him to obedience" (GS 16). Every human being is obliged to conform to "the objective norms of morality" (GS 16). Human behavior must strive for "full conformity with human nature" (GS 75). All people, even those completely ignorant of scripture and the Church, can come to some knowledge of the good in virtue of their humanity. "All this holds good not only for Christians, but for all men of good will in whose hearts grace works in an unseen way" (GS 22).

The council fathers placed great emphasis on the dignity of the person, but like John XXIII they understood dignity to be protected by human rights, and human rights to be rooted in the natural law. As Jacques Maritain wrote: "The dignity of the human person? The expression means nothing if it does not signify that, by virtue of the natural law, the human person has the right to be respected, is the subject of rights, possesses rights."[105] Dignity also issues in duties and the duties of citizenship are exercised and interpreted under the influence of the Christian conscience.

The biblical tone and framework of *Gaudium et spes* displayed an understanding of natural law rooted in Christology as well as in the theology of creation. The council fathers gave more credit to reason and the intelligibility of the good than Protestant critics like Barth would ever concede,[106] but they also indicated that natural law could not be accurately understood as a self-sufficient moral theory based on the presumed superiority of reason to revelation. Just as faith and intelligence are distinct but complementary powers, so scripture and natural law are distinct but harmonious components of Christian ethics. The acknowledgment of the authority of scripture helped to build ecumenical bridges in Christian ethics.

The council fathers knew that practical reasoning about particular policy matters need not always appeal explicitly to Christ. Yet they also held that Christ provides the most powerful basis for moral choices. Catholic citizens *qua* citizens, for example, can make the public argument that capital punishment is immoral because it fails to act as a deterrent, leads to the execution of innocent people, and legitimates the use of lethal force by the state against human beings. Yet Catholic citizens *qua* citizens will also understand capital punishment more profoundly in light of Good Friday.

The influence of *Gaudium et spes* was reflected several decades later in the two most well-known U.S. bishops' pastorals, *The Challenge of Peace* (1983) and *Economic Justice for All* (1986). The process of drafting these pastoral letters involved widespread consultation with lay and non-Catholic experts on various aspects of the questions they wanted to address. The drafting procedure of the pastoral letters made it clear that the general principles of natural law regarding justice and peace carry more authority for Catholics than do their particular applications to specific contexts. It had of course been apparent from the time of Leo that it is one thing to affirm that workers are entitled to a just wage as a general principle and another to determine specifically what that wage ought to be in a given society at a particular time in its history. The pastorals added to this realization both much wider and public consultation, a clearer delineation of grades of teaching authority, and an invitation to ordinary Christians to engage in their own moral deliberation on these critically important social issues. The peace pastoral made clear the difference between the principle of proportionality in the abstract and its specific application to nuclear weapons systems, and both of these from questions of their use in retaliation to a first strike. It also made it clear that each Christian has the duty of forming his or her own conscience as a mature adult. Indeed, the bishops inaugurated a level of appreciation for Christian moral pluralism when they conceded not only the moral legitimacy of universal conscientious pacifism but also of selective conscientious objection. They allowed believers to reject a venerable moral tradition that had been the major framework for the tradition's moral analysis of war for centuries. Some Catholics welcomed this general differentiation of authority because it encouraged the laity to assume responsibility for their own moral formation and decision making, but others worried that it would call into question the teaching authority of the magisterium and foment dissent. The bishops subsequently attempted, though unsuccessfully, to apply this consultative methodology to the question of women in the Church.[107]

Paul VI

Paul VI (1963–78) presented both the neoscholastic and historically minded streams of Catholic social teachings. Influenced by his friend Jacques Maritain, Paul VI taught that Church and society ought to promote "integral human development"[108]—the whole good of every human person. Paul VI understood human nature in terms of powers to be actualized for the flourishing of self and others. This more dynamic and hopeful anthropology placed him at a great distance from Leo XIII's warning to utopians and socialists that "humanity must remain as it is" and that to "suffer and to endure, therefore, is the lot of humanity" (RN 14). Paul's anthropology was personalist: each human being has not only rights and duties but also a vocation (PP 15). Thus *Populorum progressio* (1967) was concerned not only that each wage earner achieve physical sustenance (in the manner of *Rerum novarum*) but also that each person be given the opportunity to use his or her talents to grow into integral human fulfillment in both this world and the next (PP 16). Since this "transcendent humanism" focuses on "being" rather than "having," its greatest enemies are materialism and avarice (PP 18–19).

Paul VI understood that since the context of integral development varies across time and from one culture to the next, social questions have to be considered in light of the findings of the social sciences as well as through the more traditional philosophical and theological analysis. The Church is "situated in the midst of men," and therefore has the duty of studying the "signs of the times and of interpreting them in light of the Gospel." In addressing the "signs of the times," the Church cannot supply detailed answers to economic or social problems. She offers "what she alone possesses, that is, a view of man and of human affairs in their totality" (PP 13, from GS 4). Paul knew that the magisterium could not produce clear, definitive, and detailed solutions to all social and economic problems.

This virtue is particularly evident in Paul VI's apostolic letter *Octogesima adveniens* (1971). This letter was written to Cardinal Maurice Roy, president of the Council of the Laity and of the Pontifical Commission for Justice and Peace, with the intent of discussing Christian responses to "the new social problems" (OA 8) of postindustrial society. These problems included urbanization, the role of women, racial discrimination, mass communication, and environmental degradation. Paul's apostolic letter called every Christian to take proper responsibility for acting against injustice. As in *Populorum progressio*, it did not presume that natural law could be applied by the magisterium to provide answers to every specific question generated by particular communities. In the face of widely varying circumstances, Paul wrote, "it is difficult for us to utter a unified message and to put forward a solution which has universal validity" (OA 4). Instead, it is "up to the Christian communities to analyze with objectivity the situation which is proper to their own country, to shed on it the light of the Gospel's unalterable words and to draw principles of reflection, norms of judgment and directives for action from the social teaching of the Church" (OA 4). Whereas Leo expected the principles of natural law to yield clear solutions, Paul leaves it to local communities to take it upon themselves to apply the gospel to their own situations. Natural law functions differently in a global rather than simply European setting. Instead of pronouncing from "above" the world, now the Church "accompanies humankind in its search." The Church does "not intervene to authenticate a given structure or to propose a ready-made model" to all social problems. Instead of simply reminding the faithful of general principles, it "develops through reflection applied to the changing situations of this world, under the driving force of the Gospel" (OA 42).

It bears repeating that Paul VI's social teachings did not abandon, let alone explicitly repudiate, the natural law. He employed natural law most explicitly in his famous treatment of sex and reproduction, *Humanae vitae* (1967). This encyclical essentially repeated, in somewhat different language, the moral prohibitions given a half century earlier by Pius XI in *Casti connubii* (1930). Paul VI presumed this not to be a distinctively Catholic position—"our contemporaries are particularly capable of seeing that this teaching is in harmony with human reason"[109]—but the ensuing debate did not produce arguments convincing to the "right reason" of all reasonable interlocutors.

Humanae vitae repeated the teleological claim that life has inherent purposes and each person must conform to them. Every human being has a moral obligation to conform to this natural order. In sexual ethics, this view of nature generates specific moral prohibitions based on respect for the body's "natural functions,"[110] obstruction of which is "intrinsically evil." The key principle is clear and allows for no compromise: "each and every marital act must of necessity retain its intrinsic relationship to the procreation of human life."[111] Neither good motives nor consequences (e.g., humanitarian concern to limit escalating overpopulation) can justify the deliberate violation of the divinely given natural order governing the unitive and procreative purposes of sexual activity, by either individuals or public authorities.

Critics argued that Paul VI's "physicalist" interpretation of natural law failed to appreciate sufficiently the complexities of particular circumstances, the primacy of personal mutuality and intimacy in marriage, and the difference between valuing the gift of life in general and requiring its specific expression in openness to conception in each and every act of intercourse.[112] Another important criticism laments the encyclical's priority with the rightness of sexual acts to the negligence of issues pertaining to wider human concerns. James M. Gustafson observes that in *Humane vitae* "considerations for the social well-being of even the family, not to mention various nation-states and the human species, are not sufficient to justify artificial means of birth control."[113]

"Revisionists" like Joseph Fuchs, Peter Knauer, and Richard McCormick argued that natural law is best conceived as promoting the concrete human good available in particular circumstances rather than in terms of an abstract rule applied to all people in every circumstance.[114] They pointed to a significant discrepancy between the methodology of *Octogesima adveniens* and that of *Humanae vitae*.[115]

John Paul II

John Paul II (1978–2005) interpreted the natural law from two points of view: the personalism and phenomenology he studied at the Jangiellonian University in Poland and the neoscholasticism he learned as a graduate student at the Angelicum in Rome.[116] The pope's moral teachings and his description of current events made significant use of natural law categories within a more explicitly biblical and theological framework. One of the central themes of his preaching reminds the world that faith and revelation offer the deepest and most reliable understanding of human nature, its greatest purpose and highest calling. Christian faith provides the most accurate perspective from which to understand the depth of human evil and the healing promise of saving grace.

Echoing the integral humanism of Paul VI, John Paul asked in his first encyclical, *Redemptor hominis*, whether the reigning notion of human progress "which has man for its author and promoter, makes life on earth more human in every aspect of that life. Does it make a more worthy man?"[117] The ascendancy of technology and science calls for a proportionate development of morals and ethics. Despite so many signs of progress, the pope noted, we are forced to face the question of what is most essential: "whether in the context of this progress man, as man, is becoming truly better, that is to say more mature spiritually, more aware of the dignity of his humanity, more responsible, more open to others, especially the neediest and the weakest, and readier to give and to aid all."[118] The answer to these questions can only be reached through a proper understanding of the person. Purely scientific knowledge of human nature is not sufficient. One must be existentially engaged in the reality of the person, and particularly as the person is understood in light of Jesus Christ. John Paul's Christological reading of human nature is inspired by *Gaudium et spes*: "only in the mystery of the incarnate Word does the mystery of man take on light" (GS 22).

John Paul II's social teachings rarely explicitly mention the natural law. In fact, the phrase is not even used once in *Laborem exercens* (1981), *Sollicitudo rei socialis* (1987), or *Centesimus annus* (1991). The moral argument of these documents focuses on rights that promote the dignity of the person; it simply takes for granted the existence of the natural law. John Paul II's social teachings invoke scripture much more frequently, and in a more sustained, meditative fashion, than did that of any of his predecessors. He emphasizes Christian discipleship and the special obligations incumbent on Christians living in a non-Christian and even anti-Christian world. He gives human flourishing a central place in his moral theology, but construes flourishing more in light of grace than nature. The pope's social teachings express his commitment to evangelize the world. Even reflection on the economy comes first and foremost from the point of view of the gospel. Whereas *Rerum novarum* was addressed to the bishops of the world and took its point of departure from "man's nature" (RN 6) and "nature's law" (RN 7), *Centesimus annus* is addressed to "all men and women of good will" and appeals "above all to the social message of the Gospel" (CA 57).

John Paul II's most extensive discussion of natural law occurs not in his social encyclicals but in *Veritatis splendor* (1993), the encyclical devoted to affirming the existence of objective morality. The document sounds familiar themes. Natural law is inscribed in the heart of every person, is grounded in the human good, and gives clear directives regarding right and wrong acts that can never be legitimately violated. John Paul reiterates Paul VI's rejection of ethical consequentialism and "situation ethics." "Circumstances or intentions can never transform an act intrinsically evil by nature of its object [the kind of act willed] into an act 'subjectively' good or defensible as a choice."[119] He also targets erroneous notions of autonomy:[120] true freedom is ordered to the good and ethically legitimate choices conform to it.[121]

John Paul II's emphasis on obedience to the will of God and on the necessity of revelation for Christian ethics leads some observers to suspect that he presumes a divine command ethic. Yet the pope's ethic continues to combine two standard principles of natural law theory. First, he believed that the normative structure of ethics is grounded in a descriptive account of human nature and, second, he insisted that knowledge of this structure is disclosed in revelation and explicated through its proper authoritative interpretation by the hierarchical magisterium. Since awareness of the natural law has been blurred in the "modern conscience," the pope argued, the world needs the Church, and particularly the voice of the magisterium, to clarify the specific practical requirements of the natural law. Using Murray's vocabulary, one might say that the pope believed that the magisterium plays the role of the "wise" to the "many" that is the world. As an "expert in humanity," the Church has the most profound grasp of the principles of the natural law and also the best vantage point from which to understand their secondary and tertiary (if not also the most remote) principles.[122]

The pope, however, continued to hold to the ancient tradition that moral norms are inherently intelligible. People of all cultures now acknowledge the binding authority of human rights. Natural law *qua* human rights provides the basis for the infusion of ethical principles into the political arena of pluralistic democracies. It also provides criteria for holding accountable criminal states or transnational actors that violate human dignity by engaging, for example, in "genocide, abortion . . . deportation, slavery, prostitution . . . degrading conditions of work which treat laborers as mere instruments of profit."[123]

John Paul II applied the notion of rights protecting dignity to the ethics of life in *Evangelium vitae* (1995). Faith and reason both testify to the inherent purpose of life and ground a universal obligation to respect the dignity of every human being, including the handicapped, the elderly, the unborn, and the otherwise vulnerable. "Intrinsically evil acts" cannot be legitimated for any reasons, whether individual or collective. The moral framework of society is not given by fickle popular opinion or majority vote but rather by the "objective moral law . . . the 'natural law' written in the human heart."[124] States as well as couples, no matter what difficulties and hardships they face, "must abide by the divine plan for responsible procreation." Sounding a theme from Pius XI and Paul VI, the pope warns his listeners that "the moral law obliges them in every case to control the impulse of instinct and passion, and to respect the biological laws inscribed in their person."[125] He employs natural law not only to oppose abortion, infanticide, and euthanasia but also newer biomedical procedures regarding experimentation with human embryos. The pope's claim that "a law which violates an innocent person's natural right to life is unjust and, as such, is not valid as a law" suggests to some in the United States that *Roe v. Wade* is an unjust law and therefore properly subject to acts of civil disobedience. It also implies resistance to international programs that attempt to limit population expansion through distributing means of artificial birth control.

Natural law provides criteria for the moral assessment of economic and political systems. The Church has a social ministry but no direct relation to political agenda as such. The Church's social doctrine is not a form of political ideology but an exercise of her evangelizing mission (SRS 41). It never ought to be used to support capitalism or any other economic ideology: "For the Church does not propose economic political systems or programs, nor does she show preference for one or the other, provided that human dignity is properly respected and promoted." It does not draw from natural law any one correct model of an economic or political system, but it does require that any given economic or political order affirm human dignity, promote human rights, foster the unity of the human family, and support meaningful human activity in every sphere of social life (SRS 41; CA 43).

John Paul II's interpretation of natural law has been subject to various criticisms. First, critics charge that it stresses law, and particularly divine law, at the expense of reason and nature. As the Dominican Thomist Herbert McCabe observed of *Veritatis splendor*, "despite its frequent references to St. Thomas, it is still trapped in a post-Renaissance morality, in terms of law and conscience and free will."[126] Second, the pope has been criticized for an inconsistent eclecticism that does not coherently relate biblical, natural law, and rights-oriented language in a synthetic vision. Third, he has been charged with a highly selective and ahistorical understanding of natural law. Thus what he describes as "unchanging" precepts prohibiting intrinsic evil have at times been subject to change, for example, the case of slavery. As John Noonan puts it, in the long history of Catholic ethics one finds that "what was forbidden became lawful (the cases of usury and marriage); what was permissible became unlawful (the case of slavery); and what was required became forbidden (the persecution of heretics)."[127] Critics argue that John Paul II has retreated from Paul VI's attempt to appropriate historical consciousness and therefore consistently slights the contingency, variability, and ambiguities of historical particularity.[128] This approach to natural law also leads feminists to accuse the pope of failing sufficiently to attend to the oppression of women in the history of Christianity and to downplay the need for appropriately radical change in the structures of the Church.[129]

RECENT INNOVATIONS

The opponents of natural law ethics have from time to time pronounced the theory dead. Its advocates, however, respond by pointing to its adaptability, flexibility, and persistence. As the distinguished natural law commentator Heinrich Rommen put it, "The natural law always buries its undertakers."[130] The resilience of the natural law tradition resides in its assimilative capacity. More broadly the Catholic social tradition from its start in antiquity has been eclectic, that is, a mixture of themes, arguments, convictions, and ideas taken from different strains within Western thought, both Christian and non-Christian. The medieval tradition assimilated components of Roman law, patristic moral wisdom, and Greek philosophy. It was subjected to radical philosophical criticism in the modern period but defenders of the tradition inevitably arose either to consolidate and defend it against its detractors or to develop its intellectual potentialities through the critical appropriation of conceptualities employed by modern and contemporary philosophy. Catholic social teaching has engaged in both a retrieval of the natural law ethics of Aquinas and an assimilation of some central insights of Locke and Kant regarding human rights and the dignity of the person. Scholars have argued over whether this assimilative pattern exhibits a talent for creative synthesis or the fatal flaw of incoherent eclecticism.

Philosophers and theologians have for the past several decades made numerous attempts to bring some degree of greater consistency and clarity to the use of natural law in Catholic ethics. Here we will mention three such attempts: the new natural law theory, revisionism, and narrative natural law theory.

The new natural law theory of Germain Grisez, John Finnis, and their collaborators offers a thoughtful account of the "first principles of practical reason" to provide rational order to moral choices. Even opponents of the new natural law theory admire its philosophical acuity in avoiding the "naturalistic fallacy" that attempts illicitly to deduce normative claims from descriptive claims, or "ought" language from "is" language.[131] Practical reason identifies several basic goods that are intrinsically valuable and universally recognized as such: life, knowledge, aesthetic appreciation, play, friendship, practical reasonableness, and religion.[132] It is *always* wrong to intend to destroy an instantiation of a basic good.[133] Life is a basic good, for example, and so murder is always wrong. This position does not rely on faith in any explicit way. Its advocates would agree with John Courtney Murray that the "doctrine of natural law has no Roman Catholic presuppositions."[134] Despite some ambiguities, this position presents a formidable anticonsequentialist ethical theory in terms that are intelligible to contemporary philosophers.

The new natural law theory has been subject to significant criticisms, however. First, lists of basic goods are notoriously ambiguous, for example, is religion always an instantiation of a basic value? Second, it holds that basic goods are incommensurable and cannot be subjected to weighing, but it is not clear that one cannot reasonably weigh, say, religion as a more important good than play. This theory takes it as self-evident that basic goods cannot be attacked. Yet this claim seems to ignore Niebuhr's warning that human experience is by its very nature susceptible not only to significant conflict among competing goods but even to moral tragedy in which one good cannot be obtained without the destruction of another. Third, the new natural law theory is criticized for isolating its philosophical interpretation of human nature from other descriptive accounts of the same and for operating without much attention to empirical evidence for its conclusions. For example, Finnis opines, without any empirical evidence, that same-sex relations of every kind fail to offer intelligible goods of their own but only "bodily and emotional satisfaction, pleasurable experience, unhinged from basic human reasons for action and posing as its own rationale."[135] Critics ask: To what extent is such a sweeping generalization confirmed by the evidence of real human lives rather than simply derived from certain a priori philosophical principles?

A second interpretation of the natural law comes from those who are often broadly classified as "revisionists." They engage in a selective retrieval of themes of the natural law tradition in terms of the concrete or "ontic" or "premoral" values and "dis-values" confronted in daily life. The crucial issue for the moral assessment of any pattern of human conduct, they argue, is not its "naturalness" or "unnaturalness" but its relation to the flourishing of particular human beings. The most distinctive feature of the revisionist approach to natural law, particularly when contrasted with the new natural law theory, is the relatively greater weight it gives to ordinary lived human experience as evidence for assessing opportunities for human flourishing.[136] It holds that moral insights are best attained "by way of experience,"[137] that "right reason" requires sufficient sensitivity to the salient characteristics of particular cases, and that moral theology needs to retrieve the ancient Aristotelian virtue of *epicheia*, or equity, the capacity to apply the law intelligently in accord with the concrete common good.[138] This ethical realism, as moral theologian John Mahoney puts it, "scrutinizes above all what is the purpose of any law and to what extent the application of any particular law in a given situation is conducive to the attainment of that purpose, the common good of the society in question."[139] Revisionists thus want to revise some moral teachings of the Church so that they can be pastorally more appropriate and contribute more effectively to the good of the community.

Revisionists are convinced that there is a significant difference between the personal and loving will of God and the determinate and impersonal structures of nature. They do not believe that a proper understanding of natural law requires every person to conform to given "biological laws." Indeed, some revisionists believe that natural law theory must be abandoned because it is irredeemably wedded to moral absolutism based on "physicalism." They choose instead to develop an "ethic of responsibility" or an "ethic of virtue." Other revisionists, however, remain committed to the ancient language of natural law while working to develop a historically conscious and morally sensitive interpretation of it. Applied to sexual ethics, for example, they argue that the "procreative purpose" of sexual intercourse is a good in general but not necessarily a good in each and every concrete situation or even in each particular monogamous bond. They argue that some uses of artificial birth control are morally legitimate and need to be distinguished from those that are not. On this ground they defend the use of artificial birth control as one factor to be considered in the micro-deliberation of marriage and family and in the macro-context of social ethics.

Critics raise several objections to the revisionist approach to natural law. First is the notorious difficulty of evaluating arguments from experience, which can suffer from vagueness, overgeneralization, and self-serving bias. Second, revisionist appeals to human flourishing are at times insufficiently precise and inadequately substantive. Third, critics complain that revisionists in effect abandon natural law in favor of an ethical consequentialism based in an exaggerated notion of autonomy.[140]

A third and final contemporary "narrativist" formulation of natural law theory takes as its starting point the centrality of stories, community, and tradition to personal and communal identity. Alasdair MacIntyre has done the most to show that reason, and by extension reason's interpretation of the natural law, is "tradition-dependent."[141] Christians are formed in the

Church by the gospel story, so their understanding of the human good will never be entirely "neutral." Moral claims are completely unintelligible when removed from their connection to the doctrine of Christ and the Church, but neither can the moral identity of discipleship be translated without remainder into the neutral mediating language of natural law.

Narrativists agree with the "new natural lawyers" that we are naturally oriented to a plethora of goods—from friendship and sex to music and religion—but they attend more seriously to concrete human experiences as the context within which people come to determine how (or, in some cases, even whether) these goods take specific shape in their lives. Narrativists, like the revisionists, hold that it is in and through concrete experience that people discover, appropriate, and deepen their understanding of what constitutes true human flourishing. But they also attend more carefully both to the experience, not as atomistic and existentially sporadic but as sequential, and to the ways in which the interpretations of these experiences are influenced by membership in particular communities shaped by particular stories. Discovery of the natural law, Pamela Hall notes, "takes place within a life, within the narrative context of experiences that engage a person's intellect and will in the making of concrete choices."[142]

All ethical theories are tradition-dependent, and therefore natural law theory will acknowledge its own particular heritage and not claim to have a "view from nowhere."[143] Scripture, and notably the Golden Rule and its elaboration in the Decalogue, provided the tradition with criteria for judging which aspects of human nature are normatively significant and ought to be encouraged and promoted, and, conversely, which aspects of human nature ought to be discouraged and inhibited.

This turn to narrativity need not entail a turn away from nature. The human good includes the good of the body. Jean Porter argues that ethics must take into account the considerable prerational, biological roots of human nature and critically appropriate contemporary scientific insights into the animal dimensions of our humanity.[144] Just as Aquinas employed Aristotle's notion of nature to explicate his account of the human good, so contemporary natural law ethicists need to incorporate evolutionary accounts of human origins and human behavior in order to understand the human good.

Nor does appropriating narrativity require withdrawal from the public domain. "Narrative natural law" *qua* natural law still understands the justification for basic moral norms in terms of their promotion of the good that is proper to human beings considered comprehensively. It can advance public arguments about the human good but it does not consider itself compelled to avoid all religiously based language in the manner of John A. Ryan[145] or John Courtney Murray.[146] Unlike older approaches to the common good, it will "accept a radically plural, nonhierarchical and not easily harmonizable notion of the good."[147] Its claims are intelligible to people who are not Christian, but intelligibility does not always lead to universal assent. It thus acknowledges that Christian theology does not advance its claims on the supposition that it has the only conceivable way of interpreting the moral significance of human nature. Since morality is "under-determined" by nature, "there is no one moral system that can plausibly be presented as the morality that best accords with human nature."[148]

Critics lodge several objections to narrative natural law theory. First, they worry that giving excessive weight to stories and tradition diminishes attentiveness to the structures of human nature and thereby slides into moral relativism. What is needed instead, one critic argues, is a more powerful sense of the metaphysical basis for the normativity of nature.[149] Narrativists, like revisionists, acknowledge the need to beware of the danger of swinging from one extreme of abstract universalism and "oppressive generalizations" to the other extreme of "bottomless particularity."[150] Second, they worry that narrative ethics will be unable to generate a clear and fixed set of ethical standards, ideals, and virtues. Stories pertain to particular lives in particular contexts, and moralities shift with changes in their historical contexts. Moral norms emerging from narratives alone are inherently unstable and subject to a constant process of moral drift. Narrativists can respond by arguing that these two criticisms apply to radically historicist interpretations of narrative ethics but not to narrative natural law theory.

THE ROLE OF NATURAL LAW IN CATHOLIC SOCIAL TEACHING IN THE FUTURE

Natural law has been an essential component of Catholic ethics for centuries and it will continue to play a central role in the Church's reflection on social ethics. It consistently bases its view of the moral life and public policies, in other words, on the human good. Its understanding of the human good will be rooted in theological and Christological convictions. The Church's future use of natural law will have to face four major challenges pertaining to the relation between four pairs of concerns: the individual and society, religion and public life, history and nature, and science and ethics.

First, natural law will need to sustain its reflection on the relation between the individual and society. It will have to remain steady in its attempt to correct radical individualism, an exaggerated assertion of the sovereignty and priority of the individual over and against the community. "Utilitarian individualism" regards the person as an individual agent functioning to maximize self-interest in the market system and "expressive individualism" construes the person as a private individual seeking egoistic self-expression and therapeutic liberation from socially and psychologically imposed constraints.[151] The former regards the market as opportunistic, ruthless, and amoral, and leaves each individual to struggle for economic success or to accept the consequences of failure. The latter seeks personal happiness in the private sphere where feelings can be expressed and private relationships cultivated. What Charles Taylor calls the "dark side of individualism" so centers on the self that it "both flattens and narrows our lives, makes them poorer in meaning, and less concerned with others or society."[152]

Natural law theory in Catholic social teaching responds to radical individualism in several ways. First and foremost, it offers a theologically based account of the worth of each person as made in the image of God. Second, it continues to regard the human person as naturally social and political and as flourishing within friendships and families, intermediary groups, and larger communities. The human person is always both intrinsically worthwhile and naturally called to participate in community.

Two other central features of natural law provide resources with which to meet the challenge of radical individualism. One is the ethic of the common good that counters the presupposition of utilitarian individualism that markets are inherently amoral and bound to inflexible economic laws not subject to human intervention on the basis of moral values. Catholic social teaching holds that the state has obligations that extend beyond the "night watchman" function of protecting social order. It has the primary (but by no means exclusive) obligation to promote the common good, especially in terms of public order, public peace, basic standards of justice, and minimum levels of public morality.

A second contribution from natural law to the problem of radical individualism lies in solidarity. The virtue of solidarity offers an alternative to the assumption of therapeutic individualism that happiness resides simply in self-gratification, liberation from guilt, and relationships within one's "lifestyle enclave."[153] If the person is inherently social, genuine flourishing resides in living for others rather than only for oneself, in contributing to the wider community and not only to one's small circle of reciprocal concern. The right to participate in the life of one's own community should not be eclipsed by the "right to be left alone."[154]

A second major challenge to Catholic social teachings comes from the relation between religion and public life in pluralistic societies. Popular culture increasingly regards religion as a private matter that has no place in the public sphere. If radical individualism sets the context for the discussion of the public role of religion, there will be none. Catholic social teachings offer a synthetic alternative to the privatization of faith and the marginalization of religion as a form of public moral discourse. Catholic faith from its inception has been based in a theological vision that is profoundly corporate, communal, and collective. The gospel cannot be reduced to private emotions shared between like-minded individuals.

Catholic social teachings also strive to hold together both distinctive and universally human dimensions of ethics. There are times and places for distinctively Christian and universally human forms of reflection and dialogue, respectively. In broad public contexts within pluralistic societies, Catholic social teachings must appeal to "human values" (sometimes called "public philosophy").[155] The value of this kind of moral discourse has been seen in the Nuremberg Trials after World War II, the UN Declaration on Human Rights, and Martin Luther King Jr.'s "Letter from a Birmingham Jail." In more explicitly religious contexts, it will lodge claims on the basis of Christian commitments, beliefs, or symbols (now called "public theology").[156] Discussions at bishops' conferences or parish halls can appeal to arguments that would not be persuasive if offered as public testimony before judicial or legislative bodies. Catholic social teachings are not reducible to natural law, but they can employ natural law arguments to communicate essential moral insights to those who do not accept explicitly Christian arguments. The theologically based approach to human rights found in Catholic social teachings strives to guide Christians, but they can also appeal across religious and philosophical boundaries to embrace all those who affirm, on whatever grounds, the dignity of the person. As taught by *Gaudium et spes*, there must be "a clear distinction between the tasks which Christians undertake, individually or as a group, on their own responsibility as citizens guided by the dictates of a Christian conscience, and the activities which, in union with their pastors, they carry out in the name of the Church" (GS 76).

A third major challenge facing Catholic social teaching concerns the relation of nature and history. The intense debates over *Humanae vitae* pointed to the most fundamental issues concerning the legitimacy of speaking about the "natural law" in an age aware of historicity. Yet it is clear that history cannot simply replace nature in ethics. Since the center of natural law concerns the human good, the "is" and the "ought" of Catholic social teachings are inextricably intertwined. Personal, interpersonal, and social ethics are understood in terms of what is good for human beings and what makes human beings good. It holds that human beings everywhere have, in virtue of their humanity, certain physical, psychological, moral, social, and religious needs and desires. Relatively stable and well-ordered communities make it possible for their members to meet these needs and fulfill these desires, and relatively more socially disordered and damaged communities do not.

This having been said, natural law reflection can no longer be based on a naïve view of the moral significance of "nature." Knowledge of human nature by itself does not suffice as a source of evidence for coming to understand the human good. Catholic social teaching must be alert to the perils of the "naturalistic fallacy"—the assumption that because something is natural, it is ipso facto morally good—committed by those, like Herbert Spencer and the social Darwinians, who naively attempted to discover ethical principles embedded within the evolutionary process itself.

As already indicated above, natural law reflection always runs the risk of confusing the expression of a particular culture with what is true of human beings at all times and places. Reinhold Niebuhr, for example, complained that Thomas's ethics turned "the peculiarities and the contingent factors of a feudal-agrarian economy into a system of fixed socio-economic principles."[157] The same kind of accusation has been leveled against modern natural law theories. It is increasingly taken for granted that people are so diverse in culture and personal experience, personal identities so malleable and plastic, and cultures so prone to historical variation, that any generalizations made about them will be simply too broad and vague to be ethically illuminating. Though it will never embrace postmodernism, Catholic social teaching will need to be more informed by sensitivity to historical particularity than it has been in the past. The discipline of theological ethics, unlike Catholic social teachings, has moved so far from naïve essentialism that it tends to regard human behavior as almost entirely the product of choices shaped by culture rather than rooted in nature. Yet since human beings are biological as well as cultural beings, it is more reasonable to attend to the interaction of culture and nature than to focus on one to the exclusion of the other. If "physicalism" is the triumph of nature over history, relativism is the triumph of history over nature. Neither extreme ought to find a home in Catholic social teachings, which will have to discover a way to balance and integrate these two dimensions of human experience in its normative perspective.

A fourth challenge that must be faced by Catholic social teaching concerns the relation between ethics and science. The Church has in the past resisted the identification of "reason" with "natural science." It has typically acknowledged the intellectual power of scientific discovery without regarding this source of knowledge as the key to moral wisdom. The relation of ethics and science presents two broad challenges, one positive and the other negative. The positive agenda requires the Church to interpret natural law in a way that is compatible with the best information and insights of modern science. Natural law must be formulated in a way that does not rely on archaic cosmological and scientific assumptions about the universe, the place of human beings within it, or the interaction of human beings with one another. Any tacit notion of God as "intelligent designer" must be abandoned and replaced with a more dynamic contemporary understanding of creation and providence. Catholic social teachings need to understand natural law in ways that are consistent with evolutionary biology (though not necessarily neo-Darwinism). John Paul II's recent assessment of evolution avoided a repetition of the Galileo disaster and clearly affirmed the legitimate autonomy of scientific inquiry. On October 22, 1996, he acknowledged that evolution, properly understood, is not intrinsically incompatible with Catholic doctrine.[158] He taught that the evolutionary account of the origin of animal life, including the human body, is more than a mere hypothesis. He acknowledged the factual basis of evolution but criticized its illegitimate use to support evolutionary ideologies that demean the human person.

Negatively, Catholic social teaching must offer a serious critique of the reductionistic tendency of naturalism to identify all reliable forms of knowing to scientific investigation. "Scientific naturalism" can be described (if simplistically) as an ideology that advances three related kinds of claims: that science provides the only reliable form of knowledge ("scientism"), that only the material world examined by science is real ("materialism"), and that moral claims are therefore illusory, entirely subjective, fanciful, merely aesthetic, only matters of individual opinion, or otherwise suspect ("subjectivism"). This position assumes that human intelligence employs reason only in instrumental and procedural ways, but that it cannot be employed to understand what Thomas Aquinas called the "human end" or John Paul II the "objective human good." The moral realism implicit in the natural law presuppositions of Catholic social thought needs to be developed and presented to provide an alternative to this increasingly widespread premise of popular as well as academic culture.

In responding to the challenge of scientific naturalism, the Church must continue to acknowledge the competence of science in its own domain, the universal human need for moral wisdom in matters of science and technology, the inability of science as such to offer normative guidance in ethical matters, and the rich moral wisdom made available by the natural law tradition. The persuasiveness of the natural law claims made by Catholic social teachings resides in the clarity and cogency of the Church's arguments, its ability to promote public dialogue through appealing to persuasive accounts of the human good, and its willingness to shape the public consensus on important issues. Its persuasiveness also depends on the integrity, justice, and compassion with which natural law principles are applied to its own practices, structures, and day-to-day communal life; natural law claims will be more credible when they are seen more fully to govern the Church's own institutions.

NOTES

1. Aristotle, *Nicomachean Ethics* 5.7, 1134b18, trans. Martin Ostwald (Indianapolis, Ind.: Bobbs Merrill, 1962), 131.

2. Cicero, *De re publica* 3.22.

3. *Institutes* I,1. *The Institutes of Gaius*, Part 1, ed. and trans. Francis De Zulueta (Oxford: Clarendon, 1946), 4.

4. Alan Watson, ed., *The Digest of Justinian*, 2 vols. (Philadelphia: University of Pennsylvania Press, 1998), bk. I, 13 (no pagination). Justinian's *Digest*, bk. I, 1, attributes this view to Ulpian.

5. Justinian, *Digest* I, 1.

6. See Athenagoras, "A Plea for Christians," chaps. 25 and 35 in *The Writings of Justin Martyr and Athenagoras*, ed. and trans. Marcus Dods, George Reith, and B. P. Pratten (Edinburgh: Clark, 1870), 408ff. and 419ff., respectively.

7. See "Dialogue with Trypho the Jew," chap. 93, in ibid., 217. On patterns of early Christian response to pagan ethical thought, see Henry Chadwick, *Early Christian Thought and the Classical Tradition: Studies in Justin, Clement, and Origen* (Oxford: Clarendon, 1966), and Michel Spanneut, *Le Stoïcisme des Pères de l'Église: De Clément de Rome a Clément d'Alexandrie* (Paris: Éditions du Seuil, 1957). Tertullian provided a more disparaging view of the significance of "Athens" for "Jerusalem."

8. Chadwick, *Early Christian Thought*, 4–5.

9. For an influential modern treatment, see Ernst Troeltsch, "The Ideas of Natural Law and Humanity in World Politics," in *Natural Law and the Theory of Society: 1500–1800*, ed. Otto Gierke, trans. Ernest Barker (Boston: Beacon, 1960). A helpful correction of Troeltsch is provided by Ludger Honnefelder, "Rationalization and Natural Law: Max Weber's and Ernst Troeltsch's Interpretation of the Medieval Doctrine of Natural Law," *Review of Metaphysics* 49 (1995): 275–94. On Rom. 2:14–16, see John W. Martens, "Romans 2:14–16: A Stoic Reading," *New Testament Studies* 40 (1994): 55–67, and Rudolf Schnackenburg, *The Moral Teaching of the New Testament* (New York: Seabury, 1979). Schnackenburg comments on Rom. 2:14–15: "St. Paul's 'by nature' cannot simply be equated with the moral *lex naturalis*, nor can this reference be seen as straight-forward adoption of Stoic teaching" (291).

10. From Origen, "Commentary on Romans," cited in *The Early Christian Fathers*, ed. and trans. Henry Bettenson (New York and Oxford: Oxford University Press, 1956), 199, 200.

11. *Against Faustus the Manichean* XXII. 73–79, in *Augustine: Political Writings*, ed. Ernest L. Fortin and Douglas Kries, trans. Michael W. Tkacz and Douglas Kries (Indianapolis, Ind.: Hackett, 1994), 226; *Patrologia Latina* (Migne) 42, 418.

12. See Augustine, *De Doctrina Christiana* 2, 40; PL 34, 63.

13. See Alan Watson, ed., *The Digest of Justinian*, with Latin text, ed. T. Mommsen and P. Krüger, 4 vols. (Philadelphia: University of Pennsylvania Press, 1985); A. Watson, ed., *The Digest of Justinian*, 2 vols., rev. English-language ed. (Philadelphia: University of Pennsylvania Press, 1998).

14. See note 5, above; *Institutes* 2.1.11. See also Thomas Aquinas's adoption of the threefold distinction: natural law (common to all animals), the law of nations (common to all human beings), and civil law (common to all citizens of a particular political community). ST II-II 57, 3. This distinction plays an important role in later reflection on the variability of the natural law and on the moral status of the right to private property in Catholic social teachings (e.g., RN 8).

15. *Decretum*, Part 1, distinction 1, prologue; *The Treatise on Laws (Decretum DD. 1–20) with the Ordinary Gloss*, trans. Augustine Thompson and James Gordley, *Studies in Medieval and Early Modern Canon Law*, vol. 2 (Washington, D.C.: Catholic University of America Press, 1993), 3.

16. Ibid., Part 1, distinction 8; in *Treatise on Laws*, 25.

17. See Brian Tierney, *The Idea of Natural Rights: Studies on Natural Rights, Natural Law and Church Law, 1150–1625* (Atlanta: Scholars Press, 1997), 65.

18. See Ernest L. Fortin, "On the Presumed Medieval Origin of Individual Rights," *Communio* 26 (1999): 55–79.

19. ST I-II, 90, 4. See Clifford G. Kossel, "Natural Law and Human Law (Ia IIae, qq. 90–97)," in *The Ethics of Aquinas*, ed. Stephen J. Pope (Washington, D.C.: Georgetown University Press, 2002), 169–93.

20. ST I-II, 90, 1.

21. Ibid., I-II, 94, 3.

22. See *Phys.* II.1, 193a28–29.

23. *Pol.* 1252b32.

24. Ibid. 1.2.1253a; see also Plato, *Republic* 428e–429a.

25. ST I-II, 94, 2.

26. See ibid. I-II, 94, 2. See also Cicero, *De officiis*, I. 4; Lottin, *Le droit naturel chez Thomas d'Aquin et ses prédécesseurs*, rev. ed. (Bruges: Beyaert, 1931), 78–81.

27. *Laws*, I.xii, 33; emphasis added.

28. ST I-II, 94, 2. See also Cicero, *De officiis*, I. 4.

29. ST I-II, 94, 2.

30. *De Lib. Arbit.* I,15; PL 32, 1229; for Thomas, ST I, 22, 1–2; I-II, 91, 1; 91, 2.

31. ST I-II, 31, 7; emphasis added.

32. See ibid. I, 96, 4; I-II, 72, 4; II-II, 109, 3 ad 1; 114, 2, ad 1; 129, 6, ad 1; also *De Regno*, I, 1; *In Ethic.*, IX, lect. 10, no. 1891; *In Polit.*, I, lect. I, no. 36–37.

33. See ST I, 60, 5; I-II, 21, 3–4; 90, 2; 92, 1, ad 3; 96, 4; II-II, 58, 5; 61, 1; 64, 5; 65, 1; see also Jacques Maritain, *The Person and the Common Good*, trans. John J. Fitzgerald (Notre Dame, Ind.: University of Notre Dame Press, 1946).

34. See ST I-II, 21, 4, ad 3.

35. See ibid. I-II, 109, 3; also I-II, 21, 4; II-II, 26, 3.

36. ST II-II, 57, 1. See Lottin, *Droit Naturel*, 97; also see idem, *Moral Fondamentale* (Tournai: Desclée, 1954), 173–76.

37. See ST II-II, 78, 1.

38. Ibid. II-II, 110, 3.

39. Ibid. II-II, 153, 2. See ibid. II-II, 154, 11.

40. Ibid. I, 119.

41. Ibid. I, 92, 1.

42. Ibid. I-II, 23.

43. See Michael Bertram Crowe, *The Changing Profile of the Natural Law* (The Hague: Martinus Nijhoff, 1977).

44. See ST I-II, 91, 4.

45. Ibid. I-II, 91, 4.

46. See Yves Simon, *The Tradition of Natural Law* (New York: Fordham University Press, 1952), 61, and Servais Pinckaers, chap. 10 in *The Sources of Christian Ethics*, trans. Mary Thomas Noble (Washington, D.C.: Catholic University of America Press, 1995).

47. See Pinckaers, *Sources*, 240–53, who relies in part on Vereecke, *De Guillaume d'Ockham á saint Alphonse de Ligouri*. See also Étienne Gilson, *History of Christian Philosophy in the Middle Ages* (New York: Random House, 1955), 489–519. Michel Villey's *Questions de saint Thomas sur le droit et la politique* regards Ockham as the first philosopher to break with the premodern understanding of *ius* as objective right and to put in its place a subjective faculty or power possessed naturally by every individual human being. Richard Tuck's *Natural Rights Theories: Their Origin and Development* (Cambridge: Cambridge University Press, 1979) traces the origin of subjective rights to Jean Gerson's identification of *ius* and liberty to use something as one pleases without regard to any duty. Tierney shows that the origins of the language of subjective rights are rooted in the medieval canonists rather than invented by Ockham. See Tierney, *The Idea of Natural Rights*.

48. See Simon, *Tradition of Natural Law*, 61.

49. See B. Tierney, who is supported by Charles J. Reid Jr., "The Canonistic Contribution to the Western Rights Tradition: An Historical Inquiry," *Boston College Law Review* 33 (1991): 37–92, and Annabel S. Brett, *Liberty, Right, and Nature: Individual Rights in Later Scholastic Thought* (Cambridge and New York: Cambridge University Press, 1997).

50. See, for instance, *On Civil Power*, ques. 3, art. 4, in *Vitoria: Political Writings*, ed. Anthony Pagden and Jeremy Lawrence (Cambridge: Cambridge University Press, 1991), 40. Also Ramón Hernandez, *Derechos Humanos en Francisco de Vitoria* (Salamanca: Editorial San Esteban, 1984), 185.

51. On *dominium*, see chap. 2 in Tuck, *Natural Rights Theories*. Further study of this topic would have to include an examination of the important contributions of two of Vitoria's students, Domingo de Soto and Fernando Vázquez de Menchaca. See Bartolomé de las Casas, *In Defense of the Indians*, trans. Stafford Poole (DeKalb: North Illinois University Press, 1992).

52. See John Mahoney, *The Making of Moral Theology: A Study of the Roman Catholic Tradition* (Oxford: Clarendon, 1987), 224–31.

53. See Ernest L. Fortin, "The New Rights Theory and the Natural Law," *Review of Politics* 44, no. 4 (1982): 602.

54. See Thomas Hobbes, chap. 6 in *De corpore*.

55. Michael Sandel, *Liberalism and the Limits of Justice* (New York: Cambridge University Press, 1998), 175. An alternative to Sandel is provided by the defense of modern natural law by David Braybrooke, *Natural Law Modernized* (Toronto: University of Toronto, 2001).

56. Thomas Hobbes, *Leviathan*, ed. C. B. MacPherson (New York: Penguin), I.14, 189.

57. Ibid.

58. Ibid.

59. John Locke, chap. 9 in *The Second Treatise of Government*, ed. Peter Laslett (New York and Scarborough, Ont.: New American Library, 1960), esp. 395.

60. Chap. 11 in ibid., 314; chap. 16 in ibid., 319.

61. Chap. 131, in ibid., 398.

62. See Alasdair MacIntyre, *After Virtue* (Notre Dame, Ind.: University of Notre Dame Press, 1981, rev. ed., 1984).

63. Immanuel Kant, *Critique of Pure Reason* (1781), trans. Norman Kemp Smith (New York: St. Martin's, 1965), 23.

64. See I. Kant, *Foundations of the Metaphysics of Morals*, 1787, Second Section.

65. Jeremy Bentham, *The Principles of Morals and Legislation* (New York: Hafner, 1948), 1.

66. Leo XIII, *Aeterni patris* 31, in *The Church Speaks to the Modern World: The Social Teachings of Leo XIII*, ed. Étienne Gilson (Garden City, N.Y.: Doubleday, 1954), 50.

67. Leo XIII, *Immortale dei* (*On the Christian Constitution of States*), in ibid., 157–87.

68. Ibid., 163, number 4.

69. Leo XIII, *Libertas praestantissimum* (*The Nature of Human Liberty*), in ibid., 57–85, number 15.

70. Ibid., 66, number 15.

71. Ibid., 61, number 7.

72. Ibid.

73. Ibid., 76, number 32.

74. See ST II-II, 66, 1.

75. J. Locke, Bk. II, chap. 27. Leo was influenced in this matter by Jesuit theologian Luigi Taparelli d'Azeglio (1793–1862). See Richard L. Camp, *The Papal Ideology of Social Reform: A Study in Historical Development, 1878–1967* (Leiden: E. J. Brill, 1969), 55, 56; see also Normand Joseph Paulhus, *The Theological and Political Ideals of the Fribourg Union* (Ph.D. diss., Boston College-Andover Newton Theological Seminary, 1983).

76. See *Pol.* 1261b33.

77. See RN 52 against improper "absorption" and CA 48 on "coordination" for the common good; also EJA 124 and *Catechism of the Catholic Church* 1883. Pius's subsidiarity also provided inspiration for the "distributism" or "distributivism" of Chesterton, Belloc, and Dorothy Day.

78. In *The Church and the Reconstruction of the Modern World: The Social Encylicals of Pius XI*, ed. Terence P. McLaughlin (Garden City, N.Y.: Image, 1957), 115–70.

79. *Casti connubii*, in ibid., 136, number 54.

80. Ibid., 141, number 71.

81. See ibid., 148, number 86.

82. See ibid., 149–50, numbers 89–91.

83. It is important to note that eugenics policies were not the invention of Nazi Germany. Widespread forced sterilization of those deemed "criminally insane," "feebleminded," or otherwise "mentally defective"—often residing in public mental institutions—was practiced in the United States well before the Nazification of the German legal system. In 1926 Justice Oliver Wendell Holmes justified sterilization policies by arguing that "it is better for all the world, if instead of waiting to execute degenerate offspring for crime, or to let them starve for their imbecility, society can prevent those who are manifestly unfit from continuing their kind." Roman Catholic bishops provided the strongest opposition to the eugenics movement in the United States. See Edward J. Larson, *Sex, Race, and Science: Eugenics in the Deep South* (Baltimore: Johns Hopkins University Press, 1996).

84. Adolf Hilter, *Mein Kampf*, in *Social and Political Philosophy: Readings from Plato and Gandhi*, ed. John Somerville and Ronald E. Santoni (Garden City, N.Y.: Doubleday, 1963), 445.

85. *Casti connubii*, in *Social Encyclicals of Pius XI*, ed. T. P. McLaughlin, 140, number 68.

86. Ibid., 140, number 69.

87. Ibid., 141, number 70, citing ST II-II, 108, 4 ad 2.

88. *Summi pontificatus* (October 27, 1939) (*On the Function of the State in the Modern World*), in *The Social Teachings of the Church*, ed. Anne Fremantle (New York: New American Library, 1963), 130–35.

89. *Mit brennender Sorge* (*On the Present Position of the Catholic Church in the German Empire*), in ibid., 89–94.

90. See ibid., 91–92.

91. *Summi pontificatus*, in ibid., 131, number 35.

92. See Pius XII, "Christmas Message 1944," in *Pius XII and Democracy* (New York: Paulist, 1945), 301. See also the article in this volume by John P. Langan, "Catholic Social Teaching in a Time of Extreme Crisis: The Christmas Messages of Pius XII (1939–1945)."

93. See Drew Christiansen's Commentary on *Pacem in terris* in this volume.

94. See Reinhold Niebuhr, "Pacem in Terris: Two Views," *Christianity in Crisis* 23 (1963): 81–83; Paul Ramsey, "Pacem in Terris," *Religion in Life* 33 (winter 1963–64): 116–35; Paul Tillich, "Pacem in Terris," *Criterion* 4 (spring 1965): 15–18, and idem, "On 'Peace on Earth,'" *Theology of Peace*, ed. Ronald H. Stone (Louisville, Ky.: Westminster/John Knox, 1990). More favorable reviews of natural law in general have emerged recently, as in James M. Gustafson, *Ethics from a Theocentric Perspective*, 2 vols. (Chicago: University of Chicago Press, 1981 and 1983), Michael Cromartie, ed., *A Preserving Grace: Protestants, Catholics and Natural Law* (Washington, D.C.: Ethics and Public Policy Center/Grand Rapids, Mich.: Eerdmans, 1997), and Oliver O'Donovan, *Resurrection and Moral Order: An Outline for Evangelical Ethics*, rev. ed. (Grand Rapids, Mich.: Eerdmans, 1994).

95. David Hollenbach, *Justice, Peace and Human Rights: American Catholic Social Ethics in a Pluralistic World* (New York: Crossroad, 1988, 1990), 90.

96. Ibid., 90.

97. PT 30–43, 57–59, 75–79, 126–29, 142–45, based on Matt. 16:1–4, where Jesus rebukes the Pharisees and Sadducees for their blindness before the "signs."

98. See Johan Verstraeten, "Re-Thinking Catholic Social Thought as Tradition," in *Catholic Social Thought: Twilight or Renaissance*? ed. J. S. Boswell, F. P. McHugh, and J. Verstraeten, *Bibliotheca Ephemeridum Theologicarum Lovaneinsium*, vol. 157 (Leuven, Belgium: Leuven University Press, 2000).

99. See John O'Malley, "Reform, Historical Consciousness, and Vatican II's *Aggiornamento*," *Theological Studies* 32 (1971): 573–601.

100. See Pinckaers, *Sources*, Part 2.

101. Joseph Komonchak, "The Encounter between Catholicism and Liberalism," in *Catholicism and Liberalism: Contributions to American Public Philosophy*, ed. R. Bruce Douglass and David Hollenbach (New York: Cambridge University Press, 1994), 82.

102. See M. D. Chenu, *"La doctrine sociale" de l'église comme idéologie* (Paris: Cerf, 1979).

103. Jean-Yves Calvez and Jacques Perrin, *The Church and Social Justice: The Social Teaching of the Popes from Leo XIII to Pius XII, 1878–1958*, trans. J. R. Kirwan (Chicago: H. Regnery, 1961), 39.

104. See in this volume chapters by C. Curran, R. Gaillardetz, and M. Mich. Mich attributes the development of an inductive methodology to MM.

105. Jacques Maritain, *The Rights of Man and Natural Law*, trans. Doris Anson (New York: Charles Scribner's Sons, 1943), 65.

106. See Karl Barth, "The Command of God the Creator," chap. 12 in *Church Dogmatics*, vol. 3, no. 4, trans. A. T. Mackay et al. (Edinburgh: T. & T. Clark, 1961), 3–31. See also the debate over the "orders of creation" in Emil Brunner and Karl Barth, *Natural Theology*, trans. P. Fraenkel (London: Geoffrey Bles, Centenary, 1946).

107. See Charles E. Curran, "The Reception of Catholic Social Teaching in the United States," in this volume.

108. See Jacques Maritain, *Integral Humanism*, trans. Joseph W. Evans (Notre Dame, Ind.: University of Notre Dame Press, [1936] 1973).

109. *Humanae vitae*, number 12, in *The Papal Encyclicals 1958–1981*, ed. Claudia Carlen (Raleigh, N.C.: Pierian, 1981), 226.

110. HV, number 17, in ibid., 228.

111. HV, number 11, in ibid.

112. See Charles Curran, *Transitions and Traditions in Moral Theology* (Notre Dame, Ind.: University of Notre Dame Press, 1979).

113. James M. Gustafson, *Ethics from a Theocentric Perspective*, vol. 2 (Chicago and London: University of Chicago Press, 1984), 59.

114. Representative essays can be found in Charles E. Curran and Richard A. McCormick, eds., *Readings in Moral Theology No. 1: Moral Norms and Catholic Tradition* (Mahwah, N.J.: Paulist, 1979).

115. See Charles E. Curran, "Official Social and Sexual Teaching: A Methodological Comparison,"

in *Tensions in Moral Theology* (Notre Dame, Ind.: University of Notre Dame Press, 1988), 87–109.

116. See John M. McDermott, ed., *The Thought of John Paul II* (Rome: Editrice Pontificia Università Gregoriana, 1993). One should note that personalism has been used by progressive as well as traditionalist interpretations of Catholic ethics. A revisionist form of personalism is found in Louis Janssens's classic article, "Artificial Insemination: Ethical Considerations," *Louvain Studies* 5 (1980): 3–29.

117. *Redemptor hominis*, number 15, in *Papal Encyclicals 1958–1981*, ed. C. Carlen, 256.

118. Ibid., 256–57.

119. *Veritatis splendor*, number 81, in *The Splendor of Truth: Veritatis Splendor* (Washington, D.C.: U.S. Catholic Conference, 1993), 124–25.

120. Contrast Josef Fuchs, *Personal Responsibility: Christian Morality* (Washington, D.C.: Georgetown University Press, 1983) with Martin Rhonheimer, *Natural Law and Practical Reason: A Thomist View of Moral Autonomy*, trans. Gerald Malsbary (New York: Fordham University Press, 2000).

121. *Veritatis splendor*, number 72, in *Splendor of Truth*, 109–10.

122. See notes 95–97 above.

123. *Veritatis splendor*, number 80, in *Splendor of Truth*, 123, citing GS 27.

124. *The Gospel of Life, Evangelium Vitae: On the Value and Inviolability of Human Life* (Washington, D.C.: U.S. Catholic Conference, 1995), 70, 128.

125. Ibid., 172, number 97.

126. Herbert McCabe, "Manuals and Rule Books," in *Considering Veritatis Splendor*, ed. John Wilkins (Cleveland, Ohio: Pilgrim, 1994), 67. See also William C. Spohn, "Morality on the Way of Discipleship: The Use of Scripture in *Veritatis Splendor*," in *Veritatis Splendor: American Responses*, ed. Michael E. Allsopp and John J. O'Keefe (Kansas City, Mo.: Sheed and Ward, 1995), 83–105.

127. John T. Noonan Jr., "Development in Moral Doctrine," in *The Context of Casuistry*, ed. James F. Keenan and Thomas A. Shannon (Washington, D.C.: Georgetown University Press, 1995), 194.

128. See Charles E. Curran, *Catholic Social Teaching 1891–Present: A Historical, Theological, and Ethical Analysis* (Washington, D.C.: Georgetown University Press, 2002), 61–66.

129. See Lisa Sowle Cahill, "Accent on the Masculine," in *John Paul II and Moral Theology: Readings in Moral Theology, No. 10*, ed. Charles E. Curran and Richard A. McCormick (New York: Paulist, 1998), 85–91.

130. Heinrich A. Rommen, *The Natural Law: A Study in Legal and Social History and Philosophy*, trans. Thomas R. Hanley (St. Louis, Mo.: Herder, 1947), 267.

131. On the "is-ought" issue, see Germain Grisez, "The First Principle of Practical Reason: A Commentary on the *Summa Theologiae*, 1–2, Question 94, Article 2," *Natural Law Forum* 10 (1965): 168–201.

132. John Finnis, *Natural Law and Natural Rights* (New York: Oxford University Press, 1980), 86–90.

133. Ibid., 118–23.

134. John Courtney Murray, *We Hold These Truths: Catholic Reflections on the American Proposition* (New York: Sheed and Ward, 1960), 109.

135. *Aquinas: Moral, Political, and Legal Theory* (Oxford: Oxford University Press, 1998), 153, 151. For the major critique of this position, see Russell Hittinger, *A Critique of the New Natural Law Theory* (Notre Dame: University of Notre Dame Press, 1987).

136. See, for example, Margaret Farley, "The Role of Experience in Moral Discernment," in *Christian Ethics: Problems and Prospects*, ed. Lisa Sowle Cahill and James F. Childress (Cleveland, Ohio: Pilgrim, 1996). Whereas John Paul II identifies the normatively human with what is given in the scriptures and tradition and taught by the magisterium, the revisionist relies, *in addition to* these primary sources, on reasonable interpretations and judgments of what actually constitutes genuine human flourishing in lived human experience. Human flourishing is conceived much more strongly in affective and interpersonal terms than in strictly natural terms. One must acknowledge the qualifying phrase *in addition to* scripture and tradition to avoid the impression that this position favors experience *over* revelation or ecclesially established norms; the revisionist regards experience as one basis for selectively modifying and revising an ongoing moral tradition, not as its replacement.

137. ST II-II, 47, 15.

138. See *Nicomachean Ethics* 1137a31–1138a3, and ST II-II, 120.

139. See Mahoney, *Making of Moral Theology*, 242.

140. See Rhonheimer, *Natural Law and Practical Reason*.

141. See Alasdair MacIntyre, *After Virtue*, rev. ed. (Notre Dame, Ind.: University of Notre Dame Press, 1984); Pamela Hall, *Narrative and the Natural Law* (Notre Dame, Ind.: University of Notre Dame Press); Jean Porter, *Natural and Divine Law: Reclaiming the Tradition for Christian Ethics* (Grand Rapids, Mich.: Eerdmans/Ottawa, Ont.: Novalis, 1999).

142. Hall, *Narrative and Natural Law*, 37. Human learning takes time. Natural law is "discovered progressively over time and through a process of reasoning engaged with the material of experience. Such reasoning is carried on by individuals and has a history within the life of communities. We learn the natural law, not by deduction, but by reflection upon our own and our predecessors' desires, choices, mistakes, and successes." Ibid., 94.

143. Thomas Nagel, *The View from Nowhere* (New York: Oxford University Press, 1986).

144. See Porter, chap. 1 in *Natural and Divine Law*.

145. See John A. Ryan, *A Living Wage: Its Ethical and Economic Aspects* (New York: Macmillan, 1906).

146. See Murray, *We Hold These Truths*.

147. See John A. Coleman, "The Future of Catholic Social Thought," in this volume.

148. Porter, *Natural and Divine Law*, 141.

149. Lawrence Dean, "Jean Porter on Natural Law: Thomistic Notes," *Thomist* 66, no. 2 (2002): 275–309.

150. Cahill, "Accent on the Masculine," 86.

151. See Robert Bellah et al., *Habits of the Heart: Individualism and Commitment in American Life* (San Francisco: Harper and Row, 1985).

152. Charles Taylor, *The Ethics of Authenticity* (Cambridge, Mass.: Harvard University Press, 1991), 4.

153. Bellah et al., *Habits*, 71–75.

154. Samuel Warren and Louis Brandeis, "The Right to Privacy," *Harvard Law Review* 4 (1890): 193.

155. See J. Bryan Hehir, "The Discipline and Dynamic of a Public Church," *Origins* 14 (May 31, 1984): 40–43.

156. See Michael J. Himes and Kenneth R. Himes, chap. 1 in *Fullness of Faith: The Public Significance of Theology* (New York: Paulist, 1993).

157. Reinhold Niebuhr, *The Nature and Destiny of Man: A Christian Interpretation*, 2 vols. (New York: Scribners, 1964), 1:281.

158. See John Paul II, "Message to the Pontifical Academy of Sciences," *L'Osservatore Romano*, October 30, 1996, reprinted with responses in *Quarterly Review of Biology* 72, no. 4 (1997): 381–406. See also John Paul II, "Lessons of the Galileo Case," *Origins* 22 (November 12, 1992): 370–75.

SELECTED BIBLIOGRAPHY

Curran, Charles E., and Richard McCormick, eds. *Readings in Moral Theology No. 7: Natural Law and Theology*. New York and Mahwah: Paulist, 1991. Representative essays by moral theologians from a variety of perspectives.

Delhaye, Phillippe. *Permenance du droit naturel*. Louvain: Nauwelaerts, 1967. Historical survey of major figures in the history of moral theology.

Evans, Illtude, O.P., ed. *Light on the Natural Law*. Baltimore and Dublin: Helicon, 1965. Helpful studies in natural law from several disciplines.

Fuchs, Josef. *The Natural Law: A Theological Investigation*. New York: Sheed and Ward, 1965. Early attempt to examine the biblical basis of natural law.

George, Robert P., ed. *Natural Law Theory: Contemporary Essays*. New York: Oxford University Press, 1992. Representative of the new natural law theory.

Nussbaum, Arthur. *A Concise History of the Law of Nations*. New York: Macmillan [1947] 1954. Natural law and international law.

Sigmund, Paul E. *Natural Law in Political Thought*. Cambridge, Mass.: Winthrop, 1971. Selections of classic texts from the history of philosophy.

Strauss, Leo. *Natural Right and History*, 2d ed. Chicago: University of Chicago Press, 1965. Argues for re-examination of the normative status of nature.

Traina, Cristina L. H. *Feminist Ethics and Natural Law: The End of Anathemas*. Washington, D.C.: Georgetown University Press, 1999. Feminist reflections on natural law.

CHAPTER

3

The Ecclesiological Foundations of Modern Catholic Social Teaching

RICHARD R. GAILLARDETZ

INTRODUCTION

Catholic Christianity holds that the life and teaching of Jesus Christ has public significance and carries with it implications for social structures and for the conduct of men and women living in society. Even when many Christians in the second and third centuries adopted an adversarial stance toward the larger society, they maintained their conviction that the practice of the Christian faith had concrete social consequences. The emergence of an explicit body of doctrine referred to as Catholic social teaching from the late nineteenth century up to the present has always depended upon a set of presuppositions about the nature and mission of the Church in the world.

This chapter explores some of the ecclesiological foundations of modern Catholic social teaching by considering four distinct questions: (1) How ought we to conceive the Church's relationship to the world? (2) What are the ecclesial processes operative in the formation of Catholic social teaching? (3) What is the authoritative status of Catholic social teaching and, correlatively, what is the appropriate response of the believer to this teaching? (4) What are the implications of Catholic social teaching for the life of the Church itself?

THE CHURCH'S RELATIONSHIP TO THE WORLD

This first section addresses the most foundational of ecclesiological concerns in Catholic social teaching: how the Church is to relate to the larger society. The development of Catholic social thought in the mid-eighteenth century began in a period of ecclesiological upheaval. The various threats to the fundamental nature and structure of the Church raised by the Protestant reformers in the sixteenth century had led to a one-sided stress on the visibility of the Church. Catholic apologists like St. Robert Bellarmine saw the Church as a visible society mirroring the institutional integrity of a secular city-state. In particular, Bellarmine reacted to Luther's denigration of the visible Church by insisting that ecclesial institutions were integral to the very definition of the Church. It is during the late sixteenth and early seventeenth centuries that the Church came to be seen as a *societas perfecta*, a "perfect society." The idea was not that the Church was morally perfect but rather that it was completely self-sufficient, possessing all of the institutional resources necessary for the fulfillment of its mission.

With the Reformation, and later the Enlightenment, had come the gradual demise of Christendom, that uneasy partnership of Church and culture that could be traced back to the fourth century. The Reformation rent asunder the precious unity of the Western Church of the Middle Ages, and when the seventeenth and eighteenth centuries saw the rise of modern science, the emergence of nationalism, and the age of reason, the medieval synthesis of Church and culture was lost, replaced by suspicion and festering animosities. The Catholic Church's stance toward the world moved from a confident if often combative engagement with society to a growing siege mentality.

This ecclesiological shift plays a vital role in the development of modern Catholic social teaching. Many ecclesiastical pronouncements on "worldly affairs," condemnations of unwarranted state interference in church matters, denunciations of anticlericalism, and a repeated assertion of the state's obligation to preserve the right of Catholics to practice their faith, all reflected the Church's negative judgment on the demise of Christendom and the rise of liberalism.[1] This siege mentality would only be strengthened by the French Revolution. As T. Howland Sanks observed, "if the Age of Reason had threatened the authority of the Church in various intellectual spheres, the Age of Revolution threatened its very existence."[2]

The emergence of a Catholic social critique in the late eighteenth and early nineteenth centuries was occasioned in large part by the rise of industrialism and dramatic population shifts from rural areas to the cities. The result of these shifts was a profound sense of social dislocation and the creation of a new class, an "urban proletariat."[3] The Church was quick to recognize the potentially dangerous social consequences of these developments. While the virulent anticlericalism that came in the wake of the French Revolution abated to an extent, the tumultuous events of the nineteenth century only exacerbated the Church's defensive posture toward a world perceived as increasingly hostile to the Church. Pope Gregory XVI produced a series of condemnations of various aspects of modern liberalism, and Pope Pius IX, initially open to the liberal impulse, was shocked by the wave of nationalist revolution that swept Western Europe in 1848 and henceforward would share Gregory's substantial repudiation of liberalism.

A certain ecclesial paternalism predominated in Catholicism's engagement with the larger society. Michael Schuck has noted a common ecclesial metaphor running through papal pronouncements from Benedict XIV through the long pontificate of Pius IX: the shepherd and flock. Christ is consistently portrayed as the good shepherd:

> correspondingly, the popes represent the world as a pasture. Unlike the Enlightenment's heady optimism over a machine-like, controllable world, the popes' pastoral image imparts a cautionary worldview. Though the pasture provides nourishment and rest for the flock, it also contains "trackless places," "ravening wolves," and evil men "in the clothing of sheep."[4]

The sheep are expected to docilely heed the warnings of their shepherd the pope in avoiding the many evils of the age.

With the pontificate of Leo XIII in the late nineteenth century the Church embarked on a more positive if still quite cautious engagement with the issues of the larger world. Yet this stance was short lived. The violent reaction to modernism early in the pontificate of Pope Pius X reinforced key elements of the siege mentality preponderant since the Reformation. A largely critical stance toward society continued in the first half of the twentieth century, with the papacy issuing sharp rebukes of significant elements of modern capitalism, socialism, industrialism, and a continued program of state encroachment in church matters. Schuck observes that from Leo XIII to Pius XII one can detect in the Church's attitude toward the world a marked shift in metaphors. The pastoral metaphor of sheep/flock is replaced by the metaphor of "cosmological design" in which it is the task of the Church to see that the natural order of things, indeed all of creation, fulfill its God-given end.[5] Were it not for the effects of sin on human rationality, humankind would be able to recognize the rational order of the universe. This defect in human nature demands the guidance of church teaching to assist humanity in the recognition of the divinely willed, cosmic order of things. Not surprisingly, the specific formulation of Catholic social teaching would make much greater use of natural law theory, congenial as that theory was to a viewpoint built on the rational ordering of the cosmos. This shift in perspective would also warrant ever more expansive claims to papal authority in the affairs of the world. It would be left to the pontificate of John XXIII and Vatican II to reconceive the Church's relationship to the larger world.

Conciliar and Postconciliar Views of the Church's Relationship to the World

The encyclicals of Pope John XXIII and Vatican II's *Gaudium et spes* inaugurated a new stage in the Church's perception of its engagement with the world. Pope John's two social encyclicals *Mater et magistra* and *Pacem in terris* continued to articulate Catholic social teaching within the framework of natural law, but the tone of the documents reflected a new orientation of the Church toward the world, one characterized by a desire for positive engagement.

The spirit of these documents, along with Pope John's stirring speech at the opening of the Council, encouraged the members of the Council to establish a fresh period of interaction with the world. Yet in spite of a broad agreement among them that a new stance toward the larger world was required, significant disagreements emerged when they attempted to flesh out the specific shape of this new stance.

Vatican II

Many depictions of the fault lines of conciliar debate focus on perduring disagreements between progressive bishops open to church reform and traditionalists who were resistant to reform. However, the lines of debate regarding the document that would become *Gaudium et spes* were quite different.[6] Many bishops and *periti* belonging to the progressive camp disagreed with one another when it came to articulating an adequate exposition of the Church's relationship to the world. On the one hand, there were a significant number who adopted a more Thomistic anthropology that granted a limited autonomy to the natural order and viewed grace not so much as a divine force sent to fix what was broken as a divine principle that transcendentally elevated the natural order, bringing it to its perfection.[7] Without wishing to deny the reality of human sinfulness, those who promoted this perspective were more willing to grant the limited but still positive natural potentialities of the human person and human society, even as they acknowledged the need for these potentialities to find their fulfillment in the life of grace.

On the other hand, there were also many bishops and *periti* who advocated a more Augustinian anthropological perspective that would draw a sharp line between sin and grace. Grace was a divine force oriented toward the healing of a fundamentally broken human nature. For these council members and theologians, the natural order possessed no autonomous status, serving primarily as the arena for the working out of the drama between sin and grace in human history. These figures were quite concerned that early versions of the text seemed influenced by the neoscholastic tendency to merely juxtapose the natural and supernatural orders rather than configuring them in their constitutive relation to one another.[8] These bishops could not accept that events transpiring in the natural order could serve in any significant way as a preparation for the working of God's grace in the world.

Forty years after the promulgation of the *Pastoral Constitution*, these disputes are seen in a different light. *Gaudium et spes* has been accused of excessive optimism as regards its stance toward the world. Yet the document certainly affirmed the reality of human sin: "Often refusing to acknowledge God as their source, men and women have also upset the relationship which should link them to their final destiny; and at the same time they have broken the right order that should exist within themselves as well as between them and other people and all creatures" (GS 13). Later the document presents human history as a tale of humanity's "combat with the powers of evil" (GS 37). Nevertheless, on balance, the dominant tone is better reflected in the Council's confident assertion that "the achievements of the human race are a sign of God's greatness and the fulfillment of his mysterious design" (GS 34).

Clearly emboldened by the theology of dialogue that Pope Paul VI outlined in his first encyclical, *Ecclesiam suam*, the Council itself acknowledged the fruitfulness of a respectful dialogue with the world, and while insisting that the Church had much to offer, the Council also recognized that "it has profited from the history and development of humankind" (GS 44). A positive affirmation of the relative autonomy of the world is evident in the following passage: "That is why, although we must be careful to distinguish earthly progress clearly from the increase of the kingdom of Christ, such progress is of vital concern to the kingdom of God, insofar as it can contribute to the better ordering of human society" (GS 39). The crucial change in the English title of the document in which the conjunction *and* was replaced by the preposition *in* suggests an understanding of the Church's task to transform the world without negating the positive features of contemporary society. More important, the title presupposes a vital but hitherto neglected category for configuring the Church's relationship to the world, namely, the role of mission.

The missiological orientation of the Church to the world was already announced in the Council's *Decree on the Church's Missionary Activity, Ad gentes*: "The church on earth is by its very nature missionary since, according to the plan of the Father, it has its origin in the mission of the Son and the holy Spirit."[9] This document announces a theology of mission far removed from the late medieval and Counter Reformation view of church mission. At that time church mission was conceived as a quantitative and geographic expansion of the boundaries of the Church and "manifested itself supremely within the context of the European colonization of the nonwestern world."[10] With the new orientations of the Council, church mission became a theological imperative.

> Thus the church, at once a visible organization and a spiritual community, travels the same journey as all of humanity and shares the same earthly lot with the world: it is to be a leaven and, as it were, the soul of human society in its renewal by Christ and transformation into the family of God . . . the church then believes that through each of its members and its community as a whole it can help to make the human family and its history still more human. (GS 40)

The Council's treatment of the Church's relationship to the world sought to preserve an uneasy tension between affirming legitimate human endeavors and insisting on the world's need for transformation. This balancing act would continue in the later documents of Pope Paul VI. Pope John, Pope Paul, and the Council itself would gradually reconfigure the Church's relationship to the world with the introduction of a new metaphor, that of a "dialogical journey."[11]

The Pontificate of Pope Paul VI

Pope Paul VI offers the most developed reflections on applying the principle of dialogue to the Church's relationship to the world in his first encyclical, *Ecclesiam suam*. The pope conceives of Christian dialogue according to a series of concentric circles: the outermost circle calls for a dialogue with the entire human community; then moving inward there is the dialogue among all religious people; third, there is the dialogue among Christians; and finally, there is a dialogue within Roman Catholicism. This dialogical spirit is maintained in *Populorum progressio*, which applies the principle of dialogue to the question of suffering and poverty in the Third World. The pope calls for a new dialogue between civilizations and cultures based on the dignity of the human person and not on "commodities or technical skills" (PP 73). Such dialogue must pursue not merely economic development but integral human development.

In *Octogesima adveniens*, written in celebration of the eightieth anniversary of *Rerum novarum*, Paul VI follows *Gaudium et spes* in situating Catholic social teaching within a theology of the Church's mission to the world. He emphasizes that all Christians are to engage the problems and issues of the world today, advocating what was sometimes referred to as the Cardijn method: "observe, judge, act."[12] However, his application of this method was quite different from that of John XXIII, who also referred to it in *Mater et magistra*. For Pope John the method was a way for the faithful to apply the universal principles of Catholic social teaching to a particular situation. However, Mary Elsbernd notes that for Pope Paul VI the starting point was

> reflection on the local situation by the local Christian community. The community then becomes the locus of dialogue between the situation and its traditions, namely Scripture and social teaching, in order to bring about action. The process is not application of ahistorical principles to situations, but dialogical discernment for action, emerging from concrete situations and the Christian traditions.[13]

The pope dared to suggest that Catholic social teaching could only emerge out of specific, regionally situated dialogue with societal concerns.

Two important events during Paul VI's pontificate further refined an ecclesiological framework for understanding the Church's engagement with the world: the meeting of Latin American bishops in Medellín in 1968, and the 1971 meeting of the synod of bishops. In Medellín, Colombia, bishops from throughout Latin America gathered to assess the state of both the Church in Latin America and Latin American society in the spirit of the call for dialogue with the world found in *Gaudium et spes*. The fruit of this historic meeting was an ecclesiastical program for church renewal and a stringent critique of the unjust societal structures that were oppressing so many people in Latin America. The Medellín documents offered an unusual level of specificity to the kind of critical engagement with societal concerns that Vatican II had envisioned. These documents also provide a convenient marker for the emergence of theologies of liberation committed to furthering a biblically inspired critique of unjust social structures and an often stinging rebuke of the Church's complicity in social injustice. Liberation theologians have made a vital contribution to ongoing reflection on the Church's relationship to the world. They have noted that the salvation that God promised and that the Church is sent to announce includes the liberation of human persons from any social, political, or economic structures that would prevent them from achieving their God-given dignity.

In 1971 bishops from throughout the world gathered at a world synod to address the topic "Justice in the World." With the important statement of Medellín clearly on their minds, the bishops declared that "action on behalf of justice and participation in the transformation of the world fully appear to us as a constitutive dimension of the preaching of the Gospel, or, in other words, of the Church's mission for the redemption of the human race and its liberation from every oppressive situation" (JM introduction). This statement was also one of the first church documents to note that the Church itself has an obligation to justice in its own ecclesiastical structures and policies. I return to this important development in the final section.

Finally, both the heightened sensitivity to the integrity and plurality of human cultures evident in Paul VI's earlier writing and the liberative themes that were so pronounced in the Medellín documents are given fuller development in Paul VI's important apostolic exhortation on evangelization, *Evangelii nuntiandi*, where he reframed the task of evangelization within the necessary engagement of the gospel with diverse cultures. The pope writes that "in the mind of the Lord the Church is universal by vocation and mission, but when she puts down her roots in a variety of cultural, social and human terrains, she takes on different external expressions and appearances in each part of the world."[14] For Paul VI the modern dichotomy that had emerged between faith and culture was "the drama of our time."[15] Although the pope resisted the politicization of

Christian salvation, he also affirmed that Christian understandings of salvation do possess social and political dimensions.

The Pontificate of John Paul II

Pope John Paul II continued to develop the new direction inaugurated by the Council. At the same time, his large corpus of social teaching reflects some significant shifts in the dominant conciliar view of the Church's relation to the world. If *Gaudium et spes* had marked the beginning of a much more sophisticated treatment of the Church's engagement with human culture, this would have received new development in the pontificate of John Paul II. In 1982 the pope created the Pontifical Council for Culture. In connection with that event, John Paul II observed that "the synthesis between culture and faith is not just a demand of culture, but also of faith. . . . A faith which does not become culture is a faith which has not been fully received, not thoroughly thought through, not faithfully lived out."[16] We must also note, however, that this commitment often stood at odds with Vatican policies that reflected a deep-seated suspicion of theologies of inculturation.

Further evidence for a shift in the pontificate of John Paul II is reflected in the conclusions of the extraordinary episcopal synod convened in 1985 to assess the reception of Vatican II. While the synod offered a ringing affirmation of the teaching of the Council, it did articulate a much more cautionary assessment of *Gaudium et spes*:

> we affirm the great importance and timeliness of the pastoral constitution, *Gaudium et spes*. At the same time, however, we perceive that the signs of our time are in part different from those of the time of the council, with greater problems and anguish. Today, in fact, everywhere in the world we witness an increase in hunger, oppression, injustice and war, sufferings, terrorism, and other forms of violence of every sort. This requires a new and more profound theological reflection in order to interpret these signs in the light of the Gospel.[17]

This justifiable concern for the scope of human suffering and the pervasiveness of sinful social structures became a characteristic theme in the writing of John Paul II. Where liberation theology would stress the need to transform unjust social structures, the emphasis in the writing of John Paul II was placed more on the cultivation of a Christian personalism that speaks to the sinfulness of the human heart as the root cause of social injustice. Moreover, a more cautious but still dialogical stance toward the world was at times interrupted by a kind of apocalypticism, as with his popular but overdrawn opposition of a "culture of death" and a "culture of life."[18] This has led Thomas Shannon, borrowing the typology of H. Richard Niebuhr,[19] to suggest that John Paul II moved beyond Niebuhr's "Christ transforming culture" to an almost sectarian "Christ against culture."[20] Almost invariably, when the pope chose to interpret the "signs of the times" in his encyclicals, the analysis highlights the negative features of the world today.

Contemporary North American Perspectives

During the long pontificate of John Paul II three different theological frameworks for configuring the Church's engagement with the world emerged in North America. We might identify these as neoconservative, radical, and correlational.[21]

Neoconservative Cultural Engagement

Proponents of this form of church engagement with society share a generally positive assessment of the "American experiment" and are committed to the possibility of a fruitful conversation between Catholic belief and North American culture. The neoconservatives find much to commend in the system of democratic capitalism that has flourished in North America. For them many of the most important values held in the founding documents of the United States presuppose a Christian theism and a natural law framework and are quite congenial to Roman Catholic convictions.

Proponents of this perspective believe that the United States may have arrived at a "Catholic moment" in which a public philosophy funded by the Catholic natural law tradition can enhance the best of American values while purging it of its excesses. Scholars like George Weigel,[22] Richard John Neuhaus,[23] and Michael Novak[24] all influenced in varying degrees by the public philosophy of John Courtney Murray, would agree that the Church must participate in the formation of human culture by affirming social and political developments like democratic capitalism that are most in accord with Catholic teaching. They offer what some regard as a selective reading of the encyclicals of Pope John Paul II,[25] as affirming the compatibility between Catholic social teaching and a free market economy buttressed by a vibrant democratic polity.

Strikingly absent from the writings of these authors, however, is any sense that the "American experiment" might stand as a critique of Roman Catholicism, calling it, for example, to a greater affirmation of women's rights and the development of more democratic decision-making structures. The neoconservatives tend to overidentify the larger Catholic tradition with a set of magisterial pronouncements and to condemn any and all forms of dissent, seeing in the postconciliar Church a dangerous crisis of fidelity.

Radical Cultural Engagement

In contrast to the approach of the neoconservatives, a second view of the Church-world relationship has been inspired by the radical social witness of Dorothy Day and Peter Maurin, founders of the Catholic Worker movement, and the peace movement, which emerged, in part, in response to the Vietnam War. A number of theologians, with quite distinct perspectives, have found inspiration in the counterculturalism of these movements and their commitment to fundamental gospel values, nonviolence, and solidarity with the poor.

Some Catholic theologians and grassroots communities have also been influenced by the writing of the provocative Protestant ethicist Stanley Hauerwas. His far-ranging works combine a Barthian condemnation of Christian liberalism's determination to make the human person and not God the starting point for theological reflection, with an admiration for the prophetic witness of the free church tradition and that tradition's best-known contemporary apologist, the late John Howard Yoder.[26] The task of the Church, Hauerwas has famously insisted, is not to *have* a social ethic but to *be* a social ethic. Christians are to submit to the transformative power of communal existence in which they allow themselves to be shaped within the life and practices of the Church by Christianity's distinctive story and vision. More recently Catholic scholars like Michael Baxter,[27] Rodney Clapp,[28] Michael Budde,[29] and William Cavanaugh[30] have brought this analysis into Catholic intellectual conversation. They reject the hegemony, as they see it, of the Christian appropriation of procedural liberalism, which has resulted in the evacuation of any distinctive Christian identity from Catholic ethical thinking. They are also quite critical of capitalism and contend that Christianity has too often succumbed to the contemporary consumerist and commodifying impulses of global capitalism.

From a quite different perspective, David Schindler, editor of the English-language edition of the theological journal *Communio*, has argued for a distinctive form of engagement with contemporary North American culture.[31] He too would reject a procedural liberalism that would require Catholics to abandon their most basic religiously informed convictions in order to enter into public conversation. Rather, Schindler holds that Catholics must engage in "dialogue" only from a position that begins with the revealed truths of the Catholic faith.[32] Drawing from the *communio* theology of Hans Urs von Balthasar, Schindler would assert, against the neoconservatives, the incompatibility of Christianity and capitalism. Only a Trinitarian theology that affirms God as a communion of love is capable of transforming a culture obsessed with "having," "doing," and "making."

Yet one other example of a radical engagement with contemporary culture, born on English soil but increasingly influencing North American thinkers, is found in the writing of the Anglican theologian John Milbank. A somewhat idiosyncratic English intellectual, he advocates a postmodern, or perhaps better, countermodern view of Western civilization under the influence of the Enlightenment.[33] Milbank's wide-ranging thought is difficult to summarize, but central to his project is an attempt to reclaim a Christian meta-narrative of human flourishing that is superior to secular social theories. This "radical orthodoxy," built around a neo-Augustinian account of society in which the Church offers an exemplary form of human community, is not inclined toward any serious engagement with contemporary secular culture except by way of critique.

Correlational Cultural Engagement

The majority of Catholic moral theologians and ecclesiologists in North America approach the engagement of Church and culture from a perspective that must be distinguished from both the neoconservative and radicalist perspectives. Because I believe this third approach represents a more fruitful perspective, I explore its distinguishing features in more detail. We might characterize this approach as one of correlational cultural engagement, drawing on David Tracy's description of the theological task as that of "mutually critical correlation."[34] Tracy has offered a compelling account of the public nature of theology conceived as a dialogue between a theological appropriation of the received Christian tradition and an analysis of the contemporary human situation. He understands the theological project to be largely hermeneutical, that is, theology must draw upon an interpretation of the received Christian tradition and an interpretation of the contemporary social situation and then attempt a correlation of the two. The "mutually critical correlation" between these two interpretations will differ, often dramatically, from situation to situation. In one specific context the Christian tradition will confront prophetically the contemporary situation that occasioned the theological reflection. At another point the tradition may find much to confirm. Often it will be a combination of affirmation and critique. Nor should we assume that it will always be the tradition that does the challenging or affirming. If this critical correlation is genuinely "mutual," the received Christian tradition will also, on occasion, be confronted by an interpretation of the contemporary situation. This way of describing the Church's relationship to the world has the signal advantage of allowing for any of a number of different correlations.

This correlational approach shares with the neoconservatives a commitment to a positive engagement with North American culture. It is indebted as well to the Catholic natural law tradition. Nevertheless, a correlational approach goes beyond the construction of a public philosophy to affirm the value of the Christian theological heritage for public discourse. Those proposing a correlational cultural engagement believe that it is possible to construct not only a public philosophy but a public theology that seeks to bring the wealth of the Christian theological tradition to bear on social questions of broad import. Proponents of this view might include David Hollenbach,[35] Richard McBrien,[36] Kenneth and Michael Himes,[37] and Charles Curran.[38] Many of these figures would also insist that the engagement with the larger culture cannot be unidirectional; there is often much that the Church itself can learn from modernity. The American values of freedom, personal autonomy, and participative decision making are all values the Church would do well to adopt.

Finally, the correlational approach would balance the Thomistic commitment to the relative autonomy of the created order with the Augustinian conviction that the world stands in need of transformation. One avenue for maintaining this balance has been to appeal to the sacramentality of the Church.[39] Just as any sacrament, in order to function as such, must draw its "matter" from worldly realities, so too the Church could not function as sacrament if it were not able to acknowledge the inherent goodness of the human community. It is the cultural "matter" of this community (e.g., institutions, social conventions, and practices) that becomes within the Church, not just any set of cultural constructions but the means through which the Church can become a sign and instrument of God's saving offer to the world.[40] As the sacramentality of the Eucharist depends on the prior intelligibility of bread, wine, and the culture of the table, so too the sacramental character of the Church presupposes substantive contact points with the ordinary, human experience of community. There is, in other words, implicit in any claim to the Church's own sacramentality, a necessary affirmation of the potential goodness of the social, political, and economic communities that constitute human society. The sacramentality of the Church is capable of incorporating, then, the Thomistic tradition's affirmation of the integrity of the natural order and the potentiality that lies therein for meaningful human community apart from the life of the Church. Indeed, *Gaudium et spes* makes this connection quite clear in number 42:

> The church, moreover, acknowledges the good to be found in the social dynamism of today, especially in progress towards unity, healthy socialization, and civil and economic cooperation. The encouragement of unity is in harmony with the deepest nature of the church's mission, for it "is a sacrament—a sign and instrument, that is, of communion with God and of the unity of the entire human race." (GS 42)

At the same time, the Church, precisely as sacrament, offers to the world a vision of the world transformed, the very kingdom of God. The Church is not itself the kingdom of God, but rather it "receives the mission of proclaiming and establishing among all peoples the kingdom of Christ and of God" and in the Church's sacramentality it stands before the world as "the seed and the beginning of that kingdom."[41] So an assertion of the Church's sacramentality also incorporates the Augustinian concern that the Church's principal task is to communicate to the world a vision of its potential transformation. In the transformative memory that it maintains through its fidelity to scripture and its articulation of doctrine, in its distinctive ecclesial practices (e.g., almsgiving, acts of hospitality), and in its liturgical life, the Church sacramentalizes, that is, makes concrete for the world, God's promise of salvation and the hope for the possibility of a transfigured world. As Francis Sullivan suggests, "the church is a sign of salvation by being a holy people, since holiness consists in the love of God and of neighbor."[42]

Advocates of this correlational perspective will continue to insist that the Church must *have* a social ethic capable of addressing the pressing issues of the times. Yet, with the advocates of radical Catholicism, they will also affirm that as a sacrament of universal salvation the Church must *be* a social ethic in its distinctive communal patterns of interaction. At the heart of the liturgical movement lies the conviction of Virgil Michel and others that the liturgy, for example, should not simply be a vehicle for the message of peace and justice (as with the "peace and justice liturgies" so popular in the 1970s and 1980s), but rather the very doing of the liturgy forms the assembly into a just and peaceable community sent forth into the world.[43]

These two features—the configuration of the Church's engagement to the world as a dynamic and changing mutually critical correlation, and the affirmation of the Church's nature as a sacramental sign to the world of God's saving offer—situate the correlational model as a mediating position between the neoconservative and radical approaches. Nevertheless, those other approaches have made important contributions to our understanding of the Church's engagement with North American culture. The neoconservatives have certainly done much to encourage Catholics to enter more fully into American public life, confident that connections can be made between one's Catholic faith and civic obligation. The radical Catholic tradition brings into relief the distinctive aspects of Catholic Christian belief and stresses the way in which the moral life depends on the crucial character formation that comes from faithful discipleship and participation in the transformative practices of the Christian community.

THE ECCLESIAL PROCESS OF FORMULATING CATHOLIC SOCIAL TEACHING

In the first half of the twentieth century Catholic social teaching was drawn largely from the two major papal encyclicals, *Rerum novarum* and *Quadragesimo anno*. This was in keeping with a broader tendency to see Catholic doctrinal formulation as an exclusively papal prerogative. This reflected a trajectory of development in the understanding of authority in the Catholic Church begun with Pope Gregory XVI and coming to its term in the pontificate of Pius XII. During this period the magisterium gradually came to function as the proximate norm for church tradition. The operative ecclesiology was articulated with the greatest clarity in a 1906 encyclical of Pope Pius X, *Vehementor nos*:

> It follows that the Church is essentially an *unequal* society, that is, a society comprising two categories of persons, the Pastors and the flock, those who occupy a rank in the different degrees of the hierarchy and the multitude of the faithful. So distinct are these categories that with the pastoral body only rests the necessary right and authority for promoting the end of the society and directing all its members towards that end; the one duty of the multitude is to allow themselves to be led, and, like a docile flock, to follow the Pastors.[44]

This ecclesiology rested on a distinction first articulated by the sixteenth-century theologian Thomas Stapleton, between a teaching church (*ecclesia docens*) and a learning church (*ecclesia discens* or *ecclesia docta*). Within this framework, the learning church was reduced to a passive receptacle of that revelation given to the hierarchy. The result was a "trickle down" theory of revelation. Divine revelation was conceived as a *depositum fidei*, a collection of propositional truths in the firm possession of the magisterium. This positivistic theology of revelation too easily collapsed divine revelation into its historical mediations. Revelation was identified with a set of truths offered through apostolic succession to the hierarchy and through them, as through a conduit, to the laity, whose sole ecclesial responsibility was to accept passively the teaching of the magisterium.

Within this schema, the ecclesial processes for the formulation of Catholic social teaching, as with any church teaching, were relatively straightforward. The magisterium (practically speaking, this meant the pope) drew from the treasury of divine truths to pronounce on one or another of the ills of contemporary society. The papacy rather uncritically presupposed that it already possessed, within the deposit of the faith, all the answers to the problems of the age. Reflecting on the development of Catholic social teaching at the end of the nineteenth century, Pope Pius XI asserted that

> this grave conflict of opinions was accompanied by discussion not always of a peaceful nature. The eyes of all, as often in the past turned toward the Chair of Peter, sacred repository of the fullness of truth whence words of salvation are dispensed to the whole world. To the feet of Christ's vicar on earth were seen to flock, in unprecedented numbers, specialists in social affairs, employers, the very workingmen themselves, begging with one voice that at last a safe road might be pointed out to them. (QA 7)

This rather arrogant assertion reflected the dominant viewpoint in the Vatican up to Vatican II.

The Important Shifts Inaugurated at Vatican II

Vatican II articulated both a theology of revelation and a vision of the Church that would offer an alternative framework for considering the formulation of Catholic social teaching.

A New Theology of Revelation

The opening clause of Vatican II's *Dogmatic Constitution on Divine Revelation* (*Dei verbum*) begins by describing the task of the Council:

"hearing the Word of God reverently, and proclaiming it confidently."[45] This introduces a major theme of the constitution, namely, the primacy of the living Word of God, spoken from the beginning of creation, incarnate in Jesus of Nazareth, and proclaimed in the life of the Church. The priority of the living Word of God is further reflected in the Council's preference for speaking of truth in the singular rather than in the plural: "The most intimate truth thus revealed about God and human salvation shines forth for us in Christ, who is himself both the mediator and the sum total of revelation"[46] This theology of divine revelation begins with revealed truth understood not so much as a discrete body of information communicated in a set of propositional statements as truth communicated in the form of a relationship. God's revelation is itself, then, an event of communion and of transformation; it calls for a dialogue between God and humankind. It is a Word offered to us in love by a God whose very being is love, and it is by the power of God's Spirit that we are able to respond to that Word.

The Council affirmed that Jesus Christ was God's definitive self-expression, the Word incarnate to which there is nothing left to be added. It also affirmed, however, that this Word is received by humanity in history; it is kept alive in the living memory of the Church. As a dynamic, living Word, it speaks anew to each generation of believers. Therefore, God's Word must continue to assume new forms as it takes root in the minds and hearts of believers and in the life of the Church. This is the understanding of tradition in its most dynamic sense, as God's Word actualized in the life of the Church. The Council writes:

> The tradition that comes from the apostles makes progress in the church, with the help of the holy Spirit. There is a growth in insight into the realities and words that are being passed. This comes about through the contemplation and study of believers who ponder these things in their hearts. It comes from the intimate sense of spiritual realities which they experience. And it comes from the preaching of those who, on succeeding to the office of bishop, have received the sure charism of truth. Thus, as the centuries go by, the church is always advancing towards the plenitude of divine truth, until eventually the words of God are fulfilled in it.[47]

In this passage the Council's Christocentric theology of revelation as the living Word of God is conditioned pneumatologically as the Council recognizes the decisive role of the Spirit.

It is in the Spirit that the Church comes to *recognize* divine truth: "the holy Spirit, through whom the living voice of the Gospel rings out in the church—and through it in the world—leads believers to the full truth and makes the word of Christ dwell in them in all its richness."[48] This ability to recognize and respond to God's Word was called a "supernatural sense of the faith" (LG 12), a gift given by the Spirit to all baptized believers.

This pneumatological perspective negates any attempt to conceive of God's Word as the unique possession of any single group within the Church, including the pope and bishops. God's Word continues to abide in the whole Church through the Holy Spirit. In fact, in the Council's listing of the ways in which the Church grows in the truth, the preaching of the bishops is preceded by the role of the faithful. This represents an important expansion of the "traditioning" process of the Church.

Since the Council, new light has been shed on this "traditioning" process through consideration of "ecclesial reception," that is, the unique contribution of the whole faithful in actively appropriating church teaching and making it their own.[49] This new theology of revelation, when integrated into the renewed ecclesiology of the Council, will offer a quite different framework for understanding the formulation of Catholic social teaching.

A Renewed Ecclesiology

The two slogans that characterized the work of the Council, *aggiornamento* (an Italian word used to refer to the task to "bring the Church up-to-date") and *ressourcement* (a French word used to refer to the Council's determination to "return to the sources" of Christianity), were reflected in the Council's treatment of the Church's nature and mission. Both tasks were particularly evident in the constitution *Lumen gentium*, a document that reaffirmed some of the preconciliar developments in biblical and liturgical theology found in Pope Pius XII's encyclical, *Mystici corporis*, while moving well beyond that document in several important respects.

The Council soundly rejected the pyramidal model of the Church as a *societas inequalis* in favor of a vision of the Church as the new people of God grounded in the equality of all members by virtue of faith and baptism. This Church was indeed, as Pope Pius XII taught, the Mystical Body of Christ, but it was also a temple of the Holy Spirit in which it was the Spirit who guided the Church "in the way of all truth and [bestowed] upon it different hierarchic and charismatic gifts."[50] The Council reaffirmed the nature of the Church as an ordered communion, but it stressed the themes of collaboration and co-responsibility between the ordained and the laity. The ordained pastors were warned not to "quench the Spirit"[51] but to "foster the many and varied gifts of the laity"[52] and to recognize that the laity were entitled and sometimes even "duty bound to express their opinion on matters which concern the good of the church."[53]

The common view of the bishops as "vicars of the Roman pontiff" was decisively rejected as the Council affirmed that bishops were truly "vicars and legates of Christ,"[54] who served as "the visible source and foundation of unity in their own particular churches."[55] As members of the episcopal college, they shared with the bishop of Rome "supreme authority over the whole church."[56]

Catholic triumphalism was repudiated as the Council acknowledged that the Christian community was not only a church of pilgrims but a "pilgrim church" that was "at once holy and always in need of purification" and which must follow "the path of penance and renewal."[57] Thus, Christ summoned the Church "to that continual reformation of which she always has need, insofar as she is a human institution here on earth."[58]

The Council also redressed a century-long tendency to reduce the local church to a mere subdivision of the universal Church as the bishops asserted that it was "in and from these [particular churches] that the one and unique Catholic Church exists."[59] The Council's appropriation of a Eucharistic ecclesiology from the patristic tradition led to a much richer theological view of the local church. In each local church the faithful are "gathered together by the preaching of the Gospel of Christ," and in each local church "the mystery of the Lord's Supper is celebrated so that, by means of the flesh and blood of the Lord the whole brotherhood and sisterhood of the body may be welded together."[60] The local or particular church was the locus for the realization of the universal Church. By acknowledging the theological significance of the local church, the Council also recognized the value of each church's unique gifts to the universal communion of churches. This important insight, only imperfectly developed at the Council, along with the participation for the first time at an ecumenical council of bishops who truly came from throughout the world, led theologian Karl Rahner to assert that the "abiding significance of the Second Vatican Council" was its actualization of the Church as a true "world church."[61] As such, this new actualization would demand a need for much greater recognition of diversity and pluralism within the churches and in the churches' engagement with the world.

Gaudium et spes: New Foundations for the Formulation of Catholic Social Teaching

The wedding of the Council's theology of revelation and its renewed ecclesiology was evident in the Council's most mature document, *Gaudium et spes*. At numerous points the *Pastoral Constitution on the Church in the Modern World* offers a more modest though still substantive view of the formulation of church social teaching. "The church is guardian of the deposit of God's word and draws religious and moral principles from it, but it does not always have a ready answer to every question. Still, it is eager to associate the light of revelation with the experience of humanity in trying to clarify the course upon which it has recently entered." (GS 33) One should notice here the similarities to Tracy's mutually critical correlation. The Council suggests that church teaching ought to proceed, not from a deductive application of universal principles ready at hand, but from an association of the "light of revelation" with the "experience of humanity." A major contribution of the Council lay in its willingness to affirm what the Church has to learn from the world. For example, in its *Declaration on Religious Liberty* the Council acknowledged what it has learned from the growing consciousness in modern society of the human right to religious freedom (DH 1).

This ecclesial humility in the face of the relative autonomy of the world leads the Council to exhort the laity to take the initiative in bringing their Christian faith to bear on contemporary issues.

> For guidance and spiritual strength let them turn to the clergy; but let them realize that their pastors will not always be so expert as to have a ready answer to every problem, even every grave problem, that arises; this is not the role of the clergy; it is rather the task of lay people to shoulder their responsibilities under the guidance of Christian wisdom and with careful attention to the teaching authority of the church. (GS 43)

The liberty that the baptized possess in the engagement of contemporary problems and issues brings with it the possibility that Christians might disagree regarding particular solutions to those problems. The Council foresaw this possibility and warned:

> if one or other of the proposed solutions is readily perceived by many to be closely connected with the message of the Gospel, they ought to remember that in those cases no one is permitted to identify the authority of the church exclusively with his or her own opinion. Let them then, try to guide each other by sincere dialogue in a spirit of mutual charity and with a genuine concern for the common good above all. (GS 43)

Almost four decades removed from the Council, it is still remarkable to read these texts and to appreciate the seismic shift that took place at the Council regarding both the dominant theology of revelation and its reinvigorated ecclesiology. The implications for our understanding of the ecclesial formation of Catholic social teaching are immense.

The emerging conciliar vision suggests that the ecclesial formation of Catholic social teaching occurs not through a kind of supernaturally infused knowledge first given to the hierarchy then applied to worldly concerns, but through the dynamic interactions of the whole Church. God's Word is offered to the Church in the power of the Spirit. The Council presented the Church not as the master of the Word of God but as its servant. The Church must prayerfully "listen" for divine revelation as it is proclaimed in the scriptures, celebrated in the liturgy, critically reflected upon by the theological community, and manifested in the testimony of the *sensus fidelium*, the graced testimony of the whole people of God. The Council also acknowledged that the Church, sent into the world in mission, must bring into respectful dialogue the received Christian tradition and the insights and concerns of the larger human community. This dialogue is not to be reduced to a kind of polite formality; the Council dared to admit that in this dialogue the Church has not only much to offer but also much to learn. Although the laity is to play an exemplary role in this engagement between revelation and worldly concerns, it is the whole Church that is to participate in this dialogue as a "leaven" in the world. Finally, the Council recognized that the scope of divine revelation is not so large as to remove any ambiguity regarding the appropriate Christian response to often significant social questions.

Postconciliar Developments in the Ecclesiological Framework of Catholic Social Teaching

One of the first documents to reflect some of the ecclesiological shifts brought about at the Council was Pope Paul VI's apostolic letter

Octogesima adveniens. The crucial passage is found in number 4:

> In the face of such widely varying situations it is difficult for us to utter a unified message and to put forward a solution which has universal validity. Such is not our ambition, nor is it our mission. It is up to the Christian communities to analyze with objectivity the situation which is proper to their own country, to shed on it the light of the Gospel's unalterable words and to draw principles of reflection, norms of judgment and directives for action from the social teaching of the Church. This social teaching has been worked out in the course of history and, notably, in this industrial era, since the historic date of the message of Pope Leo XIII on "the conditions of the workers." . . . It is up to these Christian communities, with the help of the Holy Spirit, in communion with the bishops who hold responsibility and in dialogue with other Christian brethren and all men of good will, to discern the options and commitments which are called for in order to bring about the social, political, and economic changes seen in many cases to be urgently needed.

Many commentators have noted the shift to a more historically conscious methodology evident in this letter.[62] In particular, I comment on two features of this letter. First, the document's application of the Cardijn method, mentioned above, implied that it is the whole Christian community that participates in the formulation of social teaching, not simply the hierarchy, who pronounces universal principles to be applied by the laity. Second, the pope frankly acknowledged the difficulties inherent in the preconciliar model of church authority in which the papacy articulated universally binding principles. He appealed implicitly to the principle of subsidiarity, acknowledging that much of the formulation of Catholic social teaching must be undertaken by local communities.[63] The papal document presupposed the Council's move toward the concept of a "world church" that places practical limits on papal teaching and advocates more regional church responses to diverse social situations.

The 1980s saw the American bishops adopt the insights of the Council and of Pope Paul VI. By issuing several major documents concerned with social analysis, they fulfilled the pope's call for regional communities to shoulder more of the load in the formulation of Catholic social teaching. By adopting a methodology, at least with respect to the pastoral letters, *The Challenge of Peace* and *Economic Justice for All*, which incorporated open listening sessions conducted in individual dioceses and by the drafting committee itself, the bishops took seriously the assumption of both Vatican II and Paul VI that not only the hierarchy but all God's people must engage in the central processes of ecclesial discernment. In the late 1980s the American bishops began the process of formulating a new pastoral letter on women. They initiated that process by employing the same methodology (e.g., widely distributed drafts and listening sessions) used with regard to their two earlier pastoral letters on social issues. Midway in the process, however, the bishops were notified by the Vatican that the overall process being employed was unacceptable and must be abandoned. Subsequent episcopal documents promulgated by the conference have abandoned the earlier methodology.

Since that time there has been a withdrawal of support from the methodological and ecclesial approaches first explored at Vatican II and then developed under Pope Paul VI. In the final decade of the twentieth century and the initial years of the twenty-first century, we have seen a series of papal documents and Vatican instructions that reduce the ecclesial processes for the formulation of church doctrine to those tasks proper to the magisterium alone. In 1986 the Congregation for the Doctrine of the Faith published *Libertatis conscientia*, in which it specified that it was the task of Christians not to formulate church teaching but only to apply that which had already been formulated.[64] The implication was that the Church already possessed a self-contained, complete body of social teaching that needed only to be implemented by the faithful.[65]

In 1998 Pope John Paul II's apostolic letter *Apostolos suos* was issued as a response to a plea made by bishops at the 1985 extraordinary synod for a doctrinal study of the authority of episcopal conferences. The document offered a helpful historical and theological framework for considering the important role of episcopal conferences. It also offered a set of norms that granted the authority of episcopal conferences to issue binding doctrinal statements, but only under very restrictive conditions: (1) such a document may only be issued in a plenary session and not by a committee or commission; (2) it must be unanimously approved by the entire conference; or (3) it must be approved by a two-thirds majority and then receive a papal *recognitio*.[66]

It is an ancient and theologically sound principle to require a high degree of church consensus prior to the issuance of a doctrinally binding document. However, the requirement of absolute unanimity far exceeds the rules established for any other gathering of bishops, whether in regional synod or ecumenical council, in the history of the Church.[67] According to Francis Sullivan, the assumption of this document appears to be that there are only two levels of episcopal authority, that of the local bishop and that of the whole college of bishops. By requiring absolute unanimity, *Apostolos suos* creates a situation where such a document would essentially carry no more authority than that of each individual bishop, since each individual bishop within a conference would have had to assent to the teaching. The other alternative, a two-thirds majority with a *recognitio* from the Vatican, effectively shifts the authority of the document away from the episcopal conference and onto the papacy.[68]

The rejection of the American bishops' process for drafting episcopal statements, the devaluation of the role of regional episcopal conferences in the formulation of church teaching, and the insufficiently developed employment of the synod of bishops, all have occurred under the pontificate of Pope John Paul II. At the same time, John Paul II has employed a questionable approach to the issuance of papal encyclicals and other papal documents. These documents are generally written in secret by a select few drafters in or close to the Vatican. No one outside a small inner circle has the opportunity to offer input into these drafts. The documents are often very long and filled with philosophical speculation, rendering them unreadable to all but a small intellectual elite. In light of the new ecclesiological perspectives that emerged from both the conciliar documents and postconciliar reflection, this methodology must be challenged. It reflects nothing of the insight of the Council that the whole Church is the recipient of God's Word. It ignores the Council's affirmation of the coresponsibility of the college of bishops, with the bishop of Rome, for the welfare of the whole Church. It gives no place for the insight of the sense of the faithful nor does it recognize the Council's insistence that the laity play a primary role in bringing the gospel into engagement with the issues and questions of our age. Finally, this methodology ignores the important insight of Paul VI that much of the dialogue between Christian faith and the concerns of our age must be engaged at the regional and even local levels.

The full reception of the teaching of Vatican II remains incomplete. The more decentered and contextual character of Pope Paul VI's approach to the formulation of Catholic social teaching stands in tension with the often sophisticated and perceptive but fundamentally papocentric social analysis of Pope John Paul II. The unfolding of the life of the Church in the first century of its third millennium will no doubt play a determinative role in the achievement of a more comprehensive reception of conciliar teaching.

THE AUTHORITATIVE STATUS OF CATHOLIC SOCIAL TEACHING AND THE APPROPRIATE RESPONSE OF THE BELIEVER

This volume is dedicated to a study of Catholic social teaching. As was noted in the introduction, Catholic social teaching should not be equated with Catholic social ethics or Catholic social thought; both are much broader categories. Catholic social teaching includes the normative articulation of official church positions regarding social questions. A study of Catholic social teaching is in a sense a study of official pronouncements of the magisterium that function like a series of snapshots taken at given moments in history. These snapshots offer normative articulations of an always broader and more variegated tradition of Catholic social thought. These snapshots, however helpful and even necessary, can never do justice to the much richer ecclesial conversation out of which they emerged. These official teachings will tend to be conservative, often eschewing the controversial and even prophetic stand of the few in favor of positions that have some hope of achieving a broader consensus in the Church (e.g., on the question of pacifism and just war theory). They will often avoid questions related to the social scientific bases of their positions, recognizing that it would be difficult to impose normatively positions based on highly contingent social-scientific data. The necessarily conservative cast of such documents suggests a difficulty inherent in a Church committed to an authoritative teaching office. This becomes particularly evident in a comparative analysis of Catholic social teaching with documents that have emerged from the World Council of Churches. In the latter instance, the goal of such documents is not to articulate a normative position but to speak prophetically *to* rather than *for* the churches. This distinction must be kept in mind as we consider the differentiated authoritative status of Catholic social teaching.

The Catholic tradition of social teaching has met with resistance in certain quarters of the American Catholic Church. Many Catholics have taken issue with church positions on questions ranging from capital punishment to the first use of nuclear weapons. These disagreements, in turn, have raised important questions regarding the authoritative status of church teaching in general and Catholic social teaching in particular. The moral and dogmatic manuals of the nineteenth and early twentieth centuries often dealt with this question by employing a relatively sophisticated taxonomy for church teaching based on the assignment of certain "theological notes" to various doctrinal propositions.[69] Theological notes were formal judgments by theologians or the magisterium on the relationship of a doctrinal formulation to divine revelation. Their purpose was to safeguard the faith and prevent confusion between binding doctrines and theological opinion. This kind of detailed taxonomy had the advantage of making explicit an important but all too often neglected aspect of church teaching, the recognition that not all teaching was proposed, or to be received, with the same degree of authority. However, it relied on an overly propositional view of divine revelation and tended to overlook the fact that the Christian's most profound response in faith was not to a particular dogma or doctrine but to the good news of Jesus Christ crucified and risen who in the Holy Spirit offers life to the world. The decisive Christian framework for responding to any and all church teaching is not one that treats church teaching as an atomistic set of propositions, each of which demands a particular kind of assent. The decisive framework is that of Christian discipleship in which one submits to the transformative power of the gospel and the distinctive practices of the Christian tradition while bringing that dynamic tradition into critical engagement with the contemporary human situation. Still the question of assessing the authoritative status of particular formulations of Catholic social teaching cannot be avoided altogether. In the last fifteen years a more general taxonomy of church teaching has been articulated in various ecclesiastical documents.[70] The four principal categories of official church teaching that have emerged are: (1) dogma, (2) definitive doctrine, (3) authoritative (nondefinitive) doctrine, and (4) prudential admonitions and church discipline.

Basic Gradations in the Authority of Magisterial Pronouncements

Among a large and diverse body of formal doctrinal teaching are those teachings of the Church that have been proposed as divinely revealed either by solemn definition (by either pope or council) or by the ordinary and universal magisterium (the infallible teaching of the college of bishops is exercised when, while dispersed throughout the world and in communion with one another and the bishop of Rome, the bishops are in agreement that a particular teaching is to be held as definitive).[71] These teachings, known as *dogmas*, are taught infallibly and therefore are irreversible in substance. Because a dogma is divinely revealed, it calls forth from the believer an assent of faith. An obstinate and sustained repudiation of these foundational principles would ordinarily place a person at odds with the most basic of Christian teachings.

The second category, *definitive doctrine*, refers to teachings that have been "definitively proposed by the church." The believer must "firmly accept and hold" these teachings as true. It must be noted that this is a relatively new category of church teaching. In the dogmatic manuals, the staple of seminary formation before the Council, such teachings were considered part of "the secondary object of infallibility." However, their status was never the subject of a dogmatic definition. Moreover, scholars have raised significant questions regarding the scope of this category of church teaching. Definitive doctrines are generally viewed as teachings necessary to safeguard and expound divine revelation with integrity. Yet some official statements expand the scope to include any teaching connected to divine revelation by "logical" or "historical necessity."[72] Although Catholics are called "to embrace and hold as true" these teachings, the ecclesial consequences for failing to do so are unclear. In any event, this category does not come into play in any significant way in the area of Catholic social teaching.

A third category, *authoritative (nondefinitive) doctrine*, refers to those teachings that have been taught authoritatively but not infallibly by the magisterium. These teachings contribute to a fuller understanding of God's Word and its implications for the Christian life. They may emerge out of the Church's disciplined conversation between divine revelation and a critical comprehension of the pressing problems and issues of the age. Nevertheless, authoritative doctrines are those teachings which, for various reasons, the Church is either not yet ready or not able to teach definitively. Often these teachings may be too far removed from divine revelation to be subject matter for a dogmatic definition. At other times it may be that the doctrine's precise relationship to divine revelation is not yet clear. In some instances an authoritative doctrine may be a teaching that has not fully "matured" within the consciousness of the Church. Perhaps more scholarly work needs to be undertaken in evaluating its place in scripture and tradition. It may be a teaching yet to be "received" by the faithful, or it may be a teaching, which, by the nature of that with which it is concerned, *cannot* be divinely revealed (e.g., it may depend on contingent data).

Because the Church does not irrevocably bind itself to the revelatory character of these teachings, authoritative doctrines must be qualified as *nondefinitive or reversible*. In other words, the possibility of a substantive reversal cannot, in principle, be excluded. The formal description of the response that believers are to give to such teaching is an "*obsequium* of will and intellect." Essentially this means that believers must make an honest attempt to assimilate this teaching into their religious consciousness. However, since the magisterium itself admits that there is a remote possibility of error, a failure to assimilate this teaching need not separate the Catholic from full and active participation in the life of the Church.

Finally, we might note the existence of *doctrinal applications*, *prudential admonitions*, and *church discipline*. These determinations are doctrinal only in an analogous sense. Although all church teaching is in a sense pastoral in character, there are some ecclesiastical pronouncements that are explicitly pastoral, concerned not so much with the proclamation of God's Word as with offering prudential judgments regarding the soundness of theological and ecclesiological developments in the Church, or regarding concrete guidelines for Christian action.

This category also includes legislative determinations regarding the disciplinary life of the

Church, as with the requirement of mandatory celibacy for the ministerial priesthood in the Latin rite. The *prudential* character of these pronouncements and disciplinary practices must be emphasized. The Spirit certainly assists the authoritative teachers of the Church even in its prudential judgments. Nevertheless, the guarantee of the Spirit is concerned primarily with preserving the Church in fidelity to the Word, not with protecting it from unwise or imprudent disciplinary actions.[73] Catholics ought to attend respectfully to the appropriate admonitions and disciplinary decrees with a view to implementing the spirit of the law where such an implementation does not conflict with the demands of conscience.

Now we must consider how these gradations in doctrine relate to Catholic social teaching.

Gradations of Authority in Catholic Social Teaching

Catholic social teaching certainly possesses a dogmatic foundation grounded in the Decalogue and the teaching of Jesus. Yet an important passage from *Gaudium et spes* suggests that the Council was not convinced that *all* moral teaching was divinely revealed: "The church is guardian of the deposit of God's word and draws religious and moral principles from it, but it does not always have a ready answer to every question. Still, it is eager to associate the light of revelation with the experience of humanity in trying to clarify the course upon which it has recently entered." (GS 33) What is the nature of this distinction between moral principles drawn from God's Word and answers "to particular questions" that do not necessarily come from divine revelation?

Roman Catholicism has always stressed the importance of human reason in the moral life. Catholicism has insisted that there is an identifiable moral structure to the universe (we can also speak of this as a moral "law" as long as we overlook the rigorist connotations of the word)[74] and that we are capable of discovering it through rational reflection on human experience. Because of human sinfulness, this is not as easy as it might be. For that reason, in addition to the employment of our powers of reason in reflection on our experience, we may also turn to divine revelation. We believe that God's saving Word calls us to moral conversion and a life dedicated to the achievement of virtue and goodness. Therefore, at least some of what we might discover in the natural law through reasoned reflection on human experience is also confirmed in divine revelation. But does this hold for the entirety of the natural law? From the sixteenth through the nineteenth centuries it was not uncommon for theologians to teach that all of the natural law belonged to divine revelation, including the most specific of moral injunctions. Few theologians would hold this position today.

It may be helpful to distinguish between three integrally related categories of moral teachings. Of a more general nature are universal moral teachings regarding the law of love, the dignity of the human person, respect for human life, and obligation to care for the environment. These affirmations constitute the very foundation of Catholic social teaching, would generally be considered dogmatic in character, and, even though they have never been formally defined, demand of believers an assent of faith.

Most of the more specific contents of what we think of as Catholic social teaching belongs, however, to the next two levels: specific moral principles and the application of specific moral principles. Specific moral principles emerge out of the Church's ecclesial reflection upon universal moral teachings in the light of theological inquiry, the insights of the human sciences, and rational reflection on human experience. This complex ecclesial inquiry yields such specific moral principles as the affirmation of political, civic, and economic human rights; the restrictive conditions that must exist in order to justify capital punishment; the preferential option for the poor; and the prohibition of the direct taking of innocent life.

These specific moral principles generally fall within the category described above as authoritative doctrine. These are teachings that possess a provisionally binding status but are not, in principle, irreversible. The main reason for seeing such teachings as nondogmatic lies in the way in which, as these teachings attend more to specific moral issues, they are shaped by changing moral contexts and contingent empirical data. These more specific moral principles can be of great assistance in the moral life, but because they are dependent in part on changing circumstances they can only apply, as the medieval tradition put it, "in the majority of instances" (*ut in pluribus*). This dependence on changing empirical data presents a strong argument against considering such teachings as belonging to divine revelation. Consequently, it is the conclusion of many theologians that, while it is legitimate and necessary for the teaching office of the Church to propose specific moral principles for the guidance of the faithful, these teachings are not divinely revealed and cannot be taught as dogma.[75] This means that Catholics must treat these teachings as more than mere opinions or pious exhortations but as normative church teaching that they must strive to integrate into their religious outlook. However, because they are not taught as irreversible, it is possible to imagine a Catholic who might be unable to accept a given teaching as reflective of God's will for humankind and could legitimately withhold giving an internal assent to it.

At an even greater level of specificity are the concrete applications of specific moral principles. Here the dependence on changing contexts and contingent empirical data is even more pronounced than with specific moral principles. For example, the American bishops' condemnation of first use of nuclear weapons constituted a quite concrete application of specific moral principles in a particular context. The American bishops acknowledged this category in the distinction they made between moral principles and their concrete application in two of their better-known pastoral letters, *The Challenge of Peace* and *Economic Justice for All*.[76] Regarding the latter category the bishops insisted that moral applications and prudential judgments must be given "serious attention and consideration by Catholics as they determine whether their moral judgments are consistent with the Gospel."[77] Nevertheless, they admitted that Catholics might legitimately differ with the bishops regarding these moral applications and prudential judgments.

This schema for assessing the binding character of various Catholic social teachings is similar to that proposed by the American bishops except that, where the bishops wrote of two categories, moral principles and their applications, I am proposing here three categories: universal moral teachings (dogma), specific moral principles (authoritative doctrine), and moral applications. This schema or taxonomy of church teaching cannot do justice to the richness and multitextured character of Catholic social teaching. As Catholic teaching has moved from the propositional emphasis of the moral manuals to a more persuasive and dialogical style of articulating church teaching, it will not be so easy to come to a ready and certain judgment regarding the precise authoritative status of one or another particular teaching. It remains, in no small part, for the theological community to assist the whole people of God in the important ecclesial discernment necessary if Catholics are to grasp the proper demands set before them by Catholic social teaching.

CONCLUSION: THE IMPLICATIONS OF CATHOLIC SOCIAL TEACHING FOR THE LIFE OF THE CHURCH

Vatican II plainly affirmed the sacramental nature of the Church as a "universal sacrament of salvation."[78] This teaching highlights the sign value of the Church itself. This sign value extends beyond preaching and teaching to the Church's visible structures and characteristic practices. If the salvation that the Church preaches is not to be understood in a narrow and otherworldly fashion but as a genuinely "integral salvation,"[79] a salvation that attends not only to the spiritual but to the historical and social nature of the human person, then the call to justice is integral to that message of salvation. This was explicitly affirmed in the 1971 synod of bishops' statement *Justitia in mundo*:

"Action on behalf of justice and participation in the transformation of the world fully appear to us as a constitutive dimension of the preaching of the Gospel, or, in other words, of the Church's mission for the redemption of the human race and its liberation from every oppressive situation." (JM 6) As a sacramental sign and instrument of this integral salvation, the Church must not only preach justice, it must embody justice in its structures and practices. This too was acknowledged in the 1971 synodal statement: "While the Church is bound to give witness to justice, she recognizes that anyone who ventures to speak to people about justice must first be just in their eyes. Hence we must undertake an examination of the modes of acting and of the possessions and life style found within the Church itself." (JM 3)

It is, in part, because of the Church's own sacramentality that theologians both during and after the Council have debated whether it was appropriate to speak of the Church not only as a Church of sinners but, in some sense, as a sinful Church.[80] The Council did not directly address this question, though one could argue that in speaking of the Church not only as a church of pilgrims but as a pilgrim church, it had something of this issue in mind. The debate is not as esoteric as it seems. For those who oppose any attribution of sinfulness to the Church, such a claim would contradict the biblical affirmation that the Church is "the spotless bride of Christ." Others argue that to attribute sin, at least analogously, to the Church itself is only to acknowledge that the Church may possess sinful structures and practices that can vitiate the sign value and therefore the very sacramentality of the Church itself. To acknowledge unjust structures and practices in the Church is to recognize that the Church has the capacity not only to be a "universal sacrament of salvation" but also a countersign to the very message of salvation that it preaches. This is why the Council spoke of the necessity of reform and renewal in the Church:

> Christ summons the Church, as she goes her pilgrim way, to that continual reformation of which she always has need, insofar as she is a human institution here on earth. Consequently, if, in various times and circumstances, there have been deficiencies in moral conduct or in church discipline, or even in the way that church teaching has been formulated—to be carefully distinguished from the deposit of faith itself—these should be set right at the opportune moment and in the proper way.[81]

This necessary reform and renewal must include the application of the social teaching of the Church to the Church's own structures and practices.

Justitia in mundo called for fair wages for all who work for the Church and, at the same time, for the Church to administer its temporal goods in ways that bespeak its solidarity with the poor. The synod called for greater participation of the laity in church decision making and acknowledged the need for an appropriate freedom of expression and thought, advocating "a spirit of dialogue which preserves a legitimate diversity within the Church." The bishops also affirmed the need for women to have greater participation and share of responsibility in the life of the Church. Many of these themes were picked up in the American bishops' 1986 pastoral letter *Economic Justice for All*.[82] Elsewhere the American bishops have also decried the presence of racism in the Church.[83]

In the more than three decades since the 1971 statement was issued, little has been done to address the injustice that abounds in church policies and structures.[84] Communities of professed religious women have for decades served the Church for slave wages. Now they find themselves with an aging population and greatly diminished sources of income while facing soaring health care costs. The U.S. bishops' conference is to be praised for its institution of an annual collection for professed religious women's communities, but one can only wonder whether this is too little, too late to redress the economic impoverishment of the many women religious who served so selflessly for so long.

Far too many Catholic employees in diocesan offices, parishes, and schools receive considerably less than a fair wage and often work without the kind of basic contractual protection assumed in the private sector. The unionization of church employees is frequently discouraged as employees are told that their work should be viewed as a "vocation" or "ministry" that therefore cannot be compared to correlative positions in the secular business world. This avoids the fact, however, that many of these employees, unlike the clergy who often employ them, have families to provide for. Moreover, while women constitute the majority of lay church employees in both schools and parishes, they often encounter a church version of the "glass ceiling" as regards key positions for which they are canonically eligible. Standardized personnel policies, such as established procedures for job reviews, are still the exception rather than the norm.

It is also difficult to discern significant progress as regards the bishops' call for greater participation of the laity in decision-making processes. Although the 1983 Code of Canon Law has numerous provisions for lay participation in church decision making, many of these provisions are inadequately developed. Restrictions on the role granted to the laity in church decision making are justified on several grounds. Many contend that according to canon law, the laity cannot exercise the power of governance. Yet recent canonical studies have called this into question, noting historical instances in which the laity have exercised the power of governance and pointing out significant ambiguities in the current code on this question.[85]

One often hears the slogan, "the Church is not a democracy," yet almost never does one hear its necessary ecclesiological correlate, "the Church is also not an oligarchy." In fact the Church cannot be compared to any single political model for it is, uniquely, a spiritual communion constituted as such by the power of the Holy Spirit. Within the life of the Church, unlike an oligarchy, power is not to be located in a select few. Ecclesiologically, power proceeds from baptism as a gift of the Spirit and can be defined as *the capacity to fulfill one's baptismal call and engage in effective action in service of the Church's life and mission.* The power we receive through Christian initiation enables us to fulfill our calling as disciples of Jesus. We are empowered to share the good news of Jesus Christ, to pursue holiness, to love our neighbor, to care for the least, to work for justice, and to build up the body of Christ through the exercise of our particular gifts in service of the Church. Any new empowerment, beyond that oriented toward our common discipleship, must be strictly a function of our entrance into some new ecclesial relation, as occurs in sacramental ordination. Power cannot be considered apart from a concrete ecclesial relationship, whether that relationship is constituted by sacramental initiation or ordination.

If the Church is not an oligarchy it is also not a liberal democratic polity; the Church does not, and ought not, make decisions based on the aggregate majority of private opinions on a given matter. As a spiritual communion bound to discern the will of God, the Church should avoid any kind of majoritarianism. Its task is to cultivate a "holy conversation" in which each participant actualizes the *sensus fidei* (supernatural instinct for the faith) received at baptism in order to discern the will of God rather than private desires or preferences. These ecclesial discernment processes will acknowledge the indispensable role of ordained church leadership as guardians of the apostolic faith while also remaining open to the prophetic voice that so often emerges outside of established institutional structures.

Finally, while it was not expressly mentioned in *Justitia in mundo*, the principle of subsidiarity that first appeared in Catholic social teaching in *Quadragesimo anno* has been applied to the life of the Church in several church statements. Put simply, the principle of subsidiarity holds that higher levels of a society should not take on tasks and functions that can be accomplished better at lower levels. Pope Pius XII extended the sphere of application when he observed in 1946 that this principle, "valid for social life in all its grades," was valid "also for the life of the church without prejudice to its hierarchical structure."[86] The principle was not explicitly mentioned in the documents of Vatican II, though several commentators believe it is implicit in several passages.[87] The 1967 synod of bishops approved ten principles for the revision of the Code of Canon Law that explicitly mentioned the need to incorporate the principle of subsidiarity, apparently with the relationship of pope to bishops in mind.[88] The 1969 synod addressed episcopal collegiality and approved a brief statement calling for a clearer determination of the competency of the bishop as pastor of the particular church in view of the principle of subsidiarity.[89] The preface to the revised Code of Canon Law explicitly mentions the principle though there is some disagreement regarding the degree to which it was in fact integrated into the revised code.

The application of subsidiarity to the life of the Church requires that we transpose the sociopolitical principle into the ecclesiological framework determined by the integrity of the local church "in and out of which" the universal Church is manifested.[90] If we admit that, at least analogically, it can be applied to the Church, we might reformulate that principle as follows: *the pastoral authority with direct responsibility for a local community must have primary responsibility for pastoral ministry within that community and is expected to address, without external intervention, the pastoral issues that emerge there. Only when these issues appear insoluble at the local level and/or threaten the faith and unity of the Church universal should one expect the intervention of "higher authority."*

Some who view subsidiarity as strictly a sociological principle have criticized its application to the Church as inappropriate. They contend that the Church is no mere sociological reality but a spiritual communion and therefore not subject to the sociological rules that apply to other secular institutions.[91] Yet it is also possible to see subsidiarity as the concrete structural realization of what it means to say the universal Church is a communion of churches.[92] A *communio*-ecclesiology demands the preservation of the full integrity of the local church as the concrete presence of the one Church of Christ in that place. Any exercise of authority at a level beyond the local can never be undertaken in a way that undermines that church's integrity. The exercise of "higher authority" must always be a means toward preserving the integrity of the local church and its communion with the other churches. This is why one must resist the tendency to identify subsidiarity with decentralization. The latter concept starts with the rights of the higher authority to intervention and then "concedes" authority to the lower levels. The principle of subsidiarity, on the other hand, begins with the relative autonomy of local authorities and demands justification for the intervention of higher authorities. In this view, many recent curial interventions in the affairs of the local churches cannot help but be viewed as contraventions of the principle of subsidiarity.[93]

In this chapter I have addressed several basic questions regarding the proper ecclesiological framework for understanding Catholic social teaching. Yet none is more vital than the question of justice in the Church, for it goes to the very integrity of Catholic social teaching itself. In the midst of the various debates about continuity and discontinuity in Catholic social teaching, a larger truth cannot be forgotten: to the extent that the Church is seen to perpetuate unjust structures and policies, the enduring validity of its social teaching will be irrelevant. As the bishops reminded us in *Justitia in mundo*: "anyone who ventures to speak to people about justice must first be just in their eyes" (chap. 3).

NOTES

1. *Liberalism* itself is a contested term, but as used here it refers to what, from Catholicism's perspective, was a cultural perspective shaped by "the Lutheran revolt against the Church's authority and on behalf of free examination, in the naturalism of the Renaissance, in the Enlightenment's repudiation of tradition, authority and community, in the secularization of the political sphere, in the possessive individualism of capitalist economics, and in the cultural anarchy produced by an unrestrained freedom of opinion, speech, and the press. Common to all these developments was an exaltation of the individual and a definition of freedom as exemption from external constraint." Joseph Komonchak, "Vatican II and the

Encounter between Catholicism and Liberalism," in *Catholicism and Liberalism: Contributions to American Public Philosophy,* ed. Bruce Douglass and David Hollenbach (Cambridge: Cambridge University Press, 1994), 76.

2. T. Howland Sanks, *Salt, Leaven and Light: The Community Called Church* (New York: Crossroad, 1992), 99.

3. Josef L. Altholz, *The Churches in the Nineteenth Century* (New York: Bobbs-Merrill, 1967), 137.

4. Michael J. Schuck, *That They Be One: The Social Teaching of the Papal Encyclicals 1740–1989* (Washington, D.C.: Georgetown University Press, 1991), 20.

5. Ibid., 67.

6. See David Hollenbach's Commentary on *Gaudium et spes* in this volume.

7. See Komonchak, "Vatican II and the Encounter," in *Catholicism and Liberalism,* ed. B. Douglass and D. Hollenbach, 86–88.

8. See Joseph Ratzinger, "The Church and Man's Calling: Introductory Article and Chapter I," in *Commentary on the Documents of Vatican II*, vol. 5, ed. Herbert Vorgrimler, trans. W. J. O'Hara (New York: Herder, 1969), 119–20.

9. Vatican II, *Decree on the Church's Missionary Activity* (*Ad gentes*), number 2.

10. David Bosch, *Transforming Mission: Paradigm Shifts in Theology of Mission* (Maryknoll, N.Y.: Orbis, 1991), 237.

11. Schuck, *That They Be One*, 134.

12. Joseph Cardijn was a Belgian priest who in the early twentieth century played an important role in the Lay Apostolate movement.

13. Mary Elsbernd, "What Ever Happened to *Octogesima Adveniens?*" *Theological Studies* 56 (1995): 43.

14. Paul VI, *Apostolic Exhortation on Evangelization in the Modern World* (*Evangelii nuntiandi*) (Boston: Daughters of St. Paul, 1975), number 62.

15. Ibid., number 20.

16. *L'Osservatore Romano* (English-language edition), June 28, 1982, 7.

17. "Final Report," *Origins* 15, no. 27 (1985): 449.

18. See SRS 24; CA 39; *Evangelium vitae*, numbers 12, 19, 21, 24, 26, 28, 50, 64, 87, 95, 100.

19. H. Richard Niebuhr claimed that it was possible to discover in the history of Christianity five basic types for conceiving the engagement of Christ and culture: (1) Christ against culture, (2) Christ of culture, (3) Christ above culture, (4) Christ and culture in paradox, and (5) Christ transforming culture. See his *Christ and Culture* (New York: Harper and Row, 1951).

20. Thomas Shannon, "Roman Catholic Social Thought: Historical, Methodological, and Analytic Perspectives," unpublished paper presented at the Collegium Colloquium on Faith and Intellectual Life at St. John's University, Collegeville, Minn., June 21, 2000.

21. For an alternative typology, see Avery Dulles, "The Four Faces of American Catholicism," *Louvain Studies* 18 (1993): 99–109.

22. See George Weigel, *Catholicism and the Renewal of American Democracy* (New York: Paulist, 1989).

23. See Richard John Neuhaus, *The Naked Public Square: Religion and Democracy in America* (Grand Rapids, Mich.: Eerdmans, 1984), and idem, *The Catholic Moment: The Paradox of the Church in the Postmodern World* (San Francisco: Harper and Row, 1987).

24. Michael Novak, *The Spirit of Democratic Capitalism* (New York: Simon and Schuster, 1982), and idem, *The Catholic Ethic and the Spirit of Capitalism* (New York: The Free Press, 1993).

25. Especially John Paul II's CA. See Daniel Finn's Commentary on *Centesimus annus* and Charles Curran's "Reception of Catholic Social Teaching in the United States," both in this volume.

26. Stanley Hauerwas, *A Community of Character* (Notre Dame, Ind.: University of Notre Dame Press, 1981); idem, with William H. Willimon, *Resident Aliens* (Nashville, Tenn.: Abingdon, 1989); idem, *With the Grain of the Universe: The Church's Witness and Natural Theology* (Grand Rapids, Mich.: Brazos, 2001).

27. Michael J. Baxter, "'Blowing the Dynamite of the Church': Catholic Radicalism from a Catholic Radicalist Perspective," in *The Church as Counter-Culture,* ed. Michael L. Budde and Robert W. Brimlow (New York: State University of New York Press, 2000), 195–212; idem, "Reintroducing Virgil Michel: Towards a Counter-Tradition of Catholic Social Ethics in the United States," *Communio* 24 (1997): 499–528; idem, "Review Essay: The Non-Catholic Character of the 'Public Church,'" *Theology Today* 11 (1995): 243–58.

28. Rodney Clapp, "Practicing the Politics of Jesus," in *The Church as Counter-Culture*, ed. M. Budde and R. Brimlow, 15–37.

29. Michael Budde, *The (Magic) Kingdom of God: Christianity and Global Culture Industries* (Boulder, Colo.: Westview, 1997); idem, with Robert W. Brimlow, *Christianity Incorporated: How Big Business Is Buying the Church* (Grand Rapids, Mich.: Brazos, 2002).

30. William T. Cavanaugh, "'A Fire Strong Enough to Consume the House': The Wars of Religion and the Rise of the State," *Modern Theology* 11 (1995): 377–420.

31. David Schindler, *Heart of the World, Center of the Church: Communio Ecclesiology, Liberalism and Liberation* (Grand Rapids, Mich.: Eerdmans, 1996).

32. See David Schindler, "On the Catholic Common Ground Project: The Christological Foundations of Dialogue," *Communio* 26 (1996): 165–70.

33. John Milbank, *Theology and Social Theory: Beyond Secular Reason* (Cambridge: Blackwell, 1991).

34. David Tracy, *The Analogical Imagination: Christian Theology and the Culture of Pluralism* (New York: Crossroad, 1981), 374ff.

35. David Hollenbach, *Claims in Conflict: Retrieving and Renewing the Catholic Human Rights Tradition* (New York: Paulist, 1979).

36. Richard McBrien, *Caesar's Coin: Religion and Politics in America* (New York: Macmillan, 1987).

37. Kenneth R. Himes and Michael Himes, *Fullness of Faith: The Public Significance of Theology* (New York: Paulist, 1993).

38. Charles Curran, *Directions in Catholic Social Ethics* (Notre Dame, Ind.: University of Notre Dame Press, 1985), and idem, *Church and Morality: An Ecumenical and Catholic Approach* (Minneapolis: Fortress, 1993).

39. The ancient view of the Church as itself sacramental had already become a topic of renewed interest in the years prior to the Council. See Karl Rahner, *The Church and the Sacraments*, trans. W. J. O'Hara (New York: Herder and Herder, 1963); Otto Semmelroth, *Church and Sacrament*, trans. Emily Schossberger (Notre Dame, Ind.: Fides, 1965); Edward Schillebeeckx, *Christ the Sacrament of the Encounter with God*, trans. Paul Barrett (New York: Sheed and Ward, 1963). It would be affirmed explicitly in several conciliar texts. LG 1 taught that "the church, in Christ, is a sacrament—a sign and instrument, that is, of communion with God and the unity of the entire human race." In chapter 7 of that constitution, the Church is referred to as "a universal sacrament of salvation" (LG 48) and both of these texts are quoted in GS. The *Decree on the Church's Missionary Activity* (*Ad gentes*) begins with the following passage: "Having been sent by God to the nations to be 'the universal sacrament of salvation,' the church, in obedience to the command of her founder and because it is demanded by her own essential universality, strives to preach the gospel to all" (*Ad gentes*, number 1). The references in both GS and *Ad gentes* are particularly important because they suggest that the council members saw the sacramentality of the Church as crucial to the Church's fulfillment of its mission to be a leaven in the world.

40. See David Hollenbach, "A Prophetic Church and the Catholic Sacramental Imagination," in *The Faith that Does Justice*, ed. John Haughey (New York: Paulist, 1977), 234–63.

41. *Lumen gentium*, number 5.

42. Francis A. Sullivan, *The Church We Believe In: One, Holy, Catholic and Apostolic* (New York: Paulist, 1988), 123.

43. For a helpful collection of essays on the integral connection between liturgy and justice, see *Living No Longer for Ourselves: Liturgy and Justice in the Nineties*, ed. Kathleen Hughes and Mark R. Francis (Collegeville, Minn.: Liturgical, 1991). For a treatment of Virgil Michel's thought on this connection, see R. W. Franklin and Robert L. Spaeth, *Virgil Michel: American Catholic* (Collegeville, Minn.: Liturgical, 1988). See also the collection of essays, *Liturgy and Justice: To Worship God in Spirit and Truth*, ed. Anne Y. Koester (Collegeville, Minn.: Liturgical, 2002).

44. Pius X, *Vehementor nos*, number 8. English translation from *The Papal Encyclicals*, vol. 3, ed. Claudia Carlen (Wilmington, N.C.: McGrath, 1981), 47–48.

45. Vatican II, *Dogmatic Constitution on Divine Revelation* (*Dei verbum*), number 1.

46. Ibid., number 2.

47. Ibid., number 8.

48. Ibid.

49. For more on the theology of ecclesial reception, see Yves Congar, "La 'réception' comme réalité ecclésiologique," in *Église et papauté: regards historiques*

(Paris: Cerf, 1994), 229–66. For an abbreviated English translation, see "Reception as an Ecclesiological Reality," in *Election and Consensus in the Church*, *Concilium*, vol. 77, ed. Giuseppe Alberigo and Anton Weiler (New York: Herder, 1972), 43–68. For other notable studies on the topic, see J. M.-R. Tillard, "Tradition, Reception," in *The Quadrilog: Tradition and the Future of Ecumenism*, festschrift for George Tavard (Collegeville, Minn.: Liturgical, 1994), 328–43; "Reception—Communion," *One in Christ* 28 (1992): 307–22; Hermann J. Pottmeyer, "Reception and Submission," *Jurist* 51 (1991): 269–92.

50. *Lumen gentium*, number 4.

51. Vatican II, *Decree on the Apostolate of the Laity* (*Apostolicam actuositatem*), number 3.

52. Vatican II, *Decree on Priestly Ministry and Life* (*Presbyterorum ordinis*), number 9.

53. *Lumen gentium*, number 37.

54. Ibid., number 27.

55. Ibid., number 23.

56. Ibid., number 22.

57. Ibid., number 8.

58. Vatican II, *Decree on Ecumenism* (*Unitatis redintegratio*), number 6.

59. *Lumen gentium*, number 23.

60. Ibid., number 26.

61. See Karl Rahner, "The Abiding Significance of the Second Vatican Council," in *Theological Investigations*, vol. 20, trans. Edward Quinn (New York: Crossroad, 1981), 90–102.

62. See Mary Elsbernd, "What Ever Happened to *Octogesima adveniens?*" *Theological Studies* 56 (1995): 39–60. See also Shannon, "Roman Catholic Social Thought."

63. On this point, see Kenneth Himes, "The Local Church as a Mediating Structure," *Social Thought* 12, no. 1 (1986): 23–30.

64. *Libertatis conscientia*, *Origins* 15 (April 1986): 513–28.

65. See the analysis of this document in Elsbernd, "What Ever Happened," 52–53.

66. *Apostolos suos*, *Origins* 28 (July 1998): 152–58.

67. For an analysis of this document, see Francis A. Sullivan, "The Teaching Authority of Episcopal Conferences," *Theological Studies* 63 (2002): 472–93; Ladislas Orsy, "Episcopal Conferences and the Power of the Spirit," *Jurist* 59 (1999): 409–31.

68. Technically, this is not the intent of the *recognitio*. According to canon law, the *recognitio* represents nothing more than an administrative act of the Holy See confirming that a given document does not violate church teaching or current law. In practice, however, the conferral or refusal of a *recognitio* has gone far beyond the limited role intended for it in canon law to give the Vatican substantial veto authority. See Ulrich Rhode, "Die Recognitio von Statuten, Dekreten und Liturgischen Büchern," *Archiv für katholisches Kirchenrecht* 169 (2000): 433–68.

69. A typical example can be found in Ludwig Ott, *Fundamentals of Catholic Dogma*, rev. ed., trans. Patrick Lynch (St. Louis, Mo.: Herder, 1960), 9–10. See also Joseph Salaverri, *Sacrae theologiae summa*, vol. 1, rev. ed. (Madrid: BAC, 1955), 781–96. For an in-depth treatment of the role of theological notes and censures, see Sixtus Cartechini, *De valore notarum theologicarum et de criteriis ad eas dignoscendas* (Rome: Gregorian University Press, 1951). See also Harold E. Ernst, "The Theological Notes and the Interpretation of Doctrine," *Theological Studies* 63 (2002): 813–25.

70. See, for example, CDF, "Profession of Faith and Oath of Fidelity," *Origins* 18 (March 16, 1989): 661–63; idem, "Instruction on the Ecclesial Vocation of the Theologian," *Origins* 20 (July 5, 1990): 117–26. For an in-depth consideration of these distinctions, see Richard R. Gaillardetz, *Teaching with Authority: A Theology of the Magisterium in the Church* (Collegeville, Minn.: Liturgical, 1997), 101–27, 258–71.

71. See *Lumen gentium*, number 25.

72. This formulation was found in CDF, "Instruction on the Ecclesial Vocation of the Theologian," 121. The definitive study on the history of this category of church teaching is Jean-François Chiron, *L'infaillibilité et son objet: L'autorité du magistère infaillible de l'Église s'étend-elle aux vérités non révélées?* (Paris: Cerf, 1999). See also Christoph Theobald, "Le développement de la notion des 'verités historiquement et logiquement connexes avec la Révélation,' de Vatican I à Vatican II," *Cristianesimo nella storia* 21 (2000): 37–70; Richard R. Gaillardetz, "*Ad tuendam fidem*: An Emerging Pattern in Current Papal Teaching," *New Theology Review* 12, no. 1 (1999): 43–51; Bernard Sesboüé, "'A propos du 'Motu Proprio' de Jean-Paul II, *Ad tuendam fidem*," *Études* 389 (1998): 357–67; Ladislas Orsy, "Von der Autorität kirchlicher Dokumente,"

Stimmen der Zeit 216 (1998): 735–40; Joseph Ratzinger, "Stellungnahme," *Stimmen der Zeit* 216 (1998): 735–40; Francis A. Sullivan, "The Secondary Object of Infallibility," *Theological Studies* 54 (1993): 536–50.

73. Ladislas Örsy, *The Church: Teaching and Learning* (Wilmington, Del.: Michael Glazier, 1987), 76–78.

74. For a consideration of the ambiguities inherent in speaking of a moral "law," see John Mahoney, "The Language of Law," in *The Making of Moral Theology: A Study of the Roman Catholic Tradition* (Oxford: Clarendon, 1987), 224–58. See also Jean Porter, *Natural and Divine Law: Reclaiming the Tradition for Christian Ethics* (Grand Rapids, Mich.: Eerdmans, 1999).

75. See John Boyle, "The Natural Law and the Magisterium," in *Church Teaching Authority: Historical and Theological Studies* (Notre Dame, Ind.: University of Notre Dame Press, 1995), 43–62; Richard A. McCormick, *Corrective Vision: Explorations in Moral Theology* (Kansas City, Mo.: Sheed and Ward, 1994), 86–89; Franz Böckle, "Le magistère de l'Église in matière morale," *Revue théologique de Louvain* 19 (1989): 3–16; Francis A. Sullivan, "Some Observations on the New Formula for the Profession of Faith," *Gregorianum* 70 (1989): 552–54; André Naud, *Le magistère incertain* (Montréal: Fides, 1989), 77–121; Karl Rahner, "Basic Observations on the Subject of Changeable and Unchangeable Factors in the Church," *Theological Investigations,* vol. 14, trans. Edward Quinn (New York: Seabury, 1976), 3–23.

76. See *Challenge of Peace*, number 10; EJA 135, both in *Catholic Social Thought: The Documentary Heritage* (Maryknoll, N.Y.: Orbis, 1992).

77. *Challenge of Peace*, number 10.

78. *Lumen gentium*, number 48; GS 45; *Ad gentes*, number 1.

79. This understanding of the Church as a sacrament of "integral salvation" is taken from Sullivan, *The Church We Believe In*, 132–51.

80. Karl Rahner wrote two classic essays on this topic, "The Church of Sinners" and "The Sinful Church in the Decrees of Vatican II," in *Theological Investigations*, vol. 6, trans. Karl-H. and Boniface Kruger (New York: Crossroad, 1982), 253–69, 270–94, respectively. See also an earlier essay by Hans Urs von Balthasar, "Casta Meretrix," in *Sponsa Verbi*, Skizzen zur Theologie, 2 (Einsiedeln: Johannes Verlag, 1961), 203–305.

81. *Unitatis redintegratio*, number 6.

82. EJA 347–58.

83. *What We Have Seen and Heard: A Pastoral Letter on Evangelization from the Black Bishops of the United States* (Cincinnati, Ohio: St. Anthony Messenger, 1984), 20.

84. For an assessment of the Church in North America on this question, see Raymond A. Lucker, "Justice in the Church: The Church as Example," in *One Hundred Years of Catholic Social Thought: Celebration and Challenge,* ed. John A. Coleman (Maryknoll, N.Y.: Orbis, 1991), 88–100.

85. See James Coriden, "Lay Persons and the Power of Governance," *Jurist* 59 (1999): 335–47; John P. Beal, "The Exercise of the Power of Governance by Lay People: State of the Question," *Jurist* 55 (1995): 1–92; James H. Provost, "The Participation of the Laity in the Governance of the Church," *Studia Canonica* 17 (1983): 417–48; John M. Huels, "Another Look at Lay Jurisdiction," *Jurist* 41 (1981): 59–80; J. James Cuneo, "The Power of Jurisdiction: Empowerment for Church Functioning and Mission Distinct from the Power of Orders," *Jurist* 39 (1979): 183–219.

86. Pius XII made this statement in an address to newly created cardinals, *Acta apostolicis sedis* (AAS) 38 (1946): 144–45. He reaffirmed the ecclesial implications of the principle of subsidiarity in an address to the Second World Congress of the Lay Apostolate in 1957. See AAS 49 (1957): 926–28.

87. Joseph Komonchak, "Subsidiarity and the Church: The State of the Question," *Jurist* 48 (1988): 309–12.

88. For the principles themselves, see Xavier Ochoa, *Leges ecclesiae post codicem iuris canonici editae volumen III* (Rome: Commentarium pro Religiosis, 1972), 5253–75. For a discussion of their significance, see Ad Leys, *Ecclesiological Impacts of the Principle of Subsidiarity* (Kampen: Uitgeverij Kok, 1995), 89–93.

89. Cited in Leys, *Ecclesiological Impacts,* 95.

90. *Lumen gentium*, number 23. Opponents of the application of subsidiarity to the life of the Church, such as canonist Eugenio Corecco, do not attend sufficiently to the theological relationship between the local church and the universal Church, and thus fail to recognize that the Church as com-

munion is always being realized within the specificity of the local churches. See Leys, *Ecclesiological Aspects*, 187ff.

91. For a review of this argument, see Leys, *Ecclesiological Aspects*, 113–19; and Komonchak, "Subsidiarity and the Church," 336–37.

92. J. M.-R. Tillard, *Church of Churches: The Ecclesiology of Communion*, trans. R. C. DePeaux (Collegeville, Minn.: Liturgical, 1992), 275–83.

93. Some recent examples regarding curial intervention in the Church in North America would include interventions in the translations of biblical and liturgical texts, the renovations of the cathedral in Milwaukee, Wisconsin, and the American implementation of *Ex corde ecclesiae,* the apostolic constitution on Catholic higher education.

SELECTED BIBLIOGRAPHY

Baum, Gregory. *Compassion and Solidarity: The Church for Others*. New York: Paulist, 1990. A slim but insightful set of reflections on the Church as "an instrument for justice and a focus for human solidarity."

Bosch, David. *Transforming Mission: Paradigm Shifts in Theology of Mission*. Maryknoll, N.Y.: Orbis, 1991. A comprehensive study of the historical development of theologies of mission from an ecumenical perspective.

Budde, Michael L., and Robert W. Brimlow, eds. *The Church as Counterculture*. Albany, N.Y.: State University of New York Press, 2000. A collection of essays laying out the ecclesiological convictions of Catholic radicalism.

Bühlmann, Walbert. *With Eyes to See: Church and World in the Third Millennium*. Translated by Robert R. Barr. Maryknoll, N.Y.: Orbis, 1989. Offers a challenging vision of the shape of the Church in mission for the third millennium.

Gaillardetz, Richard R. *Teaching with Authority: A Theology of the Magisterium in the Church*. Collegeville, Minn.: Liturgical, 1997. Addresses basic questions regarding the teaching authority of the pope and bishops, the various gradations of church doctrine, and the appropriate response of believers to church teaching.

Himes, Kenneth R., and Michael Himes. *Fullness of Faith: The Public Significance of Theology*. New York: Paulist, 1993. The authors develop a public theology that draws on the Catholic doctrinal tradition, for example, the Trinity, original sin, the communion of saints, for resources in constructing a Catholic strategy for engagement with the world.

Hughes, Kathleen, and Mark Francis, eds. *Living No Longer for Ourselves: Liturgy and Justice in the Nineties*. Collegeville, Minn.: Liturgical, 1991. This collection of essays reflects on the role of the liturgy in shaping a Church dedicated to the work of justice.

Metz, Johann Baptist. *The Emergent Church: The Future of Christianity in a Postbourgeois World*. Translated by Peter Mann. New York: Crossroad, 1981. An important articulation of a leading political theologian who is calling the Church to emerge out of what he sees as its present bourgeois, middle-class imprisonment.

Neuhaus, Richard John. *The Naked Public Square: Religion and Democracy in America*. Grand Rapids, Mich.: Eerdmans, 1984. A neoconservative examination of the convergence of Catholic political philosophy and American democratic values.

Niebuhr, H. Richard. *Christ and Culture*. New York: Harper and Row, 1951. In this theological classic a well-known Protestant theologian identifies five consistent patterns of relating the Christian message to human culture.

Sanks, T. Howland, and John Coleman, eds. *Reading the Signs of the Times: Resources for Social and Cultural Analysis*. New York: Paulist, 1993. A collection of essays that considers the social mission of the Church from the perspective of Catholic ecclesiology and the social sciences.

CHAPTER

4 Early Modern Roman Catholic Social Thought, 1740–1890

MICHAEL J. SCHUCK

INTRODUCTION

This is an unsettling yet fascinating time for Roman Catholic Christians. Outstanding saints and notorious sinners lead the Catholic community. Ostensibly incompatible beliefs coexist among church authorities, intellectuals, and the faithful. Vocal Catholics incant an array of social justice imperatives; others listen with polite misgiving. More than a few Catholic scholars suffer magisterial censure; others applaud their fate. For some, the Roman Catholic Church is disjointed—"traditional" religious discipline and practices need retrieval. For others, the Church has regressed—recovery of the modernizing spirit of reform is imperative. At the same time, society seems unraveled by religious divisions, political violence, family breakdown, and economic uncertainty. There are people who view these times as an apocalyptic "clash of civilizations."

Such is life between 1740 and 1890, the period of early modern Roman Catholic social thought.[1] If the above description seems closer to our present time, then the importance of this early period for contemporary Roman Catholic social thought suggests itself. The characters are fascinating, the events and movements are gripping, and the ideas remain important.

But is it not true that 1740–1890 was an era of reactionary stasis in the Roman Catholic Church, symbolized by Pope Gregory XIV's *Mirari vos* on the errors of Félicité de Lamennais and Pope Pius IX's *Quanta cura* with its infamous *Syllabus of Errors?* Is it not true that Europe's economy was still predominantly agricultural, making the industrial working-class "social question" premature? And is it not true that while a few intellectuals and activists modestly anticipate social Catholicism during this period, substantive Roman Catholic social thought really only begins with Pope Leo XIII's 1891 encyclical *Rerum novarum?*

Actually, no. As Ann Swidler observes, human beings possess more cultural resources than they can use at one time.[2] Given their purposes, people select some pieces from their cultural reserve and not others. Individually and in groups, human beings combine, disassemble, retrieve, and recombine these pieces on an ongoing basis. In doing so, people shape their self-consciousness and develop what Charles Lemert calls a "native social competence."[3]

As a Church, Roman Catholics do the same. One example is the standard identification of modern Roman Catholic social thought. It goes like this: Roman Catholic social thought begins with Pope Leo XIII's 1891 encyclical *Rerum novarum*, focuses primarily on economic morality, and continues down to the present through papal texts periodically commemorating Leo XIII's "originating" text. Popes have constructed this identity with a purpose, selecting and combining pieces from Roman Catholic social thought's cultural reserve. By repeating the standard identification, Catholics reinforce the pope's position as broker of Catholic social thought, *Rerum novarum* as the *Urtext*, Europe as the epicenter, and economic morality as the principal "social question."

However, modern Roman Catholic social thought is wider and deeper than the standard identification. Between 1740 and 1890, many church officials, professional authors, academics, and grassroots leaders contribute to this thought. These faithful people struggle with a vast array of social-moral problems occasioned by not only economic crises but also the religious, political, familial, and cultural tensions of their time. Without their work, *Rerum novarum* would never have appeared.

The legacy of papal teaching is not disparaged by recognizing that more social resources exist in the Catholic community than popes can use at any given time. Communities require both historically tutored and untutored memory for survival. Recognizing a wider and deeper base for Roman Catholic social thought protects the community's memory from a forgetfulness imposed by recurrent use of the tutored and standard identification. Religious communities with strong centralized authority must particularly guard against Robert Michel's "iron law of oligarchy," ensuring that the centralized identification exercises a generative, not hegemonic, power.[4]

An exciting yet traditional aspect of intellectual labor in the Roman Catholic Church is *ressourcement*—the possibility of discovering some helpful but forgotten piece of communal memory. Who could imagine, for example, that the thought of a fifth-century pope could be retrieved and used at Vatican II to advance the idea of separation of church and state and religious freedom?[5] And given the standard identification of modern Roman Catholic social thought, who could imagine that reform-minded Catholics promoted a minimum wage, old age insurance, child labor restriction, trade union protection, and safe workplace conditions *before* Leo XIII's *Rerum novarum?*

In view of the uncanny parallels between the 1740–1890 period and the present moment, this chapter encourages reexploration of the collective Catholic memory. While doing so, however, it does not repeat the outstanding work already done by others. This includes detailed analysis of important figures such as Joseph de Maistre, Alban de Villeneuve-Bargemont, Félicité de Lamennais, Philippe Buchez, Frédéric Ozanam, and Wilhelm Emmanuel von Ketteler. Their contributions are noted, but thorough studies of these men already exist.[6] Similarly, select papal writings are discussed, but not the full range of pre-Leonine encyclical social teaching. This work has also been done elsewhere.[7]

This chapter notes the dominant movements and figures of early modern Roman Catholic social thought but also raises up lesser-known and previously unrecognized contributors. Among these are parish homilists, Central and South American intellectuals, Catholic novelists, women activists, and European artists. These figures surface by way of not only new historical studies of the period but also by two distinct approaches taken in this chapter.[8]

I accept Michael Paul Driskel's claim that social discourse includes not only written and spoken words but also visual symbols. In his view, art and architecture participate in structuring and ordering social reality. Of course, art's greater interpretive porousness makes it a comparatively elusive carrier for social ideologies—elusive, but not impossible. Driskel's work effectively shows how art can be "a means of giving concrete, visible form to a specific religious, social and political ideology."[9] On this basis, Roman Catholic social thought should include the social-moral insights encoded in what faithful Catholics paint, sculpt, and build.

In addition, I use ideas of James B. White to say that Roman Catholic social thought is also communicated through a self-conscious "repertoire of forms of action and of life."[10] For example, an incredible number of women join religious communities during this period. Their decision builds, among many other things, the most extensive orphanage network in Europe and America. Such forms of self-conscious action, though seldom articulated theoretically, should no longer be precluded as a form of Roman Catholic social thought.

Roman Catholic social thought between 1740 and 1890 can be divided into four periods. The first extends from the earliest modern papal encyclical (Pope Benedict XIV's 1740 *Ubi primum*) to Pope Pius VI's decisive break with the French Revolution in the 1791 encyclical *Charitas*. The second period treats Catholic social thought between *Charitas* and Europe's 1848 worker revolutions. The third period moves from the aftermath of these revolutions to the 1871 Paris Commune. Finally, the fourth period takes the discussion of Catholic social thought to the eve of Pope Leo XIII's *Rerum novarum*.

Like Roman Catholic social thought as a whole, early modern thinking has great variety. This point is not new but merits reinforcement. Scholars appreciating this variety typically model it on a scale from conservative to liberal to radical ideas. This makes for a complex ménage à trois. Social thinkers with comparatively right and left orientations exist at each point on the scale. Regional and national diversity further complicates the picture.

More than complex, this model can be obfuscating. A Catholic political "conservative" like Villeneuve-Bargemont is "liberal" on economic reform. Ozanam, a Catholic "liberal," is "conservative" by the standards of Enlightenment liberalism. Karl Marx calls a Catholic "radical" like Buchez "retrograde."[11]

I adopt the *ménage à trois* idea but model it differently here. The operative terms are *traditionalism*, *cosmopolitanism*, and *transformationism*. These categories signal social ideologies shaped by particular space-time coordinates. Traditionalism names an approach taken by those valuing the longstanding social customs of a particular people. Modern social changes are scrutinized with great caution. The spatial coordinate for traditionalism is typically regional and the time coordinate is long-range. It is important to Karl Vogelsang, for example, that Catholic corporatism reflects German culture and reaches back to the Middle Ages. Cosmopolitanism represents an orientation generally sanguine over the possibilities of modernity, particularly in areas where humanity's social condition can be improved. For cosmopolitans, the spatial coordinate is global and the time coordinate is the reformer's middle range. An 1862 pastoral letter by French Bishop Felix Dupanloup, for example, condemns slavery in the United States and calls for reform based on universal human rights. As used in this study, transformationism is an orientation characterized by visionary proposals and experiments urgently seeking greater equity in social structures and processes. When Pauline-Marie Jaricot acquires a blast furnace in 1844, her immediate plan is to start a model Christian town where men and women earn a living wage, children are educated, and the sick and the aged receive care. Typical of transformationism, Jaricot's spatial coordinate starts in her immediate local surroundings. And while she is realistic about planning and building, her time frame mirrors the urgency typical of social visionaries.

Actually, traditionalism, cosmopolitanism, and transformationism are age-old Christian moral orientations. One hears Tertullian's traditionalism in his classic question, what does a *particular* community like Jerusalem have to do with a *particular* community like Athens? In Clement of Alexandria's Christ *paidagogos*, one senses the cosmopolitan voice of early Christian humanism. And in John Chrysostom's *koinonia* of shared ownership, one feels the urgent and concrete plea of a transformationist. These ancient voices echo through early modern social thought, and it is good to listen because their reverberations continue down to the present.

1740–1791

The traditionalist, cosmopolitan, and transformationist orientations of Roman Catholic social thought exist in several varieties between Pope Benedict XIV's inaugural encyclical of

1740 and Pope Pius VI's break with the French Revolution in 1791. Within traditionalism, some social thinkers take a decidedly polemic approach while others pursue a more arcadian style. Cosmopolitan thinkers also vary. Some Catholics express their social cosmopolitanism in pacifistic terms; others take characteristically republican or cultural tacks. The period also offers a specifically communal form of Catholic transformationism.

Traditionalism

The foremost Catholic polemicist of the time is Abbé Nicolas-Sylvain Bergier, royal confessor and canon of the cathedral of Notre Dame in Paris. Bergier is an ardent reader of Rousseau, Voltaire, d'Holbach, and other Encyclopedists. Through multiple volumes and correspondence, Bergier presents meticulous arguments against his opponents' deism, naturalism, and rationalism. In *Quelle est la source de toute autorité?* Bergier particularly attacks the modern notion that civil authority arises from the free consent of the people. With Romans 13:1, Bergier insists: "there is no authority except from God."[12]

Though most peasant and working-class Catholics are unfamiliar with Bergier, they remain well-schooled in traditionalist polemic. As Nigel Aston states in his study of eighteenth-century French Catholicism, the faithful receive their moral instruction from the "*curé's* pulpit"—along with "announcements about taxation, poor relief, the militia ballot and other items from the wider world."[13]

Bernard Groethuysen observes the same in his study of eighteenth-century sermons. Drawing largely on the published sermons of Abbé Réguis and Jean-Baptiste Massillon, Groethuysen sees a pattern in their polemic against bourgeois materialism and secularism. According to these preachers, everyday life plays out within a cosmic conflict between the devil and God. The spiritual skirmish affects human society through the actions of two principals: the "great" and the "poor." As one homilist explains:

> He has created the rich, so that they atone for their sins by helping the poor. He has created the poor, so that they humble themselves according to the aid they receive from the rich. Like this, they have been intertwined in civil society, in order that through their mutual functions they strongly help one another, not only for the comfort of the present life, but more for their salvation and their sanctification, the one by honest generosity, the other by humble acknowledgement.[14]

Of course, the devil's role is to dissuade the rich from almsgiving and the poor from resignation. But what of the bourgeois? They are people, says Groethuysen, with no role in the drama. For the preachers, the bourgeois is a class "without mystery," an "essentially secular phenomenon, governed solely by the laws of this world"—and all the more dangerous for practicing avarice without the devil's help![15]

The period's popes share much of this traditionalist polemic but express it in a distinctly arcadian style. The word *arcadian* refers to the pastoral literary genre where images of rural life are used to communicate the innocence and serenity of simple living. A common literary device in papal texts of the time is the pastoral metaphor of a shepherd and his flock. Drawing on scriptural and patristic sources, the popes employ the sheepfold metaphor to explain everything from the person and work of Christ to the people's customary social obligations. The popes repeatedly remind their "flock" that "God's field" coexists with "'trackless places,' 'ravening wolves,' and evil men 'in the clothing of sheep.'"[16] As such, one must proceed through life with extreme moral caution.

In the encyclical *Acerbi plene doloris*, for example, Pope Benedict XIV notes how modernity is eroding worthy agricultural customs. Citing Leviticus 19:10, he insists that landlords continue leaving a portion of their fields unharvested "for the poor and for the sojourner." Benedict maintains that the landlords' *pietas* is owed the poor as both a *pia consuetudus* and a *praecepto jure*. Pope Clement XIII repeats this point in his 1756 encyclical *A quo die*. Mercy to the poor is a *fructu justitiae* required as a *praecepto jure*.

On its face, the popes' terminology confuses arcadian scriptural injunctions with philosophical rights language. In fact, arcadianism is an early expression of the eighteenth-century papacy's commitment to artistic neoclassicism. With this medium, the popes promote a natural, simple style based on Greek and Roman models to suggest how a paleochristian "golden age" might have looked—and how it might be recovered. For example, though the idyllic landscape and earthy sensibility of Giuseppe Chiari's 1707 painting *Rest on the Flight into Egypt* contrast with the stone surfaces and doctrinaire gestures of Jacques Louis David's neoclassical *The Death of Socrates*, the social encoding is related.[17] The avaricious frivolity of a modern nouveaux riche is condemned; the return to traditional, "classic" verities is enjoined. And no less than in arcadian art, the verities of classicism are linked to Christianity. In David's painting, for example, a Christlike Socrates is accompanied by twelve friends.

Throughout the eighteenth century, the papacy favors the arts for society's "moral and religious regeneration."[18] Great attention and expense is directed, for example, at reviving the Roman *Accademia di San Luca*. In addition, the popes sponsor an annual *concorsi clementini* art competition. Much is at stake in these activities. By maintaining Rome (against Paris) as art Mecca of Europe—and by elevating select art forms—the popes seek increased tourism and, by what tourists see, a fortification of "the era's faith in the status quo." Such *kapitolspolitik*, says Christopher Johns, serves the popes' "dual purpose of cultural glorification and political propaganda."[19] Like their Renaissance forebears, the eighteenth-century popes use art as a "tool of policy."[20]

Cosmopolitanism

As a cosmopolitan social thinker Abbé de Saint-Pierre construes European politics somewhat differently. Though originally published in 1713, his *Projet de paix perpetuelle* continues influencing political discussions up to the French Revolution. Saint-Pierre's *Projet* condemns war and calls for a permanent league of European nations to "renounce forever, for themselves and their successors, resort to arms as an instrument of national policy."[21]

Saint-Pierre's moral imagination is not confined to matters of international peace. He also calls for a graduated income tax in France, free public education for men *and* women, and an improved transportation system. In the process Saint-Pierre coins the term *bienfaisance*, later used in early modern social thought to differentiate individual almsgiving (*charité*) from more rational and methodical approaches to poor relief (*bienfaisance*).

Saint-Pierre's pacifistic approach differs from the more republican cosmopolitanism of other Catholic social thinkers. Sensing the value of modern civil liberties, Cardinal Barnaba Chiaramonti of Imola declares himself a citizen-cardinal, ready to abandon his traditional estates and titles. In his famous 1797 Christmas homily, Chiaramonti instructs the congregation: "fulfill faithfully the precepts of the Gospel and you will be the joy of the Republic. Be good Catholics and you will be good democrats."[22] When he is elected Pope Pius VII three years later, Chiaramonti's social perspective moves in a decidedly traditionalist direction.

Abbés Claude Fauchet and Henri-Baptiste Grégoire share Chiaramonti's enthusiasm for democracy. Before their 1791 break with Rome over allegiance to the French Constitutional Church, both bishops articulate social perspectives with wide Catholic appeal. Considering liberty, equality, and fraternity gospel ideals, Fauchet stands shoulder to shoulder with his parishioners in the 1789 capture of the Bastille. In twenty-three discourses for his Cercle social, a discussion group he forms in 1790, Fauchet highlights those elements of Rousseau's *Social Contract* compatible with Christian faith.[23] On his part, Abbé Grégoire wins a prize in 1788 from the Royal Society of Sciences and Arts at Metz for his *Essai sur la régénération physique et morale des juifs*. In his essay, Grégoire blames the cruel treatment of

European Jews on fanaticism. He suggests "that Jews be granted liberty of conscience, equality of taxation, and the right to own land."[24]

In Rome, Nicola Spedalieri, a close friend of Pope Pius VI, writes a defense of human rights in *I diritti dell'uomo*. Drawing on his earlier *Influenza della religione cristiana nella società civile*, Spedalieri believes Christian principles support natural human rights and decry political absolutism.

Across the Atlantic, the American Catholic "republican" John Carroll, first Roman Catholic bishop in the United States, enjoys American-style separation of church and state, religious freedom, and democracy. When it comes to his appointment as bishop, Carroll feels he should be voted on by his American clergy "to dissipate as much as possible the notion that American Catholicism was under foreign control."[25] Rome reluctantly agrees and Carroll wins the election—the first and last "popular election" of an American bishop. Here, as in other matters, "Carroll's approach," says Philip Gleason, "was shaped less by abstract devotion to a self-consciously adopted theoretical position than by a pragmatic, but principled, willingness to adjust to the realities of the post-revolutionary situation."[26]

However, Carroll's pragmatism has a dark side. Carroll, like the majority of North, Central, and South American bishops, tolerates slavery. From France, Abbé Grégoire sends Carroll a sermon on Catholicism and emancipation, but to no avail. While he calls for the humane treatment of slaves, Carroll never agitates for the elimination of slavery. Bishop Francis Patrick Kenrick later states the representative American position in his *Theologia moralis*: "As all men are by law of nature equal, no one is by nature a master of another; yet by the law of nations not only the dominion of jurisdiction, but also the dominion of property is granted to man over [another]: and this the old law ratified."[27] Kenrick regrets the number and condition of slaves, but rejects disobedience to the law: "Nevertheless, since this is the state of things, nothing should be tried against the laws, or be done or said that would make them carry their yoke unwillingly: but rather prudence and charity of the holy ministers [clergy] should be shown in such a way that slaves, informed by Christian custom, should offer obedience to their masters."[28]

In *The Popes and Slavery*, Joel S. Panzer argues that the American hierarchy—not the papacy—creates the moral distinction between slavery conditions and slavery as such. In 1741, Pope Benedict XIV's *Immensa pastorum* repeats Pope Paul III's 1537 *Sublimis Deus* message: native Americans are human beings, not slaves by nature; not only slavery conditions, but also slavery as such is condemned. In Panzer's view, early modern popes repeat the *Sublimis Deus* message because Catholic leaders—like those in North and South America—were "refusing to accept and teach what was contained in the antislavery documents of the Papal Magisterium."[29]

Jesuit émigrés from slave societies in Central and South America offer a "cultural" form of cosmopolitan social thought. Francis Xavier Clavijero and Francis Xavier Alegre represent Jesuits who, when exiled from Spain's colonies in 1767, bring their appreciation for native cultures back to Europe. Clavijero is angry over Europe's disdain for Mexican culture and writes the *Ancient History of Mexico*, outlining the merits of Aztec civilization. In *Arte poetica*, Alegre develops a comparative linguistic method for appreciating the cultural depth of Mexican literary history. Clavijero's and Alegre's socially conscious academic works helped pave the way for Mexican independence.[30]

Transformationism

At the same time, other Jesuits in South America and their native Guarani faithful practice a communal style of transformationism in the missionary reductions. The word *reduction* refers to these settlement communities established by the Jesuits and the Guarani since the seventeenth century. Though neither fully egalitarian nor fully democratic, the reductions nevertheless envision communities of producer-owners with town hall-style political structures. Art is an important ingredient in this attempt. Whereas official colonial churches in the capitals "used art primarily as a tool of political hegemony," the Jesuits take what Gauvin Bailey calls an "accommodationist" approach, blending their baroque tastes with the artistic traditions of the Guarani.[31]

While the Jesuit role in the reductions is clearly paternalistic, it is not autocratic. The Jesuits struggle against the colonial landlords' exploitation of the Guarani. When Spain cedes territory east of the Uruguay River to Portugal in 1750, seven reductions are put in jeopardy. Manuel Querini, Jesuit provincial of the endangered San Miguel reduction, writes to King Ferdinand VI of Spain: "the transfer imposed on the Indians of the seven pueblos, by the treaty, is against the Indians' natural right to maintain their liberty, their homes and their lands."[32]

European politics terminate Jesuit participation in the reductions after 1768. Five years later, Pope Clement XIV's *Dominus ac Redemptor* suppresses the Society of Jesus. Nevertheless, the reduction experiment animates European and American social imaginations throughout the period and down to the present day.

1792–1848

Europe and the Americas' recurrent turmoil for fifty years after the French Revolution breeds a new generation of Roman Catholic social thinkers. Earlier traditionalist polemic branches into what will be called below a more autocratic *caudillo* ideology. At the same time, the arcadian legacy survives in new romantic styles of German and French social thought. Another group of traditionalist social thinkers borrows from Abbé de Saint-Pierre and develops a *bienfaisance* approach. The cosmopolitan orientation resurfaces in its republican forms and in a novel politico-economic style. Other Catholics offer a distinctly societal form of transformationism.

Traditionalism

At the beginning of the nineteenth century, Abbé Bergier's polemic spirit survives in Joseph de Maistre and Louis de Bonald. With greater theological and sociological creativity than Bergier, both men develop panoramic social-moral interpretations of Europe's revolutionary condition. In this way, their social thought has a uniquely prognostic quality.

Joseph de Maistre is realistic about the causes of revolution in France but rejects the revolutionaries' idealistic solutions. He writes: "I could dirty twenty pages with proofs of the astonishing corruption and debasement, unfortunately only too general, which reigned in France at the moment of the Revolution."[33] But he explains in his 1809 *Essai sur le principe générateur des constitutions politiques et des autres institutions humaines* that social ideals are not simply written in constitutions; they must gradually evolve in the unwritten 'constitution' of a nation's soul. It is through this latter constitution that God's providential wisdom operates.

Joseph de Maistre is the first thinker to interpret the French Revolution as a providential act of God, a punishment for France's social corruption. According to Geoffrey Cubitt, de Maistre thought the blood of innocent Frenchmen, like that of Christ, "possessed a special expiatory significance: it was through 'the reversibility of the sufferings of the innocent to the benefit of the guilty' that collective redemption—the temporary salvation of nations in history, that of mankind in eternity—could ultimately be achieved."[34] "De Maistre's achievement," Cubitt continues, " was to formulate a theological understanding of catastrophe that turned the Revolution into part of the universal moral drama of human suffering."[35]

If de Maistre is awed by God's providential action, Louis de Bonald is impressed with God's created design for human social relationships. De Bonald details these observations in his 1796 *Théorie du pouvoir politique et religieux, 1800 Essai analytique sur les lois naturelles de l'ordre social* and 1830 *Démonstration philosophique du principe constitutif des sociétés*. In a claim that becomes characteristic of Catholic social thought, de Bonald identifies not the Enlightenment individual as the irreducible unit of society but the family. To be an individual, he says, one must participate in human *association*. Besides the *famille*, other vital associations are one's workplace (*guilde*), status group (*status*), and religion (*église*). For de Bonald, Enlightenment individualism and *étatisme* violate human individuality by contravening God's created design.

Robert Nisbet claims de Bonald's study of associations is the "first appearance of a pluralistic theory of authority in the social thought of nineteenth-century France." From this perspective, the charge that de Bonald's ideas incubate twentieth-century totalitarianism is questionable. "There remains in Bonald," insists Nisbet, "a clear strain of thought which must remove him from any real connection with . . . totalitarianism."[36]

If autocratic aims unfairly characterize the traditionalism of de Maistre and de Bonald, they do describe the period's *caudillo* form of Catholic social thought. The Spanish word *caudillo* is used here to refer to a strong military leader focused on restoring "throne and altar" political authority in society. Concomitantly, *caudilloism* promotes broad state control over education, communication, and associations.

In Central and South America, *caudillo* traditionalism surfaces in Agustín de Iturbide and Rafael Carrera. While Iturbide supports Mexican independence, he opposes Miguel Hidalgo's peasant liberation movement. By skillfully co-opting Hidalgo's success, Iturbide gains Mexico's independence from Spain but installs an autocratic—not democratic—state. In 1822, Iturbide crowns himself Agustín I, emperor of Mexico. To the south, Carrera overthrows Guatemala's liberal anticlerical government in the interests of the Creole landlords and the Church. Carrera devotes the rest of his life to spreading *caudillo* traditionalism throughout Central America—a legacy that survives down to the present.

Caudillo social thought also emerges across the ocean in Europe. At the 1814 Congress of Vienna, Klemens Metternich cements a "Holy Alliance" of European monarchs against liberal and nationalist political movements. Although a valuable balance of power is struck, Metternich requires an international network of spies and saboteurs to sustain it against liberal insurrection. In 1831, Joseph von Radowitz and Karl Jarke establish the *Politisches Wochenblatt* as a forum for Metternich-style social thought. Radowitz later outlines his ideas in *Gespräche über Staat und Kirche* as Metternich himself does in his 1848 *Mein politisches Testament*.

The message of European *caudilloism* also finds a carrier in the period's restorationist art. A well-known piece is Pierre-Narcisse Guérin's *Portrait of Henri de La Rochejaquelein*. During the French Revolution, the Vendée region supported counterrevolutionary insurrection against the Jacobin republic. One of the fallen heroes of the insurrection was Commander-in-Chief La Rochejaquelein. Guérin's painting, appearing in 1817, reinforces the idea of monarchical restoration across Europe. In the portrait, La Rochejaquelein gallantly leads his troops forward, inches away from Jacobin bayonets. On his shirt is the insignia of the Sacred Heart, understood by Catholics as "the symbol of the triumph of the Church over its enemies and a restoration of the union of throne and altar."[37]

The popes reinforce Metternich's restorationist ideology. Concerned over political restiveness in the Papal States, Pope Leo XII forms a Congregation of State to advise him on political matters. With Cardinal-Secretary of State Della Somaglia, Leo XII creates "a harsh police state, complete with press censorship, capital punishment," and secret societies that "sniffed out the slightest hints of revolution."[38] The saddest moment in this development is Pope Gregory XVI's 1832 encyclical *Cum primum*. Here, the pope supports Russian Orthodox Czar Nicholas I over the Polish Catholic struggle for independence—after 82 percent of Poland had been partitioned by a Russian "régime of political and religious repression!"[39]

Further artistic developments reinforce the popes' social perspective. In *Representing Belief: Religion, Art, and Society in Nineteenth-Century France*, Michael Driskel shows how the period's "return to the hieratic mode in the visual arts" gives "visible form" to the popes' "throne and altar" ideology. The hieratic mode designates pictorial qualities of "frontality, stasis, severity, and an emphatic reduction of pictorial illusionism."[40] The intent is to project images of timeless religious majesty and dogmatic authority. This sense of "nontime" is invoked by the popes and the monarchists to buttress the "aristocratic and 'God-given' verities of the *ancien régime*."[41]

One of the principal Catholic militants of this aesthetic discourse is Jean-Auguste-Dominique Ingres. In his painting *The Vow of Louis XIII*, for example, Ingres depicts King Louis on his knees, offering his crown and scepter *up* to the ascended frontally iconic Virgin Mary. Patricia Mainardi says Ingres's viewers throughout Europe accept his art as the embodiment of "the Church and public morality . . . of Throne and Altar."[42]

The autocratic excesses of political and artistic *caudilloism* are often mistakenly associated with the organic vision of society proposed by Catholic romantic traditionalists. As Ad Leys points out, "the concrete meaning of 'organism' is different in different authors."[43] In the case of most romantic thinkers, to describe society as an organism means to show how intermediate associations preserve—not suppress—a healthy dialectic between the individual and society.

No one articulates this dialectic better than Adam Müller. Meticulous analyst of Adam Smith's *The Wealth of Nations*, Müller rejects Smith's economic individualism while holding equal disdain for *étatiste* plans of economic production and distribution. In his 1808 *Die elemente der Staatskunst*, Müller enlists extensive research on medieval social structures to support his argument that a good society requires multiple sets of interconnected political and economic associations. As Paul Misner observes, Adam Müller exemplifies a style of traditionalist social thought that "attempted to relate modern freedoms and traditional order in creative tension."[44]

This creative tension between the individual and society is a dominant theme in the novels of Honoré de Balzac. In the story of a country doctor from his massive *La comédie humaine*, Balzac expresses his own 'romantic' traditionalism:

> Once I looked upon the Catholic religion as a cleverly exploited mass of prejudices and superstitions, which an intelligent civilization ought to deal with according to its desserts. Here I have discovered its political necessity and its usefulness as a moral agent; here, moreover, I have come to understand its power, through a knowledge of the actual thing which the word expresses. Religion means a bond or tie, and certainly a cult—or, in other words, the outward and visible form of religion is the only force that can bind the various elements of society together and mould them into a permanent form.[45]

François-René de Chateaubriand also believes this tension is best communicated aesthetically. No less a social thinker than Müller, Chateaubriand relays in his 1797 *Essai historique, politique et moral sur les révolutions anciennes et modernes* and 1802 *Le génie du Christianisme* the social benefit of a medieval neogothic *sensibilité*. Throughout his life, says Richard Fargher, Chateaubriand remains "horrified" by post-medieval Europe, where "some individuals had millions, and others subsisted in filth and squalor."[46]

In Rome, Chateaubriand's neogothic aestheticism is lived out by the Brotherhood of St. Luke. Occupying an abandoned monastery, this group of German painters revives medieval fresco technique, seeing art as the key to Europe's social and political regeneration. Recognizable throughout Rome by their long hair and robes, the members of the Brotherhood live a semimonastic lifestyle of morning housekeeping and afternoon painting. They attract many aspiring artists to their "medieval" workshop and influence later pre-Raphaelite art. Friedrich Overbeck's *Joseph Being Sold to His Brothers* represents their traditionalist neogothic style.[47]

Not all traditionalist social thinkers work from a romantic point of view. Although a devoted monarchist and nobleman, Villeneuve-Bargemont develops a *bienfaisance* form of traditionalist social thought, generating "not merely occasional legislative intervention, but systematic regulation."[48] Among Villeneuve-Bargemont's projects as a member of the French legislature are public housing, savings banks, trade schools, child labor restriction, a just wage, and agricultural cooperatives. A less well-known social thinker in Villeneuve-Bargemont's style is Spanish economist Ramón de la Sagra. In his 1840 *Lecciones de economia social* and 1849 *Aphorismos Sociales: Introducción a la Sciencia Social*, La Sagra outlines a "Roman Catholic social economy." He follows many of Villeneuve-Bargemont's proposals but is cautious—as a traditionalist—about general public education. He fears breakdown of "an inequality which is necessary and natural, but which becomes violent, forceful and dangerous when it does not correspond to a similar inequality in the intelligences of individuals."[49]

François Ledreuille wants charity organized on a more rational basis but is less sanguine about state organization than Villeneuve-Bargemont and Sagra. Indeed, French monarchist social Catholics like Ledreuille maintain a principled opposition to the republican state. Yet, for some monarchists, this does not mean opposition to socially organized charity. In Paris, Ledreuille's *bienfaisance* approach involves the organization of independent worker associations called *Maisons des ouvriers*. At Ledreuille's "homes," workers can access employment information, health care, and legal counsel.

Cosmopolitanism

A new politico-economic form of cosmopolitan social thought differs from *bienfaisance* traditionalism by rejecting the latter's noblesse oblige and monarchist tendencies. Instead, politico-economic thinkers connect economic reform to the spirit of Catholic republicanism. An early champion of this approach is Frédéric Ozanam. Supporter of both civil liberties and economic welfare, Ozanam is famous for founding the St. Vincent de Paul Society. It is important to recall, however, that Ozanam's primary motivation for starting the Society is not *charité* but putting people in direct contact with the poor. Unlike meeting the poor through an episodic and unempowering style of almsgiving, however, Ozanam wants contact through structured social service.

Few accomplish this better than Elizabeth Ann Seton. Widowed mother of five children, Seton establishes a Sisters of Charity community in Emmitsburg, Maryland, in 1809. Mother Seton and her sisters address the needs of the poor by building schools, hospitals, and orphanages. By the time of Seton's death in 1821, Sisters of Charity communities exist in twenty cities across the United States. For most of these cities, Mother Seton's sisters establish the first structured delivery of social service to the poor.

Charles de Coux and Spanish philosopher-theologian Jaime Luciano Balmes bring a heightened degree of theoretical attention to the politico-economic style of Catholic social thought. De Coux is the first occupant of the chair of political economy at Louvain, where he pursues his *Cours d'économie sociale* and *Cours d'économie politique*. Through his 1840 *Observaciones sociales, políticas, y económicas sobre las buenes del clero*, Balmes gains European attention. Both de Coux and Balmes imagine the solution to economic oppression in "the principles of democracy," which they also see as "the principles of catholicism."[50]

The legacy of pre-Revolutionary republican-style cosmopolitanism is brought forward by the famous L'Avenir group: Félicité Lamennais, Henri Dominique Lacordaire, and Charles de Montalembert. Their meld of ultramontanism and support for free press, free speech, universal suffrage, and Catholic education in France is amply documented.

Less discussed under this rubric is the work of Italian priest Vincenzo Gioberti and American bishop John England. In his 1833 letter *Della republica e del cristianesimo*, Gioberti encourages young priests to support Italian liberation from Austrian and French rule as well as unification under moderate republican principles. While exiled in Paris, Gioberti refines his Catholic republican ideas in *Del rinnovamento civile d'Italia*.

Among John England's many accomplishments is the *U.S. Catholic Miscellany*, the first Catholic newspaper in the United States. For forty years the *Miscellany* constitutes an important resource for Catholic republican social thought. In *American Catholicism*, John Tracy Ellis recounts one of England's responses in the *Miscellany* to the charge that Catholicism is incompatible with American democracy:

> to him republicanism meant that no set of men had any inherent natural right to take precedence over their fellow men and that all power to regulate public affairs of individuals, united in a special compact, was derived from the public will freely expressed by the will of the majority. "This is what we understand by *Republicanism*," said England, "and we know of no doctrine of *Catholicism*, if we must use the expression, opposed to this."[51]

In this spirit, England writes a diocesan constitution establishing a board of trustees with lay membership. This unique constitution is published in a collection of England's works from 1849 but is deleted from the 1908 edition.

Novelists and artists also express the aspirations of Catholic republicanism during the period. Important here is Victor Hugo's left-wing medievalism as expressed in his enormously successful 1831 novel *Notre Dame de Paris*. Hugo's heroes—a deformed Quasimodo and gypsy Esmeralda—stand in stark contrast to oppressive aristocrats and priests. Noteworthy, too, is sculptor Jean Duseigneur's 1831 *Roland furieux*. In this piece, the medieval Roland's struggle to free himself from captivity "symbolizes France's political dilemma" between liberals and the July Monarchy.[52]

Catholic activist republicanism also resurfaces after the French Revolution. In his famous pulpit *Grito de Dolores*—"Down with bad government. . . . Long live our most holy Virgin of Guadalupe"—revolutionary priest Miguel Hidalgo openly declares a peasant war for Mexican independence in 1810.[53] Daniel O'Connell is an equally ardent Irish republican but a committed pacifist. After effecting the Catholic emancipation bill in 1829, O'Connell writes a friend: "It is one of the greatest triumphs recorded in history—a bloodless revolution."[54] But in moving toward repeal of union with England, O'Connell calls off a "monster meeting" in Clontarf, fearing violence. His hope is to "carry the repeal of the Union without one drop of blood."[55] Generations of Irish republicans never forgive O'Connell for missing the moment when, in their view, Irish freedom could have been won by the sword.

Dramatic struggles for independence are a subject for many Catholic artists. In his famous *The Third of May, 1808*, Francisco Goya reflects the bitterness of Spain's crushed hopes for liberation as Napoleon's forces take aim on a group of Spanish peasants.[56] Though attacked for exposing clerical vices and institutional Church abuse through art, Goya remains a Christian throughout his life.

Another Catholic artist interested in republican struggles is Eugène Delacroix. In *The Massacre at Chios*, for example, Delacroix depicts a scene from the Greek war of independence. Mixing the cruel and the sensuous into the struggle for freedom, Delacroix paints a dying Greek fighter lying on a maiden's shoulder, an autocratic Turk on horseback, and a slain woman ensnarled in the rider's lariat. These "democratic and humanitarian passions" stand in stark contrast to Ingres's ultramontane aesthetic. Indeed, says Mainardi, the art public understands "the historic battle between Ingres and Delacroix."[57] On the side of Delacroix, art critic Gabriel-Desiré Laverdant writes in 1848, "art, the expression of society, manifests, in its highest soaring, the most advanced social tendencies; it is the forerunner and the revealer."[58]

Transformationism

A societal form of utopian thought also develops during this period. Unlike communal transformationists, these Catholic social thinkers seek economic *and* political transformation. Well-known is the Christian socialist *L'atélier* group, including Philippe Buchez, Anthime Corbon, Charles Chevé, Henri Feugueray, and Auguste Ott. A disciple of Sainte-Simon, Buchez promotes worker-owned and operated-producer cooperatives. The movement's newspaper *L'atélier* is the first worker-edited and -owned paper in Europe. Buchez is equally convinced that art influences social change and explains this thesis in his 1830 *Introduction à la science de l'histoire du développement de l'humanité*.[59] Buchez, says Charles Chevé, "was for a large number of young people who had imbibed democratic ideas, the providential instrument and means of their conversion to catholicism."[60]

Other societal transformationists are Nicolas de Bonneville and Adolphe Bartels. De Bonneville is a member of Claude Fauchet's Cercle social and author of *De l'esprit des réligions*. In this 1791 treatise, de Bonneville argues that "the only possible means to achieve the great social communion is to divide the estates in equal and limited parts for the children of the deceased, and leave the rest to divide among the other heirs."[61] Adolphe Bartels is the Belgian author of a Christian socialist treatise entitled *Essay on the Organization of Labor*. He believes the workers' only hope is the acquisition of political power. To assist the workers, writes Bartels, there must also be "democratic reform in the structure of the Church."[62] He propagates his ideas in the journal *Le débat social*.

1849–1871

Roman Catholic social thought between 1849 and 1871 spans the violent deaths of two Paris archbishops. Denis-Auguste Affre is shot in 1848 while mediating worker violence at the Paris barricades. Georges Darboy is taken hostage and assassinated by the revolutionary communards during the "Bloody Week" of 1871.

With one important exception, the patterns of Catholic social thought during this period replicate those of the past. Polemic, *caudillo*, romantic, and *bienfaisance* traditionalisms resurface, as do politico-economic and republican forms of cosmopolitan social thinking. Transformationism recurs as well, in both communal and societal styles. The one exception to these now-familiar approaches is the appearance of a new form of cosmopolitan social thought. This is neoscholasticism, the style that acquires—by the end of the early modern era—normative hegemony over other forms of Roman Catholic social thought.

Traditionalism

The story of Juan Donoso Cortés is typical of the era. Cortés begins his rich intellectual life espousing Catholic republican ideals. His *Lecciones de derecho politico* remains in print to this day as *A Defense of Representative Government*. However, the worker revolutions sweeping Europe in 1848 permanently alter Cortés's social perspective. No longer the sole possession of middle-class intellectuals, liberal ideas now incite the long-suffering working class. Worker revolt in Paris triggers King Louis Philippe's abdication. Even Metternich, strongman of the restoration, flees worker and student revolt in Vienna. This "pan-European simultaneity" of collapsing autocratic power has, says Isser Woloch, "no parallel until 1989."[63]

Through this experience, Cortés becomes—like de Maistre and de Bonald before him—a polemic traditionalist. He sees the revolutions as "the impending 'final dissolution' of modern civilization . . . for some unrevealed, but certainly glorious, purpose of Providence."[64] His subsequent 1851 essay *Essayo sobre el catolicismo, el liberalismo y el socialisme* analyzes the collaborative power of liberalism and socialism in undermining the Christian culture of Europe.

The 1848 revolutions also affect the social communication of Catholic artists. Before the revolutions, Louis Janmot is an enthusiastic supporter of liberal education. After the revolutions, Janmot creates *Le mauvais sentier*, a picture of two girls on a quest for education. On their right stands a haunting succession of liberal university professors. As Driskel notes, "an owl, a symbol of the malefic belief in reason, hovers over this barren route."[65]

On both sides of the Atlantic, journalists Louis Veuillot and James McMaster offer outlets for polemic traditionalism. Veuillot's *L'univers* promotes the idea that Europe is "being steadily polarized along spiritual lines," that a clash between the Christian civilization of life and the modern civilization of death is underway. Writes Veuillot: "two powers deny each other reciprocally, that is the heart of the matter."[66]

In the United States, James McMaster edits the nationally circulated *New York Freeman's Journal* from 1848 to 1886. Opponent of Catholic republicanism, secular liberalism, abolitionism, and strident nationalism, McMaster spends the first six weeks of the Civil War in jail as a seditionist. As a French enthusiast of McMaster's opinions, Louis Veuillot "termed the *Freeman's Journal* the 'best edited, best informed' Catholic paper in the United States."[67]

As this "clash of civilizations" visits the Papal States, Pope Pius IX turns to the autocratic techniques of *caudillo* social thought. In a succession of encyclicals, Pius IX decries the "sacrilegious attacks made on the civil power of the Roman Church."[68] When Napoleon suggests the pope concede to the rebels in the papal province of Emilia, Pius IX responds: "an argument of this kind . . . has no validity. Similar rebellions have often occurred in Europe and in other areas, yet anyone can see that a legitimate argument cannot be deduced from that fact to diminish civil sovereignty."[69] Possibly a degree of Pius IX's sorrow over the loss of the Papal States is mitigated by Vatican I's 1870 definition of his office as infallible.

Of course, Pius IX's condemnation of liberalism in *Quanta cura* and the *Syllabus of Errors* is of a piece with the Papal States crisis. Yet Henri Daniel-Rops observes that "neither *Quanta Cura* nor the *Syllabus* broke any new ground."[70] Pius IX's teachings are consistent with the *caudillo* style of papal thought common since Pope Leo XII.

Commentary on these social dynamics simultaneously occurs in the Catholic art community. In Hippolyte Flandrin's *Le Christ remettant les clefs à Saint-Pierre* a precise reversal of the movement noted above in Ingres's *The Vow of Louis VIII* takes place but with the same social encoding. Flandrin's work shows a dolmen-like Christ handing the eternal keys *down* to St. Peter. Completing the transaction between eternal and temporal powers, St. Peter kneels in the exact position of Ingres's King Louis.[71]

The legacy of romantic traditionalism survives in the thought of Austrian Karl von Vogelsang. In Vogelsang's mind, the Catholic romantics' idea of social change through organic, intermediate associations takes shape as "corporatism." In a corporatist society, political and economic class divisions are replaced by a federated system of representation in three vertical *Stände*: large industry, small crafts, and agriculture. This would recover, thinks Vogelsang, the redeeming qualities of medieval "egalitarianism":

> The basic principle of the feudal order is the full solidarity of all citizens, the congruence of economic, social, and political positions, the clear definition of national tasks, and a corresponding differentiation of political and social positions. Obligation to work is strictly enforced on all those who want to share in the social product which is distributed to each according to his contribution. There is no unrestricted private ownership of the means of production . . . but merely the use of the property for productive purposes. Finally, social protection is afforded all estates and individuals against the danger of degradation to the level of the fourth estate, the proletariat, which works but does not own.[72]

Also characteristic of Vogelsang's thought is the prohibition of usury. Like most German romantics, Vogelsang believes "that the medieval legislation of the Church against usury and the notion of money as 'dead' or 'unfruitful' [are] still viable, operational concepts."[73] He considers capitalist bankers the usurious oppressors of the Austrian peasants.

The underside of this emphasis on usury is anti-Semitism. Commonly, romantic traditionalist thinkers of the time associate the evils of usury with the Jewish community. John Boyer contends that "Vogelsang's anti-Semitism was both nonracial and nonviolent. He used the Jew mainly as a symbol for the 'materialism' to which Christians easily succumbed. He rejected, however, special legislation against the Jews or any form of persecution."[74]

The *bienfaisance* form of traditionalist Catholic social thought also continues during this period. Émile Keller's work represents those *bienfaisance* social thinkers seeking organized charity through social legislation. Like Villeneuve-Bargement, Keller mixes a traditionalist perspective on civil liberties with an activist approach toward economic welfare. As a delegate from the department of the

Rhine—and father of fourteen children—Keller supports a wide range of social welfare legislation. Keller's inspiration is St. Benedict, creator of what became the characteristically medieval communities of authoritative politics and egalitarian economics.

Adolph Kolping carries forward the independent association style of *bienfaisance*. A journeyman shoemaker, Kolping has the unusual opportunity to study theology at the University of Munich. Here, he comes in contact with the "Munich circle" of German Catholic romantics. From this experience, Kolping develops his *Gesellensverein* system for journeymen workers.

In Europe at this time, a journeyman travels from town to town obtaining various work experiences needed to become a master craftsman. French workers call this the *tour de France*. Kolping is shocked by the squalid living conditions and faithless workers he encounters as a journeyman. The *Gesellensverein* Kolping develops are hospices for journeymen, supplying not only food and lodging, but also recreation, craft education, and religious instruction. Thanks to Kolping, says the Jesuit Charles Plater, "an artisan who leaves one town for another finds a home waiting for him." "This movement did more than anything," Plater continues, "to weld clergy and laity together and formed the basis for social action."[75] By Kolping's death in 1865, over four hundred *Gesellensverein* operate in Germany.

Cosmopolitanism

The towering figure of politico-economic cosmopolitanism during this period is Wilhelm Emmanuel von Ketteler, bishop of Mainz. Many consider his creative combination of Catholic republicanism and economic reformism the most outstanding work of Roman Catholic social thought in the early modern era.

Possibly the most inventive element in Ketteler's thought is a translation of the romantics' organological vision of society into the principle of subsidiarity. According to Leys, Ketteler does not work from a neoscholastic framework but creatively combines the longstanding German organic idea with his positive historical experience of civil freedom.[76] One hundred and twenty years later, Ketteler's invention finds its way into article 3b of the European Union's Maastricht Treaty: "in areas that do not fall within its exclusive competence, the Community shall take action in accordance with the subsidiarity principle."[77]

Ketteler is not alone in advocating a politico-economic cosmopolitanism. Edouard Ducpetiaux of Belgium also works for civic freedom and economic reform. As a true cosmopolitan, Ducpetiaux is the first to encourage a formal international labor organization and creates an international conference for this purpose in 1856. In France, Désiré Laverdant creates the Cercle de la démocratie catholique for thinkers interested in this social approach. Indeed, Catholic politico-economic cosmopolitanism will increasingly be identified in Europe and South America as "Christian Democracy."[78]

Bishop Felix Dupanloup also has a cosmopolitan perspective, placing particular emphasis on modern liberties. In 1865, Dupanloup softens the blow of Pius IX's *Syllabus of Errors* for Catholic republicans by distinguishing the pope's theses from his hypotheses. Pius IX never formally rejects this distinction as Dupanloup's *La convention du 15. septembre et l'encyclique du 8. décembre* is read throughout Europe.

Dupanloup champions liberation movements throughout the world. He supports the ongoing struggle for freedom in Ireland. In 1862, he writes a remarkable Passion Sunday pastoral letter opposing U.S. slavery. "The unity of the human family, the principle of dignity, of equality, of freedom, of humanity among mankind," says Dupanloup, "condemns and rebukes slavery." He adds with rhetorical passion: "Is it not yet time, after eighteen centuries of Christianity, for us all to begin to practice the ever enduring law, 'Do not to another that which you would not he should do to you; and that which your brothers should do for you, do ye fore them'?"[79]

A fascinating dynamic between artists at this time reflects the distinction between republican and traditionalist Catholic social thought.

Driskel observes that an artistic commonplace for Catholic republican artists is to render Christ's crucifixion realistically. In Delacroix's 1853 *Christ en croix*, for example, Christ's arms are not strictly perpendicular to his body, but vertically extended. His body is pulling down on the impaled hands; blood flows from the lance wound and drenches his loincloth; his eyes look skyward, questioningly.[80]

Traditionalist Catholic artists do not depict the crucifixion this way. Flandrin's virtually bloodless Christ, in *La Crucifixion*, has his arms extended in a predominantly horizontal direction. Christ's loincloth is completely clean; his head rests calmly on his shoulder with eyes closed; there is no lance wound. As Driskel explains, "the arms were extended in such a way as to deny emphatically that he 'hangs' from his support, seeming instead to float in space independent of it." In doing this, Flandrin is "attempting to create a symbolic image of the 'Christ Triumphant' type, the emblematic convention of the Middle Ages" and encoding the hierarchical social message of the ultramontane aesthetic.[81]

Orestes Augustus Brownson is a cosmopolitan republican whose social thought moves in and out of ultramontane traditionalism. In his 1865 *The American Republic: Its Constitution, Tendencies, and Destiny*, Brownson argues that Catholic principles are not just *compatible* with American democracy but the *optimal* safeguard of democracy. In regular correspondence with Catholic republicans in Europe, Brownson agrees with Dupanloup's condemnation of American slavery.[82]

Elsewhere, Brownson distinguishes between "Catholic tradition" and the "traditions of Catholics." On this basis, he contends that Catholic participation in public schools does not threaten Catholic tradition while, on the contrary, Brownson says, the creation of a separate school system to protect the "traditions of Catholics" will impair Catholic participation in American democracy.[83]

Archbishop John Hughes of New York defends America's political institutions but considers Brownson's views on Catholic ethnicity and education "pure speculation." At this time, Irish Catholics in New York face nativist anti-Catholicism at the workplace and in municipal politics. For Hughes, the memory of Philadelphia's 1844 riots and killing of Catholics is fresh. Unlike Bishop Kenrick, whose advice to Philadelphia Catholics was to move away, Hughes is defiant. Andrew Greeley recounts the archbishop's warning to the mayor of New York: "if a single Catholic Church [is] burned in New York, the city [will] become a Moscow . . . 'Are you afraid,' asked the mayor, 'that some of your churches will be burned?' 'No, sir; but I am afraid that some of *yours* will be burned. We can protect our own. I come to warn you for your own good.'"[84] What Hughes's social perspective signals is the transition from Bishop Carroll and England's colonial-inspired republicanism to one influenced by immigrant Catholicism.

If an important transition in social thought occurs in America, an even more potent one develops in Europe. A neoscholastic form of cosmopolitan social thought emerges in Italy. It is the work, says Misner, "of a relatively small band of thinkers, until one of them, Gioacchino Pecci, became Pope Leo XIII" in 1878.[85]

The most important of these early "neoscholastic" thinkers are the Jesuits Aloysius Taparelli and Matteo Liberatore. Given both the eclecticism of Catholic theology in the eighteenth and early nineteenth centuries and the weakened state of "second Scholasticism," neither Taparelli nor Liberatore is educated in the Scholastic tradition. As Misner points out, they had to "teach themselves scholastic philosophy and rebuild it from scratch."[86]

Taparelli had already composed a theoretical essay on the concept of natural right in 1840. In 1850, he begins writing for the new journal *La civiltà cattolica*, the Jesuit incubator of neoscholasticism. Taparelli's important two-volume *Esame critico degli ordini rappresentativi nella società moderna* inaugurates a new era of discussion over Thomas Aquinas's theories of law and justice as applied to modern political and economic conditions.

In the course of his career, Matteo Liberatore writes over 900 articles for *La civiltà*. Though he focuses on the metaphysical dimensions of Aquinas's thought, Liberatore also relates these insights to the natural law, relations between Church and state, and the social conditions of life.

Transformationism

Catholic transformationist social thought persists between 1848 and 1871 in both its societal and communal forms. One representative of the societal approach is François Huet. Despite the excesses of the 1848 revolutions, Huet works diligently at reconciling Catholicism and socialism. In his 1853 *Le règne social du christianisme*, Huet outlines a distributivist scheme involving broad social ownership of property, cooperative enterprises, and free education. Generations of Professor Huet's students at the Belgian University of Ghent work through his ideas.[87]

Pauline-Marie Jaricot and T. Wharton Collins develop a more communal style of Catholic transformationism. Jaricot is most remembered as foundress of the Society for the Propagation of the Faith, which exists to this day. Less known is her work at creating a model Christian town in Rustrel, France. Torn by the oppression of French workers, Jaricot acquires a bankrupt iron foundry in the village of Rustrel. Her plan is to create a worker-owned and -operated factory, with profits equitably distributed in the village for food, shelter, clothing, health care, and education. She devises a "Bank of Heaven," where shares in the enterprise are sold at $20,000 each. But two fatal accidents occur at the foundry and unscrupulous financiers rob her. Jaricot's dream dies and she declares bankruptcy in 1852.

In Louisiana, lawyer T. Wharton Collins is called the "Catholic Communist labor reformer." Increasingly pessimistic over social change brought about through the labor movement, Collins develops the idea that Catholics should "live apart" from society in producer cooperatives of married couples vowed to poverty and obedience.[88] He outlines his vision in *The Eden of Labor, or the Christian Utopia*. And what is one of the prime motivators of his scheme? The eighteenth-century Jesuit reductions in Paraguay!

1872–1890

Over the next twenty years, forces external and internal to Roman Catholicism gradually narrow the range of its social thought. Externally, workers take greater interest in Marxian socialism, triggering antisocialist laws across Europe. Both phenomena contract Catholic experimentation with Christian socialism. Simultaneously, an intensified anti-Catholic *Kulturkampf* in Europe and the Americas draws Catholics closer together, socially and ideationally. Internally, Vatican I's definition of papal infallibility reinforces the pope's juridical power over determining what *officially* counts as "Roman Catholic" thought. This, combined with Pope Leo XIII's nomination of St. Thomas Aquinas as the Church's philosophic muse, delimits the intellectual latitude of faithful Roman Catholic social thinkers. Ironically, believes Rosemary Haughton, these forces create—from Vatican I to Vatican II—the "least Catholic" period in Roman Catholic history.[89]

Traditionalism

The polemic style of traditionalist social thought becomes more clandestine during this period. Louis Veuillot's *L'univers* still promotes a restored Christian monarchy in France under Bourbon pretender Comte de Chambord. However, when Veuillot and Chambord die in 1883, an opening is created for Pope Leo XIII's *ralliement* policy with the French republic.

Given the period's enhanced papal power, Pope Leo XIII's new approach toward France makes traditional legitimism and integrism less openly acceptable. In Spain, for example, a group of Catholic traditionalists led by Ramón Nocedal rejects the Carlist dynasty for its perceived concessions to republicanism. Propounding a radical doctrine of pure theocracy under a "reign of Christ," Nocedal forms an underground organization called the Integristas. As Daniel-Rops describes this recurrent "perfidy" in church history, "men who had no authority to do so took it upon themselves to track down the 'heretics'" and manipulate their downfall.[90] Variations on this cynical form of traditionalist social thought continue down to the present.

Only partially concealed are the legitimist and integrist aspirations of Catholic artists. Noteworthy here is Auguste Rodin's sculpture *The Burghers of Calais*. A monarchist enamored of medieval themes, Rodin sculpts the story of the 1347 Calasian resistance against England to, in part, rally legitimist patriotism. Albert Boime observes that the souvenir booklet for the unveiling of Rodin's work "was illustrated with Royal and Catholic symbols redolent of the medievalising fantasies of the political and cultural right wing."[91]

In Central and South America, *caudillo* traditionalism survives openly. In Ecuador, Gabrial Garcia-Moreno continues the pattern of military "throne and altar" dictatorship established fifty years earlier by Guatemalan Rafael Carrera. In 1871, Garcia-Moreno makes membership in the Roman Catholic Church a requirement for Ecuadorian citizenship. Three years later, he decrees that 10 percent of the state's yearly revenue be sent to the pope. Though assassins end Garcia-Moreno's dictatorship in 1875, Catholic *caudillo* social thinking survives.

René de la Tour du Pin is a monarchist and a soldier but he is neither a clandestine legitimist nor a *caudilloist*. While serving as French military attaché in Vienna, La Tour du Pin discovers corporatist ideas through conversation with Karl von Vogelsang and avid reading of the latter's *Vaterland* newspaper and journal *Österreichische Monatsschrift für christliche Sozialreform*. By 1881, La Tour du Pin agrees: corporatism is "the only solution to the labor question." Only a corporatist social arrangement can ensure just deliberation over wages, prices, and supply horizontally (between employees and employers) and vertically (from the local workshop to the national trade council). As La Tour du Pin explains,

> We term professional association or syndicate, the society formed with the object of defending professional interests, between people of the same status and condition; corporation, the society which unites the diverse elements of the same profession, i.e., its employers, its white collar and manual workers, in a society perfect from the professional point of view; finally, *corps d'état*, the ensemble of all the workshops where the same profession is practiced.[92]

La Tour du Pin's contribution to romantic traditionalism also includes the promotion of an international conference of Catholic social thinkers. Under the leadership of Bishop Gaspar Mermillod, this idea becomes the Catholic Union of Fribourg from which Pope Leo XIII requests input before drafting *Rerum novarum*.

Another of La Tour du Pin's collaborators, Albert de Mun, is more impressed with the *bienfaisance* style of traditionalist social thought. With the aid of Émile Keller, Maurice Maignen, and La Tour du Pin, de Mun organizes a system of worker clubs called the Oeuvre des Cercles Catholiques (OCC). The *cercles* bring employees and employers together for social interaction and dialogue over workplace problems created by economic liberalism. The journal *Revue de l'association catholique* spreads this dialogue across Europe. Eventually, de Mun's OCC becomes an important lobby in the French Chamber of Deputies for legalization of trade unions, minimum wage, health insurance, old age pensions, workplace safety, an eight-hour workday, and child labor restrictions.[93]

By 1879, most of de Mun's goals are already in practice at Léon Harmel's textile factory in the Champagne region of France. There, a board of workers with a management chairman make shared decisions about wages, shop management, social insurance, vocational training, medical care, housing, and dowries for the workers' daughters. Harmel's factory is not corporatism but a model Christian corporation. Harmel encourages this model in his 1877 *Manuel d'une corporation chrétienne*.[94]

Other *bienfaisance* social thinkers look askance at social legislation and Christian factories. For Charles Périn and Frédéric Le Play, these activities disturb the free play of supply and demand on the open market. In their view, economic laissez-faire promotes social health by increasing jobs and consumer goods. Périn already made this argument in his 1861 *De la richesse dans les sociétés chrétiennes* but broadens it in his 1880 *Les doctrines économiques depuis un siècle*. In both works, Périn believes the social benefits of an open market require the moral rectitude of employers and employees. Both parties must avoid avarice and practice charity. From this standpoint, Périn supports organized *voluntary* charity.

Le Play arrives at the same conclusion by a different route. His earlier sociological study of the European family convinces him that social health requires a moral regeneration of the family.[95] Only a return to responsible fatherhood—not state or employer paternalism—will effect this regeneration. Périn and Le Play explain their free market–moral regeneration approach in the journal *La réforme sociale*. Catholic social thinkers sympathetic to this viewpoint receive episcopal support in 1880 from the bishop of Angers, Charles-Émile Freppel. As a result, Pope Leo XIII can add input from the so-called school of Angers while preparing *Rerum novarum*.

Cosmopolitanism

A competing school of Catholic social thought is the school of Liège. This school is an expression of the period's politico-economic form of cosmopolitan social thought. Through the leadership of Archbishop Victor Doutreloux, three international conferences on Catholic social thought are held in Liège between 1886 and 1890. Though open to social Catholics of every orientation, the dominant voices are those favoring civil liberties and state intervention in social problems. Even participant Léon Harmel warms to these strategies. By his third worker pilgrimage to Rome in 1889, he is advocating worker self-determination. Now a Christian democrat, Harmel aligns with Catholic thinkers like Abbé Potter, editor of *Le pays de Liège*—the "first Christian democrat daily."[96]

A peculiar form of politico-economic cosmopolitanism surfaces in the thought of American Henry George. Society's economic problems are not the result of avaricious employers or disruptive employees but the "unearned increment" that idle landowners extract from employers and employees through land rent. If the state taxed all land rent, ample funds would be available for public use. George's "single-tax theory," as outlined in his 1879 *Progress and Poverty*, "sparked a debate around the world."[97]

Less newsworthy but more enduring is the cosmopolitan social thought expressed in the "brick and mortar" social service of religious women. Since the founding days of Mother Seton in North America and comparable women leaders in Europe, the number of communities for women religious soars. This creates not only more school teachers and alms collectors but a burgeoning array of boarding homes, foundling hospitals, reading rooms, orphanages, and homeless shelters. Close contact with the poor through service structures, explains John McGreevy, "fostered a jaundiced view of economic 'laws' explaining poverty as a consequence of bad choices."[98] Without time, interest, or permission, religious women of the period do not translate this experience into treatises on Catholic social thought. Instead, their action is the text, read by thousands of illiterate poor across Europe and the Americas.

While support for economic reform would characterize most cosmopolitan thinkers during this period, some remain particularly focused on the merits of civil liberties. In America, this is best represented in the distinct styles of John Ireland, archbishop of St. Paul, Minnesota, and James Gibbons, archbishop of Baltimore.

One-time seminarian under the supervision of French Bishop Dupanloup, John Ireland encourages expeditious "Americanization" of ethnic Catholics, experiments with public ownership of Catholic schools, and the legalization of interracial marriage. Throughout his life, Ireland celebrates American liberties unapologetically. "Republic of America," Ireland incants, "thou bearest in thy hands the hopes of the human race, thy mission from God is to show the nations that men are capable of highest civil and political liberty."[99]

No less an "Americanist" than Ireland, James Gibbons holds a position in the famous see of Baltimore that gives him de facto responsibility for holding the diverse American Church together. This responsibility requires much of Gibbons, not the least of which are patience with ethnic Catholic communities and support for parochial schools. It also calls for the kind of deft diplomacy Gibbons displays in his well-documented defenses of open-membership trade unions like the Knights of Labor and Henry George's right to propound his economic theories. Yet Gibbons is not adverse to principled prophetic action. In 1889, he celebrates the opening Mass of the first Black Catholic Congress and repeatedly insists to Catholics worldwide, "Yes, our nation is strong and her strength lies, under Providence, in the majesty and supremacy of the law, in the loyalty of her citizens to that law, and in the affection of our people for their free institutions."[100]

Of all the styles of Roman Catholic social thought between 1872 and 1890, none match the normative power of neoscholastic cosmopolitanism. Several social thinkers write from a neoscholastic approach, but none are as prodigious as Pope Leo XIII and his collaborators. In the thirteen years before *Rerum novarum*, Pope Leo XIII produces no less than nine major encyclicals on social-moral issues. These include the restoration of Thomistic philosophy (*Aeterni patris*) and discussions of socialism (*Quod apostolici muneris*), marriage (*Arcanum*), the character of political power (*Diuturnum*), the problem of freemasonry (*Humanum genus*), a Christian theory of the state (*Immortale Dei*), the nature of human freedom (*Libertas*), the moral ordering of human life (*Exeunte iam anno*), and the meaning of citizenship (*Sapientiae Christianae*).

While Pope Leo XIII's Thomistic philosophical commitment involves a metaphysic of universal first principles, it is also a form of realism encouraging particular observation of the material world. Pope Leo XIII does, in fact, have great interest in science. He formally reestablishes the Vatican Observatory in 1891, supports biblical archaeology, and insists that minor and major seminarians study physical science.

According to Michael Paul Driskel, the rise of neoscholastic realism transforms Christian art at the end of the early modern period. The earlier papal-supported "aesthetic of ultramontanism" mediated eternal truths through neoclassical images of either idyllic arcadianism or hieratic timelessness. With Pope Leo XIII, the new artistic realism "that had been slowly gaining favor within the Church" is endorsed.[101]

The works of Mihály Munkácsy and Henri Lerolle exemplify this development. Munkácsy's much admired *Le Christ devant pilate* depicts a rather unattractive but realistic Jesus surrounded by men gesturing in lifelike ways. As Driskel explains, Munkácsy was scrupulous about giving "the physiognomies, poses, and accoutrements an almost photographic fidelity to nature, something he achieved by utilizing photographs for the principal actors in the drama and for the details of the set."[102] Lerolle follows this same approach in his 1883 *L'Arrivée des bergers*. Here, shepherds enter to see the Christ child in a stable that "could have been found in any farmyard in France." Like Munkácsy, Lerolle worked from a "carefully squared photograph of an actual stable."[103]

This visual "rhetoric of reconciliation" between God and the world reflected the major transformation in Catholic thought occasioned by neoscholastic cosmopolitanism. Catholics would now see the images and concerns of their world in the realist representations of Jesus and the saints. In 1891, the realist painter Théobald Chartran is invited to execute the official portrait of Pope Leo XIII.

Transformationism

In *A Fight for God*, Henri Daniel-Rops offers a vivid description of the Paris Commune, the event that began this final period of early modern Roman Catholic social thought.

> At about seven o'clock in the evening of Thursday, 24th May 1871, six [innocent] men were taken from their cells in the Parisian jail of La Roquette, lined up against a wall and shot. They included a layman . . . and five priests [including archbishop of Paris, Georges Darboy] . . . this measure had been decided by the [socialist] Insurrectional

> Committee six weeks earlier by way of revenge for the execution of some of their own partisans who had been taken prisoner during an abortive counter attack . . . on the 25th May the Dominicans of the École Saint-Albert d'Areueil, having been allowed to escape, were shot down like rabbits on the Avenue a'Italie. On the 26th ten priests, among them three Jesuits and two Picpucians, were massacred in the Rue Haxo.[104]

The bloody events of the Paris Commune cast a shadow over all Roman Catholic social thinkers at the close of the nineteenth century. However, no thinkers were affected more than those who had earlier explored the possibility of Christian socialism. As a result, no forms of either "communal" or "societal" transformationism are conspicuous in Catholic social thought between 1872 and 1890.

CONCLUSION

Three of the most important non-Catholic sociological minds of the nineteenth century sought an explanation for their changing world in the processes of differentiation, commodification, and rationalization. Emile Durkheim keenly observed the phenomenon of differentiation—the social process whereby social units (e.g., family, church, business, school, and government) become increasingly specialized in their functions relative to one another. Karl Marx provided the classic description of commodification—the social process whereby an increasing number of objects come within the ambit of capitalist exchange relations. Max Weber had a particular interest in the process of rationalization whereby knowledge becomes increasingly identified with what is calculable, impersonal, formal, and processual.

Roman Catholics of the early modern period felt these processes in the actions of their governments, the alterations in their family life, the upheavals in their economic routines, the startling changes in cultural communication, and the unimaginable overturning of their Church's longstanding social power. And Catholics were not simply passive observers of these events. They responded. Hans Maier says, "Catholics had a hand in every upheaval in the formation of modern society."[105] The diverse and abundant expressions of Roman Catholic social thought during the early modern period was one way Catholics addressed the shocking changes and enormous complexities of their world. From this standpoint, one might see Pope Leo XIII's *Rerum novarum* as much a summary conclusion of one period of modern Catholic social thought as the beginning of another.

This is not meant to diminish the importance of *Rerum novarum*. It is important to recall that most Catholics of the early modern period did not encounter fellow religionists animated with social concern. Émile Zola no doubt captures the common experience in his novel *Germinal*. There, a desperately impoverished La Maheude and her children pass Abbé Joire on their way to beg from the wealthy mine owner, Monsieur Grégoire:

> The curé of Montsou, the Abbé Joire, came by, hiking up his cassock with the delicacy of a well-nourished cat; he was fearful of soiling his habit. He was a gentle little man who tried not to get involved in anything, so as to irritate neither the workers nor the bosses.
>
> "Good Morning, Father."
>
> Without stopping, he smiled at the children and left her standing there in the middle of the road.[106]

While Pope Leo XIII's *Rerum novarum* cannot be accurately described as inaugurating Roman Catholic social thought, the encyclical certainly made it such that fewer Catholics could, in good conscience, leave the poor "standing there in the middle of the road."

Contemporary sociologists Stephen Crook, Jan Pakulski, and Malcolm Waters believe the dynamic that shocked early modernity and became routinized in modernity has broken apart in our postmodern era. They argue that postmodernization involves a conflictual hyperextension of the modernization processes of differentiation, commodification, and rationalization. They write: "The shift from modernization to postmodernization is related to the convergence of modernizing processes on an impossible combination of hyperdifferentiation with monocentric organization."[107] In other words, differentiation now separates human beings into special interest enclaves, rationalization now socializes human beings into a global sameness, and commodification—ironically—fuels both movements. This "genuinely explosive" combination of hyperdifferentiation, hyperglobalization, and hypercommodification accounts for the "unprecedented level of unpredictability and apparent chaos" marking postmodern life.[108]

This language would surely have eluded early modern Catholics but not the experience. If Crook, Pakulski, and Waters are correct, then aspects of the social dynamics of the early modern and postmodern worlds may have more in common with each other than either have with modernity. And if that is a possibility, then early modern Roman Catholic social thought may be a fruitful source of *ressourcement* for contemporary Roman Catholic social thinkers facing the simultaneity of social factionalism, globalism, and consumerism.

The age-old Christian moral orientations of traditionalism, cosmopolitanism, and transformationism inspire multiple social insights among Roman Catholics in the early modern period. These insights are expressed in texts, speeches, artistic creations, and lives self-consciously ordered toward the construction of just social structures. Every type of Roman Catholic is involved—cleric and lay, professional academic and public intellectual, inspired leader and humble builder. All seek to enrich the Catholic social imagination. In addition to this contribution to the overall legacy of Roman Catholic social thought, early modern Roman Catholics may be uniquely speaking to our own time.

NOTES

1. For the purposes of this discussion, early modern Roman Catholic social thought spans the period from Pope Benedict XIV's 1740 retrieval of the encyclical genre up to the 1891 appearance of Pope Leo XIII's RN. For an explanation of this dating, see Michael J. Schuck, *That They Be One: The Social Teaching of the Papal Encyclicals, 1740–1989* (Washington, D.C.: Georgetown University Press, 1991), ix–xi. I want to thank my graduate assistant, Ron Wright, for his invaluable assistance in preparing the present study.

2. Ann Swidler, *Talk of Love: How Culture Matters* (Chicago: University of Chicago Press, 2001), 13.

3. Charles Lemert, *Social Things: An Introduction to the Sociological Life* (Lanham, Md.: Rowman and Littlefield, 1997), 18.

4. In his 1911 *Political Parties*, Robert Michels shows that priorities of leaders in bureaucratic organizations tend, over time, to shift from the organizational good to the preservation of the leaders' own power and influence. On the tension between highly centralized institutions and community memory, see Paul Connerton, *How Societies Remember* (Cambridge: Cambridge University Press, 1989), 14–16.

5. John Courtney Murray appealed repeatedly to the *duo sunt* of Pope Gelasius I (492–496) when arguing for the separation of Church and civil government. See, for example, John Courtney Murray, "Contemporary Orientations of Catholic Thought on Church and State in the Light of History," *Theological Studies* 10 (1949): 177–234.

6. See, for example, Aaron Abell, *American Catholicism and Social Action: A Search for Social Justice, 1865–1950* (Notre Dame, Ind.: University of Notre Dame Press, 1963); Thomas Bokenkotter, *Church and Revolution: Catholics in the Struggle for Democracy and Social Justice* (New York: Image, 1998); Frank Paul Bowman, *Le Christ des barricades* (Paris: Les Éditions du Cerf, 1987); John A. Coleman, "Neither Liberal nor Socialist: The Originality of Catholic Social Teaching," in *One Hundred Years of Catholic Social Thought: Celebration and Challenge*, ed. John A. Coleman (Maryknoll, N.Y.: Orbis, 1991); Jean Baptiste Durocelle, *Les débuts du catholicisme social en France, 1822–1870* (Paris: Presses universitaires de France, 1951); Michael Fogarty, *Christian Democracy in Western Europe, 1820–1953* (Notre Dame, Ind.: University of Notre Dame Press, 1957); Robert Kothen, *La pensée et l'action*

sociale des catholiques, 1789–1944 (Louvain, Belgium: Em. Warny, 1945); Hans Maier, *Revolution and the Church: The Early History of Christian Democracy, 1789–1901*, trans. Emily M. Schossberger (Notre Dame, Ind.: University of Notre Dame Press, 1969); Georgiana Putnam McEntee, *The Social Catholic Movement in Great Britain* (New York: Macmillan, 1927); Bela Menczer, *Catholic Political Thought, 1789–1848* (Notre Dame, Ind.: University of Notre Dame Press, 1962); Paul Misner, *Social Catholicism in Europe: From the Onset of Industrialization to the First World War* (New York: Crossroad, 1991); Joseph Moody, ed., *Church and Society: Catholic Social and Political Thought and Movements, 1789–1950* (New York: Arts, 1953); Parker Thomas Moon, *The Labor Problem and the Social Catholic Movement in France: A Study in the History of Social Politics* (New York: Macmillan, 1921); Franz H. Mueller, "The Church and the Social Question," in *The Challenge of 'Mater et Magistra,'* ed. Joseph Moody and Justice Lawler (New York: Herder and Herder, 1963); Pierre Pierrard, *L'Église et les ouvriers en France (1840–1940)* (Paris: Hachette littérature 1984); Alec Vidler, *A Century of Social Catholicism* (London: SPCK, 1964).

7. See Schuck, *That They Be One*.

8. See, for example, Nigel Aston, ed., *Religious Change in Europe, 1650–1914* (Oxford: Clarendon, 1997); Mauricio Beuchot, *The History of Philosophy in Colonial Mexico*, trans. Elizabeth Millán (Washington, D.C.: Catholic University of America Press, 1998); James E. Bradley and Dale K. Van Kley, *Religion and Politics in Enlightenment Europe* (Notre Dame, Ind.: University of Notre Dame Press, 2001); Owen Chadwick, *A History of the Popes, 1830–1914* (Oxford: Clarendon, 1998); Austen Ivereigh, ed., *The Politics of Religion in an Age of Revival: Studies in Nineteenth-Century Europe and Latin America* (London: Institute of Latin American Studies, 2000); John T. McGreevy, *Catholicism and American Freedom: A History* (New York: W. W. Norton, 2003); Hugh McLeod, ed., *European Religion in the Age of Great Cities, 1830–1930* (London: Routledge, 1995); John W. O'Malley et al., *The Jesuits: Cultures, Sciences, and the Arts, 1540–1773* (Toronto: University of Toronto Press, 1999); Frank Tallet and Nicholas Atkin, eds., *Catholicism in Britain and France since 1789* (London: Hambledon, 1996) and *The Right in France, 1789–1997* (New York: St. Martin's, 1998); Peter Wilson, *The Holy Roman Empire, 1495–1806* (New York: St. Martin's, 1999); Isser Woloch, ed., *Revolution and the Meanings of Freedom in the Nineteenth Century* (Stanford, Calif.: Stanford University Press, 1996).

9. Michael Paul Driskel, *Representing Belief: Religion, Art and Society in Nineteenth-Century France* (University Park: Pennsylvania State University Press, 1992), 11. Of course, Driskel's starting point is not new; Arnold Hauser explored the relationship between art and politics in his well-known four-volume *The Social History of Art* (New York: Vintage, 1958). Other contemporary scholars with this interest and useful to the present study include Gauvin Alexander Bailey, *Art on the Jesuit Missions in Asia and Latin America, 1542–1773* (Toronto: University of Toronto Press, 1999); Albert Boime, *Hollow Icons: The Politics of Sculpture in Nineteenth-Century France* (Kent, Ohio: Kent State University Press, 1987); Patricia Mainardi, *Art and Politics of the Second Empire: The Universal Expositions of 1855 and 1867* (New Haven, Conn.: Yale University Press, 1987); Linda Nochlin, *The Politics of Vision: Essays on Nineteenth-Century Art and Society* (New York: Harper and Row, 1989); Philip Nord, *Impressionists and Politics: Art and Democracy in the Nineteenth Century* (London: Routledge, 2000).

10. James B. White, *Justice as Translation: An Essay in Cultural and Legal Criticism* (Chicago: University of Chicago Press, 1990), xi.

11. Robert C. Tucker, ed., *The Marx-Engels Reader* (New York: W.W. Norton, 1972), 393.

12. Alfred J. Bingham, "The Abbé Bergier: An Eighteenth Century Catholic Apologist," *Modern Language Review* 54, no. 3 (1955): 349.

13. Aston, ed., *Religious Change*, 36.

14. "Il a crée le riche, afin qu'il rachète ses péchés en secourant le pauvre. Il a crée le pauvre, afin qu'il s'humilie par le secours qu'il reçoit des riches. Ils ont été comme entrelacés dans la société civile, afin que par des offices mutuels ils puissent s'entr'aider, non-seulement pour les commodités de la vie présente, mais encore pour leur salut, en se sanctifiant, les uns par une liberalité honnête, les autres par une humble reconnaissance." Sermon *Sur L'Obligation de l'aumone*, by Esprit Flechier in Henri Bremond, *Oeuvres choisies* (Paris: Librairie Bloud, 1911), 81. Translation mine.

15. Bernard Groethuysen, *The Bourgeois: Catholicism and Capitalism in Eighteenth-Century France*,

trans. Mary Ilford (New York: Holt, Rinehart and Winston, 1969), 150.

16. Schuck, *That They Be One*, 20.

17. Giuseppe Chiari's *Rest on the Flight into Egypt* can be viewed at http://www2.bc.edu/~khimes/publications/mcst/ Jaccques Louis David's *The Death of Socrates* can be viewed at http://www2.bc.edu/~khimes/publications/mcst/

18. Christopher M. S. Johns, "Papal Patronage and Cultural Bureaucracy in Eighteenth-Century Rome: Clement XI and the Accademia di San Luca," *Eighteenth Century Studies* 22, no. 1 (1988): 2.

19. Ibid., 13, 16 (number 28), 23.

20. Geoffrey Scott, *The Architecture of Humanism: A Study in the History of Taste* (New York: W. W. Norton, 1974), 31.

21. Charles Irenée Castel de Saint-Pierre, "A Project for Perpetual Peace," in *Peace Projects of the Eighteenth Century*, ed. M. C. Jacob (New York: Garland, 1974), 27.

22. Bokenkotter, *Church and Revolution*, 32.

23. Ruth Graham, "The Revolutionary Bishops and the *Philosophes*," *Eighteenth Century Studies* 16, no. 2 (1982–83), 127–28.

24. Ibid., 119.

25. John Cogley, *Catholic America* (Garden City, N.Y.: Image, 1973), 22.

26. Philip Gleason, "American Catholics and Liberalism, 1789–1960," in *Catholicism and Liberalism: Contributions to American Public Philosophy*, ed. R. Bruce Douglass and David Hollenbach (Cambridge: Cambridge University Press, 1994), 48.

27. Quoted in Kenneth J. Zanca, ed., *American Catholics and Slavery: 1789–1866* (Lanham, Md.: University Press of America, 1994), 255.

28. Quoted in Joel S. Panzer, *The Popes and Slavery* (New York: Alba House, 1996), 257.

29. Ibid., 42. Panzer also blames the early American distinction between slavery conditions and slavery as such for the misinterpretation of papal thought in John T. Noonan, Laennec Hurbon, and John F. Maxwell. Ibid., 2. If Panzer is correct, his argument would also hold for McGreevy's discussion in *Catholicism and Freedom*, 50.

30. Jesuit Family Album can be viewed at http://www.faculty.fairfield.edu/jmac/jp/jpintro.htm (downloaded December, 8, 2003).

31. Bailey, *Art on the Jesuit Missions*, 10.

32. Jesuit Family Album.

33. Paul H. Beik, "The French Revolution Seen from the Right: Social Theories in Motion, 1789–1799," *Transactions of the American Philosophical Society* 46 (1956): 64.

34. Geoffrey Cubitt, "God, Man and Satan: Strands in Counter-Revolutionary Thought among Nineteenth-Century French Catholics, " in *Catholicism in Britain and France since 1789*, ed. Frank Tallett and Nicholas Atkin (London: Hambledon, 1996), 147.

35. Ibid., 146.

36. Robert A. Nisbet, "De Bonald and the Concept of the Social Group," *Journal of the History of Ideas* 5 (1944): 323, 330.

37. Boime, *Hollow Icons*, 18.

38. Richard P. McBrien, *Lives of the Popes: The Pontiffs from St. Peter to John Paul II* (San Francisco: HarperSanFrancisco, 1997), 334.

39. Sean O'Riordan, "The Teaching of the Papal Encyclicals as a Source and Norm of Moral Theology: A Historical and Analytic Survey," *Studia Moralia* 14 (1976): 155.

40. Driskel, *Representing Belief*, 5.

41. Mainardi, *Art and Politics*, 76.

42. Ibid., 74. Ingres's painting can be viewed at http://www2.bc.edu/~khimes/publications/mcst/

43. Ad Leys, *Ecclesiological Impacts of the Principle of Subsidiarity* (Kampen, Netherlands: Uitgeverij Kok, 1995), 5.

44. Misner, *Social Catholicism*, 41. Catholic thinkers sharing key elements of Müller's thought include Friedrich von Schlegel, Karl Ludwig von Haller, Franz Xavier von Baader, and Joseph Görres. See also discussions of M. Levacher-Duplessis, Felix de La Farelle, and Eugéne Buret in Matthew H. Elbow, *French Corporative Theory, 1789–1948* (New York: Columbia University Press, 1953).

45. Honoré de Balzac, *The Country Doctor*, from Online Literature Library at http://www.literature.org/authors/de-balzac-honore/country-doctor/index.html (downloaded December 8, 2003). See also Balzac's discussion of society and the individual in Menczer, *Catholic Political Thought*.

46. Richard Fargher, "Religious Reactions in Post-Revolutionary French Literature: Chateaubriand, Constant, Mme de Staël, Joseph de Maistre," in *Religious Change*, ed. N. Aston, 263.

47. Overbeck's painting can be viewed at http://www2.bc.edu/~khimes/publications/mcst/

48. Moon, *The Labor Problem*, 21.

49. Ernst J. Brehm, "Catholic Social Economy and the Social Question in Mid-Nineteenth Century Spain: De la Sagra, et al.," in *On the Condition of Labor and the Social Question One Hundred Years Later*, ed. Thomas O. Nitsch et al. (Lewiston, N.Y.: Edwin Mellen, 1994), 203. Another important Catholic social thinker sharing Villeneuve-Bargemont's approach is Armand de Melun. See Misner's discussion of de Melun in *Social Catholicism*.

50. Vidler, *A Century of Social Catholicism*, 9.

51. John Tracy Ellis, *American Catholicism* (Chicago: University of Chicago Press, 1956), 59.

52. Boime, *Hollow Icons*, 30–31. See also the discussion of Montalembert's interest in medieval art and architecture in Driskel, *Representing Belief.* A photograph of Duseiggneur's sculpture appears in Boime, *Hollow Icons*, 32.

53. J. N. Moody et al., "Catholic Developments in Spain and Latin America," in *Church and Society*, ed., J. N. Moody et al., 744.

54. Bokenkotter, *Church and Revolution*, 99.

55. Ibid., 105. While O'Connell was a skilled, pragmatic social thinker, he did oppose slavery *in principle* in his 1843 letter to Irish Americans. See McGreevy, *Catholicism and American Freedom*, 50.

56. Goya's work can be viewed at http://www2.bc.edu/~khimes/publications/mcst/.

57. Mainardi, *Art and Politics*, 114. Delacroix's work can be viewed at http://www2.bc.edu/~khimes/publications/mcst/.

58. Nochlin, *The Politics of Vision*, 2. The view of Delacroix as a radical nonbeliever is challenged in Joyce C. Polistena's analysis of his religious and theological sources. See discussion of Polistena's "Revising Eugène Delacroix's Religious Oeuvre: Romantic Painting and Its Reintegration with Theology" in Cordula A. Grewe, "Reviving a Historical Corpse: Rewriting the Historiography of Nineteenth-Century Religious Art." Available at http://www.ghi-dc.org/bulletin27F00/b27confrelart.html (downloaded April 18, 2005).

59. The favorite artist of the Catholic socialists is Protestant Ary Scheffer. Characteristically, his 1837 *Le Christ consolateur* depicts Jesus with the socially oppressed on his right and left. Buchez and Scheffer are discussed in Joyce C. Polistena, "The Role of Religion in Eugène Delacroix's Religious Paintings: Intention and Distortion" (Ph.D. diss., The City University of New York, 1997), 145–58. Scheffer's work can be viewed in Driskel, *Representing Belief*, 37.

60. Vidler, *A Century of Social Catholicism*, 17.

61. Antiquariaat Matthys de Jongh, N. de Bonneville. Available at http://www.polybiblio.com/mdejongh/S51.html (downloaded December 8, 2003).

62. Vidler, *A Century of Social Catholicism*, 88. Another important societal transformationist during this period is Hippolyte de la Morvonnais. See discussion of la Morvonnais in Duroselle, *Les débuts*, 383–91.

63. Woloch, ed., *Revolution and the Meaning of Freedom*, 1.

64. Menczer, *Catholic Political Thought*, 159.

65. Driskel, *Representing Belief*, 41. Janmot's work can be viewed in ibid., 42.

66. Cubitt, "God, Man, and Satan," 140.

67. McGreevy, *Catholicism and American Freedom*, 70.

68. *Qui nuper* in *The Papal Encyclicals, 1740–1878*, ed. Claudia Carlen (Wilmington, N.C.: McGrath, 1981), 357.

69. *Nullis certe verbis*, in ibid., 360.

70. Henri Daniel-Rops, *The Church in an Age of Revolution, 1789–1870*, vol. 2, trans. John Warrington (Garden City, N.Y.: Image, 1967), 74.

71. Flandrin's work can be viewed in Driskel, *Representing Belief*, 125.

72. Quoted in Alfred Diamant, *Austrian Catholics and the First Republic: Democracy, Capitalism, and the Social Order, 1918–1934* (Princeton, N.J.: Princeton University Press, 1960), 58–59.

73. John W. Boyer, *Political Radicalism in Late Imperial Vienna: Origins of the Christian Social Movement, 1848–1897* (Chicago: University of Chicago Press, 1981), 176.

74. Ibid., 478, number 216.

75. Charles Plater, *The Priest and Social Action* (London: Longmans, Green, 1914), 54–55. In France, Maurice Maignen developed a *patronage* system analogous to Kolping's but with joint involvement of workers and employers. Misner explains that Maignen's joint approach was less effective than Kolping's sole focus on the workers. See Misner, *Social Catholicism*, 99–100.

76. Leys, *Ecclesiological Impacts*, 24.

77. Maastricht Treaty, *How Does the European Union Work?* (Brussels, Belgium: Office for Official

Publications of the European Communities, 1996), 13–14.

78. Misner masterfully traces the evolution of "Christian democracy" during this period in *Social Catholicism*, 80–90. Other Catholic thinkers with this cast of mind include Cardinal Louis de Bonald, Henry Maret, Peter Reichensperger, and Louis René Villermé.

79. Quoted in Zanca, ed., *American Catholics and Slavery*, 124.

80. Delacroix's work can be viewed in Driskel, *Representing Belief*, 93.

81. Driskel, *Representing Belief*, 128–31. Flandrin's work can be viewed in ibid., 129.

82. For a helpful recent discussion of Brownson, see McGreevy, *Catholicism and American Freedom*, 43–49, 66–68, 88–90.

83. In the same spirit, Brownson's lifelong friend, Issac T. Hecker, founds a religious congregation of men in 1858—the Paulists—whose mission includes communicating the spiritual value of intellectual freedom. The Paulists' important monthly journal *The Catholic World* begins publication in 1865.

84. Andrew M. Greeley, *The Catholic Experience* (Garden City, N.Y.: Image, 1969), 102, 122.

85. Paul Misner, "Antecedents of *Rerum Novarum* in European Catholicism," in *On the Condition of Labor*, ed. T. Nitsch et al., 216.

86. Ibid., 217.

87. Other new Catholic "societal" transformationists during this period are Pierre Leroux, Pierre Pradié, and Victor Calland.

88. Quoted in Aaron Abell, ed., *American Catholic Thought on Social Questions* (Indianapolis, Ind.: Bobbs-Merrill, 1968), 85.

89. Rosemary Haughton, *The Catholic Thing* (Springfield, Ill.: Templegate, 1979), 226.

90. Henri Daniel-Rops, *A Fight for God*, vol. 1, trans. John Warrington (Garden City, N.Y.: Image, 1967), 287.

91. Boime, *Hollow Icons*, 102. Photographs of Rodin's sculpture are at http://www2.bc.edu/~khimes/publications/mcst/.

92. Elbow, *French Corporative Theory*, 84, 70.

93. See Moon's discussion of de Mun's social legislation in *The Labor Problem*, 101–12, and the "Comparative Table" on 163–65.

94. Franz Brandts undertakes a similar factory experiment in Mönchengladbach, Germany. See discussion of the "Mönchengladbach orientation" in Misner, *Social Catholicism*, 181–85.

95. Le Play carries forward the sociological emphasis on the family begun by Louis de Bonald at the turn of the century. Le Play first publishes his findings in *Ouvriers européens* (1855).

96. Misner, *Social Catholicism*, 222.

97. McGreevy, *Catholicism and American Freedom*, 132. George's subsequent run for mayor of New York and the controversial involvement of Rev. Edward McGlynn in the "single-tax" campaign is well-documented.

98. Ibid., 130.

99. Greeley, *The Catholic Experience*, 155. Another important American "republican" is John Spalding, bishop of Peoria, Illinois.

100. Ibid., 180. An important Gibbons-style social Catholic thinker in Europe is Henry Edward Manning, archbishop of Westminster. The story of Daniel Rudd, former slave and president of the first Black Catholic Congress, remains to be written. Born in 1854, Rudd began the *American Catholic Tribune* in 1886, the first newspaper of its kind in the United States. It was Rudd and his *American Catholic Tribune* that first promoted the idea of a national meeting of African American Catholics. Adrienne Curry, "The History of the Black Catholic Congress Movement." Available at http://www.blackcatholicchicago.org/Archive%20Articles/0206_historyp1_nbcc.htm (downloaded December 8, 2003).

101. Driskel, *Representing Belief*, 212.

102. Ibid., 204. Munkácsy's work can be viewed in ibid., 204.

103. Ibid., 209. Lerolle's work can be viewed in ibid., 210.

104. Daniel-Rops, *A Fight for God*, 110, 112.

105. Maier, *Revolution and the Church*, 241.

106. Émile Zola, *Germinal* (New York: New American Library, 1970), 74.

107. Stephen Crook, Jan Pakulski, and Malcolm Waters, *Postmodernization: Change in Advanced Society* (London: Sage, 1992), 220.

108. Ibid., 35.

SELECTED BIBLIOGRAPHY

Abell, Aaron. *American Catholicism and Social Action: A Search for Social Justice, 1865–1950*. Notre

Dame, Ind.: University of Notre Dame Press, 1963. The first three chapters treat nineteenth-century American Catholic social thought.

———, ed. *American Catholic Thought on Social Questions*. Indianapolis, Ind.: Bobbs-Merrill, 1968. Excerpts from American Catholic social thinkers, fifteen texts pertaining to nineteenth-century thought.

Bokenkotter, Thomas. *Church and Revolution: Catholics in the Struggle for Democracy and Social Justice*. New York: Image, 1998. Very helpful, though selective, study of Catholic social thinkers since the French Revolution.

Corrin, Jay P. *Catholic Intellectuals and the Challenge of Democracy*. Notre Dame, Ind.: University of Notre Dame Press, 2002. Chapters 1–3 provide a general overview of early European social Catholicism.

Durocelle, Jean Baptiste. *Les débuts du catholicisme social en France, 1822–1870*. Paris: Presses universitaires de France, 1951. Classic study of nineteenth-century French social Catholicism.

Maier, Hans. *Revolution and the Church: The Early History of Christian Democracy, 1789–1901*. Translated by Emily M. Schossberger. Notre Dame, Ind.: University of Notre Dame Press, 1969. A particularly useful treatment of German social Catholicism.

McGreevy, John T. *Catholicism and American Freedom: A History*. New York: W. W. Norton, 2003. The first half of the book offers a fresh study of the American Catholic response to education, slavery, and labor issues in nineteenth-century America.

Menczer, Bela. *Catholic Political Thought, 1789–1848*. Notre Dame, Ind.: University of Notre Dame Press, 1962. Hard-to-find excerpts from early-nineteenth-century conservative and romantic Catholic social thinkers.

Mich, Marvin L. Krier. *Catholic Social Teaching and Movements*. Mystic, Conn.: Twenty-Third, 1998. The first two chapters treat social developments in American Catholicism before and during the publication of Pope Leo XIII's *Rerum novarum*.

Misner, Paul. *Social Catholicism in Europe: From the Onset of Industrialization to the First World War*. New York: Crossroad, 1991. Well-researched, thorough, and most current study of nineteenth-century European social Catholicism.

Moody, Joseph N., ed. *Church and Society: Catholic Social and Political Thought and Movements, 1789–1950*. New York: Arts, 1953. A compendium of valuable, though uneven, essays on social Catholicism in Europe and the Americas.

Schuck, Michael J. *That They Be One: The Social Teaching of the Papal Encyclicals, 1740–1989*. Washington, D.C.: Georgetown University Press, 1991. Chapters 1–2 cover eighteenth- and nineteenth-century encyclical social teaching.

Vidler, Alec. *A Century of Social Catholicism*. London: SPCK, 1964. Though Misner covers this material, Vidler's perspective is still enlightening.

PART

II

Commentaries

CHAPTER 5

Commentary on *Rerum novarum* (*The Condition of Labor*)

THOMAS A. SHANNON

INTRODUCTION

Rerum novarum (1891) emerged out of critical international discussions of social issues, particularly the status of workers, by a variety of Catholic clergy and laity and the organizations that they founded. The encyclical is a crystallization of many of these ideas and thus initiated the body of papal encyclicals referred to as social teaching. It was written at a time of political and economic turmoil and built on a growing sense that the Church needed to be involved in the great social issues of the day and to bring the wisdom of its tradition to bear on them. RN defended the right of private property (under attack by the socialists), argued for a living wage for workers (rather than the contract most workers could not refuse), and affirmed the right of labor to organize and, when necessary, strike (against the major industrial interests of the day). The significance of this encyclical is not only that it spoke to the issues of the day, but also that it set in motion the tradition of the popes continuing to address the social problems of the day.

OUTLINE OF THE DOCUMENT

RN confirmed the significance of a growing body of social perspectives and ideas from various members of the laity and hierarchy. The encyclical identified a number of themes that were germane to the situation of labor at the time of Leo XIII but also helped set an agenda for future analysis and commentary. The introductory section (1–13) of the encyclical sets out the agenda in fairly broad strokes. Changing economic conditions have significantly changed the nature of work as well as the conditions of labor. A primary consequence, and the focus of the encyclical, is the relation between capital and labor, employee and employer, the wealthy and the poor (14–27). Leo helps frame this by identifying the purpose of work—the ownership of property—and the role of the Church in resolving these great changes. Additionally, Leo made an extremely strong case for the necessity of private property, a rejection of socialism as an economic system.

The encyclical focuses on a number of problems of the emerging economic structure as well as responds to claims made by the socialists whom Leo understands to be destroying religion as well as initiating class warfare. Thus a strong interest is class harmony and cooperation, the right use of money by both the wealthy and the poor, and the dignity of labor and the laborer.

The solutions proposed (28–36) are of two kinds: religious and social. The religious solutions to the problems of the contemporary economy are a return to some form of the medieval guild system and the Christian religion (by which Leo means Roman Catholic) and Christian institutions, as well as respect for the plight of the poor. Institutionally, the pope identifies a number of practical responses on the part of state, employers, and workers. These include a heightened role for distributive justice, the correct use of authority, the protection of workers through regulation of hours of labor and providing a just wage, regulation of labor by children and women, as well as instilling in workers a sense of hope for the future so that they will have a foundation for perseverance in the tasks of this world.

Finally, the pope insists that such reforms, as necessary as they are, should not distract anyone from his or her real goal in life: attaining eternal happiness. Leo is insistent that while the social issues are important, even more important are the role of religion and the cultivation of piety among both employers and the employed. Should too much attention be paid to the temporal, there is danger that the eternal will be forgotten and all will be lost.

CONTEXT OF THE DOCUMENT

The Social Context

The European world of RN was one of incredible political and economic complexity. Europe was in social turmoil given the effects of the social, economic, and political transitions from late medieval feudalism to capitalism to the full expression of the Industrial Revolution. While the effects of such changes were felt first in England, the reverberations rapidly spread throughout all of Western Europe. Additionally the political scene was at least as convoluted as the economic one. Nationalism was rising, the existence of the Papal States was a serious bone of contention, and numerous revolutionary movements sponsored by socialists and the newly emerging Communists under the leadership of Marx and Engels were under way. The times indeed were revolutionary.

The Economic Context

Feudalism was a complex medieval political, social, and economic system. Its essence consisted of a set of reciprocal obligations between the various members of the social order. By the eighteenth century, all that remained were the land relations between peasant and landowner. "The full feudal authority of the lords, including political authority over such things as the administration of justice and private armies for defense and public order, had long since given way to the early modern monarchical or princely forms of a more or less centralized state authority."[1] A core economic problem was the effective control of such lands—particularly the problem of title—by arrangements made in the distant past. Yet as complex as these land arrangements were, productivity on them, combined with an absence of plagues, contributed to doubling of the European population between 1750 and 1850.[2] This population was composed of mostly single males who had to go somewhere, and thus began the great migration to towns. This surplus population, a potential seedbed of significant political and economic threats, combined with the development of a market economy to establish two key elements necessary for the Industrial Revolution.

The beginning of a market economy was the development of "cottage industries in connection with the capitalist 'putting-out' system of organizing the labor and the marketing of rural crafts, like weaving."[3] The system of putting out involved contractors estimating demand for a particular product in various markets. The at-home weavers would receive a kind of advance payment to make a product to meet the needs of the contractor. Occasionally there was a central area for preparation work for the wool or the yarn, but the work was done at home. Present in this cottage industry was a market, a kind of wage system, and some centralization of production. As Misner notes, "All that was required for the transition to industrialization after a while was to stop supplying the weavers with hand looms and start installing mechanized power looms in a large central workshop, namely the 'factory.'"[4] That and the development of a constant source of energy to power the looms came quickly enough in the form of the steam engine fueled by coal.

The major impacts of the Industrial Revolution, such as the British welfare policies that encouraged the poor to leave the countryside, were socioeconomic. The availability of jobs lured more and more to the cities. To fill these jobs, family members spent their days outside the home in the factory motivated by the lure of year-round wages as opposed to seasonal farm wages. Yet because of this surplus population, factory owners were able to get workers at continually lower wages. Because of low wages, days off were unknown and all—children included—had to work longer hours to survive. Seasonal down time on the farm was replaced by prolonged periods of unemployment. Additionally, women had to endure the sexual solicitations of the managers. Clearly, after such a twelve- to fifteen-hour day, not much time was left for family or anything else. With the spread of such conditions over most of Western Europe and the plight of the workers becoming ever more desperate, the first major social question of the Industrial Revolution was engaged.

Another component of the feudal system that continued into changing times was the sense of a fixed social hierarchy: few people were in positions of high social standing while the majority was of much lower rank. However, this social structure was not the cause of social dissent since, on the one hand, all were created and loved equally by God and, on the other hand, there was an interesting social interdependency between the classes: the poor served the needs of the rich but the rich were to care for the poor through distributing alms to them. The hope was that this social complementary and paternalistic interdependence would result in a spirit of noblesse oblige that would help smooth some of the rough edges of the beginnings of industrialization.

The historical prohibition on the practice of usury was another practice called into question by the economic necessities fueling international business, mainly the need for credit. The terms of the question changed, though, from a prohibition on charging interest by simple reason of the lending to accepting a finance charge because of the inconveniences suffered by the lender. Eventually the question of usury became moot and the credit system became an integral part of capitalism and industrialism and led to the development of the bourgeois class, the entrepreneurs of their day.[5] The rise of this class also struck a blow with far-reaching consequences at the concept of a static social order. The bourgeoisie were not content to remain in the estate to which they were born.

> This-worldly, pragmatic, rational, they could appreciate that the inequalities marking the old world would remain, but not necessarily at their expense; they came to realize, during the Revolution if not already before hand, that the social teachings of the church that they themselves rejected were all the more necessary for the common people.[6]

Noblesse oblige indeed!

The Political Context

As complicated as the developing capitalistic and industrial systems were, they almost pale in comparison to the political developments across Europe. Among the issues of concern are those of revolution, monarchy, the *Kulturkampf*, and the fate of the Papal States.

The Revolution of 1789 set the stage for Church-state relations in Europe in a particularly dramatic way. In France, for example, church property was nationalized, and persecution of institutions and individuals initiated. In Germany, the temporal authority of abbots and bishops was taken away and ecclesiastical control of many universities was lost. The goal was freedom from tradition and from the institution that most symbolized tradition, the Catholic Church.

The year 1848 saw the initiation of the revolutionary trend helped along by the failure of many areas of preindustrial manufacturing in Central Europe, a massive crop failure, the unequal legal status of employer and employee, and the cyclic nature of business that, combined with ever more aggressive competition, left many workers unemployed and homeless.[7]

Then the revolutions started.

> In January of 1848 a rebellion broke out in Sicily—it was not put down by the Bourbon regime that ruled southern Italy for over a year. Then followed the February Revolution in Paris and the rest of France, which set off a whole series of revolutions across Europe, especially in Berlin and Vienna. In Paris, Louis Philippe abandoned the throne in a panic over demonstrations that the army tried to meet with force. In Vienna, Metternich took his leave unceremoniously in the middle of March.[8]

All this and we have yet to mention Karl Marx and Frederich Engels, who published the *Communist Manifesto* in that year as well. Reality was becoming too complicated as well as too much for many people. Social chaos seemed to gain the day.

Consequently, one response, particularly in France, was a longing for a restoration of the monarchy combined with strong ultramontanist religious tendencies among many Catholics. Many of the French Catholic reformers were both royalists and progressives, a fact that frequently caused their calls for the reform of working conditions to be rejected. This led to a situation in France in which the "question of a monarchical restoration threatened not only to split the Church but to nullify the social movement."[9] The social reform movement, however, eventually proved to be a stronger ideology than restoration.

In Germany, Bismarck initiated the *Kulturkampf* (1870–82).[10] While the *Kulturkampf* was an effort to redefine German politics and culture, it was also an attempt to remove or at least diminish the role and status of the Catholic Church. Thus the May Laws of 1873 and the Emergency Laws of June 1875 "wiped out all remaining guarantees of the Prussian Constitution of 1850 which had safeguarded the Catholic Church according to the principle of 'a free Church in a free State,' a principle of the Prussian Constitution of 1859 which Bismarck had always regarded as a mere 'translation from French waste paper.'"[11] In 1872 the Jesuits were suppressed and in 1873 other religious Orders suffered the same fate. In addition to weakening the power of the Church, there was also an attempt to decouple the German Church from Rome, one example of which was the 1871 "'Muzzle Act' with an article for the supervision of pronouncements from the pulpit."[12] This unhappy state of affairs was eventually concluded after the election of Leo XIII, who initiated some changes in the Church's stance toward Germany as well as the sustained efforts of the Central Party that became a major actor in resolving the *Kulturkampf*. "This found its strongest expression in the modus vivendi between Bismarck and Rome, established first in 1882 through a Prussian legation at the Vatican and culminating in the Repeal Acts (1887) by which the Kulturkampf was finally liquidated."[13]

The Papal States, consisting essentially of central Italy, were given to the papacy by the Carolingian kings in the eighth century so that the papacy would have enough temporal resources to keep it relatively independent. While this did occur, such possessions also forced the papacy into significant temporal concerns and political entanglements. In 1809, for example, Napoleon occupied the Papal States and Pius VII barricaded himself in a Roman palace for five years. In 1848 Pius IX fled to Gaeta in Naples, where he remained in exile until 1850. In 1874 Pius IX prohibited Catholics from taking part in Italian politics by either electing or being elected through his "non expedit," a ban reversed only in 1919 by Benedict XV. During the Franco-Prussian war, Napoleon withdrew from Rome the French troops defending the papacy and on September 20, 1870, Italian troops took Rome and unified Italy, and Pius IX began his term as "Prisoner of the Vatican." Pius IX continued to ignore any and all initiatives from the Italian government. It was not until 1929 that Pius XI brought the relation of the Vatican and Italy together in a concordat with Mussolini.

All of these political events created a context in which the status of the Church, to say nothing of its role in society, was constantly questioned, if not put in jeopardy. The situation was not the best for the Church to initiate social reform, but such reform movements nonetheless made their appearance.

The Roman Catholic Social Movement

As the Industrial Revolution spread from England to Belgium, Germany, France, and Italy, so also did its devastating consequences of displaced and separated families, child labor, poor wages, inadequate housing, and dangerous working conditions. While workers frequently accepted these circumstances because of the desperateness of their situation, others began to speak out on their behalf. In England, for example, Cardinal Manning[14] argued that labor was not a commodity. He also spoke and wrote frequently on behalf of dockworkers.

Many social reformers emerged in France. Frederic Ozanam critiqued the law of supply and demand and the so-called iron law of wages because they degraded the worker. His lasting contribution was the founding of the Society of St. Vincent de Paul. Léon Harmel, a French factory owner, organized a series of clubs for workers "founded on a paternalistic basis, regarding the duties of the managerial class toward the worker as similar to those of a father to his family."[15] Each had mutual obligations to the other, particularly with the managers being trained to care for the workers' families. Additionally Harmel sponsored frequent pilgrimages to Rome to demonstrate the workers' fidelity to the Church as well as to help lobby for his cause of the working poor. Albert de Mun and René de la Tour du Pin were major contributors to the growing cause of the workers. They too formed a number of workers' clubs dedicated to God and France as well as to help hold off socialism while they sought to secure the welfare of the workers. Their task was, in du Mun's words, "to clear the Church of the charges hurled against it and without abandoning a word of this social definition to show that there are within it resources sufficient to meet all the legitimate aspirations of the worker, to satisfy all his needs, and to harmonize his material well-being with the safety of his soul."[16] The Fribourg Union was formed under the direction of Karl von Lowenstein, Count Franz Kuefstein, René de la Tour du Pin, and Louis Milcent together with Bishop Mermillod of Fribourg and met from 1885 to 1891. This group both offered a critique of the economic systems of capitalism and socialism and proposed a coherent social theory based on social justice and grounded in Thomistic philosophy. This was the system of corporatism "constituted by the natural grouping of persons according to their professional duties, rights, interests, and social functions. Only when all of these natural groupings are represented in the political arena can justice prevail in a truly 'organized corporative system.'"[17]

A continuing problem with these and other clubs like them was both the underlying paternalism of the organizers that had the effect of inhibiting the workers from rising to leadership and articulating their own agenda as well as the explicit commitment to the restoration of the monarchy. While these individuals benefited the workers by making their cause known in Rome, ultimately they were less than successful because of their inherent paternalism and focus on charity rather than justice as a means to resolve workers' grievances.

The first Catholic in Germany to speak against some of the extremes of capitalism and indeed to address directly the ideas of Adam Smith was Adam Müller in his 1809 book *Elements of Statecraft*. He opposed Smith's individualism and free-trade proposals by arguing for a reestablishment of the guild system of the Middle Ages and for a dialectic of freedom and responsibility, with the family as the central socioeconomic union. While he did engage in arguments with Smith, the rapidity of change was to render most of his ideas inoperable—other than his coining of the term *human capital*. The first major voice to address the social question in Germany was Bishop Wilhelm von Ketteler[18] of Mainz, who spoke on behalf of the needs of the workers in the heavily industrialized Rhineland. Among his lasting contributions is a set of six sermons he gave as a parish priest offering a critique of the liberal affirmation of the absolute rights of private property. He was also critical in helping to establish a key element of the Catholic social analysis: the legitimate role of the state in addressing social questions.

These are but a few of the individuals involved in ensuring that the Church attended to the needs of the workers both by practical action on their behalf and also by establishing that such action was an important dimension of the mission of the Church. These efforts saw their fulfillment in Leo XIII's speaking directly to these concerns in RN.

The Ecclesial Context

As complex and difficult as the sociopolitical context was externally, the internal ecclesial ones were no less problematic. A thematic problem was the perception of a lack of respect for authority, both civil and ecclesial. Democratic, liberal, and socialistic movements were taking hold, and monarchy—to say nothing of papal authority—was a difficult concept to sell.

The challenge to papal authority was not helped by a series of popes who were particularly weak with respect to civil and political affairs.[19] But the most sustained challenges came from various antiauthoritarian movements. Erastus, a German Protestant, rejected "all authority not emanating from conscience alone."[20] Jansenism, though mostly associated with a rejection of probabilism and the promotion of moral strictness, also championed the role of the local bishop. Though this usually focused on liturgical matters, the Jansenists also supported the political implications of local rule. Gallicanism came in two versions: aristocratic and democratic. "The aristocratic Gallicanism . . . restricted the primacy and jurisdiction of the Roman pontiff in favor of the local bishops. The democratic Gallicanism . . . asserted that Christ had conferred the power of jurisdiction on the whole ecclesial assembly."[21] Febronianism, initiated in 1763 by Johann von Hontheim of Trierin, asserted that Christ gave jurisdiction to the whole ecclesial community. However, the authority of the bishop in his diocese "was unlimited. The primacy of the Roman pontiff was simply a primacy of honor."[22] The main function of the pope was to ensure the faithful implementation of decrees of general councils. Josephinism was an Austrian use of Febronian ideas to resolve that nation's Church-state relations. Here "Emperor Joseph II began his vigorous campaign to subordinate the Church to the imperial throne and make the Austrian Church as thoroughly independent of the Holy See as a Church could be without ceasing to be Catholic."[23] These positions were augmented by the excesses of the French Revolution that almost succeeded in destroying the French Catholic Church both institutionally as well as physically. Because of these excesses, the revolutionary slogan of "Liberty, Equality, and Brotherhood" never quite took root among members of the hierarchy, even though there is an engraving from that time showing these virtues emerging from the Sacred Heart of Jesus (and depicting Pius IX liberating the Church from various monarchs)![24]

The response to this decline was the strong assertion of papal authority through the centralization of ecclesial power in the office of the papacy, a movement known as ultramontanism. The strictly ecclesial dimension of this movement included several elements. One was Pius IX's 1854 infallible definition of the Immaculate Conception that "established the precedent that, for the formal definition of Catholic dogma (an uncommon occurrence) it was sufficient that the Pope should act on his own authority, with only such consultation with the Church as might seem to him proper."[25] A second was the 1864 *Syllabus of Errors* that condemned the political, philosophical, and theological errors of the day. Bishop Dupanloup of Orléans, France, attempted to mitigate the seemingly harsh and unnuanced positions of the *Syllabus* by devising the thesis-hypothesis framework. The thesis was the ideal situation, the way things should be, such as the establishment of the Catholic Church as the official religion of a country because it was the only true Church. The hypothesis was the way things were in reality. For example, in many countries the Catholic

Church was one among many religions rather than the established religion. According to this distinction, the Church could accept this as a temporary reality, but should strive for establishment. But in reality this distinction allowed for selective application depending on the evaluation of the hypothesis by the pope. Thus the *Syllabus* constricted much of the developing Catholic intellectual life, particularly the lay congresses so popular in Germany. The third element was the convening of Vatican Council I in 1870 together with its ensuing definition of papal infallibility in the constitution *Pastor aeternus* on July 18, 1870. The developing neo-Thomistic movement that both aligned itself with the ultramontane movement and opposed German university theology also directly attacked this ecclesial independence movement, helping to conclude the process initiated by *Pastor aeternus*.

McCool identifies the two major theological tasks of theology of this period. "The first was the defense of the Catholic faith against the rationalism and the religious skepticism of the Enlightenment. The second was the presentation of positive Christian revelation in a coherent, unified system that could stand comparison with the systems of Fichte, Schelling, and Hegel without compromising the supernaturalism and the unique, historical character of positive Christian revelation."[26] This reformulation resulted in the founding of the neoscholastic movement built on the understanding of the philosophy and theology of St. Thomas and sanctioned in the encyclical *Aeterni Patris* of Leo XIII (August 4, 1879). The Jesuit, Joseph Kleutgen, the most influential of the neo-Thomists, was one of the authors of the Vatican I constitution *Dei Filius* that restated the faith and reason problematic and "it is highly probable that Kleutgen was one of the authors designated by Leo XIII to draft the encyclical *Aeterni Patris*."[27] One of his close collaborators in the neo-Thomistic movement was a fellow Jesuit, Matteo Liberatore, an editor of *La civiltà cattolica*, the major journal for this movement and the author of the first draft of RN. Liberatore focused on the "need of a sound scholastic philosophy to overcome the dangers to public order and to religious and moral life, created by false modern notions of liberty and authority."[28]

Thus during the reign of Leo XIII we have, as a heritage from Pius IX and Vatican I, a centralization of papal power and authority, and from Leo himself a centralization of thought based on the sanctioning of neoscholastic or neo-Thomistic philosophy that provided an objective and universal basis for reflection as well as a response to the errors of extreme individualism that in turn led to subjectivity. Thus a conceptual framework was set in place for responding to the problems of the modern world.

PROCESS OF FORMULATION AND AUTHORSHIP

Several streams of influence came together to produce the final text of RN. These streams consisted of the writings of Bishop von Ketteler in Germany, Cardinal Manning through his writings and involvement with the dock workers' strike in England, Cardinal Gibbons's intervention with Pope Leo XIII on behalf of the Knights of Labor in America, the work of the Roman Committee for Social Studies under the direction of Monsignor Jacobini in Italy, the Fribourg Union under the direction of Monsignor Mermillod, as well as the numerous pilgrimages of workers to Rome led by Léon Harmel and complemented by the thought of René de la Tour du Pin. Although Leo XIII was greatly impressed by the work and themes developed by Ketteler and those of the French factory owners and labor activists (defense of private property, workers' wages, the social role of the Church, workers' associations, and a role for the state in economic affairs), Misner nonetheless argues convincingly that the main influence on RN came from Matteo Liberatore, a Jesuit, a neo-Thomist, and a member of the editorial board of *La civiltà cattolica*.[29]

Part of this argument comes from the recently discovered textual history of RN. During the 1940s, Monsignor Tardini, the Vatican secretary of state, became interested in the history of RN and discovered the treasure trove of a collection of all the drafts of RN that had been preserved by Monsignor Volpini, the private secretary of Leo XIII. These drafts were then given to Monsignor Antonazzi, who prepared the manuscripts for publication.[30]

Matteo Liberatore wrote the first draft in Italian. This draft of *La questione operaia*, dated July 5, 1890, was given to Cardinal Zigliara, a friend of Leo XIII, who then wrote a second draft with the same name. These two texts were merged into an Italian draft redacted by Zigliara, Liberatore, and Cardinal Mazzella, a professor of theology at the Gregorian. This became the basis for the first Latin text *Causa est*. Then this Latin text went through five stages of redaction. Monsignor Gabriele Boccali, Leo XIII's secretary, undertook at Leo's direction a reworking of the whole text. Volpini, Mazzella, and Liberatore made other redactions to this text. This became the basis of the second Latin text *Excitatâ semel*. This text went through another editing process and became the first draft of RN, and this text went through three more edits before the final text was produced. And then on May 15, 1891, Leo XIII promulgated the final text.[31] Although Leo XIII is not mentioned in this summary, it is the case that he was in close contact with the drafters and added his own comments to the text.[32]

The other part of Misner's argument for Liberatore's influence is twofold. First is a negative argument: the absence of the distinctive notion of a corporative regime in the encyclical. This theory, derived from Von Ketteler's work by his disciple Karl von Vogelsang and further developed by Harmel, focused on a reassociation "of labor and capital in a given sector through a sort of collective self-administration, sanctioned by but not run by the state, of the sector's human and material resources."[33] This implies a total reform of the economic structure, and that perspective is absent from the encyclical. Second is his presentation of the economic influences on Liberatore that made their way into RN. Among these were little opposition to liberal economics, the acceptance of private property, an acceptance of usury in opposition to corporatist dismissal of it, and an acceptance of workmen's associations guided by owners.[34] However, in spite of this influence, Liberatore's key idea of corporatism is absent from the final draft and was replaced with the possibility of workers forming or joining unions comprised of workers only, a clear break from the corporatist model.

ESSAY

RN was written in 1891, the end of one century and the beginning of a new age. It was written in the aftermath of a genuine revolution, the Industrial Revolution that began in England with the invention of the steam engine and its application as an energy source for factories. Soon the economic and social implications of this Revolution spread throughout Western Europe with consequences that to some degree were unforeseen but indeed were understood as advantageous to capital: a steady supply of surplus labor, wages set at the lowest level possible, the need for long hours of labor by all members of a family merely to survive. Additionally, major social transitions were also effected by this Revolution: a substantive population shift from rural to urban, a shift in the family as a unit of production to a unit of consumption, the rhythm of life set by the clock and work schedule rather than by the rhythms of nature, and the uncertainty of steady employment compounded by a lack of other resources (such as a plot of land on which to grow some food). Indeed, the wake of the Industrial Revolution produced the "cupido rerum novarum"—a spirit of revolutionary change, as the phrase is translated.

Leo responded to these situations from the perspective of natural law articulated from within the context of Christendom. That is, Leo assumed the normative status of the Catholic Church within Western Europe as the institution that legitimated other social institutions as well as having the moral authority to prescribe solutions to various problems. The framework for such analysis was the natural law that also served as the foundation for civil law. Human reason was able to observe the world around it and draw from it moral principles embedded in it by its Creator. Leo, like many others in the Church, accepted natural law in the traditional framework of a predominantly static understanding of both nature and society. The natural law also helped the Church defend itself and the status quo against unwelcome forces of change. A critical assumption of Leo, for example, is that inequality within a society is a given and cannot be eliminated, though adjustments were possible. A major effort of the encyclical, therefore, is to prevent false ideas about the nature of society and social classes being given to the poor: "so in a State it is ordained by nature that these two classes should exist in harmony and agreement, and should, as it were, fit into one another, so as to maintain the equilibrium of the body politic." (15) While the encyclical is progressive in many ways, this static and ahistorical framework conditions how problems are understood and resolved, though its overriding intent is to soften some of the rigidity of class distinctions and make possible some movement among classes.

The core of the encyclical is its insistence on private property as a key element in the resolution of many of the social problems of the day. Leo argues "when a man engages in remunerative labor, the very reason and motive of his work is to obtain property, and to hold it as his own private possession." (4) Working for another for wages establishes both the intent for remuneration as well as the right to dispose of this wage. By living sparingly, the worker is able to save up to buy property and this property, as is the case with wages, is the worker's to dispose of as desired. Such a right of disposal of wages and property is seen by Leo as at the heart of ownership and constitutes a key distinction between his thought and that of the socialists who, Leo argues, transfer ownership—and, therefore, disposability—of property to the community. In actuality, however, the socialists offered a critique of the private ownership of the means of production and did not reject private ownership of personal property. This misperception weakens his arguments against socialism and also sets in motion the misstating of the Thomistic doctrine of private property as a natural right rather than a particular form of social organization of property to which people had claims.

Private Property

Leo sets out a fourfold argument for private property. First, the possession of property distinguishes us from the animals, for property allows us to go beyond the animal instincts of self-preservation and the propagation of the species to preparing for the future. Because humans do not use things exclusively in the here and now, but also plan for future use—a function of our reason, the faculty that sets us apart from the other animals—"it must be within his right to have things not merely for temporary and momentary use, as other living beings have them, but in stable and permanent possession." (5)

Second, following up on the necessity of planning, for our needs recur and demand future provision, Leo says we can "possess not only the fruits of the earth but also the earth itself; for of the products of the earth he can make provision for the future." (6) The critical issue here is that Leo sees property as a normative reality; people are entitled to own property. The question is the distribution of that property in society and the basis upon which that is done. Here the encyclical responds to two positions. Some say the state should hold all property in common, but Leo responds that "man is older than the State, and he holds the right of providing for the life of his body prior to the formation of any State." (6) Additionally, even though God has given the earth and its fullness for all to enjoy, "God has granted the earth to mankind in general; not in the sense that all without distinction can deal with it as they please, but rather that no part of it has been assigned to any one in particular, and that the limits of private possession have been left to be fixed by man's own industry and the laws of individual peoples." (7) And even if the earth is divided up among private owners, it still provides for all in that all live from what the land produces because all either are paid in produce or exchange their wages for produce.

Third, according to the law of nature,

> when man thus spends the industry of his mind and the strength of his body in procuring the fruits of nature by that act he

> makes his own that portion of nature's field which he cultivates—that portion on which he leaves, as it were, the impress of his own personality, and it cannot but be just that he should possess that portion as his own, and should have a right to keep it without molestation. (7)

Finally, Leo argues that since the family is the first natural society, within the family the father, in his capacity as head of the family, has the duty to provide for his family:

> For it is a most sacred law of nature that a father must provide food and all necessaries for those whom he has begotten; and, similarly, nature dictates that a man's children, who carry on, as it were, and continue his own personality, should be provided by him with all that is needful to enable them honorably to keep themselves from want and misery in the uncertainties of this mortal life. Now, in no other way can a father effect this except by the ownership of profitable property, which he can transmit to his children by inheritance. (10)

Class Relationships

Another core theme in the encyclical is the relation of classes, a problem seen as particularly acute because of the understanding of Leo and the society in which he lived that such hierarchical social structures and relationships were part of the very fabric of nature as well as his perception that the socialists wanted to stir up class warfare by making the poor dissatisfied with their lot. The touchstone for his analysis is that the Church "lays down precepts yet more perfect, and tries to bind class to class in friendliness and good understanding." (18) And because we are created for eternal things and life everlasting, "money and the other things which men call good and desirable we may have them in abundance or we may want [lack] them altogether; as far as eternal happiness is concerned it is no matter; the only thing that is important is to use them aright." (18) Thus even though there are social differences, in the long run such divisions are unimportant for the more critical reality is our final state in which all are fully equal before God.

Consequently, Leo argues that since each class requires and needs each other—as the parts of the body require and need the others—"so in a State it is ordained by nature that these two classes [the rich and the poor] should, as it were, fit into one another, so as to maintain the equilibrium of the body politic." (15) Additionally, "humanity must remain as it is. It is impossible to reduce human society to a level." (14) The argument here is that such differences are natural and such inequality is not disadvantageous to either the individual or the community, for "social and public life can only go on by the help of various kinds of capacity and the playing of many parts, and each man, as a rule, chooses the part which peculiarly suits his case." (14)

And such differences do not destroy the dignity of any person regardless of class position. Each has duties to the other—this was particularly true of property owners—and carrying these out in fidelity to the duties of one's state guarantees social harmony and well-being. Indeed, Leo very carefully spells out the rights and duties of each class to the other and then notes, "Were these precepts carefully obeyed and followed would not strife die out and cease?" (17)

The Church and the Poor

After noting that present wealth is not a sign of future beatitude, Leo identifies the basic rule for the right use of money: "it is one thing to have a right to the possession of money, and another to have a right to use money as one pleases." (19) Therefore, while no one is commanded to give out of what is necessary for one's household or give away what is required to maintain one's social position, "when necessity has been supplied, and one's position fairly considered, it is a duty to give to the indigent out of that which is left over." (19) On the other hand, "poverty is no disgrace, and (that) there is nothing to be ashamed of in seeking one's bread by labor." (19) Additionally, in a key sentence, Leo notes: "God himself seems to incline more to those who suffer evil; for Jesus Christ calls the poor blessed; he lovingly invites those in labor and grief to come to him for solace; and he displays the tenderest charity to the lowly and oppressed." (20) While one should be leery of reading the foundations of a preferential option for the poor into this sentence, the pope does suggest that the rich do not have a corner on salvation. Human excellence lies in one's moral quality and virtues, both of which are the common goal of all—rich or poor. Thus he argues for an equality in dignity and status before God for both rich and poor, a status that, if grounded in genuine charity, will lead to true friendship and brotherly love and, ultimately, social harmony within the structures of society as it then existed.

The Church, though rightly concerned with eternal salvation, is also concerned with the temporal needs of the poor that can be met without undermining the status quo. The Church desires that "the poor, for example should rise above poverty and wretchedness, and should better their condition in life; and for this it strives." (23) Historically, the encyclical argues, the Church has always promoted the interests and well-being of the poor. This was done primarily through church-sponsored works of charity and through the efforts of various religious congregations. The importance of such charity is shown by Leo's critique of those who propose another way: "At the present day there are many who, like the heathen of old, blame and condemn the Church for this beautiful charity. They would substitute in its place a system of State-organized relief. But no human methods will ever supply for the devotion and self-sacrifice of Christian charity." (24)

Yet Leo does argue for a twofold role for the state with respect to the poor. "The first duty, therefore, of the rulers of the State should be to make sure that the laws and institutions, the general character and administration of the commonwealth, shall be such as to produce of themselves public well-being and private prosperity." (26) However, there is a second and more critical obligation. "Among the many and grave duties of rulers who would do their best for their people, the first and chief is to act with strict justice—with that justice which is called in the schools *distributive*—toward each and every class." (27) This is an obligation not of charity but of justice, and the obligation is in proportion to one's status. Even though all contribute to the common good in their own way, there will yet be differences and inequalities because the obligation of justice is proportionate, not arithmetic. And while the contributions of the laborers are not the same as those of the ruling class or the capitalists, nonetheless, society could not proceed without the contributions of the workers. Hence "it cannot but be good for the commonwealth to secure from misery those on whom it so largely depends." (27)

The Rights of Workers

While Pope Leo recognizes that strikes are problematic because of the harm to the public good as well as business, he affirms that the workers also have interests that need protection. His main suggestion is prevention of strikes by attending to the workers' needs. Among the interests of the workers that are to be protected, Leo ranks first the workers' spiritual needs and the care for the workers' souls. In particular, Leo argues that the day of rest should not be spent in "mere idleness; much less must it be an occasion of spending money and a vicious excess, as many would desire it to be; but it should be rest from labor consecrated by religion." (32)

Then the encyclical turns to the question of the hours of work. The argument is that humans cannot be used as instruments for making money: "It is neither justice nor humanity so to grind men down with excessive labor as to stupefy their minds and wear out their bodies." (33) Rather than specifying a set number of hours, the pope argues that the time of work should depend "upon the nature of the work, on the circumstances of time and place, and on the health and strength of the workman." (33) Later he notes that the season of the year should also be factored in as well as the recognition that "work which is suitable for a strong man cannot reasonably be required from a woman or child." (33) The basic principle that Leo identifies is that "a workman ought to have leisure and rest in proportion to the wear and tear of his strength; for the waste of strength must be repaired by the cessation of work." (33)

Included in these provisions for manual labor is the argument that children should not be exposed to the working conditions of adults until their bodies and minds are sufficiently mature. Too early an exposure makes any education impossible and will destroy the promise that a child has. The pope then argues that women are not suited to participate in certain trades, "for a woman is by nature fitted for home work, and it is that which is best adapted at once to preserve her modesty, and to promote the good bringing up of children and the well-being of the family." (33) This text, of course, reflects a view of women grounded in social and philosophical frameworks that were uncritically assumed at the time.

The focus of this section of the encyclical is manual labor, the prime means of earnings for many. The intent of the pope is to ease the burden of workers, singling out in particular miners and quarry workers. The argument is that humans are not beasts of burden and are entitled by their dignity to relief from these conditions. A particular focus is child labor, one of the major sources of an easy supply of workers. While not calling for an end to the use of children in factories and mines, the pope sought to delay their entrance to such jobs until they are mature enough to handle many of the burdens. Also, he implicitly recognizes the importance of education for a child and that too early an entrance into the workforce destroys that. In a similar vein, Leo qualifies the role of women in the workplace. The argument rests on his reading of the nature of women, a reading highly conditioned by the normative status of the biological role of childbearing, a role he thinks qualifies their abilities in the workplace. However, women suffered the same physical stresses at work as men and were often additionally subjected to a variety of forms of sexual harassment. The frame of analysis and solution may be questionable, but the problems were real. The solutions to these problems were resolved in terms of the view of women at the time, but at least there is a recognition that there were problems and that they needed resolution.

An enduring contribution of RN is the discussion of the just wage. Here the pope directly attacks the prevailing model of using consent to set wages. Here the just wage was what the worker agreed to and injustice occurred either when the worker did not perform the work or the employer did not pay for the completed work. For Leo, this prevailing contract model of labor leaves important considerations out of the analysis. Because labor is necessary for self-preservation, Leo argues that work has two important characteristics. First, "it is *personal*, for the exertion of individual power belongs to the individual who put it forth, employing this power for that personal profit for which it was given. Secondly, a man's labor is *necessary*, for without the results of labor a man cannot live; and self-conservation is a law of nature, which it is wrong to disobey." (34)

The pope concludes that if a worker's labor were only personal, that is, directed only to one's own personal desires or to make a profit, then the contract model would be acceptable. But since work is also necessary for self-preservation as well as that of one's family, "each has a right to procure what is required in order to live; and the poor can procure it in no other way than by work and by wages." (34) Because the poor have no alternative but to work for their very survival, they cannot be at the mercy of the employer. Because of the desperation for jobs caused in part by a surplus of workers, workers would frequently take any salary that was offered since something was better than nothing, even though the something frequently approached nothing. Leo argues that this violates the law of nature because such a method makes it impossible for the worker to provide for the family in a reasonable way.

Thus, even though Leo sees that there should be free agreements between workers and employers concerning wages,

> nevertheless there is a dictate of nature more imperious and more ancient than any

> bargain between man and man, that the remuneration must be enough to support the wage earner in reasonable and frugal comfort. If through necessity or fear of a worse evil, the workman accepts harder conditions because an employer or contractor will give him no better, he is the victim of force and injustice. (34)

Yet even here Leo is concerned about the undue interference by the state so he argues, with a phrase hinting at corporatist motifs, that there should be some sort of society or board to mediate any disputes between workers and employers.

There is both a public and a private benefit to be obtained from Leo's position on the just wage.

> If a workman's wages be sufficient to enable him to maintain himself, his wife, and his children in reasonable comfort, he will not find it difficult, if he is a sensible man, to study economy [to learn to live within one's means]; and he will not find it difficult, by cutting down expenses, to set by a little property: nature and reason would urge him to do this. We have seen that this great labor question cannot be solved except by assuming as a principle that private ownership must be held as sacred and inviolable. The law, therefore, should favor ownership, and its policy should be to induce as many people as possible to become owners. (35)

The benefits of such ownership according to Leo are threefold: property will be more equitably divided and help eliminate the gap between rich and poor that frequently is the cause of revolution; more abundance will be produced because people work harder when the land they work is theirs; and since people are now more deeply invested in their own country through ownership, they would love their own country more and be less willing to leave it. (35) For Leo, then, the function of a just wage is not just the reasonable and frugal comfort of the family, but is directly related to one of the overarching themes of the encyclical as a whole: private property. Leo wants to ensure that the right to private ownership remains inviolate even while he recognizes that the state has some rights to qualify ownership for the public interest. And while Leo did not want to do away with the class system that he saw as natural, he did recognize that if the poor were always kept down, they would be ripe for revolutionary rhetoric or the seductive slogans of the socialists. Thus if "working people can be encouraged to look forward to obtaining a share in the land, the result will be that the gulf between vast wealth and deep poverty will be bridged over, and the two orders will be brought nearer together." (35) Even though class divisions will yet remain, their sharp edges will have been softened.

Workers' Organizations

Another significant contribution of the encyclical is its acceptance of workers' associations, the precursors of contemporary trade unions. After an allusion to the positive benefits of the older guild system, the pope calls for the adaptation of such associations to the needs of the current age. He also expresses the desire that such associations—consisting "either of workmen alone or of workmen and employers together" (36)—multiply and become effective in their activities. Leo argues that individuals have a natural right to enter societies such as these to provide mutual assistance and seek their legitimate private good. And while the state has no absolute right to prohibit their existence, it may intervene when such societies prove harmful to the state. However, all efforts should be made to prevent such suppression. The pope here alludes to instances of recent suppression of religious organizations and the seizure of property and violation of all manner of human rights.

The main danger that the pope sees in such organizations is that they will fall under the sway of leaders "whose principles are far from compatible with Christianity and the public well-being." (40) Here he sought to address the threat posed by the atheistic and/or socialist labor movements that were responding to the needs of the workers caused by abusive employers. Because of this reality, Leo lavishes praise on those Catholics who have joined forces with workers under the inspiration of correct ethical principles. To continue that same tradition, the encyclical emphasizes that such associations have a strong religious foundation and provide for religious instruction and for the proper celebration of religious feasts and reception of the sacraments. The encyclical goes on to enumerate practical matters of the organization of these associations such as honest leadership, fair administration of funds, grievance committees, help in securing continuous employment, and security for the disabled, sick, and elderly. (43) Finally, such associations founded on the principles articulated by the pope will help Christian workers make the correct decisions as well as give a sense of hope by offering a way out of many of the difficulties they experience. Through such means, workers' associations serve both the spiritual and temporal dimensions of the needs of workers and their families. And in this way, the Church will, through its indirect support of such associations, also help resolve the problems of the workers and contribute to the common good.[35]

EXCURSUS

In this section I will treat three topics that require further comment for an understanding of RN: the role of the state in social life, the view of private property, and the theory of corporatism.

Validation of the Role of the State in Resolving Social Issues

One important legacy of RN is its validation of the legitimate, though limited, role of the state in resolving social issues. Key to understanding this issue is recognizing the shift from seeing poverty as a sign of moral failure or laziness to understanding it as a by-product of an economic system; poverty has a systemic cause and is not simply a moral failure. The validation of this shift in perspective comes from ideas developed by Bishop von Ketteler. Additionally, the very nature of the social question changed from the relations between rich and poor or of how to care for the poor to

> the difficulty of reconciling the interests of the new classes of industrial bourgeoisie and the clientele on the one side with those of industrial workers on the other. . . . It was . . . a newly dominant mode of production that, though highly efficient, redounded to the benefit of the few, as it seemed, and to the social and economic decline or exploitation of a great number.[36]

The issue was not merely changing class structures or a shift of the population to the city, but rather a reorganization of society or a shift in the division of labor on a variety of levels in light of the changes forced by industrialization. A particular issue here is recognizing that the conditions of the poor are not a given, a destiny to be lived and suffered in a spirit of resignation, but rather the understanding that "the misery of the working classes as a state of things that ought not to be and can be changed for the better."[37] This shift of categories from the poor to poverty, of course, raises different questions about the role of the state.

Ketteler's maturing thought on this problem led the way to restating this question. Building on his own involvement in the labor movement in Germany and following the thought of other authors such as Friedrich Pilgram, Ketteler recognized that poverty was not exclusively a moral problem as had typically been thought, but rather a function of a changed economic system. This brought the further realization that the Church and its charitable organizations alone were not enough to respond to the problem. In coming to this conclusion, Ketteler also moved somewhat beyond the typical corporatist strategies, cooperative movements, or income redistribution efforts common at the time. The two elements in this changed position involved an acceptance of and participation in the union movement (with the proviso that Catholics guard the content of their Christian morality). Given the reforms he suggested that were noted above, he was convinced that

> without laws, without the state setting basic standards, that is, without a political consensus on a certain level of regulation, the social question could not be solved—just as it could not be solved without individual responsibility, without the beneficent influence of religion, or without an effective organization of labor to confront the power of concentrated capital.[38]

This shift in thought and redefinition of the social problem marks a critical turning point in Catholic thinking, particularly with respect to the attention given to social and economic structures, and is incorporated into RN. While affirming the limited role of government, Leo is careful to stress that "rulers should anxiously safeguard the community and all its parts." (28) This is followed up with the statement that "whenever the general interest of any particular class suffers, or is threatened with, evils which can in no other way be met, the public authority must step in to meet them." (28) Leo then gives specific examples of legitimate state interventions:

> If religion were found to suffer through the workmen not having time and opportunity to practice it; if in workshops and factories there were danger to morals through the mixing of the sexes or from any occasion of evil; or if employers laid burdens upon the workmen which were unjust, or degraded them with conditions that were repugnant to their dignity as human beings; finally if health were endangered by excessive labor, or by work unsuited to sex or age—in these cases there can be no question that, within certain limits, it would be right to call in the help and authority of the law. (29)

And then, in a sentence anticipating some elements of the later development of the principle of subsidiarity, Leo says, "the law must not undertake more, nor go further, than is required for the remedy of the evil or the removal of the danger." (29)

But the point made here is critical: relief for the condition of the workers is no longer the exclusive function of works of charity or under the sole direction of the Church. The discussion shifts from the poor to poverty, and because of this shift in the nature of the question, the state has a legitimate role in addressing these problems. Earlier in the encyclical, the pope identified the basis of this obligation: distributive justice. "Justice, therefore, demands that the interests of the poorer population be carefully watched over by the administration, so that they who contribute so largely to the advantage of the community may themselves share in the benefits they create." (27) And in this statement, Leo helped articulate and give clearer direction to efforts to resolve social questions. Given the recognition of a new state of affairs and the necessity of new responses to them on the part of both Church and state, Leo opened the door to the development of a social Catholicism articulated, in an initial way, in the context of the social and religious categories of a changing society.

Theory of Private Property

A major focus of RN is to affirm and safeguard the right to private property. This is the part of the encyclical that is a reaction to the ideology of socialism so prevalent at the time. Leo's perception was that the socialists were undercutting rights to property and were demanding a redistribution of property—and that implied the right to seize state property. Also, property was important to Leo because he saw ownership of property as the way out of poverty and a means of giving some security to the workers. One of the functions of the just wage is to provide the worker with enough of a surplus to be able to save enough to buy property.

After affirming that everyone has the right by nature to possess private property, Leo makes the following observations:

> And to say that God has given the earth to the use and enjoyment of the universal

> human race is not to deny that there can be private property. For God has granted the earth to mankind in general; not in the sense that all without distinction can deal with it as they please, but rather that no part of it has been assigned to anyone in particular, and that the limits of private possession have been left to be fixed by man's own industry and the laws of individual peoples. Now, when man thus spends the industry of his mind and the strength of his body in procuring the fruits of nature by that act he makes his own that portion of nature's field which he cultivates—that portion on which he leaves, as it were, the impress of his own personality, and it cannot but be just that he should possess that portion as his own, and should have a right to keep it without molestation. (7)

These paragraphs are key because while Leo does root the right of private property in nature, he also makes a very interesting claim about the relation of the right to property and labor.

"For every man has by nature the right to possess property as his own." (5) This statement of the theory of private property at least qualifies, if not rejects, the theory of property identified by Thomas Aquinas, a position that is ironic because it comes from the pen of the pope most dedicated to a restoration of Thomism as the perennial philosophy of Catholicism. Aquinas's position is that "a private property system of control is a social convention that *does not violate* the natural law but can be justified on grounds of practical expediency."[39] Aquinas says,

> Now, according to the natural order instituted by divine providence, material goods are provided for the satisfaction of human needs. Therefore the division of and appropriation of property, that proceeds from human law, must not hinder the satisfaction of man's necessity for such goods. Equally whatever a man has in superabundance is owed, of natural right to the poor for their sustenance.[40]

The upshot of Aquinas's position is that possession of property may not be a natural right in the way that Leo expresses it. Aquinas recognizes a claim to property that must be respected, but sees the social organization of property or its distribution as a social issue rather than a right. Thus its possession can be qualified by the needs of others.

Then Leo, two paragraphs later, identifies another argument for private property: "Now when man thus spends the industry of his mind and the strength of his body in procuring the fruits of nature by that act he makes his own that portion of nature's field which he cultivates." (7) This is a very interesting claim particularly when read in light of John Locke's theory of property in *Two Treatises of Government*. In this important work that secures the rights of the individual against government, Locke argues for three natural rights: life, liberty, and property. The preservation of property is the chief reason why individuals place themselves under government, but government does not grant the right to property. Rather, according to Locke,

> Though the earth and all inferior creatures be common to all men, yet every man has a "property" in his own "person." This nobody has any right to but himself. The "labor" of his body and the "work" of his hands, we may say, are properly his. Whatsover, then he removes out of the state that Nature hath provided and left in it, he hath mixed his labor with it, and joined to it something that is his own, and thereby makes it his property.[41]

According to Velasquez, this interesting blending of Locke and papal teaching entered Catholic teaching through the influence of the Jesuit Luigi Taparelli D'Azeglio in his book *Saggio teoretico di diritto naturale appogiato sul fatto* written in 1840.[42] Leo used this formulation to argue that property is a natural right, thereby undercutting the earlier ecclesial tradition of the priority of the communality of all property. Werhane notes that this position of Leo's does not soften the claim "that one has rights to property so long as one makes good use of that property and so long as there is enough property left for others."[43] When this is coupled with Leo's other statement that "it is a duty, not of justice (except in extreme cases), but of Christian Charity" (19) to share with the poor out of one's superfluity, a strong case would seem to be made for the inviolability of the natural right to private property as well as a strong case for individualism.

However, Werhane, in a very interesting argument, makes the case that the key to reconciling the right to ownership of property and social obligation is stewardship. Her point is that Leo links rights and obligations and that stewardship is the mediator between the two based on his distinguishing between ownership and just ownership: "Just ownership requires meeting one's obligations both to the poor and to workers."[44] In the case of the poor this requires the duty of charity or benevolence, "a matter of spiritual commitment. One need not be benevolent nor is benevolence enforceable."[45] In the case of workers, just ownership requires meeting one's obligations to one's workers, obligations that are analogous to the duties that the head of the family has to the family. A key qualification, however, is that "the encyclical, then, does not question the interests of ownership, but links those natural rights with duties of stewardship. Because stewardship is a natural obligation it is enforceable by the state when owners are negligent."[46]

This concept of stewardship, later taken up in Vatican II, provides an interesting and important resolution to the tension on the right of property set up by the juxtaposition of Thomistic and Lockean thinking in the encyclical.

> Thus *Rerum Novarum* challenges both Marxism and economic egoism. It links alienation to poor working conditions and the inability to own property rather than to the nature of work itself. The economic leveler of greed is not socialism nor the market but the obligation to expand and extend property ownership. Stewardship thus conceived as linking property with concomitant obligations implies a sense of social justice parallel to the demands of the nineteenth-century populists that safeguard individualism without sacrificing the goal of economic redistribution.[47]

Corporatism

The relation between workers and employers is one of the more critical questions in the encyclical. The publication of the encyclical was preceded by a lengthy debate on the Continent about this relation. Additionally, this debate was conducted in a context of fear of infiltration of workers' associations by socialists and/or Communists as well as concern that workers were motivated by greed and that giving workers too much power could disrupt the class system imposed by nature. Yet many realized that the conditions of the workers were in many cases truly desperate. Something needed to be done, if not out of concern for the well-being of workers, as least so that there would not be a revolution. The general frame of the debate is cast in terms of the corporatist movement and the trade union movement, that is, between organizations composed of workers and employers or organizations composed of workers alone.

Corporatism was not a single movement, but an idea developed by a variety of individuals in different countries. In many ways it was a reaction to the social and economic disruption that followed the Industrial Revolution, but it was also fed in part by a desire to restore the medieval guild system as well as strong elements of ultramontanism and restoration of the monarchy. It sought, in short, a restoration of society as it had been while attempting to come to terms with capitalism and the industrialization of the workforce.

For example, Karl von Vogelsang, an Austrian industrialist who was influenced by the ideas of Bishop von Ketteler and the romantic social thought of Adam Müller, came to see the ideal society as "one in which horizontal class divisions would be replaced by vertical, hierarchical divisions of various broad economic sectors, the three most important being large industry, the small craft trades and the shops, and agriculture."[48] The goal of this was to absorb the workers into larger elements of society, eliminate usury, introduce self-management and reduce bureaucracy, return to traditional social structures, and rely on a monarchy for self-defense.[49]

Léon Harmel, a Belgian who moved with his father to Reims, took charge of his father's factory in 1854. As owner, he worked out a four-step program for a Christian factory, a model of contemporary Christian corporatism as a replacement for the medieval system.

> First he would create a hard core of practicing Catholics, a few in each age group; around them he would form religious associations to draw in the others; the third stage was to found "economic institutions" (social institutions building on those already in place and managed largely by the workers themselves); and the fourth was to cap it all off with a worker-management organism to administer the whole complex.[50]

There are two key elements here: the heavily Catholic nature of the organization and the participation of workers in management, although a heavy dose of paternalism was added in for the workers' own good. Interestingly enough, though these ideas were seminal in the development of the corporatist model, Harmel himself gradually moved to a position of associations comprised of workers only, thus undercutting a key feature of the model.

René de la Tour du Pin, an early French convert to social reform who was aware of Harmel's early ideas, saw corporatism as consisting of social and economic reforms as well as religious and cultural ones. Each citizen would be placed in a particular category according to his or her economic role. They would then elect delegates to a national assembly. Thus the phrase "la corporation libre dans le corps d'état organise."[51] His vision saw three levels of organization: "a factory corporation, a regional mixed commission or union of half employers and half employees of the same industry would be the second level, and a 'corporative senate' elected by the mixed unions would represent the 'organized people' at the national level."[52] These sectors would be formed around four functions: "(1) religious and moral interests (education, arts, family, and personal nature); (2) public interests (public services and authorities); (3) agriculture interests; and (4) industrial and commercial interests."[53] No executive branch was apparently needed because that would come from "an emanation of the royal power, the indispensable keystone of the corporative system."[54] Yet in spite of this royalist perspective, ultimately responsible for its downfall, du Pin's corporatist theory did initiate a participatory element for workers into the larger social discussion.

Another part of the corporatist movement was the Oeuvre des circles catholiques d'ouvriers (OCCO), founded by du Pin and his colleague de Mun. The heart of the movement was the circle composed of workers who were beyond their apprenticeship. Each circle had clubrooms, a chapel, and a chaplain. Additionally,

> each circle would also have a committee recruited from the *classes dirigéantes* and divided into four sections: publicity, club activities, finances and studies. From the interactions of the two levels, that of the workers and that of the upper classes, under the benign guidance of religion, would result the restoration of the social health of France.[55]

Two elements were critical in this particular mix: first, a healthy dose of ultramontist orientation, and second, a heavy dose of paternalism: "They [the founders] regarded the working class as a whole as 'children,' at best as younger 'brothers' prone to join revolutionary movements."[56] Thus it was necessary for the Church to be an influence through chaplains and the upper classes. Though the movement grew to around 375 circles, membership suffered under the presence of a Republican government in France. The OCCO could not withstand the introduction of more democratic participatory policies.

The Fribourg Union was a series of seven meetings in Switzerland that brought together the leading Catholic proponents of corporatism to discuss and draft position papers. They shared a common belief that

> liberalism (individualism) in both the political and the economic realms had brought about nothing but grief. What they wanted to get at were the applications of associationist principles that would enable the twentieth century to enjoy the benefits that they thought the pre-Revolutionary guilds and other professional groupings had conferred upon medieval Christendom.[57]

A critical moment came for this group when, in 1888, Leo requested a report from them. They responded rapidly with papers on topics such as the dignity of labor and the laborer, minimum wages for the laborer, property ownership, opposition to economic liberalism, a willingness to appeal to the government to correct free market excesses, and the corporatist organization of society. While no particular recommendations of the Union made their way into the encyclical, its spirit and concerns certainly helped shape various directions in the encyclical.

But this was not through a lack of effort on the part of Matteo Liberatore, the author of the first draft of RN who also served as one of the redactors of subsequent editions. Liberatore himself said, "It seems evident now that the one practical remedy is to restore the old corporations of arts and trades (in English, guilds) with such modifications as the altered conditions of the times might require."[58] As he then notes, this too was the suggestion of Leo XIII in the encyclical *Humanum genus* (1884). There Leo called for using the pattern of the guilds not only as a way of aiding workers but also as responding to what he perceived as destructive sects such as the Masons, against whom this encyclical was written.[59] Liberatore continues in the defensive posture by arguing that the Revolution of 1789, combined with the later effects of the Industrial Revolution and contemporary developments in France in particular, destroyed the guilds and thus "broke the moral connection between the master and the operative. It became a mere question of buying and selling, by which the workman sells the commodity, labour, and the master buys it by paying wages. Thus paid, all relation between them ceases."[60] The conclusion that Liberatore draws is that "nothing but a return to the old Corporations can remedy the disorder. . . . It would bind him [the worker] to the master in fraternal friendship, unite their interests, bring them permanently together, and form, as it were, the organization of mutual good will."[61] Those who would study this question further are referred to the book *Manuel d'une corporation chrétienne,* authored by the one whom Liberatore calls "the incomparable Léon Harmel."[62]

And thus corporatism did make it into the first draft. "However, the cure for the difficulties of the working class should come from the workers themselves. In which way? Through the use of the corporatist model."[63] This perspective did not, however, make it into Zigliarra's draft because of his renunciation of a Christian social order in favor of professional organizations or trade unions.[64] But corporatism found its way back into the final Italian text edited by Zigliarra, Mazzali, and Liberatore. Seeking to find a remedy for workers, the text asks how this is to be done. The answer is, "principally by virtue of the corporatist model. In past times, the industrial corporatist model had some admirable accomplishments."[65] However, in the margin there is a note apparently written by Mazzali asking, "Solamente?"[66] The first Latin text *Causa est* translates this Italian sentence faithfully: "Idque virtute Collegiorum."[67] However, this phrase "Idque virtute Collegiorum" does not make it to the second Latin text *Excitâ semel.* Then ten lines later, in the *Causa est* draft we have the text: "It is gratifying to know that there are actually in existence not a few societies of this nature, but it were greatly to be desired that they should multiply and become more effective,"[68] a phrase taken from the final Italian draft. This phrase is repeated exactly in the *Excitâ semel* text. However, according to the textual notations of Antonazzi, in the penultimate draft of RN, the phrase "societies, consisting either of workmen alone, or of workmen and employers together" was inserted into the text.[69]

Thus in number 36 of the final text of RN, this sentence reads: "It is gratifying to know that there are actually in existence not a few societies of this nature, consisting either of workmen alone, or of workmen and employers together; but it were greatly to be desired that they should multiply and become more effective."[70]

The question, of course, is, Who inserted this phrase? Jarlot strongly asserts: "Evidemment, de Léon XIII personnellement."[71] His argument follows the thinking of Antonazzi, who argued in the introduction to his critical edition of the text that Leo kept a hand in the editing process.[72] Jarlot, however, suggests that a degree of influence on Leo himself might have come from the American Cardinal Gibbons, who traveled to Rome to make a direct appeal to Leo on behalf of the Knights of Labor, an organization that consisted of workers only.[73] While some of the problems of the Knights came from suspicions of Canadian bishops that it was a secret society, had the text of RN followed the corporatist position, membership in such independent unions would have been very difficult for Catholics, and the Church in the United States in particular would have been in a very untenable position with respect to labor reform. And thus the labor movement, particularly in the United States, would have had an entirely different history. The upshot of this insertion is that the encyclical supported either the organization of workers only or of workers and management combined. This support, while not necessarily implying a rejection of corporatist principles or the model of vocational groups to help solve problems in particular industries, did contribute, after many years, to the decline of the corporatist movement and its emphasis that workers should be under the protection and guidance of management and to the development of a strong labor movement under the direction of the workers themselves.

REACTIONS TO THE DOCUMENT

Given the complex world in which RN was promulgated, it is not surprising that reactions to it varied. According to Wallace, general European reaction was favorable, though response varied with ideological persuasion. The liberals of the day were more skeptical, seeing it representing a shift in allegiance from the rich to the poor. Moderates found it modestly liberal with some surprising democratic tendencies. The socialists found it wanting on many levels. But not surprising at all, "ultraconservatives criticized it for leaning so far toward the side of the poor. Revolutionaries asked bitter questions about the Pope's attitude toward property."[74] No group, apparently, was satisfied with the positions of the encyclical. All thought it was lacking in critical issues and that it surrendered too much to "the other side," whoever that might be.

Questions of exegesis did crop up: What was frugal comfort? Should a single worker receive the same salary as one with a large family? What was a legitimate amount to save for future needs? In France, apparently some bishops were less than thrilled with the document and interpreted it in light of their interests. But *Univers*, a journal faithful to the papal cause, "published in parallel columns those opinions and the words of the encyclical."[75]

One important part of the European reception of the encyclical was the ultramontanist context in which it was promulgated. Thus "twenty years after the proclamation of papal infallibility, the encyclical was presented as binding even in its details. Georges Goyau spoke of 'the social dogma of the church.'"[76] Yet, it was clear that such dogma had limits, as Archbishop Doutreloux of Liège discovered when conservative Catholics threatened an economic boycott of diocesan charities unless he curtailed a particular seminary professor because of his liberal teachings. Finally, Doutreloux prepared a pastoral letter incorporating themes of RN. Since he submitted the letter to Rome in advance of publication, others were able to use this advance notice to prepare another perspective for employers. "All this democracy, they stated, was merely the product of overeducated and underemployed minds, the rotten fruit of too much schooling; these middle-class busybodies roused discontent in 'the people' who never before dreamed that they were suffering from injustices."[77]

There was a different sensibility among some employers. However much Harmel, whose book on corporatism had been extolled by Liberatore, continued to feel a great deal of responsibility for "his" workers, he also began to see changes approaching. "In 1889, Harmel welcomed a future in which the working classes would make their voices heard by turning their numerical superiority into effective political majorities."[78] He was thus already predisposed to the direction taken by Leo XIII. Interestingly, in light of RN's publication, workers began asking if Christianity could support their demands. This resulted in the development of several study circles in the north of France organized by the workers themselves. Harmel was asked to join in and "it is a measure of his stature in the history of social Catholicism that he did not try to refashion this exotic sprout of the labor movement on Catholic soil into an object of direct pastoral concern, in accordance with the principles expressed in his *Catéchisme du Patron* (1889)."[79]

Even though Leo XIII supported the Knights of Labor and the encyclical opened the door to the union movement, particularly in the United States, Gilligan argues that in America "there was a noticeable lack of enthusiasm for its clear and powerful message."[80] Part of this was because some saw too close a relation between some of Leo's ideas and those of Karl Marx, particularly with regard to Leo's critique of substandard wages that led to deep poverty, a situation reinforced by workers' being required to sign what was called a "yellow dog" contract: "the individual worker not only signed a contract to accept what the boss cared to pay him, but agreed never to join a union and to inform on those who did."[81]

Part of the reason for the lack of reception for RN was the state of American Catholicism, particularly as Catholics were being accused of being under the influence of a foreign power and thus un-American. Additionally, few workers had hope in social reform, a sentiment enforced by the courts. Legislation favorable to workers was "immediately stricken down by court opinions that cited the sanctity of contract, or the legal inability of states to interfere with interstate commerce."[82] Then, too, not all had the opportunity of education, and an opportunity for disseminating encyclical teachings was missed, the most prominent example of which was Al Smith's famous statement during his presidential campaign, as phrased in the version by the Jesuit John Coleman: "Would someone please tell me what is an encyclical?"[83]

NOTES

1. Paul Misner, *Social Catholicism in Europe: From the Onset of Industrialization to the First World War* (New York: Crossroad, 1991), 8.

2. Ibid., 11.

3. Ibid., 13.

4. Ibid., 14.

5. For part of this development, see James F. Keenan, "The Casuistry of John Mair, Nominalist Professor of Paris," in *The Context of Casuistry*, ed. James F. Keenan and Thomas A. Shannon (Washington, D.C.: Georgetown University Press, 1995), 85–103.

6. Misner, *Social Catholicism in Europe*, 21.

7. Ibid., 73.

8. Ibid., 79.

9. Lillian Parker Wallace, *Leo XIII and the Rise of Socialism* (Durham, N.C.: Duke University Press, 1996), 296.

10. For an overview of the *Kulturkampf*, see Ronald J. Ross, *The Failure of Bismarck's Kulturkampf: Catholicism and State Power in Imperial Germany, 1871–1877* (Washington, D.C.: Catholic University of America Press, 1998).

11. Joseph N. Moody, ed., *Church and Society: Catholic Social and Political Thought and Movements, 1789–1950* (New York: Arts, 1953), 456.

12. Ibid., 457.

13. Ibid., 460.

14. For a sample of his writings, see Cardinal H. E. Manning, *The Dignity and Rights of Labour* (London: Burns, Oates, and Washbourne, 1934).

15. Wallace, *Leo XIII and the Rise of Socialism*, 190.

16. As cited in ibid.

17. Normand Paulhus, "Fribourg Union," in *The New Catholic Dictionary of Social Thought*, ed. Judith

A. Dwyer (Collegeville, Minn.: Liturgical, 2001), 405.

18. For samples of von Ketteler's writings, see *The Social Teachings of Wilhelm Emmanuel von Ketteler*, trans. Rupert J. Ederern (Washington, D.C.: University Press of America, 1977).

19. For a good overview, see H. Daniel-Rops, *The Church in the Eighteenth Century* (New York: E. P. Denton, 1964), esp. 210–41.

20. Ibid., 191.

21. Gerald A. McCool, *Catholic Theology in the Nineteenth Century: The Quest for a Unitary Method* (New York: Crossroad, 1977), 21.

22. Ibid., 22.

23. Ibid.

24. Roger Aubert, ed., *The Church in a Secularized Society* (Mahwah, N.J.: Paulist, 1978), illustration A3.

25. E. E. Y. Hales, *The Catholic Church in the Modern World* (Garden City, N.Y.: Image, 1960), 113.

26. McCool, *Catholic Theology in the Nineteenth Century*, 32.

27. Ibid., 167.

28. Ibid., 232.

29. Paul Misner, "Antecedents of *Rerum Novarum* in European Catholicism," in *On the Condition of Labor and the Social Question One Hundred Years Later*, ed. Thomas O. Nash, Toronto Studies in Theology, no. 69 (Lewiston, N.Y.: Edwin Mellen, 1991), 211–20. This article is the clearest presentation of the authorship of the document, together with an excellent summary of the main streams of influence.

30. Joseph N. Moody, "Leo XIII and the Social Crisis," in *Leo XIII and the Modern World*, ed. Edward T. Gargan (New York: Sheed and Ward, 1961), 75. For a more detailed analysis, see Georges Jarlot, "Les avant-projets de *Rerum novarum* et les 'anciennes corporations,'" *Nouvelle revue théologique* 81 (1959): 60–77. For the critical edition of *Rerum novarum*, see Giovanni Antonazzi's *L'Enciclia Rerum Novarum, Texto authentico e redazioni preparatorie dai documenti originali* (Roma: Edizione de Storia e Letteratura, 1957). In the following presentation of the development of the text, I am following Antonazzi's version, but framed with some of Misner's interpretations.

31. Antonazzi, *L'Enciclia Rerum Novarum*, 22.

32. See also Jarlot, "Les avant-projets," 62, no. 10. For further discussion of the development of the text, see 62ff.

33. Misner, "Antecedents," 212.

34. Ibid., 215–16.

35. One can find an interesting overlap in these main themes of the encyclical in the 1869 essay, "The Labor Movement and Its Goals in Terms of Religion and Morality" of Bishop von Ketteler, in which he identifies six demands of labor: wages that reflect the true value of labor; a reduction of the hours of work; provision for days of rest; a ban on labor for children of mandatory school age; the prohibition of female labor, both of mothers and young women, from factory work. See *The Social Teachings of Wilhelm Emmanuel von Ketteler*, 438–63.

36. Misner, *Social Catholicism in Europe*, 39.

37. Ibid., 40.

38. Ibid., 143.

39. Manuel Velasquez, "*Gaudium et Spes* and the Development of Catholic Social-Economic Teaching," in *Questions of Special Urgency*, ed. J. A. Dwyer (Washington, D.C.: Georgetown University Press, 1986), 197.

40. Cited in Ronald F. Duska, "The U.S. Bishops and Capitalism: An Unstable Alliance?" *Peace and Justice Studies* 1 (1989): 57–79.

41. Cited in ibid., 68.

42. Velasquez, "*Gaudium et Spes* and Development," in *Questions of Special Urgency*, ed. J. A. Dwyer, 197, no. 8.

43. Patricia Werhane, "The Obligatory Nature of Stewardship in *Rerum Novarum* and Its Relevance to the American Economy," in *Rerum Novarum: Celebrating 100 Years of Catholic Social Thought*, ed. Ronald F. Duska (Lewiston, N.Y.: Edwin Mellen, 1991), 190.

44. Ibid., 195.

45. Ibid.

46. Ibid., 196.

47. Ibid., 197.

48. Cited in Misner, *Social Catholicism in Europe*, 171.

49. Ibid.

50. Ibid., 133.

51. Ibid., 180.

52. Ibid.

53. Ibid.

54. Ibid., 179.

55. Ibid., 154.

56. Ibid.

57. Ibid., 204.

58. Matteo Liberatore, *Principles of Modern Economy*, trans. Edward Heneage Dering (New York: Benziger, 1981), 279. See also J. N. Moody, "Leo XIII and the Social Crisis," in *Leo XIII and the Modern World*, ed. Edward T. Gargan, 76.

59. Leo XIII, *Humanum genus*, in *The Great Encyclical Letters of Pope Leo XIII* (New York: Benziger, 1903), 203–4.

60. Liberatore, *Principles*, 283.

61. Ibid., 284.

62. Ibid., 294–95.

63. "Ma il rimedio ai mali della classe operaia deve venire principalmente dagli stessi lavoratore. In che modo? Mediante la Corporazione." G. Antonazzi, *L'Enciclica Rerum Novarum*, 156, lines 1599–604. (Trans. H. J. Manzari, Department of Humanities and Arts, Worcester Polytechnic Institute [WPI]).

64. Jarlot, "Les avant-projects," 61.

65. "In virtù principalmente della corporazione. Le corporacone industriale nei tempi antichi han fatto cose mirabili." Antonazzi, *L'Enciclica Rerum Novarum*, 156, lines 1602–4. (Trans. H. J. Manzari, WPI). The English translation follows the Italian text that uses the word *corporazione* in both phrases. The English translation is "association" (RN 36).

66. Antonazzi, *L'Enciclica Rerum Novarum*, no. for line 1602.

67. Ibid., 156 (lines 1602–5, column b).

68. Ibid., 158 (lines 1614–16). "Vulgo coiri eius generis societates, gratum est; optandum vero ut numero et actuosa virtute crescant."

69. Ibid., 159, no. for lines 1613–14. "societates, sive totas ex opificibus conflatas, sive ex utroque ordine mixtas."

70. Ibid., (lines 1613–16). "Vulgo coiri eius generis societates, sive totas ex opificibus conflates, sive ex utroque ordine mixtas, gratum est: optandum vero ut numero et actuosa virtute crescant." My emphasis.

71. Jarlot, "Les avant-projects," 67.

72. Antonazzi, *L'Enciclica Rerum Novarum*, 1ff.

73. Jarlot, "Les avant-projects," 73; Antonazzi, *L'Enciclica Rerum Novarum*, 44.

74. Wallace, *Leo XIII and the Rise of Socialism*, 275.

75. Ibid., 276.

76. Misner, *Social Catholicism in Europe*, 222.

77. Ibid., 225.

78. Ibid., 228.

79. Ibid., 229.

80. John J. Gilligan, "The Church and the Working Poor," in *Rerum Novarum: A Symposium Celebrating 100 Years of Catholic Social Thought*, Symposium Series, ed. Ronald F. Duska, vol. 29 (Lewiston, N.Y.: Edwin Mellen, 1991), 65.

81. Ibid., 69.

82. Ibid., 71.

83. John A. Coleman, "What Is an Encyclical? Development of Church Social Teaching," *Origins* 11 (June 4, 1981): 35.

SELECTED BIBLIOGRAPHY

Antonazzi, Giovanni. *L'Enciclia Rerum Novarum. Texto authentico e redazioni preparatorie dai documenti originali*. Roma: Edizione de Storia e Letteratura, 1957. This is the collection of the Italian and Latin drafts of RN. There is also a 1991 edition of this volume.

Bock, Edward C. *Wilhelm von Ketteler, Bishop of Mainz: His Life, Times, and Ideas*. Lanham, Md.: University Press of America, 1977. A general introduction to one of the early contributors to the social ethics tradition.

Calvez, Jean Yves, and Jacques Perrin, eds. *The Church and Social Justice: The Social Teaching of the Popes from Leo XIII to Pius XII, 1878–1958*. Translated by J. R. Kirwan. Chicago: Henry Regnery, 1961. A good overview of key themes in the encyclicals.

Coleman, John A. "What Is an Encyclical? Development of Church Social Teaching." *Origins* 11 (June 4, 1981): 34–41. An important discussion of the genre of social teaching.

Dorr, Donal. *Option for the Poor: A Hundred Years of Vatican Social Teaching*. Maryknoll, N.Y.: Orbis, 1983. An excellent thematic, historical, and ethical discussion of core themes in the encyclicals.

Duska, Ronald. "The U.S. Bishops and Capitalism: An Unstable Alliance." *Peace and Justice Studies* 1 (1989): 57–79. A thoughtful comparison between social teaching and a critical economic theory.

Duska Ronald F., ed. *Rerum Novarum: A Symposium Celebrating 100 Years of Catholic Social Thought*. Symposium Series, vol. 29. Lewiston, N.Y.: Edwin Mellen, 1991. A very helpful collection of thematic essays on RN.

Dwyer, Judith A., ed. *Questions of Special Urgency*. Washington, D.C.: Georgetown University Press, 1986. A comprehensive overview of key questions related to the social teaching of the Church.

Gargan, Edward T., ed. *Leo XIII and the Modern World.* New York: Sheed and Ward, 1961. A good orientation to the world in which RN was written and to which it was addressed.

Gargan, Edward T., and Raymond H, Schmandt, eds. "Selected Bibliography." In *Leo XIII and the Modern World.* New York: Sheed and Ward, 1961. A general bibliography of Leo XIII.

Giblin, Marie J. "Corporatism." In *The New Dictionary of Catholic Social Thought.* Edited by Judith A. Dwyer, 245–46. Collegeville, Minn.: Liturgical, 2001. A clear presentation of a key term in early Catholic social teaching.

Hales, E. E. Y. *The Catholic Church in the Modern World.* Garden City, N.Y.: Image, 1960. Excellent presentation of the historical context in which the Church was involved and to which it addressed its teaching.

Hobgood, Mary E. *Catholic Social Teaching and Economic Theory: Paradigms in Conflict.* Philadelphia: Temple University Press, 1991. A very thoughtful examination and critique of Catholic social teaching from a socialist perspective.

Jarlot, Georges. "Les avant-projets de *Rerum Novarum* and les 'Anciennes Corporations.'" *Nouvelle Revue Théologique* 81 (1959): 60–77. A discussion of some of the economic and ethical ideas that helped form a context for RN.

Ketteler, Wilhelm E. von. *The Social Teachings of Wilhelm Emmanuel Von Ketteler.* Translated by Rupert J. Ederer. Washington, D.C.: University Press of America. 1981. A collection of key writings and sermons that helped set a context for social Catholicism in Germany.

Liberatore, Matteo. *Principles of Modern Economy.* Translated by Edward Heneage Dering. New York: Benziger, 1981. A collection of the economic writings of one of the drafters of RN.

Manning, Cardinal H. E. *The Dignity and Rights of Labour.* London: Burns, Oates, and Washbourne, 1934. The writings of an early British contributor to the social teaching tradition.

McCool, Gerald A. *Catholic Theology in the Nineteenth Century: The Quest for a Unitary Method.* New York: Crossroad, 1977. A comprehensive overview of the development of Catholicism in nineteenth-century Europe.

Misner, Paul. *Social Catholicism in Europe: From the Onset of Industrialization to the First World War.* New York: Crossroad, 1991. The most thorough examination of the social and theological context out of which Catholic social teaching emerged.

——. "Antecedents of *Rerum Novarum* in European Catholicism." In *On the Condition of Labor and the Social Question One Hundred Years Later.* Edited by Thomas O. Nash, 211–20. Toronto Studies in Theology, no. 69. Lewiston, N.Y.: Edwin Mellen, 1991. A brief overview of core themes in European Catholicism that influenced the development of RN.

Moody, Joseph N., ed. *Church and Society: Catholic Social and Political Thought and Movements, 1789–1950.* New York: Arts, 1953. Solid thematic review of the relation of Catholic social teaching and political movements and ideas.

——. "Leo XIII and the Social Crisis." In *Leo XIII and the Modern World.* Edited by Edward T. Gargan. New York: Sheed and Ward, 1961. A focused discussion of how Leo XIII began to address the social issues of the day.

Paulhus, Normand. "Freibourg Union." In *New Dictionary of Catholic Social Thought.* Edited by J. A. Dwyer, 404–5. Collegeville, Minn.: Liturgical, 2001. A thorough and significant presentation of the ideas of a set of meetings that provided important thematic ideas for the development of RN.

Pope, Stephen J. "Rerum Novarum." In *New Dictionary of Catholic Social Thought.* Edited by J. A. Dwyer, 828–44. Collegeville, Minn.: Liturgical, 2001. Excellent essay that assesses the significance of the encyclical as well as examines its teaching.

Velasquez, Manuel. "*Gaudium et Spes* and the Development of Catholic Social-Economic Teaching." In *Questions of Special Urgency.* Edited by J. A. Dwyer, 173–99. Washington, D.C.: Georgetown University Press, 1986. Presentation of the thematic development of social teaching.

Wallace, Lillian Parker. *Leo XIII and the Rise of Socialism.* Durham, N.C.: Duke University Press, 1996. Accessible biography of Leo XIII.

Werhane, Patricia. "The Obligatory Nature of Stewardship in *Rerum Novarum* and Its Relevance to the American Economy." In *Rerum Novarum: A Symposium Celebrating 100 Years of Catholic Social Thought.* Symposium Series, vol. 29. Edited by Ronald Duska, 184–97. Lewiston, N.Y.: Edwin Mellen, 1991. A very interesting discussion of the concept of stewardship and how it functions in RN and its relation to contemporary American Catholic social teaching.

CHAPTER

6

Commentary on *Quadragesimo anno* (*After Forty Years*)

CHRISTINE FIRER HINZE

INTRODUCTION

Issued May 15, 1931, by Pope Pius XI to commemorate the fortieth anniversary of Pope Leo XIII's *Rerum novarum*, *Quadragesimo anno*, *Forty Years After: On Reconstructing the Social Order and Perfecting It Conformably to the Precepts of the Gospel*, recalls, develops, and sharpens four major contributions of the 1891 letter by (1) confirming the Church's solidarity with the cause of workers; (2) condemning enormous and, amid worldwide depression, worsening disparities between a rich elite and a large suffering majority; (3) clarifying the rights and mutual duties of poor and wealthy, labor and capital; and (4) pointing out a "safe road" for repairing socioeconomic ills that eschews the errors of liberal individualism and fascist or community collectivism—a spiritually grounded "reconstruction of the social order" along corporatist lines, hand in hand with "a reform of Christian morals."

In setting into motion behind *Rerum novarum* what would come to be known as "a tradition of modern papal social teaching," QA was intended to be *Rerum novarum*'s "brilliant complement and glorious confirmation."[1] QA's tone and content, however, along with its emphasis on organized lay social apostolates, bespeak a Church less marginalized and more self-consciously engaged on the stage of contemporary history than was the case in Leo XIII's day. Longer than its forerunner by a third, QA set out proposals for reform that echoed Leo's emphases on collaboration rather than class conflict and a renewal of Christian morals as prerequisite for social renewal. But, unlike its predecessor, QA is more sharply critical of existing conditions and more insistent on the need for structural change. Its description of the concepts of "social justice" and "subsidiarity," and its controversial proposal for a renovated, organic social order based on occupational groups or "orders" are also among this encyclical's original contributions.

OUTLINE OF THE DOCUMENT

QA contains an introduction, three principal divisions, and a conclusion. The introduction (1–15) recalls the nineteenth-century historical and economic conditions that occasioned Pope Leo's encyclical and describes its contributions. Forty years later, amid persisting economic injustice and altered social circumstances, Pius XI revisits the concerns that animated Leo's groundbreaking letter. Pius dedicates his encyclical to three goals that constitute QA's major divisions: (1) "to recall the great benefits which *Rerum novarum* brought to the Catholic Church and to the world at large" (16–40); (2) to vindicate Leo's social and economic doctrine against certain doubts and misunderstandings that have since arisen, and to develop more fully some of its points, especially concerning property, uplifting the proletariat, just wages, and the proper reconstruction of the social and economic order (41–98); and (3) after evaluating modern economics and reexamining the nature of socialism, "to expose the root of the present social disorder," which is spiritual, and to point out the only effective cure and way to social transformation: "a Christian reform of morals" (99–150).

CONTEXT OF THE DOCUMENT

Pope Pius XI's pontificate spanned seventeen uneasy years (1922–39) from the aftermath of World War I, to the consolidation of the Russian communist regime and the rise of fascism in Italy and Nazism in Germany, to the deterioration of the international economy into worldwide depression and accompanying political unrest. He died in February 1939, months before the outbreak of World War II. Issued at precisely the midpoint of Pius's papacy, QA was written and promulgated in a climate thick with economic and political tension, which included strained Italian-Vatican relations despite the Lateran Treaty and Concordat with the government of Benito Mussolini that had been signed in February 1929. This treaty had relinquished Vatican claims to sovereignty over the former Papal States, including Rome, officially ratifying circumstances that had obtained since 1870. The Church maintained legal jurisdiction over the territory of Vatican City, now incorporated as its own 108.7-acre state. The Lateran pacts, moreover, promised protection of church ministries in three areas especially important to Pius XI: educating youth, upholding marriage and the family, and supporting the myriad associations that constituted the lifeblood of the Church's everyday activities. The government agreed to uphold Catholicism as its state religion, to enforce Catholic marriage laws, and to leave ecclesial associations free to carry out their pastoral and educational work.

But Mussolini treated these arrangements as befit his own interests. He touted himself as protector of Italy as a Catholic state, but in June 1931 he ordered numerous Catholic organizations closed down by police on the charge that they were functioning as political rather than religious entities. Coming within weeks of QA's issuance, this crackdown marked the dissolution of whatever good faith the Concordat had represented and prompted Pius to issue a sharply worded defense (*Non abbiamo bisogno*, June 29, 1931). QA played its part in the pope's ongoing tightrope walk aimed at maintaining the Church's mission as distinct from political engagement or civil control, while using ecclesial authority and clout in ways that challenged, if circumspectly, Mussolini's totalitarian designs.

In May 1931 Catholic Action organizations sponsored a series of public "*Rerum novarum* Celebrations," culminating in a gathering of over ten thousand international delegates in St. Peter's Square for QA's promulgation.[2] It was Pius's third major encyclical in the wake of the Lateran accords, following *Rappresentanti in terra, On the Christian Education of Youth* (December 31, 1929) and *Casti connubii*, *On Christian Marriage* (December 31, 1930). Though a religious statement by a religious leader, QA pronounced on economic and political matters. Given the encyclical's ambiguous evaluation of the syndicalist-corporatist government that Mussolini had installed, it is not surprising that some interpreted the celebrations and their keynote document as a political provocation.

QA and the circumstances in which it appears reflect a complex mix of socioeconomic and religious concerns, and of intra- and extraecclesial interests evident in modern Catholic social teaching as a whole. As official social teaching, QA belongs to the Church, but a Church directed *ad extra*, striving to engage, instruct, and serve a changing world. Issuing a major social encyclical to commemorate *Rerum novarum* was an innovation: neither of Pius's two predecessors (nor his successor, Pius XII) did so. QA thus set in place a "modern tradition of Catholic social teaching" flowing from *Rerum novarum* forward.[3] Henceforth, matters such as vulnerable workers and their families, economic and political arrangements, and social justice could no longer be consigned to that stalwart minority of socially minded Catholics whose work had formed the background for *Rerum novarum*. Rather, confirming Leo's work, but developing it in light of what John XXIII would later call "the signs of the times," QA helped assure that during the century to come, the Catholic Church would treat the task of relating faith to socioeconomic concerns as an integral dimension of its mission.

Despite QA's worldly subject matter, the impetus for its issuance was intensely religious. Pius's inaugural encyclical, *Ubi arcano Dei* (December 23, 1922), had articulated the goal of his papacy: to promote "the peace of Christ under the reign of Christ." In a world torn by strife, "the problem . . . is one of goodness in living and therefore of a right estimation of values." But the real root of modern social ills is not moral but spiritual: "humanity's apostasy from God."[4] If the evils besetting modern society are to be cured, and genuine peace—which encompasses both justice and charity—attained, God's reign must be restored to the heart of each person *and* to the heart of familial, political, and economic life. While acknowledging the legitimate autonomy of civil institutions (41), Pius insists that the Church, and the gospel she proclaims, hold the necessary key to social peace and well-being—a spiritual rejuvenation that inspires individuals and institutions to dedicate themselves anew to serving the kingdom of Christ and the common good.

The practical centerpiece of Pius XI's tripartite (education, family, and socioeconomic) Christian social agenda was his vision of the movement known as Catholic Action, a religious "apostolate of the [lay] faithful, who under the guidance of the bishops, put themselves at the service of the Church and assist her in the integral fulfillment of her pastoral ministry."[5] The key elements of Catholic Action envisaged by Pius were (1) the organization and coordination of multiple sorts of lay apostolates, (2) with the guidance and assistance of the clergy and bishops, (3) in the work of infusing Christian values and spirit into all corners of public as well as (4) private life. And the most urgent arena for Catholic action in his day, Pius believed, was helping the working classes, both materially and spiritually.[6]

While professedly nonpolitical, Catholic Action was to be nothing less than the religious equivalent of an army for Christ, working to transform the social order in the image of Christ's reign.[7] Inevitably, its engagement brought Catholic Action to the brink of politics. Supporters insisted that "Catholic Action is, by definition, spiritual and not material, divine not earthly, religious not political. Abstention . . . and indifference [to politics] is a root condition of its success." But its members "are not forbidden to participate *as individual citizens* in the political life of the day"[8] to ensure government by Christian principles.[9]

Catholic social action was not new to the Church. What was new was its specification by Pius XI, the "central, essential, importance" he attached to it, and "solicitude with which he watche[d] over it."[10] Through the diverse apostolates of Catholic action, Pius believed that gospel values could permeate and transform the stuff of daily life. Catholics' participation in these apostolates was to be the essential vehicle for applying the social doctrine of the Church.

PROCESS OF FORMULATION AND AUTHORSHIP

Authorship is officially attributed to Pius XI, and this commanding pope was indeed the force behind QA. Ambrogio Damiano Achille Ratti (1857–1939) was the son of a silk weaver. Ordained in Milan in 1879, Ratti earned doctorates in theology and canon law. A skilled mountaineer, in 1888 he became the first Italian to scale Monte Rosa on the Italian side. Ratti served at the Ambrosian Library in Milan, then from 1912 as vice prefect of the Vatican Library. Named papal nuncio to the new Polish Republic in 1918, he returned to Milan in 1921 as cardinal archbishop. Ratti brought to priestly ministry a keen intellect, cosmopolitan language and diplomatic skills, obvious personal piety and integrity, and a personality that combined the zest for measured risk-taking of an expert climber with a librarian's patient attention to detail. He also displayed an aptitude for leadership. Elected Pope Pius XI in 1922, his sixty-fifth year, he embarked on a remarkably active papacy over which he exercised firm direction. "The pope, and he alone, was in command."[11] As pope, he was "independent-minded, authoritarian, and unyielding in argument."[12] "The very type of an authoritarian pope,"[13] Pius was also regarded as a man of integrity, simplicity, and personal sanctity, especially devoted to Christ the King and the Sacred Heart of Jesus, to Mary, and to "the star" of his pontificate, Thérèse of Lisieux.[14]

Pius extended Vatican influence by employing the mass media to amplify the scope and influence of traditional forms of papal communication. The first pope to use a public address system, he also inaugurated Vatican City's radio station, delivering the first ever papal radio message on February 12, 1931. In promulgating QA, in his conflicts with Mussolini's regime, and in later moves such as the issuance of the German-language encyclical *Mit brennender Sorge* in 1937, Pius took advantage of the speed with which public statements of his, as well as symbolic events such as the *Rerum novarum* celebrations, could be communicated internationally by means of the press.[15]

Above all, Pius XI was a man dedicated to promoting the reign of Christ in a troubled world. By deep personal sanctity combined with zealous communal effort, he believed that Christians could advance that reign within the social order and that problems besetting society and economy could be ameliorated. This thoroughly religious and thoroughly social (contemplative/active) agenda is distilled in the pope's motto, "The peace of Christ in the reign of Christ." It was expressed liturgically in Pius's institution of the solemnity of Christ the King as a universal church festival (*Quas primas*, December 11, 1925) and, in that same year, his canonization of St. Thérèse of Lisieux. His spiritual/social agenda animated as well his love for the missions and his appreciation for the need for native clergy (whom he ordained in unprecedented numbers) to advance the gospel amid differing cultural circumstances. This same inseparable link between spiritual reform and social renovation is reflected in QA's subtitle, *On Reconstructing the Social Order and Perfecting It Conformably to the Precepts of the Gospel.*

When Pius XI determined in 1930 to issue a major encyclical commemorating *Rerum novarum*, he bypassed Vatican offices and asked Jesuit Superior General Father Vladimir Ledochowski to appoint a drafter expert in the relevant matters. The pope demanded that the work proceed in strict secrecy; only the drafter, Father Ledochowski, and the pope were to be involved.

Ledochowski appointed forty-year-old Jesuit Oswald von Nell-Breuning, a student of the political economics of the Jesuit Heinrich Pesch (1854–1926), who had received his doctorate in theology in 1928 with a dissertation on the morality of the stock market. Though largely self-taught in economics, Pesch had a budding scholarly reputation[16] and had been invited to participate in discussions of the Konigswinter Group, among such respected political economists as Gotz Briefs, Theodore Brauer, and his fellow Jesuit Gustav Gundlach. By Nell-Breuning's later account, probably the only one provided by an actual drafter of an encyclical, he approached his daunting assignment with a confidence resting partly in his excellent Jesuit education, partly in the knowledge that had gained respect within Catholic economic circles, and partly in his ability to consult his Konigswinter colleagues, especially Gundlach, about theoretical questions pertaining to his project without actually revealing it.

But his greatest confidence was in God's guidance of the Church he served. Typically for the time, Nell-Breuning assumed that the papal teaching office could not err. "My trust was decisive. The presence of the Holy Spirit would protect the Pope. No error of mine could get into the official teaching statement."[17] This same certitude imbued Pius XI's approach to church teaching on contemporary social questions.[18]

Writing took place over several months. Meeting briefly with the pope only once, Nell-Breuning submitted drafts through Father Ledochowski, who returned them with corrections and small amendments in the pope's hand. A substantive addition concerning corporatist syndicalism was written by the pope himself and included in the document at his request, eventually comprising numbers 91–96. This section became the subject of controversy and misunderstanding, but Nell-Breuning would criticize it openly only decades later, in the changed ecclesial climate following Vatican II.

ESSAY

QA's introduction (1–15) describes the context and the scope of Leo's 1891 encyclical (3–14). Toward the end of the nineteenth century, new economic and industrial developments had split society into two classes. One, smaller group enjoyed nearly all the comforts so plentifully supplied by modern invention (a capacity of modern economy both Leo and Pius acknowledge). A second class, made up of "the immense multitude of workingmen,"[19] struggled in vain to escape dire economic straits.

This was quite satisfactory to the wealthy, who saw it as "the consequence of *inevitable and natural economic laws*"—an interpretation Pius clearly does not share.[20] Elites were content "to abandon to charity alone the full care of relieving the unfortunate" "as though it were a task of charity to make amends" for what Pius calls "*the open violation of justice*," a violation tolerated, even at times sanctioned, by the state. But workers grew increasingly unwilling to submit to these harsh conditions. Those who were not misled by revolutionary extremists nonetheless felt keenly the need for profound change. Joining them were numbers of "social Catholics," clergy and lay, who had long toiled to relieve the undeserved poverty of propertyless workers and who refused to believe that "so enormous and unjust an inequality in the distribution of the world's goods" could correspond to God's designs. Far from accepting modern social arrangements as given, Pius views these yawning economic disparities as patently unjust; the institutions and practices that support them must, therefore, be reformed (3–5).

Good people determined to promote change searched for the proper way forward. In a climate rife with conflicting opinions, "the eyes of all, as often in the past, turned toward the Chair of Peter, that sacred repository of all truth whence words of salvation are dispensed to the whole world." Throngs flocked to the "feet of Christ's Vicar on earth, . . . begging . . . that at last a safe road might be pointed out to them." Heeding their pleas, Leo prayed, considered, and sought out the best counselors. Finally, by virtue of the teaching authority divinely committed to him, Leo undertook "to address himself to the entire Church of Christ and indeed the whole human race" on the social question (6–9). Pius's grandiloquent narration exhibits his own lofty understanding of papal authority and competence. As "Supreme Shepherd" the pope is universal guardian of everything intimately related to religion; this includes the moral aspects of society and economy.

In his historic letter, Pius continues, Leo, grieving for the misery and wretchedness oppressing so many, boldly took up the cause of workingmen who had been "surrendered, isolated and helpless," to the callousness of employers and the greed of unrestrained competition (RN 2). Leo saw that neither liberalism nor socialism was capable of properly addressing the problem, and that its solution could not be found "apart from the assistance of religion and the Church" (RN 13). Basing his teaching upon "unchanging principles drawn from right reason and divine revelation," he proclaimed "as one having authority"(Pius attributes to the pope Matt. 7:29's description of Jesus), the rights and mutual duties of the wealthy and poor, of capital and labor, and the part to be taken in upholding these by the Church, by the state, and by concerned persons (10–11).

Rerum novarum, Pius observes, elicited a variety of positive reactions, especially from

Christian workingmen, who now felt vindicated and defended by the "highest authority on earth." But because Leo's encyclical so "boldly attacked and overthrew the idols of liberalism, swept aside inveterate prejudices, and was so far and so unexpectedly ahead of its time," the "slow of heart ridiculed . . . the new social philosophy," and the timid "feared to scale its lofty heights." Still others, while professing to admire its message, regarded it as a utopian ideal, desirable, but practically unattainable (12–14).[21]

Part 1: Benefits Derived from Rerum novarum *(16–40)*

Pius XI first addresses the Church's response to Leo's encyclical (17–24). *Rerum novarum*'s socioeconomic doctrine was proclaimed by Leo and his successors, "who were ever careful to adapt it to the changing conditions of the times, and who never relaxed their paternal solicitude . . . particularly in defense of the poor and weak." This inspired many scholars to work toward developing a truly "Catholic social science" aimed at adapting to modern needs "the unchanging and unchangeable doctrine of the Church."[22] Accurately or not, Pius also detects *Rerum novarum*'s imprint in many social reforms; its principles, for instance, were incorporated in the regulations protecting labor rights drawn up in conjunction with peace treaties after the Great War[23] (17–22).

Rerum novarum spurred increased ecclesial efforts in many countries to uplift working persons. Episcopal-directed programs to imbue workingmen with the Christian spirit helped awaken in them a sense of their true dignity, fostering initiative and progress. Simultaneously, many new associations sprang up where wage earners of all sorts, under the Church's direction, could give and receive mutual assistance and support (23–24).

Responses by and impact on civil authorities are also enumerated (25–28). *Rerum novarum* underscored the civil power's duty to work zealously to ensure that laws, institutions, and administration promote and produce "public well being and private prosperity" (RN 26). Adumbrating his treatment of subsidiarity in QA (78–79), Pius notes that *Rerum novarum* supported a sphere of freedom of action for individual citizens and families, but adds that this principle is only valid as long as the common good is secured and no injustice is entailed. The rulers' duty is to protect the community in its various subsectors, and "in protecting the rights of individuals they must have special regard for the infirm and needy." (25) The rich stand in less need of help; vulnerable wage earners should be cared for and protected by the commonwealth (RN 29f.).

Rerum novarum newly focused and clarified Christian directions for reform based, according to Nell-Breuning, "on principles, not patchwork." Pius XI commends the emergence since 1891 of labor law, a new branch of jurisprudence dedicated to defending the rights of working people. Though actual labor legislation does not always accord with Leo's recommendations, much in these laws has contributed to improved conditions for workers.

By Pius's account, responses to Leo's clarion call for reform also came from workingmen, employers, and capitalists alike (29–38). *Rerum novarum* underscored workers' right and responsibility to engage in "self-help," understood not individualistically but communally, what Nell-Breuning calls "associational self-help." In opposition to liberalism's tendency to focus only on the individual even as it protects the collusion and cooperation among the rich and powerful, Leo championed working persons' rights to association. Specifically, he supported union formation and participation, either by workers and employers together, or in separate groups. Ideally, Catholics ought to form explicitly Catholic unions. Where religiously affiliated unions are not a realistic option, workers may enroll in unions which, while not exclusively Catholic, do not inhibit members' loyalty to Catholic principles and practices[24] (35). A major theme for Leo XIII, echoed by Pius XI, was the necessity of such associations for bettering workers' circumstances.

Rerum novarum, Pius concludes, has proven itself "the Magna Charta on which all Christian activities in social matters are ultimately based." But after forty years, new circumstances and questions have arisen. Doubts concerning the correct interpretation of certain of *Rerum novarum*'s teachings or their implications have led to sometimes acrimonious controversies, even among Catholics. Further, new needs emerging from changed social conditions necessitate "a more precise application and amplification" of Leo's doctrine (39–40). The present encyclical undertakes this task.

Part 2: Interpretation and Amplification of Rerum novarum's *Teaching (41–98)*

In the social and economic spheres, Pius XI stresses that the Church can "never relinquish her God-given task; of interposing her authority not indeed in technical matters, for which she has neither the equipment or the mission, but in all those matters that have a bearing on moral conduct." In Pius's natural law schema, economics and morality are distinct, but inextricably related. Economic science can identify attainable material ends and means, but morally attuned reason deduces the goal and point of the whole economic order, assigned by the Creator. Economic goals find their proper place within the universal order of ends and thereby assist persons toward the final end of all, God, our highest good. A naturally discernable set of moral purposes, then, undergirds a proper understanding of economy, purposes that form part of a universal tendency toward final union with God. Because in this worldview, "conflict between two true sciences is impossible,"[25] Pius is confident that good economics and good morals go hand in hand (41–43).

The pope, observes Nell-Breuning, does not explicitly name the material goal of economics here, for "the meaning of economics should be clear to every social-minded Catholic!" That goal is welfare: "the utilization of means for satisfying material demands, so as far as possible to supply all needs and an honest livelihood, sufficient to uplift persons to . . . [a] higher level of prosperity and culture."[26]

The Right of Property (44–52)

Pius XI notes that Leo XIII's defense of the right to property led some to falsely accuse the Church of upholding the wealthier classes against the proletariat. QA's next section therefore endeavors to provide a fuller, correct interpretation of Catholic teaching on ownership.

Pius first highlights the dual aspect of ownership: it is individual *and* social. The right to own private property is given by the Creator so that individuals might provide for their own needs and those of their families, but also so that "by means of it, goods which the Creator has destined for the human race may truly serve this purpose." "Some, denying the social and public aspect of ownership, threaten to succumb to individualism." "Others," rejecting or diminishing property's private and individual character, fall into collectivism. To choose either, Pius warns, is to "rush headlong into the quicksands of . . . modernism" (45–46). Seeking a more adequate way, he echoes Leo's insistence (RN 19) that "the right of property must be distinguished from its use." Commutative justice requires that we faithfully respect the possessions of others. How one uses one's possessions, though, while not always legally enforceable, is subject to the dictates of other virtues. Pius praises civil efforts to specify duties attaching to use in light of the requirements of the common good, but he warns that in so doing one must take care not to destroy or even weaken property's individual character (47–48).

Property's social character requires that owners take into account not only their advantage but the common good. To define the duties relevant to the common good is the function of government. And, "provided that natural and divine law be observed," public authority, when necessary for the sake of the common good, may specify more precisely for property owners the licit and illicit use of their property. History witnesses to the diversity and elasticity of property arrangements, but the state's right in this matter is limited. The "natural right" to possess and transmit property privately by inheritance must be kept intact; the property of the domestic household is anterior to the commonwealth; it is unlawful to exhaust individuals' means by crushing taxes and tributes. When, within proper limits, civil authority adjusts ownership to meet the needs of the public good, the greater justice of the commonwealth that results strengthens the legitimate right to private property (48–49). Pius concludes his comments on ownership with three additional affirmations: superfluous income's use is constrained by the obligations of charity, beneficence, and liberality; entrepreneurial investment of extra income that creates employment opportunities for others is an act of liberality especially appropriate to the present day; and one's labor earns a title to ownership only "from that which a man exercises as his own master, and by which some new form or new value is produced" (50–52).

Labor and Capital (53–58)

Addressed next are questions pertaining to capital and labor. All value produced through work or ingenuity depends on the prior God-given gift of the resources of nature. Right order in applying natural resources to human need is only possible when owners and laborers recognize that because they need each other, it is unjust for either to deny the other's contribution by claiming rights to the entire product of labor. Historically, it has been easier for owners to appropriate excessive advantages to the detriment of laborers. In modern economies, this was justified by the patently specious "liberal" claim that "an inexorable economic law" led all accumulation of capital to fall to the wealthy, while "the workingman must remain perpetually . . . reduced to the minimum needed for existence"—the so-called iron law of wages. Socialists countered this claim with an equally false principle: that all products and profits beyond those needed to repair or replace invested capital belong wholly to the workingman. Pius XI takes pains to denounce a subtly misleading form of the latter view that advocates state socialization of the means of production, "an alluring poison" that the unwary may too easily be led to consume (53–55).

Pius now restates "true teaching" concerning ownership, wealth, and its distribution. Quoting Leo, he recalls that "the earth though divided among private owners, ceases not thereby to minister to the needs of all" (56). Yet not every kind of distribution of wealth and property can ensure that all will acquire what they need. Economic opportunities and the fruits of wealth must be distributed among individuals and social classes such that the common good of all is promoted. The vast disparities between the few who hold excessive wealth and the many who live in destitution thus constitute a patent, grave evil in modern society. "Each class . . . must receive his due share, and the distribution of created goods must be brought into conformity with the demands of the common good and social justice" (57–58). This God-given law is grievously violated by a "winner-take-all" capitalism wherein wealthy classes assume that they get everything and the laborer nothing. It is also violated by socialist "labor theories of value" whereby propertyless wage earners demand for themselves all the fruits of production. More directly than Leo, Pius declares that a redistribution of wealth is needed to attain the common good of all; he introduces the term *social justice* to describe the situation in which the demands of the common good are honored and met by and for all members.

Uplifting the Working Class (59–62)

Continuing, Pius XI confirms what Leo XIII saw as the necessary aim for all contemporary social effort: the uplifting of the proletariat (*redemptionem proletariorum*) (59–62). Much of the worst "pauperism" of the late nineteenth century has been alleviated, yet *Rerum novarum*'s teachings on wage justice remain relevant and badly need to be reasserted. In more wealthy and developed countries, workers are no longer universally miserable and lacking the necessities of life. But—here Pius alludes presciently to the globalization of capitalism—since Leo's day manufacturing and industry have spread dramatically, from newly colonized countries to ancient civilizations of the Far East. In these areas, the numbers of propertyless working poor have increased exponentially, and their "groans mount to heaven." Additionally, a huge army of rural wage workers suffer extremely depressed conditions and lack hope of ever having a share in the land they till. Without prompt and effective remedies, both groups "will remain perpetually sunk in their proletarian condition."

Granting that pauperism and proletarianism are not identical, Pius regards the present inequitable conditions for workers as scant improvement. "The immense number of propertyless wage earners on the one hand, and the superabundant riches of the fortunate few on the other, are an unanswerable argument that the earthly goods so abundantly produced in this age of industrialism are far from rightly distributed and equitably shared" among the various classes. To redress this situation, just limits should be set on capitalist accumulation of the fruits of production, so that an ample sufficiency of those fruits is supplied to workingmen. Present inequities must be speedily corrected lest the disaffected turn to revolutionary forces, undermining peace.

Just Wages (63–75)

Redressing present inequities requires that wage earners be empowered to acquire, by skill and thrift, "a certain moderate ownership." To do this, workers must manage to save funds beyond what is needed for everyday subsistence. Therefore, as Leo saw, the question of just wages and how to attain them is of central importance (63; cf. RN 34).

Catholic teaching, Pius notes, does not reject wage contracts as unjust *in se*, but it does insist that such contracts are subject to the demands of justice. Today, the wage contract should whenever possible "be modified somewhat by a contract of partnership" whereby "workers and executives become sharers in the ownership or management, or participate in some way in the profits."[27] Such experiments may open fresh possibilities for workers to attain "moderate ownership." But identifying what constitutes an equitable wage remains a paramount concern. This determination must take into account a number of factors (63–68).

Labor, like ownership, has a social as well as a personal or individual aspect, and in order to appraise it justly and compensate it adequately, both dimensions must be taken into account. The fruits of labor result from an intimate collaboration among laborers and capital within an organic social body that should provide the protections of a juridical social order. From labor's dual character flow three important factors that must be considered in the fixing and regulation of wages: the worker's and his family's needs; the condition of the business enterprise in question; and the exigencies of the common welfare[28] (69–75).

"In the first place, the wage paid to the workingman must be sufficient for the support of himself and of his family." Here Pius XI specifies commutative justice's requirement, that the laborer's pay for work performed be sufficient to meet his needs, with a further demand of social justice referenced to the conditions of modern wage-based economy. In premodern economies all family members contributed toward household maintenance; today families are nearly wholly dependent on wages for their material survival. Further, in a wage-based economy, women's and children's economic contributions, traditionally unpaid and made within and around the domestic household, are removed from the productive equation. To respond by making women and children into wage earners, is, however, soundly rejected by both Pius and Leo, who insist that "it is wrong to abuse the tender years of children or the weakness of women." Consistent with the gender script that permeates his 1930 encyclical on marriage and family, *Casti connubii*, Pius XI insists that mothers perform their work at home or near the home, giving their time to domestic cares. "Intolerable, and to be opposed with all our strength" is "the abuse whereby mothers of families, because of the insufficiency of the father's salary, are forced to engage in gainful occupations outside the domestic walls, to the neglect of their own proper cares and duties, particularly the education of their children." Every effort must be made, therefore, to assure that "fathers of families receive a wage adequate to meet ordinary domestic needs." If in present conditions this is not always feasible, "social justice demands" that reforms be introduced which will guarantee every adult workingman such a wage[29] (71).

Second, "the condition of any particular business and of its owner must also come into question in settling the scale of wages." It is unjust to demand wages so high that an employer cannot pay them without ruin. Yet business owners have certain responsibilities, and if a business makes a smaller profit due to bad management, lack of enterprise, or out-of-date methods, "this is not a just reason for reducing the workingmen's wages." Pius XI's next statement reflects the sad reality confronting many depressed business concerns in 1931: "If, however, the business does not make enough money to pay the workman a just wage, either because it is overwhelmed with unjust burdens, or because it is compelled to sell its products at an unjustly low price, *those who thus injure it are guilty of grievous wrong*," for it is they who deprive workers of just wages and force them to accept lower terms. (Here Pius seems to attribute to actions of unnamed, evil individuals what were likely, at least in part, systemic or structural causes for deflation and unemployment.) To confront such difficulties, Pius urges employers and workers to band together, when appropriate with the assistance of public authority, to reach collaborative solutions that will best serve all parties concerned (71–72).

Third, the wage scale must be regulated with a view to the economic welfare of the whole people. Especially in light of the "dreadful scourge" of unemployment accompanying worldwide economic depression, opportunities for work must be provided to all those who are willing and able, and wage scales and product pricing must take into account likely effects on employment. The common welfare also requires that a balance be achieved in the proportion between pay scales for different jobs. Appealing to a favorite metaphor, Pius predicts that when all this is observed, the various branches of industry will combine "into one single organism and become members of a common body lending each other mutual help and service." The economic and social order will be soundly established, and attain its purpose, only "when it secures for all and each those goods which the wealth and resources of nature, technical achievement and the social organization of economic affairs can give." Aided by an honest livelihood, people can be uplifted to "that higher level of prosperity and culture which, provided it be used with prudence, is not only no hindrance but is of singular help to virtue" (73–75).

Reconstructing the Social Order (76–97)

Turning now to QA's main subject, Pius XI takes up "the most significant and vital [topic] of this Encyclical: the re-establishment of a truly Christian social order."[30] If what Leo initiated is to be secured and advanced, and even richer benefits are to accrue to the human family, "two things are particularly necessary: the reform of institutions and the correction of morals."

With respect to institutional reform, Pius says, "it is principally the state we have in mind." The modern state has become distended, overburdened, and increasingly ineffective. This is because, in an era of individualism, the highly developed social life that historically flourished in a variety of organically linked and robust institutions (joined in a graded hierarchical order) has been "all but ruined." Absent this rich social fabric, the state was left to face the individual alone, and is now encumbered with all the burdens once distributed across the associational network. The state, to its distinct detriment, has become "overwhelmed and submerged by endless affairs and responsibilities" (76–78).

Pius XI acknowledges that in modern society, much that formerly was performed by small associations can now be accomplished *only* by large ones. Emphasizing the mutual rights and duties of individuals and small groups within large, complex social organisms, Pius enunciates the much-cited principle of "subsidiarity": Just as it is wrong to take away from individuals what by their own ability and effort they can accomplish and commit it to the community, "so, too, it is an injustice, and at the same time both a grave evil and a disturbance of right order to transfer to the larger and higher collectivity functions which can be performed and provided for by less and subordinate bodies." This is because all social activity should "prove a help (*subsidium*) to the members of the body social," but never may destroy or absorb them. The state should thus leave it to these smaller groups to settle minor problems so that it can better carry out the tasks for which it alone is qualified, such as "directing, supervising, encouraging, restraining, as circumstances suggest or necessity demands." The more faithfully this principle of "subsidiarity" is followed, and a graded hierarchical order observed between various associations, the more effective will social authority be, and the happier and more prosperous the condition of the commonwealth (79–80).

From Class Conflict to Harmony among Societal "Orders" (81–87)

Pius XI now considers specific avenues toward renewing a robust associational commonwealth. To accomplish this goal, current divisions and strife between opposing classes must be overcome. Nell-Breuning avers that it is on this controversial conception, of a move "from the confrontation between classes to the harmonious cooperation among the professions," that this whole section of QA is suspended.[31] The primary means Pius advocates is to restore and promote peaceful collaboration among cooperative groupings he calls "the Orders" (*ordine*, *ordo*).[32]

The Orders recall certain features of the medieval guilds, "binding men together not according to the position they occupy in the labor market, but according to the diverse functions which they exercise in society." Denying any natural enmity between labor and capital, Pius argues that it is, rather, natural for those who practice the same profession or trade to combine into corporate groups (*collegia seu corpora*) that are precisely the sorts of subsidiary, semiautonomous organizations that are the lifeblood of a healthy civil society (83).

Several features of these corporate bodies are highlighted. First, they are bound together *internally* by the shared effort of employers and employees who join to produce their particular goods or render their particular services, and *externally* "by the common good which all 'groups' should unite to promote, each in its own sphere." Second, the power and efficacy of these bonds will be "in proportion to the fidelity with which the individuals and the 'groups' strive to discharge their professional duties and to excel in them." Third, in these associations the common interest of the whole Order must predominate, the most important being the directing of each trade (*artis*) to the common good. Against this backdrop of unity, in cases where the specific interests of employers or employees need attention and protection, parties may deliberate separately or come to their own decisions when the matter requires. Fourth, these corporate bodies must be free associations in two senses. Members of an Order are free to select any form of organization and methods of operation consonant with justice and the common good; and no one may be coerced or required to participate in a particular Order.[33] Building up and supporting Orders as the warp and woof of a just and flourishing society is, therefore, the urgent task of every citizen (81–87).

Restoring the True Guiding Principle of Economics (88–90)

Pius XI closes this section by contrasting the benefits of such a "corporatist" economy to the errors and evils of dominant capitalist economics. Just as social unity cannot be built on class warfare, neither can the ordering of economic affairs be left to free competition. Ignoring the economy's social and moral aspects, the "individualistic school" (Pius apparently has in mind neoliberal laissez-faire interpretations of Adam Smith's "invisible hand") teaches complete state noninterference in economic affairs, on the grounds that free competition or open markets encompass "a principle of self-direction better able to control them than any created intellect." But consequences have proven abundantly that "free competition . . . though quite useful within certain limits, cannot be an adequate controlling principle in economic affairs." Still less can this guidance be furnished by the most prominent alternative to untrammeled competition, "economic supremacy." (Nell-Breuning describes this as the ascendance of "centralized capitalist control" where competition is limited by the dominance of a few corporate giants.[34]) If competition is to be adequately curbed and controlled, "more lofty and noble principles must be sought: to wit, social justice and social charity" (88).

Public institutions, therefore, ought to be imbued with the spirit and operation of justice, expressed in a juridical and social order capable of pervading all economic activity. Social charity (Nell-Breuning calls it "commonweal love") must be the soul of such an order. It is the task of the state to protect and defend it. Responding to the call to justice and charity should also lead nations to recognize their growing economic interdependence and propel them to reach agreements that will facilitate cooperation and mutual assistance. If, Pius declares, the various members of the social body are reformed, and the true guiding principle of social and economic activity—social justice animated by social charity—is reestablished, it will come to reflect, in analogous ways, the features of the Body of Christ (Eph. 4:16).[35]

Excursus and Analysis of Certain Corporatist Experiments (91–97)

These paragraphs, written in Italian in Pius XI's own hand, were given to Nell-Breuning later in the drafting process. They contain Pius's measured analysis of the strengths and liabilities of a recently inaugurated "special syndical and corporative organization," which is obviously the fascist organization in Italy. In hindsight Nell-Breuning concluded that Pius's interpolation had contained misunderstandings of fascist political organization that led to misinterpretations of the QA's entire vision for renovating the social order and jeopardized its effective reception. The social order QA depicted, inspired by the solidarism of Heinrich Pesch and the "very liberal" Gustav Gundlach, was intended to be "progressive, liberal, definitely democratic, against individualism and against statism." Yet, to Nell-Breuning's dismay, entanglement between QA's social vision and Pius's perceived approval of elements of fascism prompted disparagement of the encyclical "in the widest circles of Catholic social teaching as 'statist' or 'restorative' or 'reactionary,' etc."[36] Though Nell-Breuning tended to blame himself, this twist in reception was more likely an unavoidable result of what Paul Misner calls "the Fascist shipwreck in which QA was, willy-nilly, involved."[37]

In fact, Pius's description of "syndical and corporative" organizations contains, Nell-Breuning argues, a number of subtle (for many readers, it turned out, too subtle) criticisms, based on the principles for a just social order earlier presented. In a syndical arrangement, the state grants a single union juridical status and sole power to represent and draw up contracts between workingmen and employers. Though membership is optional, dues and taxes are levied on all in a given profession, and labor contracts drawn up by the syndicate are binding on all. These "corporations," composed of representatives of workers and employers in a trade, act as "organs of the state" and coordinate union activities in all matters. Strikes and lockouts are forbidden; when contending parties fail to agree, public authority intervenes.

Pius XI's next lines drew fire from both profascists and their opponents: "Little reflection is required to perceive advantages in the institution thus summarily described: peaceful collaboration of the classes, repression of socialist organizations and efforts, the moderating authority of a special ministry."[38] However, "there are some who fear that the State is substituting itself in the place of private initiative, instead of limiting itself to necessary and sufficient help and assistance. It is feared that the new syndical and corporate institution possesses an excessively bureaucratic and political character, and that, not withstanding the general advantages referred to above, it risks serving particular political aims" rather than contributing to the fostering of a better social order (95). "Mussolini did not take kindly to this paternal observation," Misner observes, adding, "it was perhaps the straw that broke the concordat camel's back and led to the suppression of all Catholic Action youth groups from May to September, 1931."[39]

To attain the desired social order, Pius XI avers, requires above all God's blessing and the cooperation of people of good will. The contributions of experts in various fields, guided by Catholic principles, will come not from Catholic Action per se, "which has no intention of displaying any strictly syndical or political activities," but from well-trained Catholic laypersons acting as individuals, yet assisted by the Church's guidance and training in the apostolate (96).

Finally, those pursuing this renewed order should remember that at one historical period there did exist a social order—the medieval guild system—which, though by no means perfect, corresponded in a certain measure to right reason according to the needs of that time. This system was abandoned at the onset of modernity, not due to its inability to adapt to changing needs and circumstances, but rather, Pius concludes, due to "the self-love" and "wrong-doing of men" who either refused their duty to extend this order or were lured by misconceived notions of liberty to attempt "to throw off all authority" (97). Needless to say, this last contributed to critics' conclusions that Pius was, at heart, antimodern, and that QA's was a reactionary restorationist program.

Part 3: Changes Since 1891 (98–140)

In the final part of QA, Pius XI examines contemporary economic conditions, noting changes that have taken place since the time of Leo XIII, and evaluating the recent career of socialism, capitalist economy's "sharpest accuser." He ends by examining more closely "the root of the present grave evils," and indicating the first and most necessary remedy, "a reform of morals" (98–99).

Economic Changes (100–110)

Leo XIII had chiefly in mind *that economic regime* (Pius XI consistently uses this phrase, not *capitalism*)[40] in which certain people provided the capital and others the labor jointly needed for production. As Leo's whole endeavor was to "adjust this economic system" to moral standards, it follows that the system of labor and capital is not inherently vicious. But it violates right order whenever capital employs workers or the propertyless class in ways that ignore or dishonor "the human dignity of the workers, the social character of economic life, social justice, and the common good." Though much of the world's economy remains agricultural, the "capitalistic" industrial regime's impact has become worldwide. Since its advantages, inconveniences, and vices now pervade the lives even of those living outside its ambit, to focus on recent changes in industrial economy pertains to the interests of the whole human race.

Domination Has Followed Free Competition (105–10)

In one of QA's hardest-hitting passages, Pius XI diagnoses the primary ills besetting capitalistic economy forty years after *Rerum novarum*:

> It is patent that in our days not only is wealth accumulated, but immense power and despotic economic domination are concentrated in the hands of a few, and that those few are frequently not the owners, but only the trustees and directors of invested funds, who administer them at their good pleasure. . . . This power becomes particularly irresistible when exercised by those who, because they hold and control money, are able to govern credit and determine its allotment, for that reason supplying . . . the life blood to the entire economic body, and grasping . . . in their hands the very soul of the economy, so that no one dare breathe against their will. (106)

Pius sees this accumulation of resources and power, a characteristic note of the modern economic order, as a natural result of unbridled competition that permits the survival only of the strongest—too often those who fight most relentlessly and who pay least heed to the dictates of conscience (105–7).

Such unprecedented concentrations of power breed a threefold tension: struggle for domination in the economic sphere itself; a fierce battle to acquire control of the state so that its resources and authority may be manipulated in economic struggles; and clashes between states as nations ruthlessly apply political influence to promote the economic interests of their citizens, and economic force and domination are exerted to decide international political controversies (108).

Pius XI regards as evident "the ultimate consequences of this individualistic spirit" in economic affairs. "Free competition has committed suicide" as economic dictatorship has superseded a free market. "Unbridled ambition for domination has succeeded the desire for gain," and economic life as a whole has become "hard, cruel, and relentless in a ghastly measure." Moreover, scandalous confusion of the duties and offices of civil authority and economy has produced grave evils and degraded the state. "The state which should be the supreme arbiter . . . far above all party contention, intent only upon justice and the common good, has become instead a slave, bound over to the service of human passion and greed." International relations have also been corrupted by economic nationalism or imperialism, and by a noxious international imperialism in financial affairs "which holds that where a man's fortune is, there is his country." (109)

Pius XI underscores the remedies for these great evils. Due consideration must be given to both the individual and social character of capital and labor, and the dangers of individualism and collectivism avoided. Labor-capital relations must be regulated according to strict justice, called commutative, but supported by Christian charity. Free competition, kept within just limits, and still more economic monopolies, must be brought under the effective control of the public authority in matters pertaining to the competence of the state. Public institutions within a nation must work together to conform the whole of society to the common good, "that is, the norm of social justice." Only thus can economic relations be restored to sanity and right order.

Changes in Socialism (111–26)

Since Leo XIII's day, socialism has also undergone profound changes. What was then a single system has become divided into two opposing and often hostile camps, but neither has abandoned "the principle peculiar to socialism, namely, opposition to the Christian faith."

One section of socialism has degenerated into violent communism that pursues aims inimical to Christianity: "merciless class warfare and complete abolition of private ownership." To attain these ends, Communists shrink from nothing and fear nothing, and once in power they have acted with stunning cruelty and inhumanity. Amid all this, "the antagonism and open hostility it has shown to Holy Church and even God himself are, alas! well-proven by facts and known to all."

The other, more moderate sector, still called "socialism," is much less radical in its views. It condemns recourse to physical force, and mitigates or even rejects class warfare and the abolition of private property. In many places noncommunistic socialism seems to approximate the principles and practices of Christian social reform. Just demands that certain forms of property be reserved to the state, for the sake of the common good, are compatible with Christian truth, but these are not peculiar to socialism. Those who look for nothing else, Pius XI observes, have no reason for becoming socialists. Though the question of a middle ground between Christians and socialists is often raised today, Pius concludes that whether considered as a doctrine, a historical fact, or a movement, "if it really remain socialism it cannot be brought into harmony with the dogmas of the Catholic Church" because "it conceives human society in a way utterly alien to Christian truth" (114–17). Socialism is grounded in a purely materialist philosophy that denies by definition humankind's divine origin and destiny. This leads socialist systems to falsely elevate the material aspects of life, and at times to disregard the dignity and rights of human beings in their efforts to maximize material production, abundance, and security. Thus, though socialism contains certain elements of truth, "no one can be at the same time a sincere Catholic and a true socialist." "Christian socialism" is a contradiction in terms (118–20).

Why, then, have so many Catholics deserted to socialism? Some do so believing that "the Church and those professing attachment to the Church favor the rich and neglect the workingmen and have no care for them." Pius acknowledges the "lamentable fact" that some professed

Catholics have ignored the obligations in justice and charity to their neighbors. Worse still, some, out of greed, "are not ashamed to oppress the workingman." Certain employers even abuse religion itself, cloaking their unjust practices under its name to protect themselves against the legitimate demands of their employees. The condemnable conduct of such people explains why the Church "without deserving it, may have the appearance and be accused of taking sides with the wealthy, and of being unmoved by the needs and suffering of the disinherited . . . of their natural heritage." To those who may have been misled by such appearances, Pius XI extends with "solicitude" an invitation "to return to the maternal bosom of the Church" and to join those endeavoring to reform society "according to the mind of the Church on a firm basis of social justice and social charity" (122–26).

Social Renovation (127–40)

One thing is evident: "this longed-for social reconstruction must be preceded by a profound renewal of the Christian spirit, from which so many of those engaged in economic activity have in many places unhappily departed." In Leo's words, if society is to be healed now, "in no way can it be healed save by a return to Christian life and Christian institutions" (RN 22). Only Christianity offers an effective remedy for "the excessive solicitude for transitory things, which is the origin of all vices." Christianity alone can redirect the attention of those absorbed in worldly things toward heaven—and this is urgently needed today (127–29).

Chief Present Disorder: Ruin of Souls (130–35)

In daily life, most people are nearly exclusively preoccupied with temporal upheavals, disasters, and ruins. Yet seen with Christian eyes, these are nothing in comparison with the ruin of souls. Under modern social and economic conditions, vast multitudes can only with great difficulty pay attention "to the one thing necessary, namely, their eternal salvation." The root cause of this spiritual debacle is an ancient one: the disordering of human affections resulting from original sin. Its manifestations, especially avarice and greed, take on different forms in different historical settings (130–31).

In an astute analysis of what John Paul II will later call "structures of sin," Pius XI explains that today, especially given the failure of civil authorities to uphold moral law, economic relations constitute an especially virulent breeding ground for spiritual corruption. First, a climate of economic uncertainty "demands the keenest and most unceasing straining of energy on the part of those engaged therein; and as a result, some have become so hardened against the stings of conscience as to hold all means good which enable them to increase their profits, and to safeguard against sudden changes of fortune the wealth amassed by unremitting toil." For too many, the easiest return for the least amount of labor or investment becomes the central criterion for economic decision making. Moreover, the impersonal relations, divided responsibility, and limited liability attending legal regulations on joint-stock companies lead to "greatly weakened accountability" that attenuates the influence of conscience on stockholders' quest for profits. "The worst injustices and frauds take place beneath the obscurity of the common name of a corporative firm" (132).

Another opportunity for vice springs from the moral instability and lack of discipline of large consumer groups. Pius decries the "well-calculated speculation" of those who, without seeking to provide for real needs, "appeal to the lowest human passions . . . in order to turn their satisfaction into gain" (132). Coloring all is an ethos that promotes the pursuit of self-interest above all things and through any means whatsoever. Prominent citizens and business leaders who follow this "broad way which leads to destruction" attract imitators who are drawn by their apparent success and extravagant lifestyles, and influenced by their derision of moral scruples and ability to crush more conscientious competitors (134). Multitudes of workingmen have sunk into economic self-absorption, all the more "because very many employers treated their workmen as mere tools." Owners' neglect of employees' higher interests has had a dehumanizing effect on workers, on work, on family, and on society. Bodily labor today has thus been sadly perverted: "dead matter leaves the factory ennobled and transformed, where men are corrupted and degraded" (135).

The Remedies (136–40)

The fundamental remedy for this pitiable situation must be "a frank and sincere return to the teaching of the Gospel." Principles of economics must come to reflect the true order of the divine plan, which "places God as the first and supreme end of all created activity, and regards all created goods as mere instruments under God" to be used only insofar as they help in attaining humanity's supreme end.[41] Remunerative occupations are not thereby "belittled or deemed less consonant with human dignity"; gospel-oriented priorities in fact help one see and reverence in work of all kinds the will of the Creator. In this vein, Pius affirms that those involved in economic production "are not forbidden to increase their fortunes in a lawful and just manner." Indeed, those who serve society by developing its wealth deserve their proportionate reward, provided that the laws of God and rights of the neighbor are observed. In a community infused with proper spiritual priorities, "Christian moderation" will ensure that production, acquisition, and the use of wealth are brought back to standards of equity and just distribution (136).

In effecting this transformation, charity, "the bond of perfection," must play a leading part. It is folly to pursue commutative justice and disdain the help of charity! Charity cannot substitute for justice, but justice alone can never bring about true union of hearts and minds. This union is the main principle of stability in all institutions. Without it, "the wisest regulations come to nothing." People can unite in striving for the common good only when all sectors of society are convinced "that they are members of one great family and children of the same heavenly Father," and further, one body in Christ and members of one another. In words that echo Leo's vision of a stable, hierarchical social order, Pius predicts that the rich will then treat the poor with solicitous love. Workingmen will lay aside feelings of envy and hatred, and become content and proud in "the position assigned them by divine providence in human society . . . working usefully for the common good," in the footsteps of a Savior who was content to be a carpenter (137).

The Christian struggle to renovate the social order will be arduous, but Pius XI exhorts his audience to the courage and willingness to endure befitting "good soldiers of Christ." Of paramount importance is promoting the return to faith of unhappy souls who, too entangled in temporal cares, have turned from God. And "if in the depths of even the most abandoned hearts lurk, like sparks beneath the ashes, spiritual forces of unexpected strength," surely this is much more true of the hearts of many "who largely through ignorance and unfavorable surroundings, have wandered into error!" (138–39).

Conclusion: The Course to Be Followed (141–47)

Pius concludes by appealing to bishops and laity to unite in advancing Christ's reign in "a world which in large measure has almost fallen back into paganism." In order to reach out to people of all classes, it will be necessary to identify and train from among each social rank people who will be able to win their hearts as comrades. "Undoubtedly the first and immediate apostles of the workingmen must themselves be workingmen, while apostles of the industrial and commercial world should themselves be employers and merchants" (141). In their labors, priests and lay Christians must be fortified by the Church's powerful educational, communal, and spiritual resources. Pius highlights Ignatius's *Spiritual Exercises*, a "school of the Spirit" where apostles for every state of life may be formed and inflamed with the love of Christ. He commends the *Exercises* as a "most precious means of personal and social reform . . . for the laity in general and especially for workingmen" (143). To push back contemporary forces that augur the ruin of so many souls, the world today has "sore need of valiant soldiers of Christ" who strain every sinew to preserve the human family from the social havoc that ensues when God's law is flouted. No stone must be left unturned to avert the grave misfortunes threatening human society, for "with the assistance of divine grace, the destiny of the human family lies in our hands" (144–45).

Carrying forward this mission for the renewal of society will require that all who dedicate themselves to a Christian social order find ways to unite and focus their efforts. QA closes by extending to all members of "the great Catholic family," but with special affection to artisans, to manual laborers, and to Christian employers and managers, Pius XI's apostolic blessing (146–47).

EXCURSUS

Three important aspects of Pius's teaching in QA will be briefly explored.

The Concept of Social Justice

QA has been credited with introducing *social justice* into the parlance of official social teaching. The term was introduced into Catholic social ethics by Italian theologian Luigi Taparelli D'Azeglio in the mid-1800s, ostensibly to replace Thomas Aquinas's terms *legal justice* and *general justice*, which were in danger of being misconstrued in the modern context.[42] But *social justice* apparently entered the vocabulary of official papal teaching by way of students of German solidarist Heinrich Pesch, especially Gustav Gundlach and Oswald von Nell-Breuning, QA's drafter.[43] Judged by many as a keynote of QA, social justice specified the directive principle of social institutions: "not competition but the common good."[44]

Social justice received a fuller official description in Pius XI's 1937 encyclical on atheistic communism, *Divini redemptoris*:

> Besides commutative justice, there is also social justice with its own set of obligations, from which neither employers nor workingmen can escape. Now, *it is of the very essence of social justice to demand from each individual all that is necessary for the common good.* But just as in the living organism it is impossible to provide for the good of the whole unless each single part and each individual member is given what it needs for the exercise of its proper functions, so it is impossible to care for the social organism and the good of society as a unit unless each single part and each individual member, that is to say, each individual in the dignity of his human personality, is supplied with all that is necessary for the exercise of his social functions. *If social justice be satisfied, the result will be an intense activity in economic life as a whole, pursued in tranquility and order.* This activity will be proof of the health of the social body, just as the health of the human body is recognized in the undisturbed regularity and perfect efficiency of the whole organism. (DR 52)

The common good cannot be present without social justice. For Pius XI, however, social charity is also required.[45] Social justice refers to the central and necessary set of conditions wherein each member is contributing, and thus enjoying, all that is needed for the common good. But this justice must be leavened and enlivened by the virtue of social charity or love (QA 88, 137). Arguably, the connections drawn between social justice, social charity, and the common good in QA adumbrate relationships among common good, justice, and solidarity developed later in the century by Pope John Paul II.

Stronger Critique of Liberalism and Capitalism

Though Pius continues a theme introduced in *Rerum novarum*, there is "rather more anger and ideological passion than in Leo XIII," especially in Pius's criticisms of individualism and liberal capitalism. Novak suggests that Pius XI most clearly departs from Leo XIII in "the ferocity of his attack on liberalism." It is true that, while QA presents Catholic social thought as an alternative to both liberalism and socialism, liberalism comes in for more detailed and extended criticism. Nell-Breuning writes that throughout the encyclical there runs "a scarlet thread of relentless pursuit into the last, and most secret fastnesses of the liberalist and individualist spirit."[46]

Pius sees a direct relationship between modern individualism and the most destructive features of capitalist economics. QA's harsh criticism of "capitalistic liberalism" (not free enterprise or markets per se, but capitalism as then practiced) is reflected in Pius's condemnation of vast and unjust disparities of economic power, systemic inducements to greed, and the concentration of wealth in the hands of a few.[47]

The Call for a Corporatist Social Order

Pius's rejection of liberal philosophy and economics is accompanied by his vision of a renewed corporatist social order. As seen, QA's discussion of corporatism, a version of what Pesch called "solidarism," has been read by many as a blueprint for an alternative to capitalist economy. In 1939, for instance, Charles P. Bruehl contended that "only a society vocationally organized verifies the Catholic social ideal. . . . Until we have a Corporative State . . . which integrates social groups according to function and . . . in a hierarchical whole the aim of which is the common good," society can be neither flourishing, stable, nor just.[48] A considerable sector of QA's Catholic readership understood the pope's mandate in a similar way, but critics, seeing in QA antidemocratic or even totalitarian tendencies, interpreted Pius's vision of a renovated guild system as one of the encyclical's greatest weaknesses.

For his part, Nell-Breuning worked energetically to show that QA's social vision was not a de facto endorsement of antidemocratic syndicalism, but in fact a practical and progressive alternative to both authoritarian and liberal regimes. He later summarized QA's picture of vocational organization and its selective appreciation of free enterprise: "1. Organization of society as a whole, and of economic society as a part, from the bottom up, according to the principle of subsidiarity. 2. Neutrality toward the capitalist economic system, as a system in which the worker is not the owner of the means of production. . . . 3. Complete rejection of the capitalist class society, i.e., the society centering around monopolized labor markets. . . . 4. Acceptance of the principle of competition to the extent that competition does not lead to self-destruction but can maintain itself as a superior guiding principle, owing to appropriate institutions and, as far as necessary, measures against monopolistic power."[49] In the years following World War II, some saw economic cooperative movements as a step toward the pope's envisioned system of Orders. As Raymond Miller wrote in 1947:

> While the Pope's ideal is not the cooperative commonwealth, and while practically it seems unlikely that big business will ever completely surrender to the cooperative movement, what does seem very possible is that the cooperative, if it goes far enough, will effect some kind of modification or reform of the abuses in the capitalistic system which may well end in the actual formation of the Pope's ideal, namely, the system of the "orders" or Industries and Professions.[50]

In the 1980s, some American commentators attempted to deflect Pius's harsh critique of liberalism, contending that his antipathy was directed at continental, rather than Anglo-Saxon versions. Michael Novak argues that in the latter, rights and freedoms, and many governmental checks and balances, provide legal and cultural space for an egalitarian approach to the common good that Pius XI would have approved. But QA offers little evidence that Pius was moving away from the accent on hierarchical-organic "corporate" institutions that had entered Catholicism (ironically in the era of fascism) by way of German social thought. In contrast to its Anglo-American counterparts, this approach celebrated *Gemeinschaftlich* communal ties and the *Volksgeist*, an underlying mystical bond that connected a people across class lines. Explicit papal openings to political democracy would await Pius XII and his successors.

REACTIONS TO THE DOCUMENT

Evaluations of QA in 1931 and since confirm that modern social encyclicals are somewhat like political and economic Rorschach tests:

sympathetic readers of varying positions tend to see in them the outlines of programs and principles they support, while equally diverse critics perceive the very things they oppose. This is at least partly due to the sidestepping of neat ideological categories by papal teaching, which has sought instead to maintain synthetic positions grounded in religiously based, normative understandings of personal and communal nature, flourishing, and destiny. QA's history of reception has thus been marked by conflicts of interpretation. This is evident in analyses of the encyclical's authority, of its socioeconomic critique, of its goals and intentions, and of the avenues toward change it advocates.

Authority

The pope's authority and competence to pronounce on the moral dimensions of society and economy were emphasized most strongly among Catholics sympathetic with his office and message. In June 1931, the progressive Catholic periodical *Commonweal* editorialized: "The voice of the Church, which is the voice of God, fills the whole earth, momentarily at least, through the words of Pope Pius," adding that, "in a very real sense, it is the voice of the Father of the Poor that speaks." Others, skeptical of the Church's claims, tended to call QA's authority into question. The political periodical *The Nation* responded to the pope's description of communism as the enemy of the Church and God by remarking, tongue in cheek, that when one recalls that early Christians were said to have held all goods in common, "one is reminded anew that the Catholic Church is a law unto itself." [51]

Some who read the encyclical as an unfair attack on capitalism questioned whether "a Church is within its proper sphere when it attempts to prescribe economic regulations," and concluded: "It is not the business of any Church to go so deeply into the practical application of the rules of justice." The pope himself mentioned that certain industrialists prevented QA from being read in local churches. Conversely, the Jesuit weekly *America* castigated business critics, defending Pius XI's interventions as proper and well-informed. "Does it not give [business representatives] pause . . . to reflect that the Pope in his commanding position surrounded by penetrating and able men of the world has surveyed our present social-economic structure and found it gravely wanting?"[52]

Goals and Intended Message

QA's vision for a reconstructed social order and the necessary steps to attain it remained general and in need of adaptation to different places and circumstances. But they were laid out with enough specificity to educe passionate responses from both supporters and critics.

Readers disagreed on whether QA intends to provide general principles or a specific and detailed map of the renovated social order it promotes. Misner points out that "in the absence of any express preference for democracy as a framework for human rights and social justice, QA was read differently in countries under dictatorship than in the free world." Many socially minded Catholics in countries supporting democratic policies prized QA "as an expression of important principles, not as a blueprint or even a call for 'the' Christian social order." But in nondemocratic, traditionally Catholic countries, (e.g., Hungary, Austria, and some Latin American countries) the encyclical was more often read as a specific set of prescriptions for a hierarchical, corporative, political, and economic regime. [53]

Disputes have also persisted concerning the radicality of QA's critique and of the social transformation it promotes. Some at the time, like Henry Somerville, argued that QA "points the way to an organization of industry completely different from that which is known as Capitalism. [The pope] would replace the wage system with one of industrial partnership; he would raise every trade to the status of an organized, self-governing profession; he would limit both free competition and State regulation by having industrial guilds to be organs of regulation." John A. Ryan perceived the encyclical as reformist but, like his own social ethics, sufficiently radical to confirm Ryan's own prescription for socioeconomic justice:

"the present system, greatly, in fact radically, modified." Much later, Jean-Yves Calvez, S.J. argued: "The central concern of QA was not a limited economic issue, but the problem of economic systems themselves, and Catholic social teaching moved in the direction of designing a fundamentally new type of economic organization."[54]

Many commentators have emphasized the more structural nature of QA's critique and prescriptions. In QA, writes Derek Holmes, "for the first time a Pope recommended the redistribution of national production, profit sharing and co-partnership of workers in industry." Pius XI, far more than Leo XIII, considered the need for fundamental changes in the social and economic order to correct the abuses he denounced, particularly the unfair distribution and concentrations of wealth and the exploitation of labor. O'Brien argues that, unlike *Rerum novarum*, "QA was radical, even revolutionary; it was about reconstruction; not reform." Its proposed Christian social order was religiously rooted, but also a practical response to concerns of both the right (authority, order, and stability) and the left (basic human needs, equitable distribution, and balanced power). Both perspectives "exposed the systemic failures of liberal capitalism, evident in the collapsing economies of 1931." Donal Dorr adds that QA moves beyond *Rerum novarum* to acknowledge that, while social stability is an important value, "justice ranks higher," and at times can require that major "social risks" be taken to attain it.[55] Others have perceived greater continuity with Leo's more static social worldview. Peter Hebblethwaite contends that "Pius continued the line of Leo XIII. Catholic social doctrine is envisaged as a set of principles, enunciated by the Church (actually the pope), that if acted upon, could transform the world. Unfortunately, these principles had not been heeded, and consequently the world was in a mess." This interpretation regards Pius's approach to problems as moralistic and individualistic: "There was no examination of the structuralist, built-in causes of modern problems. There was no attempt to interpret contemporary movements in the light of their Christian potential. Socialism was rejected out of hand. The result was that Catholics had to hive off into movements of their own."[56]

Readers have also debated QA's specificity and practicality. Early U.S. reactions ranged from the *New Republic*'s complaints that QA promoted a vague social vision, a "utopian pipe dream," to John Ryan's declaration that the encyclical realistically combines a clear statement of principles with a detailed presentation of practical proposals. "The Holy Father has given the world the most comprehensive, specific and adequate program of social reconstruction that we possess." Other sympathetic interpreters regarded as a binding norm the pope's hierarchical and organic picture of corporative social relations wherein cooperation superseded class struggle and each person was assured a secure place in society, but claimed that "the pope leaves the details of organizing vocational groups up to the people involved."[57]

The degree to which QA promotes a specifically religious social program has been another point of controversy. Many supporters stressed the applicability of Pius's moral message to all citizens. But others saw the encyclical as proposing an explicitly Christian social order that was ultimately inimical to a modern pluralistic society. How could differing interest groups be persuaded to subordinate group interests to the general welfare, and who would define the specific requirements of the common good? Eschewing both democratic compromise and dictatorial government, it seemed that Pius XI's new system "could only work if whole nations returned to the Church, accepted its teachings and its sanctions, and automatically and freely accepted the demands of right reason." O'Brien judges QA's Christian social order "the economic and social expression of the post-Vatican I ultramontane Church." "It could and did inspire selfless devotion to a revolutionary cause; it could and it did attract deeply compassionate and committed churchmen all over the world, but it was a utopia, and a dangerous one." Misner goes further, claiming that Pius regarded QA as a concrete design "for the only kind of society he considered fully viable, one in which the Roman Catholic Church has a recognized position as the only representative of the true religion."[58]

Means to Social Regeneration

A final dispute among readers of QA concerned the means by which Pius XI expected his program for social reconstruction to be accomplished. Most social Catholics rejoiced in and emphasized QA's support for economic, social, and political reforms. But others interpreted personal transformation and virtue as equally, if not more, important. So, the Benedictine monk Virgil Michel declared that "the social regeneration championed in [*Quadragesimo anno*] must necessarily entail a change of heart from the un-Christian individualism of the past and present." Contrary to what some seemed to assume, reconstructing society is not primarily a matter of setting up particular political or economic structures. "These must rather be an outgrowth of the general attitude of mind and philosophy of life basic to the new social order. That is why Pius XI emphasizes so strongly the moral aspects of the entire social question; and that is why he brings before our minds the spiritual and supernatural ideal of society, which we must try to realize proportionately in our natural social body."[59] Some later commentators have agreed that "Pius XI very clearly states that the reconstruction and perfection of social order cannot be brought about without the practice of virtue. Pius XI is, of course, in favor of reforming institutions but has no expectation that they will work well or ever be established unless individuals are converted from various kinds of self seeking to a serious concern with virtue."[60]

CONCLUSION

The legacy of QA has been as disputed as the text's meaning. Many would concur that, along with the notions of social justice and subsidiarity, and the inauguration of a "tradition" of papal encyclicals commemorating *Rerum novarum*, QA "divested some of the otherworldly rhetoric of *Rerum novarum*" by insisting "on a more direct, aggressive stance by the Church in the socio-political realm. . . . Christian charity alone is not a sufficient solution . . . there must be real structural change, if the Church is to cease looking like merely an extension of the capitalistic order."[61] O'Brien and Shannon, on the other hand, identify QA with a nostalgic and ultimately impotent social agenda. "On the whole, the project of Christianizing the modern social order had to be judged, at mid-century, a failure." The laudable effort to develop a body of Catholic social teaching produced powerful and perceptive criticisms of the liabilities of socialism, liberalism, capitalism, and democracy, but failed "to formulate a positive, attractive, and compelling alternative . . . They . . . did generate a pastoral approach that brought the Church closer to the suffering poor, but they never succeeded in relating to the hopes and aspirations of the working class. For all its failings, liberalism had excited new hopes and aspirations among masses of ordinary people; the Church seemed only to offer a return to a former age which many knew instinctively had been neither secure nor happy for most people."[62]

What, then, does QA bequeath to Catholic social thought? If QA's primary goal was to promote a new socioeconomic order arranged along specifically corporatist lines, Pius is rightly judged as advocating an unsuccessful, indeed largely ignored, agenda. Insofar as it promoted an explicitly Christian, even Catholic, social order from the perspective of a post–Vatican II embrace of pluralism, democracy, and Church-state autonomy, QA appears distinctly outdated. Moreover, many recent analysts have dismissed QA's critique of liberalism in light of historical developments in countries outside continental Europe while QA's universal condemnation of socialism has been modified in later encyclicals, and especially challenged by political and liberation theologians.

If QA is judged by its influence on the later development of Catholic social thought, however, the picture looks different. The encyclical articulated influential concepts such as social justice, the common good, and subsidiarity. It denounced great social and economic disparities and envisioned a multiassociational society in which the common good included everyone. Pius recognized the structural dimensions of socioeconomic evils and the need for structural reforms to redress them. He insisted that concerted response to economic suffering was a matter not only of organized charity but of social justice, and he saw a crucial need for a spiritually motivated and virtuous laity to engage in renovating culture and institutions according to the values and image of Christ's kingdom. All of this found its way into and through the paradigm shifts of Vatican II and continues to animate, in transmuted but clearly recognizable form, Catholic social teaching, thought, and action today.

NOTES

1. Joseph Husslein, *Social Wellsprings II: Pope Pius XI* (Milwaukee: Bruce, 1943), 164.

2. John Pollard, *The Vatican and Italian Fascism, 1929–1932* (Cambridge: Cambridge University Press, 1985), 138ff.

3. Paul Misner, "Catholic Labor and Catholic Action: The Italian Context of Quadragesimo Anno." *Catholic Historical Review* 90 (October 2004): 650–74.

4. Philip Hughes, *Pope Pius the Eleventh* (New York: Sheed and Ward, 1938), 110–11.

5. Quoted in Jacques Maritain, *Scholasticism and Politics*, trans. Mortimer Adler (London: Geoffrey Bles, 1940), 156. See also Hughes, *Pope Pius*, 122–27.

6. Hughes, *Pope Pius*, 124, citing a letter from Pius XI to the patriarch of Lisbon, November 10, 1933.

7. This religio-martial spirit was especially directed to youth. In Italy, organizations like the Catholic Boy Scouts were promoted as an alternative to entanglement in fascist youth groups.

8. Hughes, *Pope Pius*, 125.

9. The fine line involved here was trod by activist Catholics with mixed success, as the extent to which Italian Catholic Action continued to harbor Popular Party activities illustrates. See Pollard, *The Vatican and Italian Fascism*, 17.

10. Maritain, *Scholasticism and Politics*, 156. "Has [Pius not called] Catholic action that [which] the 'supreme Head of religion is known to prize and cherish most'? And recently he said yet again: 'Whoever strikes Catholic action, strikes at the Pope.' . . . (And he added: 'Whoever strikes the Pope, dies')." Ibid.

11. Robin Anderson, *Between Two Wars: The Story of Pope Pius XI, 1922–1939* (Chicago: Franciscan Herald, 1977), xv–xvi.

12. Pollard, *The Vatican and Italian Fascism*, 22.

13. Misner, "Social Catholicism in Italy," 20.

14. See Nadine-Josette Chaline, "La spiritualité de Pie XI," in *"Achille Ratti: Pape Pie XI*, Collection de l'école Française de Rome, Tome 223 (Rome: École Française de Rome, 1996), 159–70. See also Anderson, *Between Two Wars*, xxi–xxiv.

15. Pollard traces Pius's astute use of the media in an ongoing propaganda struggle with Mussolini from 1929 to 1931. See also Pius's later encyclical on morality and motion pictures, *Vigilanti cura* (1936).

16. See Richard Mulcahy, *The Economics of Heinrich Pesch* (New York: Henry Holt, 1952). See chaps. 4 and 6 of Michael Novak, *Freedom With Justice: Catholic Social Thought and Liberal Institutions* (San Francisco: Harper and Row, 1984), esp. 69–80.

17. Oswald von Nell-Breuning, "The Drafting of *Quadragesimo Anno*," in *Readings in Catholic Moral Theology No. 5: Catholic Social Teaching*, ed. Charles E. Curran and Richard A. McCormick (New York: Paulist, 1986), 62.

18. David O'Brien, "A Century of Social Teaching: Context and Comments," in *One Hundred Years of Catholic Social Teaching*, ed. John A. Coleman (Maryknoll, N.Y.: Orbis, 1991), 20–21.

19. QA 3. For both Leo and Pius, the paradigmatic "worker" was the "working man," laboring to support wife and children.

20. All emphases added.

21. Oswald von Nell-Breuning, *Reorganization of Social Economy: The Social Encyclical Developed and Explained*, trans. Bernard Dempsey (Milwaukee: Bruce, 1936), 24, no. 2, records excerpts from printed reactions to RN illustrating this range of opinions.

22. Note Pius's frank acknowledgment of changing circumstances and firm rejection of changes in doctrine. See ibid., 35–36, 79–88.

23. Ibid., 38–39, notes that the Treaty of Versailles, clearly the reference here, is never explicitly mentioned out of sensitivity to its international (e.g., French and German) readers, thus making this section "a masterpiece of tact." One wonders whom QA's drafter is complimenting!

24. See Husslein, *Social Wellsprings II*, 189, no. 12.

25. Nell-Breuning, *Reorganization of Social Economy*, 83; cf. John A. Ryan, *Distributive Justice*, 3rd ed. (New York: Macmillan, [1916] 1942).

26. Nell-Breuning, *Reorganization of Social Economy*, 87; see QA 75.

27. Ryan argued that complete worker justice, therefore, encompasses not only wage "sufficiency" but also "status" that allowed workers voice and influence in production processes and "sharing" of some sort in ownership, management, and profits. See Ryan, *Distributive Justice*, 303–39.

28. Nell-Breuning, *Reorganization of Social Economy*, 170ff.

29. Catholic promoters of the family living wage, in the United States most notably John Ryan, elaborated this claim by addressing questions such as why the unmarried male has a right to a family living wage, while the unmarried female does not. See J. A. Ryan, *A Living Wage* (New York: Macmillan, 1906, 1912).

30. Husslein, *Social Wellsprings II*, 205 no. 25.

31. Nell-Breuning, "Drafting of *Quadragesimo Anno*," in *Readings*, ed. C. Curran and R. McCormick, 64, quoting a statement by Cardinal Pacelli, future Pope Pius XII, in 1929.

32. Husslein, in *Social Wellsprings II*, 207–8, no. 29. See Nell-Breuning, *Reorganization of Social Economy*, 222, no. 5, and P. Misner, "Social Catholicism in Italy," 19, for remarks on the many ways this term has been translated—in French, *les ordres ou des professions*, in German, *Stande*, in English, *Industries and Professions, occupational groups, vocational groups*, or *guilds*. He holds that the least misleading way to render the term in English is by *Order*, the same word used most frequently in the Latin text.

33. Nell-Breuning explains that everyone practicing a particular trade or profession would necessarily belong to the Order for that profession and follow its rules. However, one is always free to choose a different profession or trade. See his *Reorganization of Social Economy*, 230–31.

34. Ibid., 249; see QA 105–9.

35. Husslein, *Social Wellsprings II*, 212, no. 35, underscores this, and draws out explicitly religious implications: "Religion must be acknowledged, the commands of God obeyed, and the Charity of Christ must vivify all. To think along other lines is folly, as the world should have learned by now."

36. Nell-Breuning, "Drafting of *Quadragesimo Anno*," in *Readings*, ed. C. Curran and R. McCormick, 64–65.

37. Misner, "Social Catholicism in Italy," 20. "Pius XI . . . saw the framework of a 'Latin bloc' of authoritarian states (Italy, Portugal, Spain, but also corporatist Austria with Dollfuss and Hungary with Nikolaus Horthy.)" This seemed to many in the Vatican a direction to encourage; one more reason why the (societal) "corporatism of QA became firmly identified with the policies of Fascist and authoritarian states in the European mind."

38. "Whence arose the regrettable association of Catholic social doctrine with authoritarian or fascist corporatism." Ibid., 19.

39. Ibid.

40. Husslein, *Social Wellsprings II*, 215, no. 38.

41. Husslein, *Social Wellsprings II*, 228, no. 49, remarks that here Pius XI, a devotee of St. Ignatius's *Spiritual Exercises*, alludes to the "First Principle and Foundation" that grounds them.

42. Marvin L. Mich, *Catholic Social Teaching and Movements* (Mystic, Conn.: Twenty Third, 2000), 80–81, 423–25, no. 58.

43. John F. Cronin, "Forty Years Later: Reflections and Reminiscences, 1971," in *Readings*, ed. C. Curran and R. McCormick, 73–74.

44. O'Brien, "A Century of Catholic Social Teaching," in *One Hundred Years*, ed. J. A. Coleman, 19.

45. See Mich, *Catholic Social Teaching and Movements*, 79–80; QA 88.

46. Novak, *Freedom with Justice*, 111–12; Nell-Breuning, *Reconstruction*, 20.

47. "Half the corporate assets of the nation is subject to the super-giant [corporations], which are dominated by a few men who are largely members of the big banks. . . . When the reader recalls that this situation is paralleled to a large extent in Europe, he will comprehend the truth expressed by the Pope." G. Donnelly, "The Pope and the Corporations," *America* 48 (March 1933): 549–50.

48. Charles P. Bruehl, *The Pope's Plan for Social Reconstruction* (New York: Devin-Adair, 1939), 217–18.

49. Oswald von Nell-Breuning, "Vocational Groups and Monopoly," *Review of Social Economy* 9 (September 1951): 90–91.

50. Raymond J. Miller, *Forty Years After: Pius XI and the Social Order* (St. Paul, Minn.: Radio Replies, 1947), 31–32.

51. Editor, "Father of the Poor," *Commonweal* 14 (June 3, 1931): 113–14; "Editorial," *Nation* 132 (June 1931): 597.

52. Editor, "The Encyclical and the Press," *America* 45 (13 June 1931): 221–22.

53. Misner, "Social Catholicism in Italy," 22.

54. Henry Somerville, "The Guild System," *Catholic World* 134 (November 1931): 221; Jean-Yves Calvez, "Economic Policy Issues in Roman Catholic Social Teaching: An International Perspective," in *The Catholic Challenge to the American Economy*, ed. Thomas M. Gannon (New York: Macmillan, 1987), 18.

55. J. Derek Holmes, *The Papacy in the Modern World 1914–1978* (New York: Crossroad, 1981), 79; O'Brien, in *One Hundred Years*, ed. J. A. Coleman, 19–20; Donal Dorr, *Option for the Poor: One Hundred Years of Catholic Social Teaching* (Maryknoll, N.Y.: Orbis, 1983), 74.

56. Peter Hebblethwaite, "The Popes and Politics: Shifting Patterns in Catholic Social Doctrine," in *Readings*, ed. C. Curran and R. McCormick, 267.

57. Editor, "The Pope and Labor," *New Republic* 67 (May 27, 1931): 32–33; John A. Ryan, "The New Things in the New Encyclical," *Ecclesiastical Review* 85 (July 1931): 13–14; E. DeCoursey, "Reconstruction of the Social Order," *Social Justice Review* 40 (September 1947): 152–53.

58. O'Brien, "A Century of Social Teaching," in *One Hundred Years*, ed. J. Coleman, 19. Misner, "Social Catholicism in Italy," 20, cites Pius XI's encyclical *Mortalium animos* (1928) as further evidence that "the reconquest of the modern world for Christ and Christ's Church, i.e., the Roman Catholic Church under the pope, was the explicit aim of his pontificate."

59. Virgil Michel, *Christian Social Reconstruction* (Milwaukee: Bruce, 1937), 106.

60. J. Brian Benestad, "The Catholic Concept of Social Justice: A Historical Perspective," *Communio* 11 (winter 1984): 378.

61. George E. McCarthy and Royal W. Rhodes, *Eclipse of Justice* (Maryknoll, N.Y.: Orbis, 1992), 166.

62. David J. O'Brien and Thomas A. Shannon, eds., *Catholic Social Thought: The Documentary Heritage* (Maryknoll, N.Y.: Orbis, 1992), 41.

SELECTED BIBLIOGRAPHY

Actes de S.S. Pie XI: Allocutions Actes de Dicastères, Encycliques, Motu proprio, Brèfs, etc. Texte latin et traduction française. Tome VII (1931). Paris: Maison de la Bonne Press, 1936. Original Latin text of QA and other documents issued by Pius during the same period.

Benestad, J. Brian. "The Catholic Concept of Social Justice: A Historical Perspective." *Communio* 11 (winter 1984): 364–81. Traces the background and origins of "social justice," including its use by Pius XI in QA.

Dorr, Donal. *Option for the Poor: One Hundred Years of Catholic Social Teaching*. Maryknoll, N.Y.: Orbis, 1983, 1992.Traces the development of Catholic social teaching, emphasizing QA's advocacy for social-structural transformation in order to meet the needs of the vulnerable.

Hughes, Philip. *Pope Pius the Eleventh*. New York: Sheed and Ward, 1938. A sympathetic contemporaneous treatment of Pius's papacy and QA's ecclesial context.

Misner, Paul. "Social Catholicism in Italy: *Quadragesimo Anno*, 1931," unpublished MS, February 2002. Forthcoming in P. Misner, *Social Catholicism in Europe*. Vol. II. New York: Continuum. A learned ecclesial-historical analysis of QA's background, formulation, and immediate impact.

Mulcahy, Richard. *The Economics of Heinrich Pesch*. New York: Henry Holt, 1952. English introduction to the solidarist political-economic theory reflected in QA.

Nell-Breuning, Oswald von. "The Drafting of Quadragesimo Anno." In *Readings in Moral Theology No. 5: Official Catholic Social Teaching*. Edited by Charles E. Curran and Richard A. McCormick, 60–68. New York: Paulist, 1986. A firsthand account by QA's drafter.

———. *Reorganization of Social Economy: The Social Encyclical Developed and Explained*. Translated by Bernard Dempsey. Milwaukee: Bruce, 1936. Rich and detailed commentary on QA by its drafter and key exegete.

Pollard, John. *The Vatican and Italian Fascism, 1929–1932*. Cambridge: Cambridge University Press, 1985). Illumines the political context of QA's drafting, promulgation, and reception.

Ryan, John A. *Distributive Justice*. 3rd ed. New York: Macmillan, 1942. Incorporates and discusses QA's principles and application to the U.S. economic context.

CHAPTER 7

The Christmas Messages of Pius XII (1939–1945): Catholic Social Teaching in a Time of Extreme Crisis

JOHN P. LANGAN, S.J.

INTRODUCTION

Pius XII, when he died in 1958, was widely extolled as a world leader, a trained diplomat who had led the Holy See through very difficult times into a position of international respect in the postwar world. He was also widely venerated as a man of profound piety who could serve as an impressive and persuasive image of religious dedication. His ascetic figure and his air of intellectual acuteness and detachment made it easy for millions of people, many of them non-Catholics, to see in him a universal religious authority and to look to him to articulate the demands of God's law in a time of discord, hatred, violence, and suffering. When he died, it seemed to many that the progress from death to canonization was inevitable and would be unusually speedy. In 1963, however, he became the object of critical scrutiny and widespread public debate when Rolf Hochhuth brought out his accusatory play *The Deputy*. The central issue in the assessment of Pius XII as a man and as a Christian leader and in the interpretation of his pontificate became the adequacy or inadequacy of his response to Hitler's attempt at a "final solution of the Jewish problem." Controversy has raged during the past forty years over when and in what detail Pius knew about the extermination camps, how much he should have said and done to oppose what the Nazis were doing to the Jews (as well as to the Poles, the gypsies, and many others), and to what extent he was infected by anti-Semitic elements within the Catholic tradition.

The assessment of Pius XII as an agent and leader in a time of grave crisis is a topic that calls for: (1) the sifting of vast amounts of archival information and controversial exchanges; (2) the articulation and defense of an appropriate standpoint for making judgments; and (3) the overcoming of suspicion and secrecy, of feelings and practices that stand in the way of a clear reading of his case. This is not a task that the author of this chapter has the time or the ability to accomplish. Rather, I have to ask readers to set aside their concerns about this overwhelmingly important and difficult topic (which many for good reasons will regard as the elephant in the center of the room). At the same time I have to admit that we should not set aside these concerns altogether; they form an indispensable part of the context within which we attempt to interpret the social thought of this leader of the Church in what is in many respects the darkest period of European history. My interest is not primarily in the moral dispositions and obligations of Pius XII himself but with the way he exercised his office of universal teacher of the

Church on issues of social justice in a time of extreme crisis, a time in which Rome itself was bombed and was under German occupation and in which enormous numbers of Europeans (as well as Asians and Africans and Americans) were killed. The major statements of Catholic social teaching have been issued as responses to profound and usually lengthy processes of social, economic, and political change, such as industrialization, decolonization, and globalization; the Christmas messages of Pius XII express the concerns of one pope who is teaching "under fire," so to speak, and who at the same time is drawing on a tradition of social thought that was elaborated for less troubled times.

What I propose to do here is to set forth some of the themes in the social teaching of Pius XII with particular attention to the ways in which they exhibit the developmental process at work in Catholic social teaching. One factor that complicates this task is that Pius XII, unlike his predecessor Pius XI and his successor John XXIII, did not in the nineteen years of his pontificate issue a single social encyclical. Documentary collections of Catholic social teaching commonly skip from *Quadragesimo anno* (1931) of Pius XI to *Mater et magistra* (1962) of John XXIII. The most influential vehicle that Pius XII used for expressing his understanding of Catholic social teaching and its implications for the crisis of his time was not an encyclical but a series of Christmas messages that he broadcast each year from 1939 on. There are several likely reasons for Pius's choice of the Christmas message over the encyclical as the format for expressing his social teaching. He may well have wanted to show a readiness to use the comparatively new and widely influential medium of radio, which would give him direct access to millions of people in many different countries. He may well have wanted to use a less formal and more flexible vehicle of teaching than an encyclical, one that would raise fewer questions about the ecclesial status and the reformability of what he wanted to say. In addition, because of his service as secretary of state under Pius XI, he had firsthand knowledge of the efforts that the totalitarian governments of Europe had made to prevent the distribution of the encyclicals that Pius XI had aimed at the governments of fascist Italy, Nazi Germany, and Soviet Russia in the late 1930s.[1]

While it is true that Pius did not issue "a social encyclical," the address that he gave on the feast of Pentecost, June 1, 1941, to mark the fiftieth anniversary of Leo XIII's issuance of *Rerum novarum* (1891) makes it clear that he thought highly of that encyclical and that he wanted his own teaching to be seen as a continuation of the teaching of Leo XIII and Pius XI. Pius XII affirms "the indisputable competence of the Church, on that side of the social order where it meets and enters into contact with the moral order, to decide whether the bases of a given social system are in accord with the unchangeable order which God our Creator and Redeemer has shown us through the Natural Law and Revelation."[2] In opposition to the totalitarian systems, which were at that time dominant throughout Europe, Pius XII affirmed the need for public authority "to safeguard the inviolable sphere of the rights of the human person and to facilitate the fulfillment of his duties." He also warned against any interpretation of the common good that would give to the state a power that would "determine at will the manner of his physical, spiritual, religious, and moral movements in opposition to the personal duties or rights of man and to this end abolish or deprive of efficacy his natural rights to material goods."[3] As the last line indicates, Pius was concerned in a special way about the threat of totalitarian communism with its explicit denial of private property, a position that Leo XIII had explicitly condemned. But, as the point about making property rights inefficacious makes clear, he was also concerned about the arbitrary confiscations and the comprehensive mobilization of resources carried on by the Nazis, the fascists, and assorted political thugs who did not reject property rights as such but who were intent on total social control and personal enrichment. The pope's language here and his use of such broad categories as human rights and the common good reflect the influence of Jacques Maritain[4] and point forward to the Universal

Declaration of Human Rights endorsed by the United Nations in 1949.

One proposal in the 1941 Pentecost address is particularly imaginative. It is tied in a special way to the circumstances of the war in which Germany was demanding *Lebensraum*, proposing to find it in Eastern Europe and in the lands of the Slavs. Pius starts from the special standing that *Rerum novarum* gives to property in land, the form of property "most conformable to nature" and "the holding in which the family lives, and from the products of which it derives all or part of its subsistence." Land "makes of the family the vital and most perfect and fecund cell of society, joining up in a brilliant manner in its progressive cohesion the present and future generations."[5] In the computer age, this is a view that sounds not merely idyllic and romantic but also nostalgic and archaic. But in 1941 it had a definite policy edge. For Pius goes on to acknowledge the uneven distribution of arable land among the diverse peoples and to argue for a right of voluntary emigration, a change that he sees as mutually beneficial for all the parties. He observes: "The thickly inhabited countries will be relieved, and their peoples will acquire new friends in foreign countries; and the states which receive the emigrants will acquire industrious citizens."[6] We should note, however, that Pius envisages this change as something accepted voluntarily by all parties and not as the product of conquest and coercion in the style favored by Hitler and by the Japanese in their similar expansion in East Asia. But the primary emphasis in this Pentecost address is not on the elaboration of new proposals but on the need to continue the teaching of Leo XIII and Pius XI.

THE CHURCH AND WORLD WAR II

Pius accomplished this continuity with the teaching of his predecessors primarily through the seven Christmas messages of the war years (1939–45), which, taken together, are equivalent in length to two encyclicals. One might think of them as the theological equivalent of Cornish hens with more bone than meat. No one of them has the theological range or the analytic ambitions of the major documents. A great deal of the material in these messages repeats formulas appropriate to the Christmas season and, on a more serious level, themes such as the need for law, the value of peace, the commandment that we should love one another, the consolation that faith provides in times of crisis and calamity. These are themes of timeless relevance within the Christian tradition, but they are not surprising or controversial. Along with this familiar and predictable material, there is an ongoing effort to find the right point of insertion for the Church to say something that would affirm the traditional teachings and values of Catholicism and speak effectively to a world in turmoil. This effort produces subtle changes in what is selected for emphasis as the war progresses; it is, however, carried forward in an abstract style and a cautious spirit, which link it with the style and spirit of the major social encyclicals. Here it is worth remembering the general course of the war and the different shaping events that dominated public awareness at successive celebrations of the Christmas feast: the uncertainty of the "phoney war" (1939), the year of apparently decisive Nazi victories (1940), the entry of the Soviet Union and the United States into the war (1941), the joining of the issue in North Africa and southern Russia (1942), the collapse of the Mussolini regime and the period of increasing Allied pressure, which included the bombing of Rome and the occupation of the city by the German military (1943), the liberation of France and the closing of the circle around Germany and Japan (1944), and the aftermath of Allied victory (1945).

The continuing expansion of the war meant that the Vatican had to deal with a growing number of political and military conflicts among nations that were prominent in the life of the Church. Franco-German, Polish-German, and Italian-French conflicts all involved countries that had large Catholic populations and that also had histories of serious government conflict with the Church. The Catholic population of the British Empire was quite large, even though it was a minority within the

United Kingdom itself, and ranged from the devotedly loyal (many Canadians and Australians) to the passionately hostile (Irish and Indian nationalists). The existence of large and articulate Catholic communities on both sides of the war in its initial phases made it plausible for the pope to assume a public posture of neutrality. The period of Nazi conquest vastly increased the number of Catholics subject to Hitler's rule in Austria, Czechoslovakia, Poland, Belgium, The Netherlands, and France. The Germans and the Italians, as they moved into the Balkans and into war with the Soviet Union, appealed to nationalist sentiments in such Catholic countries or regions as Croatia, Slovakia, and Lithuania, and they drew on anti-Semitic and anti-Bolshevik fears and passions. In Rome there were vivid memories of the violence directed against the Church in the Spanish civil war, at the end of which church interests were recognized and protected by a regime that had significant parallels with the fascist regimes of Germany and Italy and that was actively supported by them. In this early phase of successful aggression, the fascists and the Nazis found willing collaborators in many Catholic populations. The later phases of the war added further levels of complexity: (1) a comparatively self-contained war in the Pacific, in which China and the Western allies with their heritage of Christianity and colonialism opposed the intensely nationalistic and militaristic regime in Japan; and (2) the titanic and bloody struggle between Nazi Germany and Soviet Russia, a struggle in which there was no clearly positive outcome for the Catholic Church.

This way of thinking about the course of World War II may strike those of us who have been raised in the tradition of Churchillian rhetoric and who have been educated to regard the fate of Europe's Jews as a matter of overriding importance as an unfamiliar and rather parochial perspective. I am not interested in arguing for this Rome-centered perspective as the correct way of understanding the course of events in World War II. I am interested simply in indicating how things would look in an approach that understood Catholic concerns in terms of the interests and desires of particular Catholic communities and national movements and that saw the survival of the Catholic community as an effective international body as a major objective in efforts to stabilize the present and to shape a more just and less violent future. If we allow for the possibility of thinking from such a perspective, we can begin to understand why in the Christmas message of 1941 Pius XII says: "We love, and in this we call upon God to be our witness. We love with equal affection all peoples, without any exception whatsoever, and in order to avoid even the appearance of being moved by partisanship. We have maintained hitherto the greatest reserve."[7]

When a statement such as this is set against the background of Nazi ideology and propaganda, it can and should be seen both as a personal declaration that affirms core Christian values (the universality of God's gift of salvation, the universal scope of the love commandment) and at the same time as an expression of unwillingness to present unambiguously and specifically the implications of these values in the contemporary situation of conflict. In the preceding paragraph Pius has denounced those anti-Christian tendencies that have during the course of the war "become even more marked" so that it is clear that he is willing to enter into the denunciatory mode. He is willing to take sides in what we later on in America would call "the culture wars," but he does not want to do so in the conflicted international arena of his own time. Of course, we can all recognize the possibilities of misinterpretation, often enough deliberate and even malevolent misrepresentation, by the side that one opposes or criticizes in a conflict situation. We can also see the difficulty that taking one side in a conflict raises for the effort to present oneself as an exponent and practitioner of universal love. Such considerations may be of some relevance when one is dealing with what are apparently ordinary international conflicts, but they fail to illuminate the moral landscape when one side is practicing genocide and denying all elements of human community to people whom it represents as vermin and worthy of extermination. The notion of neutrality between those who are the practitioners and those who are the victims of genocide is morally vacuous, whatever the diplomatic and humanitarian opportunities which, for instance, a policy of neutrality between the Germans and the British might protect. Here, however, we should remember that at Christmas 1941 the policy of genocide was still in its early stages, with the activities of the *Einsatzgruppen* following on the advance of German armies to the east and before the establishment of the major extermination camps. Pius's public statements were understandably focused on the states that were carrying on the gigantic public struggle of the war and not on their more or less covert destructive activities, but one should begin to see the dangers of linking universal love and neutrality at a time when genocide was on the agenda of one side.

Pius XII and Balance

A surprising illustration of the papal effort to achieve a kind of balance between the sides in the conflict, if not neutrality in a technical legal sense, can be found at the end of the 1944 Christmas message. In a remarkable passage composed while Rome, along with nearly all of southern and central Italy, was under Allied occupation and while the Reich was preparing its last offensive in the Ardennes, Pius expresses his thanks to those governments that have assisted his relief efforts:

> And in the first place it is but just to record the immense work of assistance achieved in spite of the extraordinary difficulties of transport, by the United States of America and, with regard to Italy in particular, by His Excellency the personal Representative of the President of the Union. It is a pleasure for us to express equal praise and gratitude for the generosity of the head of the State, the Government and people of Spain, and the governments of Ireland, Argentina, Australia, Bolivia, Brazil, Canada, Chile, Italy, Lithuania, Peru, Poland, Roumania, Slovakia, Hungary and Uruguay, who have vied with one another in noble rivalry of brotherly love and charity, the echo of which will not resound in vain through the world.[8]

This was written at a time when purely prudential arguments for neutrality were no longer relevant for several reasons: (1) it was obvious that the Allies would be victorious both in Europe and in the Pacific; (2) Rome was no longer under the control of the Gestapo; and (3) Germany, once so terrifying and so apparently invincible, had been undergoing a long series of defeats on both eastern and western fronts. The acknowledgment of the preeminent role of the United States may be taken cynically as a salute to rising power, but it probably also reflects the impression made by the scale of resources mobilized by the United States during the last year or so of the war and by the generosity with which the United States was willing to respond to the needs of the devastated continent that had long conceived of itself as the center and ruler of the world. But what is more remarkable is that the second place is given to the Spanish government of Francisco Franco, a dictator who was widely despised in Britain, France, and the United Sates and who was generally regarded as a protégé of Mussolini and Hitler, even though he had refrained from entering the war on the side of the Axis. A special place is given to Ireland, a country that had maintained its neutrality to the end of the great conflict. Then the other nations follow in alphabetical order, with no effort being made to segregate Allied (Australia, Brazil, Canada, Chile, Peru, Uruguay) and Axis (Lithuania, Rumania, Slovakia, and Hungary) powers and with no effort to indicate the anomalous status of Italy and Poland. The list shows a specificity that is quite unusual in the Christmas messages and that would be even more unusual in an encyclical. It is of interest mainly as an indication of the range of states with which the Vatican had to deal and of the difficulty which the Vatican would have had in making its own the Anglo-American understanding of the war as primarily a crusade against Nazi tyranny. In fact, the heading of the paragraph in which Pius gives his list of countries to be thanked is "Crusade for Charity." He speaks of those countries that "have had a share in this crusade of charity," which clearly has to be a nonadversarial and benevolent activity.

The Mission of Christianity

As suggested earlier, the pope's adversarial energies are directed to those cultural forces in the modern world which he regards as hostile to Christian belief and to the Christian community. In the 1941 message he makes it clear that he is particularly stung by the accusation that Christianity has failed in its mission. He affirms that such an accusation could not have come from the heroic proponents of Christianity in its earlier phases or from "those noble men who initiated the Christian civilization, who saved the remnants of the wisdom and art of Athens and Rome, who united peoples in the name of Christ, and who taught wisdom and virtue, who raised the cross above the airy pinnacles and vaults of the Cathedrals, those replicas of heavenly beauty and monuments of faith and piety which still elevate their lofty and venerable towers in the midst of the ruins of Europe."[9] In Pius's view the religious failure of Europe is the work of those men who "have rebelled against that Christianity which is true and faithful to Christ and His doctrines." Pius has to acknowledge that there has been in Europe a "progressive de-christianization, both individual and social, which from moral laxity has developed into a general state of weakness and brought about the open denial of truth and of those influences whose function it is to illuminate our minds in the matter of good and evil and to fortify family life, private life and the public life of the State."[10] In place of the values of "Christian civilization," there has been a turning of human thoughts and efforts in the direction of producing material goods. As a result, Pius argues:

> We witnessed in the political sphere the prevalence of an unrestrained impulse toward expansion and mere political advantage, to the disregard of moral principles; in the field of economics the domination of great gigantic enterprises and trusts; in social life, the uprooting, and crowding of masses of the people in distressing and excessive concentration in the great cities and centers of industry and commerce, with all the uncertainty which is an inevitable consequence when men in large numbers change their home and residence, their country and trade, their attachments and friendships.[11]

The similarity of this to more recent religious denunciations of globalization is striking, which should not be surprising since many of the same pressures to internationalization, industrialization, urbanization, and intensified economic and social interaction on both national and international levels were present in both the first and last quarters of the twentieth century. As all, however, would recognize, the political context for the post–cold war period of globalization is significantly different from the divided and exhausted Europe of the Versailles settlement, and the economic circumstances of the 1990s are much better than those of the interwar period.

In his assessment of the European political scene and in his reaction to those totalitarian movements and ideologies that would exclude Christianity from public life or from modern society, Pius is willing to take a stance expressing religious opposition to culture, even though he would not use the "Christ against culture" language of H. Richard Niebuhr. Rather, as a striking passage in the 1942 message illustrates, he wants to use the manifest internal conflicts of the secular culture to bring about repentance and conversion. He writes: "In this hour of material and moral disintegration the appreciation of the emptiness and inconsistency of every purely human order is beginning to disillusion even those who in days of apparent happiness, were not conscious of the need of contact with the eternal in themselves or in society, and did not look upon its absence as an essential defect in their constitutions."[12] While his tone is not strident or venemous, it is clear that in Pius's view the world is called to learn from the Church, and there is not much room for traffic to move in the opposite direction.

The more optimistic and accepting tone found in *Gaudium et spes*, Vatican II's famous constitution on the Church and the modern world, is absent here. There is more similarity between Pius XII and John Paul II in that they see serious moral defects in the values and the organization of modern secular society. Pius characterizes the war itself as "the crumbling process, not expected, perhaps, by the thoughtless but seen and depreciated by those whose gaze penetrated into the realities of a social order which hid its mortal weakness and its unbridled lust for gain and power."[13] This is not altogether different from the denunciation of the opposing systems driven by the desire for power and for wealth that John Paul II offers in *Sollicitudo rei socialis*.

THE CHURCH AND DEMOCRACY

This negative interpretation of modern culture was more likely to be broadly persuasive in the time of Pius XII, for in the aftermath of the Great Depression and the enormous bloodshed of World War II there was, particularly in Europe, a widely shared feeling that something fundamental had gone wrong in the forces shaping the trajectory of European history. This feeling was probably less powerful in the United States, which had found a politically, if not economically, successful response to the Great Depression in the New Deal of Franklin Roosevelt; which had not suffered the violence of World War II on its own soil; and which had been at the head of the victorious coalition in the war. The sense that the modern project had failed could lead intellectuals and activists in the direction of the revolutionary destruction of the capitalist economic order with its legal and constitutional guarantees of personal liberties and limited government and its protection of bourgeois individualism, or it could lead in the direction of a return to Christian values. When the choice was posed in these terms, the Vatican response could not be in doubt. The important political conflicts of the postwar period in Europe were fought between the Christian Democrats (ranging from the moderate left to the moderate right) and the Communists (strongly antireligious) and their (usually secularist) socialist sympathizers. But the direction of Christian Democratic politics after World War II was not toward monarchical restoration or toward right-wing forms of nationalism; rather, it was toward a combination of democratic constitutional arrangements, establishment and enhancement of the welfare state, and the affirmation of traditional patterns of family life and economic life (family farms and businesses). The conflict between Communists and Christian Democrats raged on the national level, especially in France and Italy, and on the continental level, especially after the formation of NATO. It was given a distinctive shape in Germany, where Communists ruled in the East and Christian Democrats prevailed in the West. The Christian Democrats also played important roles in the decisive tasks of Franco-German reconciliation and of the construction of the institutional framework that ultimately became the European Union. In doing this, they were responding to strong internationalist elements within the Catholic social tradition. This transformation in the character and position of Catholic political involvement was carried on during the pontificate of Pius XII and clearly had his blessing and support from 1945 to 1958, the year in which the Treaty of Rome took effect and Pius himself died. It required an endorsement of the democratic structures and practices that were at the center of Western political life, even though Catholicism had previously kept a certain distance from these structures.

The elements of this transformation can be seen in various passages from the Christmas messages, but especially in the 1944 Christmas message, which takes as its theme "True and False Democracy." Pius begins by making the general point that "democracy, taken in the broad sense, admits of various forms, and can be realized in monarchies as well as in republics."[14] He also makes a contrast between healthy and unhealthy democracies, which he discusses in vitalist language. He makes a further distinction between "the people" and "the masses." He claims that "the people lives and moves by its own life energy; the masses are inert of themselves and can only be moved from outside."[15] The members of the people are persons conscious of their own responsibility and their own views, which implies a certain level of education and social maturation. The masses, on the other hand, are ready to be exploited. Pius describes this negative possibility in the following striking passage, which in 1944 would have to be seen as referring to the totalitarian regimes of Germany, Italy, and Russia in which a party rooted in the masses had taken over control of the state and of all key social organizations: "In the ambitious hands of one or of several who have been artificially brought together for selfish aims, the state itself, with the support of the masses, reduced to the minimum status of a mere machine, can impose its whims on the better part of the real people."[16] In Pius's view, "the masses are the capital enemy of true democracy and of its ideal of liberty and equality." Even though he admits the place of equality in the network of democratic ideals, Pius thinks that the life of the people is compatible with diverse forms of inequality. So he writes: "In a people worthy of the name all inequalities based not on whim but on the nature of things, inequalities of culture, possessions, social standing—without, of course, prejudice to justice and mutual charity—do not constitute any obstacle to the existence and the prevalence of a true spirit of union and brotherhood."[17] Pius here takes a conservative attitude to the existence of widespread inequality, though he does not want to compromise the dominant role of justice and charity as norms. He also opposes efforts to impose a comprehensive equality in the name of a democratic ideology or as an expression of the power and desires of the masses. It is also Pius's view that the democratic state should be "entrusted with the power to command with real and effective authority."[18] He puts particular weight on the character and responsibility of legislators or parliamentary deputies who are to form "a group of select men, spiritually eminent and of strong character, who shall look upon themselves as the representatives of the entire people and not the mandatories of a mob." The activity of the legislators in making positive law is to be conformed to "the absolute order set up by the Creator and placed in a new light by the revelation of the Gospel."[19] While Pius acknowledges that "the democratic form of government appears to many as a postulate of nature imposed by reason itself,"[20] he is clearly not about to offer a rubber stamp endorsement of whatever comes forth from the democratic political machinery. The papal endorsement of democracy, while real and significant, is qualified and cautious. It is also vulnerable on one key point, a point that the situation of ethnic and religious minorities during the post-Versailles period should have made inescapable, namely, the possibility of understanding "the people" in ethnically exclusive ways that would entrench and deepen existing forms of inequality and discrimination. The vitalistic and organicist language that Pius uses here is particularly liable to this sort of corruption, and the Nazi reliance on *das Volk* as a central theme in their internal rhetoric should have made clear how dangerous and even catastrophic this sort of language could be.

The treatment of democracy in the 1944 Christmas message, however, is an important step on the road from the classic affirmations of indifference among possible constitutional arrangements that had been characteristic of neoscholasticism and of early papal documents toward the full embrace of the procedures and values of constitutional democracy, at least in the political order, which is found in John XXIII's *Pacem in terris* and *Gaudium et spes* of Vatican II.[21] The direction and extent of change in this regard can be gauged from a passage in the 1942 Christmas message in which Pius assures his international audience that the Church "does not intend to take sides for any of the particular forms in which the several peoples and States strive to solve the gigantic problems of domestic order or international collaboration, as long as these forms conform to the law of God."[22] The strong element of continuity is the insistence that any regime must obey the law of God and the moral law that Pius, following the classic Catholic tradition, treats as making the same demands. What varies with time is the sense of the connection between specific positions in the age-old debate on the right form of constitution, positions that are imperfectly embodied in particular regimes, and the values and demands of morality as these come to be more clearly understood in an egalitarian conception of the human person as a democratic citizen. In the 1945 Christmas message, this development issues in an unqualified demand for the elimination of totalitarian regimes, which Pius denounces for their arbitrary disruptions of human community and for policies that are "contrary to the dignity and welfare of the human race."[23] The interesting point in the timing of this denunciation is that it occurs after the demise of Nazism and fascism but at a time when communism through its control of the Soviet Union, which had contributed to the Allied victory on a grand scale, was at the apogee of its public esteem. No particular regimes are discussed, but the general category of totalitarianism has effectively come to be a class with one member, namely, the Soviet Union along with its satellites in Eastern Europe.

The elimination of totalitarian states is one of the three prerequisites for a true peace which Pius proposes in his 1945 message, along with reciprocal confidence among peoples and the elimination of arbitrary censorship. Pius commends "collaboration, good will, reciprocal confidence" and deplores the presence of "the motives of hate, vengeance, rivalry, antagonism, unfair and dishonest competition" in "political and economic debates and decisions."[24] But his special concern was that the punishment of criminals and the demands for reparations should be based on moral principles and should not imitate or repeat the original offenses. Though he does not make the point explicitly, he was understandably concerned that the resolution of the war should not stand in the way of reconciliation as the war-guilt and reparations clauses of the Versailles Treaty had done after World War I. When he talks about eliminating arbitrary censorship, his concern seems not to be the civil libertarian's anxiety about the repression of personal liberties by the government, but rather the manipulation of public opinion through "one-sided judgments and false assertions." This seems to be a description of the monopoly of media and education in the totalitarian states that enabled them to mislead their populations in the direction of an aggressive nationalism.

Five Milestones toward a Better Future

The comparative modesty of the peace agenda set forth by the pope in 1945 is a reflection of the uncertainties of the time in which relations among the wartime Allies were clearly beginning to deteriorate and in which large numbers of refugees continued to be unsettled and in which there was no clear movement toward a comprehensive settlement. The 1942 message actually has a more clearly articulated vision of the future. Or, to use the metaphor that Pius himself employs, it offers us "the first five milestones" on the road to a better future.[25] These are (1) dignity of the human person, (2) defense of social unity, (3) dignity of labor, (4) the rehabilitation of juridical order, and (5) a Christian conception of the state.[26] With the possible exception of the fourth, all of these have been important and recurrent themes in Catholic social teaching.

With regard to the dignity of the human person, Pius is most concerned to achieve "the practical realization of the following fundamental personal rights: the right to maintain and develop one's corporal, intellectual and moral life and especially the right to religious formation and education; the right to worship God in private and public and to carry on religious works of charity; the right to marry and to achieve the aim of married life; the right to conjugal and domestic society; the right to work, as the indispensable means towards the maintenance of family; the right to free choice of state of life and hence, too, of the priesthood or religious life; the right to the use of material goods, in keeping with his duties and social limitations."[27] Here we can see an understandable preoccupation with affirming the right of individuals to participate in various religious activities that the totalitarian states had attempted to proscribe or restrict. Pius still formulates rights in the religious area in such a way that rights are linked to true goods and not to possibly erroneous choices. This is compatible with a more restrictive approach in which the rights of Catholics to believe and to act in accordance with religious truth enjoy higher status even while general rights to religious freedom are not clearly affirmed for nonbelievers and non-Christians. We should also note the close connections that Pius affirms among religion, family life, and work.

Second, the defense of social unity involves a rejection of materialism in social thinking and of the tendency to think of people in terms of masses or herds; in contrast, it affirms an understanding of society "as an intrinsic unity . . . which tends, with the collaboration of the various classes and professions, towards the eternal and ever new aims of culture and religion."[28] To put the matter more generally, Pius has no desire to think of the unity of society in reductionist or coercive terms. More specifically, he is concerned about the family and its role in regard to education. He denounces the public schools of the time as a source of materialism. This may be an indirect effort to denounce Nazi educational programs, but it is so general and vague that no one who was not already inclined to treat such programs with suspicion and disapproval would have any idea that this is what is intended. No connection is made between social unity and the divisive effects of racism and extreme nationalism.

The third of the milestones, the dignity of labor, is more complex and more interesting. Pius begins with a high and positive view of work when he says that "as an indispensable means towards gaining over the world the mastery which God wishes, for his glory, all work has an inherent dignity and at the same time a close connection with the perfection of the person."[29] This is a view that points forward to the view of work offered by John Paul II in *Laborem exercens* (1981). Pius explicitly links his understanding of work with the major affirmations of Leo XIII in *Rerum novarum* (1891) about the moral demands for a just wage for workers and for "an assured, even if modest, private property for all classes of society." He expects these to replace the sense of isolation felt by workers with "the assuring experience of a genuinely human, and fraternally Christian, solidarity." He goes on to make it clear that he believes there are close connections between "an intelligent and generous sharing of forces between the strong and the weak" and the possibility of "a universal pacification" in which there will no longer be "centers of conflagration and infection."[30] This again anticipates the teaching of Paul VI and John Paul II on the close connections between the achievement of economic interdependence and the establishment of peace.

The fourth major milestone that Pius proposes is "the rehabilitation of the juridical order." The major threat to the juridical order that he finds is "the profession and the practice of positivism and a utilitarianism which are subjected and bound to the service of determined groups, classes, and movements, whose programs direct and determine the course of legislation and the practices of the courts."[31] Against these tendencies and political pressures, which can be found in different forms in the totalitarian parties and in the legal realism that was offered in this period as an interpretation of the U.S. judicial system, Pius sets a conception of the juridical order as resting on the will of God and including man's "inalienable right . . . to a definite sphere of rights immune from all arbitrary attack."[32] Two of the conclusions that he draws from this conception are that "clear juridical norms . . . may not be overturned by unwarranted appeals to a supposed popular sentiment or by merely utilitarian considerations" and that the state and its subordinates are "obliged to repair and to withdraw measures which are harmful to the liberty, property, honor, progress or health of . . . individuals."[33] From this it should be a short step to condemn the Nurnberg Laws and the discriminatory anti-Semitic legislation of the Nazis and their satellites as well as the class-based and party-controlled judicial systems of the Soviet world. This text combines propositions that are clearly incompatible with totalitarian profession and practice with a vagueness of formulation that leaves people in the dark about the real shape of the problem. For one can readily concede that the pope has correctly pointed to the integrity of the judicial system as one of the key factors in preventing a state from going off the rails morally as well as to the danger presented by groups and movements that are intent on reshaping the public order according to their private agenda. But realistic commentary on political life has to recognize a crucially important division between the blatantly immoral and coercive programs of the Nazis and Communists and the efforts of various interest groups in democratic societies to influence legislation in their own favor. The undeniable presence of corruption and of efforts to work out special deals for the rich and the powerful in such democratic regimes as the Third Republic in France figured prominently in the totalitarian effort to delegitimate morally flawed democratic governments. Without wishing to apologize for corruption in democratic regimes, I would want to argue that it is the kind of evil that needs to be resisted, not eradicated, that it shows the moral vulnerability of democracies and the need for reform, not for revolution. The vagueness of the 1942 Christmas message allows the papal defense of the integrity of the juridical order to be ignored or to be used for misleading purposes. A more positive assessment, however, of the pope's position would interpret him as calling for the rule of law and for limited constitutional government in which the independence of the judiciary would be effectively protected.

The last of the milestones that Pius discusses is what he calls the "Christian conception of the State," a conception that he characterizes as "founded on reasonable discipline, exalted kindliness and responsible Christian spirit."[34] We should begin by recognizing that Pius is not making a clear call for any particular regime of Church-state relations, even though his language would seem naïve or pretentious to most advocates of political realism and could well strike Jews and other non-Christians as exclusionary and even ominous. The two main concerns that he has, as the rest of his discussion makes clear, are that the state should not set itself above the bounds of morality and that it should not deny its "essential dependence on the will of the Creator." This is a position that would appeal to those Christian conservatives who were shocked and appalled by what the Nazis were doing, to those members of the Church who were distressed by the godless character of the regimes in Germany and Russia, and to those philosophers and theologians who admired Maritain's efforts to combine the Catholic concern for the common good with an affirmation of the rights of the person and a defense of the Church against totalitarian regimes.[35] It falls short of the expectations of those whose views on these matters have been shaped by Anglo-American liberalism and by the American insistence on separation of church and state. We know from subsequent events, notably the treatment of John Courtney Murray, that Pius was not inclined to move in this liberal direction even after the restraints of the war had been removed.[36] But he concludes his discussion of this milestone with a provocative call for "the recognition and diffusion of the truth which teaches, even in matters of this world, that the deepest meaning, the ultimate moral basis and the universal validity of 'reigning' lies in 'serving.'" This alludes to a Roman collect, a prayer taken from the Mass that speaks of Christ *cui servire est regnare* (whom to serve is to reign). It prompts readers to think not in terms of dynastic and national aggrandizement but in a spirit of pastoral and democratic service. It can also be seen as an allusion to the title of the pope as "servant of the servants of God," and less clearly as an evocation of the self-presentation of Frederick the Great as "the first servant of the kingdom." But the fundamental basis for the position Pius proposes is the passage in the Gospels where Jesus draws a contrast between the rulers of the gentiles who lord it over their subjects and the servant leadership that is to be offered by the disciples. In effect, Pius asks his readers to consider a secular analogue to this religious maxim, a thought that is both an indictment of the practices and attitudes of contemporary governments and a call to conversion in the way nations are governed.

Pius XII and World War II

While it is in his 1942 address that Pius is most explicit in his treatment of the peace that should be brought about after the war, it is in his 1943 address that he offers his most explicit reflections on the war itself, which he sees as "that form of warfare that excludes all restriction and restraint, as if it were the apocalyptic expression of a civilization in which ever-growing technical progress is accompanied by an ever greater decline in the realm of the soul and of morality."[37] Like most observers at the time, Pius was appalled by the scale and the destructiveness of the conflict, which had a far greater impact on the civilian population than World War I. The Germans had occupied Rome and most of Italy after the fall of Mussolini's regime in July 1943 and the capitulation of the successor regime of Marshall Badoglio to the Allies in early September, and the Americans had bombed the city in July 1943. Pius was alarmed by the "interior decadence which, starting from the weakening and deviation of the moral sense, is hurtling ever downward towards the state where every human sentiment is being crushed and the light of reason is eclipsed, so that the words of Wisdom are fulfilled: 'They were all bound together with one chain of darkness' (Wis. 17.17)."[38] In his account of the moral aspect of the conflict, the pope here does not seem to make significant distinctions between the two sides, but later toward the end of the message he makes a plea that seems to be directed primarily toward Hitler: "In the consciousness of your power your war aims may well have embraced entire peoples and continents. The question of guilty responsibility for the present war and the demand for reparations may also lead you to raise your voice."[39] He also experiences a tension between what he calls "the duty of impartiality inherent in our pastoral ministry" and the need to secure "the triumph of the principles of far-seeing and even-minded justice and brotherhood in the questions that are so essential for the salvation of States."[40] Though he does not explicitly call for a negotiated settlement to the war, he does speak of "the task of securing agreement and concord between the warring nations" that would leave to each nation "the possibility of cooperating with dignity, without renouncing or destroying itself, in the great future task of recuperation and reconstruction."[41] This is, of course, a possibility that might be open to a post-Hitler German government, though Pius does not enter into such a precarious discussion in public. But it is reasonable to take the pope's public position as a thinly veiled criticism of the Allied demand for unconditional surrender, a demand that had been given a defining role among Allied war aims by Churchill and Roosevelt when they met at Casablanca in January 1943. This criticism is rooted in his fear that the continued destructiveness of the war will threaten the "very existence" of peoples. But, despite the horror he feels about the continuation of the war, Pius does not favor peace at any price; he explicitly warns against "the unspeakable catastrophe of a peace built on wrong foundations and therefore ephemeral and illusory."[42] Here both the failed settlement of Versailles and the shortsighted appeasement of Munich would be relevant precedents, though the pope makes no mention of either.

On the more general level of principle, Pius continues to adhere to the main lines of Catholic thought about the moral character of the state and about the justifiability of relying on force. He writes:

> A true peace is not the mathematical result of a proportion of forces, but in its last and deepest meaning is a moral and juridical process. It is not, in fact, achieved without the employment of force, and its very existence needs the support of a normal measure of power. But the real function of this force, if it is to be morally correct, should consist in protecting and defending, and not in lessening or suppressing rights.[43]

Pius here relies on the combination of moralism and realism that is characteristic of the just war tradition, which insists both that war be conducted within a moral environment shaped by just cause, right intention, and proper authority, and that at the same time it be directed to the end of true peace. But he also shares an awareness with most political observers in the second half of the twentieth century of the threat that vicious or morally unsound governments present to the rights of peoples. This awareness was to find its most influential articulation after the war in the Universal Declaration of Human Rights.

CONCLUSION

In the Christmas messages we find Pius proclaiming the basic truths of the Catholic social tradition, calling the peoples of a torn and divided world to a conversion of mind and heart and insisting on the moral substance present within even the most bitter political and military conflicts. He does not modify or surrender the principles of this tradition, but he allows his commitment to neutrality and his pastoral care for all parties to restrict his consideration of the practical implications of these principles in such a way that outside observers have reason to judge him to be complaisant or timorous in the face of overwhelming evils. This, of course, brings us back to questions about the personality and the moral character of Eugenio Pacelli, which I initially announced that I would not take up as a primary topic. But I think we also have to keep in mind the possibility that the religious tradition within which he was working made it very difficult for him to articulate an adequate response to the terrifying and radical crisis through which he was called to lead the Church. Here we are thinking about the intellectual tradition of Catholic social teaching articulated in the social encyclicals of Leo XIII and Pius XI, about a diplomatic and administrative pattern of practice that encouraged the Holy See to work with established governments and not with critical political movements, and about a pastoral attitude that systematically underestimated the capacity of local churches and of the laity to make mature moral judgments and to take responsible action.

In this regard, several factors deserve consideration. First, the papal leadership of the Church had come to rely on a style of thought that aimed at expressing universal truths that would be immune to being overturned by empirical counterexamples and that thus would not need to be changed. Clearly, this characterization of Catholic social teaching is not the whole story, and the Christmas messages show numerous efforts to address current issues. But the movement of thought and argument is generally from the normative and unchanging universal to the complexity, specificity, and epistemic vulnerability needed to draw moral conclusions about what is to be done, who is to be supported or opposed, what evils have to be tolerated or resisted. In this mode of thought, which is heavily influenced by powerful patterns in both philosophy and law, there is a high level of anxiety about mistakes that might give rise to critical questions about the general principles. We can notice how this tendency to incorrigible generality is ameliorated after Vatican II initiates discourse about "the signs of the times" and also how ready John Paul II is to discuss the events of the year 1989 in *Centesimus annus*.

Second, the Church was probably still guided to a large extent by a desire to avoid a repetition of four previous mistakes that involved moving too quickly to the overly specific and to adversarial rather than neutral stances. Two of these were mistakes largely of the Church's own making, namely, the intransigence with which the Church opposed the French Revolution and all its works and heirs, and the refusal of the popes from Pius IX to Pius XI to recognize or collaborate with the government of unified Italy. The Church was less than clear in acknowledging that it had made serious mistakes in opposing such fundamental tendencies as the widespread demands for constitutional democracy and the liberalization of society, and the movements for national self-determination that threatened the older imperial regimes in Europe. The reversal of its policies in these areas had been carried out in the 1920s by Pius XI, who broke with the monarchist right in France and who approved the Lateran Treaties, which created a new accommodation between the Vatican and the Italian state. The Lateran Treaties also encouraged an unrealistic optimism about the possibilities of reaching reliable agreements with dictators. An open exposition of an acceptable theological rationale for these transformations in the social and political stance of the Church had to wait until Vatican II, but the decisive changes had actually come in stages from Leo XIII to Pius XI. The relevant consideration for our purposes is that these were situations where the Church had suffered significant defeats and permanent losses as a result of being too closely linked with one side in a series of political contests. The Church had mistaken the historically conditioned and the temporary (its dependence on the structures of the ancien régime and its political control over central Italy) for the lastingly valid in the faith of the Christian community. When these mistakes are analyzed for the sake of avoiding similar failures in the future, one can move in two different directions: either emphasizing the content, in which case the corrective is to move toward acceptance of liberal democracy, or focusing on the form, in which case the corrective is to avoid anything like justifications of specific policy stances. If one has lived through the collapse of democratic regimes in Italy, Spain, and Germany, if one has lived through the global economic crisis of the Great Depression, and if one has witnessed the brutal Soviet repression of all forms of religious expression, the notion that the Church will find space and security for its mission through an accommodation with liberal democracy in opposition to the fascist and ultranationalist regimes may seem like a venture that has certain moral attractions but that is also politically and pastorally risky.

The third and fourth mistakes had to do with the conduct and conclusion of World War I that were primarily mistakes committed by the Allied Powers, especially Great Britain and France. The Imperial German government, while routinely arrogant and oppressive and intermittently brutal and even savage, was not guilty of more than a fraction of the atrocities that Allied propaganda blamed on it. The attribution of atrocities had a high level of plausibility because of the undeniable fact of Germany's violation of Belgian neutrality and because of the hectoring and self-aggrandizing style in which the kaiser's Germany conducted its relations with its neighbors both before and during the war. But the skepticism that grew as the excesses of Allied propaganda were uncovered after the end of the war made it much more difficult to make an irrefutable case against the vastly worse patterns of German behavior during World War II. The Vatican was, however, one of the few organizations with the ability to confirm the truth of the most serious charges, but the responsibility it had to sound the alarm was made more difficult to fulfill by the skepticism that grew in the aftermath of World War I. Somewhat similar effects resulted from the widespread perception that the peace settlement at the end of the war had failed to achieve a just resolution of the issues raised by the war and had manifested a fundamental unwillingness on the part of the Allies to modify the pursuit of their national interest and national security for the sake of justice as well as a failure to honor the principles laid out in the famous Fourteen Points of Woodrow Wilson. Echoes of this perception can be found in several passages of the Christmas messages. Any effort to recommend principles for resolving the issues raised by World War II had, if it was to find a credible reception among the German people, even those strongly opposed to the Nazis, to show a recognition of their beliefs about the injustice of the Versailles settlement. These beliefs had provided a crucial element of legitimacy to the international program of the Hitler regime. Endorsing these beliefs would run the double risk of seeming to accept the rightness of what Hitler had done on the basis of this moral outrage and of enraging the Allied powers and those neighbors of Germany that had been threatened or violated by German aggression. Failing to endorse or acknowledge these beliefs would entrench key parts of the German population in their skepticism about Allied intentions and about Vatican neutrality. Effectively undoing the consequences of these mistakes probably exceeded both the political will of the Vatican and its intellectual resources.

What Pius XII was able to articulate in his Christmas messages during this time of grave crisis was a constrained and restricted repetition of some central values of the Catholic tradition of social thought, values such as the importance of maintaining the moral character of the state. But these values could easily be seen as tautologies or platitudes, since they were not joined with a perceptive and forthright statement of the actual political and moral situation of Europe in this gravely disturbed time or with a prophetic willingness to denounce evil. Generality and neutrality prevailed over courageous commitment and principled resistance to evil. The sound the trumpet gave in the heat of battle and agony was muted and ambiguous.

NOTES

1. See Anthony Rhodes, *The Vatican in the Age of the Dictators, 1922–1945* (London: Hodder and Stoughton, 1973), for an account of the difficulties arising from the effort to publish *Mit brennender Sorge* in Germany in 1937.

2. Pius XII, "The Anniversary of *Rerum novarum*," Pentecost address, June 1, 1941, in *Major Addresses of Pope Pius XII*, ed. Vincent Yzermans (St. Paul, Minn.: North Central, 1961), 1:28.

3. Ibid., 31.

4. A concise statement of Jacques Maritain's views can be found in *The Rights of Man and Natural Law*, trans. Doris Anson (New York: Scribner's, 1943), 7–11. This is substantially identical with his *Scholasticism and Politics* (New York: Macmillan, 1940), 69–71.

5. Pius XII, "Anniversary of *Rerum novarum*," 34.

6. Ibid.

7. Pius XII, "Christianity and the World Crisis," Christmas message of 1941, in *Major Addresses*, 2:48.

8. Pius XII, "True and False Democracy," Christmas message of 1944, in ibid., 89.

9. Pius XII, "Christianity and the World Crisis," Christmas message of 1941, in ibid., 40.

10. Ibid., 41.

11. Ibid., 42.

12. Pius XII, "The Internal Order of States and People," Christmas message of 1942, in ibid., 59.

13. Ibid., 64.

14. Pius XII, "True and False Democracy," Christmas message of 1944, in ibid., 80.

15. Ibid., 81.

16. Ibid.

17. Ibid.

18. Ibid., 82.

19. Ibid., 84.

20. Ibid., 81.

21. See Heinrich Albert Rommen, *The State in Catholic Thought* (St. Louis, Mo.: B. Herder, 1945), 477–80, for a concise account of the Catholic debate on the right or best form of government and for Leo XIII's rejection of the view that the American form of constitutional democracy is "always an unsurpassable ideal for all nations and all times."

22. Pius XII, "The Internal Order of States and People," in *Major Addresses*, 2:52.

23. Pius XII, "Prerequisites for True and Lasting Peace," in ibid., 97.

24. Ibid., 96.

25. Pius XII, "The Internal Order of States and People," in ibid., 60.

26. Ibid., 60–63.

27. Ibid., 60–61.

28. Ibid., 61.

29. Ibid.

30. Ibid, 62.

31. Ibid.

32. Ibid., 63.

33. Ibid.

34. Ibid.

35. For an interesting discussion of the ways in which the American experience influenced Maritain and in which Maritain criticized European Catholicism, see John T. McGreevey, *Catholicism and American Freedom* (New York: Norton, 2003), 196–203.

36. For an account of the continuing reluctance of the Roman authorities to accept the possibility of significant alteration in church teaching in this area, see Donald Pelotte, *John Courtney Murray: Theologian in Conflict* (New York: Paulist, 1976), 51.

37. Pius XII, "Peace and the Function of Force," in *Major Addresses*, 2:66.

38. Ibid., 67.

39. Ibid., 76.

40. Ibid., 75.

41. Ibid., 76.

42. Ibid., 77.

43. Ibid., 76.

SELECTED BIBLIOGRAPHY

Chadwick, Owen. *Britain and the Vatican during the Second World War*. Cambridge: Cambridge University Press, 1986. A standard, scholarly analysis of the diplomatic relations between Britain and the Vatican

Fogarty, Gerald P., ed. *Patterns of Episcopal Leadership*. New York: Macmillan, 1989. A carefully researched, nuanced study of the multidimensional styles of ecclesial leadership in the "top down" hierarchical church.

Graham, Robert A. *Vatican Diplomacy: A Study of Church and State on the International Plane*. Princeton, N.J.: Princeton University Press, 1959. A diplomatic study of church diplomacy by one of the Jesuits responsible for the controversial but authoritative 11-volume collection Pierre Blet et al., eds. *Actes, et documentes du Saint Siege Relativs à la Seconde Guerre Mandiale*. Vatican City: Liberia Editrice Vaticana, 1965–1981.

Marchione, Margherita. *Consensus and Controversy: Defending Pius XII*. New York: Paulist, 2002. A hagiographic and model study of Pius XII followed by Jose Sanchez and Justis George Lawler, among others.

Phayer, Michael. *The Catholic Church and the Holocaust, 1930–1965*. Bloomington: Indiana University Press, 2000. A scholarly, sensitive study of Pius XI and Pius XII and their attempts to accommodate and resist Hitler. Phayer illustrates the lack of papal interest in the plight of the Jews and the attempts to nurture the Catholic presence in postwar German politics.

Pius XII. *Major Addresses*, 2 vols. Edited by Vincent Yzermans. St. Paul, Minn.: North Central, 1961. The standard collection of addresses.

Rhodes, Anthony. *The Vatican in the Age of Diplomacy, 1922–1945*. London: Hodder and Stoughton, 1973: New York: Holt, Rinehart and Winston, 1974. A scholarly study of papal diplomacy in the age of Fascism and Nazism.

Rittner, Carol, and John Roth, eds. *Pope Pius XII and the Holocaust*, London: Leicester University Press, 2002. An excellent collection of thoughtful essays that explore the controversies swirling around Pius XII and the Holocaust.

Zuccotti, Susan. *Under His Very Windows: The Vatican and the Holocaust in Italy*. New Haven, Conn.: Yale University Press, 2002. A controversial study illustrating the prudential silence of Pius XII during the war and focusing on his behavior toward the Jews of Italy.

CHAPTER

8 Commentary on *Mater et magistra* (*Christianity and Social Progress*)

MARVIN L. MICH

INTRODUCTION

Mater et magistra, Pope John XXIII's first social encyclical, signals a new era in Catholic social thought. Along with *Pacem in terris* and the convening of Vatican II, MM brought a new attitude and tone to the Church's reflection on social issues. Pope John taught and lived with an attitude of openness and dialogue, of walking with humanity. In MM he analyzed the growing complexity of social relationships in the controversial section on "socialization," offered concrete strategies in the agricultural sector, and discussed the social dimensions of private property and a just wage. It was the first encyclical to address issues of the developing nations. The laity was invited to employ the methodology "observe, judge, and act" in putting Catholic social teaching into action.

OUTLINE OF THE DOCUMENT

After an introduction, the encyclical is divided into four major sections.[1] In the initial part of John's letter he reviews the teaching of *Rerum novarum* (10–26) and some doctrinal developments during the ensuing pontificates of Pius XI and Pius XII. The key texts for these popes are QA (27–40) and the 1941 Pentecost Radio Broadcast (41–45), respectively. Following this review of previous teaching, John notes a variety of scientific (atomic energy, electronic communication), economic (modernization of agriculture, new consciousness of workers), social (social insurance programs, better basic education), and political (decline of colonialism, greater state interventions) changes that have marked recent decades. He concludes this initial section of the letter by stating that the reason for this new encyclical is "not merely to commemorate" the anniversary of RN but "to set forth the Church's teaching regarding the new and serious problems of our day" (50).

In part two of the document John examines the social teaching of Leo XIII under five major headings: private initiative and state intervention in economic life (51–58), the complexity of social life and its institutions (59–67), proper remuneration for work (68–81), justice in the workplace (82–103), and private property (104–121). Throughout this part of the letter, John is concerned to show that the fundamental elements of Leo's teaching remain important for understanding what must be done today to improve social life. At the same time it is clear that John is not content simply to restate Leo's thoughts, but to interpret his ideas for the changed situation.

The new aspects of the social question are treated in the third major section of the encyclical. First, is the papal view that various sectors of modern economies are advancing at very different rates (123–143). Of particular concern is the state of agriculture in the modern world. This leads to the second topic, the condition of rural workers and their role in economic life (144–149). John's third item is the need for richer sectors of a nation to assist those working in poor areas that are not enjoying the fruits of progress (150–156). He then extends this theme in his fourth comment when he treats the relationship between richer and poorer nations (157–177). A fifth subheading in this section briefly comments on the church's contribution to the social question (178–184). The two final sections of this part of the document discuss the relationship of population growth and economic development (185–199) and the state of international cooperation (200–211).

In the final major segment of MM, titled "Reconstruction of Social Relationships in Truth, Justice and Love," John exhorts the members of the Church to take up the challenge of social reform in the present time. He warns against the errors of inadequate philosophies of life (212–217) and offers Catholic social teaching as a sounder basis for the needed reforms (218–225). John then reminds his readers that it is not just a matter of correct ideas but correct practice (226–232), for correct principles are insufficient and "social norms of whatever kind are not only to be explained but also applied" (226). The grave danger of the age that must be avoided is that fundamental human and spiritual values will be denied (242–253). The pope closes with a call for renewed dedication to improvement of temporal concerns (254–257) and a reminder of the great gift that is membership in the body of Christ, the Church (258–265).

CONTEXT OF THE DOCUMENT

The formative forces that gave birth to Pope John's vision for the Church and MM can be traced to his early days in northern Italy and his diverse ministry as a priest and bishop. Angelo Giuseppe Roncalli was born to a poor peasant family on November 25, 1881, the fourth of thirteen children. His father was a peasant farmer in Sotto il Monte, near Bergamo, central Lombardy, in northern Italy.

His great-uncle Zaverio was active in the Catholic Action movement in the diocese of Bergamo. The bishop of Bergamo, Camillo Guindani, had pioneered "a remarkable campaign of social action" inspired by Leo XIII's *Rerum novarum*. The diocese had over two hundred associations with over forty thousand members, which included "study circles," mutual assistance projects, cooperatives, and credit banks. This is the diocese that shaped Roncalli's early thinking. "If he wanted to be a priest in the diocese his theology would have to have a social dimension. 'Uncle' Zaverio had disposed him to understand that."[2]

After his ordination Roncalli returned from the Collegio Romano to serve as secretary to the new bishop of Bergamo, Radini Tedeschi. Like his predecessor, Tedeschi was a progressive bishop and a proponent of social action. He supported a strike in 1909 and defended the Church's intervening in social issues. Bishop Tedeschi believed that "Christ's *preference* goes to the disinherited, the weak and the oppressed."[3]

In 1915, at the age of thirty-three, Father Angelo was called up as a hospital orderly; he then served as a chaplain during World War I. This experience left him convinced that "war is the greatest evil."[4]

His subsequent assignments took him outside Catholic Italy. He served as "apostolic visitor" to Bulgaria from 1925 to 1934 and as apostolic delegate to Turkey and Greece (1934–44). In these positions he gained both ecumenical and interfaith perspectives. He served with a certain "pastoral aura," responding to human need without reference to creed or ethnic tradition. In 1944 he was sent to Paris as nuncio to France, where he had contact with the worker-priest movement and the cardinal of Paris, Maurice Feltin, who also served as the president of Pax Christi. In Paris, he briefly served as the Vatican observer to UNESCO before becoming the archbishop and patriarch of Venice in 1953. "It was in France and at UNESCO that he learned that it was possible to set aside ideological barriers and address 'all men of good will.'"[5] In relating to those outside the Catholic tradition he stressed "what unites rather than what divides." His openness to others allowed him to welcome the Italian Socialist Party when they held their congress in Venice in 1957. This "opening to the left" enraged many. On the day after his election to the papacy, he delineated his two major concerns in his first radio broadcast: the *unity of the Christian Church* with special regard for the Orthodox churches and *peace in the world* "among all men of good will."

Angelo Roncalli was elected pope on October 28, 1958, a month short of his seventy-seventh birthday. He served the Church as Pope John XXIII for only four years and seven months. He died on June 3, 1963. In that short time, by the power of his personality, his words, and his actions, he changed forever the way the Catholic Church understood itself and how it interacted with the world. His impact surprised church watchers who did not expect much from this rotund peasant priest from northern Italy. Pope John gave voice to these low expectations. "Everyone was convinced that I would be a provisional and transitional Pope." He had confounded those who thought he would be a "do nothing" pontiff. "Yet here I am, already on the eve of the fourth year of my pontificate, with an immense programme of work in front of me to be carried out before the eyes of the whole world, which is watching and waiting."[6]

The "programme of work" that Pope John convened was an ecumenical council. He had already promulgated his "social" encyclical MM in May 1961, and on April 11, 1963, he would publish his "international" encyclical, *Pacem in terris*. These three major events of John's pontificate were part of his overall vision. Each of these had a powerful impact individually and as part of his vision of the way the Catholic Church defined itself and the way it reached out to secular society.[7] Historian and critic Garry Wills remarked: "The encyclicals and the council amounted to a one-two punch by the prime mover behind them both, Pope John XXIII. So effective was this initiative that it was sustained even after John died."[8]

During the four and a half years of John's pontificate, the international community experienced many diverse socioeconomic and political events, including the following: Fidel Castro's guerrillas took over Havana; John Kennedy was elected president (1959); the Organization of Petroleum Exporting Countries (OPEC) was established (1960); the United States became embroiled in Vietnam; the Berlin Wall was erected; the first human traveled in space around the earth (1961); the Cuban missile crisis brought the United States and the Soviet Union to the brink of nuclear war; Algeria won independence from France and Uganda gained independence from Great Britain in 1962. In the years prior to Pope John's election, the United States exploded the first hydrogen bomb and launched the first atomic submarine in 1952. In 1955, twenty-nine African and Asian nonaligned states condemned colonialism at the Bandung Conference. In 1956, Martin Luther King Jr. led the bus boycott in Alabama and in 1957 the Soviet Union launched *Sputnik I* and *II*. The world felt the chill of the cold war between the Soviet Union and its allies, and the United States and the North Atlantic Treaty Organization (NATO). Many U.S. Catholics were caught up in the staunch anticommunism of the McCarthy era. For many, the world was divided between the forces of freedom and the "Red Menace" of communist domination. The nonaligned nations in the third world were caught in the ideological battlefield of the first world (the United States and its allies) and the second world (the Soviet Union and its allies).

Pope John had a vision of a renewed Catholic Church to serve as an agent of Christian unity and to help society address the issues of economic injustice, the threat of nuclear war, and conflict between nations. He realized that this transformation of the Catholic Church would not be accomplished during his papacy, but he would use all his energy to advance that cause. As he lay dying he said: "This bed is an altar. An altar needs a victim. I am ready. I offer my life for the Church, for the continuation of the ecumenical council, for the peace of the world and for the union of Christians."[9]

In the chill of the cold war, Pope John announced in 1959 his intention to convene an ecumenical council to bring about *aggiornamento*, "updating" in the Church, and to change the Church's attitude toward society, becoming an agent of unity and justice. As the council plans developed, it was clear that its energies would be focused on internal issues: liturgy, the role of bishops, the nature of the Church, and so forth. MM was released in July 1961, fifteen months before the council fathers would gather in St. Peter's Basilica, and *Pacem in terris* was released between the first and second sessions of the Council on April 11, 1963. Both of these encyclicals were part of Pope John's attempt to lead the bishops and the curia to grapple with social issues in addition to the internal ecclesial issues. The role of the Church and its stance toward the world were clearly interconnected in the the mind of the pope. He helped the Catholic Church become, in the words of J. Byran Hehir, a "worldly" Church.[10] The final document of the Council, *Gaudium et spes*, the *Pastoral Constititution on the Church in the Modern World*, confirmed the "joy and hope" of Pope John. The Catholic Church was beginning to turn toward the world and its social issues with a new attitude, a positive, confident, yet humble stance.

Analysts of Pope John's work note a threefold agenda, envisioned as three concentric circles: (1) the inner circle is the renewal of the Catholic Church; (2) the next circle is the unity of the Christian churches; and (3) the outer circle is the unity and peace of humanity.[11] The ecumenical council was to be the centerpiece of this renewal of the Catholic Church. It would also reach out to other Christian churches to begin dialogue and ecumenical cooperation. Ultimately, the Council would examine how the Catholic Church could be of service to diverse communities as they addressed current social and political issues, and issues of justice and peace. Pope John's two social encyclicals would play important supporting roles in that drama. On June 28, 1961, he articulated the first two agendas of the Council: "God wills that to [the Council's] work on the condition of the Church herself, and her *aggiornamento*, after twenty centuries of life—which is the principal task—there should be added, as a result of the edification we may give, but especially by the grace of an all-powerful God, some progress towards the drawing together of Our Lord's mystical flock."[12] E.E.Y. Hales claimed that

> this third circle, the circle of world co-operation, of world peace, was growing steadily clearer and more compelling to the Pope. Somehow the light from the first circle—the circle of Catholic unity, as represented by the Council—had to spread out to clarify not only the second circle, Christian Unity, but the third circle, the Unity of Mankind.[13]

The pope's commitment to this plan was evident in his address on the Feast of Candlemas, February 2, 1962, when he signed the *motu proprio* that established October 11, 1962, as the date for the opening of the Council. Pope John pointed out, in reference to the feast day, that

> Jesus is the Redeemer of the whole human race; today He is saluted as "a light to lighten the nations," the Saviour of all the nations. To Him therefore belong not only all those who are sons of the Catholic Church, but all those who are baptized in His holy name, and also all those who are equally His by right of creation and by the saving virtue of his Precious Blood, shed for the salvation of the whole human race. . . . May this redeeming blood fall upon all men, become no longer strangers or enemies but brothers; may it strengthen their will for peace, their longing after tranquillity and well-being.[14]

The Italian Context

Part of Pope John's originality was that he presented himself from the outset as a spiritual pope and a pastor who made a clear distinction between the papacy and the republic of Italy. No longer in competition, the papacy and the republic of Italy could live together in that spirit of harmonious collaboration which he called *convivenza.* Because of this distinction, Pope John's Italian policy was marked by this spirit of harmonious collaboration, which translated into a certain "disengagement" (*disimpegno*) and "reserve" (*riserbo*). Pope John wanted the Church to withdraw from the immediate party-political battleground in which it had been caught for decades.

The veteran Vatican watcher Peter Hebblethwaite explained the importance of this papal "disengagement" for the encyclical under discussion:

> But this did not mean that he was washing his hands of Italian affairs. . . . He thought that once the Church was detached from the hurly-burly of everyday politics, it would be better placed to speak about the rights of Christians in the social and political sphere. Thus his "disengagement" made *Mater et Magistra*, his first great social encyclical, possible.[15]

Pope John's "reserve" meant, in effect, that he did not interfere in political choices that properly belonged to the electors and their chosen representatives. He would not seek to exercise jurisdiction in political matters. He was repudiating the position of some curial cardinals (Tardini, Ottaviani, and Siri) who defended the hierarchy's right and duty to issue commands in the political and social sphere. These cardinals argued that the bishops *alone* were competent to judge the legitimacy of political "coalitions" or "alliances." They believed that this was a *moral* judgment that could not be left to the whim of the faithful. Pope John did not agree with their position and he worked effectively to break their interference in Italian politics.

Pope John not only emphasized the importance of Italian politics being free from clerical control, he also expressed that freedom by his actions. For example, on August 3, 1962, he met with Aldo Moro. This meeting with a politician who was still being publicly attacked by Cardinal Siri took place on the eve of the Council. "It was a metaphor for the Pope's recognition of the political liberty of Italian Catholics."[16] Pope John's example was "more immediately influential than his encyclical *Mater et Magistra.*"[17] In this context, Hebblethwaite concluded: "So it was in Italy that *Mater et Magistra*, though addressed to the whole Catholic world, had its most immediate application."[18]

PROCESS OF FORMULATION AND AUTHORSHIP

During the first two years of his pontificate Pope John assembled a team of close personal advisors. The team included Cardinal Bea, to whom he entrusted the organization of the new Secretariat for Christian Unity, which was to play a key role in the preparation for the first session of the Council. Pope John also invited his colleagues at the Lateran University, Monsignors Pietro Pavan, lecturer in social economics, and Agostino Ferrari Toniolo, professor of comparative labor law. Lastly, John included Monsignor Sante Quadri, a senior official of the Catholic Workers' Organization (ACLI) and Monsignor Luigi Civardi, a leader of Catholic Action, who served as the pope's personal confessor. These five men were given important duties on the Council Preparatory Commissions. Four of them, excluding Cardinal Bea, were responsible for much of the drafting of MM. Because of the enthusiastic reception of MM, John kept the team together as a sort of private inner cabinet. The foursome was instructed subsequently to prepare a second major encyclical dealing with the Church's views on international order, *Pacem in terris.*[19]

The team of Italian advisors had a dominant influence on the drafting of MM. French and German influences were seen in the discussion of "socialization" in numbers 59 to 67. This section was originally written in German, probably by two Jesuit economists, Oswald von Nell-Breuning, the primary author of Pope Pius XI's encyclical, *Quadragesimo anno*, and Gustav Gundlach. The French influence on this section is from the Forty-Seventh Congress of the Semaines Sociales de France, which met in Grenoble in July 1960. The theme of the conference was "Socialisation et personne humaine." The papal view of socialization is very similar to the definition adopted by the Semaines Sociales meeting.

The original draft of MM was in Italian except for the numbers on "socialization," which were written in German.[20] The English translation of this section was controversial. The official Latin text is found in *L'Osservatore Romano*, July 15, 1961, and in the *Acta apostolicae sedis*.[21] The encyclical is dated May 15, 1961, but was released on July 15, 1961.

Although the *original* language of the text is Italian and German, the *official* language of the text is the Latin translation. This is the source of some confusion. Which text is to be considered more "authentic," the "original" Italian text or the "official" Latin text? The Latin text showed a marked preference for formally classical expressions that left doubt about their precise modern equivalents. There were discrepancies between the original draft and the official text, and the modern-language versions released by the Vatican Press Office, which added to the controversy.[22]

ESSAY

Part 1: Continuity and Discontinuity with His Predecessors (1–50)

Pope John intended to continue the line of thought established by his predecessors, especially by Pope Leo XIII's encyclical *Rerum novarum*, as he addressed the new social issues of the 1960s. Commentators see various degrees of continuity and discontinuity in MM.

The British historian and political commentator Paul Johnson emphasized MM's discontinuity: "John did his best to emphasize its continuity with previous teaching. He was not anxious to repudiate earlier popes more than was absolutely necessary. This led him into some well-meaning exaggerations, what might almost be termed a falsification of the record." Johnson held that "what John taught has really very little in common with any previous papal pronouncement."[23] Others, such as Paul-Émile Bolté and Richard Camp, argued that there is considerable continuity between Pope John's encyclical and the teaching of his predecessors. Richard Camp claimed that MM "is filled with Pius XII's spirit of humanitarian idealism coupled with a desire to be as realistic as possible; there was little in its spirit or in its letter which Pius could not have approved."[24] Finally, Donal Dorr, the Irish theologian, sees MM as continuing the direction of his predecessors and breaking new ground: "In one sense his position was by no means a radical one, nor did it represent any major departure from the direction set by earlier popes, especially by Pius XII. . . . Pope John had, in another sense, a major role to play in turning the Catholic Church in quite a different direction on social issues."[25]

Pope John changed the orientation of Catholic social teachings on a number of significant points. He believed in the distribution of power and the creation of countervailing forces to balance the enlargement of central government. He held that the media could help by spreading the truth, and by offering a variety of opinions, they could keep the power of the state in check. He supported education of the working classes beyond the level that his predecessors supported.

There are also some significant issues that are *missing* in MM that were evident in his predecessors' teachings. John did not resurrect the corporative approach of Pius XI. Pope John did not comment on the great conflicting ideologies of our times—communism, socialism, and neoliberalism.[26] The encyclical also makes no mention of monarchies. The silence of the document on these topics speaks loudly of a new direction. While the encyclical covered a number of crucial economic issues, it is also silent on other fundamental issues, including land and agrarian reform, nationalization of industries, and public health care. "There is no reference in *Mater et Magistra* to women as a group suffering particular injustices."[27] The awareness that there were injustices in many issues pertaining to women had not yet found its way into papal teaching. The role of women in society was generally viewed in terms of childbearing and rearing of children. Two years later in *Pacem in terris*, the pope noted with approval the public role that women were taking in society and their claiming their rights and duties (PT 41). Subsequent documents such as *Gaudium et spes*, *Octogesima adveniens*, and *Justitia in mundo* also supported women's rights to participate in cultural, economic, social, and political life. In 1984 the U.S. bishops addressed the question of injustices against women. They experienced turmoil among themselves and with Vatican representatives on how to analyze and address sexism in society and the Church.[28]

Michael Schuck identifies four "reversals" in papal political teaching from 1959: (1) acceptance of participatory democracy; (2) acceptance of separation of church and state; (3) a guarded acceptance of violent citizen resistance to unjust governments; and (4) the right of non-Roman Catholics to profess their religion publicly.[29] Pope John's letters and leadership contributed to all of these reversals at least indirectly and to two of them directly. Specifically, the acceptance of the separation of church and state and a new attitude toward non-Roman Catholics to profess their religion publicly are due to Pope's John's leadership.

New Content and New Tone

Not only does the *content* of the letter take the Church in a new direction, but the *tone* and *methodology* are new. The "constant refrain in comments issuing from different nations referred to the encyclical's manifestly modern tone."[30] The openness and optimism of Pope John are obvious in this letter: "the style of the present pope is characterized by its direct, familiar tone; by its concrete, realistic, positive approach to problems; by a preoccupation less with discussing doctrinal and theoretical matters than with outlining practical directives."[31] The French-Canadian Cardinal Leger captured something of Pope John's spirit: "it is a youthful spirit of confidence in the future, without yearning for the past; one that strives instead to make the best use of the opportunities of the present moment." Others noted the lack of nostalgia and the realistic tone of the letter. "What strikes one even on a first reading," noted the Belgian Jesuit Jules De Meij, "is the open, appreciative reception John XXIII accords to modern society. Nowhere does one encounter the nostalgia for outdated structures that has characterized the thinking of some Catholics in the past."[32]

MM exudes a sense of optimism and openness to the new realities. "Many passages are engaging, encouraging, cordial and affectionate (⌊numbers⌋ 85 ff., 156, 148 ff., 160, 182, 284, 236f.)."[33] The popes of the Leonine period (1878–1958) stylistically used a "double-pulsed" method of social instruction, paralleling negative judgments with positive recommendations.[34] Pope John broke with that style of teaching. While John was not afraid to identify what was wrong in society, he spent very little time focusing on it. This positive attitude was consistent with the pope's personality. He exuded a confidence that people of good will can cooperate with God's grace to address the social evils of the day.

Pope John took a different tack than his predecessors.[35] Yes, there were dangers and social evils in 1958 when he was elected to the papacy. For instance, the Catholic Church was still suffering behind the Iron Curtain and the threat of nuclear war was palpable. Pope John chose to emphasize the other side of the coin. He saw the opportunities as well as the threats of his day. He pointed to the progress and improvements that were being made. He encouraged the positive elements and highlighted the pursuit of good, even by those who were not part of Catholic circles. From his service in the Balkans, outside the Catholic community, and his time in France among those estranged from the Church, he had experienced the goodness of humanity. It is that side of humanity he chose to bring into focus. And humanity responded to his message.

A New Methodology

Pope John, with the help of his advisors who were schooled in modern sociological approaches, brought a new methodology to the development of Catholic social teachings. First of all, he abandoned completely the old dogmatic device of distinguishing between thesis and hypothesis. The thesis is the unequivocal statement that a certain concept (such as democracy) is intrinsically bad. This was qualified by the hypothesis that democracy should be tolerated where it has been accepted, and therefore, the Church is unavoidably obliged to work with the reality it rejected through a practical compromise, a modus vivendi. John regarded this distinction as evasive if not downright dishonest.[36] His "pragmatic" approach did not begin with abstract condemnations, which then had to be qualified into thin air. He chose to start from the ground up and see where different philosophies of life or ideologies shared common ground for acting together. His methodology focused on dialogue and collaboration rather than on condemnation. Some referred to this approach as an "opening to the left." It was seen as an "opening" because his approach did not begin with pointing out where the other side is wrong.

One of John's central beliefs was that, while the Church possessed the essence of truth for all time, reason and contemporary approaches must be constantly employed in reinterpreting that truth in the light of changing needs. That was the goal of Vatican II and that was the methodology of his encyclicals.

In addition to the new methodology used *within* the encyclical, MM also recommended a new methodology *as a way to implement* the Church's social teaching in society. The new methodology, developed by Joseph Cardijn, a Belgian priest who later became a cardinal, has three steps: (1) analyze the situation, (2) discern the principles and values of the faith tradition that apply, and (3) take action that is appropriate. These three steps are summarized as "observe, judge, act." We will come back to this question of implementation of Catholic social teaching and the Cardijn method at the end of this section.

Part 2: Expanding on the Tradition (51–121)

Increased State Intervention (51–58)

In this section of MM, Pope John addressed the complex question of the role of the state in promoting the common good. The context in question in Europe was that many European countries had moved toward a welfare state after experiencing the chaos at the end of World War II. "Workers were determined never again to face the deprivations of the depression years; and the breaking of the moulds that came during and after the war offered the chance to give political expression to this determination."[37] In some countries the welfare state took on a form of socialism that tried to redistribute ownership of property and wealth through very high levels of taxation on income and profits. In other European countries the redistribution of ownership was not undertaken.

During the papacy of Pius XII there had been "increasingly bitter and ideological" discussions in Catholic circles on the emerging welfare state, which was seen by some as undermining personal responsibility.[38] Pope John weighed into this debate by highlighting the importance of personal responsibility but also, as we will see in the discussion of socialization, by endorsing a "thick" role for the state in promoting the common good of the society and of every person. The pope supported an activist state in economic matters to avoid "mass unemployment" and "to facilitate for every individual the opportunity to engage in productive activity" (54–55).

Socialization (59–67)

The discussion of socialization is the most controversial section of the encyclical; it is also one of the most central themes of the letter. This question will be given an in-depth analysis in the "Excursus" section of this essay.

Common Good (65)

In this section Pope John clarified the meaning of the common good as "the sum total of those conditions of social living, whereby men are enabled more fully and more readily to achieve their own perfection" (65). The notion of the common good is a dynamic term that has never been defined "once and for all" because it depends, in part, on one's view of society. A hierarchical view of society sees the common good differently than a democratically ordered society. Pope John added his voice to the longstanding Catholic debate over whether the common good refers to a collection of "goods" or is an organizational context for human flourishing. In MM Pope John emphasized the latter.[39]

Pope John's legacy also contains a lingering tension between two complementary ways of describing the common good.[40] One approach emphasizes the common good as "a social reality in which all persons should share through their participation in it." The second approach, seen in *Pacem in terris*, emphasizes the human rights aspects of the common good: "it is agreed that in our time the common good is chiefly guaranteed when personal rights and duties are maintained" (PT 60). These are not contradictory views, but ways of expressing a dynamic concept in different social contexts.[41]

Pope John also contributed to the Catholic understanding of the common good by recognizing the inadequacy of the term if applied only within the boundaries of the nation-state. The common good is increasingly a global reality. In *Pacem in terris*, John observed that "the present [international] system of organization and the way its principle of authority operates on a world basis no longer correspond to the objective requirements of the universal common good" (PT 134–35).

The Just Wage and Workers' Participation (68–81)

Pope John expressed a "profound sadness" because he had seen "with [his] own eyes a wretched spectacle indeed—great masses of workers who, in not a few nations, even in whole continents, receive too small a return for their labor" (68). Pope John addressed an age-old injustice of workers being paid an insufficient wage.[42] In light of this reality, Pope John reaffirmed the importance of a just wage that is not determined by market forces alone. John offered four criteria: "(1) the contribution of individuals to the economic effort; (2) the economic state of the enterprises within which they work; (3) the requirements of each community, especially as regards over-all employment; finally, (4) what concerns the common good of all peoples, namely, of the various states associated among themselves, but differing in character and extent" (71).

The fourth criterion was new with MM. Pope John broadened the context for determining the just wage to include an international perspective. The tendency of the global free trade economy to move factories to regions where people will work for the least hourly wage violates this criterion of the just wage. Such a wage does not "rush to the bottom," pitting one group of workers against another, in offering work to the lowest bidder. Pope John put the just wage in a global perspective wherein the good of all people must be factored into debates about a living wage.

Pope John taught that workers are to benefit from the fruits of their labor not only by a just or living wage but also by sharing in the wealth produced by the corporation by owning shares of the company. Here, he followed the lead of Pope Pius XI, who held that the profit of the corporation should not only benefit executives and stockholders but the workers as well. The "*demands of the common good* on both the national and world levels" have an impact on setting just wages but also on determining shareholder dividends and interest. One of these demands is "that effective aid be given in developing the economically underdeveloped nations" (80).[43]

Demands of Justice in Productive Institutions of the Economy (82–103)

The encyclical next applied justice to the conditions of productivity. Pope John taught that "there is, in fact, an innate need of human nature requiring that men engaged in productive activity have an opportunity to assume responsibility and to perfect themselves by their efforts" (82). In this statement John cleared up a controversy that involved his predecessor Pope Pius XII from 1949 to 1952. The controversy focused on the question of what level of participation or codetermination was appropriate for workers in determining the policies, procedures, practices, and direction of their industries. A German conference of leaders, the Katholikentag (Catholic Day) of Bochum (north of Cologne), had asserted on

September 4, 1949, that codetermination (*Mitbestimmung*) is a "natural right." Pope Pius XII did not agree with that position and replied that "neither the nature of the labor contract, nor that of enterprise in itself necessarily comprises a right of this kind."[44] This led to a series of clarifications and warnings that resulted in "a feeling of uneasiness and hesitation" among Catholics regarding the notion of participation and codetermination.[45]

In this section of the encyclical, Pope John reexamined the problem of participation. He concluded that "we do not doubt that employees should have an active part in the affairs of the enterprise wherein they work, whether these be private or public" (91). He freed the concept of participation from the logjam of controversy.[46]

Pope John also recommended that "productive enterprises assume the character of a true human fellowship [*una communità di persone*] whose spirit suffuses the dealings, activities, and standing of all its members . . . marked by mutual respect, esteem, and goodwill" (90–91). This is a more contemporary way to speak of the essential relationality that is important for any human enterprise and that was evident in the guild system of preindustrial Europe. The values are maintained without a sense of nostalgia.

Through trade unions workers should exert their influence throughout the state and not just within their own spheres of employment. National and international authorities should represent workers. In particular, John singled out the efforts of the International Labor Organization in Geneva, Switzerland, for commendation (103).

Private Property (104–21)

Private property has been staunchly defended in papal teachings since the time of Leo XIII due in part to the denial of this right by the "socialists" of Leo's day. In fact, Pope Leo, in defending this right, overstated the importance of private property when he called it a "primary right." In the Thomistic tradition private property is seen as a derived or secondary right, not as a primary right as Leo taught. Primary rights are those that are necessary for survival—the rights to food, shelter, and clothing. One does not necessarily have to own property to have one's primary rights respected. Pope Pius XI and John XXIII recovered the Thomistic tradition and carried it forward. In that tradition, private property is a right to the extent that it serves a social function, in that it helps to promote right order in society and the stewardship of resources.

Pope John connected freedom with the right of ownership. He believed that the "exercise of freedom finds its guarantee and incentive in the right of ownership" (109). Ownership, according to the pope, "strengthens the stability and tranquility of family life, thus contributing to the peace and prosperity of the commonwealth" (112). He was optimistic that nations can rather easily expand ownership among the propertyless. He implied that economic growth that a number of nations had experienced led naturally to increased ownership. Donal Dorr sees this as an "uncritical assumption" and a "blind spot" in papal analysis and thinking.[47]

Part 3: New Aspects of the Social Question (122–211)

In this segment of the letter, the pope addresses four areas of particular concern for the Church's social mission.

Agriculture: A Depressed Sector (123–49)

Pope John addressed the problems of agriculture in Part 3 of the encyclical, which is titled "New Aspects of the Social Question." This heading signaled the broadening of the "social question" from the problems of the working class in the industrial setting to include the problems of farmers. The plight of farmers was of personal interest to Pope John, who grew up on his family's farm in northern Italy. In fact, his family shared the first floor of their house with six cows—a practice that was not uncommon in Europe at the time.[48]

While not ruling out large agro-business farms, the letter has a clear preference for family-type farms that model a community of persons. (This same approach is recommended by the U.S. bishops twenty-five years later in their pastoral letter on the economy, *Economic Justice for All* [233].)

Although long overdue, the analysis and recommendations of the section were seen by Douglas Hyde as "down-to-earth" and as "a charter for rural life."[49] Pope John was concerned about the great imbalances between agriculture and industry. He began this section with a call to improve public services in rural areas, transportation systems, water supplies, housing, medical services, and educational and professional services, as well as religious and recreational resources.

The encyclical urged the state to assist in addressing the concerns of farmers. The role of the government, while essential, does not obviate the other basic levels of voluntary organizations and the farmers' own individual initiatives. All three levels—government, voluntary organizations, and individuals—must play their part in keeping with the principle of subsidiarity. In this regard John XXIII focused more attention on the role of the state to assist farmers than any of his predecessors. He offered specific suggestions to address agricultural problems, sometimes in amazing detail.

Aid to Less-Developed Areas (150–84)

MM was the first encyclical to address the issues of international relations and economic development. Pope John opened a new chapter in economic teaching with his emphasis on equitable distribution and social solidarity between nations. "On a world-wide scale governments should seek the economic good of all peoples" (37).

With the era of colonialism coming to an end, John sensed a new opportunity was at hand. In this context, he recommended that the errors of the past be avoided, namely, that development efforts respect the indigenous cultures. He urged the developed nations to "take special care lest, in aiding these nations, they seek to impose their own way of life upon them" (170). Pope John applied this sensitivity to the Church's missionary activity as well: "[the Church] makes no effort to discourage or belittle those characteristics and traits which are proper to particular nations, and which peoples religiously and tenaciously guard, quite justly, as a sacred heritage" (181).

The pope was also very clear that the developed nations are not "more advanced" than the people in developing nations. In fact, those in the modernized world too often ignore "spiritual values," which are more important than their economic, scientific, and technological prosperity and progress (175). Pope John warned that help from the affluent nations could be a Trojan Horse—"not lacking grave dangers" (176). On a structural level MM failed to mention that Western prosperity is itself dependent on cheap labor and the raw materials that serve to keep the Third World in its poorer condition.[50] Pope Paul VI would devote more attention to the question of international economic and human development in his encyclical *Populorum progressio*, but it was Pope John who opened this new chapter in Catholic social teaching.

Population Growth and Economic Development (185–99)

Pope John argued that the interrelationship on a global scale between the number of births and available resources was not an immediate or impending crisis. He believed the resources of nature had an "almost inexhaustible productive capacity" to feed, clothe, and house humanity when linked with human ingenuity. The problem of population growth and economic development would be made unsolvable if the breakthroughs in science were used primarily for destructive purposes and a senseless arms race. Consistent with Catholic tradition he rejected any strategy that violated the procreative purpose of human sexuality. Rather, he trusted the advances in science and technology, which "give almost limitless promise for the future in this matter" (189).

In the next section Pope John explained that human dignity is essentially linked to the transmission of life in the marriage context. This dignity must be recognized. He did not address the concrete problem of human suffering and death due to overpopulation.

The pope did get specific about two concrete problems: people dying from misery and hunger due to lack of goods and the channeling of technological and economic productivity into a life-draining arms race. "Accordingly, with great sadness we note two conflicting trends: on the one hand, the scarcity of goods . . . that the life of men reportedly is in danger of perishing from misery and hunger; on the other hand, the recent discoveries of science [and] technical advances . . . are transformed into means whereby the human race is led toward ruin and a horrible death" (198). Pope John "links decisively the questions of population, economic development, and the arms race."[51] John's belief in a provident God led him to trust the means were available through the bounty of creation and human creativity to solve the population problem. The challenge before humanity was not to turn away from this destiny to a future filled with destruction, greed, exploitation, and misery.

International Order and Cooperation (200–211)

As the world was linked more closely by science and technology, nations had the potential of becoming more interdependent. Yet, at the same time the world was not a safer place because nations feared each other. Armaments were amassed to deter and defend against aggression. The cause of this state of tension and fear between nations was to be found in "differing philosophies of life" (205). The competing ideologies of the first and second worlds created an atmosphere of suspicion and mistrust. Even the attempts to articulate the "demands of justice" were frustrated because there was no agreement on the meaning of the concepts. These debates about "justice" were themselves sources of contention (206).

As stated in other sections of the encyclical, the solution to this threatening situation among nations was to recognize the moral order and moral law as established by God. Humanity needs the moral law, rooted in religion, not only to survive, but to thrive (208). John XXIII saw the tentative signs that people "are beginning to recognize that their own capacities are limited, and they seek spiritual things more intensively than heretofore." This movement toward the spiritual dimension of life provides the promise of cooperation and collaboration between peoples (211).

In this analysis Pope John reiterated the long-standing belief of his predecessors that the solution to the "social question" is found in religion and the "return" to God's moral law. Previous popes explicitly stated that this meant returning to the Catholic tradition as the most efficacious teacher of God's moral law. While Pope John believed the Catholic tradition was the way that should be followed, he did not state that belief in this encyclical. In one sense, he did not have to say that, as the letter is addressed to Catholics who are already members of the Catholic Church. He was sensitive to people of other religions or those who profess no religion by not being explicit about Catholicism as "true religion." This omission was consistent with his character of not finding fault with others. His approach left the door open for people to find their own way to religion and to a moral order consistent with God's will.

The assumption in this section is that the Christian religion itself is not one of the "differing philosophies of life." While that question cannot be fully examined here, it cannot be completely ignored. Is religion, including Christianity, somehow above the fracas of competing ideologies, or is it too often another source of dissension, conflict, and violence? History and contemporary times seem to confirm that turning to religion does not solve all our national and international dilemmas and conflicts.

Part 4: Reconstruction of Social Relationships in Truth, Justice, and Love (212–65)

Under this heading the pope addresses four items. Several of his comments may seem less striking now, decades after Vatican II, but at the time his comments on the role of the laity and a new form of spirituality were significant.

Incomplete and Erroneous Philosophies of Life (212–25)

Without naming the false philosophies of life of the time, Pope John explained the theological foundation for a true philosophy of life. As relationships have multiplied in recent times (socialization) because of advances in science and technology, it is even more important to recall the sacred dignity of each person and humanity's relationship with God: "Separated from God, man becomes monstrous to himself and others. Consequently, mutual relationships between men absolutely require a right ordering of the human conscience in relation to God, the source of all truth, justice, and love" (215). Pope John was not acerbic when he discussed incomplete and erroneous philosophies of life. Rather, he shared with the reader the truth of reality that he had come to know as a believer. He proclaimed the Church's theological centerpiece: without being rooted in God, humanity's efforts to find meaning in life are empty. Quoting Augustine, he reminded the reader, "our hearts are restless until they rest in Thee" (214).

Application of Social Teaching (226–32)

The encyclical's vision of humanity and its social principles must be applied to the systems and issues of contemporary society. The task at hand was how to get the word out through every possible means—journals, books, radio, and television. This was a difficult task, and the pope invited all people of good will to participate (221). He was realistic about the challenge, noting that living out of the social teachings is hampered by three realities: "(1) there is deeply rooted in each man an instinctive and immoderate love of his own interests; (2) today there is widely diffused in society a materialistic philosophy of life; (3) it is difficult at times to discern the demands of justice in a given situation" (229).

Because of these obstacles, people need to see the social teaching in action. It is not enough to train people in the principles; they must *experience* the Church's social teaching *in action* and have their character shaped by these principles. "We do not regard such instructions as sufficient, unless there be added to the work of instruction that of the formation of man, and unless some action follow upon the teaching, by way of experience" (231).

It is not enough to study the social teachings of the Church. This is only the beginning of the learning process, which is completed only when students of all ages are engaged in projects that transform these principles into action. The formation of a person of justice requires "getting off the couch" and working to change the neighborhood, the workplace, the local church, and the global community.

Pope John proclaimed a new pedagogical principle for the Church: actions on behalf of social justice will teach Christians how to act (232). In other words, Pope John emphasized that the Christian is not only educated *for* action but *by* action. Christian education is not complete unless it is supplemented by concrete action. "This is the first time that any pontifical document has ever brought out this interaction and dependency so clearly. This fusion of education and action fits in with Pope John's desire to give his flock a pastoral letter, a letter directed to concrete action, not to academic disputes."[52] The Pope pointed out that *a person can be formed only by action*. By applying Christian principles in concrete situations, the Christian truly comes to know what they mean, and this will lead to more informed action. A person comes to know the poor only when he or she works with or serves the poor and neglected firsthand. A believer is converted and transformed when he or she takes the risk of crossing boundaries of class and race to encounter God in the "other."

Action, inspired by Christian social thought, is a light for the world. This idea runs throughout the whole of MM and, in a sense, sums up its spirit and intent.[53] The focus on the "call to action" within the papal documents will be expanded upon in subsequent documents, especially the 1971 apostolic exhortation *Octogesima adveniens*.

Role of the Laity (233–60)

As mentioned above, MM recommended the three step—observe, judge, act—method of Cardinal Cardijn as a way to implement the Church's social teaching in society. Pope John went on to say: "it seems particularly fitting that youth not merely reflect upon this order of procedure, but also . . . follow it . . . lest what they have learned be regarded merely as something to be thought about but not acted upon" (237). In this way the pope gave a special nudge to schools and youth ministry to be engaged by Catholic social teachings and act on them.

The Cardijn methodology gives the laity and their clergy the responsibility to discern and adapt the Church's norms and teachings to the particular issues, people, and context. Pope Paul VI developed this "new" methodology in *Octogesima adveniens*. It was also picked up in the methodologies of liberation theology and the "pastoral circle" of North American social analysis.[54] The "basic Christian communities" in many Latin American countries utilized this "situated" analysis, action, and reflection. The Conference of Latin American Bishops followed this same process in formulating their analyses of pastoral and social issues in their countries. The U.S. bishops utilized this methodology in their pastoral letters on nuclear weapons and the economy.

From the *post*–Vatican II perspective, the contribution of MM in promoting the role of the laity does not seem outstanding. Yet, as a social encyclical just prior to the opening of Vatican II, Pope John's letter made a significant contribution on this topic. It established a new agenda for social encyclicals: "for the first time in a pontifical document, spirituality, temporality, and the apostolate are united in a total theological system."[55] Pope John was responsive to discussions in theological and activist circles that focused on three areas: the position of the laity in the Church, the dialogue of the Church with the modern world, and a "this world" theology. In MM Pope John picked up these three individual threads and "wove them into a theological synthesis."[56]

Pope John believed the laity have a "noble task" as they carry the Church's teaching to the heart of their temporal affairs (240–41). While this is not a new idea, it was given a new intensity in MM. For the first time in an encyclical the "instructions to the laity" are found within the encyclical itself. In previous encyclicals the practical instructions were presented in less formal addresses and audiences. By integrating the call to action within the letter, Pope John demonstrated the essential link of the laity's task to the Church's social teaching. The work of the laity is not only an integral part of the social teaching itself; it is, more specifically, the logical and practical application of the theoretical part of that teaching.[57]

An Immanent Spirituality

Pope John's encyclical transforms not only the Church's stance toward society, it also confronts a dominant characteristic of Catholic spirituality known as detachment. The Roman Catholic spirituality of the late 1950s, in general, did not take the temporal order seriously. Some would argue that "the Christian is incapable of transforming the temporal order because he cannot take it seriously."[58] Pope John moved away from a spirituality of detachment and replaced it with a spirituality of engagement that asked Christians to be creatively engaged in the world as a chief characteristic of their spiritual journey.

In this regard the Catholic Church at the time of Pope John had some catching up to do. Ironically, most of the accomplishments in the social, economic, and political arenas since the French Revolution had been brought about either in opposition to the Church or by nonbelievers. There are, of course, some outstanding exceptions to this generalization but it remains quite accurate. The result is that, in general, the Catholic Church presented itself as a conservative and reactionary actor regarding emerging social and political movements and was also perceived as such. This stance shaped not only the tone and content of the social encyclicals but also the public engagement and internal spirituality of the Catholic community.

In 1966 Peter Riga argued that "it will not be easy for the layman to change his usual notions of spirituality. . . . Like the religious and the priest, his mentality was geared more to the sacral, to the specifically supernatural elements in life, and the things of the 'world' were to be used carefully and cautiously."[59] It is still a challenge for Christians to find the proper balance between earthly engagement and heavenly expectations.

Pope John shifted Catholic spirituality by emphasizing the Christian's role in addressing the problems of this world. MM was one of the tools that he used to begin this revolution in Catholic spirituality and social action. Vatican II was another important impetus initiated by Pope John to reshape the Church's attitude toward society and the problems of "this world." *Gaudium et spes* became the charter of a new social and spiritual engagement for Roman Catholics.

Monsignor Pietro Pavan, the chief consultant of Pope John for this encyclical, claimed that the underlying motivation of the letter was to shore up personal human dignity by linking work with spirituality:

> The fundamental motive of the encyclical, ever present in the solution of these problems, can be found in the fact that we live in an age when a host of factors contribute to undermine, in man's minds, the consciousness of his own dignity as a person. For this reason, it is of primary importance that the economic world be constructed and function in such a way that men do not run the risk of sacrificing what they are to what they do; they must be inspired to love their work as a means of achieving spiritual enrichment and perfection.

Pavan then refers to number 256 of the encyclical: "That a man should develop and perfect himself through his daily work . . . is perfectly in keeping with the plan of divine Providence. . . . In concluding their human affairs to the best of their ability, they [the laity] must recognize that they are doing a service to humanity, in intimate union with God through Christ, and to God's greater glory."[60]

In these few lines Pope John began to break down the wall between everyday life and the spiritual life, a rift that *Gaudium et spes* would decry as "among the more serious errors of our age" (GS 43). Pope John offered a perspective that understood labor as enhancing personal dignity, as serving the needs of the community, and as an essential element in the spiritual journey. The personal, communal, and spiritual components were integrated into an attractive vision. (Pope John Paul II developed a fuller theology of work in his writings, especially LE.) His encyclical signaled a shift from a spirit of detachment to a spirit of engagement. This orientation continued into the next decades. It took root in a very intense way in various developing nations, where pastoral leaders, activists, and theologians pursued liberation theology, a truly "immanent and engaged" theology and spirituality.

EXCURSUS

This section will examine the topic of socialization as it is used in MM, but an adequate understanding of the topic requires some background.

A Complicated History

In MM Pope John moved in a new direction as he shaped the Church's response to the reality of ever-expanding socialization. Socialization is a central theme of the encyclical and its distinctive contribution to the development of Catholic social thought.[61] It is also its most complicated and controversial concept.[62] The controversy begins with the very word *socialization* and whether or not the word is used in the various translations. The controversy around vocabulary reflects the complex history of the concept as well.[63]

Pope Leo XIII had condemned the socialization of private property because it was one of the central tenets of Marxist socialism in the late nineteenth century. What Pope Leo condemned, Karl Marx had espoused. Marx foresaw a "progressive socialization, or social ownership, of the processes of industry . . . leading eventually to a classless society and the complete socialization of the productive system."[64] This was the initial meaning of socialization. It also explains why this extreme form of socialization had been rejected by all the popes since Leo. The form of socialism that Leo XIII condemned in *Rerum novarum* was the Marxist vision that proposed the socialization of private property. The Marxist notion of socialization meant the abolition of private property; it also meant collective ownership. Pope Leo and his successors would never accept this extreme form of socialization. Leo condemned the socialist solution for the poverty of the workers, which included the denial of the right of private property. Pope Leo maintained that the solution for the misery of the workers was to enable each person to procure the necessary property for one's needs and dignity so that the workers would not have to be "wage dependent."

In the forty years that followed Leo's condemnation of socialism and the abolition of private property it envisioned, the landscape had changed. A more moderate form of socialism emerged in addition to the militant communist socialism. Pope Pius XI had the moderate strain of socialism in mind when he said in his 1931 encyclical *Quadragesimo anno* that "it may well come about that gradually these tenets of mitigated socialism will no longer be different from the program of those who seek to reform human society according to Christian principles." He opened the door to potential collaboration with moderate socialists and gave support to a less radical form of socialization: "It is rightly contended that certain forms of property must be reserved to the state, since they carry with them a power too great to be left to private individuals without injury to the community at large" (QA 114).

Pope John XXIII, like his predecessor Leo XIII, rejected the earliest understanding of socialization. He took Pius XI's minimal openness to future collaboration with moderate socialists and expanded it.

As socialism changed over time, so did the Church's understanding of socialization. Even though this section of the encyclical was written in German, French thinking also played a formative role. It is clear that the Forty-Seventh Congress of the Semaines Sociales de France, which met in Grenoble in July 1960 while the letter was being drafted, had an impact on the text. The theme of this conference was precisely the question of socialization: "Socialisation et personne humaine." The encyclical's description of socialization as "the multiplication of social relationships, that is, a daily more complex interdependence of citizens, introducing into their lives and activities many and varied forms of association" (59), reflects the understanding of socialization at this Grenoble conference.[65]

The term *socialization* was in use among Catholic social thinkers as well, including the French Jesuits of Action Populaire and the French Dominicans connected with the Économie et Humanisme, including Paul Bigo, who a few years later would become the second editor of Pope Paul's *Populorum progressio*. The Australian bishops had also used the term in their statements.

Bartolomeo Sorge explains that the term had a general sense of "a progressive inserting of the State in the economic and social life" of the community.[66] But the term was used in different ways. He identifies three descriptions of socialization in Catholic social teaching. First, the term was synonymous with the state securing a monopoly or the ownership of specific productive sectors, which, if left to private control, would damage the common good. Second, it referred to concrete action of nationalizing a particular enterprise. In these two cases when just compensation is given for the state taking over an enterprise, such action was seen as compatible with the Church's social teachings. The third usage of the term was the total "statification" or nationalization of economic life.[67] Such usage was rare but memorable, as in the case of Pope Pius XII when he warned Austrian Catholics about the danger of "all-embracing socialization" (*allumfassende Sozialisierung*) during his radio broadcast to the Katholikentag of Vienna (Congress of Austrian Catholics) on September 14, 1952: "The person and the family must be saved from falling into the abyss into which an all-embracing socialization tends to lead them, a socialization at the end of which the terrifying image of the leviathan would become a horrible reality."[68]

The meaning of socialization changed over time as socialism evolved. The term itself also has a variety of meanings in different disciplines. For economists, especially Anglo-Saxon ones, it is synonymous with nationalization, that is, the public control and ownership of production and distribution of goods and services. In psychology and sociology, the term refers to the process by which a child gradually learns to live in society. The psychological and sociological understandings of socialization are not what is being evaluated in the encyclicals.

Socialization in MM

As mentioned above, MM described "the reality of socialization as one of the principal characteristics of our time . . . the multiplication of social relationships, that is, a daily, more complex interdependence of citizens, introducing into their lives and activities many and varied forms of association, recognized for the most part in private and even in public law" (59).

Pope John believed this trend toward "more complex interdependence of citizens" is a natural inclination for people "voluntarily to enter into association in order to attain objectives which each one desires" but is only achievable through a group effort (60). Socialization is due to this natural, human inclination to collaborate on common goals. It is also due to technical and scientific progress where cooperation leads to greater advancement in knowledge and practical application.

Contrary to Pius XI's understanding, Pope John saw socialization in a positive light—it "definitely brings numerous services and advantages" (61). Socialization helps people satisfy many personal needs such as health care, education, skills training, housing, labor, communication, and entertainment. But socialization also brings with it certain dangers because public authorities are involved in the more "intimate aspects of personal life" such as health care, education of the young, and choosing one's career. There is a tendency for a restriction of human freedom as the "rules and laws controlling and determining relationships of citizens are multiplied" (62).

While some feel that the complex social environment hinders and even nullifies personal freedom, Pope John proclaimed that personal freedom and initiative were still possible. Human beings are not becoming "automatons," as B. F. Skinner and other determinists would argue.

As state intervention increased due to the complexity of society, two important principles must guide the government's involvements: (1) public authorities must have a grasp of the *common good* and a commitment to pursue it; and (2) *intermediary bodies* must have freedom to guide themselves and not be controlled by the state (65). With the implementation of these two principles, a society will avoid the tyranny of excessive state control. Without using the word in this section, the pope was actually restating the principle of *subsidiarity*. The reality and risks of socialization are put in check by the principle of subsidiarity. In this sense, socialization, in Pope John's usage, is as much about intermediary groups and associations as it is about the role of the state.

Pope John did not naively praise socialization. Rather, he gave it his conditional blessing if two factors are kept in balance: "(1) the freedom of individual citizens and groups of citizens to act autonomously, while cooperating one with the other," and "(2) the activity of the State whereby the undertakings of private individuals and groups are suitably regulated and fostered" (66).

On this question, as on other controversial issues in modern society, Pope John did not fall into the pattern of condemning societal trends but rather invited Catholics "to abandon an attitude of passive defense in the face of growing socialization for a buoyant acceptance of the latter as a social and historical fact, and a willingness to work along with it."[69]

As discussed above, Pope John established three conditions under which socialization may be seen as a benefit to society: (1) that public authorities pursue the common good, (2) that intermediary bodies have sufficient freedom, and (3) that the freedom of individuals and groups be protected and balanced in relationship to the regulatory role of the state. If these three conditions are implemented in society, then socialization "does not necessarily mean that individual citizens will be gravely discriminated against or excessively burdened. Rather, we can hope that this will enable man not only to develop and perfect his natural talents, but also will lead to an appropriate structuring of the human community" (67).

Vatican officials continued John's positive attitude toward socialism. Two years after the release of MM, Cardinal Cicognani sent a letter to the Canadians in which he noted that socialization, "when freely and prudently actuated . . . is a source of true human progress." He went on to say that

> it is well to emphasize, in the first place, that socialization, as discussed in the encyclical letter *Mater et Magistra*, is in no way to be confused with socialism. Socialization, when freely and prudently actuated, is entirely in conformity with the social nature of man, and is a source of true human progress in every field, economic, social, moral and cultural.[70]

After this detailed examination of the meaning of socialization, it is helpful to step back from the specific word and the nine numbers devoted to it in the encyclical. Donal Dorr suggests that we see the overall approach of the encyclical: "The real issue is not whether the word 'socialisation' is the correct translation of the Latin text. Rather the issue is whether the pope is moving the Catholic Church away from its suspicion of such 'socialistic' notions as that of the Welfare State."[71]

The answer to that question in Dorr's mind is clearly "yes." Pope John moved the Catholic Church away from its suspicion of "socialistic" notions such as the welfare state. The evidence for that conclusion is found not only in the section on socialization but in the many specific recommendations of the encyclical.

The importance of MM is not found only in this new attitude toward socialization but in the articulation of specific recommendations that encourage socialization. Here is a partial listing of seven implications of socialization suggested by the letter:

- Employees are entitled to share in the ownership of the company where they work (75).
- Employees should have a say in management at the level of the individual firm and in determining policy at various levels, including the national level (92–93, 97).
- The state is to exercise strict control over managers and directors of large businesses (104).
- More state ownership is justified to promote the common good (116–17).
- The state and public authorities have taken on a greater role in addressing social problems (120).
- Public authorities must address the special difficulties of farmers (128–41).
- Specific suggestions are made in regard to tax assessment (133), credit facilities (134), insurance (135), social security (136), price supports (137), price regulation (140), and moving industry into rural areas (141).

All of these interventions by the state are necessary because modern human life is more complex and interdependent, especially in the developed nations. Economic life and political life are in such a situation that relationships of neighbor to neighbor or the small town economies are no longer sufficient. Modern economies are experienced on such a large scale that the state is needed to guide decisions so the common good is served.

Pope John did not believe that reliance on market forces alone would truly promote the common good. A country may try to keep the state involvement as low as possible as required by the principle of subsidiarity, but even in those situations Pope John believed the common good required more state "interference" than was needed in the past. "*Mater et magistra* gives a mandate for this extra involvement by the State; and the result begins to look like an encouragement to 'socialisation' in the popular sense of the word."[72]

Pope John's support of socialization is the most important effect of the encyclical because "it began the process of breaking the long alliance between Roman Catholicism and socially conservative forces."[73] Since *Quadragesimo anno* in 1931 the Church's social teachings often were used in an ideological way to support anticommunist and antisocialist efforts. Because the papal teachings had so clearly rejected socialism and emphasized the other end of the political and economic spectrum in defense of private property, the Catholic Church was perceived in many countries as defending the status quo rather than calling for structural change that would empower the poor. Pope John realized that the Church's traditional defense of private initiative and private property had come to be used in an ideological way that reinforced the current unjust distribution of wealth and resources. The Church's antisocialist stance had been used to resist structural reforms. One of the long-term effects of MM was that it made it more difficult to use Catholic social teaching in a reactionary way.[74] Pope Paul VI would continue this direction in *Populorum progressio* when he reasserted the priority of the common good over the right to property (PP 23) and his controversial criticism of unrestrained capitalism and profit (PP 26).[75]

Pope John's discussion of socialization and his lack of condemnatory statements about socialist and communist philosophies leave the reader of MM with the clear message that Pope John is opening a new chapter in Catholic social teaching and action. "By means of that encyclical he had publicly and clearly put the weight of the Church on the side of a policy of social reforms in favour of the poor and deprived, both within each country and at the international level."[76] Pope John gave his endorsement to the teaching of his mentor, Bishop Radini Tedeschi, who stated in 1909 that "Christ's *preference* goes to the disinherited, the weak and the oppressed."[77]

Socialization in the Current Setting

How are we to evaluate Pope John's interpretation of socialization some forty years later? Does it stand the test of time? If Pope John were to address that question today, it would no doubt be put in terms of the complexity of economic and social life on the international or global level. Today, socialization would be interpreted in terms of globalization. Second, the welfare state has been reevaluated, especially in the U.S. context. The resurgence of market-driven economic models, even in former socialist countries, is another change that would require a reinterpretation of socialization. As is evident in the abuses of capitalism due to greed of corporate leaders or the growing gap between the haves and have-nots even in developed countries, there is still a need for the state and states on the international level to intervene for the sake of the common good. Some type of socialization or governmental intervention is necessary to achieve a community where the basic human rights of all are respected and where all people can experience a basic level of human flourishing.

REACTIONS TO THE DOCUMENT

MM received a warm reception from many nations, groups, and individuals. "A constant refrain in comments issuing from different nations referred to the encyclical's manifestly modern tone." Readers appreciated its awareness of contemporary complexities and the use "of findings, and even of the terminology, of modern sociology." Beyond the question of terminology, one commentator pointed out its "sharp sociological insight into modern industrial society never exhibited in any previous papal pronouncement."[78]

These "modern" qualities gave it a remarkably broad appeal. As the Paris daily *Le Monde* remarked, the document "stresses action and the needs of the day. It is up-to-date and it suits the new generation, one which is not interested in academic discussion and doctrinal abstraction."[79] Readers appreciated the upbeat tone of MM: "Despite its frankness and unvarnished realism, the Holy Father's analysis never leaves an impression of nostalgia, pessimism, or weariness. The Church accepts with grace the world as it is."[80]

The reactions and responses to MM within the Church were mixed. In the short term, it did not receive an immediate, positive response.

Writing early on during Vatican II, one critic, E. E. Hales, complained that "*Mater et Magistra* had been ignored hitherto by the Council, which had no item as yet on its agenda about the Church in the Modern World."[81] Because MM had not yet caused the response the pope wanted from the council fathers, Hales reasoned that "he prepared a stronger challenge. *Pacem in Terris* would make good the deficiencies of the Council's schemas. If the Pope plunged Catholic thought, throughout the world, into the critical area of social justice and world peace, and the world responded, could the Council remain mute on these matters?"[82]

From Hales's perspective, MM did not produce immediate results in achieving the reform the Pope John desired for the Church. Pope John called his team of consultors together and put them to work again.

Writing before Vatican II concluded, Hales was not able to see that by the end of the Council in 1965 the bishops had paid attention to the message of MM, as was evident in their drafting of *Gaudium et spes*. An institution as large as the Roman Catholic Church does not change its direction quickly, even when directed by the pope. If MM was a turning point, as Dorr claims, it was a turn that took years to accomplish. Hales could not see the change that was taking place because he did not have the advantage of time. With the benefit of more time, Hales would have to agree with the American economist John Kenneth Galbraith's assessment in 1972 that "of all the changes I have seen in my lifetime, the greatest by far is the one in your church."[83]

The American Edward Duff also complained about the poor response the encyclical received during the first year. "The American Catholic reaction to *Mater et Magistra* cannot be called anything but disappointing." Duff pointed out that, while the secular press "noted it favorably (the *New York Times* printed the complete text), the American Catholic response has been apathetic." His assessment was based on a survey of the 134 dioceses in which fifty-three dioceses responded. Eighty-five percent of the dioceses reported that they had no plans for promoting the encyclical.[84]

This minimal response shows that the Church lacked the proper staff and educational programs to translate the social encyclical into effective tools for catechetical instruction and adult faith formation. Many dioceses are still wrestling with how to promote Catholic social teaching in their schools and parishes.

There was also a mixed reception among German readers. Donald Campion noted that more than one commentary called attention to a lack of enthusiasm, or even a sense of disappointment, among some German social experts. Pope John had relied more on Italian and French sources in contrast to previous popes who had turned to German and Austrian theologians.

> *Quadragesimo anno* (and even more so, many of the speeches of Pius XII) derived inspiration with respect to the problems to be treated, and even with respect to the formulations to be employed, directly from discussions carried on in German-speaking areas (Austria and Germany) . . . in the new encyclical, the social tradition of the French (and Italian) school is much in evidence.[85]

The influence of French scholars and social experts would continue during the papacy of Pope Paul VI, who relied heavily on French consultants in the writing of *Populorum progressio*.

According to Oswald von Nell-Breuning, the primary writer of *Quadragesimo anno* and a German himself, the shift to other sources was a way of introducing correctives such as bringing in a Roman-law approach and moving away from a too narrowly German interpretation of some concepts. Nell-Bruening appreciated the realistic approach of MM, which "has finally rid the Church of 'romantic' images of society and of the economy, which formerly held it prisoner." Finally, he noted with approval that "the real reason why the encyclical has met with so warm a reception in such divergent circles is . . . its intelligibility."[86]

Controversy surrounded not only specific aspects of Pope John's encyclical, but also the very authority of the pope to write on economic and social issues. Philip Land, who lectured on the encyclical in cities in the United States from coast to coast, repeatedly met the challenge: "What right has the Pope to talk about social questions?" and "Why doesn't the Pope just stick to what's in the Gospels?"[87] Some of these disgruntled Catholics were avid readers of William Buckley's journal *National Review*, which had criticized the encyclical in its July 29, 1961, editorial, calling it a "venture in triviality" and observing that "like Pius IX's *Syllabus of Errors* it may become the source of embarrassed explanations."[88] A few weeks later Buckley quipped that the phrase "Mater Si, Magistra no"—"Mother Yes, Teacher no" was "going the rounds in Catholic conservative circles."[89]

What Philip Land found ironic was that this rejection of the papal authority to teach on social matters came from the conservative side of the Church in America, while in Europe the rejection of the pope's teaching authority came from progressive Catholics. The European liberals complained: "Let the Church confine her exhortations to the Gospels and to the law of love. These are things of the spirit, and it is only things of the spirit that are or should be properly the concern of the Church. The task of civilization is purely temporal, wholly secular, and the Church has nothing at all to say about it."[90]

Long-Term Impact

While not all people in the Church heeded MM upon its promulgation, a few bishops did, including Dom Hélder Pessoa Câmara, the auxiliary bishop of Rio de Janeiro at the time. He suggested that "a special commission be established to implement *Mater et Magistra* and to study the problems raised by the modern world, especially world peace and the relationship between the industrialised and under-developed countries."[91] This led to the formation of the Pontifical Commission Iustitia et Pax, which continues to serve the bishops of the world and advises the Vatican on social issues.

Another long-term impact of MM is in the area of methodology. The inductive methodology of "observe, judge, act," which the encyclical employed and recommended for the Church, opened the door to a new way of thinking about the formation of Catholic social thought and social ministry. Pope Paul VI would expand on this in *Octogesima adveniens* in 1971. This inductive approach opened the door to regional and national articulations of Catholic social teachings that were appropriate for that region, for example, the Conference of Latin American Bishops (CELAM) and the National Conference of Catholic Bishops in the United States. Each of these episcopal conferences produced important social teachings in the decades following MM.

The inductive methodology broke the cast of a universal teaching from Rome that is applicable to every local situation. As a result, different approaches were taken by various regional and national groups of bishops, which led to a pluriformity of expressions of Catholic social thought and ministry. This diversity has been limited somewhat under the centralizing influence of Pope John Paul II.[92]

A third long-term impact of Pope John's encyclical is that the Church was challenged to ask, "With whom do we stand?" Church leaders realized that they could not plead neutrality, so they proclaimed "a preferential, but not exclusive, option for the poor." Those who took up this option quickly realized that they now had new enemies and new allies. The martyrdom of Oscar Romero, the archbishop of El Salvador, of the four American women, of the Jesuits in El Salvador, and of many other unknown local leaders, was the price that was paid by those who stood with the poor and powerless. "For the ability to see the need for such an option, the Church owes much to John XXIII and especially to the social teaching of *Mater et Magistra*."[93]

NOTES

1. In the official Latin text the four major sections are identified with roman numerals, but there are no headings or subheadings. In the unofficial translations distributed by the Vatican Press office, headings and subheadings do appear. The following

outline is in accord with the text as found in David J. O'Brien and Thomas A. Shannon, eds., *Catholic Social Thought: The Documentary Heritage* (Maryknoll, N.Y.: Orbis, 1992), 84–128.

2. Peter Hebblethwaite, *Pope John XXIII: Shepherd of the Modern World* (Garden City, N.Y.: Doubleday, 1985), 19.

3. Sean MacReamoinn, "John XXIII, Pope," in *The Modern Catholic Encyclopedia*, ed. Michael Glazier and Monika Hellwig (Collegeville, Minn.: Michael Glazier/Liturgical, 1994), 456.

4. Ibid.

5. Hebblethwaite, *Pope John XXIII*, 231.

6. Pope John XXIII, *Journal of a Soul*, trans. Dorothy White (New York: McGraw-Hill, 1964), 303.

7. Paul Johnson, *Pope John XXIII* (Boston: Little, Brown, 1974), 140.

8. Garry Wills, *Why I Am a Catholic* (Boston: Houghton Mifflin, 2002), 226.

9. Austin Flannery, "Vatican Council II," in *Modern Catholic Encyclopedia*, ed. M. Glazier and M. Hellwig, 891.

10. J. Bryan Hehir, "Presidential Address," Catholic Charities U.S.A., annual meeting, September 9, 2001.

11. E. E. Y. Hales, *Pope John and His Revolution* (Garden City, N.Y.: Doubleday, 1965), 132; P. Johnson, *Pope John XXIII* (Boston: Little, Brown, 1974), 141.

12. Hales, *Pope John and His Revolution*, 125.

13. Ibid., 132.

14. As cited in ibid.

15. Hebblethwaite, *Pope John XXIII*, 356–57.

16. Ibid., 368.

17. Ibid., 369.

18. Ibid., 363.

19. Johnson, *Pope John XXIII*, 141–42.

20. Donald Campion, "The World Wide Response," in *The Challenge of Mater et Magistra*, ed. Joseph Moody and Justus George Lawler (New York: Herder and Herder, 1963), 159.

21. *Acta apostolicae sedis* 53 (1961): 401–64.

22. The first English translation was published by *The Tablet* on July 22, 1961. The Catholic Truth Society of London did a second translation. A third British translation was done by J. R. Kirwan and released through the Catholic Social Guild. The most widely used translation is the one done by William J. Gibbons (Paulist, 1961). It was reprinted in Joseph Gremillion, ed., *The Gospel of Peace and Justice: Catholic Social Teaching Since Pope John* (Maryknoll, N.Y.: Orbis, 1976), and D. O'Brien and T. Shannon, eds., *Catholic Social Thought: The Documentary Heritage* (Maryknoll, N.Y.: Orbis, 1992).

23. Johnson, *Pope John XXIII*, 145–46.

24. Richard L. Camp, *The Papal Ideology of Social Reform: A Study in Historical Development, 1878–1967* (Leiden: E. J. Brill, 1969), 107. See Donal Dorr, "Pope John XXIII—New Directions?" in *Readings in Moral Theology No. 5: Official Catholic Social Teaching*, ed. Charles Curran and Richard McCormick (New York: Paulist, 1986), 103, for the reference to Bolté's work. Dorr's essay can also be found in his book, *Option for the Poor: A Hundred Years of Catholic Social Teaching*, rev. ed. (Maryknoll, N.Y.: Orbis, 1992), 113–46.

25. Dorr, "Pope John XXIII—New Directions?" 77.

26. Campion, "World Wide Response," 174–76, 185.

27. Vivian Bolland, "Mater et Magistra," in *The New Dictionary of Catholic Social Thought*, ed. Judith A. Dwyer (Collegeville, Minn.: Liturgical, 1994), 586.

28. See Marvin L. Krier Mich, *Catholic Social Teaching and Movements* (Mystic, Conn.: Twenty-Third, 1998), 347–84.

29. Michael Schuck, *That They Be One: The Social Teaching of the Papal Encyclicals 1740–1989* (Washington, D.C.: Georgetown University Press, 1991), 177.

30. Campion, "World Wide Response," 156.

31. Ibid., 157.

32. Ibid., 158.

33. Bolland, "Mater et Magistra," in *New Dictionary*, ed. J. A. Dwyer, 581.

34. Schuck, *That They Be One*, 91.

35. Pope John rejected the tradition of reproach and censure that had typified his predecessors. In the previous hundred years Europe and the Catholic Church had been through tumultuous times. The Industrial Revolution and laissez-faire capitalism had wrought havoc on traditional societies, leading to urban poverty and exploitation of workers. The Vatican had lost the Papal States and was hit with repeated waves of anticlericalism. The popes responded by pointing out the errors of the times

and calling for people to return to the Church. Pope Pius IX (1846–78) was the most outspoken critic of modern attitudes, including democracy, progress, modern civilization, and secularism. Pope John broke with that tradition. He followed the advice of Pius IX's contemporary, Archbishop Darboy of Paris, who wrote to Pius IX after his *Syllabus of Errors* was issued and said: "You have distinguished and condemned the principal errors of our epoch. Turn your eyes now towards what she may hold that is honorable and good and sustain her in her generous efforts." Ninety-five years later Pope John would be able to turn his eyes toward what is "good and honorable" in society. See Johnson, *Pope John XXIII*, 26.

36. Ibid., 143–44.

37. Dorr, "Pope John XXIII—New Directions?" 87.

38. Rodger Charles, *Christian Social Witness and Teaching: The Catholic Tradition from Genesis to Centesimus Annus*: vol. 2, *The Modern Social Teaching: Contexts, Summaries, Analysis* (Herefordshire, England: Gracewing/ Fowler Wright, 1998), 146.

39. Schuck, *That They Be One*, 141.

40. David Hollenbach, "Common Good," in *New Dictionary*, ed. J. A. Dwyer, 194.

41. Charles Curran points out that the Catholic tradition still has some work to do regarding the common good: "Experience reminds us that it is difficult for people—especially in more heterogeneous settings—to agree on the meaning of the common good. . . . In practice, the tendency for each person or group to pursue narrow individual or group interests makes working for the common good very difficult. The theory of the common good in the Catholic tradition runs into some obstacles and problems that have not been recognized." See C. Curran, *Catholic Social Teaching 1891—Present: A Historical, Theological, and Ethical Analysis* (Washington, D.C.: Georgetown University Press, 2002), 145.

42. This injustice continues to haunt both developed and developing nations where sweatshop conditions for many laborers is the norm. The lack of real living wages for low-income workers does not allow them to feed, clothe, and shelter their families.

43. This awareness of shareholder "corporate responsibility" has taken root in small pockets of morally minded stockholders who raise issues of the common good at stockholder meetings and moving their investments to "socially responsible" stocks and mutual funds. This has been especially effective among religious congregations and some dioceses in the United States, but it is not yet part of the social conscience of most Catholics.

44. Jean-Yves Calvez, *The Social Thought of John XXIII*, trans. George McKenzie (Chicago: Henry Regnery, 1965), 38.

45. Ibid., 37.

46. "Participation" would play a greater role in Catholic social teaching as it developed in the writings of Pope Paul VI and in the U.S. bishops' 1986 pastoral letter on the economy, *Economic Justice for All*.

47. Dorr, "Pope John XXIII—New Directions?" 85.

48. Hebblethwaite, *Pope John XXIII*, 5.

49. "*Mater et Magistra*: Rich and Poor Nations," *London Catholic Times*, July 21, 1961, 9.

50. Dorr, "Pope John XXIII—New Directions?" 85.

51. Bolland, "Mater et Magistra," 587.

52. Peter Riga, *John XXIII and the City of Man* (Westminster, Md.: Newman, 1966), 5.

53. Ibid., 216.

54. Joe Holland and Peter Henriot, *Social Analysis: Linking Faith and Justice* (Maryknoll, N.Y.: Orbis, 1983).

55. Riga, *John XXIII*, 4.

56. Ibid.

57. Ibid., 192.

58. Ibid., 22.

59. Ibid., 226–27.

60. Pietro Pavan, "The Place of *Mater et Magistra* in Papal Social Teaching," *Christus Rex* 16 (1962): 242.

61. Campion, "World Wide Response," 162.

62. For further bibliographical references, see Bartolomeo Sorge, "Socializzazione e socialismo," *Civiltà cattolica* 114 (1963): 326–37, esp. 336–37.

63. In the original version of MM, this section was written in German. The word *Sozialisierung* was not used in order to avoid using the same term that Pius XII had condemned nine years earlier. Instead, the original German text used the term *Vergesellschaftung*. See Eberhard Welty, *Die Sozial Enzyklika Papst Johannes XXIII Mater et Magistra* (Freiburg: Herder, 1961), 104, as noted by Michael Campbell-Johnston, "The Social Teaching of the Church," *Thought* 39 (1964): 382.

The New Cassell's German Dictionary, rev. ed., ed. Harold T. Betterridge (New York: Funk and

Wagnalls Co., 1971) defines both terms, *Sozialisierung* and *Vegesellschaftung*, as "socialization" and "nationalization." Linguistically, they are interchangeable.

The German translation authorized by the German bishops also avoided the term *Sozialisierung* and substituted the phrases *social life* (das gesellschaftliche Leben) or *social relations* (*die gesellschaftliche Verflechtung*) for *socialization* (*Sozialisierung*). See "Die Sozialenzyklika Papst Johannes' XXIII, *Mater et Magistra*, in "Der neue auf Anregung des deutschen Episkopats hergestellten Uebersetzung," *Herder Korrespondenz* (1961): 541ff. Noted by Sorge,"Socializzazione e Socialismo," 334, no. 20.

The Latin translation from the original German text did not use the problematic word. Rather, it employed expressions such as "the increase of social affairs" (*socialium rationum incrementa*), "the increase of social life" (*socialis vitae incrementa*), and "the increase of social activity" (*socialium rerum progressus*). The official Latin translation stayed closer to the original German text and was not influenced by the Italian version. There is some debate among commentators why the Latin text did not use *socialization* as the other Romance languages did. The Englishman J. R. Kirwan thought it was quite significant that the official Latin text "rejected the term," whereas the French Canadian Paul-Émile Bolté considered it simply a matter of avoiding a Latin neologism, that is, the necessity of creating a new expression or word.

When the Vatican issued its official translations in French, Italian, English, and Spanish through the Vatican Polyglot Press, the term *socialization* did occur, sometimes within parentheses and sometimes not. See Campbell-Johnston, "Social Teaching of the Church," 382. The Italian translation published in the *L'Osservatore Romano* (July 15, 1961) used the term *socializzazione* nine times in numbers 59–67. This same translation was used in a later collection of documents, *Pensiero sociale della chiesa oggi, Documenti di Giovanni XXIII, di Paolo VI e del Concilio Vaticano II*, vol. 1, ed. Giordani (Rome: Città Nuova Editrice, 1974), 21–34. Marie-Dominique Chenu used this translation in his book *La dottrina sociale della Chiesa: origine e sviluppo 1891–1971* (Brescia: Editrice Queriniana, 1977), 107–9. (Note the difference in numbering. The section on socialization is found in numbers 45–54 in the Italian version and 59–67 in the English version.)

The French translation by l'Action Populaire, like the German and Latin versions, avoided the term. It used phrases such as "the developments of social life" (*les developpements de la vie sociale*), "the development of social bonds" (*le developpement des liens sociaux*), and the "development of social relations" (*les developpements des relations sociales*). See *Encyclique Mater et Magistra, Traduction sur le texte latin official, Commentaire et index analytique par l'Action Populaire* (Paris: Spes, 1962), 67–80. Noted by Sorge, "Socializzazione e socialismo," 334, no. 20. The Vatican French translation, as mentioned earlier, did use the word *socialisation*.

In Spain the translation offered by the *Instituto Social Leo XIII* did not use the term *socialization* but rather *progress* (*progreso*), *growth* (*aumento*), *increase in social relations* (*incremento de las relaciones sociales*), or, more loosely, *the almost daily multiplication and development of new forms of association* (*multiplicación y desarrollo casi diario de nuevas formas de asociación*). See *Comentarios a la "Mater et Magistra"* (Madrid: BAC, 1962), 25–28, as noted by Sorge, "Socializzazione e socialismo," 334, no. 20.

The first English translation done by *The Tablet*, dated July 22, 1961, substituted *social action* for *socialization*. The English scholar J. R. Kirwan complained that "this clearly will not do; social action is already a technical term with its own established meaning." See D. Campion, "The Pope and 'Socialization,'" *America* 106 (1962): 751.

A second English translation was prepared by Harold E. Winstone for the Catholic Truth Society in London. He combines *The Tablet*'s *social action* with the Italian original's *socialization*. Thus, number 59 reads "the spread of socialisation or social action." The American Jesuit Donald Campion rightly argues that "the word 'spread' seems unnecessary here, since the Holy Father immediately defines his concept as 'the growing interdependence of men in society.'" J. R. Kirwan also did an English translation which, according to Donal Dorr, "often succeeds in expressing the underlying meaning of the text much better than the other versions, but is occasionally unacceptable." See Dorr, "Pope John XXIII—New Directions?" 105. The Kirwan text reads "the development of the network of social relationships." D. Campion and Eugene Culhane also translated the encyclical for the American Press. They retained the term *socialization*. The most widely used English translation in the United States, which reads "the multiplication of social relations," was done by William Gibbons and published by Paulist Press.

Vatican officials did not hesitate to use the word *socialization*. For instance, the official Vatican newspaper *L'Osservatore Romano* used *socializzazione* in the Italian edition from the very beginning. Cardinal Amleto Cicognani, Vatican secretary of state, used the word *socialization* twelve times when he wrote in English to the National Social Action Conference in 1963. The American Joseph Gremillion who worked in the Pontifical Commission Iustitia et Pax commented that "the Holy See shows no timidity in asserting its own meaning for the English term, which to many sensitive Americans might sound dangerously evocative of socialism." See Gremillion, *Gospel of Peace and Justice*, 25.

64. Eustas O Heideain, "Socialization," in *New Dictionary*, ed. J. A. Dwyer, 891.

65. The linkage with the Semaines Sociales is seen in the letter Cardinal Domenico Tardini, Pope John's secretary of state, sent to the Forty-Seventh Congress, which is congruent with the conclusions of that Congress and the subsequent text of the encyclical. The cardinal's letter read: "The economic, social, political and cultural movement owing to which, since the industrial and agricultural revolutions and with the progress of means of communication and transport, each man tends to become the center of a network of social relations, ever increasing in number and complexity, if not intensity." See Campbell-Johnston, "Social Teaching of the Church," 383.

66. Sorge, "Socializzazione e socialismo," 331.

67. Ibid.

68. Campbell-Johnston, "Social Teaching of the Church," 383.

69. Ibid., 387.

70. Gremillion, *Gospel of Peace and Justice*, 25.

71. Dorr, "Pope John XXIII—New Directions?" 95.

72. Ibid., 96.

73. Ibid., 96–97.

74. Ibid., 97.

75. Mich, *Catholic Social Teaching and Movements*, 158–60.

76. Dorr, "Pope John XXIII—New Directions?" 101.

77. S. MacReamoinn, "John XXIII, Pope," in *Modern Catholic Encyclopedia*, ed. M. Glazier and M. Hellwig, 456.

78. Campion, "World Wide Response," 156.

79. Benjamin Masse, "'Mater et Magistra': One Year After," *America* 105 (1961): 439.

80. Campion, "World Wide Response," 157.

81. Hales, *Pope John and His Revolution*, 156.

82. Ibid., 152.

83. Wills, *Why I Am a Catholic*, 226.

84. Edward Duff, "Catholic Social Action in the American Environment." *Social Order* 12 (1962): 313–14.

85. David Jakob, "Aktuelle Sozialprobleme: Was bringt 'Mater et Magistra' Neues?" *Orientierung* 25 (1961): 201, as cited by Campion, "World Wide Response," 160.

86. Oswald von Nell-Breuning, "Mater et Magistra," *Stimmen der Zeit*, 169 (1961): 128, 116; Campion, "World Wide Response," 176, 158.

87. Philip Land, "Pope John XXIII: Teacher," *America* 106 (1961): 149.

88. "The Week." *National Review* 11 (July 29, 1961): 38. In fairness to William Buckley, the full quote is: "It may, in the years to come, be considered central to the social teachings of the Catholic Church; or, like Pius IX's *Syllabus of Errors*, it may become the source of embarrassed explanations. Whatever its final effect, it must strike many as a venture in triviality coming at this particular time in our history."

89. "For the Record," *National Review* 11 (August 12, 1961): 77. Buckley had picked up that phrase from his friend Garry Wills, who claimed it was a play on Cuban exiles' slogan of the time, "Cuba si, Castro no." (Wills, *Why I Am a Catholic*, 47 and 45.)

90. Land, "Pope John XXIII: Teacher," 149.

91. Hebblethwaite, *Pope John XXIII*, 462.

92. Mary Elsbernd, "What Ever Happened to *Octogesima Adveniens*?" *Theological Studies* 56 (1995): 39–60.

93. Dorr, "Pope John XXIII—New Directions?" 104.

SELECTED BIBLIOGRAPHY

Bolté, Paul-Émile. *Mater et Magistra, commentaire*. 4 vols. Montreal: University of Montreal, 1964–68. Exhaustive study; may be hard to find.

Calvez, Jean-Yves. *The Social Thought of John XXIII*. Translated by George McKenzie. Chicago:

Henry Regnery, 1965. Analyzes seven themes in MM, noting its originality on the question of socialization and development.

Camp, Richard L. *The Papal Ideology of Social Reform: A Study in Historical Development, 1878–1967*. Leiden: E. J. Brill, 1969. An astute commentator, who is not Catholic, offers a progressive analysis.

Campbell-Johnston, Michael. "The Social Teaching of the Church." *Thought* 39 (1964): 380–410. Addresses theological context of MM; especially helpful on the question of "socialization."

Campion, Donald. "The World Wide Response." In *The Challenge of Mater et Magistra*. Edited by Joseph Moody and Justus George Lawler. New York: Herder and Herder, 1963. Very helpful bibliographical essay that surveys 193 articles on MM.

Cronin, John, F. *Christianity and Social Progress: A Commentary on Mater et Magistra*. Baltimore: Helicon, 1965. Former National Catholic Welfare Conference staff person reviews content and scope of encyclical; originally published in *Our Sunday Visitor*.

Dorr, Donal. "Pope John XXIII—New Directions?" In *Readings in Moral Theology No. 5: Official Catholic Social Teaching*. Edited by Charles Curran and Richard McCormick. New York: Paulist, 1986. Irish theologian focuses on MM's break with reactionary use of Catholic social teachings.

Hales, E. E. Y. *Pope John and His Revolution*. Garden City, N.Y.: Doubleday, 1965. British commentator who makes the case for the newness of John XXIII's approach in contrast to his immediate predecessors.

Hebblethwaite, Peter. *Pope John XXIII: Shepherd of the Modern World*. Garden City, N.Y.: Doubleday, 1985. Long-time Vatican watcher presents a thorough and appreciative biography of John XXIII.

Johnson, Paul. *Pope John XXIII*. Boston: Little, Brown, 1974. Focuses on Pope John as breaking new ground, a dramatic change from his predecessors.

Masse, Benjamin L., ed. *The Church and Social Progress: Background Readings for Pope John's Mater et Magistra*. Milwaukee: Bruce, 1966. The former associate editor of *America* brings together a variety of short articles.

von Nell-Breuning, Oswald. "Mater et Magistra." *Stimmen der Zeit* 169 (November 1961): 116–28. Brief commentary on encyclical with attention to German social issues and orientations.

Quinn, Karen. "Trade Unions in 'Mater et Magistra.'" *Gregorianum* 43 (1962): 268–94. Traces the continuity of MM with previous teachings on unions. Two practical recommendations of MM are analyzed, namely, collective agreements and worker representation in national and international organizations.

Riga, Peter. *John XXIII and the City of Man*. Westminster, Md.: Newman, 1966. Riga highlights the new directions in terms of lay spirituality, among other themes.

Sorge, Bartolomeo. "Socializzazione e Socialismo." *Civiltà cattolica* 114 (1963): 326–37. This journal is considered a semiofficial mouthpiece of the Vatican. Excellent listing of bibliographical resources (336–37).

——. "La 'Mater et Magistra' di fronte ai Socialismi contemporanei." *Civiltà cattolica* 114 (1963): 545–56. Sorge continues his analysis of MM, focusing on its stance toward socialism.

Thiefry, M. "L'Encyclique 'Mater et Magistra': ses caratères, synthèse de ses Enseignements," *Nouvelle Revue Théologique*," 83 (1961): 897–913, 1009–33. A discussion of the themes of the encyclical as part of the tradition of "Christian humanism."

CHAPTER

9

Commentary on *Pacem in terris* (*Peace on Earth*)

DREW CHRISTIANSEN, S.J.

INTRODUCTION

The Italian journalist Giancarlo Zizola has called *Pacem in terris* "the utopia of Pope John XXIII."[1] Zizola has a point. Though the encyclical was officially published on April 11, 1963, a few months after the Cuban missile crisis, it deals only in a limited way with the hard-minded issues of the cold war, such as nuclear deterrence. Rather, the "utopian" thesis of PT is that the positive substance of peace consists in political systems aimed at upholding and protecting human rights. Pope John, quoting himself from *Mater et magistra*, said that his new encyclical aspires to "'a world community, a community in which each member, whilst conscious of his own individual rights and duties, will work in a relationship of equality towards the attainment of the universal common good'" (125). As a platform for Catholic social action (on behalf of human rights), PT may be rivaled only by Leo XIII's *Rerum novarum*, which gave impetus to the Catholic labor movement. For following the publication of the encyclical, Catholics in Chile, South Africa, South Korea, Poland, Guatemala, El Salvador, the Philippines, Mexico, East Timor, and elsewhere marched at the forefront of human rights movements.

OUTLINE OF THE DOCUMENT

The opening paragraphs (1–7) ground the encyclical's moral argument on the order of the universe and the moral order "written in the hearts" of human beings.

Part 1 (8–45) lays out the "universal and inviolable" rights and duties of the human person, including the right to worship God according to one's conscience. "Characteristics of the Present Day" (39–45) is the first of three interpolations in the letter giving positive assessments of contemporary social trends. Here they are workers' rights, the emancipation of women, and the independence of new states.

Part 2 (46–79) traces the divine origin of political authority. It also identifies the function of government as upholding the common good, specified as safeguarding human rights and facilitating the fulfillment of duties. Numbers 75–79 contain a second survey of "characteristics of the present day," especially the importance of written constitutions and popular political participation.

Part 3 (80–129) treats the relations between states under the rubrics of truth, justice, and active solidarity. Numbers 109–19 address the need for disarmament, demand an end to the arms race, and include an earnest appeal from

Pope John for world leaders "to spare no pain or effort until world events follow a course in keeping with man's destiny and dignity" (117). Numbers 126–29, under the title "Signs of the Times," survey the demands of the human family for an end to war and the resolution of conflict through negotiation.

Part 4 (130–45) examines the relationship between persons and political communities with the world community. It sketches the growing interdependence of peoples and nations, postulates the need of a new level of political authority to address problems affecting the universal common good, and gives support to the United Nations and the Universal Declaration of Human Rights.

Part 5 (146–73) urges the participation of Catholics in public life, endorses the development of professional competence by the laity, and allows Catholics to cooperate with non-Catholics in social and economic affairs. The letter concludes with a prayer to the Prince of Peace.

CONTEXT OF THE DOCUMENT

Social Context

In 1962, the cold war was at its height. In March the Berlin Wall went up. In October, just as Vatican II began, the United States and the Soviet Union came to the brink of nuclear war over the deployment of Soviet missiles in Cuba. Behind the Iron Curtain, communist governments persecuted Catholics and bishops remained imprisoned. In Europe, especially in Italy, many worried about a possible political "opening to the left," that is, political compromises and alliances by Christian Democrats with the socialists and Communists. Within the Church and among Catholic politicians, a struggle had begun over the Church's role in politics. Would it remain the staunch opponent of totalitarianism, as it had been under Pius XII, or would it become a more independent, evangelical-minded instrument of peace, reaching out even to supposed adversaries? In each of these four areas (superpower relations, the Church's status in Eastern Europe, Italian politics, and the role of the Church in politics), Pope John's pontificate marked a transition to a new "optimistic" Vatican politics of peace.

Superpower Relations

In his last year, Pope John helped John Kennedy and Nikita Khrushchev step back from the brink of war over Cuba. Throughout the crisis and in the few months of life remaining to him, John commended the place of reason in international affairs and urged the resolution of conflict through negotiation. He led the Church out of its defensive cold war posture to a new active "diplomacy of conscience."[2] A little more than a week before his death, in the presence of the Cardinal Secretary of State Amleto Cicognani and John's frequent confidant Monsignor Angelo Dell'Acqua, Pope John professed his commitment to the Church as a servant of the whole human family. "Now more than ever," he told them, "we are called to serve man as such, and not merely Catholics; to defend above all and everywhere the rights of the human person, and not merely those of the Catholic Church."[3] A month earlier PT, often described as John's "last will and testament," had elaborated what Pope John hoped would be a new statecraft for a new age focused on the advancement of human rights.

Eastern Europe

One of the most intriguing relationships in John's short pontificate was that with Soviet president Nikita Khrushchev. The trust they exhibited toward one another opened the way to what was later called the Vatican's *Ostpolitik*, that is, its policy toward communist Eastern Europe. Always ready to see the good in others, Pope John appealed to the Soviet president's good sense. In a 1961 interview with *Pravda*, Khrushchev praised John for "[paying] tribute to reason" an attitude on which John relied upon in mediating the Cuban missile crisis. Khrushchev added, "We welcome the appeal to negotiate no matter where it comes from."[4] John appealed to the Soviet leader's good will to pursue other openings in the Soviet bloc, and Khrushchev reciprocated in the wake of the missile crisis, seeking regular, though informal, contacts with the pope.

Among the notable outcomes of this unique relationship was the commissioning of Russian Orthodox observers to Vatican II in November 1962 and the release of Ukrainian metropolitan Archbishop Josef Slipyi from the Siberian gulag in February 1963. Curial officials were suspicious of these departures. They disparaged the release of Slipyi and, when Khrushchev's son-in-law Alexis Adzhubei visited John that spring, they suppressed news of the event.

Italian Politics

Pope John carried out his Eastern diplomacy with the greatest delicacy. In Italy, however, the slightest shifts in policy were bound to stir public controversy. At issue were the Church's ties to the Christian Democratic Party and the party's role in Italian politics. Pope John was quietly encouraging the Vatican's "disengagement" (*disimpegno*) from a direct Vatican role in Italian politics. For his part, the Christian Democratic leader Aldo Moro was exploring an "opening to the left" that would permit alliances with Italian socialists and Communists. In the cold war atmosphere, these experiments worried Catholic leaders elsewhere, like John F. Kennedy and Konrad Adenauaer, and aroused the suspicion of CIA chief John McCone, a Knight of Malta. In Italy, these initiatives evoked hostility from Cardinal Giuseppe Siri, longtime president of the Italian episcopal conference, and Cardinal Alfredo Ottaviani, head of the Holy Office. The two Italians regarded John as hopelessly naïve and his policies as downright dangerous.

A showdown came in 1962 over the nationalization of the Italian power system, a key program of the center-left coalition government of Amintore Fanfani. Siri declared that with the nationalization proposal the Christian Democrats had forfeited the right to be called "Christian." John, however, accepted the advice of leading moralists, including the Lateran's Monsignor Pietro Pavan, that nationalization could be required by the common good without infringing on basic freedom. In a personally typed note to prominent industrialists, the pope declared his political neutrality. "The Holy Father," he wrote, wished "to remain outside conflicts of a political-social nature between sons whom he respects and loves with an equal measure of comprehension." He appealed to the example of "the patriarch Jacob, who, in the midst of his quarrelling sons, confined himself to watching, suffering, and keeping silent."[5]

The Church's Role in Politics

At one level, Pope John's struggles with curialists and Italian bishops were conflicts over the legacy of Pius XII, to whom John's adversaries disparagingly compared him. His policy of "reserve" and "disengagement" was markedly different from that of Pius, who had openly exploited Catholic Action and the Christian Democrats to impede communist gains in Italy. Instead, John counseled bishops to take up a more pastoral role. In a journal entry for August 31, 1961, he noted that "[bishops] are more exposed to temptations of meddling immoderately in matters that are not their business." The pope's task was to urge them to avoid controversy. "They are to preach to all alike, and in general terms, justice, charity, meekness, gentleness and the other evangelical virtues."[6] For some in the Italian hierarchy, asking bishops to refrain from interfering in politics and intrigue and to assume a wholly pastoral role was a tall order. For John, "conniving in evil in the hope that by doing so [they] may be useful to someone," as many Italian bishops were prone to do, was a mistaken pastoral strategy, even if it was done in the name of freedom and democracy.

When considering the ecclesial context, John XXIII's pontificate also represented a shift in internal Church governance from the pontifical demeanor of Pius XII to the pastoral style of the new pope. Pius, by birth a member of the papal nobility and by training an old-school diplomat, exercised his authority with exceptional formality. By contrast John displayed the bonhomie of the peasant he had been, but his pastoral style had also been informed by his own study and research. A historian of Charles Borromeo's reforms in Milan, John read regularly from patristic sources, the writings of previous popes, those of his countrymen in northern Italy, as well as other Italian Catholic reformers, gleaning from them his ideas about pastoral leadership. Though John was in no way an ideological progressive, it was his sense of history and his trust in the goodness of ordinary people that led him to alter the Church's role in Italian politics, to call the Council, and to write PT.

Aggiornamento

The existing style of ecclesiastical governance, inherited from Pius XII, required deference to the past, as evidenced by John's short-lived apostolic constitution *Veterum sapientia* (1962), which confirmed Latin as the official language of the Church. There were also many in the curia working mightily to preserve the legacy of Pius XII. Still, John was disposed to see reform as a matter of *aggiornamento,* or pastoral adaptation to the times, rather than as innovation. In a 1942 Pentecost sermon, he had already set out a decidedly pastoral view of the Petrine ministry. The pope, he wrote, "is *a sign of union* amid so many passions and conflicts of interest, and represents an *invitation* to order, gentleness and reconciliation."[7]

Ecumenism

Ecumenism was the principal arena in which the struggle between John's *aggiornamento* and curial traditionalism took place. John's first encyclical, *Ad Petri cathedram* (1959), had given uncertain signals about his attitude toward other Christians. Following the position of Pius XI, John ruled out participation in the international ecumenical movement and warned against the perils of indifferentism. The remedy for division in the body of Christ was for those separated from Rome to "return" to "the one, true Church." But to this traditional language, John added a soothing, personal touch: "When we lovingly invite you to the unity of the Church, we do not invite you to some strange house but to your own, shared paternal home . . . 'I am Joseph, your brother.'" John's desire was for unity in the bonds of charity, but his inherited thought frames and curial traditionalists—Cardinal Domenico Tardini, the secretary of state, had been the final editor of *Ad Petri cathedram*—still blocked firm moves in that direction.

For a breakthrough, John needed the aid of a fresh thinker who was at the same time an old hand in Rome. Augustin Bea, a German Jesuit, then rector of the Pontifical Biblical Institute and the principal drafter of *Divino afflante Spiritu*, Pius XII's encyclical on biblical studies, proved to be that man. Bea had resided in Rome since 1924 and had served as confessor to Pius XII. Frail-looking and six months older than John, he did not seem a threat to the curia. Nonetheless, it was Bea who presented a plan for a pontifical commission, drawn up by Lorenz Jaeger, the archbishop of Paderborn, to deal with ecumenical matters in preparation for the Council.

Because the Secretariat for Christian Unity, as it was called, opened the workings of the Council to observers from other Christian communions, Bea found himself under attack from traditionalists and particularly from Cardinal Alfredo Ottaviani, the powerful head of the Holy Office. Ottaviani cited Pius XII's encyclical *Mystici corporis* to the effect that "those divided from one another in faith and government cannot be living in the one Body so described, and by its one Spirit." Bea responded that Christ is the Head of the Body "to which each of us believers is related, to it we belong" by virtue of baptism.[8] This was the strategy with which Bea would lay the foundations for Catholic ecumenism: unity in Christ through baptism. Bea prevailed. On Christmas Day 1961, John officially convoked Vatican II. He prayed for "the return of unity and peace (to the Church), according to the prayer of Christ to the Father" and he expressed his hope that the other Christian churches would "send representatives of their communities to follow [the Council's] work at close quarters."[9] From that time on, Bea and his team at Christian Unity were at work holding meetings with leaders of other churches and hosting observers to the Council.

The Council and World Peace

The major ecclesial event of John's short pontificate was the convocation of Vatican II. Both Pius XI and Pius XII had contemplated calling a Council. John formally announced his intention to call a council to the College of Cardinals on January 25, 1959, at the conclusion of the Week of Prayer for Christian Unity. The night before the announcement he confided to his secretary, Monsignor Loris Capovilla, "The world is starving for peace. If the Church responds to its Founder and rediscovers its authentic identity, the world will gain."[10] The ties linking the Council, the gospel, and peace seem to have been constantly on John's mind. In a meeting with Venetian pilgrims in May 1962, he described the inspiration for the Council. "One thing we noted was that though everyone said they wanted peace and harmony, unfortunately conflicts grew more acute and threats multiplied," he told his audience. "Instead of issuing new warnings, shouldn't [the Church] stand out as a beacon of light? What could that exemplary light be?" It was at that point, "with ineffable confidence in the divine Teacher," he answered, "a Council."[11] Again meeting with the diplomatic corps on the eve of the Council, he explained that while the Council was a religious event, he hoped it would contribute to "peace based on growing respect for the human person and so leading to freedom of religion and worship."[12] In this sense, though PT was Pope John's own work, not that of the Council, it was nonetheless integral to his own hopes for the Council.

PROCESS OF FORMULATION AND AUTHORSHIP

In October 1962, Vatican II had just opened. So badly had relations between the United States and the Soviet Union deteriorated that for a few days, Vatican officials gave consideration to suspending the Council "to allow the bishops to return to their dioceses before the unthinkable happened."[13] One point of American-Soviet contact at the time was a meeting for scientists in Andover, Maryland, where one of the participants was *Saturday Review* editor Norman Cousins. Asked by the Kennedy White House to find a way to communicate with the Soviets, Cousins recommended appealing through the pope as a third party. Working through a priest attending the conference, Cousins determined the pope's willingness to serve as an intermediary. With the acceptance of both the Americans and the Soviets, John XXIII delivered his message on October 24, 1962. "The Pope always speaks well of all men of state," he told a group of Portuguese pilgrims, "who are concerned here, there and everywhere, with meeting among themselves to avoid the reality of war and to procure a bit of peace for humankind."[14] A message was also delivered to embassies around Rome. "We remind those who bear the responsibility of power of their grave duties," it read. "With your hand upon your heart, may you listen to the anguished cry from all points of land . . . that rises toward heaven: peace! peace! We today renew this solemn invocation. We beseech all the rulers not to remain deaf to this cry of humanity. May they do all that is in them to safeguard the peace. They will thereby keep the horrors of war from the world—a war whose consequences no one can foresee."[15]

At noon on October 25, 1962, Vatican radio reported the pope's message. Within hours, Soviet ships in the Atlantic turned around and began to return home. In December, Norman Cousins visited Khrushchev in Moscow. The Soviet leader told him, "In regard to what Pope John did for peace, his was humanistic assistance that will be recorded in history. The Pope and I can diverge on many questions, but we are united in our desire for peace."[16]

Two weeks after the crisis, on November 16, 1962, Pope John met with his doctors. From the physicians, the pope received the first word of the cancer that would kill him within the year. To the physicians he gave an early indication that he had decided to compose a letter synthesizing his thoughts on peace. John jotted down his own ideas, drawing principally on biblical and patristic sources. A drafting committee was assembled and the primary drafting was assigned to a professor of moral theology from the Lateran University, Monsignor Pietro Pavan, who had contributed to John's earlier encyclical *Mater et magistra*.[17] When Pavan entered the papal library, John startled him with his plan. "The Lord has saved us from a new disaster—war. We helped the little we could. It could be said now that when the Pope speaks of peace, men stop to listen. Can't we take up this issue with greater breadth?"[18]

Monsignor Pietro Pavan

In the 1940s and 1950s, Pietro Pavan had done for Italian Catholics what Jacques Maritain had done in the French- and English-speaking worlds in laying a theological groundwork for acceptance of freedom, democracy, and human rights. In 1943, for example, he had written, "The gospel determined the deepest social and political revolution, perhaps the most authentic social revolution of all history. . . . The fundamental relationship to God meant re-affirmation of the supreme dignity of human life; of the sanctity of marriage; of the functional character of the state and of society."[19] "The basic principle that won approval for the two papal documents [MM and PT]," wrote Pavan's biographer Franco Biffi, "was the method of freedom as the method peculiar to the human person" articulated in Pavan's social theology. Beginning in the late 1930s, however, Pavan had carried out his defense of freedom in the face of both fascist and conservative Christian opinion. Writing in the last years of Pius XII, he complained, "Many worthy people, old in years, and antiquated in ideas, have no sympathy for democracy. They think things would be much better if the opposition was silenced under a prestigious leader with a strong government and an efficient police force."[20]

In Pavan, Pope John found a collaborator who shared his trust in the created goodness of human beings. Pavan was disposed to find the light in the shadows, discerning what PT would call the "signs of the times," seeing like John the impact of history on the course of ideas, and valuing the step-by-step progress toward peace. "The ocean," he wrote, "is made of drops. And every action, however humble, if it is good, is a contribution to peace."[21]

During the drafting, the greatest controversy centered on the role of Catholics in public life. Not everyone was as convinced as Pavan or Pope John of the importance of human freedom, even in the political forum. At issue was the independence of the Catholic faithful from hierarchical supervision when they engaged in politics. Many did not share Pope John's policy of *disimpegno*. In particular, the papal theologian and Dominican Luigi Ciappi suspected the document of inclining toward liberalism and indifferentism. While the Jesuit George Jarlot, a professor at the Gregorian University and an editor of the French journal *Études*, believed the draft restored papal teaching to the level experienced during "the best days of Leo XIII," he nonetheless observed that whereas justice, truth, and charity are reliable principles for Christians in public life, "liberty is an unsure guide."[22]

Vatican consultants worried particularly about allowing Catholics to make common cause at a practical level with Socialists and Communists, a political posture seemingly at odds with the strong anticommunism of Pius XII. Jarlot, for one, wondered, "Wasn't the most urgent problem [faced by the Church] that of the Communist menace to the West and to Christian civilization?"[23] The ideological contamination that tainted the French worker-priest movement, he warned, provided reason for greater caution about such possible alliances than the draft seemed to suggest.

John XXIII himself broke the impasse, penning the distinction between the person—"who is always and above all a human being, and he retains in every case his dignity as a person"—and the philosophies to which he sometimes adheres (158).[24] Of such alliances across ideologies, John wrote, "Therefore, as far as Catholics are concerned, this decision rests primarily with those who live and work in the specific sectors of human society in which those problems arise, always, however, in accordance with the principles of the natural law, with the social doctrine of the Church, and with the directives of the ecclesiastical authority" (160).[25] Two years later the Council that John convoked took a further step and acknowledged the good done the Church by its opponents. John went further, affirming the possibility that alien ideologies might carry universal values. "Who can deny," he wrote, "that to the degree to which those movements conform to the precepts of right reason and are interpreters of the lawful aspirations of the human person, contain elements that are positive and worthy of approval?" (159). The pope, who felt he bore pastoral responsibility for nonbelievers, understood that God sometimes writes with crooked lines.[26]

At issue in the passages about Catholic participation in politics were particularly relations with people on the political left, whether communist governments in Eastern Europe, or Communists and Socialists in Italy and Latin America. Commenting on the Italian scene, Pietro Pavan remarked that political openness on the part of Catholics would mean that from now on a vote against the Christian Democrats was not a vote against the Church.[27] Jesuit Father Roberto Tucci, then editor of *Civiltà cattolica*, prophesied that the freedom for political compromise and practical cooperation with the left would have dramatic impact on political developments in Spain and Portugal as well, where the right-wing Catholic regimes of Franco and Salazar remained in power.[28]

ESSAY

The topic of PT is peace. Its opening words—*Peace on earth*—set the agenda and it closes with a prayerful appeal to the Prince of Peace. In between, it is a treatise on politics: on human rights, political authority, international relations, and the universal common good. With the possible exception of Vatican II's *Pastoral Constitution on the Church in the Modern World*, *Gaudium et spes*, PT is the fullest general treatment of political morality to be found in modern Catholic social teaching. Only the last chapters deal with issues typically conceived of as matters of peace: the relations between states and global relations. The backbone of the document is its teaching on human rights. Morality, political authority, international relations, and the world community are all interpreted in light of the rights of human beings.[29]

A CATHOLIC APPROACH TO PEACEMAKING

PT provides a distinctively Catholic approach to peacemaking,[30] focused on the realization of human rights as the substance of peaceful world order.[31] The encyclical advances the view that peace consists in the promotion, safeguarding, and defense of human rights at every level of social life, whether interpersonal, social, political, international, or global. Peace consists in the realization of the common good conceived of as the realization of rights. The sources of conflict may be found in the violation or nonrealization of rights, and implicitly war appears to be the result of political failure in the defense or implementation of rights. To complete a Catholic theology of peace today, other developments in official Catholic social theology (particularly reading of the signs of the times, such as the usefulness of nonviolence, or systematic reflection on themes like equitable development or forgiveness in peacemaking) would need to be added.[32] Nonetheless, the commitment to human rights first articulated by John XXIII and confirmed by Vatican II continues to be the backbone of the Church's commitment to peacemaking in the contemporary world.

Language and Method

Superficially the language and thought forms of PT, especially in the opening numbers (1–8), remain that of neoscholastic philosophy, the customary language of papal encyclicals from the time of Leo XIII. It begins with appeals to natural law, the order of creation, and conscience as Catholic moral theology and philosophy had done since the Middle Ages. Appeals to scripture and natural theology are made in support of essentially Christian philosophical arguments. The shift to positive theology, characterized by appeals to scriptural and patristic sources and marked by symbolic forms of argument, found in *Gaudium et spes*, for example, is not yet in evidence.[33] But important changes in both language and method are also to be found. These include (1) a shift to "rights talk," (2) experiments with "reading the signs of the times," and (3) appeals to Christian virtue as well as moral principle.

Rights Talk

Among the changes in language, the most significant is the shift to rights talk. While rights language was not foreign to late medieval and early modern Catholic ethical and political thought (see the "Excursus," below), it had fallen into disuse during the period of the Enlightenment and French Revolution until it was completely rejected by Pius IX in the *Syllabus of Errors* (1864). The late nineteenth- and early-twentieth-century Scholastic revival, with its reliance on Aquinas, had also largely neglected that phase of the tradition.[34] In the early 1960s most educated Catholics, and even more non-Catholics, assumed that natural law was consistent with the language of duties but not with the language of rights. So the encyclical's recourse to rights language itself constituted an intellectual challenge. For some it seemed a capitulation to the Enlightenment; to others it amounted to an overdue encounter with the secular (Western) world.[35]

Reading the Signs of the Times

Another methodological novelty of the letter was its assessment of current events. Customarily church documents spoke in generalities, making abstractions of contemporary social developments. Intercutting the philosophical argument of PT, however, one finds reflections on contemporary social developments that ultimately came to be known as "reading the signs of the times." Angelo Roncalli, as Pope John had been born, had been a historian, and as a social ethicist, Monsignor Pavan was a keen observer of long-term social trends.[36] The encyclical's short moral surveys of contemporary history constitute the early penetration of "historical consciousness" into papal teaching. The first two passages (39–45, 75–79) go by the title "Characteristics of the Present Day"; the last (126–29), "Signs of the Times," would give its name to the method.

Appearing at the end of their respective sections, each is a summation of the moral aspirations of the day intended to underscore the moral principles that have preceded them. The first section takes note of emergent aspirations to equality on the part of workers, women, newly independent nations, and those who have suffered racial discrimination. The second section comments on the need for bills of rights, written constitutions, and the rule of law. It also affirms the requirement for an extraconstitutional source for such rights as a way to affirm that neither human dignity nor human rights are of human or especially state devising.

Finally, the last section, "Signs of the Times," follows material on the relations between states. Here Pope John, writing within months of the Cuban missile crisis, affirms that people are becoming aware that disputes between states ought to be resolved by negotiation rather than war. He argues, from the fear of nuclear calamity, that "it is contrary to reason to hold that war is now a suitable way to restore rights which have been violated" (127). While recognizing the alleged need of nuclear weapons for deterrence, he expresses the hope that by meeting and negotiating, nations will learn "that between them and their respective peoples, it is not fear which should reign but love" (129).

Reading the signs of the times, therefore, introduced not only a historical dimension to the encyclical but also a different moral logic, not one of moral principles alone, but of attitudes, dispositions, and virtues. In some cases, the reading led to affirmation of the values discerned in the world, as in the growing sense of equality, the claiming of rights by women, workers, and racial minorities, or the opposition to war. In others, as in the attitude toward the cold war, the "signs of the times" established a dialectic between the existing political conditions and popular aspiration, with the pope putting the strategy of deterrence to question, advocating negotiations over armed conflict, and urging increased interaction among people so as to stimulate attitudes of love in public life.

Virtues for International Affairs

A similar effort to modify the language of principles by that of virtues is found in Part 3 of the encyclical, which deals with relations between states. Four organizing virtues are cited: truth (86–90), justice (91–93), solidarity (98–100), and liberty (120).[37] In fairness, it must be said that the language of these numbers remains mostly that of moral principle. But the intention of these subsections seems to stress the spirit of relationship, to discourage inequality and promote friendly relations, even communion, a term not yet restricted, as some would later argue and the magisterium would sometimes insist, exclusively to an ecclesial context. Truth, among other things, demands the recognition of the equal dignity of all peoples and mutual assistance in overcoming inequality. Justice requires that nations not pursue their own improvement at the price of oppressing others. Solidarity means recognizing that all political authority exists to fulfill the common good of the whole human family. Finally, freedom in international affairs requires nonintervention by the powerful.

Human Rights and Political Communities

Foundations (1–8)

The larger subject of PT is political morality in the sense of the basic moral principles guiding political life. Those principles are integrated around the theme of the dignity and rights of the human person. In this Copernican revolution, the realization and defense of the rights of human beings is placed at the heart of political life. The rights of persons are no longer subordinate to social groupings, as in some medieval Christian views of political theory or in modern realist theories of statecraft. Neither are rights set only as limits to predatory authority, as with some medieval theologians, like William of Ockham and Jean Gerson, and in some liberal democratic theories, like those of John Locke and James Madison. The encyclical proposes that the end of government, all government, is to uphold and implement these rights (and the fulfillment of the corresponding fundamental moral obligations). Even in international affairs, the goal is "the recognition, respect, safeguarding and promotion of the rights of human persons" (139). Because the encyclical puts the rights of persons as members of the one human family ahead of state interests (raisons d'état), Catholic political theory stemming from Pope John XXIII may be described as "cosmopolitan."[38]

First Principles

The encyclical opens with an affirmation of the primacy of the moral over the political. Politics, especially political authority, are grounded in the moral order of the universe. Here we have the ancient theme that the political order mirrors the cosmic order.[39] "Peace on earth," the encyclical opens, "can be firmly established only if the order laid down by God be dutifully observed" (1). The remainder of the first subsection (1–3) is dedicated to elaborating the theme of cosmic order, though with a contemporary humanist strain, namely, the harnessing of the order of the universe by science and technology. Appealing to ancient themes, the encyclical focuses on the human person, like Leonardo's geometric sketch of the human form, at the center of God's created order.[40]

Moral Order

The overture, as it were, begins with the cosmos and reaches a climax in the human microcosm. "The Creator of the world has imprinted in man's heart an order which his conscience reveals to him and enjoins him to obey" (5). There is an echo here of traditional appeals to natural law based, as in Romans 2:15, on appeals to conscience. But straightaway a contrast is made between the judgments of conscience in God's "more perfect creation," humanity (5), and rationalist and realist understandings of politics in which "the relations between men and States can be governed by the same laws as the forces and irrational elements of the universe" (6). This is a glancing blow aimed primarily at the materialism and determinism of Marx and perhaps, as well, at the political realism of Thomas Hobbes, Paul d'Holbach, Montesquieu, and James Madison. But "good Pope John" was not given to polemics; he moves forward to present his positive message. Still, there is a signal here that papal political theory will henceforth give less weight to realist considerations of statecraft and more to the moral limits and goals of political life.[41] If one does not look to the interests of states, where does one look for guidance on political life? To human nature.

Human Dignity

What is human nature? It is laid out in numbers 9–10, much as Pius XII had done in a 1941 radio address.[42] "Every human being is a person; that is, his nature is endowed with intelligence and free will. Indeed, precisely because he is a person he has rights and obligations. . . . And, as these rights and obligations are universal and inviolable, so they cannot in any way be surrendered" (9). Human dignity and the rights that flow from it are the first principles of his political ethics. While the framework appears to be one of natural law, natural law has been turned inside out.[43] Human nature, not nature, is the touchstone. Conscience, rather than cosmic law, is the foundation of the moral order. Rights and obligations, not just obligations, inhere in human nature, and in the political order, it appears, it is rights that have primacy, for the very end of government is to sustain such rights. Within the traditional framework of natural law and Catholic political philosophy a seismic shift has begun.

The Order of Love

Besides natural law, there is another dynamic that undergirds the Christian political philosophy of the encyclical, namely, the orientation of human beings to society in love. John hints at this dynamic in the description of the political agenda in number 7. There he notes that "the establishment of such a [world] community is urgently demanded today by the requirements of the universal common good." Elsewhere we find it in his identification of the processes of socialization, today we might say globalization, at work in the world (130), in his description of solidarity in terms of friendly relations among peoples (100), in his appeal that the law of fear that rules among nations must be supplanted by the rule of love (128–29), and his description of peacemaking as "a requirement of Love" (164). In his peroration, he writes, "Every believer in this world of ours must be a spark of light, a center of love, a vivifying leaven among his fellowmen, and he will be this the more perfectly the more closely he lives in communion with God in the intimacy of his soul" (164). Here we have evidence of a Christian hermeneutic of political life and contemporary history in which love and the unity of the human family are the heuristic tools. That is, Christian love enables one to see in ambiguous historical developments opportunities and positive accomplishments, ignored by realists, which contribute to the growing unity in the human family. Finally, Christian love provides a sort of teleology for political history, so that a global community comprehending all the world's peoples is projected as the goal of human history.[44]

A Catholic Theory of Rights

Highlighting human rights as the keystone of political life, PT constitutes a rapprochement with the Enlightenment and political liberalism. As contrasted with the *Syllabus of Errors* a century before, it affirms individual rights, democracy, and constitutional government. At the same time, it by no means embraces liberal (Anglo-American) political philosophy whole and complete. Instead, it integrates liberal ideas about rights and political freedom into a distinctively Catholic moral and political framework adapted to the essential sociability of human beings. It is, to use a contemporary philosophical designation, a "communitarian" understanding of human rights, emphasizing that human beings are persons among and with other persons, not just individuals with claims on one another, and that their full flourishing takes place in community where all flourish together. Among the characteristically "Catholic" features of the encyclical's human rights theory are: (1) the correlation of rights and duties, (2) an attitude of cooperation (and adjustment) in the implementation of rights, and (3) the assimilation of rights to the common good.

The Correlation of Rights and Duties

One of the philosophical issues that had divided the drafters of the Universal Declaration of Human Rights and the members of the United Nations, when they came to adopt the declaration, was the issue of whether, like the Bogota Declaration of 1948, it should affirm along with the stipulated rights a set of corresponding duties. The drafters of the Universal Declaration decided against doing so for pragmatic political reasons. It would have made gaining consensus for the document immensely more difficult.[45] PT, by contrast, holds to the traditional Catholic pairing of rights and duties and, after listing some primary rights and classes of rights (e.g., political freedoms), expounds a theory of rights and duties (28–37). Thus, for example, the right to life corresponds with the duty of self-preservation. The right to investigate truth, to take another case, carries with it the obligation to seek it out. The balance between rights and duties, as among rights themselves, is one of the principal ways in which Catholic thinking on human rights differs from the absolutist understanding of rights prevalent in the United States today. This difference is most evident perhaps in the abortion debate where in the Catholic understanding the right to life properly limits a woman's freedom of choice.

A Cooperative Spirit

The letter's approach to the implementation of rights is to call for a spirit of collaboration across society (31–34) just as it will call for solidarity among nations (98–100) and for international cooperation in the cause of economic development of poor nations (121–23). In any case, it is a very Catholic instinct to see human sociability and to trust its capacity to bring about change for the good. To political realists in particular, such hopes for moral behavior, especially in international affairs, appear excessively naïve. In defense of the encyclical, it may be argued that such appeals, at a minimum, help put a check on negative behavior. They also strengthen constructive social trends, and they project alternative political institutions.

An important consequence of the positive Catholic valuation of human sociality is the injunction that those who hold an advantage in any society ought to be ready to sacrifice some degree of the enjoyment of their rights for the sake of those who are deprived. The encyclical repeatedly affirms the importance of the freedom of persons and of states, urging the active assertion of rights (34–35), but it also insists that the exercise of rights ought to be consistent with the fulfillment of duties (30). Similarly, one function of government is to see that rights are coordinated so that the enjoyment of rights by some does not hinder the enjoyment of rights (or the fulfillment of duties) by others (62). Catholic social teaching would prevent situations where some people are "more equal" than others.

The limitation of rights is particularly evident in the discussion of justice among nations (91–93). There Pope John argues against the development of national resources in such a way that it "brings harm to other states and unjustly oppresses them" (92). The deprivations he had in mind are not specified, but in John's day they would have included colonialism and postcolonial exploitation. In our own day it is possible to identify such inequitable developments as the global burdens of industrial pollution, so-called free-trade regimes that are unfair to developing countries, and the transnational marketing and pricing of pharmaceutical products, especially anti-retroviral drugs employed to fight HIV/AIDS, to name just a few. Superiority, even in technical and scientific matters, rather than permitting domination of others, the encyclical argues, entails an obligation "to lend mutual assistance to others in their efforts for improvement" (87), and it imposes a duty "to make a greater contribution to the general development of the people" (88). Good fortune, even if it appears to be of one's own making, obligates.

The Common Good

The cardinal principle of traditional Catholic political theory is the common good. A concept of classical political philosophy, it was absorbed into Christian political thought by the church fathers, medieval theologians, and canonists, and transmitted via neoscholasticism into modern Catholic social teaching.[46] In his earlier social encyclical *Mater et magistra*, John XXIII had already offered a contemporary definition of the common good as "the sum total of those conditions of social living, whereby men are enabled more fully and more readily to achieve their own perfection."[47] In PT, he offers another interpretation of the common good, namely, the realization of human rights. The encyclical makes the point most clearly in treating of the relationship of human rights and the universal common good. There it reads: "The public and universal authority, too, must have as its fundamental objective the recognition, respect, safeguarding, and promotion of the rights of the human person" (139). While this definition does not displace the earlier one articulated in *Mater et magistra* and is compatible with it, "the recognition, respect, safeguarding, and promotion of the rights of the person" is the effective definition of the common good at work in the whole of the encyclical.[48]

Two egalitarian features of the common good as presented in PT deserve comment. First, while government's obligation to uphold the common good ought to be exercised "without preference for any single citizen or civic group," public authorities bear a special responsibility to "give more attention to the less fortunate members of the community, since they are less able to defend their rights and to assert their legitimate claims" (56). This anticipates what will later be known as the "preferential option for the poor." There is overt skepticism here that "the invisible hand," whether in the market or through political competition, can provide the necessary equity. Accordingly, the encyclical lends its support for government's role as an equalizer in an unequal world. At the same time, the rights content of the common good, along with the principle of subsidiarity, makes the common good a defense against the leveling equality associated with totalitarian and statist conceptions of public welfare.

The second point is a warning that the poor may not be served in societies marked by growing inequality. The common good, as John XXIII understands it, demands keeping broad inequalities in check. The spread of inequality, according to the encyclical, vitiates the realization and protection of rights. "Experience has taught us," reads number 63, "that, unless these authorities take suitable action with regard to economic, political and cultural matters, inequalities between citizens tend to become more and more widespread, especially in the modern world, and as a result human rights are rendered totally ineffective and the fulfillment of duties is compromised." One of the functions of government, therefore, is to foster relative equality in society as a means of ensuring that human rights can in fact be honored and enjoyed.

A Political Theory for New Times

The immediate occasion of the writing of PT, as we have seen, was the climactic moment of the cold war, the Cuban missile crisis, but the encyclical is not an extended reflection on nuclear war and deterrence. It is rather an examination of the substantive conditions of peace understood primarily in terms of human rights. Rights, however, are realized in political communities. Pope John saw what was hardly understood by any statesmen of the day, that human rights were not to be enjoyed only in one nation, state by state as it were, but that they had also to be supported in international relations and, even in what others did not even glimpse at the time, in transnational affairs. Accordingly, the encyclical begins to rethink international affairs in fundamental ways.

The Universality of Rights and the Attenuation of Sovereignty

The specifically political sections of PT, Parts 2 through 4, open with a traditional Catholic affirmation of the divine origin of political authority (46–52, esp. 46–47), but with a twist already found in the writings of Pietro Pavan. Because authority comes from God, the human exercise of authority is constrained. It is limited authority. Authorities must lead by persuasion rather than by instilling fear (48). No law contrary to the moral order, moreover, is binding on citizens (51).

In particular, human rights set a standard for political legitimacy. Thus, number 61 declares, "If any government does not acknowledge the rights of man or violates them, it not only fails in its duty, but its orders completely lack juridical force." Or, again, "if civil authorities pass laws or command anything opposed by the moral order and consequently opposed to the will of God, neither the laws made nor the authorizations granted can be binding on the conscience of citizens" (51). Together, these broad limits on legitimacy and the universal responsibility of political authority create a dynamic understanding of international relations that trumps sovereignty and nonintervention in the interest of protecting the rights of persons. Forty years after the release of PT, with the emergence of humanitarian intervention, war crimes tribunals, truth commissions, and the International Criminal Court, we are witnessing the world community's first steps toward the realization of the idea of such universal jurisdiction.

The cosmopolitan political theory of PT goes further still in redefining the end and scope of political authority in the service of persons. Thus, political authorities bear responsibility for the common good, that is, the realization of human rights, even outside their own societies. "We must remember," reads number 98, "that, of its very nature *civil authority exists*, not to confine its people within boundaries of their nations, but rather *to protect, above all else, the common good of the entire human family*" (emphasis this author's). The full weight of this conception of politics in which the function of all governance is the promotion of the rights of all persons is revealed in the extrapolation of the idea of the universal common good: "Like the common good of individual states, so too the universal common good cannot be determined except by having regard for the human person. Therefore, the public and universal authority, too, must have as its fundamental objective the recognition, respect, safeguarding and promotion of the rights of the human person" (139). Authorities must look beyond the limits of their own immediate jurisdiction and exercise their powers in defense of the universal common good, not just where their own nations are affected, but in the interest of the rights of all persons, especially any who lack protection. Here we have an interpretation of government that anticipates justifications for foreign policy innovations like humanitarian intervention and diplomatic engagement with human rights and religious liberty problems in other countries, initiatives that developed in dramatic ways only three decades after John wrote.

Individual States (46–79)

Part 2 (46–79) deals with "the relation between individuals and the public authorities within a single state." The text introduces the concept of the common good. Its first discussion of that topic does not deal with the role of government but of the "individual citizens and intermediary groups" to contribute to the common welfare. Thus, it should be understood that the common good is a social as well as a political principle. In so doing, the encyclical prepares the way for an understanding of the limited role of the state (65) and the principle of subsidiarity (140). Typical of the conciliating view of social life running through Catholic social teaching, persons and groups are urged to "bring their own interests into harmony with the needs of the community" (53). In similar fashion, one responsibility of government is "to coordinate social relations in such fashion that the exercise of one man's rights does not threaten others in the exercise of their rights nor hinder them in fulfillment of their duties" (62). Throughout there is an emphasis on citizen participation and the free exercise of rights and duties; the moral context for this behavior, however, is always one of mutual responsibility and accountability.

International Relations (80–129)

Having placed political life in the frame of the moral order written on the hearts of humans, Pope John postulates that "the same natural law, which governs the relations between individual human beings, serves also to regulate the relations of nations with one another" (83). With regard to the relations between states as within them, the function of authority is "the achievement of the common good" (84). In interstate relations, the encyclical addresses five problem areas: (1) inequality among nations, (2) ethnic relations, (3) migration, (4) development, and (5) disarmament.

Equality of States. Numbers 86–90 constitute a clarification of the principle of equality that should undergird the relations to states. "All states are by nature equal in dignity," possessing the same rights to existence, self-development, the means to that development, and autonomy in pursuing it (86). The encyclical addresses the inequalities of knowledge, power, talent, and wealth that lead to disparities between nations. These differences, the encyclical contends, ought not to be a justification for the advantaged "to subject others to their control in any way. Rather, they have a more serious obligation . . . to lend mutual assistance to others in their efforts for improvement" (87). Likewise, advances in science and economic development impose "the obligation to make a greater contribution to the general development of the people" (88).

Finally, in a principle very applicable to a period of free trade and globalization, the encyclical declares a principle of nonmalfeasance: "As men in their private enterprises cannot pursue their own interests to the detriment of others, so too states cannot lawfully seek that development of their own resources which brings harms to other states and unjustly oppresses them" (92). The encyclical is clear about the duties of the rich and powerful to the poor and powerless, under what the tradition will soon come to call the "principle of solidarity." It does so, however, in a moral framework that trusts in moral suasion and goodwill in public affairs, and seems to ignore the dynamics of competition and conflict in society and in international relations.

Ethnic Relations. While recognizing the aspirations of many ethnic groups to independence—aspirations church teaching and Vatican policy have often fostered—the encyclical does not see statehood as a realistic possibility for every subnational group. It goes on to exclude policies of demographic control for minority populations, especially when they entail genocide. Civil authorities are charged with the betterment of the conditions of life of these minorities and with encouraging the preservation and transmission of their cultural heritage. At the same time, minority groups are asked to refrain from excessive ethnocentric and chauvinist behavior that disparages "things common to all mankind" (97).

Refugees. A third issue taken up in Part 3 is that of refugees (103–8). The letter affirms that even in exile refugees retain the right to citizenship in the countries of which they are members. At the same time, it asserts that each person ought to have a right "to enter a political community where he hopes he can more fittingly provide a future for himself and his dependents" (108). Correspondingly, states have a duty "to accept such immigrants and to help them integrate them into itself as new members."[49] The Church's assertion of the rights of refugees and migrants generally is one of strongest in any political theory. Church teaching is almost unique in affirming the right of refugees to integration and citizenship. Founded on the belief in the unity of the one human family under God, the Church's advocacy for admission and integration of refugees and the freedom of movement of migrants puts it at odds with state-centered approaches to the movement of peoples, nation-centered conceptions of the common good, as well as nativist and racist ideologies.

Development. Appealing to the unity of the human family grounded in creation, redemption, and eschatological fulfillment, numbers 121–25 address the international role in development of poor countries. The function of development is "the attainment of a degree of economic development which will enable every citizen to live in conditions more in keeping with his human dignity" (122). At the same time that Pope John calls for developed countries to aid poor ones he also asks that they exercise restraint to show respect for the rights of smaller states and the moral values and ethnic characteristics of each people and to eschew pretensions to domination.

Disarmament and Peace. The precipitating event for the encyclical was the Cuban missile crisis, but the associated issue of arms control appears only in numbers 109–19. These eleven numbers describe the condition of fear in which the world lived in a period when "mutually assured destruction" in a massive nuclear exchange was the defense strategy of both superpowers. The goals of a moral defense policy are set out in number 112: the arms race should cease, weapons stockpiles be equally and spontaneously reduced, nuclear arms banned, and a program of disarmament undertaken in a context of mutual and effective controls. The pope writes in number 127: "in an age such as ours which prides itself on its atomic energy, it is contrary to reason to hold that war is now a suitable way to restore rights once they have been violated." If a point may be marked where Catholic teaching moves from unqualified adherence to the just war and toward advocacy of the nonviolent resolution of conflict, it may be found here.

The central pastoral message of this section is an appeal for conversion on the part of international actors. Peacemaking must "[proceed] from inner conviction." The pope continues: "the fear and anxious expectations of war with which men are oppressed" must be banished. He then comes to the heart of the matter. "The fundamental principle on which our present peace depends must be replaced by another which declares that the true and solid peace among nations consists not in equality of arms but in mutual trust alone" (113). Pope John makes a solemn appeal as vicar of Christ and "interpreter of the very profound longing of the entire human family," that everyone, but especially "those who hear the responsibility of public affairs, [spare] no pain or effort until world events follow a course in keeping with man's destiny and dignity" (117). In particular, he calls for peaceful adjustment of differences, sincerity in negotiations, and fidelity to agreements. So, the Holy Father concludes: "There is reason to hope . . . that by meeting and negotiating men may come to discover better the bonds that unite them together, deriving from the human nature they have in common; and that they may also come to discover one of the most profound requirements of their common nature is this: that between them and their respective peoples it is not fear which should reign but love" (129). (Given Pope John's reported reaction to the "cold" draft first written by Monsignor Pavan, it is quite possible that John himself was responsible for inserting the passages throughout the document attributing a role to love in political life.).

The World Community (130–45)

The Universal Common Good. One of the truly innovative concepts in PT is that of the universal common good, the central theme of Part 4, "The Relationship of Men and of Political Communities with the World Community." The empirical background for Part 4 is to be found in the evidence, already available in the 1960s, of the world's growing interdependence in commerce, communications, and transportation, what since the late 1980s has been called "globalization." From the theological side, the premise on which the pope formulates the principle of the universal common good is the unity of the human family. From the point of view of Catholic social theology, interdependence is desirable because it contributes to the historical realization of the essential unity of the human family.[50]

Historically the common good had applied to existing political entities: Greek and Italian city-states, the Roman and Holy Roman empires, the modern nation-state. The novelty of the universal common good lies in the extension of the idea to the world community, where no comparable polity exists. The encyclical's argument is that while in earlier periods the wider common good may have been served by diplomacy, summit meetings, and international agreements, in the contemporary political context there are difficult problems relating to "the security and peace of the whole world" which the interstate system by virtue of the equality of states is unable to address. As we see four decades later, treaties seem less and less able to bind signatories, including leading powers. New organizations like the World Trade Organization, founded because of an excess of big power influence, and other undertakings like the International Criminal Court or the Kyoto Protocols on global climate change are far less effective than they ought to be due to a lack of superpower commitment. Accordingly, Pope John's judgment that "both the structure and the form of governments as well as the power which public authority wields in all the nations of the world must be considered inadequate to promote the universal common good" (135) continues to hold true today.

A Universal Political Authority. Because the common good and the structures of political authority are intrinsically related, the encyclical argues, there is a need for a new form of political authority on a world scale. "Today the universal common good poses problems of world-wide dimensions which cannot be adequately tackled or solved except by the efforts of public authority endowed with a wideness of powers, structure and means of the same proportions" (137). Anticipating objections to such a world authority, John argues that its rule must be accomplished by consent and with respect for the principle of subsidiarity applied to the relation between individual states and the universal authority. The goal, the Holy Father explains, is "to create, on a world basis, an environment in which the public authorities of each state, its citizens and intermediate associations, can carry out their tasks, fulfill their duties and exercise their rights with greater security" (142). The global political authority, in other words, is in the service of subsidiarity. Its task is to supply the conditions in which other social and political units are empowered to exercise their rights and fulfill their duties.[51]

For political realists convinced of the paramount importance of national sovereignty and the realism of the international state system, the most controversial point of the encyclical is the connection it draws between the requirement of the universal common good for global political authority and the United Nations system. On the one hand, they regard support for the UN as foolishly optimistic about the capacities of human nature to devise a perfect solution to all its problems. On the other, they fear the potential for authoritarian mischief latent in the notion of universal government.

The Holy See, since PT, has continued to be supportive of the United Nations. In his 2003 World Day of Peace Message, "*Pacem in Terris*: A Permanent Commitment," Pope John Paul II commented that John XXIII "was suggesting that the vigorous defense of human rights by the U.N. organization is the indispensable foundation for the development of that organization's capacity to promote and defend international security."[52] John Paul went further, asking, "Is this not the time for all to *work together for a new constitutional organization of the human family*, truly capable of ensuring peace and harmony between peoples, as well as their integral development?"[53]

Still, too much can be made of endorsement of existing UN structures as such. The argument is an in-principle one: if there are grave problems affecting the universal common good and existing political authorities are unable to address them, then a political body ought to be devised to meet the need. As Pope John Paul II argued in his World Day of Peace Message, "This does not mean writing the constitution of a global super-state. Rather, it means continuing and deepening processes already in place to meet the almost universal *demand for participatory ways of exercising political authority, even international political authority, and for transparency and accountability at every level of public life.*"[54] It is also possible to think of other structures, outside the United Nations system, which can satisfy the need. In other words, there can be autonomous or loosely related transnational "regimes" directed at resolving given sets of problems, such as the World Trade Organization or the international financial institutions (World Bank, International Monetary Fund, etc.) do. In defense of the Holy See's endorsement of the UN, however, it ought to be noted that already the United Nations system itself is a variegated assembly of organizations and agencies involving different levels of authority, different patterns of participation, and building on the cooperation of experts from various countries and organizations. It is far from a monolithic dictatorship of the international majority.

Human Rights in the International System. In the forty years since the release of PT, human rights have played an increasingly important role in international affairs. In the last decade especially, a variety of innovations have enhanced international collaboration on human rights issues. During the 1990s the concept of humanitarian intervention gained a considerable degree of international acceptance with interventions in Haiti, Bosnia, Kosovo, East Timor, Congo, Sierra Leone, and Liberia. Truth and reconciliation commissions, in South Africa and several Latin American countries, have paved a peaceful path away from authoritarian regimes toward democratic governance, while acknowledging prior violations of human rights. War crimes tribunals have been arranged for Rwanda, the former Yugoslavia, and East Timor, and the Rome Treaty on the International Criminal Court, having been signed by the requisite sixty nations, has come into effect. The trial of former Yugoslav President Slobodan Milosevic, the Spanish indictment of former Chilean dictator Augusto Pinochet, and the withdrawal of amnesty for members of the Argentine junta have set precedents for ending impunity for heads of state and government for crimes committed under their authority. The international environment favoring human rights has moved ahead fitfully, and the institutional framework for defending human rights is a haphazard one. A universal political authority to deal with global problems and to defend rights across borders is still far from a reality. Nonetheless, the "utopia" foreseen by Pope John XXIII in PT continues to progress.

Evaluation

PT was a watershed document, signaling a new era in Catholic social teaching. With its adoption of rights thinking, it achieved a rapprochement with modern Western political thinking and opened a path for Catholics to join in the emancipation of people from despotic rulers in much of the world, especially in Catholic regions like Latin America and the Philippines, as well as for participation by the faithful in struggles for justice and peace worldwide. It also offered the Catholic Church's first clear acceptance of religious liberty. The introduction of "signs of the times" began a new style of experienced-based religious reflection to social questions, and John's appeals to trust and love gave people a new sense of the hope that the gospel can bring to public life.

In its utopianism, the encyclical tended to understate the force of sin in political life. Its appealing reliance on goodwill and human sociality did overcome some levels of cold war hostility, as Pope John's relation with Premier Khrushchev proved, but as a social ethic it was incomplete. As a result of its optimism, it failed to recognize the tensions inherent in divided societies between rights advocacy and peacemaking, and appeared to discount the hostility and conflict that the quest for human rights would provoke. John's vision of peace as a world community upholding human rights captured the end-state of a process that in lived experience would be fraught with conflict. To this day Catholic social teaching has still to suitably integrate a theory of conflict into its communitarian vision of society and its conciliating view of politics.

The Soviet Union and the cold war have passed away, but the challenge of nuclear disarmament remains urgent. In a unipolar world marked by U.S. hegemony, Pope John's commitment to the United Nations continues to be challenged, inside as well as outside the Church. While debate before the Anglo-American invasion of Iraq (2003) appeared to leave the UN weakened, in the aftermath of the war the organization seems more indispensable than ever. From nuclear disarmament to global climate change to the control of pandemic diseases and the rescue of failed states, the need for a level of political authority capable of dealing with the challenges of a globalized world becomes more evident every year. Whatever its shortcomings, John XXIII's farsighted vision of peace today remains as fresh as ever.

EXCURSUS

This excursus will consider the historical background to the encyclical's presentation of human rights according to Catholic social teaching.

Medieval and Modern Anticipations

For ordinary Catholics, as for theologians and church leaders in other Christian traditions, much of the novelty—and the appeal—of PT came in the contrast it provided with the previous century or more of Catholic teaching on politics. Because of the Church's nineteenth-century conflict with rationalism, secularism, and liberalism, most overlooked the precedents for rights thinking in earlier Catholic thought. Ignorance of a long historic Catholic rights tradition was reinforced in Catholic circles by the lack of inclusion of rights, properly speaking, in the work of Saint Thomas Aquinas, the quintessential Catholic thinker of the Middle Ages.

Conventional wisdom has tended to contrast the natural rights tradition, begun with the British social contract theories of the seventeenth and eighteenth centuries, especially Hobbes and Locke, with the supposedly duty-centered natural law theories of the Catholic Middle Ages. Enlightenment theories about natural rights, however, built on several centuries of developing Christian ideas of natural rights.[55] As early as the twelfth century, medieval jurists developed a "subjective" conception of right that served as the basis of later medieval and early modern conceptions of rights as powers inhering in persons. During the fourteenth-century controversy over Franciscan poverty, writes legal historian Brian Tierney, "all sorts of rights came under discussion—the right to acquire property, rights to establish governments and limit their powers, natural rights as distinguished from civil rights, alienable natural rights and inalienable natural rights, natural rights that were also duties, and what would later be called adventitious rights."[56] William of Ockham, the champion of primitive Franciscan poverty, moreover, elaborated a political theory in which a people retained rights, for example, to property, which their rulers could not alienate.

A third milepost in the early evolution of Catholic ideas on natural or human rights came with the conciliar movement and its premier theologian, Jean Gerson, the chancellor of the University of Paris. Conciliarism was a fourteenth- and fifteenth-century movement that sought to reform the Church "both in head and members" through the convocation of general councils. It addressed two interlinked problems: the sanctification of individual Christians and the resolution of the Great Schism (1378–1417). In the context of church reform, Gerson argued that people had natural rights to defend themselves against the abuses of those in authority. Similarly, every polity had the right to preserve itself against abuses from higher authority. Interestingly, it was because individuals possessed such rights of self-defense that the bodies to which they belonged also possessed them.[57]

The last landmark in these anticipations of modern Catholic rights theory may be found in the Spanish Scholastics. The Spanish *conquista* of the New World was the occasion in the sixteenth and seventeenth centuries for the extension of natural rights beyond Christian Europe to the peoples of the non-Christian world. The savage behavior of their own people forced Christian theologians to apply ideas of natural rights in defense of the peoples of "the Indies," thereby making explicit the universality of human rights. The Spanish Scholastics supplied later thinkers with principles of liberty, self-defense, government by consent, legitimacy, and, yes, tyrannicide.[58]

The defenders of the conquest contended that because they were in one way or another deficient, the indigenous peoples did not possess the right to self-government (*dominium*). The Dominican Francisco de Vitoria replied that every human being had the right to *dominium* because, as Saint Thomas argued, every person was master of his own acts.[59] In doing so, Vitoria worked a major shift from the ancient and medieval view that society is structured on natural inequalities to the modern view that society must uphold the fundamental equality of human beings.

One cannot conclude a discussion of the sixteenth- and seventeenth-century Spanish struggle for rights without noting another Dominican friar, Bartolomeo de las Casas. The context of his defense of the rights of the Indians was primarily that of evangelization. The conquest had been undertaken for the sake of spreading the gospel. The conquering Spaniards presumed that they could impose the faith by force. Las Casas believed that the only way to promote conversion to Christianity was by persuasion, not by the sword. Having once believed that might and strength could put an end to the abuses of the Spanish colonists, by the end of his career he concluded that Spanish rule, built as it was on violence and plunder, was utterly illegitimate.[60]

Enlightenment and Reaction

The Spanish Scholastics represented the last flowering of Christian rights thinking before the Enlightenment. Political and legal theory became the province of lay scholars whose thinking became increasingly secularized.[61] Catholic rights talk, insofar as it survived, became a self-interested attempt to guard the rights of the Church, papacy, and clergy. The culmination of the long period of Catholic reaction came with the papacy of Pius IX (1846–78). Until the revolution of 1848 reached Rome, Pius was a populist reformer. After a period of bitter exile (1848–50) following the revolution of 1848, Pius was returned to the papal throne in 1850 and maintained there by French and Austrian troops. Finally, in 1864, under pressure from conservative ultramontanes, "Pio Nono" struck out in the encyclical *Quanta cura,* with the appended *Syllabus of Errors*, against a whole family of "liberal" doctrines—rationalism, indifferentism, socialism, communism, naturalism, freemasonry, separation of church and state, liberty of press, liberty of religion—which he felt lay behind threats to the papal monarchy. The letter concluded with the notorious protestation against the proposal that "the Roman Pontiff can and ought to reconcile himself and reach agreement with progress, liberalism and modern civilization." From this point on, there seemed to be no longer room for discussion of human rights in the Roman Catholic Church.

Catholics and the Universal Declaration of Human Rights

The later Catholic social tradition was one of the formative influences in the UN Declaration of Human Rights.[62] Shortly before his death in 1878, Pope Pius IX is reported to have confessed to having failed to understand the times in which he lived. "I can see that everything has changed; my system and my policies have had their day; but I am too old to change my course; that will be the task of my successor."[63] That successor was Pope Leo XIII, whose encyclical letter *Rerum novarum* (1891), according to most church historians, opened the modern period of official Catholic social teaching.

According to legal historian Mary Ann Glendon, the early texts of modern Catholic social teaching, RN and Pope Pius XI's *Quadragesimo anno*, in part, lay behind Catholic contributions to the formation of the Universal Declaration of Human Rights in 1948. Earlier that year twenty-one Latin American countries had signed the American Declaration of the Rights and Duties of Man, also known as the Bogota Declaration. The Declaration affirmed substantive rights, like the right to education, work, and social security, which had been promoted by the existing Catholic social teaching and Christian democratic movements in Latin America and Europe.[64] Latin American participants in the drafting process also carried with them a broader understanding of rights that led eventually to the definition of social and economic as well as political rights.

Papal encyclicals also influenced some of the major drafters of the Universal Declaration, especially the Lebanese delegate Charles Malik, an Orthodox Christian. A Harvard-trained philosopher, Malik had greedily imbibed the Catholic social teaching of the day, and his writings and memoranda reflect its influence. Another important figure was the French Catholic philosopher Jacques Maritain. Though not himself a member of the Commission, Maritain served on a blue-ribbon committee appointed by the United Nations Educational, Scientific, and Cultural Organization (UNESCO) to prepare a study on "the theoretical bases of human rights." Reporting on the committee's decision, Maritain explained that agreement was possible "not on the basis of common speculative ideas, but on common practical ideas, not on the affirmation of one and the same conception of the world, of man, and of knowledge, but upon the affirmation of a single body of beliefs for guidance in action."[65]

One person who seemed to disagree with this approach was Pope Pius XII, although in a June 1941 radio address he had appealed for an international bill acknowledging the rights flowing from the dignity of the human person. But after the completion of the Universal Declaration, Pius failed to offer his encouragement, apparently because of the lack of firm foundational underpinnings for the asserted rights. For its part, the Universal Declaration opens with the affirmation that "recognition of the inherent dignity and of the equal and inalienable rights of all members of the human family is the foundation of freedom, justice, and peace in the world," a formula that corresponded to Pius's 1941 broadcast proposal.[66]

One churchman who was not put off by the lack of theoretical foundations was Angelo Roncalli, then papal nuncio in Paris. René Cassin, a distinguished French jurist and a principal drafter of the declaration, recalled receiving "on several occasions" in the fall of 1948 "discreet personal encouragements from the Papal Nuncio Roncalli."[67] Almost fifteen years later Roncalli, then Pope John XXIII, was to author PT. There he wrote of the Universal Declaration of Human Rights as "an act of the highest importance" and "a step on the path toward the juridical-political organization of all the peoples of the world" (143, 144). PT, therefore, represents the fruition of a longtime commitment by Pope John to the safeguarding and promotion of human rights as a foundation for world peace.

REACTIONS TO THE DOCUMENT

In English-speaking countries, Catholics demonstrated a considerable caution about accepting John's optimistic agenda for peacemaking through mutual trust. As *Catholic World* editor and Paulist father John B. Sheerin commented: "To us Americans, the cold war seems futile. We don't trust the Soviets, we don't believe they can be sincere in negotiations, we remember they have broken innumerable pacts and treaties."[68] The Jesuit weekly *America* prepared its readers for a careful reading of the text. The editors seemed to fear political misinterpretations of every sort.[69] Editor Thurston Davis reminded readers of how much the encyclical owed to Pius XII, but a later editorial praised it as an expression of "all mankind's authentic aspirations for lasting peace in a world order based on justice, truth, charity and freedom."[70]

Under the oblique title "Eastern Approaches," the British weekly *The Tablet* chided those to its political left: "There is a page or so about [peace and war] which gives very little comfort to unilateralists, for what it calls for is 'simultaneous' and progressive disarmament, step by step."[71] The same hectoring antipacifism can be found in the lead editorial of the same week: "So far from what [the United States and the United Kingdom] are now doing being evil, it would be gross dereliction of duty on their part if they had not used the resources they possess in order to remain on at least a level of equality with the Russians."[72]

The American Jesuit John Courtney Murray, while skeptical of John XXIII's hopes for improvements in cold war relations between the United States and the Soviet Union, nonetheless found in the "important" distinction between ideologies and movements the possible basis for a "complete and unitary Catholic doctrine of Church and State capable of prudent application in the political and religious conditions of our times."[73] Coeditor of *Christianity and Crisis* John C. Bennett went further: "*Pacem in Terris* may be the most powerful healing word that has come from any source during the Cold War." In a swipe at Cold Warriors within the Church, he added: "It calls Christians in the West away from the kind of anti-communism by which they have often been obsessed."[74]

The encyclical's endorsement of the United Nations came in for the harshest criticism and profoundest doubts. Bennett's coeditor Reinhold Niebuhr objected: "the United Nations is not so much a world government in embryo as a minimal bridge of community in a world riven by a cold war. [John's] idealism is a little too easy."[75] John Courtney Murray also demurred: "But it will not be clear to many, including myself, how this hope is concretely to be realized, given the fact that no moral or political consensus exists within the international community."[76]

Only *The Tablet* uncharacteristically allowed that it was "not utopian to seek to build [some form of world authority] on the foundations that exist there [i.e., in the United Nations.]"[77] Despite his misgivings, Murray also defended the overall optimism of the encyclical: "[John's] hope, therefore, is not a utopian idealism. It is possible of realization. . . . It is . . . a hope that no reasonable man can fail to share, no matter what the difficulties in the way may be."[78]

For secular commentators like the *New York Herald Tribune*'s Walter Lippmann, natural law represented a decided advantage in communicating with the wider world.[79] "Western man has finally found a long-sought definition of the meaning and purpose of a free society," wrote Lippmann, according to the *Catholic World*'s John B. Sheerin. "The considered opinion of this veteran columnist is [that the encyclical is] a satisfying restatement for the modern age of the central philosophy upon which the institutions of the West are based. That philosophy," said Lippmann, "is the natural law philosophy which can be held by men of widely differing theological beliefs."[80]

Among American Catholic commentators, Sheerin was exceptional in his enthusiasm for the encyclical. Unlike the letter's realist critics, Sheerin noted the progress being made in the Vatican *Ostpolitik* during John's pontificate: "There is something in the air. The presence of Russian Orthodox observers at the Council, the Soviet Press's favorable coverage of the Council, the release of Metropolitan Slipy from his 18-year imprisonment, the visit of Adshubei, Khrushchev's son-in-law, to the Vatican and his audience with the pope—all these seem to point to some imminent Vatican move to ease cold war tensions."[81] Waxing with praise, he concluded, "the amazing world acclaim that has greeted this extraordinary document also marks it out as a magna charta of peace for all humanity."

The Paulist also observed what few others noted: "The pope has established the case for religious liberty so unmistakably and unconditionally that there is little left for the Council to say on the subject, save to fill in the details of the papal outline."[82] John Courtney Murray agreed. The Jesuit resonated with Pope John and Monsignor Pavan's emphasis on freedom as "the human principle itself." He wrote: "Freedom is a basic principle of political order; it is also the political method. . . . The Pope makes clear that freedom is *the* method for the 'realization' of the order in human affairs as well as the good of order itself."[83]

Its Impact[84]

There can be no doubt that John XXIII's promotion of human rights profoundly affected Catholic teaching and practice. In 1998, on the occasion of the fiftieth anniversary of the Universal Declaration, the Pontifical Council for Justice and Peace held a World Congress on the Pastoral Promotion of Human Rights with representative witnesses from five continents. The Congress heard witnesses to the Church's human rights work from South Africa, Bosnia, Guatemala, South Korea, and Oceania.[85] In a unique move for a Vatican event, the Congress also published the results of a survey of 118 national episcopal conferences on the pastoral service of human rights.[86] Its findings were mixed. Overall the Church's pastoral activity focused primarily on socioeconomic rights to the neglect of civil and political rights. The Church's major endeavor lay in education and formation, but while human rights were part of many curricula, there was little treatment of rights in national catechisms. Nearly all bishops' conferences had some office that addressed rights questions, but there were only a few that dealt solely with human rights. In addition, there were few statements of conferences or human rights commissions that dealt exclusively with human rights. Rather, they tended to be part of statements dealing with broader economic, social, and political situations in their respective countries.

The survey questions failed, however, to convey the vitality and public importance of Catholic work for human rights, particularly in

Latin America, where the Church's influence was greatest.[87] Beginning in 1973, following the coup against Chilean president Salvador Allende, the Chilean church, particularly the archdiocese of Santiago, gave its support to the Committee for Peace, soon called the Vicariat for Solidarity, a model for human rights commissions in Latin America and elsewhere. Among its imitators were the Archdiocesan Human Rights Office in Guatemala City, Tutela Legal in El Salvador, and the Bartolomeo de las Casas and the Miguel Pro centers in Mexico.

No assessment of the impact of PT, moreover, can overlook the numbers of Catholics who have achieved recognition in the last decades of the twentieth century for their defense of human rights: Lech Welesa in Poland, Kim Dae Jung in South Korea, Corazon Aquino in the Philippines, José Zalaquett in Chile, Mairead Corrigan Maguire in Northern Ireland, Franjo Komarica in Bosnia, Michel Sabbah in Israel and Palestine, Samuel Ruiz in Mexico, and Felipé Ximenes Belo in East Timor. Among them were martyrs for human dignity such as Guatemala's Bishop Gerardi and five Protestant and Catholic staff members of the Lahore Justice and Peace Commission killed in 2002. There have also been Nobel laureates like Walesa, Kim, Corrigan Maguire, and Belo. They too are the legacy of John XXIII, men and women who have devoted and in some cases sacrificed their lives to make his utopia a reality.

NOTES

1. See Giancarlo Zizola, *The Utopia of John XXIII*, trans. Helen Barolini (Garden City, N.Y.: Doubleday, 1985), 171, 409, 440.

2. I take the phrase *diplomacy of conscience* from Monsignor Celestino Migliore, the Vatican's former under-secretary for relations with states, now the Holy See permanent observer to the United Nations. See his "Nature and Methods of Vatican Diplomacy," *Origins* 29, no. 3 (February 3, 2000): 539–43.

3. Peter Hebblethwaite, *Pope John XXIII: Shepherd of the Modern World* (Garden City, N.Y.: Doubleday, 1984), 498.

4. As cited in ibid., 393.

5. Ibid., 367.

6. Ibid., 363.

7. Ibid., 182.

8. Ibid., 382.

9. Ibid., 399.

10. Ibid., 319.

11. Ibid., 316–17. Pope John's own account of this conversation with Cardinal Domenico Tardini, his secretary of state, is somewhat problematic, for he seems to have confided his idea to Tardini and others before the January 20, 1959, meeting with Tardini. The broad outlines of what concerned the pope seem accurate but, according to Peter Hebblethwaite, the quote seems to be a conflation of several conversations over some time.

12. Ibid., 436.

13. For the account of the origins of PT, I am indebted to Zizola, *Utopia*. See also "Riscoperta della consienza, Intervista di Pietro Pavan di F. De Santis," *Corriere della Sera*, April 11, 1973.

14. Zizola, *Utopia*, 7.

15. Ibid., 8.

16. Ibid., 11.

17. Franco Biffi, in his biography of P. Pavan (*Prophet of Our Time: The Social Thought of Cardinal Pietro Pavan*, trans. Rosemarie Goldie [New Rochelle, N.Y.: New City, 1992], originally published as *I Cantico dell'Uomo* [Rome: Città Nova, 1990]), avoids stating outright that Pavan was the principal drafter of the encyclical. He acknowledges, however, "the hypothesis [that Pavan was the ghost writer] has a high degree of probability." Other authors, including Pavan himself, have been less discrete. (See especially his brief relation of "una conversazione confidenziale" in an interview with *Corriere della Sera* on the tenth anniversary of the encyclical.)

Jesuit Father Robert Tucci, now a cardinal, in a journal entry for April 16, 1963, on a meeting with Cardinal Amleto Cicognani, the secretary of state, recorded that Pavan penned the first draft; Father Luigi Ciappi, the papal theologian, did a theological revision; and Monsignor G. Zannoni oversaw the final draft with the support of personnel of the secretariat of state. He also notes that Pope John found the first draft too cold (*troppe fredda*) and added introductory passages of a biblical and hortatory nature (Tucci fax to the author, August 26, 2003).

18. Biffi, *Prophet*, 13.

19. Ibid., 8–9.

20. See ibid., 34.

21. Ibid., 61.

22. Zizola, *Utopia*, 20.

23. Ibid.

24. On John's authorship of the critical distinction, see ibid., 22.

25. Ibid., 23.

26. Two years later the Council that John convoked took a further step, acknowledging in GS the good done the Church by its opponents: "Whoever promotes the human community . . . such a one is contributing greatly to the Church community as well . . . Indeed, the Church admits that she has greatly profited and still profits from the antagonism of those who oppose or persecute her" (44).

27. See Zizola, *Utopia*, 23, for Pavan's comments on the impact of John's attitude to collaboration with non-Catholic groups on Italian politics. For an account of how intramural Vatican squabbling on this issue was resolved, see G. Zizola, "Come e nata la 'Pacem in Terris,'" in *Riposte a Papa Giovanni*, ed. G. Zizola (Rome: Coines Edizione, 1972), 19–66.

28. Hebblethwaite, *Pope John XXIII*, 363.

29. For more on the encyclical's innovative theology of human rights, see René Coste, "La première charte écclesiale des droits de l'homme," in Coste et al., *Paix sur la terre*, 95–121.

30. On the encyclical's theology of peace, see Yves Congar, "Uno shalom per il mondo," a paper delivered at a conference on the tenth anniversary of the encyclical at the Tantur Ecumenical Institute, Jerusalem. On the larger issue of the Catholic theology of peace, see U.S. Institute for Peace, Special Report, April 9, 2001, "Catholic Contributions to International Peace," esp. 2–8, a summary of Drew Christiansen's unpublished paper, "Catholic Peacemaking: From *Pacem in Terris to Centesimus Annus*."

31. For a recent statement on the role of forgiveness in peacemaking, see Pope John Paul II's January 1, 2000, World Day of Peace Statement, "No Peace without Justice, No Justice without Forgiveness" (Vatican City: Editrice Vaticana, 2000). In a recent paper delivered in the 2000 International Mennonite-Catholic Dialogue, Guatemalan Mennonite pastor Miguel Higueros offers a perspective on how the human rights work of the Guatemalan Catholic Church and particularly the Guatemalan bishops' conference made it a peace church. See Higueros, "What Is a Peace Church?" a paper prepared for the International Mennonite-Catholic Dialogue, Thomashof, Germany, November 28–December 4, 2000.

32. For the treatment of nonviolence and development in relation to peace, see, e.g., John Paul II, *On the Hundredth Anniversary of Rerum Novarum: Centesimus Annus* (Washington, D.C.: United States Catholic Conference, 1991), numbers 23, 25, 52; on justice and forgiveness, see "No Peace without Justice."

33. See particularly the summary Christological passages in GS 22, 32, 39.

34. The notable exception, of course, was the French philosopher Jacques Maritain.

35. See Coste, "La Première Charte," and Joseph Joblin, "The Church and Human Rights: Historical Overview and Future Outlook," in Pontifical Council for Justice and Peace, *Human Rights and the Church: Historical and Theological Reflections* (Vatican City: Editrice Vaticana, 1990), 11–46.

36. Zizola, "Come e nata," 23.

37. These four principles (truth, justice, solidarity, and liberty) are frequently cited in later interpretations of the encyclical, as, for example, in Pope John Paul II's 2003 World Day of Peace Message, "*Pacem in Terris*: A Permanent Commitment." But, although they may be valuable in elaborating an inchoate Catholic theology of peace, they still appear, to this reader, at least, as interpolations whose connections to the main argument of the encyclical must still be spelled out.

Also, it must be remembered that at the time people regarded the inclusion of liberty, in accord with Pavan's "method of freedom," as a controversial innovation.

38. I have taken the descriptive term *cosmopolitan* from Charles R. Beitz, *Political Theory and International Relations* (Princeton, N.J.: Princeton University Press, 1979). *Cosmopolitan* designates a political theory that gives priority to the rights of persons over state interests.

39. On the theme of morality, politics, and cosmic order, see Paul Friedlander, *Plato: An Introduction*, trans. Hans Meyerhoff (New York: Harper and Row, 1964), 29ff.

40. For Pavan's view of the central role of the human in PT, see his "L'Ordine tra gli esseri umani" in *Seminarium* 39, New Series 18, no. 1 (January–March 1988): 54–61.

41. For more recent rejection of political realism by official Catholic social teaching, see John Paul II, *Centesimus annus*, 25.

42. On Pius XII's proposal, see Mary Ann Glendon, "The Sources of Rights Talk: Some Are Catholic" *Commonweal* 128, no. 17 (October 12, 2001): 11.

43. Of course, this appeal to human (moral) reason as the heart of natural law conforms to the late medieval/early modern Catholic rights theory sketched in the "Excursus" and its belief that rights rest on the *ius naturale* as the human power of reason. The contrast I have made, therefore, is not intended to be made with the whole span of Catholic political theory, but only with the period from the mid-seventeenth century on, and especially with the century of Catholic social teaching preceding the publication of PT inaugurated by the *Syllabus of Errors* in 1864.

44. See GS 42.

45. On the Bogota Declaration and the debate over rights and duties in drafting the Universal Declaration, see M. A. Glendon, *A World Made New: Eleanor Roosevelt and the Universal Declaration of Human Rights* (New York: Random House, 2001), 140–41.

46. For an analysis of the understanding of the common good in Pope John's social teaching, see Drew Christiansen, "The Common Good and the Politics of Self-Interest: A Catholic Contribution to Citizenship," in *Beyond Individualism: Toward a Retrieval of Moral Discourse in America*, ed. Donald Gelpi (Notre Dame, Ind.: University of Notre Dame, 1989), esp. 62–72. More generally on the common good as applied to current social issues, see David Hollenbach, *The Common Good and Christian Ethics* (Cambridge: Cambridge University Press, 2002).

47. MM 65.

48. PT 56 quotes directly the definition of the common good from MM 65, and PT 64 offers its own list of policy implications of the common good parallel to those found in MM 79.

49. See also PT 25.

50. Within a few years the Council would make that theme central to the Church's own identity as a sacrament of unity. In LG 2 and in GS 42 it would soon make service of the unity of the human family one of the three principal ways in which the Church served the world.

51. In a sense Pope John has simply applied the principle of subsidiarity on a global scale. The principle is a two-edged sword. On the one side, it asserts the autonomy of smaller social and political units. On the other side, it affirms the need of these lesser units for aid or support (*subsidium*) from larger (superior) bodies to execute tasks for which they have insufficient capacity. Thus, as long as states, citizens, and intermediate associations can carry out their responsibilities, there is no need for the exercise of universal authority. But, if they prove unable to do so, worse still, if they are structurally prohibited from grappling with global problems, then a new transnational political entity is necessary. So, while the idea of a universal or transnational political authority is an expression of the Catholic belief in the one human family and by virtue of historical conditions an increasingly necessary ideal, it is an ideal conditioned and limited by the principle of subsidiarity.

52. John Paul II, "*Pacem in Terris*: A Permanent Commitment," *America* 188, no. 4 (February 10, 2003): 20. In July of the same year, following the war in Iraq, Cardinal Angelo Sodano, the Vatican secretary of state, wrote UN Secretary General Kofi Annan at the request of the pope to offer the Holy See's support for the United Nations. The 2004 World Day of Peace Message underscored the value of international law.

53. Ibid., 21.

54. Ibid.

55. See esp. Brian Tierney, *The Idea of Natural Rights: Studies on Natural Rights, Natural Law, and Church Law, 1150–1625*, Emory Studies in Law and Religion, no. 5 (Atlanta, Ga.: Scholar's, 1997). See also Quentin Skinner, *Foundations of Western Political Thought*, 2 vols. (Cambridge: Cambridge University Press, 1978).

56. Tierney, *The Idea of Natural Rights*, 93.

57. Ibid., 233.

58. Ibid., 314–15.

59. See Thomas Aquinas, *Summa theologiae* 2a 2ae, 66.1. It should be emphasized that Thomas himself did not have a concept of right in the sense used by the Spanish Scholastics. Rather, they seized on features of his anthropology to ground their own views of rights. For the debates on the fidelity or novelty of their views within the Thomistic tradition, see Tierney, *The Idea of Natural Rights*, 256–65, 274–77.

60. Tierney, *The Idea of Natural Rights*, 281.

61. The role of the Jesuit colleges, particularly in France, in the shift of intellectual leadership to secular elites is unclear. Although the style of training the Jesuit colleges had grown outmoded, they nonetheless had taught many of the philosophes, including Descartes and Voltaire, expounded a natural religion, and in their defense of the Guarani in Latin America had espoused a moral universalism admired by their own and the Church's critics. See Jean Lacouture, *The Jesuits: A Multibiography* (Washington, D.C.: Counterpoint, 1995), 263.

62. For an overview of Catholic influences on the Universal Declaration of Human Rights, see M. A. Glendon, "The Sources of 'Rights Talk,'" *Commonweal* 78, no. 17 (October 12, 2001): 11–13.

63. Cited in Alec R. Vidler, *The Church in the Age of Revolution: 1989 to the Present Day*, Pelican History of the Church, ed. Owen Chadwick (London: Hodder and Stoughton, 1961), 153.

64. See Glendon, *A World Made New*. On the Bogota Declaration, see esp. 140–41.

65. Ibid., 77–78.

66. The Universal Declaration of Human Rights (Preamble) Appendix 7, in Glendon, *A World Made New*, 310.

67. Glendon, *A World Made New*, 13

68. John B. Sheerin, "*Pacem in Terris*, Magna Carta for Peace," *Catholic World* 197, no. 1179 (June 1963): 150.

69. Editor, "Current Comment," *America* 108, no. 16 (April 20, 1963): 518.

70. Thurston N. Davis (signed 'TND'), "Of Many Things," *America* 108, no. 17 (April 27, 1963): 596, and in the same issue, the editorial "Light to the Nations," 604.

71. Editor, "Eastern Approaches," *The Tablet* 217, no. 6413 (April 20, 1963): 415.

72. Editor, "Increasing Difficulties," ibid., 414.

73. John Courtney Murray, "Things Old and New in *Pacem in Terris*," in *Bridging the Sacred and the Secular*, ed. J. Leon Hooper (Washington, D.C.: Woodstock Theological Center/Georgetown University Press, 1994), 215–52. (Originally published in *America* 108, no. 17 [April 27, 1963]: 612–14).

74. John C. Bennett, "*Pacem in Terris*: Two Views," *Christianity and Crisis* 28, no. 8 (may 12, 1963): 82.

75. Reinhold Niebuhr, "*Pacem in Terris*: Two Views," ibid., 81.

76. Murray, "Things Old and New," 251–52.

77. Editor, "Eastern Approaches," *The Tablet*, 416.

78. Murray, "Things Old and New," 252–53.

79. J. B. Sheerin reports W. Lippmann's views in "*Pacem in Terris*: Magna Carta for Peace," 148, 150. Among the other secular promoters of the encyclical was Norman Cousins, who had served as an intermediary between Pope John and Premier Khrushchev. See his "Therefore Choose Life," in *Therefore Choose Life: On 'Pacem in Terris.' The Encyclical of Pope John XXIII*, Papers on Peace, ed. Norman Cousins et al. (Santa Barbara, Calif.: Center for the Study of Democratic Institutions, 1965), 5–12.

Compared to secular readers, Protestants, who preferred scripture-based arguments in articulating social morality, were ambivalent about the encyclical's use of (a form of) natural-law reasoning. Reinhold Niebhur noted: "The significance of *Pacem in Terris* lies in the fact that for the first time, Roman Catholicism has co-opted the modern theory of 'natural rights' as an extension of its natural law theory. Hitherto Catholic theologians regarded it as a corruption of natural law theory" ("*Pacem in Terris*: Two Views," 81). The evangelical journal *Christianity Today* saw rights talk as a source of the encyclical's wide appeal. An unsigned comment described the encyclical as "masterful and historic" and ironically aimed its criticism at some of its evangelical co-religionists who trusted human nature too little. See "Pope Calls for Global Authority to Guard World Peace," *Christianity Today* 7, no. 15 (April 26, 1963): 25.

80. See Sheerin, "*Pacem in Terris*: Magna Carta for Peace," 148.

81. Ibid., 151.

82. Ibid.

83. Murray, "Things Old and New," 251.

84. How deeply John XXIII's human rights revolution affected the Church can be seen from GS, Vatican II's charter for the Church's social ministry. Part 1, chap. 4 of the *Pastoral Constitution on the Church in the Modern World* (40–44) lists the defense of human rights as one of the primary services the Church brings the world. GS also helped launch Catholics into the human rights movement. Number 90 of the pastoral constitution promoted international coordination of the Church's efforts on behalf of justice and urged "that some agency of the universal Church be set up for the worldwide

promotion of justice for the poor and Christ's kind of love for them." Three years later, Pope Paul VI founded the Commission Justitia et Pax, today known as the Pontifical Council for Justice and Peace. From its early days, the Commission took a special interest in pastoral work on behalf of human rights. See Pontifical Commission Justitia et Pax, *The Church and Human Rights*, Working Paper No. 1 (Vatican City: Commission Justitia et Pax, 1975).

85. Pontifical Council for Justice and Peace, *Human Rights and the Pastoral Mission of the Church*, World Congress on the Pastoral Promotion of Human Rights, Rome, July 1–4, 1998 (Vatican City: Pontifical Council for Justice and Peace, 1998), 45.

86. Ibid., 30–51.

87. For more on Church initiatives on human rights in Latin America, see Edward L. Cleary, *The Struggle for Human Rights in Latin America* (Westport, Conn.: Praeger, 1997).

SELECTED BIBLIOGRAPHY

Biffi, Franco. *Prophet of Our Times: The Social Thought of Cardinal Pietro Pavan*. Translation and abridgment by Rosemarie Goldie. New Rochelle, N.Y.: New City, 1992. Biffi writes a popular intellectual biography of the head of the committee that drafted PT. (Originally published in Italian as *I Cantico dell' Uomo* [Città Nova, 1990].)

Cleary, Edward L. *The Struggle for Human Rights in Latin America*. Westport, Conn.: Praeger, 1997. Cleary relates the history of Catholic advocacy for human rights in a region where Church involvement proved critical to the defense of human rights.

Coste, René, et al. *Paix sur la terre: actualité d'une encyclique*. Paris: Centurion, 1988. A collection celebrating the twenty-fifth anniversary of the encyclical, including Coste on human rights and Christian Mellon on the Catholic theology of peace.

Filibeck, Giorgio. *Human Rights in the Teaching of the Church from John XXIII to John Paul II: Collection of Texts of the Magisterium of the Catholic Church from 'Mater et Magistra' to 'Centesimus Annus'* (1961–991). Preface by Cardinal Roger Etchegaray. Vatican City: Libreria Editrice Vaticana, 1994. This authoritative analytical sourcebook on Catholic teaching on human rights includes many lesser known texts.

Glendon, Mary Ann. *A World Made New: Eleanor Roosevelt and the Universal Declaration of Human Rights*. New York: Random House, 2001. This history of the drafting of the Universal Declaration of Human Rights contains portraits of many participants besides Eleanor Roosevelt, the central figure.

——. "The Sources of 'Rights Talk': Some are Catholic," *Commonweal* 127, no. 17 (October 12, 2001): 11–13. Glendon reflects on the influence of Catholic social teaching and Catholic thinkers on the Universal Declaration of Human Rights.

Hebblethwaite, Peter. *Pope John XXIII: Shepherd of the Modern World*. Garden City, N.Y.: Doubleday, 1984. This full-length biography of Pope John XXIII by the late British journalist and Vaticanologist is rich in anecdote and telling detail.

Hollenbach, David. *Claims in Conflict: Retrieving and Renewing the Catholic Human Rights Tradition*. New York: Paulist, 1979. Hollenbach's superior analytical treatment of official Catholic thinking on human rights examines the problem of conflicting rights claims.

Human Rights: A Compilation of International Instruments. New York: UN Centre for Human Rights—Geneva, 1988. This standard source includes basic documents of international human rights law.

John Paul II. "*Pacem in Terris*: A Permanent Commitment." World Day of Peace Message, 2003. Vatican City: Editrice Vaticana, 2003. Written on the encyclical's fortieth anniversary, Pope John Paul II's message lays out a contemporary agenda for peace based on PT.

Pontifical Commission Justitia et Pax. *The Church and Human Rights*. Working Paper No. 1. Vatican City: Commission Justitia et Pax, 1975. This booklet contains historical and theological papers on Catholic human rights theory.

Pontifical Council for Justice and Peace. *Human Rights and the Pastoral Mission of the Church*. World Congress on the Pastoral Promotion of Human Rights. Rome, July 1–4, 1998. Vatican City: Pontifical Council for Justice and Peace, 2000. This conference report includes thumbnail sketches on Catholic advocacy for human rights in different regions, a general survey and evaluation of Catholic activity worldwide, and two statements by Pope John Paul II.

Pontifical Council for Justice and Peace. *The Church and Racism: Towards a More Fraternal Society.* Contribution of the Holy See to the World Conference against Racism, Racial Discrimination, Xenophobia, and Related Intolerance. Durban, South Africa, August 31—September 7, 2001. Vatican City: Pontifical Council for Justice and Peace, 2001. This study treats leading-edge issues: pardon in racial reconciliation, affirmative action as a corrective for racism, and the role of religion in human rights education.

Tierney, Brian. *The Idea of Natural Rights: Studies on Natural Rights, Natural Law and Church Law, 1150–1625.* Emory Studies in Law and Religion, no. 5. Atlanta, Ga.: Scholar's, 1997. Tierney offers a detailed and instructive history of pre-Enlightenment Catholic thinking on natural rights, revealing a rich but little-known heritage. He concludes that nearly all of what constitutes modern rights thinking was available in Catholic sources before the Enlightenment.

Zizola, Giancarlo. *The Utopia of John XXIII.* Translated by Helen Barolini. Maryknoll, N.Y.: Orbis, 1979. A leading Italian journalist and Vaticanologist recalls Pope John's papacy.

CHAPTER

10 Commentary on *Dignitatis humanae* (*Declaration on Religious Freedom*)

LESLIE GRIFFIN

INTRODUCTION

Dignitatis humanae, the *Declaration on Religious Freedom*, was the last document promulgated by Vatican II, which met in Rome from 1962 to 1965. Pope Paul VI, who succeeded Pope John XXIII in June 1963, signed DH on December 7, 1965. DH, "the only conciliar document that [was] formally addressed to the world at large on a topic of intense secular as well as religious interest,"[1] affirmed that religious freedom is the right of every human person. This teaching marked a dramatic change from the Church's earlier position that non-Catholics do not possess a public right to worship because "error has no rights."

OUTLINE OF THE DOCUMENT

The text of DH is short. It is divided into a preamble and two chapters. Opening words about dignity set the tone for the document, whose central claim is that the right to religious freedom is based on the dignity of the human person. Chapter 1 identifies the "general principle of religious freedom":

> Freedom of this kind means that all men should be immune from coercion on the part of individuals, social groups and every human power so that, within due limits, nobody is forced to act against his convictions nor is anyone to be restrained from acting in accordance with his convictions in religious matters in private or in public, alone or in associations with others. (2)

Chapter 2 examines "religious freedom in the light of revelation." It explores the scriptural and theological roots of religious freedom. Although the right is rooted in human dignity, "this doctrine of freedom is rooted in divine revelation, and for this reason Christians are bound to respect it all the more conscientiously" (9).

The coauthor of the declaration, Father Pietro Pavan, identified the "essential elements" of the document as the following:

> (1) Every human person has the right to religious freedom. (2) This right has as its object or content an immunity from coercion at the hands of individuals, social groups, or public powers. (3) The immunity is understood in two senses: (a) no one must be forced to act against his conscience in religious matters; (b) no one must be restrained—in those same religious matters—from acting in conformity with his conscience, whether privately or publicly,

whether alone or in association with others, within due limits. (4) The right has its foundation in the dignity of the human person as this dignity can be known in the light of revelation as well as through reason. (5) This right demands recognition and sanction in the constitutional law whereby society is governed.[2]

CONTEXT OF THE DOCUMENT

The College of Cardinals elected seventy-six-year old Pope John XXIII on October 28, 1958. Commentators expected that, given his age and background, he would be a transitional, "caretaker" pope who would hold the throne of Peter until a younger man assumed it. Instead, on January 25, 1959, he announced an ecumenical council (Vatican II), the first in the Roman Church since 1870, when Vatican I, which defined the doctrine of papal infallibility, was disrupted by the Franco-Prussian war and the invasion of Rome by the Italian army. Pope John supported the early drafts of DH because of his commitment to ecumenism. Upon his death in June 1963, observers wondered if his successor would support the Council, ecumenism, and religious freedom. After some delay, Pope Paul encouraged the council fathers to vote on DH during the last session of the Council.

The debates over the declaration were contentious and its passage was difficult. Since Vatican I, the Church had opposed the liberal reforms of the Enlightenment that had changed governments throughout Europe. The pope of Vatican I, Pius IX, had condemned liberalism, the separation of church and state, and free speech in the *Syllabus of Errors*. Although World War II left Pope Pius XII more sympathetic to democracy than his predecessors were, his writings provided only an ambiguous defense of religious liberty.[3] Before John's papacy, the Church had never recognized a right to religious freedom.

World War II hastened the Church's acceptance of democracy. Nonetheless, the victory of the democracies over the totalitarian governments in that war posed difficult challenges to Catholics in Europe and the United States. Christians of different denominations began collaborating in the work of social reconstruction in response to the ravages of the war. Such cooperation was important and valuable—yet also risky from the perspective of the Catholic hierarchy.[4] The Church taught that Catholicism was the one true religion. Collaboration with non-Catholics might challenge that true faith. Most worrisome was the problem of "indifferentism," which was condemned by Pope Pius IX in the *Syllabus*.[5] Indifferentism was the belief that all religions are equal, that is, indifference to the truth that Catholicism is the one true religion. Cooperation between Catholics and non-Catholics must never suggest that all religions are equal in truth.

The political aspects of this problem were more difficult than the social ones. Even after the Church accepted democracy, it could not accept the separation of church and state. When John XXIII became pope in 1958, the dominant account of Catholic church-state theory was summarized in the thesis/hypothesis distinction whose premise was that Catholicism is the one true religion. If Catholicism is the one true religion, it should be the established religion of the state. The state should establish the one true Church and govern in accordance with Catholic principles. By the 1960s, however, Catholics knew that Catholicism was not always the established religion, and that it would be difficult to gain or regain established status in some nations. The thesis stated the ideal: Catholicism should be the established religion of the state. A non-Catholic state was the "hypothesis" that had to be tolerated as an evil. Catholics could tolerate nonestablishment when they could do no better, but should change the hypothesis to thesis when they could do so.[6]

The slogan connected to the thesis/hypothesis distinction was that "error has no rights." The implications of this phrase were most severe in the realm of public worship. Catholics in the minority have the right to public worship; their religion is true. But error does not have rights to public worship. Thus non-Catholics in the minority should not have the right to public worship. Only true faiths have the right to public worship.[7]

Nowhere was the social and political problem for Catholics more pressing than in the United States. American Catholics had always confronted a tension between their American and Catholic identities. In the nineteenth century, for example, Bishop John Ireland and others had encouraged American Catholics to accept religious toleration, religious freedom, and separation of church and state as part of an accommodation to the modern world.[8] Their efforts were rebuffed by Pope Leo XIII, whose encyclicals *Longinqua oceani* and *Testem benevolentiae* renounced American separation of church and state as well as "a constellation of ideas he labeled 'Americanism.'"[9]

During World War II and in the late 1940s, the American Jesuit theologian John Courtney Murray defended "intercredal cooperation," the collaboration of Catholics and non-Catholics in the work of social justice.[10] In response, Murray's critics raised the specter of indifferentism in opposing cooperation and labeled him an Americanist.[11] Cooperation with non-Catholics might leave Catholics indifferent to the truth of their own religion.

On the political front, the Constitution of the United States requires that "Congress shall make no law respecting an establishment of religion, or prohibiting the free exercise thereof."[12] The constitutional ban on establishment contradicted the Catholic thesis that Catholicism should be the established religion of every state. Some Catholic writers identified Spain as the thesis and the United States as the hypothesis. In other words, Spain had the ideal form of government while the separation of church and state in the United States was an evil to be tolerated until it could be changed. In Spain in 1960, "after 22 years in power, Generalissimo Francisco Franco [was] still the sole, supreme authority . . . The 'Sentinel of the West,' as he like[d] to be called, [was] chief of state, head of government, protector of the church, commander in chief of the armed forces and boss of the sole political party, the Falange. . . . The very coinage proclaim[ed] him 'By the Grace of God—Caudillo Leader.'"[13]

Two years after John XXIII took the papal throne, John Fitzgerald Kennedy was elected the first Catholic president of the United States in November 1960. Kennedy's Catholicism was a contentious issue throughout the presidential campaign. Critics charged that a Catholic president would take orders from the pope, enforce Catholic teaching as law, or undermine the strict separation of church and state. The thesis/hypothesis view was useful fuel for the fire of Paul Blanshard and other critics of American Catholics. Thesis/hypothesis suggested that Catholics would seek the establishment of religion once they had the majority. Kennedy addressed these criticisms in a famous speech to Protestant ministers in Houston, in which he successfully reassured the audience that he would not take orders from the pope.[14]

Kennedy's advisors consulted with John Courtney Murray as they prepared the Houston address.[15] Murray had written about the problems of religious freedom and church and state since the 1940s. His writings defended the First Amendment and offered the most rigorous Catholic challenge to the thesis/hypothesis distinction. He demanded, "Are we to suppose that 30,000,000 Catholics must live perpetually in a state of 'hypothesis'?"[16] In the United States, his principal adversary was Joseph Fenton, professor of dogma and dean of theology at the Catholic University of America, who defended thesis/hypothesis. *Time* magazine put Murray on its cover after Kennedy's election in recognition of the intellectual work he had done to demonstrate that Catholics could be American citizens, politicians, and presidents.

In 1960, the praise of Murray occurred in *Time* and in the United States, not at the Vatican. Indeed, in 1955 Murray was ordered to cease writing about church and state by officials in Rome. In 1960, the separation of church and state and religious freedom remained contested issues within Catholicism. Outside the Church, many non-Catholics remained skeptical about the Church's commitment to religious freedom for all persons. Since the 1920s, the ecumenical movement had developed among other Christian denominations without Catholic participation; fears of indifferentism kept Catholics from full engagement in ecumenism. For example, the Church refused to send observers to the First Assembly of the World Council of Churches (WCC) in Amsterdam in 1948.[17] The WCC adopted a "Declaration on Religious Liberty" in August 1948 that demanded "adequate safeguards for freedom of religion and conscience, including the right of all men to hold and change their faith, to exercise it in worship and practice, to teach and persuade others, and to decide on the religious education of their children."[18] After the announcement of Vatican II, the WCC urged the Church to address ecumenism and Christian unity as a central issue of the Council. "Error has no rights" did not provide a firm foundation for ecumenism.

PROCESS OF FORMULATION AND AUTHORSHIP

Announced by the new pope in January 1959, Vatican II did not begin until October 1962. In the interim the Church underwent extensive preparations for the Council. Ten commissions and three secretariats were formed to study possible topics for discussion. The Central Preparatory Commission (CPC), overseen by the pope, coordinated the work of the other commissions.[19]

On the subject of religious freedom, the most important bodies were the Theological Commission (TC) and the Secretariat for Christian Unity (SCU). TC, headed by Cardinal Alfredo Ottaviani, included among its assignments the Church—*De Ecclesia*. "Church and state" fell within that category. Pope John appointed the Jesuit Cardinal Augustin Bea to head SCU. Ecumenism was a topic dear to the pope's heart; as apostolic visitor to Bulgaria from 1925 to 1934 and as apostolic delegate to Turkey and Greece from 1935 to 1944 he had become aware of the interests of Protestant and Orthodox Christians, Jews, and Muslims. SCU's focus was unity with Protestant Christians while the Commission for Oriental Churches (OR) was assigned the Orthodox churches.[20] Eventually the Orthodox Christians dealt primarily with Cardinal Bea.

SCU was a secretariat, not a commission. Accordingly, it was originally viewed as an "information center"[21] that would help other Christian churches to understand the Council, not as a drafter of documents. Cardinal Bea had other plans, however, especially once the preparatory commissions ignored the ecumenical dimensions of their topics. TC "conducted itself in sovereign independence of the SCU."[22] When SCU's authority to draft council documents was challenged, the ecumenical pope supported SCU. It prepared drafts in the preconciliar period.

The Six Drafts Debated at the Council

Once the Council started, SCU's competence was again challenged. The pope then upgraded the SCU to the status of a commission. The other commissions had their members elected at the Council, but the SCU (with its upgrading) was the only one to keep its preconciliar membership intact, with no elected members.[23]

> The Secretariat for Christian Unity was thus given an exceptional status among the conciliar commissions: it was the only one that had all its members in the preparatory phase confirmed in their position during the conciliar phase by the express will of John XXIII. Thus it was, paradoxically, an organ of the Pope that kept the ecumenical tension alive during the Council.[24]

The two bodies eventually battled over religious freedom. TC considered "Church and state" to be part of its subject, the Church; SCU saw "religious freedom" as fundamental to ecumenism, its assignment. On June 18, 1962, both groups submitted drafts to the CPC. Their perspectives differed. "The starting point of the Secretariat's text was the *dignity of the person,* seen from a moral point of view, namely, as grounded in the uprightness and integrity of conscience; the Theological Commission's starting point was constituted by the *rights of truth*."[25]

TC drafters included Rossaire Gagnebet, whose drafted condemnation of Murray and French theologian Jacques Maritain for their writings on Church and state was halted by the death of Pope Pius XII in 1958.[26] TC preferred the thesis/hypothesis account of Church and state; its draft demonstrated harshness toward non-Catholics.[27] The March 1962 TC draft recognized the state's "duty to perform religious obligations," that is, to acknowledge the Catholic Church as "the one way in which God wishes to be served and worshipped."[28] Although the state could not "coerce consciences, it could act in order to help its citizens persevere in the true faith, by restricting public displays of other religions and the spread of false doctrines."[29] "Those citizens who belong to other religions *do not have the right not to be prevented from professing these religions*; however, for the sake of common good the State may tolerate their profession."[30] Meanwhile, minority Catholics must be "completely free to profess their own religion."[31]

The SCU's Schema on Ecumenism included chapter 5 on "religious freedom." Religious freedom was of ecumenical concern because of justified skepticism by non-Catholics about the commitment of the Church to the right of non-Catholics to believe their own religion. Non-Catholics could not agree with such stark TC opposition to the right to "profess their own religion." SCU emphasized the need for tolerance and cooperation, and recognized a right to religious freedom for all human persons.[32]

Thus the TC and SCU drafts differed greatly. When the two groups met, Ottaviani insisted that SCU should not draft texts.[33] CPC could not resolve the controversy, so the pope created a special commission. "By July, 1962, Pope John created an *ad hoc* commission to reconcile the two drafts. On July 15, the Secretariat for Christian Unity, under Bea's leadership, submitted a compromise draft to the *ad hoc* commission. But on August 2, 1962, negotiations between the Secretariat and the Theological Commission collapsed."[34] The two groups did not reach agreement before the Council started.

The battle between the TC and SCU approaches continued throughout the Council. Eventually, the council fathers decided that religious freedom deserved its own declaration, separate from the topics of the Church and of ecumenism. From then on, SCU issued separate documents on religious freedom; the Council promulgated DH as a single declaration. The Church and ecumenism received their own documents, *Lumen gentium* and *Unitatis redintegratio.*

At the beginning of the Council, it appeared that the TC perspective would triumph. Joseph Fenton was invited to the first session of the Council as a personal advisor to Cardinal Ottaviani. His rival Murray was initially invited but later "disinvited," probably at the urging of Ottaviani and Egidio Vagnozzi, the apostolic delegate in Washington, D.C.[35] While Murray stayed in Woodstock, Maryland, Church and state and religious freedom were not discussed at the first session, which ran from October 11 to December 8, 1962.

The American bishops then pushed to have the topic included in the second session. At the insistence of New York's Francis Cardinal Spellman, on April 4, 1963, Murray received his invitation as *peritus*, or expert, for the next session. Already Murray was urging the bishops to confront thesis/hypothesis, to provide a sounder theoretical foundation for religious freedom, and to intervene "in defense of the American Constitutional system."[36] Pope Paul VI, who succeeded John XXIII after John's death in June 1963, opened the second session of the Council on September 29, 1963, and some debates on the Church and ecumenism began. Murray was in Rome for a November 11, 1963 meeting with Ottaviani, during which TC reviewed the SCU text. In "a glorious victory for the Good Guys,"[37] the SCU text was voted out of committee to the council floor.

From the second session to the end of the Council, six schemata on religious freedom were advanced.[38] Émile Joseph M. de Smedt, the bishop of Bruges, Belgium, presented the first schema, chapter 5 of the *Decree on Ecumenism*, to the council fathers on November 19, 1963. Ecumenism was discussed November 19 to 21, 1963, but not voted on. That left SCU with plenty of time for revision after the second session ended on December 4, 1963. During the intersession, Murray evaluated the suggestions of the council fathers about revisions of the schema.[39] In the United States, President Kennedy was assassinated on November 22.

The third session began on September 14, 1964. The American bishops were active and united in promoting religious freedom. A second schema (revised by SCU in February and March 1964) was debated September 23 to 25, 1964. Again, no vote was taken. At this point, "DeSmedt commissioned Murray as the 'first scribe' to rewrite the Declaration. This was done in collaboration with Monsignor [Pietro] Pavan, [Monsignor Jan] Willebrands, [Jerome] Hamer, and DeSmedt himself. Murray later reported that this was his and Pavan's first entrance on the work of drafting."[40] Pietro Pavan, a council *peritus*, was a priest and professor of social economy at the Lateran University in Rome. Although Murray often receives most of the credit for the declaration, Pavan deserved equal billing for DH.[41]

By the third session, the decision had been made to treat religious freedom as a distinct topic, separate from ecumenism. The third schema (the *textus emendatus*), entitled the "Declaration on Religious Freedom or on the Right of the Person and of Communities to Freedom in Matters Religious," was presented on November 17, 1964, again by Bishop de Smedt. The key theme was the dignity of the human person as the basis for a right to religious freedom. On that same day, a vote was announced for November 19. Then the conciliar intrigue intensified. One group of fathers requested that the vote be delayed until further study could be completed. In response, a group led by Cardinal Meyer of Chicago and other American bishops petitioned the pope to hold the vote. Pope Paul VI upheld Cardinal Tisserant's decision to delay the vote on the declaration until the fourth session of the Council. In this instance, Pope Paul sided with the conservative minority. "The events of this day have been referred to as 'Black Thursday' while Murray called it the 'Day of Wrath.'"[42] The third session ended on November 21, 1964. Amid the controversy, Pope Paul VI promised that religious freedom would be the first item of business in the next session.

On December 27, 1964, Pope Paul sent his private secretary, Monsignor Pasquale Macchi, and the French intellectual Jean Guitton to Toulouse to consult with the pope's old friend Jacques Maritain about the last session of the Council. Maritain was the French Thomist philosopher and theologian who had written extensively about the proper autonomy of Church and state. His early writings had influenced Murray on these questions. Now, one of Pope Paul's four questions to Maritain was about religious liberty. Pope Paul named their mutual friend, l'Abbé Charles Journet, a cardinal on January 26, 1965.[43]

Maritain returned a text about religious liberty to the pope in March 1965. His answer emphasized the political aspect of religious freedom. According to Maritain, the sacral state was a thing of the past. In the modern world, both Church and state were autonomous. "L'État n'a plus aucun titre à intervenir dans les choses de la conscience," he wrote. The state was not entitled to interfere in matters of conscience unless it were "au nom du bien commun terrestre," for the terrestrial common good (for example, to stop suicidal groups or to oppose racial persecution).[44] The state's right to intervene was limited because, in Maritain's view, "human beings, directed as they are to God, 'transcend by their nature the terrestrial and temporal order of things.'"[45]

Murray and Pavan worked on a new draft from February 18 to 25, 1965; Paulist priest Thom Stransky, French theologian Yves Congar, and Monsignor Willebrands assisted them.[46] The pope arranged a brief audience with Murray after receiving a letter from him on May 8.[47] The missive explained the argument of the DH draft, especially its choice of dignity (rather than conscience) as the foundation of the right. Murray mentioned that the French would "not like" the section on scripture and revelation because they wanted a fuller theological argument in the declaration.[48] This draft, the *textus reemendatus*, was completed by May 11. Pope Paul conveyed his approval of the document to Murray on May 28, 1965.[49]

The fourth session opened on September 14, 1965. Discussion of the fourth schema (*textus reemendatus*) began the next day and continued through September 21. Differences between the French and American bishops about the style of argument were ironed out. The French had wanted a more theological document that emphasized the rights of conscience. Maritain himself had included conscience in his remarks to the pope: "La conscience n'a pas droit à l'erreur."[50] Nonetheless, Maritain's friend, the new Cardinal Journet, made a decisive intervention on the floor in favor of the new draft.

Pope Paul also intervened. Some council fathers again tried to postpone the vote on the declaration. On September 21, the pope decided that the vote would proceed. "Paul had taken a stand."[51] The fourth schema was approved on September 21, 1965, by a vote of 1997–224. "This was one of the most decisive 'interventions' of Paul in the work of the Council. . . . The difference between Paul at the third and the fourth session was that he had by now personally studied the question in greater depth."[52] His notes show that he understood the complexities of the debate.[53] Maritain and Murray had done their teaching job well.

Although the "basic tenet of disestablishment was unalterably accepted" by the vote on the fourth schema,[54] further edits were made to the text. The bishops led the revision process; Murray was too sick to participate. A large majority accepted the fifth schema (*textus recognitus*) on October 26 and 27, 1965. The Council approved the final text, the sixth schema (*textus denuo recognitus*), on November 19, and promulgated the *Declaration on Religious Freedom* on December 7, 1965, by a final vote of 2308 to 70. Since November 1963, there had been three public debates, 120 speeches, six hundred written interventions, numerous oral and written critiques of the schemata, consultations with the council observers, and more than two thousand *modi* (suggested corrections) about DH.[55]

ESSAY

The Intellectual Sources of DH

Because the American bishops and Murray led the fight for DH, it became known as "the American schema,"[56] or even as "Murray's schema." DH shows the influence of the First Amendment of the U.S. Constitution and was "beyond a doubt, the specific American contribution to the Second Vatican Council."[57] Judge John T. Noonan has compellingly described the American sources of DH:

> The learning had been largely from the United States: from its Constitution of such extraordinary importance praised by Maritain and from the Virginian Declaration pointed to by Pavan; from its bishops who kept the issue alive as "*the* American issue" in the Council; from its theologian John Courtney Murray, who poured his energy and insight into the shaping of the new teaching. Impossible without the recent European experience and the support of bishops from around the world and the receptivity of Italian popes, the Declaration on Religious Freedom would not have come into existence without the American contribution and the experiment that began with Madison.[58]

The history of the American experiment confirms that, although the declaration marked a development in Catholic doctrine about religious liberty, "it can hardly be maintained that the Declaration [was] a milestone in human history—moral, political, or intellectual."[59] After all, the United Nations had already included the right in the Universal Declaration of Human Rights in 1948, the World Council of Churches had affirmed the right in the same year, and numerous nations (in addition to the United States) before and after 1947 guaranteed it in their constitutions.[60] As Murray acknowledged in 1966: "The principle of religious freedom has long been recognized in constitutional law, to the point where even Marxist-Leninist political ideology is obliged to pay lip-service to it. But in all honesty it must be admitted that *the Church is late* in acknowledging the validity of the principle."[61]

The Church *was* late. The popes of the nineteenth and twentieth centuries had been preoccupied with the flaws of continental liberalism and the loss of the Papal States. In 1864, Pope Pius IX condemned most liberal principles in the *Syllabus of Errors,* including the idea that "freedom of conscience and worship is every man's proper right." Pius IX also opposed the separation of church and state, criticized the public exercise of non-Catholic religions, and favored an established Catholic Church. Pius's successor, Pope Leo XIII, was much less critical of the modern world and inaugurated modern Catholic social thought. His writings recognized the autonomy of the state and its special competence, different from the Church's. Nonetheless, Leo espoused the union of Church and state as the Christian ideal. He also proposed a "conception of a paternal state with broad responsibilities and few limits placed upon it."[62]

World War II changed that vision of the state. Totalitarianism was at odds with the dignity of the human person. In his Christmas addresses during the war, Pope Pius XII praised democracy and accepted the idea of the constitutional state. On religious freedom, however, as Bryan Hehir explained, "Pius XII opened the door but he never walked through it."[63] It was Pope John XXIII who walked through that door in 1963, after the Council had started but before the council fathers agreed on DH. John issued "the first clear statement found in Roman Catholic teaching concerning a right of religious freedom"[64] in his encyclical letter *Pacem in terris* on April 11, 1963.

Pavan was the lead author of the notable encyclical, which identified an extensive list of rights of the human person. Included on the list was religious freedom: "Also among man's rights is that of being able to worship God in accordance with the *right dictates of his own conscience,* and to profess his religion both in private and in public" (PT 14) (emphasis added). The use of *rectam* (*ad rectam conscientiae*) in the Latin text, translated as "right" in the official English translation, raised an important question, however. Did *Pacem in terris* mean that the erroneous conscience had the right to public worship? "In one view, this right exists only in the case of the right and true conscience; in the other view, its existence attaches to the right conscience, whether true or erroneous."[65] Pavan "stated that the pope deliberately chose *recta* in order *not* to resolve the theological problem!"[66] The problem was left for the Council to solve.

Pacem in terris was published between the first and second sessions of the Council, before the issues of Church and state and ecumenism were discussed. This "transitional text . . . moved the Roman Catholic discussion beyond the teaching of Pius XII, yet it did not attempt the more comprehensive argument of *Dignitatis Humanae*."[67] *Pacem in terris* identified the right of religious freedom, but did not provide the theoretical foundation for it. That task was left to Murray, Pavan, and the Council. It was a monumental undertaking because of the legacy of Pius IX, thesis/hypothesis and error has no rights, which many bishops believed was the authentic and irreformable teaching of the Church. Murray, who understood the commitment of his opponents to an established church, had always urged the American bishops to prepare a theoretically sound declaration that would lay thesis/hypothesis to rest.

Alternative Bases for a Right to Religious Freedom

Although unnuanced, "error has no rights" was a useful slogan because it captured the traditional position's focus on the truth. God created an objective moral order. Within that order, the truth has rights, but error cannot have rights. Catholicism is the one true religion. As the truth, it always has rights, either to establishment (when circumstances permit) or to public worship (when they do not). Error has no right to either establishment or public worship.

For the traditionalists, the social context did not change this ideal of truth. As the Church was disestablished in Europe, they argued that Catholics had to tolerate this situation while maintaining the ideal of establishment. Although historical situations changed, the teaching of the Church remained true in all circumstances. At Vatican II, the TC, Cardinal Ottaviani, and other bishops who delayed the vote on DH supported this position.

The ecumenical movement challenged that ideal. When he introduced the first schema to the Council, Bishop de Smedt explained why ecumenists suspected Catholics of "a kind of Machiavellism": "Many non-Catholics harbor an aversion against the Church or at least suspect her of a kind of Machiavellism because we seem to them to demand the free exercise of religion when Catholics are in a minority in any nation and at the same time refuse and deny the same religious liberty when Catholics are in the majority."[68] The World Council of Churches, which had its own suspicions, urged the Council to review religious freedom. Recall that the first schema was chapter 5 of the *Decree on Ecumenism*. DeSmedt argued to the Council that religious freedom "cannot be omitted in a pastoral decree on ecumenism."[69]

The challenge to Murray and Pavan was to construct an argument about religious freedom that was rooted in tradition but distinct from the TC stance. The TC group did not bear sole responsibility for the delay in passing DH. "The advocates of religious freedom were divided among themselves" about the best "methodology and focus of argument."[70] The French preferred the more theoretical approach of the first two schemata while the Americans preferred the pragmatic argument of the third. The debates about the six schemata illustrated the difficult theoretical questions associated with Catholic recognition of a right to religious freedom, even for the right's supporters.

Murray explained that the first two schemata emphasized *freedom of conscience*.[71] The focus on conscience was not surprising, given the texts' roots in the subject of ecumenism. The starting point of SCU was the "moral, theological and ecumenical question of how Catholics relate to people who don't share their faith."[72] The *moral* answer was that individuals must not be coerced in matters of faith. "Freedom of conscience" recognized the individual right to follow the dictates of one's own conscience and offered an ecumenically sound principle.

In the first two drafts, freedom of conscience was more than a moral claim, however. According to the first two schemata, the "right of a freely followed conscience" provided the basis for a *juridical* right to the free exercise of religion. The moral right of conscience entailed the legal protection of free exercise. This right was not unlimited, however, according to de Smedt and the first schema: it "can be, at times must be, tempered and regulated for the common good."[73] Public authority (i.e., the government) orders society for the common good.

This emphasis on conscience created an analytical problem within Catholicism. It suggested that the person of sincere conscience—even if she or he were in error—possessed the right to religious freedom, including juridical recognition by the state. This argument was in tension with the traditional Catholic belief that an erroneous conscience has no rights, especially to religious freedom or the public manifestation of erroneous belief. This was the unresolved aspect of *Pacem in terris*. Moreover, the first two schemata suggested that the government could interfere with religious freedom for the common good or other purposes of society. That vision was reminiscent of the old Catholic paternalistic state that restrained erroneous religion in order to protect the common good. Yet the Church had accepted the limited constitutional state. Murray thought that the early schemata were "confused" and required a sounder basis. He and Pavan provided this foundation when they stepped in to draft the third schema.

What should the Church say about the person with the sincere but erroneous conscience? According to Murray, the logical problem with the early schemata was that one person's right to follow his or her erroneous conscience could not obligate another person to respect or honor it. A subjective belief in rightness could not provide the objective foundation for legal rights against the state. No Catholic theory could endorse "subjectivism" or "unfettered conscience." Because of this "unresolved dispute within the Church with regard to the 'rights of conscience,'"[74] a new argument was needed.

Murray explained the new argument—the change in emphasis between second and third drafts—in an article in *America* in January 1965.[75] The basis for the right to religious freedom became the objective dignity of each human person, not the subjective freedom of conscience. The ecumenical, moral, and theological bases of the first two schemata were replaced by a juridical focus in the third schema. The third text "affirmed the free exercise of religion in society to be a basic human right that . . . should be furnished with a juridical guarantee so as to become a civil or constitutional right."[76] Objective dignity provided a sounder basis than subjective conscience for this legal right to religious freedom.

In this juridical and constitutional argument, the influence of the First Amendment on Murray was evident. Like the Catholic popes and bishops, the Puritan Fathers had wanted "freedom to practice without interference the one truth faith, . . . correctly interpreted. Thus religious freedom in the 'City upon a Hill' meant freedom from error."[77] But the Founding Fathers inscribed a non-Puritan, non-Catholic, "radically different conception of religious freedom" into the U.S. Constitution.[78] Murray borrowed from them the idea that the "juridical guarantee" of religious freedom was a negative immunity from government interference, not a positive entitlement. In other words, religious freedom was a "*freedom from*"[79] coercion and restraint, not a freedom from error or a freedom for the truth to be established. "Religious freedom is a freedom from coercion; it is an immunity; its content is negative" and "twofold."[80] "First, no man is to be forcibly constrained to act against his conscience. Second, no man is to be forcibly restrained from acting according to his conscience."[81]

Within Catholic theology, this "negative" definition avoided the problems of indifferentism and the erroneous conscience. That religious belief could not be coerced did not mean that all religions were equal in the truth. Catholicism was still the one true religion. Nonetheless, the third schema did not immediately gain full support at the Council; the "French-speaking school" thought that the American argument was "superficial"[82] and not as theoretically satisfying as the argument about conscience. These disagreements between supporters of religious freedom were resolved at the fourth session of the Council.

Pope John XXIII, who *ab initio* had supported Cardinal Bea and the drafts of SCU, provided Murray and Pavan with the best argument for religious freedom before his death on June 3, 1963. They relied on *Pacem in terris* as they drafted DH since it provided the most solid basis in the tradition for the right to religious freedom. When Pavan addressed the French episcopacy about *Pacem in terris* in November 1963, during the second session, he explained that the pope

> began with facts and not ideas. The key facts [include] every man's conviction that he has a right to follow his conscience, especially in professing his religion, whether privately or publicly. *Pacem in terris* affirms this right clearly.
>
> Only God has the right to judge our conscience. The person himself must decide on religious matters, not external pressures and especially public powers, which have only one responsibility—and that is to create conditions favorable to the expression of the rights of citizens.[83]

Pacem in terris, with its undeveloped analytical framework on religious freedom, was important to the argument because the council debate was not only about Church and state, religious freedom or ecumenism, but was most importantly about the "development of doctrine," the euphemism for change in the Church's teaching. As Murray noted:

> [DH] was, of course, the most controversial document of the whole Council, largely because it raised with sharp emphasis the

> issue that lay continually below the surface of all the conciliar debates—the issue of *development of doctrine*. The notion of development, not the notion of religious freedom, was the real sticking-point for many of those who opposed the Declaration even to the end.[84]

Pacem in terris provided the best precedent for those worried about drafting a document that was faithful to the Church's prior teachings on religious freedom. Murray explained that DH's "immediate roots" were in *Pacem in terris* in his May 8, 1965, letter to Pope Paul. As he wrote, "'the line of development is clear, the schema simply presents a more explicit *enucleatio doctrinae* [encapsulating of doctrine]. The development is not only valid but necessary for today.'"[85]

The bishops were persuaded; they adopted the Murray-Pavan argument in DH on December 7, 1965. DH provided the theoretical foundation for religious freedom that was lacking in *Pacem in terris*. Within the Council, the final vote of 2308–70 demonstrated overwhelming support for religious liberty. Moreover, "we all know that the reception given to the Declaration by non-Catholics was instantly positive. It was one of the freshest breezes blowing through the Church after Pope John XXIII opened the window."[86]

The Final Text: Human Dignity and Freedom from Restraint

Like the U.S. Constitution, the "conciliar document is a brilliant politico-legal document."[87] The text is divided into a preamble and two chapters. In keeping with the focus of Vatican II on the "signs of the times," the preamble (1) identifies the awareness of the dignity of the human person and the demand for limited government as part of a new situation for the Church. In this environment, the preface first reaffirms the traditional teaching that Catholicism is the "one true religion" and so rejects indifferentism (the belief that all religions are equally true). The conscience cannot be forced to believe the truth, however; it must be immune from coercion. Finally, the preamble announces the intention of the bishops to "develop the teaching of recent popes" (1). With these words DH embraced historical consciousness over the more classical worldview of the preconciliar Church.[88]

Chapter 1 (numbers 2–8), on the "general principle of religious freedom," provides the political and juridical argument for religious freedom developed by Murray and Pavan. Number 2 includes the most important content of the declaration. First, the right is grounded, not in truth (as thesis/hypothesis had held) or conscience (the focus of the early schemata), but in the dignity of the human person, of every human person. In place of "truth has rights" or "error has no rights," DH proclaims that human dignity possesses rights.

Next, number 2 explains the nature of the right of religious freedom. The right is a double immunity from both *coercion* and *restraint*. The government may not coerce the individual conscience into belief. Nor may it restrain her or him from the practice of religion. As Murray described this twofold immunity: "First, no man is to be forced to act in a manner contrary to his personal beliefs; second, no man is to be forcibly restrained from acting in accordance with his beliefs. The affirmation of this latter immunity is *the new thing*, which is in harmony with the older affirmation of the former immunity."[89]

"The new thing." The preconciliar Church did not hold that the Church or state could coerce the individual to believe. It had already accepted the first immunity from coercion "even during the post-Reformation era of confessional absolutism. . . . The principle was gradually established that even the absolutist prince may not compel a man to act against his conscience or punish him for reasons of conscience."[90] As we have seen, however, in the preconciliar Church it *was* appropriate for the government to restrain the practice of erroneous religion. Only the true religion had the right to public worship; erroneous religions could be prohibited from public worship. Error had no rights until DH recognized the individual's immunity from *restraint* as well as *constraint*. What was new was the immunity from restraint, which, according to Murray, was "first effectively proclaimed in the First Amendment to the Constitution of the United States."[91]

Number 2 includes the affirmation that this right, with its twofold immunity, "must be given such recognition in the constitutional order of society as will make it a civil right" (2). The Church here reaffirms its support for the limited constitutional state that protects human rights and human dignity. Delineating the state's proper role, however, is a difficult task. How can any declaration both clarify that "religious freedom is not without bounds" and protect religious freedom from the state?[92] DH resolves this issue with the criterion of *public order*. DH concludes that "the exercise of this right cannot be interfered with as long as the just requirements of public order are observed" (2). Even individuals who do not seek the truth have a right to religious freedom upon which the state may not intrude unless "public order" is violated.

Note that the Council did not adopt the French or Maritainian view that the state should intervene to protect the common good. The choice of "public order" over "common good" was important to the analysis of religious liberty. Unfortunately, however, DH's treatment of public order was "vague"; "no attempt was made to specify what constituted a just public order."[93]

Number 3 offers a reminder that rights entail obligations. The right of religious freedom carries a duty to seek the truth. Nothing in DH frees Catholics of their obligations to the true Catholic faith. This argument establishes the tension between truth and freedom that became a central theme of the pontificate of Pope John Paul II.

Murray later identified within number 3 a "general and somewhat enigmatic phrase" that appears to recognize a positive role for government in promoting religion (not merely a negative role of avoiding constraint and restraint).[94] The text states that "the civil authority . . . must recognize and *look with favor* on the religious life of the citizens. But if it presumes to control or restrict religious activity it must be said to have exceeded the limits of its power" (3). Look with favor? Murray explained that the council fathers did not want to support a completely secular or laicist account of the state and so included the enigmatic passage. "One of the difficulties with the whole Declaration is that it did not want to get into the broader problem of Church and state; it simply wanted to prevent such a Declaration from appearing to favor an older laicist or secularist conception of the problem of Church and state."[95] The text's ambiguity was not lost on American commentators, however, who could interpret the wording to permit or mandate government aid to religious institutions, then a controversial issue in American constitutional law.[96]

The right of religious freedom is not merely an individual right, but a right of religious bodies (4) and families, especially in their education of children (5). The right is not absolute, however, and religious organizations must not abuse it. They ought "to avoid any action which seems to suggest coercion or dishonest or unworthy persuasion" (4). According to Murray, this paragraph permits "Christian witness" but not "proselytism,"[97] which is an abuse of religious freedom and "an infringement of the rights of others" (4).

The government has the duty to safeguard religious freedom and to provide favorable conditions for fostering religious life (6). The third paragraph of number 6 is "carefully phrased"[98] because it addresses the difficult problem of establishment. Although the First Amendment forbids the establishment of religion, DH does not. Instead, on that subject the "declaration [is] wide open to interpretation."[99] Murray and the council fathers had good theological and practical reasons to avoid the DH equivalent of the American Establishment Clause. They had no commitment to disestablish the Church from Catholic nations. In some nations, Catholics were content to keep establishment whenever it worked for the Church, and would accept it willingly wherever governments chose it.

Thus the long journey from the thesis/hypothesis distinction did not end with a renunciation of the "notion of a 'religion of the state.'"[100] During the council debates, the fathers had disagreed about the role of concordats as a means of settling Church-state relations. One group supported them while another group opposed. A third group, led by Cardinal Alfrink of Amsterdam, argued that Church-state problems "could not be solved *a priori*,"[101] but that in all circumstances the right of religious freedom must be accorded to everyone equally. This equality argument prevailed; it is reflected in number 6. Forms of government are decided by historical circumstance, not by church doctrine and not a priori. Equality of citizens is the watchword. Thus nations may maintain an establishment—or not—as long as they protect the religious freedom of all individuals and communities.

No right is absolute, and so individuals must exercise their freedom responsibly while the government must protect them from the abuse of the freedom of religion (7). The notion of a protective government is fraught with difficulty, given DH's core argument about the citizen's twofold immunity against the state. When may the government interfere with religion? DH opts for public order over common welfare. "The free exercise of religion may not be inhibited unless proof is given that it entails some violation of the rights of others, or of the public peace, or of public morality. In these cases, in other words, a public action ceases to be a religious exercise and becomes a penal offense."[102] In other cases, the government may not interfere with religious freedom, even for the common welfare. Here this declaration of freedom affirms the principle that also formed the core of Murray's juridical work: "as much freedom as possible and only as much restriction as necessary."[103] Government's intervention in the sphere of religion is very limited.

Chapter 2 (numbers 9–14) examines "religious freedom in the light of revelation" by exploring the scriptural and theological roots of religious freedom. In chapter 1, DH demonstrated that the Church has learned through reason and experience that religious freedom is required by the dignity of the human person. Chapter 2 reaffirms the consistency of this modern insight with the deposit of faith. Although the right is rooted in human dignity, "this doctrine of freedom is rooted in divine revelation, and for this reason Christians are bound to respect it all the more conscientiously" (9). In chapter 2 "two fundamental points of doctrine are developed: (1) religious freedom as a right of the person to immunity from external coercion in religious matters is not *formally* enunciated in revelation; (2) religious freedom understood in this sense has its roots in revelation."[104] This scriptural chapter softens the juridical tone of the declaration and addresses the criticism that DH was too political and juridical in style and content. This effort did not assuage Protestant critics of the declaration; they argued that the human dignity and natural law aspects of the argument were overemphasized.

From a Catholic theological rather than juridical perspective, "two doctrines are immediately relevant: 1) the freedom of the Church, both as a spiritual authority and as a spiritual community in its own right, and 2) the necessary freedom of the act of Christian faith."[105] First, as number 10 affirms quite simply, "man's response to God by faith ought to be free." God draws us to himself and we respond freely. So too the Church "convert[s] men to confess Christ as Lord, not however by applying coercion . . . but, above all, by the power of the word of God" (11).

Second, the Church must have freedom, "nothing more." "The freedom of the Church is the fundamental principle governing relations between the Church and public authorities and the whole civil order" (13). Read in conjunction with chapter 1, this sentence is of great significance. "Implicit in it is the renunciation by the Church of a condition of legal privilege in society. The Church does not make, as a matter of right or of divine law, the claim that she should be established as the 'religion of the state.' Her claim is freedom, nothing more."[106] This is the new thesis: the freedom of the Church, not the establishment of the Church. In the use of this freedom, moreover, the disciple must act "without having recourse to methods which are contrary to the spirit of the gospel" (14).

EXCURSUS

Pope John Paul II has been the most influential interpreter of DH. As Archbishop of Krakow,

Karol Wojtyla attended every session of the council. He offered written and oral interventions on religious freedom in both September 1964 and September 1965, during the third and fourth sessions. Both times he emphasized the important link between freedom and truth. Both DH and the First Amendment recognized that religious truth does not provide a sound foundation for a civil right to religious freedom. Nonetheless, as bishop and as pope, John Paul has consistently emphasized truth over freedom and accentuated the theological demands of truth over the juridical rights of freedom. Hence his papal teachings have weakened DH's juridical argument and reinstated the truth claims that plagued the preconciliar Church.

In the September 1964 intervention, Wojtyla insisted that religious freedom is not merely a negative immunity; it is freedom *for* the truth. "It was only by living in the truth that the human person was set free."[107] At the fourth session, he again stressed the connection of freedom, truth, and responsibility.[108] On September 22, 1965, he "insisted that the text should emphasize 'the responsibility to seek the truth' as much as the freedom to pursue it. He wanted it to be made clear that there were some 'limits' to religious liberty, some concessions that could not be made for fear of falling into 'indifferentism.'"[109]

Professor Rico has elucidated this conciliar stance by explaining that Wojtyla rejected religious freedom as a "mere principle of tolerance."[110] Tolerance is insufficient because

> it means too much resignation with the "status quo" and does nothing to lessen the division [within Christianity]. The objective of the ecumenical effort cannot be just greater toleration of differences, but, it should rather be, through greater incentive to the efforts to reach the truth, more progress in the acceptance of the truth by all, "for *nothing else but the truth* will free us from separations of many kinds."[111]

In other words, Wojtyla wanted the declaration to emphasize "objective, not just subjective, truth."[112] Given his position on objective truth and ecumenism, it is not surprising that Wojtyla emphasized the Church's right to evangelize when he and the Polish bishops proposed an alternative draft of *Gaudium et spes*.[113]

On this point of truth, Wojtyla was at odds with Murray. Both believed that Catholicism was true. Throughout the long drafting of DH, however, Murray had sought the best foundation for the right to religious freedom; as we have seen, he eventually rejected "conscience" and "truth" in favor of "dignity." Murray concluded that "the obligation to search after the truth" was inadequate as a basis for the right to religious freedom. "Truth" did not protect the erroneous conscience or limit the powers of the state. If religious freedom were a right of truth, for example, the public authority would be able to say to the individual:

> But, sorry to say, we judge you to be in error. For in the sphere of religion we possess objective truth. More than that, in this society we represent the common good as well as religious truth—in fact, religious truth is an integral part of the common good. . . . we acknowledge no duty on our part to refrain from coercion in your regard when in the public life of society, which is our concern, you set about introducing your false forms of worship or spreading your errors. Continue, then, your search for truth until you find it—we possess it—so that you may be able to act in public in keeping with it.[114]

Murray and the final text of DH opted for the dignity of the human person. In his commentary on the declaration, however, he acknowledged that, although the right to religious freedom is fundamental, the argument about religious freedom's intellectual foundation was not "final and decisive."[115] It awaited further inquiry within the Church. After he became pope, Wojtyla pushed the inquiry toward the foundation of truth.

At the Council, the archbishop also proposed a stronger theological argument for the declaration. Scripture and revelation must complement the natural law. "Perhaps concerned that its opponents would, in defeat, claim that the only 'authority' behind the declaration was that of human reason, Wojtyla submitted a written intervention urging that the document make an even stronger case for religious freedom as a matter of God's revealed will for the world and for human beings."[116]

Finally, in contrast to the American and Western European bishops, Wojtyla viewed DH from the perspective of the Church's oppression in communist Poland. This explains why, on September 20, 1965, he "'thundered away' against Pavan's draft" about the state's interventions to protect public order.[117] Recall that DH's description of public order suffered from "vagueness" and imprecision.[118] Bishops in communist nations did not want to give the state new excuses to interfere with religious freedom on behalf of public order. "The Poles did not like this criterion of 'public order' because it was precisely what their government used as a cloak for its arbitrary acts of repression."[119] Americans saw DH as a defense of the First Amendment, toleration, and the limited constitutional state. In contrast, Wojtyla

> saw the Decree on Religious Liberty as a weapon that could be used against the Communist regime under which he grudgingly lived. He brought the Eastern bishops to support the decree, which helped, with North American, French, Dutch, and German votes, to enable it to achieve a conciliar majority against the solid bloc of Spanish, Portuguese, and Latin Americans (and not a few Italians) who couldn't—at the time—begin to imagine their societies adopting such a program.[120]

Vatican II ended what Professor Rico has identified as the "first moment" in DH's history, namely, "Religious Freedom Replaces Established Catholicism."[121] During the reign of the pope from the communist world, he argues, DH enjoyed a "second moment" of the "Freedom of the Church against Atheistic Communism"[122] as well as a "third moment" of "The Challenges of Secularism and Relativism"[123] at the end of the cold war.

Led by John Paul II, during the "second moment" Catholics throughout the world used the universal language of DH to claim religious freedom against oppressive governments. The Church became a powerful defender of religious freedom against governments throughout the world. Hence the document became primarily a tool to employ against the power of the *state* rather than a critique of the *Church's* opposition to the civil rights of non-Catholics. "What this second moment did was to reorganize the balance of the reception of the document, putting more emphasis on what it demanded from governments than on what it committed the church to pursue and promote by example."[124] Once the focus was on the conduct of governments, it was natural for the pope to emphasize anew the subject that had been so important to him at the Council, namely, that religious freedom is freedom for the truth. Yet this proclamation of truth established an inevitable tension between the pope and the declaration.

It was the preconciliar Church's claims to truth that had caused the problem that DH had to solve. First, as Bishop deSmedt had explained, the Catholic claims of truth had offended non-Catholics. Second, as Murray and Pavan had demonstrated, truth was an inadequate foundation for a human and civil right to religious freedom. John Paul's emphasis on truth brought the debate on religious freedom full circle as DH began its "third moment" of "The Challenges of Secularism and Relativism"[125] at the end of the cold war.

First, the pope's emphasis on truth turned the ecumenical discussion away from the public rights of non-Catholic individuals and back toward the truth claims of the Catholic Church. This shift has been most evident in papal statements on ecumenism. While acknowledging the importance of ecumenism, the pope has insisted, in *Ut unum sint* and other writings, that other religions must recognize that the Catholic Church alone possesses the truth. It is difficult, however, to sustain ecumenism when one party claims to possess the absolute truth. Many non-Catholics objected, for example, when the Congregation for the Doctrine of the Faith issued the declaration

Dominus Jesus in September 2000. This instruction emphasized the evangelizing mission of the Church to spread the truth to everyone, including members of other religions. It warned that the Church was endangered by "relativistic theories which seek to justify religious pluralism" (4) and that ecumenism must never undermine the Church's "character of absolute truth and salvific universality" (4). Forgotten were DH's ecumenism and its warnings against "proselytism" (4).

Second, in the pope's teaching, this claim to absolute truth is not merely a theological statement of faith. It also forms the basis for the pope's juridical argument that the Church's truth provides the appropriate foundation for civil law. At Vatican II, Jacques Maritain had taught Pope Paul to accept the demise of the sacral state and to celebrate the autonomy of the modern state. John Murray had believed in the truth of Catholicism, but had brilliantly and persuasively convinced the Council that such truth did not form the foundation of the civil order.

John Paul does not share this commitment to autonomous civil government. Instead, most notably in his encyclical letters *Veritatis splendor* and *Evangelium vitae*, he has been a vehement critic of the "moral relativism" of democracy.[126] This defender of truth has not accepted the religious and moral pluralism that characterizes modern democracies. Pluralism is untruthful. Instead, his writings identify moral truths (on a range of topics, from abortion to capital punishment, homosexuality, marriage and social justice to contraception) that must become civil law. The result is a theory of civil law that is excessively entangled with theological doctrine.

This stance—that the Church's teachings must become established law—is reminiscent of the preconciliar "error has no rights" position; it holds that non-Catholics must be governed by Catholicism's moral teaching. In 2002, the Church reminded Catholic politicians of their moral obligation to vote the Church's positions into law without compromise.[127] Some leading American Catholic politicians have responded, however (citing President Kennedy), that this teaching contradicts their obligations to non-Catholic citizens.[128] It does. In the United States, "the Establishment Clause is intended to prevent a religious majority from using its political power to dominate the lives of nonadherents to the majority faith."[129] DH contains no comparable provision; it left the establishment topic unresolved. Hence, in interpreting DH, the pope has fought worldwide for Free Exercise (a universal right to public worship) and for establishment (of the Church's moral teachings as civil law). In other words, although DH shows the influence of the free exercise clause of the First Amendment on its drafters, neither DH nor John Paul has accepted the other half of the wisdom of the American experiment, namely, that disestablishment best protects religious freedom.

Thus in the second and third moments of DH—in battles against atheistic communism, secularism, and relativism—it became a tool against states rather than a blueprint for the Church. This outcome disappoints the predictions of the drafters, who saw in DH a commitment to freedom within the Church. In one introduction to DH, Murray predicted that "inevitably, a second great argument will be set afoot now—on the theological meaning of Christian freedom."[130] Despite the emphasis on the Church's freedom in chapter 2, Murray acknowledged that DH never addressed this question of religious freedom within the Church.[131] DH included no "theology of freedom" for Catholics. "The issue of freedom within the Church is neuralgic today,"[132] he wrote in 1966, before his death a year later.

In 1977, Pavan sketched the impact of DH on the Church's life before the First World Congress on Religious Freedom in Amsterdam. In that address he rejected the argument that DH's right of religious freedom had no implications for the internal life of the Church. If the human person has a right to religious freedom, he argued, "obviously, the right holds for Catholics as such, as members of the Church."[133] Within the Church, Pavan thought that the repercussions of DH were already evident in "a process of readjustment . . . not yet in sight of its end" that had "some fundamental tendencies," namely:

- a wider, more insistent demand, recognized by members of the hierarchy themselves, that authority should be exercised as a service
- a reduction of the punitive aspects of discipline
- a reordering of the relations between laity and hierarchy and between the various grades of the hierarchy itself, aimed at giving a more ample air of liberty—understood and lived as an exercise of responsibility—to all members of the Church, making them share more consciously and actively in its life; greater initiative and autonomy to the laity in their effort to christianize the temporal order.[134]

Pavan may have been accurate that these trends were present in the Church in 1977. Today he sounds naïve. In 1978, Wojtyla took the papal throne, and truth gained the upper hand. Since then, Murray's and Pavan's hopes for a theology of freedom and a right of religious freedom within the Church have not been realized. Pope John Paul II has championed the freedom of the Church against the state in the juridical and political realms while resisting religious freedom within the Church. The Vatican investigations of theologians and the new restrictions on academic freedom in Catholic universities identified in *Ex corde ecclesiae* confirm that truth takes priority over free theological inquiry.

REACTIONS TO THE DOCUMENT

"What now seems inevitable came close to not happening."[135] Some outsiders who had witnessed the conciliar intrigue and the delayed votes had doubted that DH would be approved. Many Christian churches had insisted that a declaration on religious freedom was essential to ecumenism. For this reason, "the entire world breathed a sigh of relief"[136] at DH's passage. "The Council's protestations of commitment to ecumenism would have met reactions of skepticism if the clarion note of liberty had not been sounded."[137]

Positive responses to DH appeared from member churches of the WCC and from nonmembers such as Southern Baptists and Pentecostals. Yet the praise was not unqualified. Despite "relief" at the declaration, many Protestants concluded that Catholics were late to the conversation and criticized DH's style of argument.[138] Although Protestant theologians noted the similarity of DH's "practical conclusions" to WCC statements on religious freedom, for example, they decided that some scriptural and theological arguments were undeveloped.[139] These responses reflected classical Protestant-Catholic disputes about theology and human nature. While invoking Reinhold Niebuhr *contra* Murray, for example, Lutheran theologian and council observer George Lindbeck remarked, "The Protestant tends to make not human dignity but human sinfulness the foundation of religious liberty."[140] Thus Protestants could agree with the "subject" and "content" of DH while disapproving its "foundations."[141]

Members of the "'free church' tradition . . . namely Baptist, Mennonites, Brethren, Disciples"[142] determined that DH had "recognized and validated" four centuries of support for religious freedom by "Protestantism's so-called radical wing."[143] Nonetheless, led by Methodist Franklin Littell, they complained that Murray had misread history, both constitutional and religious. Roger Williams was as important as Thomas Jefferson to the First Amendment. Moreover, free church support of religious liberty had been unwavering for centuries, antedating both DH and the First Amendment.[144] Littell "enter[ed] a demurrer to the notion that the discussion of religious liberty begins with the American experiment."[145]

In his initial response, Littell also commented that DH's arguments about "the nature of a just government" were inadequately developed.[146] While DH emphasized the rights of the human person and the nature of the Church, it neglected the theme that religious freedom leads to "an important breakthrough in government,"[147] indeed, that religious freedom "makes a better government."[148] Such an argument might have demonstrated a stronger commitment by the Church to constitutional government and civil rights.[149]

Professor Philip Denenfeld offered a different perspective on the constitutional argument. Although Murray had considered the declaration a vindication of the first amendment, Denenfeld argued that, unlike the Bill of Rights, DH's "primary commitment . . . is to religion, not to freedom."[150] Denenfeld had spotted the tension within the "one true religion" argument; he recognized the paradox that religious freedom was "endorsed as a human right, but tied to the conviction that its proper use will lead to a predetermined religious truth."[151] Such conflict between the values of the Constitution and DH suggested that the application of DH's juridical norms within a nation's legal system would be difficult.

Although Judge Noonan has hailed DH as a "substantial accomplishment," he also compared DH to a piece of legislation, noting that three of its "inadequacies" are due to its legislative assemblage:

> Three large inadequacies, then—the failure to deal with history, the failure to deal with the implications of an establishment, the vague and tangled treatment of the civil power's right to limit actions based on religious convictions. In its failures, the Declaration reflected its character as a document composed by a committee issuing from a legislature-like assembly.[152]

DH's inadequacies on these and other questions provided Pope John Paul II with the opportunity to interpret DH to reflect his own vision of Church and state, one rooted in Poland instead of France, Spain, or the United States.

Looking back on DH after forty years, it remains to be seen how a post–John Paul II Church will interpret and utilize the *Decree on Religious Freedom*. Nonetheless, it retains its historical importance as the document that finally engaged the Church with democracy and liberalism in the lucid, limited, and late argument of paragraph 2: that Catholics must acknowledge religious freedom as the right of every human person, a right that must be protected by the limited constitutional state.

NOTES

1. John Courtney Murray, "The Declaration on Religious Freedom," in *War, Poverty, Freedom: The Christian Response, Concilium*, vol. 15, ed., Franz Böckle (New York: Paulist, 1966), 4.

2. Pietro Pavan, "The Right to Religious Freedom in the Conciliar Declaration," in *Religious Freedom*, ed. Neophytos Edelby and Teodoro Jiménez-Urresti (New York: Paulist, 1966), 39.

3. John Courtney Murray, "The Problem of Religious Freedom," in *Religious Liberty: Catholic Struggles with Pluralism*, ed. J. Leon Hooper (Louisville, Ky.: Westminster/John Knox, 1993), 170.

4. John Courtney Murray, "Current Theology: Christian Co-operation," *Theological Studies* 3 (1942): 413–31.

5. "Indifferentism" and "Syllabus of Errors," in *The HarperCollins Encyclopedia of Catholicism*, ed. Richard P. McBrien (San Francisco: HarperCollins, 1995), 662, 1233, respectively.

6. John Courtney Murray, "Current Theology: On Religious Freedom," *Theological Studies* 10 (1949): 409–32.

7. Thomas T. Love, *John Courtney Murray: Contemporary Church-State Theory* (New York: Doubleday, 1965), 29–30.

8. Jay Dolan, *In Search of American Catholicism: A History of Religion and Culture in Tension* (Oxford: Oxford University Press, 2002), 99–107.

9. Ibid., 107–8.

10. John Courtney Murray, "Current Theology: Intercredal Co-operation: Its Theory and Its Organization," *Theological Studies* 4 (1943): 257–86.

11. Paul Hanly Furfey, "To the Editor," *Theological Studies* 4 (1943): 463.

12. U.S. Const., Amend I, §1.

13. Celestine Bohlen, "Benjamin Welles, Biographer and Journalist Is Dead at 85," *New York Times*, January 4, 2002, C10 (citing B. Welles, *New York Times Magazine*, 1960).

14. Address of Senator John F. Kennedy to the Greater Houston Ministerial Association, Rice Hotel, Houston, Texas, September 12, 1960, available at http://www.jfklibrary.org/j091260.htm (downloaded April 3, 2005).

15. Donald E. Pelotte, *John Courtney Murray: Theologian in Conflict* (New York: Paulist, 1975), 76.

16. Ibid., 38.

17. René Girault, "The Reception of Ecumenism," in *The Reception of Vatican II*, ed. Giuseppe Alberigo and Joseph A. Komonchak (Washington, D.C.: Catholic University of America Press, 1987), 137.

18. James E. Wood Jr., "Religious Liberty in Ecumenical and International Perspective," *Journal of Church and State* 10 (1968): 432.

19. Joseph A. Komonchak, "The Struggle for the Council during the Preparation of Vatican II (1960–1962)," in *History of Vatican II*, vol. 1: *Announcing and Preparing Vatican Council II: Toward a New Era in Catholicism*, ed. G. Alberigo and J. A. Komonchak (Maryknoll, N.Y.: Orbis, 1995), 171.

20. Ibid., 200, 263.

21. Ibid., 227.

22. Ibid., 287.

23. Andrea Riccardi, "The Tumultuous Opening Days of the Council," in *History of Vatican II*, vol. 2: *The Formation of the Council's Identity: First Period and Intersession: October 1962–September 1963*, ed. G. Alberigo and J. A. Komonchak (Maryknoll, N.Y.: Orbis, 1997), 44–47.

24. Ibid., 45–46.

25. Pietro Pavan, "Ecumenism and Vatican II's Declaration on Religious Freedom," in *Religious Freedom: 1965 & 1975, A Symposium on a Historic Document*, ed. Walter J. Burghardt (New York: Paulist, 1977), 7.

26. Komonchak, "The Struggle," in *Announcing and Preparing Vatican Council II*, 296.

27. Ibid., 297.

28. Ibid.

29. Ibid.

30. Pietro Pavan, "Declaration on Religious Freedom," in *Commentary on the Documents of Vatican II*, vol. 4, ed. Herbert Vorgrimler (New York: Herder and Herder, 1969), 50.

31. Ibid.

32. Komonchak, "The Struggle," in *Announcing and Preparing Vatican Council II*, 298.

33. Ibid.

34. Pelotte, *Murray*, 81.

35. Ibid.

36. Ibid., 83.

37. Ibid., 82.

38. Pavan, "Declaration," in *Commentary*, vol. 4, ed. H. Vorgrimler, 51–62.

39. Evangelista Vilanova, "The Intersession (1963–1964)," in *History of Vatican II*, vol. 3: *The Mature Council Second Period and Intersession. September 1963–September 1964*, ed. G. Alberigo and J. A. Komonchak (Maryknoll, N.Y.: Orbis, 2000), 434.

40. Pelotte, *Murray*, 94.

41. Ibid., 95.

42. Ibid., 96.

43. Bernard Doering explained to me the details of this exchange; Philippe Chenaux, *Paul VI et Maritain* (Brescia: Instituto Paolo VI, 1994), 83–86.

44. Jacques Maritain, "No. 2—La Liberté Religieuse," in *Oeuvres complètes*, vol. 16 (Fribourg: Éditions universitaires, 1982), 1086–91.

45. John T. Noonan Jr., *The Lustre of Our Country: The American Experience of Religious Freedom* (Berkeley: University of California Press, 1998), 350.

46. Peter Hebblethwaite, *Paul VI: The First Modern Pope* (New York: Paulist, 1993), 417–18.

47. Ibid., 419.

48. Ibid.

49. Ibid.

50. Maritain, "No. 2," in *Oeuvres complètes*, vol. 16, 1087.

51. Hebblethwaite, *Paul VI*, 434.

52. Ibid., 434–35.

53. Ibid.

54. John Courtney Murray, "Declaration on Religious Freedom," in *American Participation in the Second Vatican Council*, ed. Vincent A. Yzermans (New York: Sheed and Ward, 1967), 623.

55. John Courtney Murray, "Religious Freedom," in *The Documents of Vatican II*, ed. Walter M. Abbott (New York: Guild, 1966), 672.

56. Murray, "Declaration on Religious Freedom," 668.

57. Ibid., 617.

58. Noonan, *Lustre of Our Country*, 353.

59. Murray, "Religious Freedom," 673.

60. John Courtney Murray, "The Declaration on Religious Freedom," in *Vatican II: An Interfaith Appraisal*, ed. John H. Miller (Notre Dame, Ind.: Association, 1966), 565.

61. Murray, "Religious Freedom," in *Documents*, 673 (emphasis added).

62. J. Bryan Hehir, "*Dignitatis Humanae* in the Pontificate of John Paul II," in *Religious Liberty: Paul VI and Dignitatis Humanae*, ed. John T. Ford (Brescia: Istituto Paolo VI, 1995), 170.

63. Ibid.

64. Ibid., 169.

65. John Courtney Murray, "The *Declaration on Religious Freedom*: A Moment in Its Legislative

History," in *Religious Liberty: An End and a Beginning*, ed. J. C. Murray (New York: Macmillan, 1966), 26.

66. Thomas F. Stransky, *Declaration on Religious Freedom of Vatican Council II* (New York: Paulist, 1966), 20, no. 11.

67. Hehir, "*Dignitatis Humanae*," in *Religious Liberty*, ed. J. T. Ford, 170.

68. Émile Joseph de Smedt, "Religious Liberty," in *Council Speeches of Vatican II*, ed. Hans Kung, Yves Congar, and Daniel O'Hanlon (Glen Rock, N.J.: Paulist, 1964), 238.

69. Ibid., 237–38.

70. John Courtney Murray, "This Matter of Religious Freedom," *America* 112 (January 9, 1965): 42.

71. Murray, "A Moment," in *Religious Liberty*, ed. J. C. Murray, 16.

72. Ibid., 16; de Smedt, "Religious Liberty," in *Council Speeches*, ed. H. Kung et al., 240.

73. de Smedt, "Religious Liberty," in *Council Speeches*, ed. H. Kung et al., 243.

74. Murray, "A Moment," in *Religious Liberty*, ed. J. C. Murray, 26.

75. Murray, "This Matter," 40–43.

76. Ibid., 40.

77. Frank Lambert, *The Founding Fathers and the Place of Religion in America* (Princeton, N.J.: Princeton University Press, 2003), 3.

78. Ibid.

79. Ibid., 40 (emphasis added).

80. Murray, "A Moment," in *Religious Liberty*, ed. J. C. Murray, 27–28.

81. Murray, "This Matter," 40 (emphasis added).

82. Ibid., 42.

83. Henri Fesquet, *The Drama of Vatican II: The Ecumenical Council June, 1962–December, 1965*, trans. Bernard Murchland (New York: Random House, 1967), 256.

84. John Courtney Murray, "Meaning of the Document," in *Declaration on Religious Liberty and Declaration on the Relationship of the Church to Non-Christian Religions*, ed. John Courtney Murray and Robert A. Graham (New York: America Press, 1966), 4.

85. Hebblethwaite, *Paul VI*, 420.

86. J. Robert Nelson, "The Ecumenical Reception of the *Dignitatis Humanae* Declaration of the Second Vatican Council," *Ecumenical Trends* 24 (May 1995): 67.

87. Victor G. Rosenblum, "The Conciliar Document: A Politico-Legal Excursus," in *Religious Liberty: An End and a Beginning*, ed. John Courtney Murray (New York: Macmillan, 1966), 110.

88. Murray was influenced by Bernard Lonergan's "contrast between historical and classical consciousness." John Courtney Murray, "Appendix: Toledo Talk," in *Bridging the Sacred and the Secular*, ed. J. Leon Hooper (Washington, D.C.: Georgetown University Press, 1994), 334.

89. John Courtney Murray and Robert A. Graham, eds., *Declaration on Religious Liberty and Declaration on the Relationship of the Church to Non-Christian Religions* (New York: America Press, 1966), 10, no. 5 (emphasis added).

90. Murray, "This Matter," 40.

91. Ibid.

92. Noonan, *Lustre of Our Country*, 350.

93. Ibid.

94. Murray, "Declaration on Religious Freedom," in *Vatican II: Interfaith Appraisal*, ed. J. H. Miller, 579.

95. Ibid., 580.

96. Rosenblum, "The Conciliar Document," in *Religious Liberty*, ed. J. C. Murray, 112.

97. John Courtney Murray, "Annotations to 'Religious Freedom,'" in *Documents*, ed. W. M. Abbott, 682–83, no. 10.

98. Ibid., 685, no. 17.

99. Noonan, *Lustre of Our Country*, 351.

100. Murray, "Annotations," in *Documents*, ed. W. M. Abbott, 685, no. 17.

101. Pietro Pavan, "Repercussions of the Declaration 'Dignitatis Humanae' in the Life of the Church," *First World Congress on Religious Freedom* (March 21–23, 1977): 56.

102. Murray, "Annotations," in *Documents*, ed. W. M. Abbott, 686, no. 20.

103. Murray, "This Matter," 40.

104. Pavan, "Right to Religious Freedom in the Conciliar Declaration," in *Religious Freedom*, ed. N. Edelby and T. Jiménez-Urresti, 49.

105. Murray, "This Matter," 41.

106. Murray, "Annotations," in *Documents*, ed. W. M. Abbott, 693, no. 53.

107. George Weigel, *Witness to Hope: The Biography of Pope John Paul II* (New York: HarperCollins, 1999), 164.

108. Ibid., 165.

109. Peter Hebblethwaite, *Synod Extraordinary: The Inside Story of the Rome Synod November–*

December 1985 (Garden City, N.Y.: Doubleday, 1986), 16–17.

110. Herminio Rico, *John Paul II and the Legacy of Dignitatis Humanae* (Washington, D.C.: Georgetown University Press, 2002), 105.

111. Ibid., 106 (emphasis added).

112. Ibid.

113. Ibid., 107–12.

114. John Courtney Murray, "Arguments for the Human Right to Religious Freedom," in *Religious Liberty: Catholic Struggles with Pluralism*, ed. J. Leon Hooper (Louisville, Ky.: Westminster/John Knox, 1993), 235.

115. Murray, "Annotations," in *Documents*, ed. W. M. Abbott, 680, no. 7.

116. Weigel, *Witness to Hope*, 165.

117. Hebblethwaite, *Synod*, 17.

118. Noonan, *Lustre of Our Country*, 350.

119. Hebblethwaite, *Synod*, 17.

120. Thomas Cahill, *Pope John XXIII* (New York: Penguin, 2002), 219.

121. Rico, *John Paul II*, 4.

122. Ibid., chap. 1.

123. Ibid., 12.

124. Ibid., 10.

125. Ibid., 12.

126. I develop this argument in detail in Leslie Griffin, "Evangelium Vitae: Abortion," in *Readings in Moral Theology, No. 10*, ed. Charles E. Curran and Richard A. McCormick (New York: Paulist, 1998), and "Good Catholics Should Be Rawlsian Liberals," *Southern California Interdisciplinary Law Journal* 5 (1997): 297.

127. Congregation for the Doctrine of the Faith, *Doctrinal Note on Some Questions Regarding the Participation of Catholics in Political Life*, November 24, 2002, available at http://www.usccb.org/dpp/congregation.htm (downloaded April 3, 2005).

128. Michael Paulson, "Catholic Politicians Warned on Dissent," *Boston Globe*, January 17, 2003.

129. Steven G. Gey, "When Is Religious Speech Not 'Free Speech'?" *University of Illinois Law Review* 2000, no. 2 (2000): 390.

130. Murray, "Meaning of the Document," 5.

131. Murray, "Declaration on Religious Freedom," in *War, Poverty, Freedom*, 4.

132. Ibid., 5.

133. Pavan, "Repercussions," 53.

134. Ibid.

135. Noonan, *Lustre of Our Country*, 352.

136. Jerald C. Brauer, "Religious Freedom as a Human Right," in *Religious Liberty*, ed. J. C. Murray, 45.

137. Nelson, "The Ecumenical Reception," 67.

138. Wood, "Religious Liberty," 434.

139. Nelson, "The Ecumenical Reception," 69.

140. George Lindbeck, "Critical Reflections," in *Religious Freedom: 1965 & 1975*, ed. W. J. Burghardt, 53.

141. Ibid., 52.

142. Nelson, "The Ecumenical Reception," 72.

143. Ibid.

144. Ibid. See also Franklin Littell, "The Significance of the Declaration on Religious Liberty," *Journal of Ecumenical Studies* 5 (winter 1968): 333.

145. Littell, "Significance," 333.

146. Franklin Littell, "A Response," in *Documents*, ed. W. M. Abbott, 699.

147. Ibid.

148. Ibid., 700.

149. Francis J. Canavan, "The Catholic Concept of Religious Freedom as a Human Right," in *Religious Liberty*, ed. J. C. Murray, 79.

150. Philip S. Denenfeld, "The Conciliar Declaration and the American Declaration," in ibid., 120.

151. Ibid.

152. Noonan, *Lustre of Our Country*, 351.

SELECTED BIBLIOGRAPHY

Alberigo, Giuseppe, and Joseph A. Komonchak, eds. *History of Vatican II*. 3 vols. Maryknoll, N.Y.: Orbis, 1995, 1997, 2000. A thorough history of the Council that explains how DH was drafted.

Murray, John Courtney. "This Matter of Religious Freedom." *America* 112 (January 9, 1965): 40–43. This and the following essays explain how the lead drafter of DH developed the argument about religious freedom.

——. "The Declaration on Religious Freedom." In *War, Poverty, Freedom: The Christian Response, Concilium*, vol. 15. Edited by Franz Böckle. New York: Paulist, 1966.

——. "The Declaration on Religious Freedom." In *Vatican II: An Interfaith Appraisal*. Edited by John H. Miller. Notre Dame, Ind.: Association, 1966.

——. "The Declaration on Religious Freedom: A Moment in Its Legislative History." In *Reli-*

gious Liberty: An End and a Beginning. Edited by J. C. Murray. New York: Macmillan, 1966.

——. "Declaration on Religious Freedom: Commentary." In *American Participation in the Second Vatican Council*. Edited by Vincent A. Yzermans. New York: Sheed and Ward, 1967.

——. "Religious Freedom." In *The Documents of Vatican II*. Edited by Walter M. Abbott. New York: Guild, 1966.

Nelson, J. Robert. "The Ecumenical Reception of the *Dignitatis Humanae* Declaration of the Second Vatican Council." *Ecumenical Trends* 24 (May 1995): 67–72. A good account of DH's reception in Protestant churches.

Pavan, Pietro. "Declaration on Religious Freedom." In *Commentary on the Documents of Vatican II*, vol. 4. Edited by Herbert Vorgrimler. New York: Herder and Herder, 1969. An explanation of DH's argument by its codrafter.

——. "Ecumenism and Vatican II's Declaration on Religious Freedom." In *Religious Freedom: 1965 & 1975: A Symposium on a Historic Document*. Edited by Walter J. Burghardt. New York: Paulist, 1977. An explanation of DH's argument by its codrafter.

——. "Repercussions of the Declaration 'Dignitatis Humanae' in the Life of the Church." *First World Congress on Religious Freedom* (March 21–23,1977): 52–64. Coauthor's reflections on the impact of DH after twelve years.

——. "The Right to Religious Freedom in the Conciliar Declaration." In *Religious Freedom*. Edited by Neophytos Edelby and Teodoro Jiménez-Urresti. New York: Paulist, 1966.

Regan, Richard J. *Conflict and Consensus: Religious Freedom and the Second Vatican Council*. New York: Macmillan, 1967. Best book-length treatment of DH's development.

Rico, Herminio. *John Paul II and the Legacy of Dignitatis Humanae*. Washington, D.C.: Georgetown University Press, 2002. Most recent book-length treatment, important for its analysis of DH's role in the Church of Pope John Paul II.

CHAPTER 11

Commentary on *Gaudium et spes* (*Pastoral Constitution on the Church in the Modern World*)

DAVID HOLLENBACH, S.J.

INTRODUCTION

Gaudium et spes (*Pastoral Constitution on the Church in the Modern World*) is one of the four major constitutions of Vatican II. Promulgated on December 7, 1965, the last day of the Council, it embodied John XXIII's desire that the Council should address the challenges facing the Church in the mid-twentieth century in a way that was above all pastoral. The constitution's common Latin name, *Gaudium et spes* (joy and hope), sounds the leitmotif of its whole message: "The joys and the hopes, the grief and anguish of the people of our time, especially those who are poor and afflicted, are the joys and hopes, the grief and anguish of the followers of Christ" (1).[1] In light of these realities, the document makes a major new contribution to modern Catholic social teaching by presenting more explicitly developed theological grounds for the Church's social engagement than are found in the earlier social encyclicals. The Church is concerned with all human struggles for life with dignity, with building up the solidarity of the human community, and with the humanization of all human activity and work. GS also presents practical aspects of Catholic social teaching in the familial, cultural, economic, political, and international spheres. Overall, it can be regarded as the most authoritative and significant document of Catholic social teaching issued in the twentieth century.

OUTLINE OF THE DOCUMENT

The introduction presents a schematic reading of the situation of the human race today (the "signs of the times") and states the Council's goal of interpreting contemporary conditions "in the light of the Gospel" (4). Deep social changes have raised new questions that must be addressed in ways that respond to humanity's desire for a life that is full, free, and worthy of human nature. GS voices the Council's conviction that Christ and the Church can respond to these questionings.

Part 1 addresses "The Church and the Human Vocation." Chapter 1 treats "The Dignity of the Human Person" as the focus for the Church's concern in the social, economic, political, and cultural domains. The Church is concerned with the promotion of human dignity, for this dignity reflects the creation of men and women in the image of God and their redemption by Christ. Chapter 2, titled "The Human Community," treats the communal or social dimensions of the human vocation. Disciples of

Christ must be especially concerned with building up solidarity, for human dignity can only be attained in community with others. Thus, the pursuit of equality and justice requires a morality that goes beyond individualism to an ethic grounded in participation in community. Chapter 3 argues that concern for human dignity means that the humanization of all human activity and work is part of Christian discipleship. It affirms that the cultural, scientific, and technological labors of humanity should enjoy a rightful autonomy from the Church and that social development must be distinguished from the establishment of God's kingdom. These social and cultural achievements, however, make genuine contributions to the building up of God's reign. Chapter 4 explicitly addresses the interaction of the Church with society, showing how the Christian community can both contribute to and learn from domains of life often regarded as secular.

Part 2 deals with more specific areas of social life in which "problems of special urgency" are discerned. Chapter 1 treats marriage and family life. Chapter 2 deals with the significance of culture for the mission of the Church. Chapter 3 addresses aspects of social and economic life, especially the significance of work and economic development in poor countries. Chapter 4 treats political life and chapter 5 the international dimensions of politics, such as the promotion of peace, the dangers of war, and the building up of an international community. The themes treated in the chapters of Part 2 will be dealt with selectively here.[2] The document ends with a conclusion stressing how the gospel can illuminate the entire human enterprise through dialogue between Church and world, and how this dialogue will in turn enable the Church to serve humanity in love.

CONTEXT OF THE DOCUMENT

Because GS seeks to relate the faith of the Church to the signs of the times, its analysis of the contemporary contexts is particularly important.

Social Context

The half century preceding the calling of Vatican II was a tumultuous time.[3] Two bloody world wars were waged from 1914 to 1919 and from 1939 to 1945. The two dominant images from World War II—the atomic bombing of Hiroshima and Nagasaki and the Holocaust—are still echoed in contemporary moral consciousness and broader public policy debates. The use of nuclear weapons by the United States initiated an arms race of unprecedented expense and terror; the Holocaust revealed the depths to which human evil could descend. Images of these events are seared into our historical memories. Indeed, the twentieth century may well qualify as the bloodiest hundred years in all of human history.

Yet out of this darkness arose a modest hope: the United Nations was formally established in 1945 as a successor to the failed League of Nations proposed after World War I. Though the UN remains a fragile institution with limited abilities to achieve its goals, it has played an active role in resolving some of the world's problems through debate, persuasion, and, to a limited extent, peacekeeping activities, on occasion including the enforcement of the peace by military means. The promulgation of the Declaration of Human Rights in 1948 was a particularly bright moment in articulating the dignity of the person as a normative standard to which all cultures and nations should be held accountable.

The issue of human dignity arose in a particular way in the United States during the mid-1950s as a result of the civil rights movement. Begun in nonviolent protest of discrimination against African Americans in schools, transportation, and other public places, it ignited a moral movement that resulted in significant gains in voting rights as well as helping to dismantle the system of desegregation and the Jim Crow laws that supported it. The struggle created deep controversy through its challenge to entrenched cultural systems based on racial distinctions. The outcome was some progress toward a more just society in the

United States and a new visibility for basic human rights.

Tensions between the Soviet Union and the United States, begun as the World War II alliance ended and as the Soviets tested their own atomic bomb, intensified in 1952, when the Soviets tested a hydrogen bomb and accelerated the arms race. In 1957, the Soviets put the first satellite, *Sputnik*, into space. Its sustained orbiting of Planet Earth suggested to many that the United States was lagging behind the Soviets in science and, therefore, in military technology as well. This provided further impetus to the arms race and influenced the military policies and overall budgets of the two superpowers, as well as those of other countries who wanted to keep up. The policies that resulted sought to deter war through threats of Mutually Assured Destruction (MAD).

Other important social movements were also unfolding during the same period. In the late 1950s and early 1960s, many African nations achieved independence from European colonial powers, signaling the waning of the age of empire. In 1959, Fidel Castro's revolution in Cuba established the first communist country in the Western Hemisphere, just a few miles from the coast of the United States. Also in the early 1960s, the Organization of Petroleum Exporting Countries (OPEC) was established by many of the major oil producers of the world. The Berlin Wall, built in 1961, was a vivid symbol of the tensions and hostilities of the cold war. The wall remained standing for nearly thirty years as a constant reminder of these tensions. The West saw it as a powerful sign of the failure of the communist system. In 1962, immediately after the beginning of Vatican II, the entire world was horrified by the prospect of impending nuclear conflagration when Soviet missiles and missile bases were discovered in Cuba. War was averted after three days of extraordinary tension when Soviet ships carrying more missiles to Cuba reversed course. Agreement was reached that the missile silos would be dismantled by the Soviet Union and that the United States would remove its missiles from Turkey.

In Vietnam, the United States picked up where France had left off with its intervention in that country's civil war. This engaged the United States militarily in Vietnam from the early 1960s to 1975. The conflict was seen by the United States as a war against communist expansion. The war deeply divided American society and was accompanied by highly visible protests. The antiwar movements of the 1960s and 1970s were accompanied by challenges to traditional cultural values, in both the United States and Western Europe. These cultural challenges largely occurred after the Council had concluded, but reactions to them had a notable influence on the way the impact of the Council was interpreted by some bishops and theologians.

Thus the Council was convoked in years when many in the West were experiencing new levels of prosperity, with new hope for human rights and for the overcoming of poverty in a world beginning to see new relations with emerging nations. As the Council opened, the world was mostly at peace. Yet it was also the time of the deep political tensions of the Cold War. All lived in the shadow of the Holocaust and many under the constant threat of nuclear annihilation. It was a time of profound political, economic, and cultural shifts, some achieved through bloody wars and independence movements and others through slow and complex political processes. Change was the order of the day, and the critical questions concerned who would direct this change and to what ends. The Council sought to present a Christian framework for response to these questions in GS.

Ecclesial Context

Following the intellectual and cultural shocks of the Enlightenment, the French Revolution, Marxism, and Darwinism, the Church had taken a stance of resistance to almost all of the movements characteristic of modern society and culture. This resistance was symbolized most graphically by Pius IX's declaring himself a prisoner of the Vatican, never to leave its grounds during the remainder of his papacy. Intellectually, this rejection of modernity was epitomized by Pius IX's *Syllabus of Errors* (1864), a set of condemnations intended to shore up the ramparts of an embattled Catholicism against modern ideas of progress and freedom that were seen as secularist threats.

This opposition to modern intellectual movements of the world beyond the Vatican was continued within the Church because of the fear that such movements were influencing clergy and professors of theology. Modernism, as this movement was called by the popes, was seen as presenting a grave danger to the Church because of its acceptance of the possibility and indeed the reality of change in Christian doctrine and its call to adapt the Christian community's self-understanding to the requirements of the intellectual currents of modern times. Pius X carried this fight forward in his encyclical *Pascendi dominici gregis* (1907) when he condemned those who affirmed the possibility of adaptation of doctrine: "they are seen to be under the sway of a blind and unchecked passion for novelty, thinking not at all of finding some solid foundation of truth, but despising the holy and apostolic traditions."[4]

This encyclical also established censors in each diocese for all publications as well as an elaborate reporting system—the Council of Vigilance—which was to meet with the bishop every two months. Reports were then to be made every three years to Rome. Years of censorship and rigorous monitoring of scholarship followed. Creative explorations on the relations between Catholic tradition and modern thought, such as those that had been launched by the theologians now known as the Tübingen school and by a number of biblical scholars, came to a halt. It is not unfair to say that the overall effect was to force creative scholarship by Catholic thinkers to the margins of the Church or beyond them.

In the face of this retrenchment and anti-intellectualism, a number of French-speaking theologians began a sustained effort in the 1930s to revive the intellectual life of the Church by addressing problems of the day from a theological perspective. These included Yves Congar, Henri de Lubac, Jean Daniélou, Marie-Dominique Chenu, Gustave Thils, and others. De Lubac's study, titled *Catholicism: Christ and the Common Destiny of Man*, stressed that Catholic faith is essentially a social faith. It is social not merely in its applications to the institutions of this-worldly life, but in itself and in its essence. Awareness of this social quality of faith "should have made the expression 'social Catholicism' pleonastic."[5] In a similar vein, works such as Gustave Thils's *Theology of Earthly Realities* and Yves Congar's *Lay People in the Church* stressed the continuities between the kingdom of God and the social life in earthly history in innovative ways. These efforts came to be called the *théologie nouvelle*. The work of these theologians and of others pursuing parallel projects, such as Karl Rahner in Germany and Edward Schillebeeckx in The Netherlands, laid the groundwork for GS.[6]

At the time, negative reaction to this work by official church leadership resulted in the removal of some of these theologians from their teaching positions and the withdrawal of their articles and books from circulation. During the same period, however, some hope in the possibility of openness to new intellectual currents was raised by Pius XII's 1943 encyclical *Divino afflante Spiritu*. The encyclical validated some of the work of the Catholic biblical scholars of the day by affirming the importance of the study of biblical texts in their original languages and with contemporary textual methods. Such hopes were dampened somewhat by Pius XII's 1950 encyclical *Humani generis*, which specifically addressed some of the continuing issues arising from the new theology. Pius XII stated the limits to innovation in theological thought in unambiguous words: "If the Supreme Pontiffs in their official documents purposely pass judgment on a matter up to that time under dispute, it is obvious that the matter, according to the mind and will of the same pontiffs, cannot be any longer considered a question open to discussion among theologians" (29). But *Divino afflante Spiritu*'s acceptance of new forms of critical biblical scholarship had opened the door for significant theological developments. These bore fruit at the Council, both in its discussion of the role of the Bible in the life of the Church and by making possible a more biblically grounded approach to the Christian social vision.

PROCESS OF FORMULATION AND AUTHORSHIP

GS was very much a document written in committee, with all the strengths and drawbacks of such a process. In fact, numerous committees, subcommittees, and literally hundreds of people participated in drafting the document over the four sessions of the Council held from October to December 1962 and September to December 1963, 1964, and 1965.

The drafting of the document began remotely with the preparation of two documents before the Council: a more theoretical and doctrinal one prepared by the Council's Theological Preparatory Commission and a more practical one drafted by the Preparatory Commission on the Apostolate of the Laity. The tension between the more theological, doctrinal approach of the former and the more applied, issue-oriented approach of the latter persisted throughout the drafting process and indeed among the different interpretations of GS in the decades after the Council. A month before the Council opened, John XXIII stated his hope that in response to the needs of the underdeveloped countries, the Church "wishes to be the Church of all, and especially the Church of the poor."[7] A pastoral letter by Cardinal Léon Joseph Suenens on the eve of the Council resonated with John XXIII's desires for the Council. Suenens's ideas helped shape the allocution with which the pope opened the Council, calling for explicit attention to the needs of the world. During the Council itself, Cardinal Lercaro argued in a powerful and influential speech during the first session that a central theme of the Council should be the Church as the Church of the poor. Dom Hélder Câmara, then auxiliary bishop of Rio de Janeiro, continually pressed the question of how the Church was going to respond to the problems of the poor in developing countries. Hélder Câmara also saw the importance of the episcopal conferences in the Church's future response to these urgent topics. He initiated contact with Suenens and this led to their continued collaboration on these matters.[8] In addition, Cardinal Montini, who was soon to become Pope Paul VI, addressed the first session with a strong speech calling the Council to address the Church's role in society. By the end of the first session it had become clear that many of the most important leaders of the Council strongly favored producing a document that would address the realities of the contemporary world.

The first texts of what became GS produced within the Council itself emerged during February and March 1963 from discussions of a Mixed Commission composed of members of the Theological Commission and the Commission for the Apostolate of the Laity. This group produced the outline of what came to be known as Schema 13. A second text, developed between March 14 and April 24, 1963, was influenced by the publication of John XXIII's encyclical letter *Pacem in terris*. The worldwide reception of *Pacem in terris* showed the importance of identifying and commenting on the signs of the times as well as the power of certain forms of a natural law language that was not specifically biblical or theological. Monsignor Pietro Pavan, who was known to have played a major role in drafting *Pacem in terris*, was actively involved in several of the committees that helped produce these drafts of the conciliar document, as was Josef Fuchs, a moral theologian who had written a significant work on natural law theory. Others who had worked on more explicitly biblical and theological approaches to the Church's involvement in the world, such as Bernard Häring, Marie-Dominique Chenu, and Henri de Lubac, were also deeply involved, foreshadowing the complex blend of biblical, theological, and natural law approaches found in the final text of GS.

Two more drafts were produced in the late spring of 1963, chiefly through the work of the Mixed Commission. During this time it was also decided to involve laypeople in the drafting process, and they were the ones who insisted on going forward with a discussion of marriage and the family despite the belief of some of the clerical participants that the time was not ripe for this. In addition, ecumenical influence on the document began at this time through the influence of Lukas Vischer of the Faith and Order section of the World Council of Churches. Vischer urged that the theme of the Lordship of Christ should receive significant emphasis and not be confused with the requirements of natural law.

What is called Interim Text A was drafted in Cardinal Suenens's city of Malines, Belgium, in September 1963. This revised text had a sharper theological focus on how the gospel points toward the kind of world that Christians should be helping to build. It was sent to the Conciliar Secretariat for distribution to the bishops at the second session of the Council. Interim Text B, drafted in Zurich in February 1964, emphasized biblical, theological, and sociological interpretations of urgent problems and the pastoral need of responding to them. A second Zurich text emerged after a process of revision that extended from February to November 1964. The debate of this text on the floor of the third session of the Council highlighted four clusters of issues: (1) the urgency of explicitly addressing the reality of atheism; (2) the need to better explain that the Church speaks about earthly realities because of the requirements of the gospel itself; (3) a set of issues touching the human person and the family, including the controversial matter of birth control; and (4) matters relating to culture, development, and peace, including the question of the morality of nuclear weapons.

Between November 1964 and January 1965, this text was redrafted by several of the conciliar commissions, producing what is called the Ariccia text, which was itself widely discussed and revised from January and September 1965 between the third and fourth sessions of the Council. Ten subcommissions guided the Ariccia draft through four more iterations under the skilled leadership of Monsignor Gérard Philips. Of considerable importance was the decision that the genre of the text would be that of a pastoral constitution as opposed to a dogmatic constitution, for this permitted explicit attention to the "signs of the times" and the more concrete practical problems facing the Church. The outcome of all this discussion and revision was titled *Schema XIII: Constitutio pastoralis de ecclesia in mundi huius temporis*, and was approved by Paul VI for discussion at the fourth session of the Council. It totaled 122 pages, seventy-nine of which were text.

The debate on this text from September 14 to 24, 1965, resulted in five hundred single-spaced pages of comments that collected the responses and amendments from all the bishops of the Council. The proposals for revision were then dealt with by the ten subcommissions between October 17 and 20. The resulting final text of 151 pages was submitted to the council fathers on November 12. Debate on the text resumed on November 15 and resulted in another round of amendments, though support for the basic structure of the document remained strong. Specific points of contention were the treatments of atheism, marriage, and war. Debate continued, and on December 7 the vote was taken on the final text. Of 2391 votes cast, 2309 were positive (*placet*), 75 negative (*nonplacet*), and 7 invalid. Thus GS became the teaching of the ecumenical Council.

ESSAY

GS launched the Roman Catholic Church on a new path in its involvement in social and political affairs. The fact of church involvement in such affairs, of course, is nothing new. For example, the special place granted the Church in the Roman Empire by Constantine, the investiture controversy of the Middle Ages, and the history of the Papal States all show that the Church has been no stranger to the world of politics in the past. Similarly, the Church has long been deeply involved in responding to pressing social ills through Christian service. Direct efforts to aid the poor, as well as hospitals, orphanages, and schools, have historically been part of the Church's understanding of its own mission. Since the Council, however, the mode of the Church's engagement in social and political life has entered a distinctive new phase whose contours are still in the process of taking shape.

Signs of the Times

GS played a major role in setting the Church on this new course. This contribution emerged from the Council's reading of the social situation the human community was facing (the "signs of the times") and its formulation of a direction for the Church's response to this situation in light of the gospel. The Council's interpretation of its context is sometimes criticized for being overly optimistic about the direction of the social trends. The Council did indeed see notable positive developments in the social and cultural situation, and it regarded these as grounds for hope. For example, the Council noted that the human race has achieved unprecedented wealth, that there is a growing aspiration for freedom among peoples everywhere, and that people increasingly value the unity of the human family as well as communication across national and cultural boundaries. Nevertheless, the Council clearly recognized that the human community that benefits from these positive developments is also deeply wounded. It pointed to a number of negative signs, including widespread hunger and disease, a widening and unjust gap between rich and poor nations, new forms of enslavement through social and psychological manipulation by the media, and political control by authoritarian regimes (4–9). These realities are accompanied by deep ideological rifts that threaten genuinely communicative social and political discourse. In other words, increasing consciousness of the divisions between nations, classes, races, and ideological groups has had a corrosive effect on the unity of human self-understanding. Thus the Council's reading of its social context was of two minds, certainly not naïvely optimistic.

This ambivalence in the reading of the prevailing social situation led the Council to point to a deeper uncertainty and ambivalence within the human spirit itself. Social uncertainty generates an interior sense of anxiousness "about current developments in the world, about humanity's place and role in the universe, about the meaning of individual and collective endeavor and finally about the destiny of nature and of humanity" (3). This anxiety is the result of a loss of confidence in the lasting worth of human projects and ideas occasioned by the discovery of the historicity and therefore contingency of all things human. Though our age is a period of genuine social transformation brought about by human intelligence, it is also an age in which people recognize that their desires and decisions are deeply shaped by their social and historical context. Thus they can become uncertain of whether their undertakings have lasting significance.

The tensions that are experienced in contemporary culture are, therefore, not simply material contradictions explainable by means of physical or mechanical analogies. They exist within the human spirit itself. This conflict or dichotomy is characterized as one between the drive of the human spirit toward values worthy of wholehearted commitment and the shifting and limited values of historical existence. In the words of GS: "The dichotomy affecting the modern world is, in fact, a symptom of the deeper dichotomy that is rooted in humanity itself. It is the meeting point of many conflicting forces. As created beings, people are subject to many limitations, but they feel unlimited in their desires and their sense of being destined for a higher life" (10). This inner spiritual dynamic leads to a tension between a transcendent drive to deeper meaning and the fragility and contingency of all social and cultural values. This tension had a significant influence on the way the Council framed its discussion of the relation of Christian faith to social life.

On the one hand, the quest for meaning can be focused on a historically limited value in a way that falsely absolutizes this value. The result would be a kind of idolatry or enslavement to limited goods that the Council saw as an aspect of some forms of unbelief and atheism. Authentic belief in God can thus set people free, leading to a genuine humanism that works for the betterment of the human condition through social justice. On the other hand, the Council was very much aware that the growth of unbelief in the West has often been motivated more by the desire to affirm the human than to deny God. Therefore, if Christians live in ways that suggest that faith detracts from humanistic commitment, they bear responsibility for the growth of unbelief. Forms of religion that lead to withdrawal from historical engagement in the struggle for human well-being are a temptation and indeed a manifestation of sin. The Council thus made one of its rare negative judgments when it condemned the separation of faith from social engagement:

> It is a mistake to think that, because we have here no lasting city, but seek the city which is to come, we are entitled to evade our earthly responsibilities; this is to forget that because of our faith we are all the more bound to fulfill these responsibilities according to each one's vocation. But it is no less mistaken to think that we may immerse ourselves in earthly activities as if these latter were utterly foreign to religion, and religion were nothing more than the fulfillment of acts of worship and the observance of a few moral obligations. One of the gravest errors of our time is the dichotomy between the faith which many profess and their day-to-day conduct. (43)

Thus both the hopes for human advancement that the Council discerns in contemporary culture and the possible distortions of these hopes set the framework for the Council's presentation of its vision of the social mission of the Church.

Theology and Natural Law

A distinctive contribution of this vision is its explicitly theological nature. J. Bryan Hehir, an astute interpreter and practitioner of the Church's social ministry, has argued that "the decisive contribution of Vatican II was to provide a description of the Church's role in the world which was properly theological and ecclesial in tone and substance."[9] Hehir's point is evident if one compares Part 1 of GS with the social encyclicals issued by the popes from Leo XIII to John XXIII. These earlier social teachings were almost exclusively framed in concepts and language of the natural law ethic of Scholastic philosophy. One searches in vain the writings of the popes during the hundred years before the Council for careful consideration of the biblical, Christological, eschatological, or ecclesiological basis of the Church's social role. All of these are presented at least schematically in Part 1 of GS. At the same time, the Council's desire to speak to the larger society led it to continue to appeal to arguments based on human understanding. Explicitly religious arguments were thus joined with an appeal to reasoned reflection on human experience, that is, to appeals based on natural law. The Council's effort to forge such a linkage was based on the hope that a Christian humanism is possible—a hope that one can articulate a vision that is both faithfully Christian and also intelligible to those outside the Christian community. The document set forth this hope in its first paragraph, when it said that "nothing genuinely human fails to find an echo" in the hearts of Christians, that the Christian message of salvation is addressed to "all humanity," and that their faith leads Christians to "cherish a feeling of deep solidarity with the human race and its history" (1).

Both Faith and Reason

The first three chapters of Part 1 of GS all have a similar structure. Each begins with themes drawn from a theology of creation, supports these themes with philosophical warrants grounded in reason and natural law, goes on to consider the distortions introduced into the created order by human sin, and finally concludes with a discussion of how Christ heals these distortions and how Christian faith leads to a distinctive perspective on the theme under discussion. In this way, the Council seeks to ground its vision of the social role of Christians firmly in central religious convictions of the Christian tradition, while keeping open a path to an understanding of the human condition that can be shared with those outside the Church.

Thus, chapter 1 grounds its understanding of the dignity of the human person on the affirmation in the book of Genesis that human beings are created in the image and likeness of God (12). This scriptural theme is accompanied by several philosophical perspectives. The dignity of men and women is seen in the ability of the human intellect to transcend the material universe, enabling humans to "share in the light of the divine mind." Dignity is also expressed in the call to obedience to conscience, and in the capacity for freedom as a key manifestation of the worth of human beings (15–17). Respect for this transcendent dignity of human beings is at the heart of the Council's social teaching, and the duty to show this respect is supported by both theological and secular, philosophical warrants.

The argument attends to the more negative aspects of the social scene when it notes how human beings abuse their freedom through mistreatment of one another. This distorts people's hearts and minds as well as the patterns of social life they share together. Theology calls this distortion sin—a rising up against God that simultaneously fractures a proper relation with other creatures. Because a distorted relation with God and one's neighbor is at the heart of sin, a restoration of a proper relation with God and neighbor is needed to overcome it. Thus, the Council argues that the revelation of God in Christ is finally the central norm shaping its perspective both on what it means to be human and on the right patterns for life together in society. In the words of the Council: "it is only in the mystery of the Word made flesh that the mystery of humanity truly becomes clear. . . . Christ the new Adam, in the very revelation of the mystery of the Father and of his love, fully reveals humanity to itself and brings to light its very high calling" (22). The Council, therefore, appeals both to scriptural revelation and theology and to human experience interpreted and understood by reason to develop its understanding of moral life in society.

In chapter 2 of Part 1, GS makes a similar appeal to both theological and philosophical warrants in treating the central importance of social life and communal solidarity for the realization of human dignity. Theologically, the Genesis account of creation suggests that "God did not create men and women as solitary beings. . . . [Their] partnership constitutes the first form of communion between people" (12). People were not created by God simply as individuals but with a need and destiny for community. God's salvation is not offered to humans simply as individuals. Rather, it comes to them as a "people" formed into a social unity who together serve God in holiness (32). All nations have been created as one family, and all people are called to solidarity with each other by the commandment to love one's neighbor as oneself (24). These biblical and theological insights into the communal nature of the human vocation are also warranted by philosophical reasoning as old as Aristotle's affirmation that human beings are social animals. Such philosophical reflection suggests both that "humanity by its very nature stands completely in need of life in society" and that the human person "ought to be the beginning, the subject and the object of every social organization." Regrettably, the orientation to solidarity is distorted and frustrated by human sin. The Council anticipates later discussions of social sin when it states that people "are often turned away from the good and towards evil by the social environment in which they live and in which they have been immersed since their birth." Distorted economic, political, and social structures can be a social inducement or occasion of sin. At a deeper level, however, sin is rooted in the human heart where "selfishness and pride" originate and go on to "contaminate the atmosphere of society as well." The aid of grace is needed to help overcome these distortions (25), and this grace is offered to all persons in Christ. Thus, "the communitarian character [of the human vocation] is perfected and fulfilled in the work of Jesus Christ" (32). In addition, the Council sees the deepest significance of the communal aspects of the human vocation in the way human interrelationships reflect the unity of the three divine persons in the Trinitarian life of God. This Trinitarian theological ground of human sociality "has opened up new horizons closed to human reason" (24). GS, therefore, envisions the theological aspects of human dignity in community as simultaneously confirming, healing, and fulfilling on a higher level what reason and experience reveal about these fundamental concepts of social ethics.

The Council's understanding of the relations between faith and reason and between Church and society can thus be called "transformationist."[10] It envisions Christ and his disciples as affirming all that is truly human in social life. At the same time, Christian faith calls the followers of Jesus to work to overcome whatever is distorted by injustice or oppression. Faith also opens up a vision of human fulfillment in union with God in God's kingdom that goes beyond what can be naturally expected. Thus, GS does not oppose or reject what is human but seeks to transform and ennoble it through a genuinely Christian humanism. This transfomationist vision means that Christians should affirm the great achievements of human culture while also being deeply engaged in the struggles to overcome injustice and to heal the brokenness of the world. Efforts to transform the world, therefore, not simple affirmation or simple rejection, should characterize the Christian stance toward the secular domains of culture, politics, and society.

In this vein, chapter 3 of Part 1 of GS affirms the human and religious significance of worldly activity. It sees human creativity in the social, economic, political, and cultural domains as continuations of the creative activity of God. Indeed, when people work in ways that are in line with what work is meant to be, "they can rightly look upon their work as a prolongation of the work of the creator" (34). This human activity deserves respect in its own right, not simply as a backdrop for more obviously religious activity such as prayer. Human activities in secular domains possess a "rightful autonomy." Science, politics, and culture have a legitimate integrity that the Church must respect. The Church does not control them, as if theology were the sum total of knowledge or as if ecclesial life could substitute for vigorous human activity in the full sweep of scientific, political, and cultural activity. The Christian humanism envisioned by the Council calls the Church to be a partner with the many other forces that seek to create a more human, and therefore more Christian, world. Collaboration rather than control should be the Church's mode of operation in society.

Chapter 4 carries this argument forward in explicit reflection on what the Christian community can learn from the secular world and what the secular world can learn from the Church. It argues that the Church must listen to the many voices of the larger social and cultural domains while it also seeks to shape these domains in accord with Christian and human values. The relation of Church to society is neither oppositional nor one of identity; it is a relation of mutual interaction and dialogue. Thus, the constitution states that the Church "profits from the experience of past ages, from the progress of the sciences, and from the riches hidden in various cultures, through which greater light is thrown on human nature and new avenues to truth are opened up" (44). There are no purely religious answers to scientific questions. When the Church respects the integrity of the scientific endeavor it is respecting the handiwork of God. The same is true of social life: there are no purely religious answers to most of the questions that arise in political or economic life. For this reason, no one should expect pastors "to have a ready answer to every problem, even every grave problem, that arises" (43). In fact, different members of the Church may sometimes reach different conclusions about the action called for by Christian faith in a given situation since Christian answers to complex social problems cannot be simply deduced from theological first premises.[11] Serious encounter with the multiple dimensions of the human experience and attentive dialogue with the natural and social sciences are essential in the formation of a Christian response.

At the same time, the legitimate autonomy of science, culture, and politics does not mean that they are somehow independent from all relationship to the God who is their creator and redeemer. Politics and all social activity have an ultimate relation to God in whose presence they unfold, who heals their brokenness, and in whose light their ultimate significance becomes clear (36–38). Though the Church's mission is religious and not directly political, the Christian community does, then, have a responsibility to help shape public life in accord with created human nature and in a way that is open to ultimate fulfillment in God's kingdom (42). The recognition of both the autonomy of earthly affairs and the properly religious mission of the Church, therefore, does not mean the earthly and heavenly cities are radically separate from each other. The fact that the Church's mission is religious rather than political does not mean that the Church is an otherworldly community with no role in public life. Quite the contrary. Christian eschatological hope should strengthen involvement in the work of social transformation, not weaken it. As GS put it: "Far from diminishing our concern to develop this earth, the expectation of a new earth should spur us on" (39). Building the earth is not in competition with the coming of God's reign but can contribute to it.

Revising the Tradition of the Social Encyclicals

Some significant differences exist between this conciliar model of the relation between Church and society and the approach of the social encyclicals from *Rerum novarum* to *Pacem in terris*. The earlier encyclicals relied almost exclusively on a natural law approach based on philosophical rather than biblical and theological categories. This natural law method was in line with the Catholic tradition's high estimate of the power of human reason to discover at least the outlines of God's design for social life through reflection on human experience. This neoscholastic approach to the complementarity of faith and reason put the Church in a position to declare that anyone who rejected the popes' conclusions about the proper ordering of society was not only unfaithful but also unreasonable. For this essentially apologetic strategy to be effective, it was necessary to avoid direct and explicit appeal to biblical and theological perspectives in proposing the Catholic vision of social life. Thus, in the words of Johann Baptist Metz, modern Catholic social teaching before the Council did not seek to mediate between faith and society but rather to defend the Christian tradition against the corrosive currents of modernity. This defense "was carried on just in front of the fortress Church, on the territory of pure social ethics" (i.e., strictly natural law ethics).[12] The Catholic insistence on the complementarity of faith and reason thus ironically came to be interpreted in a way that saw them moving on two parallel tracks only extrinsically related to each other. Faith and reason were not envisioned as interacting or transforming each other. In the same way, Church and society were not seen as in dialogue to the mutual benefit of both. Affirmation that morality was grounded in natural law and reason thus turned into an affirmation of the Church's privileged insight into what is truly human. This put the Church in a strong position to assert its views even when others argued that their experience and reasonableness pointed to other conclusions.

During the decades immediately prior to the Council, it became increasingly clear that this solution to the problem of the relation of the Church and the surrounding culture was both socially and theologically unsatisfactory. On the social level, the early encyclicals had Western Europe implicitly in mind as the "world" to which the Church's mission was to be directed. Further, they assumed that this world shared a unified intellectual heritage in which Christianity and culture had been harmoniously synthesized. When Vatican II convened, it had become clear to many of the bishops and the theologians who advised them that this understanding of the context of the Church's mission was no longer accurate (if it ever was fully accurate). Differences of class, race, economic status, and political tradition had made the West far from a unified society with a harmoniously integrated culture. When the full global scope of the Church's social mission was considered it became even clearer its context was no longer a single and unified culture. As GS put it:

> The world is keenly aware of its unity and of mutual interdependence in essential solidarity, but at the same time it is split into bitterly opposing camps. We have not yet seen the last of bitter political, social, and economic hostility, and racial and ideological antagonism, nor are we free from the spectre of a war of total destruction. If there is a growing exchange of ideas, there is still widespread disagreement in competing ideologies about the meaning of the words which express our key concepts. (4)

Thus, cultural pluralism and social conflict were more adequate descriptions of the context of the Church's social mission at the time of the Council than the organic model of society assumed by neoscholasticism. The Council was also very aware of the methodological specialization of modern intellectual life and that this reality had increasingly led to competing conceptions of the human person.

GS took up these challenges of pluralism with great seriousness, and it saw them as a call to revise the rather complacent self-confidence that had come to mark some aspects of the social teaching of the modern popes. The dangers of loss of common meaning for basic moral terms and incomplete views of the person brought about by methodological specialization are not only dangers that beset those who are intellectually obtuse, morally of bad will, or religiously unfaithful, as earlier social encyclicals sometimes seemed to assume. Christian thought must itself grapple with the uncertainties of the Council's own intellectual and cultural moment in history. These challenges must be addressed in the theological effort to clarify the Church's social mission and in the task of formulating the orientation and norms of a Christian social ethic.

During the decades preceding the Council, a number of Catholic theologians had been at work seeking to respond to fundamental social questions in ways that spoke to the context of modern pluralism and skepticism from the explicit perspective of Christian belief. Far from abandoning the Catholic conviction about the complementarity of faith and reason, these theologians sought to appropriate the meaning of this complementarity more thoroughly. They sought to mediate the meaning of Christianity to a modern pluralistic and often conflictual society and to appropriate the positive values of this society into the life and thought of the Church. For example, thinkers such as John Henry Newman, Maurice Blondel, Pierre Teilhard de Chardin, Henri de Lubac, Edward Schillebeeckx, and Karl Rahner (each in a different way) argued that God's grace is not extrinsic to human experience, understanding, society, or culture. Grace is immanent within history, beckoning it to transformation and redemption. It was but a short step from this retrieval of a more authentic understanding of the relation of nature and grace to the conclusion that the response of Christians to grace in faith should have a transformative and redemptive impact on history, society, and culture. It had become clear, as Metz put it a decade after the Council, that the task of expounding the theology of the Church's social mission "has to be carried on by using the very substance of the Christian faith."[13] The social mission is not a propaedeutic to or an extension of the Church's real purpose but is integral or essential to that purpose. The work of these theologians led the Council to adopt an explicitly theological approach to the social mission of the Church in the world. They formed the Council's teaching that the Church's social mission flows from the heart of Christian faith.

Thus, there is a significant tension in the Council's approach to the relation of faith and reason that affects its understanding of the role of the Church in society. On the one hand, GS affirmed a distinctively Christian theological foundation for its ethic and an epistemology based on revelation through which this ethic can be known. This leads to stressing the importance of the distinctive religious identity of the Christian community and how it contributes to and sometimes contrasts with the cultures it encounters. On the other hand, in continuity with the natural law tradition, GS sought to engage all persons of good will in the pursuit of a universal ethic or common morality that will be normative in all cultures and for all religious communities. The Council seems to want to have it both ways.[14] Is such a position coherent?

Universality through Dialogue

Several interpretations of the relationship between universalist and particularist sources could explain the twofold approach discernable in GS. First, one could affirm that universal moral standards are in principle knowable by all persons but that in practice revelation is needed because of the limitations of human understanding and the mind's further distortions by sin. Following this approach, most people will need the assistance of revelation and grace if they are to know and live by the natural law in the concreteness of their lives. This position can be found in Augustine and Thomas Aquinas in the Catholic tradition and especially in the work of John Calvin in the Protestant tradition. The disadvantage of this approach is that it sometimes fails to attend sufficiently to the way the sinfulness of the Christian community itself casts doubt on strong claims that Christians have privileged knowledge of the universal human good. Second, one could argue that the authoritative teaching office of the Roman Catholic Church guarantees that the magisterium is capable of discerning and teaching the universally normative natural law in ways that are preserved by the Holy Spirit from sinful distortions. This stance, however, risks undermining the claim to provide a common morality for a pluralistic world by suggesting that only the teaching office of the Roman Church can in practice know what that universal morality is.

Neither of these approaches to the tension between universality and particularity was fully adopted by the Council, though there are hints of both of them in GS. Rather, the Council's approach can be characterized as a form of what can be called "dialogic universalism."[15] Following postmodern critiques of the Western Enlightenment, this approach acknowledges that reason is embedded in history. Rational inquiry is deeply shaped by the tradition within which the inquirer has been educated. Neither the questions addressed by rational discourse nor the thought patterns available to address these questions are the products of a kind of pure reason that is somehow independent of the particularities of the historical and cultural location of the one doing the reasoning. This dependence of rational inquiry upon tradition is evident not only in ethics and theology but in other domains of knowledge as well. At the same time, a dialogically universalist orientation is fully committed to respect for the dignity of those outside the communal tradition of the inquirer, in this case, those who are not Christian. This respect generates a commitment to dialogue across the boundaries of diverse communities as an essential expression of Christian commitment to the gospel.

Following such an approach, the gospel and the ways the gospel has been historically appropriated and understood in the Christian tradition were the starting point for the Council's effort to contribute to the pursuit of a common morality. At the same time, the Council called for these received convictions to be brought into active encounter with visions of the human good held by other communities, with other religious or cultural traditions, with different, non-Western histories. Thus, the pursuit of an understanding of the Church's role in modern society should seek both to be faithful to the gospel and to be engaged with those who are different through dialogue. This commitment to dialogue calls for showing genuine respect toward those outside the Christian community, but it does not imply relativism. In fact, the commitment to dialogue and mutual inquiry would be pointless if one were to adopt a relativist stance. Serious engagement in dialogue makes sense only if one is convinced that there is a truth about the human good that must be pursued and that makes a claim on the minds and hearts of all persons.[16] The Council committed itself to such dialogue in pursuit of a more adequate understanding of that truth within the Christian tradition itself and as a way of contributing to a deeper understanding of the truth claims of Christianity by those outside the Church. The commitment to such dialogue helps create a genuinely universal community. It will lead both to a transformation of the world by its encounter with the gospel and to transformation of the Church by Christian encounters with diverse societies and cultures.

Thus, when GS gave new emphasis to the particularity of the Christian theological understandings in developing its approach to social life, this did not lead it to reject the Catholic tradition's pursuit of universal moral standards that apply cross-culturally and across religious traditions. But this universalism was conceived as the outcome of inquiry and dialogue, not as already in full possession by the Church. Universal norms are to be discovered, not simply to be proposed to or imposed upon others. As GS put it in a reprise of the first three chapters of Part 1, "All we have said up to now about the dignity of the human person, the community of men and women, and the deep significance of human activity, provides a basis for discussing the relationship between the church and the world and the dialogue between them" (40). The Church has learned in the past from all the sciences, from diverse philosophies, and from differing cultures. It must continue to do so today (44). This stance of dialogue was broadened by other documents of the Council that advocated significant new initiatives in inter-Christian ecumenical dialogue and in dialogue with the other great world religions.[17]

GS thus saw commitment to dialogue as both a demand of Christian faith and a requirement of reasonableness. It is simultaneously an expression of fidelity to the gospel and of respect for the other. Christian faith entails care and respect for all persons, and respect for their dignity means listening to their interpretations of the human good. Further, Christian love calls for the building up of the bonds of solidarity among all persons, and such solidarity requires efforts to understand those who are different, to learn from them, and to contribute to their understanding of the good life as well. This can be called a commitment to "intellectual solidarity."[18] It is a stance that expresses reasonableness, but avoids the dismissal of historical traditions and communal particularities that sometimes characterized the approaches to natural law in the earlier social encyclicals. It takes the diverse traditions and cultures of the world seriously enough both to listen carefully to them and to respond with respect. This is a reasonableness that expects both to learn and to teach through the give-and-take of dialogue. For Christians such dialogue, therefore, embodies a dynamic interaction between the biblical faith handed on to them through the centuries of Christian tradition and the reason that is a preeminent manifestation of the *imago Dei* in all human beings.

Justice and Human Rights

This dialogic and dynamic linkage of faith and reason had implications for a number of more specific moral questions that arise in public life. First, it influenced the Council's approach to the broad area of justice and its implications for an ethic of human rights. GS brought Catholic tradition into dialogue with the orientations of modern consciousness, but to the extent that Western "modernity" is identified with the emergence of the autonomous person or "self," the Council was at least as critical as it was adaptive. For the Council strongly emphasized the social nature of the person and stressed the implications of sociality for its understanding of justice. It challenged all individualistic interpretations of human dignity and justice for both empirical and normative reasons. Empirically, "one of the most striking features of today's world, and one due in no small measure to modern technical progress, is the very great increase in mutual interdependence between people" (23). John XXIII's *Mater et magistra* called this growth in interdependence "socialization," and GS repeated the use of that term (25). Socialization describes a social process in which technological and other social changes lead to more complex patterns of social interaction, expressed in new forms of association and richer patterns of organizational interaction. The Catholic tradition has always stressed the social nature of the person, but, in the Council's view, contemporary patterns of social interdependence are more tightly woven than in earlier, perhaps simpler, times.

The Common Good and Solidarity

These newly emergent empirical conditions make the normative ideas of the common good and of solidarity increasingly important for an adequate understanding of justice today. The Council echoed Aquinas's position that justice requires a commitment to the common good by all citizens of a society. For Aquinas, the premier moral virtue is justice, which directs a person's actions toward the good of fellow human beings. Because human beings are simultaneously individuals and participants in the common life of the civil community, virtuous citizens ought to seek not only their own individual good but also the larger good of the community. Thus justice directs the activity of individual citizens and of smaller groups in society to the common good of the community as a whole.[19] Today, because of the process of socialization, such commitment to the common good has become even more important than in the days of Aquinas or the earlier social encyclicals. Further, the increasingly international scope of human interdependence today generates obligations of justice that reach across borders and that call for new manifestations of global solidarity. GS strongly stressed the obligations of justice that flow from these new forms of international interdependence: "All must consider it their sacred duty to count social obligations among their chief duties today and observe them as such. For the more closely the world comes together, the more widely do people's obligations transcend particular groups and extend to the whole world. This will be realized only if individuals and groups practice moral and social virtues and foster them in social living" (30). This stress on the importance of the common good for the meaning of justice flows directly from the Council's conviction that we "need to transcend an individualistic morality" (30). It calls for an ethic that stresses active solidarity and enables all persons to participate in the life of the human community in ways that befit their dignity.

This conviction also has significant influence on the way the Council conceives of human rights. John XXIII's encyclical *Pacem in terris* was published during the Council and it had gone well beyond earlier openings by Pius XII to lead the Catholic Church to a dramatic change of direction on the matter of human rights. *Pacem in terris* moved the leadership of the Church from a position of staunch opposition to modern rights and freedoms to activist engagement in the global struggle for human rights. This shift was one of the most dramatic reversals in the long history of the Catholic tradition. *Pacem in terris* advocated this shift while also reaffirming the Catholic tradition's strong emphasis on the need for commitment to the building up of the common good. This was particularly evident when *Pacem in terris* affirmed the social and economic rights that are in considerable tension with the individualistic understanding of the person characteristic of the modern liberalism frequently associated with human rights in the West. John XXIII, however, did not develop in any depth the understanding of the human person that made it possible for him to link human rights with the more solidaristic understanding of the person characteristic of the Catholic tradition. The Council took up that task in a somewhat more developed way.

Human Rights and Interdependence

GS begins its discussion of human rights in the midst of its treatment of the growing interdependence of persons. Thus its approach diverges in significant ways from the individualistic understandings of human rights that predominate in the United States and in the Western liberal tradition. The key point of divergence is the Council's insistence that rights be understood in light of the social nature of the human person and in a framework of solidarity. This stress on the communal rather than individualist grounding of rights leads contemporary Catholic discussions of constitutional democracy and market capitalism to diverge in notable ways from liberal, individualistic approaches to political and economic life.

Within the framework of the common good, GS affirms that persons possess a "sublime dignity" that must be protected by respect for "rights and duties [that] are universal and inviolable" (26). These rights include persons' "right to act according to the dictates of conscience and to safeguard their privacy, and rightful freedom, including freedom of religion" (26). Support for the right to religious freedom was further developed in an unambiguous way in the Council's *Declaration on Religious Freedom*, which stated: "The right to religious freedom is based on the very dignity of the human person as known through the revealed word of God and by reason itself" (2). Where the rights to these freedoms are not respected, persons are treated neither as the gospel requires nor as reasonableness demands.

Following the lead set by John XXIII's *Pacem in terris*, therefore, GS affirmed the rights that have been classically defended by the liberal democratic tradition of the West and that are enshrined in the Bill of Rights of the Constitution of the United States.

That these rights are not understood in an individualistic way is evident since GS follows John XXIII in also affirming social and economic rights that are more difficult to justify on liberal and individualistic grounds. These include the rights to "access to all that is necessary for living a genuinely human life: for example, food, clothing, housing, . . . education, work" (26). Rights, in other words, can be understood as "the minimum conditions for life in community," as the U.S. bishops described them in their 1986 pastoral letter *Economic Justice for All* (79). Basic goods such as food and work are essential for a dignified life in community, so respect for human dignity implies that persons have rights to these goods. In the same way, being able to speak freely, to express one's beliefs in public, and to participate actively in political life are requisites of living in community with dignity. These rights, therefore, are not merely immunities that protect individuals and their zone of privacy against encroachment by society or the state. They are positive claims to be able to participate actively in the life of the community, through speech, expression of one's deepest convictions, and efforts to influence the political direction of the common life. The freedoms of belief, speech, and political participation, therefore, are among the concrete expressions of the Council's strong commitment to dialogue and to what we have called intellectual solidarity. Where these freedoms are denied, dialogue is impossible and ideological conflict likely. Thus duties to respect all human rights—those known as civil-political rights as well as those called social-economic-cultural rights—are duties of solidarity. In the view advanced by GS, therefore, protection of human rights and the advancement of the common good are mutually correlative, not opposed to each other. It was this linkage of the idea of human rights with the common good that enabled the Catholic tradition to see that support for human rights did not require abandonment of the tradition's deep sensitivity to the importance of communal solidarity for human flourishing. Thus, the Council affirmed a development of the Church's social doctrine begun by Pius XII and John XXIII. This development has made the Catholic community of the postconciliar period one of the world's most vigorous advocates of human rights. It has put the Church in the forefront of the worldwide struggle for human rights, from Poland to the Philippines, from Central America to South Africa.[20] This is surely among the most important contributions of the Council to the social mission of the Church.

GS also advanced the Church's understanding of human rights by its strong statements on the equality of all human beings. As recently as Leo XIII, Catholic social teaching affirmed that the equal dignity of all persons as images of God did not necessarily translate into equality in society. It could be compatible with a stratified society governed by unequal rights.[21] The Council rejected this position. Though it acknowledged the evident fact that persons are not identical in their physical, intellectual, or even moral qualities, it strongly affirmed equality of human rights. In its words, "any kind of social or cultural discrimination in basic personal rights on the grounds of sex, race, color, social conditions, language or religion, must be curbed and eradicated as incompatible with God's design" (29). It singled out denial of equal rights to women and excessive economic disparity as particular violations of this fundamental equality. It also singled out some of the gravest violations of human dignity for particular condemnation, including genocide, abortion, torture, arbitrary imprisonment, slavery, prostitution, the selling of women and children, and degrading working conditions (27). These violations harm their victims, of course, but the Council's understanding of the social framework of human rights led it to note that they harm society as well, including those who commit these crimes.

The Council thus set a large agenda before the nations of our interdependent world. Its solidaristic understanding of the human good demands that commitment to human rights not be limited to the promotion of the political freedoms prized in the West but must also include a commitment to economic justice in global, regional, and national markets. Human rights should not be turned into a banner under which a battle between "the West and the rest" is fought today. From the perspectives of both Christian fidelity and respect for those outside the Christian community, human rights are the most basic requirements of genuine solidarity in the economic as well as the cultural and political fields. Despite the great scope of this agenda, it can give substantive guidance for the direction in which the Church wants to encourage social, political, and economic institutions to move.

The Council saw respect for human rights as an implication both of a social understanding of human nature and of Christian love. Following its understanding of the complementary relation of faith and reason, commitment to justice and human rights is rooted in the Christian faith itself and also in a common morality that can, at least potentially, be known by all. GS declared that the Church proclaims human rights "in virtue of the gospel entrusted to it" while at the same time affirming that it "holds in high esteem the dynamic approach of today which is fostering these rights all over the world" (41). The Council's approach, therefore, links Church and world in a mutually transformative relationship. The religious mission of the Church has important social, cultural, and even political implications, and the shape of this mission must be discerned in dialogue with the societies and cultures that are the context of this mission. GS's treatment of justice and human rights thus set the Church on a path that is still unfolding. Since the Council there has been both progress and retreat along this path. Adequately addressing the future will call for renewed commitment to the agenda set by Vatican II.

A Fresh Appraisal of War

The Council also brought about significant developments in the Church's official approach to issues of war and peace. Several aspects of the Council's teaching will be noted here. Recent church teaching on the issue of war and peace is treated more fully elsewhere in this volume.[22]

Just War and Nonviolence

Most notable is GS's dramatic statement that the proliferation of scientifically advanced weapons with enormously destructive potential calls for "a completely fresh appraisal of war" (80). In a footnote to this statement, the Council refers to John XXIII's statement that "in this age of ours which prides itself on its atomic power, it is irrational to believe that war is still an apt means of vindicating violated rights" (PT 127). This sounds like the renunciation of the tradition of just war, which has held that the sinfulness of the fallen human condition in history can justify resort to force under carefully specified conditions. Indeed, the fresh appraisal of war by the Council did lead church teaching to give a new and stronger support to nonviolent approaches to the struggle for justice. In the words of the Council: "We cannot fail to praise those who renounce the use of violence in the vindication of their rights and who resort to methods of defense which are otherwise available to weaker parties too" (79).

This statement is in notable contrast with Pius XII's statement in 1956 that conscientious objection to all war is not a position legitimately open to Catholics.[23] Pius XII's position followed from his natural law–based argument that some human goods are so important that Christians can have a right and "even an obligation" to defend such goods. It can be legitimate to defend the innocent against unjust aggression and there is "a duty not to abandon a nation that is attacked."[24] It seems clear that the Council did not intend to commit the entire Church to a pacifist position that rejects all use of force as morally unacceptable. This is evident in GS's reaffirmation that "governments cannot be denied the right to legitimate defense once every means of peaceful settlement has been exhausted." The Council also affirmed that soldiers can make genuine contributions to peace as long as they abide by the moral standards for the just use of force

(79). Thus, the Council did not abrogate the earlier tradition's commitment to defending innocent people and nations against injustice. It did suggest, however, that such defense could be achieved nonviolently, in a way that Pius XII had not envisioned. This is clear in the Council's support of nonviolent resistance to injustice provided the renunciation of force does not abandon the protection of the rights of others and of the community (78). The supposition here is that nonviolence can be effective in resisting injustice in some and perhaps many circumstances. Thus, the support for nonviolence in GS does not abandon the commitment to justice that has been characteristic of the just war approaches to conflict. For this reason the Council's approach did not entirely satisfy those who see a Christian commitment to nonviolence as more fundamental than concerns about effectiveness in the pursuit of justice.[25]

The Council's "fresh reappraisal of war" does, however, make more evident than has often been the case in the past that the norms of just war are to be interpreted very strictly. The "just war theory" has often been confused in the popular mind with the view that war is simply to be expected and is quite frequently a morally legitimate undertaking. The Council's teaching, however, makes it clear that peace is the condition that should be expected when people live in accord with the moral order with which God has invested the created world. Also, peace flows from life in accord with the love of neighbor taught by Jesus and from the reconciliation promised by the death and resurrection of Christ. Thus, both natural law and the revelation known by faith lead Christians to "join with all peace-loving people in pleading for peace and trying to achieve it" (78). This orientation to peace is the context of the Council's praise of those who renounce violence. A Christian approach to the use of force, therefore, must begin from what the U.S. Catholic bishops have called a "presumption against war" (CP 71). The just war tradition itself begins from a commitment to peace and legitimates the use of force only in carefully defined circumstances: when it is necessary to secure justice, when it can be pursued proportionately, as a last resort, and with morally legitimate means. If these norms are followed with care, war may be necessary in some circumstances but it is always an exception to the preferred nonviolent route to justice. So the Council fully agrees with St. Augustine's sad acknowledgment that even justified war is a form of "misery."[26] It should be pursued with deep regret and only when strictly necessary.

War's Means

GS also sought to restrain war through restatement of the limits on the means that can be legitimately used even in a justified conflict and through application of these norms to contemporary forms of conflict. It forcefully stated the classic *jus in bello* norm of noncombatant immunity in a way that was directed at modern war: "Any act of war aimed indiscriminately at the destruction of entire cities or extensive areas along with their population is a crime against God and man himself. It merits unequivocal and unhesitating condemnation" (80). This "declaration" is one of a very small number of explicit condemnations issued by the Council, a fact that reinforces the seriousness with which the bishops took the question. It is a direct application of the just war norm of discrimination to contemporary total war, both conventional and nuclear. It does not, however, settle the hard cases about nuclear war-fighting that have emerged in policy debates in the decades since the Council. Can there be a discriminate and proportionate use of nuclear weapons, particularly smaller "tactical" nuclear weapons? Can there be a use of nuclear weapons that will succeed in achieving a form of justice that proportionately outweighs the damage the weapons cause? Can there be a use of nuclear weapons that can remain within human control and therefore satisfies the just war demand that war must be limited and conducted by legitimate authority? The Council did not analyze these questions with the detail that would be needed to answer them satisfactorily. The incomplete discussion of such matters in GS put these questions on the agenda of both Church and society for the years after the Council. They were taken up by several conferences of bishops in Western countries in the 1980s, particularly the bishops of England and Wales, France, the Federal Republic of Germany, and, most notably, the United States.[27]

The Council's discussion of the moral limits on the means that may be legitimately used in war was not restricted to the indiscriminate use of nuclear weapons against cities. It also condemned the use of force aimed at peoples on the basis of race, ethnicity, or nationality. The Council's condemnation of indiscriminate force also applies to terrorism and to those forms of covert or guerrilla war that fail to respect the lives of innocent civilians. "Such actions must be vehemently condemned as horrendous crimes." These judgments continue to have notable relevance to contemporary warfare in which ethnic, religious, and even genocidal conflict have regrettably reemerged as more frequent occurrences than they had been in the years of the cold war. In the face of these forms of war, GS reminded soldiers that orders from higher authority do not excuse the commission of such actions. It called for disobedience if authorities issue commands to undertake such actions: "The courage of those who fearlessly and openly resist those who issue such commands merits supreme commendation" (79).

GS also discussed at some length the question of deterrence of war by the threat to use nuclear weapons. This question was strongly controverted at the Council and was not resolved to the satisfaction of many participants in the discussions. It, too, remained on the agenda of the Church and was taken up in the decades after the Council by several bishops' conferences. The Council acknowledged the dangers inherent in the possession of nuclear weapons for purposes of deterrence and appealed for a reversal of the arms race. It did not, however, reach a specific conclusion on the morality of deterrence as such. In its words:

> Since the defensive strength of any nation is considered to be dependent upon its capacity for immediate retaliation, this accumulation of arms, which increases each year, likewise serves, in a way heretofore unknown, as deterrent to possible enemy attack. Many regard this procedure as the most effective way by which peace of a sort can be maintained between nations at the present time. (81)

After the Council, especially in the mid-1980s, pointed questions continued to be raised about whether securing "peace of a sort" through the threat of mass destruction built into the nuclear deterrent was morally justified.

Since the debate of the 1980s these concerns have remained alive, but they have assumed new forms. The new questions that have emerged include how to respond morally to the proliferation of nuclear weapons, whether deterrence is an adequate stance in the face of those who may possess chemical and biological weapons, and whether preventative action can be morally justified under certain circumstances to disarm states or terrorist organizations that may possess weapons of mass destruction or who may be prepared to use destructive forms of unconventional warfare to achieve their aims. The Council's call for a fresh appraisal of war did not resolve these questions. But it did move them to a position high on the agenda of the Christian community in the years following the Council. They remain central to the Church's social mission today. Christians who continue to explore the moral questions contained in these issues and who take action based on their religious and ethical conclusions are continuing to carry forward the legacy of GS.

EXCURSUS

The Council's consideration of the Church's relation to the modern world was influenced in a special way by the extraordinary participation of bishops from virtually every corner of the world. This was an ecumenical council unlike any other in history in that its participants came from countries around the world and from societies where all of the great world religions play significant roles. Thus the Council's experience of the challenges facing the Church was strongly shaped by the way voices within it spoke in the languages and accents of many peoples of the world. This experience was one of the most fundamental influences of Vatican II on the Church's understanding of its role in society. It led Karl Rahner to assert that the Council was "in a rudimentary form still groping for identity, the Church's first official self-actualization as a world Church."[28] The global presence of the Church, of course, was not new at the Council. Missionary activity had brought Christianity into contact with many societies and cultures of the world, especially in the days when missionaries accompanied European explorers and colonizers. At the Council, however, the challenge was to engage the diverse societies, cultures, and religious traditions of the world in a manner marked by mutual respect.

Becoming a truly world Church raised important issues that the Council began to tackle and that have been further addressed in subsequent years. The first of these was the need to respond strongly to global economic injustice. From the first, many bishops had called the Council to address the realities of poverty in the world and to become a "Church of the poor." The Council responded by presenting a vivid description of the inequalities marring the global economic picture. It stated that while a minority can live sumptuously, the vast majority "are deprived of the bare necessities" and "have to live and work in conditions unworthy of human beings." The situation shows "contempt for the poor" (63). GS's response to these conditions in Part 2, chapter 3, was mostly a reprise of the ethical approach to justice found in earlier social encyclicals. It presupposed a natural law-based ethic. The treatment of private property, however, placed notably greater stress than did Leo XIII on how the right to private ownership is limited by the duty to respond to the needs of the poor. In particular, GS recalled the biblically informed teachings of several theologians of the patristic era on the Christian obligation to aid the poor. It also recalled Thomas Aquinas's position that those in extreme need can legitimately take what they need from those who have more than enough. It also went notably beyond St. Thomas and the earlier social encyclicals in affirming the obligation to aid the poor does not apply merely to one's "superfluous goods." The duties of justice are to be measured by the needs of the poorest and by what is necessary to bring about the development that will free the poor from their plight (69). This approach is a clear anticipation of what came to be called the "preferential option for the poor" in social theology and ethics after the Council. It was one of the strongest effects of the burgeoning consciousness of being a genuinely global Church in a world marked by deep inequality and poverty. The Council did not develop this approach in depth, but the discussion it opened had important consequences in subsequent years.

A second consequence of the incipient awareness of the global nature of the Church was in the Council's treatment of culture. The presence of Asian, African, and Latin American participants highlighted the need to avoid viewing Christianity as a European religion to be exported to the rest of the world along with European culture. The challenge now was to relate Christianity to the diverse cultures of the world in ways that respected their differences and avoided domination or manipulation in the name of the gospel. Taking these diverse cultures seriously had important effects on the Church's understanding of its social role and its approach to social teaching. It led to an awareness of how different cultures and religious traditions influence what people see as reasonable interpretations of the human good and reasonable demands of social morality (4). Thus, one can discern in some of the texts of Vatican II an incipient emergence of what has since come to be called the postmodern suspicion of universalism. Indeed, there are hints in GS that reason does not have a single meaning that can provide univocal answers to the basic moral questions of society. For example, in its treatment of culture in Part 2, chapter 2, GS acknowledges that the plurality of cultures leads to different scales of values, different forms of behavior, and a different way of organizing social institutions (53).

This recognition of the importance of cultural differences raises important challenges to the conviction that reason can lead to the discovery of a natural law that makes the same demands on all persons. Thomas Aquinas had recognized that an adequate approach to natural law should recognize that only the most general principles of morality are the same for all persons, that more detailed moral demands can vary from culture to culture, and that specific moral rules can sometimes change through history.[29] Thomas's flexibility in this regard, however, had not always been characteristic of the earlier encyclicals of modern social teaching of the Church.

GS took notable steps in its recognition of cultural differences, and these had important consequences for its social teaching. On a very basic level, the Council presented its normative ethical conclusions with a deepened epistemological humility. This is evident in its readiness to distinguish its convictions about core ethical values from the multiple ways these values can be realized in diverse cultures and historical periods. At the very center of these core values is the Council's unequivocal affirmation of the dignity of the human person. This dignity is a transcendent principle that should be protected in every culture and historical period. This dignity is only achieved, however, in the midst of the concrete particularities of different cultures and historical periods. Therefore, sensitive discernment of the requirements for living with dignity in particular historical and cultural settings will be required if church social teaching is to be both reasonable and truly humane (GS 14, 23, 25). This calls for an intellectual humility that avoids premature closure of inquiry and unwarranted certainty. For example, the precise form of family life, economic organization, or structure of government may legitimately vary from one society to another. The forms these relationships will take in the concrete can only be determined in the context of a wise analysis of the patterns and institutions of a historical and cultural milieu.

On the other hand, the Council did not conclude that all the norms of social ethics are now up for grabs. The requirements of justice and basic human rights continue to make genuine moral claims across cultures. For example, though the patterns of family life may differ from one culture to another, to deny persons the right to form a family would be to deny them an essential dimension of the human personality. Similarly, though patterns of political life may legitimately differ, to deny persons the right to participate in some way in the political governance of their community would be oppressive and unjust. The Council thus sought, again in an incipient way, to combine serious attention to cultural diversity with a continuing claim that the requirements of human dignity and justice make transcultural demands. Today the need for a deeper understanding of how to relate genuine commitment to inculturation with a strongly held belief in the unity of the human family remains very much on the agenda of the Church's developing social thought.

A third consequence of the Council's acknowledgment of the significance of cultural and religious differences was its readiness to speak about the basis of social morality in explicitly theological ways. The Council implicitly recognized that cultural and religious traditions can have significant influence on what is held to be reasonable. Basic religious questions can emerge in the effort to clarify what forms of social life and politics are reasonable. The Council stated some of these questions this way: "What is humanity? What is the meaning of suffering, evil, death which have not been eliminated by all this progress? What is the purpose of these achievements, purchased at so high a price? What can people contribute to society? What can they expect from it? What happens after this earthly life is ended?" (10). These questions are primarily concerned with what it is to be fully human and thus what forms of life men and women should pursue. Answers to such anthropological questions have consequences for an understanding of social life. Since such answers have important religious dimensions, the distinction between a reason-based natural law approach to social morality and a more explicitly theological approach to social ethics is not a sharp one. Thus the Council concluded that "the mission of the Church will show itself to be supremely human by the very fact of being religious" (11).

This stress on the religious and theological aspects of the Council's approach to social life is a consequence of its readiness to acknowledge the impact of cultural and religious traditions on the way one reasons and on the way human nature is understood. The particularity of religious and cultural traditions is thus in tension with the aspiration to identify at least some basic social norms that are universally applicable. Once again, the Council made a beginning in the effort to address this tension. It did so through its repeated emphasis on an approach to dialogue in which the Christian community begins from its own distinctive beliefs but goes on to engage those who are different. This engagement itself opens up a vision of a genuinely universal human community. The challenge of relating the distinctiveness of a Christian vision of social morality to a common morality shared by all who are human has remained central in postconciliar Catholic moral and social thought.

REACTIONS TO THE DOCUMENT

The perspectives on social life presented in GS have been carried forward in the postconciliar teaching of the magisterium and in a variety of movements in theology. The content of these subsequent developments can be grouped under the commitment to justice for the poor and the relation between the gospel and inculturation.

The Council suggested in an unsystematic way that matters of justice should be adjudicated in light of their effect on the poor. The Conference of Bishops of Latin America (CELAM) elaborated on this theme in considerably greater depth at its 1968 meeting in Medellín, Colombia, convened to address the role of the Church in "present-day transformation of Latin America in the light of the Council." Following the lead of GS, the Latin American bishops had "undertaken to discover a plan of God in the 'signs of the times.'"[30] Looking at the Latin American social reality, they saw the vast majority of people "beset by misery" and by "injustice which cries to the heavens." This poverty is caused by "unjust structures" and is the result of social patterns that can be called forms of "institutionalized violence."[31] In the face of these injustices, the gospel itself calls the entire Church to a new commitment to solidarity with the poor who are the victims of such injustice. This commitment was subsequently named the "preferential option for the poor" at the 1979 CELAM meeting in Puebla, Mexico.[32] The option for the poor has since become a leitmotif in Catholic social thought on the level of the magisterium, in social theology and ethics, and in much of the Church's pastoral discourse. The same is true of Medellín's use of the term *liberation*, which Gustavo Gutiérrez's work *A Theology of Liberation* canonized as the name of what has surely been the most influential school of theology to emerge during the post–Vatican II period.[33]

The way Latin American Christians developed themes from GS in terms of the option for the poor, structural injustice, and solidarity in the struggle for liberation had notable influence in the Church in other parts of the world also. The regional churches of both Africa and South Asia, in different ways, have come to stress how the Christian vocation is a call to solidarity with the poor in their struggle to overcome the plight of deprivation and marginalization.[34] In the United States, the Catholic bishops' 1986 pastoral letter, *Economic Justice for All*, also made the option for the poor central to its teaching.[35] At the same time, the pope and officials of the Holy See expressed alarm that these liberation emphases were being developed in Latin America in ways that borrowed too heavily from Marxism. They also feared compromise of the Council's distinction between the gospel and political ideology, and they were concerned that the liberation struggle could illegitimately draw Christians into support for violence.[36] Major thinkers such as Gutiérrez wrote vigorous restatements of their views that sought to show again how liberation theology was deeply rooted in the gospel and in no way fell into the alleged compromises. Such expositions appear to have been persuasive, for the Holy See tempered its critique and took a more positive stance toward the liberation theology approach in a subsequent instruction.[37] As a result of these initiatives and clarifications, the option for the poor and commitment to the liberation of the marginalized have become truly central themes in postconciliar Catholic social thought. There can be little doubt that this has been one of the most important overall impacts of GS on the subsequent life of the Catholic Church throughout the world.

GS's call for dialogue with the diverse cultures and religious traditions of the world has also had notable impact on Catholic social thought in the years since the Council. In the face of the post–cold war reemergence of violent conflicts among cultural and religious communities in a number of parts of the world, the Council's call for dialogue and solidarity across cultural and religious boundaries has grown in its relevance for social and political life. Pope John Paul II has intensified the Council's commitment to eliminate anti-Semitism from the Church, and he has taken dramatic steps in pursuit of a new relation with the Jewish people.[38] In the same vein, John Paul II has several times convened leaders from the world's major religious traditions at Assisi to pray for world peace, thus seeking to set an example of religion as a source of peace and justice rather than conflict and division. The theological grounding of such interreligious cooperation for peace and justice remains a matter of serious contention within the Church[39] and some theologians have been censured for their positions on these matters. Nevertheless, dialogue with the other religions in the pursuit of human solidarity and justice has entered into the mainstream of Catholic life and thought due to the combined initiatives taken in GS and in the Council's *Declaration on the Relation of the Church to Non-Christian Religions* (*Nostra aetate*). In a similar way, call to dialogue with culture has had important consequences for the Church in Africa, Asia, and South America, where engagement with traditional and popular cultures is leading to new ways of formulating the church's social role.[40] These efforts at interreligious understanding and inculturation have only just begun in the decades since the Council. But one can predict with a certain confidence that they will have significant impact in the long term.

In the decades since the Council, of course, there have been serious disputes about the direction and pace of change in the Church's relation to social, political, and cultural life. The controversies surrounding liberation theology and dialogue with non-Christian religions are but two examples. These controversies are often characterized as conflicts between progressives and conservatives. Joseph Komonchak has proposed an analysis of the postconciliar tensions that is considerably more helpful than one based on the liberal versus conservative stereotype. He has suggested that the approaches that have sometimes come into conflict might be better understood in a more explicitly theological way. Komonchak sees the tension as arising between a style of theological thinking that can be called broadly Augustinian and one that can be called broadly Thomist. The Augustinian approach, which can be found in the writings of thinkers such as Cardinal Joseph Ratzinger, draws a sharp, unmediated distinction between the domains of sin and grace, of natural reason and faith. The natural world is destined for fulfillment in the supernatural, but it does not have a solidity of its own. Thus the Church's encounter with the world is seen as a case in point of the fundamental contest between grace and sin. The domain of the natural, which would include much of culture, the sciences, politics, and economic life, has value only to the extent that it is oriented to and subsumed under the domain of ultimate, supernatural meaning.[41] Such an Augustinian approach, therefore, will be highly suspicious that movements like liberation theology risk subordinating the transcendence of the gospel to this-worldly categories by granting an undue value to politics. This approach will also be inclined to downplay what Christians can learn from non-Christian cultures or religions. Rather, it will stress how these cultures and religions need to be corrected and fulfilled by the gospel. In other words, this Augustinian style leads to a suspicious and critical stance toward the world. It will expect the transformative influence of the gospel on society to be accompanied by considerable conflict. Those with this theological orientation, therefore, will not be surprised if the Church needs to assume a countercultural stance toward the world fairly often.

The Thomist approach, on the other hand, sees nature as having a certain created autonomy that differentiates it from both grace and sin. Sin contradicts or falls short of nature, and grace heals and fulfills nature. But nature is not itself sinful, and grace does not abolish or destroy the significance of nature. Thus, the fact that a certain domain of society, politics, or culture is not yet transformed into the fullness of the kingdom of God does not by that very fact put it in opposition to the gospel. Komonchak points out that this kind of differentiation enabled Thomas Aquinas to reach out to the new world confronting the Church in the thirteenth century as it encountered Aristotelian philosophy and Arab science. In a similar way, Thomists such as Rahner and Chenu were able to reach out to the world faced by the Church at the time of the Council and after it.

An important contribution of Komonchak's analysis, therefore, is the way it shows that the interpretation of the relation of the Church to the world is ultimately a theological matter, both in GS and in the reception of this document after the Council. There are, of course, elements of both the Augustinian and Thomist styles in GS. Nevertheless, it is impossible to deny the Council's clear commitment to reciprocal dialogue with culture and its acknowledgment of the legitimate though limited autonomy of culture. This stance of openness and of readiness for dialogue seems basic in the text of GS and it sets the framework within which the struggle against sin and toward fulfillment in the kingdom of God is seen. For this reason, the Council's basic theological stance implies that social justice and critical solidarity across religious and cultural boundaries must remain integral aspects of the religious mission of the Church. This will remain the major contribution of GS to the unfolding tradition of Catholic social thought.

NOTES

1. All references here to documents of Vatican II, including those to GS, are from the translations in Austin Flannery, ed., *Vatican Council II: Constitutions, Decrees, Declarations*, completely revised translation in inclusive language (Northport, N.Y.: Costello, 1996).

2. A number of these themes are treated in greater depth in other chapters in this volume. Marriage and family are treated in the commentary on FC; the significance of economics and work in the discussions of RN, QA, and LE; and aspects of the discussion of peace and international politics in the commentaries on PT and CP.

3. Thomas A. Shannon played a major role in the drafting of both this and the following sections of this chapter.

4. Pius X, *Pascendi dominici gregis*, number 13, in *The Papal Encyclicals*, 5 vols., compiled by Claudia Carlen (Raleigh, N.C.: Pierian, 1990), 3:76.

5. Henri de Lubac, *Catholicism: Christ and the Common Destiny of Man*, trans. Lancelot C. Sheppard and Elizabeth Englund (San Francisco: Ignatius, 1988), 15. The French original was published in 1947.

6. For a helpful study of the theological developments that led up to Vatican II, see Mark Schoof, *A Survey of Catholic Theology, 1800–1970*, trans. N. D. Smith (Glen Rock, N.J.: Paulist Newman, 1970).

7. John XXIII, "Radio Message of September 11, 1962," in *Council Daybook, Vatican II, Sessions 1 and 2*, ed. Floyd Anderson (Washington, D.C.: National Catholic Welfare Conference, 1965), 19.

8. Charles Moeller, "History of the Constitution," in *Commentary on the Documents of Vatican II*, vol. 5, ed. Herbert Vorgrimler, trans. W. J. O'Hara (New York: Herder and Herder, 1969), 1–76, at 10–11. Much of the information in this section is based on this account of the formulation of the text of GS.

9. J. Bryan Hehir, "Church-State and Church-World: The Ecclesiological Implications," *Proceedings of the Catholic Theological Society of America* 41 (1986): 56.

10. The term is H. Richard Niebuhr's. See "Christ the Transformer of Culture," chap. 6 in his *Christ and Culture* (New York: Harper and Row, 1951).

11. See Karl Rahner, "On the Theological Problems Entailed in a 'Pastoral Constitution,'" in *Theological Investigations* 10, trans. David Bourke (New York: Herder and Herder, 1973), 303.

12. Johann Baptist Metz, *Faith in History and Society*, trans. David Smith (New York: Seabury, 1980), 18–19.

13. Ibid., 19.

14. The same dual approach is present in the recent writings of John Paul II. See, for example, his encyclicals *Veritatis splendor* and *Evangelium vitae*.

15. I originally used this phrase in my *Claims in Conflict: Retrieving and Renewing the Catholic Human Rights Tradition* (New York: Paulist, 1979), 131. What is said here is a development of that earlier discussion.

16. See Alasdair MacIntyre, chap. 18, in *Whose Justice? Which Rationality?* (Notre Dame, Ind.: University of Notre Dame Press, 1988). See also chap. 10 in his *Three Rival Versions of Moral Enquiry: Encyclopaedia, Genealogy and Tradition* (Notre Dame, Ind.: University of Notre Dame Press, 1990), which relates this treatment of how traditions develop to the task of the university.

17. See Vatican Council II, *Unitatis redintegratio* (*Decree on Ecumenism*) and *Nostra aetate* (*Declaration on the Relationship of the Church to Non-Christian Religions*).

18. See my "Afterword: A Community of Freedom," in *Catholicism and Liberalism: Contributions to American Public Philosophy*, ed. R. Bruce Douglass and David Hollenbach (Cambridge and New York: Cambridge University Press, 1994), 334, and chap. 6 in my *The Common Good and Christian Ethics* (Cambridge and New York: Cambridge University Press, 2001).

19. Thomas Aquinas called the form of justice that orients citizens to the service of the common good both "general justice" and "legal justice." See *Summa theologiae* II-II, q. 58, art. 6. Pius XI called it "social justice" in *Divini redemptoris*, no. 51, and the U.S. bishops called it "contributive justice" in EJA 71.

20. Samuel Huntington has observed that since the mid-1960s the Catholic Church has become one of the most vigorous actors promoting human rights on the global stage and that, as a result, a large number of countries with Catholic cultures have moved from authoritarian to democratic regimes. He attributes these developments to the influence of Vatican II. See S. Huntington, "Religion and the Third Wave," *National Interest* 24 (summer 1991): 29–42.

21. See, for example, Leo XIII's 1878 encyclical *Quod apostolici muneris*, 1.

22. See T. Whitmore's chapter in this volume.

23. Pius XII, Christmas message 1956, in *The Major Addresses of Pius XII*, vol. 2, ed. Vincent A. Yzermans (St. Paul, Minn.: North Central, 1961), 225.

24. Pius XII, Christmas message 1948, in *The Major Addresses of Pius XII*, 2:125.

25. See Lisa Sowle Cahill, *Love Your Enemies: Discipleship, Pacifism, and Just War Theory* (Minneapolis, Minn.: Fortress, 1994), 211–13. For a critical pacifist reading of the treatment of war in GS, see esp. chap. 5 in James W. Douglass, *The Non-Violent Cross: A Theology of Revolution and Peace* (New York: Macmillan, 1968).

26. St. Augustine, *The City of God*, trans. Henry Bettenson (New York: Penguin, 1984), Book XIX, chap. 7, 861.

27. The approach of the U.S. bishops is treated elsewhere in this volume. See the essay by Todd Whitmore, "U.S. Catholic Approaches to Peace and War."

28. K. Rahner, "Toward a Fundamental Theological Interpretation of Vatican II," *Theological Studies* 40 (1979): 717.

29. Thomas Aquinas, *Summa theologiae*, I-II, q. 94, arts. 4 and 5.

30. CELAM, *The Church in the Present-Day Transformation of Latin America in Light of the Council*, vol. 2, trans. Division for Latin America (Washington, D.C.: U.S. Catholic Conference, 1973), 25.

31. Ibid., 40–41, 61.

32. CELAM, *Evangelization in Latin America's Present and Future: Final Document of the Third General Conference of the Latin American Episcopate*, esp., Part 4, chap. 1, in *Puebla and Beyond: Documentation and Commentary*, ed. John Eagleson and Philip Scharper (Maryknoll, NY: Orbis, 1980), 264–67.

33. Gustavo Gutiérrez, *A Theology of Liberation: History, Politics and Salvation*, trans. and ed. Caridad Inda and John Eagleson (Maryknoll, N.Y.: Orbis, 1973).

34. For a western African perspective, see Jean-Marc Éla, *African Cry*, trans. Robert R. Barr (Maryknoll, N.Y.: Orbis, 1986), and from a South Asian standpoint, Felix Wilfred, *Asian Dreams and Christian Hope: At the Dawn of the Millenium* (Delhi: ISPCK, 2000).

35. National Conference of Catholic Bishops, *Economic Justice for All: Pastoral Letter on Catholic*

Social Teaching and the U.S. Economy (Washington, D.C.: U.S. Catholic Conference, 1986), esp. numbers 86–92.

36. These were central concerns in the *Instruction on Certain Aspects of the "Theology of Liberation"* issued by the Sacred Congregation for the Doctrine of the Faith, August 6, 1984 (Washington, D.C.: U.S. Catholic Conference, 1984).

37. Gutiérrez restates his position in "Introduction to the Revised Edition: Expanding the View," in his *A Theology of Liberation*, rev. ed. (Maryknoll, N.Y.: Orbis, 1988). The Holy See's more receptive stance is contained in the Congregation of the Doctrine of the Faith, *Instruction on Christian Freedom and Liberation*, March 22, 1986 (Washington, D.C.: U.S. Catholic Conference, 1986).

38. See Pontifical Commission for Religious Relations with the Jews, "We Remember: A Reflection on the *Shoah*," March 16, 1998. Available online at http://www.vatican.va/roman_curia/pontifical_councils/chrstuni/documents/rc_pc_chrstuni_doc_16031998_shoah_en.html. Many of John Paul II's addresses during his Jubilee Pilgrimage to the Holy Land in 2000 dealt with Jewish-Christian relations. They are available on the Vatican Web site.

39. See the Declaration of the Congregation for the Doctrine of the Faith, *Dominus Jesus: On the Unicity and Salvific Universality of Jesus Christ and the Church*, August 6, 2000, available at the Vatican website. For theological discussions of this declaration, see Stephen J. Pope and Charles Hefling, eds., *Sic et Non: Encountering Dominus Iesus* (Maryknoll, N.Y.: Orbis, 2002).

40. See Robert J. Schreiter, *Constructing Local Theologies* (Maryknoll, N.Y.: Orbis, 1985), and Thomas Bamat and Jean-Paul Wiest, eds., *Popular Catholicism in a World Church: Seven Case Studies in Inculturation* (Maryknoll, N.Y.: Orbis, 1999).

41. Joseph A. Komonchak, "Vatican II and the Encounter between Catholicism and Liberalism," in *Catholicism and Liberalism: Contributions to American Public Philosophy*, ed. R. Bruce Douglass and David Hollenbach (Cambridge: Cambridge University Press, 1994), 87. Komonchak has developed this analysis of tensions regarding GS during and after the Council at greater length in his "Le valutazioni sulla *Gaudium et Spes*: Chenu, Dossetti, Ratzinger," in *Volti de Fine Concilio: Studi di Storia e Teologia sulla Conclusione del Vaticano II*, ed. Joseph Doré and Alberto Melloni (Bologna: Il Mulino, 2000), 115–53.

SELECTED BIBLIOGRAPHY

Alberigo, Giuseppe, Jean-Pierre Jossua, and Joseph A. Komonchak, eds. *The Reception of Vatican II.* Translated by Matthew J. O'Connell. Washington, D.C.: Catholic University of America Press, 1987. Surveys the response to the Council in the subsequent two decades; especially valuable for the Latin American reception in liberation theology.

Dulles, Avery. "Vatican II: The Myth and the Reality." *America* 188, no. 6 (February 24, 2003): 7–11. Argues for almost total continuity between Vatican II and the tradition that preceded it. Contrast this essay with the sharply different perspective of John O'Malley noted below.

Hehir, J. Bryan. "The Church in the World: Responding to the Call of the Council." In *Faith and the Intellectual Life: Marianist Award Lectures*. Edited by James L. Heft. Notre Dame, Ind.: University of Notre Dame Press, 1996. A valuable treatment of the impact of theology on social thought at the Council.

McDonagh, Enda. "The Church in the Modern World (*Gaudium et Spes*)." In *Modern Catholicism: Vatican II and After.* Edited by Adrian Hastings. New York: Oxford University Press, 1991. A solid, brief analysis of the key ideas of the document.

O'Malley, John W. "The Style of Vatican II." *America* 188, no. 6 (February 24, 2003): 12–15. Stresses invitational style and commitment to dialogue as significant emphases of the Council as a whole, parallel to the interpretation of GS presented in this chapter.

Vorgrimler, Herbert, ed. *Commentary on the Documents of Vatican II*, vol. V, "Pastoral Constitution on the Church in the Modern World." Translated by W. J. O'Hara. New York: Herder and Herder, 1969. The best treatment of the drafting of the document is in the first chapter by Charles Moeller.

CHAPTER 12 Commentary on *Populorum progressio* (*On the Development of Peoples*)

ALLAN FIGUEROA DECK, S.J.

INTRODUCTION

Populorum progressio vigorously asserted the connection between Christian faith and the pursuit of economic justice for all. Pope Paul VI took the term *development* in its social and economic sense and sought to link it intimately with a Christian understanding of the human person in community. Grounding his vision in the gospel message itself and in the spirit of Catholic social thought, he took seriously the social science findings regarding the appalling and morally unacceptable material conditions in which human beings live around the globe. He took the concept of solidarity first expressed by Pope John XXIII, invested it with richer significance and urgency, and established it as a fundamental and distinctively Catholic norm of social and economic justice.

The appearance of Pope Paul VI's "magna carta on development" in 1967 gave renewed impetus to the strong social justice concerns of Pope John XXIII's pontificate and of Vatican II. Twenty years later Pope John Paul II recognized the importance of this encyclical and revisited it in his *Sollicitudo rei socialis*, in which he praised, updated, and expanded on his predecessor's seminal work. Pope Paul VI's analysis and teachings, his method, and many of his conclusions in PP continue to resonate even now in the early years of the third millennium.

OUTLINE OF THE DOCUMENT

The introduction (1–5) presents the background for the Church's concern for socioeconomic development.[1] In the five paragraphs of this section Paul VI stresses the urgent need to confront the reality of poverty in the world. He links this concern to the tradition of Catholic social teaching beginning with Leo XIII and most recently extending to his immediate predecessor John XXIII. The reality of poverty, the pope affirms, makes a claim on the consciences of all humanity, especially the affluent—a reference to be further developed in the document's teaching on solidarity.

Part 1 consists of thirty-seven numbers (6–42). An overview of the problem of worldwide underdevelopment is provided in numbers 6 to 11. The pope describes the situation in terms of various factors affecting it such as education, negative and positive influences of colonialism, and the deleterious effects of laissez-faire economics. There are growing inequalities in wealth, power, and access to food among nations and entire continents. As a result, there is a growing sociopolitical unrest exacerbated by generational differences and sharp contrasts between traditional and industrialized cultures. This fuels an unhealthy populism that leads only to bloodshed, totalitarianism, and more misery.

Numbers 12 to 21 trace the Church's response to the challenge. The pope recalls the historical involvement of the Church in the promotion of human progress at various local levels through humanitarian institutions like schools. The dimensions of poverty are so great today, however, that progress at the local level is not enough. There must be a concerned international effort to address the challenges of underdevelopment, and the Catholic Church is uniquely situated to make a contribution since it promotes a truly "global vision of man and of the human race" (13). At the heart of this vision is the idea that authentic development is not just a matter of economics. It is a matter of humanity. The purpose of economic development is to help people move from less human to more human conditions of life.

Numbers 22 to 33 stress a Catholic vision of development. The material wealth of the world exists in order to meet the legitimate needs of life such as food, shelter, and access to health care and education. The right of private property is subordinate to this higher end. Liberal capitalism goes too far when it fails to respect the social purpose of private property. Planned economies like the socialist ones are not the answer either. Government must learn to collaborate in the search for appropriate means to advance the human development of all, especially the poorest of the earth. This requires creative innovations and an honest assessment of means and ends on the part of governments and international organizations.

Numbers 34 to 42 insist on the need for economics and technology to serve human development. Economic growth and social advancement go together, as do availability of food and access to education. The document seeks to integrate all these factors under the unifying vision of a Christian humanism.

Part 2 consists of forty-four numbers (43–87). The obligations of the more affluent nations toward those in need are outlined in numbers 43 to 60. These involve a better distribution of wealth through aid of various kinds, charity, and more equitable trade relations. Numbers 61 to 70 stress the central role of solidarity among nations. This means guaranteeing more equality of economic opportunity, the end to racist and nationalistic policies, and more international cooperation.

Numbers 71 to 84 remind readers about the humanistic underpinnings of the pope's vision of economic justice. The struggle for development must be grounded in the love of persons and of God. Technological and material advances are important, but the ultimate grounding must never be forgotten. Paul VI ends with an appeal in which he directly connects the struggle for economic justice with the pursuit of lasting peace in the world. He invites all people to consider what their personal role might be in the attainment of this noble mission.

CONTEXT OF THE DOCUMENT

Pope Paul VI's encyclical PP was published on March 26, 1967, less than two years after the conclusion of Vatican II, during a time of new and exhilarating social, economic, and cultural advances on a global scale. Rapid communications along with increased travel and interaction among the peoples of the earth were generating an unprecedented global awareness. The Catholic Church, no less than governments and peoples throughout the world, were acknowledging, even celebrating these changes—mostly for the good, it was thought—brought about by new technologies and by ever-expanding communications media. The United Nations declared this the "Decade of Development," a period of economic expansion, industrialization, and international trade previously unknown in human history with repercussions in every corner of the globe.

The world, however, had become more dangerous than ever before in history, divided between East and West along sharp lines set in motion at the end of World War II. This was ominously demonstrated in the early years of the 1960s by two cold war confrontations—the Cuban missile crisis and the Berlin Wall—that brought the United States and the Soviet Union to the brink of nuclear annihilation. Never before and never since has the world come so close to Armageddon.

The United States and its Western allies were enjoying years of unequaled economic expansion. In the West it became clear that the United States was consolidating as well as broadening its hegemony in several spheres of human endeavor such as industry, science, and technology. The Soviet bloc for its part was also enjoying a time of consolidation and showed signs of being a force to contend with, not only militarily but in the areas of science and culture as well. The rivalries of the cold war, the arms and the space races, exciting technological advances, and competing ideological visions characterized the decade of the 1960s. In the United States that decade was truly a time of high drama punctuated by the assassinations of John F. Kennedy in 1963 and of his brother Robert and Dr. Martin Luther King Jr. in 1968.

In the 1950s the world had been viewed in terms of allegiances along the lines of economic systems, capitalist or socialist/communist. The so-called iron curtain separating Eastern Europe from the West was emblematic of this deep rupture. In the 1960s that chasm widened and spread. The world was divided into thirds: the First World made up of Western Europe, North America, Australia, and Japan; the Second World consisting of the Soviet Union, its several Eastern European satellites, and Communist China; and the third world, the so-called developing nations of Africa, Asia, and Latin America. Many of these countries, particularly in Africa, were just emerging from the shackles of colonial rule. There was excitement and hope mixed with considerable apprehension regarding how they would prosper as independent nations. Within this global arrangement the spotlight kept moving south to the third world, where cold war rivals invested considerable economic, propaganda, and military assets in the hope of acquiring new clients and expanding their strategic interests. The Vietnam War, a deadly, futile exercise dictated by cold war logic, began in the dawning years of the decade and dragged on until the mid-1970s.

Pope John XXIII convened Vatican II, what many have called the greatest ecclesial event of the twentieth century. His temperament and manner responded ideally to the opportunities of the times, to the heady changes, and to the risks of the late 1950s and 1960s. His personality was in many ways "larger than life."[2] He opened a new chapter in Catholic social thought. His first encyclical, *Mater et magistra*, clearly acknowledged the emerging phenomenon of global, social, and economic advancement and interdependency. His attitude was one of optimism with regard to the encouraging changes and opportunities of the times.

Pope John saw the need to build upon but also move beyond the static principles of the Church's social teaching formulated in the thought of his predecessors going back to Pope Leo XIII. In a hint of what he was to do for the Church itself, Pope John looked at the global socioeconomic, political, and cultural realities dialogically and with openness. He acknowledged the specter of a nuclear holocaust and seized the occasion to use the Petrine ministry, especially its symbolic capital, to play a constructive leadership role in world affairs. While clearly building on the insights of his predecessors, Pope John's approach to the formulation of teaching tended more toward the inductive. He acknowledged the Church's received traditions but gave much attention to modern realities that required new reflections and formulations of teaching more in accord with social science analysis and less dependent on traditional philosophical or theological frameworks. His was a serious effort to establish a wide-ranging dialogue with the human and social sciences as a starting point for reflection in the formulation of the Church's social teaching.[3]

One way to understand the fresh air that Pope John was letting into the Church is in terms of his vision of dialogue with the modern world and with the culture of modernity. This attitude was to have profound implications for Vatican II, for the inner life of the Church, its self-understanding, and renewed commitment to its pastoral mission.[4] Inextricably linked to this attitude was an outward-looking vision that sought to put an end to the centuries-old fortress mentality of Roman Catholicism. This meant that the Church must pay attention to the "signs of the times" as the human and social sciences reveal and explain them and as a more contemporary theology illuminates them. At the heart of this "turn to the world" is a respect for the proper autonomy of the secular, a renewed theological vision, and a Christian humanism that stressed dialogue, human dignity, and solidarity in pursuit of the common good.

Pope John's secretary of state and trusted colleague Giovanni Battista Montini was handed the responsibility of finishing what Pope John had begun and, more important, of putting this remarkable vision into practice. The internal church politics of the time that led up to Montini's election as pope were quite complex. Some kind of rift had occurred between Pope Pius XII and Montini in the years just before Pope Pius's death. Given that Montini was a faithful servant of Pius XII and his veritable right-hand man especially in matters of diplomacy, it is not clear why Pope Pius treated him so strangely. In 1954 Montini was suddenly made archbishop of Milan, the largest archdiocese of Italy and a rather troubled one at that. But he was never made a cardinal by Pius XII, something that Pope Paul's biographer Peter Hebblethwaite calls "unprecedented and unintelligible."[5] Pope Pius XII was ill for the last four years of his pontificate and spent considerable time in bed. Many people at the Roman Curia had begun to see Montini as *papabile* even though he was not yet a cardinal. Cardinal Roncalli actually wanted the conclave of 1958, which ended up electing him, to instead elect Montini, even though the cardinals would have had to have gone outside the conclave to do it since Montini was not yet a member of the College of Cardinals.[6] When Roncalli became pope, he immediately made Montini a cardinal. There was no doubt that Montini was Pope John's candidate to succeed him. The main opposition to Pope John XXIII came from within the Roman Curia among a group of conservative Italian cardinals. Peter Hebblethwaite maintains that they most likely lobbied Pius XII to send Montini away to Milan and not make him a cardinal.[7]

Underlying this tension was concern regarding certain progressive tendencies in Montini. This fear was exacerbated when Montini quickly got on the bandwagon of reform that Pope John unexpectedly launched by calling for a "pastoral" ecumenical council. In the responses to the surveys made in preparation for the Council very few bishops seem to have had any idea of what a "pastoral" ecumenical council would be.[8] There was a meeting of the minds, however, between Pope John and Cardinal Montini with regard to ecclesial, social, and global visions. The social and global vision showed itself first in Pope John's *Mater et magistra* and *Pacem in terris* and was picked up by Vatican II itself, especially in *Gaudium et spes*[9] and then substantially elaborated and developed by Pope Paul in *Populorum progressio*, *Octogesima adveniens*, and *Evangelii nuntiandi*. The bishops of the world for their part embraced this vision in *Justice in the World*, the document of their 1971 Synod. These five documents constitute the classic Vatican II and post–Vatican II formulation of Catholic social teaching before the emergence of Pope John Paul II, who took these principles and substantially reaffirmed and expanded them, giving them his own inimitable stamp.

Montini had a markedly different personality from that of Pope John. A more refined and studious person, he suffered in comparison with his predecessor in the sense that he was not nearly as affable or winning in manner. The Italians used the word *amletismo* to describe Montini. This referred to his Hamlet-like indecisiveness and tendency toward depression.[10]

Pope John died at the end of the Vatican Council's first session. The second session was directed by Montini, who took the name Pope Paul VI. In taking this name he signaled that his pontificate was to be profoundly activist along the lines of Paul the Apostle's tireless activities on behalf of proclaiming the gospel message. Vatican II's vision of a Church on the move in ongoing and productive dialogue with the world was affirmed perhaps more than anywhere else in *Gaudium et spes*, the *Pastoral Constitution on the Church in the Modern World*, a document vigorously supported by the new pope and produced with him presiding at the Council. As never before, a humanistic understanding of the Church's purpose, identity, and mission was asserted in terms of an anthropological concept of culture. Its second chapter stresses this understanding of culture's role in the life of the Church. The third chapter outlines a fundamentally humanistic vision of socioeconomic life, asserting that it has to do ultimately with the service of each and every human person.

In subsequent Catholic teaching—social, theological, and pastoral—the concept of culture, at the heart of the humanist vision of influential thinkers like Jacques Maritain, became a highly influential lens for renewing and deepening the Church's self-understanding. This humanism grounded in a profound respect for the human person and his or her culture provides solid criteria for analysis of social, economic, and political realities.[11] Pope Paul VI loses little time in getting to it. PP, his third encyclical letter, is precisely on socioeconomic life. Some have called it Catholic social teaching's Magna Carta on development.

The newly elected pope came from a comfortably established middle- to upper-middle-class family. He was formed from his youth in the social teachings of the Church as they were expressed in the Italian Catholic Action movement and in what contemporaries called "social Catholicism."[12] As a young priest Giovanni Battista Montini showed a keen interest in the service of youth and of the poor. While schooled as a career Vatican diplomat he found time to be involved in outreach to the poor. This orientation was especially exemplified in his ministry as archbishop of Milan from 1954 to 1962. He took up the challenge of winning back working-class people who had come under the influence of the burgeoning Italian Communist Party. During those years he traveled widely and became familiar with the economic misery of the peoples of Africa and Latin America. He even invited Saul Alinsky, a Russian American Jew and founder of a style of community-based social action in the United States, to visit Milan and advise him on how to support the workers' struggles for a better life.[13]

In PP Paul VI considers the concrete effect of economic decisions on the poor as the privileged place to begin ethical reflection on the state of social and economic affairs. In the face of this, Pope Paul goes further than ever before in proposing "solidaristic egalitarianism" as a fundamental principle for political economy. Albino Barrera, a specialist in theology and economics, follows Peter Groenewegen and defines political economy as "the field of study that deals with the distribution of the benefits and burdens of the common productive effort and is much broader in scope than the term 'economics' because it encompasses history, theory, moral values, and policy."[14] Accordingly, Paul VI takes an enlightening political and economic approach to development by placing the issue in context and articulating its linkages to history, theory, moral values, and policy.

PROCESS OF FORMULATION AND AUTHORSHIP

It is said that the main inspiration for PP came from the writing of the French Dominican Louis-Joseph Lebret, who edited a review on economics and Christian humanism.[15] Dominican Vincent Cosmao, founder of the Centre Lebret Foi et Developpement, writes:

> The elaboration of *Populorum Progressio* began on the occasion of the First United Nations Conference on Trade and Development (UNCTAD, Geneva, 1964) where Lebret, spokesperson for the Holy See's delegation, presented the idea for the need of a new international economic order. Lebret intensely participated in the event and was, along with Che Guevara, the most applauded speaker at the plenary session. Within this context Lebret began to write a document on the development of peoples at the request of Paul VI.[16]

Behind the scenes here is certainly Jacques Maritain, whose humanism greatly inspired both Lebret and Giovanni Battista Montini, later to become Pope Paul VI.[17] In addition to Lebret, commentators have suggested that Monsignor (later Cardinal) Pietro Pavan, who was closely involved in the writing of *Pacem in terris* for John XXIII, was the real author or perhaps the final editor of PP. Pavan had worked with John Courtney Murray on Vatican II's statement on religious liberty, *Digni tatis humanae*.[18] Pavan was interviewed in an article in *The Tablet* in which he stated that the original language of PP was French.[19] It is also said that Barbara Ward-Jackson, the British international economist, and Jesuit Georges Jarlot provided inspiration and ideas for the encyclical.[20] Judging from Cosmao's assertion above to the effect that Lebret "began to work on the writing project soon after the 1964 UN Conference on Trade and Development," it can safely be said that the main writer was Lebret, but others also participated, especially Pietro Pavan, since Lebret died in 1966 before the final draft was written.

In Pope John XXIII's thought as well as in that of his successor, the influence of Cardinal Joseph Cardijn is unmistakable. Cardijn was a revered Flemish priest who, beginning just before World War I, followed a lifelong vocation of linking faith with life. For him that meant focusing on the reality of workers, especially their material conditions. For decades Cardijn's Young Christian Workers inspired the lower socioeconomic class in many Catholic countries, especially in Europe and Latin America.[21]

The impact of the work of social activists like Cardijn upon Pope Paul's generation is undeniable. Similarly, the research and writings of thinkers like Lebret were well received in Rome during the pontificates of Pope John XXIII and his successor Pope Paul. Of great relevance, however, in assessing how the encyclical came about, and the immediate motivation for it are the pope's travels both as archbishop of Milan and in his first years as pope. His address to the General Assembly of the United Nations in October 1965 already gives a clue regarding the immediate inspiration for PP. That address focused on global poverty, the urgent need for a more equitable distribution of the world's wealth, and the connection between economic justice and world peace. His thoughts are undoubtedly influenced by the intensity of his recent experiences in India. There and in other third world travels Montini was personally exposed to the dire, intolerable realities of hunger, disease, and illiteracy.[22]

ESSAY

Paul VI begins the encyclical by providing a brief analysis of the status of integral development among the peoples of the world. Full, integral human development involves freedom from misery and provision for subsistence, health, and fixed employment (6). It means that people somehow can assume responsibility for their lives without fear of oppression. This concept of integral development also means that people have an adequate level of security—physical, economic, social, and cultural—so that their dignity is guaranteed. Access to education is a central concern here. These telling words get to the heart of the document's message: "to seek to do more, know more and have more in order to be more: that is what men aspire to now when a greater number of them are condemned to live in conditions that make this lawful desire illusory" (6).

Development, Culture, and Modernity

According to the pope, important resources have been provided by "the means inherited from the past" even though he believes they are inadequate to the enormity and urgency of the problems. He seemed to be acknowledging the drive toward human development rooted in the Western culture of modernity. He affirms here the ambiguity of the legacy of colonialism. On the one hand, previously colonized peoples have often been forced to maintain one-crop agricultural policies and one-commodity trading. On the other, these nations have been provided with scientific and technological resources that can and do contribute to human development by "diminishing ignorance and sickness" and by making better communication and improved living conditions possible (7). But the pope quickly adds that all of this is inadequate. The bottom line is that the prevailing economic system if left to itself simply serves to "widen the differences in the world's levels of life . . . rich peoples enjoy rapid growth whereas the poor develop slowly" (8). He insists that *the imbalance is on the increase.*

Human misery and underdevelopment are worldwide phenomena. The glaring inequality shows itself in terms of material scarcity as well as in political powerlessness and lack of participation in any kind of decision making for growing numbers of human beings. The conflict is exacerbated by the encounter of traditional cultures with that of modernity. The previously affirmed traditional worldviews that emphasized family, community, hierarchy, and religion seem rigid, out of place, and ineffective in the modern world with its emphasis on individual advancement, technological progress, and scientific positivism. Paul VI suggests here that a serious conversation needs to take place regarding the positive and negative aspects of the drive toward modernity.[23] The complete development of humanity depends on rethinking the way traditional cultural values change under the influence of modernity: "In effect, the moral, spiritual and religious supports of the past too often give way without securing in return any guarantee of a place in the new world" (10).[24]

The Option for the Poor

Paul VI grounds the Church's concern about human development directly on the message of Jesus Christ, whose mission is universal but focused in a special way on the poor (PP 12ff.). So too is the Church's mission. This assertion is an early formulation of and suggests the need for "a preferential option for the poor," an idea that will continue to develop in Catholic social teaching. The Latin American bishops at Medellín and third world liberation theologians subsequently gave form and substance to this initial formulation. Other church documents during the pontificate of Paul VI—*Octogesima adveniens*, *Justitia in mundo*, and *Evangelii nuntiandi*—repeated this special focus on the materially poor. The option for the poor, as it came to be called, derives from the principle of solidarity that Paul VI outlined. Here he lists the many ways in which the Church has opted for the poor in history through the building of schools, hospitals, and other institutions that contributed to their material advancement. He acknowledges the frequent failures of missionaries to respect the native cultures, but insists that over all, the Church brought about or at least contributed to many aspects of human development among the peoples it evangelized (12). But the point now is that neither the Church, the state, nor any other individual institution can effectively confront the enormity of such worldwide human misery alone and think that they will prevail. There must be a concerted effort organized at the highest levels of world leadership. Nevertheless, the Church has something very important to offer at this time of truly global urgency: its insight into human nature and its global vision of the human person and of the human race (13).

Development Rooted in Christian Humanism

Paul VI stresses the essential link between humanism and development. His conviction about the importance of this link is evident when he quotes from a study of the dynamics of development by Louis-Joseph Lebret. The pope quotes Lebret's words: "'We do not believe in separating the economic from the human, nor development from the civilizations in which it exists. What we hold important is man, each man and each group of men, and we include the whole of humanity'" (PP 14). The affirmation of the humanistic significance of development also shows the prolonged and deep influence that Maritain had on Montini, and through him on a great deal of the Church's subsequent social teaching. This influence dates from the 1930s to the time of Maritain's death in 1973. Two of the philosopher's works are especially relevant in this regard: *True Humanism* (1936) and *The Person and the Common Good* (1946). The spirit of this humanism is captured in this quotation from the 1938 translation of *True Humanism:*

> This new humanism, which has in it nothing in common with bourgeois humanism, and is all the more human since it does not worship man, but has a real and effective respect for human dignity and for the rights of the human person, I see *as directed towards a socio-temporal realization* of that evangelical concern for humanity which *ought not to exist only in the spiritual order, but to become incarnate* . . . It is not to the dynamism or the imperialism of race, or of class, or of nation, that it asks men to sacrifice themselves: it is for the sake of a better life for their fellows and for the concrete good of the community of human individuals, so that the humble truth of brotherly love may advance . . . *to the permeation of the social order and the structures of common life.*[25]

The pope further proposes the notion of human life as a vocation that everyone has. Each person has his or her attributes that call for development. Education and other opportunities enhance that process. Ultimately, it is a question of growing in humanity, "becoming more a person, being more, rather than having more" (15). But the pope insists that the humanism proposed by the Church is transcendent, that is, the fullest expression of human development is found in a person's union with Jesus Christ. This development is also social. It is not a question of isolated, individual development but rather through solidarity each and every individual is linked, whether he or she knows it or not, to all other human beings. Therefore, we have a duty toward all others. Development is always personal and communal, not just one or the other. What works against the proper balance between the personal and communal aspects of human development is materialism. It leads people, whether they are rich or poor, to think only about themselves. Here and throughout the encyclical Paul VI affirms what Marvin L. Mich, following the lead of Peter Riga, calls an "immanent spirituality" proposed by John XXIII in *Mater et magistra.*[26]

Development as a Spiritual Task

In numbers 14–21 the pope spends some time discussing the nature of materialism. In this connection he says that avarice is the most obvious form of moral underdevelopment for both nations and individuals. It becomes "stifling," hardens people's hearts, closes their minds, and makes self-interest rather than friendship the driving force behind human interactions. The pope proposes the need for wisdom, not just technological know-how, as a remedy to the materialism that creates such an obstacle to human development. This wisdom has to do with the pursuit of "higher values" such as friendship and love, prayer and contemplation. What is always at stake here, he reminds us again, is a movement from less human conditions to more human ones (20).

By less human conditions the pope means material poverty, the lack of the basic needs for human life, and moral poverty characterized by selfishness. The rich may, in this sense, be poor. The less human conditions refer to those of political and economic oppression that reveal themselves in the exploitation of workers and unjust business dealings. By more human conditions he means moving from material poverty to the possession of what one needs to live with dignity, the overcoming of dangers to health and social security, educational advancement, and the acquiring of cultural benefits. Truly human conditions develop even further, according to the pope, when people begin to respect the dignity of others, freely adopt a simpler, materially poorer way of life, and come to view the common good as greater than their own individual advancement. The turning away from violence and the pursuit of peace in all dealings with others exemplifies the movement from less to more human conditions of life. Human life in the most profound sense is crowned by a relationship with God that affirms God as the source and finality of all that is (21). In all of this Paul VI follows the lead of his predecessor John XXIII in proposing the "observe, judge, act" paradigm of pastoral reflection.[27]

The "observe, judge, act" method he put into practice was enthusiastically received as a simple but powerful way to help those on the margins connect their faith with real life, specifically with the social, economic, and political reality. Undoubtedly this simple but seminal framework for pastoral reflection was echoed in the methodology of Vatican II, especially in *Gaudium et spes*, but also in much of Paul VI's writings. The method flowered from 1970 to 1990 when it was enthusiastically taken up by liberation theology and adopted by local Latin American, African, and Asian churches. The U.S. Catholic bishops adopted the method for the *encuentro* processes, three national gatherings of Hispanic leaders over two decades.[28]

The Social Purpose of Material Possessions

Pope Paul VI strongly affirms the insistence on the universal destination of created things consistent with the Church's social teachings. In numbers 22–24 he discusses the human right to private possessions, subordinating it to the principle that God created everything on earth for the use of every human being. The pope insists that "it is a grave and urgent social duty to redirect them (property and commerce) to their primary finality" (22). This affirmation of the social purpose of private property is still the strongest to be found in Catholic social teaching. It is interesting to note the development of this basic theme. Pope Leo XIII began with an insistence on the right that all persons have to personal possessions. Adopting Thomas Aquinas's approach to the question of private property, Pope Leo was especially concerned with opposing Marxist views on that issue. When Pope Pius XI returned to this theme again in *Quadragesimo anno* he highlighted the social purpose and duty inherent in the possession of private property. In PP Pope Paul VI *inverted* his predecessors' approach to the topic by placing the social function before the individual right to private property. In asking the question about the actions that flow from an awareness of global poverty and economic injustice the pope chose to make the topic of the proper role of private property absolutely central.

The encyclical makes some strong assertions in numbers 22–24 about (1) the universal destination of all created things; (2) the demands made by the poor who lack what they need to live with dignity on those who possess more than what they need; and (3) common practices regarding the disposition of land and the investment of financial resources that often do not reflect an awareness of their negative effect on the common good.

Development, Industrialization, and Work

Paul VI then reflects in numbers 25–28 on industrialization's contributions and deficiencies in regard to the promotion of a truly human development. He begins by pointing out the positive contributions of industrialization to human progress. But he quickly moves to the basic issues underlying the conduct of industrial development, namely, the profit motive, unfettered competition, and private ownership of the means of production as an absolute right. The pope asserts in no uncertain terms that "the economy is at the service of man." Yet he reminds the reader that the evils are not inherent to industrialization per se but rather they inhere in *a type of capitalism*. Labor and industry can and do contribute to human development, but a defective capitalist system negates the great potential of industrialization for human advancement. While previous social documents of the Church tended to balance critiques of liberalism or free market capitalism with equal or stronger critiques of collectivism, this encyclical tilts more in the direction of a critique of the type of capitalism currently practiced. The pope repeats *Quadragesimo anno*'s reference to "the international imperialism of money," a systemic *cause* of socioeconomic underdevelopment rather than a remedy for it (26).

In the formulation of key issues affecting appropriate responses to the challenge of underdevelopment the pope devotes two substantial numbers to the place of work. He recalls Pope John XXIII's reflections on the transcendent role of meaningful work in a humanistic and Christian vision of the person (28). Pope John Paul II returns to this theme, expanding and deepening it, fourteen years later in *Laborem exercens*.

Reflection and Action

The urgency of the task to be done influences the actions undertaken in response (29). The pope cautions all those concerned about the bad effect of too much hastiness, how it can create a lack of balance and lead unwittingly to violence and disruption in the lives of many. He speaks out against the temptation to revolutionary action and discards it as an option in almost all cases. He opts for reform. Yet, in a somewhat passing observation that received a great deal of press subsequently and became the source of confusion, the pope mentions the possibility that revolutionary action may be admissible "where there is manifest, long-standing tyranny which would do great damage to fundamental personal rights and dangerous harm to the common good" (31).[29] One could argue then and now that there are several regimes in the world that fit that description.

What Paul VI calls for here is the need for all possible resources to be applied in response to the immense challenges posed by human misery and underdevelopment throughout the world. Concrete action like divesting oneself of wealth in the cause of redistributing resources, if only a gesture, is still a meaningful one. He cites the thoughts of Chilean Bishop Manuel Larraín in this connection (32).

In numbers 33–42 the encyclical gets down to specific responses to the enormous challenges of underdevelopment. The pope begins by saying that a laissez-faire attitude toward the resolution of underdevelopment is totally unacceptable. Even programs at the intermediary level are important, but they are not adequate. The response must come from the highest level of the states, regional associates of governments, and the entire international community.[30] Without explicitly mentioning it, Paul VI seems to be mindful of the principle of subsidiarity that Leo XIII first articulated and Pius XI stressed anew. In this section Pope Paul suggests that if ever there was a reality whose scope and urgency required the engagement of the highest echelons of government at the level of the state and international bodies it was global poverty (33).

What Matters Is the Human Person

For Pope Paul the bottom line must always be how the measures taken to address global poverty affect the human person. He lays out that thought in detail in numbers 33–42. The actions taken must result in more equality, less discrimination, and less social, economic, and political oppression. At the same time those actions must contribute to the flowering of what is best and deepest in human beings, that which goes beyond the purely economic or material, that is, the spiritual side of the human person and community. Development also has as much to do with social matters as with economic ones. More money alone is not the answer. Social organization requires that wealth be equitably distributed.

More technology by itself is not the answer either. Technocracy, the pope reminds us in the age of atomic weaponry's "assured mutual destruction," can breed evils comparable to those generated by capitalism's historical excesses. Economic progress depends on social progress in the form of more access to literacy and other forms of education. It also involves the proper ordering of family life, which influences the ability of people to pursue their human development. Striking a balance here, Pope Paul mentions the possibility that the family in traditional cultures may indeed exercise at times a negative role, holding people back from their proper development: "The family's influence may have been excessive to the detriment of the fundamental rights of the individual" (36). He is aware of the growing struggle between traditional third world cultures and the worldwide culture of modernity whose principal paradigms are American. In this context of tension the pope calls for give and take but also insists on the preservation of a certain basic Christian value: the natural, monogamous, and stable family.

Development and Population

Another social issue affecting human development is demographics. The pope acknowledges the impact demography has on economics and therefore on human development when the population surpasses available resources. Paul VI supports a limited concept of family planning. He refers to "radical means" to limit births. One can imagine he means measures such as abortion, infanticide, mass sterilization, and artificial contraception. He suggests that there are traditional means that may be sanctioned, such as limiting births by the practice of abstinence and other traditional, noncontraceptive means. He punctuates this section by insisting that the ultimate norm of judgment in these matters must always be individual conscience "enlightened by God's law authentically interpreted" (37). One year later Paul VI published *Humanae vitae*, an extensive and authoritative interpretation of sexuality and family planning. This document promptly became his most controversial work. Indeed, it can be argued here in passing that the generally negative, strident, and ongoing reaction to this encyclical for the rest of his pontificate, especially in Western European and North American contexts, distracted significantly from the positive reception of all his other teachings, including those on social justice.

Collaboration, Ideology, and Action

In PP 40 the pope recalls the role that professional organizations such as trade and credit unions play in promoting socioeconomic development. These groups and movements may be made up of people with diverse religions, ideologies, and interests, but they can all play a part in supporting efforts to address the causes of poverty. In this Paul VI makes a distinction in how ideology is understood. The first to make this distinction was John XXIII in *Pacem in terris:*

> It is, therefore, especially to the point to make a clear distinction between false philosophical teachings regarding the nature, origin, and destiny of the universe and of man, and movements which have direct bearing either on economic and social questions, or cultural matters or on the organization of the state, even if these movements owe their origin and inspiration to these false tenets . . . the movements, precisely because they take place in the midst of changing conditions, are readily susceptible of change. Besides, who can deny that those movements, insofar as they conform to the dictates of right reason and are interpreters of the lawful aspirations of the human person, contain elements that are positive and deserving of approval? (PT 159)

Paul VI's encyclical suggests that the Church and Christian people will find themselves collaborating with movements of various ideological stripes and that this pluralism should not necessarily hold them back from active collaboration in the cause of development. Concretely, Christians may find themselves working along with socialists and even Communists whose materialistic and atheistic doctrines are abhorrent. Yet the specific social movement in which they are involved is legitimate. The theme of ideology came up again in a subsequent encyclical, *Octogesima adveniens*, where the pope pulled away somewhat from the notion that Christians can cooperate with Marxists. In an earlier number of PP (26) Pope Paul VI criticizes some doctrines and the underlying philosophy of liberal capitalism: the profit motive as key consideration, a concept of ownership of the means of production that accepts no limitations, and the abuses that underlie the "woeful system" of the industrial age.

Echoed here as well is the idea of subsidiarity in the sense that intermediate bodies and movements have a legitimate role to play along with governments and international agencies in responding to the challenges of development.[31] Paul VI reaffirms here what John XXIII observed regarding "socialization."[32] He also notes that as long as Christians are not forced to deny their religious commitments or to support unjust actions that oppress others, they may engage in all manner of cooperative effort.

The Encyclical's Originality and Subsequent Influence

Paul VI warns the underdeveloped nations about the bad example given them by the wealthy ones: identifying development with material and technological advancement alone, and practically denying the world of the spirit, human transcendence, by attending only to earthly affairs. Once again he speaks of a *complete* humanism. This powerful humanistic thread in Catholic social teaching goes to the heart of this encyclical's concept of development and accounts for its distinctive contribution, what Pope John Paul II later refers to as its *originality* in *Sollicitudo rei socialis* (5–7). Subsequent writings of Paul VI, especially *Octogesima adveniens* and *Evangelii nuntiandi,* further elaborate the implications of both the humanist orientation of the Catholic social teaching and the Church's self-understanding and identity. Paul VI takes the anthropological concept of culture as elaborated in *Gaudium et spes* (53–62) and makes it the lens through which the Church views human reality (social, economic, and political) as well as its own identity and mission. Culture refers precisely to humanity, how humanity is understood and how it functions. Pope John Paul II takes this humanist thread and weaves it even more securely into the contemporary magisterium through the inspiration of Emmanuel Mounier's personalism as well as through his use of phenomenology as a philosophical method for reflection on human and Christian existence in the world.[33]

Catholic social teaching since John XXIII had noted and reflected upon the reality of interdependence among nations and peoples of the modern world. Paul VI makes a significant leap by elaborating the response that people of goodwill must make to this reality. He uses the word *solidarity*, which, as Kenneth R. Himes maintains, is "a term that defies neat definition in Catholic social teaching." The *Catechism of the Catholic Church* compares solidarity to "social charity." It hearkens back to a Catholic idea about organic society and natural sociality that played a role in the corporatism that inspired the social teaching of the Church in the first half of the twentieth century. Himes succinctly expresses the evolution of the concept:

> Solidarity . . . moves interdependence to another level, beyond acknowledging the fact of interdependence. Solidarity shapes the response we should have to interdependence, evoking within us a desire to build a common life. As a virtue, solidarity, in the words of John Paul II, is not a feeling of vague compassion but a "firm and persevering determination to commit oneself to the common good."[34]

Arguably, Pope Paul made here the most significant assertion of the entire encyclical: "There can be no progress toward complete development of man without the simultaneous development of all humanity in the spirit of solidarity" (43). He goes on to insist that solidarity means that the rich nations must be concerned about the poor ones. They must show that concern in practical ways, such as giving direct aid, establishing fairer trade relations, and seeing to it that no one is left behind as development advances (44). Paul VI invokes the figure of Lazarus, who ate the crumbs that fell from the master's table. He compares Lazarus to the poor nations. He insists that "Lazarus sit down at table with the rich man" (47). Solidarity applies to nations and blocs of nations as well as to individuals. "No nation," he tells the reader, "can claim . . . to keep its wealth for itself alone" (48).

The encyclical then proceeds to emphasize the inequity in trade relations among rich and poor nations, and suggests that the results of many development efforts that take the form of financial and/or technical assistance are "nullified" by unbalanced trade relations. The rich countries trade in costly and sophisticated manufactured products and technologies while the poor nations have only relatively inexpensive agricultural products and raw materials. In this situation "what is given them with one hand, was being taken away with the other" (56). Moreover, the trade in raw materials, unlike that of first world products, is subject to wild fluctuations that leave developing countries at the mercy of the market. As a result, poor nations become poorer and the rich ones richer. Free trade by itself is therefore not the answer to socioeconomic inequities. While not without merits, free trade as the rule in international commerce and as the "fundamental principle of liberalism" is directly challenged by Catholic social teaching. Paul VI quotes his predecessor

Leo XIII in *Rerum novarum* to the effect that mere consent in a contract between two parties that are extremely unequal does not make a *just* contract (59). He insists that laws of the marketplace alone cannot be the guiding principle of trade relations; rather, trade relations are subject to the demands of social justice (61).

The pontiff, however, is not suggesting that the free market be eliminated. Rather, he wants it to be regulated in such a way that social justice is achieved. That means leveling the playing field so as to establish conditions of equality. This involves regulating prices, assuring that certain types of production are pursued and new industries fostered.[35]

Threats to Development

Turning to other sources of injustice at the international level, the encyclical points to nationalism and racism. Nationalism can be rooted in a people's sense of their great achievements and their antiquity. It can also show itself in the context of independence recently attained that requires the fostering of a sense of national identity for the sake of a still fragile unity. In both cases nationalism can become an excuse for not embracing other people, not exercising a "universal charity," and isolating one nation from another. Commercial and cultural development requires just the opposite: the combining of efforts in a wide range of financial, technical, and educational areas (62). The extreme imbalances in the distribution of the world's wealth require not only a redistribution of that wealth but also a commitment to providing poor nations with the means of production necessary to move out of poverty. This means that the level of international collaboration must increase dramatically. Each nation must attain a sense of responsibility for all nations. The goal in all of this is creating the conditions whereby all peoples can become "artisans of their destiny."

Paul VI goes on in Part 2 of PP to boldly assert that "the world is sick" (66). The source of this sickness is not just the "unproductive monopolization of resources" in the hands of a few, but rather the lack of a real sense of unity among individuals and nations. This lack is opposed to solidarity and universal charity that ought to characterize human relations. This is manifested in the treatment of foreign migrant workers who are often not appropriately welcomed in their host countries. Hospitality toward strangers is a fundamental expression of the solidarity and universal charity to which the pope is referring. Within the context of immigration, moreover, he notes that immigrant youth are often alienated from their culture as they assimilate to the new one. This process must be monitored lest important spiritual values of their cultural heritage be jettisoned (68). Businesses that begin to function in developing countries need to respect the communitarian ethos of traditional cultures rather than presume that all peoples share in the more individualistic ethic of Western cultures. Pope Paul proceeds to list several practical measures that will guarantee the respectful treatment of workers in the developing countries by first world businesses operating in the third world. He signals the need for international codes of conduct that were being proposed at the time.

In the task of pursuing a complete human development, the ability to enter into healthy dialogue with others is essential. That is the way to draw people and nations together in solidarity. That dialogue must first of all be based on the human person, not on commodities or things (73). Technicians are more than that; they are educators, Paul VI reminds his readers. What is at stake is not just material advancement but, more pertinently, human development. In proposing the task of service to those in need across international borders, the pope makes a special appeal to youth. He notes a rising number of human development projects that focus the energy of youthful volunteers on service to the poor. Perhaps he is thinking of the Peace Corps established by President John F. Kennedy in the early 1960s.

Development and Peace

The pope ends this section by relating the struggle for human development to issues of war and peace. The catching and felicitous subtitle given this final section is "Development is the new name for peace." It has become a common refrain for social justice workers ever since. The pursuit of peace requires a war on poverty, human misery, and inequality. Given the dimensions of the challenges faced by such extensive poverty in the world, the pope suggests that a universal order of justice must be recognized. Endorsing the United Nations in a most unequivocal way, he repeats the question first posed in his 1965 speech before that body: "Who does not see the necessity of thus establishing progressively *a world authority*, capable of acting effectively in the juridical and political sectors?" (78). The encyclical challenges the idea that this is utopian and dismisses those who would deny the need that slow but sure steps can be taken in the direction of a more interconnected world of solidarity. The author mentions the underlying motivation for such a vision in biblical theology, in the doctrine of the body of Christ. "What is at stake," we are reminded, "is the peace of the world and the future of civilization" (80).

EXCURSUS

A number of issues emerge that merit further reflection as one looks more carefully at the encyclical. The first is the novel approach taken to the very concept of development. In the 1950s it became clearer that the redistribution of the world's wealth was not the only way to address worldwide poverty. The social teaching of the Church had simply assumed that redistribution was the more obvious way to go. Reflection upon the sustained economic development in Europe and North America began to suggest that poverty could be more effectively addressed by means of productivity. All boats, as it were, would rise with the tide of development. In effect, the rich could keep their goods but the poor would also gain the benefits of there being more goods to go around than ever before. Pope Paul VI certainly did not abandon the idea of redistribution and he seized on the idea of economic growth as offering a real way out of global poverty. But he added something to it. For one thing, he stressed the idea of integral development; for another, he raised the issue of asymmetrical power relations in the quest for development. This eventually led to a recognition of the need in Catholic social thought to confront the *political* order as well as the economic one. In this encyclical he simply refused to take the prevailing notion of *economic* development as the appropriate starting point for a serious and adequate discussion of development. He insisted that in addition to economic development there must also be a furthering of humanity broadly understood. Economic growth by itself does not respond to the broader concept of integral development. The humanistic concept adds key elements to the notion of economic development: concerns regarding culture, the family, human rights and dignity, and the effect on the environment. The document lays down criteria that judge the authenticity of human development. True human development must be evaluated by the larger framework provided here. That framework goes beyond purely economic criteria and asserts that development is ultimately a matter of ongoing humanization.

Subsequent analyses and events, however, demonstrated that there are serious limits to making integral development, even this broad, humanistic understanding of it, the principal focus of the world's response to poverty. Neocolonialism is implicated as a major obstacle in this regard. The Latin American bishops took the thought of Paul VI quite seriously and immediately discovered that an awareness of how *politics* influences development was lacking. In their watershed document of Medellín they talked less about "development" and more about "liberation." For they realized that the main obstacles to development of any kind in Latin America are the prevailing, oppressive, nondemocratic, and nonparticipatory political structures. So it seemed to them that the first task in the struggle against poverty is not economic but political in nature. Indeed, the very word *development* became problematical in the 1970s and beyond. It became identified with dependency and neocolonial international economic policies. Interestingly enough, it can be said that the response given to PP by Latin

American bishops, other third world leaders, and liberation theologians moved Pope Paul VI to balance his vision. He officially added the word *liberation* to the ecclesial vocabulary and made it—the struggle for complete, human development that requires sociopolitical as well as economic changes at the structural level—an essential component of evangelization, the Church's identity and mission. Eight years after PP's publication, in arguably the most influential of his writings, *Evangelii nuntiandi*, Paul VI puts development squarely within the context of liberation. Speaking of the many people represented by the bishops who attended the 1971 synod in Rome, the pontiff wrote:

> peoples, as we know, engaged with all their energy in the effort and struggle to overcome everything which condemns them to remain on the margin of life: famine, chronic disease, illiteracy, poverty, injustices in international relations and especially in commercial exchanges, situations of economic and cultural neo-colonialism sometimes as cruel as the old political colonialism. The Church, as the Bishops repeated, has the duty to proclaim the liberation of millions of human beings, many of whom are her own children—the duty of assisting the birth of this liberation, of giving witness to it, of ensuring that it is complete. This is not foreign to evangelization.[36]

The recognition of the Church's role in the promotion of liberation came about when the dialogue around PP, the document of Medellín, and other ecclesial reflections gradually led to the realization that development really is a political problem as well as an economic or even broadly humanistic one. This realization led in turn to the issue of how to approach political change. What model of political change is the most relevant and effective? Clearly, Pope Paul VI in PP continues to insist on a consensus model:

> a revolutionary uprising—unless there is question of flagrant and long-standing tyranny which would violate the fundamental rights of the human person and inflict grave injury on the common good of the State—produces new injustices . . . and provokes people to further destructive outrage. (31)

Donal Dorr analyzes this text and concludes that "the statement as it stands does not encourage people to use violent means to overcome injustices, even in extreme circumstances." He goes on to say, "the encyclical *implies* that there may well be situations in our world today where revolution might be permissible."[37] This matter was to take on more significance after the Medellín conference in 1968. In applying the principles of Catholic social teaching, and particularly PP, the Latin American bishops insisted on linking issues of development with the broader issues of socioeconomic and political or structural liberation. The seed that eventually led to John Paul II's emphasis on "structural sin" is found here. In the next twenty years significant popular political movements arose, some of them supported by revolutionary guerrilla fighters. The more radical stance taken by the Latin American bishops was undoubtedly a source of considerable concern to Paul VI, who in his next letter, *Octogesima adveniens*, tried to moderate what he considered the excesses that critics were blaming on him and Latin American bishops.

Dorr notes that Pope Paul VI can ultimately be criticized for failing to acknowledge the role that conflict plays in social change. It is one thing to discourage revolutionary action; it is another to avoid conflict in general. There cannot be dialogue leading to consensus when the parties in the supposed dialogue are unequal. Some way must be found for the rich and powerful to yield something to the poor and powerless. This rarely occurs in an irenic manner.[38]

As reported above, Pope Paul VI invited the famous community organizer Saul Alinsky to Milan to advise him on ways to respond to the gains communist-led labor unions and the Communist Party were making in his archdiocese, the largest in Italy. Alinsky's approach to political participation was based upon a positive evaluation of conflict in society and politics. While Alinsky's principles and the Church's social teachings were undoubtedly in agreement about the fundamental right people have to participate in decisions affecting their lives, they part ways in their attitude toward conflict. Alinsky welcomed it as necessary. Indeed, according to him, the failure to appreciate how to enter into and transform conflictive situations, the "rules for radicals," is one of the main causes of oppression in the world.[39]

Alinsky came upon this positive evaluation of conflict in the context of a democratic republic, the United States. Perhaps the inability of Pope Paul VI to deal more easily with the reality and necessity of conflict in his approach to social justice issues is that he knows that the vast majority of the world's poor and powerless do not live in democratic republics. Consequently, they must be much more cautious than citizens, albeit poor and downtrodden, of democratic regimes. Speaking out about the most elementary rights means persecution and even instant death in many places of the world. The pope may have judged it unwise to go beyond the consensus model given the very real dangers that talk about confrontations can pose for the poor in many regimes. One might ask those who wish to propose confrontational models for political change, now with the benefit of hindsight, what benefits were obtained for the poor and powerless, what human development came about as a result of the years of conflict in Central America during the 1980s. The answer remains ambiguous.

Pope Paul VI's emphasis on integral development itself underwent development in the last three decades of the twentieth century. The collapse of the socialist world in the early 1990s gave a new impetus to development talk based on the assumption that had first fascinated so many world leaders concerned with the plight of the poor, namely, the prospect of the free market's productivity lifting everyone out of poverty. Latin American theologian José Comblin comments on this at the end of the twentieth century:

> Production is the great myth of the bourgeoisie; the work ethic was created for no other reason than to foster production. Certainly, production has increased astonishingly throughout the twentieth century, reaching levels that no one would have imagined. Societies are governed in such a way as to increase their production. All this is true, but production—at least as it is presently being implemented—does not resolve the problems of dire poverty, the basic needs of a good portion of the population, or unemployment. . . . This emphasis on production enables a minority to accumulate even greater wealth. Any reforms, any proposals for redistribution, are considered impossible because they would keep production from rising. Production has thus become an idol to which the lives of whole peoples are sacrificed.[40]

Comblin notes that the problem of global poverty is still viewed basically as an economic issue and not as one of complete human development despite how Paul VI would have it in PP. This reluctance to frame properly the issue of poverty and human development is not served by the prevailing bourgeois ethics of the Western world. This ethic presupposes that equity and justice will come about as the result of the pursuit of *individual* rights. What is lacking here, according to Comblin, is an option for the poor (rather than for economic, production) and an ethic of solidarity rather than one of individual rights.[41]

In contrast to Comblin's view from the third world is that of social ethicist Albino Barrera, whose perspective is more first world and technical. He offers a critique of the Church's social teachings from the point of view of globalization and the information economy. While he is speaking of the tradition in general, his observations bear directly on Pope Paul's vision in PP and subsequent writings. Barrera suggests that a globalized information-based economy will exacerbate the problem of relative inequality. He claims that the Catholic social teaching of the past one hundred years is deficient because (1) it promotes an uncritical egalitarianism that does not grasp the inseparability of wealth-income creation from its distribution; (2) it is too abstract and fails to give concrete particulars from which guidelines can be developed; (3) its approach toward egalitarianism is ahistorical, disregarding the peculiarities and challenges in the actual situations, in experience; and (4) it proposes a kind of cure-all egalitarianism that looks at the issue only from the point of view of distribution of shared resources and outcomes.[42]

Barrera suggests that these matters have to be incorporated into future formulations of the Church's social teachings. The contemporary context was already hinted at in *Mater et magistra* when John XXIII noted the changed nature of property, dividing it between material and immaterial. The information age makes that distinction increasingly relevant. The drive toward distributive justice requires an analysis of equity in terms of access to both tangible and intangible goods. He proposes linking the principle of participation to equity, particularly in regard to access to these intangible properties.[43]

REACTIONS TO THE DOCUMENT

Peter Hebblethwaite in his in-depth biography of Paul VI observes that the encyclical was especially well received in France. Perhaps that is because a great deal of the inspiration for it, as noted above, came from Père Lebret, whose journal had been disseminating this humanistic vision of development in the French-speaking world. Hebblethwaite quotes François Perroux of the College of France, who called PP "one of the greatest texts of human history."[44] The encyclical builds on the goodwill generated by Pope Paul's 1965 speech to the United Nations. It struck a cord in the minds of many thoughtful people who were seeking insight regarding the global extent of poverty and what to do about it. This encyclical addressed that reality and provided a powerful if at times high-minded vision of where to go next. The growing awareness of dreadful living conditions for so many human beings throughout the world found a response in this encyclical.

This was especially true in Latin America, where Pope Paul's social vision in this encyclical was right on target. The encyclical gained more notice there than anywhere else. The Latin American bishops moved ahead with the effort to apply its insights in their own document of Medellín.[45] For similar reasons, it was well received by other bishops and political leaders in other parts of the third world. According to Hebblethwaite, what made the encyclical so timely was that it addressed all men and women of goodwill and acknowledged the reality of "spaceship earth" and the logical need for true solidarity among human beings living on this fragile craft.[46] It appealed to those seeking a balance between collectivism and individualism, and among legitimate human diversities in the form of nation, culture, language, and ethnicity.[47]

Nevertheless, there were strong negative critics, particularly in the English-speaking world. The *Wall Street Journal* led the attack:

> Pope Paul's encyclical lends the mantle of religion to certain ideas which are profoundly secular in origin, and advocates programs of a type now undergoing widespread reappraisal by their one-time secular sponsors. . . . The trouble with making religious tenets of this warmed-over Marxism is that it is highly unlikely to help the bulk of poor nations which suffer not from an excess of capitalism, but from a paucity of it. . . . It is both curious and sad that these mistaken attitudes toward foreign aid should now be advanced from the realm of religion. For the realm of history, as more people are starting to recognize, shows that they impede rather than advance the development of peoples.[48]

The review given the encyclical by Michael Novak writing many years after its publication was anything but positive. He thought it was "naive and lacking in humility," very abstract, and overly emotional. Novak contended that the pope "lashed out" at unrestrained liberal capitalism, condemning it as a "woeful system." Novak suggested that the problem with this encyclical is that the pope depended too much on the thought of third world development intellectuals.[49] The encyclical was not well received among supporters of the free market economy because the pope trenchantly criticized it. These proponents claim that he was misinformed regarding the facts of economic development and how markets work. They maintain that the encyclical tilts too much in the direction of state intervention in the development process, and that it naïvely assumes that centralized authority can do more than experience has shown to ameliorate economic inequality. Novak and others feared that Paul VI was playing with fire because his views would only incite the poor to rebellion.[50]

Writing two decades after the publication of PP, Robert Royal produced one of its more trenchant critiques. In hindsight Royal detects a murkiness in the pope's language that contributes to what Royal calls a vague developmentalism that took too much for granted and borrowed excessively from prevailing and now outmoded developmental theories.[51] Royal is more sympathetic to John Paul II's take on development in *Sollicitudo rei socialis*, which is more solidly grounded on the facts of development and, in contrast to Paul VI's fledgling effort, enjoys the benefit of two decades of experience and evaluation of the thorny question of economic development.

The encyclical was also criticized from the more radical left for being too beholden to "developmentalism." A vigorous critique of developmentalism actually arose around the time of PP's publication. As mentioned earlier, the United Nations had designated the 1960s as the First Development Decade. World leaders were taken by the idea that the unprecedented productivity of the age would provide the opportunity to eliminate poverty once and for all. Peter Henriot reflects on the controversy around the word *development*:

> The use of the word "development" stirs mixed reactions in many scholarly and political circles. And is usually seen as both a goal and a process, an end and a means. . . . In the 1960's, largely influenced by the thinking of economists such as Rostow, development was viewed as a linear process marked by "stages" . . . as measured primarily by economic growth rates. . . . More radical economists, many from the Third World, challenged this narrow notion . . . as being inadequate and misleading.[52]

Certainly PP at the time of its publication was one of the first major critiques of the prevailing and inadequate notions of development. The fact, however, that at the end of the day it accepted the term and did not propose a clear practical alternative leading to the implementation of its exalted vision ironically made it susceptible to criticism for falling into a soft kind of developmentalism.

Dissatisfaction with the word *development* was voiced by Latin American economists and liberation theologians in what came to be called the "theory of dependency."[53] Gustavo Gutiérrez, writing four years after the publication of PP, described the theory of dependency in these words:

> The underdevelopment of the poor countries, as an over-all social fact, appears in its true light: as the historical by-product of the development of other countries. The dynamics of the capitalist economy lead to the establishment of a center and a periphery, simultaneously generating progress and growing wealth for the few and the social imbalances, political tensions, and poverty of the many.[54]

Many third world social activists and liberation theologians became uncomfortable with the unanalyzed and uncritical use of the term *development* without first dispelling the notion that in its concrete historical manifestation it is the solution to endemic poverty when, in fact, it is a major part of the problem. André Gunder Frank spoke ironically of "the development of underdevelopment."[55]

The humanist thrust of Catholic social thought, however, in later years received a powerful boost from the wide and deep application of the anthropological concept of culture in John Paul II's writings. Pope John Paul gives his predecessor's orientation a Christological and incarnational twist and expands on it in his first encyclical, *Redemptor hominis,* where he makes the remarkable statements "for the Church all ways to God lead to the human person" and "the human person is the primary route the church must travel in fulfilling its mission."[56]

While the humanistic current in PP has been strengthened by Pope John Paul II, it is not clear whether its strong critique of liberal capitalism has been sustained or softened. In a review of Michael Novak's *The Catholic Ethic and the Spirit of Capitalism*, John Attarian recalls the Polish pope's treatise titled *The Acting Person* and suggests that the Church's social teaching is now more sanguine about capitalism:

> John Paul had long been impressed by "the human being's most arresting characteristic": his or her capacity to originate action; that is, to imagine and conceive of new things and then do them. He found in creative acts the clue to human identity. . . . Every woman and every man has been created in the image of the Creator, in order to help co-create the future of the world. . . . Thus man is endowed with an inalienable right to creative initiative, whence follows the religious case for the free economy.[57]

Michael Budde, on the other hand, maintains that the Catholic Church in the period after Vatican II and under the leadership of Pope John Paul II continues to be one of the few worldwide institutions that regularly offers a critique of the prevailing capitalist system. Budde holds that the single most important change now well under way in worldwide Catholicism is precisely its transition from an institution rooted in Europe and North America to one massively engaged in the least developed nations of the world. That means that the emphasis on solidarity is not only a theoretical matter grounded in social ethics but a practical matter vital to the concerns of the Church's primary constituencies.[58] If Budde is correct, these trends reinforce the critical stance toward liberal capitalism taken by Pope Paul in PP.

More than thirty years after PP's publication, the renowned Bengali humanistic economist Amartya Sen has built a brilliant career around the elucidation of a mature and nuanced concept of development. A winner of the Nobel Prize in Economic Sciences in 1998, Sen takes an approach that is generally compatible with Pope Paul's. These are just a few of the important points of contact between the two: insistence on the ethical, philosophical underpinnings of one's notion of development, and a clear focus on the issues of poverty, inequality, and social choice and action.[59]

Nevertheless, circumstances extraneous to the encyclical itself had a negative effect on its reception, especially in the developed English-speaking world. First, writers like Michael Novak may have found the document's grounding in French intellectual culture with its philosophical bent and its tendency (arguably) toward high-sounding generalizations to be a put-off. Second, the uproar caused by *Humanae vitae* less than a year later took away from the serious study and discussion of this document in the developed nations. Nevertheless, as Peter Henriot affirms, this encyclical plays a central role in the elaboration of the concept of development in the Church's social teaching: "The most complete statement in Catholic social teaching of this integral development is found in Pope Paul's *Populorum Progressio*. This teaching is updated and elaborated in John Paul II's *Sollicitudo Rei Socialis*. These are the two major Catholic social teaching documents on development."[60]

Pope Paul's encyclical also makes substantial contributions to the discourse in the Church's social teaching regarding the purpose of economic life, which is for people and for enhancing being, not having. It affirms basic principles and takes the discussion to new levels of insight. The encyclical certainly contributed to the remarkable flowering of ecclesial reflection and action that took place in Latin America throughout the 1970s and 1980s. It contributed to the rise of liberation theology and the basic ecclesial communities in Latin America, Africa, and Asia. This certainly constitutes one of the more original, extensive, and influential applications of Catholic social teaching ever achieved. This legacy continues to influence Christians throughout the world, especially in the least developed nations. Issues that arise in PP, such as the need for equity in trade relations between rich and poor nations, the immorality of the arms race, and the social purpose of property, are as crucial today in the age of globalization as they were when Pope Paul first articulated them. As such, this encyclical represents a significant milestone in the ongoing elaboration of Catholic social teaching.

NOTES

1. Michael Walsh and Brian Davies provide a useful outline in *Proclaiming Justice and Peace: Papal Documents from Rerum Novarum to Centesimus Annus* (Mystic, Conn.: Twenty-Third, 1991), 221–23. I have followed its major divisions here.

2. P. Hebblethwaite, *John XXIII: Pope of the Council* (London: Geoffrey Chapman, 1984).

3. Drew Christiansen discusses Pope John's significant shift in method in some detail in his Commentary on *Pacem in terris* in this volume.

4. Marcello de Carvalho Azevedo outlines the nature of this encounter in *Inculturation and the Challenges of Modernity* (Rome: Gregorian University Press, 1982), 30ff.

5. Hebblethwaite, *Paul VI*, 278.

6. Loris F. Capovilla, ed., *Giovanni XXIII, Lettere 1958–1963* (Rome: Edizioni di Storia e Letteratura, 1970), 40.

7. Hebblethwaite, *Paul VI*, 271–72, 278.

8. Preparatory Survey for Vatican II in *Acta et Documenti Concilio Vaticano II Apparando*, Series I, Antepraeparatoria (Vatican City: Editrice Vaticana, 1960–61).

9. See David Hollenbach's Commentary on *Gaudium et spes* in this volume.

10. Hebblethwaite, *Paul VI*, 8.

11. See Alan Figueroa Deck, "Culture," in *New Encyclopedia of Catholic Social Thought*, ed. Judith A. Dwyer (Collegeville, Minn.: Liturgical, 1994), 256.

12. See Hebblethwaite, *Paul VI*, 27.

13. Marion K. Sanders, *The Professional Radical: Conversations with Saul Alinsky* (New York: Harper and Row, 1965), 9. Sanders writes, "During numerous stays in local jails he (Alinsky) wrote *Reveille for Radicals*—a personal credo which Jacques Maritain called 'epoch making.' Maritain who subsequently became a warm, personal friend, introduced Alinsky to the Archbishop of Milan—now Pope Paul VI—with whom he spent a week in Italy discussing the Church's relationship with local communist unions." See also Hebblethwaite, *Paul VI*, 260–80.

14. Albino Barrera, *Modern Catholic Social Documents and Political Economy* (Washington, D.C.: Georgetown University Press, 2001), 2; Peter Groenewegen, "Political Economy and Economics," in *The New Palgrave Dictionary of Economics*, ed. John Eatwell, Murray Milgate, and Peter Newman (London: Macmillan, 1987).

15. Lebret had been present at the Second World Congress of the Lay Apostolate in Rome in 1957. Giovanni Battista Montini, later Pope Paul VI, helped organize the first Congress in 1951. See Peter Hebblethwaite, *Paul VI: The First Modern Pope* (New York: Paulist, 1993), 271–72. Cited in the text of PP is Lebret's "Dynamique concrete du développement" (Paris: *Économie et Humanisme*, Les Éditions Ouvrières, 1961), 28.

16. Vincent Cosmao, "*Populorum Progressio*, 30 Ans Après," *Foi et Développement*, Bulletin of the Centre Lebret, nos. 250/251 (February–March 1997). Translation of the French text graciously provided by Marguerite Gendron.

17. Jacques Maritain was the French ambassador to the Holy See during John XXIII's pontificate. He spent much time during those years with the pope and his trusted colleague Montini. An example of Maritain's "new humanism" is clearly present in PP 20. The influence of Maritain's humanism on the thought of Montini was a red flag for a conservative group of cardinals that included Pizzardo, Ottaviani, and Siri (their candidate for pope in the conclave that elected John XXIII). Some Jesuits in Rome acted as "attack dogs" for these prelates. Vaillancourt notes that Jesuit Antonio Massineo attacked Maritain in *Civiltà Cattolica*, the semiofficial Roman journal. See Jean-Guy Vaillancourt, *Papal Power: Study of Vatican Control over Lay Catholic Elites* (Berkeley: University of California Press, 1980), 74.

18. Hebblethwaite, *Paul VI*, 417.

19. "Monsignor Pavan Elucidates," *The Tablet* 221 (April 8, 1967): 392.

20. See Barbara Ward, "Looking Back on *Populorum Progressio*," in *Official Catholic Social Teaching, Moral Theology, No. 5*, ed. Charles E. Curran and Richard A. McCormick (New York: Paulist, 1986), 131. See also Georges Jarlot, "L'Église et le developpement, l'enciclique *Populorum Progressio*," *Études* 326 (May 1967): 674–88.

21. A. Arbuthnott, *Joseph Cardijn: Priest and Founder of the Y.C.W.* (London: Darton, Longman, and Todd, 1966); also Joseph Cardijn, Cardinal, *Laymen into Action*. Trans. by Anne Heggie. (London: Chapman, 1964). Originally published as *Laïes en premières lignes* (Paris: Éditions Universitaires).

22. Cardinal Agostino Casaroli, Paul VI's secretary of state, as reported by Hebblethwaite, stated that the pope started a dossier on "human development" immediately after returning from his visit to India. See manuscript of Casaroli's sermon in Brescia Cathedral of September 24, 1984, as reported in Hebblethwaite, *Paul VI*, 14.

23. M. de C. Azevedo, *Inculturation and the Challenges of Modernity*, 30–52. Also from a distinctively Latin American perspective sociologist Pedro Morandé discusses underlying issues in the process of modernization in *Cultura y Modernización en América Latina* (Santiago: Pontificia Universidad Católica de Chile, 1984).

24. Richard R. Gaillardetz in his chapter in this volume outlines a way to approach the encounter between the Church and cultures using David Tracy's concept of "mutually critical correlations." This method may also be useful for addressing the pope's concern about modern Western culture's encounter with Asia, Africa, and Latin America.

25. J. Maritain, *True Humanism*, trans. Margaret Adamson (London: Charles Scribner's Sons, 1938), xvii. Emphases mine. Later translations of this work changed the title to *Integral Humanism*, a more literal rendering of the French original, *Humanisme Intégral.*

26. See the Commentary on *Mater et magistra* by Marvin L. Mich in this volume.

27. See ibid., where Mich develops the pastoral-theological synthesis in Pope John XXIII's writings. He cites the use Pope John made of Cardinal Cardijn's method.

28. Allan Figueroa Deck, *The Second Wave: Hispanic Ministry and the Evangelization of Cultures* (Mahwah, N.J.: Paulist, 1989), 120–32.

29. For a cogent analysis of Catholic teaching regarding revolutionary violence with references to Paul VI's views in PP, see Charles E. Curran, *Catholic Social Teaching: 1891–Present: A Historical, Theological, and Ethical Analysis* (Washington, D.C.: Georgetown University Press, 2002), 162–63. John Langan explores the implications of this teaching in the context of Latin American popular uprisings in "Violence and Injustice in Society: Recent Catholic Teaching," *Theological Studies* 46 (1985): 685–99.

30. The realization that nongovernmental organizations, NGOs as they are called, have an important if not critical role to play in resolving serious social issues throughout the world had not yet been reached. The collapse of communism and the decline in centrally planned economies, together with the rise of more fledgling democratic regimes in the world, are examples of how circumstances have changed since 1967. The pope's point, however, is still quite valid: given the scale and urgency of the challenges, governments and the highest level of public order are essential players in the resolution of the most serious endemic socioeconomic inequities.

31. Pope Pius XI spoke of subsidiarity in QA 79. This principle of Catholic social teaching suffers from considerable ambivalence. It seeks to restrain centralizing and bureaucratic tendencies that are often identified with the political left, especially socialism, while encouraging a certain pluralism of options, diversity, and sharing of power, traits that are often not the hallmark of rightist conceptions of order.

32. See Mich's Commentary on *Mater et magistra* in this volume.

33. Emmanuel Mounier, *Personalism*, trans. Philip Mairet (Notre Dame, Ind.: University of Notre Dame Press, 1952). See also D. Wolf, "Emmanuel Mounier, Catholic of the Left," *Review of Politics* 22 (1960): 324–44. For Mounier's influence on Wojtyla, see George Huntston Williams, *The Mind of John Paul II* (New York: Seabury, 1981), 147ff.

34. Kenneth R. Himes, *Responses to 101 Questions on Catholic Social Teaching* (New York: Paulist, 2001), 38; John Paul II, SRS 38.

35. Père Lebret, perhaps the pope's main source of inspiration here, had spoken out about the need for energetic efforts to level the playing field in a commentary he wrote on GS. See L.-J. Lebret in *La Chiesa del mondo contemporaneo: commento alla costituzione pastorale "Gaudium et Spes,"* ed. H. de Reidmatten et al. (Brescia: Queriniana, 1966), 224.

36. Paul VI, *Evangelii nuntiandi*, number 30.

37. D. Dorr, *Option for the Poor* (Maryknoll, N.Y.: Orbis, 1992), 193.

38. See Christine Gudorf's Commentary on *Octogesima Adveniens* in this volume, where this matter is pursued in depth.

39. Saul D. Alinsky, *Reveille for Radicals* (New York: Vintage, 1946), 132.

40. José Comblin, *Called for Freedom: The Changing Context of Liberation Theology* (Maryknoll, N.Y.: Orbis, 1998), 157.

41. Ibid., 162–63.

42. Barrera, *Modern Catholic Social Documents*, 190.

43. Ibid., 191.

44. François Perroux, "L'encyclique de la Résurrection," in *L'Église dans le monde de ce temps*, 3, 202–3 as cited in Hebblethwaite, *Paul VI*, 483, n. 4.

45. *Iglesia y Liberación Humana, Los Documentos de Medellín* (Barcelona: Editorial Nova Terra, 1969).

46. Paul VI's ideal of a solidaristic world is more under attack than ever. See the writings of Australian ethicist Peter Singer, "The Singer Solution to World Poverty," September 5, 1999, available on Brandeis University web page at www.brandeis.edu/departments/philosophy/philosophy.html. For a nonscholarly but well-written attack on the entire notion of solidarity, see Garret Hardin, "Life Boat Ethics: The Case against Helping the Poor," *Psychology Today* 8 (September 1974): 38–43, 124–26. For a more thoughtful contemporary view of solidarity without using the term, see Wendell Berry's essay, "The Idea of a Local Economy," *Harper's* 304 (April 2002), 15–20.

47. Positive evaluations of the encyclical are found in the Catholic press: *National Catholic Reporter* (April 5, 1967): 3; *The Tablet* 221 (April 7, 1967): 367; *Commonweal* 86 (April 14, 1967): 108; Mary McGrory, *America* 116 (April 15, 1967): 552; Philip Burnham, *Triumph* 2 (May 1967): 10; José de Broucker, *New Blackfriars* 48 (1968): 540. The secular press is more critical.

48. *Wall Street Journal*, March 30, 1967, 14.

49. Michael Novak, *The Development of Catholic Social Thought* (New York: Harper and Row, 1984), 134, 140.

50. Hebblethwaite, *Paul VI*, 485.

51. Robert Royal, "Populorum Progressio," in *Building the Free Society: Democracy, Capitalism and Catholic Social Teaching*, ed. George Weigel and Robert Royal (Grand Rapids, Mich., and Washington, D.C.: Eerdmans and the Ethics and Public Policy Center, 1993), 115–31.

52. Peter Henriot, "Who Cares about Africa? Development Guidelines from the Church's Social Teaching," ed. Oliver F. Williams and John W. Houck, *Catholic Social Thought and the New World Order* (Notre Dame, Ind.: University of Notre Dame Press, 1993), 209.

53. The classic formulation of the theory of dependency is found in Fernando Henrique Cardoso and Enzo Faletto, *Dependency and Development in Latin America*, trans. Marjory Mattingly Urquidi (Berkeley: University of California Press, 1979). See also Frank Bonilla and Robert Girling, *Structures of Dependency* (Palo Alto, Calif.: Nairobi, 1973).

54. Gustavo Gutiérrez, *Theology of Liberation: History, Politics, and Salvation*, trans. and ed. Caridad Inda and John Eagleson (Maryknoll, N.Y.: Orbis, 1973), 84ff.

55. André Gunder Frank, "The Development of Underdevelopment," in *Latin America: Underdevelopment or Revolution* (New York: Monthly Review, 1969).

56. John Paul II, *Redemptor hominis,* number 14. The personalist and phenomenological currents in John Paul II's humanism are clearly revealed in *The Acting Person*, a work of phenomenological anthropology, the fruit of his teaching at the Catholic University of Lublin. His thought is an intensification and wider development of Pope Paul VI's humanism with similar, if less explicit, underpinnings in Catholic intellectual culture of pre– and post–World War II Europe. See Karol Wojtyla, *The Acting Person*, trans. Andrzej Potocki (London: D. Reidel, 1969).

57. See John Attarian's review of Michael Novak's work in *The Acton Institute's Journal* 4, no. 1 (January–February 1994).

58. Michael L. Budde, *The Two Churches: Catholicism and Capitalism in the World System* (Durham, N.C.: Duke University Press, 1992), 126–33.

59. See Ajit Kumar Sinha and Raj Kumar Sen, eds., *Economics of Amartya Sen* (New Delhi: Vedams Books of India, 2000).

60. Henriot, "Who Cares about Africa? in *Catholic Social Thought and the New World*, ed. O. F. Williams and J. W. Houck, 210.

SELECTED BIBLIOGRAPHY

Antoncich, Ricardo. *Christians in the Face of Injustice.* Maryknoll, N.Y.: Orbis, 1987. This book exemplifies the approaches and concerns of a longtime student of Catholic social teaching in the Latin American context. Since Latin America became a significant dialogue partner with Rome and other centers of Catholic thought at the time of PP's appearance and later in the period of its dissemination, Antoncich's monograph is a helpful resource.

Azevedo, Marcello de Carvalho. *Inculturation and the Challenges of Modernity*. Rome: Gregorian

University Press, 1982. Azevedo provides a cogent framework for discussing the social and cultural implications of the Church's dialogue with modernity. It provides excellent background information relevant to PP's orientation toward development in the modern world.

Barrera, Albino. *Modern Catholic Social Documents and Political Economy*. Washington, D.C.: Georgetown University Press, 2001. Barrera reviews Catholic social teaching in light of history and current social-ethical concerns using data and issues raised by a wide range of supporters and critics of the tradition.

Baum, Gregory, and Robert Ellsberg, Jr., eds., *The Logic of Solidarity: Commentaries on Pope John Paul II's Encyclical "On Social Concern."* Maryknoll, N.Y.: Orbis, 1989. A collection of wide-ranging interpretations of solidarity, a central theme of PP, by recognized experts in the field.

Bayer, Richard C. *Capitalism and Christianity: The Possibility of Christian Personalism*. Washington, D.C.: Georgetown University Press, 1999. This original study takes the critique of capitalism in PP and other ecclesial documents and reviews and interprets that critique from the point of view of the influence of personalism on the thought of Pope John Paul II.

Budde, Michael L. *The Two Churches: Catholicism and Capitalism in the World System*. Durham, N.C.: Duke University Press, 1992. From the angle of political science, Budde's is an early and provocative assessment of the growing identification of worldwide Catholicism with the hopes and aspirations of the poor as emphasized in the call for integral development and the demands of solidarity enunciated in PP and subsequent Catholic social teaching.

Comblin, José. *Called for Freedom: The Changing Context of Liberation Theology*. Maryknoll, N.Y.: Orbis, 1998. This longtime student of Latin American liberation theology and social thought provides one of the better evaluations of the reception given to PP and other documents by liberation theologians. He assesses the state of affairs after the fall of worldwide communism.

Cosmao, Vincent. *Changing the World*. Maryknoll, N.Y.: Orbis, 1984. Cosmao was one of the main players in the elaboration of Catholic social teaching in the 1960s and 1970s. His reflections on the role of transformative action echo PP's urgent call for a faith that does justice.

De Vries, Barend A. *Champions of the Poor*. Washington, D.C.: Georgetown University Press, 1998. An interesting and original evaluation of Judeo-Christian social values including those of the Church from the point of view of an experienced international economist. He discusses various approaches to development.

Dorr, Donal. *Option for the Poor*. Maryknoll, N.Y.: Orbis, 1992. Dorr provides a rich and thoroughly researched commentary on the social teaching of the Church with emphasis on the option for the poor. The commentary on PP is excellent.

Hebblethwaite, Peter. *Paul VI: The First Modern Pope*. New York: Paulist, 1993. A highly skilled biographer and world-class journalist with years of firsthand experience in Rome has written the definitive English-language biography of Paul VI.

Sinha, Ajit Kumar, and Raj Kumar Sen. *Economics of Amartya Sen*. New Delhi: Vedams Books from India, 2000. A detailed overview of the rich teachings of an accomplished contemporary international economist whose vision in some ways affirms and also challenges the Church's understanding of development.

Williams, Oliver F., and John W. Houck. *Catholic Social Thought and the New World Order*. Notre Dame, Ind.: University of Notre Dame Press, 1993. A collection of essays by a broad range of experts focusing on how Catholic social teaching will fare in the world after the fall of communism. A critical issue is how development as understood in PP continues to be the central question in the quest for economic and social justice in an age of globalization.

CHAPTER 13 Commentary on *Octogesima adveniens (A Call to Action on the Eightieth Anniversary of* Rerum novarum)

CHRISTINE E. GUDORF

INTRODUCTION

Octogesima adveniens, the apostolic letter of Paul VI to Cardinal Maurice Roy, president of the Pontifical Commission for Justice and Peace, issued May 14, 1971, marked the eightieth anniversary of Leo XIII's *Rerum novarum.* As in previous anniversary documents following Leo's encyclical, OA initially reviewed the social teaching that had been developed in *Rerum novarum*'s trajectory and then proceeded to examine recent changes in the world that required further development in the Church's social teaching. Virtually all analysts agree that the most distinctive innovations in OA revolved around a pronounced shift from economic to political perspectives in the pursuit of justice, accompanied by a related shift from claims of universal authority in the magisterium to expectations that solutions emerge from local contexts.

OUTLINE OF THE DOCUMENT

At the outset of the letter, Paul VI takes note not only of the general yearning for justice and peace on the part of people but of a wide diversity of situations throughout the world (1–7). He acknowledges that "in the face of such widely varying situations it is difficult for us to utter a unified message and to put forward a solution which has universal validity. Such is not our ambition, nor is it our mission" (4).

In the next section of the document (8–21) the pope recounts what he views as the new social problems. These include urbanization; the situation of youth, women, and workers; the virulence of discrimination; and the problem of emigration from poorer lands. Two fundamental human aspirations are evident in the face of these problems: the desire for equality and the desire for participation (22–41). These basic aspirations grow ever stronger under the influence of better education and increased flows of information. The pursuit of these twin goals requires legislation but that alone is insufficient. Also needed are democratic-type societies; although various democratic models have been tried, none is fully adequate. Christians ought to contribute to the search for a proper political order.

As people seek to build a good society it must be remembered that all ideologies are ambiguous. The pope notes that many are attracted to the currents of socialism, and it is possible to decide on a commitment to socialism that does not compromise Christian values. History demonstrates that marxism has evolved, creating different levels. These levels remain linked, however, and discernment is required when considering marxist ideology (32–34). At the same time, support for liberalism demands discernment as well, for at root this ideology exalts human autonomy in a manner that is ill-advised (35).

In protest against the failed promises of these ideologies there has been a renewed attraction to utopias. There is the promise but also the temptation to reductionism present in modern science. Christians must beware of this risk even as they collaborate in the widening of human liberty through scientific advances. When considering the idea of progress, an ambiguity should be noted. Not only does the search for progress too often focus on quantitative, material progress, but it also opens people to dissatisfaction.

Christians must address these new problems forthrightly (42–47). The most important duty in the realm of justice is to allow each country to promote its own development in a framework of cooperation free of domination, either economic or political. The aim of any political activity should be the common good. Such political action is an expression of the contemporary person's demand for greater sharing in responsibility and in decisionmaking. It is true that decisions are more and more complex, but this ought not "slow down the giving of wider participation in working out decisions, making choices, and putting them into practice" (47).

In the final section of the letter, Paul issues a call to action (48–52). For the pope it is vital that each person conscientiously make decisions about the actions in which she or he is called to participate. There is no set formula: "in concrete situations, and taking account of solidarity in each person's life, one must recognize a legitimate variety of possible options" (50).

CONTEXT OF THE DOCUMENT

OA renewed hope in many that the fresh air of Vatican II was still blowing through the higher elevations of the Church. What some interpreted as OA's central themes—"the historically constituted nature of the social teaching of the church, the role of the local community and the difficulty as well as the undesirability of a single universal papal message or solution to problems"[1]—seemed to continue and even further develop the impressive openness of Vatican II, which had ended six tumultuous years earlier.

The major contribution of OA to Catholic social thought was an insistence that the dignity of human beings and their ongoing humanization require a universal participation in politics broadly understood, specifically in participation in decision making toward the common good. The timeliness of this message was undeniable. Trends in economics and in politics both necessitated a new, broader, more inclusive sharing of responsibility in the face of new situations that traditional structures of power were not equipped to address.

By 1971 the globalization of capital, which Paul VI had in *Populorum progressio* so clearly recognized as problematic for economic justice, had made the political mechanisms that previous social teaching had advocated for controlling capital in the past—national labor unions and laws—insufficient. Also, many new nations had come into being, often with new multiethnic and multicultural constituencies for which previous state models were not appropriate, and for whom the global economy did not provide basic justice. Many parts of the world seemed mired in crisis: within the three-year period immediately preceding OA, Paul VI had addressed the Paris student uprisings, political assassinations in the United States, the Six Day War, the Vietnam War, the invasion of Czechoslovakia, and the genocide in Biafra.[2]

In the social arena as well, increased mobility and education had loosened traditional social structures, bringing demands from many new groups for a voice in decision making. All sectors of society, not only the Church, were forced to rethink questions of decision making, power, and authority. Thus the questions raised in OA were major issues of the day outside as well as inside the Church.

OA's focus on decision making in the contemporary world was an innovation in the ecclesial context. Four years earlier, *Populorum progressio* had posed the problems of global poverty and injustice; in OA Paul attempted to reformulate the relationship of faith, the Church, and the papal role to the struggle against poverty and injustice. James Finn has described the specific theme of the document as the use of political power:

> In *Populorum progressio* Paul VI focused on an economy that "is in the service of man." Here [in OA] he asserts that, though economic activity is necessary, "the need is felt to pass from economics to politics. . . . each man feels that in the social and economic field, both national and international, the ultimate decision rests with political power" (#46). It is with that appreciation of political power in mind that Paul VI considers the many grave problems of our time: political power, its proper use, and its potential for abuse. This is the document's binding theme.[3]

Many analysts attributed the liberation flavor of OA to Paul's trip to Medellín in 1968 and to his relationship with liberationist Latin American prelates, such as the Franciscan archbishop of São Paulo, Evaristo Arns. The episcopal conference of Latin America (CELAM) had been invigorated by the Vatican II theme directing the local churches to develop by addressing challenges to the gospel within their local situations. At Medellín, the bishops had issued a radically new message, one that broke with hundreds of years of ecclesial history in Latin America and evoked the memory of those colonial bishops who had crusaded, largely unsuccessfully, for the cause of the Indians in the sixteenth and early seventeenth centuries. The Medellín conference was led by the Brazilian bishops, many of whom had been radicalized by the vicious campaign of human rights abuses that followed the 1964 military coup that had not spared priests, religious, and even bishops. These Brazilian bishops were supported by a group of European-educated Latin American liberation theologians committed to the themes and process of Vatican II.

The Medellín documents insisted that the Church become a Church of the poor, that the primary issue for the Church in the Latin American context was the crushing poverty of the majority, and that this could only be addressed by recognizing the structural injustice that characterized the continent and undermined hopes for social and individual peace.[4] The emphasis at Medellín on the necessity for the Church to address the issue of poverty resonated with Paul's urgent cry for justice for poor nations in *Populorum progressio* (1967), but that document had concentrated on the role of the Church in pointing out the unjust reality and providing motivation for attacking the problem. It did not move the Church beyond its traditional magisterial role. The Medellín documents seemed to propose that the Church take the side of the poor, which would pit the Church in Latin America against the entrenched elites with whom the Church had been allied virtually since the Conquest more than four centuries earlier.

PROCESS OF FORMULATION AND AUTHORSHIP

In Latin American quarters and elsewhere, the release of OA was often interpreted in terms of Pope Paul responding to Medellín. That OA was not merely Paul's personal response to Medellín is clear since the first draft of OA was actually written by Maurice Cardinal Roy, the president of the Pontifical Commission for Justice and Peace, to whom the letter was addressed. But the letter is reputed to have gone through a number of drafts in which Paul took a personal hand.

ESSAY

Though OA can easily be read as a point-by-point response to the themes that were emerging from Latin American theological and episcopal quarters, it was also relevant to what was happening in other areas of the world as well. In many parts of the world, increased mobility and education had loosened traditional social structures, bringing demands from many new groups for a voice in decision making. All sectors of society, not only the Church, were forced to rethink questions of decision making, power, and authority.

Pope John XXIII had recognized that the conditions of modern life had changed, and that changes in both roles and structures were now required in order to produce justice. But Paul VI had lived through the 1960s. He had experienced the global tide of social and political revolution in virtually every area of human life, and had a much stronger sense that not only had the conditions in which peoples lived changed, but peoples themselves had changed in ways that began to make inherited understandings obsolete. New potential in human beings had come to light, linked to new aspirations. Paul, more than John, had an elemental sense of what we have come to call the constructed nature of human identity. He presented equality and participation, for example, as fundamental human aspirations that have been provoked and supported by the conditions of contemporary life (OA 22). Aspirations to equality and participation are expressions of human dignity; this is why they are fundamental to humans. But they have taken shape historically and developed over time amid the changing conditions of human life into concepts and forms that would have been totally alien to premodern peoples. With this same sense of some plasticity in human nature responding to the conditions in which it finds itself, Paul expresses his worry that belief in progress has become so strong that it can both obscure the Christian necessity to face the eschatological mystery of death and bring about large-scale deception and dissatisfaction (41). In fact, the very urgency for dealing with the problems of justice in the world is this connection between the conditions in which people live and the kind of persons that they become (10–12).

When Paul presided over the concluding session of Vatican II, he also presided over the most massive changes in Catholic theology since the Council of Trent four hundred years earlier. At the time of Trent, the vast majority of human persons did not face personal decisions about where they would live and die, which religion to follow, which gender or sexual orientation to claim, which nationality or occupation to adopt, which social class to strive for. All of these aspects of personal identity were given at birth; later most persons were assigned by parents either a spouse or a religious habit. For the married, there was little or no choice of whether to have children, or how many to have. All of these assignments were for life, and individual choice played little or no role in them. By the pontificate of Paul VI, individuals in much of the world made personal choices of locality, education, occupation, class, sexual identity, marital status, spouse, family size, and often even nationality. Faced with such a burden of responsibility for self-creation, modern individuals demanded greater and greater degrees of freedom and participation in decision making. Thus, the questions raised in OA were major issues of the day outside as well as inside the Church.

Not an Encyclical, but an Apostolic Letter

Mary Elsbernd interpreted Paul's decision to issue OA as an apostolic letter instead of in the encyclical form used by virtually all his predecessors[5] as suggesting "Paul's awareness of the importance of human experience or a historically conscious methodology."[6] She supported this interpretation by noting that after *Humanae vitae* (HV) in 1968 (and perhaps in part due to the response to it) Paul never again in the last ten years of his pontificate issued another encyclical.[7]

There are, of course, a number of other interpretations. It has been suggested that Paul issued OA as an apostolic letter so as to not preempt the discussion in advance of the 1971 bishops' synod, which was to address the question of justice in the world. Number 6 does read: "It will moreover be for the forthcoming synod of bishops itself to study more closely and to examine in greater detail the Church's mission in the face of grave issues raised today by the question of justice in the world." (6) Thus the decision might be a bow to collegiality with the bishops.

On the other hand, it is tempting to interpret this decision to issue OA as an apostolic letter as signaling its more provisional, less universal, and less authoritative nature, since such a message is so clearly a key theme of the letter itself. However, such an interpretation has the effect of suggesting that Paul consciously matched the level of authority of the document to the message of the document, raising the question as to whether such conscious intent preceded, or developed in the aftermath of, HV.

Disclaiming Authority and Power

Without a doubt the single most striking aspects of OA when it was issued were its initial disclaimers on authority and power. Charles Curran, noting these disclaimers, wrote that OA "reflects a heightened awareness of historical consciousness and the need for a more inductive approach."[8] Before Paul, Catholic social doctrine, which had consisted principally of papal social encyclicals, especially *Rerum novarum* and its anniversary documents, had been taught in the Church as the definitive solution to the social problems of the (developed) world.

Leo XIII had confidently written of the role of the Church in confronting the social problem of labor, claiming that "no practical solution of this question will ever be found without the assistance of religion and the Church. It is we who are the chief guardian of religion, and the chief dispenser of what belongs to the Church, and we must not by silence neglect the duty that lies upon us" (13). He acknowledged that rulers of states, employers, the rich, and workers themselves had some role in resolving the problem, but concluded that "all the striving of men will be in vain if they leave out the Church" (13).

Pius XI had been only slightly more restrained when he claimed that it was his right and his duty to deal authoritatively with social and economic problems in *Quadragesimo anno*: "For the deposit of truth entrusted to us by God, and our weighty office of propagating, interpreting and urging in season and out of season the entire moral law, demand that both social and economic questions be brought within our supreme jurisdiction, insofar as they refer to moral issues" (QA 41).

By contrast, Paul's treatment of papal social teaching authority is radically different. Paul began by expressing his confidence that the Spirit is at work in Christian communities throughout the world: "On all the continents, among all races, nations and cultures, and under all conditions, the Lord continues to raise up authentic apostles of the gospel" (2). Because Paul saw the Spirit of the Lord at work in the world, he saw neither the Church nor the papacy as the only source of answers to the social justice problems of the world. He went on to speak of hearing the cries of distress and hope on his recent journeys to Africa, Latin America, India, and the Middle East. He recognized the universal desires for justice and peace and the particularity and complexity of local social problems. Then he pronounced the most oft-quoted lines of OA:

> In the face of such widely varying situations it is difficult for us to utter a unified message and to put forward a solution which has universal validity. Such is not our ambition, nor is it our mission. It is up to the Christian communities to analyze with objectivity the situation which is proper to their own country, to shed on it the light of the Gospel's unalterable words and to draw principles of reflection, norms of judgment, and directives for action from the social teaching of the Church. . . . It is up to these Christian communities, with the help of the Holy Spirit, in communion with the bishops who hold responsibility and in dialogue with other Christian brethren and all men of good will, to discern the options and commitments which are called for in order to bring about the social, political and economic changes seen in many cases to be urgently needed. (4)

This passage contains a number of distinct but complementary innovative elements. First, it says that definitive answers must come, not from the papacy, but from local church communities—from the laity—working with their bishops, other Christians, and non-Christians of goodwill. These communities first analyze the situation and then discern the options and commitments called for, based on their observation of the signs of the times. Second, the passage portrays the Church's teaching on social issues as developing through time—being "worked out in the course of history"—and thus presumably never being finished. It also deliberately and consistently uses less authoritative language for that magisterial teaching, calling it not the Church's social "doctrine" but rather the Church's social "teaching."[9] This is very different from previous papal statements in which social teaching is depicted as authoritative papal statements expressing unchanging and complete principles fully contained in the gospel. So alien had the concept of developing Church teaching been in the Catholic Church that for at least half a century students and faculty at Catholic seminaries have joked about the tendency for popes to introduce documents that reversed the teachings of their predecessors with the words "in continuity with the teachings of my predecessors . . ."

Third, Paul not only renounced exclusive papal responsibility for resolving global injustice, but in the spirit of conciliar collegiality, assigned to the forthcoming synod of bishops, representing all the local churches of the world, the responsibility for doing the detailed study of how the Church should respond to global injustice. Later parts of the document dealing with participation and responsibility also echoed this theme of decentralizing power in the Church and sharing it not only between pope and bishops but also between whole Christian communities and clerical hierarchies.

Human Aspirations to Equality and Decision Making

The other major substantive innovation occurs in Paul's treatment of fundamental human aspirations to equality and decision making beginning in number 22:

> While scientific and technological progress continues to overturn man's surroundings, his patterns of knowledge, work, consumption, and relationships, two aspirations persistently make themselves felt in these new contexts, and they grow stronger to the extent that he becomes better informed and better educated: the aspiration to equality and the aspiration to participation, two forms of man's dignity and freedom.

Recognition of this innate aspiration to equality had been a long time coming in the Church, even within modern social teaching. Leo XIII had written in *Rerum novarum* that humanity must remain as it is, that hierarchy is natural and "all striving against nature is in vain. There naturally exist among mankind innumerable differences of the most important kind; people differ in capability, in diligence, in health, and in strength; and unequal fortune is a necessary result of inequality in condition" (14). Leo presented such inequality as being a positive good for individuals and communities. Using an organic model of society in which there are many functions and roles to be carried out, some high and some low, Leo insisted it is in the interests of all that all roles and functions, even the lowly, be performed. Furthermore, he argued that as a result of sin, human labor had become punitive, and thus the difficulties of even lowly labor must be accepted as the painful expiation of human sin: "for the consequences of sin are bitter and hard to bear, and they must be with man as long as life lasts. To suffer and endure, therefore, is the lot of humanity, let men try as they may, no strength and no artifice will ever succeed in banishing from human life the ills and troubles which beset it" (14).

Leo was not the last of a dying papal breed in this respect. Pius XI in *Divini redemptoris* wrote: "It is not true that all have equal rights in civil society. It is not true that there is no lawful social hierarchy."[10] Pius XII in his first encyclical in 1939 wrote: "Mankind, by a divinely appointed law, is divided into a variety of classes." He further clarified this statement in his Christmas address of 1945:

> In a nation worthy of the name, inequalities among the social classes present few or no obstacles to their brotherly union. We refer,

> of course, to those inequalities which result not from human caprice, but from the nature of things—inequalities in intellectual and spiritual growth, with economics, with differences in individual circumstances, within, of course, the limits prescribed by justice and mutual charity.[11]

After Paul VI it would be impossible for any pope to consider gross economic inequalities or many other differences in individual circumstances as solely or even principally due to "the nature of things," rather than also to the workings of human institutions such as global capitalism and the nation-state.

John XXIII provided a bridge between earlier popes and Paul VI on these themes. While John's first encyclical had quoted both Leo XIII (above) and this Christmas message of Pius XII on the inevitability of classes as founded in nature,[12] his *Mater et magistra* not only advocated, as had Pius XII, that whenever possible workers share in the direction of economic enterprises, but went further. John added that the greater amount of responsibility desired today by workers in productive enterprises "not merely accords with the nature of man but also is in conformity with historical developments in the economic, social and political fields" (93).

There is not necessarily an inconsistency between insistence on human inequality and hierarchy on the one hand and, on the other hand, insistence on some degree of participation in decision making even for those most lowly, given John's recognition that historical developments, such as universal education, have created in the masses' greater capacity for sharing in responsibility. But if sharing in responsibility is necessary to both satisfy human nature and develop it, as John stated and Paul later explicated, then traditional understandings of radical inequality in which some rule and others follow orders are clearly foregone.

Paul took the next step by recognizing in OA that increased capacity for participation in decision making itself indicates a kind of equality, in that if all groups are becoming more and more capable of responsible decision making, then human potential is open-ended and not necessarily fixed at different unequal levels. Rather than identify inequality as a part of nature, Paul insisted that equality was founded in the dignity that is the essential component of human nature. Moreover, he recognized the aspiration to equality as a form of human dignity and freedom, opening the possibility that other shared human aspirations could in the future be understood as forms of human dignity and freedom, for example, as in the aspiration of women to equal roles in the Church.

Even more compelling than the papal shift on equality is Paul's related emphasis on participation. In area after area, Paul called on all humans to accept shared responsibility for ending injustice and creating justice. The condition for this sharing of responsibility is human equality, which he perhaps overgenerously read back into John's statements on participation.[13] In number 41, for example, Paul speaks of the pursuit of progress in the world and comments: "The quality and the truth of human relations, *the degree of participation and of responsibility*, are no less significant and important for the future of society than the quantity and variety of the goods produced and consumed." In contemporary controversies within social, political, and economic organizations about how "participation" or even "participation in decision making" should be interpreted, many still prefer to interpret participation in terms of consultation: all must be consulted, their opinions heard, before those in authority can make a decision. It is very difficult to interpret Paul's use of participation in this weak sense because he so often, as in the above quote, links participation to the exercise of responsibility.[14] Responsibility only accrues to those who decide, who exercise power. In fact, it is largely by making decisions and living with the results that humans learn to make responsible decisions.

Number 47 of OA shifts the treatment of participation in decision making from the economic realm in which John treated it to the political realm: "The passing to the political dimension also expressed a demand made by the man of today: a greater sharing in responsibility and in decision making. This legitimate aspiration becomes more evident as the cultural level rises, as the sense of freedom develops and as man becomes more aware of how, in a world facing an uncertain future, the choices of today already condition the choices of tomorrow." Paul reminds his readers that John in *Mater et magistra* stressed that exercise of responsibility is a basic demand of human nature, a concrete exercise of human freedom, and a path to human development which, in economic life and particularly in enterprise, should be ensured. Paul then went on to say that such responsibility should extend to the social and political spheres, where "a reasonable sharing in responsibility and in decisions must be established and strengthened." While he admitted that the situations calling for decisions are increasingly complex and that the consequences involve risk, "these obstacles must not slow down the giving of wider participation in working out decisions, making choices and putting them into practice." Paul insisted that modern forms of democracy must be devised to balance increasing technocracy so that every person could not only become informed and express himself or herself, but also exercise shared responsibility.

Thus in OA Paul VI built on John XXIII's earlier call for worker participation in decision making in economic enterprises by demanding not only citizen participation in democratic political decision making, but also universal participation in decision making in the social sphere. Moreover, Paul believed that participation in decision making, and the consequent sharing of responsibility for the condition of humans and their world, should continue to expand because, he insisted, participation in decision making is the "path to his [a human being's] development."

Pluralism of Christian Options

Having read Paul's insistence on universal participation in decision making throughout OA, one is not surprised to find near the end of the letter a statement on the legitimate pluralism of Christian options. For if all Christians, and indeed all humans, must participate in decision making and accept responsibility for their decisions and actions, then it would be naïve to expect that all Christians will interpret the situation in similar ways. It is unlikely that all Christian consciences will reach the same conclusion on decisions and actions, much less that all peoples of different faiths will agree on what should be done: "In concrete situations, and taking account of solidarity in each person's life, one must recognize a legitimate variety of possible options" (50). Paul says that the same Christian faith can lead to different commitments. He calls for an openness to experimentation, for openness to working with those with different political options, for mutual understanding of others' positions and motives, and a willingness to critically examine one's own behavior and its correctness. Such openness, he says, can lead to a more profound charity that is not naïve but recognizes the challenges, and yet "believes nonetheless in the possibility of convergence and unity" (50).

It is amazing that Pope Paul can speak with this level of confidence in "the possibility of convergence and unity" at the same time that he reminds his audience of not only the complexity and diversity of different situations, but also of the very different commitments that Christians of good faith can make when faced with those different situations. No longer was unity among members of the Church to depend upon obedience to the direction of local bishops within Catholic Action or on specific universal directives within papal teaching. Nor were Catholics who were victims of injustice any longer to protect themselves from conflicts with political power only by withdrawal to prayer, as Leo XIII's *Quod apostolici muneris*[15] had recommended. Evans points out that

> citizen involvement in the area of political affairs, so strongly endorsed by Paul VI, was utterly discouraged by many of his predecessors. Even in the face of structural injustices inflicting pain and threatening the dignity of ordinary people, these victims of societal injustices were not encouraged to seek changes in the social or political systems that were causing human suffering. On the contrary, prayer was presented as an

alternative to the kind of action that might change the unjust situation.[16]

In OA the Catholic layperson was instead urged to claim an active and independently chosen role in transforming the world in the direction of justice through collaborative action. The suspicion of democratic politics as a field of activity for Christians, which had bedeviled the Church since the French Revolution, seemed to have dissolved.

Elements of Theological Innovation

If most of the innovations in OA are concerned with understandings of the human person, decision making, participation, and responsibility, it is nevertheless the case that there are elements of theological innovation as well. The most important of these is the recognition of the preferential option for the poor as a gospel teaching, a recognition that seems to have become part and parcel of ongoing social teaching. The first reference to a preferential option for the poor found in Catholic social teaching occurs in OA: "In teaching us charity, the Gospel instructs us in the preferential respect due to the poor and the special situation they have in society: the more fortunate should renounce some of their rights so as to place their goods more generously at the service of others" (23).

Within liberation theology, the preferential option for the poor is closely connected with the epistemological privilege of the poor. While the preferential option for the poor demands that all Christians, the rich and the poor alike, share and live out in action the divine priority for alleviating the suffering of the poor, the epistemological privilege goes a step further. It insists that the poor have a privilege in knowing, that is, a privilege in knowing God and in knowing certain aspects of the world relevant to the alleviation of poverty. The poor who struggle against the alienation and despair of poverty tend to be more dependent on God for daily survival and more aware of the divine presence. They live in the place—poverty—where God has taken preferred root in order to support and comfort the afflicted.

Paul VI does not take up this claim on behalf of the poor that they tend to be closer to God than the nonpoor. The aspect of the epistemological privilege of the poor that he addresses in OA concerns the experience that the poor have of the workings of power in the world. In situations of domination, the powerless always know the powerful better than the powerful understand the powerless. The colonized know the colonizer better than the colonizer knows the colonized; slaves know owners better than owners know slaves; women have known men better than men have known women; and workers know bosses better than bosses know workers. Such knowledge is often a necessary condition for survival, certainly for thriving. Thus, in the project of eliminating poverty, the experience of the poor within the structures of poverty is a valuable resource for the project. They know who benefits from poverty, who structures and maintains poverty. Paul validates this claim, this epistemological privilege of the poor, throughout OA in his demand for universal participation in decision making in all areas of human life. While *Populorum progressio* laid out the needs of the poor around the world and called upon the rich to cooperate in alleviating those needs, OA insists that the task of creating a just social order requires the political empowerment of all, including the poor themselves, who cannot be—and will not be—merely the recipients of justice, but must instead be agents of justice.

Pope Paul's travels to India and Latin America seem to have brought the plight of the world's poor into the center of his thought, not only causing him to write *Populorum progressio*, but influencing many aspects of his thinking. He touched the world of the poor to the point that he understood something of both their pain and their urgency. This experience helped him in his confrontation with liberation theology, whose demands on the Church were often rejected by bishops and cardinals as too radical and strident. Paul here responded to the liberation theologians and bishops that the preferential option for the poor was not merely a new political ideology out of Latin America, but was, in fact, the teaching of the gospel itself. *Populorum progressio* had made an eloquent plea for the poor, calling all to recognize their growing masses and the severity of their plight and to organize to meet their needs in both charity and justice. But here in OA Paul moved further toward the case made by the liberation theologians, who argued for the preference for the poor as constitutive of the gospel, for a reorientation of the Church itself to give the cause of the poor center stage. While Paul does not directly address the latter claim, he did effectively deny both that the cause of the poor was one of the Church's concerns among many equally important ones and that the cause of the poor was the central concern of states, organized social groups, and individuals, but not the central concern of the Church itself. If God the Father, Jesus Christ, and the Gospel teachings all demonstrate a preferential option for the poor, then all Christians, and the Church as the body of Christ and the community of Christians, must evidence this same preference for the poor.

During the subsequent pontificate of John Paul II, opposition to the politics of liberation theology characterized papal diplomacy, episcopal appointments, and teaching. But this one central tenet of liberation theology, the preferential option for the poor, continued to be affirmed as constitutive of the gospel, though it was often qualified by a reminder that the preference of both Yahweh and Jesus Christ for the poor, the suffering, the marginalized, and the despised was not an exclusive preference, and that God loves all.[17] Nevertheless, since Paul it has never been denied that God's preference for the poor obliges humans to give first priority to meeting the basic needs of the poor. This is, of course, directly connected with Paul's claim that human dignity required participation in decision making. When Paul claimed in *Populorum progressio* that charity was not enough, that the poor required the creation of structures of justice, he realized that the creation of those structures of justice would not happen without the participation of the poor themselves in the construction process. Participation of all in decision making is the procedural justice that is absolutely necessary for the creation of substantive social justice. Perhaps, then, it has been the failure to implement the participation of all in the decision making of both states and the Church itself that has prevented both Church and nations from better implementing the preferential option for the poor.

A number of other lesser innovations were set out in OA as well. Paul's treatment of urbanization as a new social problem, for example, was the most expanded and eloquently moving analysis of urbanization in church documents to date. But his treatment of urbanization was not accompanied by any significant innovative response on the part of the Church. Bernard Evans pointed out another innovation, that this document is one of the first Church documents to mention the environmental problem.[18] But its lens for understanding and assessing environmental crisis was very anthropocentric, which limited the consequences of recognizing it as a problem.[19] That is, Paul points out that the risk in human destruction of nature is that the human race will itself become "the victim of this degradation" in a human future that "may well be intolerable" (21). There is no note here that what is being destroyed—creation—is sacred, and is not humans' to destroy, but belongs to God. Despite the criticism that humanity has overextended its power, there is no expression in OA of the interdependence that characterizes all the elements of creation.

A similarly narrow, traditional perspective undermines a seeming progressive shift when Paul approaches the problem of women's roles and rights. He assumes that equality "to participate in cultural, economic, social and political life" (13) can and should simply be added to the "proper" traditional domestic roles of women without revision of the domestic roles of both women and men. Papal mention of urbanization, environment, and women's roles as social problems may have served to validate others in rethinking Christian approaches to these issues, but it was not accompanied by any specific response to them. In the case of women's rights, the dual nod to women's traditional family role under patriarchy and to the application of liberal rights to women served to validate both patriarchal traditionalists and feminist reformers in the Church, about which more will be said later.

At least one significant and relatively well-developed innovation emerged, understood at the time as a major contribution by some and as a dangerous deviation by others, and that was the treatment of ideology, socialism, and communism. While these related themes had long been discussed and were relevant to movements and discussions within Europe, this section of OA was usually interpreted as a papal response to Latin American liberation theologies that had emerged to world acclaim in 1968 with the CELAM meeting at Medellín. Paul appeared to be hesitant to support the liberation current, not only when he quoted John XXIII on how movements and ideologies, including socialism and communism, develop and change in history, but also when he went on to add that while caution is necessary in discerning links between Marxist analysis and Marxist ideology, some aspects of Marxism may be useful tools for Christians regardless of their objectionable roots (32–34).

In Latin America, most worker and student movements had long been Marxist in their orientation, and many opposition parties were similarly connected to different strains of Marxism. By 1971 liberation theologians were recognized as having called the Church in Latin America from its historic alliance with governments and parties of the elites toward a new solidarity with the poor, among whom the most politically organized sectors were Marxist. A key attraction of socialism for Latin American Catholic advocates for the poor was the idea of social ownership of the means of production on a continent in which the richest 10 percent owned the vast majority of land and other resources.[20] The Marxist elements with which liberation theologians were aligned were engaged in democratic electoral processes, as illustrated most clearly in the election of Salvador Allende in Chile in 1970.[21] The argument of the liberation theologians was that Marxism was valuable not as ideology, but as a tool for analyzing reality, for recognizing injustice and how to address it.[22] Paul seemed to agree cautiously, with reservations.

Since Catholic social teaching had treated socialism beginning with *Rerum novarum* (and other Church documents had done so even before it[23]) and continued to treat socialism in the anniversary documents following its publication, for Paul to treat it here was an example of continuity. His greater openness to Marxist socialism in OA compared to his predecessors was also a continuation of a more recent openness in the Church, perhaps most publicly signaled when John XXIII received Soviet leader Nikita Krushchev's son-in-law and relations between the Church and Eastern European nations began to thaw in the 1960s. One very telling aspect of Paul's greater openness to Marxist socialism in OA is that he spoke of the development of socialism*s* (31ff.)—in the plural, recognizing the many divisions and permutations of socialism present in the world. Paul wrote that sometimes socialism represented a continual struggle against domination and exploitation, sometimes the exercise of political power in a single-party state, sometimes an ideology based on historical materialism and the denial of transcendence, and sometimes a scientific approach to social and political realities. None of his papal predecessors had treated socialism as having this degree of complexity.

Though John XXIII had theoretically opened the door to Christian collaboration with socialists in social justice projects and Paul VI had spoken approvingly of such collaboration in *Populorum progressio*, none of Paul's predecessors had recognized that any tool, any personal adoption, of socialism could possibly offer Christians more use than danger.[24] Thus, though John and Paul in *Populorum progressio* had clearly differed from the stance of Pius XI, who had clearly forbidden any Catholic adoption of or affiliation with Marxism in any form, OA took yet another step away from Pius XI by proposing the possibility that, with careful discernment, Christians might find some Marxist tools, such as social analysis, useful in the work of social justice.

EXCURSUS

The failure to implement OA has been well recognized. The title of Mary Elsbernd's article in *Theological Studies* tells the tale: "Whatever Happened to *Octogesima adveniens*?" OA, says Elsbernd, "held that Catholic social teaching had been worked out in history, i.e., that Catholic social teachings are historically constituted, that the local Christian community contributed to the development of Catholic social teachings, and that a single universal message is not the papal mission."[25] In contrast, John Paul II "stresses the continuity of Catholic social doctrine [not "teaching" but "doctrine"] back to the gospel itself in a kind of unbroken chain."[26] John Paul, she says, sees the fundamental inspiration, the principles of reflection, the criteria of judgment, and basic directives for action as all proceeding from the gospel. In fact, the *Catechism of the Catholic Church* issued under John Paul II actually reverses this teaching of Paul's, insisting that the message of social teaching is a single universal message.[27]

Elsbernd notes that John Paul II never cites OA 4, which denied that it was the papal mission to put forth a solution to social problems that had universal validity.[28] Moreover, when John Paul II did make four references to development of church doctrine in *Laborem exercens*, "the text makes clear that it is the magisterium itself that brings about the 'development' by bringing up to date 'ageless Christian truth.' The people, the historical situation and the activities of practitioners apply the teaching but do not shape its development."[29]

Clearly one major reason for the failure to implement the innovative approaches in OA has been the person of John Paul II. But understanding him as the only obstacle is to indulge in an unwarranted cult of personality. The obstacles to implementing a historically conscious understanding of social teaching go beyond John Paul. They were present in Paul VI himself, and in the Council, and throughout the self-understanding of Christian communities as well. Despite the seamlessness that seemed apparent to so many appreciative Latin American liberationists and European and North American progressives at the time, OA itself does contain a number of clues to its subsequent lack of influence.

Before pursuing those clues, however, it is necessary to identify a concern of OA that disappeared from the public screen due to an unforeseen historical change: the collapse of the communist bloc. Since the demise of Soviet communism, the capitalist turn in China and Vietnam, and the foundering of communist Cuba and North Korea in poverty and famine, the triumph of Western capitalism has discredited Marxism throughout most of the globe, despite the continuing, and many two-thirds world residents would say, the increased, need for structural economic justice on a global scale. Consequently, the openness of OA to Christians using the tools of Marxism has become, at least for the time being, largely an interesting historical footnote.

The first clue to the failure of the methods and style of OA to be enacted throughout the Church, one that by hindsight is glaringly obvious, is that the context for all of Pope Paul's insistence on participation in decision making within the document was the socioeconomic-political world. Never did he make this claim with reference to matters internal to the Church itself, but always with a view to Christians working "in the world." Thus, the preferential option for the poor was binding on both the Church and all Christians, but Paul does not indicate any ways in which the Christian laity can participate in the Church's decision making on behalf of the poor. An underlying split in reality between the Church and the world seems to have characterized his thought.

Perhaps the clearest indication within the text itself that the document's statements on human dignity's demand that humans participate in decision making were never intended to involve intra-Church decision making is that in the very number in which Paul denies that the papal mission is to supply universal answers to social problems, he refers to "the light of the Gospel's unalterable words" (4). This comes in startling contrast to the language of historicity, development, trends, complexity, and newness. It evokes the language of past social teaching, a language of timeless truth, permanent, unchanging teaching, and divinely established natural orders of hierarchy. The implication here is that, while Paul recognized that Catholic social teaching had developed and continued to develop due to historical change and human consciousness of history, other aspects of Church teaching, beginning with the gospel itself, are outside, and unaffected by, the historical process. This is, of course, difficult to accept with regard to the structure of, roles within, and teachings of the Church whose development can be traced historically. But it is also difficult to accept since biblical scholarship has demonstrated over a century that, while "words" may be unalterable, their meanings are not, and that it is the meanings of the gospel message to which Christians should adhere, not to the words themselves.

The Distinction between the Historical and the Natural/Revealed

OA is not unsullied by the split that exists between the method and assumptions that govern papal thinking on the Church as opposed to the method and assumptions that govern its thinking since Vatican II on other human institutions. This split was to become entrenched in the following decades, and has been most often described as the split between methods used to deal with faith and medical/sexual issues on the one hand and social teaching on the other. Charles Curran explains the origins of the split using the example of Vatican II's treatment of religious liberty. In the nineteenth century religious liberty had been condemned in papal teaching, so the question for the Council was how the twentieth-century Church could accept religious liberty. The answer eventually given was that the historical circumstances changed so much as to justify a different teaching on the part of the Church. "As a result the papal social teaching has an historical hermeneutic to justify change and development which is not present in the sexual and medical teaching. In order to support its teaching in the sexual and medical areas, the papacy continues to cite the older teachings of Pius XII, which emphasized the more classicist approach not open to development and change."[30] Curran notes that significant methodological differences exist between the papal approach to sexual/medical issues on the one hand and social issues on the other. Curran and other commentators point out that teachings that involve the Church as institution, including the roles of laity, clergy, and religious, questions of orthodoxy, issues of due process, and many more, are treated like sexual/medical issues, with reference to legal, even juridical, norms justified with reference to unchangeable formulations of what is understood as eternal truth, rooted in revelation, whether that revelation occurs through nature, Scripture, or tradition. These norms assume that creation is static. Therefore, both human sexuality and the basic structures of the Church itself are fixed forever by the will of God. All the other aspects and capacities of human beings except their sexuality are dynamic and historically developing, just as all other human communities except the Church community are called by God to support universal participation in decision making in order that human beings grow in responsibility and love.

There can be no question of a contradiction between asserting that participation in decision making in economic, social, and political affairs is a requirement of human dignity, and that the exclusion of the laity from decision making within the Church itself is ongoing. There is a contradiction between assertions of episcopal collegiality that assume that truth and wisdom emerge from collaboration of concerned and responsible bishops, and assertions of papal authority that assume that absolute truth and authority are instilled within whoever is elected pope. The seeds of this contradiction ran through the entire work of Vatican II because its work was, almost inevitably, a series of compromises between divergent understandings both of the human person and of the nature of the Church. Paul VI saw his own role in the Council as preserving the unity of the Church by facilitating precisely these compromises between the liberals led by bishops such as Léon-Joseph Cardinal Suenens of Belgium and the conservatives led by a group of curial cardinals such as Cardinal Alfredo Ottaviani of the Congregation for the Doctrine of the Faith. The result of such compromises was to preserve the contradictions. This was both Paul's achievement and his shortcoming.

During the Council, for example, Paul VI had listened to the traditionalist minority who saw the doctrine of collegiality in chapter 3 of *Lumen gentium* as "dangerous modernism and incompatible with Vatican I"[31] and its proclamation of papal infallibility, and who had attempted to appease their concerns by insisting on adding to the document the *Nota praevia*, an initial note governing the entire document. From the start it informed readers that the treatment of collegiality in *Lumen gentium* and in Vatican II as a whole did not in any way signal "a receding from the peak of papal authority asserted by Vatican I."[32] For the bishops of the majority, the insertion of the *Nota* served to dissuade them of their initial high expectations of papal understandings of collegiality.

Similarly, Paul ignored collegial power sharing in his executive decision to eliminate discussion of birth control from the Council's sessions on the pastoral constitution and in his later proclamation of *Humanae vitae* without first consulting the bishops of the world. When the very pope who authored a document urging universal participation in decision making as a requirement of human dignity is unwilling to share responsibility for the formulation of church teaching with his fellow bishops, succeeding popes are unlikely to be willing to share responsibility for the development of Catholic social teaching and practice with the laity and their communities.

If in Vatican II the Church opened its door to historicity, Paul nevertheless attempted to preserve some small space for stasis. OA thus contains at least some hints prefiguring the later gulf that developed between the methods and assumptions governing papal thought on the Church itself, its internal governance, its teaching on sexuality, and, to a lesser extent, its interpretation of scripture and tradition, as opposed to its teaching on the world, its politics, culture, economics, and interrelationships as revealed by the sciences. This gulf widened under John Paul II, but it began with Vatican II and Paul VI himself.

Ambivalence on Women's Roles

Paul's proclivity for attempting to preserve both church unity and tradition at the same time that he acknowledged the need for change in the direction of greater justice led to a mixed signal to and about women, at two levels. Though he advocated the equality of women "to participate in cultural, economic and social life," Paul never indicated how such participation could and should be integrated with previous papal understandings of women's role as the heart of the home, dedicated to motherhood and domesticity, as described so eloquently by Pius XII. Paul can justly be taken to task by women as justifying the "double burden" that modernity has assigned to women who share economic, political, and social responsibility with men, but retain principal and often exclusive responsibility for the care and welfare of children and for domestic work. Paul seems oblivious to the need in justice for women's participation in cultural, political, and economic responsibility to be balanced by men's sharing in domestic and childcare responsibility.

At the same time, Paul seemed unable to understand that his justification for women's—and all humans'—right to participate in cultural, political, and economic responsibility could serve equally well to justify women's participation in new roles in the Church, roles that involved participation in decision making. In *Ministeria quaedam*, issued *motu proprio* on August 15, 1972, and again in his 1976 *Inter insigniores* (*Declaration on the Question of the Admission of Women to the Ministerial Priesthood*),[33] he excluded women first from being acolytes and lectors and then from being ordained as priests in the Roman Catholic Church. In *Ministeria quaedam* the exclusion was especially jarring in light of the context of the document, in that Paul claimed, in continuity with the opening of the Church to the world at Vatican II and its increased emphasis on the Church as community, to be opening these roles to the nonordained by virtue of their baptism:

> Mother Church earnestly desires that all the faithful should be led to that full, conscious and active participation in liturgical celebra-

> tions which is demanded by the very nature of the liturgy. Such participation by the Christian people as "a chosen race, a royal priesthood, a holy nation, a purchased people" (1 Pt 2, 9) is their right and duty by reason of their baptism. In the restoration and promotion of the sacred liturgy, this full and active participation by all the people is the aim to be considered before all else.[34]

But number 7 of the new norms summarily excluded women from becoming lectors and acolytes despite their baptism.[35] Paul's continuation of women's exclusion from ordination was made simply incomprehensible to many, given his words in OA, because, according to canon law, governance in the Church is reserved to the ordained.[36] Thus, in excluding women from ordination, Paul was excluding them not only from sacramental administration, but also from all governance in the Church, despite his understanding that participation in decision making, sharing in responsibility, and equality are aspects of basic human dignity.[37]

Visionary Document

Perhaps the best explanation for the failure of OA's reception and implementation is that it was a visionary document ahead of its time. The admission of new groups to equal power and status, whether racial, ethnic, class, or gender groups, seldom occurs based on acceptance of visions or principles alone. Humans usually require evidence of equality in order to grant it, and the more personal the evidence, the more convincing it is. As movements of the poor around the world successfully organize to gain political, economic, and cultural power, they not only inspire other powerless groups to do so, but also demonstrate to the elites in power that the poor are also capable of negotiating power and are perhaps not so different after all. Many of the social transformations under way today were barely beginning in Paul's lifetime. This was especially true in the Church, where the severe shortage of priests for over a quarter century since Paul has created, of necessity, new roles for laywomen and laymen, many formerly exercised only by priests. Much of the laity has become convinced that both laymen and laywomen can exercise pastoral care, theological expertise, and responsible decision making in parishes and dioceses precisely because they have experienced laypeople doing these very things on the "emergency basis" created by the priest shortage.

The movements that prompted Paul's visionary letter have multiplied, not abated. The poverty that existed in the developing world in 1971 now encompasses many millions more people than it did then. Poor war refugees and migrants now not only constitute large communities in the developing world, but also constitute significant poor racial and ethnic minorities in the most developed nations in the world. The fall of communist states and the simultaneous collapse of Eastern European economies, together with the collapse of Asian economies in 1997–98 added many millions more to the ranks of the desperately poor who have little participation in the decision making that affects their condition. Nor is the current militancy and resurgence in the Muslim world unrelated to the failure of most Muslims to receive support for their aspirations for participation both in the prosperity of the developed world and in political and economic decision making within their native countries. Given all these trends, we can therefore expect that Catholic social teaching will again revisit the teachings of OA, which will then provide precedents for some future pope to proclaim new changes "in continuity with the teaching and practice of our brother, Paul."

REACTIONS TO THE DOCUMENT

Reactions to OA were mixed. Both Catholics and the rest of the world had been fed a steady stream of innovative church documents in the previous six years, beginning with the documents of the Council itself, then *Populorum progressio*, *Humanae vitae*, Medellín (CELAM), and OA. The storm of controversy over HV that still endured in 1971 distracted many from further attention to OA. For others, it seemed not so new a focus, but merely a continuation of *Populorum progressio*; many failed to understand the shift from analysis of social injustice to methods for addressing that injustice. For yet others, the brevity of the letter, and the fact that it was not an encyclical, seemed to diminish its importance.

Within the institutional Church, the effect of OA was incremental, further increasing the pressure for the creation of mechanisms to deal with social justice issues. Throughout the 1970s there were thousands of justice and peace organizations established within dioceses and parishes in addition to the newly forming parish and diocesan councils that also dealt with justice issues. Thousands of new books and periodicals dealing with justice and peace were published. Catholic social justice lobbying groups were established to deal with local issues of poverty, racism, and violence, as well as with international and global issues of injustice, as in South Africa, Latin America, and the dwindling war in Southeast Asia.

While the essentially innovative nature of Pope Paul's approach to justice in OA seems clear and relatively consistent yet today, we know from hindsight that the innovative approach of OA never took root. It has had a very limited impact on the way that the official Church acts either internally or externally in the world, and has effectively become a dead letter in the domain of the hierarchy.

NOTES

1. Mary Elsbernd, "Whatever Happened to *Octogesima adveniens?*" *Theological Studies* 56 (1995): 39–60.

2. Ibid., 41–42.

3. James Finn, "Beyond Economics, Beyond Revolution: *Octogesima adveniens*," in *Building the Free Society: Democracy, Capitalism and Catholic Social Teaching*, ed. George Weigel and Robert Royal (Grand Rapids, Mich., and Washington, D.C.: Eerdmans and the Ethics and Public Policy Center, 1993), 151–52.

4. See the five documents from Medellín in Alfred T. Hennelly, ed., *Liberation Theology: A Documentary History* (Maryknoll, N.Y.: Orbis, 1990), 89–120.

5. The exception to the rule is Pius XII, who issued his 1941 anniversary document as a radio address, probably due to the war. See "The Anniversary of Rerum Novarum," in *The Major Addresses of Pope Pius XII*, vol. 1, ed. Vincent Yzermans (St. Paul, Minn.: North Central, 1961), 26–36.

6. Elsbernd, "Whatever Happened," 41.

7. Ibid.

8. Charles E. Curran, *The Catholic Moral Tradition Today: A Synthesis* (Washington, D.C.: Georgetown University Press, 1999), 149.

9. While many commentators, Catholic Web sites, and even John Paul II have used the terms *social doctrine* and *social teaching*—even in John Paul II *social magisterium* (CS 2)—as synonymous, theological approaches have often distinguished the terms, understanding *social doctrine* as indicating more authority, as an essential element of evangelization. The debate around these terms is complicated and has changed over time. In the period leading up to and following Vatican II, the term *social teaching* was preferred by those theologians and commentators who applauded the more inclusive approach to social decision making advocated in OA while *social doctrine* was preferred by traditionalists as emphasizing papal authority. However, as Whitmore points out, some conservatives later defended their dissent from later encyclicals of John Paul II stressing economic rights by asserting that their dissent was only from "social teaching" and was not to be compared with liberals dissent from *Humane vitae*, which was doctrine. See Todd David Whitmore, "The Loyal Dissent of Neo-Conservative Economics, Part 2," *The Observer*, October 16, 1998, http://www.nd.edu/~cstprog/19981016.htm.

10. Pius XI, *Divini redemptoris*, *Acta apostolica sedis* (AAS) 29 (1937): 81.

11. Pius XII, *Christmas address*, AAS 37 (1945): 14.

12. Christine E. Gudorf, *Catholic Social Teaching on Liberation Themes* (Washington, D.C.: University Press of America, 1980), 40.

13. Paul VI's interpretation of John XXIII's MM 91–97, noted in OA 47, assumes that the continued emphasis on the need for participation is based in natural human equality, but MM 97–98 gives the reason for implementing participation in decision making: "But it should be emphasized how neces-

sary, or at least very appropriate, it is to give workers an opportunity to exert influence outside the limits of the individual productive unit, and indeed within all ranks of the commonwealth. The reason is that individual productive units, whatever their size, efficiency, or importance within the commonwealth, are closely connected with the overall economic and social situation in each country, wherein their own prosperity ultimately depends."

14. For a discussion of the development and implications of the theme of participation in decision making, see Christine E. Gudorf, "Probing the Politics of Difference: What's Wrong with an All-Male Priesthood?" *Journal of Religious Ethics* 27, no. 3 (1999): 382–87.

15. Leo XIII, *Quod apostolici muneris* (*On Socialism*, 1878), in *The Church Speaks to the Modern World: The Social Teachings of Leo XIII*, ed. Etienne Gilson (Garden City, N.Y.: Doubleday, 1954), 189–99.

16. Bernard Evans, "*Octogesima adveniens*," in *The New Dictionary of Catholic Social Thought*, ed. Judith A. Dwyer (Collegeville, Minn.: Liturgical, 1994), 687.

17. See Congregation for the Doctrine of the Faith, *Instruction on Christian Freedom and Liberation*, in *Liberation Theology*, ed. A. T. Hennelly, 461–97.

18. B. Evans, "*Octogesima adveniens*," in *New Dictionary of Catholic Social Thought*, ed. J. A. Dwyer, 685.

19. Ibid.

20. Gustavo Gutiérrez, *A Theology of Liberation: History, Politics, and Salvation*, trans. and ed. Caridad Inda and John Eagleson (Maryknoll, N.Y.: Orbis, 1973), 111–12; "Declaration of the 80 [1971]," in *Christians and Socialism: The Christians for Socialism Movement in Latin America* (New York: Orbis, 1975), 3. The "Declaration of the 80" was published one month before OA; while the English translation of Gutiérrez included references to OA, the original Spanish edition was published only a few months after OA, and written months before.

21. While this was true on the whole, there were some exceptions. But the options of Christians such as Camillo Torres, a priest of Colombia (Orlando F. Borda, *Subversion and Social Change in Colombia*, trans. J. D. Skiles [New York: Columbia University Press, 1969)], and Néstor Paz, a Christian student in Bolivia (N. Paz, *My Life for My Friends: A Guerilla Journal of Néstor Paz, Christian*, trans. and ed. Ed Garcia and John Eagleson [Maryknoll, N.Y.: Orbis, 1975)], for armed struggle were early, rare, and routinely rejected by liberation theologians as failing to meet conditions for the just use of violence, principally the expectation of success, but often proportionality and last resort as well.

22. "Declaration of the 80," 4.

23. In the late nineteenth century a number of papal documents condemned socialism and communism, beginning with Pius IX's *Qui pluribus* in 1846 and including his *Syllabus of Errors* of December 8, 1864. Leo XIII included socialism among the evils of the day addressed in his first encyclical, *Inscrutabili*, in 1878, and then issued an entire encyclical condemning socialism, *Quod apostolici muneris*, in 1878. See chap. 3 in Gudorf, *Catholic Social Teaching*.

24. Some commentators, for example, Finn in "Beyond Economics, Beyond Revolution," ignore both the development in the doctrine before John XXIII, John's innovations, and the shifts between Paul VI and John XXIII, and instead read Paul's cautions about the dangers of Marxist ideology and praxis as general condemnations of Marxism later vindicated by the fall of the Soviet Union.

25. Elsbernd, "Whatever Happened," 40.

26. Ibid.

27. *Catechism of the Catholic Church*, no. 2032.

28. Elsbernd, writing in 1995, in "Whatever Happened," 50.

29. Ibid.

30. Charles E. Curran, *History and Contemporary Issues: Studies in Moral Theology* (New York: Continuum, 1996), 112.

31. Henry Chadwick, "Paul VI and Vatican II," *Journal of Ecclesiastical History* 41, no. 3 (1990): 466.

32. Ibid. Chadwick also adds that through the addition of the *Nota*, the traditionalist minority were brought to support the document so that it became a consensus document of the Council, which was a continuous goal of Paul's.

33. *Inter insigniores* (*Declaration on the Question of the Admission of Women to the Ministerial Priesthood*), in *Women Priests*, ed. Leonard and Arlene Swidler (New York: Paulist, 1977).

34. Paul VI, *Ministeria quaedam*, August 15, 1972, AAS 64 (1972): 530; trans. *The Pope Speaks* 17 (1972): 256.

35. "In accordance with the venerable tradition of the Church, installation in the ministries of lector

and acolyte is reserved to men." Paul VI, *Ministeria quaedam*, 553; trans. *The Pope Speaks* 17 (1972): 261.

36. *Code of Canon Law*, trans. Canon Law Society of America (Washington, D.C.: Canon Law Society of America, 1983), c. 129.1.

37. Gudorf, "Probing the Politics of Difference," 398–400.

SELECTED BIBLIOGRAPHY

Coleman, John A. *One Hundred Years of Catholic Social Thought: Celebration and Challenge*. Maryknoll, N.Y.: Orbis, 1991. Unusually inclusive approach to social teaching; articles by Coleman and Hehir deal directly with OA.

Curran, Charles E., and Richard A. McCormick, eds. *Readings in Moral Theology No. 5: Official Catholic Social Teaching*. Mahwah, N.J.: Paulist, 1986. Most relevant to OA are essays by Hehir and Hebblethwaite. Hebblethwaite presents Paul VI as presiding over the death of (authoritarian, universalist) Catholic social doctrine, and John Paul II as resurrecting it; Hehir presents John Paul as developing Vatican and post-Vatican social teaching, grounding them theologically and biblically.

Elsbernd, Mary. "Whatever Happened to *Octogesima adveniens*?" *Theological Studies* 56 (1995): 39–60. Illustrates the striking failure of later social teaching to develop OA themes, attributing the failure to John Paul II's vision of the Church.

Evans, Bernard F. "*Octogesima adveniens*." In *The New Dictionary of Catholic Social Thought*. Edited by Judith A. Dwyer, 683–92. Collegeville, Minn.: Liturgical, 1994. Excellent analysis of the document, concentrating on the five new themes developed: the aspiration to participation, the preferential respect due the poor, the need to move from economics to politics, the call to action, and the plurality of options.

Finn, James. "Beyond Economics, Beyond Revolution: *Octogesima adveniens*." In *Building the Free Society: Democracy, Capitalism and Catholic Social Teaching*. Edited by George Weigel and Robert Royal. Grand Rapids, Mich., and Washington, D.C.: Eerdmans and the Ethics and Public Policy Center, 1993. Conservative interpretation and critique of OA; leans heavily on the assumptions and approaches of earlier social teaching.

Gudorf, Christine E. *Catholic Social Teaching on Liberation Themes*. Washington, D.C.: University Press of America, 1980. Treats OA as giving cautious approval of most of the major themes of liberation theologies and their approaches to politics while encouraging experimentation in the attempt to create justice.

Hebblethwaite, Peter. *Paul VI*. New York: Paulist, 1993. In-depth portrait of Paul VI as misunderstood and torn between allowing, even encouraging, development of multiple participative forms of both Church and solidarity with the poor within different global contexts, and refusing to risk either cracks in the unity of the church or abrupt breaks with tradition.

CHAPTER

14 Commentary on *Justitia in mundo* (*Justice in the World*)

KENNETH R. HIMES, O.F.M.

INTRODUCTION

Justitia in mundo was a statement produced by the bishops assembled at the 1971 Roman synod held during the fall of that year. Authorized for publication on November 30, the actual text was first published in Italian on December 9. Among the important aspects of the document was the role that bishops from the poorer regions of the world played in its formulation. As with the papal encyclical *Populorum progressio*, there was an intentional effort to describe the social question from the vantage point of those who live in nations with widespread and serious poverty. The document takes as its starting point the reality of systemic injustice in the world and the need for Christians to join with one another and all persons of good will to overcome injustice. There is an emphasis on the mission of the Church being concerned not simply with personal conversion but with the social transformation of the world. In this regard the bishops asserted a right to development. Notable, too, was the self-criticism that church leaders engaged in as they described the mission of the Church in a world scarred by economic underdevelopment. In many ways the document was a call to action more than a doctrinal statement; the bishops were concerned with stirring up a new resolve to eliminate the social evils caused by injustice. Yet, despite its brevity, the biblical and theological reflection explaining why the Church must take up the struggle to achieve justice in temporal life has proven significant. Finally, the fact that the document emerged as a consensus statement from an assembly representing the worldwide episcopate created additional interest in the social teaching of the Roman Catholic Church.

OUTLINE OF THE DOCUMENT

Unlike papal and conciliar documents the synod statement is not divided by numbered paragraphs. The official format of the document is an introduction, with three major parts and a concluding section.

In the introduction the bishops assert that they have gathered together to question themselves about the mission of the Church to promote justice in a world marked by profound injustices. The conclusion of this section is the oft-quoted sentence that "action on behalf of justice and participation in the transformation of the world fully appear to us as a constitutive dimension of the preaching of the Gospel" (introduction).

The first major section of the document is an overview of the situation in the world meant to highlight illustrations of justice and injustice. The bishops identify a "tremendous paradox" in the modern world: never before have there been so many forces and resources available to promote human unity, yet the divisions and tensions within the human family appear to be increasing. This is the "crisis of universal solidarity" (1.1).

Confronted with the injustice and oppression that mark international life the remedy is a "right to development" without which new forms of colonialism between rich and poor will appear (1.2). Among the many who are disadvantaged in this world there are "silent, voiceless, victims" who deserve particular attention.

The most overtly theological part of the document is the second major section that describes the motivation and meaning behind the Church's work for justice. Appealing to both the Old and New Testaments, the bishops assert that love of God and love of humankind are intimately bound together (2.1). Yet the religious mission of the Church does not give it special competence in formulating particular solutions to injustice. Individual Christians must fulfill their right and duty to promote the common good (2.2).

In the final major part of the document the bishops provide guidance and encouragement for enacting the commitment to justice. Of note is the call for the Church itself to practice justice in both internal and external activities (3.1). This part of the bishops' statement emphasizes the need to educate for justice and endorses methodologies that awaken the consciences of believers. There are also calls for the local and regional churches to work cooperatively, especially for rich and poor churches to develop networks of mutual action. The theme of cooperation is extended to include ecumenical and inter-religious activities (3.2–4). This third part also lists eight proposals for international action that would build a more just world.

The final closing words of the document are a statement of belief and hope that the transformation of the created order, already begun in the paschal mystery of Christ, will continue in the alleviation of injustice and oppression.

CONTEXT OF THE DOCUMENT

Social Context

Without question, the desperate situation of the poor nations of the world was the setting for the second ordinary synod held in Rome in 1971. For many bishops this was the new social question, replacing Leo XIII's earlier formulation of the issue as being the situation of the working class in the newly industrialized European nations. Now the social question was put into a global context. As the bishops stated in the beginning of the document, "we have . . . been able to perceive the serious injustices which are building around the world of humanity a network of domination, oppression and abuses which stifle freedom and which keep the greater part of humanity from sharing in the building up and enjoyment of a more just and more fraternal world" (introduction).

At its beginning, one observer of the synod identified four components of the "somber background" for the episcopal gathering: (1) "the growth of huge power blocs" (led by the United States and the Soviet Union) engaged in a rivalry that occasioned huge military expenditures; (2) "the inequitable distribution of the world's resources" as a result "either of deliberate exploitation or a consequence of patterns of world trade" and the imbalance of power; (3) the explosion of population, much of it in the poorer nations, with growth being double that of the nineteenth century; and (4) environmental damage due to pollution caused by human agents and societies.[1]

According to one of the experts invited to address the synod, "75% of the world's resources are controlled and consumed by the third of humanity" who live in technologically advanced nations where most of the people are Christian. Add to this the claim that a number of the wealthier nations at the time were "less concerned, less inventive in their approach to world development," and the situation appeared to many as a crisis among the poor.[2] This predicament was all the more disappointing when one considers that there had been considerable optimism about the possibility of improving matters when the United Nations had declared the decade of the 1960s as the Decade of Development. The failure of that effort led to the designation of the 1970s as the Second Decade of Development. By then, however, there was considerably less innocence among development advocates about the challenge of the task.

One of the consequences of the above reading of the state of affairs was the worry that "the incapacity of the existing structures to meet the demand of those who want justice and more participation forces the latter into opting for violence."[3] Paul VI had warned of this danger in his 1967 encyclical, *Populorum progressio*, and now the bishops were taking up the question of international justice in a climate that was pessimistic, though not despairing, about the prospects for effecting peaceful and significant change. Amid this somber atmosphere, the bishops were well aware of the viewpoint expressed by Cardinal Maurice Roy at the opening of their deliberations: "*Gaudium et Spes* reminded the People of God that Christians should not be considered as a community separated from the rest of the world."[4]

Ecclesial Context

The word *synod* derives from the Latin *synodus*, a crossroads where military and civil governors of the provinces of the Roman Empire gathered to discuss concerns and policies for implementing the instructions of the emperor. Once the Church spread to various regions of the world its leaders imitated the imperial practice, holding meetings of bishops to discuss mutual concerns of doctrine and discipline. The practice of calling such synods likely was in effect by the latter part of the second century.[5]

The recent history of episcopal synods dates from the time of Vatican II. During the preparation for the Council some bishops indicated a desire to see a permanent body created whereby bishops could exercise their role within the universal Church. No consensus on the matter was attained, however, until after Paul VI announced at the beginning of the fourth session of the Council on September 14, 1965, that he was going to create a synod of bishops.[6] Thus, although it is viewed as a vehicle for collegial reflection by the bishops the synod is, strictly speaking, not a representative arm of the episcopal college but an advisory body under the pope convoked to assist him in his role as head of the college.[7]

Different types of synods—general or special—refer to whether the purpose is to address concerns of the universal Church or of a particular region(s), for example, the Church in Africa. General synods can be ordinary or extraordinary, distinguished mainly by the rules governing membership. Ordinary synods have a majority of delegates elected by episcopal conferences while extraordinary synods, meant to address issues of urgency, have norms governing membership that permit a more rapid convocation of the bishops because the majority of members serve *ex officio* and a lengthy process to elect delegates is unnecessary.[8] General synods have usually met after intervals of two to four years.[9]

The 1971 meeting was the first synod to be held in the auditorium custom-built for that purpose. The auditorium is above the papal audience hall in a building next to St. Peter's Basilica that was designed by Pier Luigi Nervi at Paul VI's request. In attendance at the opening session of the 1971 synod were 190 bishops (142 elected to represent local episcopal conferences, including 4 from the United States) as well as 25 papal appointees, 14 representatives from the Eastern churches, 19 heads of curial offices, and 10 members of the Union of Superiors General (representing male religious orders). In sum, there were 210 members of the synod. There were also 28 priest observers and 8 lay observers, 4 of whom were women.

Significant for this assembly was that more than half of the bishops came from countries of the third world. At Vatican II the European bishops were the dominant voice but at this synod "the bishops of the Third World were heard from in an unprecedented proportion."[10] It was the first time leaders of churches in poor nations had a formal opportunity to dialogue about justice with members of the curia and bishops from the wealthy nations.[11]

Synods differ from ecumenical councils in two important ways. First, councils usually meet over the course of several years in various sessions; this permits extended reflection on topics and facilitates wide consultation beyond the membership. Synods are convened for a brief period of time in one session, usually little more than a month, thus greatly increasing the pace at which work must be done. The 1971 synod lasted thirty-eight days, from September 30 until November 6, but only the second half of the synod, from October 19 until the close, was devoted to the topic of justice. During the prior sessions the synod addressed the issue of priestly ministry.[12]

Second, synods are consultative not deliberative, although the pope may confer decision-making authority upon a synod if he so desires. At the 1971 meeting, Archbishop Wladyslaw Rubin, general secretary of the synod, indicated that although the synod had only a consultative character, nevertheless, the bishops should take their role seriously because what they said would be heard. It was understood by all in attendance that the pope was using the general secretary to send a message to the bishops.[13]

Also important for understanding the ecclesial context of the 1971 synod was the fact that at the extraordinary synod of 1969 the assembled bishops had voted for three proposals: (1) bishops should urge clergy and laity to give their support "to all initiatives designed to promote justice with regard to the poor nations"; (2) the various episcopal conferences should assist the pope in "establishing a fund for the progress of poor countries"; and (3) the Pontifical Commission Justitia et Pax (Justice and Peace) should suggest methods for educating and resolving the problem of the poor nations.[14] Thus, many bishops came to the meeting with the plight of the world's poor already a topic of concern within episcopal circles.

PROCESS OF FORMULATION AND AUTHORSHIP

It is difficult to understand the writing of JM without some knowledge of the synod's procedures and process.

At the Vatican an office of the synod is presided over by a general or permanent secretary appointed by the pope. He is assisted by a Council of the General Secretariat of the Synod of Bishops composed of bishops, twelve of whom are elected by their fellow bishops and three others appointed by the pope. This group usually meets two or three times a year for several days at a time. They function until a new general synod begins. A small group of priests and laypersons assists this group with staff work but it is the Council of the Secretariat that makes decisions about the synod, subject to papal approval. The Council goes out of existence with the opening of a synod and is reconstituted at the end of a synod.

Among the tasks of the Council is to determine the topic of the synod. Once that is done, various experts may be recruited to assist the Council in drawing up a preliminary document (*lineamenta*) with the aim of stimulating discussion and eliciting responses from episcopal conferences worldwide as well as some other audiences. Based on the responses received, the staff of the secretariat, along with selected experts, often drawn from Roman universities, develops a working paper (*instrumentum laboris*) for the synod. This latter document, a refinement of the topic, is sent to all the synod delegates and also made public. The hope is to stimulate wide discussion and interest within the body of the Church on the synod's work.

Prior to the opening of the synod the pope appoints both a *relator* and a special secretary. A *relator* plays an important role because he gives the opening report on the topic to the assembly, not just repeating the working paper; he also helps to facilitate synod discussions and consensus on synod conclusions. The *relator* is assisted by the special secretary, an expert on the topic of the synod who works throughout the synodal process, collecting all the written comments of participants after plenary and small group discussions and putting them in some sort of coherent order. This summary forms the basis for the final voting. After the vote the special secretary works with the general secretary to prepare the final report of the synod's conclusions to the pope.

Synod sessions typically follow one of two formats: plenary and small group. The plenary sessions are given over to what is loosely called debate. The pope appoints president(s) to chair the plenary meetings.[15] At the first session the general secretary provides a review of the preparation for the synod and the work of the secretariat since the previous synod. Then the *relator* gives his paper. The delegates then have a short period of time allotted to give their views on the topic. These interventions usually are seven- to eight-minute speeches prepared in advance, sometimes addressing the preparatory document but not always. Due to the advance preparation, each speaker delivers his remarks with no necessary connection to the preceding speaker's remarks. Interruptions or spontaneous intervention from the floor are not allowed. Thus, there is little genuine argument nor any methodical analysis of an issue. Over the course of several days it often is possible, however, to discern recurring themes or concerns among the speeches.[16] The list of speakers is made up of those who asked to speak. At the 1971 synod there were eighty-two such speeches over the course of several days of plenary sessions. Following the speeches it is the task of the *relator* to summarize the main points.

The other format for sessions is small group discussion (*circuli minores*) organized by language. These groups use the *relator*'s summary as a starting point for their conversations. Each group convenes and then elects its own moderator and group *relator* who eventually will report back in a plenary session on the group's discussion. Often it is in these groups that much of the work of a synod gets done, as the reports from the small groups can greatly shape the final document. At the 1971 synod the participants were divided into 12 groups using one of 7 languages: Latin (1 group), English (3), French (3), Italian (1), Spanish and Portuguese (3), German (1).[17]

The final days of a synod are often hectic as a drafting committee works to put together a document for the delegates to review and vote upon. Votes follow the format of *placet* (approve), *non placet* (oppose), *placet iuxta modum* (approve with reservation), and abstention. Any reservation must be submitted in writing. Then all proposed amendments are reviewed by the drafting committee. Because the goal is consensus the tendency is to drop controversial amendments. The final draft is then voted upon once again by the entire body of the synod. At the 1971 synod the process was so rushed and difficult that subsequent synods have not sought to issue their own document but have instead voted on a list of recommendations that are then given to the pope for his reflection. Often the pope will use the material as a basis for an apostolic letter or encyclical on the theme of the synod.[18] The 1971 synod, however, did formulate its own statement on justice in the world.

As this overview of the process suggests, it is difficult to go back and determine just who is responsible for directly influencing the document of a synod. Participants themselves are not always in agreement as to just who originally wrote a particular paragraph or sentence that found its way into the final statement. At the synod of 1971 we do know that besides the bishops and official delegates there were other significant figures who played a large part in the production of JM.

As a result of the proposals concerning poor nations endorsed by the 1969 extraordinary synod, the Vatican secretariat of state set up an ad hoc committee in the spring of 1970 to study how to enact the decisions. This ad hoc committee, in turn, requested the Pontifical Commission Justitia et Pax to provide a working paper on the issue of justice for the poor nations. This was done on short notice and made available shortly before Christmas of the same year. Deliberation about the topic led Paul VI to decide that the theme of justice in the world would be added to the previously announced synod's agenda of priestly ministry. It seemed that the pope wanted more episcopal input and guidance as to how the Church should enact its social mission.

Archbishop Rubin, the general secretary, relied upon staff members of Justitia et Pax to put together an early version of the *lineamenta*. After discussion within the Council of the General Secretariat of the Synod of Bishops, the document was revised, discussion questions were added, and the text, "Elements for a Reflection on Justice in the World," was distributed to the episcopal conferences and other ecclesial bodies for feedback.[19] More than sixty official responses came back which, despite their differences, demonstrated points of convergence on the need to denounce injustice in the world, address injustice in the Church, develop a theology for the Church's involvement in social justice, and propose new strategies to educate people for justice.[20]

While the document was in the hands of the bishops, the staff at Justitia et Pax, working under its chair, Monsignor Joseph Gremillion of Louisiana, produced several pamphlets related to the theme of justice in the world that examined demographic aspects of global poverty, listed available social justice resources, and presented existing episcopal documents from various regions of the world. The last element was quite significant because it put the statements of the Latin American bishops' meeting at Medellín, Colombia, into the hands of the worldwide episcopacy. Those 1968 statements from Medellín were far in advance of other episcopal conferences' comments on the topic of social justice.

After receiving the responses to the *lineamenta*, Archbishop Rubin and Bishop Ramon Torrella Cascante, the vice president of Justitia et Pax and special secretary for the synod, asked the staff of Justitia et Pax to sift through the replies to the *lineamenta* and formulate a draft of the *instrumentum laboris*. Archbishop Theopist Alberto y Valderrama of the Philippines, who was the *relator* for the synod, also relied upon staff at Justitia et Pax for assistance in crafting his opening address.[21]

On October 19, 1971, following the delivery of the *relator*'s address, the synod debate on justice in the world began. Examination of the topic continued through eleven plenary sessions and four days of small group meetings until October 30, when discussion and voting on a draft document started. On each of the first three days of plenary sessions one of the experts (*periti*) attending the synod gave a major address that sparked discussion and reflection.[22] Particularly influential was developmental theorist Barbara Ward (Lady Jackson), the first woman to address a synod, who analyzed the gap between rich and poor nations.[23] Following the speeches of the *periti* came the brief, prepared remarks of those bishops who had asked for a time slot to speak. The plenary sessions ended with the beginning of small group meetings on October 25 that continued for four days, followed by two days of the groups reporting back to the full assembly in plenary sessions.[24] Then the voting on a draft document began.

From the evening of October 30 through November 2 the drafting group[25] produced, after four prior versions, a document (*textus prior*) that was presented on November 3 to the synod's delegates. On November 4 the document was voted upon section by section. The next day the revised text (*textus emendatus*) was distributed and a final vote was taken on November 6. As special secretary, Torrella Cascante was chair of the drafting committee.[26] In many cases the work of the drafters was closer to that of being a redactor or editor rather than author because the drafting committee worked with a text that had been revised and amended many times by many people. It is fair to conclude, therefore, that while the actual formulation of JM involved the work of a small committee it was a document of the entire synod of bishops.[27]

ESSAY

Before examining the statement according to the headings proposed in the outline, there are three topics to consider regarding the overall document.

Methodology

The brevity of the synod statement as well as its purpose—less a doctrinal statement than a call to action—precluded any extensive development of a methodology. Nonetheless, there is a three-step method evident both in the format of the document and in the introduction to JM. It is a method that can be called "contextual" in the sense that the starting point for theological reflection is an attempt to understand the concrete setting in which reflection takes place.[28] As one analyst describes the method, "a genuine effort is made to begin from the real situation in the world, in order to discern there 'the signs of the times,' the specific ways in which God is speaking to today's world and calling people to respond."[29] One might say the "sign of the times" that appeared most glaring to the bishops was "the serious injustices which are building around the world" (introduction).

Important for the message of the synod, however, was that the methodology employed did not rest with citing the existence of injustice. According to Philip Land, a consultant to the synod and a contributor to the work of the drafting committee, "the effort to be contextual led further to recognizing the need to search deeper into the underlying structural causes of injustice."[30] Part 1 of the document provides the analytical reading of the global context. The problem that the bishops observed was not due to happenstance, bad luck, or the evil actions of a few individuals. Rather, they perceived "a network of domination, oppression, and abuses that stifle freedom and keep the greater part of humanity from sharing in the building up and enjoyment of a more just and more fraternal world" (introduction). Thus, in Part 3 the remedial actions suggested by the bishops to overcome the situation, while not ignoring the need for personal conversion, consisted largely of calls for new and/or reformed international structures and policies.

Before formulating their proposed remedies, however, a second methodological step was necessary. Theological reflection upon the situation meant the bishops had to "have listened to the Word of God that we might be converted to the fulfilling of the divine plan for the salvation of the world" (introduction). The bishops did not assemble as a convention of social theorists but understood that they were gathered "in communion with all who believe in Christ" and they wished to open their "hearts to the Spirit who is making the whole of creation new." Their aim was to speak as religious leaders, as people charged with the task of ecclesial leadership, and so "we have questioned ourselves about the mission of the People of God to further justice in the world" (introduction). It was through theological reflection upon the signs of the times that the bishops sought to articulate the social implications of the Church's religious mission. Part 2 of JM is the theological rationale for why the mission of the Church includes a commitment to establishing a more just order within and between nations.

In following their method the synod delegates assumed a posture of dialogue, wherein listening was as important as speaking. Dialogue with the wider world was pursued chiefly through two means: the presence at the synod of laypersons with expertise in various aspects of development and the input of various national justice and peace commissions through the comments of the Pontifical Commission Justitia et Pax. The lay experts were present throughout the synod and they participated actively in the small group discussions.[31] Three of them delivered papers at plenary sessions on consecutive days of the synod.[32] Meanwhile comments from numerous diocesan and national justice and peace commissions worldwide were presented in the paper distributed by the pontifical justice and peace commission. In this way the wisdom to be gleaned from human experience and the study of social scientists found its way into the synod hall.

Another form of dialogue occurred among the bishops themselves. Although the plenary sessions did not lend themselves to open discussion, the series of speeches taken as a whole provided a general sense of the concerns of the Church in the various regions of the world. Bishops unfamiliar with the situation in another continent or culture heard firsthand reports of the experiences of injustice. Often these speeches suggested the interconnection between the benefits to one region of the world at the expense of others. Even more significant were the dialogues that took place in the small group sessions. "Bishops from rich countries heard plain talk about the forms of domination their countries exercise. Bishops from developing countries heard experts tell them that economic domination is only a partial explanation of poverty."[33] The makeup of the synod, with elected delegates representing all the various episcopal conferences, confronted individuals with the eye-opening diversity of experience present within the universal Church.

Influences

When reading the document several influences are evident. First, there is the impact of Paul VI's 1967 encyclical letter *Populorum progressio* and his apostolic exhortation *Octogesima adveniens* issued just months prior to the synod in May 1971. *Populorum progressio* was specifically addressed to the issue of international justice and his exposition of "integral development" encouraged the synod's claim that human persons possess a right to development (PP 14–21). The impact of *Octogesima adveniens* on the synod can be seen in three points: (1) Paul's forthright call for the elimination of "flagrant inequalities" between nations, (2) the papal encouragement to bishops for local and national churches to develop their own strategies to achieve justice, and (3) a belief that just development requires each nation to be able to chart its own course with the support of others but free from domination by others (OA 2, 4, 43). In this light, it is correct to characterize the synod statement as "a response to the Pope's request for advice on what the Church must do to serve better the cause of justice in the world."[34] Throughout the synod, references were regularly made to Paul's documents; they had a clear influence on the delegates and the synod statement.

Another significant influence upon the bishops and their statement was the meeting of the Conference of Bishops of Latin American (CELAM) in Medellín, Colombia, in 1968. The method adopted by the synod of reading the signs of the times, reflecting upon God's revelation, and devising pastoral strategies for action was central to the Medellín documents. And the language of domination, colonialism, oppression, and liberation was the vocabulary of Medellín. This is not to say that the Latin Americans spoke with one voice, for there were divergences among them,[35] but the tone, methodology, and outlook of JM are reflective of the documents of CELAM.

Although not an explicit influence upon the authors of the synod statement, it is hard to imagine JM or any of the previously mentioned documents without *Gaudium et spes*, the *Pastoral Constitution on the Church in the Modern World*. That document popularized John XXIII's phrase *reading the signs of the times*. More than any specific expression it was the *Pastoral Constitution* that reconceptualized the Church's relationship to the world. The need for engagement with humankind's aspirations and troubles, the posture of dialogue when encountering the empirical sciences, the linkage of human advancement with the religious mission of the Church, the theological foundation for speaking of a church with a social mission—all this was expressed in *Gaudium et spes*.[36] Although more immediate influences upon the synod are apparent, the *Pastoral Constitution* must be considered among the most significant.

Key Themes

There are three major themes that are central to the document: (1) the right to development, (2) the connection between Christian faith and justice, and (3) strategies for acting on behalf of justice in our time. The first theme borrows an expression initially used by Paul VI in a speech to the International Labor Office in Geneva on its fiftieth anniversary. Paul spoke there of a "common right of people to their integral development."[37] The bishops did not employ the modifier *integral* because they went on to explain what they meant by development; it is clear they were in accord with the views of Paul VI and John XXIII[38] that development was more than economic. Regarding the second theme, the connection between the Christian faith and justice, the synod's way of articulating how faith relates to justice turned out to be the most debated aspect of the document, not at the synod itself but in subsequent years. When treating the third major theme of the document, strategies for justice, the bishops placed great emphasis on education for justice as well as the need for reformed international institutions and agreements. This latter point was in keeping with the prevailing view of many of the Latin American bishops, as well as Paul VI in *Populorum progressio*,[39] that the problems of poverty and underdevelopment among poor nations were intimately linked to the structure and workings of the global economy. Notable in the document is that under this last theme there is also forthright self-criticism by the bishops in regard to justice as it is practiced by and within the Church.

Analysis of the Document

With the above comments about influences, methodology, and major themes as prefatory, the document will be analyzed following the outline provided in the second section of this commentary.

Introduction

The bishops begin by putting the ecclesiological theme up front: "we have questioned ourselves about the mission of the People of God to further justice in the world." It is not simply as good citizens, workers, or employers that Christians must consider the demands of justice. Rather, it is explicitly as disciples that the task of justice must be examined. And the point is not to determine the vocation of a specific individual acting alone but to assess what is asked of the Church *qua* Church. So the bishops are interested in examining how the work of justice is to be related to the corporate mission of the Church.

In their opening remarks the bishops also establish that they see the world as marked by "serious injustices" and as a place where the majority suffers while only a minority enjoys freedom, security, and economic well-being. Not claiming to speak as social scientists employing technical analyses of the world, the bishops speak as pastors sensitive to the needs of the people they serve. Without dismissing the contribution of experts the bishops maintain the reality of injustice is clear enough that people of goodwill are "able to perceive" the severity of the problem.

Nevertheless, there is cause for hope. Something is at work that gives rise to "a new awareness which shakes [people] out of any fatalistic resignation" and encourages them to work for their own and others' betterment. These "forces which are moving the world in its very foundations are not foreign to the dynamism of the Gospel."

Two aspects of this connection between the gospel and movements for social change ought to be noted. First, the bishops see the drive to bring about justice as a manifestation of the Holy Spirit's power at work. It is the Spirit who releases people from the bondage of "personal sin and from its consequences in social life." In the document sin is seen as personal but because individuals live in society their actions have "ripple effects" that spread out to others. There are social consequences to personal sin.[40]

The second aspect is the wording that the bishops used to describe the connection between the movement for justice and the gospel. The final sentence of the introduction reads: "Action on behalf of justice and participation in the transformation of the world fully appear to us as a constitutive dimension of the preaching of the Gospel, or in other words, of the Church's mission for the redemption of the human race and its liberation from every oppressive situation." Although not much debated at the synod itself, the claim that acting for justice was "a *constitutive* dimension of the preaching of the Gospel" became a controversial issue later.

Were the bishops putting the work of justice on a par with the preaching of the Word and the celebration of the sacraments as being definitive of the Church? Or were the bishops simply making the point that working for justice is not merely an ethical implication of discipleship but something at the very center of Christian life? The synod's language became a flashpoint for those who disagreed about how much emphasis should be given to the social mission of the Church. Arguing against "constitutive" was a way of diminishing the import of the social mission while defending "constitutive" became a badge for those who supported social activism.

Opposition to heightening the import of the social mission of the Church was not due to indifference about social injustice, however, but reflected a concern that the mission of the Church not be reduced to *horizontalism*. This term expressed a fear that the message of the gospel might lose its transcendent and religious dimension and become equivalent to a human project for social change. Indeed, the synod statement included the phrase "redemption of the human race" alongside the newer expression "liberation from every oppressive situation" as a way "to avoid the danger of excessive 'horizontalism.'"[41] By their insertion of the more traditional language of "redemption" the bishops signaled that the Church's message and hope transcends the category of time and looks toward what God will do, not what humans will achieve in history.[42]

A reasonable conclusion to draw concerning the discussion over "constitutive" is that the bishops assembled at the synod were trying to make a point: justice is at the heart of gospel life, it is an essential human response to proclamation of the good news. Thus, the social mission is a particular and necessary element of the overall religious mission. Working for justice is central and indispensable to the Church's preaching and witnessing to the gospel. The social mission can never be viewed as optional or peripheral to the religious mission.[43]

Part 1. Justice and World Society

The very title of the section indicates that the frame of reference for the bishops is global. The unit of analysis will not be the nation-state or a geographic region but the entire world situation.

1.1 Crisis of Universal Solidarity

This section of the document is the bishops' statement of the "signs of the times," their perception of what is happening in the world around them. The word that the bishops use to describe the situation is *paradox*, for there are forces, powerful on both sides of the paradox, working for unity and promoting division. On the one hand, people are aware of their common origin as one family; human beings have a sense that they are linked together in terms of their common destiny as a race, and even are developing a shared responsibility for the world.

On the other hand, the document provides a dismal account of "the forces of division and antagonism" that only seem to be gaining in strength. Notable in this regard is the technology of weaponry. The arms race is seen as a pernicious threat to humankind. Yet it is not solely weapons technology that creates disunity, for industrial technology "favors the concentration of wealth, power and decision-making in the hands" of a few.

The document acknowledges that many persons wished that economic growth would spread to include all who are presently suffering, but the synod gathering concludes that "this has been a vain hope." Without providing details the bishops cite a number of causes for the failed promise of development: rapid population growth, lack of agrarian reform, urbanization, unemployment. The result is a great rise in the numbers of "'marginal' persons [who are] ill-fed, inhumanly housed, illiterate and deprived of political power as well as the suitable means of acquiring responsibility and moral dignity."

There is in this section of the document two competing, if not contradictory, theses. There is the belief that the separation of haves and have-nots is due largely to advanced technology, the accompanying skills of production, and the reaping of the benefits restricted to a minority. Alongside the technology thesis the bishops mix in statements that indicate support for the dependency theory so prevalent among Latin American thinkers at the time. This approach to the economics of development sees a core group of wealthy nations that dominate an unjust international economic system. Poor nations, according to dependency theorists, are kept on the periphery of global economics through forms of economic colonialism that control various key factors like capital investment and trade relations. Systematic marginalization keeps people from attaining their rightful share in the goods of the earth. The process of marginalization, therefore, has both domestic and international roots in the minds of the document's authors.[44]

Particularly striking is the formulation of a different kind of argument about exploitation tied to an emerging ecological awareness. The bishops assert that "the demand for resources and energy by the richer nations, whether capitalist or socialist," and the effects of pollution by these same countries make it impossible for the poorer nations to see them as a model for development. The environmental costs of development as practiced by the rich nations mean "it is simply not possible for all parts of the world to have the kind of 'development' that has occurred in the wealthy countries."[45] The bishops do not expand upon the argument, but implicitly suggest rich nations have achieved their present state of wealth, at least in part, by the way they have abused the earth's resources. Nations that developed first in the industrial era took more than their fair share of what belongs to all. For rich nations not to make amends by more adequate sharing of resources and by assistance in formulating new paths to development amounts to the rich now exploiting the poor as well as the earth.

1.2 Right to Development

In modern Catholic social teaching there is an intimate connection between human dignity and human rights. Put simply, human rights give specificity to the language of human dignity; they articulate the freedoms, the goods, and the relationships that are expressive of a person's dignity. The right to development is one of the major themes of the document and in this subsection the bishops explain what they mean by development, provide a critique of mistaken notions of development, and warn of obstacles to genuine development.

It is evident that the synod did not view the right to development as one more right alongside other rights. Instead, "the right to development must be seen as a dynamic interpenetration of all those fundamental human rights" to which both persons and nations aspire (PT 11–27).[46] It can be understood as an overarching category that includes many of the particular human rights endorsed by the Church. Or, put differently, the right to development is shorthand for a group of fundamental rights that, taken together, constitute the framework and substance of a just social order. Satisfaction of these basic rights can serve as an objective criterion for measuring development.

There is also a subjective component to development. A first step in development is for the person to be conscious of his or her dignity and to desire the actualization of those rights proper to that dignity. In this regard the bishops refer to a passage in *Progressio populorum* where Paul VI states, "it is the design of God" that all persons "develop and fulfill" themselves, "for every life is a vocation" (PP 15). This sense of a divinely inspired vocation to achieve authentic personhood grounds the right to development. Absent the subjective awareness of one's dignity and worth, true development fails to occur, even if one's material lot improves.

Such self-consciousness is itself a good that makes the struggle for development worthwhile even if there is limited success in attaining all that a person seeks. "By taking the future into their own hands through a determined will for progress, the developing peoples—even if they do not achieve the final goal—will authentically manifest their own personalization."

Following immediately upon the above comment the bishops observe there is a role for "a certain responsible nationalism" in the pursuit of development. "Responsible nationalism" does not promote aggression but affirmation, a coming together of people to create a sense of shared history and communal culture; it forges an identity of a people. Nationalism in the episcopal vocabulary represents the collective dimension of a will to development. It is a group's awareness of the call to progress.

Responsible nationalism should promote both the objective and subjective components of development. The objective side is economic growth and prosperity that raises standards of living. The subjective component of development requires attention to how decisions about, and the benefits of, development are shared. In other words, the bishops believed in "the necessity—within the political system chosen—of a development composed both of economic growth and participation." This last word had great significance since participation was deemed "a right which is to be applied both in the economic and in the social and political field."

Economic participation means contributing to the material well-being of oneself and others and sharing in the benefits of economic prosperity. Social and political participation indicates that decision making cannot be in the hands of elites who act for the masses but the grassroots must have a say in determining the process and goals of a nation's development. Once again, the concern for the subjective component of authentic development is evident: a demand that persons take responsibility for their own identity and progress. This is impossible without the right to participate in the formulation and execution of strategies for development.[47]

The bishops were not naïve about the difficulties standing between the poor and development. In particular, they single out "social structures" that are "objective obstacles" to progress. There are "systematic barriers" that "oppose the collective advance" of the majority of people. The bishops did not believe the path to development began at a neutral starting-point. Poor peoples and nations confront "conditions of life created especially by colonial domination" that leave them "the victims of the interplay of international economic forces." These passages exhibit a social analysis similar to dependency theory when describing the situation of the poor nations.

Without referring to any particular individual or organization the bishops state their opposition to a certain approach to development: "the concept of evolution must be purified of those myths and false convictions which have up to now gone with a thought-pattern subject to a kind of deterministic and automatic notion of progress." This refers to those development theorists who believe nations follow necessary "stages of growth" and foresee seemingly natural advancement for the poorer nations as they move on to industrialization. The reference may also respond to John XXIII's optimism in *Mater et magistra* where he thought there might be a transformation in poor regions of the world in a manner akin to Europe's rebuilding with the aid of the Marshall Plan after World War II. Just ten years after John's encyclical, the bishops are less sanguine for they perceive serious obstacles that stand in the path of true development. And so what is necessary is "liberation through development."[48]

1.3 Voiceless Injustices

Because an essential part of the liberation process is the active role of the subject in his or her own development there is a particular victim of injustice who merits special attention. This subsection calls attention to "those persons and nations which because of various forms of oppression and because of the present character of our society are silent, indeed voiceless, victims of injustice." Voiceless victims, effectively marginalized by deliberate intent or historical circumstance, endure a unique disadvantage, for they cannot correct their own plight and it is unnoticed by others. This is the particular pain of the truly marginal; they cannot participate in social affairs so as to correct or even call for the correction of their situation. The ecclesiastics gathered at the synod believed that the Church's "action is to be directed above all" at this special category of victims.

The bishops comment on particular groups who compose the class of voiceless victims. First to be mentioned are migrants, those who for economic reasons leave their homeland and take up residence in a foreign country where "they are often obliged to lead an insecure life or are treated in an inhuman manner." The second group cited is refugees, those forced from their homeland because of persecution, the basis of which may be racial, ethnic, or tribal.[49] What unites both groups is that they often have little or no legal standing within their host country and so are easily discriminated against or exploited.

As might be expected, the bishops have a deep concern for those who suffer persecution for reasons of faith. The statement on religious freedom at Vatican II, *Dignitatis humanae*, made clear that the Church understands freedom regarding religious belief to be fundamental to the protection of human dignity.[50] Other categories of voiceless victims include those who suffer torture at the hands of the state, especially political prisoners and prisoners of war denied the protections of the Geneva Convention. The bishops mention in this subsection threats to human life (abortion) and dignity (manipulative communications media) as well as the broad category of those neglected by family and society: the elderly, orphans, the sick. The material, while not unimportant nor without its moral urgency, does demonstrate that the 1971 synod did not always stay focused on the particular problem of development of the poor nations as proposed by the prior synod of 1969. The broad theme of justice in the world meant, in effect, "the consideration of almost any situation of injustice which a particular bishop felt intensely about."[51]

1.4 The Need for Dialogue

This epilogue to Part 1 of the statement is indicative of a persistent tendency in Catholic social teaching. Again and again in the documents there is a commitment to bring about social change through nonconflictual means. There is a belief that people can sit down and reason out a mutually satisfactory resolution, though mediators may be necessary to assist people to overcome conflicts.

Part 2. The Gospel Message and the Mission of the Church

The material presented in the two subsections of Part 2 comprises the second major theme of JM, namely, the connection between religious faith and justice.

2.1 The Saving Justice of God through Christ

This subsection provides only a schematic outline of a theological argument. In just two sentences the authors indicate their understanding that the Old Testament reveals a God who is "the liberator of the oppressed and the defender of the poor." Behind this statement was the special emphasis that many Latin American theologians gave to the exodus event and the writings of the classical prophets. Viewed in this way, Yahweh demonstrates both a constant concern for the Hebrew people during their sufferings and a demand that the Hebrews remember how God cared for them so that they, in turn, would not neglect others who suffer. Because Yahweh's very nature is to be just it becomes necessary for those who would truly know God to practice justice. Otherwise the risk is that a false god replaces Yahweh, the faithful and just God.

In the paragraphs that address the New Testament materials the bishops understand Jesus as carrying this Old Testament theme forward. "Christ united in an indivisible way the relationship of humanity to God and the relationship of persons to other persons." The text recalls both the Lucan passage, where Jesus reads from Isaiah in announcing his ministry as bringing about God's justice on behalf of the needy, and the Last Judgment scene of Matthew, where Jesus identifies with the least of his brothers and sisters. In this brief treatment the bishops indicate that they see "the Church's social mission on behalf of justice is ultimately grounded in the nature of God as disclosed in the Hebrew Scriptures and in the actions and teaching of Jesus as recounted in the Christian Scriptures."[52]

The bishops then proceed to the claim that the history of the Church, beginning with the early church of the New Testament, affirms "faith in Christ, the Son of God and the Redeemer, and the love of neighbor constitute a fundamental theme" of discipleship. From Paul's writing to the present there is a consistent emphasis that a Christian's "relationship to his neighbor is bound up with his relationship to God" and "the love of God . . . is shown to be effective in love and service of people." The bishops conclude that "Christian love of neighbor and justice cannot be separated. For love implies an absolute demand for justice. . . . Justice attains its inner fullness only in love."

Embedded in the few sentences of the bishops is much of the structure of Catholic moral theology. Some further explanation of the Catholic perspective may be useful at this point. If the tradition is to avoid the charge of "works righteousness"—the claim that people can earn God's grace by good deeds—the relationship of morality to faith must be understood as a grateful response to what God has already done. Christians know they are loved first and, transformed by that experience, are led to respond in kind. Moral action, similar to worship, is a response to the realization of God's goodness, mercy, and love. Those who love God seek to love what God loves. So the moral life is not driven by the human effort to please God. Its motivation is gratitude and joy at being loved; it is a response of the beloved to the lover.

Love, however, cannot be seen as a sentiment without content. Love, in the Catholic moral tradition, includes the content of justice. A person cannot love others and then deny them basic rights; justice, then, is at least a minimum measure of love's content. On the other hand, a strictly measured accounting of what is due a person by right falls short of what is needed for true communion. A person must be willing to offer friendship, forgiveness, self-sacrifice, and self-giving as well as justice if a relationship is to be characterized by love. As the bishops put it, true love requires at least justice—"love implies an absolute demand for justice"; but love also requires more—"justice attains its inner fullness only in love."

Moral activity is intimately connected to the religious mission of the Church, for without the lived witness of disciples the proclamation of the gospel becomes less persuasive. In the present age, where people are crying out for liberation from suffering and oppression, the people of God cannot ignore the voices of their brothers and sisters while preaching a salvation that lies beyond history. Rather, the bishops affirm "the mission of preaching the Gospel dictates at the present time that we should dedicate ourselves to the liberation of human beings even in their present existence in this world." This is so because without a moral commitment to effective liberation "the Christian message of love and justice . . . will only with difficulty gain credibility" among the people of our age. So the religious mission of the Church is fatally undercut if the social mission does not receive proper emphasis.

2.2 The Mission of the Church, Hierarchy, and Christians

In the words of one of the key figures in the drafting of the text, as the synod progressed the bishops began to ask themselves: "Are we not in danger of asking too much of the Church in the stamping out of injustice? Is it her competence to achieve justice? . . . And who or what, in any case, is the Church? Are we not in danger of making the Church responsible for political options" made by individual members?[53]

These questions did not evoke quick and ready replies but the document provides some points that offer direction. First, the bishops affirm not only the right but the duty of the Church to proclaim justice and denounce injustice. This is because the religious message of preaching the gospel includes a call to repentance and conversion "to the love of the Father, universal brother and sisterhood and a consequent demand for justice in the world." This initial affirmation is followed by the bishops' clarification of the Church's role.

Those assembled at the synod did not maintain that the Church alone is responsible for justice in the world. There is a specific responsibility of the Christian community owing to its "mission of giving witness before the world of the need for love and justice contained in the Gospel message." But this obligation does not mean that the Church should "offer concrete solutions in the social, economic and political spheres for justice in the world." The competence of the Church does not extend that far, for there are a host of technical judgments and historically conditioned choices contained in developing specific solutions and policy recommendations. In such matters the Church cannot claim special expertise. Instead, the role of the Church is better understood as "defending and promoting the dignity and fundamental rights" of persons. The community of faith contributes to the work for justice by insisting that the basic human rights of persons and groups not be neglected and that these rights be contained in any satisfactory plan for addressing specific injustices. But the formulation of such plans is not the direct role of the Church.

The bishops point out the duty of church members to contribute to the common good of society and the importance of acting in temporal matters with care and commitment, thereby giving good witness. Finally, there is a reminder that individual Catholics cannot claim to be acting in the name of the Church in any sort of official way as they choose specific options in social life, though there is a sense in which their actions do reflect upon the Church and its witness to the wider world.

This entire section of JM had a significant impact because of the episcopacy's strong support for linking the social mission of the Church with the religious mission. Many Christians took encouragement to commit themselves further to justice and peace activities. Although the actual case was presented succinctly, the direction in which it pointed was sufficient orientation for readers to see in the document a growing support among church leaders for social ministry.

Part 3. The Practice of Justice

In the longest section of the document there are various ideas and suggestions, grouped under five headings, for how the Church might put into effect the mandate to bring about justice. This entire section comprises the third great theme of the synod statement, action on behalf of justice.

3.1 The Church's Witness

From the beginning of the process of preparation for the synod, the theme of the Church's own practice of justice was present. Already in the early drafts of the *lineamenta* the argument was made that the Church had to be just in its own life in order to witness successfully to justice in the world.[54] When the various episcopal conferences responded to that preparatory document there was strong support for "addressing justice within the Church itself."[55] The working paper, or *instrumentum laboris*, also included a paragraph on justice within the Church, as did the opening speech (*relatio*) of Archbishop Valderrama.[56] Although lacking somewhat in specifics, this section reflects the feeling of many synod members that action for justice was needed in the internal affairs of the Church.

Though critics have charged that focusing on justice within the Church was a "kind of escapism," such was not the case. A synod observer noted "the most eloquent speeches" on this topic "came from those hierarchies which had analyzed the wider social problems most carefully and were prepared to adopt radical solutions." So the motive behind this concern was not to avoid dealing with larger questions of social justice but the belief that "the Church must be just before preaching justice to others."[57]

Two concerns were addressed under this heading of the Church's witness to justice: rights within the Church and the use of temporal goods. With regard to the first of these items, rights in the Church, there was great interest in talking about respect for human rights in the life and practices of the ecclesial community. In the small working groups long lists of abuses by the Church were formulated but the document provides only a few characteristic ones. Treatment of church workers is mentioned with the accompanying issues of fair wages, opportunities for advancement, social security, and access for laypersons to positions of power over administrative and financial matters. Issues of due process were also cited as a concern, especially in marriage cases, and there was acknowledgment that the Church ought to defend a "right to suitable freedom of expression and thought," including the right of all to be heard so as to preserve "legitimate diversity" in the life of the Church. This would include establishment of forums such as pastoral councils and diocesan synods in order that there be a "spirit of dialogue" in the faith community.

Noteworthy in this treatment of rights in the Church was the discussion of the role of women. Several bishops spoke up strongly on the question of promoting the rights of women.[58] Indeed, in the synodal discussion of concern for rights within the Church the topic of women "came out on top" in the judgment of one observer.[59] Yet the final document expressed the concern in just two sentences, one calling for women to "have their own share of responsibility and participation" in Church and society and a second sentence proposing a commission to study the role of women in the Church.[60] The first sentence has a nuance that may not be obvious to all readers. What is translated in the English as women having their "own" share of responsibility is the Latin word *propria*, which means "due" or "proper." Their "own" share while not terribly inaccurate is not quite the same. More significant is that *propria* was substituted for *aequalis* (equal) before the final vote on the text. There was a fear that, read within the context of the first half of the synod's debates about ministerial priesthood, a statement that women have equal rights and responsibilities in church life might be interpreted as endorsement of the ordination of women. And so *aequalis* became *propria* in the Latin text.[61]

Use of temporal goods was the second topic treated under justice within the Church. Since their own conference in Medellín, Colombia, the Latin American bishops had concluded that a hallmark of the Church should be its solidarity with the poor. Avoiding anything that might be open to a charge of materialistic excess was an important sign of the sincerity of the Latin Americans' newly articulated preferential option for the poor.

Due to the presence of the Church in so many different societies and cultures it was a difficult task for the drafters of the document to include the variety of strategies being urged by individuals or groups of bishops from the same region. Instead the document addresses three areas, offering two general norms and two questions for reflection. The document speaks to the use of goods by the hierarchy of the Church, the situation of Christians in poor nations, and, lastly, Christians in rich countries. The first norm for the Church's leadership is that the use of material goods should never permit "that the evangelical witness which the church is required to give becomes ambiguous." While it not always easy to discern what temporal goods are necessary for the sake of effective ministry and what should be avoided for the sake of witness, a second general norm is "our faith demands of us a certain sparingness in use," for the mission of the Church is to proclaim "good news" to the poor.

When the bishops turn their attention to the situation of believers living in poor nations the question is posed "whether belonging to the Church places people on a rich island within an ambient of poverty." At times this has been the situation of foreign missionaries who come from wealthy regions of the world to poor settings and, despite an admirable zeal to minister, find that continuing or even approximating the standards of life to which they are accustomed within their homeland leaves them in a privileged position. A second problem is that entrance into and participation in the life of the Church may entail notable improvement in a person's material situation with access to church institutions and resources that other native inhabitants lack. Both of these cases were on the minds of the bishops when they posed their question.

In the matter of Christian believers in rich nations the synod delegates were mindful of the challenge that Barbara Ward asked the bishops to give to well-off disciples. And so the question posed was "whether our life style exemplifies that sparingness with regard to consumption which we preach to others as necessary" so that the less fortunate may have a greater share in basic goods. For Ward it was a failure of distributive justice that so much of the earth's resources were directed to a minority of the world's population while others lacked essentials for living. Her hope for the Church located in the rich countries was "a modesty of living" that rejected high rates of consumption.[62] This was more than asceticism; it was respect for the demands of justice.

Before the material on the Church's witness to justice within its own life, at the very outset of this subsection, is a brief and "underdeveloped"[63] paragraph about violence and conflict. While not explicitly excluding all recourse to violence the bishops indicate a clear preference for nonviolent methods of resolving social ills. The synod statement notes an important witness of Christians is that "there are sources of progress other than conflict, namely love and right." This latter term may seem an odd word to employ but it is one possible interpretation of the Latin *ius*. The interpretation given by Phil Land, who was present at the drafting committee's meetings, is that "right" in this context stood for a social order that provides "a reasonable degree of justice together with procedures of law permitting the resolution of conflicts" through means that do not require violent force to bring about change.[64]

3.2 Educating to Justice

This subsection begins with the claim that the practical contribution that the believer makes to the cause of justice in the world is "acting like the leaven of the Gospel" in the daily settings of family, school, work, and public life. Leaven is a source of change; what it mixes with is transformed. This image provides the context for understanding what the synod means by education. For the synod, education to justice cannot mean following the traditional methods of teaching. Too often societies "allow the formation only of the person desired by that order." The result is not a person capable of promoting social change but an individual who will rest content with the values and customs inherited.

The new method of education called for by the synod had several characteristics. First, education for justice was concerned with "a renewal of heart, a renewal based on the recognition of sin in its individual and social manifestations." Whereas traditional education reached only the head, imparting ideas, the goal of education to justice was conversion and therefore it must be more holistic than a one-sided intellectual approach. Second, the education discussed at the synod had as its "principal aim . . . to awaken consciences to a knowledge of the concrete situation and . . . to secure a total improvement." A third characteristic was that education for justice "is deservedly called a continuing education for it concerns every person and every age." This is an ongoing process leading people to become "decidedly more human." Fourth, education for justice was education in solidarity; it must affirm the unity of humankind and bring people to work on behalf of that affirmation. Fifth, the content of this education to justice—respect for human dignity and the principles of Catholic social teaching—provided a reflection upon how the gospel can promote human dignity throughout the social order.

During the synod debate Cardinal Flahiff caught the sense of the group in remarks summarized by a reporter at the synod: "academic knowledge was not enough to break out of [the] . . . enslavement to systems." Rather, the education being called for was akin "to the biblical notion of knowledge—experience shared with others—to substantiate the basic principle that only knowledge gained through participation is valid."[65] Such education to justice has close affinities with methods that are called "conscientization" or consciousness-raising. It is a method of learning meant to promote social change by leading people to critical reflection upon and awareness of the reality they experience and then to develop pastoral strategies that transform the reality.[66]

The final paragraph of this subsection introduces the idea that the liturgy of the Church can "greatly serve education for justice." Although more suggestive than adequately developed, this linking of liturgy and justice corrects a significant omission in the conciliar constitutions on liturgy (*Sacrosanctum concilium*) and on the Church in the modern world (GS). Neither of those documents even alluded to the connection between liturgy and justice. For the bishops at the synod one of the key ingredients in the new education for justice is the liturgy. In this matter as throughout the entire treatment of education the synod follows the path set out by Medellín.

3.3 Cooperation between Local Churches

What might be called the two minor motifs in Part 3 are collaboration between local churches (diocesan or national) and ecumenical cooperation. In both cases the treatment is brief and not particularly notable when compared to the other three areas included in this third section: justice in church life, education for justice, and international action.

In a certain sense this short subsection could be considered part of the first realm of action, the witness to others of the Church's own life. The key point is that the relationships between the various churches—local dioceses as well as national or regional churches—should demonstrate that bonds of charity and solidarity are hallmarks of the Christian community. Sharing of resources is a good in itself for the life of the Church. It presumes that the resources of any individual church are really a part of the common patrimony of the universal Church.

The expectation was that churches in wealthier areas of the world would share generously with those churches in poorer regions. In doing so, however, there should not be any conditions that restrict the legitimate "autonomy and responsibility" of the receiving churches "in the determination of criteria and the choice of concrete programs" for which the funding is used. In sum, the same warning applies to the wealthier churches as to wealthier nations when they offer economic assistance to poor counterparts. There is always the risk of paternalistic and self-serving aid programs that do not foster genuine development.

3.4 Ecumenical Cooperation

This material might appear almost as an afterthought if one were unaware of how the document was written. During the synod's discussion of the working paper, Cardinal Jan Willebrands, president of the Secretariat for Christian Unity (the Vatican's chief ecumenical officer), faulted the document as a "regression from Vatican II" for it did not make clear the need for ecumenical cooperation.[67] Other bishops noted the absence of ecumenical observers at the gathering and the clear need for joint Christian witness to justice and international development. Philip Land maintained that behind the few sentences in the final document "are numerous declarations in the general assembly. Church spokesmen from every continent repeatedly and in the name of their Episcopal Conferences endorsed ecumenical cooperation."[68] Inclusion of this theme, therefore, reflects a widely held view among the hierarchy assembled in Rome that the ecumenical dimension not be overlooked.

Furthermore, it is significant to note that while the statement calls "first and foremost" for cooperation in "securing human dignity and the individual's fundamental rights, especially the right to religious liberty," it goes beyond joint activities at the practical level. "Collaboration extends also to the study of the teaching of the Gospel insofar as it is the source of inspiration for all Christian activity." This directly responds to the urging of Willebrands: "Collaboration with separated brethren is not limited to concrete actions, but extends to the common study of evangelical principles for the promotion of justice."[69] This takes the ecumenical agenda beyond shared moral concerns to discussions of underlying theology and spirituality.

3.5 International Action

The material presented restates many of the recurring themes heard in the plenary speeches and within the small group discussions. The eight proposals all address the great issue of justice in international life. Thus, here the delegates focused upon the issue that the 1969 extraordinary synod had said urgently required further study and action, namely, the plight of the poor countries of the world.

It comes as no surprise that the synod strongly supports the United Nations and its related agencies. The Catholic Church has long been an active participant in that body and the Church's criticisms of the UN tend to be along the lines that it is not strong enough organizationally to fill the need that exists. Quite opposite the complaint one hears in the United States about the UN trying to do too much or the unfounded anxieties of those who see in the UN some sort of world government destined to eradicate national sovereignty, the Catholic Church's major regret about the UN is that it does not do enough and is hampered by the factions or blocs representing the interests of the powerful.

After words of recognition for all those efforts already occurring in the Church to assist the poor, the bishops "urge Catholics to consider well" eight propositions. Four of the first five speak to UN-related matters. The synod calls for ratification of the UN Declaration of Human Rights by all governments (number 1). There is also support for UN efforts to limit the arms trade, end the arms race, encourage disarmament, and support nonviolent forms of conflict resolution. Connected to this latter point the bishops encourage each nation to give legal recognition to a right of conscientious objection (number 2).[70] In addition, the delegates recognized "the importance of the specialized agencies of the United Nations," those dealing with matters like agriculture, health, education, housing, urbanization, and unemployment. A particular concern was voiced over the situation of food for children of poor regions (number 5).

The bishops, in this fifth proposition, allude to the problem of population growth. Undoubtedly, this was a touchy question, due to Paul VI's encyclical *Humanae vitae* in 1968 and the subsequent uproar still present within the Church in 1971. The approach taken was to quote Paul himself, not from *Humanae vitae* but from his earlier statement in *Populorum progressio*, where he acknowledged the legitimate role of governments in limiting birth rates as long as this was done by "suitable measures . . . in conformity with the moral law" (PP

37). This was said with an eye toward policies in China and other nations that coerced couples to prevent or abort pregnancies.

Proposition 3 was a direct statement of support for the aims of the Second Development Decade sponsored by the UN and the work of the UN Conference on Trade and Development. Among the specific goals of the Second Development Decade were agreements on specific percentages of the income of rich nations to be dedicated to assist poor nations, better prices for raw materials shipped from poor to rich nations, and the opening of markets in the rich nations to the cheaper goods of the poorer nations. This led to the next proposition (number 4) that went beyond the role of the UN to the entire range of economic agreements and institutions governing the international economy. Here the bishops called attention for redress of the "concentration of power" that permitted rich nations to follow a practice of "*de facto* exclusion" of poor nations "from discussions on world trade and . . . monetary arrangements."

Proposition 6 supported the development efforts of individual donor nations but suggested that multilateral approaches were preferable to unilateral ones and that either method should preserve the rightful role of the receiving nations in determining priorities for investment.

The seventh proposition gave further evidence that the Church was growing in its awareness of the environmental movement. The bishops were forthright in stating those "already rich are bound to accept a less material way of life, with less waste, in order to avoid the destruction of the heritage which they are obligated by absolute justice to share with other members of the human race."

Appropriately, the final proposition frames the document by returning to the first major theme of JM, the right to development. In order for that right to be exercised three things are necessary: people must be allowed to seek development according to their own cultural heritage; people ought to "be able to become the principal architects" of their own development; and every person must be permitted and able to contribute to the common good. Evident in these conditions is the emphasis that bishops and theologians of Latin America brought to discussions of development—it must be a process directed by the poor as active subjects of their own liberation.

3.6 Recommendations of the Synod

This word is addressed to all the members of the hierarchy, calling upon local churches and episcopal conferences to act upon the vision and recommendations of the synod, perhaps by setting up centers for research to develop pastoral plans. The synod delegates also express the wish that ongoing agencies and offices, like the Pontifical Commission Justitia et Pax and the Council of the Secretariat of the Synod, will continue to develop the ideas and goals of the delegates as expressed at the synod.

This last comment was not as uneventful as it might appear. For a long period of time the diplomatic corps of the Vatican, under the secretariat of state, was the dominant voice in passing along information regarding the state of affairs in the various nations of the world. As might be expected, this voice tended to reflect the voices of elites in these nations who moved in the circles of leadership, whether that be ecclesiastical, governmental, commercial, or cultural.

One of the developments resulting from *Populorum progressio* was the establishment of the Pontifical Commission Justitia et Pax (PP 5). That body, in turn, encouraged the creation of justice and peace commissions at the level of episcopal conferences and dioceses. What was evolving by 1971 was a new network of communication between the Vatican and local churches, only this time the information was more reflective of the grassroots interests of pastoral agents working with the poor. Support for Justitia et Pax at the synod was a boost to the development of this new network.[71] The British commentator Arthur McCormack believed that the synod "enhanced the role of the Pontifical Justice and Peace Commission" and that the discussions among the bishops "should give great impetus to the work of the over forty national justice and peace commissions in existence throughout the world and the forty others which are in progress of formation."[72]

Part 4. A Word of Hope

The concluding section of the document is a brief comment on two points: the source of Christian hope and the implications of this hope for the work of justice. It is not a fully developed reflection but, as is the case with other sections of the document, a sketch or outline of a proper treatment.

The foundation of the Christian's hope is what God has begun and continues to do in the paschal mystery of Christ: the life, death, and resurrection of the Lord. By being in the midst of the poor, sharing in the suffering and oppression of the least of the brothers and sisters, the Church lives the Passion of Christ. The work of the people of God to transform the situation of the poor is an initial stage, a foreshadowing of the glorious transformation that God is preparing for all creation. The community of faith, then, finds hope in the belief that human efforts, however weak or inadequate, to attain justice and peace will be brought to completion in the "new earth" that God has promised.

Consequently, the hope in ultimate fulfillment to be wrought by God in Christ is not a distraction from human effort but an encouragement since "the radical transformation of the world in the Paschal Mystery of the Lord gives full meaning" to human efforts. It is not that all must be done by dint of human action; it is enough that human action for justice provides the soil for the coming reign of God "to take root" in human hearts. Thus, the work of justice is not a project doomed to fail because of human inadequacy but a means whereby we "cooperate with God to bring about liberation from every sin and to build a world which will reach the fullness of creation" as God's plan is revealed in Christ who is the firstfruit of all creation.

EXCURSUS

According to Charles Murphy, "the document Justice in the World is easily the most reprinted publication issued by the Pontifical Commission for Justice and Peace, and the sentence most quoted"[73] was "Action on behalf of justice and participation in the transformation of the world fully appear to us as a constitutive dimension of the preaching of the Gospel, or, in other words, of the Church's mission for the redemption of the human race and its liberation from every oppressive situation." This sentence was a rhetorically forceful ending to an introduction that was intended to establish "the central issue that the synod bishops sought to address and clarify," which was the relationship of the ministry of justice or the social mission to the overall religious mission of the Church.[74]

The key word to understand within the sentence is *constitutive*. It is, as Murphy suggests, "a strong, arresting term."[75] The reason it is seen as the key word is because it places the social mission at the very heart of any description of the Church. As a result, the sentence became the oft-quoted "legitimation for a whole series of new initiatives in social and political life by Roman Catholics."[76]

It is curious that at the time of the synod the passage did not receive much attention.[77] Each section of the document was voted upon separately and the introduction received fewer unfavorable votes (nine) than any other section of the document. The document was written under a very tight deadline and there was not an opportunity for long and contentious debate in favor of or in opposition to any particular part of the document. The goal of the document's drafters, therefore, was to get consensus and, as Reese notes in his examination of synod procedures, generally one obtains consensus by dropping controversial passages.[78] It is reasonable to conclude, given the presence of the sentence and the lack of opposition to the passage in the delegates' voting, that the sentence was not perceived to be controversial at the time. This is supported by the fact that John Harriott, one of the better informed journalists writing an early post-synod evaluation, never even mentions the final sentence for either praise or criticism.[79] Murphy, who has studied the synod carefully on this matter, further observes that while "the term 'constitutive' to describe the relationship of the preaching of the gospel and the work of justice is a new one, certain equivalent or approximate theological expressions from other sources can be found."[80]

In trying to assess the issue at stake in the subsequent debate over the passage it is necessary to first clarify what the drafters of the document meant by what they said and, second, to determine, as much as is possible, what the delegates understood by the sentence given their overwhelming support of it.[81] One interpretation of the term *constitutive* is "that which is most fundamental and pertains to the very definition of a being, making it to be what it is."[82] Murphy suggests an equivalent expression in English would be *essential* while a word such as *indispensable* does "not seem to be adequate to communicate the force of the word."[83] That *essential* is an equivalent term finds support by the fact that at the synod the German and Dutch translations of the document used *essential*, not *constitutive*, and there was no objection raised about the preference of one for the other.

After the synod, as the debates about its work began, Ramon Torrella Cascante, the special secretary for the synod, maintained that *essential* was not the apt equivalent for *constitutive* and proposed the term *integral* as a better choice. The drafters, he said, wanted to convey that work for justice is not simply an ethical conclusion drawn from the gospel but that there is a close internal relationship. Torrella's reasoning is that *integral* is the better expression "because working for justice is more on the level of the credibility of the gospel in the circumstances of today than of its essence." His point is not to downplay the import of justice or to make it a mere option for disciples but the concern is "to avoid the danger of reducing the mission of the Church to a mere temporal project by mixing the divine initiative with the human response."[84] Use of *essential* suggests that without the temporal project's success the Church is somehow defective in its very core.[85]

Three key staff members to the synod, the Jesuits Juan Alfaro and Philip Land and the Dominican Vincent Cosmao, however, dispute the reasoning of Torrella and others who support it. Alfaro explains his position using a more biblical than Scholastic mind-set. For him God's justice as seen in the proclamation of Jesus requires the human response to the gospel. "If justice is conceived in the biblical sense of God's liberating action which demands a necessary human response . . . then justice must be defined as of the essence of the gospel itself."[86] Land maintains that *integral* weakens the meaning of *constitutive* and is not acceptable. Cosmao, the original author of the draft version of the introduction and the particular passage under scrutiny, also challenges Torrella's later gloss on *constitutive*. In sum, of those involved in the process that are on the record, three of the major drafters of the synod statement disagree with one of the others. Furthermore, while Torrella had an important official role in the synod process as special secretary it is questionable whether he actually played a role equal to Alfaro, Cosmao, and Land in the detailed formulation of the drafts and final text.[87]

At the 1974 synod on the topic of evangelization Torrella, who was appointed by Paul VI as a delegate, made important comments both prior to the synod and in two interventions. In his first set of remarks at the synod he emphasized the need to make explicit the link between justice and evangelization, avoiding any false dichotomy. During his second intervention he emphasized the significance of avoiding a simple identification of justice and evangelization. He went on to say that the synod of 1971 understood "constitutive dimension" as "integral part." Torrella acknowledged that *integral* is not as strong a term as *essential*, for *integral* refers to "something which accompanies, but need not be present, that is, strictly speaking, a true proclamation of the gospel could take place without action for justice."[88] *Integral* indicates "something that is not absolutely essential to the life of the Church but pertains rather to its fullness."[89] For that reason *integral* is the better way to understand *constitutive* rather than the word *essential*.

The other drafters, however, continue to challenge Torrella's explanation of *constitutive*. Land finds Torrella's choice of *integral* confusing. "If you say something is an integral part, it could be either a substantial part or an accidental part. No one wanted to say that justice is an accidental part of the gospel." Alfaro agrees, maintaining Torrella weakens the 1971 document by introducing an "unnecessary complication." He argues that a constitutive or integral part is not the same thing. "This was not the thinking of the drafting group. It is to introduce another term altogether."[90]

It is instructive to grasp how Cosmao, Land, and Alfaro explain their understanding of *constitutive*. For Cosmao, who chose the word originally, *constitutive* means "the preaching of the gospel 'occurs' by means of its action on behalf of justice." To proclaim the gospel, when interpreted with an eye toward the Old Testament, is to proclaim that God intervenes in history for the purpose of realizing justice. To work for justice, therefore, is "a very condition for the truth of the faith."[91] Land notes that in regard to Cosmao's choice of words, "Alfaro had different language, as I did. Same thing but different language to express the idea."[92] Murphy reports, "Alfaro believes the use of the scholastic term 'constitutive' was unfortunate. . . . It would be better to use another type of vocabulary and say that in the proclamation of the gospel we cannot forget the proclamation of justice and the duty to practice justice." According to Alfaro, that was the sense of the group working to draft the text. They "used Cosmao's term 'constitutive' not in a strict scholastic sense but in a much broader way. 'Constitutive' means, for Alfaro, that justice is an essential aspect of the gospel."[93] Alfaro, as he did in his memorandum on justice and liberation in scripture distributed during the synod, prefers to use biblical language that stresses the indivisibility of love of God and love of neighbor and an understanding of justice as required by love. When seen this way, "justice must be defined as of the essence of the gospel itself" since justice "conceived in the biblical sense of God's liberating action . . . demands a necessary human response."[94]

When one reads the document with an awareness of the background events, the following explanation appears plausible, perhaps probable. *Constitutive* is not being used in a strictly technical sense but rhetorically to signal an intimate connection between justice and the gospel. It is a connection that is far more than a simple moral implication. It is at the very core of the gospel. The biblical framework for discussing the relationship is the key to understanding the meaning of the document.[95] When Alfaro authors a booklet *Theology of Justice in the World*, published by the Pontifical Commission for Justice and Peace, he never alludes to *constitutive* to explain his position.[96] It is not the word but the mind-set the word expressed that is significant, and the intent is to suggest a more intimate connection, than in previous magisterial statements, between justice and the Church's mission. This is clear from what all the drafters have publicly stated, including Torrella.

What did the delegates, as distinct from the drafters, believe they were saying? Beside the likelihood that Alfaro's biblical theology was influential among the bishops, there is the additional evidence of the German- and Dutch-language versions of the text. In both cases *essential* was used in place of *constitutive*. It is fair to conclude, therefore, that the synod was making a powerful claim that the ministry of justice is of the very essence of the Church's mission. Finally, Cosmao suggests a third piece of evidence for the strong sense of *constitutive* as *essential* when he relies upon the reception of the document and that "Churches in the Third World have recognized themselves in this phrase of the synod."[97]

Cosmao, however, goes too far when he claims that the phrase "became a key part of the pontificate of Paul VI." For the pope evidently had some discomfort with the phrase. Although he allowed the release of the synod document to the general public, the pope "did not give it papal approval as he did the statement on the priesthood," the other document of the synod.[98] Over the years he commented favorably upon JM but never alluded to or quoted the controversial passage of the introduction. At the opening of the 1974 synod on evangelization, Paul VI stated that there was a need for a "better and more supple" explanation of the relationship between justice and evangelization. One can fairly conclude, therefore, that Paul VI had reservations about the 1971 synod's formulation. John Paul II twice quoted the sentence of the 1971 synod but in one case used the word *indispensable* and on the other occasion used *integral* instead of *constitutive*.[99]

In light of the papal reaction one can imagine that, as time passed, Torrella Cascante, and others might have had second thoughts about the phrase "a constitutive dimension." Certainly it is reasonable to revisit the work of a synod and reconsider the best way to describe the relationship of the Church's social mission to its religious mission. But those second thoughts ought not to be read back into the original document as some seem to have done. Based on the evidence available there is a good case to be made that the synod of 1971 understood *constitutive* as *essential* and viewed this as a proper expression of how justice is to be understood in the work of the Church.

Three years later, when the 1974 synod took up the question, neither the pope nor the bishops wanted to lose the basic thrust of JM—justice is not adequately understood as being an ethical obligation derived from the gospel but rather is intimately caught up in the very proclamation of God's liberating action and the human response to that good news.[100] There was a concern, however, that "even generous Christians . . . in their wish to commit the Church to the liberation effort are frequently tempted to reduce her mission to the dimensions of a simply temporal project."[101] This was the horizontalism issue, the identification of the mission of the Church with social reform and temporal progress in attaining justice. So Paul VI made clear that evangelization must always contain "a clear proclamation that, in Jesus Christ, the Son of God made man, who died and rose from the dead, salvation is offered to all people, as a gift of God's grace and mercy." This salvation is not "immanent" and "restricted to the framework of temporal existence and completely identified with temporal desires, hopes, affairs, and struggles, but a salvation which exceeds all limits" for it is "a transcendent and eschatological salvation."[102]

As the 1975 apostolic letter *Evangelii nuntiandi* teaches, however, evangelization cannot be interpreted as simply spiritual in nature, for it is inextricably linked to the manifestation of God's reign in the historical processes of political, economic, and cultural life. "Between evangelization and human development—development and liberation—there are in fact profound links." The links are of an anthropological order (the person to be evangelized "is not an abstract being but is subject to social and economic questions"); a theological order ("one cannot dissociate the plan of creation from the plan of Redemption"); and an evangelical order ("how in fact can one proclaim the new commandment without promoting in justice and in peace the true, authentic advancement of the person?").[103] The fear of horizontalism was present among some church leaders, and *Evangelii nuntiandi* spoke to that concern with its explicit claim that the Church has a religious mission that goes beyond human action for justice. At the same time, Paul VI was equally clear that he was not willing to back away from an ecclesial engagement with the world for the purpose of building a more just and peaceful order.

JM is a bridge between the preconciliar papal teachings on the Church's social mission and postconciliar ecclesiology. Whereas much of the pre–Vatican II teaching presumed the Church had a role to play in creating a more just world there was not a developed rationale for the social mission. With *Gaudium et spes* the underlying principle was explained.[104] The bishops in their 1971 statement six years later used strong and direct language to affirm the conciliar teaching on the social mission. Without the ministry of justice "the church would not be true to itself or to its vocation."[105] Although later debates swirled around the 1971 synod's formulation expressing that conviction, it remains as an abiding legacy of the synod that the social mission is now widely understood to be at the heart of ecclesial self-understanding.

REACTIONS TO THE DOCUMENT

There is a measure of difficulty in separating reactions to the document from reactions to the overall experience of the 1971 synod. The latter event underwent some harsh criticism on the matter of process as well as on the results of the first half of the synod that addressed the ministerial priesthood.[106] In Italy, most press reaction was critical. The Vatican correspondent for Milan's *Corriere della Sera* wrote that the synod concluded "with a balance sheet in the red." JM was judged to be lacking "even some of the pungency of the latest social encyclicals." In France, the correspondent for *Le Monde* believed the synod was "dull from beginning to end." And as for the work on justice, the lack of explicit and specific references to situations of injustice was deemed a "victory for Vatican diplomacy against the spirit of prophecy." In Germany, the Roman correspondent for *Frankfurter Allgemeine Zeitung* "noted faults of procedure, in particular the synod's failure to conclude its deliberations on justice in the world." As a result, he predicted not much would come of all the paperwork except "a trickling outlet in an article on justice in *L'Osservatore Romano*." The theologian René Laurentin, writing in *Le Figaro*, suggested that "the majority" of participants in the synod regarded it "as a setback" and saw the cause as the ineffectual organization of the meeting's agenda and procedures. Laurentin did distinguish between the two documents on priesthood and global justice, generally being favorable to the latter. He understood the differences between the two documents as an example that two differing theologies were at work in the synod, neither of which was consistently developed by the delegates.[107]

Even those favorably disposed to the document on justice were critical of the synod's methods: "no concern for the good name of the Church can conceal the fact that the last week of the Synod was, to speak English, a shambles. That does not mean failure, though it was touch and go. . . . It is not normal for an important text to have to be re-written twice in two days. . . . It is folly to have a commission working on amendments till 3 a.m. before rushing round to the Vatican printers."[108]

Overall, however, it is fair to say that JM received less criticism than the means used to bring it about and that it was judged a document worthy of study and discussion within the Church. One expert commentator on Catholic social teaching has written, "though relatively brief, it is one of the most important statements on social justice ever issued by Rome."[109] A number of reasons can be provided for that conclusion.

Marvin Mich has listed five contributions of JM to the tradition of Catholic social teaching: (1) the plainly expressed commitment that the work of justice is "constitutive" to the life and work of the Church; (2) the use of a social analysis that "acknowledged and named structural injustice"; (3) a dialogical style of teaching that "did not offer ready-made answers drawn from Catholic natural law tradition but issued an invitation to listen to what God is speaking today"; (4) an emphasis that justice must begin at home and the Church must itself be just; and (5) an energetic plea for "effective education for justice."[110] He believes that, taken in concert with the papal exhortation *Octogesima adveniens*, the synod statement was "a catalyst for the local churches" to develop a significant social ministry.[111]

The British writer John Harriott has made several of the same points as Mich but cites additional reasons why the document is "in many important respects . . . an advance even on *Populorum Progressio* or *Octogesima Adveniens*."[112] He points out that "the liberation" of the human person "in Christ and in society is no longer regarded purely as *metanoia*, an inner spiritual conversion." Now other conditions, including material ones, are also included. Second, the document defends the right to development so that "concern for the poorer nations is not a work of charity but of justice." A third contribution is that "for the first time the role of the priest and of the Church in political life have been openly discussed." This should encourage local churches to make political judgments on their own. In line with this idea is a fourth item of note: bishops have been awakened to their larger role beyond the diocese; they see "that they themselves are responsible not only for the Church but for the good of the whole human family." A fifth advance is that nationalism, which had been seen only negatively, "is now acknowledged to be in certain circumstances a necessity for development" as long as it is "responsible." Finally, Harriott believes that the synod debates have conclusively demonstrated the value of outside experts offering bishops insight and advice on matters where specialized knowledge is necessary. In several of his remarks it should be noted that Harriott has gone beyond what can accurately be claimed for the actual text of the document and has included the broader experience of the synod.

Though not an impartial commentator, Philip Land, who played a large role in the writing of the document, has assessed what he considers its contributions to Catholic social teaching. First, he believes that the Church does not set itself apart from the rest of humankind in the quest for justice but realizes that it, too, must be subject to scrutiny as to the justice of its inner life and practices. Second is the method of reading the signs of the times, which led the synod participants to see injustice not simply in human hearts but in the institutions and structures of nations and the international order. A third benefit of the document is that the statement about work for justice being constitutive to preaching the gospel "should remove any lingering doubt" that "justice is not only a moral exigency but an essential activation of the faith." Finally, two other items of note, according to Land, are the emphasis upon education as formation, not merely imparting information, and the document's awareness of the validity of political struggle and the reality of conflict in working for justice.[113]

From the distance of several decades, theologian Ronald Hamel finds the document important for questions raised even if not satisfactorily answered. "What, for example, is the relation between liberation and salvation? Who are the primary agents of change, and what are acceptable methods of bringing it about? . . . Is the use of violent force and revolution ever justified?"[114]

Finally, Arthur McCormack, a scholar of development and population issues, cites what to my mind is the most important consequence of the synod document. He observed that JM, passed by overwhelming support of the synod, put the Church clearly and publicly on the side of those working with the poor and marginalized for an end to oppression and achievement of social justice. "The Synod has put the theme of justice, and especially social justice and concern for this world, into the very centre of the church's life." He further noted that those bishops already working closely with the poor came away "heartened to realize they were not alone." More significant than any scholarly response to the document was the upsurge in interest in matters of global justice that occurred within ecclesial circles. Numerous religious institutes, lay communities, and diocesan efforts were instigated that made international justice a priority for a substantial number of Catholics in the United States. McCormack is correct, I believe, to see the lasting consequence of JM to be the subsequent rise of personal commitment by church members to matters of global justice.

NOTES

1. John F. X. Harriott, "Justice in the World," *Month* 3, second series (October 1971): 104.

2. Barbara Ward, "Structures for World Justice," *The Tablet* 225 (October 30, 1971): 1061.

3. Kinhide Mushakoji, "A Crisis of Growth in World and Church," *The Tablet* 225 (November 6, 1971): 1084.

4. Cardinal Maurice Roy, "How the Church Can Act," *The Tablet* 225 (November 6, 1971): 1085.

5. Francis X. Murphy, "The Roman Synod of Bishops 1971," *American Ecclesiastical Review* 165 (October 1971): 74.

6. The formal institution of the synod took place the next day in *Apostolica sollicitudo*, issued *motu proprio*. The establishment of the synod, therefore, was an act of the pope and not an official act of the Council that eventually followed his lead and incorporated Paul's ideas in the document *Christus Dominus*, the conciliar decree on the pastoral office of bishops. See *Decree on the Bishops' Pastoral Office in the Church* (*Christus Dominus*), in *The Documents of Vatican II*, ed. Walter M. Abbott (Piscataway, N.J.: New Century, 1966), 396–429.

7. Mathew Kiliroor, "The 1971 Synod of Bishops on 'Justice in the World'" (S.T.D. diss., Katholieke Universiteit Leuven, 1988), 46. Kiliroor notes that the selection of the topics of a synod, although done by bishops assigned to the ongoing

advisory council of the synod, must be approved by the pope. It is the pope who sets the agenda of the synod and decides about the circulation of preparatory materials. The pope also presides over the synod, in person or through his delegate. All officers of the synod are appointed by the pope and act in his name.

8. The canon law governing the nature, role, and structure of the synod is found in canons 342–48. A helpful commentary is John G. Johnson, "The Synod of Bishops," in *New Commentary on the Code of Canon Law*, ed. John Beal, James Coriden, and Thomas Green (New York: Paulist, 2000), 454–63.

9. The synod of 1971 was the third general synod and the second ordinary one. It followed the ordinary general synod of 1967 called to complete remaining details of Vatican II and the extraordinary general synod of 1969 convoked to discuss collegiality.

10. John F. X. Harriott, "The Difficulty of Justice," *Month* 5 (January 1972): 9.

11. See Donal Dorr, *Option for the Poor*, rev. ed. (Maryknoll, N.Y.: Orbis, 1992), 228; Marvin Mich, *Catholic Social Teaching and Movements* (Mystic, Conn.: Twenty-Third, 1998), 191.

12. For many people, at least those outside the synod, the discussion on priesthood was actually about the narrower issue of celibacy and whether the Roman Church would permit a change in the discipline of priestly celibacy. A number of observers noted that after the discouraging tone of the first half of the synod several bishops entered into the sessions on justice in a pessimistic mood while others were pleased simply to be able to address a new topic. See Philip Land, "Oral History of Phil Land," transcribed and edited by Judy Mladineo, unpublished and on file at the Center of Concern, Washington, D.C., 58; Andrew Greeley, "After the Synod," *America* 125 (November 20, 1971): 424–26.

13. Peter Hebblethwaite, "The Future of the Synod," *Month* 5 (January 1972): 3.

14. See Harriott, "Justice in the World," 104.

15. The three presidents of the 1971 synod were Cardinals Duval (France), Munoz Vega (Ecuador), and Wright (United States).

16. Harriott, "The Difficulty of Justice," 11.

17. "The Church in the World," *The Tablet* 225 (October 2, 1971): 961.

18. For the recounting of the synod's process, I have relied upon Thomas Reese, *Inside the Vatican* (Cambridge, Mass.: Harvard University Press, 1996), 42–65, and Kiliroor, "The 1971 Synod," 53–108.

19. Land, "Oral History," 40.

20. Ronald Hamel, "Justice in the World," in *The New Dictionary of Catholic Social Thought*, ed. Judith Dwyer (Collegeville, Minn.: Liturgical, 1994), 496.

21. Land, "Oral History," 41.

22. On October 20 Barbara Ward spoke on structures of injustice and remedies; on October 21 Candido Mendes de Almeida addressed development and the problems of the marginalized; and on October 22 Kinhide Mushakoji analyzed the need for new structures that permitted participation as well as the need to develop nonviolent strategies for social change. The full texts of these three speeches have never been published although they are contained in the archives of Justitia et Pax. Excerpts from B. Ward and K. Mushakoji appeared in *The Tablet* 225 (October 30, 1971): 1061–62; (November 6, 1971) 1084–85.

23. Also influential was a consultant who did not speak before the assembly. Juan Alfaro, professor of systematic theology at the Gregorian University in Rome, had prepared an eight-page memo "'*Iustitia Dei*,' '*Iustitia et Liberatio hominis*' *in Sacra Scriptura*" that was widely circulated among synod members. This reflection on divine justice and human justice and liberation provided the delegates with a biblical basis for understanding justice as integral to the Christian life.

24. Although they could not vote, all the lay experts participated in the small group discussions and bishops often utilized their insights in a group's report.

25. There were twenty-four members of the drafting group: Munoz Vega, representing the three presidents, Rubin as general secretary, Torrella as special secretary, Valderrama as synod *relator*, the twelve *relators* from the small groups, and various assistants associated with Justitia et Pax. See Kiliroor, "The 1971 Synod," 102.

26. Though several episcopal members of the drafting group were intimately involved in the process the key persons, working in either French or English, responsible for sections of the text were: Vincent Cosmao (introduction and conclusion), Barbara Ward and Candido Mendes de Almeida (Justice and World Society), Juan Alfaro (The Gospel Message and the Mission of the Church), Jean Canivez, Philip Land, and Barbara Ward (The

Practice of Justice). Bishop Torrella was the overseer of the entire process. For background on this final part of the process, see Kiliroor, "The 1971 Synod," 102–5; also Charles Murphy, "Action for Justice as Constitutive of the Preaching of the Gospel: What Did the 1971 Synod Mean?" in *Readings in Moral Theology*, vol. 5: *Official Catholic Social Teaching*, ed. Charles Curran and Richard McCormick (New York: Paulist, 1986), 152–53; and Land, "Oral History," 41–42. Note the comment of Donal Dorr: "The actual text owed very much to a few key people working in or with the Pontifical Commission for Justice and Peace. This Commission had been established by Paul VI in 1967, and by 1971 it was at the height of its power. It had become the focus in Rome for fresh approaches and deep commitment on social justice questions." *Option for the Poor*, 229.

27. Final votation on the document, done by section, demonstrated the wide approval. Of 199 possible votes the lowest affirmative vote was 161 for the section on the practice of justice with the highest approval being 176 for the conclusion. In sum, no section of the statement received less than 80 percent approval from the bishops.

28. The broad outline of the method was familiar to many students of Catholic social teaching. In the 1930s a Belgian priest, Joseph Cardijn, developed a three-step method of "observe, judge, act" that he popularized in his work with many small groups of lay Catholics. This three-step approach encouraged observation of what was happening in a given situation, formulating a preliminary judgment or evaluation of the situation in light of one's faith, and, finally, devising a plan of action to improve the situation. This last point was critical since Cardijn's aim was not to form discussion groups but to develop groups of laity committed to acting in the world on the basis of their faith. His "observe, judge, act" method was the approach of a large number of lay groups placed under the umbrella-title of Catholic Action.

29. Dorr, *Option for the Poor*, 229.

30. Philip Land, *An Overview* (Vatican City: Pontifical Commission for Justice and Peace, 1972), 12.

31. Ibid.

32. Barbara Ward (Lady Jackson), an English economist, spoke on "Planetary Justice"; a political scientist, Candido Mendez de Almeida of Brazil, addressed the topic "Development and Structural Marginalization"; and Kinhide Mushakoji, a Japanese expert on disarmament, provided a paper on "The Universal Aspiration to Participation."

33. Land, *Overview*, 13.

34. Ibid., 10.

35. One of the significant differences among the Latin Americans was the approach to reform. John F. X. Harriott, a journalist covering the synod, noted a split between those who wanted to continue to work with societal elites to bring about change and those who wanted to break decisively with the past and put the Church on the side of grassroots or popular groups. On the side of "top-down" reform were the bishops of Colombia, Venezuela, and Argentina while the bishops of Chile and most of the Brazilians favored a different approach that bypassed the political, economic, and military aristocracies in favor of organizing those who were marginal and oppressed. "Difficulty of Justice," 12. See also Mich, *Catholic Social Teaching and Movements*, 192, and Land, *Overview*, 69.

36. See the Commentary on GS by David Hollenbach in this volume.

37. Land, *Overview*, 42.

38. See the Commentary on MM by Marvin Mich in this volume.

39. See the Commentary on PP by Allan Figueroa Deck in this volume.

40. Later treatments by theologians, and even the papal magisterium, of the way sin infects society will go further in describing how sin becomes embodied in the very structures of a society and culture. A clear and succinct treatment of the evolution of the idea of social sin can be found in Mark O'Keefe, *What Are They Saying about Social Sin?* (New York: Paulist, 1990). More detailed analyses of how the theme of social sin has developed and can be understood can be found in Adam DeVille, "The Development of the Doctrine of 'Structural Sin' and a 'Culture of Death' in the Thought of John Paul II," *Église et Théologie* 30 (1999): 307–25; Joseph McKenna, "The Possibility of Social Sin," *Irish Theological Quarterly* 60 (1994): 125–40; Mark O'Keefe, "Social Sin and Fundamental Option," *Irish Theological Quarterly* 58 (1992): 85–94.

41. C. Murphy, "Action for Justice," in *Readings*, ed. C. Curran and R. McCormick, 153.

42. The "Excursus" will review how the ongoing concern over horizontalism was continued at the

1974 synod on evangelization and explain Paul VI's position in the debate.

43. R. Hamel, "Justice in the World," in *New Dictionary of Catholic Social Thought*, ed. J. A. Dwyer, 496.

44. See Land, *Overview*, 39–41.

45. Dorr, *Option*, 231.

46. See the commentary on PT by Drew Christiansen in this volume. John Paul II also provided a listing of human rights in paragraph 13 of his speech on October 2, 1979, before the United Nations General Assembly. See *Origins* 9 (October 11, 1979): 262.

47. The synod participants were well aware that Paul VI had a few months earlier cited movements for equality and for participation to be "two forms of human dignity and freedom" (OA 22). See the Commentary on OA by Christine E. Gudorf, in this volume.

48. The word *liberation* first used by the Latin American bishops at their Medellín meeting is used in a positive sense at the synod. Some in the hierarchy, however, felt that the word was too closely associated with a form of Marxist social analysis that ought not be endorsed. The expression *liberation through development* reflects a compromise between the Latin American bishops and others. Dorr suggests that "In Latin America the word 'development' was irretrievably associated with a model of economic growth that widened the gap between rich and poor . . . in other parts of 'the South'—especially in the newly independent countries of Africa—'development' was still a positive word." See *Option*, 230. The synod statement's wording is an effort to account for both perspectives.

49. Refugees are understood to be a special class of involuntary migrants who have been forced to flee because of extreme danger or serious threat of danger due to political or other conditions.

50. See the Commentary on DH by Leslie Griffin in this volume.

51. Arthur McCormack, "The Synod and World Justice," *The Tablet* 225 (November 20, 1971): 1115.

52. R. Hamel, "Justice in the World," in *New Dictionary*, ed. J. A. Dwyer, 497.

53. Land, *Overview*, 20.

54. Philip Land of Justitia et Pax was a key figure in writing materials at the early stages of the preparatory process. Land recounts a meeting of the bishops who made up the Council of the General Secretariat of the Synod of Bishops to which he was asked to present a draft of what would become the *lineamenta*. The draft included a paragraph that eventually wound up in the final synod statement, with the phrase: "anyone who ventures to speak to people about justice must first be just in their eyes." As a result, it was noted that the Church must engage in self-examination about its practice of justice. At that meeting an Italian curial official, Cardinal Pericle Felici, stated: "The Church does not have any injustices." There was silence. "Nobody speaks. Nobody speaks!" Land recalled, and then "with the little bit of courage I had," he replied: "Your Eminence, I really believe if we cannot say that the Church has injustices, we should not have a document." A discussion ensued and in a vote the paragraph in question was supported by everyone on the Council except Felici. See Land, "Oral History," 40.

55. Hamel, "Justice in the World," in *New Dictionary*, 496.

56. No surprise that the *relatio* kept the theme of justice in the Church since it was written by Land, and "it was delivered as I wrote it." Land, "Oral History," 41.

57. Harriott, "Difficulty of Justice," 14.

58. Cardinal Bernard Flahiff of Winnipeg and Archbishop Leo Byrne of Minneapolis/St. Paul gave floor speeches on this topic that led to substantive discussion within the small groups. See Land, *Overview*, 27.

59. Harriott, "Difficulty of Justice," 15.

60. This latter was a suggestion made by Cardinal Flahiff and it was to be a commission that included appropriate representation of women, both lay and vowed religious.

61. The Latin in the original amendment called for "*aequalem cum viris partem*" for women. This was changed to "*propriam partem responsabilitatis et participationis*." See M. Kiliroor, "The 1971 Synod," 95 and no. 295.

62. Ward, "Structures for World Justice," 1062.

63. Hamel, "Justice in the World," in *New Dictionary*, 499.

64. Land, *Overview*, 24.

65. As reported in Harriott, "Difficulty of Justice," 13.

66. For more extensive commentary on this subsection, see Mary Linscott, *Education and Justice* (Vatican City: Pontifical Commission for Justice and Peace, 1972).

67. As reported in Harriott, "Difficulty of Justice," 11.

68. Land, *Overview*, 57.

69. As quoted in Harriott, "Difficulty of Justice," 11.

70. On this question Bishop Gran of Oslo, Norway, had urged, on behalf of the Scandinavian Episcopal Conference, in his plenary speech that conscientious objection be seen as a moral obligation in some instances and that the teaching of *Gaudium et spes* in this area be remembered in discussions of violence. See Peter Hebblethwaite and John F. X. Harriott, "Synodal Diary—2," *Month* 5 (January 1972): 21.

71. It is not clear, however, that subsequent developments have continued to favor such networks. From the Vatican side, the influence of the secretariat of state has led to some diminishment of the role of Justitia et Pax. From the side of the local churches, a new generation of bishops with different pastoral priorities, budget constraints, governmental pressures, and in some cases outright repression from local political and military agents has led to a decline in the work of justice and peace offices.

72. McCormack, "The Synod and World Justice," 1115.

73. Murphy, "Action for Justice," 159.

74. Hamel, "Justice in the World," in *New Dictionary*, 496.

75. Murphy, "Action for Justice," 151.

76. Ibid.

77. Donal Dorr writes that the passage "was not considered unusually new or daring when it was presented in draft form to the Synod." Although "soon after the Synod the passage became very controversial—and most of the debate focused on the word 'constitutive.'" Dorr, *Option*, 238.

78. Reese, *Inside the Vatican*, 58.

79. Harriott, "Difficulty of Justice."

80. Murphy, "Action for Justice," 160. He cites DH and the *instrumentum laboris* for the 1974 synod as examples of these "other sources."

81. Murphy's essay along with the transcript of Land's oral history were very valuable for understanding the viewpoints of major figures involved in the drafting of the statement.

82. Murphy, "Action for Justice," 160.

83. Ibid., 161.

84. As quoted in ibid.

85. "Those who rejected the word 'constitutive' argued that this word should be used only of something that can never be absent without the Church failing to be itself; whereas, they claimed, the Church, without ceasing to be Church, may at times find itself so restricted by political authorities that it is totally prevented from undertaking 'action on behalf of justice.'" Dorr, *Option*, 239.

86. Murphy, "Action for Justice," 163.

87. This last comment is based on reading Land's "Oral History."

88. Torrella as quoted by Murphy, "Action for Justice," 156.

89. Dorr, *Option*, 239.

90. Land and Alfaro as quoted in Murphy, "Action for Justice," 156.

91. This is Murphy's summation of Cosmao based on correspondence between the two. See ibid., 153.

92. Land, "Oral History," 41.

93. Murphy, "Action for Justice," 157.

94. Ibid., 162.

95. Another indication that language was not being used with the precision of Scholastic philosophy is Land's observation years later that the document consistently speaks of "justice" without any modifier like *social* or *distributive*, or other common distinctions in Catholic moral reasoning. He believes the explanation for the unmodified use of justice is that the synod teaching reflects "the biblical inspiration of the discussion rather than the academic concern for definition." Philip Land, *Catholic Social Teaching* (Chicago: University of Chicago Press, 1994), 101–2.

96. Juan Alfaro, *Theology and Justice in the World* (Vatican City: Pontifical Commission for Justice and Peace, 1973).

97. As quoted in Murphy, "Action for Justice," 159.

98. Reese, *Inside the Vatican*, 58.

99. Murphy, "Action for Justice," 164–65, no. 8.

100. What is not addressed in this commentary is another strand of the debate that was occasioned by the 1971 synod. Some of the critics of JM were people who wished to downgrade the importance of a synod's role. During the synod itself there was confusion among delegates as to just what their role was. Some seemed to believe that the synod was a sort of mini-council with juridical and doctrinal authority. Others, especially members of the Vatican curia, wanted to reaffirm that the synod had a consultative role—its function was simply to advise the pope, who was free to heed or ignore the advice offered. Challenging the use of the word *constitutive*

was a way of questioning the authority of the synod and its teaching role. The point was to demonstrate that a pope could put aside the formula of a synod in favor of another means of expression if he so chose. As with many other aspects of church life in the late 1960s and early 1970s, the question of authority was a backdrop. For some it was the question behind the question of how to describe the social mission of the church. See Dorr, *Option for the Poor*, 239–40.

101. Paul VI, *Evangelii nuntiandi* (Vatican City: Vatican Polyglot, 1975), number 32.

102. Ibid., 27.

103. Ibid., 31.

104. See David Hollenbach's Commentary on GS in this volume.

105. Hamel, "Justice in the World," in *New Dictionary*, 496.

106. Not untypical in the American press was the comment of Andrew Greeley: "The Church looks ridiculous to nonbelievers as its leaders offer pontifical advice to virtually every other human institution about the need for justice and freedom, but show precious little interest in reforming their own institution." He also maintained "the Synod was a more humiliating experience for the Church than anything since '*Humanae Vitae*.'" See "After the Synod," 424.

107. The survey of press reaction in the above paragraph is based on a report in "The Church in the World," *The Tablet* 225 (November 20, 1971): 1129–30.

108. Peter Hebblethwaite, "Synod Chronicle: 5," *The Tablet* 225 (November 13, 1971): 1104.

109. Dorr, *Option*, 240.

110. Mich, *Catholic Social Teaching and Movements*, 192–94.

111. Ibid., 195.

112. All quotations in the paragraph are taken from Harriott, "Difficulty of Justice," 17–18.

113. Land, *Overview*, 58–60.

114. Hamel, "Justice in the World," in *New Dictionary*, 500.

SELECTED BIBLIOGRAPHY

Alfaro, Juan. *Theology of Justice in the World*. Vatican City: Pontifical Commission for Justice and Peace, 1973. This booklet by a key advisor at the synod provides a fine summary of the theological vision behind the document.

Dorr, Donal. *Option for the Poor*. Rev. ed. Maryknoll, N.Y.: Orbis, 1992. An excellent survey of Catholic social teaching, this volume provides a brief analysis of the synod statement.

Hamel, Ronald. "Justice in the World." In *The New Dictionary of Catholic Social Thought*. Edited by Judith A. Dwyer. Collegeville, Minn.: Liturgical, 1994. A clearly written treatment of the synod statement that provides a concise, well-done exposition and analysis.

Harriott, John F. X. "Justice in the World." *Month* 3 (October 1971): 104–9.

——. "The Difficulty of Justice." *Month* 5 (January 1972): 9–18. Two short articles by a British journalist who was an on-the-scene observer of the synod.

Kiliroor, Mathew. "The 1971 Synod of Bishops on 'Justice in the World.'" S.T.D. diss., Katholieke Universiteit Leuven, 1988. An excellent scholarly treatment of the synod that also provides a detailed analysis of the theme of justice in Catholic social teaching.

Land, Philip. *Justice in the World: An Overview*. Vatican City: Pontifical Commission for Justice and Peace, 1972. A booklet that offers a synopsis of the synod document with commentary by one of the key staff persons at the synod.

Linscott, Mary. *Education and Justice*. Vatican City: Pontifical Commission for Justice and Peace, 1972. Another booklet in the series published by Justitia et Pax following the synod, it explains the theory of education for justice that was influential among liberation thinkers.

Mich, Marvin. *Catholic Social Teaching and Movements*. Mystic, Conn.: Twenty-Third, 1998. A readable yet serious examination of Catholic social teaching and its impact on social action that contains a fine chapter on the synod document.

Murphy, Charles. "Action for Justice as Constitutive of the Preaching of the Gospel: What Did the 1971 Synod Mean?" In *Readings in Moral Theology*, vol. 5. Edited by Charles E. Curran and Richard A. McCormick. New York: Paulist, 1986. A balanced and well-researched essay on how to interpret the meaning of *constitutive* and understand the ensuing controversy after the synod.

CHAPTER 15

Commentary on *Familiaris consortio* (*Apostolic Exhortation on the Family*)

LISA SOWLE CAHILL

INTRODUCTION

Familiaris consortio (1981) was composed by John Paul II after the conclusion of a universal synod of bishops that met in Rome in 1980 to discuss marriage and family issues. This document attempts to address modern social challenges to family life, such as the increase in divorce, changing roles of women, the acceptance by many Catholics of artificial contraception, the pluralism of models of marriage and family in different cultures, and economic pressures on families, especially those in the developing world. The pope defends traditional Catholic teaching that upholds heterosexual, indissoluble procreative marriage as the norm, and rejects artificial birth control, reaffirming the teaching of his predecessor Paul VI (*Humanae vitae*, 1968). John Paul II sees men and women as having different psychological characteristics and hence complementary social and familial roles, but he nonetheless defends the equality of women in family and society. He envisions the family as a "domestic church," having a fundamental role in the spiritual formation of family members and fulfilling a mission to serve the common good, especially society's poor and vulnerable members.

OUTLINE OF THE DOCUMENT

There are four main parts to the papal letter. In the introduction and part one of the text there is a description of the context of the family today. Looking at the cultural dimension of the context there are both good and bad factors to note. Positive aspects include greater attention to the dignity of women, to the quality of interpersonal relationship in marriage, and to responsible procreation and education of children. Negative aspects include lack of spousal interdependence, problems between parents and children, divorce, purely civil marriages, abortion, sterilization, and a "truly contraceptive mentality." Huge disparities between rich and poor countries and families are unjust.

The second part of the letter develops a theology of the family. The human vocation to love is fulfilled through marriage or celibacy. "Total self-giving," both physical and personal, defines the former relationship. Christian marriage and family are communions of persons that reflect God's love and build up the Church. The family is a "domestic church" and a "school of deeper humanity." (This concept of domestic church will be a major contribution of this document.) Although human sexuality is a "great value," it can be renounced "for the sake of the kingdom of God." The celibate person witnesses to the kingdom of heaven as the ultimate value, and becomes "spiritually [rather than physically] fruitful." Therefore, the Church "has always defended the superiority of this charism to that of marriage."

The third part of the letter treats five specific family issues. First is gender, and the pope declares that women and men have "equal dignity and responsibility." Women should have access to public roles, but their most valuable role is motherhood; fathers also have an important family role. Violence and discrimination against women are repudiated. Following these comments the focus moves to children and the elderly who ought to receive special protection as they are among the most vulnerable members of family and society. The third topic of this part of the letter is the procreation and education of children; the teaching on artificial contraception in the 1968 papal encyclical *Humanae vitae* is defended as correct. Also noted is that parents have rights and duties with regard to the religious and moral education of their children and deserve the aid of the Church and the state in meeting their parental responsibilities.

The final two topics that are treated in this part of the letter are the family and society and the family as domestic church. The family is the first cell of society, and should look outward by dedicating itself to social service as "hospitality." The rights of the family are defended against society and state, including the international order. The family communicates Christ's love, not just to family members, but to society. Parents and children communicate the gospel to each other, a mission rooted in the sacrament of marriage and in the Eucharist. The Christian family also serves the world.

Pastoral Care of the Family is the title of part four of the letter. Preparation for marriage, support for marriages and families, and care for those in mixed marriages and canonically "irregular situations" are the subtopics treated. Regarding marriage preparation, pastoral ministers are encouraged to take it seriously, but without creating an impediment to the celebration of marriage. It should be seen as an opportunity to evangelize couples.

Priests, bishops, the parish, other married couples, and associations of families all contribute to the pastoral care of families. Mention is made of families in especially difficult circumstances, such as single-parent families, families with members in prison, geographically separated families, families suffering discrimination, and families suffering from addiction or illness.

In the case of mixed marriages, the emphasis is on strengthening the faith of the Catholic partner while living with respect and harmony, and, in cases where both parties are Christian, enjoying the grace of the sacrament of marriage. Divorced Catholics who have not remarried need intensive support from the community, as do those with no natural family. Those who have remarried or are living in other situations outside sacramental marriage are offered a measure of pastoral understanding while exhorted to convert to the Church's ideals.

In the conclusion of the letter there is no reiteration of any condemnations, but the pope speaks of "joy and conviction" in relation to the inner resources and mission of the Christian family. The Holy Family, which suffered many difficulties, is offered as a model.

CONTEXT OF THE DOCUMENT

The decades leading up to and following Vatican II were tumultuous ones for families and for society in general. In the 1960s and 1970s, Western postindustrial societies were undergoing a gender as well as a sexual revolution that brought women (at least white middle-class women) out of the domestic confines of the nuclear family and introduced them into broader social roles.[1] In the process, the link between women's sexuality and reproduction was loosened. One result was greater social and sexual equality for women. But negative consequences included increased expectation of women's sexual availability, less social protection of women's childrearing roles and indirectly of children, and more general uncertainty about how to redefine the family in ways to incorporate sexual and gender equality with consistent care for children.

While many feminists celebrated the coming end to patriarchal exploitation of women's free domestic labor in the family,[2] others noted that women of color had a long history outside the home, defined themselves in terms of an extended family as well as the nuclear unit, and were still far from enjoying the social freedom from exploitation that many white women optimistically anticipated.[3] The liberal model centered on individual rights of family members was also problematic.[4] Still other commentators noted changes in family forms and male and female roles with alarm, lamenting the "breakdown" of the family, danger to children, loss of women's special status, and threatened alienation of men from family responsibilities.[5]

Gaudium et spes (*Pastoral Constitution on the Church in the Modern World*), *Humanae vitae* (the 1968 "birth control encyclical" of Paul VI), and the writings of John Paul II all affirm in principle the equality of spouses in marriage, see sexual intercourse as a form of "mutual self-gift," and give up ranking the ends of marriage. Whereas in the past procreation was seen as the primary end and love a secondary one, the ends of procreation and love of spouses are treated as equal from the 1960s on. At the same time, papal writings continue to defend certain specific conclusions about sexual and marital ethics that were originally developed on the assumptions that women should be subordinate to men, and that the primary purpose of sex, marriage, and family is to bear and nurture children. These norms include prohibitions of contraception and divorce, as well as of sexual intercourse and childbearing outside of marriage, norms that protect the status of permanent monogamous heterosexual marriage as a central organizing structure of society.

One of the most important developments since the Council had been an explosion of international attention to the population problem and the consequent widespread recognition that demographics are tied to economic development. Debate ensued about whether, at what level, and under what conditions birth control should be used to address the plight of women, couples, and families living in poverty. During this time, a lay-led movement in favor of natural family planning (NFP) was making strides in advocacy for the effectiveness and attractiveness to couples of periodic continence as a means of controlling family size.[6]

Before a consideration of the immediate synod and process that resulted in FC, some key texts in *Gaudium et spes* and *Humanae vitae*, as well as in some earlier writings of John Paul II, will be examined. These set the stage for the language and issues of the later document. Linking the welfare of society with that of the family, *Gaudium et spes* calls the family a "community of love" and rejects as distorting "disfigurements" practices like polygamy, divorce, "free love," and "illicit" birth control as well as "modern economic conditions" and the pressures of overpopulation.[7] The focus of the discussion about how to protect marriage and family is on the "sanctity" of the "marriage covenant of mutual love" by which a man and a woman "render mutual help and service to each other through an intimate union of their persons and of their actions." Marital love is also called "a mutual gift" and "mutual self-bestowal."[8] Without going into concrete details (to be addressed by *Humanae vitae*), this conciliar document specifies that "responsible transmission of life" has to follow objective norms based on "the nature of the human person," church authority, and "divine law."[9] The Christian family "springs from" the marriage covenant, and manifests Christ's presence and the nature of the Church "by the mutual love of the spouses, by their generous fruitfulness [procreation], their solidarity and faithfulness, and by the loving way in which all members of the family work together."[10] *Gaudium et spes* is traditional in that it regards the (nuclear) family as "the foundation of society," and urges public authorities to protect and support it, so that it can fulfill its proper function of educating children. The cooperation of both parents is necessary for this task, but younger children "need the care of their mother at home. This domestic role of hers must be preserved, though the legitimate social progress of women should not be underrated on that account."[11]

Humanae vitae was written primarily to address the controverted question of birth control and is best known for its reassertion of the traditional prohibition of all "artificial" forms. For present purposes, it is also of interest for its presentation of the relation of sex, love, and procreation in marriage, and for its endorsement of "responsible parenthood" in view of personal, marital, and family welfare. Paul VI speaks simply of the "two meanings of the conjugal act," the unitive and the procreative, without ranking them. Only by expressing these meanings can sexual intercourse preserve "true mutual love," an affirmation the author believes to be "deeply human and reasonable," that is, not based on church authority alone.[12] Presenting the "natural" structure of the sex act as a minimal criterion of respect for the procreative meaning, Paul VI goes on to outlaw "artificial" birth control, but to advocate the "natural" means of confining sex to infertile periods[13] as a possible expression of "responsible parenthood" in view of the duties of spouses toward themselves, their families, and society.[14]

Although Paul VI had counseled pastoral understanding in the application of *Humanae vitae*, it prompted a debate, even crisis, over magisterial credibility on marriage and family issues that was still quite alive ten years later when John Paul II was elected pope.[15] Although FC was authored near the beginning of his papacy, it had already been preceded by a series of Wednesday audience talks at the Vatican in which the new pontiff developed his "theology of the body."[16] In a personalist interpretation of natural law, John Paul II links the interpersonal meaning of sex with embodiment by saying that the body itself has a "nuptial meaning" realized in the "self-gift" of intercourse between two committed partners.[17] He reaffirms the idea of *Humanae vitae* that a true gift of self through sex requires not only a permanent monogamous commitment but also openness to procreation expressed as noninterference in the biological structure of the sex act. Whatever the merits of this argument against birth control, it furthers the tendency of Catholic teaching since mid-century to give greater recognition to gender equality and to the foundational character of love for marriage and family. It also provides the basis for limits on sex outside marriage and on divorce. By closely connecting embodiment with love and commitment, it represents an attempt to retain a definition of family as founded in some important way on biological kinship and marriage, even though family and marriage are increasingly understood as interpersonal love relationships.[18]

Considered overall, the documents produced from the time of the Council up until 1980 reflect a shift toward gender equality and a prioritization of love in marriage and family while still maintaining traditional teachings about individual behavior related to the unity of family. The key underlying concern is that sexual behavior not lead to irresponsible procreation. This primarily excludes childbearing outside the established social institutions (marriage and family) whose main traditional purpose had been to systematize the generational and kin relationships that undergird other social institutions such as child care and education, the transmission of property, and (until modern times) material production, government, and religion. Teachings that keep procreation in the proper setting include the monogamy and indissolubility of marriage, and parental responsibility for children ("responsible parenthood") within marriage. Although traditional institutional forms of marriage and family have reflected patriarchy and furthered ecclesial control over the laity,[19] modern changes and their implications for family life should not be underestimated. Even before John Paul II arrived on the scene, official teaching on matters relating to the family had already been notably influenced by changing cultural experiences.

PROCESS OF FORMULATION AND AUTHORSHIP

Some of the resulting stress points noted above were behind the convocation of the 1980 synod of bishops to study the theme "On the Role of the Family."[20] This topic was chosen as a result of worldwide consultation with bishops, who suggested marriage and family more frequently than any themes as the subject of the fifth general synod.[21] One pressing issue was to hold together change and continuity, incorporating both lay expertise and respect for church authority. The former had raised the possibility that the center of the standard norms about sex and marriage could no longer hold. Add to this cause for controversy the expansion of the Council's "modern world" into an ever more obviously pluralistic cultural environment, and it is easy to see why the synod of bishops that met to debate family teaching was decidedly fractious. The decision to choose "family" as the synod theme made it possible to avoid confronting sexual ethics directly, as well as recognizing that sex and marriage have social ramifications that cannot be completely captured by talking about them in interpersonal terms. However, it also becomes the occasion of lively debate about the supposed "universality" of the magisterium's prior conclusions on family-related topics.

Many bishops from North America and Europe arrived at the synod wanting to address the crisis around "nonreception" of *Humanae vitae* in their countries and the need for new pastoral approaches. But bishops from the developing and underdeveloped countries communicated a great aversion to an "antilife" mentality that attempted to foist population control on poorer peoples, often through government propaganda and sanctions, especially in Asia. Asian bishops usually ministered to families in a religious minority who might want to rely on church support to resist birth control programs. Bishops from Asia and Latin America in particular were concerned about structural poverty and the despair that results from survival in conditions of misery and inhumanity.[22] African bishops endorsed their cultures' traditional valuing of vitality and fertility, presented marriage as a communal rather than interpersonal affair, and raised polygamous marriage as an issue of inculturation.[23] Poised to resist any calls for contraception, the Catholic Church now had to bring its theology and ethics of the family in line with its growing commitment to a "preferential option for the poor," and to address a range of economic and social issues relating to family life, including divorce and remarriage, mixed marriages, the inculturation of marriage customs and rites, the connection of sacramental marriage to faith, the situation of couples living together without marriage, and the need for sex education and marriage preparation.

Since the end of the Council, four general synods of bishops had already been convened on the themes of church authority, priesthood and world justice, evangelization and catechesis. The fifth general synod on the theme of family life, like its predecessors, proceeded through a number of steps intended to encourage participation toward eventual consensus among the world's bishops. About one and a half years before the synod met, a proposal in a standard format known as the *lineamenta* was sent by the Vatican's General Secretariat for the Synod to the world's bishops for study and response. On the basis of their reactions, another type of document, the *instrumentum laboris*, would be drawn up to serve as the basis of discussion at the synod itself. Meanwhile, bishops' conferences worldwide were organizing consultations of various types on the synod theme in order to discern the needs and outlooks of the local churches.[24] These produced position papers from many bishops' conferences around the world, including nations in Africa, Asia, Latin America, and North America. The first week of the month-long synod was devoted to interventions from individual bishops. At the synod there was a preponderance of European representation because of the numbers of Vatican officials and representatives of religious orders present. The majority of representatives from bishops' conferences, however, were from the third world. About thirty lay *auditores* (listeners) were also included, among whom spokespersons of the Natural Family Planning movement were disproportionately represented. Following the general interventions, there was a division into language groups.[25]

The most difficult part of the synod was reportedly the drawing up of a set of forty-three "Propositions" and a final "Message" of the synod to the Christian families of the world. At each stage of the synod, the content had to become narrower and more focused, with predictable tensions between "upward" movements from the delegates and "downward" ones from Vatican authorities who consolidated information and viewpoints. For example, when it was suggested to the bishops that they might submit to the pope a list of restricted propositions rather than an unlimited collection of their much more disparate interventions, most appeared to feel they could hardly refuse. Similarly, the final message was entrusted to a small committee that had to negotiate between one faction that wanted to adhere to doctrinal precedent and another that desired a more pastoral approach. The problem was resolved, not too satisfactorily, by noting pastoral concerns in the first and last paragraphs, and devoting the body of the message to doctrine, though at a very general level. Hence the propositions might be said, over the final message, to be more representative, however imperfectly, of the deliberations and concerns of the bishops present.[26]

Among the suggestions contained in the propositions are that the Church undertake further study with regard to the following points: whether the validity of the sacrament of marriage requires faith; pastoral care for the divorced and remarried, including the possibility of a rite of second marriage similar to that of the Eastern churches; promotion of the equality and rights of women within the Church; inculturation of marriage rites; a "fuller, more organic and more synthetic explanation" of marriage and human sexuality; study and promotion of scientifically sound methods of regulating fertility; the phenomenon of "experimental marriages."[27] The pope, however, prepared his own conclusions, taking into account at his own discretion the specific concerns represented by the bishops present at the synod.

A "Closing Homily" was delivered by John Paul II in which, like the *lineamenta*, he invoked the "eternal plan of God" in settling marriage and family controversies. He addressed four specific problem areas: divorce and remarriage, the "law of gradualism" as a pastoral tool in interpreting *Humanae vitae* flexibly, inculturation, and the roles of women. John Paul II reiterated that divorced and civilly remarried persons must lead celibate lives if they wish to approach the sacraments; that spouses must adhere exactly to the teaching against birth control, even endeavoring to persuade recalcitrant partners of its obligatory nature; and that culturally specific marriage customs must remain in communion with the universal Church. He furthermore voiced the view that a mother should devote herself fully to her family (not to any outside profession) if the family is to live "rightly," but did not take up the questions of social exploitation of women and the roles of women in the Church.[28] FC, a relatively long document, followed a little over a year after the conclusion of the synod, a year in which John Paul II had survived an attempt on his life and produced another encyclical, *Laborem exercens* (*On Human Work*). FC reflects convictions expressed in the closing homily, but it also indicates that further reflection, nuancing, and balancing of concerns had occurred.

ESSAY

In the decades preceding FC, Catholic leaders voiced concern about the erosion of Catholic family norms under the pressures of modern societies. Some of the concerns of John Paul II, as well as the positive view of the family as an important locus of Christian formation and as an agent of Christian social engagement, can be appreciated against the backdrop of earlier teaching. Responding to early-twentieth-century feminist movements and a trend toward greater acceptance of divorce and birth control, Pius XI's encyclical *Casti connubii* (1930) sought to reinstate a traditional hierarchical view of indissoluble marriage oriented primarily toward the birth and education of children, even while accepting that marriage is an intimate personal union.[29] Pius XI granted that love is "the chief reason and purpose of matrimony."[30] Yet he still thought "honourable and trusting obedience" of the woman to the man[31] was a precondition of marital fidelity, and ranked procreation and mutual help as primary and secondary ends, both of marriage and of sexual acts.[32] He worried that if a woman refuses to see motherhood as her primary calling or "descends from her truly regal throne to which she has been raised within the walls of her home," "the good of the family and the right ordering and stability and unity of home life" would be lost.[33]

Some continental theologians, influenced by phenomenological philosophy, debated whether this approach, in particular the subordination of love to procreation as the meaning of sex and marriage and the foundation of the family, was still credible in light of the experience of married couples. Foremost among these was Herbert Doms, who interpreted marriage as the "two-in-oneship" or community of life of the couple. In this relationship, sexual acts express love and lead to procreation.[34] Doms recommended that the language of primary and secondary ends be abandoned. He fell under the cloud of a 1944 decree of the Holy Office that condemned "certain modern writers" who "either deny that the primary end of marriage is the generation and education of children, or teach that the secondary ends are not essentially subordinate to the primary end, but are equally principal and independent."[35] The significance of this debate for the family is that interpersonal relations of love are gaining in significance as the basis of family relations and family-centered spirituality, beginning with marriage.

Two decades later, Vatican II abandoned the language of primary and secondary ends, and treated "conjugal love" and "the transmission of life" as though they were equal, requiring not ranking but "harmonization."[36] This innovation came in on the wave of John XXIII's openness to "the modern world" and his call and that of the Council for increased inclusion of the laity in discernment of Catholic life and teaching. The personal experience of married couples, and by extension family members, became a new source for the theology and social ethics of family life. As *Gaudium et spes* noted, even women "claim for themselves an equity before the law and in fact."[37] Changing and more equal roles of women made it newly possibly for sexual intercourse to be viewed, even by ecclesiastical spokesmen, as fundamentally an expression of marital mutuality and love. This changed perspective on the meaning of sex established a different framework for the analysis of sexual ethics, marriage, and ultimately family, than that which had obtained less than a generation earlier in *Casti connubii*. Families would be measured not only by their effectiveness in raising children to be productive members of church and society, but by the quality of their internal relations of love.

The content of FC can be considered in four categories, corresponding roughly but not exactly to the structure of the document (topics resurface at various points). These categories are: theological-ethical foundations, domestic church, gender, and sexual and marital ethics. These topics will here be treated primarily in view of their importance for a social perspective on the family.

Theological-Ethical Foundations

FC brings social realities of family life into contact with two specifically Christian and Catholic sources, and one source that is central to Catholic social ethics but also connects the Catholic view of the family with public and interreligious discourse. These sources are inherited Catholic teaching, scripture, and natural law. The relevance and interdependence of these sources are indicated in the final sentence of the introduction. Here the pope states that "the family is the object of numerous forces that seek to destroy it or in some way to deform it," making the Church urgently aware of its "mission of proclaiming to all people the plan of God for marriage and the family, ensuring their full vitality and human and Christian development, and thus contributing to the renewal of society and of the people of God" (3). Evident from this phrasing is the pope's intention to reveal a "plan of God" on the basis of distinctively Christian sources, but also to interpret these in such a way that they can speak to the "human" realities of family life and contribute to the renewal of society as well as of the Church.

The role of past official teaching in defining the parameters of FC and establishing the direction and degree of change has been discussed above. Theological authorities like John Chrysostom, Tertullian, Augustine, Ambrose, and Aquinas are occasionally cited, but most citations of tradition refer to ecclesial documents since Vatican II, most extensively those produced by the Council or authored by John Paul II himself. (*Casti connubii* does not appear.) The importance of authoritative teaching for assessing the family today is indicated in the conclusion of the document, which asserts that "the church knows the path by which the family can reach the heart of the deepest truth about itself. The church has learned this path at the school of Christ and the school of history interpreted in the light of the Spirit" (86). Clearly, in the pope's mind the Church has a privileged position in interpreting both scripture and the reality of the family itself; the "school of history" that yields doctrinal formulations of belief has also refined the Church's perspective on the true meaning of family life. The challenge the document faces is to reconcile past teaching, current Catholic theology, and scripture, and to bring all these to bear in a social ethics of the family that makes sense and is persuasive in the larger social and multicultural context John Paul II aims to address.

Scripture, especially the New Testament and the example and teaching of Christ, as well as the biblical creation accounts, are cited liberally throughout FC. There is no extended exegesis of any particular text. In fact, direct quotations are infrequent. Paraphrases and allusions provide a point of departure for the pope's own theology. The first sentence of Part 2, "The Plan of God for Marriage and the Family," is illustrative. "God created man in his own image and likeness; calling him to existence through love, he called him at the same time for love" (11; a footnote references Gen. 1: 26–27). The conclusion of the document exhorts Christians to follow Christ, bearing the cross and expressing generosity toward others, and holds up Mary, Joseph, and Jesus as examples (86).

The two most important theological uses of scripture in FC are the grounding of the unity of spouses in creation and the development of a sacramental theology of marriage from the idea, derived from Ephesians 5:32–33, that Christ is the bridegroom of the Church. The created union of man and woman is seen to be the ground of indissoluble marriage, the only place where total physical (i.e., sexual) and personal (i.e., through sex) self-giving is possible. The reference to creation gives the idea of the permanence of marriage a comprehensive basis, in human nature as such, not just in Christian faith. It also helps establish on the same basis the ideas that artificial birth control and sex outside marriage are unacceptable because they are a distortion of the true meaning of love and are dangerous to the institution of the family and societies everywhere. Marriage is of its very nature "a covenant of conjugal love" in which "man and woman accept the intimate community of life and love willed by God himself" (11). For the baptized, the covenant "is elevated and assumed into the spousal charity of Christ, sustained and enriched by his redeeming power" (13). Hence, "the Church has solemnly taught and continues to teach that the marriage of the baptized is one of the seven sacraments of the New Covenant" (13). This, of course, is a conclusion derived from Catholic tradition, not one necessarily demanded either by a strictly human understanding of marriage nor by the analogy of Ephesians 5:32–33 itself in which husbands are simply told to love their wives as Christ loved the Church. While one purpose of viewing marriage as a sacrament is to bring it under the control of church authority and canon law, which set high standards for the marriage relationship,[38] another effect is to present marriage and ultimately family life as special spheres of God's presence in ordinary life.[39] Love, shared accomplishments and suffering, forgiveness, and healing in family relationships can all communicate the redeeming presence of Christ, especially when marriage is a freely chosen and personal covenant.

FC perhaps uses arguments from human nature and the natural moral law most effectively in delineating the social role of families and the interdependence of families and other social institutions. As will be discussed below, "far from being closed in on itself, the family is by nature and vocation open to other families and to society" (42). Certain social contributions are to be expected from families, and families in turn have certain rights and deserve certain supports from the societies in which they live and at the international level.

Family as Domestic Church

The characterization of the Christian family as a domestic church is certainly the most innovative and distinctive contribution of FC to Catholic social teaching. John Paul II did not invent this metaphor, but he uses it here to envision all families as having an important evangelical role, to make the social justice mission of the family central to its identity, and to ground that mission in a family spirituality. Particularly important and characteristic of Catholic social tradition is the emphasis on the contribution to and participation in the common good, here seen from the perspective of families.

The domestic church metaphor finds its immediate predecessor in the Council's *Lumen gentium* (*Dogmatic Constitution on the Church*), which, however, envisions its meaning primarily in terms of the transmission of Catholic belief. "The family is, so to speak, the domestic Church. In it parents should, by their word and example, be the first preachers of the faith to their children" (11).[40] Earlier usages of this and similar metaphors, such as "small church," "church in miniature," or "church of the home," go back to patristic thinkers, including John Chrysostom and Augustine, and find Protestant parallels, especially in Puritan writings.[41] As summarized by Michael Fahey, the use of the domestic church image helps counterbalance an emphasis on the nature of marriage as contract present in canon law since Trent, and helps "reappropriate the notion that the Christian couple and their children participate in an ongoing sacramental reality through which they are sanctified and invited to participate actively in the outward mission of the church, especially through service and hospitality."[42] The promulgation of this vision of the family was able to capitalize on the Christian Family movement, which had emerged as a social and religious support network for Catholic families, often with large numbers of children who helped one another in times of stress, cultivated an interdependent relation with clergy, and reached out to neighbors and community members in need. Some vivid examples are given by economist Charles Wilber and his wife Mary Ellen, who illustrate economic proposals with stories about taking in friends whose house had burned down, and providing for the seven children of neighbors who were suddenly taken off to jail.[43]

The conception of families as domestic churches also fits well with the social tradition's principle of subsidiarity by which smaller, more local communities operate in a sphere correlated with but relatively independent from "higher" authorities and larger, more inclusive collectivities (37).[44] This is true of the family in its relation to both the Church and the state. First of all, parents "through the witness of their lives are the first heralds of the Gospel for their children." Parents provide a basis for religious education by praying with their children, reading scripture, and participating with them in the sacraments and the life of the Church (39, 57–62).[45] Second, parents have a responsibility for moral education and education for citizenship that coordinates with but is not replaced by educational institutions outside the home. The pope seems particularly concerned about sex education as the responsibility and right of parents (36–37). He also mentions "ideologies opposed to the faith" that may be taught in some cultures and should be resisted by parents, with the support of pastors (40). Opportunity for schooling, including the right to choose education in conformity with religious faith (40), should be supported for families by both Church and state.

In order for the family to fulfill its ecclesial and social obligations, certain conditions are necessary. The pope realizes that these conditions are sorely lacking in many societies and reiterates several rights of the family affirmed by the synod bishops. These include the right to marry, the right to have children and to educate them as one sees fit and in consistency with one's own religious beliefs and cultural values, the right to political and economic security, the right to housing, the right to protection from drugs and pornography, the right to emigrate for a better life, and the right of the elderly to a worthy life and death.

Although the family is rooted in natural bonds of kinship and marriage, it is the Christian family specifically that "constitutes a specific revelation and realization of ecclesial communion" so that it can even be termed a "domestic church" (21, citing *Lumen gentium*, number 11) or a "church in miniature" (49, also citing *Lumen gentium*, number 11). The family imitates Christ's self-giving love for the human race, communicating Christ's love to others, so that the family itself becomes "a saving community" (49). The love between husband and wife and among family members participates in "the prophetic, priestly, and kingly mission" of Christ and his Church. These missions undergird the nature of the Christian family as a gospel community, a community in relation to God, and a community in service of others (50, 63). These missions are rooted in baptism, though strengthened by the grace of the sacrament of marriage (52). By making baptism foundational for Christian family sacramentality, the theology of FC makes it possible to envision unmarried adults as sharing in the mission of domestic church along with spouses. Just as all persons, married or not, are born into families, so all Christians are baptized into the family of the Church, whether or not they receive the sacrament of marriage. FC recognizes that family has an extended intergenerational meaning and validity that precedes and goes beyond the married couple and the nuclear family.

Importantly, the pope does not see the family as merely reflecting higher-order values, charisms, or functions that are realized more perfectly by the Church as a whole. From the other side, the love of spouses and of all family members, including their ability to survive hurtful interactions and find reconciliation, should "be extended to the wider circle of the ecclesial community of which the Christian family is a part. Thanks to love within the family, the Church can and ought to take on a more homelike or family dimension, developing a more human and fraternal style of relationships" (64).[46]

An essential note is sounded in connecting the family to Catholic social tradition. The family is given the role of being "a school of deeper humanity" where there is "mutual service every day" and "a sharing of goods and sorrows" (21), a role that eventually is to extend beyond family boundaries in service to a more humane society. This indeed is the characteristic emphasis in John Paul II's vision of the family. Christian families "recognize with faith all human beings as children of the same heavenly Father" (41). The family is "the most effective means for humanizing and personalizing society"; it is "the first and irreplaceable school of social life, an example and stimulus for the broader community of relationships marked by respect, justice, dialogue and love" (43).

The family thus has a social and political role that goes far beyond procreation and the education of its own children. A theme of the document is the practice of hospitality in imitation of Christ (44). However, not stopping at charity, the pope encourages families to work for structural reforms. He quotes the synod's closing message in saying that the Christian family "'is not closed in on itself, but remains open to the community, moved by a sense of justice and concern for others, as well as by a consciousness of its responsibility toward the whole of society'" (64). The family's commitment to the hungry, poor, old, sick, disabled, drug addicted, ex-prisoners, and those without families, especially abandoned children and orphans (41), leads it to social engagement and "active and responsible involvement in the authentically human growth of society and its institutions" extending to the international level (47–48).

Gender Roles

It has already been noted that official Catholic teaching since the 1960s, following on theological trends emerging since at least the 1930s, has come increasingly to regard women and men as equal partners in a spousal relationship constituted primarily by mutual love. At the same time, it has defended a procreative norm for marital sexuality that eliminates what for many couples are the most effective and least stressful means of birth control. The recommended method is Natural Family Planning (NFP), a system of periodic abstinence from sexual relations, based on the detection of fertile and infertile periods in the woman's menstrual cycle. This is done by methods such as recording body temperature and testing cervical mucus. The reliability of these methods has been improved over the past few decades, but for many couples NFP techniques provide very imperfect indicators of the likelihood of pregnancy. Due to biological conditions, natural methods are more reliable for some couples than for others. Moreover, NFP requires that couples refrain from sexual intercourse for several days each cycle. Some but by no means all couples find that cooperatively practicing NFP enhances the love and mutuality of the marriage relationship. As a result of the absoluteness with which the prohibition against artificial contraception is proposed, if not always observed, the quality of the marital relationship can suffer. The ability of the woman to assume roles beyond maternity and domesticity may be compromised if she has little control over the prospect of pregnancy.

A related issue is the understanding of gender equality that is employed to underwrite a mutual love relation in marriage and the sharing of responsibilities by men and women in marriage, family, church, and society. FC and other papal writings have repeatedly affirmed that men and women have distinct personalities that are equal but complementary. A subsequent section here treats critical reactions to this framework in more depth. The present exposition of FC focuses on development, nuances, and possible implications of the pope's thought as presented in this document.

Traditionally, all members of society have been regarded by Catholic social teaching as having reciprocal rights and responsibilities, and as entitled to participate in the common good. However, the ways in which this is true for women and men differ, as is so evident in an encyclical like *Casti connubii*. The primary functions of women are to be wives and mothers; men assume public political and economic roles outside the home; and the socioeconomic status of women is dependent on that of their male family members, especially their husbands.

In his closing homily for the Synod on the Family, John Paul II had begun to change this picture somewhat. Propositions submitted by the bishops had affirmed the equality of the sexes, based on Genesis 1:27 and on the actions of Christ, had identified types of exploitation of and discrimination against women, had upheld women's dignity and equality both inside and outside the home, and had affirmed an interchangeability of roles between husband and wife. The bishops also affirmed the feminine characteristics of women and their different cultural expressions, and had called for greater appreciation and enhancement of these qualities.[47] Many bishops are accustomed to cultural situations in which women, even in their maternal and domestic roles, enjoy much less status than that ascribed to women in liberal democracies, and even in so-called democratic states the reality of women's situation does not always match idealistic rhetoric or even the law. Moreover, domestic violence and the sexual exploitation of women are even more rampant in some cultures than in others and tend to be exacerbated by economic stress. In his homily John Paul II repeats the point of the bishops that women not be forced to work outside the home. He seems to link closely a woman's dignity as "daughter of God" with her vocation "as a wife and as a mother." He certainly expects that in most cases women will remain in the home for the good of the family.[48]

FC expands and develops this framework, according greater independence to women and flexibility to women's roles, devoting more attention to the roles of men in the family, and more explicitly repudiating injustices to women. This is a trajectory that was to be followed in the pope's subsequent writings about women. FC devotes four sections to these topics. The pope begins by recalling that a family is "a communion and community of persons," then goes on to "underline the equal dignity and responsibility of women with men." Some biblical support for this point is offered: the creation of women and men with "inalienable rights and responsibilities"; the role of Mary as Mother of God; the actions of Jesus in calling women as followers and friends, and appearing on Easter "to a woman before the other disciples"; "the mission entrusted to women to carry the good news of the resurrection to the apostles"; and the words of Paul (Gal. 3:28) that "'there is neither male nor female; for you are all one in Christ Jesus.'" Although John Paul II maintains a relatively traditional model of men's and women's roles within the traditional family, he is also influenced by the changing roles of women in modern societies, and is concerned about fair treatment of women in family and society.

Proceeding to the implications for women and society, the pope observes that historically "a widespread social and cultural tradition has considered women's role to be exclusively that of wife and mother, without adequate access to public functions, which have generally been reserved for men" (23). To the contrary, he concludes that the equality of the sexes "fully justifies women's access to public functions." The pope seems to want it both ways, however, when he continues, "On the other hand, the true advancement of women requires that clear recognition be given to the value of their maternal and family role, by comparison with all other public roles and all other professions." Work in the home is also a vocation to be included under a "theology of work," one equal in value to any other. The pope cautions that women must not renounce their true femininity to imitate the male role. Yet he also, and rather surprisingly, calls on the Church itself to promote the equal vocations and rights of women "in her own life," "as far as possible" (23).

Within the family, fatherhood is an important role for men, though not necessarily their most important. Cultural biases may discourage men from being as invested in their families and less involved in the education of children than their mother, but the absence of fathers harms family relationships and should be reversed. Yet a father should not be an "oppressive" power, indulging the phenomenon of "machismo," or a wrong superiority of male prerogatives that humiliates women (25). The fatherhood of God is held up for male imitation though the possible patriarchal and authoritarian ramifications of male emulation of divine authority are moderated if not removed by references to the friendship between spouses and their sharing of tasks in the family (25).

Overall, FC presents a much more egalitarian picture of gender roles than previous official sources, reflecting cultural trends toward more symmetrical families and more women's employment outside the home, for vocational as well as economic reasons.[49] There is no question that the pope assumes an "equal but different" model of the sexes. Nonetheless, he moves much further than any previous pontiff in drawing men into domestic responsibilities and in affirming women's right to roles outside the home as well as fair treatment in that capacity. Taking his lead from the synod bishops, he also names prevalent and intolerable forms of violence against women that deprive women of even basic humanity and rights. A substantial number of offenses are traced by the pope to the attitude that a woman is a "thing" or a mere "object of trade." Some items named are pornography, prostitution, and discrimination against childless wives, widows, separated or divorced women, and unmarried mothers (24).

Sexual and Marital Ethics

Sexual behavior in and around the limits of marriage is at least as prominent a topic in FC as the social responsibilities implied by the identification of the family as a domestic church or by the assertion that women have rights that are often ignored. Sexual ethics is connected to social ethics in this document through the idea that immoral or irresponsible sexual behavior undermines the family, and with it, the stability and orderliness of society. The two major topic areas of sexual morality are birth control and the normativity of marriage as the sole appropriate context of sexual and procreative activity.

The dependence of FC on *Humanae vitae* has been treated above. The later document essentially repeats the teaching of that encyclical, citing it explicitly in the body of the text (29, 32). Like Paul VI, John Paul II makes the argument that

> the innate language that expresses the total reciprocal self-giving of husband and wife if overlaid, through contraception, by an objectively contradictory language, namely, that of not giving oneself totally to the other. This leads not only to a positive refusal to be open to life, but also to a falsification of the inner truth of conjugal love, which is called upon to give itself in personal totality. (32)

In contrast, the rhythm method represents total self-giving. The pope asserts that married couples will corroborate this view, for "the couple comes to experience how conjugal communion is enriched with those values of tenderness and affection which constitute the inner soul of human sexuality in its physical dimension also" (32). Not everyone will be convinced,[50] but the pope offers the Church's pastoral support to "couples in difficulty" over this teaching while accepting no compromise in regard to compliance (33, 35). Couples are reminded that the mission of the Christian life involves the cross before the resurrection (34). The pope also develops the social ramifications of an "anti-life" mentality, which are said to include exaggeration of the dangers of population growth and coercive public programs of contraception, sterilization, and abortion (30).

The sexual ethics of FC suffers from a tension between a focus on individual behavior as a way to resolve concerns about marriage and family as essentially social institutions and the more fully social approach suggested by the "domestic church" metaphor for the family. For instance, although the document as a whole discusses many ways in which parents are responsible for children and to larger communities, the only moral absolutes about "responsible parenthood" have to do with not using artificial birth control. Another example is the use of the indissolubility of sacramental marriage as the linchpin of a response to the diverse effects that changing cultural expectations and experiences of sexual relationships, commitment, and parenthood are having on the institution of the family. And although confirmation in the experience of married couples is invited, the point of departure for the positions of FC on sexual ethics is not experience but the teaching of *Humanae vitae*.

Although the mission of the family is rooted in baptism, it seems to be the sacrament of marriage that provides the most specific guidance for the family responsibilities of married couples and decides the ideal in light of which various family forms can be judged (38, 56). Many of these are covered in the document's concluding part, on pastoral care of the family. The sacrament is conferred on the couple by the Holy Spirit at the celebration of the marriage ceremony (19). The liturgical celebration gives a social and communal expression to the ecclesial nature of the covenant made in marriage between two baptized persons. This celebration should be based on the free consent of the couple, without impediments, and in observation of the prescribed canonical form for the marriage rite (67). The marrying couple receives "the gift of a new communion of love" even if they are not fully aware of it at the time (19, 68). Baptized persons seeking a church marriage by that very fact are said to "consent to what the Church intends to do when she celebrates marriage" (68). From that time forward, there exists an indissoluble unity of one man and one woman (20).

Preparation for the celebration of marriage is therefore very important. Marriage preparation is a gradual and lengthy process that begins in childhood, continues in the formation of young people, and culminates in the weeks and months immediately preceding the wedding. Episcopal conferences are encouraged to establish specific programs of marriage preparation in cooperation with married couples and families. Although couples should universally be required to participate in marriage preparation programs, neither omission of such preparation nor a questionable level of faith (as exhibited, for instance, by infrequent participation in the sacraments) should be an impediment to the celebration of marriage. The process of preparing for marriage as well as the celebration of marriage in the Church can be the occasion of evangelization of those being married (66, 68). Couples living in mixed marriages have special needs. Care must be taken that the faith of the Catholic party is supported and not endangered, but such marriages and their celebration can also be occasions of ecumenical cooperation, for instance, through an interfaith wedding ceremony. Catholics in merely civil unions are not to be admitted to the sacraments, however (82).

Of much greater concern are unions that do not meet the criterion of marriage at all. Cohabitation before marriage or "trial marriages," more or less permanent unions in the absence of any civil or religious institutional bond, and remarriages after divorce are all unacceptable (80–84). The section on divorced and remarried persons differentiates among various situations, acknowledging a difference between those who have tried to save their marriages, those who have been abandoned, and those who are at fault for the destruction of a marriage. The fact that some persons are certain in conscience that their first marriage was never valid is also conceded, as is the fact that some remarry to provide a better home for their children. All these are encouraged to regard themselves as members of the Church, to attend Mass, and to bring up their children in the Catholic faith. However, countering pastoral and theological movements advocating that the sacraments be available to such persons, the pope reaffirms that they must not be admitted to eucharistic communion. Not only would this create confusion about whether the Catholic Church accepts divorce, it would fail to respect "the fact that their state and condition of life objectively contradict that union of love between Christ and the Church which is signified and effected by the Eucharist." Their only alternatives are to separate or to live together in complete abstinence from sexual relations (84). Whether indissolubility comes irreversibly into existence at the point of the marriage ceremony; whether the marriage of baptized persons is always a sacrament, no matter what their level of faith; and whether heterosexual monogamous marriage is the sole form of sexual commitment that can be the foundation of a family have been huge topics of debate in the decades since the publication of FC. Some of this controversy will be taken up below.

EXCURSUS

Several topics deserve further comment and will be treated under three headings: the equality of women; marriage and family structures; social, cultural, and economic factors.

The Equality of Women

Many feminist theologians have objected to a complementarity model of gender because it seems to limit women's social contributions to motherhood and domesticity within the home while discouraging men from meeting similar responsibilities and finding fulfillment in parent-child intimacy. Of even greater concern, it holds up an ideal of self-sacrificial love for women that can result in inequity and injustice in family and social relationships.[51] Christine Gudorf objects to the modern papacy's ultimately confining romanticization of motherhood and insists on an equal partnership of men and women in reproducing and nurturing human life. Without this equality, she believes, male church leaders, through the sacramental system, will continue to compete with women for power over roles such as birthing, feeding, reconciling, and healing, and women will continue to be excluded from more public and political sources of power.[52] Christine Hinze has criticized the sexual division of labor that devalues women's work in the home, excludes women from other kinds of work, and makes women dependent on male wage earners for their support. While the social encyclicals' ideal of a "family living wage" seems to benefit women and children within the family unit, it concedes too much to a market economic model and fails to register the many contributions adults make to the common good through a variety of activities outside the current structure of wage labor.[53]

A full assessment of feminist critiques related to the content and aftermath of FC is far beyond the scope of the present discussion.[54] It is important, however, to note at least briefly how the pope's own thinking has developed on these issues, moving beyond FC but also retaining many of its ambiguities and stress points. Two writings are particularly significant in this regard. These are his 1988 apostolic letter *Mulieris dignitatem* and his 1995 "Letter to Women" in preparation for the UN Fourth World Conference on Women in Beijing.[55] The first of these is on one level a sustained argument for a complementarity schema of male and female identity in which women's dignity hinges on a unique vocation quintessentially realized in Mary the Mother of God. Women have a special "genius" deriving from the nature of femininity, which consists in a vocation to love. "*Woman can only find herself by giving love to others*." "The moral and spiritual strength of a woman is joined to her awareness that *God entrusts the human being to her in a special way*"[56] and this entrusting is what determines her femininity and her role.

On the one hand, the pope might be interpreted as respecting and prizing in women a sensitivity to human vulnerability that he has experienced to be a part of the personalities of many women he has known. On the other hand, he explains what might de facto be qualities of many women as what he terms an "ontological" and hence necessary condition of being female. He does not address the possibility that women's "nurturing" characteristics might reflect adaptation to social expectations, nor does he respond to the critique of many feminists that the service role expected of women results in disproportionate sacrifice for others by women as compared to men. This not only plays into asymmetrical compromise of women's welfare, but also seems to exclude equal participation by men in the ideal of self-sacrificial love embodied for all Christians not by Mary but by Christ. Although the pope has never explicitly endorsed the submission of women to men, the "headship" or authority of men over women in the family or society, or any other explicitly hierarchical arrangement of adults in the family, a feminist concern is that elevation of certain "feminine" qualities as invariant attributes of women can have the same practical effect.

The 1995 "Letter" repeats the complementarity model of "ontological" differences between men and women, and again applauds the "genius" of women as consisting in "affective, cultural, and spiritual motherhood."[57] Nevertheless, three points move this writing further along the path of women's equality than earlier treatments of the topic by the pope. First, for apparently the first time in magisterial teaching, women's work outside the home is praised as a vital cultural contribution, not just tolerated as an unfortunate economic necessity. Along with special expressions of gratitude to wives, mothers, daughters, sisters, and women religious, the pope exclaims, "Thank you, women who work! You are present and active in every area of life—social, economic, cultural, artistic and political."[58] Second, he goes on to praise "the great process of women's liberation," noting difficulty in its accomplishment and the courage of women who persisted in defending their own rights. The pope even apologizes personally for the "objective blame" for oppression of women that rightly falls on "not just a few members of the Church"—"for this I am truly sorry."[59] Careful readers will not miss the fact that the pope spares the "objectively guilty" parties from any imputation of intentional wrongdoing and refrains from calling them "representatives" of the Church, far less from holding the institution as such to account. Nonetheless, his endorsement of the right of women to seek equality by resisting practices that church leaders may have helped put into place should not be minimized.

Finally, the pope in no uncertain terms upholds equal rights of women ("equal pay for equal work," "fairness in career advancement," "equality of spouses with regard to family rights"),[60] and condemns discrimination against women. He especially condemns sexual abuse. "The time has come to condemn vigorously the types of sexual violence which frequently have women for their object and to pass laws which effectively defend them from such violence."[61] Although the pope has maintained consistency with the basic gender assumptions of FC, it is apparent that he has also moved toward greater sympathy with and support for women's struggle against specific social disadvantages that constitute Catholic feminists' primary complaint against the "equal but different" approach to gender.

Marriage and Family Structures

An initial point is the framework of value within which the Church sees the status of marriage in general. FC follows the tradition in giving celibacy a higher rank than marriage since celibate persons supposedly can dedicate their lives more wholeheartedly to the service of God, Christ, Church, and fellow humanity. However, this connection of celibacy with Christian commitment has been shadowed by a tendency to see marriage as inferior because it involves sex and sexual passions that are in turn associated with the degrading effect of the body on spiritual experience and goals (see 1 Cor. 7). Since Vatican II in particular, the Catholic Church has shown more appreciation for worldly vocations, among them marriage. The value of marriage as a school of love and devotion is reflected in the treatment of love as a purpose of marriage just as important as procreation. However, there remains a tension: even though the status of marriage as a Christian vocation has risen, it is still in theory regarded as inferior to celibacy and, in practice, is regulated by very strict control of its forms and structures.

Two critical questions concern the essential forms of marriage and family: Is "indissolubility" a realistic, useful, and theologically adequate way to understand the nature of the commitment between a man and a woman who bring together and enlarge families through marriage and parenthood? Is permanent procreative heterosexual union the only valid foundation on which families can be built?[62] Once again, the scope of the potential discussion of these issues is very large and the literature concerning them is not limited to, nor does it even focus on, FC. The first of these questions does bear directly on the content and structure of that document, however, because the response FC makes to diverse and changing patterns of family life is constructed on the premise that indissoluble marriage is the norm. Hence other relationships like cohabitation before marriage and remarriage after divorce are treated not as possible developments in the understanding or practice of "marriage" but as anomalies in light of the assumed standard.

Some theologians have suggested that this standard follows from a problematic contractual view of marriage in which consent and the celebration of the marriage ceremony, followed by sexual consummation, bring into being a graced and irreversible bond whose existence is able to outlast the demise of a real experiential union of the couple. An alternative understanding of the sacramentality of marriage would see it as a progressive reality, one that might be attained and perhaps lost over time, and in relation to the quality of a relationship in which existentially the grace of the sacrament is offered. It has also been argued that a sacrament does not "automatically" occur in the absence of any explicit faith intention by the spouses to marry in a sacramental way.[63] Bernard Cooke depicts indissolubility as more a "guiding ideal" and eschatological goal than an absolute modality that characterizes every marriage relation of Christians from the wedding day forward.[64] The factual dissolution of many marriages of Christians, as well as the progressive formation of relationships that in some cultures are recognized in stages rather than in one definitive ceremony,[65] are experiential evidence that the sacramental theology of marriage deserves reconsideration in light of a more historical, diachronic, and incremental view of human commitments and of divine action in and through them.[66] Some of this discussion has continued to occur around the topics of cohabitation and marriage preparation, and the suggestion by some that Church and society might consider instituting a "betrothal" period and ceremony, seen as a formal phase in the creation of the marriage relationship.[67]

Another set of issues concerns family structure. The focus on indissoluble marriage as the key foundation of families reinforces the image of the family as a nuclear, consensual, or contractual unit rather than as an intergenerational consanguineous network with much more flexible lines of interdependence and boundaries. It also makes questionable or at least marginal the family experiences of single parents, heterosexual couples living together and possibly raising children without marriage, and same-sex unions, with or without children. On the other hand, monogamy and indissolubility create a horizon against which couples can seriously undertake a commitment to partnership "for better or worse, until death do us part." Although John Paul II includes all families within the purview of his evangelical call, he clearly has in mind firm norms for acceptable types of family relationships. This firmness is diminished somewhat in messages of the U.S. bishops, for instance, who have defended economic support for all families, and who have called on the local church and Catholic families, especially parents, to support gay and lesbian family members.[68]

One important question here is whether all types of family are equally geared to provide for the well-being of members, especially children. On this point the high divorce rate in the United States and Europe has been rightly criticized, notwithstanding the fact that divorce is a sometimes necessary option to end harmful relationships.[69] Economic factors may play an important part in the difficulty some couples have in making and sustaining a marital commitment,[70] and economic difficulties can be exacerbated for women and children when they lose male economic support after a divorce.[71] Many authors hold up the advantages two-parent families can provide for children, and argue in favor of greater long-term investment of fathers in commitment to mothers and children.[72]

These concerns and ideals, however, do not preclude the validity, resilience, and effectiveness of many types of family structure that come into being as persons strive in particular circumstances to form interpersonal relationships, increase mutuality, function productively in society, and care for dependents, including the elderly and the ill as well as the young. Catholic social tradition confirms and values the reciprocity of personal rights and obligations with communal networks of support and participation. As far as families and their welfare are concerned, a flexible approach that highlights the interdependence of family welfare with the support of other social bodies and institutions seems most appropriate. Although there continues to be controversy within Catholicism about the normative desirability and acceptability of various nontraditional unions, FC can support consensus at the practical level about social and pastoral support for all existing families, so that they can contribute to as well as participate in the benefits of the common good.

Social, Cultural, and Economic Factors

The bishops in attendance at the Synod on the Family were well aware of the diversity in family and marital forms and experiences that result from geographical location, national and ethnic identity, and economic status. Although the pope strove to bring all Catholics and even all cultures together under one ideal of permanent, monogamous, heterosexual, procreative marriage, he did allow for significant cultural differences in the embodiment of this ideal, and was particularly aware of economic and political stresses on marriage and family life.

Authors writing about the family from the standpoints of a variety of racial, ethnic, and cultural groups challenge other Catholics and the Church to rethink some of their assumptions about what a family is and how it functions. Some of these challenges go back to the question of family structure and require an imaginative expansion of "domestic church" beyond the nuclear model. The synod on the church in Africa, held in Rome in 1994, stimulated renewed debates about inculturation of Catholic teaching on marriage and family, particularly in regard to "progressive marriage" (marriage in stages, by gradual agreement of the participating families) and polygamy.[73] Toinette Eugene, writing of ministry by and to black Catholic families in the United States, also takes exception to the idea that the nuclear family is the norm. Precisely as an extended family, the black family is church. Identifying "black love" as "the chief attribute of black family," Eugene calls for a prophetic spirituality of family life that "can inspire parents, children, and other relatives in their extended groupings" to embody love and justice through a "willingness to include prodigal children, outcasts, the pariah, the stranger, and even the oppressor within the folds of its embrace."[74] Hispanic interpreters of family also move beyond the individual-based nuclear model to affirm the importance of community and to emphasize the need for the Church to support the social empowerment of all families through participation in "mediating institutions" between the person and the state. This is especially important for families from populations whose interests and welfare have not always been well served by the dominant culture.[75]

This is even more true in the era of economic globalization. In their 1994 pastoral letter on families, the Peruvian bishops identify threats to the family from a "culture of death" that includes "poverty, the humiliating contrasts, terrorist violence that displaces and uproots thousands of families, and generalized unemployment: this dramatic reality makes gravely difficult and even impedes a large sector of our population from depending on the means for adequate education and formation of their children."[76] The Brazilian theologian Marcio Fabri notes that, among families of the third world such as landless peasants and *favela*-dwellers, the struggle for survival and basic needs leads to a cultivation of a socially based spirituality of solidarity and mutual help.[77] Reviewing the conditions and problems of families in Africa, Asia, and Latin America, Enrique Dussel inquires whether the European–North American modern "nuclear" family could not benefit by greater receptivity to forms of family in other cultures. After all, "the spiritual riches of family structures that still survive in the Peripheral World . . . represent actual ways in which family experience is lived *by the greater part of humankind*."[78] Local family customs must not be negated, but can be remodeled in light of the gospel by the Christian subjects themselves who live within them.

Some questions that require further discernment in the decades to come are whether the newer views of sex and marriage that FC strives to accommodate provide an adequate basis for the defense of older norms; whether the "complementarity" model of gender equality defended by FC provides full equality for women, useful though it may be for the maintenance of traditional norms; whether acceptable family structures are confined to the model in which kin groups are aligned through the heterosexual procreating couple; and whether the experiences and values of non-European cultures are adequately reflected in the model of marriage and family that FC upholds. These questions have all been posed repeatedly in one form or another since the 1960s as part of a movement to open up sexual and marital teaching that seemed authoritarian and distant from the real lives of married people and their families, and much more so from the experiences of those living in other kinds of sexual and familial relationships.

As FC and similar documents are considered anew at the beginning of the twenty-first century, the cultural contexts have changed substantially from those in place at the time of Vatican II. In North Atlantic postindustrial societies, the repressive sexual ethos of the 1950s has been replaced by a milieu in which sex is promoted, even marketed, with few boundaries, and in which the flexibility and fluidity of family structures can result in inadequate parental, social, and economic support for children. Meanwhile, in an increasingly "globalized" world, non-Western cultures offer critiques of the same priority given to individual rights, liberty, and conscience that once motivated many "liberalizing" changes in gender, sex, marriage, and family in so-called first world societies, both inside and outside the Roman Catholic Church. Moreover, taken to the level of global economics and politics, the Euro-American emphasis on individual rights has turned into a model for unconstrained corporate behavior that has had pernicious effects on the survival of families in other parts of the world. Critics from the latter cultures have rightly asked whether first world advocacy for family planning measures is a way to avoid the costs of genuine development and a redistribution of economic assets. Setting aside the looming social issues of starvation and war, the ability of marriages and families to remain intact and support women and children is often endangered or made impossible when traditional societies and means of livelihood are disrupted, for example, when young adults, especially men, leave their families to seek urban employment or emigrate abroad to find work.

FC represents a "bridge" document in modern Catholic social teaching. On one side are approaches to family that funnel assessment of the family as a social institution through norms about individual sexual and procreative behavior. On the other side, an emerging approach gives equal or even greater precedence to social conditions that determine the possibility of family welfare and the well-being of individual members within the family. A major challenge for future Catholic social teaching about families will be to develop an understanding of family that allows for structural pluralism while establishing some normative parameters. The challenge will be to balance the value of family as a community and social institution with the rights of individual family members, and also allow for genuine gender equality while upholding commitment to and protection for children.

REACTIONS TO THE DOCUMENT

The reactions to FC have been generally favorable, though not unqualifiedly so. It must be conceded that, of its various champions, some have taken its content in opposite directions, emphasizing different elements to different effect. There are those who simply comb it for points of consistency or inconsistency with previous teaching on sexual ethics and divorce, rejecting or affirming it on that score alone. FC's more important focus, the concept of family as a domestic church in service to the common good, has gained a certain following among bishops and theologians. The metaphor has not particularly caught on at the popular level, perhaps because of its seeming abstractness, and also because some fear (perhaps wrongly) that its main import is disciplinary rather than evangelical.[79]

One group of commentators has celebrated FC's development of John Paul II's "theology of the body," especially the "nuptial meaning of the body," to give a more holistic, personalist, and appealing context for the affirmation of *Humanae vitae* and related teachings. They tend to see the document as providing protection for Catholic family values and forms against the incursions of an increasingly secular and hostile society. For example, the American Family Institute in Washington, D.C., convened a symposium almost immediately after the appearance of FC. In its published papers, Carlo Caffarra praises this apostolic exhortation because it "affirms that marriage and the family are rooted in a universal truth about mankind, a truth that is independent of any particular social or cultural context."[80] Such thinkers concur in the pope's view that sex, marriage, and family will only be positive and fulfilling realities if lived out according to Catholic teaching. Adrzej Poltawski denies that the pope's insistence on the teaching of the Church about "marriage and family, abortion and contraception" is designed to "torment" Catholics and suggests instead that it arises "out of a profound vision of the human person," and "is designed to show them the only way to true self-fulfillment and real happiness."[81] Additional works that provide commentary and praise in a similar vein are *Pope John Paul II and the Family* with a foreword by Cardinal Terence Cooke who was present at the synod, and a collection of articles edited by Richard M. Hogan and John M. LeVoir titled *Covenant of Love: Pope John Paul II on Sexuality, Marriage, and Family in the Modern World*.[82] Calling FC a "brilliantly written work,"[83] Hogan and LeVoir adopt a sacramental view of the human body and argue that the pope's theology represents the integration of the bodily and the personal through marriage, marital sexuality, and family. Only "deeds in accordance with the truth" can bring couples and families joy and peace.[84] Authors in this first category prize FC in part because, while defending established norms, it does contextualize them in a more complete view of the person as moral agent in interpersonal and social relationships. There continue to be some younger Catholics who, while not adhering to magisterial teaching on sex and birth control out of guilt or fear, find in it a radical framework for Christian commitment in a sexually chaotic world.[85]

Another set of commentators focuses on the domestic church metaphor and advocates an approach to marriage, family, and sexuality that has more in common with the flexible and outward-looking model of Catholic social teaching than of traditional "moral theology" (focused on individual decision making about specific actions) and of past sexual teaching in particular (focused on avoiding sins). Authors in the first and second categories tend to share a positive appreciation for the pope's theology of the family, as epitomized in the domestic church concept, since it grounds the practices and social action of the family in spirituality, evangelical identity, and prayer. But thinkers in the second category tend to give greater emphasis to "the preferential option for the poor" and related efforts toward service and structural change in defining the identity of the Christian family. They call attention to unjust and discriminatory conditions that inhibit some families from achieving their own well-being and full participation in the common good of society.

Reactions to FC that hinge on the domestic church address both the spiritual and the social dimensions of this concept of the family. Florence C. Bourg provides a comprehensive survey of literature on the topic, setting responses in the context of endeavors by the U.S. and Australian bishops' conferences, a synod of African bishops, the Catholic Theological Society of America, and both Catholic and Protestant research projects on religion and the family.[86] As Bourg notes, an early response linking spirituality and social commitment to the family was Mitch and Kathy Finley's *Christian Families in the Real World*.[87] Bourg's own work on this connection emphasizes the sacramentality of the Church as mediating an experience of God, and the family as an instantiation of church.[88] These and similar authors agree that the domestic church image can help empower families within the Church and nurture a sense of mission for social justice that carries forward the tradition of Catholic social teaching in an era in which the laity assume an ever more important role in church renewal, evangelization, and social action.[89]

A stimulus to further appropriation of a family spirituality and social justice commitment was the 1994 UN "Year of the Family." The pope authored a "Letter to Families" centered on the domestic church as helping to create a "civilization of love," but in which he also expressed concern about the "breakdown of the family" in modern cultures.[90] This letter focuses attention primarily on the need to sustain the unity and permanence of marriage, the countercultural education of children, the responsibility of both parents for nurturing children, and the commitment of spouses and families to protect human life at every stage.[91] In the previous year, the U.S. Catholic bishops had released a pastoral message titled *Follow the Way of Love* in which they addressed families directly and included all families as bearers of the gospel, not just families conforming structurally to Catholic marriage norms. Christian families, based in faith and prayer, are described as accomplishing the work of domestic churches. "You welcome the stranger, the lonely one, the grieving person into your home. . . . You act justly in your community when you treat others with respect, stand against discrimination and racism, and work to overcome hunger, poverty, homelessness, illiteracy."[92] The U.S. bishops also published a 1992 letter in response to the problem of domestic abuse, exhorting church representatives and ministers to aid women who are victims.[93]

The 1994 *Catechism of the Catholic Church* includes a brief section on domestic church after its presentation of the sacrament of marriage. It explicitly includes single persons within the Church's concept of family, and associates the family with "the priesthood of the baptized," but barely even alludes to the social mission of the family.[94]At the very least, this omission not only fails to carry through on a major contribution of FC but endangers the ability of that document to serve as a positive inspiration for families in the future. Reactions that minimize the socially radical mission of the Christian family are not numerous and do not seem to have been widely influential, even though the political orientations of various commentators have varied.

A third set of respondents, overlapping to some extent with the group interested in domestic church, discusses whether and in what way indissoluble sacramental marriage as defined in FC is the sine qua non of Christian family life.[95] Some of these, however, are more concerned about a pastoral response to divorce based on an adequate understanding of the nature of the marriage relationship than with the relation of marriage and family to Catholic social ethics. Their critiques may be motivated as much by the 1983 code of canon law as by the Synod on the Family and FC, and thus do not bear as directly on the reception of FC. Some of their concerns have been treated in the previous section.

The diversity of responses to FC was partly captured in a twentieth anniversary symposium sponsored by the U.S. Conference of Catholic Bishops. Societal changes in views and practices of marriage were a significant topic, as was the related problem of effective ministry to Catholic couples and families. But rather than focusing on cultural breakdown or rejection of Church teaching, conference participants sought more attractive and effective ways to present pro-life convictions and to defend the permanence of marriage while continuing to reshape the tradition in line with Vatican II.[96] Responses from the perspectives of women's equality and challenges of globalization and cultural diversity will also play a part in the continuing interpretation of FC.

NOTES

1. Stanley L. Saxton, Patricia Voydanoff, and Angela Ann Kukowski, eds., *The Changing Family: Views from Theology and the Social Sciences in Light of the Apostolic Exhortation Familiaris Consortio* (Chicago: Loyola University Press, 1984).

2. Barrie Thorne and Marilyn Yalom, eds., *Rethinking the Family: Some Feminist Questions* (Boston: Northeastern University Press, 1992).

3. See, for example, Maxine Baca Zinn, "Family, Race, and Poverty in the Eighties," in ibid., 71–90.

4. Ada Maria Isasi-Diaz, *En La Lucha: A Hispanic Women's Liberation Theology* (Minneapolis: Augsburg Fortress, 1993).

5. James Hitchcock welcomed FC out of a perception that at the time, "even in religious circles, the depth of the family's crisis is often minimized or denied, partly perhaps out of naiveté but partly because it is easier to introduce revolutionary changes into society if people do not appreciate how truly revolutionary they are." See James Hitchcock, "Catholic Social Thought and Family Policy: John Paul II's *Familiaris Consortio*," in *The Family in the Modern World*, ed. Carl A. Anderson and William J. Gribbin (Washington, D.C.: American Family Institute, 1982), 29.

6. Jan Grootaers and Joseph A. Selling, *The 1980 Synod of Bishops "On the Role of the Family": An Exposition of the Event and an Analysis of Its Texts* (Leuven: Leuven University Press and Uitgeverij Peeters, 1983), 194. See also John J. Billings, M.D., "Love and Life within the Family: Part One," and Evelyn L. Billings, M.D., "Love and Life within the Family: Part Two," in *Faith and Challenges to the Family*, ed. Russell E. Smith, *Proceedings of the Thirteenth Workshop for Bishops, Dallas, TX* (Braintree, Mass.: The Pope John XXIII Medical-Ethics Research and Education Center, 1994), 163–81.

7. GS 47. For the text, see David J. O'Brien and Thomas A. Shannon, eds., *Catholic Social Thought: The Documentary Heritage* (Maryknoll, N.Y.: Orbis, 1998), 166–237.

8. GS 48. Similar phrases occur elsewhere, esp. number 49.

9. Ibid. 50.

10. Ibid. 48.

11. Ibid. 52.

12. Paul VI, *Humanae vitae* (*On the Regulation of Birth*) (New York: Paulist, 1968), number 12.

13. HV 16. This actually represents another innovation in the tradition, hearkening back to Pius XII. In his 1951 "Address to the Midwives" [*Acta Apostlicae Sedis* 53 (1951): 835–54], Pius XII accepted periodic continence to avoid pregnancy whereas prior to that time sexual intercourse for any intention other than procreation was regarded as not fully justified or even sinful.

14. HV 10.

15. The ongoing controversy generated from the majority of self-identified Catholics not accepting an absolute ban on contraception is the reason that HV is often held up as an example of church teaching that is nonauthoritative by virtue of "nonreception."

16. See John Paul II, *Original Unity of Man and Woman: Catechesis on the Book of Genesis* (Boston: St. Paul Editions, 1981) and his *Blessed Are the Pure of Heart: Catechesis on the Sermon on the Mount and Writings of St. Paul* (Boston: St. Paul Editions, 1983). See also Richard M. Hogan and John M. LeVoir, *Covenant of Love: Pope John Paul II on Sexuality, Marriage, and Family in the Modern World* (San Francisco: Ignatius, 1985), 39–70.

17. John Paul II, *Original Unity*, 110–20. See the section on John Paul II's personalist philosophy in the Commentary on *Laborem exercens* by Patricia Lamoureux in this volume.

18. Refer also to the *Code of Canon Law*, trans. Canon Law Society of America (Washington, D.C.: Canon Law Society of America, 1983), esp. canons 1055, 1057, 1095, and 1096, in which contractual language for marriage is being gradually though incompletely replaced by covenant and partnership language applied to the entirety of the relationship. For a discussion, see Ladislas Orsy, *Marriage in Canon Law: Texts and Comments, Reflections and Questions* (Wilmington, Del.: Michael Glazier, 1986).

19. Some of these criticisms will be taken up in the "Excursus."

20. The major source for this history of the synod is J. Grootaers and J. A. Selling, *The 1980 Synod of Bishops "On the Role of the Family."*

21. Ibid., 69.

22. Ibid., 93–94.

23. Ibid., 71–72, 90.

24. Ibid., 79–80.

25. On the preparation process and constitution of representation at the synod, see also David M. Thomas, "Introduction," in *Changing Family*, ed. S. L. Saxton et al., xi–xvii.

26. Grootaers and Selling, *1980 Synod of Bishops*, 68–77, 130.

27. Ibid., 292–93.

28. Ibid., 298–301.

29. The specific impetus behind this encyclical was the decision of the Anglican Church at the 1930 Lambeth Conference to accept artificial birth control. *Casti connubii* also followed upon and reiterated the main themes of the first papal encyclical on marriage, Leo XIII's *Arcanum divinae sapientiae* (1880). Leo XIII began the social encyclical tradition with *Rerum novarum* (1891).

30. Pius XI, *Casti connubii* (*On Christian Marriage*), in *Official Catholic Teachings: Love and Sexuality*, ed. Odile Lombard (Wilmington, N.C.: McGrath, 1976), 31.

31. Ibid., 47.

32. Ibid., 42.

33. Ibid., 48.

34. Herbert Doms, *The Meaning of Marriage* (New York: Sheed and Ward, 1939), 25–26. Originally published as *Vom Sinn und Zweck der Ehe* (Breslau: Ostdeutsche Verlagsanstalt, 1935).

35. The decree is cited in full by John C. Ford and Gerald Kelly, *Contemporary Moral Theology 2: Marriage Questions* (Westminster, Md.: Newman, 1964), 27–28. The ideas for which Doms fell under suspicion were largely incorporated in later Catholic teaching.

36. GS 49–51.

37. Ibid., 9.

38. Brennan R. Hill, "Reformulating the Sacramental Theology of Marriage," and Michael G. Lawler, "Marriage and the Sacrament of Marriage," in *Christian Marriage and Family: Contemporary Theological and Pastoral Perspectives*, ed. Michael G.

Lawler and William P. Roberts (Collegeville, Minn.: Liturgical, 1996), 3–21, 22–37, respectively.

39. Maureen Gallagher, "Family Life as Sacrament," Michael D. Place, "*Familiaris Consortio*: A Review of Its Theology," and Mary G. Durkin, "Love and Intimacy: Revealing God in Intimate Relationships," in *Changing Family*, ed. S. L. Saxton et al., 5–13, 23–46, 51–62, respectively.

40. At the Council the inspiration for the inclusion of this metaphor in LG was Bishop Pietro Fiordelli of Prato, Italy, who had been involved in the Christian Family movement. See Michael A. Fahey, "The Christian Family as Domestic Church at Vatican II," in *The Family*, ed. Lisa Sowle Cahill and Dietmar Mieth (London: SCM; Maryknoll, N.Y.: Orbis, 1995), 85–92.

41. See Florence Caffrey Bourg, "Domestic Church: A Survey of the Literature," *INTAMS Review* 7 (autumn 2001): 182–91; and F. C. Bourg, *Where Two or Three Are Gathered: Christian Families as Domestic Churches* (Notre Dame, Ind.: University of Notre Dame Press, 2003). See also Lisa Sowle Cahill, *Family: A Christian Social Perspective* (Minneapolis: Augsburg Fortress, 2000), 47–82.

42. Fahey, "Christian Family as Domestic Church at Vatican II," in *The Family*, ed. L. S. Cahill and D. Mieth, 91.

43. Charles K. Wilber and Mary Ellen Wilber, "The Economy, the Family, and Social Justice," in *Changing Family*, ed. S. L. Saxton et al., 71–72. See also "Appendix A: An Overview of the Christian Family Movement," in ibid., 77–78.

44. See entry on QA by Christine Firer Hinze in this volume.

45. John Paul II mentions that a catechism to assist Catholic families had been requested by the synod bishops, who are invited to contribute to its preparation. For the outcome, see *Catechism of the Catholic Church*, trans. U.S. Catholic Conference (Liguori, Mo.: Liguori, 1994).

46. On this and other ecclesiological implications of the domestic church, see Joann Heaney-Hunter, "Domestic Church: Guiding Beliefs and Daily Practices," and William P. Roberts, "The Family as Domestic Church: Contemporary Implications," in *Christian Marriage and Family*, ed. M. G. Lawler and W. P. Roberts, 59–78, 79–90, respectively.

47. Grootaers and Selling, *1980 Synod of Bishops*, 275.

48. Ibid., 301. The portion of the homily on women is quoted directly.

49. See Patricia Voydanoff, "Changing Roles of Men and Women: The Emergence of Symmetrical Families," and Dana V. Hiller, "Sex Equality, Women's Employment, and the Family," in *Changing Family*, ed. S. L Sexton et al., 125–37, 109–24, respectively.

50. The sociologist Andrew Greeley invokes the "spectacle of a group of elderly unmarried men pontificating easily and freely about the problems of marriage, sex, and family life without any need to listen to those who are married, have families, and experience sexual intimacy." *Los Angeles Herald Examiner*, January 16, 1982, sec. B8, as cited in *Pope John Paul II on the Family*, ed. Michael J. Wrenn (Chicago: Franciscan Herald, 1983), xxvii.

51. Secretariat for Family, Laity, Women and Youth, *Marriage and Family Life Symposium*, August 2001 (Washington, D.C.: U.S. Conference of Catholic Bishops, 2001). See http://www.nccbuscc.org/laity/marriage/symposium.htm to access symposium materials (downloaded March 12, 2004).

52. Christine E. Gudorf, "Encountering the Other: The Modern Papacy on Women," in *Feminist Ethics and the Catholic Moral Tradition*, ed. Charles E. Curran, Margaret A. Farley, and Richard A. McCormick (New York: Paulist, 1996), 66–89. For an opposite viewpoint, defending gender complementarity as the necessary consequence of male and female embodiment, see Francis Martin, *The Feminist Question: Feminist Theology in the Light of Christian Tradition* (Grand Rapids, Mich.: Eerdmans, 1994). See also Elizabeth A. Johnson, ed., *The Church Women Want* (New York: Crossroad, 2002). This volume contains contrasting essays on male and female complementarity by Sara Butler, Elizabeth A. Johnson, and Colleen M. Griffith.

53. Christine Firer Hinze, "Bridge Discourse on Wage Justice: Roman Catholic and Feminist Perspectives on the Family Living Wage," in *Feminist Ethics*, ed. C. E. Curran et al., 511–40.

54. Many provocative and incisive discussions can be found in Curran, Farley, and McCormick's *Feminist Ethics*.

55. John Paul II, *Mulieris dignitatem* (*On the Dignity and Vocation of Women*) (Washington, D.C.: U.S. Catholic Conference, 1988) and his "Letter to Women," *Origins* 25 (1995): 137, 139–43.

56. John Paul II, *Mulieris dignitatem*, number 30.

57. John Paul II, "Letter to Women," numbers 7, 9–10.

58. Ibid., number 3.

59. Ibid., number 6, number 3.

60. Ibid., number 4.

61. Ibid., number 5.

62. For a review of literature on these and related topics, see the essays on marriage, sex and eros, and homosexuality by Lisa Sowle Cahill, Peter Black, and James F. Keenan, respectively, in *Theological Studies* 64, no. 1 (2003). These essays cover literature from the mid-twentieth through the very early twenty-first centuries, and engage some voices from non-Western cultures.

63. See Michael G. Lawler, *Secular Marriage, Christian Sacrament* (Mystic, Conn.: Twenty-Third, 1985), 66, on the marriages of so-called baptized nonbelievers.

64. Bernard Cooke, "Indissolubility: Guiding Ideal or Existential Reality?" in *Commitment to Partnership*, ed. W. P. Roberts, 64–75.

65. Michael J. Wrenn reports on a 1980 article from the *East Asian Pastoral Review* in which it is said that eighteen bishops at the synod raised the question of "dynamic progressive marriage." See *John Paul II and the Family*, ed. M. J. Wrenn, xxi.

66. See also Kevin T. Kelly, *Divorce and Second Marriage: Facing the Challenge* (Kansas City, Mo.: Sheed and Ward, 1997); Lawler and Roberts, eds., *Christian Marriage and Family*; and M. G. Lawler, *Marriage and Sacrament* (Collegeville, Minn.: Liturgical, 1993).

67. In 1999, the U.S. Bishops' Committee on Marriage and Family released *Marriage Preparation and Cohabiting Couples: An Information Report on New Realities and Pastoral Practice*. This report attempted to confront realistically the problem of bringing couples already living together to a strong commitment to sacramental marriage. A debate on pastoral care and on implications for seeing marriage as definitively beginning at the marriage ceremony was published in *INTAMS Review* 6 (spring 2000) with articles by Lisa Sowle Cahill, Hubert Winisch, and Pierre-O. Bressoud. A defense of a period of betrothal in which sexual relations would be permitted is offered by the Anglican theologian Adrian Thatcher in *Marriage after Modernity: Christian Marriage in Postmodern Times* (Washington Square, N.Y.: New York University Press, 1999). See the affirmative review by Michael Lawler, *INTAMS Review* 6 (spring 2000): 132–34.

68. See National Conference of Catholic Bishops, *Economic Justice for All: Pastoral Letter on Catholic Social Teaching and the U.S. Economy* (Washington, D.C.: National Conference of Catholic Bishops, 1986); and National Conference of Catholic Bishops Committee on Marriage and Family, "'Always Our Children': Pastoral Message to Parents of Homosexual Children," *Origins* 27 (1997): 285, 287–91.

69. For an endorsement of gender equality, the importance of a vocation outside the home for both women and men, and a social view of family responsibilities, along with a strong negative reaction to divorce, see Julie Hanlon Rubio, *A Christian Theology of Marriage* (New York: Paulist, 2003).

70. William Julius Wilson, *When Work Disappears: The World of the New Urban Poor* (New York: Vintage, 1996).

71. Mary Ann Glendon, *Abortion and Divorce in Western Law* (Cambridge, Mass.: Harvard University Press, 1987).

72. Five articles in the *Josephinum Journal of Theology* 9 (winter–spring 2002) treat the roles of fathers from a Catholic perspective. A similar concern about fatherlessness motivates Don S. Browning, Bonnie J. Miller-McLemore, Pamela D. Couture, K. Brynolf Lyon, and Robert M. Franklin, *From Culture Wars to Common Ground: Religion and the American Family Debate* (Louisville, Ky.: Westminster/John Knox, 1997).

73. See Emmanuel Martey, "Church and Marriage in African Society: A Theological Appraisal," in *Christian Perspectives on Sexuality and Gender*, ed. Elizabeth Stuart and Adrian Thatcher (Grand Rapids, Mich.: Eerdmans; Herefordshire, England: Gracewing Fowler Wright, 1996), 199–210; and Elochukwu E. Uzukwu, *A Listening Church: Autonomy and Communion in African Churches* (Maryknoll, N.Y.: Orbis, 1996).

74. Toinette M. Eugene, "African American Family Life: An Agenda for Ministry within the Catholic Church," *New Theology Review* 5 (May 1992): 40–41.

75. Ernie Cortes, "Reflections on the Catholic Tradition of Family Rights," in *One Hundred Years*, ed. J. A. Coleman, 155–73.

76. Peruvian Pastoral Conference, "The Family:

Heart of the Civilization of Love," *Catholic International* 5 (June 1994): 270.

77. Marcio Fabri dos Anjos, "Building a Spirituality of Family Life," in *The Family*, ed. L. S. Cahill and D. Mieth, 97–109.

78. Enrique Dussel, "The Family in the 'Peripheral World,'" in ibid., 59. See also Kabasele F. Lumbala, "The Church as Family in Africa," in ibid., 93–98.

79. This opinion is expressed by the German theologian Norbert Mette: "Instead of the family being evaluated in its original independence, the term 'domestic church' is used in an attempt to requisition the family for the institution in a lofty way. The 'spiritual packaging' conceals nothing less than the expectation that the 'Catholic family' is a reliable place for the reproduction of the church, and moreover functions as an advance bulwark of the 'fortress of God' against tendencies towards liberalization and pluralization." See "The Family in the Teaching of the Magisterium," in *The Family*, ed. L. S. Cahill and D. Mieth, 81.

80. Carlo Caffarra, "Marriage and Family in the Thought of Karol Wojtyla," in *The Family in the Modern World*, ed. C. A. Anderson and W. J. Gribbin, 59.

81. Adrzej Poltawski, "Person and Family in the Thought of Karol Wojtyla," in ibid., 57.

82. Wrenn, ed., *Pope John Paul II and the Family*. For Hogan and LeVoir, *Covenant of Love*, see note 16, above.

83. Hogan and LaVoir, *Covenant of Love*, 12. A similar orientation is reflected in the proceedings of a conference held for the U.S. bishops. See Donald G. McCarthy, ed., *The Family Today and Tomorrow: The Church Addresses Her Future* (Braintree, Mass.: The Pope John XXIII Medical-Moral Research and Education Center, 1985).

84. Ibid., 305.

85. An example is a young Catholic feminist, married and a parent, who claims that natural birth control allows women more control over their bodies and respects the sacred design of sex. See Jennifer Popiel, "Necessary Connections? Catholicism, Feminism and Contraception," *America* 181 (November 1999): 22–26.

86. Bourg, "Domestic Church: A Survey of the Literature."

87. Mitch and Kathy Finley, *Christian Families in the Real World: Reflections on a Spirituality for the Domestic Church* (Chicago: Thomas More, 1984). See also Wendy Wright, *Sacred Dwelling: A Spirituality of Family Life* (New York: Crossroad, 1989); James and Kathleen McGinnis, "Family as Domestic Church," in *One Hundred Years of Catholic Social Thought*, ed. John Coleman (Maryknoll, N.Y.: Orbis, 1990), 120–34; and Michael G. Lawler, *Family: American and Christian* (Chicago: Loyola, 1998).

88. Bourg, *Where Two or Three Are Gathered.*

89. McGinnises, *Family as Domestic Church*, 129.

90. John Paul II, "Letter to Families," *Origins* 23 (March 1994): 637, 639–59.

91. Similar concerns are reflected in Smith, ed., *Faith and Challenges to the Family*.

92. U.S. Bishops, "Follow the Way of Love," *Origins* 23 (December 1993): 436.

93. Bishops' Committee on Marriage and Family Life and Bishops' Committee on Women in Society and in the Church, *"When I Call for Help": A Pastoral Response to Domestic Violence against Women* (Washington, D.C.: U.S. Catholic Conference, 1992).

94. *Catechism of the Catholic Church*, nos. 1655–66.

95. See, for example, Joann Heaney-Hunter, "Living the Baptismal Commitment to Sacramental Marriage," in *Christian Marriage and Family*, ed. M. G. Lawler and W. P. Roberts, 106–22; and William P. Roberts, ed., *Commitment to Partnership: Explorations of the Theology of Marriage* (New York: Paulist, 1987).

96. See Margaret A. Farley, "The Church and the Family: An Ethical Task," *Horizons* 10 (1983): 50–71.

SELECTED BIBLIOGRAPHY

Anderson, Carl A., and William J. Gribbin, eds. *The Family in the Modern World.* Washington, D.C.: American Family Institute, 1982. Treats the thought of Karol Wojtyla (Pope John Paul II) as providing perennially valid insights into marriage, family life, family policy, and the dignity of the person in the family.

Bourg, Florence Caffrey. *Where Two or Three are Gathered: Christian Families as Domestic Churches.* Notre Dame, Ind.: University of Notre Dame, 2003. Treats family spirituality and commitment to the common good, emphasizing baptism (not marriage) as establishing membership in the domestic church.

Cahill, Lisa Sowle, and Dietmar Mieth, eds. *The Family*. London: SCM; Maryknoll, N.Y.: Orbis, 1995. Critical Catholic perspectives on the family from the United States, United Kingdom, Europe, Latin America, and Africa.

Grootaers, Jan, and Joseph A. Selling. *The 1980 Synod of Bishops "On the Role of the Family": An Exposition of the Event and an Analysis of Its Texts*. Leuven: Leuven University Press and Uitgeverij Peeters, 1983. Detailed history of the synod with extensive attention to politics and international representation.

Lawler, Michael G., and William P. Roberts, eds. *Christian Marriage and Family: Contemporary Theological and Pastoral Perspectives*. Collegeville Minn.: Liturgical, 1996. A variety of innovative perspectives on marriage, divorce, family spirituality, and the domestic church.

McCarthy, Donald G. *The Family Today and Tomorrow: The Church Addresses Her Future*. Braintree, Mass.: The Pope John XXIII Medical-Moral Research and Education Center, 1985. Social change, migrants, family violence, health, aging, parental education of children, and so on are treated according to magisterial teaching.

Rubio, Julie Hanlon. *A Christian Theology of Marriage and Family*. Mahwah, N.J.: Paulist, 2002. Treats issues of marriage, parenthood, and social justice work from the perspective of a young "two-career" Catholic family today.

Saxton, Stanley L., Patricia Voydanoff, and Angela Ann Kukowski, eds. *The Changing Family: Views from Theology and the Social Sciences in Light of the Apostolic Exhortation Familiaris Consortio*. Chicago: Loyola University Press, 1984. Essays on sacramentality, intimacy, economics, gender roles, employment, and the Christian Family movement, with a progressive slant.

CHAPTER

16 Commentary on *Laborem exercens* (*On Human Work*)

PATRICIA A. LAMOUREUX

INTRODUCTION

Laborem exercens was published on September 14, 1981, to commemorate the ninetieth anniversary of *Rerum novarum*. This third encyclical of John Paul II offers the most comprehensive treatment of human work in the corpus of Catholic social teaching.[1] While John Paul deals with this issue in "organic connection" with the tradition, he aims to endow work with new meaning and purpose. The essence of the encyclical's teaching is the human person considered in the context of the experience of work. It centers on and revolves around two key notions: work is for the person, not the person for work; and labor has priority over capital. The enduring legacy and challenge of this encyclical is its positive vision of human labor as a sharing in the activity of the Creator, and the responsibility of men and women to collaborate in the ongoing creation and re-creation of both self and the world of work.

OUTLINE OF THE DOCUMENT

The encyclical begins with an Introduction (1–3) and is structured around four main sections: Work and the Human Person (4–10); Conflict between Labor and Capital in the Present Phase of Human History (11–15); Rights of Workers (16–23); Elements for a Spirituality of Work (24–27).

The Introduction makes the point that at least since *Rerum novarum* the Church's social teaching has been concerned with the question of human labor. For John Paul II, however, work is considered to be "the essential key to the whole social question" when viewed from the perspective of human good (3).

As the pope begins his treatment of the meaning of work and its relation to the human person he proposes that the biblical grounding for the meaning of work is the Genesis story. In his reading of the first book of the Bible, John Paul maintains that it is by their labor that men and women participate in God's creative activity, that they shape themselves and the world (4).

As he develops his theology of human labor the pope emphasizes the priority of the subjective over the objective dimensions of work (5–7). That is, the proper subject of work is the human person who takes priority over the sort of work being done. The right order of values is threatened when the person is viewed as an instrument of production or as a form of merchandise to be bought and sold.

Two other points are made in this first major section. First, is the importance of worker solidarity; in order to achieve social justice in various parts of the world, there is a need for new movements of solidarity of the workers and with the workers (8). Secondly, the value of work ought to be appreciated. Work is good in the sense of corresponding with human dignity, as a condition for enabling a family's material support, and as the basis of cultural and social life (9–10).

The second major segment of the encyclical treats the conflict between labor and capital. This conflict has historical roots in the ideological conflict between liberalism and Marxism (11). What cannot be lost in this debate is the priority of labor over capital (12–13). Human labor takes precedence over the means of production. Labor is always a primary efficient cause while capital is an instrumental cause.

It is also asserted that the right to private ownership is subordinated to the right to common use, to the fact that goods of the earth are meant for everyone (14). In this sense, labor is given priority over ownership. In keeping with John Paul II's philosophical orientation, he appeals to a personalist argument that in human labor the worker is aware of working not only for others but primarily for oneself (15).

While much of the preceding material reflects the originality of John Paul's thinking, the third section is closer to many of the classical themes that Catholic social teaching has exhibited when defending the rights of workers. The traditional rights of workers to employment, a just wage, and to unionize must be defended in the context of human rights (16). The rights of workers, however, must be considered in view of the relationship between the employer, direct and indirect, and the worker (17).

The first and basic right of workers is the right to work (18); this is essential to protect the dignity of human labor. Respect for workers' rights constitutes the fundamental criterion for shaping the economy. In keeping with earlier teaching, a just wage is considered a concrete and key means of assessing the justice of any socioeconomic system (19). Finally, when discussing the rights of workers, it is clear that labor unions are necessary to secure the rights of workers and to ensure participation in the workplace (20).

In the closing section of the letter the pope offers a reflection on the need for a spirituality of work. Labor's spiritual dimension arises from the worker's participation in God's ongoing story of creation and in the paschal mystery (24–27).

CONTEXT OF THE DOCUMENT

LE was written in response to profound social changes in the world since the Industrial Revolution in Europe and the United States that exerted an impact on the dignity and rights of workers. John Paul identifies several of these new conditions and problems that have tremendous impact on the world of work and that require a reordering and adjustment of structures of the economy and the distribution of work. He notes the developments in technology and the widespread introduction of automation, the increase in the cost of energy and raw materials, limitations of the earth's resources, and the growing awareness of environmental degradation. Furthermore, labor problems such as unemployment in vulnerable sectors of the domestic economy are complicated by the growth of multinational corporations that can move productive capacities from high-wage unionized locations to developing countries where unions tend to be restricted or outlawed. Thus, in LE, the issue of human work is a worldwide phenomenon that has national, international, and transnational dimensions.[2]

In addition, LE is occasioned by a crisis of meaning of work combined with a more fundamental crisis of values in contemporary society. John Paul II surveys a world in which the primary threat and new tragedy of human labor is a growing and all-pervasive materialistic civilization, a universal atmosphere and public opinion that favors exaggerated material consumption. This distorted social context is primarily due to material progress being stressed over human needs along with the all-consuming drive for efficiency and profit.

Another factor to be considered in regard to the social context of the document is the situation in Poland, particularly the tensions that were present between the trade union movement, Solidarity (*Solidarnosc*), and the Polish communist government. Solidarity was launched during the Gdansk shipyard strike, August 14–31, 1980. On August 20, John Paul delivered a message to Polish church leaders in support of the strikers' demands. An agreement signed on August 31 provided for independent self-governing trade unions. The newly installed Communist Party leader Stanislaw Kania attempted to derail the Solidarity movement, and the leadership of the Soviet Union tried to remove it forcibly. The pope intervened with an unprecedented letter to Leonid Brezhnev in which he stated his defense of Polish sovereignty and nonnegotiable support for Solidarity.[3]

As the first quarter of 1981 unfolded and Solidarity struggled to carry out its social revolution, John Paul met with a Solidarity delegation at the Vatican (January 15–18, 1981). In his public remarks he described Solidarity as a different kind of revolution. He stated that a commitment to the "moral good of society" was the "cornerstone" of Solidarity's work and the beginning of any "real progress" in national renewal.[4] The first Solidarity National Congress opened in Gdansk on September 5, 1981, the same day the Soviet Union began massive military and naval exercises in the Baltic region. Growing disagreement among the delegates over a long-festering issue—the extent to which Solidarity should engage in political activity—marked the Congress. LE appeared in the midst of the Congress, which concluded on October 7, 1981.

Vatican sources maintain the encyclical is not a direct commentary on these tensions. Others claim the pope's solidarity with the Polish workers is "the socio-political base on which the encyclical is built";[5] that LE is John Paul's "philosophical defense of the Solidarity movement";[6] and that "the Polish political scene seems to condition what John Paul II says about trade unions."[7] It is at least plausible that for this "Slavic Pope"[8] with a "fierce Polish nationalism"[9] the Polish situation was very much on his mind while formulating the encyclical. At the same time, it would be too narrow and simplistic an interpretation of LE to suggest that it is directed solely to the tensions in Poland. Rather, this situation along with profound changes in the world of labor and the crisis of meaning of work occasioned the document.

John Paul's visits to Mexico, Poland, and Italy, especially during the first year of his papacy (1979), provided the opportunity for personal contact with various sectors of the world of labor and with the concrete reality of workers' complex and multiform needs. He spoke frequently of being profoundly affected by his contact with rural, domestic, and migrant workers, and working-class families, and on many occasions expressed sensitivity to their labor problems and to their legitimate aspirations. He repeatedly affirmed workers' rights, especially the fundamental right of workers to create organizations to defend and promote their own interests, as well as their obligation to contribute responsibly to the common good. In the speeches John Paul gave to these primarily industrial and agricultural workers, he articulated two basic ideas or fundamental concepts found in LE: the inviolable dignity of the worker and the spiritual dimension of human work, seen as a vocation of service to God and others. As the pope stated in a homily in Poland and has repeated on numerous occasions, the problems of human labor cannot be fully solved without the gospel.[10]

The nine-day papal visit to Poland in June 1979 was more politically charged than the other trips. The situation in Poland had become critical—socially, economically, and politically. Communist economic mismanagement, government corruption, and political repression had created an explosive climate. Thus, John Paul not only directed his speeches to workers, but he wanted to strengthen the morale of Polish society and to bring hope for what he saw as difficult years ahead. The pope did not intend to precipitate a rebellion, but rather he anticipated an evolutionary process toward a peaceful transition to democracy. The presence of this Polish pope in the midst of fervently devout Catholic compatriots, however, played some role in accelerating the march of events, at least in terms of the national psychology.[11]

In addition to John Paul's travels, his first two encyclicals—*Redemptor hominis* and *Dives in misericordia*—provide the ecclesial context for his reflection on human work. In these documents, the pope expounds his integral humanist vision and manifests the Christocentric structure of his theological anthropology primarily through themes of the mystery of the redemption of Christ (*Redemptor hominis*) and the normative significance of mercy (*Dives in misericordia*). Readers of the encyclical on human labor are invited to look at the "social question" with an understanding of the human person and his or her relationship with a merciful and forgiving God in light of the gift of redemption.

The pope's theological anthropology is influenced by the Christocentric perspective crystallized in *Gaudium et spes*. Essentially, humanity is understood in light of Jesus Christ, who is the perfection of what it means to be human. Perhaps the *Pastoral Constitution*'s most significant impact upon John Paul II's teachings, though, was of an indirect nature. Karol Wojtyla was among the bishops who participated in all four conciliar sessions and debates surrounding the drafting of *Gaudium et spes*. In many respects, the *Constitution* confirmed the importance of ideas pursued in his own writings, but it also contributed to the evolution of the future pope's thought.[12] There is ample evidence in LE of the fruits of the Council's impact on John Paul's theology of human labor.

PROCESS OF FORMULATION AND AUTHORSHIP

The substance of LE is the unique contribution of John Paul himself to the social teaching of the Church. The encyclical was originally scheduled for promulgation on May 15, 1981, to commemorate the ninetieth anniversary of *Rerum novarum*, but it was delayed by the assassination attempt of May 13 by Mehmet Ali Agca in St. Peter's Square during the pope's weekly general audience. He revised the document while recuperating in the hospital and during his convalescence at his summer residence, Castel Gandolfo (27).

John Paul seems to have brought his own distinctive experience as a manual worker to bear in reflecting on the issue of human labor. At the stone quarry of Zakrzowek and Solvay furnaces in Borek Falecki, where he worked while his country was under brutal Nazi occupation, Karol Wojtyla was introduced to a new, difficult, and dangerous world of the industrial laborer—the *robotnik*, as he was called in Polish. The quarry was a cold pit hundreds of feet deep in which workers mined limestone and shoveled it into miniature railway cars at the bottom of the pit. Working along with these laborers, the young Wojtyla came to know intimately "their living situations, their families, their interests, and their human worth."[13] He was struck by the innate dignity of these workers expressed in their friendliness, self-sacrifice, and generosity.

Karol Wojtyla later reflected something of this work experience in his "industrial" poetry. Particularly poignant are the images of work contained in poems published under the collective title "The Quarry." It is in part an ode to the beauty and spiritual depth of labor. A stanza from one of these poems offers a glimpse of the pope's profound vision of work that prefigures LE:

> Listen, when cadences of knocking
> hammers so much their own
> I transfer into our inner life, to test the
> strength of each blow—
> Listen: electric current cuts through a river
> of rock—
> Then the thought grows in me day after
> day,
> The whole greatness of this work dwells
> inside a man.[14]

In addition to his work experience, John Paul's philosophical background influenced the categories that constitute the basis of his convictions in LE. His early intuitions about the root crisis of the modern age—a crisis in the very idea of the human person—which began in his late teenage years under Nazi occupation, developed philosophically at the Catholic University of Lublin. From 1951 to 1953 Wojtyla studied phenomenology, personalism, and existentialism under the direction of the Catholic phenomenologist Roman Ingarden. He concentrated on the work of Emmanuel Mounier, Gabriel Marcel, Martin Buber, and above all Max Scheler, who was the focus of Karol Wojtyla's second dissertation.[15] While his writings reveal the influence of the phenomenology of Scheler, John Paul remains in the neo-schololastic tradition in which he was trained. Scheler's phenomenological method and Thomas Aquinas's ethics and metaphysics of being were incorporated, in different ways, into his personalist philosophy of the moral agent.[16] Scholars differ about whether to interpret John Paul's thought as fundamentally phenomenological, borrowing elements from Thomism, or as metaphysical and Thomistic, expanding Thomism with insights from phenomenology. It is not necessary to resolve this debate, but only to recognize that in writing LE he brought both a phenomenologal method and a Thomistic philosophy to the task. Since his election as pope in October 1978, John Paul II has consistently demonstrated a personalist vocabulary, style, and approach to problems.

ESSAY

In LE's introduction, John Paul states that he considers work to be the "essential key" to the "social question if we see it from the point of view of human good" (3). The *social question* is a classic expression born with the problem of labor in the industrial age and addressed by previous popes. For example, *Rerum novarum* focused on the working class; *Quadragesimo anno* expanded the horizon from the working class to the whole nation; *Mater et magistra* and *Octogesima adveniens* advert to the "new proletariat," today's poor in the world. As the tradition develops and is confronted with new problems and issues, labor is seen as integral to world peace and development, to the international equilibrium between industrialized nations and the third world. By focusing on the single issue of human labor, LE marks a shift from the recent tendency in Catholic social teaching to broaden the agenda. Nonetheless, John Paul II has a far more expansive and inclusive view of the meaning of work than his predecessors did.

The encyclical goes beyond *Rerum novarum*'s focus on manual labor to include industrial, agricultural, clerical, scientific, service-oriented, intellectual work, as well as care of the family. Work is more than paid employment; it is about who we are as well as what we do and produce. This broad view of work includes the myriad possibilities of how one can participate in society, contribute to the common good, and develop one's potential. Throughout the encyclical, the meaning of human labor unfolds in a circular way, as John Paul employs various elements of a phenomenological method, shifting from one perspective to another, intertwining biblical, philosophical, and theological perspectives. The method contributes to the frequent criticism that the document is repetitious.

Three additional methodological points are worth noting. First, John Paul II does not start his reflection on human work with an analysis of society or with sociological or economic data, although these are acknowledged to be necessary elements in any good ethical methodology. Rather, the Bible, particularly the Genesis story (1:26–28), is the starting point and "guiding thread" of this "gospel of work" (12). The selection and interpretation of biblical texts, however, are influenced by the pope's own experience. That is to say, from the experience of the quarry and the manual labor he did at the Solvay chemical company, Karol Wojtyla came to understand firsthand that work touched the very essence of the human being. Thus, LE illustrates the important point commonly made in ethics that elements of experience and the concept of the human good discovered in the Bible are interdependent.

Another aspect of the encyclical's methodology is the connection between scripture and natural law. Like *Gaudium et spes*, there is a movement in the encyclical away from a predominant reliance on natural law methodology to its placement in an explicitly theological framework. John Paul asserts that the meaning of work as a fundamental dimension of the person is discoverable through the natural sciences, but "the source of the Church's conviction is above all the revealed word of God, and therefore what is a conviction of the intellect is also a conviction of faith" (4). Principles of natural law such as justice, human rights, solidarity, participation, and the common good are placed within the framework of revelation, but these norms are accessible to reason for all people.

Finally, LE's methodological structure is open to new meanings and new problems of work because the analysis of human labor is done at the foundational, not prescriptive level—the dignity of the human person. The encyclical proposes some general values that underlie particular teachings on social issues, especially the primacy of the subjective over the objective dimensions of work and the priority of labor over capital. There is, however, room for specification by other disciplines and for disagreement about concrete applications and policies. The strengths of this approach are twofold. It properly recognizes the competence and responsibility of others in the development and implementation of the Church's social teaching.[17] It is also open to a wide spectrum of flexible interpretation within particular historic and cultural settings.

With these methodological points as prefatory, LE can be analyzed according to four main themes: theological anthropology of work, the priority of labor over capital, rights of workers, and a spirituality of work.

Theological Anthropology of Work

At the core of LE and the context for understanding John Paul's agenda for social ethics is his theological anthropology. The human person has long been at the center of Catholic social thought and the pope's emphasis on this theme places him squarely in line with the teaching of, for example, Pius XII's Christmas addresses, John XXIII's *Pacem in terris*, and the conciliar documents *Dignitatis humanae* and *Gaudium et spes*. The important insight of this encyclical is the integral connection between the person's self-realization and human labor.

Key to John Paul's theological reflection on the human person is the image of God found in the first chapter of Genesis. The human person is created in the image of God and is appointed to have dominion over all living things. This does not imply exploitation of nature, but rather humankind is called to share in God's governance of the universe, to be the guardians or stewards of nature, entrusted with responsibility for conserving and preserving creation (4). Since the focus is on Genesis 1:26–28, human labor is understood to be a mandate from God before sin entered the world. Work is viewed not as one of the curses of original sin, but positively as a participation in God's continual creative activity. At the same time, while recognizing limitations of capabilities, the human person in some way continues to develop and to perfect that activity as he or she "advances further and further in the discovery of the resources and values in the whole of creation" (25). Even those who engage in the most monotonous, menial, or toilsome types of work, what Christine Firer Hinze calls "dirty work,"[18] are participating in the creative activity of God.

A dynamic interrelation exists between God's action as Creator and the human activity of work. People are called and invited to participate in and carry on God's work daily in the workplace, as *Gaudium et spes* stated, "to be a partner in the work of bringing God's creation to perfection" (67). Workers also have a responsibility to join with God in fashioning both the world and themselves, in effect being "co-creators" with God.[19] Basically, this means that creation is a continuing process, sustained through God's power and love in cooperation with men and women.

The Preeminence of the Subjective Dimension of Work

To further define the meaning of human work, the encyclical distinguishes between objective and subjective dimensions of labor. The source of the dignity of work is found primarily in the subjective dimension (human agency), not in the objective one (type of work done). The fundamental principle of LE is that work is for the person, not the person for work (6). Almost the entire encyclical can be viewed as a meditation on, and drawing out the implications of, this statement. The subjective aspect—the self-realization of men and women through their labor—conditions the ethical nature of work. The priority of the subjective does not mean objective content is irrelevant, but that work has an ethical value of its own, linked to the worker as a person, a conscious and free subject capable of self-determination (6). Simply put, the use of the word *conscious* here and elsewhere in the encyclical (4) means that the person is aware of the significance or insignificance of her actions and capable of self-determination no matter what kind of work it may be.

The basis for determining the value of human labor is not primarily the kind of work being done, but the fact that the one who is doing it is a person. It is the human person who organizes, creates, and bears accountability for the work that is being done, what the pope calls the "transitive" sense of work, that is, objects produced by labor such as agricultural products, manufactured goods, and technology (4). We should note that the encyclical defines the limits of technology by its impact on workers, but it does not acknowledge its limitations on other aspects of the created order such as the environment.

The objective aspect of work expresses humankind's dominion over the world and the ensuing material progress. The concept of dominion, though, refers in a certain sense to the subjective dimension of work more than the objective one (6). That is to say, while the laborer is involved in making, creating, or producing some external object, in the final analysis it is the person from whom the work proceeds who is always work's ultimate object. The *imago Dei* motif is brought forward to emphasize that in work human beings must remain true agents and that both the means of production and the fruits of labor must serve those who work. Thus, as David Hollenbach states: "a major theological contribution of the encyclical . . . lies in the grounding it provides for a very positive evaluation of human work through the interpretation of the *imago Dei* as expressed in the subjectivity of workers."[20]

While drawing upon *Gaudium et spes*'s teaching on human activity and self-development through work (GS 67), John Paul deepens the conciliar understanding of why the worker's subjective dimensions are more important than objective aspects. Work is a fundamental way that people exercise the distinctive human capacity for self-expression and self-realization. Work is not only for one's self; it is also for one's family and for the benefit of the entire human family. Furthermore, work enables people to contribute to the well-being of the larger community and it includes all forms of social participation and contributions to the common good. These three "spheres of values" are always important for human work in its subjective dimension and should govern the activities of the many different communities and institutions that make up society (10; see also EJA 97, 98). If the division and organization of labor become unjust, that is, if the subject character of workers is violated, both the family and nation are harmed. Thus, human labor is both a personal and social activity; it is the mark of a person within a community of persons and should also contribute to building human community.

The "error of economism" occurs when labor is valued only in accordance with its economic purpose; materialism gives primacy and superiority to material factors over the spiritual, placing the person in a subordinate position (13). The pope makes an implicit link between "economism" and "materialism" inasmuch as economic perspectives are associated with tendencies to view human work solely in terms of production and consumption.[21] This distorted order of values is seen whenever work's subjective dimension is trivialized or negated (7). When human labor is viewed only objectively, or when the objective dimension is given a higher value than the subjective, work that is economically unproductive, for example, raising children, participating in voluntary associations, and caring for the elderly, tends to be devalued. Moreover, exploitation occurs whenever economic activity is organized in such ways that there is a denial of subjectivity or a moral failure to recognize the worker's personhood. It is the reversal of means and ends, the use of persons as instruments. While exploitation can result from workers receiving inadequate wages or oppressive working conditions, the fundamental degradation of the worker occurs when personal satisfaction and incentives to creativity and responsibility are lacking (5).

Labor becomes alienating when men and women are denied participation in the work enterprise.[22] The conditions must be present for participation so that, through work, people can gain a fuller experience of their own humanity. Social structures must be evaluated in the light of this basic criterion: Do they create the conditions for the development of participation? Do they obstruct participation and destroy the basic fabric of human existence and activity that must always be realized in common with others?

Priority of Labor over Capital

Before presenting the argument for the priority of labor over capital, the encyclical discusses the "great conflict" that has existed between them since *Rerum novarum*. What John Paul refers to is the socioeconomic class conflict between liberalism (the ideology of capitalism) and Marxism (the ideology of scientific socialism and communism) (11). The pope criticizes both the "unabashed competitiveness" of capitalism as well as Marxist collectivism for separating capital from labor in the sense that the person is subordinated to either profit or class (11). The error of industrial capitalism was to set up capital over against and in opposition to labor, a problem that is repeated whenever the person is treated as an instrument rather than a subject (13). Marxism transformed the conflict into a "systematic class struggle conducted not only by ideological means, but also and chiefly by political means" (11).

The encyclical does not opt for any particular socioeconomic order as the correct one, unlike previous encyclicals that tried to set up a "third way" between extremes of capitalism and socialism, that is, Leo XIII's Christian philosophy and Pius XI's Christian society. LE points out the structural inadequacies of each system (7, 8, 11, 14). For example, the encyclical's teaching on property ownership differs from that of both Marxists and liberal capitalists. Unlike Marxists, the moral legitimacy of the private ownership of productive goods is accepted. Unlike liberal capitalism, though, this is not seen as an absolute right. The "invisible hand" of the market is not to be trusted to harmonize conflicting interests, as some classical economists suggest. Nor will the free market alone solve the problem and "evil" of unemployment (18). The encyclical also differs from Marxism in its interpretation of class conflict. That is to say, the confrontation of workers with the capitalist class is not due to historical necessity or to forces beyond personal option. On the contrary, it emerges from the realization of situations of injustice in the workplace and the awareness that only in solidarity with others can workers gain the power to change the situation.[23]

The encyclical draws upon and develops the theme in Catholic social teaching that there is no intrinsic opposition between labor and capital. The opposition between capital and labor that occurred in history is a contradiction because they are "inseparably linked" (13). Capital, as accumulated labor, is "the result of work and bears the signs of human labor" (12). Yet, labor is distinct from and prior to capital because all capital is the result of human work. All capital is produced by past labor and the means of production are merely instruments of the collective wisdom of the community. Thus, both those who work and those who manage the means of production or who own them must be in some way united. This is reminiscent of Leo XIII's argument that the wealth of nations originates from the labor of workers. Capital and labor are integrally related to each other, and these two classes should exist in harmony and agreement. "Each requires the other; capital cannot do without labor, nor labor without capital" (RN 15). In LE the conflict is largely due to a distorted view of work, for the "fundamental structure of work" is that it first and foremost unites people. In this consists its social power: the power to build a community (20). This does not mean a complete harmony of interests among various groups that participate in the economic process, but the encyclical emphatically rejects the notion of a total conflict between them.

John Paul refutes the antagonism between labor and capital by first recalling that the principle of the priority of labor over capital has always been taught by the Church. Capital is always subservient to labor because of the fundamental claim of human dignity based upon the doctrine of creation. The encyclical states: "the principle of the priority of labor over capital . . . directly concerns the process of production: In this process labor is always a primary efficient cause, while capital, the whole collection of means of production, remains a mere instrument or instrumental cause" (12).

There are several points to consider in order to understand the import of the principle of labor over capital in the encyclical. First, in most instances in the encyclical, capital refers to the machines and natural resources that the capitalists own and use in production as well as the whole collection of means by which natural resources are appropriated and transformed (12). John Paul also speaks of capital as groups of persons, "the small but highly influential group of entrepreneurs, owners or holders of the means of production" (11). In both definitions, labor represents ordinary workers in the economy who lack the means of production and who share in the process of production solely by their labor. It is, however, capital in the former sense—the "whole collection of instruments . . . that is subordinate to labor" (12).

At one point (11) the encyclical appears to associate entrepreneurs with those who own and control capital, but later it suggests that entrepreneurs simply represent the owners of capital. They may not be owners themselves, but rather use the capital of others (14). Yet, entrepreneurs have much at stake, for they not only organize and manage a business undertaking, but also assume risk for the sake of profit. When discussing the development of unions, a distinction is made between entrepreneurs and the owners of capital. The pope observes that "modern unions grew up from the struggle of the workers . . . to protect their just rights vis-à-vis the entrepreneurs and the owners of the means of production" (20). Thus, even though John Paul is critical of those who own and control capital when they subordinate workers to the pursuit of maximum profit, he is not necessarily caviling with entrepreneurs. In fact, in other writings that treat the theme in more depth, entrepreneurs are praised for their creativity, initiative, and ingenuity. At the same time, the pope emphasizes the responsibilities of entrepreneurs and owners of capital to create work, an important element in achieving the common good.[24]

Second, the encyclical concludes the priority of labor over capital based on value criteria, not market or class analysis. John Paul wants to ensure that each person, regardless of the type or nature of work, is the fundamental value around which work processes are organized. The primary basis of the value of work is the human person, not the principle of "maximum profit" or the differentiation of people into classes according to the kind of work done. It is excessive or inordinate profit that is problematic, though, not reasonable or legitimate profit. The encyclical makes explicit what many economists deny—that there are values behind economics (7).

Third, the encyclical connects the priority of labor to property ownership. The only legitimate title to the possession of property, whether in the form of private or collective ownership, is that it "should serve labor and thus . . . should make possible the achievement of the first principle of this order, namely, the universal destination of goods and the right to common use of them" (14). Claims by individuals upon material resources are worthy of response, but no claim is absolute, for the goods of the earth belong to all. "Christian tradition has never upheld this right as absolute and untouchable. On the contrary, it has always understood this right within the broader context of the right common to all to use the goods of the whole creation: The right to private property is subordinated to the right to common use, to the fact that goods are meant for everyone" (14).

Essentially, this principle is grounded in the mystery of creation, which places limitations on ownership because Yahweh is the Lord of creation and thus the only true owner (12). Furthermore, John Paul's perspective follows the Thomistic tradition, which views private property as a "derived or secondary right." Primary rights—the right to food, shelter, and clothing—are those that are necessary for survival. One does not necessarily have to own property to have one's primary rights respected. Private property is a "right" to the extent that it serves a social function, in that it helps to promote right order in society and the stewardship of resources. For Aquinas, private property serves the well-being of humans; the social arrangement of private property cedes priority to the right of all to benefit from the resources of the material world.

Fourth, the priority of labor over capital rests on the personalist argument that workers must have a participatory role in the workplace, sharing in responsibility and with opportunities for creativity and self-initiative (15). Worker participation can assume different forms in different economic systems, such as sharing in decision making and profits, and can be aided by mediating structures such as labor unions. The workplace should be structured to promote the development of workers and to enable them to "know that in his work, even on something that is owned in common, he is working 'for himself'" (15). Bureaucratic centralization prevents this from happening because the person is not really the subject of work. John Paul recommends attention be given to the many proposals put forward by the magisterium: joint ownership of the means of work, sharing by workers in management and/or profits of businesses, and shareholding by labor (14, references to GS 68 and QA 29). Several schemes of ownership may be quite legitimate as long as they respect the requirements of meeting the needs of all. When the pope speaks of "socialization . . . of certain means of production," he does not mean state ownership of the means of production, but broadening ownership in accordance with the principle of common use and the personalist argument (14, 7).

Rights of Workers

LE defends traditional rights of workers to employment, to a just wage, and to form workers' associations in the context of human rights. The encyclical stresses that all these rights belong to agricultural workers (21), disabled persons (22), and emigrants (23). In Catholic social teaching, rights are rooted in human dignity, which is more fundamental than any specific human right. Human dignity makes claims on others that it be recognized and respected. Human rights are the moral imperatives that express the more specific context of these claims. Also, because of the essentially social nature of humankind, the uniqueness and dignity of the person always exists in the context of relations in a larger community. It is in the context of human rights properly understood, promoted, and guaranteed in and through the existence of commonality and solidarity that we should read the encyclical's treatment of workers' rights. Work is viewed as "a right which proves to be just because it is being claimed for others . . . and precisely in that is a sign that it is part of the creative activity of God."[25]

While John Paul offers a more complex vision of solidarity than we find in the writings of previous popes, situating rights language in the context of solidarity is not new. Rather, solidarity serves as the "deep theory" of recent Catholic social teaching.[26] As Philip Land remarked in his reflections on over a half a century of work on official church teaching, "rights are possessed, shared, promoted, guaranteed in and through the existence of commonality, communal being, and solidarity."[27]

It is helpful to recognize the different ways solidarity is defined in this encyclical. Of the nine times *solidarity* is used in number 8 and the one reference in number 20, different aspects of the reality of solidarity are described—as an attitude, a virtue, and a principle. Solidarity is mainly considered as an attitude, an outward direction toward other persons, their needs, and structures of society. For example, the encyclical refers to a "great burst of solidarity between workers," "movements of solidarity," and a world "marked by great solidarity." Solidarity, a natural consequence of human relationality, is the primary authentic attitude toward society that signifies a constant readiness to accept one's share in the community and to serve the common good. It is an attitude of a community in which the common good properly initiates participation, and participation in turn properly serves the common good, fosters it, and furthers its realization.

At the same time, solidarity as a virtue is implied because it refers to the effect of solidarity on the individual's moral growth. As a Christian virtue, it requires a "firm and persevering determination to commit oneself to the common good" (SRS 38). Solidarity has a particular reference to the personalist value of an action. That is, the first end of solidarity as a virtue is the goodness of the person who acts. "When the attitude of solidarity consistently directs the will toward the realization of the common good, it becomes habitual, taking on the characteristics of a virtue, and enabling the will to spontaneously direct participation to the common good."[28]

Solidarity also means a moral obligation that should be the guiding influence in people's lives and their decision making. When the encyclical refers to the solidarity that must be present whenever it is called for by social injustice, the "call to solidarity" and "solidarity that must never be closed to dialogue and collaboration," the term seems to be used as a general principle. As a principle linked with the right to work, this means "we can demand our own right to work all the more that this guarantees the possibility of the right to work of others."[29]

In addition, the encyclical considers rights of workers in view of the direct and indirect employers. The "direct employer" is the person or institution with whom the worker enters directly into a work agreement. Workers have a right to enter into a work contract with the direct employer, to seek work most suited to one's talents, and to freely change jobs. The concept of the indirect employer is one of the more distinctive and effective elements in the encyclical. It refers to many different elements that influence employment and conditions of employment. The indirect employer "includes both persons and institutions of various kinds and also collective labor contracts and the principles of conduct which are laid down by these persons and institutions and which determine the whole socioeconomic system or are its result" (17). This comprises such things as labor legislation, labor unions, transportation systems, child care, job training, and, in particular, government.

The concept of indirect employer reminds us that the responsibility for the disadvantaged and marginalized in society does not lie solely with federal or state governments. Along with the state, businesses, managers, and other social forces have a duty to create conditions in which individuals can realize their right as well as their duty to work. To be without work is to be deprived of the most fundamental means of self-realization. Not only does unemployment harm the individual and his or her family materially, but also without participation in the productive process, individuals are unable to share in the work of creation. For this reason LE appeals to the indirect employer to take every kind of initiative to make it possible for the right to work to be implemented. Furthermore, the notion of indirect employer is not limited to agencies within any particular state. Account must also be taken of links between individual states that create mutual dependence (17). While some commentators have interpreted the concept of indirect employer as a radical indictment of developed countries and their economic systems, its main thrust is more basic. As Robert Destro points out, "In a global economy one cannot evade the moral responsibility for the welfare of workers in other countries by the simple expedient of pointing the finger at the local plantation or sweatshop owner. If one enjoys the fruits of others' labor, one must assume some degree of moral responsibility for their welfare."[30] Indirect employer implies that responsibility for the injustices that mark our world cannot be evaded because there are numerous bodies that have some degree of complicity in these injustices.[31] All people have some level of responsibility for creating a just society and for the laws that govern the workplace. Establishing an ethically correct labor policy, one that respects workers' rights to work, to a just wage, and to form labor associations, the influences of both direct and indirect employers must be taken into consideration.[32]

Right to a Just Wage

The encyclical states that remuneration for work is not only the most important way for securing a just relationship between worker and the employer, but it is also the concrete and "key means" of assessing if a socioeconomic system is functioning justly (19). That is because wages are the most common means by which people have access to the goods of creation. A presumption of Catholic social teaching is that an able-bodied person will obtain these basic goods and necessities of life as the fruit of one's labor or in exchange for it. LE affirms the principle found throughout Catholic social teaching that workers are entitled to at least enough remuneration so that they and their families can live with dignity and in modest comfort. The document emphasizes this point, though, in stating that "above all" the family is the means of verifying if the system is functioning justly. A family wage is described as "a single salary, given to the head of the family for his work, sufficient for the needs of the family without the other spouse having to take up gainful employment outside the home" (19). In addition, John Paul realizes that the market sets the parameters for wages and, consequently, the family wage cannot be determined outside the productive/distributive system in which it finds itself. Wages cannot, however, be determined solely through the market dictated by laws of supply and demand. That is because "implicit in the market wage is the idea that wages can fall below the level necessary to support a family; hence, denying the principle of common use."[33]

While the encyclical contains the strongest statement we find in Catholic social teaching on just wage, it presumes but does not explicate some essential points developed by John Paul's predecessors. For example, *Rerum novarum* emphasized that the poor and helpless—the industrial workers—had a claim to special consideration because the rich population had many ways of protecting themselves and were less in need of help. In addition, there is a certain floor below which a worker's compensation should not fall. Complex factors subject to change will enter into the calculation of what that minimum level will be, and it has to be flexible and in accord with economic realities. Nevertheless, Leo XIII argued that to pay less than a just minimum was to exploit the poverty and misery of the workers and to deprive them of a fair return on their labor (RN 16–17, 34).[34]

Pius XI expanded Leo's teaching on just wages in three ways. First, he added a concern for the state of business and its owners, expressing a firm's capacity for survival as a factor to consider in setting the scale of wages. Second, if it is not feasible in the present state of society to pay a worker a wage sufficient to support him and his family in decent comfort, then social justice demands that "social provisions" or societal reforms be introduced to guarantee every adult workingman such a wage. Third, just wages have to be in accord with requirements of the common good. The wage level should be arrived at with the public economic welfare in mind. A "reasonable relationship" between different wages is to be considered as well as a reasonable relationship between prices obtained for products of various economic groups. Wages should be determined in such a way as to offer the greatest number of opportunities of employment and of securing for workers a suitable means of livelihood (QA 70–74).[35]

While *Mater et magistra* does not treat the issue of just wage as extensively as the preconciliar popes, it does add two new aspects to understanding the meaning of wage justice: the individual's contribution and the need to consider the common good of the entire world economy. Furthermore, the norms of justice and equity must be strictly observed. These standards are absolute and unchanging, but the measure in which they are applied in concrete cases will change considering resources, which vary in quantity and quality among different peoples and in different times (MM 68–72).

LE gives a new twist to the notion of family wage with the proposal that family allowances or grants should be given to mothers devoting themselves exclusively to their families. It should not be necessary for both spouses to be employed outside the home in order to maintain a family's well-being (19). Implied in this legitimate interest in the well-being of the family is the belief that women are by nature primarily guardians of children and the home. Thus, "it is fitting that they should be able to fulfill their tasks in accordance with their own nature." And it is "wrong from the point of view of the good of society and of the family for her to have to abandon these tasks in order to take up paid work outside the home" (19).

One of the important lessons history teaches in regard to the concept of family wage is that it is a historically constructed image, a relative and not an absolute standard with both cultural and social biases. It contains messages about what some people perceive to be just and fair. In the name of justice, though, the family wage has perpetuated gender inequality and a patriarchal view of the family. Inherent in this concept is an ideal that envisions men as the breadwinners and women as caretakers of the home and family. While LE calls for freedom of choice for women to enter the job market or stay at home, it perpetuates these biases with the ideal of motherhood.

Work inside the home, particularly the care of children, is rightly to be valued as equal to public forms of participation and employment. However, as Lisa Sowle Cahill points out, it is not clear to what extent, if any, these important human endeavors ought to be assigned on the basis of sex, or the degree to which "masculine" and "feminine" gender differences are extended to nature beyond physical differences between the sexes.

Sociological studies indicate that culture may be at least as influential as biology in determining social conceptions of appropriate traits and behavior of men and women. Rather than reinforcing traditional gender roles, it is preferable to encourage both sexes to develop the full range of virtues appropriate to humanity. Moreover, "it is important to keep in mind when defining male and female roles that humanly fulfilling work which contributes to the social whole does not belong only to men, nor the fullness of self-giving for others only to women."[36]

LE does call for a "social re-evaluation" of the mother's role, of the work connected with it, and of the need that children have for parental care, love, and affection in order to develop into responsible and morally mature persons (19). While the encyclical avoids an exclusively masculine interpretation of the breadwinner role, the implication remains that the male is indispensable as the provider of material needs for the family and is not fundamentally meant for the domestic role. Furthermore, the pope affirms the right of women, like men, to labor outside the home, and he appeals for equal treatment of women and for work arrangements that support parental responsibilities.

Yet there is no account of *Pacem in terris*, which refers to "the entry of women into public life" and "women's growing sense of their dignity as human persons" as positive "signs of the times." The vision of women presented in LE seems almost oblivious to the dramatic changes and movements that have occurred in the world of women and work. Moreover, the encyclical fails to recognize the systemic nature of sexism and unequal wages that persist in the workplace. Nevertheless, the pope makes a crucial point in stating that care of the family is as important as laboring in the marketplace, and neither parent should be forced to abandon these responsibilities to take up paid work outside the home. The encyclical challenges any public policy that forces a mother to work outside the home, especially when there is inadequate child care or insufficient compensation, or that leads them to deeper poverty.

The encyclical concludes this section by noting that there are other "particular" rights, along with remuneration for work, which must be considered when determining the correct relationship between worker and employer. These include various social benefits that ensure the life and health of workers and their families—the right to a pension and social benefits, especially health care, which "should be easily available for workers and as far as possible be cheap or even free of charge," ample time for rest, and the right to a safe working environment (19).

The Right of Association

The encyclical reaffirms Catholic social teaching's long tradition of support of workers' right to organize and the moral necessity of unions to ensure the exercise of this right. Moreover, LE provides the strongest affirmation of labor unions to be found in Catholic social teaching with the claim that unions are not just legitimate or important, but an "indispensable element of social life" (20). The notion of indirect employer helps to provide a rationale for this indispensability. The use of the word *indispensable* is stronger than Paul VI's statement that unions have an "important" role (OA 14).

The essence of Catholic social teaching on labor unions that the encyclical proffers is that people have a natural right to participate in the decisions affecting their lives and a right to free association. The right of workers to form unions or other associations to secure their rights is a specific application of the more general right of association. The right to organize is based in the personal and necessary character of work and also in human sociality. The state does not have a right to forbid workers' associations, but they can be regulated. Workers should have the freedom to form associations that will secure their just rights within the framework of the common good of society. If properly oriented toward the common good, unions present an opportunity for solidarity with all workers.

The encyclical calls for new movements of solidarity of workers and with workers whenever they are degraded or exploited. Because of its mission—fidelity to Christ as a "church of the poor" (8)—the Church is called to support solidarity among workers. John Paul specifically mentions the need for solidarity among groups of people who may have had a privileged position in the past but now find themselves in a "proletariat situation." These would include some categories of working "intelligentsia" (8). The point is that the proletariat is no longer confined to those who work with their hands, but refers to industrial workers as well as all men and women working in industries. Thus, "Marxist descriptions are no longer adequate to describe the present reality."[37]

Even if it is because of their work needs that people unite to secure their rights, the "ethical vocation" of labor unions is to move beyond the struggle for improving their own circumstances and to promote solidarity and social justice.[38] In a spirit of solidarity, unions are to use their power not only for their own self-interest, but also for the good of the whole society, especially those who are weakest and marginalized. When the pope states that "it is characteristic of work that it first and foremost unites people," he recognizes the important role of unions in promoting worker participation, which is necessary, though may be insufficient, to achieve that unity (20).

Union activity may enter the sphere of politics to accomplish its goals, but "unions do not have the character of political parties struggling for power"; they should not become political parties or have too close links with them. Political involvement is limited to those issues essential for unions to pursue their proper purpose (20). While the pope seems to have the Polish situation in mind, this is a valid and important general principle for all labor unions. When organized labor is too closely aligned with a political party, there is a danger of its losing its essential and primary aim, which is to defend and protect the dignity and rights of the worker. In addition, when organized labor devotes too much time and resources to political activity, it runs the risk of neglecting other aspects of its mission such as organizing and monitoring internal union practices. And when labor is too closely aligned with a particular political party, it may not only be co-opted, but unions can also become irrelevant when the opposing party is in power, thus losing their potential to be effective advocates for just labor legislation. Application of the principle in concrete situations or different contexts, though, requires prudential judgment to determine when it is appropriate for unions to become politically involved, what is exactly meant by being "too closely linked," or what legislation should be supported to protect workers' dignity and rights.[39]

Strikes are regarded as legitimate in the labor struggle, but must be undertaken under appropriate conditions and within just limits. Essentially, they should be a last resort to promote workers' rights. Collaboration through collective bargaining is an essential means of securing cooperation between workers and employers as well as achieving social justice. Even in conflictual situations, unions should engage in some form of constructive opposition "for the good of social justice, not for the sake of 'struggle' or in order to eliminate the opponent" (20). While the word *struggle* is used several times when the pope addresses the role of trade unions, it is qualified by the language that it is a struggle "for" justice rather than "against" other people or classes (20). Instead of evoking images of divisiveness, solidarity suggests that the primary thrust of workers' activity is toward unity and community. This does not eliminate the possibility of confrontation with those who try to maintain situations and structures that dehumanize the worker, but it calls for dialogue and collaboration as the primary way to address injustice (8). The pope's reluctance to concede the necessity of struggle that involves conflict is indicative of the persistent tendency in Catholic social teaching to bring about social change through nonconflictual means.[40] Additionally, he may be trying to avoid connotations of the word *struggle* that could be associated with Marxist analysis.

Elements for a Spirituality of Work

In this final section, John Paul's meditation on the "gospel of work" reaches its apex. Since work in its subjective aspect is always a personal action, it follows that the whole person, body and spirit, participates in it. The Church has a duty to bring out the human and moral value of work and to foster a spirituality of work so that through their labor people may come closer to God, participate in God's salvific plan for humankind and the world, and deepen their friendship with Christ (24). The encyclical proposes a vision of the spiritual life that is not limited to prayer, contemplation, or worship, but includes work. A similar, and more explicit, connection between the work of the laity and the spiritual life, though, is found in *Mater et magistra*. As Marvin Mich points out, the encyclical "signals a dramatic shift of spirituality from a spirit of detachment to a spirit of engagement." John XXIII provides an "integrating perspective" of labor as enhancing personal dignity, serving the needs of the community, and being essential to the spiritual journey toward God.[41]

The gospel of labor in LE opens work to a spiritual interpretation that has three essential elements drawn from *Gaudium et spes* and applied to the world of work. First, aspects of the theme of creation introduced earlier (4) are reiterated: made in God's image, people have been given dominion over the earth, and in daily work they participate in God's creative activity. Work is a vocation to which human beings have been called "from the beginning." Here the pope adds that people share in the activity of the Creator and imitate God in both working and resting (25). While there is no extended reflection on leisure, the encyclical affirms its importance with respect to a person's divine calling to participate in God's creative activity. That is to say, leisure is a safeguard against becoming completely bound up in work and neglecting to give thanks and praise to God for the gift of life.

Second, a spirituality of labor draws from the experience of Christ, a "man of work" who had an appreciation and respect for human work. Moreover, it is in the context of the proclamation of the reign of God that Jesus' words and images of labor are to be understood. So, too, in contemporary situations, human work is significant and reflective of God's presence through the right and just ordering of human life. The "glimmer of new life" that the mature Christian discovers through work contributes not only to "earthly progress," but also to the development of the reign of God.

Third, the Christological emphasis in a spirituality of labor is also seen in consideration of the "sweat and toil" that accompanies human work. John Paul recognizes the distasteful, even painful aspects of work, but does not limit his perceptions to so narrow a focus. Experientially, even the most mundane and repetitious work can provide fulfillment and contribute to personal, familial, and human good. The encyclical deals with the toilsome aspect of work in two ways. First, despite the toil, work is a "bonum arduum" (9). A reference is made to Thomas Aquinas's meaning of the human good and virtue to support the claim that even in the most burdensome kinds of work, labor is a difficult good.

Work is a good thing for humankind because through work the human person not only transforms nature (the creative aspect), but also achieves fulfillment and becomes even more human (9). This is a self-realizing moral good that the pope associates with the development of virtue in the Thomistic sense. The moral virtues are the dispositions that enable individuals to sustain a course of activity and to pursue the human good that perfects them as human beings. To become "more of a human being," one must act in accordance with virtue. At the same time, realization of the moral good for which humankind was created requires acting in accordance with what it means to be a good human being. The greatest value of a worker's actions lies in her or his capacity to contribute to the struggle to achieve self-fulfillment and the common good by developing morally virtuous habits. For this reason work in itself is a good thing for people.[42] Workers should to be able to participate in the workplace in such a way, though, that they have the freedom to develop the virtues that are appropriate to work such as industriousness and solidarity.[43]

A second aspect is that the toil of work has spiritual significance as a participation in the cross of Christ: "By enduring the toil of work in union with Christ crucified for us, man in a way collaborates with the son of God for the redemption of humanity. He shows himself a true disciple of Christ by carrying the cross in his turn every day in the activity that he is called upon to perform" (27). Reiterating a theme that permeates *Redemptor hominis*—that Christ reveals what it means to be truly human, and this includes suffering love—John Paul suggests that Jesus is one with humanity through the suffering and toil that accompany human labor. Seen through the perspective of faith, work achieves its fullest meaning as part of the paschal mystery. The difficulties of labor are a way of following and sharing in the salvific and redeeming cross of Christ. As the paschal mystery involves both the cross of Christ and the resurrection, so, too, human work involves both weariness and a "new good," an announcement of "the new heavens and the new earth" (27).

EXCURSUS

The plethora of reactions and controversy surrounding the encyclical can be attributed, at least in part, to the particular stance of the interpreter, that is, political, economic, and feminist. While these various perspectives provide important insights, they tend to overlook or pay insufficient attention to the philosophical lens through which John Paul views the question of human labor. Along with the "gospel of work," his personalist philosophy provides a stance from which to offer a critique on any political or economic system.[44] The pope's theological anthropology is grounded in the mystery of creation and the revelation of God in Jesus Christ. This anthropology discloses a spiritual dimension of the person within the philosophical framework of the person revealed in action.

John Paul's Personalist Philosophy

There are a variety of ways to interpret the concept of personalism, but essentially it can be used to characterize any philosophy that asserts the primacy of the distinctive reality and worth of the person. Many twentieth-century thinkers were known as personalists. Immanuel Kant's philosophy can be called personalist to the extent that he made the notion of the person central in his ethics. The existentialism of Kierkegaard was a personalist outcry against Hegelian thought, which threatened to submerge transcendence and the distinctive identity of the person in monistic idealism. Even an atheistic existentialist like Sartre was concerned with the authenticity of personal life in at least some aspects.

John Paul's personalist philosophy is rooted in the classical Christian tradition of Thomas Aquinas. Thomistic personalism lies at the basis of his ethics, his anthropology, and his major pronouncements since the beginning of his papacy.[45] Karol Wojtyla expressly acknowledged the Thomistic influence on his notion of personalism in the preface to his philosophical magnum opus, *The Acting Person*. He describes his task as one of explaining human nature through a phenomenological analysis of the person in action. This text will serve as the basis for explaining three key aspects of the pope's notion of personalism that permeate LE.[46]

First, Karol Wojtyla explores the relationship between action as *actus humanus* and action as experience.[47] That is, the issue is not just the metaphysical objectification of the human being as an acting subject, as the agent of acts, but the "revelation of the person as a subject experiencing its acts and inner happenings, and with them its own subjectivity."[48] While "being is prior to action" (action follows existence) and the person is prior to and more fundamental than the value of the action, it is in actions that the person manifests him or her self.[49] In the encyclical, this occurs through all types of work-acts. Every work-action, no matter how marginal or burdensome, involves self-determining choices and thus either confirms or diminishes self-realization.

The second essential aspect of John Paul's Thomistic personalist philosophy undergirding the encyclical is the notion of human activity as simultaneously transitive and intransitive. Wojtyla states that human activity is "transitive insofar as it tends beyond the subject, seeks an expression and an effect in the external world, and is objectified in some product. It is intransitive, on the other hand, insofar as it remains in the subject, [and] determines the subject's immanent quality of value."[50] While John Paul refers to transitive action in the encyclical (4), and does not use the word *intransitive*, it is clear that he intends this meaning in light of his description of "transitive" and "intransitive" dimensions of action in *The Acting Person*.[51] The intransitive is implied in the encyclical when the pope discusses the subjective sense of work (4, 6, 25).

What is meant by intransitive is that all human actions have an inescapable inner effect that morally shapes the person. Human labor's intransitive effect begins when workers utilize their unique capacities as conscious subjects to make choices about an external object. In the process, each person simultaneously makes a self-determining decision. Self-realization through work does not mean doing whatever one desires to do, but attaining that which is in accord with one's "calling" to be a person and in accord with the common good. The emphasis is upon the link between a person's status as the subject of work and personhood. "Not only does work assume significance beyond its objective effects . . . but . . . the human subject's work-acts are always acts of the person."[52]

The third aspect of the pope's notion of personalism worth noting is that to be self-possessed presupposes consciousness, which is an "intrinsic and constitutive aspect . . . of the acting person."[53] By conscious thought is meant that human beings, having free will, are able to deliberate on the relation between means and ends, and thus have responsibility for their actions. This presumes the conscious person is aware of the significance or insignificance of her or his actions and is capable of self-determination. The importance of recognizing what the pope means by the term *conscious* used in the encyclical (4, 6) is that it helps to explain the optimistic view of even the most seemingly mundane and trivial kinds of work. It also points to the need for consciousness-raising or what liberation theologians refer to as "conscientization," when people lack the sense of being self-possessed, self-governing, and self-determining. Consciousness-raising enables workers to recognize when they are treated as objects rather than subjects, to take responsibility for their actions, and to transform oppressive work situations. In the process of transforming the situation, a new, more human, and self-determining person may be created.[54] Thus, in order to "work for oneself" (to possess and fulfill the self), consciousness-raising may be needed to enable the laborer to engage in self-determining activity.

In sum, when a personalist hermeneutic is used to interpret the encyclical, it cannot be claimed as a Marxist, socialist, or capitalist manifesto. At the same time, if workers are self-possessed (purposive and deliberative), self-governing, and self-determining, if they are able to achieve self-realization through work-acts, then a variety of political or economic systems may be acceptable. It is not the intent of the encyclical, though, to make this determination.

Challenges for the Future

LE provides a good foundation and several building blocks for developing an ethic of discipleship in the workplace. The challenge for the future is to construct an edifice that more closely reflects the reign of God, one that promotes justice for workers, fosters solidarity, and enables workers to become virtuous and self-determining. There are several elements of the encyclical's ethic of human labor that contribute toward achieving this goal and that present challenges for the future. There are other aspects that require further development. We begin with the problematic areas.

First, LE's ethic of human labor is grounded in scripture, which is meant to provide guidance for disciples in the workplace. In some cases, though, the lack of careful exegesis of a text leads to missing the point of what the text meant in its early form. For example, there is a reference to the Tower of Babel in connection with the example of the worker as "builder" (26, number 52). But as David Hollenbach points out, the Tower of Babel is actually a story about the division of humankind caused by human society's alienation from God and from one another. Furthermore, the pope's selective use of the creation story to interpret work's theological significance relies almost exclusively on the Priestly source and neglects the Yahwist tradition. The Priestly account is quite optimistic about the ability of human beings to form bonds of solidarity and to achieve harmonious cultural and societal integration. Yahwistic theology, on the other hand, is more attuned to the "riddles and conflicts" of human behavior, and the "mistakes and muddles" present in the human heart. Because achievements of human creativity can lead to rebellion against God and actions that harm persons and communities, the Yahwist account of creation is needed along with the Priestly narrative to formulate a balanced biblical theology of work.[55]

Some legitimate criticisms have also been made of the encyclical's linkage of the toil of work and the cross of Christ. Arguments center around three points: (1) the cross of Christ is not just a symbol of life's difficulties, but a unique and specific instance of suffering; (2) to equate the "toil" of work with the sufferings of Christ without attending to its causes in particular cases can lead one to overlook social injustice; and (3) John Paul's "co-redemptive" view of the toil of human labor seems to imply that the more unpleasant work is, the more fully it is a participation in Christ's sufferings, and, paradoxically, the more redemptive it is.[56] In short, the treatment of Genesis and of the cross suggests the encyclical's ethic of human labor needs a critical theory of biblical interpretation.

Second, an ethic of human labor requires more attention to social sin and structures than the encyclical provides. There is a danger that the very positive and optimistic view of work that flows from the mystery of creation can bestow a false aura of religious legitimacy to social structures that contribute to work that is meaningless or dehumanizing. There are alienating patterns of work and international distribution of labor that threaten human dignity. While the encyclical points to the role of socioeconomic systems in the priority of labor (12) and the problem of unemployment (18), it does not sufficiently or critically address the relation between subjectivity and social structures. LE does not treat the way that unjust labor systems negatively impact consciousness and one's sense of personhood. The challenge is to create the conditions that make it possible to offer work that satisfies the requirement of self-realization and that enables participation in the workplace. The magnitude of this challenge can be seen in light of globalized capitalism and its impact on the world of work and the character of workers. A sense of insecurity and helplessness is unavoidable when businesses close and corporations move to another part of the world to seek cheaper wages and union-free environments without adequate consideration of the effects on workers left behind.

Third, an ethic that gives priority to labor over capital must acknowledge and address the tension that exists between this harmonious ideal and conflictual reality. Defining what is reasonable or legitimate profit, determining the responsibility of employers and employees to the common good, or establishing democracy in the workplace are divisive issues. They cannot be resolved simply by stating that the fundamental structure of work is that it first and foremost unites people, or declaring that the priority of labor over capital has always been taught by the Church. Also, conflict is unavoidable when solidarity is linked with the right to work. For example, when there is high unemployment, to whom is the right to work granted—to one person in a family, to single people, to the most disadvantaged, to men, to immigrants? This issue also becomes more complex in the context of globalization. Solidarity with disadvantaged workers in less developed nations often conflicts with solidarity among working people in the United States. Another thorny issue concerns how the legitimate right to organize as well as the right to strike and the right to a just wage are to be exercised in practice in accord with the principle of solidarity, especially when dialogue and collaboration break down.

Positively, the encyclical's broad definition of work and appreciation for all types of work moves us away from the differentiation of people into classes according to the kind of work done,[57] and the erroneous distinction often made between "work of the hands and minds" and "labor of our bodies." As these two broad types of work tend to be defined, labor is a human activity that implies pain and toil whereas the "work of our hands and minds" connotes a more creative kind of human activity. Historically, the work of our hands and minds has been valued more highly, and thus rewarded more richly, than the labor of our bodies.[58] Furthermore, in accord with this broad definition, work within the home is to be honored as much as work in the marketplace since it is sharing in God's creative activity. And those who care for the family deserve just remuneration because of their contribution to the building up of society. This viewpoint provides a challenge to current welfare-to-work policy in the United States that requires able-bodied welfare recipients to work regardless of family needs and without provisions for adequate child care. This expansive view of labor also contains some ambiguity about what actually counts as work. For example, are actions on behalf of justice work? Is painting that one does as a hobby but with intent to sell considered work? Are spiritual practices that require discipline and persistence part of human labor? While the encyclical does not address these questions, it is clear that the definition of work is contrary to any economic analysis that considers labor solely as a commodity whose value is determined by the supply and demand of labor in a competitive market.

In addition, the encyclical expands the scope of labor unions. That is, the dominant interest of labor unions should extend far beyond the customary concerns of unions with job security, wages, benefits, and workplace conditions. Their primary concern and "indispensable" role is to enable working peoples throughout the world to be brought effectively into the forum of decision making about what forms of production might be most conducive to the welfare and advancement of all life.[59] This presents a challenge to create democratic communities in the workplace that foster participation and enable creativity. Individuals become self-governing through habit, by repeatedly and regularly engaging in acts of self-government. Democracy is endangered when people do not have direct responsibility for making the day-to-day decisions about the order of their lives. This also has serious implications for public life, for if citizens spend much, if not most, of their lives in work situations that are not participatory and undemocratic, then it is unlikely they will engage in robust critical dialogue in civic society. Thus, creating democratic communities in the workplace is an important challenge for labor and society.

Finally, the encyclical proffers a vision of work as "transformative vocation." That is, work is a way men and women collaborate in the ongoing creation and re-creation of self, the workplace, and the world.[60] This stance, grounded in John Paul's "gospel of work," theological anthropology, and personalist philosophy of action, implies that workers are to be viewed not merely as employees or resources, but as agents who should be fully respected as partners in a cooperative enterprise. With this transformative vision of labor, the encyclical reflects a basic assumption of liberation theology that the "ontological vocation" of each human person is to be a subject who acts upon and transforms the world. In so doing, there is growth toward a fuller and richer individual and collective life. This is the encyclical's most important challenge for the future.

REACTIONS TO THE DOCUMENT

Reactions to LE in the United States and other parts of the world ranged from praise for its "great relevance and impressive freshness"[61] to criticisms that it was "a bit old hat"[62] and "essentially irrelevant."[63] It was characterized as "the most amazing papal document" issued in nearly 500 years,[64] and the "most important document ever devoted to social teaching of the Church by a sovereign pontiff."[65] Even when it was criticized for being too long and repetitious or for its lack of collegiality in authorship,[66] the encyclical was lauded for being a "refreshing and even exciting" contribution to Catholic social teaching.[67]

In the United States the encyclical was viewed positively by some as a rich and thoughtful document that interprets the "social question" in light of the signs of the times while remaining faithful to the social doctrine of the past. It was seen as bringing together in an "authoritative way" the general teaching on problems affecting the place of work. Offering general principles that can be endorsed in secular society in a period of "rampant relativism" was viewed as a necessary and important contribution.[68] On the other hand, the encyclical was criticized by others as utopian. Unlike Pope Paul VI's turn to the local churches to discern the signs of the times, John Paul II offers an ideal vision for the renewal of society.[69] The encyclical was also favorably assessed for its concern with transnational issues and for the debate it engendered about national and international policies.[70]

From the perspective of organized labor, LE provided moral and religious support for many of the developments in labor management relations. The pope spoke directly to issues that confronted leaders of American business and labor such as quality of work programs, workers' participation in managerial decisions, and employer-employee cooperation for labor cost reduction. Confronted with weak, even antilabor legislation and employer opposition to unions, the encyclical's endorsement of unions as "indispensable" and its support of worker solidarity gave "trade unionists great heart."[71]

The cacophony of reactions from women in the United States and abroad tended to be mostly negative. In addition to the almost universal disdain for the dominance of sexist language in the encyclical, much of the criticism focused upon the pope's view of the proper and principal role of women as mothers. While recognizing the positive implications of the concept of a "social re-evaluation of the mother's role," the primary mission of a mother as a homemaker negates the view of a woman as a human person with needs, wants, rights, and responsibilities independent of her relationship to husband and children.[72] Some of the strongest reactions to John Paul's view of women emerged in the Italian press. LE was seen as taking a step backward in contrast to John XXIII's welcoming the entry of women into public life. The encyclical was attacked as "absurd" in its references to women and doomed to failure in its efforts to "push women back into the home." The fundamental critique was that "for the role of man, work is an instrument of self-realization; for the role of woman, it is only a 'bitter necessity.'"[73]

Other reactions to the encyclical outside the United States were mixed. *The Tablet* commented that while the encyclical does not break new ground, it does "bring to life in today's context a series of principles often obscured by language they were written in."[74] Oswald von Nell-Breuning called attention to John Paul as a worker; unlike previous popes, he could speak to the subject of work from his own experience.[75] René Coste commented on the pope's methodology of using both faith and reason in reflecting on the depth of the human person at work, which he considered to be "the most interesting, stimulating, and, in the long term, fruitful aspect of LE."[76] Marie-Dominique Chenu applauded John Paul's positive theology of labor, but noted that the overall situation of humankind calls for a more realistic interpretation. The Paris Protestant weekly *Réforme* found nothing new politically in the encyclical. An editorial stated that the encyclical's recommendation of a "third way" as a solution of social problems, while a noble goal, is based on a false analysis. And the "petrified argumentation" of the encyclical is based on natural law theology overflowing with postulates, "tricky exegeses," and clichés.[77]

In Latin America the encyclical received wide coverage and mostly positive reactions in response to what was perceived as a clear attempt by John Paul to interweave concerns of the Third World with papal social teaching on labor. LE was seen to be in continuity with the Puebla Documents of the Third Assembly of the Latin American Bishops.[78] The encyclical was praised for several elements that resonated with a theology of liberation: the inductive methodology from the situation and praxis of work and the workers;[79] the spirituality of work; the call for a "church of the poor"; and its "liberating theology," that is, the liberation of the poor, the priority of the worker over capital, and solidarity with the workers.[80] In addition to these points of convergence with liberation theology, Gustavo Gutiérrez commended the encyclical for the challenge it poses to address social injustices, particularly the responsibility to change economic structures that violate rights of workers.[81]

The theology of work in LE was also viewed as important and relevant to the South African situation, particularly the core concepts of the dignity of the human person and the notion of work as co-creation. The hope was that these themes and the "spiritual tone" of the encyclical would encourage creativity and responsibility, and would help to rescue Africa from economic secularism and materialism. In addition, with its emphasis on the priority of the subjective over objective dimensions of labor, the encyclical provided a principle to help African policy makers strike a balance between rigid capitalism and extreme collectivism. The concept of indirect employer could help African leaders recognize that some problems in labor and productivity are controlled by factors beyond the worker and his or her direct employer.[82]

While the encyclical received scant attention in the Asian press, it was viewed positively by those who saw its potential to shed new light on the concept of human work as a subjective experience that enhances human dignity and self-realization. The reactions could be summarized as hopeful that the concept of the human person would be a "powerful liberating force in the development of Asia. Its profound theological roots and connotation are too often slurred over in the thinking of Asian Catholics."[83]

In Poland there was an enthusiastic response to the encyclical in part because it was authored by a Polish pope and also because it seemed to support a convergence of ideas with *Solidarność*. Of vital importance to the Polish people, especially for the fledgling Solidarity movement, was LE's support of free associations of workers and its description of unions as "indispensable." Poles also found in the encyclical an inspiration to improve society and to create a new social order. The spirituality of work, especially the emphasis on the connection of toil with the cross and resurrection, was "crucially expressive" of the situation in Poland.[84]

One of the most controversial aspects of the encyclical is whether it favors a Marxist, socialist, or capitalist system to achieve its vision of human labor. Or does it provide a "third way" between the extremes of capitalism and socialism, implying an opening toward democratic socialism?[85] Some Marxists read the encyclical as an indictment of capitalism.[86] Gregory Baum has noted that "Catholics who have followed the recent shift to the left in the Church and have acquired socialist sympathies are delighted with the encyclical and understand it as confirmation of the direction in which they have moved."[87] Michael Novak, on the other hand, sings praise for this "brilliant encyclical" as a defense of private property.[88] Some economists have interpreted LE as misrepresenting capitalism and displaying "the evidently invincible determination of the Church not to understand capitalism."[89]

It is unsurprising that various commentators on the left and right would seek to find in LE some passage or section to support their positions. What remains beyond dispute, however, is the papal insistence that workers are to be seen as transformative actors, capable not only of changing the objective world by their labor but, in so doing, becoming also fully human subjects whose dignity and vocation must be respected.

NOTES

1. The first two encyclicals are *Redemptor hominis* (1979) and *Dives in misericordia* (1980).

2. J. Bryan Hehir, "A New Era of Social Teaching," *Commonweal* 108 (October 23, 1981): 585, 607.

3. George Weigel, *Witness to Hope: The Biography of Pope John Paul II* (New York: HarperCollins, 1999), 403–7.

4. Lech Walesa, *A Way of Hope: An Autobiography* (New York: Henry Holt, 1987), 164–65.

5. Gregory Baum, *The Priority of Labor: A Commentary on Laborem Exercens, Encyclical Letter of Pope John Paul II* (New York: Paulist, 1983), 74.

6. Weigel, *Witness to Hope*, 421.

7. Ronald Preston, "Pope John Paul II on Work," *Theology* 86 (January 1983): 19–24.

8. George H. Williams, *The Mind of John Paul II* (New York: Seabury, 1981), 11, 45. Williams notes that John Paul refers to himself as the "Slavic Pope."

9. Eric O. Hanson, *The Catholic Church in World Politics* (Princeton, N.J.: Princeton University Press, 1987), 345.

10. Romano Rossi, *The Social Teaching of John Paul II: Human Labour* (Vatican City: Pontifical Commission for Justice and Peace, 1981), 19.

11. Tad Szulc maintains the pope's presence "unquestionably" played a part in accelerating events in his native country. In *Pope John Paul II: The Biography* (New York: Scribner, 1995), 307.

12. Samuel Gregg, *Challenging the Modern World: Karol Wojtyla/John Paul II and the Development of Catholic Social Teaching* (Lanham, Md.: Lexington, 1999), 45.

13. Pope John Paul II, *Gift and Mystery* (New York: Doubleday, 1996), 21–22.

14. Karol Wojtyla, "Material," in *Easter Vigil and Other Poems*, trans. Jerzy Peterkiewicz (New York: Random House, 1979), 25.

15. Wojtyla's dissertation on Max Scheler led to the first of his philosophical books: *The Possibility of the Foundation of Christian Ethics on the Philosophy of Max Scheler*. His first doctoral thesis was titled "Problems of Faith in the Writings of St. John of the Cross." It reflected his concern with atheism in personalist circles in the period of the 1940s.

16. See Ronald Modras, "The Thomistic Personalism of Pope John Paul II," *Modern Schoolman* 59 (January 1982):117–27; and "The Moral Philosophy of John Paul II," *Theological Studies* 41 (1980): 683–97.

17. Richard McCormick, "*Laborem Exercens* and Social Morality," in *Official Catholic Social Teaching, Readings in Moral Theology, No. 5*, ed. Charles E. Curran and Richard A. McCormick (New York: Paulist, 1986), 219–32.

18. Christine Firer Hinze, "Dirt and Economic Inequality: A Christian-Ethical Peek under the Rug," *The Annual: Society of Christian Ethics* 21 (2001): 45–62.

19. While John Paul II does not use the word *co-creation*, it is clearly implied. See *Co-Creation and Capitalism: John Paul II's Laborem Exercens*, ed. John W. Houck and Oliver F. Williams (Washington, D.C.: University Press of America, 1983).

20. David Hollenbach, "Human Work and the Story of Creation," in ibid., 65.

21. Gregg, *Challenging the Modern World*, 114–15.

22. Wojtyla, "Participation or Alienation?" in *Person and Community: Selected Essays*, trans. Theresa Sandok, O.S.M. (New York: Peter Lang, 1993), 206. See also *Redemptor hominis*, number 15, where the

pope states that people are "under threat" from what they produce, from manual labor, the work of the intellect, as well as the tendencies of the will. What this manifold activity too often yields, and in unforeseeable ways, "is not only subjected to 'alienation,' in the sense that it is simply taken away from the person who produces it, but rather it turns against man himself, at least in part, through the indirect consequences of its effects returning on himself" (15).

An interesting point here is that John Paul clearly is using a Marxist term and his comment is reminiscent of Marx's writing on alienation, such as the following from *Economic and Philosophic Manuscripts of 1844*:

> "What then constitutes the alienation of labor? First the fact that labor is external to the worker, i.e., it does not belong to his essential being. . . . He is at home when he is not working, and when he is working he is not at home. His labor is therefore not voluntary, but coerced; it is forced labor. . . . Lastly, the external character of labor for the worker appears in the fact that it is not his own, but someone else's, that it does not belong to him, that in it he belongs not to himself, but to another. . . .
>
> We have considered the act of estranging practical human activity, labor, in two of its aspects. 1. The relation of the worker to the product of labor as an alien object exercising power over him. . . . 2. The relation of labor to the act of production within the labor process. This relation is the relation of the worker to his own activity as an alien activity not belonging to him.

23. Baum, *Priority of Labor*, 29. It should be noted that there are thinkers within the Marxist tradition whose views on some issues are close to those of Pope John Paul II, that is, a nondeterminist view of history and the role of human responsibility, that human solidarity is more basic than the class struggle. While there are differences between the pope's view on work and the worker and "critical" Marxists, there seems to be room for dialogue. See Donal Dorr, *Option for the Poor: A Hundred Years of Catholic Social Teaching* (Maryknoll, N.Y.: Orbis, 1992), 308–11.

24. In CA, the pope discusses the contributions and responsibilities of the owners of capital and entrepreneurs in more depth. See the Commentary on *Centesimus annus* by Daniel Finn in this volume. For an examination of the theme of entrepreneurship in Catholic social teaching, see Francis Hannafey, "Entrepreneurship in Papal Thought," *Louvain Studies* 26 (2001): 217–44.

25. Dietmar Mieth, "Solidarity and the Right to Work," in *Concilium* 160 *Unemployment and the Right to Work*, ed. Jacques Pohier and Dietmar Mieth (New York: Seabury Press, 1982), 58–65.

26. Michael J. Himes and Kenneth R. Himes, *Fullness of Faith: The Public Significance of Theology* (New York: Paulist, 1993), 169. The authors borrow the expression *deep theory* from Drew Christiansen, "On Relative Equality: Catholic Egalitarianism after Vatican II," *Theological Studies* 45 (1984): 651–75. Christiansen in turn borrowed this phrase from Ronald Dworkin, *Taking Rights Seriously* (Cambridge, Mass.: Harvard University Press, 1977).

27. Philip S. Land, *Catholic Social Teaching: As I Have Lived, Loathed, and Loved It* (Chicago: Loyola University Press, 1994), 72.

28. Kevin P. Doran, *Solidarity: A Synthesis of Personalism and Communalism in the Thought of Karol Wojtyla/Pope John Paul II* (New York: Peter Lang, 1996), 160. On the various ways of describing solidarity, as a principle, attitude, or virtue, see 192–93.

29. Mieth, "Solidarity and the Right to Work," 63.

30. Robert Destro, "Work: The Human Environment," in *Building the Free Society: Democracy, Capitalism, and Catholic Social Teaching*, ed. George Weigel and Robert Royal (Grand Rapids, MI: Eerdmans, 1993), 178.

31. Dorr, *Option for the Poor*, 291–94.

32. Determining one's moral responsibility for workers in other countries or complicity in the injustices that mark our world is a complex and controversial matter. In the Catholic tradition, the category of cooperation with evil guides deliberations about whether to perform an act that contributes to the morally objectionable action of another. It covers cases in which people are confronted with a decision about whether they should perform an action that in some way assists another's morally objectionable activity. As M. Kathleen Kaveny convincingly argues, however, this principle needs to be supplemented by a new category—appropriation of evil—that better illumines problems such as purchasing clothing made in sweatshops located in developing countries. The

category of appropriation of evil "covers the 'mirror image' situations in which agents wonder whether they can *take advantage* of the fruits or byproducts of someone else's wrongful acts in order to facilitate their own morally worthwhile activity." See "Appropriation of Evil: Cooperation's Mirror Image," *Theological Studies* 61, no. 2 (2000): 218–330.

33. Michael Naughton, *The Good Stewards: Practical Application of the Papal Social Vision of Work* (Lanham, MD: University Press of America, 1992), 76.

34. See "The Rights of Workers" in Thomas Shannon's Commentary on *Rerum novarum* in this volume.

35. See "A Just Wage" in Christine Firer Hinze's Commentary on *Quadragesimo anno*.

36. Lisa Sowle Cahill, "Women, 'Respect for Life,' and the Church in the United States," *Social Thought* 13 (1987): 74–86. See Cahill's Commentary on *Familiaris consortio* in this volume.

37. Dorr, *Option for the Poor*, 307.

38. Gregory Baum, "Laborem Exercens," in *The New Dictionary of Catholic Social Thought*, ed. Judith A. Dwyer (Collegeville, Minn.: Liturgical, 1994), 523.

39. Peter Hebblethwaite questions the relevance of the encyclical's viewpoint for those situations where unions are constitutionally linked with Western socialist parties. See "The Popes and Politics: Shifting Patterns in 'Catholic Social Doctrine,'" in *Religion and America: Spiritual Life in a Secular Age*, ed. Mary Douglas and Steven Tipton (Boston: Beacon, 1983), 190–203. See also P. Hebblethwaite, "The Pope and the Unions," *The Tablet* 12 (April 1986): 368–69.

40. See the first section of the Commentary on *Justitia in mundo* by Kenneth Himes in this volume.

41. See the section titled "An Immanent Spirituality" in Mich's Commentary on *Mater et magistra* in this volume.

42. Gregg, *Challenging the Modern World*, 90.

43. Naughton, *Good Stewards*, 82.

44. Wojtyla was part of a Catholic movement in Poland that used personalist philosophy to criticize both these political and economic systems.

45. Modras, "The Thomistic Personalism of Pope John Paul II," 117–27. See also Ronald Lawler, "Personalism in the Thought of John Paul II," in *Catholic Social Thought and the Teaching of John Paul II, Proceedings of the Fifth Convention (1982) of the Fellowship of Catholic Scholars*, ed. Paul L. Williams (Scranton, Pa.: Northeast, 1982), 2–18; John Hellman, "John Paul II and the Personalist Movement," *Cross Currents* 30 (winter 1980–81): 409–19. K. Wojtyla, *The Acting Person*, ed. Anna-Teresa Tymieniecka, trans. Andrezej Potocki, *Analecta Husserliana* 10 (Dordrecht, Holland: D. Reidel, 1979), vii, xiii–xiv.

46. For a clear and concise summary of John Paul II's philosophical framework as it is expressed in *The Acting Person*, see Gerard Beigel, *Faith and Social Justice in the Teaching of Pope John Paul II* (New York: Peter Lang, 1997), 9–32.

47. Wojtyla, "Thomistic Personalism," in *Person and Community*, 166.

48. Wojtyla, "Subjectivity and the Irreducible in the Human Being," in *Person and Community*, 213.

49. Wojtyla, *The Acting Person*, 10–11.

50. Wojtyla, "Constitution of Culture," 516, quoted in Gregg, *Challenging the Modern World*, 104. See also Gerald A. McCool, "The Theology of John Paul II," in *The Thought of John Paul II: A Collection of Essays and Studies*, ed. John M. McDermott (Rome: Pontifical Gregorian University, 1993), 29–53.

51. Ibid., 150–51.

52. Gregg, *Challenging the Modern World*, 87, 103.

53. Wojtyla, *The Acting Person*, 31.

54. Paulo Freire, *Pedagogy of the Oppressed* (New York: Seabury), 51–52.

55. Comments on LE's treatment of the creation story in Genesis are drawn from David Hollenbach, "Human Work and the Story of Creation: Theology and Ethics in *Laborem Exercens*," in *Co-Creation and Capitalism*, 63–75.

56. See Philip West, "Cruciform Labor: The Cross in Two Recent Theologies of Work," *Modern Churchman* 28, no. 4 (1986): 9–15; Stanley Hauerwas, "Work as Co-Creation: A Critique of a Remarkably Bad Idea," in *Co-Creation and Capitalism*, 50–51; John Howard Yoder, *The Politics of Jesus* (Grand Rapids: Eerdmans, 1972).

57. Gregory Baum maintains that one of the benefits of this wide definition of labor is that it overcomes the classical Marxist view that the industrial proletariat is a single wealth-producing class and as such a singular organ of social reconstruction. See *Priority of Labor*, 13–14.

58. William E. May, "Theology of Work," in *New Dictionary of Catholic Social Thought*, ed. J. A. Dwyer, 991.

59. Douglas Sturm, "The Labor Question and Energetic Democracy: On Moving toward a Larger Selfhood," *Soundings* 82, nos. 3–4 (1999): 425–33.

60. Ibid., 427.

61. Fernando Charrier, "Labour and Capital," *L'Osservatore Romano*, October 19, 1981, 8, 11.

62. Quote from historian Valeria Castronova and economist Francesco Forte *L'Espresso* (September 25, 1981), in McCormick, "*Laborem Exercens* and Social Morality," 219.

63. William F. Buckley, Jr. "The Encyclical and the Unions," *National Review* 33 (October 16, 1981): 1228–29.

64. Quote by Malachi Martin, *Prince George's Journal* (October 9, 1981) as cited in R. McCormick, "*Laborem Exercens* and Social Morality," in *Official Catholic Social Teaching*, 219.

65. Quote from Michael Schooyans, *La libre belgique* (September 23, 1981), in ibid., 220.

66. Comments of Philip Land and George Higgins reported in *Washington Post*, October 24, 1981, C10.

67. Editorial, "The Pope's Third Way," *The Tablet* 235 (October 3, 1981): 955–56.

68. Editorial, "Work Is for Man, Not Man for Work," *Time* 118 (September 28, 1981): 59.

69. Peter Hebblethwaite, "Labor Encyclical: Worker, Not Capital Key to Moral Order," *National Catholic Reporter* 17 (September 25, 1981): 1, 32.

70. Hehir, "A New Era of Social Teaching," 585, 607. See also editorial, "Good News of Work," *Commonweal* 108 (October 9, 1981): 548–49.

71. Thomas R. Donohue, "*Laborem Exercens*: A Comfort and a Challenge to U.S. Labor," *Origins* 18 (April 29, 1982): 730–38.

72. Andrea Lee and Amata Miller, "Women in the Workplace: Challenges and Opportunities," in *Co-Creation and Capitalism*, 214–16.

73. Quote from *Panorama* (September 28, 1981) as cited in Carl Marzani, "The Vatican as a Left Ally?" *Monthly Review* 34 (July–August 1982): 1–42.

74. Editorial, "The Pope's Third Way," 955–56.

75. R. McCormick, "*Laborem Exercens* and Social Morality," in *Official Catholic Social Teaching*, 220, no. 16.

76. René Coste, "*Laborem Exercens*: dans une perspective europeène," in *Rerum Novarum, Laborem Exercens Symposium 2000* 3–5/IV (Rome: Justitia et Pax, 1982), 263.

77. Quoted in Ludek Broz, "Encyclical on Human Labor," *Communio Viatorum* 24, no. 4 (1981): 269–71.

78. Antonio Quarracino, "*Laborem Exercens* Y Doctrina Social De La Iglesia Una Perspectiva Latinoamerican," in *Symposium 2000*, 204.

79. Javier Querejazu, *La moral social y el Concilio Vaticano II* 62 (Vitoria: Editorial Eset, 1993), 240.

80. *Commentario, Juan Pablo II: Sobre El Trabajo Humano* (San José, Costa Rica: Departmento Ecuménico de Investigaciones, 1982), 59–67.

81. Gustavo Gutiérrez, "El Evangelio del Trabajo," in *Sobre el Trabajo Humano*, ed. Centro de Estudios y Publicaciones (Lima, Peru: CEP, 1982), 43–63.

82. Francis A. Arinze, "The Encyclical *Laborem Exercens* in the African Context," in *Symposium 2000*, 225.

83. Aloysius Fonseca, "*Laborem exercens* from an Asian Perspective," in *Symposium 2000*, 237.

84. Bohdan M. Cywinski, "*Laborem Exercens* et la doctrine sociale vues dans le contexte des pays de l'Europe de l'Est," in ibid., 302.

85. Paul G Schervish, "Is John Paul II a Socialist?" *In These Times* no. 5, vol. 38 (October 6, 1981): 7; Carl Marzani, "The Vatican as a Left Ally?" *Monthly Review* 34 (July–August 1982): 1–42.

86. Arthur F. McGovern, "Pope John Paul II on 'Human Work,'" *Telos* 16 (winter 1983–84): 215–18.

87. Gregory Baum, "John Paul II's Encyclical on Labor" *Ecumenist* 20/1 (1981): 1–4. Baum maintains that the pope draws upon certain Marxist insights, but "opens them up, overcomes their rigidity, expands them toward new meaning."

88. Michael Novak, "The Pope's Brilliant Encyclical," *National Review* 33 (October 16, 1981): 1210.

89. Daniel Seligman, "Unfair to Capitalism," *Fortune* 104 (November 2, 1982), 63. See also Maryann O. Keating and Barry P. Keating, "The Crossroads between John Paul II's Social Vision and Conservative Economic Thought," *International Journal of Social Economics* 25/11–12 (1998): 1790–1802.

SELECTED BIBLIOGRAPHY

Baum, Gregory. *The Priority of Labor: A Commentary on Laborem Exercens, Encyclical Letter of Pope John Paul II*. New York: Paulist, 1982. This commentary offers an interpretation of the encyclical that is critical of capitalism and sympathetic to socialism.

Doran, Kevin P. *Solidarity: A Synthesis of Personalism and Communalism in the Thought of Karol Wojtyla/Pope John Paul II*. New York: Peter Lang, 1996. This analysis of solidarity is important to understanding a key theme in the thought of John Paul II.

Gregg, Samuel. *Challenging the Modern World: Karol Wojtyla/John Paul II and the Development of Catholic Social Teaching*. Lanham, Md.: Lexington, 1999. This is a scholarly and comprehensible treatment of the connection between John Paul II's preconciliar writings, particularly moral-anthropological themes, and many teachings developed in his encyclicals.

Hobgood, Mary E. *Catholic Social Teaching and Economic Theory: Paradigms in Conflict*. Philadelphia: Temple University Press, 1991, esp. 173–86. From the perspective of the social sciences, this book offers a scholarly analysis of the encyclical that is critical of its treatment of socialism and too favorable view of capitalism and first world perspectives.

Houck, John W., and Oliver F. Williams, eds. *Co-Creation and Capitalism: John Paul II's Laborem Exercens*. Washington, D.C.: University Press of America, 1983. This collection of essays contains analyses of the encyclical from scholars in the field of theology, ethics, philosophy, and economics, as well as labor and management.

Pontificia Commissio Justitia et Pax. *Rerum Novarum Laborem Exercens 2000 Symposium 3–5/IV*. Rome: Justitia et Pax, 1982. The importance of this collection of papers is twofold: the two encyclicals are the reference point; and it contains essays from each of the five major continents as well as an Eastern European perspective.

CHAPTER

17 Commentary on *Sollicitudo rei socialis* (*On Social Concern*)

CHARLES E. CURRAN

KENNETH R. HIMES, O.F.M.

THOMAS A. SHANNON

INTRODUCTION

John Paul II issued his seventh encyclical, *Sollicitudo rei socialis* (*On Social Concern*), to commemorate the twentieth anniversary of Paul VI's encyclical letter on development, *Populorum progressio*. Consequently, like Paul's letter, John Paul's document focused on the issue of human development. The ensuing twenty years since the publication of *Populorum progressio* found the poor of the world still desperate. John Paul's aim was to name the obstacles to development, point out false meanings of development, articulate a vision of authentic human development, and lay down some guidelines for implementing the vision.

One major aspect of the encyclical was a reflection on the state of the world as seen along the axis of North and South rather than East and West. By looking at the world from the perspective of North-South, a shorthand expression for examining the global situation with the categories of rich and poor nations, John Paul suggested the human family had reached a crisis stage in the relationship between the minority rich and majority poor.

John Paul's reading of the existing global situation was a substantial part of the papal letter. In his analysis he opposed both the "logic of the blocs," that is, the superpower conflict, as well as the societal structures that hinder the exercise of initiative. These latter obstacles to development exist across the political spectrum of totalitarian regimes on the left as well as authoritarian regimes of the right. Creating cultures of participation and democratic institutions along with the moral virtue of solidarity provided a needed remedy. The goal was authentic human development. For those who already enjoyed a measure of prosperity and freedom there was the danger that cultures prone to consumerism exhibited a false form of development, one the pope called "superdevelopment."

OUTLINE OF THE DOCUMENT

The encyclical is divided into seven chapters, including an introduction and a conclusion. As is the custom with papal encyclicals, the document is organized by numbered paragraphs. At the outset the pope explains that he wrote this encyclical to commemorate the 1967 encyclical *Populorum progressio* by Paul VI, a document whose teachings "retain all their force as an appeal to conscience" twenty years later (4).

John Paul interprets the document of his predecessor as one "which applies the teachings of the Council" (6) to the "specific problem of the development and the underdevelopment of peoples" (7). Paul's contribution to the Church's social teaching is summarized by the claim that "development is the new name for peace" (10).

In the third chapter, the longest of the letter, John Paul provides a personal overview and interpretation of the world situation in the late 1980s. The papal perspective is "rather negative" (13) because the gap between rich and poor is wide and getting worse.

Chapter four presents a critique of consumerism as a false form of development (28). Both nations and individuals have a right to full development (32) and this requires an accurate reading of the specific needs of both people and their communities (33). Such needs reach far beyond simply the material to include cultural and spiritual needs as well. The Church, too, has an obligation to contribute to human development. This includes not only teaching but could also require the sale of some church possessions to alleviate human suffering (31).

Next John Paul offers a theological interpretation of the situation (35–40). The two major themes of this chapter are sin and solidarity. With regard to poverty and want, "the true nature of the evil which faces us" is "a moral evil, the fruit of many sins which leads to structures of sin" (37). Solidarity is the appropriate response to the fact of interdependence and the need to overcome the gap between rich and poor (38–39).

In the penultimate chapter entitled "Guidelines for Development" (41–45) the pope makes explicit "that Church does not have technical solutions to offer" those seeking to overcome underdevelopment but authentic development cannot be reduced to a "technical problem" (41). Catholic social teaching is not an ideology meant to serve as a "third way" between capitalism and Marxism. Rather, it is a branch of moral theology meant to "guide Christian behavior" in a complex social order (41). "The option or love of preference for the poor" is the central guideline that inspires our choices (42). It should lead disciples to a series of conclusions about international trade, global financial systems, technology transfer, private property, and other elements of development planning (42–45).

The letter concludes with the acknowledgment that "the Church well knows that no temporal achievement is to be identified with the kingdom of God," for all human achievements "simply reflect and in a sense anticipate" God's reign that comes in its fullness at the end of time. Such a future "expectation can never be an excuse for lack of concern for people" in their present personal and social contexts (48).

CONTEXT OF THE DOCUMENT

The declared purpose of SRS was to commemorate PP, the earlier document of Paul VI on development. In the twenty years between the documents, the commitment of the papacy to advance human development had not altered. What had changed, however, was the setting in which development was to take place. For this reason, an understanding of the new context in which John Paul II wrote his letter is important.

Social Context

The world of the late 1980s exhibited two profound cleavages betraying the unity of the human family. One divide was between the Soviet Union and the nations of the Warsaw Pact and on the other side the United States and the countries of NATO. The acceleration of the arms race by both superpowers heightened tensions around the world, sometimes even to the discontent of their own allies. For many commentators and analysts this was the divide that claimed their attention.

John Paul II, however, was among those observers who saw a more worrisome gap within the human family. This was the growing chasm between rich and poor nations, as well as between rich and poor within nations, described by many as the North-South division, as well as a division between first world (wealthier nations) and third world (poorer nations). In SRS the pope also takes note of a "fourth world," pockets of extreme poverty within the wealthier nations (14; number 31). Particularly disappointing was that even though by the late 1980s there had already been more than two decades of concentrated attention given to the issue of development by the United Nations, the situation in most cases had worsened. This dramatic contrast between extremes of rich and poor living on the same planet, but seemingly in different "worlds," focused the pope's attention.

Yet the other division—East versus West—could not be ignored. This is especially so for a Polish pope who so deeply opposed the stifling presence of the Soviet Union and the Communist Party in his native land. Yet while certainly sympathetic to the political and cultural freedoms of the West, the pope was not willing to view the superpower conflict as one-sided. He perceived a "bipolar deadlock in which the world is left hanging" and a "destructive war of attrition between East and West" found the great powers "in a long-term deadlock" from which "neither could liberate itself."[1] This situation left the superpowers absorbed with their own conflict while the majority of the poor nations were viewed either as peripheral to geopolitics or merely as pawns in a game of superpower chess.

As a result, John Paul II placed substantial blame for the lack of authentic development upon the wealthy nations, seeing them as "a direct obstacle to the real transformation of the conditions of underdevelopment." He went on to note, however, that there was a sign of hope in "processes which might mitigate the existing opposition" (22). This may well be a reference to the Treaty on Intermediate Nuclear Forces (INF) that was signed in Washington, D.C., in December 1987. By that treaty President Ronald Reagan and Mikhail Gorbachev, the general secretary of the Soviet Union, eliminated an entire class of missiles and launchers from their arsenals.

In part, we can attribute the INF Treaty to the movement called "perestroika." This Russian term referred to the program of economic restructuring Gorbachev initiated in 1985. The program, ultimately, did not adequately address the depth and extent of reform required for the health of the Soviet economy. Among its outcomes, however, was a significant attempt to reduce military spending. This entailed serious efforts at nuclear arms reduction, the eventual withdrawal of the Soviet army from its war in Afghanistan, and the promotion of what was humorously called the "Sinatra doctrine," a reference to the popular song "My Way" by the famous singer. Gorbachev proclaimed a policy of lessened Soviet intervention in the internal affairs of fellow communist countries, thereby allowing them to pursue economic reform on their own terms. In the future, each Warsaw Pact nation could announce "My Way" of reform. This was particularly important for Poland, which was already evolving in unorthodox ways for a communist nation with the emergence of the Solidarity labor movement.

Further notable aspects of the social setting of the document were the general unrest and tragedy occurring in the Middle East: Iran and Iraq were engaged in a war that turned into a bloody slaughter for both populations; the first "intifada" or uprising erupted among Palestinians in opposition to the policies of Israel; and in Lebanon there were numerous acts of terrorism undermining the civic life of that war-ravaged nation.

ECCLESIAL CONTEXT

Travel, so central to the agenda of John Paul's papacy, plays an important role in understanding SRS. Two papal trips in 1987, one to Chile, Argentina, and Uruguay in Latin America, and the other to Poland, were of particular significance. In April 1987, John Paul II visited Chile, an overwhelmingly Catholic nation that was under the oppressive control of General Augusto Pinochet and a military regime established in a coup d'état in 1973. According to one eyewitness, during a papal Mass held in Santiago on April 3 a major disturbance broke out nearby. "Anti-government protestors clashed with police during a hit-and-run riot that lasted throughout the service and left nearly thirty persons badly injured. The air in Parque O'Higgins smelled of tear gas, not incense, and guns instead of bells sounded in the distance." The pope was visibly reluctant to be rushed away from the scene, even as his security personnel tried to get him away from the disturbance. It was "by far the worst violence during any of his public appearances."[2] In the mind of at least one Vatican official, John Paul later decided to go ahead with a new social encyclical "because he felt that Catholics like those who kept with him in Parque O'Higgins deserved clear direction from the church on how to find a way out of the turmoil and poverty around them."[3]

Among the lessons the pope apparently drew from his Latin American trip was that twenty years after *Populorum progressio* the "United States has failed to promote economic and political development in Latin America."[4] Coupled with this was the belief of Cardinal Josef Ratzinger, prefect of the Congregation for the Doctrine of the Faith (CDF), that the United States had become overly materialistic and morally insensitive to the plight of the world's poor. Ratzinger was skeptical of a liberal capitalist system as the blueprint for genuine development.[5]

Later that spring John Paul visited his homeland of Poland. There he encountered the unrest and yearning for change among the Polish people that had marked the entire decade of the 1980s. This was the third papal trip to Poland and by this time the signs of social change were abundantly clear.[6] The trade union movement Solidarity was operating quite publicly, relations between the Vatican and the Polish government had warmed considerably since the early years of the pontificate, and the Soviets were signaling their willingness to permit Poles to undertake reforms. The transition from a bureaucratic state-controlled economy to a more open market-based system promised to be difficult and there was anxiety mixed with hope about the eventual outcome. John Paul worried over the fate of those who had become dependent upon the security of the old economic system and now would have to survive in a different context. The pope was also aware that much of Poland's economic misery was due to the inefficiencies and lack of freedom found in the old communist system.

What the two trips demonstrated was the reality of underdevelopment and that the problem took more than one form. Both Chile and Poland were troubled nations but each in its own way: the former suffered from the injustices of a right-wing military regime; the latter struggled under the power of a communist empire. The firsthand experience of the pope inspired his interest in addressing the issue of human development by naming the obstacles to it and contrasting authentic development with its false forms.

John Paul was keenly aware of the trends toward interdependence and interconnectedness that are facets of globalization. He sought to fashion an appropriate ecclesial response to these trends, one that would foster human development. The answer appeared, in his mind, to be for the Church to promote the virtue of solidarity. The need for this virtue loomed large in a world characterized by division between "haves and have-nots." Solidarity was the Church's message for the social ills of an international system now twenty years older than when Paul VI wrote *Populorum progressio.*

In addition to the impact of the papal trips, other elements contributed to the climate in which the new encyclical was formulated. In 1984 and again in 1986 the CDF had issued instructions on liberation theology. The first document, "Instruction on Certain Aspects of the 'Theology of Liberation,'" was exceptionally critical of the ideas and activities associated with this largely Latin American movement. A second statement titled "Instruction on Christian Freedom and Liberation" was understood by many persons, including several Latin American church leaders, as a more conciliatory assessment of liberation theology.[7]

The second instruction corrected the one-sidedly negative treatment given liberation theology in the first. Acknowledgment of the movement's positive aspects came after the Brazilian bishops visited the Vatican during a series of *ad limina* visits and the pope heard their comments, many of them supportive of liberation theology. Indeed, four days after the second instruction was published, John Paul sent a letter to the Brazilian hierarchy in which he described liberation theology as "not only timely but useful and necessary."[8] Furthermore, after the first CDF instruction evoked protests about its harsh assessment of liberation theology the pope himself "promised on several occasions to present eventually the positive side of this theology, and he finally did with this encyclical."[9]

John Paul's reflection upon the plight of the poor was not limited to the Latin American experience and liberation theology. During 1987, Vatican officials concerned with foreign affairs prepared a report on the state of Africa with a particular spotlight on the war-torn nation of Angola. The report attributed a portion of the blame for Africa's poverty to the fact that it was often the battleground for proxy struggles between East and West. Toward the end of 1987, the president of Angola, José Eduardo Dos Santos, visited the Vatican and met privately with the pope. President Dos Santos explained that despite its rich natural resources, Angola remained poor due to civil war between a Soviet- and Cuban-supported government and an insurgency movement backed by South Africa and several Western nations. This kind of information led the pope and other Vatican officials to the view "that neither East nor West provides poor nations with a model for real moral and material development."[10]

The African situation, along with the Poland trip, strengthened the conviction of John Paul that many people needed liberation. Wanted was a liberation theology that addressed situations beyond the Latin American context. *Sollicitudo rei socialis* is John Paul's framework of a liberation theology built upon the idea of human development that could be utilized in various cultural contexts. For this reason the fourth section of the encyclical (27–34) is devoted to sketching an outline of "authentic human development."

PROCESS OF FORMULATION AND AUTHORSHIP

John Paul followed "a different process" from that of his first six encyclicals to produce this document. This letter "was the result of elaborate consultations and discussions within the Roman Curia."[11] Earlier in 1987, John Paul had considered writing a letter on the twentieth anniversary of *Populorum progressio*, but it was not until after his trip to Poland in June that he began in earnest to formulate his seventh encyclical.

During the early summer the pope wrote in longhand a schema that became *Sollicitudo rei socialis*. "More than a simple outline but much less than a first draft, it laid out the basic ideas of the document in chunks of prose."[12] Several senior curial officials commented upon the ideas. Then the schema was given to the Pontifical Commission Justitia et Pax, where it was developed into a first draft. The resulting document was circulated within the curia by the Secretariat of State, headed by Agostino Casaroli. Among those reported to have offered comments were Achille Silvestrini, the head of the Council for the Public Affairs of the Church (the Vatican's Foreign Office), and Josef Tomko, prefect of the Congregation for the Propagation of the Faith (office for missionary activities). A revised draft was then put together in reaction to the comments.

This process was repeated several times: draft prepared, draft circulated and commented upon, revision. Each time the pope reviewed the revised edition.[13] As a result of this method the French Cardinal Roger Etchegaray, president of Justitia et Pax, and Archbishop Jorge Maria Mejia, the Argentinian secretary of the Commission, had influential roles in the formulation of the text. The Commission had also elicited a global survey of bishops on the status of development since *Populorum progressio* and the pope was apprised of the result. John Paul also had various conversations with visitors to the Vatican, including Michael Camdessus, director general of the International Monetary Fund, and bishops attending the 1987 synod.[14]

At the beginning of Advent, in late November, a complete, though not finalized, draft was prepared. Oversight of the process now shifted from Justitia et Pax to the Secretariat of State. Final revisions to the text continued well past Christmas and the New Year. Although dated December 30, 1987, so as to be a twentieth anniversary commemoration, publication did not occur until mid-February 1988.[15]

Despite the collaborative nature of this document it is clear that the encyclical reflects the views of John Paul and carries his authority. As George Weigel observes, "drafting assistance does not compromise the teaching authority of a papal document," for an encyclical gets "its authoritative 'form' from the Pope's signature . . . without which any draft is just that: a draft."[16]

ESSAY

While John Paul II wrote SRS in 1987 to commemorate the twentieth anniversary of Paul VI's encyclical *Populorum progressio*, it also afforded him the opportunity to make a wide-ranging statement about the state of the world when viewed from the perspective of the poor. He did this by viewing the world from the perspective of North-South and from an inner analysis of what he calls the "logic of the blocs" that grounds his critique of both liberal capitalism and communism. This sets up his critique of elements of developmental theory and his advocacy for the virtue of solidarity as the new name for development.

Analysis of the Document

In the introduction, John Paul identifies two objectives: one is to pay homage to *Populorum progressio* and the other is to "reaffirm the *continuity* of the social doctrine as well as its constant *renewal*" (3). The constancy of the doctrine is shown in five ways: "in its fundamental inspiration, in its 'principles of reflection,' in its 'criteria of judgment,' in its basic 'directives for action,' and above all in its vital link with the Gospel of the Lord" (3). The renewal of the doctrine is demonstrated by its adaptations to the changes in historical circumstances and the changes in the lives of people and society. The purpose of this current encyclical is to extend the teachings of *Populorum* to today's world, particularly with respect to the concept of development.

In "Reflections on *Populorum Progressio*," John Paul discusses the originality of *Populorum progressio*. In general, he praises the encyclical because it both applies the teachings of Vatican II and responds to the appeal of the Council to address the issues of poverty and underdevelopment, which the pope notes are part of the grief and anxiety of the world.

John Paul lists three points that demonstrate the originality of *Populorum progressio*. First is the very fact the document addresses a seemingly secular topic, the social and economic issues of development. Paul VI continued the work begun in *Rerum novarum*. However, by revealing the moral and cultural dimensions of economic questions, he shows the social doctrine to be an application of the Word of God to the people of today. This doctrine offers "'principles for reflection,' 'criteria of judgment,' and directives for action'" (8). The second point of originality is described as breadth of outlook that, while affirming the international dimensions of the social question, highlights the reality of interdependence between the conduct of rich nations and underdevelopment within poor nations (9). Additionally, Paul VI insists that development is not simply an economic question, one that can be resolved by increasing the number of goods and seeking better distribution. Third, *Populorum progressio* was a very "original contribution to the social doctrine of the Church in its totality and to the very concept of development" (10). Here Paul recognized that the demand for justice was an international demand and that the use of huge sums of money for the arms race was a major roadblock to peace. All of this leads John Paul to offer his encyclical as a continuing reflection on the concept of development, "a concept that has a permanent and contemporary value" (10).

"Papal Perspective on the World Situation" presents a review of the events of the current world as the initial stage for developing the teaching of Paul VI. After stating that hopes for development are far from being realized even after two decades of development, John Paul begins by describing several negative characteristics of our age and their causes.

The first of these is the widening gap "between the areas of the so-called developed North and the developing South" (14). Surveying general economic indexes of levels of food, water, shelter, life expectancy, and hygiene, for example, suggests a growing gap between the two groups. Additionally, there are differences of culture and value systems that make the "*social question much more complex*, precisely because this question has assumed a universal dimension" (14). Here the pope notes that within our one world there are four worlds and that such a reality threatens the unity of the world and the human race.

Even more serious for the pope are cultural issues such as illiteracy, the difficulty of obtaining a higher education, the inability to participate in developing one's own nation, exploitation, and discrimination. The denial of the right of economic initiative also has two important cultural implications: first, a destruction of the creative subjectivity of the individual citizen, and second, a denial of the subjectivity of the individual nation, particularly as this affects its sovereignty (15). The cause of these problems stems "at least in part" from "a *too narrow idea* of development, that is, a mainly economic one" (15).

John Paul then turns to signs of underdevelopment and notes three critical ones: the housing crisis, unemployment/underemployment, and international debt. The underlying issue is ironically the availability of capital that developing nations borrowed to invest in development projects. However, servicing the debt led to exporting the very capital they now need to develop their countries. Thus development has "turned into a *counterproductive mechanism*" and led to "*aggravated underdevelopment*" (19).

The political roots of this are found in the "*existence of two opposing blocs*, commonly known as the East and the West" (20). The Western bloc is centered on liberal capitalism and the Eastern on Marxist collectivism. This ideological difference led to military opposition in the form of cold war tensions and proxy wars. The opposition between the two blocs is not because of two different levels of development "but rather between two *concepts* of the development of individuals and peoples, both concepts being imperfect and in need of radical correction" (21). Thus, the Church adopts a critical stance to both, asking how they "favor or promote a true and integral development of individuals and peoples in modern society" (21).

The developing countries, whether in the East or West, focus on economic development alone with the consequence that instead of promoting autonomous behavior, the culture turns people into machines. The temptation to imperialism in the form of neocolonialism becomes stronger. Questions of security dominate each nation's agenda and the divisions between them become "a *direct obstacle* to the real transformation of the conditions of underdevelopment in the developing and less advanced countries" (22). John Paul argues that the West turns to selfish isolation and the East ignores its duty to cooperate in relieving human misery. Such desertion of moral duty by both sides finds serious application in the arms trade. "While economic aid and development plans meet with the obstacle of insuperable ideological barriers, and with tariff and trade barriers, *arms* of whatever origin circulate with almost total freedom all over the world" (24). This is coupled with the stockpiling of atomic weapons that reveals a focus on death rather than development.

The consequences that flow from this are imbalances in the world economy that have led to a serious refugee problem, continued despair that breeds the sources of terrorism, and a systematic campaign against birth as a response to demographic pressures. There are positive signs, however, that the pope holds up. Among these are an increasing awareness of human dignity and human rights among more and more peoples, a movement sanctioned by the Universal Declaration of Human Rights, and other efforts of the United Nations.[17] Additionally, a growing number are convinced of the interdependence of all peoples and a consequent need for true solidarity. Further positive signs of hope are a growing respect for life and the recognition that peace is indivisible, an increasing awareness of the ecological movement, and some self-sufficiency in food and industrialization in a few third world countries. These positive developments are supported by many international organizations and thus constitute signs of hope for all peoples.

In "Authentic Human Development," John Paul begins with a critique of false notions of development. Those who see it as automatic and limitless understand development from the Enlightenment perspective, that of economic and social development. A further evolution of this perspective is what the pope terms *superdevelopment*: "an *excessive* availability of every kind of material goods for the benefit of certain social groups" (28). Because there is no horizon other than material possessions, people in this mind-set soon find themselves slaves of their possessions and of immediate gratification. Consumerism holds sway and dissatisfaction soon sets in.

Since the mere accumulation of goods does not ultimately satisfy persons, it is, therefore, necessary to develop a moral understanding of development. Here John Paul turns to a distinction used by Paul VI: having and being. Having objects can perfect the subject only if they contribute to the "realization of the human vocation as such" (28). It is not "having" as such that is the ethical impediment to development but "possessing without regard for the *quality* and the *ordered hierarchy* of the goods one has. *Quality and hierarchy* arise from the subordination of goods and their availability to man's 'being' and his true vocation" (28). Although development has an appropriate economic dimension, the key element is the interior dimension grounded in the bodily and spiritual nature of the human. Hence, while God created humans superior to all other beings and has given humans the duty of cultivating and watching over the earth, at the same time, humans "must remain subject to the will of God, who imposes limits upon his use and dominion over things" (29). By the subordination of material possessions, human dominion, and use of the image of God revealed in the human person, true transcendence is achieved. This transcendence is social and is accomplished "within the framework of *obedience* to the divine law and therefore with respect for the image received" (30). The present stage of development "is to be seen as a moment in the story which began at creation, a story which is constantly endangered by reason of infidelity to the Creator's will, and especially by the temptation to idolatry" (30).

When facing the reality of underdevelopment and superdevelopment, the response of the Church is to relieve the misery and suffering of others by responding not only from its abundance but also from its necessities. One must respond out of the hierarchy of values, particularly the pope notes, "when the 'having' of a few can be to the detriment of the 'being' of many others" (31). This is a duty that falls on each person, on societies and nations, and in particular on the Church and other ecclesial communities. This duty is both internal to each nation as well as international so that all can reach their true destiny. This focus must include the promotion of human rights as a source of the full development of the human, a development that includes political, social, and personal rights as well as economic ones. Thus "development must be achieved within the framework of *solidarity* and *freedom*, without ever sacrificing either of them under whatever pretext" (33). Thereby one achieves what Paul VI referred to in *Populorum progressio* as a civilization of love.

John Paul concludes this section with a final and new element in development, the ecological. This section is significant because, though brief, it is the first major discussion of ecology in an encyclical. The pope makes three points. First, one cannot simply use the earth and other entities, living or not, with impunity. Creation has its own innate dignity, quite apart from its instrumental value to humans. One must take into account "the *nature of each being* and of its *mutual connection* in an ordered system, which is precisely the 'cosmos'" (34). Second, because natural resources are limited, one cannot use them as if one held absolute dominion over them. Finally, one must take into account the quality of life that comes from industrialization. Even on the ecological level, therefore, development requires respect for moral demands.

"Theological Interpretation of the Situation" presents a theological reading of modern problems. The core of this section is an analysis of the "*moral causes* which, with respect to the behavior of individuals considered as *responsible persons*, interfere in such a way as to slow down the course of development and hinder its full achievement" (35). With that the pope begins his analysis of structures of sin. John Paul writes: "The sum total of the negative factors working against a true awareness of the universal *common good*, and the need to further it, gives the impression of creating, in persons and institutions, an obstacle which is difficult to overcome" (36). These obstacles may be called structures of sin and are linked first to the particular acts of individuals who introduce these structures, consolidate them, and consequently ensure their difficulty of removal. These structures then become the source of other sins that, in turn, influence the actions of others. In this perspective the pope notes two attitudes and actions in particular that are typical of sinful structures: "on the one hand, the *all-consuming desire for profit*, and on the other, the *thirst for power*, with the intention of imposing one's will upon others" (37). These attitudes are more problematic when they are absolutized and when they are indissolubly united. They may reflect the perspectives not only of individuals, but nations or blocs. For the pope, "hidden behind certain decisions, apparently inspired only by economics or politics, are real forms of idolatry: of money, ideology, class, technology" (37).

John Paul engages in this theological analysis to ensure our awareness of the moral evil, the fruit of many sins, that is the true reality we must face. The path to overcoming such evil is long and complex because of human frailty and because of changing circumstances. Hence, all the more reason to focus on moral and spiritual attitudes when people seek the common good. Christians, in particular, must see interdependence as a moral reality and solidarity as a virtue.

The key point here is solidarity that leads each member in a society to recognize each other as a person. Solidarity helps us "to see the 'other'—*whether a person, people, or nation*—not just as some kind of instrument, with a work capacity and physical strength to be exploited at low cost and then discarded . . . but as our 'neighbor,' a 'helper' to be made a sharer, on a par with ourselves" (39). Solidarity leads to various obligations. The influential, possessing a greater number of goods, should be ready to share them. Weaker parties ought not be negative but should do what they can for the good of all. Intermediate groups must "not selfishly insist on their particular interests, but respect the interests of others" (39). Echoing his predecessor's comment that "development is the new name for peace" (PP 87), John Paul proposes that solidarity is a veritable synonym for development.

> In this way, the solidarity that we propose is the path to peace and at the same time to development. For world peace is inconceivable unless the world's leaders come to recognize that interdependence in itself demands the abandonment of the politics of blocs, the sacrifice of all forms of economic, military, or political imperialism, and the transformation of mutual distrust into collaboration. This is precisely the *act proper* to solidarity among individuals and nations. (39)

The first part of "Guidelines for Development" looks to the Church's contribution. This will not be a technical solution, but a proclamation of the Church's social doctrine, defined as a "'set of principles for reflection, criteria for judgment, and directives for action' proposed by the Church's teaching" (41). The pope states explicitly that the Church's social doctrine is not a third way between liberal capitalism and Marxist collectivism. Neither is it an ideology. Rather, social doctrine is "the *accurate formulation* of the results of a careful reflection on the complex realities of human existence, in society, and in the international order, in the light of faith and the church's tradition" (41). Social doctrine thus leads to a ministry of evangelization in which evil is condemned yet the proclamation of the good news is more important.

An important element of this social teaching is "the *option* or *love of preference* for the poor. This is an option, or *special form* of primacy in the exercise of Christian charity, to which the whole tradition bears witness" (42). Such love is not only personal but also social. One insight of this social dimension to charity is the recollection that the goods of the world were originally meant for all. Although private property is "*valid and necessary*, it does not nullify the value of this principle. Private property is under a 'social mortgage,' which means that it has an intrinsically social function" (42).

The final part of this section looks to areas that are in particular need of reform. John Paul II identifies these as the reform of the international trade system, which is mortgaged to protectionism and increasing bilateralism; the freedom of the world monetary and financial system, today recognized as inadequate; the question of technological exchanges and their proper use; the need for a review of the structure of the existing international organizations, in the framework of an international juridical order (43).

Reform will be effected only by changing unjust structures, particularly political institutions, and replacing them with democratic and participatory ones. This will require the collaboration of all in a spirit of solidarity and interdependence, both locally and internationally. Not addressed specifically is the question of means by which to do this. The lack of specificity as to the question of how reform ought to be pursued is not surprising. It is in keeping with the reserve that recent popes have exhibited concerning specific political and economic strategies. Although some earlier documents of Catholic social teaching proposed particular solutions, there has been a reticence since John XXIII to go into detail when discussing the means of reform. As with SRS, recent papal statements endorse certain goals—less inequality—and propose broad norms to guide reform—participation—yet refrain from endorsing particular means. Undoubtedly one reason for this is to avoid going beyond the Church's competency as a moral teacher. Another motive is to prevent the Church from becoming identified with a particular political or economic ideology.

In the conclusion of SRS, John Paul acknowledges the significance of liberation as a central category of analysis and a first principle of action. Development must include "the *cultural, transcendent and religious dimensions* of man and society," and false notions of development that slight these dimensions are not "conducive to authentic liberation. Human beings are totally free only when they are completely *themselves*, in the fullness of their rights and duties. The same can be said about society as a whole" (46).

Obstacles to liberation are sin and the "*structures* produced by sin as it multiplies and spreads" (46). Despite the power of sin, the Church has confidence in humanity and knows that men and women will seek the dignity of the human person through peaceful political means. And though no particular temporal achievement can be identified with the reign of God, "all such achievements simply *reflect* and in a sense *anticipate* the glory of the kingdom" (48). And for the Christian, a fuller sense of God's reign is discovered in the celebration of the Eucharist by which we are "called to discover, through this sacrament, the profound *meaning* of our actions in the world in favor of development and peace; and to receive from it the strength to commit ourselves ever more generously" (48).

Assessment

Overall, John Paul II succeeds in raising critical questions about poverty, development, and solidarity. These issues are thematically present in the corpus of Catholic social teaching and the pope here focuses on new dimensions of these issues. Of great importance in the document is his challenging of the ideology of the blocs and his critique of development theory, particularly its capitalistic form of "superdevelopment." Yet he is equally critical of regimes that stifle freedom, creativity, and human flourishing. No one receives favored treatment or escapes criticism as the pope casts his critical eye over the problems of the world, especially that of poverty. What is clear in SRS is the continuing commitment of the Church to the cause of the poor of the world; questions continue to be raised as to the causes of and remedies for that situation.

While John Paul uses ideas from *Populorum progressio* to refocus our attention on the plight of the world's poor and to identify causes of poverty both internationally and nationally, there remain issues for debate: the methodology of SRS, how social structures are evaluated, the relation of individual sin to social sin and to what the pope calls structures of sin, and how solidarity is to be achieved between the classes.

The term *social doctrine* deserves special attention here, particularly because of the way in which John Paul references *Populorum progressio* and *Octogesima adveniens* but also because the term itself has been subject to considerable debate since M. D. Chenu's description of social doctrine as an ideology.[18] Part of the debate is a translation issue: sometimes the generally consistent use of the Latin term *doctrina* is variously translated as teaching or doctrine, and this suggests a possible change in meaning. The more important issue is the function of the term and how John Paul II uses it. Of critical significance is the pope's reference to paragraph 4 in *Octogesima adveniens.* This paragraph is a clear rejection of the formulation of universal solutions to social issues being provided by the papacy and an affirmation of the role of the local church in formulating this teaching. While not necessarily a rejection of universal or general principles, the document of Paul VI certainly focuses on the role of the local church in addressing local problems. Likely, it seems his aim was to have a two-way dialogue between the local church and the universal Church. Some commentators have pointed out the failure of the documents of Catholic social teaching to give enough importance to and learn from what has occurred in the various local churches. Such a criticism seems valid and in keeping with the proposal of Paul VI.

Continuing in this vein, Mathew Kiliroor notes that with regard to the practice of local churches determining their pastoral agenda SRS signals a different approach: "An important, active role which Pope Paul VI had allocated with the re-found ecclesiology of *communio*, namely that of drawing principles of reflection, norms of judgment and directives for action, seems to be taken back. This has serious implications if it is inspired by an ecclesiological conviction of centralization."[19]

Additionally the document of the Congregation for Catholic Education, "Guidelines for Teaching the Church's Social Doctrine in Forming Priests," provides clear evidence, particularly with an early reference to SRS, that the methodology in that letter retreats significantly from the more historically conscious methodology of *Populorum progessio* and *Octogesima adveniens.* There is a return to a pre–Vatican II method of the development of universal principles that are then applied to concrete particular solutions. This document of the Congregation, while by no means a definitive interpretation of SRS and its methodology, maintains that candidates for ordination are to learn the social doctrine so that they are "capable of applying it in pastoral activity in its entirety, as formulated and presented by the Magisterium of the Church."[20] Then the document notes that the magisterium "intervenes in this field [social teaching] with a doctrine that all the faithful are called upon to know, teach, and apply."[21] This social doctrine has three components. First is the theoretical, "an organic and systematic reflection in its social documents. . . . These are permanent ethical principles, not changeable historical judgments." Second is the historical dimension in which "the use of principles is framed in a real view of society and inspired by an awareness of its problems." Finally, there is the practical dimension that is "the effective application of these principles that are in practice by translating them concretely into the ways and to the extent that circumstances permit or require."[22] With respect to the method of "observe, judge, act" referred to by John Paul II, the Congregation notes that the role of judging, described as an intermediate step, is a "function proper to the Magisterium of the church."[23]

Elsbernd notes three critical shifts among others that sum up this change in methodology. First is a transfer from the community to the magisterium with respect to participation in the development of social teaching. Second, the starting point for the development of social doctrine has moved from the local situation to the "permanent principles of Catholic social doctrine." And third, "in considering the contribution of history, a shift occurred from history as a constitutive dimension of social teaching to an awareness of historical contingencies in the application of social teaching."[24]

Despite the frequent appeals to both *Progressio populorum* and *Octogesima adveniens*, John Paul II seems to be using a pre–Vatican II methodology, one that affirms universal principles developed by the hierarchical magisterium and applied by the hierarchical magisterium to particular situations. This seems to reflect a shift from a methodology rooted in historical consciousness to one that is more transcendental and independent of particular historical and cultural events. It is also much more reflective of a centralized ecclesiology, as noted by Kiliroor. Such a shift has profound implications for the role of the local church in the development of social doctrine.

Another aspect of the methodology adopted by the pope is found in chapter 5 of the document, where he provides a theological reading of the present social situation. This is a new development in Catholic social teaching, reflecting the evolution of postconciliar social teaching as more biblically grounded and reliant upon the theological tradition in addition to the insights of natural law philosophy. In his very first encyclical, *Redemptor hominis*, John Paul II demonstrated his conviction that Christology was the proper theological foundation for a truly humanistic ethic and that the Church's mission in support of human dignity and the defense of human rights stemmed from its understanding of the meaning of the Christ-event.[25]

It is possible to read this use of theological language in a social encyclical as the adoption of a more confessional, less socially engaged approach. However, the encyclical is explicitly addressed to all people of good will; its other sections speak to a broad audience. In the conclusion the pope reiterates his desire to speak to "all men and women without exception" (47), and even in chapter 5 there is expressed the hope that "also men and women without an explicit faith would be convinced that the obstacles to integral development are not only economic but rest on more profound attitudes" (38). Thus, it does not appear that the reason for employing theological language in this chapter is a retreat into confessionalism.

Rather, it appears that because the pope is taking into account the dual nature of his audience, the wider world and the Church, he is employing a method that has been called "public theology," that is, "the effort to discover and communicate the socially significant meanings of Christian symbols and tradition."[26] By providing an explicitly theological rendering of the world situation, John Paul is speaking to those who accept the Christian message and wish to make the connection between their faith and the teaching of SRS and other documents of Catholic social thought. It is also useful to explain to people outside the Christian community the deeper motivation and rationale for the Church's public role. Utilization of public theology is a noteworthy methodological development in the papal formulation of social teaching.

EXCURSUS

SRS has made solidarity a central and foundational part of Catholic social teaching. The encyclical uses the term *solidarity* twenty-seven times. In three subsequent encyclicals of John Paul II's, two—*Centesimus annus* and *Evangelium vitae*—also put a heavy emphasis on solidarity, but *Veritatis splendor* uses the concept comparatively infrequently.

Basic Understanding

What is the basic meaning of solidarity? John Paul II's most concentrated and developed discussion of solidarity comes in his theological reading of modern problems (38–40), but he also sees solidarity as a fundamental call for all humanity. In our world today there is a growing recognition of the interdependence among individuals and nations. Interdependence, however, is more than just the factual situation that we recognize today. Interdependence becomes a moral category when we are aware of it as a system determining relationships in the contemporary world in its economic, cultural, political, and religious elements. The correlative response to interdependence as a moral category is the moral attitude or virtue of solidarity.

For John Paul II, solidarity is not just "vague compassion or shallow distress at the misfortunes of others" but rather "a firm and persevering determination to commit oneself to the common good; that is to say to the good of all and of each individual, because we are all really responsible for all" (38). Solidarity is a Christian virtue forming a central part of conversion, but it is also a duty and a virtue for all humankind. John Paul II hopes that all women and men without explicit faith also recognize that integral development rests on profound spiritual attitudes that define each individual's relationship with self, with neighbor, and with even the remotest human communities and with nature itself. People are called to work for the common good or the full development of the whole individual and of all women and men.

Solidarity must be exercised within each society and within international society (39). Solidarity calls for the members of society to recognize each other as persons and not simply as instruments or means. Solidarity opposes any exploitation, oppression, and annihilation of others. Above all, on a societal level, solidarity calls for the Church and all to take their place beside the poor and to satisfy the just demands of the poor without losing sight of the common good. The stronger need to share with and be responsible for the weaker. The weaker, while claiming their legitimate rights, must also contribute to the moral fabric and the good of all and not merely adopt a passive attitude toward the common good.

Solidarity is most important on the international level. International interdependence must be transformed into the virtue of solidarity by recognizing that the goods of creation exist to serve the needs of all so that what human industry produces by processing raw materials through human work must serve equally for the good of all. Solidarity opposes any form of imperialism or hegemony of the rich and powerful nations over the poor nations. The international system must rest on the foundation of the equality of all peoples and the necessary respect for their legitimate differences. SRS uses solidarity to support its central thesis that the two blocs of East and West have produced the danger of war and an excessive preoccupation with security to the detriment of the autonomy, well-being, and even territorial integrity of the weaker nations in their sphere of influence.

SRS thus sees solidarity as a central principle and virtue of Catholic social teaching. "Solidarity . . . is the path to peace and at the same time to development" (39). Here, John Paul II builds on concepts developed by his predecessors. Paul VI said that development is the new name for peace (PP 87). Pius XII's motto was "Peace as the fruit of justice." But John Paul II now understands "Peace as the fruit of solidarity" (39). Thus solidarity is central and fundamental in John Paul II's Catholic social teaching. From the Christian perspective, solidarity strives to overcome the structures of sin that are radically opposed to peace and development. John Paul II adopts the concept of the structures of sin from liberation theology, but he places more emphasis on the relationship of sinful structures to individual intentionality and responsibility, whereas liberation theologians emphasize the role of societal forces.[27]

An analogous use of solidarity finds a much more limited place in SRS. This is the solidarity within different groups, especially the oppressed and marginalized. Among positive signs in the contemporary world "are the growing awareness of the solidarity of the poor among themselves, their efforts to support one another, and their public demonstrations on the social scene which, without recourse to violence, present their own needs and rights in the face of the inefficiency or corruption of the public authorities" (39). The two different understandings of solidarity lead to two different methodological approaches. Liberation theology begins with the solidarity of the poor and marginalized among themselves. Such an approach begins from the bottom up with the solidarity of the poor and marginalized among themselves, recognizes the role of praxis, and gives greater significance to conflict and power in overcoming sinful social structures. As is well known, John Paul II is sympathetic to the goals of liberation theology but critical of some aspects of it (46). All agree that John Paul II does not use a liberationist model. His encyclicals on social teaching employ a different methodology that moves from the top down. His primary understanding of solidarity fits in very well with his methodology. As a universal teacher in the Church, he is proposing a teaching document for all. His concern is the Church universal and the world in general. As a philosopher, he tends to discuss human issues from a broad human perspective. For him, solidarity is a fundamental concept that all humankind and Christians should agree upon and put into practice. Solidarity should influence the lives of persons, nations, and the world. Notice here the move from an agreed understanding of moral truth to practice. Such an approach by its very nature downplays the role of conflict and power in social life. Thus, John Paul II's primary understanding of solidarity as a central and fundamental duty and virtue for social life fits in very well with the methodological approach he uses. At the same time, he distances himself from the method of liberation theology that strongly insists on the solidarity of the poor and marginalized among themselves.[28]

There is a marked difference between SRS and the earlier *Laborem exercens* with regard to the understanding of solidarity, but both encyclicals follow the same method of moving from agreed-upon concepts to practice. The word *solidarity* appears ten times in *Laborem exercens*, nine times in paragraph 8, which is entitled "Worker Solidarity." Since *Rerum novarum* the Church has recognized the need for worker solidarity in overcoming the degradation and exploitation of the human person as the subject of work. Whenever such degradation and exploitation occur even today, there is need for such worker solidarity. Obviously, John Paul II here uses the word *solidarity* to show his support for the solidarity movement in Poland that was then playing such a central role in political change in that country. *Centesimus annus* explicitly mentions the solidarity movement in Poland as the decisive factor in the dramatic changes that occurred in that country (23).

Number 20 of *Laborem exercens* uses *solidarity* in the broader sense of human solidarity to situate and better understand the role of worker solidarity and the struggle for justice. This is not a struggle against others or to eliminate an opponent but a struggle for social justice and the common good. The workers' struggle for their rights must always be "a constructive factor of social order and solidarity." Even paragraph 8, without using the word *solidarity* in the broader sense, recognizes that solidarity of workers must never be closed to dialogue and collaboration with others.

Thus, in *Laborem exercens*, John Paul II insists on worker solidarity and recognizes some role for power and conflict, but insists on seeing worker solidarity in the broader context of human solidarity. In accord with this understanding, *Laborem exercens* uses the same methodological approach that has characterized all John Paul II's social encyclicals. He moves from agreed-upon concepts of the human person and the priority of labor over capital to action for social justice, the common good, and broader human solidarity.

Further Explanations

There is no doubt that John Paul II's insistence on the centrality and importance of solidarity is a new emphasis in Catholic social teaching. But there still exists great continuity both with previous documents of Catholic social teaching and with Karol Wojtyla's writings as a philosopher before he became pope.

Wojtyla already discussed solidarity in *The Acting Person*. The treatment is quite similar to that found in SRS. Solidarity is an attitude that is based on the reality that human beings live and act together. It is therefore always related to the common good. Solidarity is the attitude of a community in which the common good conditions and initiates participation, and at the same time it calls for the constant readiness of each person to accept and to realize one's share in the community because of membership in the community. The nonauthentic attitudes of conformism and noninvolvement work against solidarity. Solidarity also calls for the need for opposition in a community, but this is constructive opposition based on the common good or the good of other persons.[29]

Solidarity has appeared before in Catholic social teaching. In fact, SRS, which was written on the twentieth anniversary of *Populorum progressio*, cites that encyclical in speaking about the duty of solidarity that involves both individuals and nations. Advanced nations have an obligation to help developing nations (SRS 9; PP 48).

In the very first encyclical of his pontificate, Pope Pius XII in 1939 maintained that the first of the pernicious errors of our day is the forgetfulness of the law of solidarity and charity that is based on our common origin and the equality of all human begins.[30] According to René Coste, solidarity constitutes one of the great themes of *Gaudium et spes* and is mentioned explicitly in numbers 4, 31, 57, and 85. Again, the emphasis is on a human solidarity in the service of the common good that includes the international common good.[31] *Populorum progressio* also gives a significant role to solidarity. The second part of the encyclical bears the title, "The Development of the Human Race in the Spirit of Solidarity" (43). Here the emphasis is on human, social, and world solidarity.

Redemptor hominis, John Paul II's first encyclical, refers to solidarity in the broad sense twice in number 16. Mention has already been made of the emphasis on workers' solidarity in *Laborem exercens*. John Paul II's "Message for the Celebration of the World Day of Peace," January 1, 1987, foreshadowed the centrality and importance of solidarity found in SRS. The title of this message is "Development and Solidarity: Two Keys to Peace."[32] Thus John Paul II's emphasis on solidarity is not something totally new in Catholic social teaching but its centrality and basic importance are indeed new.

John Paul II would be the last one to claim that he is adding a new concept, principle, duty, or virtue to Catholic social teaching. He has consistently maintained, as he does in the beginning of SRS, that Catholic social teaching has continuity because it remains identical in its "principles of reflection, criteria of judgment, and basic directives for action" (3). *Centesimus annus* insists that solidarity has been one of the fundamental principles of Catholic social teaching even though popes have used different words to describe it. Leo XIII used *friendship*; Pius XI, *social charity*; and Paul VI, the *civilization of love* (10).

Catholic social ethics, which is broader than Catholic social teaching, because of its Thomistic background has always insisted on an anthropology recognizing both the dignity of the human person and the fact that human persons are social and political by nature. Each person is called by God to work in various communities and in harmony with all others for the common good.[33] SRS expresses this reality by insisting that genuine development must be achieved within the framework of freedom and solidarity (33).

Wojtyla learned from phenomenology the need to present Catholic theology and teaching in a more meaningful and attention-grabbing way for people today. This seems to be a significant factor in his making solidarity such a basic and central concept. The meaning of solidarity is very clear for all. In addition, solidarity is a helpful term for the two audiences that Catholic social teaching and John Paul II address in their social encyclicals: Catholics and all people of good will. Here is a single word understood well by both audiences. All human beings can appreciate the interdependence of the world in which we live and the need to respond to that interdependence in a spirit of solidarity. But John Paul II insists that solidarity is also a Christian virtue with many points of contact with Christian charity. Solidarity in this understanding has dimensions of total gratuity, forgiveness, and reconciliation. The neighbor is a living image of God the Father, redeemed by Jesus, and placed under the action of the Holy Spirit. Going beyond human and natural bonds involving all humankind, Christian faith gives us another model for the unity and solidarity of all God's children (40).

From the Christian perspective, solidarity provides one word that brings together elements of charity and justice that enter into the Christian understanding of relationships in our interdependent world. Theologians have debated for years about the exact meaning of love and of justice and of the relationship between the two.[34] Solidarity provides an appealing understanding of our Christian relationship to others in this world while bypassing all the controversies of the past.

John Paul II refers to solidarity in various ways: as a principle, an attitude, a duty, and a virtue. In one sense solidarity is all of these. Here again note the value and advantage of a concept that can be used in all these significant ways. However, it seems both from his understanding in SRS and from the understanding of moral theory in general that primacy should be given to solidarity as a virtue.[35]

One of the underdeveloped aspects of Catholic social teaching is the role of the virtues. Although Catholic moral theology gives a central role to the virtues[36] the focus on structures and institutions in Catholic social teaching has often led to the neglect of virtue theory in the literature that is the subject matter of this volume. It is refreshing, therefore, to find John Paul giving such a central role to the virtue of solidarity. One might raise the concern that the emphasis on solidarity as a virtue, like John Paul's use of other religious language, might lead to a displacement of the centrality of justice and the common good in Catholic social teaching. Does this signal a withdrawal from the Church's commitment to speak in language and appeal to arguments that resonate with all persons of good will, not just Christian believers? In the writing of John Paul this does not appear to be the case. It is evident that throughout SRS the virtue of solidarity is closely linked to the themes of the common good and justice, not used in opposition to them or as a device to supplant them. Recall the papal definition of solidarity as "a firm and persevering determination to commit oneself to the common good" (38).

Use of solidarity as a virtue in SRS underscores a theme that is often overlooked in Catholic social teaching: the need for a change of heart as well as a change of structures.[37] Indeed, without a change of heart on the part of the well-to-do nations and their inhabitants it is difficult to imagine that appeals to the norms of social justice and the common good will receive a serious hearing. Self-interest alone will never suffice to motivate the rich to change structures for the benefit of the poor. This is why John Paul observes that even nonbelievers must recognize that a profound change in attitude is needed if the situation of the world is to be improved (38).

SRS has thus made solidarity a central and fundamental concept in Catholic social teaching, which is congenial with the method of going from the common acceptance of a moral truth to how persons should act. Although solidarity has not added new content as such to the tradition of Catholic social teaching, it has provided an appropriate new concept that is readily understandable not only by Christians but by all people of goodwill.

REACTIONS TO THE DOCUMENT

To understand a good deal of the response to SRS, it must be remembered that it was written in the context of the waning years of a decades-long struggle between communism and the West. Many in the West had invested themselves in winning the conflict on all levels, including the moral level. So when John Paul II used the "logic of the blocs" as an analytical device it appeared to some as if he were treating the Soviet Union and the United States as equals. This outraged many in the United States who maintained that the struggle with communism was a deeply moral conflict and that the Soviet Union was the moral villain. It was, therefore, predictable that those who had staked out strong positions against the Soviet Union during the cold war would read the encyclical differently than those who put the encyclical in the context of North-South relations.

William Buckley, a lay author and former editor of *National Review*, thought the document to be "heart-tearingly misbegotten." He saw the pope adopting a "Tweedledum-Tweedledee view of the crystallized division between the visions of Marx, Lenin, Mao Tse-tung, and Pol Pot over against those of Locke, Jefferson, Lincoln and Churchill."[38] An editorial in the *New Republic* titled "Papal Gull" described John Paul as an "apostle of moral equivalence."[39] An editorial in *America*, however, saw Buckley and other critics as wrong and viewed the encyclical more positively, reading it not from the perspective of the superpower conflict but from that of the forty-one nations classified as "least developed" by the United Nations.[40] The editors of *Commonweal* described the papal letter as a "wide ranging and compelling analysis of the continuing lag in third-world development." They went on to note that some of what was said would be "painful" for Americans to read but the encyclical provided "honest criticism . . . to which we must attend."[41] Writing in the same journal, a former U.S. ambassador applauded the encyclical for its "trenchant criticism of the role of the superpower blocs."[42] An editorial in *New Oxford Review* praised the pope for his moral criticism of both West and East, acknowledging different bases for criticism of the two superpowers, but defending the accuracy of seeing both sides as morally flawed.[43]

Those who took offense at the papal teaching believed the document was guilty of being too evenhanded in the treatment of the superpowers. According to the papal critics a necessary distinction between East and West had to be made, the Soviet side being far more morally flawed, whatever truth lay in criticisms of the United States. Defenders of the encyclical did not see the charge of moral equivalence as fair since the pope on several occasions in the document indicated his support for democracy, religious freedom, free markets, and economic self-initiative. At the same time, supporters of the papal position pointed out that on a practical basis, from the perspective of the poor, both East and West presented inadequate views of development—repressive collectivism and excessive consumerism, respectively—as well as preoccupation with an arms race that misallocated resources away from human development.[44]

Those critics who accused the pope of endorsing moral equivalence seem to have missed an important aspect of the document: the different perspective that John Paul II brought to the discussion of development. "He is concerned in the encyclical with the way the East-West conflict is exported to the detriment of the poor South."[45] Certainly, it was a mistake to think that a pope from communist Poland was blind to the failing of the Soviet regime and its client states. Nor were supporters of the document fairly described as proponents of moral equivalence. The crucial divide was the issue of which axis was given precedence in looking at the world's plight, North-South or East-West. From the perspective of the poor, the viewpoint taken by the pope and supporters of the encyclical, both superpowers deserved criticism for their treatment of the world's poor countries and people. Outside the orbit of the superpowers this was easier to grasp, but for those Americans caught up in the struggle against communism it was hard to see the world from the perspective advocated by John Paul.[46]

Another criticism of SRS was made by the *New York Times* columnist William Safire, who viewed the pope as trying to win favor with third world nations by use of "the rhetoric of resentment." A U.S. representative to the United Nations also wondered whether it was fair to put all the blame for poverty at the feet of the rich nations.[47] In response, however, one Catholic journalist observed that a closer reading of the encyclical did not remove all blame for their plight from the poor nations themselves.[48]

Without doubt the churches of the third world received the encyclical warmly. They saw it as an accurate rendition of the world they knew. For example, the Jesuit Bishop Francisco Claver wrote: "the encyclical is right on target as far as we in the Philippines are concerned."[49] This reaction was not surprising since during the process of writing the document many bishops from the third world offered input, and the pope himself began to read the theological literature emerging out of Latin America and other poor regions.[50] Richardo Antoncich, a Latin American theologian well-versed in Catholic social teaching, believed that SRS would "touch a special nerve" in his part of the world because a "great deal of the theological reflection that has developed in Latin America over the course of the two decades since Medellín now appears in the encyclical."[51]

This last comment challenges those like Richard Neuhaus who wanted to see in the papal statement a rejection of liberation theology. He suggested that the letter "no less than eight times invokes the 'instructions' of the

Congregation for the Doctrine of the Faith, with their rigorous strictures aimed at Liberation Theology."[52] The difficulty with this argument is that Neuhaus failed to notice that all the references were to the second instruction, the one that was interpreted by almost every Latin American theologian as being far more receptive to liberation theology than the first document of the CDF.

In England the Catholic weekly *The Tablet* acknowledged that the letter was "likely to cause equal dismay" in those places that dismissed Paul VI's encyclical. But the editorial viewed the document as balanced in its criticism of rich nations. The bottom line "message of the encyclical is that there can and must be change" in the way the poor of the world are treated.[53] The Jesuit journal *The Month* published two articles of commentary on the document that reflect concerns of scholars of Catholic social teaching. Paul Lakeland sees the letter as "clearly an important and intelligent document."[54] Among several wise observations, Lakeland notes that key ideas of liberation theology, option for the poor and sinful social structures, have been utilized by John Paul, and his thinking about ecology moves beyond the anthropocentric vision of *Laborem exercens* to a more "creationist" view that refuses to treat all of creation as merely instrumental goods for human use.[55] Indian Catholic theologian Mathew Kiliroor suggests that the document reflects an unnecessary preoccupation with demonstrating the "constant" character of the social teaching. He also comments on the centralizing tendencies behind John Paul's use of the term *social doctrine* in the encyclical. Kiliroor, like Lakeland, is supportive of the general message of the encyclical but focuses his comments on the way John Paul presents the teaching.[56]

Additionally, concerns have been raised about two other issues in the encyclical: its methodology and the term *social doctrine*. The methodology of SRS has been both praised and criticized. In the judgment of Philip Land and Peter Henriot, the methodology of SRS is "a major contribution . . . to the development of Catholic social teaching." In their opinion the document's methodology will enrich the social tradition for years to come.

> Experientially in touch with today's reality through a reading of the signs of the times, analytically focused on the global structure of underdevelopment, theologically sensitive to both tradition and scripture, and pastorally open to whatever system respects authentic human development, the encyclical demonstrates an approach to social teaching that will have long-term consequences.[57]

Other commentators have seen it quite differently. Denis Goulet notes, for instance, that "the methodology it employs differs sharply from that found in other works located in this stream. *On Social Concern* is evidently not an exercise in social analysis, but a sermon."[58] Goulet argues that John Paul derives his primary analysis of development from theological sources and does not engage that analysis with other methods to give a structural evaluation of development. This judgment is shared by William K. Tabb: "Moral exhortation in this mode is badly needed but it is also insufficient."[59] It is insufficient because "a prophetic statement that the rich should give to the poor as a matter of charity or justice must also explore the sources of their riches."[60] Donal Dorr also agrees with this assessment: "What is lacking is a social analysis which would take more seriously the causes of the class structure in society and which would then go on to examine ways in which tensions between the different classes can be overcome or lessened."[61]

Finally, Mary Hobgood argues that the encyclical "departs significantly from Paul's teaching by failing to appropriate or even acknowledge important liberation dimensions both of Paul's analysis of capitalism and Paul's understanding of the process of social change."[62] In Hobgood's reading of the text, John Paul places too much emphasis on individual choice, failing to understand that "socioeconomic systems are systems of social relations that specify certain relations between persons and groups, and preclude others."[63] Hobgood concludes that the encyclical is a major departure from mainstream Catholic social teaching because it ignores "structural criticisms concerning the causes of poverty, and by disregarding radical prescriptions of what might be done about poverty."[64]

In sum, it can be said that SRS elicited two negative reactions. One came from those who thought the pope had been unduly critical of the West by treating it no better than the East in the superpower conflict. The other criticism came from theologians and church leaders who saw in John Paul's methodology a tendency to backtrack from a more inductive method that underscored the role of local Christian communities. This was in accord with the centralizing policies that have marked his papacy. Despite these criticisms there was also a widespread sense that John Paul II refocused attention on the plight of the poor around the globe and had used his moral voice for those who often are voiceless.

NOTES

1. Maciej Zieba, *The Surprising Pope: Understanding the Thought of John Paul II*, trans. Karolina Weening, interviews conducted by Adam Pawlowicz (Lanham, Md.: Lexington, 2000).

2. Robert Suro, "The Writing of an Encyclical," in *Aspiring to Freedom*, ed. Kenneth Myers (Grand Rapids, Mich.: Eerdmans, 1988), 161.

3. Ibid., 162.

4. Ibid., 168.

5. Ibid., 168–69.

6. Tad Szulc, *Pope John Paul II: The Biography* (New York: Scribner, 1995), 408–10.

7. Congregation for the Doctrine of the Faith (CDF), "Instruction on Certain Aspects of the 'Theology of Liberation'" (Vatican City: Vatican Polyglot, 1984), and idem, "Instruction on Christian Freedom and Liberation" (Washington, D.C.: U.S. Catholic Conference, 1986). It is significant for understanding this encyclical to recall that the second, more positive, treatment of liberation theology is cited eight times in SRS while the first document is not cited at all.

8. John Paul II, "Pope's Letter to Brazil's Bishops," *Origins* 16, no. 1 (May 22, 1986): 14.

9. Suro, "Writing of an Encyclical," 162.

10. Ibid., 168.

11. George Weigel, *Witness to Hope: The Biography of John Paul II* (New York: HarperCollins, 1999), 557, 558.

12. Suro, "Writing of an Encyclical," 163.

13. Ibid., 164.

14. Ibid., 165.

15. Suro speculates that one explanation for the uneven nature of the letter is that Archbishop Giovanni Battista Re, a former member of the secretariat of state, had moved to another department of the curia. Re was a gifted editor and his absence during the final editing may explain the awkward organization and arrangement of material in certain parts of the letter. See "Writing of an Encyclical," 166.

16. Weigel, *Witness to Hope*, 557.

17. Throughout his papacy John Paul II has been warmly supportive of the United Nations. In SRS the UN is mentioned five times (12, 17, 26 [twice], 33) and documents of the organization are cited twice in footnotes (36, 47). The references are the only ones to non-Catholic sources cited in the encyclical. Though John Paul is aware of criticisms that the UN has not been effective in bringing about the needed reforms, he is unwilling to dismiss the UN and other international organizations that he believes "have worked well for the benefit of peoples" (43). In his appreciation for the work of the United Nations, John Paul II is in accord with his predecessors.

18. Marie-Dominique Chenu, *La "doctrine sociale" de l'Église comme idéologie* (Paris: Cerf, 1979).

19. Mathew Kiliroor, "'Social Doctrine' in *Sollicitudo Rei Socialis*," *The Month* 21, second series (1988): 712. Cf. also Mary Elsbernd, "What Ever Happened to Octogesima adveniens?" *Theological Studies* 56 (1995): 39–60.

20. Congregation for Catholic Education, "Guidelines for Teaching the Church's Social Doctrine in Forming Priests," *The Pope Speaks* 24 (1988): 293.

21. Ibid., 295.

22. Ibid., 297–98.

23. Ibid., 298.

24. Elsbernd, "What Ever Happened to *Octogesima Adveniens*?" 59.

25. John Paul II, *Redemptor hominis* (Vatican City: Vatican, 1979). See in particular numbers 8–17.

26. David Hollenbach, "Editor's Conclusion," in David Hollenbach, Robin Lovin, John Coleman,

J. Bryan Hehir, "Theology and Philosophy in Public: A Symposium on John Courtney Murray's Unfinished Agenda," *Theological Studies* 40 (1979): 714. For an extended treatment of public theology within the Catholic tradition, see Michael J. Himes and Kenneth R. Himes, *Fullness of Faith: The Public Significance of Theology* (New York: Paulist, 1993).

27. Gregory Baum, "Structures of Sin," in *The Logic of Solidarity: Commentaries on Pope John Paul II's* Encyclical "On Social Concern," ed. Gregory Baum and Robert Elsberg (Maryknoll, N.Y.: Orbis, 1989), 110–17.

28. Mary Hobgood, "Conflicting Paradigms in Social Analysis," in *Logic of Solidarity*, ed. G. Baum and R. Elsberg, 167–85; G. Baum, "Structures of Sin," in ibid., 117–23.

29. Karol Wojtyla, *The Acting Person*, trans. Andrzej Potocki (Boston: D. Reidel, 1979), 283–97; see also Kevin P. Doran, *Solidarity: A Synthesis of Personalism and Communalism in the Thought of Karol Wojtyla/Pope John Paul II* (New York: Peter Lang, 1996), 123–67.

30. Pope Pius XII, *Summi pontificatus*, number 35, in *The Papal Encyclicals, 1939–1958*, ed. Claudia Carlen (Wilmington, N.C.: McGrath, 1981), 10. This same excerpt from Pope Pius XII is cited in *Catechism of the Catholic Church*, number 1939.

31. René Coste, "*Solidarité*," in *Dictionnaire de Spiritualité* 14 (Paris: Beauchesne, 1990), 1000–1001.

32. Available on the Internet at http://www.vatican.va/holy_father/john__paul_ii/messages/peace/ (downloaded July 7, 2003).

33. Charles E. Curran, *Catholic Social Teaching 1891–Present: A Historical, Theological, and Ethical Analysis* (Washington, D.C.: Georgetown University Press, 2002), 127–36.

34. E.g., Timothy P. Jackson, *The Priority of Love: Christian Charity and Social Justice* (Princeton, N.J.: Princeton University Press, 2003).

35. Marie Vianney Bilgrien, *Solidarity: A Principle, an Attitude, a Duty or the Virtue for an Interdependent World?* (New York: Peter Lang, 1999).

36. A systematic treatment of the virtues in Catholic moral theology can be found in C. E. Curran, *The Catholic Moral Tradition Today: A Synthesis* (Washington, D.C.: Georgetown University Press, 1999), 110–36.

37. Curran, *Catholic Social Teaching 1891–Present*, 45–48.

38. William F. Buckley, "What Is the Pope Saying?" *National Review* 40 (March 18, 1988): 17–18.

39. Editor, "Editorial," *New Republic* 198 (March 14, 1988): 5–7.

40. Editor, "The 'Solidarity' Encyclical," *America* 158 (March 12, 1988): 251.

41. Editors, "*Sollicitudo Rei Socialis*," *Commonweal* 115 (March 11, 1988): 131–32.

42. Robert E. White, "Blaming the Villains, Not the Victims," *Commonweal* 115 (October 21, 1988): 555.

43. Editor, "Neither East Nor West: On the Pope's Radical New Encyclical," *New Oxford Review* 15 (April 1988): 2–5.

44. John W. Donohue, "A Lever to Move the World," *America* 159 (October 8, 1988): 211–12.

45. Editors, "A Charter for the Human Family," *The Tablet* 242 (February 27, 1988): 231.

46. Roland Faley nicely described the challenge for U.S. citizens: "It is not difficult for most people to recognize a Communist regime as repressive and therefore morally objectionable. More difficult for many to see is how capitalism, a system that has brought so much to so many, can also be guilty. And yet that is the reality." See "Pope as Prophet: The New Social Encyclical," *America* 158 (April 30, 1988): 449.

47. As reported in Donohue, "A Lever to Move the World," 211. Even one author who warmly endorsed the document stated he "would have hoped the encyclical had said more" about the culpability of governments in the poor nations. After all, there are "totalitarian regimes that exist quite apart from the superpowers" and the "poor of the world are abused by their own governments," not just the rich nations. See Faley, "Pope as Prophet," 449.

48. Ibid., 211. On this point see number 44 of the encyclical, where the pope cites an array of reforms that poor nations should consider.

49. See Francisco Claver, "*Sollicitudo Rei Socialis*: A View from the Philippines," in *Logic of Solidarity*, ed. G. Baum and R. Elsberg, 202.

50. Suro reports that during the summer of 1987 John Paul II read several works of liberation theology. See "Writing of an Encyclical," 162.

51. Richardo Antoncich, "*Sollicitudo Rei Socialis*: A Latin American Perspective," in *Logic of Solidarity*, ed. G. Baum and R. Elsberg, 211.

52. Richard Neuhaus, "*Sollicitudo* Behind the Headlines," in *Aspiring to Freedom*, ed. K. Myers, 136.

53. Editors, "A Charter for the Human Family," 231.

54. Paul Lakeland, "Development and Catholic Social Teaching: Pope John Paul's New Encyclical," *The Month* 21 (June 1988): 708.

55. Ibid., 710, 708.

56. Kiliroor, "'Social Doctrine' in *Sollicitudo Rei Socialis*," 711–14.

57. Philip S. Land and Peter J. Henriot, "Toward a New Methodology in Catholic Social Teaching," in *Logic of Solidarity*, ed. G. Baum and R. Ellsberg, 74.

58. Denis Goulet, "The Search for Authentic Development," in ibid., 130.

59. William K. Tabb. "John Paul II and Fidel Castro," in ibid., 157.

60. Ibid., 158.

61. Donal Dorr, *Option for the Poor: A Hundred Years of Catholic Social Teaching*, rev. ed. (Maryknoll, N.Y.: Orbis, 1992), 332.

62. Mary E. Hobgood, "Conflicting Paradigms in Social Analysis," in *Logic of Solidarity*, ed. G. Baum and R. Ellsberg, 174.

63. Ibid., 175.

64. Ibid., 168.

SELECTED BIBLIOGRAPHY

Baum, Gregory, and Robert Ellsberg. *The Logic of Solidarity: Commentaries on Pope John Paul II's* Encyclical "On Social Concern." Maryknoll, N.Y.: Orbis, 1989. A solid collection of essays by a variety of scholars from theology as well as the social sciences who examine the encyclical's methodology and significance as well as its actual teaching.

Bilgrien, Marie Vianney. *Solidarity: A Principle, an Attitude, a Duty or the Virtue for an Interdependent World?* New York: Peter Lang, 1999. An in-depth study of the meaning of solidarity that shows the complexity of its modern usage.

Dorr, Donal. *Option for the Poor: A Hundred Years of Catholic Social Teaching*. Rev. ed. Maryknoll, N.Y.: Orbis, 1992. The first half of chapter 13 is devoted to the author's assessment of the encyclical with special concern for the papal understanding of solidarity.

Myers, Kenneth, ed. *Aspiring to Freedom*. Grand Rapids, Mich.: Eerdmans, 1988. A collection of essays from an ecumenical group of authors that examines the background to the letter as well as its impact on the wider political and economic setting.

CHAPTER

18 Commentary on *Centesimus annus* (*On the Hundredth Anniversary of* Rerum novarum)

DANIEL FINN

INTRODUCTION

Pope John Paul II issued *Centesimus annus* on the one hundredth anniversary of *Rerum novarum*, the great 1891 encyclical of Pope Leo XIII, the first major statement of modern papal social thought. John Paul addresses both the dramatic changes undermining communism in Eastern Europe and the necessary choices by newly liberated nations concerning alternative economic systems. More thoroughly than any of his predecessors, he engages the arguments surrounding Western capitalism. He condemns Eastern European socialism but holds out hope for capitalism if it accords with the requirements of justice. He criticizes the consumerist culture in the West and the tendency of capitalism to take unfair advantage of working people. His encyclical is a strong call for both personal and institutional renewal.

OUTLINE OF THE DOCUMENT

The encyclical comprises six chapters and an introduction. At the outset the pope states that this new document will be a "re-reading" of *Rerum novarum*. In chapter one he then comments upon Leo's earlier letter and makes three points. First, there were, in fact, many morally appalling "new things" that Leo faced in 1891. Second, in addressing the social question, Leo was right to maintain that the Christian view of the person generates the correct picture of society. And, finally, Leo opposed both socialism and liberalism in his time.

Chapter two is a presentation of what John Paul sees as the "new things" of today. He notes the collapse of communism and sees the underlying weakness of socialism to have been an anthropological error: subordination of the person to the socioeconomic mechanism. When this is done the autonomy of the person disappears and the "subjectivity" of society is thwarted. The Church also opposes the idea of class struggle even though it affirms conflict in the struggle for social justice.

The state must respect a legitimate sphere of autonomy in economic life. This is true even though the state must construct a "juridical framework" for economic life. Two principles to guide the state in this regard are subsidiarity and solidarity.

The pope also notes that a proper understanding of freedom is not to be equated with self-love but obedience to the truth. He concludes this chapter with criticisms of consumerism and the arms race and a defense of human rights and aid to poor nations.

Chapter three is a review of the remarkable year 1989, which saw the collapse of the U.S.S.R. and its political bloc. John Paul observes that several things contributed to this collapse: the violations of workers' rights, the inefficiency of a command economy, and the utopian desire to eliminate all evil. Most markedly, the collapse of communism was due to the spiritual void of atheism.

The central arguments of the encyclical are contained in chapter four, which discusses private property, free markets, and capitalism after the demise of socialism. According to the papal viewpoint there is a real but not absolute right to private property. God gave the wealth of the earth for the sustenance of all; this is the principle of "the universal destination of the earth's goods." Fundamentally, possessions should be considered as "common to all." This is true even for new forms of property associated with modern work, such as know-how, technology, and skills.

Today's market economy exhibits both positive aspects (freedom, initiative, prosperity) and violations of justice (marginalizing the poor, mistreatment of workers, domination of things over people). It is true that the market is the most efficient economic mechanism, but this is true only for "solvent" needs (backed by purchasing power) and for marketable resources (not the environment).

Should capitalism be the goal? The papal response to the question is twofold: if by capitalism is meant the responsible exercise of economic freedom and a positive role for business the answer is yes; however, if capitalism is equated with freedom unrestrained by a proper and strong juridical framework, the answer is no. Socialism's failure does not mean that a blind trust in markets is now acceptable. The private ownership of the means of production can be a service to workers, but it is legitimate only if it serves the cause of work and workers. The Church has no economic model of its own to present, but it is concerned with the moral dimensions of economic life. In that regard, the pope notes the evil of consumerism and the harm it does to families and the environment.

Chapter five of the letter moves the focus to the relationship of state and culture. There is an endorsement of democracy coupled with a reminder that authentic freedom only exists in the truth. The state is the institution that is oriented to the common good and is to be guided by subsidiarity and solidarity. The existence of a healthy civil society with a generous number of social organizations helps maintain the "subjectivity of society." A consequence of this approach that the pope outlines is his criticism of the social assistance state and an impersonal bureaucratic approach to meeting the needs of the neighbor. He advocates smaller-scale welfare assistance for the needy.

In the final section there is a reminder that the human person is the way that the Church must follow and advocate. One danger of the collapse of "real socialism" is that it will keep Western nations from changing their own economic institutions. A proper economic system will be shaped by the preferential option for the poor which is to help entire peoples enter into productive economic life. Finally, the pope calls for a commitment to change lifestyles and sinful structures so that justice may be attained.

CONTEXT OF THE DOCUMENT

After decades of decennial anniversary encyclicals celebrating and extending the work of Pope Leo XIII in *Rerum novarum*, it was nearly certain that Pope John Paul II would publish another in 1991, for the one hundredth anniversary of the original. Even its title, *Centesimus annus*, was predictable. However, no one could have anticipated the radical change in the social context of this document, coming as it did in the midst of the dramatic transformation of communism in the Soviet Union and Eastern Europe. In addition, this pope was no mere observer of events. Because John Paul himself was understood to be an important catalyst of these changes, his encyclical was guaranteed from the beginning to draw the attention of leaders of academy, embassy, factory, and favela.[1]

Karol Wojtyla grew up under the heavy hand of Polish communism. As a manual laborer, a teacher, and later a bishop in Krakow, Wojtyla knew firsthand the terrible problems the Polish people faced in both their personal and public lives. Thus it is no surprise that once he became Pope John Paul II, this intellectual churchman, committed to a more just economic system, would attend carefully to the world historical events unfolding in his homeland and elsewhere in Eastern Europe as he wrote this new encyclical.

Poland, of course, was not simply one of the nations of Eastern Europe in the process of throwing off the Soviet Union. It was the leader in this movement. And the primary impetus within Poland for this transformation was a labor union named Solidarity, based at a shipyard. While intellectuals, businesspeople, and students played a role, there is little doubt in history—and little doubt in John Paul's own assessment—that working people, organized to accomplish morally worthy goals, were at the heart of the transformation that the world so badly needed.

The revolution within Poland occurred in a nonviolent manner, a tactic that may have been necessary in the face of overwhelming state police power, but a tactic nonetheless that was endorsed by Bishop Wojtyla and the Catholic Church. Thus, in the reflections of a pope in an encyclical on the hundredth anniversary of *Rerum novarum*, the Polish transformation stands as the model of the sort of politically effective movement to which even a Roman pontiff could give general support without appearing to be politically biased.

This dramatic series of events still unfolding at the time of the publication of *Centesimus annus* presented an occasion for the Church's message, truly a *kairos* (an opportunity) that exceeded even the timeliness of *Rerum novarum*. In the face of the immense social and economic transformations—and widespread suffering of ordinary people—caused by the Industrial Revolution, Leo XIII had ample reason to begin his famous encyclical with the claim that the historic results "of new things" (*rerum novarum*) were revolutionizing the world. The Church needed to make a response to the "social question," to offer a strategy for hope. But while the social and economic context within which Leo operated had been simmering for 150 years, John Paul was facing a novelty of developments over the prior two or three years, a tumultuous change from the stability of the cold war scenario that had been in place since the end of World War II. Thus, given both his own personal involvement in Poland and the historic opportunity being taken up at that very moment by a dozen or more nations rethinking their political and economic institutions, the pope had an unprecedented opportunity for a constructive contribution to ongoing public debate and struggle.

The ecclesial context of this encyclical also was significantly different from that of Leo's original. It will be helpful to attend to two separate dimensions. The first is the care with which church leaders had engaged the ongoing developments in the secular world. The Church and its popes had, over the previous century, developed a greater sense of humility about its own mission and insight than had characterized the early encyclicals in this century-long tradition. On the one hand, both *Rerum novarum* and *Quadragesimo anno* (written by Pius XI in 1931) demonstrated an unfortunate lack of careful attention to the secular arguments they criticized. The most significant error in this regard was the presumption by both of these popes that socialism universally called for the end of all forms of private property. As Leo put it: "The main tenet of socialism [is] the community of goods" (RN 12). And in his effort to celebrate the importance of his predecessor's work, Pius XI made the outlandish claim that in Leo's day "the eyes of all, as often in the past, turned toward the Chair of Peter, sacred repository of the fullness of truth whence words of salvation are dispensed to the whole world" (QA 7), something that surely raised the eyebrows of those Catholics of the day who realized regretfully that most eyes looked in other directions.

Later popes, such as John XXIII and Paul VI, were more aware of the limits of the

Church's insights into what are not simply moral but also technical economic and political matters.[2] John Paul himself has deepened this awareness,[3] declaring in the introduction that it "does not fall per se within the Magisterium's specific domain" to "pass definitive judgments" on historical developments (3). One can only surmise that corresponding to this growing sense of humility, and perhaps producing it, was a greater awareness of the subtleties of the arguments about economic and political matters in the secular arena.

A prominent part of this shift in the Church's attitude about its own advice to the secular world was the change in the content of that advice over the century. Leo and Pius had quite openly expressed their admiration for the older medieval approach to the organization of economic life, primarily based on the guild system.[4] As Leo put it, "in no other way can [society] be cured but by a return to the Christian life and Christian institutions" (RN 22). In the older guild system, the responsibility for the morality of economic life was located primarily in this organization of producers in each line of artisanship. Similarly, following the economic analysis of the nineteenth-century Jesuit economist Heinrich Pesch,[5] Pius argued for an organization of the modern economy based on corporatism, where workers, managers, and owners in each industry would form an organization to deal with any problems there (QA 82).

Unfortunately for this proposed solution, the world was at the time developing along other lines. The great struggles of workers against abuse by their employers were not being resolved by industry-specific conversations among workers, managers, and owners. Instead they were being structured by national governments, pressed by democratic majorities to legalize trade unions as countervailing forces against corporations.[6] Once governments set up the rules for these negotiations, the period of bloody struggles between unions and management in Europe and the United States shifted to an economic struggle of heavyweights.[7] Beginning with Pius XII, papal documents acknowledged this development. Thus, when John Paul set out to write his encyclical, the general format of the advice had been set by both encyclical tradition and world history. He does not propose new institutions the way Leo XIII and Pius XI had, but instead talks about both the values to be incorporated and the role of the state in setting up the structures of economic and political life.

In doing so, John Paul exhibits that very Catholic tendency toward "mediation." Most fundamentally, as Charles Curran has put it, this aspect of Catholic theology recognizes "that the gospel, faith, and grace cannot deny or go around the human but are mediated in and through the human. The gospel does not provide a shortcut which avoids the human and supplies rather direct and easy answers to complex social problems."[8] By recognizing that the way of the gospel is through the human person, and that this involves complexities addressed by the various sciences, Catholic social thought strives to avoid two kinds of mistakes: the claim that the Church has no competence in economic issues, and the opposite extreme, that Christian faith or the Bible can provide neat answers to complicated and contingent economic questions.[9] As Richard Gaillardetz describes it in greater detail,[10] the Church and the world are engaged in "a mutually critical correlation."

A second important dimension of the ecclesial context for CA was the quarter century of theological developments concerning the relation of faith and economic life that had taken place since Vatican II. Three among these deserve mention here: liberation theology, the neoconservative defense of capitalism, and the publication of detailed responses to economic issues by various national episcopal conferences.

Liberation theology arose out of a conviction on the part of Gustavo Gutiérrez and a number of other Latin American theologians educated in Europe or the United States that a first world theology does not fit the realities of their people.[11] Rather, building on but extending recent themes in much mainstream theology, these theologians began with three central insights. The first is that theology is a secondary task, a task of reflection on an already existing life of faith. This means that theology can only be done after lived participation in the life of a Christian community. The second is that the example of Jesus requires identification with and commitment alongside of the poor and marginalized in society. The third is that the work of God in history has been a work of liberation. As Gutiérrez has argued, this liberation extends from the exodus (which is too often spiritualized away from its economic and political reality) to the mission of Jesus, bringing freedom to captives and hope to the forlorn, and on to the work of God in our day. In the Latin American context, this has meant identification with the poorest sectors of society and commitment to working with them in the process of liberation. This commitment embodies the "preferential option for the poor," a phrase that within a decade began appearing in episcopal and papal documents.

Liberation theologians' critique of capitalistic abuses and endorsement of socialism brought tension with church authorities, as did their encouragement of "base ecclesial communities," which many bishops viewed with suspicion as undermining the traditional parish structure. Most problematic was their appreciation of Marxist analysis,[12] a far more respectable academic and political option in Latin America than in the United States, or even in Europe. They argued that the "developed" nations were keeping most of the rest of the world underdeveloped, thus rejecting the "developmentalism" espoused by the United Nations and even, in their view, much church teaching.[13]

Although it began in Latin America, liberation theology was endorsed by Christian movements for social transformation in Africa, Asia, and the developed world. It has had important impacts on theological developments among women and racial and ethnic minorities in most parts of the globe. It generally received support, ranging from enthusiastic to respectful, among academics in North America and Europe.

A second important development prior to CA was the effort on the part of conservative Catholics to construct a moral defense of capitalism. Prior to the 1970s there were many religiously motivated critiques of the capitalist system, but few attempts to articulate a religious defense in its favor. At the same time, however, there was a nearly 300-year history of secular theorizing about the advantages of freedom, markets, and self-interested activity in economic life.

Central to the argument was a description of the economic system as only one element of a three-part social system referred to as "democratic capitalism" by Michael Novak, the most prominent proponent of this point of view. Together, economic markets, political democracy, and the institutions of "the moral-cultural system" acted as checks and balances for each other. Thus, while a free economy left people, Christians and others, free to make choices that are good or bad from a moral point of view, it was the responsibility of culture (especially the churches), and not the government, to counteract the bad ones and encourage the good. Most well-intentioned advocates for the poor wrongly emphasized the redistribution of goods as the key to addressing poverty. Neoconservatives pointed out in response that the prosperity of the industrialized countries must almost in its entirety be attributed to the productivity of their citizens, and not to the exploitation of the poor nations of the world, even though abuse does at times occur.

Theologically, neoconservatives saw the need for the Church to shift away from its historic aversion to commerce and recognize that, if backed by strong cultural institutions, virtuous behavior, and an appropriately restrained political system, the market is by far the best economic arrangement for human flourishing and deserves ecclesiastical endorsement.

Although definitely a minority opinion in academic and church institutions, this neoconservative movement received significant appreciation and support in secular conservative circles, and growing respect and support from church people.

The third development in the ecclesial context of CA was the drafting of pastoral letters and other documents on economic life by numerous national conferences of Catholic bishops around the world.[14] Though these universally exhibited heavy dependence on the encyclical tradition, their existence stood as a kind of local approbation and encouragement to John Paul as he prepared to extend this tradition in new directions.

In summary, both the ecclesial and social contexts for CA were significantly different from those of *Rerum novarum*. The most fundamental similarities, however, stand out as well: the suffering of so many in the world, the Church's vision of hope, and the courage of a pope to work to bring the two together.

PROCESS OF FORMULATION AND AUTHORSHIP

With the publication of *Solicitudo rei socialis* in 1988, delayed past its official 1987 date commemorating the twentieth anniversary of *Populorum progressio,* there was some discussion on the Pontifical Council for Justice and Peace as to whether another encyclical should be issued on roughly the same topic a mere three years later. Would John Paul have anything significantly new to say? Still, the hundredth anniversary of *Rerum novarum* was important enough that at least some document commemorating the anniversary seemed appropriate.[15] A draft was prepared within the Council, centering on the issues of property and other themes brought forward from Leo's encyclical. However, these subdued expectations were dramatically altered by the events that transformed the pope's homeland in 1989.

In August of that year a Catholic intellectual, Tadeusz Mazowieki, was elected prime minister of Poland. By early October, Mazowieki's finance minister, Leszek Balcerowicz, announced detailed plans to convert the nation to a market economy, even though, he announced, the nation would temporarily undergo problems of tight money, unemployment, and bankruptcies on the way to a prosperous market-based economy.[16] These events clearly drew the pope's attention. The drafting of a relatively minor anniversary document was taken over by the Vatican secretary of state and the pope himself by the time the Polish government implemented these reforms in early 1990. This direct involvement by the pope also entailed efforts to engage the best of contemporary economic thinking on the issues.

Jorge Mejía, vice president of the Pontifical Council for Justice and Peace at the time, reports the pope himself proposed that the Council organize a symposium of leading economists to help the Church and the pope develop an informed perspective on the economic prospects for Eastern Europe at the time. With the help of Italian economists Ignazio Musu and Stefano Zamagni, the Council invited and got agreement from nearly twenty internationally known economists to present answers to a list of detailed questions developed by the Vatican. Fifteen economists participated in the gathering in November 1990, which included a lunch with John Paul in the papal residence.

These were economists of international recognition, including Protestants, Catholics, Jews, and others.[17] The fundamental themes of the conversation developed in two directions: the relation between economic systems and ethics (including issues of the government's role in the economy, efficiency, and distributive justice) and the problems of economic development (including problems in the transition from central planning to greater reliance on markets).[18] As J. C. de Pablo has put it, the economists told the pope "that capitalism works and communism doesn't, that developing nations have no alternative but to join themselves with the first world, that the Pope should express a preference for the poor, that the distribution of investment spontaneously generated in capitalism is morally intolerable for its inequality, and that the economist's vision of *homo economicus* is completely inadequate as a theory of the human person."[19] At the end of the session, the pope told the group he was deeply impressed by the concern these economists showed for the moral dimensions of economic life.

Jorge Mejía has described this effort as part of "the well-known concern of the Holy Father that the documents of the Holy See be seriously and rigorously scientific when they refer in any way to science."[20] This consultation represents the most thoroughgoing interaction of a pontiff with economists in the effort to improve the content of church teaching; it bodes well for the ongoing improvement in the quality of Catholic social teaching.[21]

In spite of such care in the drafting process, it is peculiar that several ideas centrally important to John Paul's earlier work do not appear in CA. In his 1981 encyclical, *Laborem exercens,* John Paul employed the ideas of the "priority of labor over capital" and the "indirect employer,"[22] but neither of these appears in this later encyclical. The notion of the "structures of sin" is mentioned only once (38). Nonetheless, this document clearly demonstrates an organic development and basic continuity in John Paul's vision of the world.

There is little doubt that several persons were involved in the drafting of CA, though details on this will likely not be made public during John Paul's own lifetime. Nonetheless it is clear, according to Jorge Mejía, that there was no "ghost writer" in the usual sense of that term. John Paul made very clear to those assisting him what he wanted to say, often writing parts himself in Polish first, and exercised a complete and active oversight in the process.[23]

ESSAY

CA addresses a large number of issues concerning the relation of faith and economic life. Most are treated in more than one place in the document. As a result it will be helpful to consider the key issues thematically rather than in accord with the organization of the document.

The Tradition of Catholic Social Thought: Rerum novarum

Deference to predecessors is fundamental to the genre of literature known as the papal encyclical. Beyond this predictable dimension of CA, however, Pope John Paul II is authentically wrestling with *Rerum novarum,* the famous work of his predecessor Leo XIII, and as he himself puts it, he proposes a "rereading" of that document (3). Recognizing Leo's work as part of the Church's tradition, John Paul cites Matthew 13:52 to explain that, like Leo, he is acting as the householder who "brings out of his treasure what is new and what is old" (3).

John Paul recalls that Leo was reacting not only to new developments in the economic life of the world but also to "a new conception of society and of the state, and consequently of authority itself" (4). John Paul points to capital after the Industrial Revolution as a new form of property and wage labor as a new form of work. He argues that their interaction has transformed economic reality. He thereby implicitly acknowledges that the modern world, in bringing forth these developments, requires a new orientation of the Church's social thought.

From John Paul's point of view, Leo began at the proper starting point for theological access to these worldly issues: the view of the human person. From this point, about which the Church has considerable confidence, it can make a constructive statement about new and more complicated issues of economic and political life in the modern world. As John Paul puts it, "from the Christian vision of the human person there necessarily follows a correct picture of society" (13). Further evidence for the centrality of this controlling methodological principle is that it appears not only in the opening chapters when John Paul discusses Leo's work, but it is also the title of the final chapter of CA: "Man is the Way of the Church."

Consistent with encyclical style over the ages, John Paul does not cite those parts of *Rerum novarum* that history has proved to be unhelpful. Thus there is no mention of Leo's hope that new economic institutions, a "third way," might come to characterize the economic world and provide the moral guidance for economic life. (Pius XI later developed this hope with an endorsement of corporatism, the organization of workers, managers, and owners in each industry.[24]) At the same time, however, John Paul celebrates and lists at length numerous teachings of Leo that remain critical today. He cautions that "the church has no models to present," no "third way" that, after the work of Leo and Pius, Catholics had for decades hoped could offer the world an alternative structure.

The right to private property is essential, including private ownership of the means of production, but it is not an absolute right, as it falls under the limitation of "the universal destination of the earth's goods" (6). This way of conceiving of private property is so important that it becomes the title and focus of chapter 4, the longest in CA, in which John Paul analyzes capitalism and markets. Similarly, John Paul cites various rights of human persons that Leo endorses. These include the right to form private associations (including professional associations, trade unions, and a wide variety of other social or political organizations), the right to limitation on working hours, to legitimate rest, and—especially for women and children—the right to be treated differently with regard to the character and length of the work day.

John Paul explicitly cites Leo's argument that workers have the right to a just wage, which cannot be defined as the market wage. As Leo argued, the right to subsistence and the obligation of the worker to support self and family is so strong that not even the consent of workers can guarantee the justice of a wage if it is not sufficient (34). The inequality in power between workers and corporations is so large that workers may be forced by circumstance to agree to a wage that is not just (8). In this regard, John Paul extends further than Leo the traditional moral skepticism of the Church about market relationships. As John Paul puts it, a "purely pragmatic" relation between employers and employees, one "inspired by a thorough-going individualism," is unacceptable in a moral economic system and was "severely censured" in Leo's work. John Paul asserts that "even today one finds instances of contracts between employers and employees which lack reference to the most elementary justice" in regard to such things as working hours, working conditions, and the employment of children or women. He notes that Leo, in spite of his condemnation of the socialist state, holds that governments everywhere have the "strict duty" of preventing such injustices and actively seeking distributive justice to rectify these situations (8).

John Paul notes Leo's criticism of both socialism and liberalism and his argument for a national government that avoids the mistakes of both an overly collective and overly individualistic orientation. The state has the obligation to defend the rights of individuals, especially of the poor, who rarely have the political access to argue for this on their own. Leo opposed Marxism in his insistence on the rights of individuals, but equally opposed the liberal view of the state that would eliminate the government's role as guarantor of distributive justice. As John Paul puts Leo's view, "the mass of the poor have no resources of their own to fall back on, and must chiefly depend on the assistance of the state" (10).

John Paul acknowledges Leo's recognition of this social connectedness among persons and classes in society. What Leo called "friendship" (and what Pius XI called "social charity") John Paul says is "what we nowadays call the principle of solidarity" (10). In this, John Paul extends and deepens the notion of "solidarism," developed by nineteenth-century European Catholics and endorsed by Heinrich Pesch.[25] Undergirding this obligation of all to solidarity are, in his view, both the teachings of Jesus about concern for the poor as well as the fundamental rights arising from the dignity of the human person created by God (30).

Clearly, John Paul is building his own statement about economic life on the foundation crafted by his nineteenth-century predecessor.

The Human Person

From John Paul's perspective, the person is the entry point of Catholic social thought into ongoing economic debates. "The Church has no models to present" in the ongoing debate about economic and political institutions (43), but it has much to say about the dignity and character of the human person (*Redemptor hominis*, number 10). And since there is in the world "the fruitful activity of many millions of people" who are working for economic justice, "these people represent a great movement for the defense of the human person and the safeguarding of human dignity" (3). Thus, what the Church has to say about the human person is vividly important in the ongoing efforts to transform the world.

John Paul bases this concern for each person in both Christology and the doctrine of creation, for the human is "the only creature on earth which God willed for its own sake, and for which God has his plan, that is, a share in eternal salvation" (53). For this reason the Church has taken up "the social question" for the sole purpose of caring and taking responsibility for humanity, the mission "entrusted to her by Christ himself" (53). Like Christ, the Church must engage the mystery of incarnation and redemption in developing its social doctrine (RH 8–10). This effort is always in service to the Church's "religious and transcendent mission" on behalf of humanity, but it must never abandon the particularities of the struggles of daily economic life (55).

This does mean, however, that the Church's social teaching will avoid the reductionism of both left and right. Where Marxists reduce the religious standing of humanity to the thin shell of secular status, many on the political right ignore the dehumanizing effects of subsistence wages, demeaning working conditions, or the cult of consumerism among the prosperous.

John Paul spends considerable time and effort in this encyclical on an analysis of economic institutions, and with good reason. But equally important, he stresses that those social and economic institutions must not be used as an excuse for failing to heed Christ's call. "Man receives from God his essential dignity and with it the capacity to transcend every social order so as to move towards truth and goodness" (38).

The love which God has shown for humanity, and which the Trinitarian relationship demonstrates within the life of God, represents a call to communion and solidarity for all people in this world. As John Paul quotes Vatican II's *Pastoral Constitution on the Church in the Modern World*, "it is through the free gift of self that man truly finds himself" (GS 41). This "capacity for transcendence" is quintessentially human, though the forces of sin tempt individuals and groups to opt for selfish aims. In this, of course, Leo XIII was right: we will not find a solution to the social question aside from the gospel message of love of neighbor (RN 13).

Private Property

John Paul's reliance on the Catholic interpretation of private property is at the center of his analysis of economic life in the modern world. Only the notion of the dignity of the human person is appealed to more frequently than the teaching on private property.

John Paul begins with an endorsement of Leo's affirmation of "the natural character of the right to private property" (30). In doing so, however, John Paul notes that Leo's arguments in favor of private property played a particularly important role in his predecessor's efforts to oppose socialism in the late nineteenth century. John Paul tactfully does not note that Leo XIII and Pius XI represent the high water mark of individualism in the trajectory of Catholic views on private property.[26] As Ernest L. Fortin has said, their views "always smacked of something like *fin-de-siècle* capitalism."[27]

Leo was faced with many "new things" brought about by the tremendous cultural transformation wrought by the Industrial Revolution. Uncounted numbers of people in the industrializing nations of Europe were uprooted from their traditional agricultural setting and lived in hastily created urban slums that offered neither the physical nor cultural and spiritual security of a previous era. This, of course, led Leo to criticize the greed of wealthy industrialists. In response to such abuses came the rise of trade unionism, but this was predominately the work of antireligious parties and organizations on the political left. Church membership in Europe dropped off dramatically. The departure of the working class from the churches was less attributable to socialist agents of persuasion within the union movement than to the cultural dislocations that broke up families and severed traditional religious ties. The pope, however, was left with no other guilty party to point to than the anticlerical socialists and this deeply influenced his view of the world situation of his day. The result was that Leo proposed a view of private property more individualistic than that of the medieval or early church.

Prior to the Industrial Revolution, Catholic teaching on property had not changed much since the early days of the patristic period. The fathers of East and West, such as Clement of Alexandria, Ambrose of Milan, Augustine, and

John Chrysostom, all agreed on the basics. God had given the earth to humanity to meet the needs of all. As Ambrose put it, "Not from your own do you bestow upon the poor man, but you make return from what is his. For what has been given as common for the use of all, you appropriate to yourself alone. The earth belongs to all, not to the rich. . . . Therefore you are paying a debt, you are not bestowing what is not due."[28] The standard patristic formulation was that if I have more than I need and you have less than you need, I have an obligation to share my surplus with you.

A millennium later, Thomas Aquinas retained this basic formula and incorporated it into a full-blown theory of natural law, rooted, as was the patristic doctrine, in an insight into God's intention in creating the world. For Thomas, every creaturely thing was created with a purpose from God, and fulfilling that purpose was the essence of that thing's "natural law." Thomas's view of private property was based in this analysis.

For Thomas, there were two dimensions of the question of private property: first, the procuring and dispensing of goods and second, the use of goods.

Thomas argued that procuring and dispensing material objects is in general best handled by individuals who have individual responsibility and control over those things. He gave three now-famous reasons for this conviction.[29] The first was that people are more careful to produce or otherwise obtain something that would be theirs personally than if, following the procurement, it were to be owned by everyone in common. The second is that human affairs will be more orderly if particular persons are charged with taking care of particular things; people should take care of their own things. The third reason Thomas gives is that with private procuring and dispensing of property there will be greater peace, as there will be no disputes as to who has authority over which things.

All this sounds like a strong endorsement of an individualistic view of ownership, but the second dimension of property that Thomas then identifies is the actual use of the things in question. Here Thomas teaches that when it comes to use, everyone should possess things "not as their own, but as common" so that the owner is "ready to communicate them to others in their need." That is, although the owner of an object has the authority to decide its use, that person does not have the authority to use it in any way he or she wishes. Rather, the nature of material things can only be fulfilled if they meet human needs, in accord with God's creative intention. Thus, if I were to horde bread in my pantry beyond my own needs and if you did not have sufficient food, I would be under obligation to share my bread with you. Thomas goes on to argue that if the need is urgent due to some imminent danger and there is no other possible remedy, the needy may take the property of the well-to-do without this being morally wrong.[30]

In sum, while Thomas recognizes that the invention of private property by humans was a wise and prudent thing to do (he describes it as a useful human addition to natural law, like the invention of clothing),[31] his limitations on the rights of ownership conflict with the typical modern view of a more absolute control over property by owners.

Leo XIII made reference to Thomas's work in the footnotes of *Rerum novarum*, but he clearly downplayed Thomas's notion of the common use of material goods. In his concern about the threat posed by atheistic socialists he proceeded to condemn what he mistakenly believed to be the rejection of all private property in socialism (RN 1). In fact, of course, very few socialists ever called for the common holding of all goods. Marxists, for example, only condemned private ownership of the means of production: the tools, machines, and (especially) factories that produce other goods in the industrialized world. And apparently because he overestimated this threat to the Catholic doctrine of property, Leo described that doctrine in somewhat more individualistic terms than Thomas had endorsed.

Leo stressed that private ownership is part of the natural law. His successor, Pius XI, went even further in arguing that it was "given to man . . . by the Creator himself" (QA 45). Thomas, of course, had stressed its correspondence with the natural law but made clear equally that it was a human construction that, presumably, might not have occurred had humans found it less helpful.

As a result, Leo and Pius acknowledged more subtly than Aquinas the obligations of property owners toward those whose needs were unmet. Leo describes this as a "duty, not of justice (except in extreme cases), but of Christian charity" (RN 19), and Pius speaks of it as "the grave obligations of charity, beneficence and liberality" (QA 50). While these are obligations of any good Christian, they are not, in the works of Leo and Pius, as intimately related to the doctrine of property, even though that is clearly the position of the early church and Thomas Aquinas.

For his part, John Paul II, following several of his more recent predecessors, insists on stronger obligations for property owners, and stronger restrictions on their prerogatives, than did Leo or Pius. This means that the economic efficacy and the moral adequacy of markets must be evaluated in light of the conviction that the goods of the earth are destined for all humans and not simply for the prosperous.

Equally important is a subtler shift of the argument from the right *of* private property toward the right *to* private property, as John Paul phrases it in the opening sentence of chapter 4, the most important section of his encyclical. Not only do those who own property have a right to it but all persons have a claim on property, a right to have sufficient amounts of it to maintain themselves and those for whom they have responsibility.

It is additionally significant that John Paul stresses the universal destination of material goods and not simply the right of individuals to food, clothing, shelter, and the other elements essential to life. Rights language is itself a development of the modern world. There was, of course, a basic notion of a right in the premodern world, but it was a claim held by a person in a particular office, as the right of the lord of the manor or the rights of the bishop of Paris. The notion that all persons shared any single claim ("human rights") was only introduced in the late premodern era and only came to be widely employed and acknowledged in the modern age. It is important to note, however, that in spite of the widespread modern conviction that political rights to noninterference (such as the right to free speech or assembly) are more basic and better warranted than economic rights (such as the right to food or shelter), it was the latter kind of right that first appeared in Western intellectual discourse.[32]

Thus, Aquinas did not speak about the rights of individuals to food, clothing, or shelter. When Thomas asserted that a person in urgent and desperate need could morally take goods without permission, he argued that if the wealthy man did not share those goods with the needy, he was violating not the right of the poor man but the nature of those goods (which is to meet human needs), contravening God's intention in creation.

The development of rights language in philosophical ethics and moral theology attended a general cultural shift of focus in the modern world to the individual. Perhaps most vivid here is the change in political life that understands individual persons—all citizens—as holding the ultimate political authority in a nation, with their political leaders having legitimacy only if supported in office by a majority of the citizens. Nearly everyone in the premodern world would have found this claim incredible. This transition occurred for a number of reasons about which scholars speculate. The point here is that in light of this modern shift of the focus of inquiry away from various holistic presumptions and onto the individual person, one can reinterpret the Thomistic relationship between the desperately poor man and the thing he takes from the rich man. From the point of view of the rich man, it is the nature of the bread that is violated if it is not shared. From the point of view of the poor man, there is an implicit claim (called a "right") on the bread embodied in God's intention that all persons, rich and poor, have sufficient food to eat. As David Hollenbach has put it, rights "specify the most fundamental demands of the common good."[33] Thus while Thomas did not use the language of rights, it is not unfair that contemporary moral theology translates his work into the language of rights, as long as the source of those rights is understood as God's intention, both in creating humans as having an irrepressible dignity and in creating material goods to meet human needs.

Many popes of the last half century have cited a long list of rights that all persons have due to their dignity as children of God.[34] Rights language, however, is not without its dangers, because in contemporary civic discourse, rights are often presumed to exist without any reference to an origin in God. Similarly, others have made the claim that rights exist only if the government of the nation says they exist, a sort of positivist view of rights. As James Schall has indicated, in this regard John Paul stakes out his arguments against both Marxism and philosophical liberalism. Although he concludes that John Paul appears "inconsistent and illiberal" to many on this issue, Schall observes that both the source of rights and the conviction that there is a truth that transcends our knowledge of it distance this pope and the tradition of Catholic social thought from the dominant secular academic perspectives of the modern world.[35]

John Paul II has indeed employed rights language[36] but uses it less frequently in the encyclical literature than some of his predecessors, perhaps in light of the problems just cited.[37] Thus his reliance on the notion of the universal destination of goods stresses the idea underlying the right of individuals to the goods they need, but puts the stress where Aquinas put it: on God's creative intention for the goods needed, with somewhat reduced emphasis on the claims of individuals.

At the same time, John Paul extends the argument beyond that of Aquinas in his stress on human work. In Thomas's day, of course, as throughout the premodern world, the wealthy held that status almost universally because they owned large tracts of land. As John Paul puts it, "at one time the natural fruitfulness of the earth appeared to be, and was in fact, the primary factor of wealth, while work was, as it were, the help and support for this fruitfulness" (31). Both mineral and agricultural wealth are quite obviously the gifts of God. It was simply presumed in the premodern world that the doctrine of property applied quite directly to all wealth because, as Augustine once put it, it was "found" here on the earth by the wealthy.[38]

However, today there is a growing awareness that much of the wealth of the world is not simply found in nature but is the result of human work and ingenuity, transforming simpler natural resources into more helpful products whose value far exceeds that of the natural resources embodied in them. Thus, as John Paul puts it, "in our time, the role of human work is becoming increasingly important as the productive factor both of non-material and of material wealth" (31). Here the social character of work becomes critically important, as very little of the great wealth of the modern world would have been possible were it not for this inherent sociality of labor. Machines, skills, scientific knowledge, and various sorts of intellectual property are impossible without the sort of social cohesion that human work makes feasible. John Paul goes on to argue that human knowledge and insight are critical to modern wealth. Without naming it, he praises entrepreneurship as the ability to foresee needs of others and to combine various factors of production to meet those needs (32).

At the same time this attention to work broadens the requirement faced by the well-to-do to assist those without. As David Hollenbach has argued, John Paul's inclusion of skills and technology within the property doctrine means that the universal destination of goods requires "the participation of others in this network of solidarity." Without this inclusion, the ownership even of this intellectual property "has no justification."[39] Not only do goods have a universal destination but a moral society will be structured in such a way that education, skill formation, and access to technology will be available to all and not simply to the privileged[40] (32 and 34).

As a result John Paul condemns those situations in developing nations where "large foreign companies" are "unwilling to commit themselves to the long term development of the host country" (20). While the aggregate data for a nation may show economic growth, a large number of poor and marginalized citizens are often left out of this process, or, as the pope puts it elegantly, "economic development takes place over their heads" (33). He uses the strongest language of the whole encyclical when he describes the injustice visible in the struggle for survival of untold millions of persons in the developing world: "These are situations in which the rules of earliest period of capitalism still flourish in conditions of 'ruthlessness' in no way inferior to the darkest moments of the first phase of industrialization" (33). The solution will not be easy but it must include, according to John Paul, bringing "the great majority of people in the third world" into the benefits that can be experienced only with sound education and good health care systems that will prepare the poor for productive roles in their societies. This will require debt relief for third world nations (35).

The pope also insists on the opening of the markets of the industrialized world to products coming from developing nations (33). This is, of course, a shameful necessity in light of the rhetoric of free trade heard so often from the United States and other Western governments. In making this appeal, John Paul II follows the lead of John XXIII in *Mater et magistra*. There he rejected the policy of "import substitution" in developing countries and instead encouraged their participation in trade with the industrialized world.[41] It is clear that John Paul agreed with the advice of nearly all the economists he had met with when he argued "that the chief problem is that of gaining fair access to the international market" (33).[42]

John Paul concludes his lengthy treatment of property with two particular implications. The first concerns the ownership of the means of production. On the one hand, this ownership is an important service to society because it produces jobs for ordinary workers. On the other hand, this purpose of capital ownership, in creating jobs that pay a wage sufficient to ensure that the goods of the earth are accessible to all, means that ownership becomes illegitimate if it contravenes this goal. As John Paul put it quite precisely,

> Ownership of the means of production, whether in industry or agriculture, is just and legitimate if it serves useful work. It becomes illegitimate, however, when it is not utilized or when it serves to impede the work of others, in an effort to gain a profit which is not the result of the overall expansion of work and wealth of society, but rather is the result of curbing them or of illicit exploitation, speculation or the breaking of solidarity among working people. (43)

As if to make the point undeniable, John Paul adds a sentence immediately following: "Ownership of this kind has no justification, and represents an abuse in the sight of God and man" (43).

This specification of the responsibility of owners of capital toward workers is a far better explanation than "the priority of labor over capital" that played so central a role in *Laborem exercens* ten years earlier (LE 12). That earlier phrase did not distinguish between capital as machines and capital as financial ownership of machines.[43] Jean-Yves Calvez has argued that one of the fundamental problems today is "unequal capitalism" where the prerogatives of capital leave ordinary workers "almost completely" dependent.[44] In CA, John Paul clearly brings owners of capital into the conversation as *part* of the firm. In the pope's words, a business is "a community of persons who in various ways are endeavoring to satisfy their basic needs, and who form a particular group at the service of the whole society" (35).

The last concrete implication of this doctrine of property concerns the right to a job. Beginning with the presumption that each individual has an obligation to work to support self and dependents, John Paul argues that "the obligation to earn one's bread by the sweat of one's brow also presumes the right to do so" (43). He says that economic policies that "do not allow workers to reach satisfactory levels of employment" are unjustifiable from an ethical perspective (43). Thus, while John Paul sides with capitalists against socialists in the right of persons to own the means of production, he sides with socialists against the typical capitalist perspective in his assertion that such ownership of the means of production is morally illegitimate if it does not preeminently serve work and workers.

Subsidiarity and Solidarity

Often in encyclicals, a pope will take pains to affirm what is good and to criticize what is bad on both sides of a contentious issue in the world. John Paul does this in several ways in *Centesimus annus*, but one of the most clear is his conscious linking of two principles: subsidiarity and solidarity.

The principle of subsidiarity, first articulated by Pius XI in *Quadragesimo anno*, is a statement about the relation of individuals and smaller groups to larger regional or national governments that have the legal power to intervene locally.[45]

Pius explained that it is "gravely wrong to take from individuals what they can accomplish by their own initiative and industry and give it to the community." In addition it is similarly unjust "to transfer to the larger and higher collectivity functions which can be performed and provided for by lesser and subordinate bodies" (QA 79). John Paul's own general description of the principle (48) refers only to the latter concern for relationships among communities of higher and lower orders. This description is somewhat peculiar because whereas Pius applied the principle to relationships among organizations (principally between the national state and subordinate groups), John Paul explicitly uses the notion of subsidiarity to warrant economic freedom for individuals in the market. He describes the state as having an indirect contribution to numerous economic goals "by creating favorable conditions for the free exercise of economic activity, which will lead to abundant opportunities for employment and sources of wealth" (15). Government should not arrogate to itself what individuals can properly do among themselves.

Correspondingly, John Paul insists on the principle of "solidarity," a term that appears fifteen times in the document. He describes it as "one of the fundamental principles of the Christian view of social and political organization" (10), even though he acknowledges that the term itself is a recent one in Catholic social thought.[46] He does not define solidarity but it clearly includes both a moral empathy of each toward all others, especially of the well-to-do toward the poor and weak, as well as concrete action in support of this commitment. As Matthew Lamb describes it, the notion of solidarity emphasizes "society and economy as ontologically and ethically oriented toward cooperation and harmony."[47] The pope describes the activity of the state as directly contributing to the achievement of economic goals "by defending the weakest," by limiting the autonomy of powerful employers, and by ensuring minimum support for the unemployed (15). As Charles Strain puts it, "from a solidaristic perspective the concept of equal opportunity which promises each, swift or lame, a chance to race from a mythically identical starting line permits an intolerable degree of social Darwinism."[48] John Paul's conviction of the centrality of cooperation and mutual commitment embodied in solidarity also stands behind his endorsement of nonviolence and his critique of the "insane" arms race among the world's great powers (18).

"Solidarity" is, of course, the name of the labor union in the pope's homeland of Poland that, more than any other organization, brought down the communist state there not long before the writing of this encyclical. As he puts it, "the great upheavals which took place in Poland" occurred "in the name of solidarity" (23). Clearly this identification with a historically effective labor organization of worldwide fame transforms the term *solidarity* into a more politically active and self-consciously transformative notion than is the case for either Leo's *friendship* or Pius's *social charity* (10).

The interplay of the two principles of subsidiarity and solidarity sets the stage for John Paul's careful moral assessment of capitalism. Where subsidiarity argues for the respectful recognition of individual economic initiative, solidarity calls for strong communal action to prevent abuses and ensure the common good.

Society, the State, and the Common Good

Central to John Paul's analysis, and indeed to all Catholic social thought, is the important distinction between society and the state. The state is the governmental apparatus of a nation, something distinct from, though ideally arising out of, the society that constitutes the nation. John Paul's view of the relation of society and government is thoroughly Catholic and rooted in the tradition, even though he himself adds an important element of analysis to it.

Like his more recent predecessors, John Paul endorses democracy. As he puts it, "the Church values the democratic system inasmuch as it ensures the participation of citizens in making political choices, guarantees to the governed the possibility both of electing and holding accountable those who govern them, and of replacing them through peaceful means when appropriate" (46). This is a sort of pragmatic endorsement of the democratic system, and not one that is convinced the majority always knows best. In fact, John Paul notes that with the prevalence of abortion and other problems in many nations, democracies "seem at times to have lost the ability to make decisions aimed at the common good" (47). Thus the Church "respects the legitimate autonomy of the democratic order" (47) at the same time as it insists that the state remain committed to the common good.

To understand this view it is helpful to recall some differences between the far left and far right in debates about the role of government in economic life. The traditional Marxist analysis attributed nearly all the evils of economic life to the faulty economic institution of private ownership of machines and factories. From this perspective government is a rather unproblematic tool that, once controlled by working people, would simply eliminate the economic problems without causing any of its own. Voices on the far right of this debate, often libertarian, understand most of the problems of economic life as created by governments. From this perspective the persons who run governments, whether bureaucrats in communist nations or elected officials in democracies, are doing so to pursue their self-interest and thus will set up laws and organize economic and political structures in ways that inevitably serve their own interests by assisting one group of citizens (the supporters of their own political party) to the detriment of all others. Here the presumption is that if we could simply pull the government out of its constant intervention in economic life, the interplay of individuals in the market would provide for better outcomes, even for the poor, than occur with state activity.

John Paul's approach to the nature of the state and its role in economic life corrects misinterpretations from both the right and the left, basing this perspective on a Catholic view of the individual person and society. The fact that the human person is inherently social means that all economic activities are essentially social interactions as well. He makes this clear in his treatment of human labor, but beyond that John Paul stresses the critical importance of the various organizations within which the people of a society relate to each other, at times in small voluntary groupings and, at the extreme, within the national state. Unlike classic Marxism, which sees little difficulty in working out those relationships once the distorting influence of capitalism is removed, John Paul is deeply aware of the importance and challenge of establishing vital "intermediate communities" that vary in size from local social and cultural groups to much larger economic and political organizations (49). These arise from the social nature of the human person and, when well structured and led, they serve the common good, which is to say they serve both the interests of the individual members of the group as well as society as a whole.

Similarly, although libertarians and others on the right of the political spectrum celebrate such voluntary intermediary groups, John Paul distances himself from them in his conception of "the subjectivity" of society, a theme that he first developed in his earlier encyclical letter, *Sollicitudo rei socialis* (15). Libertarians such as Frederich Hayek have argued for "methodological individualism," the conviction that there exist in social life only individuals who gather in various groupings to accomplish their goals.[49] This leaves the whole idea of "society" as an illusion, or at best simply a shorthand for the interactions of individuals. On the contrary, John Paul is aware that groups and societies are organic wholes and actually have a life of their own that not only arises out of the self-understanding of their members but reciprocally has influence on those members' understanding of themselves and their world. It is a form of "subjectivity" that needs to be recognized. John Paul goes so far in his understanding of the subjectivity of society as to say that a society can be alienated, something that would happen "if its forms of social organization, production and consumption make it more difficult to offer this gift of self and to establish this solidarity between people" (41). Thus, he argues that communism not only attempted to destroy the subjectivity of the individual person but also the subjectivity of society, by forbidding the existence of the panoply of groups that characterize vibrant democratic life (13).

For John Paul, the state, when things are working as they should, expresses the society's values and aspirations. As Russell Hittinger put it, "the state is an instrument of, rather than the substance of, human solidarity."[50] Ideally, the national government is informed by the vitality and ideas of the many voluntary associations within society and prudently structures the rules of economic, political, and social life in accord with the common good. For John Paul, democracy "above and beyond its rules, has in the first place a soul" consisting in "fundamental values." He calls for "a state conceived, therefore, as a service of synthesis, of protection, of orientation for civil society, with respect for it, its initiatives and values . . . democracy understood as participative management of the state through specific organs of representation and control in the service of the common good."[51]

While he does not explicitly analyze the common good in CA, it is clear that it includes two fundamental dimensions: the well-being of every person and the provision of those "common goods" that are necessary for the thriving of both individual and society. These he describes as "the natural and human environments" (40), and would include such things as environmental health and the many institutions of society so often taken for granted, such as schools, churches, hospitals, police, courts, and museums.[52]

Given this perspective on society, government, and the common good, John Paul's view of the role of government in economic life makes perfect sense. Government is neither the savior of the worker nor the villain in an economic story. Rather, as he puts it, the state has the responsibility of structuring "the juridical framework within which economic affairs are to be conducted" (15). This juridical framework would entail the various laws that structure human interaction, whether in the market or in daily life, including a large number of prohibitions against abusive behaviors. Here he builds on the teaching of Pius XI, who argued that both state and society have a role here: they must "build up a juridical and social order able to pervade all economic activity" (QA 88). Thus, John Paul supports markets' opportunities to make and respond to offers but insists "that the market be appropriately controlled by the forces of society and by the state, so as to guarantee that the basic needs of the whole society are satisfied" (35). Like all useful "instruments of social organization," markets must be structured, "orienting them according to an adequate notion of the common good in relation to the whole human family" (58). With a later clarification, John Paul argued that "it is essential that political activity assure a balanced market in its classical forms by applying the principles of subsidiarity and solidarity, according to the model of the social state. If the latter functions moderately, it will also avoid a system of excessive assistance that creates more problems than it solves." What is needed is "the harmonization of the 'demands of the economy' with the demands of ethics."[53] John Paul is committed to establishing participation of the currently marginalized.

In doing so, the government must respect the two principles of subsidiarity and solidarity. That is, in accord with subsidiarity, it must set up the rules of the economic game so as to ensure security and "individual freedom and private property, as well as a stable currency and efficient public services" (48). It must also encourage creative and free economic activity that will lead to jobs and economic well-being for ordinary people. At the same time, the principle of solidarity requires that the state oversee and direct "the exercise of human rights in the economic sector" (48). The state has only secondary responsibility here, as this function ought to be addressed by various institutions within society, but the state stands as facilitator and the ultimate guarantor of such rights. In addition, out of this same solidaristic concern, the state has the duty to intervene "when particular monopolies create delays or obstacles to development" (48). When necessary, the state should temporarily play a much stronger role in the direction of economic life, "a substitute function," when social sectors or business systems are too weak or just getting under way (48).

In general, then, the state is to set up the legal conditions under which institutions will harmoniously conduce to the common good, but it must be ready to intervene when necessary in defending the most vulnerable in society by limiting the power of the powerful in economic life (15). It is both "possible and right" to "organize a solid economy which will direct the functioning of the market to the common good" by "adequate interventions" (52).

In addressing the government's obligations concerning the welfare of its citizens, the encyclical includes a strong critique of the "social assistance state" (48). Arguing from the principle of subsidiarity, John Paul criticizes "a loss of human energies and an inordinate increase of public agencies" that bring about thick bureaucracies and wasteful spending. He endorses a reliance on society, rather than the state, in meeting these unmet needs because they are "best understood and satisfied by people who are closest to them and who act as neighbors to those in need" (48). A number of commentators have asked whether the multitude of functions assigned to the state by John Paul in other parts of the document conflict with his criticism of big government here.[54] A possible resolution is to interpret John Paul as calling not for a change in the government's responsibilities, but in the manner in which government provides services. It is important to note, as Kenneth Himes has pointed out, that this is a critique of excessive government bureaucracy from a communitarian and not a libertarian point of view. That is, John Paul does not argue for ending government responsibility here but argues for a more "human scale" and the use of "alternative delivery systems," in the midst of the abiding conviction that not only material needs but spiritual ones as well must be addressed.[55]

John Paul also broadens the view of society and its need for governance beyond national boundaries, and cautions that this will be costly for the prosperous. He calls for "a concerted worldwide effort to promote development, an effort which also involves sacrificing the positions of income and of power enjoyed by the more developed economies" (52). He cites a growing awareness that the "increasing internationalization of the economy ought to be accompanied by effective international agencies which will oversee and direct the economy to the common good" (58). As Jorge Mejía has phrased it, "'the state,' or rather the states, should develop a form of sovereignty that does not hinder, but on the contrary, facilitates the true exercise of universal solidarity."[56] Following John Paul's logic, this will also require the development of a much more robust sense of "subjectivity" of the international community. Several recent developments in the interaction of governments and nongovernmental organizations (NGOs) concerning environment, trade, debt, and a number of other issues are encouraging.

Capitalism and Markets

One of the central questions of the encyclical, and surely its most widely reported theme, is whether following the collapse of Soviet communism "capitalism" should be viewed as "the victorious social system" and whether capitalism should be the goal for the nations of Eastern Europe as they decide upon the rules for economic activity within their borders (42). Although John Paul uses the term *capitalism*, he acknowledges that it is often a problematic one, and thus offers three alternatives to speak about: "a business economy," "a market economy," or "a free economy." Nonetheless, he gives what he calls an "obviously complex" answer to the questions about the status of capitalism.

In a famous paragraph that is frustrating for its ambivalence, John Paul answers both yes and no. That is, "capitalism" *is* the model that should be proposed across the world if that term means the positive role of business and the market and private property along with the consequent responsibility taken for the means of production and the incentive to human creativity. These, of course, are the positive sides of capitalism and John Paul openly affirms them. However, he says that the answer must be "No" if by "capitalism" we mean a system where economic freedom is supreme and economic action is not limited by "a strong juridical framework" that places economic life "at the service of human freedom in its totality," which must include the ethical and religious core of freedom (42).

We should note that John Paul's treatment of socialist alternatives to capitalism is given far less careful attention than his critique of capitalism itself. He dismisses "the Marxist solution" (42) as having failed in the world, by which he clearly seems to mean Soviet communism. There are, of course, many other versions of socialism, including the varieties of democratic socialism embodied in various European nations in the twentieth century. In this regard John Paul II continues in the tradition of Leo XIII and Pius XI in not attending as carefully as he should to arguments from the left.

In any case, John Paul lays out stringent conditions for the endorsement of a market economy. As we will see, in contrast to some who claim he gives a blanket endorsement of capitalism, John Paul criticizes "a radical capitalist ideology" that would have government no longer attempt to address problems and that instead "blindly entrusts their solution to the free development of market forces" (42).

Earlier in the document John Paul addresses the "free market" in a similar manner. He reports that "it would appear that . . . the free market is the most efficient instrument for utilizing resources and effectively responding to needs" (34). But he immediately notes that there are two major problems with this appearance. The first is that the market takes note only of the needs of those consumers who have purchasing power to enter the market and buy the things they need. The very poor do not possess the price of admission to enter the realm of prosperity that the well-to-do enjoy. Second, not all resources are marketable, meaning for example, that a literally free market would lead to tremendous environmental despoliation because both producers and consumers would ignore those social costs that are not included in the price of the product but are nonetheless imposed on society and the ecosphere.

Thus, John Paul notes that Catholic social teaching "recognizes the positive value of the market and of enterprise," but nonetheless points out that these need to be oriented toward the common good. From this point, two conclusions flow. The first is that individuals involved in enterprise and other forms of economic activity have a personal moral responsibility to further the common good (43). Second, the market itself can only be oriented toward the common good by the interplay of society and governmental decision, including through the proper definition of the juridical framework.

In spite of his many reservations about the abuses that attend to poorly regulated markets today, John Paul recognizes that an essential part of improving the economic well-being of peoples in the third world is participation in "the international market." There must be "fair access" (a critique of first world protectionism) and development must stress improving the skills of ordinary workers (33). John Paul here exhibits his agreement with advice universally proposed by the group of economists from whom he earlier sought counsel.

It is essential to recall that the whole of John Paul's analysis of markets and capitalism occurs within chapter 4, titled "Private Property and the Universal Destination of Materials Goods." This quite vividly subordinates his prudential endorsement of markets to more fundamental commitments.

Consumption, the Goal of Life, and a Commitment to Transformation

In spite of all the attention in both popular press and academic treatises given to the pope's discussion of economic institutions, his treatment of the meaning of economic life for the human person is more fundamental. Not only is this an arena about which the Church has great confidence in its teachings, but the promise of prosperity is worthwhile only if it conduces to the true fulfillment of the person in relation to God.

Crucial here is the problem John Paul calls "the phenomenon of consumerism" (36). In prosperous societies, new "needs" for the human person arise that often run counter to human fulfillment. The problem can be avoided only if this process "subordinates his material and instinctive dimensions to his interior and spiritual ones" (36). John Paul does not mention modern advertising by name but he points out that "if . . . direct appeal is made to his instincts . . . then consumer attitudes and lifestyles can be created which are objectively improper and often damaging to his physical and spiritual health" (36). He calls for an economic system that possesses "criteria for correctly distinguishing new and higher forms of satisfying human needs from artificial new needs which hinder the formation of a mature personality." He adds that "a great deal of educational and cultural work is urgently needed" (36). "It is not wrong to want to live better; what is wrong is a style of life which is presumed to be better when it is directed toward 'having' rather than 'being'" (36). Alienation is the result (41). And even in the developing nations where the large majority are poor, "the dazzle of an opulence which is beyond their reach" leads many to forsake traditional values and institutions and move to overcrowded cities where neither their economic nor spiritual needs are met (33).

For exactly these sorts of failings, the family and marriage suffer greatly. People too easily "consider themselves and their lives as a series of sensations to be experienced rather than as a work to be accomplished" (39). This in turn leads to abuses such as abortion, campaigns against childbearing, and state control of family decisions (39). John Paul cautions that these family-related concerns are not so much directed against the economy but primarily "against an ethical and cultural system." Here are examples where culture "absolutizes" economic life, allowing production and consumption concerns to dominate more important values (39). It is not only in communism but in capitalism as well that things dominate people (33).

The solution is to recognize that the various concerns about freedom of the individual must be rooted in "the totality of freedom," which is a moral and ultimately religious reality. With a nod to liberation theology, John Paul identifies the goal as "integral human liberation (26).[57] The solution to alienation is self-transcendence, giving oneself "to other persons, and ultimately to God, who is the author of his being and who alone can fully accept his gift" (41). Forgetfulness of the true goal of life will inevitably lead to emptiness and alienation. As David Schindler has put it, without a vibrant and deep-seated dependence on God, "efforts at moral and political and economic reform risk merely reinstating our problems, however much these efforts may bring about external improvements or short-term gains."[58]

Most of CA is dedicated to clarifying the conceptual issues concerning the relation of faith and economic life. Nonetheless, it is clear that John Paul intends not simply an academic illumination but also an incitement to action on the part of his reader. In this he challenges both individuals and groups.

The individual is challenged to "a change of lifestyles" and to different models of consumption. This must be accompanied by a greater concern for the marginalized. "Justice will never be fully attained unless people see in the poor person who is asking for help in order to survive, not an annoyance or a burden but an opportunity for showing kindness and a chance for greater enrichment" (58).

Such a commitment to individual transformation will entail "specific ethical and religious values, as well as changes of mentality, behavior, and structures" (60). Here the pope makes an eloquent appeal for personal change and, invoking Mary the Mother of Jesus, prays that "her maternal intercession accompany humanity toward the next Millennium in fidelity to him" (62).

At the same time, John Paul clearly calls for a commitment to the transformation of groups, larger institutions, and "the established structures of power which today govern societies" (58). In the only mention in the encyclical of a likely negative reaction from some of his readers, John Paul cautions that "too many people live, not in the prosperity of the Western world, but in the poverty of the developing countries amid conditions which are still 'a yoke little better than that of slavery itself.'" The Church, he says, "continues to feel obliged to denounce this fact with absolute clarity and frankness, although she knows that her call will not always win favor with everyone" (61).

As we have seen, in premodern times, the Church's doctrine of property required the prosperous to share directly with the needy, but today moral responsibility includes an additional commitment. "It is not merely a matter of 'giving from one's surplus,' but of helping entire peoples which are presently excluded or marginalized to enter into the sphere of economic and human development" (58). Clearly, "helping entire peoples" is not just the work of individuals but of larger organizations and of national governments. Thomas Aquinas taught that "whatever can be rectified by reason is the matter of moral virtue."[59] In the modern world, we recognize that larger institutional problems can indeed be rectified or at least improved by concerted action, and as a result John Paul argues that we have the obligation to work with others to make the needed changes.

This will only happen if both national and international structures change. John Paul cautions that increasing globalization of the economy "ought to be accompanied by effective international agencies which will oversee and direct the economy to the common good, something that an individual state, even if it were the most powerful on earth, would not be in a position to do" (58).

The need for clearer understanding and institutional transformation is indeed a challenge, but one absolutely essential to the mission of the Church on earth. It is to just such a transformation that John Paul calls his readers.

EXCURSUS

CA is a critically important document in the history of Catholic social thought because it both preserves the tradition and pushes it forward in significant new ways. It articulates a stronger appreciation for economic markets than had any earlier papal document. At the same time, however, more than a few of its readers have been irritated, if not actually confounded, by the document's tendency to leave important questions unanswered at critical junctures. These require further work.

Several of these issues concern the proper interplay of government control and freedom within markets. This issue presents itself in several contexts, but two aspects deserve special mention here.

The first is the reality of globalization. Within any one nation, efforts to prevent most abuse within economic life depend on the legal prohibition of those abuses by government. Without any world government and with relatively weak international institutions, there is no assurance that the solutions historically available at the national level can be sustained at an international level today. This is particularly problematic because international economic competition places a downward pressure on the level of legislated morality within individual nations, as multinational firms have the option of moving operations to other nations with less restrictive laws.

A second obvious question concerns John Paul's view of the layoff of workers by large corporations. Especially in the United States more than in Europe, capitalist firms enjoy the right to terminate workers permanently in many situations and to lay them off temporarily if that serves the interests of the firm. As we have seen, however, John Paul made clear that the ownership claim of stockholders over the assets of the corporation only has moral validity if it "serves human work." Part of John Paul's concern here would be the moral commitment to the common good of the individual managers running a firm. Equally essential though would be the juridical framework constructed by the state that would set the rules for terminations and layoffs.

John Paul has asserted that "full employment of the labor force should be the first priority of any social organization."[60] Few will doubt that a corporation in danger of going bankrupt has the right to terminate unproductive investments, leaving workers unemployed. However, more typical in the market system is the effort by corporations to prevent the reduction of profits by a similar process. John Paul has not explicitly said that layoffs are immoral, and since they are so fundamental to the capitalist market system, it is hard to imagine him producing a blanket condemnation of them. At the same time, however, it is equally hard to imagine how the pope could offer moral approbation to layoffs by a profitable firm since this would seem to violate his strong presumption that the whole moral justification of the ownership of capital is the production of work. Requiring stockholders to give up profits rather than lay off workers would seem to comport better with John Paul's view of private property. In any case, there is a clear need for further development in his thinking at this juncture.

Looking at this question more broadly, we can see that business layoffs are simply a subset of the broader issue of the exercise of self-interest in economic life, an issue John Paul does not address in CA or the rest of his writings. This is peculiar since the defense of self-interest has been part of the argument in favor of markets and capitalism at least since Bernard Mandeville published his *Fable of the Bees* three hundred years ago.[61] The Church, of course, has to face several complexities in addressing self-interest, the most important of which is the claim by Jesus that love of neighbor is the essence of a life of discipleship. Nonetheless, it is equally clear that an appropriate form of self-interest can be a proper moral response even for Christians. To take but one example, few Christians would turn down a job they had sought simply because it would serve their own interests and harm the interests of the next best candidate in the pool of applicants. Economists have long argued that even the simplest economic exchange is in essence a gain-seeking transaction by both the buyer and the seller.[62] The appropriate question, of course, is: When and in what circumstances might Christians morally advance their own interests?

Looking even more broadly, we are taken on to a set of questions concerning John Paul's evaluation of markets and capitalism. He says, as we have seen, that if markets operate properly, and people are treated as ends and not means, markets and capitalism are a good thing. On the other hand, if they are abusive of people and undermine basic human values, then they are a bad thing. What is left, of course, is for John Paul to answer the question: Are markets as they exist in reality good or bad from the point of view of Catholic social thought? However, even this question is poorly phrased, for it puts too much focus on economic institutions without recognizing their interplay with democratic, cultural, and personal characteristics in the broader society.

A far better question would be to ask: Under what conditions might Catholic social thought trust markets to produce just outcomes? Markets allow, though they do not require, individuals to pursue their interests in proposing offers to others or in accepting offers made. This question asks: Under what conditions might we trust that this interplay of self-interest in markets will conduce to a just situation?

This is a better formulation of the issue at hand because those conditions will include not only the way markets themselves are structured but also the noneconomic institutions and cultural patterns within which markets operate in any particular society. Although John Paul does not ask this question explicitly, he does provide a set of principles that offer the substance of an answer.

It is helpful, then, if we think of the fundamental issue of the status of capitalism and markets as entailing four separate elements in the moral context of markets, or what might be called "the moral ecology of markets."[63]

The first element is the "juridical framework," which defines those behaviors that are permitted in economic life and that are prohibited or regulated. John Paul endorses the importance of individual economic initiative, entrepreneurship, education for increased productivity, the development of science and technology, and private property, including the ownership of the means of production. Among those activities that the juridical framework should eliminate are unsafe working conditions, treating women and children in the work world the same as men, the seeking of profit by owners of capital by means of reducing the opportunities for work, destruction of the natural environment, and efforts to prevent workers from organizing themselves in the workplace. Although John Paul does not specify what he understands the requirements of a just wage to imply concretely, the government's role as "indirect employer" (LE 17) would fall under its obligation to establish the juridical framework for market interactions.

In addition to the actual structuring of markets themselves, there are three other elements we can identify as present in John Paul's evaluation of a market system. The first of these is the provision of essential goods and services to those who through no fault of their own are unable to provide them for themselves. This, of course, is the essence of the requirement of distributive justice and a crucial part of the meaning of solidarity, so central to John Paul's message. The pope is particularly concerned about the status of the unemployed who, though willing and able to work, are unable to find gainful employment. Employers have a strong obligation to their employees but when there is no employer for an able-bodied worker, both society and the state must recognize their obligation in meeting needs.

The next essential requirement for a morally adequate economic system is the moral conviction that grounds the behavior of individuals and groups. The juridical framework can require or prohibit certain behaviors, but John Paul recognizes what Thomas Aquinas argued centuries earlier: that the law cannot prohibit all evil actions for fear that many good things will be eliminated in the process.[64] Thus, even if there exists a market that is properly constituted and a social system that provides for the vulnerable, if individuals and groups did not behave with fundamental moral virtue, the economic world would be a vicious place in which to live and the economic system would fail. Thus, John Paul often appeals to business leaders in his homilies, as he did in Poland in 1997: "Do not let yourselves be deceived by visions of immediate profit, at the expense of others. Beware of any semblance of exploitation."[65] John Paul identifies a number of virtues that, at its best, the market system sees exercised by the individuals who act within it. These include "diligence, industriousness, prudence in undertaking reasonable risks, reliability and fidelity in interpersonal relationships, as well as courage in carrying out decisions which are difficult and painful but necessary" (32).

The final element that in John Paul's analysis must be present if markets are to receive any sort of moral approbation is the presence of a vital "subjectivity" of society (SRS 15). By this he means a vibrant interaction of a large number of groups and associations in which members strive to achieve their ends as well as the common good. The absence of a vibrant "civil society" simply allows the powerful greater sway. For this reason critics of totalitarian communism on the right have made the same endorsement of civil society as have critics of corporate hegemony on the left.

John Paul did not explicitly ask under what conditions markets might be morally endorsed, but his implicit answer would seem to entail these four elements: the proper definition of markets through the construction of the juridical framework, provision for the needs of those unable to provide for themselves, the moral comportment of both individuals and groups, and the presence of an energetic civil society. No one of these alone can guarantee the morality of an economic system, but the four together come as close to an assurance as is possible. Of course, simply naming the four elements leaves a number of questions and real political debates that have to occur to resolve each one. But we can say that if all four were indeed resolved in accord with the standards of Catholic social thought, then although individuals would still suffer from misfortune or from mistakes they have made, the ensuing problems would not be evidence of injustice. The economic system could then merit a kind of conditional moral approbation from the perspective of Catholic social thought.

Of course, Catholic social thought does not provide such precise answers that there would not be serious debates among people of good will as to whether this or that resolution of the four elements is more faithful to the tradition. Moving the public debate to that stage, however, would be a great advance. Although the human person will no doubt remain "the way of the church," the movement of Catholic social thought toward this kind of structural analysis will be a helpful development.

A second set of issues surrounds the important development that John Paul makes in the Catholic doctrine of property when he recognizes the difference in the character of wealth today when compared with the premodern world. As human work becomes "increasingly important as the productive factor of both non-material and material wealth" (31), Catholic social thought is implicitly challenged to make adjustments in its understanding of the logic of its view of private property. In the ancient world it was presumed that wealth came from "the natural fruitfulness of the earth" (31), and a true appreciation of the role of human ingenuity and hard work in the production of wealth did not arise until the modern world. That consciousness came in response to an immense shift in the character of wealth, but it now provides a more accurate description even of primitive wealth, as labor was essential there too.

John Paul begins this development in his insistence on the social character of human labor, both in its origin in the person as a gift from God (31) and in its embodiment in social networks, without which no individual's work would be more than minimally productive (31). The Church now needs the work of moral theologians to further develop such ideas and to integrate the various warrants for the responsibilities of property owners. Only the ungrateful could ignore the debt that the economically successful owe to typically unacknowledged multitudes of unnamed others who came before them, but Catholic doctrine on property needs to make clearer the differences in warrant and prerogatives that attend to the ownership not of naturally occurring objects but of the products of human creativity. Considerable theoretical work is yet to be done, not only in biblical theology and ethical sources but in careful scientific work, in both social and natural sciences.

These concerns and opportunities for further development, however, do not detract from the importance of CA or the thought of Pope John Paul II. Rather, they demonstrate that the pope, as any good householder, not only brings out of the storehouse what is old and well known but also, in light of changing world circumstances, what is new, always in faithful continuity with that which came before. In doing so, John Paul meets the standard he sets for the Church's social teaching as an effective means of evangelization: "As such, it proclaims God and his mystery of salvation in Christ to every human being, and for that very reason reveals man to himself" (54).

REACTIONS TO THE DOCUMENT

CA received a lively reaction in both the popular press and scholarly circles. The most frequent response was appreciation and praise. This was particularly strong among neoconservatives in the Catholic Church. From this perspective, the encyclical represented a much-needed shift of ecclesial attention toward the advantages of markets, individual effort, and human creativity. John Paul's strong condemnation of "real socialism" as well as his stern warning against the excesses of the welfare state were celebrated as setting the agenda not only for the industrialized world but in particular for the economies in transition from Soviet domination. At the same time, neoconservatives tended to read the document as providing more support for their positions than more centrist scholars felt appropriate.

Michael Novak, perhaps the best known of the Catholic defenders of capitalism, lauded the document as "the great Magna Carta for the twenty-first century" and as "the fullest and best [encyclical] in the whole tradition."[66] Novak salutes the pope because "he supports a type of 'reformed capitalism.'"[67] He is appreciative that the pope "now proposes" this model for the nations of formerly communist Eastern Europe and the third world. Acknowledging the pope's call for limitations on capitalism, Novak holds up two as critically important. The first is "a judicial framework that protects other fundamental liberties besides economic liberty." And the second is the need to ground all liberties in a "moral and religious core."[68]

In commenting on the pope's teaching concerning markets, James Schall argues that John Paul "has affirmed that the outlines of prosperity, how it is produced and conserved, is [*sic*] now basically known in the productive economies. What remains is for bureaucratic dangers of the welfare state and the total control of the Marxist tradition to be confronted and removed."[69] Schall celebrates the shift of debate in religious discourse about poverty away from "exclusive discussion of distribution" and toward the more realistic awareness that "this production is primarily a responsibility of individual peoples and nations themselves."[70]

Richard John Neuhaus asserts that in CA "the Pope offered an extended moral-theological argument in favor of 'the new capitalism.'" He sees the pope's criticism of capitalism as being directed toward an "unbridled capitalism" that is "unchecked by culture, morality and just regulation." From this perspective, John Paul has endorsed capitalism; his reservations are appropriate but secondary. As Neuhaus puts it, "the market economy comes with a price, and the Pope is deeply concerned about unemployment, social dislocation, and 'the whole ultra-liberal, consumerist system which is devoid of values, and introducing it with the power of propaganda.'"[71] According to Neuhaus, the pope's encyclical teaches that "the poor of the world are not oppressed because of capitalism, . . . but because of the absence of capitalism." He describes the pope as adamant in insisting on more freedom in the economy, not less, so that the pope is convinced that "state interventions, . . . no matter how well intended, almost always turn out to be oppressive and stifling."[72] In a similar vein, Robert A. Sirico asserts that John Paul II and CA "endorse capitalism as essentially in accord with Christianity."[73]

British economist Ronald Preston reviewed the encyclical with general approval but found it wanting in several areas: a simplistic view of socialism and Marxism as represented only by Eastern European communism, a generally inadequate analysis of power in economic life, an absence of criticism of economic injustice in the Church itself, and an overly simple critique of the welfare state, given the many tasks that John Paul clearly assigns to the national government.[74] Jonathan Luxmoore and Jolanta Babiuch, in an article in the British journal *The Tablet*, have gently chided the pope for overrating Leo XIII's insight about state and society and for a failure "to make sensible distinction between socialism past and present."[75]

Stanley Hauerwas, who was quite critical of John Paul's earlier encyclical *Laborem exercens*, reacted with praise for CA. He reiterates his objection that the popes in the encyclical tradition following *Rerum novarum* "felt obliged to make their peace with modernity and in particular liberalism." He values the countercultural stance of John Paul though he clearly prefers the spirit of *Rerum novarum* and Leo's "insistence that the foremost social witness of the Church for the world is worship of God."[76]

Gennadios Limouris, an Orthodox priest of the Ecumenical Partriarchate, has expressed general approval of the encyclical, with a special appreciation for the notion of solidarity. However, he cautions against a "monolithic" approach to economic problems across the globe and recommends a stronger liturgical connection in the Church's work for justice in the world.[77]

An editorial in *America* was broadly appreciative, but provided gentle chiding for the pope's statement that exploitation in the forms analyzed by Marx had been overcome in Western society and for his broadening of the preferential option for the poor to include spiritual poverty as well.[78] Marx clearly analyzed many forms of exploitation that John Paul himself decries; by adding to the notion of the preferential option those members of the wealthy class who are "spiritual paupers," the pope empties the concept of the preferential option of "its specific and historic content." As Patrick McCormick has put it in another context, "shall we be for both Lazarus and Dives?"[79]

Other commentators have been also appreciative of the encyclical but critical of its interpretation by those farther to the right. John Pawlikowski has argued that, in an effort to claim John Paul's patronage for their project, neoconservatives have too easily ignored the ways in which John Paul disagrees with their positions. Pawlikowski argues that in the months and years following the early round of excessive statements from neoconservatives, John Paul proceeded to reiterate his own refusal to endorse capitalism.[80] For example, John Paul has condemned "the selfish demands inherent in current economic models."[81] As Pawlikowski puts it, "John Paul II's critique undercuts the triumphant language about capitalism" in the writings of North American neoconservatives.

In a critique of Michael Novak and his claim that "we are all capitalist now, even the Pope,"[82] Todd Whitmore has argued that John Paul endorses important elements that Novak rejects or ignores: economic rights, the moral relevance of the gap between rich and poor, the various limits on private property, and, of course, John Paul's explicit statement that he rejects capitalism's ideology.[83] Charles Wilber argues that Novak, along with William Simon and Robert Sirico, has misinterpreted the pope's encyclical to endorse a free-market capitalism that Catholic social thought has condemned along with socialism for over a century. Wilber argues that the "socially regulated capitalism" endorsed by John Paul calls for a stronger government oversight of economic life than Novak would allow.[84]

John Langan has written appreciatively of the good work of neoconservatives such as Novak and Neuhaus but has chided them for two important faults in their claim that John Paul supports their positions. The first is that they, like many secular neoconservatives, "trade in the antistatist rhetoric that has been the common currency of American and British politics." Neuhaus, Langan points out, goes so far as to contradict the pope, who asserts that the national state is a community "of higher order."[85] Second, Langan accuses them of naiveté in their presumption that the institutions of the moral-cultural system are independent of the economic order and thus act as a sort of check and balance on it. As he points out, some of the largest institutions shaping American culture (television networks, large entertainment conglomerates, etc.) are primarily profitable economic corporations. These are likely to have far more negative influence than the intellectuals whom neoconservatives so often blame for the emptiness of our culture. These firms certainly are inclined "to regard intellectual products in terms of their profitability rather than in terms of their intrinsic value or their conformity to moral norms."[86] Stefano Zamagni has argued that only an uncritical understanding of markets forgets that markets themselves "slowly but inexorably" undermine both norms and social conventions necessary for responsible economic life.[87]

There is a long list of elements essential to John Paul's view that receive either little attention or rather explicit redefinition in the work of those who claim him under the banner of capitalism. Included here are his strong endorsements of labor unions and of the role of government in reducing the power of employers. Similarly, the pope's notion of universal destination of material goods and its relation to solidarity typically go unexamined. In one of the rare neoconservative treatments of the theme, John S. Barry argues that Augustine and Aquinas and the whole of Roman Catholic tradition support private property and that the combination of private property and free exchange is the best way to reinforce the Church's teaching on the universal destination of goods.[88] Unfortunately, at no point in his analysis does Barry note Augustine's teaching on the obligation of the well-to-do toward the needy or Aquinas's doctrine of common use of all private property. Neither does he mention the various economic rights arising from the universal destination of goods that John Paul includes in his analysis.

Whereas neoconservatives argue that John Paul's critique of consumerism and relativism is a criticism solely of modern culture and not the economy, David Hollenbach argues that "on this level, a consumer society is one in which the spirit of the marketplace has leached into the sphere of politics, culture, and religion."[89] Similarly, we might observe that in supporting the pope's opposition to relativism in contemporary life, neoconservatives have numerous times criticized the work of Richard Rorty and James Schlesinger, but they overlook the analogous belief of Milton Friedman and many other conservative and libertarian advocates of freer markets, whom neoconservatives often consider as allies and rarely criticize.

What we see is that the themes emphasized by many commentators correspond to their prior commitments and thus demonstrate that the careful reader must assess them judiciously. Jorge Mejía provided an important caution to readers shortly after the encyclical's publication. He points out that following the publication of an encyclical, there is a process of "reception" of the document by the Church. This is, as he puts it, "an important ecclesial and therefore theological endeavor," whereby the contents of the document are "appropriated by the church and by each member in the church, each one according to his or her own situation and own ecclesial responsibility."[90] Importantly, Mejía warns against any "partial or selective reading of the text" or "one aimed at serving particular purposes." He adds that "in our day, we have been witness to more than one such reading."[91]

Selective reading seems to be the only way that Michael Novak could come to the perspective that "the encyclical *Centesimus annus* does everything that many of us had hoped for from some Church authority."[92] Thus, for example, Novak carefully quotes the pope's caution about the right to work and other human rights in the economic sector: "Primary responsibility . . . belongs not to the state but to individuals and to the various groups and associations which make up society" (48). This, Novak asserts, does away with the notion of the right to work implicit in Marxism and even the Humphrey-Hawkins Right to Work legislation in the United States. Novak's longstanding position, of course, is that the state should not guarantee such ill-conceived "rights."[93] It is, however, at least peculiar that Novak neglects to mention the topic sentence of the paragraph that appears immediately preceding the one he quotes: "Another task of the state is that of overseeing and directing the exercise of human rights in the economic sector" (48). Clearly, John Paul's view of the role of the state in economic rights is more nuanced than Novak leads his readers to believe.

Whereas neoconservatives have interpreted CA as endorsing the fundamental economic and political system in place in the United States, the British theologian Frank Turner asserts that CA "sometimes reads like an unusually well-written Labour manifesto."[94] Hollenbach notes that its proposals are "certainly closer to the program of the Labour Party than they are to laissez faire or libertarian objectives."[95] Elsewhere Hollenbach has argued that the social market economy of Germany "most closely resembles what Pope John Paul's letter describes."[96] As he puts it, "in my judgment, the principles it lays out call for major changes both in the domestic arrangements presently in place in the United States as well as in the global marketplace."[97] Marciano Vidal has gone so far as to say that if an economic system were to exhibit the restrictions that John Paul articulates in CA, there is doubt whether that system ought to be called "capitalism" at all.[98]

How, then, should one interpret the various claims and counterclaims as to whether John Paul has indeed endorsed "capitalism" or "some form of capitalism"? The best way to answer this question is to step back and ask what this is all about. If what is at stake is the difference between the economic system of the United States and the former Soviet Union, there is little doubt that the former is far less objectionable to John Paul than the latter. Much talk about capitalism and socialism in the United

States over the past fifty years has construed the debate as exactly this difference. The problem, of course, is that almost no one in the United States, and certainly no one among the major political parties that are involved in such debates, has ever actually advocated Moscow-style communism for the United States. Claiming to have the pope on your side in this dichotomy would be irrelevant to real economic issues at stake today.

The real debates that occur within the United States and other industrialized nations concern differences of opinion across a much narrower range of the ideological spectrum. The narrowest of ranges characterize the main options debated in the United States, classically between Democrats and Republicans. But even in Europe the debates are largely between what might be called democratic capitalists and democratic socialists. Thus the differences really at stake might be characterized as ranging from U.S. democratic capitalism to Swedish democratic socialism. While John Paul's assertion of various balancing principles such as subsidiarity and solidarity clearly exclude Soviet communism and North American libertarianism, they leave him open to allowing for a variety of structures as long as each nation attends to its obligations. Some elements of his vision, of course, can only be established through the state's juridical framework, and in the case of the United States, perhaps the most important example here is the need in John Paul's view for a stronger legal status for workers and labor unions in the face of corporate power. In any case, it is clear from both CA and John Paul's later writings that he has not given a blanket approval to the U.S. economy as it exists, and it will be an ongoing challenge to moral theologians and social ethicists, from across the political spectrum, to work out what his vision means for changes in government and society.

It may be an effective tactic in what has come to be called "the culture wars" to quote selectively those parts of John Paul's work that support one's own perspective and to ignore those that critique it. However, this misleads public discourse and undermines the subjectivity of society that John Paul wants to encourage.

NOTES

1. J. Bryan Hehir, "Reordering the World: John Paul II's *Centesimus Annus*," *Commonweal* 118, no. 12 (June 14, 1991): 393–94.

2. See, for example, Paul VI, OA 4.

3. For a more detailed discussion of John Paul's sense of limits of competence, see Gabriel J. Zanotti, "Economy and Culture in the Thought of John Paul II," *Logos* 1, no. 2 (1997): 76–89.

4. See Thomas A. Shannon's analysis of corporatism in his commentary on *Rerum novarum* in this volume.

5. For an introduction to the work of Pesch, see *Heinrich Pesch on Solidarist Economics: Excerpts from the Lehrbuch der Natinal Okonomie*, trans. Rupert J. Ederer (Lanham, Md.: University Press of America, 1998).

6. In Europe, there was another factor leading to the demise of corporatism: a distorted version of it was adopted by several heavy-handed governments as a way to control the economy, undermining the original idea. For further discussion, see Marie J. Giblin, "Corporatism," in *The New Dictionary of Catholic Social Thought,* ed. Judith A. Dwyer (Collegeville, Minn.: Liturgical, 1994), 246.

7. For a description of the shift from the solidarist to a "meliorist" strategy for dealing with economic injustices in the workplace, see Franz Herman Mueller, *The Church and the Social Question* (Washington, D.C.: American Enterprise Institute for Public Policy Research, 1984).

For a brief discussion of the Fribourg Union and other continental influences on Leo, see Normand J. Paulhus, "Social Catholicism and the Fribourg Union," *The Society of Christian Ethics, Selected Papers* (1980): 63–88.

8. Charles E. Curran, *Toward an American Catholic Moral Theology* (Notre Dame, Ind.: University of Notre Dame Press, 1987), 177.

9. Ibid.

10. See in this volume "The Ecclesiological Foundations of Modern Catholic Social Teaching" by Richard Gaillardetz, esp. the section titled "A Mediating View of the Church's Engagement with the World."

11. See, for example, Gustavo Gutiérrez, *A Theology of Liberation: History, Politics, and Salvation*, trans. and ed. Caridad Inda and John Eagleson (Maryknoll, N.Y.: Orbis, 1973).

12. See, for example, Congregation for the Doctrine of the Faith, "Instruction on Certain Aspects of the Theology of Liberation," *Origins* 14, no. 13 (September 13, 1984).

13. Ibid.

14. For a commentary on activities in the United States, see "The Reception of Catholic Social and Economic Teaching in the United States" by Charles E. Curran in this volume.

15. Conversation with Jean-Ives Calvez, New York City, April 20, 2002.

16. "Poland Details Economic Change," *New York Times*, October 7, 1989, 2.

17. The economists were Kenneth J. Arrow, Stanford University; Anthony B. Atkinson, University of London; Parta Dasgupta, Stanford University; Jacques H. Dreze, Université Catholique de Louvain; Peter J. Hammond, Stanford University; Hendrik S. Houthakker, Harvard University; Robert E. Lucas Jr., University of Chicago; Edmond Malinvaud, Collège de France; Ignazio Musu, Università degli Studi di Venezia; Jeffrey D. Sachs, Harvard University; Amartya Sen, Harvard University; Horst Siebert, The Kiel Institute of World Economics; Witold Trzeciakowski, Warsaw; Hirofumi Uzawa, Tokyo University; and Stefano Zamagni, Università degli Studi di Bologna. For the published version of the responses, see Pontifical Council for Justice and Peace, *Social and Ethical Aspects of Economics: A Colloquium in the Vatican* (Vatican City: Vatican, 1992).

18. Jorge Maria Mejía, "Aspects of the Preparation and Reception of *Centesimus Annus*," in *Centesimus Annus: Assessment and Perspectives for the Future of Catholic Social Doctrine*, ed. John-Peter Pham (Vatican City: Vatican, 1998), 46.

19. J. C. de Pablo, "Lo que los economistas le dijeron al papa," *Criterio* 56 (May 12, 1994): available at http://www.depabloconsult.com.ar/aplicaciones/escritos-56.htm: section 6.

20. Mejía, "Aspects of Preparation and Reception," 44.

21. A second symposium of economists was hosted by the Council in January 1993. Its focus was world development. For an account of the issues and questions posed by the Council and the response of the twelve participants, see Pontifical Council for Justice and Peace, *World Development and Economic Institutions* (Vatican City: Vatican, 1994).

22. See the section titled "Priority of Labor over Capital" in Patricia Lamoureux's Commentary on *Laborem exercens* in this volume.

23. Conversation with Jorge Cardinal Mejía, Rome, April 29, 2002.

24. For further discussion, see M. J. Giblin, "Corporatism," in *New Dictionary of Catholic Social Thought*, ed. J. A. Dwyer, 244–46. See also the "Excursus" in Christine Firer Hinze's commentary on *Quadragesimo anno* in this volume.

25. For a further description, see Franz H. Mueller, "Solidarism," in *New Dictionary of Catholic Social Thought*, ed. J. A. Dwyer, 906–8.

26. For a treatment of the distance between Leo XIII and Thomas Aquinas on private property, see Charles E. Curran, *Catholic Social Teaching, 1891–Present: A Historical, Theological, and Ethical Analysis* (Washington, D.C.: Georgetown University Press, 2002), 175–79.

27. Ernest L. Fortin, "'Sacred and Inviolable': *Rerum Novarum* and Natural Rights," *Theological Studies* 53, no. 2 (1992): 216. Fortin's essay provides a helpful summary of the novelties to papal thought presented by Leo in his treatment of private property.

28. Ambrose, *De Nabuthe,* 11 PL 14: 747, as quoted in Charles Avila, *Ownership: Early Christian Teaching* (Maryknoll, N.Y.: Orbis, 1983), 66.

29. Aquinas, *Summa theologiae* [ST] II-II, q. 66, a. 2.

30. Ibid., II-II, q. 66, a. 7.

31. Ibid., I-II, q. 94, a. 5.

32. For a discussion of premodern precedents to rights language, see Brian Tierney, *The Idea of Natural Rights: Studies on Natural Rights, Natural Law and Church Law, 1150–1625* (Atlanta: Scholars, 1997).

33. David Hollenbach, "Common Good," in *New Dictionary of Catholic Social Thought*, ed. J. A. Dwyer, 193.

34. For example, John XXIII in PT (1963) and Paul VI in PP (1967).

35. James V. Schall, "The Teaching of *Centesimus Annus*," *Gregorianum* 74, no. 1 (1993): 32–36.

36. John Paul II, "Address to Fiftieth General Assembly of the United Nations Organization," (October 5, 1995): nos. 2–3, www.vatican.va/holy_father/john_paul_ii/speeches/1995/october/documents/hf_jp-ii_spe_05101995_address-touno_en.html (downloaded March 12, 2004).

37. For an extended discussion of rights in Catholic social thought, see Julie Clague, "'A Dubious Idiom and Rhetoric': How Problematic Is the Language of Human Rights in Catholic Social Thought?" in *Catholic Social Thought: Twilight or Renaissance?* ed. Jonathan S. Boswell, Frank P. McHugh, and Johan Verstraeten (Leuven: Leuven University Press, 2000), 125–40.

38. Augustine, Sermon 124, 5, 5, PL. 38:686, as found in Avila, *Ownership*, 119.

39. David Hollenbach, "Christian Social Ethics after the Cold War," *Theological Studies* 53, no.1 (1992): 86.

40. J. M. Mejía, "*Centesimus Annus*: An Answer to Unknowns and Questions of Our Times," *Ecumenical Review* 43 (October 1991): 401–10.

41. For a more complete description of Pope John's views, see chap. 2 in Albino Barrera, *Modern Catholic Social Documents and Political Economy* (Washington, D.C.: Georgetown University Press, 2001).

42. See, for example, Robert E. Lucas Jr., "Reactions to the Five November Conferences," in Pontifical Council for Justice and Peace, *Social and Ethical Aspects of Economics: Colloquium in the Vatican* (Vatican City: Vatican, 1992), 77. See also the report of the oral comments of Jeffrey Sachs by Edmond Malinvaud, ibid., 90.

43. See "Priority of Labor over Capital" in Lamoureux's Commentary on *Laborem exercens* in this volume.

44. Jean-Yves Calvez, "Things Old and New: Catholic Social Thought in Retrospect and Prospect," in *Catholic Social Thought*, ed. J. S. Boswell, F. P. McHugh, and J. Verstraeten, 10.

45. See "The Reconstruction of the Social Order" in Hinze's Commentary on *Quadragesimo anno* in this volume.

46. See Commentary on *Solicitudo rei socialis* by Charles E. Curran, Kenneth R. Himes, and Thomas A. Shannon in this volume.

47. Matthew L. Lamb, "Solidarity," in *New Dictionary of Catholic Social Thought*, ed. J. A. Dwyer, 909.

48. Charles R. Strain, "Concerning New Things and Old: A Reading of *Centesimus Annus*," *Word and World* 12, no. 4 (1992): 365.

49. Frederich Hayek, "Scientism and the Study of Society," *Economica,* M.A. 9–11 (August 1942, February 1943, February 1944): 267–91, 34–63, 27–39.

50. Russell Hittinger, "Making Sense of the Civilization of Love: John Paul II's Contribution to Catholic Social Thought," in *The Legacy of Pope John Paul II,* ed. Geoffrey Gneuhs (New York: Crossroad, 2000), 83.

51. John Paul II, "What Church Social Teaching Is and Is Not," address in Riga, Latvia, *Origins* 23, no. 15 (September 23, 1993): 257.

52. For a helpful distinction between a procedural and a substantive view of the good in common good, see "The Future of Catholic Social Thought" by John A. Coleman in this volume.

53. John Paul II, "Toward a Balanced Well-Regulated World Market," address to the Pontifical Academy of Social Sciences, April 25, 1997, *Origins* 27, no. 3 (June 5, 1997): 43.

54. See, for example, Hehir, "Reordering the World," 394.

55. Kenneth R. Himes, "The New Social Encyclical's Communitarian Vision," *Origins* 21, no. 10 (August 1, 1991): 167.

56. Mejía, "*Centesimus annus*: An Answer to Unknowns and Questions of Our Times," 408.

57. It is interesting to note that the footnote for this phrase refers to the second response/correction to liberation theology by the Congregation for the Doctrine of the Faith, the one that speaks more favorably about liberation theology.

58. Schindler, "Reorienting the Church on the Eve of the Millennium: John Paul's New Evangelization," in *Legacy of Pope John Paul II*, ed. G. Gneuhs, 108.

59. Aquinas, ST II-II, q. 58, a 8.

60. John Paul II, "The Influence of Labor Unions," address to Workers in Buenos Aires, April 10, 1987, *Origins* 16, no. 45 (April 23, 1987): 797.

61. Bernard Mandeville, *The Fable of the Bees* [1705] (Oxford: Claredon, 1924).

62. For a careful analysis of "gain-seeking" by a personalist Catholic economist, see chap. 7 in Peter L. Danner, *The Economic Person: Acting and Analyzing* (Lanham, Md.: Rowman and Littlefield, 2002).

63. Daniel Finn, "John Paul II in the Moral Ecology of Markets," *Theological Studies* 59, no. 4 (1998): 662–79.

64. Aquinas, ST I-II, q. 91, a. 4.

65. John Paul II, "The Necessity of Jobs, the Meaning of Work," homily at Legnica, Poland, *Origins* 27, no. 6 (June 26, 1997): 89.

66. Michael Novak, "The Hundredth Year," *Crisis* 10 (May 1992): 2–3.

67. M. Novak, "Capitalism with a Heart," *Crisis* 9 (May 1992): 21.

68. Ibid.

69. Schall, "The Teaching of *Centesimus Annus*," 38.

70. Ibid.

71. Richard John Neuhaus, quoting John Paul II as reported in a published interview by Polish journalist, Jas Gawronski, in R. J. Neuhaus, "John Paul's 'Second Thoughts' on Capitalism," *First Things*, no. 41 (March 1994): 66.

72. R. J. Neuhaus, "The Pope, Liberty, and Capitalism: Essays on *Centesimus Annus*," *National Review* 43, no. 11 (June 24, 1991): 5–9.

73. Robert A. Sirico, "The Pope, Liberty, and Capitalism: Essays on *Centesimus Annus*," *National Review* 43, no. 11 (June 24, 1991): 12–13.

74. Ronald H. Preston, "*Centesimus Annus*: An Appraisal," *Theology* 95 (1992): 405–16.

75. Jonathan Luxmoore and Jolanta Babiuch, "The Pope's Balancing Act," *The Tablet* 260 (June 28, 1997): 826–28.

76. Stanley Hauerwas, "In Praise of *Centesimus Annus*," *Theology* 95 (1992): 416–17.

77. Gennadios Limouris, *Ecumenical Review* 43 (1991): 420–29.

78. Editorial, "*Centesimus Annus*," *America* 164, no. 20 (May 25, 1991): 555–56.

79. Patrick McCormick, "That They May Converse: Voices of Catholic Social Thought," *Cross Currents* 42, no. 4 (1992): 527.

80. John T. Pawlikowski, "Government and Economic Solidarity: The View from the Catholic Social Encyclicals," *Bridges: An Interdisciplinary Journal of Theology, Philosophy, History, and Science* 7, nos. 3–4 (2000): 288ff.

81. John Paul II, "The World's Hunger and Humanity's Conscience," address to the UN International Conference on Nutrition, *Origins* 22, no. 28 (December 1992): 475.

82. M. Novak, *The Catholic Ethic and the Spirit of Capitalism* (New York: The Free Press, 1993), 101.

83. Todd David Whitmore, "John Paul II, Michael Novak, and the Differences between Them," *Annual of the Society of Christian Ethics* 21 (2001): 215–32.

84. Charles K. Wilber, "Argument that the Pope Baptized Capitalism Holds No Water," *National Catholic Reporter* (June 7, 1991): 10.

85. John Langan, "Ethics, Business, and the Economy," *Theological Studies* 55, no. 1 (1994): 112–14.

86. Ibid., 113.

87. Stefano Zamagni, "Hacía una economía civil," *Criterio* (Buenos Aires) 70, no. 2205/6 (October 16, 1997): 28.

88. John S. Barry, "On the Universal Destination of Material Goods," *Religion and Liberty*, Acton Institute 10, no. 1 (January–February 2000): 5–7.

89. Hollenbach, "Christian Social Ethics after the Cold War," 93.

90. Mejía, "*Centesimus Annus*: An Answer to Unknowns and Questions of Our Times," 403.

91. Ibid.

92. M. Novak, "The Pope, Liberty, and Capitalism: Essays on *Centesimus Annus*," *National Review* 43, no. 11 (June 24, 1991): 10–11.

93. M. Novak, "The Rights and Wrongs of 'Economic Rights': A Debate Continued," *This World* no. 17 (spring 1987): 42–52.

94. Frank Turner, "John Paul II's Social Analysis," *The Month* 24 (August 1991): 347.

95. Hollenbach, "Christian Social Ethics after the Cold War," 90.

96. Hollenbach, "The Pope and Capitalism," 591.

97. Hollenbach, "Christian Social Ethics after the Cold War," 90.

98. Marciano Vidal, "La sospechosa cristianización del capitalismo: Juicio ético al capitalismo a partir de la encíclica *Centesimus Annus*," *Persona y Sociedad* 7 (1993): 116.

SELECTED BIBLIOGRAPHY

Barrera, Albino. *Modern Catholic Social Documents and Political Economy*. Washington, D.C.: Georgetown University Press, 2001. An economically and theologically astute overview of official Catholic thought on economic life.

Boswell, Jonathan, Frank McHugh, and Johan Verstraeten. *Catholic Social Thought: Twilight or Renaissance?* Leuven, Belgium: Leuven University Press, 2000. A helpful collection of European perspectives on Catholic social thought.

Curran, Charles E. *Catholic Social Teaching: 1891–Present: A Historical, Theological, and Ethical Analysis*. Washington, D.C.: Georgetown University Press, 2002. An examination of both the method and content of Catholic social teaching.

Danner, Peter L. *The Economic Person: Acting and Analyzing*. Lanham, Md.: Rowman and Littlefield, 2002. An economic, philosophical, and implicitly Catholic view of economic life.

Dwyer, Judith A., ed. *The New Dictionary of Catholic Social Thought*. Collegeville, Minn.: Liturgical, 1994. A wealth of thematic essays on issues in Catholic social thought.

Hollenbach, David. "Christian Social Ethics after the Cold War." *Theological Studies* 53 (1992): 75–93. A survey of issues following the fall of the Soviet Union.

Pham, John-Peter, ed. *Centesimus Annus: Assessment and Perspectives for the Future of Catholic Social Doctrine*. Vatican City: Libreria Editrice Vaticana, 1998. Essays from a conference in Rome organized by the Acton Institute.

Pontifical Council for Justice and Peace. *Social and Ethical Aspects of Economics: Colloquium in the Vatican*. Vatican City: Libreria Editrice Vaticana, 1992. The collection of statements written by economists prior to their meeting with John Paul II in November 1990.

Vidal, Marciano. "La sospechosa cristianización del capitalismo: Juicio ético al capitalismo a partir de la encíclica *Centesimus annus*." *Persona y Sociedad* 7 (1993). A Latin American critique of one-sided interpretations of John Paul's evaluation of capitalism.

Weigel, George, ed. *A New Worldly Order: John Paul II and Human Freedom*. Washington, D.C.: Ethics and Public Policy Center, 1992. An insightful collection of (mostly neoconservative) responses to CA on social and economic order.

PART

III

Reception and Future of the Tradition

CHAPTER

19 The Reception of Catholic Social and Economic Teaching in the United States

CHARLES E. CURRAN

INTRODUCTION

The term *Catholic social teaching*, according to Pope John Paul II, refers to papal encyclicals and other documents issued since the 1891 encyclical of Pope Leo XIII, *Rerum novarum*, which deal with labor, social, and economic issues (CA 2).[1] Although there is no official canon or list of the documents of Catholic social teaching, general agreement exists on the major documents belonging to this tradition as illustrated in the documents studied in this volume. Catholic social teaching is a much narrower concept than Catholic social thought or Catholic social ethics.

This chapter examines the reception and influence of Catholic social teaching in the United States. Both developments in Catholic self-understanding and the evolving changes in U.S. society and culture have affected the way in which these documents have been received in the United States. Significant changes both in Catholic ecclesiology, especially at Vatican II, and in the cultural and social issues facing the United States in the 1960s ushered in a distinctively new context. This chapter considers two different time periods—from the beginning of Catholic social teaching in the late nineteenth century to the 1960s and the period from the 1960s to the present.

BEFORE THE 1960s

The influence and reception of Catholic social teaching in the United States involves three different factors or sources: the teaching and documents of the bishops of the United States, the theological and more theoretical writings on Catholic social ethics in general, and the practical and pastoral involvements of Catholics.

Teaching of the U.S. Bishops

Before 1919 there were no letters or teaching documents from the bishops as a whole because the U.S. bishops did not have any perduring national organization. The U.S. bishops first formed a national organization in 1917 to coordinate the Catholic support for the war effort. This organization became the National Catholic Welfare Conference (NCWC) in 1923 and has gone through subsequent changes, especially at the time of Vatican II.[2]

The most famous document coming from NCWC was the "Bishops' Program of Social Reconstruction" issued by the administrative board of the NCWC in February 1919. This document dealt with reconstruction plans for justice and peace after World War I; proposed eleven recommendations, ten of which were ultimately put into practice in the United

States; but also pointed out three long-term defects in the present system that needed continuing attention: inefficiency and waste in production and distribution, insufficient incomes for the majority of workers, and unnecessarily large incomes for a small minority of privileged capitalists.[3] This sixteen-page document in contemporary format contains only one reference to papal teaching—the encyclical *Rerum novarum* of Leo XIII.[4]

What explains the lack of extensive citations from papal documents in the earliest and perhaps most significant document coming from the U.S. bishops dealing with social justice in the first half of the twentieth century? Many influences are at work here. With regard to papal teaching in general, its role or importance was somewhat less in the early twentieth century than it was to become in subsequent years. In the case of social teaching in particular, there existed only one document (*Rerum novarum*) and not a body of Catholic social teaching. Likewise, the 1917 program addressed the broad U.S. audience as well as Catholics and perhaps purposely did not appeal that much to authoritative church teaching. The first draft of the document came from the typewriter of John A. Ryan, the foremost theoretician of Catholic social ethics at the time, and was not originally intended as a document to be issued by the bishops.[5]

The first pastoral letter of the U.S. bishops in the twentieth century in 1919, however, differs markedly from the "Bishops' Program of Social Reconstruction" with regard to the use of papal teaching. The six-page section on "Industrial Relations," in this sixty-three-page document, starts by citing *Rerum novarum* and begins each of its separate sections with a citation from Leo XIII, thus making the encyclical the primary source for the teaching in this area.[6] The different audience and subject matter of this document help to explain the different emphasis on papal teaching. As a pastoral letter the document is addressed to all members of the Catholic Church in the United States and not directly to non-Catholics. This long document also deals with the whole life of the Catholic Church in the United States, including its internal and devotional life as well as its relationship to the broader U.S. society and the problems facing that society.

One should see the statements of the U.S. bishops on industrial relations in the period between 1919 and 1950 in the light of the bishops' statements and documents on other issues. In his 1952 book, Raphael Huber collected the various letters, resolutions, and statements of the U.S. bishops from the period of 1919 to 1951 and included only eighty-two documents. Less than ten of the statements deal with issues of industrial relations. Here too there is a tendency in addressing the broader American society to downplay the teaching of the popes and to appeal to sources that all the people in the United States readily accept. See, for example, the 1947 statement, "Secularism," and the 1951 statement, "God's Law: The Measure of Man's Conduct."[7]

The Depression in the 1930s focused much attention in the United States on industrial relations. From the Catholic perspective, the issuance of the new encyclical by Pope Pius XI in 1931 added another authoritative voice to the solution for industrial problems. Now the Church had two encyclicals dealing with this issue. Thus, in the decade of the 1930s, the U.S. bishops frequently addressed the problems of the Depression and gave primary place to the solutions proposed by the papal encyclicals. These various statements include: "Statement on Unemployment" (1930); "Statement on the Economic Crisis" (1931); "Statement on the Present Crisis" (1933); "Statement in Defense of the Rights of Workers to Organize" (1934); "Statement on the Christian Attitude on Social Problems" (1937); "Statement on Industrial and Social Peace" (1938); "Statement on the Church and Social Order" (1940).[8] In the eyes of the U.S. bishops the encyclicals of Leo XIII and Pius XI proposed solutions for the industrial problems that existed in the United States in the 1930s. In the 1940 statement of the administrative board, "Church and Social Order," the bishops insist on the role of the Church "as the teacher of the entire moral law and more particularly as it applies to man's economic and social conduct in business, industry, and trade. To make our pronouncements authentic and to interpret truly the mind of the Church, we follow closely the teachings of our late lamented pontiff, Pope Pius XI."[9]

In this document the U.S. bishops strongly urge the United States to put into practice the principles found in this papal teaching.[10] Here the bishops stress the right of workers to organize, the right of workers to receive a living wage as a minimum requirement of justice, the need for federal and state appropriations and intervention to bring about justice and relief from the present crisis, and a more equitable sharing of the goods of creation. In proposing a just social order, the bishops insist that the papal principles and understanding are a *via media* between individualism on the one hand and collectivism or communism on the other. Economic liberalism wants no interference whatsoever on the part of government and insists on no restrictions upon individual initiative and personal enterprise. The government is limited to the function of a policeman or umpire in enforcing private contracts with no responsibility for promoting justice and the common good. On the other extreme, collectivists and communists desire to centralize all power in the state and to socialize all resources including private property.

The bishops in accord with the teaching in *Quadragesimo anno* want to overcome the opposition between capital and labor and build a more organic society. Human society must be seen as an organic entity based on analogy with the human body in which all the parts work for the good of the whole. We all belong to the same social organism, but unfortunately that social organism has been dismembered and broken up with different groups such as capital and labor seeking their own good and not the common good of all. The encyclical calls for new functional structures called occupational groups or vocational groups. These occupational groups well illustrate economic democracy at work and avoid the opposite extremes of laissez-faire capitalism and government dictating all economic policy. Labor and capital, together with the blessing and limited help of government, will thus form these public groups that determine production, prices, and wages in a particular industry, while an overall council coordinates and directs the individual industries to make sure they work for the common good. Thus, labor, capital, consumers, and government work together for the common good and replace the primary role of the free market.

In the 1930s, the bishops were also worried that communist leaders in the United States might take advantage of the chaos to introduce their approach, which masqueraded as the champion of the downtrodden, the archenemy of capitalistic abuses, and the redeemer of the poor and the working classes. Such atheistic communism failed to recognize the basic God-given dignity of the individual person. The United States needed to respond to the problems of the Depression in accord with the principles of papal teaching to avoid a radical takeover by Communists.[11] This theme of the danger of communism on both the national scene and especially the international scene would become quite prominent in the rhetoric of the U.S. Catholic bishops in the 1950s.[12] However, this topic extends well beyond the limited question of industrial relations being treated here.

New issues came to the fore in the 1940s and 1950s with World War II and its aftermath. In this period the U.S. bishops at their annual plenary meetings issued no statements or pastoral letters on industrial relations as such. As one might expect, they addressed the issues of the day including war, peace, communism, the cold war, and the family, and in 1958 condemned "enforced segregation" of Negroes.[13] However, the bishops had already forcefully made the point that in the area of industrial relations the papal encyclicals, especially *Rerum novarum* and *Quadragesimo anno*, provide the principles to bring about justice in this area and even a plan for a just social order based on the industry councils.

Theologians and More Popular Writings

The writings of Catholic theologians and commentators on socioeconomic issues in the United States in the first sixty years of the twentieth century show a trajectory that gave an increasingly important role to papal teaching and encyclicals, culminating in these sources becoming the primary and principal sources for Catholic social thought. Likewise by the 1960s, the mainstream of Catholic writing on socioeconomic issues in the United States basically followed the same approach as the papal documents: a heavy natural law basis, a moderate reforming stance, a working together with all others for the common good, and an emphasis on change of structures rather than change of heart.

John A. Ryan (1869–1945), an archdiocesan priest of St. Paul in Minnesota, was the foremost exponent of Catholic social thought in his role as professor at the Catholic University of America from 1915 to 1939 and the most visible spokesperson for Catholic social thought in his role as director of the Social Action Department (SAD) of NCWC, one of the four original departments of NCWC founded in 1919. Ryan was a prolific author throughout his life, but he did his more academic and scholarly publishing early, especially *The Living Wage* (1906) and *Distributive Justice* (1916).[14] In these two monographs Ryan gives practically no attention to papal documents. *Distributive Justice*, in its almost 450 pages, mentions Leo XIII's *Rerum novarum* in only three places![15] However, by the 1930s papal encyclicals constitute the primary source for Ryan's ethical analysis of socioeconomic issues.[16] Four factors influence this change. First, in his role as director of the SAD, Ryan's charge called for him to make official church teaching known and applied. Second, papal teaching became more important in the life of the Catholic Church in general as the century progressed. Third, by 1931, there were now two papal encyclicals dealing with industrial relations. Fourth, Ryan himself had often been attacked by others within the Roman Catholic Church as being too advanced and liberal in his social positions, but many saw the new 1931 encyclical as a papal vindication of Ryan's positions. Ryan defended himself by calling upon the teaching of the popes.

Throughout his over four decades of publishing, Ryan remained basically consistent in his approach to Catholic social ethics. He employed a natural law methodology, proposed a constantly reforming position rejecting radical reconstruction, called for some government intervention to promote justice, worked with many groups and associations outside the Church for social change, and emphasized the change of structures while neglecting the change of heart.[17]

Three somewhat different Catholic approaches to the social problem emerged in the period before 1940 in more popular Catholic writings. These approaches addressed a very Catholic audience from the perspective of a triumphalistic Catholic ecclesiology. The German American Catholics under the leadership of Frederick P. Kenkel, in their journal *Central Blatt and Social Justice* which reached a peak circulation of eight thousand in 1913, were more negative than Ryan in their view of the U.S. economic scene and called for more radical change in the social order based on the corporatist theory proposed by German Catholics, especially the Jesuit Heinrich Pesch. Corporatism called for a system analogous to the guild system of the Middle Ages and similar to the vocational groups proposed later by Pius XI as a middle road between the extremes of socialism and capitalism. As quite conservative Catholics, they referred to papal teaching but their primary source was Pesch and the German writers associated with him.[18]

Paul Hanly Furfey (1896–1992), a priest-professor of sociology at the Catholic University of America, wrote significant popular works in the 1930s, especially *Fire on the Earth* (1936), calling for a radical Christian personalism in opposition to the existing mores and institutions of U.S. society and life. *Fire on the Earth* explains the theoretical basis of the Catholic Worker movement founded by Dorothy Day. Furfey advocated a supernatural sociology (in opposition to the natural law approach of others), a literal and radical interpretation of the New Testament, and strategies of separation, nonparticipation, and bearing witness in relation to the existing ethos and culture in the United States. However, in the very first paragraph of *Fire on the Earth* Furfey appeals to *Quadragesimo anno*'s call for a return to genuine Christian life as a justification for his very different approach.[19]

Virgil Michel (1890–1938), a Benedictine monk of St. John's Abbey, Collegeville, Minnesota, with very broad philosophical and theological interests, wrote often on social issues, including a commentary on *Quadragesimo anno* in which he explains the problems of capitalism and the need for a reconstruction of the social order based on the encyclical's call for occupational groups. Addressing primarily a Catholic audience, he insists this more substantive change calls for a basic change of heart that could only take place in and through a living participation in the liturgy. He cites Pope Pius X to justify his emphasis on bringing together social change, change of heart, and active participation in the liturgy.[20]

Joseph Casper Husslein (1873–1952), a Jesuit priest, associate editor of *America*, and professor and founder of the School of Social Service at St. Louis University, was a prolific popular writer on social justice beginning with his 1912 *The Church and Social Problems*. He even wrote a 1924 book for the SAD of NCWC on *The Bible and Labor*. His writings well illustrate the trajectory described in this section of gradually making the papal encyclicals the primary source for his teaching. In 1931 he published *The Christian Social Manifesto*, which was a commentary on *Rerum novarum* and *Quadragesimo anno*. In 1940 and 1942 he first published under the general title of *Social Wellsprings* two different books bringing together the important encyclicals of Leo XIII and Pius XI.[21] For the later Husslein, the papal encyclicals constituted the primary and governing source for Catholic social thought.

John F. Cronin (1908–94), a Sulpician priest who taught in seminaries and served as the assistant or associate director of the SAD of NCWC from 1948 to 1967, wrote often on Catholic social thought.[22] His *Social Principles and Economic Life* (1959), based on an earlier work and later revised to include the encyclicals of John XXIII, served as a textbook in many Catholic colleges and universities. All seventeen chapters begin with extended citations from appropriate papal (and occasionally episcopal) documents, especially *Rerum novarum* and *Quadragesimo anno*. Thus Catholic social thought involves a commentary on, and an application of, papal documents. In this book, Cronin follows the natural law approach, adopts a reforming and not a radical approach to the social order, and insists on institutional and structural change while downplaying to a great extent the role of change of heart.[23] Writing in 1971, Cronin criticized his own naïve hermeneutic of the papal documents for failing to recognize their historical and cultural conditioning and also pointed out the limited and fundamentalist ecclesiology of the times.[24]

Thus, by 1960, the Cronin book illustrates that Catholic social thought in the United States became almost identified with the teaching of the papal social encyclicals as giving the principles for guiding and overcoming the problems still existing in the socioeconomic order.

Practical Influence of the Social Encyclicals

The SAD, despite a very small staff, tried to disseminate the ideas of the social encyclicals and to show how these principles should affect pastoral life. This department strongly supported labor and union organizing with occasional criticisms about corruption and the failure to organize industrial workers in earlier times. The SAD in the 1920s, for example, started the Catholic Conference on Industrial Problems, which sponsored conferences dealing with industrial issues in light of Catholic teaching. The department also ran conferences, short courses, and lectures to train priests to work in the labor apostolate and help in the work of labor schools in many areas of the country. Later the department issued a monthly bulletin, *Social Action Notes for Priests*. In many ways the department was the center for Catholic social action with some areas such as family life, rural life, and international relations eventually becoming separate entities within NCWC.[25]

Beginning in the 1940s George G. Higgins, a Chicago priest, worked in SAD and continued the work of Ryan and his hard-working associate, Raymond A. McGowan. In keeping with the history of the department, Higgins concentrated primarily on industrial relations but he became the most influential figure in broader Catholic social action in the United States during this period. Higgins, like his associate, John F. Cronin, championed the cause of Pius XI's occupational or vocational groups and was even able to influence some labor leaders to support this plan. However, by the 1960s Higgins and Cronin realized that there was no possibility for such institutions coming into existence in the United States.[26]

In addition to the SAD, the NCWC since 1922 housed the National Council of Catholic Women, organized to provide a voice for Catholic women and to address problems of unemployment and unjust industrial practices. The Council sought a living wage for men and women, particularly working mothers.[27]

The social encyclicals inspired four significant pastoral involvements within the Church. First, many dioceses and Catholic colleges and universities established labor schools with the practical goal of acquainting Catholic workers with the social teaching of the Church about labor and industrial problems. A special effort was made to overcome the possible inroads of communist influence in labor unions. The labor schools aimed at both training leaders for the movement and a broader dissemination of Catholic social principles to all involved. Some were basic schools existing on a parish level while more specialized technical courses were given on a diocesan level or at a college or university. In 1948, over forty dioceses had such labor schools or related projects.[28]

Second, individual priests, basing their approach on the encyclicals, were collectively known as "labor priests" because of their strong support for workers and labor unions even though they often approached things in different ways. As early as the second decade of the century, Peter Dietz worked tirelessly in support of the AFL and other labor unions, but his attempt to found a national organization of Catholic workers was unsuccessful.[29] Later figures include Charles O. Rice of Pittsburgh, John P. Boland of Buffalo, Francis J. Haas, later the bishop of Grand Rapids, Michigan, and many others.[30] From the 1953 movie *On the Waterfront*, many Americans became familiar with the antiracketeering crusade of Jesuit Father John Corridan in New York.[31]

Third, the Association of Catholic Trade Unionists came into existence in New York City in 1937 to help Catholics influence their unions to act in accord with Catholic principles and especially to overcome the danger of communist influence in unions. The group published *Labor Leader* and had about eleven chapters throughout the United States in its prime before its demise in the 1960s.[32]

Fourth, the Jesuit general told U.S. Jesuits to start something similar to the existing Jesuit centers of social research and action in Europe so as to inspire their educational apostolate with a commitment to papal social teaching. The Institute of Social Order, headquartered most of its life in St. Louis, came into existence as such a center publishing a journal known since 1951 as *The Journal of Social Order* that continued until 1963.[33]

Two significant intellectual associations began under the impulse of papal social teaching. The American Catholic Sociological Society began in 1938 with its journal *The American Catholic Sociological Review*, first published in 1940 with the primary goal of applying the principles of Catholic social teaching as found in the encyclicals to the U.S. scene. The association did not want to cut itself off from the academic study of sociology in the United States but definitely wanted to bring Catholic principles to bear on the understanding of society. At its height the society had nearly five hundred members. A few years later some Catholic scholars founded the Catholic Economic Association with its journal *Review of Social Economy* with the same basic purpose as the American Catholic Sociological Society. Both groups ceased to exist as such in the 1960s.[34]

The apostolate of Catholics in the labor and intellectual realms sprang from the understanding of "Catholic action." According to the popes, Catholic action was "the participation of the laity in the apostolate of the hierarchy."

The pope and the hierarchy proposed the social teaching with its principles and then laypeople carried these principles out in practice in their own respective areas. The role of the laity was to Christianize the social order through their efforts in their own fields in the light of the social teaching of the Church.[35]

Thus by 1960 the papal social encyclicals had become identified with Catholic social thought and significantly influenced the role of elite lay Catholic leaders who tried to implement this papal teaching especially in the labor movement and in the intellectual movements dealing with sociology and economics. The average Catholic, however, knew little or nothing about the social teaching of the encyclicals.

FROM THE 1960s TO THE PRESENT

By the end of the 1960s the associations, structures, and institutions associated with the social encyclical tradition in the United States were no longer extant. The encyclicals were no longer taught in Catholic colleges. The Association of Catholic Trade Unionists, the American Catholic Sociological Society, and the American Catholic Economic Association no longer existed as such. No new generation of labor priests came to the fore; labor schools and colleges ceased to exist. The social encyclicals with their emphasis on industrial relations no longer played a significant role in the life of the Catholic Church in the United States. John Cronin pointed out "that the golden era of Catholic social thought, beginning in 1891, had ended by 1971."[36]

Cronin's statement needs to be nuanced. Catholic social thought and action had not seen their best days. Catholic social teaching, understood as the encyclicals on industrial issues, and most of the theoretical and pastoral approaches associated with these encyclicals, definitely experienced a sharp decline.

Dramatic developments in U.S. society and in the Church helped to explain this abrupt change in the role of the encyclicals in U.S. Catholicism. First, the issues of industrial relations no longer seemed that significant or important. With greater economic growth and relative prosperity in the post–World War II era, the centrality of the problems associated with industrial relations had already moved off center stage. Catholics in general moved into the middle class and improved their economic state. Now, quite more pressing issues came to the fore. Race and segregation became a prominent issue in this country. A 1958 statement of the U.S. bishops finally condemned "enforced segregation."[37] The justifiable protest of African Americans came to the fore in the 1960s. Many middle-class white Christians in this country had trouble even with the nonviolent approach of Martin Luther King Jr. Black power advocates, however, could not accept such a gradual and nonviolent approach. The problem of racial segregation and prejudice sparked urban riots that spread across the country in the mid- and late 1960s. America's cities were burning. At the same time, opposition to the Vietnam War continued to escalate. The country was seriously divided over the morality of the U.S. involvement in Southeast Asia. Not only did the content of the social issues change but also the way in which they were addressed. A more angry and heated tone on the part of the protesters came to the fore. The 1960s ushered in a completely new situation in the United States.

Second, the understanding of how to deal with these new issues also changed. The papal encyclicals, to their credit, called for structural and institutional change. Such change should come about through rational discussion and living out the teaching of the Church. Part of the problem for the Church in the 1960s, especially in dealing with race and urban problems, came from the fact that Catholics were no longer the poor and the victims. How to help those who were not Catholic and bring about real social change presented new problems and called for new solutions. The U.S. bishops learned some things from their Protestant sisters and brothers but also from the experience of the Catholic Church in the United States, which in the 1940s and 1950s had cautiously supported community organizing efforts as illustrated especially by the support of the archdiocese of Chicago for Saul

Alinsky's work. The idea was for the poor to organize themselves to work for justice for their neighborhoods. In 1970 the U.S. bishops inaugurated their Campaign for Human Development (CHD), which called for an annual collection in all Catholic churches throughout the country that would then be used to fund community self-help projects and organizations involving the poor throughout the country. Notice here that the Church did not teach others what to do; rather, it tried to empower the poor to change their own situations. Obviously CHD would not be able to accomplish much, but it definitely indicated a different way for the Church to deal with social problems.[38]

Third, significant changes at Vatican II (1962–65) also contributed to the demise of the importance and influence of the social encyclicals in the United States. Vatican II insisted on the primacy of scripture in the life, liturgy, and theology of the Church and especially in the discipline of moral theology. The papal social encyclicals, including the two in the early 1960s written by John XXIII (*Mater et magistra* in 1961 and *Pacem in terris* in 1963), employed a natural law methodology and gave practically no importance to the scriptures.

More significantly, Vatican II changed the understanding of the Church. The laity were no longer second-class citizens who participated in the apostolate of the hierarchy by carrying out in their lives the principles and truths that were taught by the pope and bishops. The Church is the whole people of God, not just the hierarchy. All of the baptized are called to perfection, not just religious and clergy. The laity should not expect pastors of the Church to have answers to all the problems facing the world.[39]

Fourth, a new breed of Catholic social activists appeared on the scene in the light of these dramatic changes both in U.S. society and in the Church. The old breed insisted on long-term education based on Catholic social teaching and the structural change that could come about as a result. The new breed was more impatient; appealed to a more scriptural approach; and insisted on direct action, prophetic witness, and the need for the Church to take stands on these controversial issues and become directly involved in social change. Their primary interests were peace, poverty, and race. In this context the labor encyclicals afforded little or no help.[40]

New Situations and a New Approach

All these reasons help to explain why the social encyclical tradition, with its approach to industrial relations that had become quite a prominent aspect of Catholic life in the 1950s, did not really survive after the 1960s. However, a somewhat different focus and role for encyclicals and official church documents on the socioeconomic order began to appear after the 1960s and took on its own important role in the life of the Catholic Church in the United States. What brought about this development and renewed interest in Catholic social teaching?

First, the issues confronting U.S. society and the world were truly moral issues affecting the lives of all. The problems were not only national but international. Churches as such had to deal with these issues. Recall the heavy church involvement across the board in the United States in the issues of race and peace. The leaders of the Catholic Church could not be silent in such circumstances.

Second, Vatican II, in *Gaudium et spes* (*Pastoral Constitution on the Church in the Modern World*), insisted that the "split between the faith which many profess and their daily lives deserves to be counted among the more serious errors of our age" (GS 43). *Justitia in mundo* (*Justice in the World*), the document from the 1971 synod of bishops, maintained: "Action on behalf of justice and participation in the transformation of the world fully appear to us as a constitutive dimension of the preaching of the Gospel, or, in other words, of the Church's mission for the redemption of the human race and its liberation from every oppressive situation" (JM, introduction). Thus, after Vatican II the social mission of the Church was more central and more important than it had been previously.

Third, as a result of Vatican II national conferences of Catholic bishops came into existence throughout the world. The United States with its NCWC had been a pioneer in this matter, but now many held that the national bishops' conferences had a mandate to teach for the Church in their local areas.[41] The U.S. bishops after this time took an even more public role in dealing with social issues.

Fourth, the social encyclical tradition itself developed. The post–Vatican II encyclicals tried to incorporate without total success a more scriptural approach to the issues. Above all, the documents moved away from a primary focus on industrial relations but even *Quadragesimo anno* in 1931 talked about a broader reconstruction of the social order and the need for social justice. Beginning with *Mater et magistra* in 1961, with a strong assist from Paul VI's *Populorum progressio*, the documents now recognized that the socioeconomic problem was worldwide. The plight of the third and fourth worlds came in for important consideration in these and subsequent documents. Catholic social teaching now dealt with issues of justice, peace, and poverty in a worldwide perspective.

Fifth, the popes themselves tied their post–Vatican II encyclicals into both the earlier social encyclical tradition beginning with *Rerum novarum* and into the *Pastoral Constitution on the Church in the Modern World*. The fact that new documents appeared on anniversaries of the original two documents in 1971, 1981, and 1991 made people more conscious of the tradition as a whole. Pope John Paul II has insisted on calling this tradition the social teaching of the Church (CA 2). Thus, from the viewpoint of the papal magisterium this body of authoritative teaching, including the earlier documents, constitutes the social teaching of the Church and has an important role to play in the life of the Church.

Sixth, the ecclesiology of Vatican II changed the role that official hierarchical documents played in the life of the Church. In the pre–Vatican II era, the encyclicals were the primary source of such teaching. Theologians commented on the teachings and the laity put these teachings of the encyclicals into practice in their daily lives. The process was from the top down. After Vatican II, Catholic theologians and commentators on the social scene recognized that Catholic social ethics or Catholic social thought was broader than the documents of Catholic social teaching. Activists often initiated new approaches and movements so that Catholic social action came from the bottom up as well as from the top down. The official documents, while still important, did not play the same role they had in the pre–Vatican II Church.

What about the reaction of the rest of the Church? The reception of papal and authoritative hierarchical teaching in the Roman Catholic Church, especially after the discussion and dissent occasioned by *Humanae vitae*, the 1968 encyclical condemning artificial contraception for spouses, has not been as automatic and uncritical as in the pre–Vatican II Church. Some U.S. Catholics, in theory and practice, have criticized and disagreed with aspects of this teaching. However, the whole Church has received these social documents and given them an important role. Courses in Catholic social teaching now exist in Catholic colleges and universities. Collections of and commentaries on these documents have been published. The whole Church has received these documents because they appear to address significant problems in an insightful and convincing manner, but theologians and commentators are more critical in analyzing these documents. This background sets the stage for a study of the reception of Catholic social teaching in the post-1960s in this country.

Teaching of the U.S. Bishops

The U.S. bishops' conference played a much greater role in dealing with social issues as a result of the new emphasis on national conferences of bishops. In addition, on the U.S. scene, many Catholic activists had chided the U.S. bishops for dragging their feet and failing to address, in a timely manner, the issues of race, urban unrest, and the war in Vietnam. Recall that other churches had been involved in these issues in a much earlier and stronger fashion. These two factors help to explain the greater involvement of the U.S. bishops in the 1966–80 timeframe.

The most innovative involvement of the U.S. bishops in this timeframe involves the Call to Action Conference in Detroit in 1976. Pope Paul VI's 1971 apostolic letter, *Octogesima adveniens*, titled in English *A Call to Action*, ended with a fresh and insistent call to action for laity to renew the temporal order. The U.S. bishops led by Cardinal John Dearden called for a national Catholic meeting in Detroit in October 1976 on the occasion of the U.S. Bicentennial to examine how the Church should work for liberty and justice for all in our society. The two-year preparatory period included parish discussions throughout the whole country on the theme of the meeting, six hearings throughout the country in which a committee of bishops listened to experts and people who were involved in community work and social action on the local level, and finally written reports from special committees taking into account the above data and dealing with eight specific issues: church, nationhood, family, personhood, neighborhood, humankind, ethnicity and race, and work. Each of these documents ended with recommendations to be voted on at the meeting in Detroit.[42]

The Detroit meeting involved 1340 voting delegates, more than 100 of whom were bishops, and many observers. Generally speaking the delegates tended to be people involved in social action in the Church and thus had a more reform agenda. The resolutions and recommendations passed by the group included the call for change in a number of existing Catholic Church teachings and practices. Although the process itself was far from perfect, the enthusiasm of the delegates was perceptible throughout the hall. However, the U.S. bishops, precisely because of the controversial nature of many resolutions calling for change in existing Catholic teaching and practice, ultimately did not accept much of what the conference had asked for. Never again did the bishops of the United States sponsor a meeting in which Catholics voted on particular issues and resolutions.[43] However, in some of their subsequent teaching documents, they did employ broad and extensive dialogue.

After Vatican II the U.S. bishops issued many statements covering a multitude of social issues and raised some controversy.[44] The bishops were criticized by some for making too many statements, for being too specific, and for adopting too many partisan positions.[45] In the 1980s Cardinal Joseph Bernardin popularized the metaphor of the "consistent ethic of life" to justify the bishops' involvement in a wide variety of social issues such as abortion, human rights, international relations, Central America, poverty, and nuclear war and deterrence.[46] An analysis and criticism of the role of the bishops lies beyond the parameters of this study.

In this context one would expect the bishops to deal with the economic issues facing the country and the world. In 1975, at their annual meeting, the bishops issued a short statement, "The Economy: Human Dimensions." This document justified the Church's interest in this subject; explained the pertinent teaching of the Church or what today we call Catholic social teaching; discussed the three issues of unemployment, inflation, and the distribution of income and wealth; and concluded with policy directives in these matters.[47] This statement, like many similar statements and documents coming from the bishops' conference, did not attract that much attention either within or outside the Church.

1986 Pastoral Letter

At their annual meeting in November 1980, the U.S. bishops were discussing a pastoral letter on Marxism. Some bishops then suggested that they should write a similar letter on capitalism. At that meeting, they decided to write two new pastoral letters: one on capitalism and one on nuclear war and deterrence (which was ultimately given priority). Archbishop Rembert Weakland of Milwaukee became chair of the five-bishop committee with staff members from the U.S. Catholic Conference and others to draft the pastoral on capitalism. Early on, the committee decided against a theoretical discussion of capitalism as being inappropriate. In the light of *Octogesima adveniens*'s call for local churches to analyze their own situation in the light of Catholic social teaching, the committee adopted that approach. The committee followed closely the successful methodology employed by the committee writing the peace pastoral. The committee held meetings with invited theologians, economists, sociologists, congressional staffers, social justice leaders, business leaders, labor leaders, and farmers. In addition, they welcomed all correspondence. Following the example of the peace pastoral, the committee made public all its drafts so as to broaden the discussion and involve as many people as possible. The committee purposely decided not to issue its first draft before the November 1984 presidential election in order to keep the document out of partisan political debate.[48]

The first draft was issued in November 1984, the second in October 1985, and the third in June 1986, with the bishops approving and issuing the final document in November 1986. Some changes occurred in the drafting process, but these changes were more in the nature of adjustments and refinements and were not substantial. The first draft bore the title *Catholic Social Teaching and the U.S. Economy*. The final version used this as the subtitle after the title *Economic Justice for All*. Thus, the bishops gave pride of place to Catholic social teaching and relating the principles of this teaching to the U.S. scene.[49]

Economic Justice for All contains five chapters. The first involves a reading of the signs of the times and a justification for church involvement in questions of the economy. Chapter 2 develops the Christian view of the economy with a biblical section followed by ethical norms and priorities for the economy. Chapter 3 deals with four economic issues: employment, poverty, food and agriculture, and the U.S. economy and developing nations. Chapter 4 calls for "A New American Experiment" involving the cooperation and participation of all including the government in national and international cooperation. Chapter 5 emphasizes the Christian commitment to love and to practice justice in the world and also challenges the Church including its role as an economic actor, for example, paying a living wage. In brief, the economic pastoral calls for the just participation of all, especially the poor and the marginalized in the economy, what an early draft called "economic democracy."

Catholic social teaching is the basis for the pastoral letter and thus heavily influences it. Like Catholic social teaching the pastoral letter addresses two audiences: the people of the Church and the broader public debate about what is good for the country.[50] The approach of the letter, like that of Catholic social teaching, is reforming rather than radical. Catholic social teaching, while often negative about certain aspects of capitalism, never condemned it as intrinsically evil. Catholic social teaching claims today not to endorse any one economic system but to propose principles to reform existing systems. The pastoral follows such a "pragmatic and evolutionary" approach that it claims it is also in keeping with the "American pragmatic tradition of reform" (EJA 131).

The pastoral, however, departs from Catholic social teaching in two areas. The drafting committee recognized the need to incorporate a more scriptural approach than that found in the earlier documents of Catholic social teaching with their natural law basis.[51] The document is not entirely successful in integrating scripture into the whole approach, but Catholic ethicists themselves have also been unsuccessful in integrating scripture into Catholic social ethics. In addition, the fact that the bishops also tried to address the broader pluralistic U.S. public means the document by definition cannot integrate scripture into its whole approach. Second, in keeping with the earlier peace pastoral, the economic pastoral goes beyond the principles found in Catholic social teaching and makes prudential judgments about what should be done. Such judgments in the letter do not carry the same teaching authority as the "statements of universal moral principles and formal church teaching" and are open to debate (135).

According to the pastoral, "the fundamental moral criterion for all economic decisions . . . is this: They must be at the service of *all people, especially the poor*" (24). "Human dignity, realized in community with others and with the whole of God's creation, is the norm against which every social institution must be measured" (25). Such a criterion relies on the universal destiny of the goods of creation to serve the needs of all and the preferential option for the poor. All human beings have a right to a minimally decent human existence.

The pastoral letter develops an anthropology that stresses both the dignity of the individual person and the social nature of the person who is called by one's very being to live together in various communities such as the family and the political order. (Note these are communities in an analogous sense because the family is quite different from the political order.)[52]

In such an understanding, both society and government are something natural, necessary, and good, but government is also limited. The Catholic approach thus sees itself in opposition to the two extremes of collectivism and individualism. Collectivism so emphasizes the collectivity that it fails to recognize the dignity of the individual person, whereas individualism so emphasizes the individual that it fails to give enough importance to the community.

Based on love, solidarity, and our common humanity, we are called to live in a political community that strives for the common good of the community itself. The common good, by definition, also redounds to the good of the individual person. Thus, clean air is good for the community and good for individual persons. So too not only individual poor people but society as a whole and all other people in society are better off if we can eliminate poverty. Individualism sees only individual goods; collectivism only collective goods; but the common good avoids these two extremes.

Government, however, is also limited. It is only one part of the political society that includes individual persons; basic natural societies like the family and even the neighborhood; a whole host of voluntary societies such as corporations, nonprofit groups, professional organizations of every type, and churches; and, finally, the government on the local, state, and federal levels. The principle of subsidiarity calls for the higher level to encourage and help the lower level to do everything possible, and the higher level intervenes only to do what the lower level cannot accomplish. Look at housing in the United States. People are encouraged to own their own homes. Habitat for Humanity builds houses for some people. The government intervenes in a number of ways such as the tax break on mortgages that helps families to own their own homes, but at times the local government must also intervene and build public housing for others.

Thus the government has a limited but important role to play with regard to making sure the economy exists for the common good that includes the basic good of all individuals. In chapter 4 the bishops propose a "new American experiment" involving a partnership of all involved, including the government, to work for the common good and the need for some planning in order to bring this about.

The common good involves the participation of all in the life of the community, including its economic life as well as justice and human rights for all. Justice in the Catholic tradition involves three types of justice: commutative, distributive, and legal or contributive. These three types correspond to three different relationships: individuals to individuals, society to individuals, and individuals to society (68–76). Since we are members of the civil and political community, distributive justice deals with how society distributes its goods and burdens to individuals. Individualism claims that we are free to acquire as many material goods for ourselves as we can, provided that all start in a fair position. Distributive justice, according to the pastoral, maintains that society must make sure that all its members have a sufficiency of material goods to live a minimally decent human existence. A basic minimal wage, for example, is not necessarily what employer and employee agree upon but what gives the worker enough to live a minimally decent life. In distributing burdens, those who have more have an obligation to give more to the community, thus the pastoral calls for progressive taxation (202). Legal or contributive justice (this term adds something to the Catholic social teaching approach) involves the obligation of the individual to society especially in terms of the obligation of the individual to contribute to society and society's need to facilitate that participation. The pastoral remains true to its anthropological foundations in calling not only for civil and political rights such as freedom of religion, speech, and the press, but also social and economic rights such as the right to life, food, clothing, shelter, medical care, and basic education (79–84).

Individualism is very strong in the United States. The pastoral goes against this individualism in its insistence on a more communitarian understanding of human existence, the option for the poor ("the poor have the single most urgent economic claim on the conscience of the nation" [86]), the important but limited role of government in the economy, distributive and contributive justice, and economic rights.

The pastoral wisely recognizes that Catholic social teaching also challenges the Church in its educational mission and above all in its life as an economic actor with many different employees. The Church should be exemplary in living up to its own principles (339–58).

Space does not permit an elaboration of the four specific issues considered in depth in the pastoral letter. A brief overview of the approach to poverty will serve as an illustration of how the other issues are handled (170–215). At the time of the pastoral, the official governmental definition recognized that one out of every seven Americans is in poverty. In addition, there is great economic inequality and uneven distribution of wealth and income, with 28 percent of the total net wealth held by the richest 2 percent of families. Poverty especially affects children, women, and racial minorities. Unfortunately there are too many misunderstandings and stereotypes of the poor; for example, others in our society receive much greater government subsidies than the poor. The bishops propose the following elements of a national strategy for dealing with poverty: a healthy economy is the best way to prevent poverty; discriminating barriers against women and minorities should be removed; self-help programs for the poor should be supported by both the private and the public sectors; the tax system should be reformed in terms of more progressive taxation; education for the poor must be strengthened; all programs for the poor should support and strengthen the family. A thorough reform of the nation's welfare system and income support program is necessary to ensure adequate levels of support for the poor with a goal of making them self-sufficient through gainful employment when possible.

Reaction to the Pastoral

Criticism of the pastoral came from both the left and the right. Gregory Baum, the eminent Canadian theologian and sociologist, lamented that the U.S. bishops were much less radical than the more recent statements of the Canadian bishops.[53] Liberation theologians who call into question the capitalist system itself disagreed with the pastoral. Rembert Weakland, with an obvious twinkle in his eye, put Cardinal Joseph Ratzinger in the same category as the liberationists because he had a "deep distrust of the capitalist system, especially as manifested in the United States."[54]

Within U.S. Catholicism, the strongest negative reaction from the right came from Catholic neoconservatives such as Michael Novak, George Weigel, and later Richard John Neuhaus (a Lutheran who became a Roman Catholic). The Catholic neoconservative movement began in the 1970s but became stronger and more forceful in the next decade. Catholic neoconservatives describe themselves in terms of their understanding of the Church, of the U.S. system and its role in the world, and of their intellectual predecessors.[55]

With regard to the Church, Catholic neoconservatives disagree with the liberal understanding of the Church as found in many theologians and even church institutions in the United States with their complaint that the primary problem in the Church is a crisis of authority and a recognition of the need for dissent within the Church. For the neoconservatives the problem is a crisis of faith. The liberals claiming to carry on the spirit of Vatican II have gone too far. The neoconservatives strongly support the pontificate of Pope John Paul II. They claim even many departments and offices of the U.S. bishops' conference and many bishops themselves have accepted the liberal approach. In the 1980s especially, the neoconservatives stressed a significant difference between the U.S. bishops and Pope John

Paul II. In this light, they strongly criticized both pastoral letters and the positions taken by the U.S. bishops on Central America.[56] Neoconservatives emphasize the need for a new ecumenism embracing a dialogue with the conservative, evangelical, and fundamentalist Protestant churches rather than with the mainline Protestant churches.

While not uncritical, Catholic neoconservatives are quite supportive of the U.S. political and economic systems while fearful that the Catholic liberal establishment has been too critical of the United States and naïve in its appreciation of movements associated with Marxism, especially liberation theologies. Catholic neoconservatives stress the interconnectedness and necessary linking together of the cultural, political, and economic orders so that democratic capitalism offers the best hope for overcoming poverty in the world.

From an intellectual perspective, Catholic neoconservatives appeal to the legacy of John Courtney Murray and Jacques Maritain, who strongly defended democracy and the American experiment as well as the realism of Reinhold Niebuhr that opposed the progressive illusions of Protestant liberalism. The neoconservatives with their insistence on the intimate connection between the political and economic orders want the U.S. Catholic Church to recognize today the benefits of capitalism just as the Catholic Church recognized the value of democracy and religious freedom based in great measure on the work of John Courtney Murray.

Michael Novak, a prolific author, has been the strongest voice for Catholic neoconservatism in the economic realm beginning with his monograph, *The Spirit of Democratic Capitalism* (1982).[57] Novak defends capitalism on theological, philosophical, and economic grounds as the best political economic system for the world today. He criticizes much of the earlier Catholic social teaching for stressing distribution rather than creativity and the production of wealth. John Paul II, however, has corrected this emphasis by insisting on the need for co-creation and entrepreneurship.[58]

Novak was the driving force behind and primary writer of *Toward the Future*, an analysis of Catholic social teaching and the U.S. economy, published by a lay group just before the first draft of the bishops' pastoral and proposed as an alternative approach to the one expected from the bishops.[59] Novak also responded to the drafts of the pastoral letter. His criticism of earlier drafts still holds for the final document that did not change substantially from the first draft. The pastoral letter puts too much emphasis on distribution and not enough on the creation of wealth. The bishops say far too little about the causes of wealth. The pastoral does not give enough importance to individual responsibility at all levels in the economy, including the poor. The letter is too accusatory about the causes of poverty and acts as if wealth rather than poverty were the natural condition of human beings before the advent of capitalism. The bishops fail to give enough importance to sin and consequently fall into a soft utopianism. Likewise, they endorse too many specific proposals.[60]

Novak strongly objects to the concept of economic rights in the first draft because it undermines the American idea of the limited state. Instead Novak insists the American concept of "equal opportunity for all" is just as effective in actually helping the poor.[61] Later he recognizes that John Paul II does have a concept of human rights, but Novak gives a rather minimal interpretation to such rights.[62] The vast majority of Catholic social ethicists in the United States, however, reject the neoconservative approach.

My own criticisms of the pastoral letter stem primarily from its total acceptance of Catholic social teaching and the failure to add to that tradition from the broader Catholic social ethics tradition and the U.S. Catholic experience. The letter does not deal with some more theoretical but very significant concepts in the U.S. economy, such as the profit motive, the role of markets, and the possible dehumanizing aspects of technology. Catholic social teaching itself fails to address these issues.

Like Catholic social teaching, the pastoral emphasizes the need for just structures, but it fails to give enough importance to the need for a change of heart and the social justice mission of the baptized in their daily lives. More needs to be said about the spirituality of those working for social change. The virtues and attitudes of the just person receive no in-depth development.

The pastoral letter belongs to the genre of teaching that obviously appeals to the reason and goodwill of others. Such an approach challenges the elite and the leaders to put into practice the principles proposed in the teaching. The letter pays little or no attention to the role of power. Power can never be absolutized, but is an important aspect in changing social structures. Also, power recognizes that change comes also from below and not merely from the top down. Here too the U.S. Catholic experience has something to contribute based on its own experience with community organizing and the Campaign for Human Development. Community organizations attempt to bring poor, disaffected, and marginalized people together to work for the betterment of their own neighborhood in terms of schools, public services, job creation, and safety. Here the approach is from the bottom up and often employs some conflictual tactics.[63] In practice the U.S. Catholic Church has recognized a role of power in bringing about structural change but not in the theoretical exposition of the pastoral.

The narrow focus of the letter, in keeping with Catholic social teaching, fails to appreciate the role of what I call prophetic shock minority groups in the Church.[64] These groups propose a more radical witness by focusing on one important aspect of human existence. In this case, groups like the Catholic Worker, with a significant influence beyond their small numbers, have contributed much to the life of the Catholic Church by their witness to voluntary poverty. These prophetic shock minorities, by bearing witness to one virtue such as peace or poverty, play a role analogous to religious life in the Church. Such an approach reminds the whole Church of the danger of materialism and of economic power. Thus, the pastoral letter would have been improved if it had attempted to add to Catholic social teaching from the broader Catholic social ethics tradition and the social experience of the U.S. Church.

Effect and Influence of the Pastoral

The pastoral letters of the U.S. bishops in the 1980s on nuclear war and deterrence and the economy had a greater effect on the American public in general and the Catholic Church in the United States than any other documents coming from the U.S. bishops. The primary reason comes from the unique and public way in which these letters were written and discussed. Past episcopal documents were often drafted by one person and after a somewhat pro forma discussion were voted on and accepted by the bishops as a whole. In the case of the two pastorals in the 1980s, the committees held public hearings involving many experts both Catholic and non-Catholic. Also, the drafts were not only discussed by the committee and the bishops but were made public and discussed at large. Such an approach truly involved many more people inside and outside the Church in the discussion.

Other factors also contributed to the importance given to these pastoral letters. The quality of the letters gave them credibility in the eyes of many. While critical of some U.S. positions, they gave a coherent and rational explanation for their criticisms and their proposed solutions. The timing was also good. These two significant issues were high on the agenda and radar screen of the country as a whole. The U.S. Catholic bishops also were taking on a role that mainstream Protestants had played in earlier U.S. society and culture. The Social Gospel, in the early twentieth century, and the later Niebuhrian realism had a great influence on U.S. culture and public policy. WASP culture played an important role in U.S. life, but the WASP influence and the role of mainstream Protestantism were in decline by the 1980s.[65] The economic pastoral thus made people outside and inside the Catholic Church more aware of Catholic social teaching and its application in U.S. life. The broader public debate, however, since it is in the nature of news, has a very short life span.

The pastoral letter and Catholic social teaching, as well as Catholic social ethics in the United States, have had little effect on philosophical ethics and political science worlds in this country. A number of factors help to explain this lack of influence. First, the academy in the United States tends to exist behind the walls of academic disciplines. University life has become more driven by individual disciplines and departments. Despite much talk about interdisciplinary approaches, the great complexity of each discipline forces one deeper within the confines of that particular discipline. The academic reward system in the university world tends to emphasize one's standing in the discipline. In many colleges and especially universities today the commitment of the academician to one's discipline is stronger than the commitment to one's institution. Political philosophy and political science, like all academic disciplines, often exist in their own intellectual cocoons. Without doubt, a secularistic antipathy to religion also contributes something to the isolation of the Catholic social tradition from contemporary philosophical social ethics and political science. However, other problems exist from the viewpoint of the Catholic tradition itself. Many Catholic ethicists (myself included) write primarily for a Catholic audience that at times might expand to a Christian ecumenical or religious interfaith milieu. Many people in the United States see the role of the Catholic Church as a political actor trying to have its positions enshrined in law and public policy and not primarily as an intellectual interlocutor engaged in public dialogue about what is best for the country. Thus, before and even after the pastoral letter on the economy, the Catholic social tradition has had little or no influence on political philosophy and science.

Christian and religious ethics ever since Vatican II have been more attentive to Catholic social teaching, and the bishops' pastoral letter engaged many other Christian and religious ethicists in their discussion about public policy in the United States.[66] As is to be expected, the greatest influence of the economic pastoral and its application of Catholic social teaching was on Catholic scholars. Many Catholic academic institutions, such as Georgetown University, the University of Notre Dame, DePaul University, Catholic Theological Union, and the Woodstock Center at Georgetown University, published books based on symposia held at their institutions.[67] The pastoral on the economy definitely stimulated Catholic theologians and scholars to pay more attention to Catholic social thought in general and Catholic social teaching in particular. The bishops here provided excellent leadership for Catholic theologians and scholars in recognizing the important role of Catholic social teaching.

Since the economic pastoral in 1986, the U.S. bishops have very occasionally issued documents on the economy, but they were in the older format of statements drafted in private and approved at the national meeting of the bishops without much dialogue or discussion. For example, at the 1995 meeting the bishops issued a four-page document marking the tenth anniversary of the economic pastoral with a threefold perspective of looking back, looking around, and looking ahead.[68] A year later at their annual meeting they adopted a very short ten-point "Catholic Framework for Economic Life."[69] These two documents obviously presented Catholic social teaching, but their import was nil as far as both the Church and the wider U.S. society are concerned.

Nothing the bishops have done since 1986 has come close to the impact made by their pastoral letters on peace and the economy. What happened to explain this fact? First, the issue of the economy is not the only social issue facing U.S. society, so one should not expect the bishops to address these issues that often. But deeper problems exist. The U.S. bishops, after 1986, never again issued a pastoral letter based on the methodology of broad hearings and public drafts. Why did the process not continue?

The bishops attempted to write another pastoral letter following the same format and methodology with regard to the role of women in the Church, an obviously controversial issue in the Roman Catholic Church. The committee proposed four drafts but opposition came from all sides, especially women on the one side and the Vatican on the other. In the end, the bishops scrapped the whole idea of such a pastoral letter. Thus, the last attempt to follow the newer format was an abysmal failure.[70]

Other ecclesial factors have also contributed to a lesser role played by the U.S. Catholic Bishops' Conference. The Vatican has publicly downplayed the role of national conferences of bishops as having an official teaching office in the Church. There is no doubt that the Vatican has tried to curtail the role that bishops' conferences have played, not only in the United States, but also throughout the world.[71] Some maintain that a broad consultation detracts from the teaching authority of bishops. More conservative bishops have been appointed in the last two decades who were more willing to go along with such a policy. In addition, the cardinals in the United States as a body have exercised a much greater public role and thus overshadowed the role of the national conference of bishops. Thus, it is not a surprise that the U.S. bishops in the 1990s issued no pastoral letters following the format of the peace and economic pastorals in the 1980s. Unfortunately, the bishops abandoned what had been their most effective teaching tool.

Theologians

As mentioned, Vatican II introduced significant changes that greatly altered the life of the Catholic Church in general and the approach of Catholic social teaching in particular. These same changes significantly affected Catholic moral theology and Catholic social ethics. Social ethics is a part of moral theology that also includes personal morality, sexuality and marriage, and medical ethics or bioethics. Vatican II called for newer approaches in moral theology with emphasis on a greater role for scripture, the universal call to holiness, a more significant attention to the signs of the times with a corresponding need for a more inductive methodology, and a recognition of a greater philosophical pluralism with regard to dialogue partners for theology. As a result, those in the United States who had been leaders in moral theology before Vatican II, because of age and these significant changes, no longer played an important leadership role in moral theology. Newer and younger moral theologians had to come along to fill the vacuum. In the immediate post–Vatican II period in the United States (and in the whole Catholic world) the primary moral issue concerned the official Catholic teaching on contraception and other issues of sexuality and marriage. Medical ethics, or bioethics as it was later called, also shared the spotlight. Thus, it took some time for a new generation of Catholic social ethicists and moral theologians in the United States to come to the fore and to begin publishing on matters of social and economic ethics.[72]

It was not until the late 1970s and early 1980s that the first scholarly monographs on Catholic social ethics appeared with the work of David Hollenbach,[73] John Coleman,[74] and Charles Curran.[75] The late 1970s also saw an increase in the number of articles dealing with issues concerned with Catholic social teaching. J. Bryan Hehir, as a staff person for the bishops' conference from 1973 to 1992, strongly influenced the social documents and positions taken by the U.S. bishops, and he also contributed many articles and speeches dealing with Catholic social teaching and the broader area of Catholic social ethics.[76] Two centers also contributed to a renewal of Catholic social ethics in general and its relationship to Catholic social teaching: the Woodstock Theological Center, started by the Society of Jesus at Georgetown University in 1974,[77] and the Notre Dame Center for Ethics and Religious Values in Business, founded in 1978.[78] Thus, before the first draft of the economic pastoral, Catholic social ethics was coming to life again, but there can be no doubt that the writing of the economic pastoral contributed greatly to the growth of Catholic social ethics dealing with political and economic issues.

Within the parameters of this essay, one cannot pretend to give a history of Catholic social ethics in the latter part of the twentieth century in the United States or to cover all the people who have contributed to this endeavor. The contributors to this volume include many of those who have been involved. Our focus in this short section is how Catholic social ethics has dealt with Catholic social teaching. As has already been pointed out with regard to the neoconservative approach, there are a number of different approaches within Catholic social ethics so that one cannot speak of a monolithic discipline. The contributors to this volume propose a critical correlation between the gospel and the U.S. ethos involving four different perspectives on Catholic social teaching: a historical critical hermeneutic in discussing Catholic social teaching with a corresponding recognition of great historical development within the body of Catholic social teaching; the realization that Catholic social ethics in the United States involves much more than Catholic social teaching; some criticisms of Catholic social teaching; and the critique of Catholic neoconservatives by the majority of other social ethicists.

First, as mentioned previously, John Cronin, in 1971, perceptively pointed out how he and his earlier colleagues failed to use a critical historical hermeneutic in discussing papal documents.[79] Subsequent Catholic ethicists such as John Coleman have brought such an approach to their understanding of Catholic social teaching. The European perspective of the papal author very much colored the teaching as well as the tendency toward triumphalism in the Catholic Church at the time.[80]

Catholic social teaching claimed to be a body of eternal and unchangeable moral principles and truths. In fact, it is a myth to portray the teaching as an unchanging body of truths. Tremendous development has occurred since the time of Pope Leo XIII. Leo had a very paternalistic and even authoritarian notion of society. All recognize the growing importance that Catholic social teaching gave to freedom, equality, and participation in the light of its twentieth-century opposition to communism. The attitude toward socialism and Marxism developed over time, with John XXIII fostering an opening to the left with his distinction between false philosophical teachings and historical movements that were originally based on these teachings. This opened the door to the possibility of dialogue with communist countries that differed strongly from the previous anathema of socialism and communism. Many critics have pointed out that Leo XIII's understanding of private property was not a faithful exposition of the teaching of Thomas Aquinas because it tended to absolutize the individual aspect of private property. However, subsequent popes, without acknowledging error in the previous position of Leo XIII, proposed a more nuanced understanding of private property by insisting on the social as well as the individual aspects of property. Vatican II, as related before, greatly affected the methodological approach to Catholic theology in general and to Catholic social ethics by calling for a greater role for scripture, a close connection between faith or theology and daily life, and a more inductive methodology emphasizing the signs of the times. Later documents of Catholic social teaching have moved in this direction, but commentators have also pointed out how John Paul II moved back from the greater historical-mindedness found in the documents of Paul VI.[81]

Second, Catholic social ethics in the United States no longer sees itself as simply exegeting and applying Catholic social teaching to the U.S. Catholic scene. Catholic social ethics in the United States is much broader and more inclusive than just considerations of Catholic social teaching. A good number of social ethicists in this country developed their own understandings and approach without being totally dependent on Catholic social teaching. Likewise, on a more practical level, as Marvin L. Krier Mitch has pointed out, many grassroots movements of different stripes have come into existence in the United States in an attempt to deal with social issues.[82]

The U.S. scene is going to raise issues and require responses that are pertinent to its own historical and social circumstances. What is the proper way for the Church to address public issues in the United States in the light of the First Amendment and the U.S. ethos? Theologians have analyzed and offered a critique of the approach taken by the U.S. Catholic bishops especially in their period of great activity in the 1980s. One controversy concerns the way in which the Catholic Church should address the broader society. Should the Church speak a language accessible to all other citizens as the older natural approach had done, or is a biblical narrative and foundation necessary to sustain a lasting commitment in this area? Most contemporary Catholic social ethicists also disagree with the neoconservative claim that John Courtney Murray's thought is the basis for their neoconservative position.[83] Catholic scholars are in dialogue with philosophers and political scientists about the proper role of religion and the Church in public political life.[84] Catholic social ethicists in the United States thus generally recognize that Catholic social teaching involves only one part of what comprises the whole of Catholic social ethics in the United States today.

Third, Catholic theologians since Vatican II, despite opposition from the Vatican authorities, have understood their own theological role in terms of analyzing and criticizing papal documents. This also holds for the documents of Catholic social teaching. Catholic feminists have criticized Catholic social teaching from a feminist liberation perspective beginning with the published doctoral dissertation of Christine Gudorf in 1980.[85] Amata Miller,[86] Mary Hobgood,[87] and others have criticized Catholic social teaching from a feminist perspective although these feminists themselves do not all take the same approach. Christine Firer Hinze has moved beyond the feminist hermeneutic of suspicion to a hermeneutic of recovery by trying to bring together a feminist approach and the traditional support of Catholic social teaching for a living wage.[88] Many other criticisms have also been developed. Just as in the case of reaction to the economic pastoral letter, so too critics from both the left and the right have disagreed with aspects of Catholic social teaching.

Fourth, many Catholic social ethicists have disagreed with the Catholic neoconservative position already mentioned. Yes, Catholic social teaching recognizes "the fundamental and positive role of business, the market, . . . and human creativity in the economic sector," but in the same encyclical John Paul II calls for economic freedom to be circumscribed within a strong juridical framework pointed toward the common good (CA 42). Many commentators point to these and other statements of the pope to disprove the neoconservative position of Michael Novak with regard to the pope and capitalism.[89] Daniel Finn has criticized Catholic social teaching for basing the social dimension of property and material goods on the intention of the Creator in making all things. Finn, like the neoconservatives, insists that human creativity has brought about the great increase of material goods in our world, but he strongly argues for the social aspect of material goods produced by such human creativity.[90] Todd Whitmore has maintained that Michael Novak's position differs substantially from that of John Paul II and that Novak actually dissents from the papal teaching, especially on such questions as economic rights.[91]

Catholic neoconservatives are not the only ones who have strongly disagreed with the approach taken by the U.S. bishops. A small group of younger scholars have called for the Church to be more countercultural.[92]

Thus, Catholic social ethics in the last few decades continues to recognize an important role for Catholic social teaching, but the role of Catholic social ethicists is not simply to repeat and apply that teaching but also to analyze and criticize it in the light of a broader Catholic social ethics.

Practical Influence of Catholic Social Teaching in the Life of the Church

To assess the practical influence of Catholic social teaching in the life of the Church adequately would require a broad and deep sociological analysis of what is actually taking place in Catholic parishes and institutions in the United States. Such an analysis is impossible here. Also, such an analysis at this time after Vatican II is more difficult than it was in the pre–Vatican II period with its understanding of Catholic social action as the participation of the laity in the apostolate of the hierarchy. After Vatican II the social mission of the Church involves all its members working for social justice in their own circumstances and places. Often the initiative comes from below. Perhaps the most significant development in the social mission of the U.S. Catholic Church, as mentioned earlier, has been the support of community organizations and the work of the Campaign for Human Development.

The postconciliar Church has recognized that working for justice is a constitutive dimension of the gospel and the mission of the Church. Liturgy and preaching have a strong justice dimension.[93] Justice and peace commissions, human development committees, and similar groups exist in most dioceses and in many parishes. The economic pastoral did more to make Catholic social teaching better known in the Church than any other teaching effort by the U.S. bishops. Schools on all levels of Catholic education and also religious education show a concern for social justice. In all these efforts, Catholic social teaching obviously plays a part but only a part in the guidance of such activity. However, one still very often hears the lament that Catholics in the pew on Sunday seldom hear anything about Catholic social teaching.[94]

Catholic social teaching itself has evolved and changed since 1891. This chapter has tried to show the various ways in which this evolving Catholic social teaching has been received and interpreted in the United States in the twentieth century.

NOTES

1. These documents can be found in a number of different sources. The best-known collection is David J. O'Brien and Thomas A. Shannon, eds., *Catholic Social Thought: The Documentary Heritage* (Maryknoll, N.Y.: Orbis, 1992).

2. For the origins of the NCWC, see Elizabeth McKeown, *War and Welfare: American Catholics and World War I* (New York: Garland, 1988).

3. Administrative Committee of the National Catholic War Council, "Bishops' Program of Social Reconstruction," in *Our Bishops Speak, 1919–1951*, ed. Raphael A. Huber (Milwaukee: Bruce, 1952), 243–62.

4. Ibid., 259.

5. Francis L. Broderick, *The Right Reverend New Dealer: John A. Ryan* (New York: Macmillan, 1963), 104–8.

6. The Hierarchy of the United States, "Pastoral Letter of 1919," in *Our Bishops Speak*, ed. R. A. Huber, 46–51.

7. The Hierarchy of the United States, "Secularism," in ibid., 137–45; Administrative Board of the National Catholic Welfare Conference, "God's Law: The Measure of Man's Conduct," in ibid., 368–75.

8. All these letters are found in Huber, ed., *Our Bishops Speak.*

9. Administrative Board of the National Catholic Welfare Conference, "Church and Social Order," in ibid., 326.

10. Ibid., 324–43.

11. Administrative Board of the National Catholic Welfare Conference, "Christian Attitude on Social Problems," in ibid., 314–18.

12. John F. Cronin, *Social Principles and Economic Life*, rev. ed. (Milwaukee: Bruce, 1964), 106–22.

13. See Hugh J. Nolan, ed., *Pastoral Letters of the United States Catholic Bishops*, vol. 2: *1941–1961* (Washington, D.C.: U.S. Catholic Conference, 1984).

14. For the biography of Ryan, see Broderick, *Right Reverend New Dealer.*

15. John A. Ryan, *Distributive Justice* (New York: Macmillan, 1916), 64–66, 306–9, 377.

16. John A. Ryan, *A Better Economic Order* (New York: Harper and Brothers, 1935).

17. For my analysis and criticism of Ryan's social ethics, see Charles E. Curran, *American Catholic Social Ethics* (Notre Dame, Ind.: University of Notre Dame Press, 1982), 26–91.

18. Ibid., 133–71.

19. Paul Hanly Furfey, *Fire on the Earth* (New York: Macmillan, 1936).

20. Virgil Michel, *Christian Social Reconstruction* (Milwaukee: Bruce, 1937); *The Social Question: Essays on Capitalism and Christianity* (Collegeville, Minn.: St. John's University Press, 1987). See also R.W. Franklin and Robert L. Spaeth, *Virgil Michel: American Catholic* (Collegeville, Minn.: Liturgical, 1988).

21. For different perspectives on Husslein, see Peter McDonough, *Men Astutely Trained: A History of the Jesuits in the American Century* (New York: The Free Press, 1992), 50–64; Stephen A. Werner, *Prophet of the Christian Social Manifesto: Joseph Husslein, S. J., His Life, Work, and Social Thought* (Milwaukee: Marquette University Press, 2001).

22. For a biography of Cronin, see John Timothy Donovan, "Crusader in the Cold War: A Biography of Father John F. Cronin, S. S. (1908–1994)" (Ph.D. diss., Marquette University, 2000).

23. John F. Cronin, *Social Principles and Economic Life* (Milwaukee: Bruce, 1959).

24. John F. Cronin, "Forty Years Later: Reflections and Reminiscences," in *Readings in Moral Theology No. 5: Official Catholic Social Teaching*, ed. Charles E. Curran and Richard A. McCormick (New York: Paulist, 1986), 69–76.

25. H. W. Flannery, "Social Movements, Catholic," in *New Catholic Encyclopedia* 13, 331–32.

26. For Higgins's own story, see Monsignor George Higgins with William Bole, *Organized Labor and the Church: Reflections of a Labor Priest* (New York: Paulist, 1993); also *Social Catholicism: Essays in Honor of George Higgins, U.S. Catholic Historian* 19, no. 4 (2001).

27. Patricia Ann Lamoureux, "Justice for Wage Earners," *Horizons* 28 (2001): 222–25.

28. John F. Cronin, *Catholic Social Action* (Milwaukee: Bruce, 1948), 75–88; McDonough, *Men Astutely Trained*, 98–108.

29. Mary Harrita Fox, *Peter E. Dietz, Labor Priest* (Notre Dame, Ind.: University of Notre Dame Press, 1953).

30. Patrick J. Sullivan, "Monsignor George G. Higgins: The Labor Priests' Priest," *U.S. Catholic Historian* 19, no. 4 (2001): 103–18.

31. James T. Fisher, "The Priest and the Movie: On the Waterfront as Historical Theology," in *Theology and the New Histories*, 1999 Annual Publication of the College Theology Society, 44, ed. Gary Macy (Maryknoll, N.Y.: Orbis, 1990), 167–85.

32. For different views of the Association of Catholic Trade Unionists, see Neil Betten, *Catholic Activism and the Industrial Worker* (Gainsville: University Presses of Florida, 1976), 124–45; and Douglas P. Seaton, *Catholics and Radicals: The Association of Catholic Trade Unionists and the American Labor Movement from Depression to Cold War* (Lewisburg, Pa.: Bucknell University Press, 1981).

33. McDonough, *Men Astutely Trained*, 295–318.

34. E. J. Ross, "American Catholic Sociological Society," *New Catholic Encyclopedia* 1, 399; Thomas F. Devine, "The Origins of thc Catholic Economic Association," *Review of Social Economy* 2 (1944): 102–3.

35. Cronin, *Catholic Social Action*, 42–44.

36. Cronin, "Forty Years Later," in *Readings in Moral Theology No.5*, ed. C. E. Curran and R. A. McCormick, 76.

37. Catholic Bishops of the United States, "Discrimination and Christian Conscience," in Nolan, *Pastoral Letters*, 201–6.

38. Lawrence J. Engel, "The Influence of Saul Alinsky on the Campaign for Human Development," *Theological Studies* 59 (1998): 636–61.

39. For a more popular account of Vatican II and its documents, see Timothy O'Connell, ed., *Vatican II and Its Documents: An American Appraisal* (Wilmington, Del.: Michael Glazier, 1986); for an in-depth analysis, see the five-volume study, Giuseppe Alberigo and Joseph A. Komonchak, eds., *The History of Vatican II*, 3 vols. (Maryknoll, N.Y.: Orbis, 1995, 1997, 2000), 2 vols. forthcoming.

40. George G. Higgins, "Historical Resumé of the Teaching, Policy, and Action of the Church and Social Mission," in *Metropolis: Christian Presence and Responsibility*, ed. Philip D. Morris (Notre Dame, Ind.: Fides, 1970), 145–50.

41. Thomas J. Reese, ed., *Episcopal Conferences: Historical, Canonical, and Theological Studies* (Washington, D.C.: Georgetown University Press, 1989).

42. Available on the Internet at http://www.cta-sa.org/whobishconference/bishindex.html (downloaded July 1, 2004).

43. For an evaluation of the Call to Action Conference ten years later, see the special issue of *Commonweal* 113 (December 26, 1986).

44. J. Brian Benestad and Francis J. Butler, eds., *Quest for Justice: A Compendium of Statements of the United States Catholic Bishops on the Political and Social Order, 1966–1980* (Washington, D.C.: U.S. Catholic Conference, 1981).

45. J. Brian Benestad, *The Pursuit of a Just Social Order: Policy Statements of the U.S. Catholic Bishops, 1966–1980* (Washington, D.C.: Ethics and Public Policy Center, 1982).

46. Joseph Cardinal Bernardin et al., *Consistent Ethic of Life*, ed. Thomas G. Feuchtmann (Kansas City, Mo.: Sheed and Ward, 1988).

47. U.S. Catholic Conference, "The Economy: Human Dimensions," in Benestad and Butler, *Quest for Justice*, 263–69.

48. For the development of the pastoral, see Rembert Weakland, "Church Social Teaching and the American Economy," *Origins* 13 (1983): 447–48; "Where Does the Economic Pastoral Stand?" *Origins* 13 (1984): 753–59; "The Economic Pastoral and the Signs of the Times," *Origins* 14

(1984): 394–96; "The Economic Pastoral: Draft Two," *America* 153 (September 21, 1985): 129–32; "How to Read the Economic Pastoral," *Crisis* 4 (1986): 27–34.

49. For the three drafts and the final version of the pastoral, see *Origins* 14 (1984): 337ff.; 15 (1985): 257ff.; 16 (1986): 33ff.; 16 (1986): 410ff.

50. *Economic Justice for All* has been published in many places, including *Origins* 16 (1986): 410ff.; D. J. O'Brien and T. A. Shannon. eds., *Catholic Social Thought*, 572–680; and a 1986 publication of the National Conference of Catholic Bishops.

51. Weakland, "How to Read the Economic Pastoral," 27–29.

52. My synthesis proposed in this and the following paragraphs comes from "Chapter 2: The Christian Vision of Economic Life," numbers 28–126.

53. Gregory Baum, "A Canadian Perspective on the U.S. Pastoral," *Christianity and Crisis* 45 (1985): 516–18.

54. Rembert G. Weakland, "The Economic Pastoral Letter Revisited," in *One Hundred Years of Catholic Social Thought: Celebration and Challenge*, ed. John A. Coleman (Maryknoll, N.Y.: Orbis, 1991), 203.

55. The following description of Catholic neoconservatives is based on their own self-understanding. See especially Michael Novak, "Neoconservatives," in *New Dictionary of Catholic Social Thought*, ed. Judith A. Dwyer (Collegeville, Minn.: Liturgical, 1994), 678–82; George Weigel, "The Neoconservative Difference: A Proposal for the Renewal of Church and Society," in *Being Right: Conservative Catholics in America*, ed. Mary Jo Weaver and R. Scott Appleby (Bloomington, Ind.: Indiana University Press, 1995), 138–62.

56. George Weigel, "When Shepherds are Sheep," *First Things* 30 (1993): 34–40.

57. Michael Novak, *The Spirit of Democratic Capitalism* (New York: Simon and Schuster, 1982).

58. Michael Novak, "Creation Theology," in *Co-Creation and Capitalism: John Paul II's Laborem Exercens*, ed. John W. Houck and Oliver F. Williams (Washington, D.C.: University Press of America, 1983), 17–41.

59. Lay Commission on Catholic Social Teaching and the U.S. Economy, *Toward the Future: Catholic Social Thought and the U.S. Economy* (New York: Lay Commission on Catholic Social Teaching and the U.S. Economy, 1984).

60. Michael Novak, "4 Views of the Bishops' Pastoral: The Lay Letter and the U.S. Economy: A Panel Discussion," *This World* 10 (winter 1985): 112–16; "Toward Consensus: Suggestions for Revising the First Draft, Part I," *Catholicism in Crisis* 3 (March 1985): 7–16.

61. Michael Novak, "Economic Rights: The Servile State," *Catholicism in Crisis* 3 (October 1985): 8–15.

62. Michael Novak, "The Rights and Wrongs of 'Economic Rights': A Debate Continued," *This World* 17 (spring 1987): 43–52.

63. Engel, "The Influence of Saul Alinsky on the Campaign for Human Development."

64. Jacques Maritain used the term *prophetic shock minorities* to refer to those groups that provide and provoke the leaven or energy that political democracy needs. See Jacques Maritain, *Man and the State* (Chicago: University of Chicago Press, 1956), 139–46.

65. William Lee Miller, *The First Liberty: Religion and the American Republic* (New York: Knopf, 1986), 288–89.

66. E.g., Charles R. Strain, ed., *Prophetic Visions and Economic Realities: Protestants, Jews, and Catholics Confront the Bishops' Letter on the Economy* (Grand Rapids, Mich.: Eerdmans, 1989); David Hollenbach, "Liberation, Communitarianism, and the Bishops' Pastoral Letter on the Economy," and Gregory Baum, Ruth Smith, and Robert Benne, "Replies to David Hollenbach," *The Annual of the Society of Christian Ethics* (1987): 19–54; Charles P. Lutz, ed., *God, Goods, and the Common Good: Eleven Perspectives on Economic Justice in Dialog with the Roman Catholic Bishops' Pastoral Letter* (Minneapolis: Augsburg, 1987).

67. R. Bruce Douglass, ed., *The Deeper Meaning of Economic Life: Critical Essays on the U.S. Catholic Bishops' Pastoral Letter on the Economy* (Washington, D.C.: Georgetown University Press, 1986); John W. Houck and Oliver Williams, eds., *Catholic Social Teaching and the United States Economy: Working Papers for a Bishops' Pastoral* (Washington, D.C.: University Press of America, 1984); Strain, *Prophetic Visions*; John Pawlikowski and Donald Senior, eds., *Economic Justice: CTU's Pastoral Commentary on the Bishops' Letter on the Economy* (Washington, DC: Pastoral, 1988); Thomas M. Gannon, ed., *The Catholic Challenge to the American Economy: Reflections on the U.S. Bishops' Pastoral Letter on Catholic Social*

Teaching and the U.S. Economy (New York: Macmillan, 1987).

68. National Conference of Catholic Bishops, "A Decade after 'Economic Justice for All': Continuing Principles, Changing Context, New Challenges," *Origins* 25 (1995): 389–93.

69. National Conference of Catholic Bishops, "Catholic Framework for Economic Life," *Origins* 26 (1996): 370–71.

70. Marvin L. Krier Mich, *Catholic Social Teaching and Movements* (Mystic, Conn.: Twenty-Third, 1998), 357–70.

71. John Paul II, "Motu Proprio: The Theological and Juridical Nature of Episcopal Conferences," *Origins* 28 (1998): 152–58.

72. Charles E. Curran, *Moral Theology at the End of the Century*, the Père Marquette Lecture in Theology 1999 (Milwaukee: Marquette University Press, 1999).

73. David Hollenbach, *Claims in Conflict: Retrieving and Renewing the Catholic Human Rights Tradition* (New York: Paulist, 1979).

74. John A. Coleman, *An American Strategic Theology* (New York: Paulist, 1982).

75. Curran, *American Catholic Social Ethics*.

76. For Hehir's analysis of the U.S. bishops' social mission, see J. Bryan Hehir, "The Church and the Political Order: The Role of the Catholic Bishops in the United States," in *The Church's Public Role: Retrospect and Prospect*, ed. Dieter T. Hessel (Grand Rapids, Mich.: Eerdmans, 1993): 176–97.

77. Available on the Internet at http://www.georgetown.edu/centers/woodstock/ (downloaded July 2, 2004). An early publication of this Center was John C. Haughey, ed., *The Faith that Does Justice: Examining the Christian Sources for Social Change* (New York: Paulist, 1977).

78. Available on the Internet at http://www.nd.edu/~ethics/ (downloaded July 2, 2002).This Center has published many symposia dealing with Catholic social ethics edited by John W. Houck and Oliver F. Williams.

79. Cronin, "Forty Years Later," in *Readings in Moral Theology No. 5*, ed. C. E. Curran and R. A. McCormick, 73.

80. John A. Coleman, "Development of Church Social Teaching," *Origins* 11 (1981): 33ff.

81. Charles E. Curran, *Directions in Catholic Social Ethics* (Notre Dame, Ind.: University of Notre Dame Press, 1985), 5–69.

82. Krier Mich, *Catholic Social Teaching*.

83. Charles E. Curran and Leslie Griffin, eds., *The Catholic Church, Morality, and Politics: Readings in Moral Theology No. 12* (New York: Paulist, 2001).

84. David Hollenbach, *The Common Good and Christian Ethics* (Cambridge: Cambridge University Press, 2002); Michael J. Perry, *The Idea of Human Rights: Four Inquiries* (New York: Oxford University Press, 2000); Paul Weithman, *Religion and the Obligations of Citizenship* (Cambridge: Cambridge University Press, 2002).

85. Christine E. Gudorf, *Catholic Social Teaching on Liberation Themes* (Lanham, Md.: University Press of America, 1980).

86. Amata Miller, "Catholic Social Teaching: What Might Have Been if Women Were Not Invisible in a Patriarchal Society," in *Rerum Novarum: One Hundred Years of Catholic Social Teaching*, ed. John Coleman and Gregory Baum (London: SCM, 1991), 21–47.

87. Mary E. Hobgood, *Catholic Social Teaching and Economic Theory: Paradigms in Conflict* (Philadelphia: Temple University Press, 1991).

88. Christine Firer Hinze, "Bridge Discourse on Wage Justice: Roman Catholic and Feminist Perspectives on the Family Living Wage," *The Annual of the Society of Christian Ethics* 11 (1991): 109–32.

89. E.g., David Hollenbach, "The Pope and Capitalism," *America* 164 (June 1, 1991): 591; Monsignor George Higgins, *Subsidiarity in the Catholic Social Tradition: Yesterday, Today, and Tomorrow*, Albert Cardinal Meyer Lecture (Mundelein, Ill.: Mundelein Seminary, 1994), 29–39.

90. Daniel R. Finn, "Creativity as a Problem for Moral Theology: John Locke's 99 Per Cent Challenge to the Catholic Doctrine of Property," *Horizons* 27 (2000): 44–62.

91. Todd David Whitmore, "John Paul II, Michael Novak, and the Differences between Them," *Annual of the Society of Christian Ethics* 21 (2001): 215–32.

92. Michael L. Budde and Robert W. Brimlow, eds., *The Church as Counterculture* (Albany: State University of New York Press, 2000); Michael J. Baxter, "Notes on Catholic Americanism and Catholic Radicalism: Toward a Counter-Tradition of Catholic Social Ethics," in *American Catholic Traditions: Resources for Renewal*, ed. Sandra Yocum Mize and William Portier, College Theology Society

Annual Volume 42 (Maryknoll, N.Y.: Orbis, 1997), 53–71.

93. Anne Y. Koester, ed., *Liturgy and Justice: To Worship God in Spirit and Truth* (Collegeville, Minn.: Liturgical, 2002); Walter J. Burghardt, *Preaching the Just Word* (New Haven, Conn.: Yale University Press, 1996).

94. Peter Henriot, Edward De Berri, and Michael Schulteis, *Catholic Social Teaching: Our Best Kept Secret*, centenary ed. (Maryknoll, N.Y.: Orbis, 1992).

SELECTED BIBLIOGRAPHY

Coleman, John A., ed. *One Hundred Years of Catholic Social Thought: Celebration and Challenge*. Maryknoll, N.Y.: Orbis, 1991. A collection of essays on Catholic social thought dealing with its development, the family, work, and peace, especially in the light of the U.S. experience.

Cronin, John F. *Catholic Social Principles: The Social Teaching of the Catholic Church Applied to American Economic Life*. Milwaukee: Bruce, 1950. The application of Catholic social teaching to American life and its influence on American Catholic social thought in the first half of the twentieth century.

Curran, Charles E. *American Catholic Social Ethics: Twentieth-Century Approaches*. Notre Dame, Ind.: University of Notre Dame Press, 1982. A study of five significant American Catholic approaches to social ethics in the twentieth century.

Gannon, Thomas M., ed. *The Catholic Challenge to the American Economy: Reflections on the U.S. Bishops' Pastoral Letter on Catholic Social Teaching in the U.S. Economy*. New York: Macmillan, 1987. A wide-ranging collection of essays from many different perspectives on the bishops' pastoral letter.

Himes, Michael J., and Kenneth R. Himes, *Fullness of Faith: The Public Significance of Theology*. New York: Paulist, 1993. The authors show how grace, sin, the Trinity, and other theological concepts play a public role in a pluralistic society.

Hollenbach, David. *The Common Good and Christian Ethics*. Cambridge: Cambridge University Press, 2002. Shows how the concept of the common good as found in the Catholic tradition can contribute to American public life and policy.

Mich, Marvin L. Krier. *Catholic Social Teaching and Movements*. Mystic, Conn.: Twenty-Third, 1998. From a historical perspective the book discusses Catholic social teaching and grassroots movements that arose in the United States.

Novak, Michael. *Catholic Social Thought and Liberal Institutions: Freedom with Justice*, 2nd ed. New Brunswick, N.J.: Transaction, 1989. Brings together theology and economics to show that Catholic social thought supports liberal institutions in the cultural, political, and economic realms.

CHAPTER

20

The Reception of Catholic Approaches to Peace and War in the United States

TODD D. WHITMORE

INTRODUCTION

There are many ways to organize a commentary on American Catholic approaches to peace and war. Perhaps it is best to begin by noting the late Cardinal Joseph Bernardin's comment regarding the 1983 pastoral letter *The Challenge of Peace: God's Promise and Our Response*: "It is perhaps the most important and timely letter ever to come from the American Hierarchy in its nearly two centuries of existence."[1] Even severe critics of the document have regarded it as a "watershed."[2] Certainly if one measures the number and range of responses to the various statements of the American Catholic bishops, Bernardin's assessment appears to be right on target. In writing CP the bishops made a cover story in *Time* magazine and repeated front-page news across the nation. Responses to the different drafts of the document came not only from the media but also from members of Congress, the presidential administration, and the Vatican. The significance of the document in American Catholic history is unquestioned. The present commentary, therefore, is organized around CP as a kind of interpretive pivot point with attention to both precursors and subsequent responses. This will help limn the shifts in the trajectory of the American Catholic response to the teaching on war and peace.

Before discussing the American Catholic response, it is necessary to say a word about official teaching on war and peace. While historically Christian theorists have backed crusades as well as the just war tradition and pacifism as options for responding to conflict, by the modern era Catholic teaching has considered only the latter two options to be legitimate. Early Christianity tended toward nonviolence, in part because violence appeared to be a violation of charity and in part because participation in the military involved worship of Caesar, which constituted idolatry. In the fourth century the emperor Constantine made Christianity the official religion of the Holy Roman Empire, and in so doing engendered a Christianity more closely aligned with the state and thus with war-fighting. Official Christianity dealt with this development socially and ecclesiologically by designating a certain class of persons—those who were members of religious orders—to witness to the kingdom of God through their nonviolence and, with a few exceptions, this social and ecclesial division held in practice. While there were a number of lay movements espousing nonviolence, official Catholicism generally frowned on them. As late as 1956, in his Christmas address, Pope Pius XII stated that laypersons could not be conscientious objectors to what state and Church deemed a just war.

The just war tradition itself was never formally declared Catholic doctrine but achieved the force of history by the accrual of writing and teaching over time. In its Christian context, the just war tradition first found articulation in the writings of St. Ambrose and St. Augustine in the fourth and fifth centuries and was later refined by St. Thomas Aquinas (1225–74), Francisco de Vitoria (1486–1546), and Francisco de Suarez (1548–1617). It arose out of the attempt to answer the questions of whether war itself could be conducted as a legitimate means for pursuing peace and, if so, under what moral limitations. The various principles of the just war tradition are statements of the limits that must be placed on war-fighting if the latter is ever to have peace as its true end. The principles are divided into those that must be met in order to engage in war in the first place (*jus ad bellum*) and those that must be met in the conduct of war itself (*jus in bello*).

Under the *ad bellum* rubric fall a number of principles that must be met before there is recourse to armed force. First, there must be a "just cause." While the meaning of this criterion may seem obvious, the tradition in the modern era has limited what can count as a just cause, allowing only wars of self-defense and humanitarian intervention, while ruling out wars of retribution, which was once considered a just cause. Second, the war must be declared by a "legitimate authority" or "competent authority," making unlawful all war declared by private individuals. Third, there must be "right intention" in going to war, a correct aim or goal such as self-defense. This principle concerns not the psychological state of the authority declaring war but the objective purpose of the war. Fourth, recourse to war must be a "last resort." All reasonable means of nonviolent conflict resolution must be exhausted before recourse to arms. Fifth, there must be a "reasonable chance of success" or "probability of success" if the resort to violence is not to be gratuitous. Here, success is more than military victory; it includes the restoration of a proximate peace that is the aim of a just war. Sixth, there must be a "proportionality" between the overall destruction of the war and the good that the war seeks to achieve. Here, the danger is in escalating the interpretation of the evil against which one is fighting and so rationalizing the escalation of violence beyond what is truly proportionate.

There are two *in bello* criteria that must be met during the conduct of war. The first is, again, proportionality. Here, the focus is on the proportionality, or lack thereof, of specific tactics in a war. For instance, it is possible to hold that the Persian Gulf War of 1991 was, overall, a just war, while saying that the bombing of retreating Iraqi soldiers on the road to Basra was, among other things, disproportionate. Second, the conduct of war must recognize "noncombatant immunity" or "discrimination." Those persons not directly involved in the war-fighting effort are not to be victims of its violence.

Vatican II (1962–65) declared that while nations must use lethal force if necessary to defend its borders, individuals within any given nation can legitimately be pacifist. As we will see, this declaration both was in response to and further enabled the living practice of nonviolence by Catholics.

This chapter attends to the ways in which American Catholicism has responded to the teachings on both the just war tradition and nonviolence by first of all examining two sets of precursors to CP. The first set involves the changes in the bishops' own account of the issues of war and peace. It is important to note here that what first of all changes is not a moral judgment about whether war is right or wrong, but what the bishops have taken to be morally relevant at all in their account of war. In earlier statements, what was most relevant was the need to convey, in the face of nativism, that Catholics, too, are good Americans. Moral calculus of the kind more common today, with judgments in light of the just war tradition, was simply not present. It is only later that greater presence of the United States on the world stage and of Catholics in the United States occasioned a more outward-looking moral lens, one honed less by internal ecclesial worries than a broad political and social theory. This chapter describes the shift in terms of a move from internally driven nationalism to outward-looking critical patriotism.

The second set of precursors comes under the heading of the rise of the Catholic peace movement. Beginning particularly with the Catholic Worker movement and broadening out to include other constituencies, the Catholic peace movement has helped to legitimize nonviolent methods of conflict resolution and social change. Without this witness, much of what is in CP would not have been conceivable. Both of these considerations—the turn to a wider political and social context and the rise of peacemaking—play themselves out in the debate over the contents of CP, with the former concern articulated from the political and ecclesial right and the latter from the left. The present chapter illuminates how the bishops take up these concerns in their letter and how, in turn, the concerns continue to shape what has come after.

FROM INTERNALLY DRIVEN NATIONALISM TO OUTWARD-LOOKING CRITICAL PATRIOTISM: THE BISHOPS, 1792–1976

The attitudes toward and views of war and peace in early American Catholicism were shaped more by domestic concerns than by questions of foreign policy or international relations. American nativists questioned whether Catholics, with their allegiance to the pope, could be loyal Americans. The bishops responded that indeed Catholics could be, even to the point of the loss of life in war on behalf of the United States. Here, the issue of war arises not as a moral question about the legitimacy of taking another person's life on behalf of the state but as a statement marking the boundaries, or the lack thereof, of American Catholic loyalty to the United States. The issues addressed in the early official documents—for instance, the "necessity of vocations to the priesthood," "support of the church," and "attendance at Sunday Mass"[3]—are primarily internal to the Church in its American domestic setting. When the issue was war, therefore, the effort was to show that this particular church is loyal to this particular nation.

Two sample documents reflecting the concern to demonstrate Catholic loyalty to the United States exhibit earlier and later statements of this internally driven nationalism. In 1884, the bishops of the Third Plenary Council of Baltimore wrote that they were well acquainted with the "laws, institutions, and spirit" of both the Church and the nation, and declared "no antagonism" between them. The Catholic, according to the document, is "at home" in the United States, and the "right-minded" American "nowhere finds himself more at home than in the Catholic Church." The bishops knew that combat in war and the willingness to sacrifice one's life was the test case of Catholic loyalty. Therefore, they went on to uphold that if the country's well-being is "imperilled," then "our Catholic citizens will be found to stand forward, as one man ready to pledge anew 'their lives, their fortunes, and their sacred honor.'"[4] Similarly, in April 1917, just before the United States entered World War I, Cardinal James Gibbons spoke for the American Catholic bishops and church when he claimed, "The primary duty of a citizen is loyalty to country. This loyalty is exhibited by absolute and unreserved obedience to his country."[5] That August, the bishops established the National Catholic War Council to help organize the American war effort.

Catholic participation in the war itself, however, brought about a shift in viewpoint. The perspective of the bishops and the American Catholic Church became less driven by internal concerns and more directed to the world events themselves. The Administrative Committee of the National Catholic War Council began to focus on wider considerations and, with the aid of John A. Ryan, wrote the 1919 *Program of Social Reconstruction*, which became one of the plans most discussed by national political leaders in their efforts to rebuild Europe after the war. In keeping with this wider perspective, in 1919 the bishops changed the name of the council to the National Catholic Welfare Council (and, in 1923, to the National Catholic Welfare Conference).[6] In the bishops' *Pastoral*

Letter of 1919, nativism in the United States still existed, but the bishops viewed the Church's main adversary to be secularism (101, 161–62). The section on "The Church in our Country" makes no mention of nativism. The combination of U.S. power and at least some release from domestic concerns about nativism allowed the bishops to turn outward: the document has an entire section on international relations, a first for the bishops.

Nationalism is still present in the document. The letter cites the 1884 Third Plenary Council document pledging the "lives" of Catholics to the nation quoted above and discusses Catholic support for the nation (69–72). Even with such nationalism, however, there are indications of the beginnings of a movement away from an unquestioning attitude and toward a critical patriotism. Under a section titled, "The Lessons of the War," the document refers to "the destruction of life and the consequent desolation," the "spiritual suffering," and "the moral evil, the wrong whose magnitude only the searcher of hearts can determine" (79). Though the just war principles are not used explicitly, it is clear that the document holds there to have been a just cause and legitimate authority in fighting. Still, the bishops went on to state contrition. The document highlights that people and nations acted in such a way that "sin abounded" in their "loosening of passion and the seeking of hate." As a result, not only human rights, but the "law of God" was "openly disregarded." Therefore—the document now moving, significantly, from the third-person to the first-person plural—"we" must come before God "with contrite hearts" and beseech God to "continue his mercies toward us" so that we "may atone for our past transgressions and strengthen the bond of peace with a deeper charity" (80).

The principles of the just war tradition, and thus a more precise grammar for the moral assessment of warfare, began to enter explicitly into the American Catholic discussion through pamphlets published by the Catholic Association for International Peace (CAIP). As early as 1922, when he heard about England's Catholic Council for International Peace, John A. Ryan sought to start a similar organization in the United States. He and his assistant, Raymond McGowen, brought together fifty people in 1925 for an initial meeting, and an official organizational meeting followed in 1927. Ryan wrote a working paper for the latter meeting, and its published pamphlet title, *International Ethics*, indicated the outward-looking thrust of the organization, the first of its kind for Catholics in the United States. Later pamphlets issued through the organization criticized nationalism and put forward the just war theory framework.[7]

It was precisely through such pamphlets, together with the lobbying of political leaders, that CAIP sought during its forty years of existence to influence American Catholic response to war and peace. From the beginning, CAIP's ties to the bishops were close. Ryan was director of the National Catholic Welfare Council's Social Action Department, where McGowen was again his assistant. The Council provided the office space and much of the funding for CAIP. Later leaders in CAIP—for instance, Monsignor George Higgins—kept the close ties. When the National Catholic Welfare Conference became the U.S. Catholic Conference (USCC) in 1967, CAIP was formally folded into the USCC's Commission for World Justice and Peace. In the interim, CAIP produced statements and pamphlets on the full range of conflicts, including the Spanish-American War, World War II, the Korean War, the cold war with its possibility of nuclear exchange, and the Vietnam War.

Still, through World War II, the language of the just war tradition remained uncommon, and the bishops both unquestioningly backed entrance into the war and were silent during the carpet bombings over Germany, the fire bombings of Japan, and the dropping of the atomic bombs. It took the Jesuit John C. Ford, in a 1944 article in *Theological Studies* titled "The Morality of Obliteration Bombing," to reintroduce the just war language, and he did so in a way that did not merely buttress present policy. Ford assessed the strategy of obliteration bombing and its effects in detail and found that it violated the principle of noncombatant immunity. He defined obliteration bombing as "the strategic bombing, by means of incendiaries and explosives, of industrial centers of population, in which the target to be wiped out is not a definite factory, bridge, or similar object, but a large section of the whole city." His own calculations determined that two-thirds to three-quarters of city inhabitants were noncombatants. To interlocutors who argued that there are no noncombatants in modern war, he provided a list that included a variety of occupations—for instance, librarians, social workers, and musicians—and vocations in life—for example, priests, nuns, and mothers—that he found to be certainly noncombatants "according to natural law." In reply to the argument that the direct targets are military ones and that the loss of civilian life is indirect or collateral, he argued that it is precisely the military effects that are collateral. "The evil effect is first, immediate, and direct, while any military advantage comes through and after it in a secondary, derivative, and dependent way." Against the argument that there is a proportionately grave cause to engage in the bombing, Ford countered that the probability of achieving the good desired is highly speculative, and even debated within the military itself, while the evil unleashed is certain and devastating. Having addressed possible objections, he concluded that obliteration bombing "is an immoral attack on the rights of the innocent."[8]

What is noteworthy here is not simply that Ford wrote an article critical of the policy of obliteration bombing when the bishops were, by and large, silent.[9] Perhaps most significant is that, while he found the policy morally reprehensible, he also felt that he could not advise confessors to deny absolution to a bombardier in the sacrament of penance because there was insufficient guidance from the Church to find the bombardier culpable. Ford quotes an earlier article of his stating, "The application of our moral principles to modern war leaves so much to be desired that we are not in a position to impose obligations on the conscience of the individual, whether he be a soldier with a bayonet or a conscientious objector, except in cases where violation of the natural law is clear."[10] Given that the bishops again had allowed the just war tradition to fall largely into disuse, and that they had not said much, if anything, on the specific practice of obliteration bombing and whether it violated the just war norms, the priest had to absolve the bombardier, even if the latter took part in direct attacks on hundreds of thousands of civilians.

A number of factors explain the bishops' silence, including continued nativism, heightened now by wartime, which put a premium on Catholic loyalty to the nation, and the press of a war where American soil was bombed and the opponent in Europe was formidable. Still, Ford's assessment is accurate. There was little, if any, reference to the moral limits on war-fighting in the bishops' statements of this era. On the contrary, the bishops appealed to what Ford called "proportionately grave cause" to overlook the norms. On the eve of American entrance into World War II, in a document titled "The Crisis of Christianity," the administrative board of the National Catholic Welfare Conference called the situation "the most serious crisis since the Church came out of the catacombs." The twin threats were Nazism and communism. The bishops supported "wholeheartedly" the administration and urged "respect and reverence for the authority of our civil officials which has its source in God."[11] Soon after the onset of the war, Archbishop Edward Mooney, the chair of the administrative board of the NCWC, speaking on behalf of the Conference, wrote a letter to President Roosevelt indicating that the bishops were conscious of their "responsibilities." Like the bishops at the entrance of the United States into World War I, the letter quotes the 1884 Third Plenary Council pledging the "lives" and "fortunes" of Catholics in the war effort.[12]

What differentiates the documents during World War II from earlier documents, however, is that, given the experience of World War I and after, there developed a more outward-looking perspective as reflected in the bishops' repeated insistence on the establishment, once the war was over, of a peace based on justice. This is evident in the December 1941 letter to Roosevelt. The letter includes a mix of boosterism—"We will do our part in the national effort to transmute the impressive material and spiritual resources of our country into effective strength"—and internationalism—"not for vengeance but for the common good, not for national aggrandizement but for common security in a world in which human rights shall be safeguarded."[13] References to an international order, even a central international institution, based on justice run throughout the documents during World War II.[14] To be sure, the just war criteria are rarely mentioned. The *ad bellum* criteria are assumed to have been met and, given the references to the supremacy of the crisis and no mention of the obliteration and atomic bombing, the *in bello* criteria appear to be set aside without comment for reasons of proportionately grave evil, an argument that John Ford himself found unconvincing.[15]

The documents during World War II read as if the bishops were hoping that, if the world could just get through this particular conflict, then it would be possible to construct an international order where actions like obliteration and atomic bombing are unnecessary. The documents immediately following the war, where the bishops first mention atomic weaponry, support this reading. There is no condemnation of the United States's use or possession of these weapons, but there is recognition of the horror of such warfare and conviction that an international order preventing use is of the utmost urgency. The first bishops' document after the close of the war, written in 1945, states, "The war is over, but there is no peace in the world. . . . Are we going to give up this ideal of peace? If, under the pretext of false realism, we do so, then we shall stand face to face with the awful catastrophe of atomic war."[16] This is the bishops' first mention of atomic weaponry.

The problem is that while Nazism is defeated, the other of the two threats, communism, remains. During the cold war the bishops issued numerous documents against communism and the persecution that takes place in communist countries. It appears again, then, that the magnitude of the perceived threat led to a willingness to set aside the just war criteria, at the very least the *in bello* principles, and this was coupled with the hope that an international order would make war-fighting unnecessary. Modern war, especially nuclear war, the bishops wrote in 1956, would be "a nightmare of unimaginable horrors. It can only annihilate; it has no power to solve our problems." Every moral means must be used to "avoid the final arbitrament of nuclear warfare." Still, such warfare may be necessary to resist "naked aggression."[17] If deemed necessary, atomic war would be fought, and apparently without limits.

The structure of the bishops' presentation is much like Michael Walzer's idea of "supreme emergency"; under normal circumstances we are bound by the moral principles, but in an emergency we are "under the rule of necessity" and "necessity knows no rules."[18] Walzer argues explicitly that while the outcome of World War II was in question, the obliteration bombing is justifiable under necessity and that nuclear deterrence afterward is a "permanent supreme emergency." The bishops' silence on obliteration bombing and their hope for an international peace indicates a tacit supreme emergency moral reading of World War II but, like Walzer, with communism and the advent of nuclear weapons, they found themselves in a seemingly permanent emergency. The bishops went beyond Walzer, however, in their willingness to countenance the actual use of nuclear weapons even though such would unleash the "nightmare of unimaginable horrors." The only statement of limitation they offered in the 1950s was one line calling for "reductions in armament."

It would again take a theologian writing in *Theological Studies* to bring just war analysis to the question of the armed conflict of the day. John Courtney Murray's "Remarks on the Moral Problem of War" undertook such analysis of nuclear weapons. Murray is sometimes criticized for allowing the use of nuclear weapons,[19] and it is true that he argued that nuclear weapons can be made to be proportionate and discriminate. What is less often recognized is that, in light of the just war tradition, he made two moves that would be less conceivable for the bishops of the 1940s and 1950s. The first was his insistence that the international conflict is "not easily and simply defined." The problem was not first and foremost West versus East but rather the problem ran deeper. "The line of rupture is not in the first instance geographic but spiritual and moral; and runs through the West as well as between East and West. It cannot be a question of locating on 'our' side of the rupture those who are virtuous and intelligent, and, over against 'us,' those who are evil and morally blind." This way of depicting the crisis serves as a bulwark against the supreme emergency argument that in an armed conflict there can be a proportionately grave evil allowing the suspension of the just war norms in our conduct. Murray's second move built on the first. He insisted that if the just war criteria cannot be met, then the moral nation must be willing to surrender. After supporting government study regarding surrender, he went on to state that we must "reckon with the possibility of failure and be prepared to accept it. But this is a moral decision, worthy of a man and of a civilized nation. It is a free, morally motivated, and responsible act, and therefore it inflicts no stigma of dishonor." Unlike the bishops, who articulated fear of nuclear annihilation but, without discussing moral limits on use, allowed it to go forward, Murray found that such annihilation, "even of the enemy," would be "worse than injustice; it would be sheer folly." Murray's aim was to "fit the use of violence into the objective order of justice," and if the violence of modern war could not so fit, then he saw that nations must prepare for and be willing to surrender. Either way, Murray held that the just war language must shape the debate and action, and not be set aside, regardless of felt exigency. The just war tradition's value, according to Murray, resided precisely in "its capacity to set the right terms for rational debate on public policies bearing on the problem of war and peace in this age."[20]

It is in their responses to the Vietnam War that the bishops themselves began to draw upon the just war tradition in a more explicit and full-bodied manner. While doing so did not mandate the articulation of positions over against U.S. policy, it did allow the bishops to have some critical distance on the nation. A number of influences played a role in this shift from nationalism, however outward-looking, to critical patriotism. These influences include Murray and other just war theorists; the Catholic peace movement, which will be discussed below; and the documents of Vatican II, particularly the *Pastoral Constitution on the Church in the Modern World* (GS), which undertook a "fresh appraisal of war."

In the early documents on Vietnam—"Peace and Vietnam" (1966), "Resolution on Peace" (1967), "Resolution on Peace" (1968)—the bishops "conscientiously support the position of our country in the present circumstances." However, the bishops also called upon all U.S. citizens to discern the question, and they backed the legal recognition of conscientious objection. Again, as recently as 1956, Pius XII had declared that conscientious objection was not an option, and the bishops previously made no mention of it. However, Vatican II changed the teaching, and the bishops, noting their debt to *Gaudium et spes*, followed the Council. While they themselves may have judged the war to be justifiable, the bishops recognized that others may legitimately come to different conclusions. Moreover, they warned that there are moral limits to war; they called for negotiation for peace and an end to the arms race.[21]

Human Life in Our Day issued in 1968 served as a turning point. The first thing to note is that, while certainly retaining a loyalty to nation, the bishops clearly rejected nationalism. Pursuit of the "universal common good" will be possible only, the document claims, when people "have rejected the tenets of an exaggerated nationalism" (148). It is precisely their ownership of the just war tradition that allowed the bishops to make such a claim. They went on to say that "frequently conscientious dissent reflects the influence of the principles which inform modern papal teaching, the Pastoral Constitution, and a classical tradition of moral doctrine in the Church, including, in fact, the norms for the moral evaluation of a theoretically just war" (145). The grounding in *Gaudium et spes* is thorough. The just war criteria are explicit. Moreover, the bishops moved beyond mere enumeration to the application of principles to specifics, with reference to, for instance, antiballistic missile systems and the Selective Service Act. Three areas of application are worth noting: nuclear war, the Vietnam War, and the exercise of conscience.

With regard to nuclear warfare, the bishops condemned the use of nuclear weapons and allowed deterrence, rejecting unilateral disarmament (106–7), all positions that anticipate those of CP. With respect to the Vietnam War, the bishops noted their previous support of U.S. policy (135) but then went on to raise questions that reflected a deep skepticism. "In assessing our country's involvement in Vietnam, we must ask: Have we already reached or passed the point where the principle of proportionality becomes decisive? How much more of our resources in men and money should we commit to this struggle, assuming an acceptable cause or intention? Has the conflict in Vietnam provoked inhuman dimensions of suffering?" (137). This pattern of moral reasoning, with its recourse to moral principles to raise questions reflecting a profound skepticism regarding U.S. policy, will be repeated in CP in the bishops' treatment of the idea of limited nuclear war (157–61).

The treatment of the role of conscience received its own section. It was here that the bishops stated explicitly what is evident in the treatment of the specific uses of force: the rejection of blind nationalism in favor of a critical patriotism. There are "political, social, cultural and like controls not necessarily in conformity with the mind and heart of the Church" (147). As before, the bishops supported participation in the military as a legitimate vocation. There is also support for conscientious objection (150). The bishops went further to support selective conscientious objection based on just war norms, and therefore called for modification of the Selective Service Act to accommodate selective conscientious objector (SCO) status. Again, both Vatican II and the work of John Courtney Murray were influential here. Murray's case is particularly interesting because he thought that the Vietnam War was just, yet he argued forcefully that conscientious application of the just war tradition can lead to a different conclusion and that such reasoning ought to be legally recognized and respected in the context of conscription. At the request of President Johnson, Murray served on a commission investigating SCO. While the commission rejected Murray's proposal to recognize SCO status, his reasoning influenced the bishops.[22]

The bishops subsequently made further statements leading up to CP in all three of the above areas. The bishops addressed more fully the problem of nuclear weapons by moving to set limits not only on their use but also on their possession. "As possessors of a vast nuclear arsenal, we must also be aware that not only is it wrong to attack civilian populations, but it is also wrong to threaten to attack them as part of a strategy of deterrence." This idea that it is wrong to threaten to do what it is wrong to do, now officially stated, would influence key conclusions of CP. In addition, in light of more evidence, they moved from raising skeptical questions to making a firm pronouncement against the Vietnam War. "At this point in history, it seems clear to us that whatever good we hope to achieve through continued involvement in this war is now outweighed by the destruction of human life and of moral values which it inflicts." Finally, they wrote a separate and emphatic document on conscientious objection and selective conscientious objection. "We should regard conscientious objection and selective conscientious objection as positive indicators within the Church of a sound moral awareness and respect for human life." The bishops moved beyond calling upon the state to recognize these exercises of conscience and put much of the burden on the Catholic community. Catholic organizations should provide draft counseling, information, and "meaningful employment" for the conscientious objector.[23] Until that time, the provision of conscientious objector services was assumed to be the task of the small collection of groups constituting the Catholic peace movement and, given that it is not possible to understand CP without regarding the contribution of these persons and groups, this commentary now turns to consider them.

THE CATHOLIC PEACE MOVEMENT IN THE UNITED STATES

Alongside and, more often than not, over against the testimony of the bishops is that of what perhaps can best be called the Catholic peace movement, a loose collection of Catholic persons, groups, and organizations from the 1930s to the present. Their witness differs from that of the bishops in a variety of significant ways. Given that it is a loose collection, the movement avoids easy characterization. However, because it is for the most part a relatively small movement, the set of interpersonal and interorganizational relationships does form a web with identifiable patterns, and it is helpful to note some of its characteristics, particularly as they contrast with those of the bishops' documents, before detailing the history.

While the numbers of persons who have been actively involved in one or another aspect of the Catholic peace movement may seem to be small, there are both historical and theoretical reasons for giving their witness extended treatment. Historically, members of the peace movement explicitly debated the question of war and peace in terms of both the just war and pacifist traditions decades before the bishops drew on these traditions. As we have seen, the bishops of World War II made virtually no mention of even the just war norms. As we will see, the most dramatic division in the peace movement came during World War II, and the debate was carried out precisely in terms of the just war versus pacifism. In other words, while the bishops concerned themselves largely with assuring the public of Catholic allegiance to the American cause, members of the peace movement were key bearers of what are now the legitimate options in the Catholic tradition regarding the use of force, both pacifism and the just war tradition. Moreover, even since World War II, when the Catholic peace movement became largely pacifist, its influence has extended far beyond those who would designate themselves pacifist.

From the theoretical standpoint, the bishops themselves state in CP that pacifism and the just war tradition are "complementary" traditions within Catholicism, each equally valid for individuals. In addition, while CP holds that nation-states must use lethal force if necessary to defend its borders, *The Harvest of Justice is Sown in Peace*, which the bishops wrote for the tenth anniversary of the former document, raises the question of whether nonviolence "should have a place in the public order with the tradition of justified and limited war." As we will see, John Paul II's focus on the successful nonviolent social changes in Europe indicates that he shares this view. From both historical and theoretical perspectives, then, it is important not to marginalize the peace movement by describing it as involving a way of life only for persons who want to go beyond what is otherwise required by the Catholic tradition.

This chapter mentions three key characteristics that distinguish the approach of the peace movement from that of the bishops. The first difference of note is in the sources drawn upon and the modes of presentation. The Catholic peace movement makes much more direct and frequent appeal to scripture than do the bishops. With some exceptions the bishops cite scripture only rarely in the documents leading up to CP.[24] They refer more frequently to American sources, such as the Constitution or the statements of the president of the United States. Moreover, when the peace movement does refer to scripture, it focuses much more on the life and specific sayings of Jesus, particularly Luke's Sermon on the Plain and Matthew's Sermon on the Mount, than do the bishops' documents. In part this is because much of the focus of peace movement theology has been on the imitation of Christ, and the details as well as the general trajectory of Jesus' life form the primary source material. Building upon that base, writing from the peace movement also frequently appeals to the early church fathers and the saints because of their interpreted historical and spiritual proximity to the Jesus of the scriptures.

Second, the more direct appeal to scripture and the life of Jesus lends itself to a different prioritizing of audiences than with the bishops. From World War I on, the documents of the bishops implicitly seek—and in CP this becomes an explicit intent—to speak to the American public generally, particularly policy-makers, as well as Catholics, and to both primarily on the level of policy. The peace movement speaks first of all to those who might listen with specifically Christian ears, so to speak, whether they are Christian in name or not. To the extent that members of the peace movement speak to policy—and they do so frequently—it is to policy where it intersects the daily lives of people. This is why by far the policy issue that has received the most attention in the peace movement is the draft: this is where war first and most directly exerts an impact on the lives of specific Americans. Moreover, while members of the peace movement have testified before government officials, the most prominent form of testimony in relation to the government is civil disobedience. Above all, the peace movement sets the message of peace in the context of the reading of the life and sayings of Jesus, which call the Christian to perform the works of mercy (see Matt. 25) because Jesus' message is first of all to those who are poor and excluded.

Third, the focus on scripture and the centrality of the hard sayings of Jesus leads to quite different conclusions about the permissibility of war than those reached by the bishops. While far from all members of the Catholic peace movement are pacifist, the majority and the most influential are. Members of the peace movement sometimes engage the language of the just war tradition, but since World War II this is most often to demonstrate how the destructive capacity of modern war has made a just war infeasible and therefore, though this does not necessarily follow, that the just war tradition itself is irrelevant.

Any account of the Catholic peace movement must begin with Dorothy Day (1897–1980) and the Catholic Worker movement. The peace movement as described above takes its shape from her life and writings. One commentator states that the Catholic peace movement up until 1965 "turns out to be, in significant measure, an interpretation of the social outlook, religion, and ideas of this one person."[25] Another judges that Day is "the one person most responsible" for the rise of American Catholic pacifism.[26] Therefore, it is important to set out, however briefly, aspects of Day's life, even the pre–Catholic Worker years, for methodological reasons internal to the Catholic Worker approach. The emphasis in its theology is on modeling one's life after Christ and the saints, and Day is the informal "saint" and model for the Catholic Worker movement. More recently, Cardinal John O'Connor urged her formal canonization.

Day's early life gave little indication that she would have this kind of influence. She took up socialist journalism and a bohemian lifestyle, the latter of which left in its trail abortion, suicide attempts, divorce, and an out-of-wedlock child. While Day had metaphysical leanings from early on, it was the birth of her daughter Tamar that prompted her to convert to Catholicism. Baptized in December 1927, Day continued her journalistic work over the next five years but, on her own account, lacked much direction.

In December 1932 she met Peter Maurin, an itinerant French lay preacher. Maurin sought to make the social teaching of the Church accessible to the layperson by transforming the teaching into extended verse in what he called "Easy Essays." In these essays he put forward a social theory that emphasized the responsibility of individual persons for the common good. "The Catholic worker believes / in the gentle personalism of traditional Catholicism. / The Catholic Worker believes / in the personal obligation of looking after the needs of our brother. / The Catholic Worker believes / in the daily practice/ of the works of mercy."[27] Maurin and other Catholic Workers drew much of their philosophy of personalism from the work of Emmanuel Mounier and his journal *L'Ésprit*. The emphasis on the action of the person-in-community rather than the government led to the adoption of a Christian version of "anarchism," not as a call for social chaos but as a part of a theologically informed social theory which held that action by individual persons in community in imitation of Christ and motivated by the Holy Spirit is the best way to Christianize the social order.

If the Catholic Worker movement was indeed to reach the worker, it had to have not only a general social theory, however theological; it also needed a specific program of action. Maurin's essays outlined this as well, calling for round-table discussions, houses of hospitality, and farming communes.[28] Maurin also had the idea of starting a newspaper, and this fit well with Day's journalistic expertise. Day edited and published 2500 copies of the first issue of the *Catholic Worker* on May Day 1933, and the movement was born. By 1940 there were 185,000 readers per issue—more people than were reading bishops' documents. The houses of hospitality offered meals and often lodging to the poor. Those who offered the hospitality themselves practiced "voluntary poverty," marked off from destitution by allowing enough material goods for simple sufficiency but eschewing all other goods as superfluous. By 1941, the houses of hospitality had multiplied from the one in New York City to thirty-two houses in twenty-seven cities.

There is debate in Catholic Worker historiography concerning the influence or lack thereof of Peter Maurin's ideas, but even if one grants that the three-part program of round-table discussion, houses of hospitality, and farming communes, in addition to the idea of a newspaper, were initially his, it is clear that Day directed these efforts, and in doing so suffused them with the spirituality that would shape much of the Catholic peace movement. Hers was a spirituality built around traditional devotions, for instance, daily Mass and the *Te Deum*, in a way that emphasized the imitation of Christ. She writes in her autobiography, "I know it seems foolish to try to be so Christ-like—but God says we can—why else his command, 'Be ye therefore perfect.'"[29] Where she departed from most traditionalists, however, was in her conviction that the Christ to be imitated is to be found in the poor and the outcast. They are "our brothers in Christ. They are more than that; they are Christ, appealing to you."[30] The central directive of the Christian life is, therefore, to love and identify with the poor and the outcast. In this way, individual Christians participate in the Mystical Body of Christ.

In the economic sphere, identifying with the outcast manifested itself primarily through the particular works of mercy of offering food and shelter. With regard to the issue of war and peace, it above all meant that of visiting those in jail, protesting the laws that put them there, and often joining them through acts of civil disobedience. The early years focused primarily on the economic issues, but there was some activity with regard to war and peace. The *Catholic Worker* criticized Mussolini's invasion of Ethiopia in 1935, and was one of the few Catholic voices not supporting Franco in Spain. Day wrote during the Spanish Civil War that imitating Christ meant turning away from the use of force, and that Christ's followers must be willing to suffer martyrdom. "Christ is being crucified every day. Shall we ask him with the unbelieving world to come down from the Cross? Or shall we as His brothers joyfully 'complete the sufferings of Christ?'"[31]

There were early and articulate adherents of the just war tradition in the Catholic Worker movement, but tensions with pacifists were there from the beginning. Paul Hanly Furfey articulated a pacifist stance in the early years and Arthur Sheehan denounced the just war tradition as inadequate to address the violence of modern war.[32] The prospect of America's entrance into World War II divided the Catholic Worker community. Day wrote an open letter in August 1940 to all of the houses of hospitality setting out pacifism as the stand of the movement. That same month there was a Catholic Worker retreat shaped around the pacifist theme, and the just war adherents did not feel free to speak.[33] Some of the nonpacifist houses closed immediately afterward. By 1945 the number of houses had dropped from the high of thirty-two to ten. Circulation of the newspaper dropped by 85,000. Still, the debate is significant since it was just about the only Catholic debate in just war and pacifist terms going on in the United States at the time.

The Catholic Worker movement continued to be virtually the only association of the Catholic peace movement through World War II, and its focus was on the draft and aiding conscientious objectors. Because the Roman Catholic

Church is not one of the historic peace churches like those of the Quakers, Brethren, and Mennonites, it proved difficult for Catholic men to be granted conscientious objector status. In fact, the hierarchical magisterium weighed in against recognizing C.O. status. Those Catholic men, then, who did receive such status by the draft board found no support from the institutional Church. Unlike the peace churches, the Catholic Church did not run or financially support a Civilian Public Service Camp for objectors. Rather, these activities were carried out by the Catholic Worker and an organization, the Association of Catholic Conscientious Objectors (ACCO), headed up by the Catholic Worker Arthur Sheehan. Given the simple lifestyle of the Catholic Worker movement and therefore the lack of significant funds, the objectors in the Catholic "Camp Simon," as it was called, lived in extreme conditions of poverty.[34] When Bishop John Peterson of New Hampshire disowned objector status as an acceptable Catholic stand, the Selective Service determined that ACCO could no longer sponsor a camp. The decision had fortunate side effects in that the objectors then worked in a variety of settings, like hospitals, where the conditions were much better and the work more worthwhile.

In the postwar years, the Catholic Worker continued both to develop the theoretical underpinnings of its activity and to participate in acts of protest and civil disobedience. Two key figures in this period were Robert Ludlow on theoretical development and Ammon Hennacy with regard to continuing protest. In the early 1950s Day wrote that Ludlow had been "the theorist of our pacifism for the past five years." Ludlow's novel contribution was to link Catholic Worker love of the outcast in a violent society with Mahatma Gandhi's idea of nonviolent truth, or *satyagraha*: "Love proceeds from truth and Gandhi proceeded in love to the very end for he proceeded in truth . . . And he could proceed in love because he could proceed without violence."[35] Hennacy is known not for his theoretical contributions but for the boldness of his acts of civil disobedience. During World War II he advocated the nonpayment of war taxes and became a migrant farm worker in order to live out his convictions. His most successful civil disobedience effort drew in many others against compulsory air-raid drills. In 1953 and 1954 he protested alone, but in 1955 when the drills became compulsory, he was joined by twenty-eight people. By 1960 over a thousand persons protested, and in 1961 the number jumped to 2500, forcing an end, by declaration of the Kennedy administration, to air-raid drills.[36] This is a key instance where the Catholic peace movement has had a direct and significant effect on public policy on the national level.

Two factors combined to broaden the Catholic peace movement beyond the Catholic Worker functioning virtually alone. The first is the rise in the destructive capacity of nuclear weapons and the second is the Vietnam War. In each case, the Catholic peace movement broadened both by members of the Catholic Worker cooperating with non-Catholic peace organizations and by the Catholic peace movement itself branching out to include Catholic persons and organizations not directly affiliated with the Catholic Worker. Although the first act of cooperation with other groups came in 1946, expanded cooperation began with the Committee for Non-Violent Action (CNVA), where Day, Hennacy, and another Catholic Worker, Ed Turner, served on the executive committee. In August 1957, twelve CNVA protesters, including Catholic Workers, were arrested for crossing into the Atomic Energy Commission's nuclear test site in Nevada. This and similar acts of protest, driven by the urgency of the development of the hydrogen bomb, broadened the base and appeal of the Catholic peace movement.

Two key developments further broadened the peace witness within the Catholic community, this time beyond the pacifist conviction. The first was the entrance of the Trappist monk Thomas Merton into the conversation, with the publication of his collection of essays on nuclear war titled *Disputed Questions*, where he directly takes on John Courtney Murray's view that such war can remain limited. However, Merton consciously did not term himself a pacifist, and in the 1968 *Faith and Violence* he explicitly refused to condemn the use of force by oppressed peoples.[37] Second, in 1962, both pacifist and just war activists formed the Catholic peace organization Pax. Directed by Eileen Egan, Pax acted not through protest and civil disobedience, but through lobbying within the Church, an activity more in line with the Catholic Association for International Peace (CAIP). Pax would serve as a beneficial intermediate organization: while it was not strictly pacifist, it did counter CAIP at several points, including working behind the scenes at Vatican II to have words condemning obliteration bombing and attending to the morality of deterrence written into the Council's *Pastoral Constitution on the Church in the Modern World* (GS). In 1971 Pax became Pax Christi U.S.A., a member of the worldwide Pax Christi organization.

Activity in response to the Vietnam War continued the trends of intercredal cooperation and Catholic participation by persons who were not associated with the Catholic Worker and often not pacifist. The Catholic Worker, together with the Fellowship of Reconciliation and the War Resisters League, was an early participant in antiwar protests, and as with World War II, the focus was on the draft. In November 1962, the Catholic Worker Tom Cornell led twenty-five others in the burning of their draft cards. In November 1965, Catholic Workers and other draft-age resisters burned their cards in front of 150,000 assembled people in New York City. Day and A. J. Muste of CNVA were featured speakers. In ensuing actions, young men from an array of backgrounds destroyed over 3500 of their draft cards, giving rise to what was called "The Resistance."[38] What differed from World War II was that this time around formal conscientious objection, if not the burning of draft cards, was recognized and supported by the bishops. Vatican II had declared that conscientious objection was a legitimate option for individuals. Later, when James Forest wrote the booklet *Catholics and Conscientious Objection*, it came with Cardinal Spellman's imprimatur. Moreover, the Catholic Association for International Peace, so closely aligned administratively with the bishops, aided Catholic men seeking objector status.

The rise of the Ultra-Resistance further diversified the cause. In November 1967, Philip Berrigan, a Josephite priest, David Eberhardt, Thomas Lewis, and James Mengel broke into the Customs House in Baltimore, Maryland, and poured blood on selective service files. Six months later, Berrigan was joined by his brother, Daniel, a Jesuit, and seven others and entered Selective Service Board No. 33 at Catonsville, Maryland. The group took draft records and burned them outside using homemade napalm. Daniel led the group in praying the Our Father while they awaited arrest.[39] A debate arose in the *Catholic Worker* regarding whether the Berrigans' actions, directed toward the destruction of property but not people, constituted nonviolence. Daniel Berrigan also helped the ecumenical development of the Catholic peace movement by playing key roles in the establishment of both Clergy and Laity Concerned About Vietnam (CALCAV), which he cochaired with Rabbi Abraham Heschel and the then Lutheran pastor Richard John Neuhaus, and in the Catholic Peace Fellowship, which formed an association with the Protestant-dominated Fellowship of Reconciliation.

The number of Ultra-Resistance actions performed between 1968 and 1972 range in estimate from fifty-three to 250.[40] Troop withdrawal from Vietnam led to a decline in actions after 1972. The later rise of the nuclear threat, however, brought a revival of Ultra-Resistance tactics. The most significant of these was the "Plowshares" action, which took place in King of Prussia, Pennsylvania, in September 1980. Daniel and Philip Berrigan together with six others broke into the General Electric plant and, in a dramatization of Isaiah 2:4 and Micah 4:3 calling persons to "beat swords into plowshares," damaged the nose cones manufactured for Mark 12A nuclear warheads. There would be an estimated thirty to forty similar actions over the next decade.

We can see, then, that there have been two major trends in the Catholic peace movement since its inception in the 1930s. The first is its broadening beyond the Catholic Worker movement and ethos. The second, however, is the influence of the Catholic Worker on the peace movement and beyond, such that by the 1960s the bishops were explicitly affirming the right to conscientious and selective conscientious objection. While the Catholic Worker movement was far from the sole factor in this development, it was a significant one. When the bishops craft CP, they take care to note Dorothy Day's impact on American Catholic responses to war and peace (117). We turn, then, to this pastoral letter and its critics.

THE CHALLENGE OF PEACE: GOD'S PROMISE AND OUR RESPONSE AND ITS CRITICS

We have seen that there are two sets of precursors to CP. There is first of all the development of the bishops' own thought from an inwardly driven nationalism that failed to place limits on the use of force to an outwardly looking internationalism that envisioned a just world political order where any conduct of war, if necessary, would be restrained by the applied criteria of the just war tradition. There is also, significantly, a Catholic peace movement with a more direct appeal to scripture and a focus on the practices of smaller groups. While the former precursor is predominant in CP, the influence of the latter is evident. Moreover, critiques of the final version of the document tend to come from either one of these two strands of Catholic reflection on war and peace. Therefore, the present commentary will detail CP in light of these critiques in order to show how the document takes up their concerns and projects them into the future. Attention cannot be given to the whole of the literature on CP. Therefore, this commentary will focus on two representatives of the critiques: George Weigel and Quentin Quesnell.

The first critique, indebted to a particular vision of international order similar to that of the bishops in the 1940s and 1950s, is best articulated by George Weigel in his book *Tranquillitas Ordinis: The Present Failure and Future Promise of Catholic Thought on War and Peace*. His primary criticism is that the bishops do not adequately place the analysis of nuclear weapons in their appropriate political context, that is, in "the peace of *tranquillitas ordinis*, of rightly ordered dynamic political community." The book proceeds in three sections. The first details the appropriate "heritage," traceable, in Weigel's account, to Augustine, with modern examples being the American bishops up through the 1950s and John Courtney Murray. The second section describes the "abandonment" of the heritage with the chief malefactors being the bishops' statements from the Vietnam era forward, including CP. These later documents, Weigel argues, have abdicated the task of placing the question of the limits of the use of force in its appropriate political context. CP is not so much a peace pastoral, therefore, as it is a "weapons pastoral." This turn in their teaching "amounted to a virtual abandonment of the heritage as Murray would have understood it."[41]

The invocation of Murray is noteworthy, and it is helpful to look more closely at it in order to be precise about Weigel's presentation. In the third section of his book, Weigel sets out his own constructive proposal based upon his understanding of the "heritage." Here he cites the World War II bishops and Murray to back the statement that the "chief obstacle" to progress toward peace is the Soviet Union. Therefore, any constructive proposal must begin by opposing the Soviets. "Anticommunism, then, is the entry point."[42] However, we have already seen that, according to Murray, the "line of rupture is not in the first instance geographic but spiritual and moral; and it runs through the West as well as between East and West." The upshot for Murray of having a vision larger than anticommunism is that there is force to his claim that there are moral limits to war-fighting such that if these limits cannot be met, then the United States must surrender. Interestingly, Weigel himself quotes this passage from Murray but then leaves it behind.[43] What is left is an aggressive appeal to change the Soviet Union without any real working out, despite passing reference to proportionality and discrimination, of the limits to war-fighting in a clash between the then superpowers. Correspondingly, unlike in Murray there are certainly no references in Weigel to the obligation to surrender if a nation cannot adhere to the moral limits.

It would appear, then, that the "heritage" that Weigel belongs to is not that of Murray but indeed that of the bishops of the 1940s and 1950s, whose emphasis on anticommunism made any references to the just war tradition rare and without bite. If one takes the heritage to include Murray—and, before that, Augustine, who also held that while some political arrangements are better than others, the sins of the City of Man run through all human arrangements—then it appears to be Weigel who has done the abandoning. What allows Murray, and Augustine before him, to keep critical distance even on their own opposition to oppressive regimes is their well-developed theology, something missing in *Tranquillitas Ordinis*. However, if we set aside the way Weigel's lack of developed theology and consequent extreme anticommunism distort his project, what remains is an important concern that the analysis of war be placed within the context of political analysis.[44]

The second critique of CP argues for a more central role for scripture in shaping the document, and is given careful treatment in Quentin Quesnell's article "Hermeneutical Prolegomena to a Pastoral Letter," which is also helpful because it shares many of the perspectives and judgments of the Catholic peace movement.[45] First of all, he makes the case that after the early section in CP specifically addressing scripture, the bishops fail to make scripture a factor in the rest of the document. Quesnell does the counting: 283 paragraph numbers follow the section on scripture, and they contain only eight biblical quotations, three of which are part of a quoted papal document. Scripture, he concludes, does not influence the rest of the document.[46] Moreover, Quesnell argues, what the bishops do highlight in the biblical section itself is a rather watered down interpretation of what scripture requires of Christians. Consonant with the Catholic peace movement, he points to the centrality and the specificity of the hard sayings of the Sermon on the Plain (Luke 6:17–49) and the Sermon on the Mount (Matt. 5:1–7:28), for instance, "Do not resist one who is evil. But if anyone strikes you on the right cheek, turn to him the other also." The bishops, in contrast, hold that scripture provides no specific directives, only a general vision. The biblical section, according to Quesnell, "seems to conclude little more than that peace is ultimately desirable and the not exactly astounding revelation that the Bible thinks peace is better than war."[47] Quesnell himself concludes that the bishops must have made a prior "decision" to so limit the interpretation of scripture. Such decisions themselves are unavoidable; the problem with the document is that the criteria guiding that decision are opaque on first reading.[48]

Quesnell, like the peace movement's personalism, places emphasis on reaching those open to hearing the gospel in its unadulterated form and gives attention to government policy as something impacted primarily through persons hearing the gospel in the context of their specific lives and vocations. "The decision for Catholics reading the pastoral is not whether nuclear wars shall be begun or what targets the Pentagon will pick out. The actual decision for Catholics will be whether to cooperate with the actions being taken in their name by their democratically elected government."[49] Christians influence governmental policy best simply by following the gospel. "If all Catholics did become conscientious objectors, a quarter of the potential armed forces would be cut off."[50] Quesnell also makes the judgment that many people in the peace movement make, that when attention is turned to the just war tradition and policy, the former is found to be no longer relevant given the magnitude of the violence of the latter. "In its time and at its best, just-war theory was the answer of reason to certain difficult situations."[51] However, war, even an ostensibly just one, is "no longer a reasonable solution to anyone's problems."[52] Most fundamentally, the issue goes beyond the modern nonutility of the just war tradition because the latter "never was the Gospel."[53]

When the secular press responded to the various public drafts of CP, it focused primarily on the specific conclusions and recommendations of the bishops, particularly the debate over one word, whether the bishops should call for a "halt" in the development and production of nuclear weapons or only a "curb" in such activity. This extremely narrow focus is unfortunate because it misses the document's *theological* analysis, and thus the bishops' own understanding of the proper perspective on the questions of the day. The subsections on the possession and use of nuclear weapons constitute fifty-eight of the document's 339 paragraph numbers, between one-fifth and one-sixth of its content, and do not come until the 122nd number. The theologically oriented discussion of biblical peace, at sixty paragraph numbers, is the first major section, and much more space, seventy-four numbers, is given to the section on peace building. In order to give an adequate account of the analysis in CP along with the critiques of the document, then, it is necessary to view the document in its entirety.

After an introduction of four paragraphs citing the threat that nuclear weapons pose to humanity and the responsibility of the bishops as Catholic leaders and citizens to respond, the document proceeds in four major sections. In the first section (5–121), the bishops set out the scriptural understandings of peace and follow that by detailing the moral options—the just war tradition and pacifism—that have developed in the Christian tradition in light of the biblical understandings. The second major section (122–99) applies the criteria of the just war tradition to the question of the use and possession of nuclear weapons. The third and longest section (200–273) moves beyond the question of the conduct of war to that of constructing a peaceful and just political order. Finally (274–329), the bishops move beyond policy to address members of the faith community in the context of their specific professional and personal vocations. A brief conclusion (330–39) follows.

In the first major section, that on scripture, the bishops find two complementary understandings of peace, that of right relationship with God, neighbor, and creation at all times, and that of the fullness of peace that comes at the end of history (27 and 55). In the first understanding, the bishops take great care to point out that the right relationship is not simply with God but also with neighbor in a way that, while theological, is also political. They note that in the Old Testament "the individual's personal peace is not greatly stressed. The well-being and freedom from fear which result from God's love are viewed primarily as they pertain to the community and its unity and harmony" (32). The bishops, following the Old Testament, apply the term *covenantal fidelity* to this understanding of peace that is at once theological and political. "Living in covenantal fidelity with God had ramifications in the lives of the people. It was part of fidelity to care for the needy and helpless; a society living with fidelity was one marked by justice and integrity" (34). When the bishops turn to the New Testament (39–54), they highlight the coming of the Messiah. At first, it appears that the bishops focus on the obligation of the specific directives in the New Testament. Jesus' words and actions are to guide us (44–49), and he "refused to defend himself with force or with violence" (49). However, when this gift of peace is passed to the disciples (52ff.), they know that it is "not yet fully operative in the world" (53). Even though it may be "visible" to others, the living out of the fullness of peace by Christians is limited to "within their own communities" (53).

Already, it is possible to engage aspects of Weigel's and Quesnell's critiques. With regard to Weigel's criticism, note the bishops' stress that biblical peace is also political: it involves a covenant that requires a just order. Weigel reads this part of the bishops' analysis out of their document. He twice claims that the peace as right relationship in the document is only that of a "personal right relationship with God," not including the important "and neighbor" and the arrangements of justice that this latter relationship requires. In other words, Weigel appears to assume that because the bishops take a theological starting point that it must necessarily not be a political one, and it is this assumption that in part allows him to make the claim that the bishops do not place the analysis of weapons in adequate political context.

Quesnell's concern that the bishops avoid or deflect the hard sayings of Jesus finds contact already in the bishops' shift from emphasizing Jesus' specific directives to stressing that this peace is not yet fully operative in the world. Other parts of this first section of the document reinforce the pattern. The bishops both generalize the biblical message and delay its full force. They generalize it when they say that the scriptures "contain no specific treatise on war and peace" (28). Rather, the vision of peace "provides us with direction for our lives and holds out to us an object of hope, a final promise, which guides and directs our actions here and now" (29; see also 55). In other words, scripture, by itself, provides us no specific directives but offers an interpretive context within which—or a horizon against which—to reason about and respond to war and peace. This vision can be "progressively realized" (20). The bishops delay the full force of the biblical understanding of peace by separating out peace as right relationship with God and neighbor from peace as eschatological reality. They refer to the tension between the two as "the 'already but not yet' of Christian existence (62). God's reign is "already" here (peace as right relation with God and neighbor), but "not yet" fully realized (peace as eschatological hope). Much of Christian pacifism can be read as reversing the two elements of peace to read, "not yet, but already." The kingdom of God is not yet fully manifested in the world, but Christians should act, both within their own communities and with others, as if the kingdom of God is fully present, even if this leads to suffering at the hands of others.[54]

On this read of CP, however, it is not necessarily the case that the theology of the biblical section is simply left behind in the rest of the document and that this makes it for the most part a just war document. Rather, what makes it a just war document is the theological decision made early on and then carried through to the rest of the document: the stress on "not yet" allows for taking human life in the interim between Christ's resurrection and his return. Quesnell argues that everyone's reading of scripture, including his own, is supported by prior decisions. In the bishops' case, it is shaped by a prior theological decision regarding how to relate the fullness of Christ's promise to present history. (Pacifists must make similar kinds of decisions.) It remains to be seen whether the relative lack of biblical references in the remainder of the document evidence the end of the influence of theology or the influence of a particular theology that allows warfighting. The test will be whether one can distinguish what comes in the remainder of the document from secular approaches.

The first distinguishing result of the theological analysis shows up when the bishops turn to the various options for living out the biblical peace in human history (66–121). The main theme that the bishops draw from the previous scriptural analysis is a "positive" understanding of peace that is "not merely the absence of war" (68–70; drawing from GS 78). From this positive understanding of peace, the bishops establish a "presumption against war" and the "principle of legitimate self-defense" (71–79). This view differs from the dominant modern view of peace—a minimalist one—as the absence of overt conflict, and an understanding of war as, in Von Clausewitz's words, the mere "continuation of politics by other means."[55] In the minimalist view there is no presumption against war. Thus the biblically based understanding of peace, although not a pacifist understanding, still marks the bishops off from the predominant understanding of peace.

The bishops argue that both just war theorists and pacifists can affirm the presumption against war and self-defense. The two subtraditions differ, however, in their strategies regarding such defense of peace. "It is the *how* of defending peace which offers moral options" (73). Pacifist and just war theorists differ simply with regard to "their perception of how the common good is to be defended most effectively." The two therefore have a "complementary relationship" (74; see also 120). On this view, the differences between just war theorists and pacifists are not theological, they are only strategic.

Yet, on closer examination, it is here that the bishops spell out the key implication of the theological decisions made in previous paragraphs. The "already, but not yet" perspective leverages the position that it is legitimate to take human life. Nonviolent conflict resolution "best reflects the call of Jesus both to love and to justice." However, the presence of "aggression, oppression, and injustice" in the world "also serves to legitimate the resort to weapons and armed force in defense of justice." Therefore, while Christians must still claim that love is "the only real hope for human relations," they must "accept that force, even deadly force, is sometimes justified" (78). Here, the bishops invoke the "not yet" status of the reign of God to back the permissibility, even responsibility, of taking life on behalf of the state. Their previous theological decision shapes the moral parameters of what they deem acceptable. On close reading, then, the differences between the just war tradition and pacifism are not merely strategic but are at bottom theological.

The just war predominance of the document is evident in the claim that individuals can be pacifist but nations must, if necessary, use lethal force for defense (75–76). The bishops qualify their just war stance both by affirming that individuals can be pacifist and by stressing the presumption against war in the just war tradition such that nonviolent means of conflict resolution receive emphasis (77–78). Here, the influence of the peace movement is in evidence. Still, the discussion of the just war criteria (80–110) precedes and is much more extensive than the discussion of "the value of nonviolence" (111–21) and the application of just war principles to the use and possession of nuclear weapons (Part 2; 122–99) precedes the nonviolent means for pursuing peace (Part 3; 200–273).

One reason for the predominance of the just war logic is that the bishops seek to speak even to those who do not share the biblical vision (16–19). The basis of this claim is the natural law argument that all people have "a law written" on their heart "by God" (17). This law provides general moral norms—"universally binding moral principles" (9)—that set parameters on legitimate moral discussion. It is evident that the norms of the just war tradition, "e.g. noncombatant immunity and proportionality," make up those parameters (9). Therefore, all persons, religious or not, must not exceed those norms. Pacifism is legitimate because it is more restrictive than the just war tradition. There can be legitimate disagreement both within and outside the Church in the application of the just war principles to specific cases of the use of force, though again, "the differences should be expressed within the framework of Catholic moral teaching," that is, the just war framework (8–12).

We saw earlier how the bishops of the 1940s and 1950s so emphasized the problem of communism that they seemed willing to countenance the use of nuclear weapons that exceeded the just war norms. We interpreted their approach in terms of Michael Walzer's idea of "supreme emergency," where the presence of an extreme political threat allows suspension of the universal principles. The bishops do not allow supreme emergency because the just war principles are ultimately grounded in the reality of God (15). Supreme emergency, suspending all rules on behalf of a human cause, is a form of idolatry. Given Weigel's affinities with the bishops of the 1940s and 1950s—the thin theology, the extreme anticommunism, and the unwillingness to discuss in any detail how just war principles limit the use of nuclear weapons—questions can be raised concerning whether his work steps outside of the just war tradition as well.

The bishops in CP are quite willing to draw on the just war principles to discuss the limits on the use and possession of nuclear weapons, and the second major section of the document (122–99) takes up this task. Analysis of this section also reveals other ways in which the theologically developed positive understanding of peace set out in the scriptural section informs the rest of the document.

With regard to the possible use of nuclear weapons, the bishops address three main categories: counter-population bombing, the first use of nuclear weapons, and the possibility of limited nuclear war in response to an opponent's first use of the weapons. When they address counter-population nuclear warfare, the bishops apply the principle of noncombatant immunity to conclude that "under no circumstances" may parties carry out such warfare (147). They apply the principle of proportionality to the first use of counter-force nuclear warfare (150–56) and conclude after careful consideration: "We do not perceive any situation in which the deliberate initiation of nuclear warfare, on however restricted a scale, can be morally justified" (150). The bishops apply proportionality again when addressing limited second strike counter-force nuclear warfare in order to raise a number of probing questions such as: "Would leaders have sufficient information to know what is happening in a nuclear exchange" and "How 'limited' would be the long term effects of radiation?" In light of the unanswerability of these questions, the bishops conclude that they are "highly skeptical" of the proportionality and thus legitimacy of such use. "The burden of proof remains on those who assert that meaningful limitation is possible" (159).

The bishops' responses to these three areas of the use of nuclear weapons further the conversation with Weigel and Quesnell. First, the bishops' explicit condemnation of counter-population bombing is a departure from the bishops of the 1940s and 1950s who remained, with few exceptions, silent on the matter, leaving it to John C. Ford to apply the just war principle of noncombatant immunity to the practice. Despite the importance of Ford's article, Weigel makes no reference to it in the 395 pages of text in *Tranquillitas Ordinis*. This further underscores the similarities between the earlier bishops and Weigel.[56] Second, *pace* Quesnell, the influence of the biblically underpinned positive understanding of peace is in evidence in this section. The positive understanding of peace backs the presumption against war discussed earlier. If peace is simply the absence of overt conflict, then there is no such presumption; war is but the continuation of politics by other means. Now note that in the second case (limited first use) and third case (limited second use) that the bishops make against the use of nuclear weapons, they do not argue that it is knowable with certainty that such uses would escalate beyond proportionality. This is why there is an apparent weakening of their rejection of use as they proceed from the first case ("under no circumstances") to the second ("We do not perceive any situation . . .") to the third case ("we will continue to be highly skeptical . . ."). However, in light of the biblically undergirded presumption against war, and in the absence of determining evidence, the presumption remains that such use is immoral. The burden of proof regarding the likely limits of war is on those who seek to argue that the war would be limited and just. In contrast, if there is not a presumption against the use of force, the absence of determining evidence concerning the likelihood of limits does not make a war or tactic immoral; both first and second use counter-force nuclear war would be judged generally allowable.[57] This is one important difference that the bishops' biblical understanding of peace makes.

Another difference is evident when the bishops address deterrence (162–99). The bishops offer their "strictly conditioned moral acceptance" of deterrence. That is to say, deterrence is allowable only under certain limits. There are three main limits. First, there must be ongoing negotiations for disarmament. Second, in the meantime the United States needs only enough nuclear weapons such that there is a "sufficiency" to deter the opponent; there is no need for "superiority" or more weapons than the opponent. Third, the United States ought to take "independent initiatives" in the effort to reduce nuclear arms, that is, in order to prompt disarmament it ought to make some reductive moves apart from negotiation even if the opponent does not immediately follow. This set of conditions has interesting policy implications. While the bishops claim disarmament is bilateral, the conditions they set imply unilateral disarmament down to the level of sufficiency, then bilateral after that, with the United States taking time-limited unilateral initiatives in reduction to prompt further reduction by all parties. Here, the biblically backed positive understanding of peace as right relationship with God and neighbor is in evidence in that the only justifiable deterrence is one that moves in the direction of disarmament (right relationship). If peace is simply the absence of overt conflict, one can argue for an arms race because, it is believed, only the race for "superiority" and the threat of mutual assured destruction can assure the absence of overt conflict. This latter position was that of both superpowers before the end of the cold war.

James Castelli has shown how the positions on the use of nuclear weapons and on deterrence are interrelated. Given that, as Castelli points out, the bishops in an earlier document state that it is immoral to threaten to do what it is immoral to do, once the bishops in writing CP accept deterrence, they cannot absolutely close the possibility of a moral use of nuclear weapons. If the use of such weapons were absolutely immoral, so would be their possession for purposes of deterrence and the threat that implies. This is why the bishops' language shifts from "under no conditions" with regard to counter-population bombing to the somewhat weaker language of "we do not perceive any situation" of moral use and "we will continue to be highly skeptical" when the issue is counterforce targeting. What remains is what J. Bryan Hehir has called a "cubic centimeter of ambiguity" in the bishops' "no" to the use of nuclear weapons. Without such ambiguity, the bishops would have had to say absolutely "no" to deterrence as well.

Moreover, Castelli sets out how the bishops made a policy decision prior to the writing of the document that shaped their response to deterrence. In the two years leading up to the bishops' meeting that started the process of writing CP, a significant number of bishops made public stands in favor of unilateral disarmament. However, early on in the meetings of the ad hoc committee appointed to draft the document, Cardinal Joseph Bernardin, the chair of the committee, set out the ground rule that the document could not come out in favor of unilateral disarmament. In part this was the result of his concern that the bishops not go further than the popes and Vatican II had up to that point, which was to allow deterrence as a kind of interim ethic. In part it was the result of Bernardin's own political judgment. In both cases, a policy conclusion delimited the moral deliberation from close to the very start of the process.[58] To the extent that this is true, *pace* Weigel, the bishops placed the analysis of war too much within the *immediate* political context.

In the third major part of CP (200–273), the bishops move beyond the question of war-fighting to that of building peace. Such peace-building is based on "the Scriptures and the theology of the Church." The bishops quote John Paul II: "Peace is not just the absence of war. It involves mutual respect and confidence between peoples and nations." The bishops detail specific steps both to reduce the danger of war and to shape a peaceful world. With regard to the former, they call for accelerated efforts for arms control, reduction, and disarmament, including a "halt" to the testing, production, and deployment of nuclear weapons (204). Much of the secular press focused on this one word because it coincided with the aims of the "nuclear freeze" movement of the time. The bishops also call for multilateral controls of the conventional arms trade and for efforts to develop nonviolent means of conflict resolution. When the bishops turn to "shaping a peaceful world," they stress the theological truth of the unity of the human family as the core truth of Catholic teaching on the world order, an order that recognizes the full array of rights and duties. The bishops "have no illusions about the Soviet system of repression and the lack of respect in that system of human rights" (250) and highlight the "glory" of the United States in "the range of political freedoms its system permits us" (252). Yet, like John Courtney Murray, they also recognize that the line of rupture is not in the first instance geographical but spiritual and moral, thus their emphasis on the theological unity of the human family. It is in light of this unity that the bishops call for a political authority with the wherewithal "to shape our material interdependence in the direction of moral interdependence" (241). The bishops follow the popes in specifically supporting the United Nations (267–69).

As in the previous sections, we can illuminate this part of CP through exchange with Weigel's and Quesnell's critiques. It is in fact here that Weigel's critique, suitably modified to limit its internal distortions, has some bite. He writes that it is only "two-thirds through the pastoral letter" that the bishops turn to "shaping a peaceful world."[59] Once they attend to the matter, the bishops, unlike Weigel, view it correctly, with U.S.-Soviet differences placed in the context of the theological unity of the human family, but Weigel is right in arguing that they should have placed this section earlier in the document. CP should have proceeded from the scriptural section to the one on peaceful world order, in the context of which the bishops would also address the option of the just war tradition and pacifism. This ordering of sections would have highlighted that the theological peace of "covenantal fidelity" is also a political peace and not simply a "personal relationship with God," as Weigel insists. In addition, such an ordering would have made clearer that the positive understanding of peace developed in the scriptural section *requires* a section detailing the policies necessary to shape a peaceful world, thus addressing in part Quesnell's concern that the theology gets left behind. Under a minimalist understanding of peace as merely the absence of overt conflict, a section on shaping a peaceful world would be unnecessary.

In the final section of the document (274–329), the bishops turn to address the faithful in the context of their various personal and professional vocations. After discussing the general need for educational programs in the formation of conscience for linkage between the various "life" issues such as abortion and war, and for prayer and penance, the bishops offer guidance to a variety of groups, including priests, educators, parents, youths, and people in the military profession, in the defense industries, in science, in the media, and in public office. If Weigel would have the bishops place the political order section earlier in the document, Quesnell would have them put this section there, immediately after the scripture section. The first audience, for Quesnell and the peace movement generally, is people in the specific context of their own lives, and only after and through that is it government policy.[60] Still, like the section on shaping a peaceful world that is of concern to Weigel, the bishops do address people in their specific vocations, even if not as early in the document or as extensively as Quesnell might have it.

Later documents from the bishops take many of these critiques into consideration. While not as a group "neoconservative" like Weigel or pacifist like Quesnell, the bishops do much more to place their analysis of war in a large political and economic context, one marked by peacemaking. We turn now to these later documents.

THE PRIMACY OF PEACEMAKING: THE BISHOPS AFTER CP

There are a variety of reasons that the bishops' documents after CP exhibit closer attention both to the broader political and economic context and to the theory and practice of peacemaking. The first of these is that the bishops are responding to critics such as Weigel and Quesnell. In this practice the bishops are following the listening style that informed CP itself. The second reason is that the bishops' documents after CP are also a continuation of the trajectory of the tradition. Weigel is correct in arguing that Augustine and the major figures following him placed war-fighting in its political context. The bishops demonstrate that contextualization much more fully in their more recent documents. They are quite explicit on this point in *The Harvest of Justice Is Sown in Peace*, written in 1993 on the tenth anniversary of CP. They focus "less on particular weapons and wars and more on a broader context of violence which still pervades our communities, our country, and our world."[61] The third reason for the focus on the political and economic context and on peacemaking is the opportunity afforded by world events. Both John Paul II and the American bishops repeatedly cite the end of the cold war and the role peaceful resolutions played in bringing that end about as signs of hope that the use of nonviolent means of conflict resolution on behalf of a just political order is now more possible than at any time in modern history. The second and third reasons just stated, that is, the bishops' continuation of the trajectory of the tradition and the role of recent peaceful resolutions, require more extensive comment. Therefore, the rest of this commentary will elaborate on these two points, attending to the specific U.S. conflicts—the two major engagements with Iraq and the response to terrorism and the bombing of the World Trade Center—in this context.

The bishops align themselves with the tradition in placing the discussion of peace in the context of a just political order. The question arises as to what constitutes such an order. The contemporary benchmark is John XXIII's 1963 document *Pacem in terris* (*Peace on Earth*). Both John Paul II and the American bishops cite this document as informing their perspective. *Pacem in terris* makes two basic claims. The first is that peace depends on a just political order. The second is that the just political order recognizes the full range of rights. At the time of John XXIII's writing, the political world was divided into those who affirmed what are called civil and political rights (e.g., the right to vote and the right to worship according to one's own beliefs) and those who affirmed social and economic rights (e.g., the rights to work, to a just wage, and to health care). *Pacem in terris* makes clear and explicit that the Catholic tradition holds that the just political order depends on the affirmation of both kinds of rights.

John Paul II concurs with John XXIII on the issue of rights in his World Day of Peace Message of 1999. After setting out the *imago Dei* doctrine as the theological basis for a transcendent human dignity, John Paul argues that this unified theological and anthropological center backs the objective "universality and indivisibility of human rights." He elaborates: "Human rights are traditionally grouped into two broad categories, including on the one hand civil and political rights and on the other economic, social, and cultural rights. . . . All human rights are in fact closely connected, being an expression of different dimensions of a single subject, the human person. The integral promotion of every category of human rights is the true guarantee of full respect of any individual right."[62]

Neoconservative writers such as George Weigel and Michael Novak reject the idea of economic rights. Therefore, while Weigel is correct in arguing that the question of war-fighting ought to be placed in the context of the question of a just political order, the political order he has in mind is quite different from that put forward by Catholic social teaching as represented by John XXIII and John Paul II. Indeed, neoconservative rejection of economic rights may even qualify as formal dissent.[63]

The attention given by John Paul II and the American bishops to economic rights in relation to the conditions for peace is linked to their judgment that one of the key factors contributing to the outbreak of violence, though far from the only factor, is the gap between rich and poor. They draw the connection between economic disparity and violence from their own observations and from earlier church documents. Vatican II's *Gaudium et spes* states: "If peace is to be established, the primary requisite is to eradicate the causes of dissension among men. Wars thrive on these, especially on injustice" (83). In *Populorum progressio* Paul VI warns without advocating: "When whole populations destitute of necessities live in a state of dependence barring them from all initiative and responsibility, and all opportunity to share in social and political life, recourse to violence, as a means to right these wrongs to human dignity, is a grave temptation" (30). He adds: "Excessive economic, social, and cultural inequalities among peoples arouse tensions and conflicts, and are a danger to peace" (76). John Paul II makes clear in *Sollicitudo rei socialis* that this point has transnational relevance when he says that "the social question has acquired a worldwide dimension" because "the demand for justice can only be satisfied on that level." He then immediately clarifies his point in terms of the rich-poor gap. "To ignore this demand could encourage the temptation among victims of injustice to respond with violence, as happens at the origins of many wars. People excluded from the fair distribution of goods originally destined for all could ask themselves: why not respond with violence to those who treat us first with violence?" (10).

John Paul continues this theme of the rich-poor gap in the post–cold war years. In a January 1991 address to the Vatican diplomatic corps issued after the United States had increased troops in Saudi Arabia but before it engaged Iraq, he states: "How can one fail to mention at this point the great barrier which continues to separate rich peoples from poor ones? This widening gap and the frustration of millions of our brothers and sisters who live without hope for the future does not only constitute an imbalance, but also represents a threat to peace." In January 2003, prior to the second large deployment of troops to Iraq, John Paul writes that only solidarity will overcome conflict, and that the duty of solidarity requires addressing living conditions that are "scandalously unequal." The pope repeats this emphasis on the role of the duty of solidarity in overcoming injustice in his statement on terrorism after 9/11.[64] In contrast, the neoconservative Michael Novak claims that the gap between rich and poor is not morally relevant, indeed, that it is "improper to concentrate on 'the gap' alleged to exist" between the rich and the poor.[65]

The American Catholic bishops follow John Paul II's lead both in *The Harvest of Justice Is Sown in Peace* and in their response to the destruction of the World Trade Center, "Living with Faith and Hope after September 11." *Harvest* provides an entire section on the role of economic development in the establishment of peace. Here the bishops observe that "the modern world is more and more illustrative of the story of the rich man and Lazarus, with an ever-widening gap between the world's haves and have-nots." Like the pope, they make clear that economic disparity is far from the only factor in violence and that, in their words, "no grievance, no matter the claim, can legitimate what happened on September 11." Still, they, like John Paul II, go on to point out how the "grinding poverty amid plenty" is one of the key "sources of deep resentment and hopelessness which terrorists seek to exploit for their own ends."[66]

The focus on the full range of human rights as the appropriate economic and political context for consideration of the use of force is so central to John Paul II and the American bishops that they both allow for and even urge humanitarian intervention in the case of severe rights violations. Behind their concern is the understanding of peace as right relation with neighbor. The pope insists that "states no longer have a 'right to indifference.'"[67] Such indifference is grounded in the view of peace as the absence of overt conflict: nations can be indifferent to the suffering *within* other nations as long as there is no conflict *between* them. This is hardly right relation with neighbor, however. John Paul insists that humanitarian intervention is "obligatory where the survival of populations and entire ethnic groups is seriously compromised. This is a duty for nations and the international community."[68] The American bishops point out that while state sovereignty is a good that in general enhances order in the modern world, it is not an absolute good. The unity of the human family and the dignity of all persons have priority in those instances where there is conflict between these goods and that of state sovereignty. In keeping with the presumption against the use of force, both the bishops and the pope affirm that nonviolent means of intervention have priority over violent means. However, both also do not rule out the use of force in certain instances. In the bishops' words, "Military intervention may sometimes be justified to ensure that starving children can be fed or that whole populations will not be slaughtered."[69]

John Paul II and the American bishops' attention to the implications of the nonviolent revolutions that helped bring about the end of the cold war, the second of our concluding themes, is also worth noting further. In the January 1991 address on Iraq quoted above, the pope asks the Vatican diplomatic corps to "first of all give thanks to 'the Lord of history,' in whom we 'live and move and have our being' (Acts 17:28), who has willed an in-depth transformation of Europe which, perhaps for the first time, is not the result of war." When John Paul goes on in the same document to address the situation in Iraq, he states that "true friends of peace know that now more than ever is the time for dialogue, for negotiation and for affirming the primacy of international law. Yes, peace is still possible; war would be a decline for all humanity." In his view, "a peace obtained by arms could only prepare new acts of violence."[70] In the January 2003 document quoted above, John Paul also asks: "And what are we to say of the threat of a war which could strike the people of Iraq?" He goes on to cite Europe, which has through nonviolent means "succeeded in tearing down the walls which disfigured her." In light of such examples, the pope notes: "It is therefore possible to change the course of events once good will, trust in others, fidelity to commitments and cooperation between responsible partners is allowed to prevail." He repeats his warning made prior to the previous Iraq engagement. "No to war! War is not always inevitable. It is always a defeat for humanity." Like John Paul II, the bishops cite Europe as an example of a just political order wrought by nonviolence. "We watched with awe the courage and faithfulness of Solidarity and other movements for freedom in Eastern Europe." They also note the example of the Philippines and certain movements in Central America.[71]

Three consequences follow from John Paul II and the American Catholic bishops' recognition that the fact of such successful efforts creates the obligation to further seek out nonviolent resolutions to conflict situations. The first consequence is the strengthening of the presumption against war at the heart of the just war tradition. The presumption has long been in place. J. T. Delos has expertly shown how it functions in Augustine's thought. The very form of the war question posed by Aquinas in the *Summa theologiae*—"Whether it is *Always* Sinful to Wage War?"—underscores the presumption. Now the fact of successful nonviolent conflict resolution means that arguments in favor of war have a much stronger burden of proof to establish in order to override the presumption. War is, as we have seen in John Paul's words, a "decline" or "defeat" for humanity and can "only prepare new acts of violence." That is why he urges "No to war!" He elaborates: "War itself is an attack on human life, since it brings in its wake suffering and death." Therefore, "war is never just another means that one can choose to employ for settling differences between nations." War, for the pope, is first of all to be presumed not to be a viable moral response. Such an approach separates the pope from secular views that follow Carl von Clausewitz's dictum that war is merely "a continuation of politics by other means." The bishops concur with the pope. They state that recent history, both good and bad, "reinforces and strengthens for us the strong presumption against the use of force."[72]

Both John Paul II and the bishops are clear that the strengthening of the presumption against the use of force does not mean that they are pacifist. In fact, both indicate that, under certain circumstances, there may be an obligation to go to war. Political leaders have responsibility for the common good, and in certain carefully circumscribed situations that responsibility may include exercising their authority to declare war. The presumption against war may be, on occasion, overridden. What the strengthened presumption does, in combination with the fact of successful nonviolent revolutions, is make the just war tradition a resource that is much more likely to condemn a particular instance of war—for instance, the Vatican's condemnation of U.S. engagement with Iraq in 2003—than to justify it. In particular, the presumption leads to an underscoring of the criterion of last resort and a focused emphasis on the question of whether all nonviolent means of conflict resolution have indeed been tried and exhausted. Such an emphasis takes the pope and the bishops in the opposite direction from recent discussions of "preventive war," such as in U.S. justification for armed engagement with Iraq in 2003, where war is a *first* resort to conflicts that a country thinks *might* happen.

Both George Weigel and Michael Novak argue that the 2003 U.S. armed engagement with Iraq is justifiable, and examining key aspects of their arguments illuminates how they depart from the pope and align with U.S. policy. Weigel denies that he is arguing for "preventive war." However, he is clear that he rejects the idea of a presumption against war, stating that instead the just war tradition begins "with moral obligations: the obligation of rightly constituted public authorities to defend the security of those for whom they have assumed responsibility." Neither John Paul II nor the bishops, however, would disagree on the centrality of certain obligations on the part of public officials. Their point is that the presumed form of obligation, that is, the proper form unless overridden by specific extenuating circumstances, is that of nonviolent rather than violent conflict resolution. Weigel wrongly concludes that the obligation to "defend security" blots out the primacy of nonviolent means of conflict resolution. Moreover, according to Catholic social teaching the highest obligation of public officials is to the common good, which is a broader concept than Weigel's "security." The idea of security, taken alone, carries historical connotations of a presumption in favor of *armed* conflict resolution. Weigel's rejection of the presumption against war aligns him with secular theorists who draw on Clausewitz's view that war is simply "a continuation of politics by other means." Here, there are no theoretical obstacles to "preventive war" because war, no different in kind from any other political means, might achieve one's political objectives. Therefore, while Weigel claims to have met the criterion of last resort, his rejection of the tradition's presumption against war means that his criterion of last resort is weak and that his theory as a whole is open in principle to "preventive war."[73]

Michael Novak was dispatched by the U.S. administration to argue its cause to the Vatican, which had made clear that U.S. engagement at that time would be unjust. Like Weigel, Novak says that he is following the just war tradition and that his view of the 2003 conflict with Iraq "has nothing to do with any new theory of 'preventive war.'" After examining the specifics of the case on the possibility of an Iraqi attack on the United States, however, he warns: "Those who judge that the risk [of such an attack] is low and therefore allow Saddam to remain in power will bear a horrific responsibility if they guessed wrong."[74] What this sentence indicates is that, for Novak, the use of armed force is indeed a "guess," a question about what Iraq *might* do. In other words, it involves the engagement of preventive war, regardless of the name by which it is called. It appears, then, that Novak as well as Weigel, therefore, is out of step with John Paul II not just on the specific conflict in question but on the presumption against the use of force and the meaning of the just war tradition as a whole.

The second consequence of the successful nonviolent movements of the late twentieth century is the elevation of nonviolent means of conflict resolution in Catholic theory on conflict. This commentary earlier noted how Vatican II broke new ground in affirming that individual Catholics can legitimately be pacifist. CP followed suit but also stressed that nation-states must defend their people with force if attacked. In *The Harvest of Justice Is Sown in Peace*, however, the bishops explicitly go beyond their position stated just ten years earlier. They note the "new importance" of nonviolence: "Although nonviolence has often been regarded as simply a personal option or vocation, recent history suggests that in some circumstances it can be an effective public undertaking as well." The bishops quote John Paul II's emphasis in *Centesimus annus* on "the nonviolent commitment of people" who have refused "to yield to the force of power" but have nonetheless "succeeded time after time." The bishops themselves go on to query: "One must ask, in light of recent history, whether nonviolence should be restricted to personal commitments or whether it also should have a place in the public order with the tradition of justified and limited war." The bishops are clear that the obligation to nonviolence on a public level does not deny the right and duty to use armed force as a last resort, but the obligation to nonviolence does "raise the threshold for the recourse to force."[75]

The third and final consequence of the recognition of the successful nonviolent efforts is an increased attention to the specific virtues and practices necessary to carry out such activities. Thus, while the bishops call for increased attention to nonviolence as a viable public—and not simply individual—political response, they and John Paul II are aware that it has not first of all been public officials who have headed the nonviolent efforts or made them possible. Here the pope, who already in *Sollicitudo rei socialis* discusses the "virtue" of solidarity, and the bishops move beyond Weigel's narrow emphasis on the obligations of public officials. In *The Harvest of Justice Is Sown in Peace*, the bishops discuss the "vocation of peacemaking," the "virtues and vision for peacemakers," and "peaceable virtues" before turning to the policy discussion. In doing so, they display the concern that Quentin Quesnell raises in his response to CP: people first of all engage policy through their practice of particular virtues (and vices) in their various everyday vocations. Both John Paul II and the bishops are aware that it has been less through recognized political leaders than through the actions of everyday people in their vocations, for instance, the workers in the Solidarity movement, that the nonviolent efforts have become successful, and that if there is to be further success Catholic teaching must attend not only to the obligations of recognized political leaders but to those of the rest of us as well. In Catholic teaching, all people, and not just political leaders, are responsible for the common good since the common good, according to John Paul II, is "the good of all and of each individual" where "we are all really responsible for all."[76]

NOTES

1. Hugh Nolan, ed., *Pastoral Letters of the United States Catholic Bishops*, vol. 4 (Washington, D.C.: U.S. Catholic Conference, 1983), 2.

2. George Weigel, *Tranquillitas Ordinis: The Present Failure and Future Promise of American Catholic Thought on War and Peace* (Oxford: Oxford University Press, 1987), 257.

3. John Carroll, "Pastoral Letter," May 28, 1792, in *Pastoral Letters*, vol. 1, ed. H. Nolan, 16–27. 4. Third Plenary Council of Baltimore, "Pastoral Letter," December 7, 1884, in ibid., 215–16.

5. From John Tracy Ellis, "American Catholics and Peace: A Historical Sketch" (Washington, D.C.: U.S. Catholic Conference, 1970), 25; reprinted from *The Family of Nations*, ed. James S. Rausch (Huntington, Ind.: Our Sunday Visitor, 1970).

6. The term *council* had specific canonical implications that the bishops wanted to avoid.

7. John A. Ryan, *International Ethics* (Washington, D.C.: Catholic Association for International Peace, 1927); Carleton J. H. Hayes, *Patriotism, Nationalism and the Brotherhood of Man* (Washington, D.C.: Catholic Association for International Peace, 1930); Cyprian Emmanuel, *The Ethics of War* (Washington, D.C.: Catholic Association for International Peace, 1932).

8. John C. Ford, "The Morality of Obliteration Bombing," in *War in the Twentieth Century*, ed. Richard B. Miller (Louisville, Ky.: Westminster/John Knox, 1992), 152–53, 159, 164–65, 169–70; reprinted from *Theological Studies* 5 (1944): 261–73, 308–9.

9. Ford writes: "The Catholic hierarchy of the United States have not offered any joint opinions that I know of on the morality of the present bombing strategy." He does cite the bishop of Seattle, Gerald Shaughnessy, as an example of an individual bishop who had condemned the policy. See ibid., 172.

10. Ibid., 144, citing John C. Ford, "Current Moral Theology," *Theological Studies* 2 (1941): 556.

11. Administrative Board of the National Catholic Welfare Conference [NCWC], "The Crisis of Christianity," November 14, 1941, in *Pastoral Letters*, vol. 2, ed. H. Nolan, 28, 32–33.

12. Edward Mooney, "Catholic Support in World War II," December 22, 1941, in ibid., 36.

13. Ibid.

14. See, for instance, the following statements of the NCWC administrative board: "Victory and Peace," November 14, 1942; "The Essentials of a Good Peace," November 11, 1943; "A Statement on International Order," November 16, 1944; and "Between War and Peace," November 18, 1945, all in *Pastoral Letters*, vol. 2, ed. H. Nolan.

15. The only reference to a just war criterion that I could find was to last resort, and it is simply to indicate that the criterion has clearly been met. When the documents discuss the need for "moral safeguards for youth in military service," they are referring to safeguards in the area of sexual and personal ethics not related to policy. See NCWC administrative board, "Victory and Peace," nos. 2 and 15, in *Pastoral Letters*, vol. 2, ed. H. Nolan, 38, 40.

16. NCWC administrative board, "Between War and Peace," no. 1, in *Pastoral Letters*, vol. 2, ed. H. Nolan, 62.

17. Catholic Bishops of the United States, "A Statement on Freedom and Peace," no. 24, in *Pastoral Letters*, vol. 2, ed. H. Nolan, 218.

18. Michael Walzer, *Just and Unjust Wars: A Moral Argument with Historical Illustrations* (New York: Basic, 1977), 251–83.

19. See, for instance, Patricia McNeal, *Harder Than War: Catholic Peacemaking in Twentieth-Century America* (New Brunswick, N.J.: Rutgers University Press, 1992).

20. John Courtney Murray, "Remarks on the Moral Problem of War," in *War in the Twentieth Century*, ed. R. Miller, 249, 260–61; reprinted from *Theological Studies* 20 (1959): 40–61.

21. See National Conference of Catholic Bishops [NCCB], "Peace and Vietnam," nos. 12, 3, and 9, in *Pastoral Letters*, vol. 3, ed. H. Nolan, 74–76. For an earlier statement on conscription that makes no reference to the possibility of conscientious objection, see the 1950 document, NCWC administrative board, "Statement on Compulsory Peacetime Military Service," in *Pastoral Letters*, vol. 2, 106. The bishops were against peacetime conscription and tried to set limits on it but did not support conscientious objection. This is in keeping with Pius XII at the time.

22. John Courtney Murray, "War and Conscience," in *A Conflict of Loyalties*, ed. James Finn (New York: Pegasus, 1968), 19–30.

23. NCCB, "To Live in Christ Jesus," November 11, 1976, no. 100, in *Pastoral Letters*, vol. 4, ed. H. Nolan, 192; NCCB, "Resolution on Southeast Asia," November, 1971, no. 3, in *Pastoral Letters*, vol. 3, ed. H. Nolan, 289; U.S. Catholic Conference, "Declaration on Conscientious Objection and Selective Conscientious Objection," October 21, 1971, no. 11, in *Pastoral Letters*, vol. 3, ed. H. Nolan, 285.

24. The most evident exception is in National Conference of Catholic Bishops, "To Live in Christ Jesus" (Washington, D.C.: U.S. Catholic Conference, 1976).

25. Mel Piehl, *Breaking Bread: The Catholic Worker and the Origin of Catholic Radicalism in America* (Philadelphia: Temple University Press, 1982), x–xi.

26. McNeal, *Harder Than War*, x.

27. Peter Maurin, "What the Catholic Worker Believes," in *Easy Essays* (Chicago: Franciscan Herald, 1984), 76–77.

28. Maurin, "Purpose of the Catholic Worker School," in ibid., 36.

29. Dorothy Day, *The Long Loneliness* (San Francisco: HarperSanFrancisco, 1980), 34.

30. Dorothy Day, "And There Remained Only the Very Poor," in *Dorothy Day: Selected Writings*, ed. Robert Ellsberg (Maryknoll, N.Y.: Orbis, 1992), 94. See also Day, "Room for Christ," in ibid., 94–97.

31. Day, "The Use of Force," in ibid., 77–78.

32. See, for instance, Paul Hanly Furfey, "Christ and the Patriot," in *A Penny a Copy: Readings from the Catholic Worker*, ed. Thomas C. Cornell, Robert Ellsberg, and Jim Forest (Maryknoll, N.Y.: Orbis, 1995), 19–20. On Arthur Sheehan, see Piehl, *Breaking Bread*, 194.

33. For an account of the debate between just war adherents and pacifists in the Catholic Worker movement, see Francis J. Sicius, "Prophecy Faces Tradition: The Pacifist Debate during World War II," in *American Catholic Pacifism: The Influence of Dorothy Day and the Catholic Worker Movement*, ed. Anne Klejment and Nancy L. Roberts (Westport, Conn.: Praeger, 1996), 65–76.

34. Gordon Zahn, who was himself an objector during World War II, has written an account of life in Camp Simon. See his *Another Part of the War: The Camp Simon Story* (Amherst: University of Massachusetts Press, 1979). Also see his *War, Conscience and Dissent* (New York: Hawthorn, 1967).

35. Day, *Long Loneliness*, 266. Robert Ludlow, "St. Francis and His Revolution," in *A Penny a Copy*, ed. T. Cornell, R. Ellsberg, and J. Forest, 88–92. See also, "Pax," in ibid., 58–59, and "Revolution and Compassion," in ibid., 66.

36. See Piehl, *Breaking Bread*, 214–15.

37. Thomas Merton, *Disputed Questions* (New York: Farrar, Straus, 1960) and his *Faith and Violence* (Notre Dame, Ind.: University of Notre Dame Press, 1968).

38. See McNeal, *Harder Than War*, 148.

39. For a detailed biography of Philip and Daniel Berrigan, see Murray Polner and Jim O'Grady, *Disarmed and Dangerous: The Radical Lives and Times of Daniel and Philip Berrigan* (Boulder, Colo.: Westview, 1997).

40. McNeal, *Harder Than War*, 197.

41. Weigel, *Tranquillitas Ordinis*, 357 and 284.

42. Ibid., 371–72.

43. Ibid., 126.

44. Weigel is not wrong in pointing out the horrors committed in the name of the Soviet Union, only in his heightening of anticommunism to the extent that it is the "point of entry" in pursuing peace. The strength of Murray's theology allowed him to keep focused on the "rupture" running through West as well as East. For descriptions of Soviet horrors, see Anne Applebaum, *Gulag: A History* (New York: Doubleday, 2003).

45. Quentin Quesnell, "Hermeneutical Prolegomena to a Pastoral Letter," in *Peace in a Nuclear Age: The Bishops' Pastoral Letter in Perspective*, ed. Charles J. Reid Jr. (Washington, D.C.: Catholic University of America Press, 1986), 3–19.

46. Ibid., 5.

47. Ibid., 5

48. Ibid., 7–10.

49. Ibid., 15.

50. Ibid., 17.

51. Ibid., 17–18.

52. Ibid., 19.

53. Ibid., 18.

54. For a clear treatment on the theological differences between the just war tradition and pacifism, see Lisa Sowle Cahill, *Love Your Enemies* (Minneapolis: Fortress, 1994).

55. Carl von Clausewitz, *On War*, trans. J. J. Graham (New York: Penguin, 1983).

56. Weigel mentions Ford only in a one-sentence endnote. See Weigel, *Tranquillitas Ordinis*, 410, number 98.

57. This is the case, for instance, in James Turner Johnson's *Can Modern War Be Just?* (New Haven, Conn.: Yale University Press, 1984). Johnson acknowledges that "no one knows" whether nuclear war would escalate, but because he rejects the presumption against war, he allows the use of nuclear weapons.

58. On the statements of various bishops in favor of unilateral disarmament and Bernardin's foreclosure of the position, see Jim Castelli, *The Bishops and the Bomb: Waging Peace in a Nuclear Age* (Garden City, N.Y.: Image, 1983).

59. Weigel, *Tranquillitas Ordinis*, 273.

60. Though Quesnell does not draw on them, there are reasons internal to Catholic social teaching for starting where he does. These reasons are summarized in the principle of subsidiarity, which insists that the building of the social order begins with the smaller "intermediate" groups such as families, neighborhoods, and parishes.

61. NCCB, *The Harvest of Justice Is Sown in Peace*; reprinted in *Origins*, 23, no. 26 (December 9, 1993): 463.

62. John Paul II, "Message of His Holiness Pope John Paul II for the Celebration of the World Day of Peace," number 3. Available at http://www.vatican.va/holy_father/john_p. . .21998 xxxii-world-day-for-peace_en.shtml (downloaded January 1, 1999).

63. On dissent in neoconservative thought, see Todd David Whtimore, "John Paul II, Michael Novak, and the Differences between Them," in *Annual of the Society of Christian Ethics* 21 (2001): 215–32.

64. John Paul II, "War, a Decline for Humanity," *Origins* 20, no. 33 (January 24, 1991): 531; "The International Situation Today," *Origins* 32, no. 33 (January 30, 2003): 544; and the Anniversary Statement on 9/11; "To Fight Terrorism, Go to Its Root Causes," http://www.zenit.org/english/audience (downloaded March 13, 2004). See also "Overseeing the Postwar Gulf," *Origins* 20, no. 41 (March 21, 1991): 668.

65. Michael Novak, *The Catholic Ethic and the Spirit of Capitalism* (New York: The Free Press, 1993), 153; Lay Commission on Catholic Social Teaching and the U.S. Economy, *Toward the Future: Catholic Social Thought and the U.S. Economy* (New York: Lay Commission on Catholic Social Teaching and the U.S. Economy, 1984): 49.

66. NCCB, *Harvest of Justice*, 456; U.S. Conference of Catholic Bishops, "Living With Faith and Hope after September 11," *Origins* 31, no. 25 (November 29, 2001): 415, 417.

67. John Paul II, "Address to the Diplomatic Corps," *Origins* 22 (January 16, 1993): 587.

68. John Paul II, "Address to the International Conference on Nutrition," *Origins* 22 (November 28, 1992), 475.

69. NCCB, *Harvest of Justice*, 461.

70. John Paul II, "War, a Decline for Humanity," *Origins* 20, no. 33 (January 24, 1991): 527, 530.

71. John Paul II, "The International Situation Today," *Origins* 32, no. 33 (January 30, 2003): 544. NCCB, *Harvest of Justice*, 464.

72. J. T. Delos, "The Sociology of War and the Theory of Just War," *Cross Currents* 8 (1958): 248–66; Thomas Aquinas, *Summa theologiae*, IIa

IIae, Q. 40, A. 1 (emphasis added); John Paul II, "The International Situation," 544; John Paul II as quoted by Celestino Migliore, "Preventing a Possible War in Iraq," *Origins* 32, no. 38 (March 6, 2003); John Paul II, "The Pope's Letters to Bush and Hussein," *Origins* 20, no. 33 (January 24, 1991): 534–35; NCCB, *Harvest of Justice*, 454.

73. George Weigel, "The Just War Case for the War," *America* 188, no. 11 (March 31, 2003): 8.

74. Michael Novak, "An Argument That War against Iraq Is Just," *Origins* 32, no. 36 (February 20, 2003): 593, 596.

75. NCCB, *Harvest of Justice*, 455. The bishops are quoting John Paul II, CA 23.

76. John Paul II, SRS 38.

SELECTED BIBLIOGRAPHY

Bainton, Roland. *Christian Attitudes toward War and Peace*. Nashville: Abingdon, 1960. This is the classic historical treatment of how Christians have responded to the issue of war and peace.

Cornell, Thomas C., Robert Ellsberg, and Jim Forest, eds. *A Penny a Copy: Readings from the Catholic Worker*. Maryknoll, N.Y.: Orbis, 1995. A variety of the contributors to the newspaper have their best articles here.

Day, Dorothy. *Dorothy Day: Selected Writings*. Edited by Robert Ellsberg. Maryknoll, N.Y.: Orbis, 1992. This is the best collection of Day's shorter writings.

Miller, Richard B., ed. *War in the Twentieth Century: Sources in Theological Ethics*. Louisville, KY: Westminster/John Knox, 1992. This volume brings together classic writings on war and peace. It includes John C. Ford's "The Morality of Obliteration Bombing" and John Courtney Murray's "Remarks on the Moral Problem of War."

National Conference of Catholic Bishops. *The Challenge of Peace: God's Promise and Our Response*. Washington, D.C.: U.S. Catholic Conference, 1983. This most read document on war and peace gives the most thorough treatment on just war and pacifism.

———. *The Harvest of Justice Is Sown in Peace*. Washington, D.C.: U.S. Catholic Conference, 1993. The U.S. bishops follow up CP with this tenth anniversary document that goes beyond its predecessor.

Nolan, Hugh, ed. *Pastoral Letters of the United States Catholic Bishops*. 6 vols. Washington, D.C.: U.S. Catholic Conference, 1983. These volumes contain all of the documents of the Catholic bishops from 1972 to 1983.

CHAPTER

21 The Future of Catholic Social Thought

JOHN A. COLEMAN, S.J.

INTRODUCTION

The title of this chapter subsumes several inquiries. Does Catholic social thought deserve a future? Not so long ago important Catholic voices suggested that the tradition was spent, had come down to us too much from on high, or had been ideologically misused. Any future for Catholic social thought will depend on a critical reading of the tradition. To answer this first inquiry, an effort must be made to understand the Catholic social tradition of thought and action, what it tried to do and on what grounds we judge that, on balance, it was an invaluable resource for Catholicism's—partially justly—ambivalent encounter with the modern world. Does it contain treasured elements that we want to bring forward into the future?

A second inquiry about the future of Catholic social thought looks to how one might bring the tradition forward to our own changed social and cultural settings and vastly altered sociological context, now more pluralistic (even within the Church) and more global. The conceptual understandings of social Catholicism grew out of reactions to nineteenth- and early twentieth-century phenomena of the rise of the democratic liberal state, the industrial revolution, and the welfare state. Adjusting these conceptual understandings to the new economic realities of globalization and its attendant consequences—mass migrations, the attenuation of state sovereignty, information technology, capital transfers across national borders, multinational corporate structures, and so forth—is a large task facing the future of Catholic social thought.[1] But, of course, no vital tradition ever remains stagnant. Any tradition should include a lively argument about how it is to move forward in changed economic, political, and cultural circumstances.

A final subset of questions asks: How does one bring the tradition of social Catholicism into a more vigorous dialogue with contemporary thought in ways which may show its relative wisdom, at least in some respects, compared to other competing modes of thought and praxis? And if the classic sociological and institutional carriers of social Catholicism have been vastly altered, what new cultural and institutional bearers/forgers of the tradition may be designed? Each of these three inquiries will be addressed.

IN WHAT DID THE TRADITION OF SOCIAL CATHOLICISM CONSIST?

Any serious assessment of the tradition of modern social Catholicism must come to grips with the following main themes. First, social Catholicism was always much more than "official Catholic Social Teaching" as found in the encyclicals and bishops' pastorals. Unofficial social thought and action profoundly fed into and was spawned by the "high" tradition as an originating charter. The tradition's major purchase on contemporary thought was also always more through the unofficial vehicles of independent social thought (e.g., the writings of Jacques Maritain, Emmanuel Mounier, Barbara Ward, John Courtney Murray, Heinrich Rommen) and the social movements (labor unions, journals of opinion, political parties, spiritual social justice movements, such as Pax Christi or the Catholic Worker movement) which it generated than through the official teaching itself, which got, at best, a respectful nod and, then, lay largely dormant. Notoriously, official Catholic social teaching was dubbed "our best kept secret."[2]

Second, for most of the period, from 1891 to 1965, official Catholic social thought was an essentially Eurocentered project with some ideological misuses. Yet it espoused an underlying distinctive anthropology that can be described as communitarian liberalism, and it allowed for alternative carriers in non-European settings. Third, the tradition was never really a "secular" modern project, untouched by motifs that came from the Bible and religious thought. Nor was the tradition ever fully a self-enclosed system. It engaged in a continuous subterranean dialogue with Marxist and liberal thought, both of which have left their imprint on social Catholicism. Each of these points needs to be parsed more closely.

Always More Than "Official Catholic Teaching" as Found in the Encyclicals

My own first encounters with social Catholicism came not from encyclicals but from my father who was a labor union official. My father's admiration for labor priests and his enthusiastic approval of courses at American Catholic universities that trained labor leaders spilled over into our household. When I was a boy, the rhetorical evocations of Leo XIII's *Rerum novarum* and Pius XI's *Quadragesimo anno* were aimed at eliciting ongoing church support for post–World War II San Francisco stevedores on strike or in arguing for the justice of health care and pension schemes for workers.

In my high school years, I came in contact with a Catholic Worker house, where we students helped serve on a soup line. At the Catholic Worker, I discovered the personalist communitarianism (influenced by Emmanual Mounier and Eric Gill) of Dorothy Day and her confrere Peter Maurin, himself a latter day *detritus*, thrown up upon American shores, from Le Sillon in France, which emerged as a French Catholic social movement in response to *Rerum novarum*.[3]

When later, as a Jesuit seminarian, I finally read and studied the papal social encyclicals through 1965, I tended at first (with the exception of *Pacem in terris*) to regard them as a kind of "background music," spiritual reading or motivational starters essentially, to evoke sufficient ecclesial justification to become involved in the Catholic Inter-Racial Councils, the civil rights movement, the farm workers' movement of César Chavez for unionization, and the antiwar movement during the period of the Vietnam War. Much more than the encyclicals, with their bloated Latinate ecclesiology-speak and their somewhat above-the-fray generalizing principles, I found the writings of unofficial thinkers within the tradition of social Catholicism cogent and engaging. Jacques Maritain's classic treatise, *Man and the State*, John Courtney Murray's *We Hold These Truths*, Barbara Ward's *The Rich Nations and the Poor Nations*, and the writings of Josef Pieper became for me, more than the encyclicals, the founding documents for a vision of social Catholicism in action.[4] These writers, akin to what Jean-Yves Calvez claims to have tried to do with his own magisterial *The Church and Social Justice*, or Charles Curran does in his recent book, *Catholic Social Teaching*, attempted to unlock a hitherto missed, or frequently hidden, unity in Catholic social thought.[5] They connected together and showed the contemporary relevance, in a way more compelling and coherent than the encyclicals had ever achieved in their episodic appearances over lapses of years, of such key Catholic concepts as human dignity, solidarity, subsidiarity, the common good, and distributive justice. They turned the often sprawling or merely evocative concepts of the encyclicals into a system of social thought.

The New Catholic Encyclopedia states that *Rerum novarum*, the first of the great social encyclicals, "marked the bestowal of significant papal approval on the then emergent Catholic social movement."[6] As Gordon Zahn has noted, this "opened the way to the further emergence and development of a wide range of other new Catholic social movements on a scale almost certainly beyond the eminent author's expectations," including the aforementioned Le Sillon movement in France and the emergence of Catholic labor unions in The Netherlands and Belgium.[7] Zahn insists further that

> the importance of that "bestowal" should not be minimized. Whatever else the encyclical achieved or did not achieve, it represents a distinct, though not yet dramatic, breakthrough that opened the way to that proliferation of social activity by predominantly lay-staffed and directed organizations that characterizes so much of Catholic social action today.[8]

Zahn privileges what he calls "Catholic social thought from below." He suggests that we read "official teaching" as primarily a response to earlier emergent Catholic social movements for reform, justice, and social betterment, and then see the official encyclical documents as, substantively, charter documents for subsequent Catholic-based social action. The most significant contributions made by or in the name of the church, for example, were movements supporting programs for economic justice, opposing the evils of racism and/or anti-Semitism, denouncing the strategies or kinds of weapons of modern war, and championing the priority of conscience. "All of these originated from 'below', from individuals and movements which, at first, were denied official recognition and support and obliged to overcome official suspicion and outright opposition. Later, often much later, these would become formally proclaimed policies of the church."[9]

If we take Zahn's principle as a hermeneutic lens to read even high "official" Catholic thought, we might read the encyclicals in a very different light. Behind and antedating *Rerum novarum* lay the developed economic conceptual thought of the Fribourg circle around Cardinal Gaspard Mermillod, the working-class pilgrimages to Rome of Leon Harmel, pressure for support for the laboring classes from the Opera dei Congressi in Italy, England's Cardinal Manning's championing of the London dock strikers, Baltimore's Cardinal Gibbons's interventions in Rome to prevent a condemnation of the American Knights of Labor as a secret society. Between the paragraphs of the document, one finds a careful balancing act, adjudicating between Catholic movements in Austria of romantic medievalists who rejected capitalism as immoral and espoused a Catholic variant of a labor theory of value in land (following Joseph Goeres and Karl von Vogelsang) and the ameliorators in Germany (such as the Solidarist School of economics around Heinrich Pesch and Bishop von Ketteler) who sought reform within an accepted capitalist framework. "Official" teaching did not suddenly emerge as some virgin birth, unrelated to the real Catholic social movements to which it responded.[10] Again, *Quadragesimo anno* hides, under its relatively unhistorical and transcultural conceptual language, much of its deep indebtedness to the close collaboration of its author, the Jesuit Oswald von Nell-Breuning, with German Catholic labor unions and the Center Party. Behind the encyclical also lies the thinking of the remarkable network of economists, historians, and moral theologians of the interdisciplinary seminar, the Koningswinter Circle, and, more largely, the socioeconomic thought of the Munchen-Gladbach school.[11]

Sections of this encyclical, especially the part devoted to the question of Catholics voting for labor parties, are quite specific to Germany. The remarks about socialism in *Quadragesimo anno*, that "no one can be at the same time a sincere Catholic and a true socialist," even a mitigated, democratic, non-Marxist socialist who, in Pius XI's words, has come gradually to hold tenets of reconstructed socialism "no longer different from the program of those who seek to reform human society according to Christian principles," were largely aimed at a small group of religious socialists in Germany (QA 120–26). These had urged collaboration between Catholics and socialists and threatened to siphon off some Catholic votes from the Center Party. Cardinal Bourne had to gain an exemption from this stricture in the English-speaking world since so many Catholics in Britain and Australia actually voted for the socialist labor parties. To understand another section of *Quadragesimo anno*, one that seems patient of a fascist interpretation of corporatism, the reader has to go behind the text to delicate relations between the Vatican and Mussolini's government.[12]

Later papal teaching also shows sensitivity to Catholic social movements from below, especially in Germany, Italy, and France. In response to a *Katholikentag* in Bochum in Germany in 1949, Pius XII showed a decided coolness toward workers' co-determination schemes in industry decisions. John XXIII in *Mater et magistra* reversed Pius's decision on this point. National councils bridging both labor and capital became key planks of the European Christian Democratic Parties in the Netherlands, Belgium, and Germany. The idea for "socialization" in *Mater et magistra* (59–67) seems to have been originally broached in a Semaine Sociale held in Grenoble in 1960. Clearly, John XXIII's famous opening to the left and cooperation with socialism in *Pacem in terris* (158–59) was closely articulated with moves by the Italian Christian Democratic Party to find new support for Italian socialist and Marxist groupings.

Nor is the social teaching of John Paul II unrelated to unofficial Catholic social movements. His long and often tortuous move toward the embrace of a "preferential but not exclusive love for the poor," as found in *Sollicitudo rei socialis* (42), makes no sense without a prior knowledge of the rise of liberation theology and the base community movement in the Latin American Church. As Peter Hebblethwaite has shown, portions of *Laborem exercens* make sense only in a Polish context of the rise of Solidarity as a struggle to de-link the Communist Party's monopoly over the labor movement, especially the sections that insist that labor unions "do not have the character of political parties struggling for power; they should not be subjected to the decision of political parties or have too close links to them" (LE 20). This "preferential but not exclusive love for the poor" made little sense, however, certainly as a universalizable tenet of Catholic social thinking, in the American, British, or continental context.[13] Even in the American context, a former official of the AFL-CIO, speaking in Rome after the publication of *Laborem exercens*, could only expostulate: "It is our involvement in politics that enables us to work for a government which will 'act against unemployment' and plan for providing work for all."[14]

Clearly, no robust exegesis of "official" encyclical teaching is possible that cuts it off from broader social movements to which it responds or which it evokes. Hence, we need a more encompassing term to enfold both "official" encyclical teaching (which cannot be simply privileged in ways that totally cut it off from unofficial thought and action) and the unofficial thought and movements. My own usage has always been to refer, more generally, to what I term *social Catholicism*. Naturally, this broader unity should show up in curricular material on social Catholicism. I could not conceive of teaching a course on social Catholicism without reference to historical works covering unofficial Catholic movements for justice and democracy, such as Paul Misner's *Social Catholicism in Europe* or Thomas Bokenkotter's *Church and Revolution: Catholics in the Struggle for Democracy and Social Justice*.[15] In courses on social Catholicism, especially for the more recent post–Vatican II period, papal encyclicals would be read as crystallizations of the wider social struggle and, moreover, be juxtaposed to episcopal social teaching in countries such as Chile, the United States, Canada, Kenya, and the Philippines.

A Eurocentric Project with Ideological Misuses Yet Still with Validity

The British writer Peter Hebblethwaite, in commenting on these issues, tends to dismiss the "official" encyclical tradition as primarily an ideological defense of the institutional interests of the Church. His sympathies lie entirely with M. D. Chenu's ground-breaking study, *La "doctrine sociale" de l'Église comme idéologie*. "By placing *doctrine sociale* in quotes, Chenu is suggesting that it is a figment; by calling it ideology, he is saying it is unacceptable."[16] Catholic social doctrine (CSD), as conceived and articulated in the 1930s, tended to lecture the world from the outside. It often stated abstract, atemporal principles that ignored the diversity of situations. It was, too frequently, nostalgic for a sort of vanishing rural, peasant world. It downplayed or ignored the fact of class conflict, which it tried to gloss over with a concept of the harmonious collaboration of all social classes. Dictators, such as Franco in Spain, Salazar in Portugal, and Vargas in Brazil, could even claim that they were implementing CSD. Hebblethwaite's summary judgment on CSD in the 1930s reads as follows: "The difficulty of CSD was this: it could fly so high in the stratosphere of principles that, from above, the whole landscape was flattened out and no details could be perceived or—more rarely—it could hew so close to the ground that its particular statement was too localized to be applicable elsewhere."[17]

There is no question in my mind that much if not most of official Catholic social thought, as found in the encyclical tradition, was tied to an essentially Eurocentered project and involved, at times, ideological misuse. Clearly, Anglo-Saxons could never have quite understood an emphasis in earlier social teaching on specifically confessional unions and political parties. They also never felt the same pincer movement from frequently rabid, anticlerical, organized political constellations of liberals on one flank and socialists on the other. It may well be, as Chenu claims, that the hiving-off of Catholics into separate confessional movements was wrong-headed: "To divide the labor movement in order to evangelize it was to make an error about the Gospel. For the real task was not to create a separate Catholic workers' group but to bring the Church to birth within the workers' movement as it actually existed."[18] In historical context, however, the Church's option seems much more understandable. Both liberalism and socialism, in the European contexts, were decidedly anticlerical.

Some severe cautions are called for before we issue blanket dismissals of official papal social thought and action as simply ideological, hopelessly abstract, and totally Eurocentered. It is worth recalling that it was social Catholics—and not socialists—who first introduced legislation in Germany and France regulating work hours, controlling the labor of minors, and supporting government subventions for the unemployed and aged. Nor were the Christian Democratic Parties in Europe, on balance, less helpful for forging a humane and democratic modern welfare state than their socialist counterparts. I, for one, retain a relatively balanced positive judgment, overall, of postwar Christian Democratic Parties in Europe, at least into the 1980s.[19] I also think the Chilean Christian Democratic Party of Eduardo Frei (and its reinstitutionalization after the Pinochet dictatorship) an arguably credible vehicle for ordered justice.[20]

Nor did the mainly Eurocentered official Catholic teaching neglect some larger global issues of world peace, disarmament, decolonialism, trade, debt and aid, and development concerns, as found in the series of remarkable papal encyclicals from *Pacem in terris* through *Populorum progressio* down to *Solicitudo rei socialis*. At times, this papal voice anticipated later movements of consensus around these sets of issues. Surely, only some more balanced judgment that social Catholicism, whatever its ambiguities, contributed to a more just and peaceful and democratic world—with a conspicuous concern for human rights, social participation, and human dignity—would lead us, in the first place, to questions about bringing the tradition forward into a new future in changed settings. Moreover, whatever a retrospective view on confessionally separate organizations may now yield, the Catholic unions, welfare institutions, and parties did serve as relatively effective social carriers for injecting the ideas and strategies of social Catholicism into the modern European setting. Not from nowhere (nor for ill!) did the European community just by accident fall upon the twin, decidedly Catholic, slogans of "the common good" and "subsidiarity" as the key catch phrases for conceiving of the European community as a true community and not just a trading bloc. It was a Catholic, Jacques Delors, longtime president of the European Union, who pushed these twin concepts for a Europe as a community of nations. It would be nearly unthinkable, for example, that those two concepts would serve as equally conspicuous slogans for social thought and policy in the more individualistic North American context.

Yet there is a bite in Louvain ethicist Johann Vertraeten's comments about the future of Catholic social thought, even in Europe. The earlier Catholic labor unions and Christian Democratic Parties have either merged into a secular grouping or are in disarray. As Verstraeten sees it, social Catholicism cannot survive without the discovery or creation of a new bearer of that tradition.

> When the social context in which Catholic social tradition concretizes itself becomes radically different from the past, when the classic forms of Catholic social movements disappear or become secularized, Catholic social thought would become meaningless, if it would maintain its original form and content without fundamental reinterpretations and adaptations.[21]

The Anthropological Core of the Tradition

We need to attend, somewhat, to the anthropological core of social Catholicism, what I like to call its communitarian liberalism, with its distinctive categories. Perhaps there is significant overlap with some other traditions of political and social thought on any given conceptual element, but the constellation and interpenetration of concepts is distinct: of human dignity, solidarity, subsidiarity, social justice, the option for the poor, the common good, justice as including a robust right to participatory voice, and so forth. Undoubtedly, social Catholicism represents a particular set of shared understandings about the human person, social goods, and their distributive arrangements. The anthropology of social Catholicism points to finitude, the social nature of the human, human autonomy and its concomitant responsibility, a sense of the human as both a product of original sin yet redeemed and called, in a vocation, to transform the material and social world. Even the notions of freedom in social Catholicism get tightly linked to a deep metaphor of human solidarity so that, as Michael J. Schuck has insisted, "Catholic social thinkers as a whole have retained a distinct understanding of freedom, equality, rights and justice in the modern world."[22] The four essential marks of sound Catholic social thought—distributive justice and the notions of solidarity, human dignity, subsidiarity, the preferential option for the poor—are ultimately connected and linked and indeed cannot be understood independently of each other.

Whether we see this unique Catholic constellation as the historic product of a determined social location in modern European history that wedged the practicing Catholics between the natural social and political constituencies of classic liberalism and Marxism, as I once tried to argue, or we locate the uniqueness in a theological anthropology (and, perhaps, we do not have to choose totally between these two alternatives), I have no doubt of the unique constellation of Catholic anthropological assumptions.[23] I was recently convinced once again of this uniqueness by an excellent book by Brian Stiltner, *Religion and the Common Good: Catholic Contributions to Building Community in a Liberal Society*.[24]

Stiltner engages in a wide-ranging conversation with the thought of John Locke, Ronald Dworkin, John Rawls, Michael Walzer, Michael Sandel, Alasdair MacIntyre, and Charles Taylor. (The latter two are prominent Catholic philosophers with sympathies for a kind of communitarian liberalism.) Stiltner himself characterizes social Catholicism's core notion of the common good as a theory of "communal liberalism." It is a liberalism inasmuch as modern Catholicism espouses procedures and norms for the protection of human rights and champions freedom and pluralism as positive social goods in their own right. It is a "'communal'" liberalism because it suggests a political theory that justifies policies of freedom, tolerance, and pluralism by reference to the good of the political community and its subcommunities, not only by reference to the rights of individuals."[25]

Drawing on the work of Jacques Maritain in his classic treatise, *The Person and the Common Good*, Stiltner argues that we exist in and for communities (which are not, as some strands in liberal theory often have it, merely instrumental for personal autonomies). The very human capacity for the engagement with community is itself a positive perfection of personality. The dignity of persons can be realized only in community, and genuine community, in its turn, can only exist where the substantial freedom and the dignity of the human person are secured. Hence, Catholic notions of the dignity of the human person, based on both human needs and human moral agency, get linked to the common good. But these concepts of dignity and freedom protect against any one-sided smothering of human agency by the tradition. They are the reason Stiltner denominates the Catholic theory of the common good as a communal "liberalism." I return to this notion of the common good later, but let me round out the evocation of Stiltner's remarkable work by his formulation of the Catholic notion of the common good, which, insists Stiltner, is both a procedural and a substantive good.

The modern Catholic conception of the ideal common good involves the mutually beneficent relation of social actors (labor, capital, agriculture, consumers, governmental agents) oriented toward supporting and nourishing diverse and good institutions. This ideal requires procedures for cooperation and dialogue within a pluralistic democratic framework and substantive norms such as defending human dignity through legally anchored rights that provide opportunity for access to participation in society's common life through both its public and voluntary institutions. "The broad definition of the common good in modern Catholic writings is beneficial because it is flexible enough to accommodate developments in moral sensibilities and to be applied to various socio-political contexts. It is also specific enough to guide political and social choices within a pluralistic, liberal society."[26]

A characteristic modern liberal complaint about any notion of the common good can be found in John Rawls's viewpoint in his book, *Political Liberalism*: "A public and workable agreement on a conception of the good can be maintained only by the oppressive use of state power."[27] Here, Catholic notions of subsidiarity guarantee pluralism in any deliberative democratic discourse about public goods and shared interests. For subsidiarity is, fundamentally, a plea for pluralism. As Stiltner reminds us:

> The plurality of associations is a consequence of human finitude and a guard against *hubris*. In sum, pluralism is central to the common good because different communities center on the pursuit of different components of the complex human good; because institutional diversity facilitates extensive participation in social life [a strong element of the Catholic component of the good society is, after all, justice as participation]; and because no one association [one presumes Stiltner includes here also the Church] can claim to be a perfect community.[28]

In sum, in the Catholic understanding, the search for the common good takes place within and not against the experience of plurality. Questions about the common good can only be ruled out, as Rawls tried to do, if a firmer notion of a deliberative, as opposed to a mere interest-balancing adversarial democracy, is also ruled out.[29] Do we just broker the demands of competing interest groups or can we actually deliberate together? As David Hollenbach notes: "A good community is a place where people are genuinely interdependent on each other through participation in, discussion concerning, and decision making about their common purposes."[30]

But those who see a distinctive and valuable anthropological constellation around a notion of communal liberalism (or, if you prefer, personalism) cannot rest content with this splendid legacy taken alone. For Johann Verstraeten forces us to face head-on the Weberian point: ideas have impact in history and on society only through a distinctive institutionalization and carrier units (what Max Weber called *trager* groups). If the older forms of these have been lost, eclipsed, or secularized, there is no way that a mere evocation of the splendid Catholic anthropology will have much contemporary impact on politics or social policy. Like liberalism, critical theory, feminism, and other political viewpoints, social Catholicism will need vehicles that bring it, with legitimacy and credibility, into the policy arenas.[31] Only through a set of institutions will Catholicism generate the sort of middle axioms to guide social policy that flow from its unique anthropological legacy.

A Complex Ambivalent Relationship with Secular Thought

One major shift in Catholic social thought that occurred between the papacy of John XXIII and that of John Paul II focuses on the reintroduction of more explicitly theological elements into the natural law tradition, which drove much of the papal teaching from Leo XIII through John XXIII. Verstraeten alludes to this shift when he claims that we have to overcome a crisis in contemporary social Catholicism by appealing for inspiration not only "from other traditions of interpretation and inquiry but from a living relation to the text of the Bible." He suggests that Catholic social thought contains powerful, biblically inspired "root metaphors which change our pre-reflective fundamental understanding of social reality."[32] Surely, solidarity that is rooted in both God's covenant in creation and God's universal salvific will for redemption, as well as in our common solidarity in the sordidness of sin, is one such metaphor. And the preferential option for the poor, which is not a distillate of reason alone but flows from the biblical God's option for the poor, serves as a second rich root metaphor in the imagination of social Catholicism.

Lurking beneath the modern Catholic reliance upon natural law, with its emphasis on rational method, clarity, and certainty, remains a residual appeal to biblical foundations. What Thomas Gilby said of Aquinas's ethical teaching in the *Summa* is no less true of *Rerum novarum*: "That it is integrated in *sacra doctrina*. The teaching of the gospel revelation and its full import can be appreciated only when it is read as a living part of this organic whole."[33] To be sure, when less guarded, classic social Catholicism in the pre–Vatican II period veered, on the surface at least, toward a tendency to overstress its philosophical aspect.

Larger issues about the role of scripture in Christian social ethics and the retrieval of a distinctively Catholic notion of natural law would each take an entirely separate chapter to explore in full. I am much informed in my response to these two issues by Jean Porter's study, *Natural and Divine Law: Reclaiming the Tradition for Christian Ethics*, and her unpublished paper, "Catholic Social Thought and the Natural Law Tradition."[34]

Porter is quite dubious about the modern project (from Pufendorf in the seventeenth century to modern attempts by John Finnis and others), whether secular or Catholic, of finding a purely autonomous natural law that is said to generate a universally valid morality that would be recognized, as such, by all rational persons.[35] She shares, with Alasdair MacIntyre, a sense that all reason is tradition-dependent and historically specific.[36]

> I am not persuaded by those who claim to isolate a "tradition-independent" core of the natural law tradition because every such account that I have seen appears to me to be either philosophically implausible or so abstract as to be without much theoretical force. Secondly, and more fundamentally, this claim simply does not seem to me to do justice to what we know about the evolution of the natural law tradition.

Yet Jean Porter is no more enamored of the currently popular idea of a purely Christian morality (perhaps most strongly associated in recent years with the work of John Milbank).[37] "A purely Christian morality which is self-contained, self-justifying and unintelligible to everyone else seems to me to be as unrealistic as the Enlightenment ideal of a universal morality, which is its mirror image."

Medieval theology (both in its theologians and in canonists such as Gratian) took up a tradition, largely pre-Christian in origins, of the Stoic natural law. Yet the medieval Scholastics expressed their distinctive concept of the natural law in terms derived from both Patristics and classical sources (principally Cicero). The Scholastics said of the natural law that it was a product of reason.

> Yet at the same time, they interpreted reason itself in theological and, ultimately, scriptural terms. That is why they did not hesitate to draw on Scripture as well as rational arguments in order to determine the concrete content of the natural law, and it is also why they did not attempt to derive a system of natural law thinking out of purely natural data or rationally self-evident intuitions.

It is only the modern exponents of natural law who attempt to do this, and their project seems to have failed. It is the theologically informed medieval notion of natural law rather than its modern, semiautonomous, rational variant in some forms of social Catholicism, which Porter wants to revive. She sees the medieval natural law tradition (and the residues of that tradition that passed over to social Catholicism in the nineteenth century) as less "secular," "modern," or purely "natural" than appears.

> While the scholastics do ground their account of the natural law in naturally given aspects of human existence, these natural givens are interpreted within a framework of theological convictions. The scholastics appeal to scriptural and theological concepts to determine which aspects of human nature should be given greatest weight morally and to guide their formulation of specific moral judgments. This process of theologically guided interpretation, in turn, led to the emergence of a social doctrine which still provides the basis for Catholic social teachings.

The validity of Porter's account becomes readily apparent in two central Catholic natural law propositions that form an integral part of social Catholicism: human dignity and private property. Catholic notions of a radical moral equality, inherent in its appeals to human dignity, imply the theological notion of the human as an *imago Dei*. It simply may be impossible, as the legal scholar Michael J. Perry argues, to ground a concept of the sacred inviolability of the human conscience and will (despite Kantian and neo-Kantian efforts to do so) on purely rational appeals to autonomous moral agency.[38]

Similarly, the Catholic natural law account for private property becomes inextricably enmeshed with the patristic *dictum* that the earth is intended, in God's creative purposes, for the sustenance of all persons, which puts a social mortgage on any purely private concept of property. Only if we engage in totally tendentious dichotomous thinking that assumes (1) *either* there is a morality grounded in human nature as the product of autonomous practical reasoning or we have nothing but purely contingent and culturally bound moral codes, and that (2) *either* we can establish a purely Christian morality derived solely from biblical narrative or we must fall back on some variant of a universally valid morality derived from the Enlightenment—only with such dichotomies do we land in hopeless *aporia*. But an alternative to these dichotomies exists. Rather sensibly, Jean Porter suggests that matters are much more complex than these dichotomies would suggest.

The tradition of the natural law is not an exclusively or distinctly Christian tradition. Many of its elements are clearly pre-Christian in origin. Jews, secularists, and Muslims have espoused their own variants of natural law. Yet the natural law was adopted by early Christian thinkers for specifically theological reasons and transformed by this appropriation into a distinctively Christian variant of the doctrine. Thus, this Christian tradition of natural law cannot be said to generate a universally valid morality which would be instantly recognized as such by all rational persons. But neither is it so fundamentally tradition-bound as to be unintelligible to nonbelievers or those in other traditions. There are overlapping conceptual elements with other traditions of thought. Because it is grounded in a construal (albeit a theologically informed one) of our common humanity and shaped by genuine (if contextualized) moral reasoning, we have every reason to expect it to be intelligible even to those whose religious and cultural traditions differ from ours. As Jean Porter sees it:

> Even though the natural law is a historically specific tradition of enquiry, it does have points of entrée into public discourse, both in our own society and in the wider forum of the world community. It does not offer us a universally valid morality or even a systematic program for moral enquiry. Nonetheless, it does offer us starting points for dialogue, together with a set of moral ideals to which we [Catholics] are committed, and which we can offer to others as attractive and persuasive ideals.

It would be difficult to see a future variant of social Catholicism as a retrieval of classic social Catholicism if it rejected the notion of natural law altogether or reinterpreted it in such general terms that it becomes the equivalent, reductively, to moral reason as such. This would be tantamount not to some retrieval of the tradition but to the start of an entirely new tradition of social thought. In so doing, we would run the risk of cutting ourselves off from a tradition of moral reflection that has played a central role in Catholic social thought.

To be sure, the distinctively modern conception of an autonomous natural law that dominated some strands of Catholic moral thinking until Vatican II stands in need of some fundamental revisions. It has to deal much more with the Council's call for a renewed attention to the scriptural roots of ethics (which a retrieval of the more medieval sophisticated use of natural law addresses) and to the very historicity ingredient in the notion of human nature. A totally unchanging human nature seems difficult to accept. Yet, as Jean Porter argues:

> In my view, this [i.e., "by and large, Catholic theologians have gone beyond critical revision to reject the idea of natural law altogether or to reinterpret it in very general terms equivalent to moral reason, *tout court*"] is an unfortunate development; all the more so since new developments in medical technology and family relations have led to a wide-spread reconsideration of the moral status of human reason in the wider society. The time has come for a Catholic retrieval of the natural law tradition.

Encounters with Marxism and Liberalism

It has always struck me how many seminal voices in social Catholicism diligently studied the classic Marxist texts: von Ketteler with the socialist Lasalle; Maritain, Chesterton, and Dorothy Day, who brought socialist backgrounds to their conversions; von Nell-Breuning and Mounier, who also pored over their Marx. Their intent was not simple refutation; they emulated aspects of their adversary. Moreover, even in a context mainly of polemics, extensive engagement in dialogue with an alternative mode of thinking begins to seep into one's own categories.

On the other side, an extensive dialogue—again, not only polemical—with liberal thought lies behind the work of Maritain and Murray. Clearly, the postwar Catholic human rights strategy, first enunciated in the encyclical tradition by John XXIII but long anticipated by unofficial Catholic participation in postwar debates in UNESCO and the discussions over the UN Charter of Rights, owes much to this dialogue with liberalism. Selectively, social Catholicism has incorporated elements from these two competing modern ideologies, even if, generally, basing them on distinctively Catholic philosophical and theological grounds. All the major liberal liberties are there, even if they get supplemented in ways not usually found in liberalism, by a corresponding positive notion of social rights to subsistence more akin to the Marxist tradition.[39]

This inner dialogue within the tradition of social Catholicism with liberalism and socialism and its renewal through this dialogue means that social Catholicism does not lack even now for interesting secular interlocutors sympathetic to many elements in the Catholic constellation of social thought. Others besides Catholics see themselves as communitarian liberals. They can and do provide allies for social Catholics on policy issues.[40] Moreover, the long, two-sided, sometimes polemical, sometimes sympathetic dialogue of social Catholicism with both liberal and Marxist social thought, and social Catholicism's subsequent refining of its own thought as a result of this dialogue, puts a brake on any too robust claims for an utter uniqueness to the conceptual apparatus of the Catholic tradition. Sometimes, an overly aggressive emphasis on Catholic distinctiveness can actually feed into making social Catholicism more peripheral to contemporary discourse than it needs to be. If, on balance, we think the tradition of social Catholicism worthy of retrieval and bringing forward into the future, we need also to face a second question about what will serve as its institutional carriers.

NEW CHALLENGES AND CONTEXTS FOR BRINGING THE TRADITION FORWARD INTO THE FUTURE

Three issues in particular feed into discussions about a possible newly grounded retrieval of social Catholicism: (1) the changed economic and political context of a more interdependent world (especially after the cold war) and globalization; (2) the changed ecclesial climate for understanding and enacting social Catholicism since Vatican II; and (3) the collapse or inner secularization of older social carriers of the tradition, which forces us to imagine new forms of institutionalization and social carriers for the tradition. I address each of these briefly.

Globalization

The classic corpus of social Catholicism assumed the sovereign nation-state, although from John XXIII on it pressed for international and regional institutions to anchor a more global common good. Classic social Catholicism dealt with issues of interclass conflict and cooperation and distributive justice largely within the context of national, relatively self-contained economies. Clearly, the end of the cold war and the new globalization force social Catholicism, as they do the whole world, to rethink its received economic categories. Luckily, the new economic phenomena of transnational capital and global finance allow social Catholicism, itself embodied in a transnational Church, to address these changed realities with fresh energies, relatively unencumbered by polemical freights.[41] What might be some of the resources it can bring to the debate about globalization?

The reality and directionality of globalization are much debated. Some simply applaud its current contours as the wave of the future. Others oppose it as a new form of savage capitalism, a free market international integration that actually causes social disintegration in the developing world. There are immense tensions in the new global interconnections. On the one hand, those in a position to influence the design and operation of an emerging global order have a responsibility to ensure that it satisfies basic requirements of justice. Among the new challenges that globalization brings are conflicts with "the traditional view that the international order is a normatively neutral domain whose rules lie beyond the competence of individuals, nations or international actors to alter—a view supported by the 'realist' model of international relations as a struggle for power which tends to encourage an abdication of responsible politics at the international level."[42]

Globalization promises to offer new avenues for wealth creation and development in the poorer nations. It holds out the possibility of an integrated economy and an integrated system of information to make the world one global village. But it also carries threats as well as promises, for both developed and undeveloped nations. The main political challenge from globalization is the eroding of the traditional functions of the nation-state without clear alternatives to its welfare and regulatory functions, "most important its role of securing social justice through welfare programs and, thereby, undermining the legitimacy of democratic decision-making within the nation-state."[43] It also threatens to give rise to global interdependences in which there is an increasing mismatch between the set of agents who make the economic decisions and those who have to live with the ecological, cultural, and social consequences of such decisions. We can expect, for some time, contestations about the impact of globalization.

Yet the global reach of telecommunications and newsgathering institutions makes economic, environmental, health, and security crises—as well as human rights violations—instantaneously public. Pressure on international actors can be generated to deal with these issues in a humane and democratic fashion. There resides a hope that, in the long run, these global developments around the emergence of international nongovernmental movements and information technology "may contribute to the emergence of a global civil society of nongovernmental organizations, transnational networks, movements and the like, and a corresponding global public opinion that could generate pressure for transnational political initiatives to address structural inequities in the global political order."[44] So, globalization remains fraught with both promise and peril.

Bryan Hehir has recently suggested that while globalization has its own logic, it does not have its own ethic. In some sense, those who evoke the term *globalization* insist that it is about going faster, farther, and further in making the world one economic and information society. But to what ends? With what consequences? With whose democratic input? These are the questions the tradition has resources to pose forcefully.

In bringing social Catholicism forward to address a new globalized economic, military, and political order, the teaching will have to address new social actors and new issues. In brief, any viable international order will address three different layers of issues. First, an international order must address security and military issues under new conditions of international forces of terrorism. While the nation-state remains, and will remain, an important actor in this arena, recent debates about terrorism and war suggest new limits to the sovereign state. In Kosovo and elsewhere, we have argued that humanitarian interventions can be justified in the name of the common good. Faced with genocide and crimes against humanity, most of the world (with the United States as an exception) now veers toward an International Criminal Court as a necessary mechanism to punish crimes against humanity. Much of the debate about the 2003 war in Iraq involved the need for the UN's control or crucial mediation on forging a military/security order against terrorism. It cannot be the unilateral imposition by one imperial nation of its blueprint for a world order that serves its interests.

Second, an international order must address the issue of political economy. Here the state remains a residual actor but there is a profound mix of new transnational actors in financial and productive markets for goods and services. At present, some agencies (the International Bank, the International Monetary Fund, the World Trade Organization) provide some sense of an ordered mechanism for decisions. But as recent critiques of these organizations have shown (I am thinking of the work of economists such as Amartya Sen and Joseph Stiglitz or the scathing critiques of the financier George Soros), these agencies have not always taken sufficiently into account any sense of an option for the poor, subsidiarity (the respect for the autonomous input of organizations of civil society), or any broader sense of the common good.[45] One task of social Catholicism is to devise a more coherent account of the proper role and limits of states, international organizations, and nonstate actors (corporations, unions, nongovernmental organizations) in promoting an international common good. Catholic concerns for workers should alert the tradition to the *lacunae* ingredient in a growing protection of property (real, capital, and intellectual) worldwide, without corresponding concern and protection for rights of workers.

Third, an international order must address the issue of thinking globally. Since Catholic social thought has always thought institutionally, there is a deficit in the present world order of globalization to deal with a range of issues: health and disease, migration of labor, the rights of workers, the environment. Increasingly, nonstate actors, so-called NGOs (nongovernmental organizations), play an important role in debates about globalization. How should we conceive of their moral place in thinking about an international common good? Clearly, social Catholicism has begun to enter these debates. Church groups were vigorously present in the fall of 2002 for the Johannesburg UN Summit on Sustainable Development. The Vatican and other church groups have played key roles in the Jubilee movement to reduce debt in Third World countries. It is too soon to give a settled blueprint for how social Catholicism will address the new questions of globalization, but these questions are decidedly a key part of the agenda for its development in the twenty-first century. However, precisely because it is a well-organized transnational institution with roots, membership, and social and educational institutions in every continent, the Catholic Church itself, as a global actor, seems poised to have important information, insights, and resources to address many of the growing issues of globalization.

The Changed Ecclesial Climate

Gaudium et spes introduced a new ecclesial element that made clear that official social teaching could not be overly privileged against unofficial forms of social Catholicism: "With the help of the Holy Spirit, it is the task *of the entire people of God*, especially pastors and theologians, to hear, distinguish and interpret the many voices of our age, and to judge them in the light of the divine word" (GS 44). Vatican II also changed some of the metaphors of the Church. No longer "over against the world" or representing a fortress besieged by a fundamentally hostile world, the Church joins all men and women of good will in seeking justice and the common good. Cooperative efforts and not just distinctively Catholic struggles are called for. Vatican II tended to define the social task as Paul VI put it in his encyclical, *Populorum progressio*, as throwing the light of the gospel on the social questions of our age. The "signs of the time," then, could no longer be discerned universally. They had to be studied on the local level. Finally, in his remarkable apostolic letter, *Octogesima adveniens*, Paul VI declared:

> In the face of such widely varying situations, it is difficult for us to utter a unified message and put forward a solution which has universal validity. Such is not our ambition, nor is it our mission. It is up to the Christian communities to analyze with objectivity the situation which is proper to their own country, to shed on it the light of the Gospel's unalterable words and to draw principles of reflection, norms of judgment and directives for action from the social teaching of the Church. It is up to these Christian communities, with the help of the Holy Spirit, in communion with the bishops who hold responsibility and in dialogue with other Christian brethren and all men of good will, to discern the options and commitments which are called for in order to bring about the social, political and economic changes seen in many cases to be urgently needed. (OA 4)

Many thought that these words of Paul VI sounded the death-knell for international social Catholicism. I do not agree. The Vatican still has an indispensable role to play to help elucidate and propagate the more generalized principles of reflection, norms of judgment, and directives for action (as John Paul II did in his encyclicals on work and on the market). Clearly, Paul VI's call for ecumenical and even wider solidarities in investigating and addressing social questions does justify a broad role indeed for unofficial Catholic action. It suggests limits, by subsidiarity, on any overly intrusive Vatican interference in local discernments of the signs of the times and the public policies to address them. Palpably, the bishops of the United States saw these words as a mandate for their very particular treatments of U.S. nuclear policy and of the American economy in the

1980s. More recently, the bishops of the Pacific Northwest and of western Canada have found their own voice to address development and ecological issues along the Columbia River Watershed.[46] Larger global issues, frequently lost to the purview of more local efforts or too caught up in perduring national self-interests, still justify a more international approach to global economic issues such as one finds in *Sollicitudo rei socialis*

Clearly, as Charles Curran has suggested, we need to address not just the content but the style of international church social teaching. He argues that such Vatican documents should: (1) raise questions we all can and must grapple with; (2) show in the documents a genuine dialogue with others outside the Church; (3) build on national and international documents of regional or national bishops' conferences; (4) arise out of a process of consultation, akin to the hearings used by the American bishops' pastoral letters of the 1980s; and (5) represent and listen to the excluded and marginal voices.[47]

Sociological Carriers of the Tradition

A vital tradition is brought forward only as it really addresses the new questions or signs of the times. A tradition of social thought is challenged to translate this address, beyond large generalities couched in anthropological assumptions, into policy and middle-axioms to guide policy studies, advocacy, and social choices. Briefly stated, policy generation usually stems from institutions that have both a legitimate interested stake in the outcomes of and an expertise and experience to bring to questions of social policy and national legislation. In the United States, the Catholic vehicles to translate social Catholicism into middle-level policy are essentially rooted in five institutional realities.

1. The U.S. Conference of Catholic Bishops (USCCB) has a service and advocacy bureaucracy that serves the U.S. bishops. It maintains close liaison with and on occasion seeks to correlate closely with the nationwide networks of Catholic institutions. The Bishops' Conference service bureaucracy maintains an active lobbying arm that testifies before Congress at every level of some legislative bills' career, suggests at times specifically worded amendments to legislation, and enters into alliances with other lobby groups to affect policy. Many of these lobbying efforts, to be sure, are addressed to protecting the self-interest of Catholic institutions or highly salient Catholic moral issues such as abortion and the protection of marriage. But the Bishops' Conference has also widely engaged in debates on foreign policy, immigration, penal law, foreign aid and welfare, and health care reforms. To justify episcopal support for their middle-level yet often quite specific policy advocacy, the Bishops' Conference's lobbyists need to show a close connection to anthropological presuppositions of social Catholicism. Outside observers of Washington lobby groups give the Bishops' Conference high marks for its serious research, access, impact, and effectiveness, at least among American religious lobbies.[48]

2. Twenty-eight of the separate state units maintain a State Catholic Conference, serving the conference of bishops for that state, which also lobbies state legislatures, enters into formal and informal coalitions, and works on amending bills on education, health, welfare, immigration, and penal policy. In Maine and Maryland, for example, the State Catholic Conferences drafted the welfare bills that were adopted by the state legislatures. In California and Washington, the state conferences played key roles in opposing successfully referenda that would have allowed physician-assisted suicides of the terminally ill. They have also worked strongly to extend health care benefits to the poor.[49]

3. The large national networks of Catholic social institutions (schools, hospitals, charities) wield considerable clout during debates about public policy. Catholic schools represent the largest non-public school system in the country and have shown interest in policy questions, for example, about vouchers and about ways inner-city schools can facilitate minority advancement to higher education. A helpful recent development has been the attempts to provide a systematic introduction to Catholic social

thought throughout the Catholic school curriculum. At a number of Catholic universities, specialized centers (e.g., The John Ryan Center for Catholic Social Thought at the University of St. Thomas in St. Paul, Notre Dame's Kroc Center for International Peace, the University of Santa Clara's Markula Center for Ethics and Policy) now focus on bringing forward the Catholic social tradition and applying it to concrete policy. Attempts have been made to link Catholic social thinking to business and law school curricula at universities.

Catholic hospitals similarly represent over 10 percent of all hospitals and in some places, like California, the Catholic health care system is the largest in the state. Catholic Charities U.S.A. (and its local affiliates) is the largest nongovernmental dispenser of social welfare services in the United States. Each of these national networks of Catholic institutions has engaged, in the last decade or so, in serious ongoing reflections on their Catholic identity in a pluralistic setting of service. Each of these institutional systems, especially Catholic Charities U.S.A., has tended to link its Catholic identity rather closely to the Catholic tradition of social thought as it touches issues of service, the common good, pluralism, and human dignity. Catholic Charities U.S.A. arguably wielded a seminal public policy voice on the issue of welfare reform. In a relatively recent book on the welfare reform debates, Thomas Massaro shows how the anthropology of social Catholicism gets translated into middle-level policy axioms by the USCCB, State Catholic Conferences, and Catholic Charities U.S.A.[50] Similar studies might show much the same for the Catholic engagement on issues of immigration reform, housing, health care, the death penalty, and penal reform.

4. Other groups, such as diocesan peace and justice offices, autonomous associations such as PAX Christi USA, Network (an autonomous Catholic lobbying group, founded by religious sisters, for the issues of the poor), The Center of Concern, The Catholic League for Civil Rights, and others, also enter this institutional mix as carriers of social Catholicism. I remember clearly, during the debates among the bishops that led up to their adoption of their pastoral on peace, how Pax Christi members, meeting in a group, carefully monitored the draft texts and pressed the bishops, in some cases with success, for emendations in the text more favorable to their nonviolent social stands. Again, we see in this example ways in which unofficial social Catholicism and more official forms mesh. As another example, the Los Angeles archdiocese's Peace and Justice Commission has played key roles in a number of issues: (1) the attempt at gaining a living wage ordinance in Los Angeles; (2) debates about the ethical issues involved in a referendum to allow parts of the city of Los Angeles to secede; (3) public debate/discussion with the president of the World Bank about the Jubilee Justice Debt relief program for the poorest debtor nations.

5. The four major national networks of church-based community organizing groups (all four of Catholic provenance) work to empower local citizens to hold their elected officials accountable for the deliverance of social services (e.g., garbage collection, neighborhood clinics, and housing rehabilitation), police protection, public safety, and democratic participative access. Most of the church-based national community-organizing networks (despite their interdenominational and interfaith constituencies) appeal to elements of social Catholicism—human dignity, subsidiarity and local control, the common good—to make their case in public. While mainly local in scope, in some places the church-based community organizing groups have effectively moved state or municipal governments to enact living-wage statutes, reform access to low-cost housing, or enable charter schools under parental control.[51]

In sum, while many of the earlier carriers for social Catholicism have collapsed or become secularized, vehicles still exist to help turn the anthropology of this tradition into concrete policy initiatives. Building upon currently existing vehicles and imagining even further alternatives—coalitions with labor, ecumenical efforts as combating sweatshops, organizing with social agencies for welfare reform—allows social Catholicism sufficient carriers to move it toward the future.

CATHOLIC SOCIAL THOUGHT IN DIALOGUE WITH CONTEMPORARY THOUGHT

A final task for the future of Catholic social thought will envision new ways to relate it to other competing modes of thought and praxis. One presumes that—without, God help us, any triumphalism—proponents of social Catholicism will try to evince the relative superiority of the tradition in addressing certain policy questions. I want to offer brief comments on three concepts within social Catholicism that call for more such dialogue and development: (1) Catholic personalism; (2) exclusionary norms that set the rules of public discourse as necessarily neutral as to any determinative conception of the good and, also, necessarily, secular; and (3) the concept of the common good.

Catholic Personalism

Over time, our public discourse in the liberal democracies has come increasingly to rest on an expansive and unnuanced account of personal autonomy that often decouples rights and responsibilities or denies any shared or public goods. The Catholic insistence on a communitarian or solidaristic understanding of the person serves to correct the imbalance of modern market economies, often driven by a reductionist notion of the person as an isolated individual consumed with maximizing self-interest. This one-sided emphasis on personal autonomy almost always lets choice trump commitment. It is inherently tradition eroding. Moreover, an atomistic and individualistic notion of rational choice theory, perhaps inadequate even to explain the markets that served as its original focus, has moved aggressively into the arenas of jurisprudence and social policy, and is being used as an explanatory theory for understanding in the social sciences.

By contrast, I do not think it is only by chance that two of the most forceful exponents of a more communitarian understanding of the self among contemporary political philosophers are the prominent Catholic voices of Alasdair MacIntyre and Charles Taylor.[52] Social Catholicism has something unique and definite to offer to contemporary liberalism to help it move into a more communitarian set of correctives for its notion of a disembedded autonomous self. It will need to press this issue in dialogue precisely because the policy implications of a one-sided sense of personal autonomy may be eroding any more robust sense of community in modern society.[53]

Exclusionary Norms of Public Discourse

A set of political philosophers, especially in the Anglo-Saxon world, notably Richard Rorty, John Rawls, and Ronald Dworkin, have been promulgating norms of "public reason" that demand that this reason be totally secular, construed entirely in procedural terms, and divorced from any substantive sense of the good or of human flourishing.[54] It strikes me that this notion of public reason, put forth by the "procedural liberals," stacks the deck against those who would speak from their comprehensive doctrines, constraining them before they speak with the condition that their arguments should be "reasonable," that is, construed according to the Rawlsian or some equivalent method. The opponents of this putatively "neutral" secular reasoning in public are correct, it seems to me, in seeing that it is neither quite as neutral nor as purely procedural as it claims. The neutralists smuggle in their highly particular conception of the good of unencumbered agents, privileging choice over commitments or tradition.[55] To be fair, however, to what dialogue on this issue can, in fact, achieve, John Rawls tended to backtrack somewhat in his last years, allowing some (it still strikes me as too restricted) "public" role for religion in the public square, precisely because of a contested yet civil conversation with those who are religious about his thesis.[56]

Social Catholicism should make common cause with adherents of other religious groups and with those many, if not legion, liberals who think that a genuine deliberative democracy should not impose gag rules on voices in public. Nor should some ideal of "public reason" dictate, in advance, what kind of reorientation of nonpublic reasons might be permitted to have an effect on "public" (i.e., in this construal, explicitly secular) reason and the content of justice. Many of the now "secular" concepts of the West, after all, came originally from a religious provenance. Even today some people have been evoking some notion of "societal forgiveness," whose origin is undoubtedly religious, as a "secular" concept for the healthy or good society. If Rawls's usually stated stringent rules for exclusively secular reason in public obtained, such a transfer from particular religious discourse to a more general secular usage would never be warranted, perhaps with some real social losses. Just because "the preferential option for the poor," for example, is ineradicably religious does not preclude it being urged in policy discussion, or its adoption (perhaps for secular resonance) by those who do not share the biblical source.

Clearly, Catholic social thought should be well poised to claim the right of religious language to a legitimate access to open public discourse. The Vatican II document on religious liberty insisted that it belongs to the very notion of religious freedom that religious bodies should be able to expound policy proposals in public that show the implications of their beliefs for social action and policy. It is possible, as José Casanova has argued, for there to be a public religion (which follows the rules of a deliberative democracy and helps to anchor the institutions of civil society) in the modern world.[57]

Even many liberals see the moves of the procedural liberals to ban all religious discourse from the public arena as a betrayal of the deepest liberal principles, related to freedom of speech. People should speak in public deliberations from their deepest motives and insights. Naturally, in order to persuade, they need to translate their religious concepts into terms that are meaningful and intelligible (which is not the same as per se secular or persuasive). But they do not need, as the procedural liberals have been increasingly insisting, to put gag rules on their biblical metaphors or to excise what evangelicals in America who are facing this stricture refer to as "Christianese." If all reason is tradition dependent, then religious thinkers, so long as they construe an ideal of true reason that remains, at least in principle, public and open to debate and genuinely intends to reach beyond the circle of fellow believers, need not and should not abandon their tradition as the very price of taking part in public discourse. But social Catholicism also needs to move out of a ghetto and speak vigorously with secular strands of jurisprudence and policy thought.

The Common Good

The retrieval of the concept of the common good in contemporary society is more fraught with peril than Catholics usually acknowledge. The common good can be defined as those societal and economic conditions that (1) guarantee access to any goods that are, as such, public goods; (2) enable true social participation in the goods of society, even goods that are not per se public; (3) establish the possibility for (at least minimal) human flourishing both as individuals and in one's fated or chosen groups. The common good is seen as an ensemble of enabling conditions for the societal flourishing of human potential. It is an institutional reality. But many of our contemporaries are often wary of appeals to the common good either because the definition of public goods is always contested or contestable, or because power is unequal in society so that alleged "common good" arrangements are, often, class-privileged institutional settings, or because pluralism and freedom are viewed as inalienable values in themselves. Jane Mansbridge speaks to these dangers inherent in an evocation of a common good. She notes how the public good is a dangerous concept. When people act in their own self-interest they inhabit a terrain in which everyday experience gives them relatively reliable messages on what is good for them. To speak of a public good is to ask them to leave this terrain for one in which, because uncertainty about its meaning and contours is far greater, authoritative others often play a far greater role in suggesting what the public good should be.

Two sources of influence pose dangers in discussions of the public good. On the one hand, individuals and groups who appeal to the exclusivity and hatred that may be a shadow part of their group loyalty are dangers to a capacious sense of the public good. Their sense is too restricted and exclusive. On the other hand, those who hold privileged positions can use force and the threat of sanction as well as appeal to their unequal resources to promote their variant of what constitutes the public good. We need a healthy suspicion of both dangers whenever we hear evocations of "the public good." Yet, in the end, Mansbridge insists that "neither the dangers nor the necessity of ongoing contest over the very meaning of the words should lead us to discard appeals to the public good. In an extraordinarily large number of contexts, human beings need, in order to cooperate, some concept of a public good. We must learn to live with, even welcome, a concept that remains continually in contest."[58]

Many contemporary liberals have been persuaded by Isaiah Berlin's argument in his classic essay, "Two Concepts of Liberty," that goods are plural, nonhierarchical, and often in tragic conflict.[59] They do not see how we can construe a notion of *a* or *the* common good. Goods are simply plural, perhaps radically antagonistic, and cannot be aggregated, let alone conjoined in some larger sense of overall public purpose and good.

It strikes me that some common ground can be found between the modern Catholic notion of the common good and some modern liberal virtue theorists who do accept, albeit in a thin way, some notion of human flourishing. Brian Stiltner's treatment of the common good insists that the common good "is not the province of any particular group [presumably, he includes the Church] but of the whole political society."[60] Catholic treatments of the common good typically vacillate between thicker notions of human flourishing and the more modest insistence that it refers to the goods we as common citizens determine together as those that will serve as our public goods and institutional arrangements for the flourishing of a common citizenry. The common good looks both to some objectivity of the good and concomitant societal consensus. A putative blueprint for the common good that seriously divides the society and ceases to be common may not continue to be a genuine *societal* good. Consensus remains a constitutive part of any notion of the common good. Hence, we may need to appeal, as Catholics in public discourse, to a thinner notion of the common good that reaches less to total human flourishing than, precisely and restrictively, to the virtues necessary to flourish in our common life together as citizens, whatever our own tradition's more thick account of human flourishing.[61]

In any event, much work will be needed to reappropriate in contemporary settings the Catholic notion of the common good. Catholics may have to confront a more robust pluralism of the good than they have hitherto entertained to engage those liberals who: (1) accept an *objective* sense of the good; (2) refuse to always privilege the right over the good; and yet (3) accept a radically plural, nonhierarchical, and not easily harmonized notion of the good. It may be wise, following John Courtney Murray, to distinguish between the two concepts of the common good and public order. The first is not a monopoly of the state. The second is that portion of the common good which is appropriate for the ends and goals of the state. It has real content but is less thick than a full concept of the common good which, in its richest notion, includes our communion in the life of the Trinity.[62] In pluralist societies, the law may not be able realistically to enshrine all of the common good. By talking about the public order, social Catholicism can restrict the common good to issues of common citizenship virtue and the institutional arrangements for a human flourishing in pluralistic societies.

If, in the first two dialogues above, the learning curve may go primarily from social Catholicism toward liberalism, in this last dialogue, I still think Catholics may have to learn more about a more robust pluralism of the good from the liberals. Yet there are liberals who can join us in a discussion of a substantive common good. I have in mind, for example, Philip Selznick's idea of the common good as profoundly systemic, "not *reducible* to individual interests or attributes yet *testable* by its contribution to personal well-being."[63] Selznick insists that the common good is served by institutions that provide collective public goods, such as education, a healthy environment, and public safety. The strength or weakness of these institutions is a communal attribute, not an individual one. Moreover, it is not in everyone's interest to support such institutions. They might, indeed, be better off, as individuals, if they did not have to pay taxes for a school or other services they will not use but which remain important for society as a whole. But Selznick adds that

> a major collective good is social integration. . . . When social integration is measured . . . the measure will take into account, at least indirectly, individual attitudes, behaviors, opportunities and affiliations. And a *connection* is likely between personal and social integration. People can live more coherent lives and have more coherent personalities when they belong to coherent social worlds."[64]

Catholics may need to learn from liberals a greater hermeneutic of suspicion about misuses of appeals to the common good; a deeper appreciation of the perduring, legitimate, and conflicting pluralism about the nature of the good in modern societies; a better recognition that the pursuit of the common good is not always a panacea. Catholics may also need to add a crucial word to their lexicon of social thought when discussing the common good, one quite unusual in Catholic social discourse: *interest* (i.e., self- and group interest). Although the common good may not, as Selznick notes, be in the interest of all individuals, any appeal to the common good, unless it be hopelessly moralistic and abstract, must take the legitimate role of interest into account. Catholic social thought typically remains overly sanguine that, at the end of the day, doctrines and conflicts (and goods) can be harmonized. But in reality opinion is divided and these divisions will show up in conflicts over moral, religious, and political issues.

No theory can eliminate the conflictual elements from life. Nor should Catholic proponents of the common good expect to do so. Those who urge a commitment to the common good, however, do not despair in advance of the possibilities, as Mansbridge urges, of achieving some real, if limited, consensus about what we will consider public good and which goods and institutional arrangements we will pursue in common as fellow citizens. The language of the common good evokes consensus on some issues and operates as a bridging nexus between self-interest and the interests of others, perhaps akin to what Alexis de Tocqueville once referred to as "self interest rightly understood," that is, a marriage of my interests with more common ones. At the end of the day, at least in our situations of modern, pluralist democracies, I do not think the Catholic notion of the common good can be much more robust than that. Brian Stiltner helps us, at any rate, to see the issues we may need to address for the future of Catholic social thought, with liberals and others, if we want to talk about a common good. Different interpretations will, in fact, perdure, so different people can and will mean quite different things in appealing to the common good. It matters greatly, for example, to know whether an appeal to the common good appeals to the good of every member of the society, including myself, or to some social good that transcends and supersedes individual goods. It matters, when parsing common good language, if each subcommunity within a society has its own common good. Do these conflict with the common good of the whole society? And, if so, how will such conflicts be adjudicated? It matters whether people think a democratic society can have a common good only in a narrowly procedural sense, by making the political process open to all on an equal basis (surely a social good), or whether it can share a more substantive common good wherein citizens experience unity around a shared set of religious, or more likely, moral values.[65]

In summary, social Catholicism is a rich tradition that deserves a future. Its anthropological presumptions can, if put into policy, make for a more humane society. The carriers for the tradition are more fragile (and too tightly, probably, tied to the ecclesial authorities, in general) than previously, but enough remain to move the tradition forward by addressing new issues of important public policy and imagining and fostering new institutional carriers for it. Substantively, a dialogue between social Catholicism and the regnant political philosophies in contemporary pluralist societies should enrich both parties to the dialogue. Such dialogue might, just perhaps, make Catholic social teaching more than "our best kept secret."

NOTES

1. Kenneth Himes, "Globalization's Next Phase," *Origins* 32 (May 23, 2002): 17, 19–22.

2. Peter Henriot, Joseph Holland, and Edward Berri, *Our Best Kept Secret* (Washington, D.C.: Center of Concern, 1978). See my earlier essay, "Retrieving or Re-Inventing Social Catholicism," in *Catholic Social Thought: Twilight or Renaissance*? ed. Jon S. Boswell, Frank McHugh, and Johann Verstraeten (Leuven, Belgium: Leuven University Press, 2000), 265–92.

3. Dorothy Day, *The Long Loneliness* (San Francisco: Harper and Row, 1981); Peter Maurin, *Easy Essays* (West Hamlin, W.Va.: The Green Revolution, 1971).

4. Jacques Maritain, *Man and the State* (Chicago: University of Chicago Press, 1951); John Courtney Murray, *We Hold These Truths* (New York: Sheed and Ward, 1960); Barbara Ward, *The Rich Nations and the Poor Nations* (New York: Norton, 1962); Josef Pieper, *Justice*, trans. Lawrence E. Lynch (New York: Pantheon, 1955).

5. Jean Yves Calvez, *The Church and Social Justice* (Chicago: Henry Regnery, 1961); Charles E. Curran, *Catholic Social Teaching: A Historical, Theological and Ethical Analysis* (Washington, D.C.: Georgetown University Press, 2002).

6. *The New Catholic Encyclopedia* (New York: Publishers Guild, 1967), 12:386.

7. Gordon Zahn, "Social Movements and Catholic Social Thought," in *One Hundred Years of Catholic Social Thought*, ed. John A. Coleman (Maryknoll, N.Y.: Orbis, 1991), 44.

8. Ibid., 48.

9. Ibid., 53. For confirmation of G. Zahn's theory in work for justice on race relations where the unofficial Catholic movements predated episcopal authoritative teaching, see John LaFarge, *The Catholic View Point on Race Relations* (Garden City, N.Y.: Hanover House, 1956).

10. For much of this history, see Paul Misner, *Social Catholicism in Europe* (New York: Crossroad, 1991).

11. See the references to Oswald von Nell-Breuning and to QA in *The New Dictionary of Catholic Social Thought*, ed. J. A. Dwyer, 676–78, 802–13.

12. O. von Nell-Breuning, "The Drafting of *Quadragesimo Anno*," in *Official Catholic Social Teaching*, ed. Charles E. Curran and Richard A. McCormick (Mahwah, N.J.: Paulist, 1986), 60–68. The relevant passage was QA 93, which seems to suggest a corporatist order under the direction of the state. See also the Commentary in this volume on QA by Christine Firer Hinze.

13. Peter Hebblethwaite," The Popes and Politics: Shifting Patterns in Catholic Social Doctrine," in *Official Catholic Social Teaching*, ed. C. E. Curran and R. A. McCormick, 264–83.

14. Thomas R. Donahue, "From *Rerum Novarum* to *Laborem Exercens*: A United States Labor Perspective," in ibid., 384–410, esp. 404. See the commentary on LE in this volume by Patricia A. Lamoureux.

15. Thomas S. Bokenkotter, *The Church and Revolution* (New York: Doubleday, 1998).

16. Hebblethwaite, "The Popes and Politics," 265.

17. Ibid., 268.

18. M. D. Chenu, *La "doctrine sociale" de l'église comme idéologie* (Paris: Cerf, 1979), 22.

19. David Hanley, *Christian Democracy in Europe: A Comparative Perspective* (London: Pinter, 1994).

20. Michael Fleet, *The Rise and Fall of Chilean Christian Democracy* (Princeton, N.J.: Princeton University Press, 1985); Brian Smith, *The Church and Politics in Chile* (Princeton, N.J.: Princeton University Press, 1982).

21. Johann Verstraeten, "Rethinking Catholic Social Thought as a Tradition," in *Catholic Social*

Thought: Twilight or Renaissance, ed. J. S. Boswell, F. McHugh, and J. Verstraeten, 64.

22. Michael J. Schuck, "Modern Catholic Social Thought," in *New Dictionary of Catholic Social Thought*, ed. J. A. Dwyer, 611–32, esp. 631.

23. John A. Coleman, "Neither Liberal Nor Socialist: The Originality of Catholic Social Teaching," in *One Hundred Years of Catholic Social Thought*, ed. J. A. Coleman, 25–42.

24. Brian Stiltner, *Religion and the Common Good* (Lanham, Md.: Rowman and Littlefield, 1999).

25. Ibid., 47.

26. Ibid., 10.

27. John Rawls, *Political Liberalism* (New York: Columbia University Press, 1993).

28. Stiltner, *Religion and the Common Good*, 178.

29. Jane Mansbridge, *Beyond Adversary Democracy* (Chicago: University of Chicago Press, 1980).

30. David Hollenbach, *The Common Good and Christian Ethics* (New York: Cambridge University Press, 2002), 42.

31. For liberalism, critical theory, feminism, and religious voices in dialogue, see Nancy Rosenblum and Robert Post, eds., *Civil Society and Government* (Princeton, N.J.: Princeton University Press, 2002). I contributed an essay to this volume entitled, "A Limited State and a Vibrant Society: Christianity and Civil Society," 222–54.

32. J. Verstraeten, "Rethinking Catholic Social Thought as a Tradition," in *Catholic Social Thought*, ed. J. A. Boswell, F. McHugh, and J. Verstraeten, 67. See also the chapter, "The Bible and Catholic Social Teaching: Will This Engagement Lead to Marriage?" by John Donahue in this volume, where he considers scripture as a background to Catholic social thought.

33. Thomas Gilbey, *Principles of Morality* (Oxford: New Blackfriars, 1958), xxi.

34. Jean Porter, *Natural and Divine Law* (Grand Rapids, Mich.: Eerdmans, 1999), and her "Catholic Social Thought and the Natural Law Tradition," unpublished paper presented at the *Commonweal* symposium, "American Catholics and the Public Square," New York City, May 12–14, 2000. All quotations in this subsection without reference are drawn from this paper. It is available online at http://www.catholicsinpublicsquare.org/papers/spring2000commonweal/porter/porterprit.htm (downloaded March 14, 2004). See also the chapter in this volume by Stephen Pope, "Natural Law in Catholic Social Teachings."

35. John Finnis, *Natural Law and Natural Rights* (New York: Oxford University Press, 1980).

36. Alasdair MacIntyre, *Whose Justice? Which Rationality?* (Notre Dame, Ind.: University of Notre Dame Press, 1988).

37. John Milbank, *Theology and Social Theory: Beyond Secular Reason* (Oxford: Basil Blackwell, 1991).

38. Michael J. Perry, *The Idea of Human Rights* (New York: Oxford University Press, 1998).

39. Catholic human rights development is treated in D. Hollenbach, *Claims in Conflict* (New York: Paulist, 1979).

40. Some representative communitarian liberal allies for Catholics could be Philip Selznick, *The Moral Commonwealth* (Berkeley: University of California Press, 1992); William Galston, *Liberal Purposes: Goods, Virtues and Diversity in the Liberal State* (New York: Cambridge University Press, 1991); and Amatai Etzioni, *The Spirit of Community: Rights, Responsibilities and the Communitarian Agenda* (New York: Simon and Schuster, 1994).

41. José Casanova, "Religion, the New Millennium and Globalization," in *Sociology of Religion* 62, no. 4 (2001): 415–41. See also the chapter on the global common good in Hollenbach, *The Common Good and Christian Ethics*, 212–44. I am also indebted for the direction of my remarks about globalization in the text to an oral presentation by Bryan Hehir, "Catholic Social Thought and Globalization," Loyola Marymount University, October 29, 2002.

42. Ciaran Cronin and Pablo De Greif, "Normative Responses to Current Challenges of Global Governance," in *Global Justice and Transnational Politics: Essays on the Moral and Political Challenges of Globalization*, ed. P. de Greif and C. Cronin (Cambridge, Mass.: MIT, 2002), 1. The entire volume is a helpful and balanced treatment of the promise and perils of globalization.

43. de Greif and Cronin, eds., *Global Justice and Transnational Politics*, 22.

44. Ibid., 2. See also Margaret Keck and Kathryn Sikkink, *Activists beyond Borders: Advocacy Networks in International Politics* (Ithaca, N.Y.: Cornell University Press, 1998).

45. For Amartya Sen, see *Development as Freedom* (New York: Knopf, 1999); George Soros, *Open Society: Reforming Global Capitalism* (New York: Public Affairs, 2000); Joseph Stiglitz, *Globalization and Its Discontents* (New York: Norton, 2002).

46. Bishops of the Northwest and Western Canada, "The Columbia River Watershed: Caring for Creation and the Common Good," *Origins* 30 (March 8, 2001): 609–19.

47. For the changed ecclesial climate for doing Catholic social thought, see Curran, *Catholic Social Teaching*, 119–20, and the chapter in this volume by Richard Gaillardetz, "The Ecclesiological Foundations of Modern Catholic Social Teaching."

48. The lobbying efforts of the U.S. Catholic Conference are treated in Thomas S. Reese, *A Flock of Shepherds* (Kansas City, Mo.: Sheed and Ward, 1992). An outside look at the effectiveness of the Conference's lobbying can be found in Allen Hertzke, *Representing God in Washington* (Knoxville: University of Tennessee Press, 1988).

49. For a treatment of strengths and weaknesses in lobbying efforts at the level of State Catholic Conferences, see Edward Dolejsi, "Coalitions: Collaboration and Compromises," in *American Catholics and Civic Engagement*, ed. Margaret O'Brien Steinfels (Lanham, Md. 2004: Sheed and Ward). Dolejsi is the director of the California Catholic Conference.

David Yamane, a sociologist at the University of Notre Dame, is currently finishing a book on his research on State Catholic Conferences. He provides some of the data in his essay, "The Bishops and Politics," *Commonweal* 130 (May 23, 2003): 17–20.

50. Thomas Masarro, *Catholic Social Teaching and United States Welfare Reform* (Collegeville, Minn.: Liturgical, 1998). I treat lobbying efforts by Catholic Charities U.S.A. in my essay, "American Catholicism, Catholic Charities U.S.A and Welfare Reform," in *Religion Returns to the Public Square: Faith and Policy in America*, ed. Hugh Heclo and Wilfred McClay (Baltimore: Johns Hopkins University Press, 2003), 229–67.

51. For church-based community organizing, see Mark Warren, *Dry Bones Rattling* (Princeton, N.J.: Princeton University Press, 2001), on the Industrial Areas Foundation in Texas; Richard Wood, *Faith in Action* (Chicago: University of Chicago Press, 2002), on another church-based community organizing group known as Pico; and Stephen Hart, *Cultural Dilemmas of Progressive Politics* (Chicago: University of Chicago Press, 2001), on another church-based community organizing group in the Midwest known as Gamaliel.

52. Charles Taylor, *Sources of the Self* (Cambridge, Mass.: Harvard University Press, 1989); Alasdair MacIntyre, *Dependent Rational Animals* (Chicago: Open Court, 1999), and idem, *After Virtue* (Notre Dame, Ind.: University of Notre Dame Press, 1984). In *Dependent Rational Animals*, MacIntyre seems to suggest that the common good inheres only in civil society and is not a prerequisite of the state.

53. This is the complaint lodged by Robert N. Bellah et al. in their study of expressive individualism in America, *Habits of the Heart* (Berkeley: University of California Press, 1985).

54. Ronald Dworkin, *A Matter of Principle* (Cambridge, Mass.: Harvard University Press, 1983).

55. Michael Sandel, *Liberalism and the Limits of Justice* (New York: Cambridge University Press, 1998).

56. John Rawls, "The Idea of Public Reason Revisited," *University of Chicago Law Review* 64 (1997): 765–807, esp. 768, 776, 785–87.

57. José Casanova, *Public Religions in the Modern World* (Chicago: University of Chicago Press, 1994).

58. J. Mansbridge, "On the Contested Nature of the Good," in *Private Action and the Public Good*, ed. W. W. Powell and E. S. Clemens (New Haven, Conn.: Yale University Press, 1998), 17.

59. Isaiah Berlin, "Two Concepts of Liberty," in *Four Essays on Liberty*, ed. Isaiah Berlin (New York: Oxford University Press, 1988), 118–72.

60. Stiltner, *Religion and the Common Good*, 75. Galston, *Liberal Purposes* is a major exponent of virtue theory among liberal thinkers.

61. Michael Walzer, *Thick and Thin: Moral Argument at Home and Abroad* (Notre Dame, Ind.: University of Notre Dame Press, 1994) argues that we need to use thinner notions of the good when we are dealing with pluralistic attempts to achieve consensus and cooperation. Just how thin they have to be remains still a matter of debate.

62. Curran, *Catholic Social Teaching*, 228–29, 241–43 treats of the distinction between the common good and public order.

63. Selznick, *The Moral Commonwealth*, 537.

64. Ibid.

65. Stiltner, *Religion and the Common Good*, 180. I treat the question of the common good at greater length in my essay "Pluralism and the Renewal of the Catholic Sense of the Common Good" in *American Catholics and Civic Engagement*, ed. Margaret O'Brien Steinfels (Lanham, Md.: Sheed and Ward, 2004). Other treatments can be found in Curran, *Catholic Social Teaching*, 235–36, 240–43. Hollenbach's *The Common Good and Christian Ethics* is presently the best-rounded treatment of the topic.

SELECTED BIBLIOGRAPHY

Boswell, Jon S., Frank McHugh, and Johann Verstraeten, eds. *Catholic Social Thought: Twilight or Renaissance?* Leuven, Belgium: Leuven University Press, 2000. Essays on the future of Catholic social thought.

Coleman, John A. *One Hundred Years of Catholic Social Thought*. Maryknoll, N.Y.: Orbis, 1991. Essays applying Catholic social thought to the issues of economics, family, and war and peace.

Curran, Charles E. *Catholic Social Teaching: A Historical, Theological and Ethical Analysis*. Washington, D.C.: Georgetown University Press. The best single one-volume treatment of Catholic social teaching.

Curran, Charles E., and Richard McCormick, eds. *Official Catholic Social Teaching*. Mahwah, N.J.: Paulist, 1986. A useful compilation of historical and theological essays on Catholic social teaching.

Dywer, Judith A., ed. *The New Dictionary of Catholic Social Thought*. Collegeville, Minn.: Liturgical, 1994. An indispensable reference work.

Hollenbach, David. *The Common Good and Christian Ethics*. New York: Cambridge University Press, 2002. An excellent retrieval of the notion of the common good.

Schuck, Michael. *That They Be One: The Social Teachings of the Papal Encyclicals, 1749–1989*. Washington, D.C.: Georgetown University Press, 1991. Very good overall treatment of the historical settings and the theological unity of papal social thought.

Stiltner, Brian. *Religion and the Common Good*. Lanham, Md.: Rowman and Littlefield, 1999. A creative address of social Catholicism to contemporary non-Catholic notions of person and society.

CONTRIBUTORS

Lisa Sowle Cahill is J. Donald Monan Professor of Theology at Boston College.

Drew Christiansen, S.J., is an associate editor of *America* magazine.

John A. Coleman, S.J., is Charles Casassa Professor of Social Values at Loyola Marymount University, Los Angeles, California.

Charles E. Curran is Elizabeth Scurlock University Professor of Human Values at Southern Methodist University, Dallas, Texas.

Allan Figueroa Deck, S.J., is executive director of the Loyola Institute for Spirituality in Orange, California, and adjunct professor at Loyola Marymount University, Los Angeles, California.

John R. Donahue, S.J., is Raymond E. Brown Distinguished Professor of New Testament Studies (Emeritus) at St. Mary's Seminary and University, Baltimore, Maryland.

Daniel Finn is William E. and Virginia Clemens Professor of Economics and the Liberal Arts and professor of theology at St. John's University, Collegeville, Minnesota.

Richard R. Gaillardetz is the Thomas and Margaret Murray and James J. Bacik Professor of Catholic Studies at the University of Toledo in Ohio.

Leslie Griffin holds the Larry and Joanne Doherty Chair in Legal Ethics at the University of Houston Law Center.

Christine E. Gudorf is professor of Christian ethics and chair of the Religious Studies Department at Florida International University.

Kenneth R. Himes, O.F.M., is chair of the Theology Department at Boston College.

Christine Firer Hinze is associate professor in the Theology Department at Marquette University, Milwaukee, Wisconsin.

David Hollenbach, S.J., holds the Margaret O'Brien Flatley Chair in Catholic Theology at Boston College.

Patricia A. Lamoureux holds the Richard and Barbara Fisher Chair in Social Ethics at St. Mary's Seminary and University, Baltimore, Maryland.

John P. Langan, S.J., holds the Joseph Bernardin Chair of Catholic Social Thought at Georgetown University in Washington, D.C.

Marvin L. Mich is director of social policy and research in the Catholic Family Center of Catholic Charities, Diocese of Rochester, New York.

Stephen J. Pope is associate professor in the Theology Department at Boston College.

Michael J. Schuck is associate professor in the Department of Theology at Loyola University of Chicago.

Thomas A. Shannon is professor of social ethics, Department of the Humanities and Arts, Worcester Polytechnic Institute in Massachusetts.

Todd D. Whitmore is associate professor of social ethics in the Theology Department at the University of Notre Dame, South Bend, Indiana.

INDEX